Horace

HORACE

THE ODES AND EPODES
C. H. MOORE

THE SATIRES AND EPISTLES
E. P. MORRIS

DEPARTMENT OF EDUCATION
LELAND STANFORD JUNIOR UNIVERSITY

NEW YORK ∴ CINCINNATI ∴ CHICAGO
AMERICAN BOOK COMPANY

597625
c

Morris and Morgan's Latin Series

EDITED FOR USE IN SCHOOLS AND COLLEGES

UNDER THE SUPERVISION OF

EDWARD P. MORRIS, M.A.,

PROFESSOR OF LATIN IN YALE UNIVERSITY

AND

MORRIS H. MORGAN, PH.D.,

PROFESSOR OF CLASSICAL PHILOLOGY IN HARVARD UNIVERSITY

VOLUMES OF THE SERIES

Essentials of Latin for Beginners. Henry C. Pearson, Teachers College, New York. 90 cents.

A School Latin Grammar. Morris H. Morgan, Harvard University. $1.00.

A First Latin Writer. M. A. Abbott, Groton School. 60 cents.

Connected Passages for Latin Prose Writing. Maurice W. Mather, formerly of Harvard University, and Arthur L. Wheeler, Bryn Mawr College. $1.00.

Caesar. Episodes from the Gallic and Civil Wars. Maurice W. Mather, formerly of Harvard University. $1.25.

Cicero. Ten Orations and Selected Letters. J. Remsen Bishop, Eastern High School, Detroit, Frederick A. King, Hughes High School, Cincinnati, and Nathan W. Helm, Evanston Academy of Northwestern University. $1.25.
Six Orations. $1.00.

Selections from Latin Prose Authors for Sight Reading. Susan Braley Franklin and Ella Catherine Greene, Miss Baldwin's School, Bryn Mawr. 40 cents.

Cicero. Cato Maior. Frank G. Moore, Columbia University. 80 cents.

Cicero. Laelius de Amicitia. Clifton Price, University of California. 75 cents.

Selections from Livy. Harry E. Burton, Dartmouth College. $1.50.

Horace. Odes and Epodes. Clifford H. Moore, Harvard University. $1.50.

Horace. Satires. Edward P. Morris, Yale University. $1.00.

Horace. Satires and Epistles. Edward P Morris, Yale University. $1.25.

Horace. Odes, Epodes, and Carmen Saeculare, Moore. **Satires and Epistles,** Morris. In one volume. $2.00.

Pliny's Letters. Albert A. Howard, Harvard University.

Tibullus. Kirby F. Smith, Johns Hopkins University.

Lucretius. William A. Merrill, University of California. $2.25.

Latin Literature of the Empire. Alfred Gudeman, University of Pennsylvania.
Vol. I. Prose : Velleius to Boethius $1.80
Vol. II. Poetry : Pseudo-Vergiliana to Claudianus $1.80

Selections from the Public and Private Law of the Romans. James J. Robinson, Hotchkiss School. $1.25.

Others to be announced later.

HORACE

THE ODES, EPODES

AND

CARMEN SAECULARE

EDITED, WITH INTRODUCTION AND COMMENTARY,

BY

CLIFFORD HERSCHEL MOORE, Ph.D.
PROFESSOR OF LATIN IN HARVARD UNIVERSITY

NEW YORK ·:· CINCINNATI ·:· CHICAGO
AMERICAN BOOK COMPANY

COPYRIGHT, 1902, BY
EDWARD P. MORRIS AND MORRIS H. MORGAN.

ENTERED AT STATIONERS' HALL, LONDON.

MOORE, HORACE.

W. P. I

MEMORIAE PATRIS

PREFACE

In preparing this edition of Horace's lyrical poems, I have had in mind the needs of freshmen and sophomores. The introduction is intended to give the necessary information as to the poet's life and writings. The text is the vulgate, although in some passages I have preferred the better manuscript tradition. As young students require no little help if they are to understand as well as translate the Epodes and Odes, I have not limited my commentary to the baldest aids, but have tried to give such assistance in interpretation as may help students to some appreciation of Horace's art and charm. The best illustrations naturally are furnished by the poet's own works; but I have endeavored to show his relations to his Greek models by quoting from them as freely as my space and judgment allowed. To all the more difficult Greek passages I have appended translations, both for the benefit of those who cannot call themselves *docti sermones utriusque linguae*, and in the hope that these translations may secure the originals more attention than students generally give to them. I have further given a number of quotations from the later Latin poets to indicate in some degree the ready acceptance which Horace's skillful phrases found among his successors. In writing my notes I have drawn freely on the fund of illustrative material which is now common property; like every other editor, I am indebted to Keller and Holder's first volume; and I have used most of the important foreign annotated editions, especially Orelli's fourth edition, and those of Schütz, Kiessling, and Mueller. Although for obvious reasons I have avoided consulting any American edition, I am aware that my debt to Professor Smith's excellent book, which I have used in my teaching for some years, must be greater than I know. In the three or four places where I have detected direct indebtedness, I have acknowledged it.

The notes to the earlier Epodes are rather full, as I firmly believe that at least Epodes 1, 2, 7, 9, and 16 should be read before the Odes; but since many teachers do not hold this view, I have adapted my commentary on the first book to meet the needs of beginners there also.

I am under obligations to many for criticism and help. My thanks are especially due Miss S. H. Ballou, Instructor in the University of Chicago, for the valuable assistance she gave me in the earlier part of my work; also to Professor Morris, who kindly gave me the benefit of his criticisms on my notes to the first two books of the Odes; but above all to Professor Morgan, whose suggestions and criticisms have been of the greatest value at every stage. Notice of errors and suggestions of every kind will be gratefully received by me.

CLIFFORD HERSCHEL MOORE.

HARVARD UNIVERSITY,
June 1, 1902.

CONTENTS

	PAGE
MAPS:	
Central Italy	10
The Valleys of the Anio and the Digentia	50
INTRODUCTION:	
Horace's Life, Works, and Characteristics	11
Manuscripts, Scholia, and Editions	25
Metres	35
Syntax	45
ODES, BOOKS 1–3	51
BOOK 4	331
CARMEN SAECULARE	388
EPODES	398
INDEX TO FIRST LINES	464

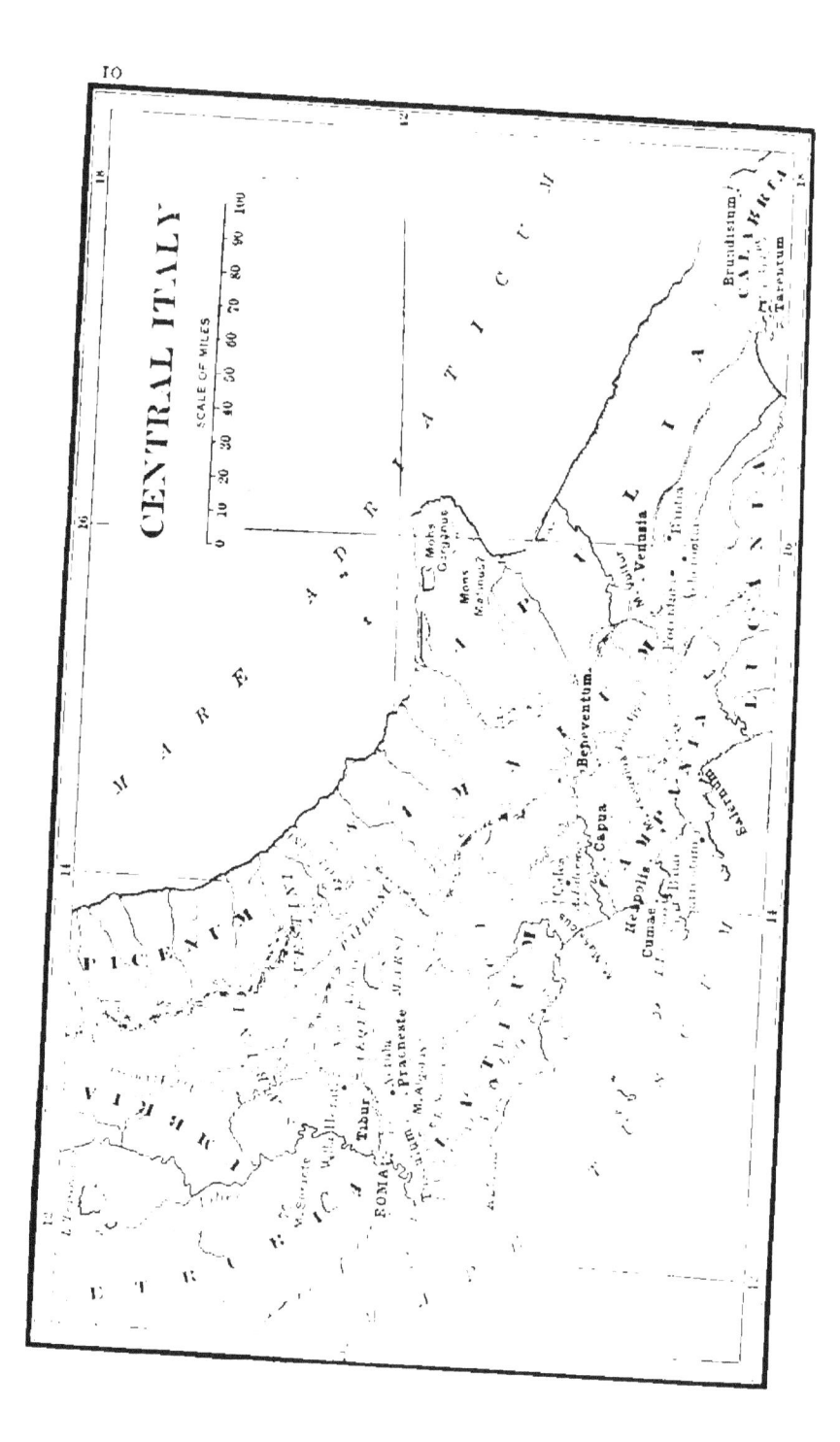

INTRODUCTION

1. Early Life and Education. — Quintus Horatius Flaccus was born Dec. 8, 65 B.C., at Venusia, a colony founded in the time of the Samnite Wars, on the borders of Apulia, near Lucania. His father had been a slave, but was free at the time of Horace's birth, so that the son was *ingenuus*. His mother is never mentioned, and it is probable that she died while the child was too young to remember her. His father was by profession a *coactor*, a collector of moneys for goods sold at public auctions, who by his thrift acquired a property sufficient to provide his son with the best education obtainable in his time. In later years Horace paid a most sincere tribute of gratitude to his father's devotion and sagacity. From him he learned a rude but practical code of morals, and it is undoubtedly to his influence that we may attribute the poet's marked characteristics of moderation, temperance, and self-control; to his father's training was also due Horace's habit of observing men and manners, which bore fruit in the shrewd and searching comments on life which have endeared him to many generations of men.

Up to the age of nine or ten Horace enjoyed such education as the local school in Venusia afforded. Then his father, whose sole ambition was to provide his son with the best education that could be had, unselfishly gave up his business at Venusia, and took the boy to Rome. Here he gave him proper attendants, provided him with suitable dress that he might not be ashamed among his high-born and wealthy schoolfellows, and with rare devotion attended the boy himself as *paedagogus*.

During the next nine or ten years Horace received the ordinary literary and rhetorical training; under the rod of the schoolmaster Orbilius, whom he has immortalized with the adjective *plagosus* (*Epist.* 2, 1, 70), he studied Latin literature, reading the works of Livius Andronicus and other old Roman poets, for whom he apparently felt little admiration; his studies also included the *Iliad* and probably other Greek classics, and we can hardly doubt that this early study of Greek literature roused that enthusiasm for it which lasted all his life.

In his twentieth year Horace went to Greece to finish his studies at Athens, which had become a kind of university town to which it was the fashion for young men of his generation to resort. Among his fellow students were Cicero's son, Marcus, and M. Valerius Messala. During the next two years he heard lectures by the leaders of the various philosophic schools, without being seriously attracted by any one system. Speculative thought had little interest for him, or indeed for his fellow countrymen in general: questions relating rather to conduct interested the Roman mind, and while Horace never gave himself up to any system of ethics, Epicureanism attracted him at first; on growing older he turned more and more to the teachings of the Stoics, as the Stoic maxims and paradoxes in his odes abundantly testify; yet no one had a keener sense than he for what was absurd in Stoic practice. His good sense always tempered his philosophy, and in all matters of conduct he steered a middle course. It is also most probable that during his stay in Athens he continued his study of the Greek poets, particularly of Archilochus and the early lyricists, especially Alcaeus and Sappho, who afterward became his chief models. At this time he was ambitious to excel in Greek verse, but wisely forsook the practice later; yet his consummate skill in handling his own language must have been due to his early exercises in Greek. By studying in Athens he had further the negative advantage of escaping the influence of Alexandrianism which prevailed at Rome and affected all contemporary poets. There, too, he made many friendships which lasted him through life.

In the autumn of 44 B.C. Brutus came to Athens, where the people received him with enthusiasm as a liberator. The young Roman nobles and Horace as well were attracted to his cause. Why the freedman's son was given the office of military tribune in the conspirators' army — a position for which he had no training — it is hard to say, and the appointment not unnaturally aroused envy at the time. It is probable, however, that Horace had already made some reputation among his fellow students as a skillful versifier, and Brutus' love of literature induced him to prefer the youth. Of Horace's military service we know little; his writings show a familiarity with some islands of the Aegean and the famous cities of Asia, which was probably gained at this time, and it is certain that he shared in the defeat at Philippi in 42 B.C. No doubt he gave as good an account of himself during his two years of service as his fellows; the ironical description of his flight at Philippi (*C.* 2, 7, 9 f.) is imitated from Archilochus and Alcaeus, and is not to be taken seriously.

The defeat of the conspirators' cause brought a crisis to Horace's life, and at the age of twenty-three taught him the meaning of the vicissitudes of fortune; it seems also to have cured him of any political or social ambitions he may have cherished. He gradually accepted the new order of things, at first despairing of the state; but later, after the battle of Actium had freed Rome from external dangers, he enthusiastically proclaimed the permanence of the Empire and celebrated the beneficence of Augustus' rule. But his entire life after his experience at Philippi was that of a man of letters, who mixed much with men rather as an observer than as a participant in their life. His later history falls into three periods of about ten years each: first, from his return to Rome to 29 B.C., the period during which he published his two books of *Satires* and the collection of *Epodes;* second, 29–19 B.C., the period of his maturity, in which his genius reached its height. During these ten years he published the first three books of *Odes* (23 B.C.) and the first book of the *Epistles* (20 B.C.). Of his personal history during the last decennium (19–8 B.C.) we know but little. He was less productive than in the two previous periods, publishing only the *Carmen Saeculare* (17 B.C.), the fourth book of *Odes* (after 13 B.C.), and the two literary epistles, which, with the *Ars Poetica*, form a second book of *Epistles*.

2. **Return to Rome.** — The general amnesty granted by Octavian after the battle of Philippi allowed Horace to return to Italy. His father evidently died before his return, and he came back to find that Venusia, where his estate was situated, had been included in the districts assigned to the veterans of the victorious army, so that he was thrown on his own resources. His means sufficed to buy him a position as clerk to the quaestors, by which his support was secured. In his leisure he turned to writing Latin verses.

Horace had now at the age of twenty-four acquired considerable experience in the good and ill fortunes of life, and had lived through some important national crises. During his school days in Rome he had seen the rupture between Caesar and Pompey, and was old enough to understand something of the serious danger to the state which it involved; Caesar's supreme position was well established before he went to Athens, and he had had a part in the final struggle between the would-be 'liberators' and the dictator's successors. While he never after showed any desire to have a share in politics, it is most probable that these experiences of his early manhood caused him to think and feel earnestly on matters of state, so that in later life, when he had heartily accepted the new régime, he expressed himself on subjects touching the well-being of the nation with a warmth which no other theme except personal friendship called forth. He lived to see the national dangers removed, the Empire firmly established, and to enjoy the blessings of peace under the rule of Augustus.

3. The Satires. — As has been said above, Horace had practiced Greek verses in the courses of his studies. He now turned to composition in his native language. When he began to write, Varius Rufus was the epic poet of the day, having won that position by his epic poem on the death of Julius Caesar, published before 39 B.C.; Asinius Pollio was distinguished in tragedy; and Vergil was beginning to be known for his bucolic poems. The field of satire as practiced by Lucilius (ca. 180–103 B.C.), comments in verse on the most miscellaneous topics, appealed to Horace, and in the leisure which his official duties left him he began to write in hexameters after the manner of his model. He understood that politics could no longer be frankly treated, and, with few exceptions, he avoided personal attack; but his nature and training had made him a keen observer of the life about him. This life he chose for his subject, and handled its different phases in the familiar tone of a man of the world; he always speaks as one of the company at whose weaknesses he laughs, never preaching or setting himself up as superior to his fellow-mortals. Horace was blessed with a keen sense of humor as well as clear insight, so that these sketches have always been held in high esteem, not only for their cleverness and wit, but also because no other works in Latin literature give us such vivid pictures of the actual life in which the author shared. While Horace made a great advance on the metrical art of his model, he never called his satires poetry. His own name was *sermones*, 'familiar talks,' and he declared that they were only distinguished from prose by the rhythm. They were written at various times during the decennium following his return, and many were undoubtedly known before they were gathered together into books. The first book was published before 33, the most probable date is 35/34; the second in 30 B.C.

4. The Epodes. — At the time when he began to write satire, Horace also attempted to introduce into Latin a new form of verse, the epodic couplet, consisting of two verses, the second of which forms a refrain (*epōdus*, ἐπῳδός) to the first. In this he was a conscious imitator of Archilochus, who, in the seventh century B.C., had perfected this form in iambic measure, and used it as the sharpest weapon of personal attack. The name which Horace, following Archilochus, gave his verses — *iambi* — can apply properly to only the first ten of the seventeen in the present collection. The remaining seven are in different measures, but only one, the seventeenth, lacks the epodic form; so that in time the name *Epodes* drove out Horace's designation. While Horace shows himself equal to his model in form, he exhibits little of the passion ascribed to Archilochus. Eight epodes show the invective spirit, two exhibit a coarseness of thought and expression which does not appear later, but others have nothing aggressive in them. The first, for example, is a plea to be allowed to accompany Maecenas to Actium; the ninth is a song of joy over the victory gained there; the seventh and sixteenth deal with the conditions of the state; the second is an idyl on the joys of country life; and the others have little of the invective spirit. They were written at various times between 40 and 31 B.C.; the sixteenth is probably to be referred to the earlier date, and the ninth is later than the battle of Actium, Sept. 2, 31 B.C.

5. Horace and Maecenas. — Horace's verses brought him into notice soon after his return, and gained him the friendship of Vergil and Varius, who introduced him to Maecenas, apparently in the spring of 38 B.C. Nine months later, in the winter of 38/37 B.C., Maecenas invited him to join the inner circle of his friends. From this time Horace was free from material cares; and about the year 33 B.C. he received from his patron a farm in the valley of the Digentia, among the Sabine hills, which was thereafter his favorite home and constant source of happiness. Maecenas was already at this time the trusted friend and adviser of Octavian. In 36 B.C., when Octavian set out from Rome for his campaign against Sextus Pompey, and in 31 B.C., during the final struggle with Antony and Cleopatra, Maecenas was left as his representative with almost complete power; and with the exception of a temporary estrangement in 23 B.C., when he indiscreetly betrayed to his wife Terentia the discovery of the plot which her brother, Licinius Murena, was forming against Augustus, he remained the emperor's most trusted adviser. Naturally, when Augustus' position was firmly established, Maecenas was to a certain extent displaced by the members of the imperial family; but the friendship between him and Augustus continued to the end. With all his opportunity and power, Maecenas declined political preferment, and remained a 'knight' throughout his life. He had a native taste for literature, was a master of the Greek language, and wrote some mediocre verses himself; but it was by his wise patronage of men of letters that he won a permanent place in the grateful memory of men. He had no doubt a political purpose in his patronage also, for he saw that literature might be used to support and establish the new régime. Yet he imposed no fettering conditions on those to whom he gave his favor: we know (*Epod.* 14) that he urged Horace to publish his Epodes; that Vergil wrote the Georgics at his suggestion; that he advised Propertius to undertake some larger themes; but nowhere is there any hint that he ever exacted any return for his favor which would not have been spontaneously made. Of the circle he gathered about him, Vergil, Horace, and Propertius achieved most permanent fame. Others were L. Varius Rufus, Plotius Tucca, Quintilius Varus, Domitius Marsus, and C. Melissus. Maecenas' favor assured Horace the friendship of these and many others besides that of Octavian, so that after 37 B.C. he had entrance into the best society of his time. His friendship with Maecenas was commingled with gratitude to him for the material aid he had given; but the relation between the two men had so genuine a basis that Horace could accept Maecenas' gifts without hesitancy, aware that his friendship was a full return in Maecenas' mind. His acceptance, too, involved no loss of independence, and in many passages he makes it clear that he would readily resign all the benefits conferred on him rather than lose his freedom in the slightest degree.

6. The Odes. — The second period of Horace's literary activity, 29–19 B.C., was devoted chiefly to lyric composition. He had long been a student of Greek poetry, and the models he now followed were chiefly Alcaeus and Sappho (600 B.C.), whose measures he adopted as his own, and from whose works he drew many themes. While these two poets had the greatest influence on him, still, as the notes to the odes will show, we find evidence of the influence of Homer, Pindar, Bacchylides, Anacreon, Stesichorus, and the three tragedians. He drew also from the Alexandrians, but chiefly from Callimachus and Theocritus. Yet he followed no model slavishly, and even in his closest studies from the Greek, he made the themes his own. The earliest ode to which a date can be assigned with certainty is 1, 37, written in 30 B.C., on hearing of the death of Cleopatra. A few may have been written before this, but not many. For seven years Horace gave himself almost exclusively to lyric verse. His mastery of form and language was now complete, and his developed taste set a high standard of perfection. The eighty-eight lyrics which belong to this period were never equaled in variety and perfection among the Romans, and alone would entitle their author to the immortality he has enjoyed. Many of these odes, — Horace called them simply *carmina*, — especially those addressed to friends, were privately circulated before they were collected into the present three books; these were published in 23 B.C., as is clear from internal evidence.[1]

---

[1] The young Marcellus died at the end of 23 B.C., but it is hardly probable that Horace would have published the reference to him in 1, 12, 45 f. in its present form after his death; further, in 2, 10 (and possibly 3, 19), Horace mentions Licinius Murena, the brother-in-law of Maecenas, who was involved in a conspiracy against Augustus in the latter half of 23 B.C. The publication must have been earlier than the discovery of this plot. The latest reference is to the death of Quintilius Varus in 1, 24, which Hieronymus records in 23 B.C.; and it is probable that 1, 4, in which L. Sestius is addressed, was written about July, 23 B.C., when Sestius entered on his office as consul suffectus.

7. **Arrangement and Character of the Odes.** — In arranging his lyrics for publication, Horace placed at the beginning eleven odes, each in a different metre, illustrating all the measures employed by him in the three books with the exception of the unique rhythms in 2, 18; 3, 12.[1] Within this group certain other principles of arrangement can be detected. The first word is Maecenas, and the opening poem virtually dedicates the three books to their author's friend and patron, to whom he had already inscribed his *Satires* and *Epodes*. The second ode celebrates Octavian as the divine restorer of order in the state; the third is a farewell poem to Vergil; the fourth is addressed to Sestius, consul in the year of publication. The others are arranged to secure variety in subject as well as measure, a principle that is observed generally throughout the three books, so that grave themes are relieved by light, and a succession of similar metres is for the most part avoided. The second book opens with an ode to Asinius Pollio, celebrating his literary powers and touching sadly on the Civil Wars of which Pollio was about to undertake a history. In the first six odes of the third book, Horace comes forward as the teacher of the new generation, and deals earnestly with the problems and dangers of the state. This is the largest group of odes on related themes, and the Alcaic metre is used in all; but, as if to avoid wearying his reader, Horace did not insert another ode in the same measure until the seventeenth. He had also some regard for chronological sequence, but this was always subordinate to the principle of variety. Each book, too, has certain characteristics. In the first there are a larger number of studies from the Greek than in the other two; about half the odes are on themes of love and wine; nowhere is any serious philosophy of life presented; and only five (2, 12, 14, 35, 37) show deep concern with the state. As if to emphasize his character as the singer of light themes, and at the same time to offset the serious notes in odes 35 and 37, Horace

---

[1] The tenth ode, while in Sapphic measure like the second, still exhibits certain metrical peculiarities.

placed at the end of his book the dainty verses, *Persicos odi, puer, apparatus*, which picture him at ease and free from care.

The odes of the second book show more reflection, a deeper sense of the poet's personal relationship to his friends, a more serious and a graver attitude toward life. His didactic odes here lay stress on wise conduct, and the checking of untoward desires, rather than on the means of securing enjoyment. The twenty odes, with two exceptions, are composed in the Alcaic and Sapphic measures.

In the third book, Horace appears as the poet of the new Rome established by Augustus. He shows a conscious pride in his position as the priest of the Muses, and his didactic odes have a graver and severer tone; yet he relieves his serious themes here, as in the other books, by lighter and charming verses nowhere excelled. The unity of the entire collection he emphasized by the form of his epilogue in which he repeats the lesser Asclepiadic measure used in the opening ode of the first book, but not elsewhere in the first three books. With proud assurance he claims that by his verse he has defeated death itself and won immortal fame.

8. The First Book of Epistles. — With the publication of his odes, in 23 B.C., Horace seems to have felt that his great work was done, and for some years he wrote no lyrics; he did, however, return to his earlier habit of recording in verse his observations on life and manners, *sermones*, which he now presented in the form of epistles. In some the epistolary form is only a cloak, but others are genuine letters, one a letter of introduction. Some offer a practical philosophy of life, others give rules of conduct, still others celebrate the delights of quiet country life, one is in praise of wine. The opening letter is to Maecenas, and announces Horace's intention to abandon poetry and devote himself to philosophy. The collection, twenty epistles in all, was published after the middle of 20 B.C.

9. The Carmen Saeculare and Fourth Book of Odes. — Horace was not allowed to desert the lyric muse. The death of Vergil in

19 B.C. left him the chief poet of his day, and even those who had long scoffed at the freedman's son were at last ready to acknowledge his preëminence. His position received official recognition in 17 B.C. from the Emperor, who commissioned him to write a hymn for the great Secular festival of that year. A little more than two years later, at the personal request of Augustus, he celebrated the victories of the young Neros, Tiberius and Claudius, over the Alpine tribes; in two other odes he sang the praises of the Emperor's beneficent rule. With these he joined eleven other lyrics, mostly reminiscent of his earlier themes; two of them, however, hymn the power of poesy. He published the collection in 13 B.C. It was not dedicated to Maecenas, as all his earlier publications had been; such dedication would have been out of place in a book the most important odes of which celebrated the imperial house. The significant fact is that, while Horace was ready to serve Augustus with his art, he did not dedicate the book to him. That his friendship with his patron was unbroken is abundantly proved by the eleventh ode in honor of Maecenas' birthday.

10. The Second Book of Epistles. — Soon after the publication of the first book of epistles, a young friend of Horace, Julius Florus, asked him for some new lyrics. In answer Horace wrote another epistle, in which he says that he has renounced lyric verse; he is too old for it; the distractions of the city prevent composition, and careful work is no longer appreciated; he will therefore devote himself to philosophy, and seek that golden mean which alone can bring happiness.

We hear from Suetonius that Augustus chided Horace for having failed to address any of his *sermones* to him. This reproach Horace could not neglect, and about 14 B.C. he wrote an epistle to the Emperor, in which he discussed popular taste in literary matters, and defended the modern school to which he belonged against those who had a blind admiration only for the ancient and ruder literature. These two epistles he united with a third addressed to the Pisones, father and two sons, naturally putting the letter to

Augustus in the first place, and published the three about 13 B.C. This third epistle is of uncertain date, but probably written about 19-17 B.C. It is a didactic treatise on the art of poetry, but deals chiefly with dramatic poetry, and with the qualifications — genius and hard work — essential for the poet. The common name, *Ars Poetica* (or *De Arte Poetica Liber*), in all probability was not given it by Horace, but became attached to it before Quintilian's day. By Hadrian's time the epistle had become separated from the two with which it was originally published, and formed the tenth book in an edition of which the four books of *Odes*, with the *Carmen Saeculare*, the *Epodes*, the two books of *Satires*, and two of *Epistles* were the first nine. In the Mss. it regularly follows the *Odes*; H. Stephanus in the sixteenth century restored it to its original position.

11. Chronological Table of Horace's Works. —

Satires, Book 1	35-34 B.C.
Epodes	30
Satires, Book 2	30
Odes, Books 1-3	23
Epistles, Book 1	20
Carmen Saeculare	17
Odes, Book 4	ca. 13
Epistles, Book 2	ca. 13

12. Last Years and Death. — Of the last years of Horace's life we know nothing. Maecenas died in the spring of 8 B.C.; his dying charge to the Emperor, *Horati Flacci ut mei esto memor*, bears witness to the unbroken friendship between the two men. Horace survived his patron but a few months, dying after a brief sickness at the close of the same year. He was buried near the tomb of Maecenas on the Esquiline.

13. Personal Characteristics. — Horace has left us at the close of his first book of *Epistles* an interesting description of himself at the age of forty-four : —

> *corporis exigui, praecanum, solibus aptum,
> irasci celerem, tamen ut placabilis essem.*

"Short in stature, prematurely gray, fond of the sun, quick to take offense, but readily appeased." This agrees with the account given in Suetonius' life, where we are told that the Emperor joked the poet on his short, stout figure. In Horace's later years his health was poor. While fond of mixing with society, he had a greater love for quiet country life, and against the protests of Maecenas spent much time on his Sabine farm or at his beloved Tibur. Praeneste, Baiae, and Tarentum were also favorite places of residence. He remained a bachelor, and was never deeply moved by love. Of all his flames named in his verses, only Cinara was certainly a creature of flesh and blood. The rest existed in his fancy only, or were borrowed from some Greek.[1] While he can sing very prettily of love, his verses have none of Catullus' fire; they were for Horace pretty works of art, but did not spring from his own passion. Likewise when he calls his friends to a carouse, we may be sure that temperance, not license, was the chief feature of his *comissatio*.

The subjects of his verse, whether lyric or *pedestris*, as he calls his muse in a passage in his *Satires*, were of the most varied sort; hardly a feature of the life about him was left untouched, and more proverbial sayings bearing on the ways and weaknesses of men have been drawn from Horace's works than from those of any other Latin writer. Certain aspects of nature appealed to him; and in a number of odes he shows the deepest interest in the welfare of the state. While he frequently shows a jovial spirit, yet there is, especially in the *Odes*, a melancholy that constantly reappears and overshadows his merrier moods. Many of his lyrics deal with death and the cheerless grave; and his philosophy of enjoyment and moderation has more in it of resignation than of eager anticipation. Horace does not show that pathetic melan-

---

[1] See Gildersleeve in *Am. Jour. of Phil.*, 18, 121 f.

choly which characterizes Vergil's poetry; his melancholy is personal, that of a sensitive individual, who has learned not to expect too much of this life, and has no hope beyond. Yet Horace avoids intruding his melancholy on his audience, as he shrinks from preaching, even in his most earnest moods.

The highest enthusiasms and deepest feelings were not given to Horace; but this very fact has in no slight degree made him a place in the affections of ordinary men, who feel that he is one of them.

14. Fame. — While Horace never gained among his contemporaries the honor enjoyed by Vergil, whose imperial epic appealed to the pride, as well as the imagination, of the Romans, still he lived to see himself pointed out by the passers on the street as the lyric poet of Rome, a fact to which he refers in *C.* 4, 3, 22 f., not without a touch of pride. Augustus' requests (cf. § 9), too, show the position in which Horace stood. Many lesser poets honored him as their master and model, but their verses have all disappeared; also the spurious works which Suetonius says were circulated under his name. His poems were early used in schools, certainly before Quintilian's day; in Juvenal's time, busts of Vergil and Horace adorned schoolrooms; so that for nearly nineteen centuries the works of Horace have formed part of liberal education in western Europe. Learned criticism and interpretation by grammarians began at least as early as Nero's reign. But the best proof of Horace's influence in antiquity is to be seen in the numerous reminiscences, conscious and unconscious, of his verses that are found in almost every Roman writer after him. In the commentary of this book only a few such reminiscences are quoted, but enough to suggest how constantly his phrases reappear in later writers. In fact no other Roman poet but Vergil influenced posterity to any like degree. Even in the period of readjustment, which we call the Middle Ages, the works of Horace were still read in schools, especially the *Satires* and *Epistles*, and verses of moral import were learned by heart; the *Odes* and *Epodes* were less used, and the *Carmen Saeculare* not unnaturally was almost entirely neglected.[1] Yet the number of Mss. earlier than the thirteenth century — nearly twenty date from the eighth, ninth, and tenth — attest the esteem in which all the works were held in mediaeval cloisters.

In the Renaissance and modern times Horace's popularity has been great. Over seventy editions, partial or complete, were printed before 1500. There have been many would-be imitators of Horace's lyric verse in the last four centuries, but no better proof of the perfection of his art can be found than in the marked inferiority of all attempts, both ancient and modern, to repeat his measures. It is not exaggeration to say that no one since Horace's day has written Latin Alcaics or Sapphics that deserve to be compared with their models. Naturally Horace's influence on modern writers of lyric verse has been marked. To illustrate this here is not possible, but there is hardly a lyricist who has not felt his spell. Among contemporary English writers, Austin Dobson's methods and verses remind us most of the Roman bard. Yet Horace's lasting popularity is attested, not so much by literature, as by the regard in which men of varied pursuits hold him. His wisdom, his moderation and good-humored satire, coined into perfect form, have won him an unique place in the affections of mankind.

15. Manuscripts, Scholia, and Editions. (*a*) **Mss.** — There are more good manuscripts of Horace preserved than of any other Latin writer except Vergil; they number about 250, dating from the eighth (or ninth) to the fifteenth century. All seem to come from a common early archetype, but the cross lines of tradition are so numerous that it is impossible to classify them satisfactorily. The most important are : —

(1) *Codex Blandinius Vetustissimus*. This manuscript was formerly in the Abbaye de St. Pierre on Mt. Blandin, near Ghent, but was burned when the Abbey was destroyed by fire in 1566. It was one of the four manuscripts borrowed from the monastery

---

[1] On Horace in the Middle Ages, see the interesting monograph by M. Manitius, *Analekten zur Geschichte des Horaz im Mittelalter*, Göttingen, 1893.

in 1565, and collated for his edition of Horace by Cruquius (Jacques de Crusque), professor at Bruges. He states in his edition of 1578 that this manuscript dated from the seventh century, and the readings which he gives from it show that, whatever its age, it was of prime importance for the text. Keller and Holder deny its very existence, and charge Cruquius with falsehood, but the evidence against them is such that we cannot doubt the existence and value of the codex. Cruquius was at times careless, but his account can in the main be accepted.

(2) *Codex Bernensis* 363, in the city library at Bern, Switzerland; written by an Irish scribe in the ninth century. The best single extant manuscript of Horace. Reproduced in photographic facsimile under the direction of De Vries, 1897.

(3) *Codex Sueco-Vaticanus* 1703, in the Vatican Library, written in the ninth century.

These two manuscripts are considered by Keller to be the most important; some claim high rank for others, especially *Parisinus* 7900 A, *s.* IX/X; *Parisini* 7974 and 7971, *s.* X; *Parisinus* 7972, *s.* IX/X, and *Leidensis* 28, *s.* X; but in establishing the text the readings of Cruquius' '*Vetustissimus*' are ordinarily of first importance.

For a description of the other manuscripts, reference may be made to the critical edition by Keller and Holder, 2 vols., Leipsic, 1864–1870; vol. 1 in 2d ed., 1899.

(*b*) **Scholia**. — Comment on the works of Horace began in the first century of our era, with brief introductory notes, giving in each case the name of the person addressed, the metre, and a brief notice of the contents and character of the poem. Under Nero, M. Valerius Probus prepared a critical edition of Horace's works. Among early commentators were also Modestus and Claranus, who flourished apparently in Domitian's reign; to the time of Hadrian belong the *Life*, by Suetonius, which is preserved in a fragmentary condition, and the edition in ten books (cf. p. 22), by Q. Terentius Scaurus. Under the Antonines, Helenius Acro wrote an explanatory commentary.

The work of all these commentators has been lost, save in so far as it is incorporated in the following scholia : —

(1) The scholia of *Pomponius Porphyrio*, a grammarian of the third century apparently, who devoted himself chiefly to grammatical and rhetorical interpretation.

(2) The scholia which bear the name of *Acro*. This collection was drawn from many sources, one of which was Porphyrio, from whom much was taken. Acro's name was not attached to these scholia until the fifteenth century.

(3) The scholia of the *Commentator Cruquianus*. These are the comments gathered together by Cruquius from many sources, and are of slight value.

(*c*) **Editions.** — The place and date of the *editio princeps* is unknown, but it was published in Italy before 1471. Bentley's edition in 1711 made a new era in Horatian criticism. Of the modern critical and explanatory editions, the following are important : —

Keller and Holder, *editio maior*, 2 vols. Leipsic, 1864-1870 ; vol. 1 (*Odes, Epodes, and C. S.*) in 2d ed. by Keller, Leipsic, 1899 ; *editio minor*, 1878. Keller, *Epilegomena zu Horaz*, Leipsic, 1879-1880, is also important for its collection of variant readings and discussion of them.

Orelli, 4th ed. by Hirschfelder and Mewes, 2 vols., with Latin commentary and complete word index, Berlin, 1886, 1892.

Kiessling, 2d ed., 3 vols. Berlin, 1890-1897 ; vol. 1 in 3d ed., 1898.

Wickham, *Odes and Epodes*, 3d ed. Oxford, 1896 ; *Satires and Epistles*, 1891.

L. Müller, *Satires and Epistles*, Leipsic, 1891-1893. *Odes and Epodes*, 1900.

The scholia are not yet fully available in good editions. A beginning has been made by Keller and Holder, *Porfyrionis commentum rec. A. Holder*. Innsbruck, 1894. The scholia of the Commentator Cruquianus are now best printed in Keller and Holder's large edition, vol. 1, 2d ed., pp. 343-370.

16. Translations and Important Books. — No classical author has been translated more often than Horace. Among the better complete translations of the *Odes* and *Epodes* into English are the following : —

SIR THEODORE MARTIN, *The Odes of Horace translated into English verse*, 2d ed., London, 1861.

JOHN CONINGTON, *The Odes and Carmen Saeculare of Horace*, 3d ed., London, 1865.

LORD LYTTON, *The Odes and Epodes of Horace*, London, 1869.

W. E. GLADSTONE, *The Odes of Horace translated into English*, New York, 1894.

C. W. COOPER, *Horace's Odes Englished and Imitated by Various Hands*, London, 1880.

Among books useful for criticism, interpretation, and illustration, the following may be named : —

W. Y. SELLAR, *Horace and the Elegiac Poets*, Oxford, 1892.

This is the most important single book in English on Horace.

J. W. MACKAIL, *Latin Literature*, pp. 106-119, New York, 1900.

This is a work of real genius, the best short history of Latin literature.

ANDREW LANG, *Letters to Dead Authors*, pp. 223-234, London, 1886.

GASTON BOISSIER, *The Country of Horace and Vergil;* translated by D. H. Fisher, London, 1896.

SCHREIBER-ANDERSON, *Atlas of Classical Antiquities*, London, 1895.

BAUMEISTER, *Denkmäler des klassischen Altertums*, 3 vols., Munich, 1889.

17. Language and Style. — Horace was well aware that his poetic genius was not great; but he possessed a highly cultivated sense for poetic form and fitting expression, and a fondness for his art, which led him to take infinite pains in the elaboration of his verses. With wise judgment he therefore chose commonplace themes and treated them with all the grace his taste and skill could give. He shows little deep thought or intense feeling; his verses are either exercises suggested by Greek lyrics, commonplaces of philosophy, Stoic or Epicurean, pretty but passionless treatment of themes of love, and society verse. Some tributes to friends show greater feeling, as do certain odes dealing with interests of state; yet in this latter class some seem like perfunctory verses written to please. In his later odes, in which he celebrates Augustus as the restorer of peace and prosperity, he exhibits a warmth of sentiment that he does not show elsewhere in the poems which concern the imperial house. Yet if his themes are commonplace, his treatment of them is so unapproachably felicitous that his phrases have become part of the world's vocabulary. Horace, therefore, deserves the high place he occupies in men's regard, not for his poetic inspiration, but because he has given beautiful and permanent expression to ordinary truths, which are of universal concern.

His vocabulary is not large, partly because the Latin language in comparison with the Greek is poor in words, partly because he chose to be restrained and moderate in statement; and the difficulty of using the Alcaic and Sapphic measures in Latin doubtless restricted the range of expression. He occasionally repeats a happy phrase, either exactly or with slight variation. His admiration for the Greeks never led him to violate the genius of his own language; he did not attempt long compounds, avoided Greek words for the most part, and seldom used a construction that was foreign to the Latin idiom.

The study of Horace's style, therefore, is chiefly concerned with the art with which he formed his phrases and fitted them to his measures. The following paragraphs deal briefly with the *Order of Words*, *Prosody*, *Metres*, and *Syntax*.

18. Order of Words. — An inflected language admits greater freedom in the arrangement of words than is possible in one which is uninflected, so that an idea is often held in suspense until it has been brought into relation with associated ideas. It is therefore necessary for the student to learn to carry in his mind incomplete ideas through groups of words of varying length. Such groups are common to both prose and poetry; but in prose they are usually brief, combinations of three words being most frequent, e.g. *ab exiguis profecta initiis*, although larger groups are not unknown. But in poetry the arrangement and grouping of words is much more highly developed. The following examples illustrate the more common arrangements in Horace's lyrics, which the student must train himself to grasp as units.

19. Groups of three words: —

   1, 1, 1 *atavis* edite *regibus*
   1, 15, 8 *regnum* Priami *vetus*
   1, 22, 22 *terra* domibus *negata*
   2, 5, 12 *purpureo* varius *colore*
   2, 7, 2 *Bruto* militiae *duce*

It should be noticed that in these groups the first and third words agree grammatically and inclose the word they modify; and that the places of adjective and noun are varied at pleasure. In the following larger groups the relation of the words is shown by varying type so far as possible.

20. Groups of four words may have the following great variety of arrangement: —

   2, 3, 9 *pinus ingens* **albaque populus**
   2, 6, 5 *Tibur* **Argeo** *positum* **colono**
   1, 24, 9 **multis** *ille* **bonis** *flebilis*
   1, 19, 11 f. **versis** *animosum* **equis** | *Parthum*
   2, 8, 11 f. **gelidaque** *divos* | **morte** *carentis*
   1, 1, 22 ad **aquae** *lene caput* **sacrae**
   1, 12, 22 f. **saevis** *inimica virgo* | **beluis**
   3, 8, 13 f. **cyathos** *amici* | *sospitis* **centum**
   4, 1, 4 f. **dulcium** | *mater saeva* **Cupidinum**

(a) Often a verb or verbs form part of the group, *e.g.:* —

   1, 1, 34 **Lesboum** *refugit tendere* **barbiton**
   1, 5, 9 te *fruitur credulus* **aurea**

21. Larger groups show more complicated structure: —

    1, 14, 14 f. nil **pictis** *timidus navita* **puppibus** | fidit
    1, 14, 19 f. *interfusa* **nitentis** | vites *aequora* **Cycladas**
    1, 22, 17 f. **pigris** ubi *nulla* **campis** | *arbor* **aestiva** recreatur **aura**
    1, 28, 19 f. **nullum** | *saeva* **caput** *Proserpina* fugit
    2, 3, 11 f. quid **obliquo** laborat | *lympha fugax* trepidare **rivo**?
    2, 4, 11 f. tradidit **fessis** *leviora* tolli | *Pergama* **Grais**.
    2, 11, 11 f. quid **aeternis** *minorem* | **consiliis** *animum* fatigas?
    2, 12, 2 f. nec *Siculum mare* | **Poeno** *purpureum* **sanguine**
    3, 1, 5 f. *regum timendorum* in **proprios greges** | **reges** in **ipsos** *imperium est Iovis*
    3, 1, 16 **omne** *capax* movet *urna* **nomen**
    3, 5, 21 f. vidi ego *civium* | *retorta* **tergo** *bracchia* **libero**

1, 9, 21 is an unusually complex group: —

    latentis *proditor* intimo | *gratus* **puellae** *risus* ab angulo.

Horace frequently employs position and arrangement to secure emphasis or other rhetorical effect.

22. Emphasis is obtained by placing the word to be emphasized at the beginning of a strophe or a verse, or before a caesura: —

    1, 18, 3 *siccis* omnia nam dura deus proposuit
    1, 34, 1 *parcus* deorum cultor et infrequens
    2, 9, 9 f. *tu* semper urges flebilibus modis | Mysten ademptum

23. Often the word in this position comes at or near the end of its sentence: —

    1, 28, 5 f. animoque rotundum | percurisse polum *morituro*
    2, 9, 15 ff. nec impubem parentes | Troilon aut Phrygiae sorores | *flevere semper*
    4, 9, 25 f. vixere fortes ante Agamemnona | *multi*

24. Often the words which agree grammatically are widely separated, gaining emphasis from their positions, and at the same time binding the sentence to which they belong into a single word group: —

    1, 1, 14 *Myrtoum* pavidus nauta secet *mare*
    1, 2, 39 f. acer et Marsi peditis *cruentum* | voltus in *hostem*

Also 3, 4, 9-12.

> *me fabulosae* Volture in Apulo
> nutricis extra limina Pulliae
> ludo fatigatumque somno
> fronde nova *puerum palumbes*

Observe that the entire strophe is bound into a single group by the two initial and final words.

25. Occasionally a number of emphatic positions are employed in a single strophe or other closely connected group : —

> 2, 10, 9 ff. *saepius* ventis agitatur *ingens*
> pinus et *celsae* || *graviore* casu
> decidunt turres feriuntque *summos*
> fulgura montis

26. Emphasis is also secured by placing contrasted words in juxtaposition : —

> 1, 6, 9   *tenues grandia*
> 1, 3, 10   qui *fragilem truci* commisit *pelago ratem*

27. Also by placing words in similar or opposite positions in the verse or strophe : —

> 1, 1, 9 f. illum si *proprio* || condidit *horreo* | quicquid de *Libycis* || verritur *areis*
> 1, 26, 2 f. tradam *protervis* || in mare Creticum | portare *ventis* ||
> 2, 2, 23   quisquis *ingentis* || oculo inretorto | spectat *acervos*.
> 2, 3, 1 f. aequam memento rebus *in arduis* | servare mentem, non secus *in bonis*
> 2, 10, 13 **sperat** *infestis* || **metuit** *secundis*

Also in 1, 10, where the initial *te, te, tu* of the second, third, and fifth strophe emphatically repeat the *Mercuri* of the first strophe. Cf. likewise 2, 9, 1.9.13.17 *non semper, tu semper, at non, flevere semper.*

28. Emphasis is further secured : —
(*a*) By immediate repetition in the same clause : —

> 2, 17, 10 *ibimus ibimus,* utcumque praecedes.
> Epod. 4, 20 *hoc hoc* tribuno militum.

(*b*) By immediate repetition at the beginning of a new clause (*anadiplosis*) : —

> 3, 16, 15 ff.　　　　　　　　　　subruit aemulos
> reges *muneribus;* ‖ *munera* navium
> saevos inlaqueant duces.

(*c*) By repetition at the beginning of successive clauses (*anaphora*), often with the added emphasis of position : —

> 1, 2, 4 ff.　*terruit* urbem,
> 　　　　　　*terruit* gentis, grave ne rediret
> 　　　　　　saeculum Pyrrhae

> 2, 4, 3 ff.　serva Briseis niveo colore
> 　　　　　　*movit* Achillem;
> 　　　　　　*movit* Aiacem Telamone natum

> 3, 3, 65 ff.　*ter* si resurgat murus aeneus
> 　　　　　　auctore Phoebo, *ter* pereat meis
> 　　　　　　excisus Argivis, *ter* uxor
> 　　　　　　capta virum puerosque ploret

Cf. also 1, 10, 1.5.9.17; 1, 12, 53.57-59; 1, 35, 5.6.9.17.21; 2, 9, 1.9.13.17.

29. Often the anaphora serves as a connective : —

> 1, 5, 9 f.　*qui* nunc te fruitur credulus aurea,
> 　　　　　*qui* semper vacuam

POSITION OF PRONOUNS, PREPOSITIONS, ETC.

30. Horace often makes his point by a reference to himself or his own experience, and introduces his concrete examples by *me*, etc., in an emphatic position : —

> 1, 1, 29 f.　*me* doctarum hederae praemia fontium
> 　　　　　　dis miscent superis, *me* gelidum nemus

> 1, 5, 13 f.　*me* tabula sacer | votiva paries indicat
> 1, 22, 9　　namque *me* silva lupus in Sabina

31. An important word or words may displace a relative or interrogative pronoun or a particle at the beginning of a clause : —

[§§ 31-37]   INTRODUCTION

    1, 2, 7   omne *cum* Proteus pecus egit
    1, 2, 18 f.   vagus *et* sinistra | labitur ripa
    1, 7, 15   albus *ut* ... deterget nubila ... Notus
    1, 22, 17   pigris *ubi* nulla campis | arbor aestiva recreatur aura
    1, 18, 3   siccis omnia *nam* dura deus
    2, 6, 6   sit meae sedes *utinam* senectae
    3, 1, 17 f.   destrictus ensis *cui* super impia | cervice pendet

Likewise *-que* may be forced from its natural position by the requirements of the metre: —

    2, 19, 32   ore pedes tetigit*que* crura

32. A dissyllabic preposition sometimes follows its noun: —

    3, 3, 11   quos *inter* Augustus recumbens

33. Sometimes the preposition is placed next the verb: —

    2, 16, 33   te greges centum Siculaeque *circum* | mugiunt vaccae
    3, 27, 51 f.   utinam *inter* errem | nuda leones

PROSODY

The following points in the prosody of Horace's lyrics should be noted: —

34. The prosody of certain proper names varies: *Ētrusco* 1, 2, 14; 3, 29, 35, *Ĕtrusca Epod.* 16, 4 and 40; *Dīanam* 1, 21, 1, *Dīana* 3, 4, 71; *Prōserpina* 1, 28, 20, *Prŏserpina* 2, 13, 21; *Ōrionis* 1, 28, 21, *Ŏrion Epod.* 15, 7; *Ītalos* 3, 30, 13, *Ĭtalo* 2, 7, 4; *Āpūliae Epod.* 3, 16, *Ăpŭli* 2, 42 and usually.

35. The final syllable of the present and perfect indicative active in the thesis occasionally retains its archaic long quantity in Books 1–3: *perrupīt* 1, 3, 36; *manēt* 1, 13, 6; *ridēt* 2, 6, 14; *timēt* 2, 13, 16; *arāt* 3, 16, 26; *figīt* 3, 24, 5. It is once long in the arsis before the caesura 3, 5, 17 *perirēt* ‖ *immiserabilis*.

36. In *Epod.* 9, 17 *vertĕrunt* occurs, but elsewhere in the lyrics the third person plural of the perfect indicative always ends in *-ērunt*.

37. A final syllable ending in a short vowel is not made long by two consonants at the beginning of the next word.

38. Synizesis occurs in *anteit* 1, 35, 17; *antehac* 1, 37, 5; *Pompei* 2, 7, 5; *vietis Epod.* 12, 7; *dehinc Epod.* 16, 65; probably also in *pueris* 2, 18, 34 (cf. § 56); *laqueo Epod.* 2, 35 (cf. § 58); *inferius* 5, 79; *mulierculum* 11, 23 (cf. § 58).

39. Hardening of vocalic i to a consonant is found in *consilium* 3, 4, 41 and *principium* 3, 6, 6. In both these cases the final syllable is elided.

40. Syncope occurs frequently in the perfect indicative forms. Also in *puertiae* 1, 36, 8; *lamnae* 2, 2, 2; *periclo* 3, 20, 1; *surpuerat* 4, 13, 20; *repostum Epod.* 9, 1; *vincla* 9, 9 and 17, 72. Possibly in *pav(i)dum Epod.* 2, 35 and *pos(i)tos* 2, 65 (cf. § 58).

41. Dialysis occurs only in *siluae* 1, 23, 4 and *Epod.* 13, 2.

42. Elision is confined chiefly to short syllables; in his earliest lyrics Horace apparently tried to avoid it altogether, but later he was less careful. There is no elision in the Second Archilochian Strophe of *Epod.* 13 or in the hexameters of *Epod.* 16. With the exception of *me*, *te*, and a single case of *iam*, *Epod.* 17, 1, monosyllables are never elided.

43. Hiatus is found after the monosyllabic interjections *o* and *a*, which naturally cannot be elided. Also in *capiti inhumato* 1, 28, 24, *Esquilinae alites Epod.* 5, 100, *Threicio Aquilone* 13, 3; and between the *cola* of Dactylo-Trochaic verses (cf. § 64 ff.). Also in *male ominatis* 3, 14, 11, if the reading be correct.

METRES

44. Logaoedic Verses. — The greater number of the *Odes* are in logaoedic rhythms, consisting of trochees $(-\smile)$, irrational spondees $(->)$, and cyclic dactyls $(\smile\smile\smile \text{ or } -\smile\smile)$.[1] The mu-

---

[1] Elementary Latin prosody and the lyric metres of Horace are satisfactorily treated in the school grammars commonly used. A brief account is given here solely for convenience, and no attempt is made to provide the elementary knowledge which must be gained from the grammars. One point, however, may be noted. The common method of marking an irrational spondee $(->)$ leads pupils to think that it is not to be distinguished from a trochee,

[§§ 44-48]

sical time is ⅜. While Horace adopted his measures from the Greeks, he is more strict than his models in certain points. He always uses an irrational spondee in place of a trochee before the first cyclic dactyl ($->|\smile\smile$, and not $-\smile|\smile\smile$); and if an apparent choriambus $\smile\smile|\llcorner$ [1] is followed by a second apparent choriambus in the same verse, the caesura regularly separates the two.

The following logaoedic verses are used by Horace:

45. The *Adonic*:

$$\angle\smile\,|\,\angle\,\smile$$
terruit | urbem
(This may also be read $\angle\smile\,|\,\angle\,|\,\angle_\wedge$)

46. The *Aristophanic*:

$$\angle\smile\,|\,\angle\,\smile\,|\,\angle\,>$$
Lydia | dic per | omnes
(This may also be read $\angle\smile\,|\,\angle\,\smile\,|\,\angle\,|\,\angle_\wedge$)

47. The *Pherecratic* (read as a syncopated tetrapody catalectic):

$$\angle\,>|\;\angle\smile\;\smile\,|\,\angle,\angle_\wedge$$
grato | Pyrrha sub | an|tro

48. The *Glyconic*:

$$\angle\,>|\;\angle\smile\smile|\,\angle\;\smile|\angle_\wedge$$
sic te | diva potens Cy|pri

i.e. that both equal ♩♩; whereas the irrational spondee must be represented in musical notation by ♩·♩·. Furthermore the musical equivalent of the cyclic dactyl, as commonly expressed, $\smile\smile$ = ♩·♩♩, is hardly correct; it should rather be ♩·♩·♩·. In the schemes as here given the form $\smile\smile$ is used when the caesura does not fall within the foot or falls between the two short syllables, $\smile\|\smile$; when the caesura occurs after the long syllable the foot is written $-\|\smile\smile$.

[1] This combination was regarded by the later Roman writers as a choriambus, $-\smile\smile-$, and many still give the name 'choriambic' to metres in which this succession of syllables occurs.

49. The *Lesser* (decasyllabic) *Alcaic*:

$$\acute{-}\cup\,|\,\acute{-}\,\cup\,|\acute{-}\,\cup\,|\acute{-}>$$
flumina | constite|rint a|cuto

50. The *Greater* (hendecasyllabic) *Alcaic*:

$$\check{\,}\,\colon\acute{-}\,\cup\,|\acute{-}>\,\|\,\acute{-}\cup\,|\acute{-}\,\cup\,|\acute{\cup}_\wedge$$
per:mitte | divis || cetera | qui si|mul

In Books 1–3 the anacrusis is usually long; in Book 4 always so. In 1, 37, 14; 4, 14, 17 diaeresis is neglected; caesura occurs after a prefix in 1, 16, 21 *ex*||*ercitus;* 1, 37, 5 *de*||*promere;* 2, 17, 21 *in*||*credibili*.

51. The *Lesser Sapphic*:

$$\acute{-}\,\cup|\acute{-}\,>|\acute{-}\,\|\,\cup\cup\,|\acute{-}\,\cup|\acute{-}>$$
iam sa|tis ter|ris || nivis | atque | dirae

In Books 1–3 the masculine caesura is regularly used; in the *Carmen Saeculare* and Book 4 the feminine caesura is more frequently allowed, *e.g.*:

$$\acute{-}\,\cup\,|\acute{-}>|\,\acute{-}\cup\,\|\cup|\acute{-}\,\cup|\acute{-}>$$
Phoebe | silva|rumque || po|tens Di|anae

52. The *Greater Sapphic*:

$$\acute{-}\,\cup|\acute{-}>|\acute{-}\,\|\,\cup|\acute{-}\,\|\,-\,\,\cup|\acute{-}\cup|\acute{-}>$$
te de|os o ro Syba|rin || cur prope|res a|mando.

Or we may write the second half of the verse as a syncopated tetrapody catalectic:

$$\|\,\acute{-}\cup\cup\,|\,\acute{-}\,\cup\,|\,\acute{-}\,|\,\acute{\cup}_\wedge$$

It should be observed that this corresponds with the Aristophanic verse (cf. 46).

53. The *Lesser Asclepiadic*:

$$\acute{-}\,>\,\acute{-}\,\cup\,|\acute{-}\,\|\,\acute{-}\cup\cup\,|\,\acute{-}\cup|\acute{\cup}_\wedge$$
Maece nas ata vis || edite | regi bus

C. 1, 1; 3, 30; 4, 8.

In 4, 8, 17, caesura is disregarded, but the text is in doubt; in 2, 12, 25 caesura occurs after the prefix in *de torquet*.

§§ 54-56] INTRODUCTION

54. The *Greater Asclepiadic*:

$$\overset{\angle}{}\;>\;|\;\overset{\angle}{\smile}\;\smile\;|\overset{\angle}{}\;\|\;\overset{\angle}{\smile}\;\smile\;|\overset{\angle}{}\;\|\;\overset{\angle}{\smile}\;\smile\;|\overset{\angle}{}\;\smile\;|\overset{\angle}{\smile}\;{}_\wedge$$
Nullam | Vare sa|cra ‖ vite pri|us ‖ severis | arbo|rem.

C. 1, 11, 18; 4, 10.

It should be observed that this differs from the preceding rhythm (53) in having a syncopated dipody ‖ $\overset{\angle}{\smile}\;\smile\;|\overset{\angle}{}$ | inserted between the two tripodies. In 1, 18, 16, caesura occurs after the prefix in *per‖lucidior*.

Iambic and Trochaic Verses. — The following iambic and trochaic verses are used by Horace:

55. The *Iambic Dimeter*:

$$\overset{\times}{}\;\overset{\angle}{}\;\smile\;\overset{\angle}{}\;|\;\overset{\times}{}\;\overset{\angle}{}\;\smile\;\overset{\angle}{}$$
$$>\;\overset{\angle}{\smile}\;\smile\;\smile\;\overset{\angle}{\smile}\;\smile\;|$$

Or in anacrustic form :[1]

$$\overset{\times}{}\;:\;\overset{\angle}{}\;\smile\;\overset{\angle}{}\;\overset{\times}{}\;|\;\overset{\angle}{}\;\smile\;\overset{\angle}{}\;{}_\wedge$$

The irrational spondee may be substituted in the first and third feet. Resolution of the thesis is found in four verses (*Epod.* 2, 62; 3, 8; 5, 48; 15, 24), and then is limited to the first foot for the apparent dactyl, $>\;\smile\;\smile$; while tribrachs may be used in the first two feet, *e.g.*:

$$>\overset{\angle}{}\smile\overset{\angle}{}|\;>\;\|\overset{\angle}{}\smile\smile$$
Oblivio | nem sensibus Epod. 14, 2.

$$\smile\overset{\angle}{}\smile\smile\smile|\;>\overset{\angle}{}\;\smile\;\smile$$
videre prope·rantis domum Epod. 2, 62.

$$>\overset{\angle}{\smile}\smile\smile\overset{\angle}{}|\;>\;\|\overset{\angle}{}\smile\overset{\angle}{}$$
ast ego vicis|sim risero Epod. 15, 24.

56. The *Iambic Trimeter Catalectic*:

$$\overset{\times}{}\;\overset{\angle}{}\;\smile\;\overset{\angle}{}|\overset{\times}{}\;\|\overset{\angle}{}\;\smile\;\overset{\angle}{}|\smile\overset{\angle}{}\;-{}_\wedge$$
trahuntque sic·cas ‖ machinae | carinas.

Or with anacrusis :

$$\overset{\times}{}\;:\;\overset{\angle}{}\;\smile\;\overset{\angle}{}\;\overset{\times}{}\;\|\overset{\angle}{}\;\smile\;\overset{\angle}{}\;\smile\;|\overset{\angle}{}\;\overset{\angle}{}\;{}_\wedge$$

---

[1] Whenever iambic verses occur in logaoedic or composite rhythms, they are to be written with anacrusis.

In C. 2, 18, 34 possibly resolution occurs in the second foot *regumque pueris*, > ⏑ ⏑ ⏑ —, unless, as is probable, we should read by synizesis, *pueris* (cf. 38).

57. The *Pure Iambic Trimeter*: —

⏑ — ⏑ — | ⏑ ‖ — ⏑ — ⏑ — | ⏑ — ⏑ —
suis et ip|sa ‖ Roma vi|ribus ruit

58. The *Iambic Trimeter* (with substitutions and resolutions): —

⏓ — ⏑ — | ⏓ ‖ — ⏑ — | ⏓ — ⏑ —
⏑ ⏑ ⏑ ⏑ ⏑ ⏑ | ⏑ ‖ ⏑ ⏑ ⏑ ⏑ ⏑ |
> ⏑ ⏑   > ‖ ⏑ ⏑
⏑ ⏑ —   ⏑ ⏑ —

Epod. 17. The caesura occurs after the prefix in *im ‖ plumibus*, *Epod.* 1, 19; and *in ‖ aestuet*, *Epod.* 11, 15. The irrational spondee is not infrequently substituted in the first, third, and fifth feet; the tribrach is used chiefly in the second and third feet, rarely in the first and fourth; the dactyl is found in the first foot, rarely in the third; and the anapaest is possibly to be read in the first foot twice (*Epod.* 2, 35 *pavidum*, 65 *positos*) and three times in the fifth (*Epod.* 2, 35 *laqueo*, 5, 79 *inferius*, 11, 23 *mulierculum*); yet some of these cases may be read by synizesis as iambs (cf. 38).

Examples of trimeters with various substitutions: —

⏑ — ⏑ — | > ‖ — ⏑ — | ⏑ — ⏑ ⏑
per et Dia|nae ‖ non moven|da numina

> — ⏑ ⏑ ⏑ | > ‖ — ⏑ ⏑ ⏑ | > — ⏑ ⏑
vectabor hume|ris ‖ tunc ego ini|micis eques.

> — ⏑ ⏑ — | ⏑ ‖ — ⏑ — | > — ⏑ —
Canidia par|ce ‖ vocibus | tandem sacris

> — ⏑ — | > ‖ — ⏑ ⏑ — | > — ⏑ ⏑
optat quie|tem ‖ Pelopis in|fidi pater.

⏑ ⏑ — ⏑ ⏑ ⏑ | ⏑ ‖ — ⏑ — | ⏑ ⏑ — ⏑ ⏑
pavidumque lepo|rem et ‖ advenam | laqueo gruem,

⏑ — ⏑ —
or *pav(i)dumque, laqueo* (cf. 38, 40).

§§ 59-65]   INTRODUCTION

59. The *Euripidean*: —

$$\text{× } - \cup - \cup\,|\,- \cup \cup \wedge$$
non ebur ne|que aureum

60. The *Nine-syllable Alcaic*: —

$$\times\,:\,-\,\cup\,|\,-\,>\,|\,-\,\cup\,|\,-\,\cup$$
sil|vae la|boran|tes ge|luque

This consists of two trochaic dipodies with anacrusis. The second foot is always irrational.

Dactylic Verses.

61. The *Lesser Archilochian*: —

$$-\cup\cup\,|\,-\cup\cup\,|\,-\wedge$$
arbori|busque co|mae

62. The *Dactylic Tetrameter catalectic*: —

$$-\overline{\cup\cup}\,|\,-\overline{\cup\cup}\,|\,-\cup\cup\,|\,-\cup\wedge$$
saeva ca|put Pro|serpina | fugit

In C. 1, 28, 2 a spondee is found in the third foot.

63. The *Dactylic Hexameter*: —

$$-\overline{\cup\cup}\,|\,-\overline{\cup\cup}\,|\,-\,\|\,\overline{\cup\cup}\,|\,-\overline{\cup\cup}\,|\,-\overline{\cup\cup}\,|\,-\,\smile$$

The feminine caesura in the third foot is occasionally found, and the masculine caesura sometimes falls in the fourth or second foot. The four cases of spondees in the fifth foot are due to proper names (*C.* 1, 28, 21; *Epod.* 13, 9; 16, 17 and 29).

Dactylo-trochaic Verses.

64. In these the *cola*, rhythmical sentences, are separate; so that the verses are compound, having a change of time ($\frac{3}{4}$ to $\frac{2}{4}$, or *vice versa*) within them. Syllaba anceps is allowed at the end of the first colon in the *Iambelegus* and *Elegiambus*.

65. The *Greater Archilochian* (a dactylic tetrameter acatalectic + a trochaic tripody): —

$$-\overline{\cup\cup}\,|\,-\,\overline{\cup\cup}\,-\,\|\,\overline{\cup\cup}\,-\,\cup\cup\,\|\,-\,\cup\,|\,-\,\cup\,|\,->$$
solvitur | acris hiems|| gra ta vice || veris | et Favoni.

The caesura is found regularly after the third thesis, and a diaeresis after the dactylic colon. The fourth foot is always a dactyl.

66. The *Iambelegus* (a trochaic dimeter catalectic with anacrusis + a lesser archilochian) : —

$$\text{≍}:\overset{\prime}{-}\cup\mid\overset{\prime}{-}\ \ \text{≍}\mid\overset{\prime}{-}\ \cup\mid\underset{\smile}{\prime}\parallel\overset{\prime}{-}\cup\cup\mid-\ \cup\ \cup\mid\overset{\prime}{-}\wedge$$
tu:vina | Torqua|to mo|ve ‖ consule | pressa me|o.

No substitutions but those indicated are allowed in the first colon; and spondees are not allowed in the second.

67. The *Elegiambus* (the cola of the Iambelegus reversed) : —

$$\overset{\prime}{-}\cup\cup\mid\overset{\prime}{-}\cup\cup\mid-\underset{\wedge}{\ }\parallel\text{≍}:\overset{\prime}{-}\cup\mid\overset{\prime}{-}\ \text{≍}\mid\overset{\prime}{-}\ \ \cup\mid\overset{\prime}{-}\wedge$$
scribere | versicu.los ‖ a:more | percus|sum gra|vi.

STROPHES

Most of the *Odes* are arranged in stanzas or strophes of four verses each; in a few the distich or the single verse is the metrical unit. In the *Epodes*, with the exception of the seventeenth, which is written in iambic trimeters, the epodic distich (cf. 4) is the unit.

The lyric strophes used by Horace are these: —

68. The *Alcaic Strophe* — two Greater Alcaics (50), one Nine-syllable Alcaic (60), and a Lesser Alcaic (49) : —

$$\begin{array}{ll} \text{≍}:\overset{\prime}{-}\cup\mid\overset{\prime}{-}>\parallel\overset{\prime}{\smile}\cup\mid\overset{\prime}{-}\cup\mid\underset{\smile}{\prime}\wedge & \text{1-2} \\ \text{≍}:\overset{\prime}{-}\cup\mid\overset{\prime}{-}>\mid\overset{\prime}{-}\cup\mid\overset{\prime}{-}\text{≍} & 3 \\ \overset{\prime}{\smile}\cup\mid\overset{\prime}{\smile}\cup\mid\overset{\prime}{-}\cup\mid\overset{\prime}{-}\text{≍} & 4 \end{array}$$

This strophe is the most frequent; found in *C.* 1, 9. 16. 17. 26. 27. 29. 31. 34. 35. 37; 2, 1. 3. 5. 7. 9. 11. 13. 14. 15. 17. 19. 20; 3, 1–6. 17. 21. 23. 26. 29; 4, 4. 9. 14. 15. In 2, 3, 27 and 3, 29, 35 there is elision at the end of the third verse.

69. The *Sapphic Strophe* — three Lesser Sapphics (51), and an Adonic (45) : —

$$-\cup\,|\,-\,>\,|\,-\,\|\,\smile\,|\,-\cup\,|\,-\,\times \quad \text{1-3}$$
$$-\cup\,|\,-\,\times \quad \text{4}$$

After the Alcaic the most frequent strophe; found in *C.* 1, 2. 10. 12. 20. 22. 25. 30. 32. 38; 2, 2. 4. 6. 8. 10. 16; 3, 8. 11. 14. 18. 20. 22. 27; 4, 2. 6. 11; *C. S.* The feminine caesura is found in a few cases (cf. 51). In a number of strophes Horace follows Sappho in treating the third and fourth verses as one, so that in three places (*C.* 1, 2, 19; 1, 25, 11; 2, 16, 7) words run over from one verse to the next as now printed; elision at the end of the third verse is found, 4, 2, 23 and *C. S.* 47; hiatus between the verses occurs but four times (*C.* 1, 2, 47; 1, 12, 7 and 31; 1, 22, 15); and in most cases the dactyl of the fourth verse is preceded by a spondee at the close of the third.

Elision occurs three times also at the end of the second verse (*C.* 2, 2, 18; 2, 16, 34; 4, 2, 22).

70. The *Greater Sapphic Strophe* — an Aristophanic verse (46) followed by a Greater Sapphic (52) : —

$$-\cup\,|\,-\cup\,|\,-\,\times$$
$$-\cup\,|\,-\,>\,|\,-\,\|\,\smile\,|\,-\,\|\,-\cup\,|\,-\cup\,|\,-\,>$$
C. 1, 8.

71. The *First Asclepiadic Strophe* — a Glyconic (48) followed by a Lesser Asclepiadic (53) : —

$$-\,>\,|\,-\cup\,\cup\,|\,-\,\cup\,|\,\overset{\smile}{-}_\wedge$$
$$-\,>\,|\,-\cup\,\cup\,|\,-\,\|\,-\cup\,\cup\,|\,-\,\cup\,|\,\overset{\smile}{-}_\wedge$$

C. 1, 3. 13. 19. 36; 3, 9. 15. 19. 24. 25. 28; 4, 1. 3. Elision at the end of the Glyconic is found 4, 1, 35.

72. The *Second Asclepiadic Strophe*—three Lesser Asclepiadics followed by a Glyconic:—

$$\text{—} > | \text{—} \cup \cup | \text{—} | \text{—} \cup \cup | \text{—} \cup | \text{—}_\wedge \quad 1\text{–}3$$
$$\text{—} > | \text{—} \cup \cup | \text{—} \cup | \text{—}_\wedge \quad 4$$

C. 1, 6. 15. 24. 33; 2, 12; 3, 10. 16; 4, 5. 12.

73. The *Third Asclepiadic Strophe*—two Lesser Asclepiadics, a Pherecratic (47), and a Glyconic:—

$$\text{—} > | \text{—} \cup \cup | \text{—} \| \text{—} \cup \cup | \text{—} \cup | \text{—}_\wedge \quad 1\text{–}2$$
$$\text{—} > | \text{—} \cup \cup | \text{—} | \text{—}_\wedge \quad 3$$
$$\text{—} > | \text{—} \cup \cup | \text{—} \cup | \text{—}_\wedge \quad 4$$

C. 1, 5. 14. 21. 23; 3, 7. 13; 4, 13.

74. The *Iambic Strophe*—an Iambic Trimeter (58) followed by an Iambic Dimeter (55):—

$$\cup \text{—} \cup \text{—} | \cup \| \text{—} \cup \text{—} | \cup \text{—} \cup \text{—}$$
$$\cup \text{—} \cup \text{—} | \cup \text{—} \cup \text{—}$$

Epod. 1–10.

75. The *First Pythiambic Strophe*—a Dactylic Hexameter (63) followed by an Iambic Dimeter (55):—

$$\text{—} \cup \cup | \text{—} \cup \cup | \text{—} \| \cup \cup | \text{—} \cup \cup | \text{—} \cup \cup | \text{—} \smile$$
$$\cup \text{—} \cup \text{—} | \cup \text{—} \cup \text{—}$$

Epod. 14 and 15.

76. The *Second Pythiambic Strophe*—a Dactylic Hexameter followed by a Pure Iambic Trimeter:—

$$\text{—} \cup \cup | \text{—} \cup \cup | \text{—} \| \cup \cup | \text{—} \cup \cup | \text{—} \cup \cup | \text{—} \smile$$
$$\cup \text{—} \cup \text{—} | \cup \text{—} \cup \text{—} | \cup \text{—} \cup \text{—}$$

Epod. 16.

77. The *Alcmanian Strophe*—a Dactylic Hexameter followed by a Dactylic Tetrameter (62):—

$$\text{—} \cup \cup | \text{—} \cup \cup | \text{—} \| \cup \cup | \text{—} \cup \cup | \text{—} \cup \cup | \text{—} \smile$$
$$\text{—} \cup \cup | \text{—} \cup \cup | \text{—} \cup \cup | \text{—} \smile$$

C. 1, 7. 28; *Epod.* 12.

78. The *First Archilochian Strophe* — a Dactylic Hexameter followed by a Lesser Archilochian (61) : —

$$-\cup\cup\,|\,-\cup\cup\,|\,-\,\|\,\cup\cup\,|\,-\cup\cup\,|\,-\cup\cup\,|\,-\,\vee$$
$$-\cup\cup\,|\,-\cup\cup\,|\,\stackrel{\cup}{-}\,\overline{\wedge}$$

C. 4, 7.

79. The *Second Archilochian Strophe* — a Dactylic Hexameter followed by an Iambelegus (66) : —

$$-\cup\cup\,|\,-\cup\cup\,|\,-\,\|\,\cup\cup\,|\,-\cup\cup\,|\,-\cup\cup\,|\,-\,\vee$$
$$\stackrel{\vee}{:}\,-\cup\,|\,-\stackrel{\vee}{\,}\,|\,-\cup\,|\,\stackrel{\cup}{-}\,_{\wedge}\|\,-\cup\cup\,|\,-\cup\cup\,|\,\stackrel{\cup}{-}\,\overline{\wedge}$$

Epod. 13.

80. The *Third Archilochian Strophe* — an Iambic Trimeter followed by an Elegiambus (67) : —

$$\stackrel{\vee}{\,}-\cup\,-\,|\,\stackrel{\vee}{\,}\,\|\,-\,\cup\,-\,|\,\stackrel{\vee}{\,}\,-\,\stackrel{\cup}{\,}$$
$$-\cup\cup\,|\,-\cup\cup\,|\,\stackrel{\cup}{-}\,_{\wedge}\|\,\stackrel{\vee}{:}\,-\cup\,|\,-\stackrel{\vee}{\,}\,|\,-\cup\,|\,\stackrel{\cup}{-}\,_{\wedge}$$

Epod. 11.

81. The *Fourth Archilochian Strophe* — a Greater Archilochian (65) followed by an Iambic Trimeter Catalectic (56) : —

$$-\cup\cup\,|\,-\cup\cup\,|\,-\,\|\,\cup\cup\,|\,-\cup\cup\,\|\,-\cup\,|\,-\cup\,|\,-\,\vee$$
$$\stackrel{\vee}{:}\,-\cup\,-\,\stackrel{\vee}{\,}\,|\,-\cup\,-\cup\,|\,\stackrel{\cup}{-}\,\stackrel{\cup}{\,}$$

C. 1, 4.

82. The *Trochaic Strophe* — a Euripidean (59) followed by an Iambic Trimeter Catalectic : —

$$-\cup\,-\cup\,|\,-\cup\,\stackrel{\cup}{-}\,_{\wedge}$$
$$\stackrel{\vee}{:}\,-\cup\,-\,\stackrel{\vee}{\,}\,\|\,-\cup\,-\cup\,|\,\stackrel{\sqsubset\,\cup}{-}\,_{\wedge}$$

C. 2, 18.

83. The *Ionic System* — pure *Ionici a minore*, $\cup\cup--$, in verses of ten feet : —

$$\cup\cup--|\cup\cup--|\cup\cup--|\cup\cup--|\cup\cup--$$
$$\cup\cup--|\cup\cup--|\cup\cup--|\cup\cup--|\cup\cup--\,.$$

C. 3, 12. Diaeresis occurs at the end of most feet.

SYNTAX

The following paragraphs deal briefly with the constructions in the lyrics of Horace, which depart most from prose usage.

THE ACCUSATIVE

84. The perfect passive participle is used as a middle with a direct object, sometimes accompanied by an instrumental ablative: 1, 1, 21 *membra . . . stratus,* 'stretching his limbs.' 1, 2, 31 *nube candentis umeros amictus,* 'wrapping thy shining shoulders in a cloud.' 3, 8, 5 *doctus sermones,* 'learned in the lore.'

85. The common prose use of the accusative neuter of adjectives of number or amount is extended to other adjectives which express the manner of the action: 1, 22, 23 *dulce ridentem, dulce loquentem,* 'sweetly smiling, sweetly prattling.'

86. The object accusative is used with many verbs which were ordinarily intransitive before Horace's time: 2, 13, 26 ff. *sonantem . . . plectro dura navis, dura fugae mala, dura belli,* 'sounding with his plectrum the hardships of the sea, the cruel hardships of exile, the hardships of war.' 4, 12, 5 *Ityn flebiliter gemens,* 'sadly mourning Itys.' 4, 13, 19 *spirabat amores,* 'breathed forth love.' *Epod.* 14, 11 *flevit amorem,* 'wept his love.'

THE DATIVE

87. The dative of agent is used with the perfect participle: 1, 32, 5 *barbite Lesbio modulate civi,* 'lyre tuned by Lesbian citizen.' Also with verbs expressing feeling or perception: 1, 1, 24 f. *bella matribus detestata,* 'wars which mothers hate.' Rarely with present passives: as 3, 25, 3 f. *quibus antris audiar?* 'by what grottoes shall I be heard?'

88. The dative of place, as well as of person, is used to denote the direction of motion: 4, 4, 69 f. *Carthagini iam non ego nuntios*

[§§ 88-94]   INTRODUCTION

mittam superbos, 'no longer shall I send proud messengers to Carthage.' Cf. 1, 24, 15 *num vanae redeat sanguis imagini?* 'would the blood return to the empty shade?'

89. The dative is also used with verbs expressing union, comparison, difference, etc.: 1, 1, 15 *luctantem Icariis fluctibus Africum,* 'the Afric struggling with the Icarian waves.' 1, 1, 30 *me . . . dis miscent superis,* 'make me one with the gods above.' 1, 24, 18 *nigro compulerit gregi,* 'has gathered to his dark flock.'

THE GENITIVE

90. An adjective is often modified by a partitive genitive: 1, 10, 19 *superis deorum,* equivalent to *superis deis* in prose. 1, 9. 14 *quem fors dierum cumque dabit,* equivalent to *quemcumque diem.*

91. In imitation of a Greek construction, a genitive is used modifying a neuter plural adjective: 2, 1, 23 *cuncta terrarum,* 'all the world.'

92. The objective genitive is used with a larger number of adjectives than in prose: 1, 3, 1 *diva potens Cypri,* 'goddess that ruleth Cyprus.' 1, 34, 2 f. *insanientis sapientiae consultus,* 'adept in a mad philosophy.' 2, 6, 7 *lasso maris et viarum,* 'weary of journeys by sea and land.' 3, 27, 10 *imbrium divina avis,* 'bird prophetic of storms.' 4, 6, 43 *docilis modorum,* 'taught the strains of.'

93. In a few cases the genitive of 'specification' is used: 2, 22, 1 *integer vitae,* 'pure in life.' 3, 5, 42 *capitis minor,* 'inferior as an individual' = 'deprived of civil rights.' And once 2, 2, 6 the genitive is almost causal: *notus animi paterni,* 'known for his paternal spirit.'

94. The objective genitive is used with verbs of ceasing, wanting, etc., in imitation of the Greek construction: 2, 9, 18 *desine querellarum,* 'cease thy plaints.' 3, 17, 16 *famulis operum solutis,*

'the servants freed from toil.' 3, 27, 69 *abstineto irarum*, 'give up thy wrath.'

THE ABLATIVE

The simple ablative, without a preposition, is used somewhat more freely than in prose.

95. The simple ablative is used to express the place where an action occurs: 1, 2, 9 *summa haesit ulmo*, 'clung in the top of the elm.' 1, 9, 10 f. *ventos aequore fervido deproeliantis*, 'winds struggling over the yeasty deep.' 1, 32, 8 *religarat litore navim*, 'anchored his ships off the shore,' also belongs here.

96. Once in the *Odes* the ablative of agent is used without a preposition: 1, 6, 1 f. *scriberis Vario . . . Maeonii carminis alite*, 'thou shalt be sung by Varius, that bird of Maeonian song.' With this we may compare *Epist.* 1, 19, 2 *carmina, quae scribuntur aquae potoribus*, 'verses written by teetotalers,' although most editors and grammarians regard *potoribus* as dative of agent. While the phrase *Vario . . . alite* approaches the ablative absolute, the difference between it and such cases as *S.* 2, 1, 84 *iudice laudatus Caesare* must not be overlooked.

97. The instrumental ablative is found once with a verbal noun: 3, 4, 55 *truncis iaculator*, 'he who threw trunks of trees.'

98. With *muto* and a direct object the ablative is used to denote both that which is given and that which is received in exchange; the context alone shows the relation: 1, 17, 1 f. *Lucretilem mutat Lycaeo*, 'exchanges Lycaeus for Lucretilis.' The opposite 1, 16, 25 f. *ego mitibus mutare quaero tristia*, 'I seek to substitute kind feelings for bitterness.'

'TRANSFERRED' ADJECTIVES

99. An adjective which naturally expresses some quality of a person or thing is sometimes transferred to an object or action which is associated with that person or thing: 1, 3, 38 ff. *neque | per nostrum patimur scelus | iracunda Iovem ponere fulmina;* 1, 15, 33 f. *iracunda . . . classis Achillei.*

THE ἀπὸ κοινοῦ CONSTRUCTION

100. Occasionally a word is so placed with reference to two other words that it may grammatically be connected with either, while logically it is necessarily so connected: 2, 11, 11 f. *quid aeternis minorem | consiliis animum fatigas?* In this *consiliis* belongs equally to *minorem* and to *fatigas*.

THE VERB

101. A singular verb is frequently used with two or more subjects: 3, 16, 29 ff. *rivus aquae silvaque . . . segetis certa fides . . . fallit.*

102. The future indicative is occasionally used with permissive or hortatory force: 1, 7, 1 *laudabunt alii claram Rhodon*, 'others may praise,' etc.; 1, 12, 57 ff. *te minor latum reget aequus orbem*, etc., 'let him rule,' etc.

103. The perfect is used like the Greek gnomic aorist, to express what has always been true or customary, *i.e.* a general truth or customary action: 1, 28, 20 *nullum saeva caput Proserpina fūgit*, 'cruel Proserpina never passes by (*i.e.* never has, and therefore, by implication, never does pass) a mortal.'

PROHIBITIONS

104. Horace occasionally employs the archaic form of prohibition, consisting of the imperative with *ne:* 1, 28, 23 *ne parce harenae*, 'spare not the sand.'

Occasionally a circumlocution is employed: 1, 9, 13 *fuge quaerere*, 'avoid asking'; 1, 38, 3 *mitte sectari*, 'give up hunting.'

INFINITIVE

105. The 'historical' infinitive is found but once in the *Epodes*, not in the *Odes: Epod.* 5, 84 *puer iam non . . . lenire verbis impias*, 'the boy no longer tries to move the wretches by words.'

106. The 'exclamatory' infinitive is found but twice in the *Epodes*, not in the *Odes: Epod.* 8, 1 *rogare te*, etc., 'the idea of your asking!' 11, 11 f. *contrane lucrum nil valere candidum | pauperis ingenium?* 'to think that against mere gold the purity of a poor man's character has no power!'

107. The infinitive of purpose is found occasionally: 1, 2, 7 f. *pecus egit altos | visere montis*, 'he drove the flock to visit the high mountains'; 1, 12, 2 *quem sumis celebrare?* 'whom dost thou take to celebrate in song?' 1, 26, 1 ff. *tristitiam et metus | tradam protervis in mare Creticum | portare ventis*, 'gloom and fear will I give to the bold winds to carry to the Cretan sea'; *Epod.* 16, 16 *malis carere quaeritis laboribus*, 'you seek to escape,' etc.

108. The infinitive is used with a large variety of adjectives to complete their meaning: 1, 3, 25 *audax omnia perpeti*, 'with courage to endure all'; 1, 10, 7 *callidum . . . condere*, 'skilled to hide'; 1, 15, 18 *celerem sequi*, 'swift in pursuit'; 1, 35, 2 *praesens . . . tollere*, 'with power to raise'; 3, 21, 22 *segnes nodum solvere*, 'slow to undo the knot'; 4, 12, 19 *spes donare novas largus*, 'generous in giving new hope'; etc.

109. The passive infinitive is also used as a verbal noun in the ablative: 1, 19, 8 *lubricus adspici*, 'dazzling;' 4, 2, 59 *niveus videri*, 'white in appearance.'

THE PARTICIPLE

110. The future active participle is often used to express purpose, readiness or ability, and prophecy, being equivalent to a clause: 1, 35, 29 *iturum Caesarem*, 'Caesar, who proposes to go'; 2, 6, 1 *Septimi, Gadis aditure mecum*, 'Septimius, thou who art ready,' etc.; 4, 3, 20 *O mutis quoque piscibus donatura cycni . . . sonum*, 'O thou who couldst give,' etc.; 2, 3, 4 *moriture Delli*, 'Dellius, who art doomed to die.'

THE VALLEYS OF THE
ANIO AND THE DIGENTIA

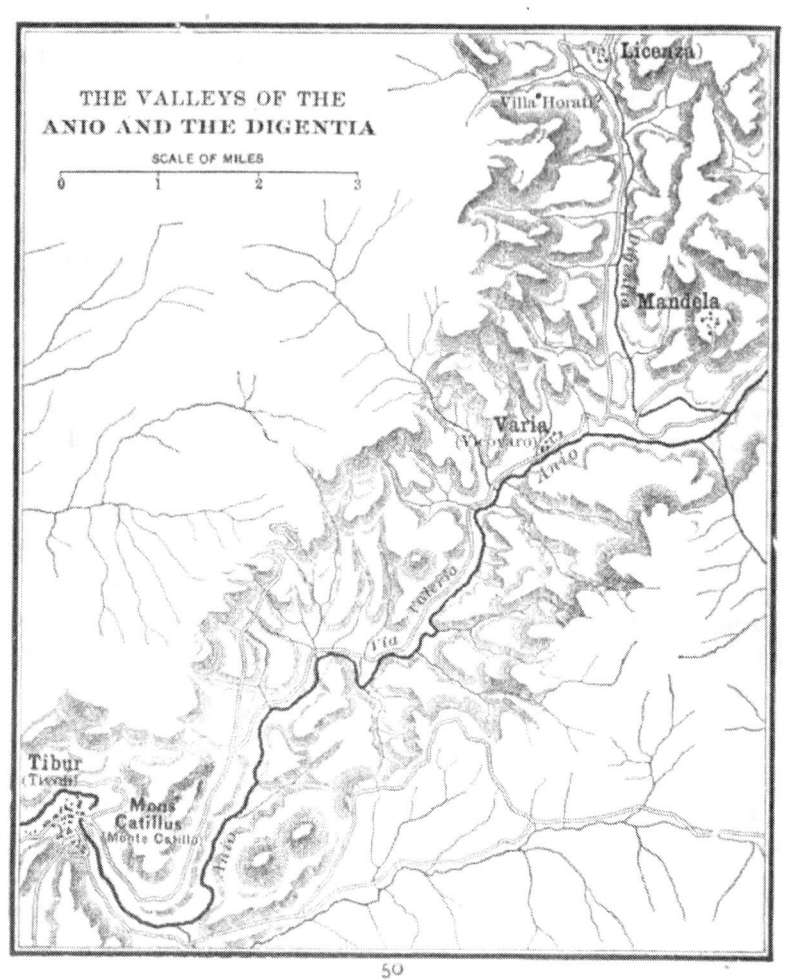

HORATI CARMINA

LIBER PRIMVS

I

This ode forms the prologue to the three books of lyrics published by Horace in 23 B.C. After the first two lines addressed to Maecenas, which virtually dedicate the whole collection to him, Horace rehearses the various interests of men, that at the end he may present his own ambition. 'Some men seek fame in athletic games or in politics (3-8), others have lower aims — riches, ease, war, or hunting (9-28) ; but as for me, I have the loftiest aim of all, Maecenas — to wear the ivy wreath and be the Muse's dear companion (29-34).' The ode was clearly written after the collection was fairly complete; that is, not long before the actual publication. Metre, 53.

Maecenas atavis edite regibus,
o et praesidium et dulce decus meum:

1. **Maecenas**: for Maecenas' position at Rome and Horace's relations with him, see Intr. 5. — **atavis**: *ancestors*, in a general sense, in apposition with **regibus**. — **edite regibus**: Maecenas was descended from an ancient line of princes of the Etruscan city of Arretium. Horace and his contemporaries emphasize the contrast between their patron's noble birth and the equestrian rank he preferred to keep at Rome. Cf. 3, 16, 20 *Maecenas, equitum decus* and note; 3, 29, 1 *Tyrrhena regum progenies*; S. 1, 6, 1 ff.; Prop. 4, 9, 1 *Maecenas, eques Etrusco de sanguine regum*. This habit is referred to by Martial 12, 4, 1 f. *quod Flacco Varioque fuit summoque Maroni | Maecenas atavis regibus ortus eques.*

2. **o et**: monosyllabic interjections are ordinarily not elided. Intr. 42. — **praesidium . . . decus**: not merely a formal compliment, for there is a warmth in the second half of the expression that is com-

Sunt quos curriculo pulverem Olympicum
collegisse iuvat metaque fervidis
5 evitata rotis, palmaque nobilis
terrarum dominos evehit ad deos;
hunc, si mobilium turba Quiritium

parable to the feeling expressed in *Epod*. 1. Cf. the more formal phrase 2, 17, 3 f. *Maecenas, mearum | grande decus columenque rerum*; also *Epist*. 1, 1, 103 *rerum tutela mearum*. Vergil makes a similar acknowledgment of his obligation, *G*. 2, 40 f. *o decus, o famae merito pars maxuma nostrae, | Maecenas*. Horace's phrase proved a striking one and is frequently adopted by later writers.

3 ff. Note how Horace secures variety in the expressions by which he designates the various classes: **sunt quos, hunc, illum**, etc. He has also arranged his typical examples with care, contrasting one aim in life with the other, and in each case bringing out the point which would be criticised by one not interested in that particular pursuit.

— **sunt quos ... iuvat**: equivalent to **aliquos iuvat**. Cf. v. 19 **est qui**. The indicative with this phrase defines the class, rather than gives its characteristics. — **curriculo**: from *curriculus, chariot*. — **Olympicum**: *i.e.* at the great games held every four years at Olympia in Elis. Yet Horace probably uses the adjective simply to make his statement concrete. Cf. note to v. 13. He is speaking here of athletic contests in general.

4. **collegisse**: *to have raised in a cloud*. Cf. *S*. 1, 4, 31 *pulvis collectus turbine*. — **meta**: the turning post at the end of the *spina*, which was the barrier that ran through the middle of the circus, and round which the horses raced. See Schreiber-Anderson's Atlas, pl. 31, 1 and 2, for illustrations of the race course.

5. **evitata**: *just grazed*. The skill of the charioteer was shown in making as close a turn as possible about the *meta* without meeting disaster. — **palmaque**: equivalent to **quosque palma**. The palm, which was the regular prize for the Olympic victor from the time of Alexander, was adopted by the Romans about 293 B.C. Livy 10, 47, 3 *translato e Graecia more*. — **nobilis**: with active meaning, modifying **palma**, *the ennobling*.

6. **dominos**: in apposition with **deos**. The victory exalts the victors to heaven, where dwell the rulers of the world. Cf. 4, 2, 17 f. *quos Elea domum reducit | palma caelestis*.

7 ff. Political ambition. — **hunc**: sc. *iuvat*. — **mobilium**: *fickle*; cf.

certat tergeminis tollere honoribus;
illum, si proprio condidit horreo
10   quicquid de Libycis verritur areis.
Gaudentem patrios findere sarculo
agros Attalicis condicionibus
numquam demoveas, ut trabe Cypria
Myrtoum pavidus nauta secet mare;

Epist. 1, 19, 37 *ventosa plebs.* —
tergeminis: the three necessary steps in the republican *cursus honorum*, the curule aedileship, praetorship, and consulship.

9 f. **proprio**: with **quicquid**, referring to the avarice which is frequently connected with great wealth. For the expression, cf. 3, 16, 26 f. *si quicquid arat impiger Apulus | occultare meis dicerer horreis.* — **Libycis**: Africa, especially the fertile district of *Byzacium* about Utica and Hadrumetum, was at this time the granary of Rome; later, Egypt became the most important source of supply.

11 ff. A modest establishment, in contrast to a great estate in Africa.—**patrios**: in this word there is a suggestion of contentment and calm security. as in *Epod.* 2, 3 *paterna rura.* This security is again contrasted with the vicissitudes and perils of the sailor.—**sarculo**: a hoe used for stirring and loosening the soil. It suggests the small farm that Horace has in mind, too small to make it worth while to use a plow. — **Attalicis condicionibus**: *with the terms a prince could offer; regiis opibus,* says Porphyrio. The Attali, kings of Pergamon, were famous for their wealth. In 133 B.C. King Attalus III, at his death, bequeathed his kingdom, with his treasures, to the Romans. This lent to his name the glamour of wealth which we associate with the name of Croesus.

13. **demoveas**: potential subj., — *you could never allure.*— **trabe**: *bark.* The part is used for the whole. Cf. Verg. *A.* 3, 191 *vela damus vastumque cava trabe currimus aequor;* Catull. 4, 3 *natantis impetum trabis.* — **Cypria**: Horace regularly employs a particular rather than a general adjective. thereby making his expressions more concrete and his pictures more vivid—a device learned from the Alexandrine poets. So we have in the following verse **Myrtoum**, 15 **Icariis**, 19 **Massici**, 28 **Marsus**; and often.

14. **pavidus**: especially applicable to the landsman turned sailor. —**secet mare**: a common figure from Homer's day. Cf. *Od.* 3, 173 ff. αὐτὰρ ὅ γ᾽ ἡμῖν | δεῖξε, καὶ ἠνώγει πέλαγος μέσον εἰς Εὔβοιαν τέμνειν.

15   luctantem Icariis fluctibus Africum
      mercator metuens otium et oppidi
      laudat rura sui : mox reficit ratis
      quassas, indocilis pauperiem pati.
      Est qui nec veteris pocula Massici
20   nec partem solido demere de die
      spernit, nunc viridi membra sub arbuto
      stratus, nunc ad aquae lene caput sacrae.
      Multos castra iuvant et lituo tubae
      permixtus sonitus bellaque matribus
25   detestata.   Manet sub Iove frigido

15 ff. Against the struggles of the sea, the trader sets the peaceful quiet of his native country town; yet it has this roseate hue for him only when he is in the midst of danger.

16 f. oppidi rura: 'the country districts surrounding the village in which he was born.' — mox: his fear quickly passes, and he returns to his old pursuit of money getting.

18. pauperiem: *a life of small estate*; not to be confused with *egestas* or *inopia*. Cf. I, 12, 43 f. *saeva paupertas et avitus apto | cum lare fundus*, also Sen. *Epist.* 87, 40 *non video quid aliud sit paupertas quam parvi possessio.* — pati: with indocilis. Intr. 108.

19 ff. Between the merchant (15-18) and the soldier (23-25) is inserted an example of the man who gives himself over to a life of ease and enjoyment, to cups of good old wine and the noonday siesta. — Massici: a choice wine from Mt. Massicus, on the southern border of Latium. — solido ... die: *uninterrupted, unbroken; i.e.* for such strenuous men as the merchant or the soldier, who give their days to trade or arms. Cf. Sen. *Epist.* 83, 3 *hodiernus dies solidus est: nemo ex illo quicquam mihi eripuit.*

21 f. stratus: a middle participle, — *stretching his limbs*, etc. Intr. 84. — sacrae: for the fountain heads of streams were the homes of the water divinities. Cf. Sen. *Epist.* 41, 3, *magnorum fluminum capita veneramur, ... coluntur aquarum calentium fontes.*

24 ff. matribus: dat. with detestata; *abhorred*. Cf. *Epod.* 16. 8 *parentibusque abominatus Hannibal.* — manet: equivalent to *pernoctat.* — sub Iove: *under the sky.* Jupiter is often used by the poets for the phenomena of the sky. Cf. Enn. *Epich. Frg.* 6 M. *Istic est is Iúpiter quem dico; quem Graecì vocant | áerem, qui véntus est et núbes, imber póstea | átque ex imbre*

venator tenerae coniugis immemor,
seu visa est catulis cerva fidelibus,
seu rupit teretis Marsus aper plagas.
Me doctarum hederae praemia frontium
dis miscent superis; me gelidum nemus
Nympharumque leves cum Satyris chori
secernunt populo, si neque tibias
Euterpe cohibet nec Polyhymnia
Lesboum refugit tendere barbiton.
Quod si me lyricis vatibus inseres,
sublimi feriam sidera vertice.

frigus, ventus póst fit, aer dénuo.
— **tenerae**: *young.*

28. teretis: *stout, close twisted.*

29. me: note the emphatic position of this word here and in the following verse. Against the background of other men's aims, Horace now places his own ambition. — **doctarum ... frontium**: *i.e.* of poets, the σοφοὶ ἀοιδοί, taught by the Muses. — **hederae**: sacred to Bacchus, on whose protection and favor the poets depend. Cf. *Epist.* 1, 3, 25 *prima feres hederae victricis praemia*, and Verg. *E.* 7, 25 *pastores, hedera nascentem ornate poetam.*

30. miscent: *make me one with.* Cf. Pind. *Isth.* 2, 28 f. Ὀλυμπίου Διὸς | ἄλσος · ἵν' ἀθανάτοις Αἰνησιδάμου | παῖδες ἐν τιμαῖς ἐμείχθεν.

32 f. secernunt: *set apart.* The poet must rise superior to common folk and common things to fulfill his sacred office. — **Euterpe ... Polyhymnia**: Horace follows the Greeks of the classical period in not ascribing to each muse a special department of literature or learning.

34. Lesboum: Lesbos was the home of Alcaeus and Sappho, Horace's chief models among the earlier Greek lyricists.

35 f. vatibus: applied to poets as inspired bards. Horace may mean specifically the nine great lyric poets of Greece. **vates** was the earliest word for poet among the Romans, but was displaced by the Greek *poeta* until the Augustan period. Cf. Verg. *A.* 6, 662 *quique pii vates et Phoebo digna locuti.* — **sublimi feriam**, etc.: a proverbial expression from the Greek τῇ κεφαλῇ ψαύειν τοῦ οὐρανοῦ. Cf. Ovid *Met.* 7, 61 *vertice sidera tangam*, and Ausonius' imitation of Horace, 3, 5, 52 P. *tunc tangam vertice caelum.* Also Herrick's 'knock at a star with my exalted head,' and Tennyson's lines, *Epilogue*, 'Old Horace? "I will strike," said he, | "The stars with head sublime."'

2

'We have been terrified enough with snow and hail, with lightning and with flood, portents that show Heaven's wrath and threaten ruin to our impious state. What god will come and save us? Apollo? Venus? Mars? or Mercury? Aye, thou art already here. Remain long among us, enjoy triumphs, the name of father and of chief; check and punish the Medes, divine leader Caesar.'

While the first ode of the collection dedicates the poems to Maecenas, the second is a declaration of loyalty and devotion to the emperor. The first six strophes review the portents that followed on the murder of Julius Caesar. Cf. Porphyrio's comment on the opening words, — *post occisum C. Caesarem, quem Cassius et Brutus aliique coniurati interfecerunt, multa portenta sunt visa. Haec autem omnia vult videri in ultionem occisi principis facta et poenam eorum, qui bella civilia agere non desinebant.* With v. 25 Horace turns from the sins of the Romans to the means of help. The following three strophes call on Apollo, Venus, and Mars in turn to save their people. Finally, v. 41 ff., Horace appeals to Mercury, who has taken on an earthly form, that of the emperor. The ode culminates with v. 49 ff., the direct appeal to Octavian; but the identification of Octavian with Mercury is not fully announced until the last word of the ode.

The choice of the gods invoked was undoubtedly determined by the subject of the ode. Apollo was the patron divinity of the Julian gens; his first and only temple at Rome to the time of the one built by Augustus was dedicated in 431 B.C., by Cn. Julius (Livy 4, 29); the members of the gens sacrificed to him at Bovillae, according to an ancient rite, *lege Albana* (*C.I.L.* 1, 807), and Octavian believed that the god had especially favored him at the battle of Actium. Cf. Prop. 5, 6, 27 ff., *cum Phoebus linquens stantem se vindice Delon | . . . adstitit Augusti puppim super et nova flamma | luxit in obliquam ter sinuato facem.* Verg. *A.* 8, 704, *Actius haec cernens arcum intendebat Apollo.* Venus, *mater Aeneadum,* as *genetrix* was the especial protectress of Julius Caesar. Augustus is himself called (*C. S.* 50), *clarus Anchisae Venerisque sanguis.* Mars is naturally appealed to as the father of Romulus' people. The final identification of the emperor is especially interesting, for it bears on the social and economic relations of the times. Under Octavian, with the restoration of peace, trade improved and prosperity returned, so that nothing could be more natural than to regard the man who was bringing this about as the incarnation of the god of trade.

The Pompeian dedicatory inscriptions quoted by Kiessling admirably

CARMINA [1, 2, 6

illustrate the growth of this identification, at least in the Campanian city. In three of these records (*C.I.L.* 10, 885-887), he first two of which can be dated 14 B.C., the persons attached to the cult of Mercury are called *ministri Mercurii Maiae;* then no. 888, of uncertain date, has *ministri Augusti Mercuri Maiae;* and finally nos. 890-910, beginning with 2 B.C., have only *ministri Augusti.* Later, the conception of Augustus as identical with Apollo prevailed.

The date of composition falls between the return of Octavian from the East in 29 B.C. (cf. v. 49, *magnos — triumphos*) and Jan. 13th, 27 B C., when his imperium was renewed, and he received the new title, Augustus. The most probable date is late in 28 B.C., when Octavian's suggestion of giving up his power (Dio C. 53, 4, 9) may well have awakened fears of the return of civil strife. Metre, 69.

> Iam satis terris nivis atque dirae
> grandinis misit pater, et rubente
> dextera sacras iaculatus arcis
>   terruit urbem,
>
> 5   terruit gentis, grave ne rediret
> saeculum Pyrrhae nova monstra questae,

1 ff. the repetition of -is is striking and may suggest the hiss of the storm. Cf. *Il.* 21, 239, κρύπτων ἐν δίνῃσι βαθείῃσιν μεγάλῃσι. Snow and hail are not unknown at Rome in winter, but an especially severe storm might well pass for a portent. — dirae: *portentous*, with both nivis and grandinis, marking them as *prodigia*. The word is especially used of things of bad omen. — pater: used absolutely, *the all-father.* Cf. 3, 29, 43 ff. *cras vel atra | nube polum pater occupato | vel sole puro.* — rubente dextera: *his red right hand; i.e.* glowing with the thunderbolt. Cf. Pind. *O.* 9, 6 Δία . . . φοινικοστερόπαν.

3. iaculatus: transitive, *striking at.* — arcis: specifically the two heights of the Capitoline hill, on the northern one of which was the arx proper, on the southern the temple of Jupiter Capitolinus; hence sacras. However, Horace may mean in general the summits of Rome's seven hills. Cf. Verg. *G.* 2, 535 *septemque una sibi muro circumdedit arces.*

4 f. terruit . . . terruit: note the anaphora by which the sentences are connected. Cf. 2, 4, 3 ff. *serva Briseis niveo colore | movit Achillem; | movit Aiacem.* Intr. 29. — gentis: *mankind.*

6. saeculum Pyrrhae: *i.e.* the deluge from which Pyrrha with

omne cum Proteus pecus egit altos
visere montis,

piscium et summa genus haesit ulmo,
nota quae sedes fuerat columbis,
et superiecto pavidae natarunt
aequore dammae.

Vidimus flavum Tiberim retortis
litore Etrusco violenter undis

her husband Deucalion alone escaped to repeople the earth. For the story see Ovid *Met.* 1, 260 ff. — nova: new, and therefore *strange*.

7. omne: *of every sort*. — Proteus: the shepherd of the sea who tends Neptune's flocks. Cf. Verg. *G.* 4, 395 *armenta et turpis pascit sub gurgite phocas*.

8. visere: infinitive of purpose. Intr. 107. Cf. 1, 26, 1 ff. *tristitiam et metus | tradam protervis in mare Creticum | portare ventis*.

9. summa ulmo: cf. Ovid *Met.* 1, 296 *hic summa piscem deprendit in ulmo*. The description may have been suggested by Archilochus *Frg.* 74, 6 ff. μηδεὶς ἔθ' ὑμῶν εἰσορῶν θαυμαζέτω, | μηδ' ὅταν δελφῖσι θῆρες ἀνταμείψωνται νομόν | ἐνάλιον καί σφιν θαλάσσης ἠχέεντα κύματα | φίλτερ' ἠπείρου γένηται, 'No one among you should ever be surprised at what he sees, not even when the wild beasts take from the dolphins a home in the sea and the echoing waves of the deep become dearer to them than the firm mainland.'

11 f. superiecto: sc. *terris*; *the whelming flood*.

13 f. vidimus: *i.e.* with our own eyes, in the period between Caesar's murder and the date of writing. — flavum: the fixed epithet of the Tiber. Cf. 1, 8, 8 *cur timet flavum Tiberim tangere*, and 2, 3, 18 *villaque, flavus quam Tiberis lavit*; also Verg. *A.* 7, 31 *multa flavus arena*. It has been adopted by the modern poets. — retortis ... undis: a glance at the map of Rome will show that the bend in the river above the island would naturally throw the Tiber's stream, in time of flood, over the Velabrum between the Capitol and Palatine, and thence into the Forum proper. — litore: abl. of separation. litus is frequently equivalent to *ripa*; *e.g.* Virg. *A.* 8, 83 *viridique in litore conspicitur sus*. The popular belief, however, seems to have been, that such floods were caused by waves or tides driving back the waters of the river. Cf. Ovid *Fast.* 6, 401 f. *hoc, ubi nunc fora*

15   ire deiectum monumenta regis
          templaque Vestae,

      Iliae dum se nimium querenti
      iactat ultorem, vagus et sinistra
      labitur ripa Iove non probante u-
20   xorius amnis.

sunt, udae tenuere paludes, | amne redundatis fossa madebat aquis.

15 f. **deiectum**: supine of purpose. — **monumenta regis**: the Regia, the official residence of the pontifex maximus, built according to tradition by Numa. Cf. Ovid *Fasti* 6, 263 f. *hic locus exiguus, qui sustinet atria Vestae, | tunc erat intonsi regia magna Numae,* and Plut. *Numa* 14, ἐδείματο πλησίον τοῦ τῆς Ἑστίας ἱεροῦ τὴν καλουμένην Ῥηγίαν. — **templaque Vestae**: at the foot of the Palatine. For an account of the temple and of the house of the Vestal Virgins, the atrium Vestae, see Lanciani, 'Ancient Rome in the Light of Recent Discoveries,' p. 134 ff. The foundations of this temple are only twenty-six feet above the mean level of the Tiber. That the ancient accounts of the flooding of the Forum are not exaggerated was shown by the flood of December, 1900, which rose quite as high as the one Horace describes. There is an especial significance in the mention of the Regia and the temple of Vesta, for they were both connected with the most ancient and sacred traditions of the Romans. Within the temple of Vesta were the *pignora imperii* on whose preservation, it was believed, the Roman empire's existence depended. With the plurals **monumenta** and **templa**, cf. 3, 27, 75 *tua nomina* for *nomen.*

17. **Iliae**: the mother of the twins Romulus and Remus. Horace here, as in 3, 3, 32, according to Porphyrio, follows the older tradition represented by Ennius. This made Ilia the daughter of Aeneas and sister of Iulus, from whom the Julii derived their line. After the birth of the twins she was thrown into the Tiber in punishment for her infidelity to her Vestal vows, but was saved by the river god and became his wife. — **nimium**: with **ultorem**; the river is over eager to avenge his bride's complaints. Cf. **uxorius**, below.

19 f. **ripa**: ablative denoting the route taken, *over the bank.* But cf. *Epod.* 2, 25 *ripis, between the banks.* — **u|xorius**: Intr. 69. Horace here follows the example of Sappho, who frequently treated the third and fourth verses of this strophe as one, e.g. *Frg.* 2. 3 f. ἄδυ φωνεύ || σας ὑπακούει; 11 f.

Audiet civis acuisse ferrum,
quo graves Persae melius perirent,
audiet pugnas vitio parentum
  rara iuventus.

25 Quem vocet divum populus ruentis
imperi rebus? Prece qua fatigent
virgines sanctae minus audientem
  carmina Vestam?

ἐπιρρόμ || βεισι δ' ἄκουαι. Other examples in Horace are 1, 25, 11 *inter* || *lunia*; 2, 16, 7 *ve* || *nale*. In the third and fourth books this is avoided. For the careful arrangement of the words in 18–20, see Intr. 21.

21-24. Civil strife with its disastrous results: 'the second generation will hear with wonder the story of their fathers' wanton wickedness.' Notice that the strophe forms a single group of words that must be understood as a whole. Intr. 24. By the suspension of the subject of the principal verbs until the end, Horace produces a highly dramatic effect.

— civis: in the sense of fellow citizens, 'that citizens sharpened sword against citizens.' — graves Persae: the troublesome enemies of the Romans. Crassus' disaster at Carrhae was still unavenged, and the Roman standards had not yet been returned. — perirent: imperfect subj. of unfulfilled obligation, *ought rather to have perished.*

23 f. vitio parentum rara iuventus: the civil wars of 48–31 B.C. cost so many lives that Italy did not recover its population for many generations, if indeed it ever did. Cf. Verg. *G.* 1, 507 f. *squalent abductis arva colonis* | *et curvae rigidum falces conflantur in ensem*; also Lucan 7, 398 f. *crimen civile videmus* | *tot vacuas urbes*, and 535 ff. A modern parallel is the depopulation of France by the Napoleonic wars.

25 ff. Horace now turns from the portents sent by the gods, outraged at the nation's crime, to seek for some divine aid; for against divine wrath human resources are of no avail. — ruentis: *rushing to ruin.* This strong word is a favorite with Horace. Cf. *Epod.* 7, 1 *quo, quo scelesti ruitis* and n. — rebus: dat. with vocet, *call to aid.* — fatigent: *importune.*

27. minus audientem: a euphemistic phrase. Vesta turns a deaf ear to the supplicating prayers (carmina) of the Virgins, for she is offended at the murder of Caesar, the pontifex maximus, who

Cui dabit partis scelus expiandi
30 Iuppiter? Tandem venias, precamur,
nube candentis umeros amictus,
    augur Apollo;

sive tu mavis, Erycina ridens,
quam Iocus circum volat et Cupido;
35 sive neglectum genus et nepotes
    respicis, auctor,

heu nimis longo satiate ludo,
quem iuvat clamor galeaeque leves
acer et Marsi peditis cruentum
40   voltus in hostem;

had charge of her worship. Cf. Ovid *Fast.* 3, 698 f. *meus fuit ille sacerdos. | sacrilegae telis me petiere manus.* With minus intimating a negative, cf. *Epod.* 5, 61 f. *minus | venena Medea valent;* and the similar use of *male* 1, 9, 24 *male pertinaci.*

29. partis: equivalent to *munus*, a technical word corresponding to our 'part' in play, 'role,' etc. — scelus: the sin of fratricide.

30. tandem: 'since prayers have so long been of no avail.' Cf. neglectum genus, v. 35 below. —precamur: parenthetical; venias is grammatically independent of it.

31 f. nube ... numeros amictus: the Homeric νεφέλῃ εἰλυμένος ὤμους, *Il.* 5, 186; for the construction of a middle participle with the acc., cf. 1, 22 *stratus.* Intr. 84. —Apollo: for the sig-

nificance of Apollo here, see introductory note to this ode.

33 f. sive tu mavis: sc. *venias.* —Erycina ridens: *laughing* (φιλομμειδής) *queen of Eryx.*— Iocus: *Mirth*, the Greek Κῶμος, with Cupido the regular companion of Venus. Cf. Plaut. *Bacch.* 113 *Amór, Volúptas, Vénus, Venústas, Gaúdium, Iócus, Lúdus.*—circum: postpositive. Intr. 33.

35 f. neglectum: cf. n. to v. 30. — auctor: the appeal is to Mars as the author of the Roman race.

37. ludo: 'the cruel sport of war.' Cf. 2, 1, 3 *ludumque Fortunae.*

38 ff. For the skillful arrangement of the words, see Intr. 21, 24. —clamor: *the battle shout.*— lēves: *smooth.*— Marsi: the Marsi were a mountain folk living in central Italy, east of Rome. They were noted for their bravery. Cf. Verg. *G.* 2, 167 *genus acre virum,*

sive mutata iuvenem figura
ales in terris imitaris almae
filius Maiae, patiens vocari
 Caesaris ultor,

45 serus in caelum redeas diuque
laetus intersis populo Quirini,
neve te nostris vitiis iniquum
 ocior aura

tollat; hic magnos potius triumphos,
50 hic ames dici pater atque princeps,

Marsos. Appian, *B. C.* 1, 46 has the proverb οὔτε κατὰ Μάρσων οὔτε ἄνευ Μάρσων γενέσθαι θρίαμβον.

41. **mutata . . . figura**: *i.e.* 'putting off the divine for a human figure.' — **iuvenem**: this word gives the first hint of the point toward which Horace has been working, that is, that Octavian is a god come down to save the state.

42. **imitaris**: *dost take on the form of.*

43 f. **vocari**: dependent on **patiens**. Intr. 108. — **Caesaris ultor**: Octavian declared his chief object in life to be the punishment of Caesar's murderers. Suet. *Aug.* 10 *nihil convenientius ducens quam necem avunculi vindicare. Mon. Anc.* 1, 9 *qui parentem meum interfecerunt, eos in exilium expuli iudiciis legitimis ultus eorum facinus et postea bellum inferentis rei publicae vici bis acie,* and also Ovid *Fast.* 3, 709 f. *hoc opus, haec pietas, haec prima elementa fuerunt | Caesaris, ulcisci iusta per arma patrem.*

45 f. This possibly gained especial significance from Octavian's sickness in 28 B.C. Some years later Ovid offered a similar prayer, *Met.* 15, 868 ff. *tarda sit illa dies et nostro serior aevo, | qua caput Augustum, quem temperat, orbe relicto | accedat caelo.*

47. **vitiis**: modifying **iniquum**.

49. **triumphos**: *i.e.* new and greater triumphs than the three celebrated in 29 B.C. Cf. Suet. *Aug.* 22 *triumphos tris egit, Delmaticum, Actiacum, Alexandrinum, continuo triduo omnes.* A triumph over the troublesome Orientals (v. 51) was at this time especially desired.

50. **pater atque princeps**: not official designations, but titles of reverence and loyalty. — **pater** as divine protector, cf. 1, 18, 6 *Bacche pater;* **princeps** as the first citizen.

neu sinas Medos equitare inultos
te duce, Caesar.

Augustus was officially named *pater patriae* in 2 B.C.

51. **Medos**: the Orientals are **Persae** (v. 22), **Medi**, or **Parthi** indifferently in Horace.—**equitare**: *ride on their raids*.

52. The last line contains the climax of the ode. It is Caesar who divinely leads and protects the state. With the position of the last two words cf. 4, 6, 43 f. *reddidi carmen docilis modorum | vatis Horati.*

3

A *propempticon*, or farewell poem, to Vergil. 'Ship that bearest Vergil to Greece, deliver him safe, I pray. (1-8.) That mortal was overbold who first dared tempt the sea (9-24); of old man stole fire from Heaven and by that act brought on himself disease and early death (25-33); he essays the air itself and does not shrink to pass the very bars of Acheron (34-36). Nothing is safe from him; through pride and sin he still calls down the wrath of Jove.' Cf. with this the ill-natured propempticon to Mevius, *Epod.* 10.

Vergil's only voyage to Greece, so far as we know, was in 19 B.C., four years after the first three books of the Odes were published. Therefore we must believe that a visit to Athens was at least planned by him before 23 B.C. or that Horace is here addressing another Vergil than the poet. The second alternative can be rejected. No other Vergil could have been called by Horace *animae dimidium meae* without receiving mention elsewhere, save possibly 4, 12, 13. For Horace's relation to Vergil, see Intr. 5; Sellar's *Virgil*, pp. 120-126.

It is remarkable that after the first eight verses which contain the propempticon proper, Horace, who was usually so tactful, should quickly revert to the old philosophical and theological notions of the sinfulness of human enterprise without observing how out of place such ideas were here, when Vergil was just about to show such enterprise by undertaking this voyage.

It is probable that the form of the propempticon was suggested by a poem of Callimachus, of which two verses are preserved. *Frg.* 114 ἆ ναῦς, ἆ τὸ μόνον φέγγος ἐμὶν τὸ γλυκὺ τᾶς ζοᾶς | ἅρπαξας, ποτί τυ Ζανὸς ἱκνεῦμαι λιμενοσκόπω. . . . 'O ship that hast snatched from me my life's one sweet light, in name of Zeus, guardian of harbors, I beseech.' ... Statius' poem, *Silvae* 3, 2, is chiefly an expansion of Horace's verses. In modern poetry we may compare Tennyson's verses, *In Memor.* 9, 'Fair ship, that from the Italian shore | Sailest the placid ocean plains | With my lost Arthur's loved remains, | Spread thy full wings, and waft him o'er.' Metre, 71.

> Sic te diva potens Cypri,
> sic fratres Helenae, lucida sidera,
> ventorumque regat pater,
> obstrictis aliis praeter Iapyga,
> 5   navis, quae tibi creditum
> debes Vergilium, finibus Atticis

1. sic: expressing the condition on which the prayer is made: 'on this condition may Heaven and the winds favor thee, namely, that thou deliverest Vergil safe.' Here **sic** is expanded in the optative subj. **reddas** and **serves**. Often an imperative or a conditional sentence follows. *E.g. Epist.* 1, 7, 69 f. '*sic ignovisse putato | me tibi, si cenas hodie mecum.*' Similarly in English, *e.g.* Tennyson, *In Memor.* 17, '*So* may whatever tempest mars | Mid-ocean, spare thee, sacred bark;' and the formula in oaths, '*So* help me God.'

—**diva potens Cypri**: Κύπρου μεδέουσα, *Venus marina*, the protectress of sailors. Cf. 3, 26, 5. 9; 4, 11, 15. For the objective genitive with **potens**, cf. 1, 6, 10 *lyrae musa potens;* 1, 5, 15 *potenti maris deo, i.e.* Neptune.

2. Castor and Pollux. It was believed that the presence of these two guardians of sailors was attested by the electrical phenomenon known to us as St. Elmo's fire. Cf. 1, 12, 27 ff.; Lucian *Navig.* 9 ἔφασκεν ὁ ναύκληρος τινα λαμπρὸν ἀστέρα Διοσκούρων τὸν ἕτερον ἐπικαθίσαι τῷ καρχησίῳ καὶ κατευθῦναι τὴν ναῦν; Stat. *Silv.* 3, 2, 8 ff. *proferte benigna | sidera et antemnae gemino considite cornu | Oebalii fratres;* and in English, Macaulay, *Regillus,* 'Safe comes the ship to haven | Through billows and through gales. | If once the great Twin Brethren | Sit shining on the sails.' On coins a star is represented over the head of each of the heroes.

3 f. ventorum...pater: Aeolus, who is *Od.* 10, 21 ταμίης ἀνέμων.
—**Iapyga**: the wind blowing from the west or northwest across Iapygia, as Apulia was anciently called, was favorable for voyages to Greece.

5 ff. Vergil is like a treasure intrusted to the ship, and therefore owed by it. Note the emphasis on **Vergilium** before the **caesura**.—

reddas incolumem precor
et serves animae dimidium meae.
Illi robur et aes triplex
10   circa pectus erat, qui fragilem truci
commisit pelago ratem
primus, nec timuit praecipitem Africum
decertantem Aquilonibus
nec tristis Hyadas nec rabiem Noti,
15   quo non arbiter Hadriae
maior, tollere seu ponere volt freta.

finibus: dat. with reddas, *deliver.*
—animae dimidium meae: a proverbial expression of affection. Cf. 2, 17, 5 *te meae partem animae;* Meleager *Anth. Pal.* 12, 52 Νότος, ὦ δυσέρωτες, | ἥμισύ μευ ψυχᾶς ἅρπασεν Ἀνδράγαθον.

9 ff. Horace now turns to reflections on the rash presumption of mankind that seem to us extravagant; but man's attempt to subdue the sea may well have been thought impious in a primitive age. These verses reflect this ancient feeling. See intr. n. Cf. Soph. *Antig.* 332 ff. πολλὰ τὰ δεινά, κοὐδὲν ἀνθρώπου δεινότερον πέλει· | τοῦτο καὶ πολιοῦ πέραν πόντου χειμερίῳ νότῳ | χωρεῖ, περιβρυχίοισιν | περῶν ὑπ' οἴδμασιν. 'Wonderful things there are many, and yet none more wonderful than man. This marvelous creature, driven by the stormy south wind, crosseth even the gray sea, passing half buried through the wave that would ingulf him.'

—robur et aes triplex: translated by Herrick 'A heart thrice wall'd with Oke, and brasse, that man | Had, first, durst plow the Ocean.' Horace was imitated by Seneca *Med.* 301 ff. *audax nimium qui freta primus | rate tam fragili perfida rupit | terrasque suas post terga videns | animam levibus credidit auris.*

12 f. praecipitem Africum: *the headlong Afric wind,* the Sirocco; called *Epod.* 16, 22 *protervus.* — Aquilonibus: dative; cf. 1, 15 *luctantem Icariis fluctibus Africum.*

14. tristis Hyadas: bringing rain and so 'gloomy.' Cf. Verg. *A.* 3, 516 *pluviasque Hyadas,* and of the Auster (Notus) *G.* 3, 279 *pluvio contristat frigore caelum.* — Noti: equivalent to *Auster.*

15. arbiter: *ruler;* cf. 3, 3, 5 *Auster | dux inquieti turbidus Hadriae.*

16. ponere: equivalent to *componere.* Observe the use of the single seu in an alternative statement.

Quem mortis timuit gradum,
  qui siccis oculis monstra natantia,
qui vidit mare turbidum et
20   infamis scopulos Acroceraunia?
Nequiquam deus abscidit
  prudens Oceano dissociabili
terras, si tamen impiae
  non tangenda rates transiliunt vada.
25 Audax omnia perpeti
  gens humana ruit per vetitum nefas.
Audax Iapeti genus
  ignem fraude mala gentibus intulit.

17. mortis . . . gradum: for the conception of death as stalking abroad and pursuing men, cf. v. 33 below; 1, 4, 13; 3, 2, 14.

18. siccis oculis: *i.e.* 'unterrified.' A man who is not moved by the awful terrors of the sea, lacks all reverence for Heaven's power and is prepared to defy the very gods. Cf. Milton, 'Sight so deform what heart of oak could long | Dry eyed behold?'

20. Acroceraunia: the long promontory on the northwest of Epirus, which had an ill repute (infamis scopulos) with sailors because of the number of shipwrecks there.

21 f. nequiquam: emphatic, *in vain it is that*, etc. — prudens: *in his wise providence.* — dissociabili: *estranging*; active as 1, 1, 5 *nobilis*.

23 f. impiae . . . rates: the ships are reckless of Heaven's displeasure, since they bound over the water which God has ordained should not be touched (non tangenda . . . vada).

25 ff. Three examples of human recklessness follow the general statement: the theft of fire (27–33), Daedalus' attempt on the air (34 f.), Hercules' invasion of Hades (36). — audax . . . audax: emphatic anaphora, Intr. 28c. — perpeti: dependent on audax. Intr. 108. — ruit: *rushes at random*, characterizing the recklessness of man, as *transiliunt* does in v. 24. — vetitum: sc. *a diis*.

27. Iapeti genus: Prometheus. Cf. Hes. *Op.* 50 ff. κρύψε δὲ πῦρ· τὸ μὲν αὖτις ἐὺς παῖς Ἰαπετοῖο | ἔκλεψ' ἀνθρώποισι Διὸς πάρι μητιόεντος | ἐν κοίλῳ νάρθηκι. λαθὼν Δία τερπικέραυνον. For

CARMINA [I, 3, 38

Post ignem aetheria domo
30   subductum macies et nova febrium
terris incubuit cohors,
    semotique prius tarda necessitas
leti corripuit gradum.
    Expertus vacuum Daedalus aera
35 pennis non homini datis;
    perrupit Acheronta Herculeus labor.
Nil mortalibus ardui est;
    caelum ipsum petimus stultitia, neque

genus, equivalent to 'child,' 'descendant,' cf. *S.* 2, 5, 63, *ab alto demissum genus Aenea,* i.e. Octavian; and collectively of the Danaids, *C.* 2, 14, 18 *Danai genus.*

29 ff. **post ignem... subductum**: *after the theft of*; **subductum** is equivalent to *subreptum.*
— **macies et nova febrium... cohors**: the legend has been preserved to us by Serv. ad Verg. *E.* 6, 42 (*ob Promethei furtum*) *irati di duo mala immiserunt terris, febres et morbos; sicut et Sappho et Hesiodus memorant.*
— **incubuit**: *brooded over.* Cf. Lucr. 6, 1143 (he is speaking of sickness), *incubuit tandem populo Pandionis omnei.*

32 f. Note the cumulative force of **semoti** and **tarda**: 'inevitable death was far removed and slow in its approach.' Before Pandora came men lived, according to Hesiod *Op.* 90 ff. πρώην μὲν ζώεσκον ἐπὶ χθονὶ φῦλ' ἀνθρώπων | νόσφιν ἄτερ τε κακῶν καὶ ἄτερ χαλεποῖο πόνοιο, | νούσων τ' ἀργαλέων, αἵτ' ἀνδράσι κῆρας ἔδωκαν.
— **prius**: with both **semoti** and **tarda**. Intr. 100.
— **necessitas leti**: the Homeric Μοῖρα θανάτοιο.

34 f. Cf. Verg. *A.* 6, 14 f. *Daedalus, ut fama est, fugiens Minoia regna, | praepetibus pennis ausus se credere caelo.* — **non... datis**: *i.e. non concessis,* implying that wings were forbidden man.

36. **perrupit**: for the quantity, see Intr. 35. — **Herculeus labor**: for the use of the adjective, cf. 2, 12. 6 *Herculea manu* and the Homeric βίη Ἡρακλείη.

37. **ardui**: *steep and hard,* modifying **nil**. Cf. Petron. 87 *nihil est tam arduum, quod non improbitas extorqueat.*

38. In his blind folly man attempts to emulate the Giants, who with brute force tried to storm the citadel of Heaven. Cf. 3, 4, 49–60, 65, and nn.

per nostrum patimur scelus
40   iracunda Iovem ponere fulmina.

40. iracunda ... fulmina: the transference of an epithet from the person to the action or thing is not uncommon. Cf. 1, 12, 59 *inimica fulmina*; 1, 15, 33 *iracunda classis Achillei*; *Epod.* 10, 14 *impiam Aiacis ratem.* Intr. 99.
—**ponere**: equivalent to *deponere*.

4

'The earth is freed from winter's thrall; Venus leads her bands, the Nymphs and Graces dance; Vulcan stirs his fires (1-8). Now crown thy head with myrtle and with flowers, now sacrifice to Faunus. Life is glad and lures one on to hope (9-12). But Death is near at hand, my Sestius: to-morrow Pluto's dreary house will shut thee in; no delight in wine or love is there (13-20).'

To L. Sestius Quirinus, probably a son of the P. Sestius whom Cicero defended. He was a partisan of Brutus, and very likely Horace's acquaintance with him began with the time of their service together in Brutus' army. Later Sestius accepted the new order of things without giving up his loyalty to Brutus' memory, and was appointed consul suffectus (July-December, 23 B.C.) by Augustus. Cf. Dio Cass. 53, 32.

Few of the odes are more skillfully planned. The underlying thought is one expressed by Horace in many forms: 'the world is pleasant and offers many joys; take them while you may, for death is near.' With this Book 4. Ode 7 should be compared. The verses are apparently based on a Greek model, possibly the same as that of Silentarius in the *Anth. Pal.* 10, 15; or did Silentarius follow Horace? ἤδη μὲν ζεφύροισι μεμυκότα κόλπον ἀνοίγει | εὖρος εὐλείμων θελξινόοιο χάρις· | ἄρτι δὲ δουρατέοισιν ἐπωπλίσθησε κυλίνδροις | ὁλκὰς ἀπ' ἠιόνων ἐς βυθὸν ἑλκομένη. 'Now the grace of charming spring which brings back fair meadows opens the bay that roars under Zephyrus' blasts. Only yesterday did the merchantman glide on the rollers, drawn down from the land to the deep.' The date of composition is uncertain, but cf. v. 14 and n. which may fix the date at 23 B.C. The position here gives Sestius, who was consul in 23, the fourth place in honor after Maecenas, Augustus, and Vergil. Metre, 81.

Solvitur acris hiems grata vice veris et Favoni,
 trahuntque siccas machinae carinas,
ac neque iam stabulis gaudet pecus aut arator igni,
 nec prata canis albicant pruinis.
5 Iam Cytherea choros ducit Venus imminente luna,
 iunctaeque Nymphis Gratiae decentes

1. **solvitur ... hiems**: 'the fetters of winter are broken.' Cf. 1, 9, 5 *dissolve frigus*, and the opposite Verg. *G.* 2, 317 *rura gelu claudit hiems.* — **vice**: *succession*. So *Epod.* 13, 7 *benigna ... vice*. Note the alliteration in v*ice veris et Favoni*; cf. v. 13. — **Favoni**: the harbinger of spring (*Zephyrus*). Cf. Lucret. 5, 737 *veris praenuntius ... graditur Zephyrus*.

2. **siccas**: from their winter position, high on the shore.

3 ff. The whole world feels the pleasant change — the beasts, man, and the very divinities themselves.

5 f. The contrast between Venus and her band of Nymphs and Graces on the one side with glowing Vulcan and his workmen on the other is carefully planned. Venus is here the goddess of regeneration, at whose coming the world wakes into life. Cf. Lucret. 1, 5 ff. *te, dea, te fugiunt venti, te nubila caeli | adventumque tuum, tibi suavis daedala tellus | submittit flores, tibi rident aequora ponti | placatumque nitet diffuso lumine caelum.*

— **Cytherea**: *of Cythera*. For this use of a local adjective modifying the name of a divinity, cf. 3, 4, 64 *Delius et Patareus Apollo.* — **choros ducit**: the concept is probably borrowed from the Hom. *Hymn to Apollo*, 194 ff. αὐτὰρ ἐϋπλόκαμοι Χάριτες καὶ ἐΰφρονες Ὧραι | Ἁρμονίη θ᾽ Ἥβη τε Διὸς θυγάτηρ τ᾽ Ἀφροδίτη | ὀρχεῦντ᾽ ἀλλήλων ἐπὶ καρπῷ χεῖρας ἔχουσαι.
— **imminente luna**: the night when no mortals are abroad, is the gods' favorite time to visit the earth. Cf. Stat. *Silv.* 1, 1, 94 f. *sub nocte silenti, | cum superis terrena placent.* — **iunctae**, etc.: *hand in hand*; cf. 4, 7, 5 f. *Gratia cum Nymphis geminisque sororibus audet | ducere nuda choros.* — **Gratiae**: Seneca *de Benef.* 1, 3 has given us an accurate description of the regular representation of the Graces in early painting and sculpture, *tres Gratiae sorores manibus implexis, ridentes, iuvenes et virgines, soluta ac pellucida veste*; in later art they are represented as nude, with their arms about one another's shoulders. Cf. Baumeister, pp. 375-6. — **decentes**: *comely*; the word is transferred to English poetry, *e.g.* Milton *Il Pens.* 'Over thy decent shoulders drawn.'

alterno terram quatiunt pede, dum gravis Cyclopum
  Volcanus ardens visit officinas.
Nunc decet aut viridi nitidum caput impedire myrto,
10 aut flore terrae quem ferunt solutae;
nunc et in umbrosis Fauno decet immolare lucis,
  seu poscat agna sive malit haedo.
Pallida mors aequo pulsat pede pauperum tabernas
  regumque turris. O beate Sesti,
15 vitae summa brevis spem nos vetat incohare longam.
  Iam te premet nox fabulaeque manes

7. alterno ... quatiunt pede : *i.e.* in rhythmic dance; cf. 1, 37, 1 *nunc est bibendum, nunc pede libero | pulsanda tellus.* — gravis : equivalent to *laboriosas, toilsome.* — ardens : 'glowing in the light of the fire.' Some editors prefer to regard it as a transferred epithet which would naturally belong to officinas : with the verse, cf. Apoll. Rhod. 3, 41 ἀλλ' ὁ μὲν ἐς χαλκεῶνα καὶ ἄκμονας ἦρι βεβήκει.

9 f. nitidum : *shining*, with unguent; cf. 2, 7, 7 *nitentis...capillos.* — caput impedire myrto : *entwine.* Cf. Stat. *Silv.* 4, 3, 68 *crinem mollibus impeditus ulvis.* — terrae ... solutae : cf. v. 1, above.

11 f. Fauno : the kindly god of Nature whose festival fell on Feb.

12. — agna ... haedo : instrumental abl.

13. Note the p five times repeated. — pulsat pede : for the custom of knocking with the foot, cf. Plaut. *Most.* 453 *pulsando pedibus paene confregi hasce ambas (fores)*, also Callim. *Hymn to Apollo*, 3 καὶ δήπου τὰ θύρετρα καλῷ ποδὶ Φοῖβος ἀράσσει.

14. turris : the houses of the great (regum) with many stories, in contrast to the one-story dwellings (tabernas) of the poor. — beate : *blessed by Fortune*; with almost concessive force. Some wish to see in this word a reference to Sestius' consulship.

15. summa brevis : *brief span.* — incohare : used properly, as here, of entering on an undertaking that cannot be fulfilled. Cf. Sen. *Epist.* 101, 4 *o quanta dementia est spes longas incohantium.*

16 f. iam : *presently.* With the future *iam* often expresses confidence in the result; cf. 2, 20, 13 f. *iam Daedaleo notior Icaro | visam gementis litora Bosphori.* — fabulae : in apposition with manes, *the spirits of the dead.* The phrase is imitated by Pers. 5, 151 f. *cinis et manes et fabula fies;* cf. also Callim. *Epig.* 13, 3 f. ὦ Χαρίδα, τί τὰ νέρθε; πολὺ σκότος. αἱ δ' ἄνοδοι τί; | ψεῦδος. ὁ δὲ Πλούτων; μῦθος. ἀπωλό-

et domus exilis Plutonia; quo simul mearis,
   nec regna vini sortiere talis
   nec tenerum Lycidan mirabere, quo calet iuventus
20   nunc omnis et mox virgines tepebunt.

μέθα. 'Charidas, what is below? Deep darkness. But what of the passages upward? All a lie. But Pluto? Only talk. Then we're lost.' — **exilis**: *unsubstantial, dreary*. — **simul**: equivalent to *simul ac*, as regularly in Horace.

18 ff. In the last three verses Horace calls back the pleasure of wine and love, and reminds his friend that he must enjoy these delights while he may. Death will soon deprive him of them. — **regna vini**: the presidency of the drinking bout was determined by lot or by dice. Cf. n. to 2, 7, 25 *quem Venus arbitrum dicet bibendi?* — **talis**: properly 'knuckle bones' which would ordinarily fall on the longer sides; the highest throw (*iactus Veneris*) was when each rested on a different side. — **Lycidan**: a name invented for the occasion.

5

To a coquette: 'What slender innocent enjoys thy smiles to-day, Pyrrha? Alas, he does not yet suspect that thou art fickle as the sea; thy smile lures on his love to shipwreck. Thank Heaven I escaped: in Neptune's temple I hang my dripping clothes as votive gift.'

The perfected simplicity of this ode can best be tested by an attempt to alter or transpose a word, or by translation. Even Milton's well-known version is inadequate. Metre, 73.

Quis multa gracilis te puer in rosa
   perfusus liquidis urget odoribus
      grato, Pyrrha, sub antro?
      Cui flavam religas comam,

1 f. **gracilis ... puer**: *stripling*. — **multa ... in rosa**: *lying on many a rose*; as in Sen. *Epist.* 36, 9 *in rosa iacere*. Cf. also *Eleg. in Maec.* 1, 94 f. *victor potiatur in umbra, | victor odorata dormiat inque rosa*; Cic. *de Fin.* 2, 65 *potantem in rosa*. — **urget**: *courts*.

3 f. **Pyrrha**: Πυρρά, a fictitious name. 'the auburn haired'; cf. **flavam**. — **religas**: *i.e.* in a simple knot. Cf. 2, 11, 23 *in comptum Lacaenae | more comam religata*

5   simplex munditiis? Heu quotiens fidem
    mutatosque deos flebit et aspera
       nigris aequora ventis
          emirabitur insolens,

       qui nunc te fruitur credulus aurea,
10   qui semper vacuam, semper amabilem
          sperat, nescius aurae
             fallacis. Miseri quibus

nodum. With the question, cf. *Anth. Pal.* 5, 227 εἰπὲ τίνι πλέξεις ἔτι βόστρυχον, ἢ τίνι χεῖρας | φαιδρυνέεις ὀνύχων ἀμφιτεμὼν ἀκίδα; • 'Tell me for whom wilt thou still dress thy curling locks, or for whom wilt thou make fair thy hands and trim thy nails' sharp points?' (*i.e.* so that they may not be used to scratch in case of a quarrel between thee and thy new lover. Cf. v. 17 f. of the following ode).

5 f. simplex munditiis: *plain in thy neatness* (Milton). **munditia** denotes a natural beauty and elegance that is unadorned; Pyrrha has chosen studied simplicity in dress. — **fidem**: sc. *mutatam* from the following **mutatos**; therefore equivalent to *perfidiam*, as the context shows. — **mutatos deos**: *i.e. adversos*: cf. Prop. 1, 1, 8 *cum tamen adversos cogor habere deos.*

7. nigris: belonging naturally with **aequora**, as 'darkened' by the gusts of wind, but here transferred to **ventis**; cf. 1, 3, 40. *iracunda fulmina.* Intr. 99. The comparison of a coquette to the sea is very old. Cf Semonides of Amor-

gos, *Frg.* 7, 37 ff. ὥσπερ θάλασσα πολλάκις μὲν ἀτρεμής | ἕστηκ᾽ ἀπήμων, χάρμα ναύτῃσιν μέγα, | θέρεος ἐν ὥρῃ, πολλάκις δὲ μαίνεται | βαρυκτύποισι κύμασιν φορευμένη. | ταύτῃ μάλιστ᾽ ἔοικε τοιαύτη γυνή. 'As the sea ofttimes is motionless and harmless, a mighty joy to sailors in the summer season, and yet ofttimes doth rage, driven to and fro with loud roaring billows. This sea it is that such a woman is most like.'

8. emirabitur: found only here in classical Latin. The prefix is intensive. Cf. the Greek ἐκθαυμάζειν. — **insolens**: used here in its original meaning of *unaccustomed, poor innocent.*

9. credulus aurea: note the force of the juxtaposition; cf. 1, 6, 10 *tenues grandia.* — **aurea**: a common designation of perfection; cf. the Homeric χρυσέη Ἀφροδίτη. In present-day English it is seldom applied to persons, but cf. Shakspere, *Cymbeline,* 4, 2 'Golden lads and girls all must | As chimney sweepers, come to dust.'

10 f. vacuam: *fancy free,* to all the world but him. — **aurae**: re-

intemptata nites : me tabula sacer
votiva paries indicat uvida
15   suspendisse potenti
vestimenta maris deo.

turning to the metaphor of v. 6 f.; cf. 3. 2, 20 *arbitrio popularis aurae*.

13. **intemptata nites**: still keeping up the figure of the glittering sea, untried and treacherous. Cf. Lucret. 2, 559 *subdola cum ridet placidi pellacia ponti*. — **tabula sacer**, etc.: the ancient custom of dedicating in the shrine of a divinity a picture (**tabula**) can still be seen in Roman Catholic churches, especially in Europe. Shipwrecked sailors sometimes hung up the garments in which they had been saved as offerings to Neptune, Isis, or other divinity. Cf. Verg. *A.* 12, 766 ff. *forte sacer Fauno foliis oleaster amaris | hic steterat, nautis olim venerabile lignum, | servati ex undis ubi figere dona solebant | Laurenti divo et votas suspendere vestes.* For votive offering of various sorts, see Schreiber's Atlas, pl. 15.

— **potenti . . . maris deo**: cf. 1, 3, 1 *diva potens Cypri*; 6, 10 *imbellisque lyrae Musa potens*; and Plaut. *Trin.* 820 *salsipotenti . . . Neptuno*.

6

'Varius, who vies with Homer, shall sing thy exploits, Agrippa. The deeds of heroes and tragic themes are all too great for my weak powers: I will not detract from Caesar's fame and thine. Only wine and lovers' quarrels are suited to my verse.'

Addressed to M. Vipsanius Agrippa, Augustus' 'Minister of War' and greatest general; he defeated Sextus Pompey at Naulochus, 36 B.C., and was commander at Actium, 31 B.C. Apparently Agrippa, or Agrippa's friends, had suggested to Horace that he celebrate the general's exploits in verse. This ode is Horace's skillful apology and should be compared with similar expressions, 2, 12; 4. 2. 27 ff.; *S.* 2, 1, 12; *Epist.* 2, 1, 250 ff. In each case, however, while declaring his unfitness for the task, he describes deeds of war, yet briefly, not in an elaborate poem. Here by his manner of declining, he pays Agrippa the highest tribute as well as compliments his friend Varius. The date of composition is after 29 B.C., when Agrippa returned from the East. Metre, 72.

Scriberis Vario fortis et hostium
victor Maeonii carminis alite,
quam rem cumque ferox navibus aut equis
    miles te duce gesserit.

5   Nos, Agrippa, neque haec dicere nec gravem
    Pelidae stomachum cedere nescii

1. **scribēris**: expressing assurance; different from *laudabunt alii* of the following ode, which is equivalent to *others may praise* (if they wish). The real subject of the verb is 'thy brave deeds and victories,' (*tu*) **fortis et hostium victor**. — **Vario**: frequently taken as abl. abs. with **alite** to avoid the apparent solecism of the abl. of agent without *ab*. This is as unnecessary as to change **alite** to the dat. *aliti*. For the abl. of agent without *ab*, cf. *Epist.* 1, 19, 2 *carmina . . . quae scribuntur aquae potoribus*. Intr. 96.

Lucius Varius Rufus was the intimate friend of Horace and Vergil. With Plotius Tucca he was the latter's literary executor, and at Augustus' command published the *Aeneid* in 17 B.C.; before the publication of the *Aeneid* he was reckoned the chief epic poet of the period. *S.* 1, 10, 43 f. *forte epos acer | ut nemo Varius ducit*. His posthumous fame, however, seems to have been based on his tragedies, especially his *Thyestes*. Quint. 10, 1, 98, *Varii Thyestes cuilibet Graecarum comparari potest*. He brought out this play not long after 31 B.C., according to the didascalia, *Thyesten tragoediam magna cura absolutam post Actiacam victoriam Augusti ludis eius in scena edidit. Pro qua fabula sestertium deciens accepit.*

2. **Maeonii carminis alite**: *i.e.* the equal of Homer, who, according to tradition, was born at Smyrna in Lydia, anciently called Maeonia; cf. 4, 9, 5 *Maeonius Homerus*. — **alite**: for 'bird' in the sense of 'poet,' cf. 4, 2, 25 *Dircaeum . . . cycnum* of Pindar, and 2, 20 entire.

3. **quam rem cumque**: this tmesis is common in Horace (*e.g.* 1, 7, 25 *quo nos cumque feret . . . fortuna*) and not unknown in prose: Cic. *pro Sest.* 68 *quod iudicium cumque subierat*.

5 ff. With the following, cf. the Anacreontic verses 23 θέλω λέγειν Ἀτρείδας, | θέλω δὲ Κάδμον ᾄδειν· | ἁ βάρβιτος δὲ. χορδαῖς | ἔρωτα μοῦνον ἠχεῖ. — **nos**: the plural of modesty, so v. 17 below. The singular of the first person is ordinarily used in the lyric poems, the plural being found only here and 2, 17, 32; 3. 28, 9; *Epod.* 1, 5. For the emphatic position, see Intr. 22. — **haec**: 'thy

nec cursus duplicis per mare Vlixei
nec saevam Pelopis domum

conamur, tenues grandia, dum pudor
imbellisque lyrae musa potens vetat
laudes egregii Caesaris et tuas
culpa deterere ingeni.

Quis Martem tunica tectum adamantina
digne scripserit aut pulvere Troico

exploits,' taking up **quam rem
. . . gesserit,** above. — **dicere**:
sing, in contrast to **scribere**, v. 1,
used of epic composition. Cf.
loqui 3, 25, 18. — **gravem Pelidae
stomachum**: *i.e.* the *Iliad*; *Il.* 1,
1 μῆνιν ἄειδε, θεά. Πηληϊάδεω
Ἀχιλῆος. — **cedere nescii**: Intr.
108. Cf. Verg. *A.* 12, 527, *nescia
vinci pectora*.

7. **cursus duplicis . . . Vlixei**:
the *Odyssey*; *Od.* 1, 1 ἄνδρα μοι
ἔννεπε, Μοῦσα, πολύτροπον, ὃς
μάλα πολλὰ | πλάγχθη. Horace
humorously shows his own unfitness for epic song by translating
μῆνις by **stomachus**, *bile*, and
πολύτροπος by **duplex**, *wily*. —
Vlixei: from a (non-existent)
nominative *Vlixeus*, formed after
the Sicilian dialectic Οὐλίξης,
Ὀλίξης.

8. **saevam Pelopis domum**: Tantalus, Pelops, Atreus, Thyestes,
Agamemnon, Orestes, etc. The
bloody history of this house was
a favorite tragic theme; we have
still extant Æschylus' Trilogy,
Sophocles' *Electra*, Euripides'
Orestes, Electra, and two *Iphigenias*. The verse is a compliment
to Varius' genius for tragedy, as
vv. 5-7 are to his position as epic
poet.

9. **tenues grandia**: in agreement with **nos** and **haec**. Notice
the forceful juxtaposition. Cf. 1,
3, 10 *fragilem truci*; 1, 5, 9 *credulus aurea*; 1, 15, 2 *perfidus hospitam*. — **lyrae musa potens**: cf. n.
to 1, 5, 15 f

11. With great skill Horace
associates Agrippa's glory with
that of Caesar. — **egregii**: Horace applies this adjective only
to Caesar among the living, and
among the dead to Regulus, 3, 5,
48 *egregius exul*. — **deterere**: *to
impair*, properly 'to wear off the
edge.'

13 ff. The answer to this question is of course, 'only a second
Homer, a Varius.' The following
themes are naturally selected from
the *Iliad*. — **tunica tectum adamantina**: cf. the Homeric χαλκοχίτων, χαλκεοθώραξ. χάλκεος
Ἄρης. — **pulvere . . . nigrum**: cf. 2,

15   nigrum Merionen aut ope Palladis
      Tydiden superis parem?

      Nos convivia, nos proelia virginum
      sectis in iuvenes unguibus acrium
      cantamus vacui, sive quid urimur,
20   non praeter solitum leves.

1, 22 *duces non indecoro pulvere sordidos*. — **Merionen**: charioteer to Cretan Idomeneus and one of the foremost fighters of the Greeks. — **ope Palladis ... parem**: Horace had in mind *Il.* 5, 881-884 (Ares speaks) ἢ νῦν Τυδέος υἱόν, ὑπερφίαλον Διομήδεα, | μαργαίνειν ἀνέηκεν ἐπ᾽ ἀθανάτοισι θεοῖσι. | Κύπριδα μὲν πρῶτον σχεδὸν οὔτασε χεῖρ᾽ ἐπὶ καρπῷ, | αὐτὰρ ἔπειτ᾽ αὐτῷ μοι ἐπέσσυτο δαίμονι ἶσος.

17 ff. Contrasted with the tragic and epic themes are drinking bouts and lovers' quarrels, fit subjects for Horace's *imbellis lyra*. — **nos ... nos**: for the anaphora, see Intr. 28c. — **sectis...unguibus**: and hence harmless. Cf. the Greek verses quoted on 1, 5, 3. — **vacui**: *fancy free*; 1, 5, 10. — **sive quid**, etc.: for the omission of the first sive, cf. 1, 3, 16. — **urimur**: *i.e.* with love. — **non praeter solitum**: *i.e.* 'after my usual fashion.' — **leves**: with the subject of **cantamus**.

7

This ode is very similar in construction to the fourth, in which the first twelve verses are given to the praise of spring, the remainder of the ode to the exhortation to enjoy life while we may; in this, 1-14 celebrate the charm of Tivoli, 15-32 urge the value of wine as a releaser from care. This second part again falls naturally into two divisions: the general exhortation (15-21), and the concrete example (21-32). The connection between the two parts of the ode is so slight that as early as the second century some critics regarded them as separate poems, and they so appear in some manuscripts, but that the two parts belong together was recognized by Porphyrio, who notes on v. 15 *hanc oden quidam putant aliam esse, sed eadem est; nam et hic ad Plancum loquitur, in cuius honore et in superiori parte Tibur laudavit. Plancus enim inde fuit oriundus.*

L. Munatius Plancus, who is here addressed, had a varied military **and political** career. He was a legate of Julius Caesar; in 43 B.C. as governor of Gaul he founded Lugdunum (Lyons) and Augusta Rauracorum (Augst near Basel); he was later the friend of Antony and was intrusted by him with the government of Asia and Syria, but Antony's relations with Cleopatra drove him in 31 B.C. to take sides with Octavian. It was he who proposed in January, 27 B.C., that Octavian be given the title Augustus. Of Horace's relations to him we know nothing beyond what this ode tells us, and as little of the special occasion for the poem. The date of composition is uncertain, but verses 26 ff. were hardly written before 29 B.C., for they seem to show acquaintance with Verg. *A.* 1, 195 ff. Metre, 77.

Laudabunt alii claram Rhodon aut Mytilenen
aut Epheson bimarisve Corinthi
moenia vel Baccho Thebas vel Apolline Delphos
insignis aut Thessala Tempe.

1. **laudabunt alii**: *others may praise* (if they will); the antithesis is **me**, v. 10. For this use of the future, cf. Verg. *A.* 6, 847 ff. *excudent alii spirantia mollius aera . . . tu regere imperio populos, Romane, memento.* — **claram**: *famous*, or possibly *sunny*. So Lucan 8, 247 f. *claramque reliquit | sole Rhodon.* The adjective belongs equally to **Rhodon, Mytilenen, Epheson**, which are closely connected by **aut . . . aut**, the following places being more loosely attached by **ve . . . vel . . . vel**. Rhodes (Catull. 4, 8 *Rhodum . . . nobilem*) famous for its commerce, its schools of rhetoric and philosophy, and its art: Mytilene, capital of Lesbos, the city of Alcaeus and Sappho (Cic. *de lege agr.* 2, 40 *urbs et natura et situ et descriptione aedificiorum et pulchritudine in primis nobilis*); Ephesus, the chief city of the province of Asia. The same three cities are named by Mart. 10, 68, 1 f. *cum tibi non Ephesos nec sit Rhodos aut Mitylene, | sed domus in vico, Laelia, patricio.*

2. **bimaris**: ἀμφιθάλασσος. Corinth, destroyed by Mummius 146 B.C., restored by Julius Caesar, from its position on the isthmus enjoyed two harbors, Cenchreae on the Saronic and Lechaeum on the Corinthian Gulf. Cf. Ovid. *Trist.* 1, 11, 5 *bimarem . . . Isthmon.*

3 f. Bacchus according to one tradition was the child of Theban Semele. Cf. 1, 19, 2 *Thebanae . . . Semelae puer.* Delphi was the seat of Apollo's greatest shrine on the mainland of Greece. — **insignis**: modifying both **Thebas** and **Delphos**. — **Tempe**: acc. neuter plur.; famed for its beauty. Cf. Eurip. *Troad.* 214 ff. τὰν Πηνειοῦ σεμνὰν χώραν, | κρηπῖδ' Οὐλύμπου

5   Sunt quibus unum opus est intactae Palladis urbem
        carmine perpetuo celebrare et
    undique decerptam fronti praeponere olivam;
        plurimus in Iunonis honorem
    aptum dicet equis Argos ditisque Mycenas.
10   Me nec tam patiens Lacedaemon
    nec tam Larisae percussit campus opimae
        quam domus Albuneae resonantis

καλλίσταν, | ὄλβῳ βρίθειν φάμαν ἤκουσ' | εὐθαλεῖ τ' εὐκαρπείᾳ. 'I have heard that Peneus' sacred district, Olympus' footstool most fair, is weighted with great fortune and goodly increase.'

5 f. **sunt quibus**: cf. 1, 1, 3 *sunt quos*. — **unum opus**, etc.: *only task*, i.e. poets who devote themselves to singing in 'unbroken song' (**perpetuo carmine**) the glorious history of Athens, the city of the virgin goddess (**intactae Palladis**). Some critics take **perpetuo carmine** to mean epic in contrast to lyric poetry, but this is not necessary.

7. The poets sing of all the legend and history that belongs to Athens, and so their work is compared to a garland made of olive leaves plucked from every part (**undique**) of the city. The same comparison was made by Lucret. 1, 928 ff. *invatque novos decerpere flores | insignemque meo capiti petere inde coronam, | unde prius nulli velarint tempora musae.* — **olivam**: sacred to Athena.

8. **plurimus**: *many a one.* — in **Iunonis honorem**, etc.: cf. *Il.* 4, 51 f. (Hera speaks) ἤτοι ἐμοὶ τρεῖς μὲν πολὺ φίλταταί εἰσι πόληες, | Ἄργος τε Σπάρτη τε καὶ εὐρυάγυια Μυκήνη.

9. **aptum . . . equis Argos**, etc.: *Il.* 2, 287 ἀπ' Ἄργεος ἱπποβότοιο, 7, 180 πολύχρυσος Μυκήνη. See Tsountas and Manatt, *The Mycenean Age*, Index, s.v. *gems*, for the treasure found at Mycenae.

10. **me**: emphatic contrast to alii v. 1. Cf. 1, 1, 29. — **patiens**: *hardy.* Cf. Quintil. 3, 7, 24 *minus Lacedaemone studia litterarum quam Athenis honores merebuntur, plus patientia ac fortitudo*.

11. **Larisae . . . campus opimae**: Thessaly was famed in antiquity for its grain. Cf. *Il.* 2, 841 Λάρισα ἐριβῶλαξ.

12 ff. Tibur (Tivoli), beloved in antiquity as in modern times for its beauty, is situated on the edge of the Sabine Mountains, overlooking the Campagna. The Anio flows round the foot of Mount Catillus (Monte Catillo still) and then falls to the valley in a number of beautiful cascades and rapids (therefore **Albuneae resonantis**;

et praeceps Anio ac Tiburni lucus et uda
  mobilibus pomaria rivis.
15 Albus ut obscuro deterget nubila caelo
  saepe Notus neque parturit imbris
perpetuos, sic tu sapiens finire memento
  tristitiam vitaeque labores
molli, Plance, mero, seu te fulgentia signis
20 castra tenent seu densa tenebit
Tiburis umbra tui.   Teucer Salamina patremque

praeceps Anio). For Horace's affection for Tivoli, see Sellar p. 179 f. — **domus Albuneae**: a grotto in which there was an ancient Italian oracle; hence the name of the last of the Sibyls. Cf. Verg. *A.* 7, 82 ff. *lucosque sub alta | consulit Albunea, nemorum quae maxuma sacro | fonte sonat.*

13 f. Tiburni: Tiburnus, grandson of Amphiaraus, the Argive seer; according to tradition he was banished with his brothers Coras and Catillus, and became with them the founder of Tibur. Cf. 2, 6, 5 *Tibur Argeo positum colono.* Catillus gave his name to the mountain behind the town; but was also associated with the town itself. Cf. 1, 18, 2 *circa mite solum Tiburis et moenia Catili.* — **lucus**: a sacred grove, distinguished from *nemus*, the more general word. — **uda mobilibus**, etc.: the Anio with its restless streams (**mobilibus rivis**) irrigated the adjoining orchards (**pomaria**). Cf. Prop. 5, 7, 81 *pomosis Anio qua spumifer incubat arvis.*

15 f. The only connection between the preceding and that which follows is **Tiburis umbra tui**, v. 21. 'You and I love Tibur beyond all other places; the thought of that spot reminds me of thee; learn the lesson of an easy life wherever thou mayest be.' It must be acknowledged that the connection is very slight. We may have here in reality a combination of two 'fragments' which Horace never completed. Cf. introductory n. to 1, 28. — **albus Notus**: the south wind usually brought rain (*nubilus Auster*); but sometimes clearing weather (**albus**, λευκόνοτος), and wiped (**deterget**) the clouds from the sky. — **parturit**: *breeds*. Cf. 4, 5, 26 f. *quis (paveat) Germania quos horrida parturit | fetus.*

17. perpetuos: cf. v. 6 above. — **sapiens**, etc.: *be wise and remember.*

19. molli: *mellow.*

20. tenent ... tenebit: notice change in tense.

21 ff. Again the connection with the preceding is slight, but the pointing of a general statement

cum fugeret, tamen uda Lyaeo
tempora populea fertur vinxisse corona,
  sic tristis adfatus amicos:
25 'Quo nos cumque feret melior fortuna parente,
  ibimus, o socii comitesque!
Nil desperandum Teucro duce et auspice Teucro;
  certus enim promisit Apollo

(17-20) by a mythological illustration is a favorite device of Horace. This particular story is found only here: Teucer's father, Telamon, refused to receive him on his return from Troy, since he had failed to bring his brother, Ajax, with him; therefore Teucer sought a new home in Cyprus, where he founded a city, named after his birthplace. The tale was a familiar one from Pacuvius' tragedy, *Teucer*, which was much admired. Cf. *Frg.* 12 R. (which is a part of Telamon's reproach) *ségregare abs te aúsu's aut sine illo Salaminam íngredi, | néque paternum aspéctum es veritus, quom aétate exacta índigem | líberum lacerásti orbásti extínxti, neque fratrís necis | néque eius gnati párvi, qui tibi in tutelam est tráditus?* Cic. *Tusc.* 5, 108 refers to the story, *itaque ad omnem rationem Teucri vox accommodari potest: 'Patria est, ubicumque est bene.'*

22 f. cum fugeret: *when starting to exile.*—tamen: 'in spite of his trouble.'—Lyaeo: *the releaser*, Liber, Λύαιος.—populea: sacred to Hercules. Cf. Verg. *A.* 8, 276 *Herculea bicolor . . . pōpulus umbra;* Theocr. 2, 121 κρατὶ δ' ἔχων λεύκαν, Ἡρακλέος ἱερὸν ἔρνος. The appropriateness of Teucer's honoring Hercules at this time lies in the character of Hercules as a traveler (3, 3, 9 *vagus Hercules*) and leader (Xen. *Anab.*, 4, 8, 25 ἡγεμών), to whose protection Teucer might naturally intrust himself when starting on this uncertain journey. Furthermore it was in company with Hercules that Telamon took Troy (cf. Verg. *A.* 1, 619 ff.) and captured Hesione, who became Teucer's mother.

25. quo . . . cumque: cf. n. to 1, 6, 3.—melior parente: *kinder than my father.* Cf. Telamon's reproach quoted on v. 21 above.

27. Teucro . . . Teucro: note that the substitution of the proper name for me . . . me appeals to their loyalty.—duce et auspice: formed from the technical Roman phrase; cf. Suet. *Aug.* 21 *domuit autem partim ductu, partim auspiciis suis Cantabriam.*

28 f. The reason for his confidence.—certus: *unerring, true,*

ambiguam tellure nova Salamina futuram.
30   O fortes peioraque passi
mecum saepe viri, nunc vino pellite curas;
cras ingens iterabimus aequor.'

νημερτής.— **ambiguam . . . Salamina**: *a Salamis to dispute the name* (Wickham); *i.e.* when Salamis was named, one could not tell which was meant, the old or the new. Cf. Sen. *Troad.* 854 *hinc ambigua veram Salamina opponunt.*

30 ff. Cf. *Od.* 12, 208 ὦ φίλοι, οὐ γάρ πώ τι κακῶν ἀδαήμονές εἰμεν,

Verg. *A.* 1, 198 f. *o socii, neque enim ignari sumus ante malorum,* | *o passi graviora, dabit deus his quoque finem.* — **nunc**: to-day, while yet you may.

32. **ingens**: *boundless.* — **iterabimus**: *sail again.* Cf. *Od.* 12, 293 ἠῶθεν δ' ἀναβάντες ἐνήσομεν εὐρέι πόντῳ.

8

'Lydia, in Heaven's name, why wilt thou kill Sybaris with love? He no longer takes part in manly sports on the Campus Martius, but hides as did Achilles on the eve of Troy.'

The same theme — the weakening of a youth by love — was adapted by Plautus *Most.* 149 ff. from a Greek comedy, *cór dolet, quóm scio, ut nunc sum atque ut fuí:* | *quó neque indústrior dé iuventúte erát* | *. . . dísco, hastís, pilá, cúrsu, armis, equó . . . .* The date of composition is unknown. It is probably a study from the Greek, and is Horace's single attempt to write in the greater Sapphic stanza. Metre, 70.

Lydia, dic, per omnis
    te deos oro, Sybarin cur properes amando·

1. **Lydia**: (Λύδη) a common poetic name for the heroine in amatory poetry from the time of Antimachus; cf. 1, 13, 1; 25, 8. — **per omnis te deos oro**: the usual order in appeals. Cf. Ter. *And.* 538 *per te deos oro*; also in Greek, Soph. *Phil.* 468 πρός νύν σε πατρός, . . . ἱκνοῦμαι.

2 f. **Sybarin**: the name is chosen to fit the effeminacy of the youth. Cf. the Eng. 'Sybarite.' — **cur properes**, etc.: *i.e.* 'what possible motive can you have for ruining the boy so quickly?' The rhetorical form of the question, as well as its content, implies that Lydia is doing wrong; no answer is expected. — **amando**: in meaning equivalent to an abstract noun. Cf. *Epod.* 14, 5 *occidis saepe rogando*, 'by questioning.'

perdere, cur apricum
oderit campum, patiens pulveris atque solis.
5 Cur neque militaris
inter aequalis equitat, Gallica nec lupatis
temperat ora frenis?
Cur timet flavum Tiberim tangere? Cur olivum
sanguine viperino
10 cautius vitat neque iam livida gestat armis
bracchia, saepe disco,
saepe trans finem iaculo nobilis expedito?

4. **campum**: the Campus Martius was the favorite place of exercise for the young Romans. — **patiens**: *when he once endured.* Sun and dust are the two tests of manly endurance. Cf. Symmach. *Or.* 1, 1 *ibi primum tolerans solis et pulveris esse didicisti*; Tacitus, *Hist.* 2, 99, thus describes the demoralized condition of the German troops in 69 A.D. *non vigor corporibus, non ardor animis, lentum et rarum agmen, fluxa arma, segnes equi; impatiens solis, pulveris, tempestatum.*

5 ff. Two centuries later Philostratus wrote *Epist.* 27 οὐχ ἵππον ἀναβαίνεις, οὐκ εἰς παλαίστραν ἀπαντᾷς, οὐχ ἡλίῳ δίδως σεαυτόν. — **militaris**: modifying **aequalis**, *with the martial youth of his own age*; *i.e.* in the exercises described 3, 7, 25 ff. *quamvis non alius flectere equum sciens | aeque conspicitur gramine Martio, | nec quisquam citus aeque | Tusco denatat alveo.* — **Gallica . . . ora**: equivalent to *ora equorum Gallorum.* The best cavalry horses came from Gaul. — **lupatis . . . frenis**: bits with jagged points like wolf's teeth, serving the same purpose as the Mexican bit of the 'cowboy.' Cf. Verg. *G.* 3, 208 *duris parere lupatis.*

8. Swimming in the Tiber was a favorite exercise; cf. 3, 7, 27 quoted on v. 5 above, and Cic. *pro Cael.* 36 *habes hortos ad Tiberim, quo omnis iuventus natandi causa venit.* For the adjective *flavum*, cf. n. to 1, 2, 13. — **olivum**: used by wrestlers to anoint the body. — **sanguine . . . viperino**: thought to be a deadly poison. Cf. *Epod.* 3, 6 *cruor viperinus.*

10. **livida**: with bruises received in his sports with discus and javelin. — **gestat**: notice the force of the frequentative. Cf. *equitat* v. 6. — **trans finem**: the winner with discus and javelin was he who threw farthest. Cf. Odysseus' throw *Od.* 8, 192 f. ὁ (δίσκος) δ' ὑπέρπτατο σήματα πάντων | ῥίμφι θέων ἀπὸ χειρός.

Quid latet, ut marinae
   filium dicunt Thetidis sub lacrimosa Troiae
15 funera, ne virilis
   cultus in caedem et Lycias proriperet catervas?

13 ff. A post-Homeric legend told how Thetis, at the outbreak of the Trojan war, knowing the fate that awaited her son, Achilles, if he went to Troy, hid him in maiden's dress among the daughters of Lycomedes, king of Scyros. (Cf. Bion 2, 15 ff. λάνθανε δ' ἐν κώραις Λυκομηδίσι μοῦνος Ἀχιλλεύς, | εἴρια δ' ἀνθ' ὅπλων ἐδιδάσκετο, καὶ χερὶ λευκᾷ | παρθενικὸν κόρον εἶχεν, ἐφαίνετο δ' ἠΰτε κώρα. 'But Achilles alone lay hid among the daughters of Lycomedes, and was trained to work in wools, in place of arms, and in his white hand held the bough of maidenhood, in semblance a maiden.' (Lang.) Here he was discovered by Ulysses, who came in disguise as a peddler bringing wares intended to attract the attention of girls; there were also in his pack some weapons, by handling which Achilles betrayed himself. The story is told by Ovid *Met.* 13, 162 ff.; cf. Statius *Achilleis* 2, 44 f. The discovery is shown in two Pompeian wall paintings, one of which is reproduced in Baumeister, no. 1528.
— **sub ... funera**: *on the eve of*; cf. *sub noctem*. — **cultus**: *dress*.
— **Lycias**: the Lycians were the Trojans' chief allies against the army of the Greeks.

9

'The world is bound in the fetters of snow and ice. Heap high the fire to break the cold; bring out the wine. Leave all else to the gods; whate'er to-morrow's fate may give, count as pure gain. To-day is thine for love and dance, while thou art young.'

The first two strophes at least are based on an ode of Alcaeus of which we still have six verses; the setting only is Italian. Alc. *Frg.* 34 ὔει μὲν ὁ Ζεύς, ἐκ δ' ὀράνω μέγας | χείμων, πεπάγασιν δ' ὑδάτων ῥόαι. | ... κάββαλλε τὸν χείμων', ἐπὶ μὲν τίθεις | πῦρ, ἐν δὲ κίρναις οἶνον ἀφειδέως | μέλιχρον, αὐτὰρ ἀμφὶ κόρσᾳ | μαλθακὸν ἀμφι(βαλὼν) γνόφαλλον. 'Zeus sends down rain, and from the sky there falls a mighty winter storm; frozen are the streams. Break down the storm by heaping up the fire; mix sweet wine ungrudgingly, and throw round thy head sweet lavender.' The last four strophes are apparently Horace's own. The theme is the same as that of *Epod.* 13.

The ode clearly suggested to Tennyson the lines, *In Memor.* 107, 'Fiercely flies | The blast of North and East, and ice | Makes daggers at the sharpen'd eaves, . . . But fetch the wine, | Arrange the board and brim the glass, || Bring in great logs and let them lie, | To make a solid core of heat; | Be cheerful-minded, talk and treat | Of all things ev'n as he were by.'

Thaliarchus (v. 8) is only a person of Horace's fancy, although the name was in actual use, as is shown by inscriptions. The ode is evidently a study and not an occasional poem: while it probably belongs to Horace's earlier attempts at lyric verse, the skill with which it is written has won admiration from all critics. Metre, 68.

Vides ut alta stet nive candidum
Soracte, nec iam sustineant onus
silvae laborantes, geluque
flumina constiterint acuto.

5   Dissolve frigus ligna super foco
large reponens, atque benignius

1. The point of view is apparently the neighborhood of Tivoli, from which Soracte can be seen some twenty miles to the west of north; while Soracte is the highest peak (2000 feet) visible from this vicinity, it is not ordinarily the most conspicuous mountain. Snow is seldom seen on it, and so Horace seems to choose this rare phenomenon to suggest extreme cold weather. — **ut**: interrogative. — **nive candidum**: cf. Macaulay, *Regillus*, 'White as Mount Soracte | When winter nights are long.'

3 f. **laborantes**: with the burden of the snow; cf. 2, 9, 7 f. where the high wind is the cause of the wood's distress, *Aquilonibus | querqueta Gargani laborant.* — **flumina constiterint**: this degree of cold is not known to the Campagna. Horace here follows Alcaeus πεπάγασιν δ' ὑδάτων ῥόαι. — **acuto**: *biting, sharp.* Cf. Pind. *P.* 1, 38 f. νιφόεσσ' Αἴτνα, πανέτης | χιόνος ὀξείας τιθήνα, 'nurse of the biting snow the whole year through.'

5. **dissolve frigus**: cf. 1, 4, 1 *solvitur acris hiems*, and n. — **foco**: the common hearth in the middle of the atrium.

6. **reponens**: 'keeping up' the supply of wood; **re-** implying a duty to replace what the fire consumes; cf. red*dere*. — **benignius**: *without stint*, ἀφειδέως; the comparative is not opposed to the positive **large** in any sense, but is simply emphatic.

deprome quadrimum Sabina,
  o Thaliarche, merum diota.

Permitte divis cetera; qui simul
stravere ventos aequore fervido
deproeliantis, nec cupressi
  nec veteres agitantur orni.

Quid sit futurum cras fuge quaerere, et
quem fors dierum cumque dabit lucro

7. **deprome**: *broach*. Sabine wine was but ordinary 'vin de pays' which would be well aged in four years. Horace means 'a roaring fire and good *vin ordinaire* will give us warmth and cheer.' Yet the age — four years — may have been a commonplace of poets; cf. Theoc. 7, 147 τετράενες δὲ πίθων ἀπελύετο κρατὸς ἄλειφαρ. 'And it was a four-year-old seal that was loosened from the mouth of the wine jars.' Likewise 14, 15 f. ἀνῷξα δὲ βίβλινον αὐτοῖς | εὐώδη, τετόρων ἐτέων, σχεδὸν ὡς ἀπὸ λανῶ. 'And I opened for them Bibline wine, four years old, fragrant almost as when it came from the wine press.' — **Thaliarche**: Θαλίαρχος; this suggests the master of the drinking bout, *arbiter convivii*. Cf. n. to 1, 4, 18. — **diota**: δίωτος: the two-handled amphora in which the wine was stored in the apotheca.

9 f. **cetera**: *all else*, in contrast to the present moment and its joys. Cf. *Epod.* 13, 7 f. *cetera mitte loqui; deus haec fortasse benigna | reducet in sedem vice*, and Theog. 1047 f. νῦν μὲν πίνοντες τερπώμεθα, καλὰ λέγοντες · | ἄσσα δ' ἔπειτ' ἔσται, ταῦτα θεοῖσι μέλει. 'Now let us take our delight in drinking, speaking words of fair omen; whatever shall come tomorrow is only Heaven's care.' Cf. also the passages quoted on v. 13 below. — **qui simul**, etc.: the following illustrates the power of the gods. — **simul**: *i.e. simul ac*; cf. 1, 4, 17, and n. — **stravere**: so στορίννυμι, in the same connection *Od.* 3, 158 ἐστόρεσεν δὲ θεὸς μεγακήτεα πόντον.

11 f. The cypresses of the garden are contrasted with the ash trees of the mountains.

13 ff. Common Epicurean sentiments. Cf. the Anacreontic τὸ σήμερον μέλει μοι | τὸ δ' αὔριον τίς οἶδεν; and Philet. *Frg.* 7 K. τί δεῖ γὰρ ὄντα θνητόν, ἱκετεύω, ποιεῖν | πλὴν ἡδέως ζῆν τὸν βίον καθ' ἡμέραν | εἰς αὔριον δὲ μηδὲ φροντίζειν ὅ τι | ἔσται: 'For what should I who am mortal do, I pray thee, save live pleasantly day by day,

15   adpone, nec dulcis amores
          sperne puer neque tu choreas,

        donec virenti canities abest
        morosa. Nunc et campus et areae
          lenesque sub noctem susurri
20   composita repetantur hora;

        nunc et latentis proditor intimo
        gratus puellae risus ab angulo

and have no anxiety for what may come on the morrow?'—**fuge**: shun, cf. 2, 4, 22 *fuge suspicari.* — **fors**: personified, *Dame Fortune.* — **dierum**: connect with **quem . . . cumque.** For the tmesis, cf. 1, 6, 3. — **lucro appone**: in origin a commercial expression; 'carrying to the profit account.' Cf. Ovid, *Trist.* 1, 3, 68 *in lucro est quae datur hora mihi.*

16. **puer**: 'while thou art young.'— **tu**: in disjunctive sentences the subject pronoun is often reserved for the second member as here, giving emphasis to the charge. Cf. *Epist.* 1, 2, 63 *hunc frenis, hunc tu compesce catena*; and Iuv. 6, 172 *parce precor, Paean, et tu depone sagittas.*

17. **virenti canities**: notice the forceful juxtaposition; cf. n. to 1, 5, 9. — **virenti**: sc. *tibi.* Cf. *Epod.* 13, 4 *dum virent genua.*

18 ff. **morosa**: *crabbed.* — **nunc**: 'while thou art young,' repeating **donec virenti**, etc. The Campus Martius and the public squares (**areae**) were natural trysting places. In our climate we have little idea of the way in which Italian life, from business to lovemaking, is still carried on in the squares (*piazze*) of the towns and cities. — **lenes . . . susurri**: cf. Prop. 1, 11, 13 *blandos audire susurros.*

21 ff. **nunc et**: the anaphora weakens the violence of the zeugma by which this strophe is connected with **repetantur**, *be claimed*; the opposite of *reddere.* cf. n. on *reponens*, v. 6, above. The skillful arrangement of the verses is striking and cannot be reproduced in an uninflected language; like an artist, Horace adds to his picture stroke after stroke, until it is complete. Each idea in the first verse has its complement in the second:—

latentis   proditor   intimo
   | | |
puellae   risus   ab angulo
                                Intr. 21.

pignusque dereptum lacertis
aut digito male pertinaci.

23 f. The girl is coquettish. Porphyrio quotes Verg. *E.* 3, 65 *et fugit* (sc. *puella*) *ad salices et se cupit ante videri.* Cf. also Maximian's verses written in the sixth century A.D. *Eleg.* 1, 67 ff. *et modo subridens latebras fugitiva petebat,|non tamen effugiens tota latere volens, | sed magis ex aliqua cupiebat parte videri, | laetior hoc potius, quod male tecta fuit.* — **pignus**: *pledge*, either ring or bracelet. — **male**: a weak negative with **pertinaci**, like *minus*, *feebly resisting*. Cf. 1, 2, 27, and n.

10

The Italian Mercury was early identified with the Greek Hermes, but was chiefly worshiped by the Romans as the god of trade. This ode is a hymn to Mercury with the varied attributes of his Greek parallel: he is celebrated as the god of eloquence (λόγιος), of athletic contests (ἀγώνιος), the divine messenger (διάκτορος), the inventor of the lyre (μουσικός), the god of thieves (κλέπτης), the helper (ἐριούνιος), and the shepherd of the shades (ψυχοπομπός), who restrains them with his golden wand (χρυσόρραπις). That this ode is based on a similar ode by Alcaeus is expressly stated by Porphyrio, *hymnus est in Mercurium ab Alcaeo lyrico poeta*, who adds on v. 9 *fabula haec autem ab Alcaeo ficta*; furthermore Pausanias (7, 20, 5) informs us that Alcaeus treated in a hymn the theft of cattle from Apollo, but Menander (*de encom.* 7) says that the chief theme of the hymn was the birth of the god, so that we may safely conclude that Horace's treatment of his original was free. Unfortunately but three verses of Alcaeus' hymn are preserved, *Frg.* 5 χαῖρε Κυλλάνας ὁ μέδεις, σὲ γάρ μοι | θῦμος ὕμνην, τὸν κορυφαῖς ἐν αὔταις | Μαῖα γέννατο Κρονίδᾳ μιγεῖσα. Metre, 69.

Mercuri, facunde nepos Atlantis,
qui feros cultus hominum recentum

1 ff. facunde: as λόγιος, god of speech, expanded in the following **qui ... voce formasti**; cf. Mart. 7, 74, 1 *Cyllenes caelique decus, facunde minister*, and also *Acts* 14, 12 'And they called ... Paul, Mercury, because he was the chief speaker.' — **nepos Atlantis**: cf.

voce formasti catus et decorae
more palaestrae,

5   te canam, magni Iovis et deorum
nuntium curvaeque lyrae parentem.
callidum quicquid placuit iocoso
condere furto.

Te boves olim nisi reddidisses
10 per dolum amotas puerum minaci
voce dum terret, viduus pharetra
risit Apollo.

Ovid's appeal, *Fast.* 5, 663 *clare nepos Atlantis, ades*, and Eurip. *Ion* 1 ff., where Hermes speaks, Ἄτλας ... ἔφυσε Μαῖαν, ἥ μ' ἐγείνατο | Ἑρμῆν μεγίστῳ Ζηνί. — **cultus**: *manners*. — **recentum**: 'newly created'; *i.e.* mankind in its infancy, described by Horace, *S* 1, 3, 100 as *mutum et turpe pecus*. By the gift of language (**voce**) and the institution (**more**) of 'grace-giving' athletic sports Mercury raised men out of their early brute condition. An inscription (Orelli 1417) in his honor reads *sermonis dator infans palaestram protulit Cyllenius*. — **catus**: an archaic word defined by Varro *L. L.* 7, 46 as *acutus*, the opposite of *stultus*.

6. **nuntium**: so he is called Verg. *A.* 4, 356 *interpres divom*. — **lyrae parentem**: cf. Arnold's *Merope* 'Surprised in the glens | The basking tortoises, whose striped shell founded | In the hand of Hermes the glory of the lyre.'

7 f. **callidum**: with the dependent infinitive **condere**. Intr. 108. Hermes is called Eurip. *Rhes.* 217 φηλητῶν ἄναξ. — **iocoso**: *sportive*.

9 ff. According to the Homeric hymn to Mercury 22 ff. it was on the very day of the god's birth that he perpetrated this theft as well as invented the lyre. The Scholiast to *Il.* 15, 256 tells the same story Ἑρμῆς ὁ Διὸς καὶ Μαίας τῆς Ἄτλαντος εὗρε λύραν καὶ τοὺς Ἀπόλλωνος βόας κλέψας εὑρέθη ὑπὸ τοῦ θεοῦ διὰ τῆς μαντικῆς· ἀπειλοῦντος δὲ τοῦ Ἀπόλλωνος ἔκλεψεν αὐτοῦ καὶ τὰ ἐπὶ τῶν ὤμων τόξα· μειδιάσας δὲ ὁ θεὸς ἔδωκεν αὐτῷ τὴν μαντικὴν ῥάβδον, ἀφ' ἧς καὶ χρυσόρραπις ὁ Ἑρμῆς προσηγορεύθη. ἔλαβε δὲ παρ' αὐτοῦ τὴν λύραν. — **olim**: 'long ago in thy childhood.' — **nisi reddidisses**: the sentence stands in 'informal' indirect discourse, the apodosis being contained in **minaci voce**: Apollo said, threateningly, 'if you do not give back my

Quin et Atridas duce te superbos
Ilio dives Priamus relicto
Thessalosque ignis et iniqua Troiae
    castra fefellit.

Tu pias laetis animas reponis
sedibus virgaque levem coerces
aurea turbam, superis deorum
    gratus et imis.

cattle (*nisi reddideris*, fut. perf. ind.), I'll ...,' his threat being interrupted by an involuntary laugh at seeing himself robbed (**viduus**) of his quiver. — **risit**: used in obligatory sense, *had to laugh*; emphatic from its position. Intr. 22.

13 ff. This strophe summarizes the twenty-fourth book of the *Iliad*, in which is told how Priam, under Hermes' direction, came into the Greek camp bringing great ransom for Hector's body, how he kissed the hand of his son's slayer, and carried back the corpse. This example of Hermes' power to protect and aid mankind forms an easy transition from the story of his clever theft (7-12) to a mention of his highest functions, as ψυχοπομπός (17-20).

— **quin et**: regularly used in transition to a more striking statement, or, as here, to a higher theme. Cf. 2, 13, 37; 3, 11, 21. — **dives**: with the treasure he carried to ransom Hector's body. — **Thessalos ignis**: specializing the watch-fires as belonging to Achilles' troops. — **fefellit**: *went all unnoticed past*.

17. tu: note the effective anaphora whereby the **Mercuri** of the first strophe is repeated in the initial word of the second, third, and fifth (**te** ... **te** ... **tu**); in the fourth the initial **quin et** pushes the pronoun (**duce te**) to the middle of the verse. Intr. 28c. — **reponis**: *dost duly bring to the abodes of the blest*, or possibly '*restorest to*,' under the conception that the souls returned to their former homes. For this force of re- cf. 1, 3, 7 *reddas*, and n. to 1, 9, 6. — **sedibus**: abl. Intr. 95.

18 f. virga ... aurea: the κηρύκειον presented by Apollo, with which Mercury rules men and the shades alike. Cf. *Il.* 24, 343 f. εἵλετο δὲ ῥάβδον, τῇ τ' ἀνδρῶν ὄμματα θέλγει | ὧν ἐθέλει, τοὺς δ' αὖτε καὶ ὑπνώοντας ἐγείρει. The familiar caduceus with which Mercury is often represented is of later origin. — **levem ... turbam**: *flitting crowd*; εἴδωλα καμόντων. — **coerces**: as a shepherd. Cf. 1, 24, 16 ff. *quam* (sc. *imaginem*) *virga semel horrida* | *non lenis precibus fata recludere,* | *nigro compulerit Mercurius gregi,* and *Od.* 24, 1 ff.

II

'Leuconoe, give up trying to learn the secrets of the future. Be wise, do thy daily task, and live to-day; time is swiftly flying.' This is simply a variation of the theme (1, 9, 12 ff.), *quid sit futurum cras, fuge quaerere, et | quem fors dierum cumque dabit, lucro | appone.* Probably a study from the Greek, possibly of Alcaeus, as are 1, 18, and 4, 10, the two other odes in the same measure. Metre, 54.

> Tu ne quaesieris, scire nefas, quem mihi, quem tibi
> finem di dederint, Leuconoe, nec Babylonios
> temptaris numeros. Vt melius quicquid erit pati,
> seu pluris hiemes seu tribuit Iuppiter ultimam
> 5 quae nunc oppositis debilitat pumicibus mare

1. **tu**: emphasizing the requests to his imaginary Leuconoe, whose name is chosen for its pleasing sound. By the collocation, **quem mihi, quem tibi**, Horace represents her as dear to him. — **ne quaesieris**: archaic and colloquial for the ordinary *noli* with the infinitive. — **scire nefas**: parenthetical. Cf. *Epod.* 16, 14 *nefas videre*: and for the thought as well, Stat. *Theb.* 3, 562 *quid crastina volveret aetas scire nefas homini.*

2 f. **nec**: with *temptaris*, continuing the prohibition, for the more common *neve*. — **Babylonios . . . numeros**: *the calculations of the*, etc., employed in casting horoscopes. After the conquests of Alexander, astrologers made their way to Greece from the east in large numbers and had established themselves in Rome as early as the second century B.C., where they did a thriving business among the superstitious.

They had become a nuisance as early as 139 B.C. when the praetor peregrinus, Cornelius Scipio, banished them; but they still continued to practice their art throughout the republic and especially under the empire, in spite of many attempts to rid Italy of them. Cf. Tac. *Hist.* 1, 22 *genus hominum potentibus infidum sperantibus fallax, quod in civitate nostra et vetabitur semper et retinebitur.*

— **ut**: cf. *Epod.* 2, 10 *ut gaudet decerpens pira.* — **hiemes**: of years, equivalent to *annos*; cf. 1, 15, 35 *post certas hiemes.*

5 f. **oppositis debilitat pumicibus mare Tyrrhenum**: pumices is used of any rocks eaten by the waves; cf. Lucret. 1, 326 *vesco sale saxa peresa.* Sidon. Apoll. 10, 27 *prominet alte | asper ab assiduo lympharum verbere pumex.* The description given, however, is hardly appropriate to the Tuscan Sea, in the region

Tyrrhenum. Sapias, vina liques, et spatio brevi
spem longam reseces. Dum loquimur, fugerit invida
aetas; carpe diem, quam minimum credula postero.

best known to Horace. — **sapias**: *be sensible*, expanded in what follows. With the sentiment, cf. 1, 7, 17 *sapiens finire memento tristitiam.* — **vina liques**: to free the wine from sediment it was poured from the amphora through a cloth (*saccus*) or strainer (*colum*). — **spatio brevi**: 'for our life's span is brief;' opposed to **spem longam**. Intr. 26. — **reseces**: *cut short.*

7. **dum loquimur ... fugerit**: note the force of the fut. perf. Cf. Lucret. 3, 914 f. *brevis hic est fructus homullis;* | *iam fuerit neque post umquam revocare licebit.* Also Iuv. 9, 128 f. *dum bibimus, ... obrepit non intellecta senectus.*

8. **diem**: *the flitting day*, equivalent to '*primo quoque die fruere*,' according to Porphyrio, who adds that the figure is taken from picking (*carpere*) fruit, '*quae carpimus ut fruamur.*' Cf. Lucil. 39, 51 M. *hiemem unam quamque carpam;* Mart. 7, 47, 11 *fugitiva gaudia carpe.* The spirit of the last line is also expressed in *Epist.* 1, 4, 12 f. *inter spem curamque, timores inter et iras | omnem crede diem tibi diluxisse supremum;* likewise by Persius, 5, 151-53, who expands Horace's verse, *indulge genio, carpamus dulcia, nostrum est | quod vivis, cinis et manes et fabula fies, | vive memor leti, fugit hora, hoc quod loquor inde est.*

— **credula**: of foolish confidence, cf. 1, 5, 9 *qui nunc te fruitur credulus aurea.*

12

'What hero, demigod, or god, dost thou prepare to sing, O Muse? Whose name shall echo on Helicon, on Pindus. or on Haemus' height, where Orpheus charmed all nature with his strains? (1-12). Of gods first surely father Jove; then his daughter Pallas, then Liber. Diana, and Phoebus (13-24). The demigod, Alceus' grandson, will I celebrate, and the twin brothers, who guard sailors from the angry sea (25-32). Then the great Romans, Romulus, Tarquin, Cato, and the long line of heroes after them (33-44). Marcellus' fame is growing; the Julian star outshines the rest (45-48). Father and guardian of men, in thy care is mighty Caesar, greatest of all the Roman line. May his rule be second to thine only; may he conquer the Parthians and the remotest Eastern peoples, and rule the wide wide world; still shall he be thy subject, for thou, thou only shalt ever be Lord of Olympus, the Punisher of crime (49-60).'

This ode, like the second of this book, is in honor of Augustus, who is celebrated as greatest of all the long line of Roman heroes, the vicegerent of Jove. The mention of Marcellus (46) makes it probable that the date of composition was either 25 B.C., when Marcellus was married to Augustus' daughter Julia and adopted as the Emperor's son, or in any case between that date and Marcellus' death in 23 B.C. The opening verses were suggested by Pindar's ode in honor of Theron (*O.* 2) which begins ἀναξιφόρμιγγες ὕμνοι, | τίνα θεόν, τίν' ἥρωα, τίνα δ' ἄνδρα κελαδήσομεν: Horace proceeds, however, in very different fashion from Pindar, who answers his question at once: 'Of the Gods, Zeus; of demigods, Heracles; of men, Theron the victor.' Metre, 69.

> Quem virum aut heroa lyra vel acri
> tibia sumis celebrare, Clio,
> quem deum? Cuius recinet iocosa
>   nomen imago
>
> 5   aut in umbrosis Heliconis oris
> aut super Pindo gelidove in Haemo?

1. **heroa**: *demigod.* — **lyra ... tibia**: the Greek rhapsodist accompanied his recital with the lyre, and it is said (Cic. *Tusc.* 4, 3) that in early times the Romans sang their songs in honor of their ancestors (*laudationes*) to the music of the tibia. — **acri**: λιγείῃ, λιγυρᾷ; of the high clear notes of the pipe. The epithet is praised by Quintilian 8, 2, 9 *proprie dictum est, id est, quo nihil inveniri possit significantius.* — **sumis**: *choose*, as subject of thy song; used with similar dependent infin. *Epist.* 1, 3, 7 *quis sibi res gestas Augusti scribere sumit?* — **Clio**: while Horace does not often distinguish the Muses, it is possible that here Clio is invoked in her peculiar character as Muse of History.

3 f. **iocosa ... imago**: *sportive echo.* Cf. 1, 20, 6 *iocosa ... Vaticani montis imago.*

5 f. Three homes of the Muses: Helicon in Boeotia, Pindus in Thessaly, Haemus in Thrace. At the foot of Helicon was the village of Ascra, in which there was a shrine of the Muses (μουσεῖον) and a guild of poets of which Hesiod (eighth century B.C.) was the most famous. The mountain was also famed for the springs of Hippocrene and Aganippe. Pindus was between Thessaly and Epirus; likewise a haunt of the Muses. Haemus was the seat of an early cult of the Muses and the traditional home of a Thracian school of poetry. Cf. Verg. *E.* 10, 11 f. *nam neque Parnasi vobis iuga, nam neque*

Vnde vocalem temere insecutae
   Orphea silvae,

arte materna rapidos morantem
   fluminum lapsus celerisque ventos, 10
blandum et auritas fidibus canoris
   ducere quercus.

Quid prius dicam solitis parentis
   laudibus, qui res hominum ac deorum,

Pindi | ulla moram fecere, neque Aonie Aganippe. — oris: the borders of.

7 f. **temere**: *blindly*, being spellbound by Orpheus' music. For the story of Orpheus' power, cf. Apoll. Rhod. 1, 28 ff. φηγοὶ δ᾽ ἀγριάδες, κείνης ἔτι σήματα μολπῆς, ἀκτῆς Θρηικίης Ζώνης ἔπι τηλεθόωσαι | ἑξείης στιχόωσιν ἐπήτριμοι, ἃς ὅγ᾽ ἐπιπρὸ | θελγομένας φόρμιγγι κατήγαγε Πιερίηθεν. 'But the wild oaks — even to-day memorials of that song — grow on Zone, the Thracian promontory, and stand there in rows close together; the oaks that Orpheus charmed with his lyre and brought down from Pieria.' Also Shakespere, *Henry Eighth* 3, 1 'Orpheus with his lute made trees, | And the mountain tops that freeze, | Bow themselves when he did sing: | To his music, plants and flowers | Ever sprung; as sun and showers | There had made a lasting Spring.'

9 ff. Cf. 3, 11, 13 f. *tu potes tigris comitesque silvas | ducere et rivos celeris morari.* — **materna**:

i.e. of Calliope. — **blandum . . . ducere**: for the dependent infinitive Porphyrio compares 1, 10, 7 *callidum condere.* — **auritas**: proleptical, 'with charm to give ears to the oaks and draw them after him.'

13-24. The Gods. Notice that Horace in taking up his examples reverses the order of v. 1 ff. **virum . . . heroa . . . deum**.

13. **solitis parentis laudibus**: the customary beginning from the time of the Homeric rhapsodists. Cf. Pind. *N.* 2, 1 ff. ὅθεν περ καὶ Ὁμηρίδαι | ῥαπτῶν ἐπέων τὰ πόλλ᾽ ἀοιδοὶ | ἄρχονται. Διὸς ἐκ προοιμίου. And Aratus *Phaen.* 1 f. ἐκ Διὸς ἀρχώμεσθα . . . . τοῦ γὰρ καὶ γένος ἐσμέν. Also Verg. *E.* 3, 60 *ab Iove principium.* The formula indicates the beginning of a loftier strain than usual, of a song that may be compared with that of Thracian Orpheus.

— **parentis**: cf. v. 49 *pater atque custos*, and 1, 2, 2 *pater*.

14. **qui res**, etc.: cf. Venus' address. Verg. *A.* 1, 229 f. *o qui res hominumque deumque | aeternis regis imperiis.*

15   qui mare et terras variisque mundum
         temperat horis?

     Vnde nil maius generatur ipso,
     nec viget quicquam simile aut secundum;
     proximos illi tamen occupavit
20   Pallas honores,

     proeliis audax; neque te silebo
     Liber, et saevis inimica virgo
     beluis, nec te, metuende certa
         Phoebe sagitta.

15 f. **mundum**: *heavens*, in contrast with **mare, terras**. — **horis**: *seasons*. Cf. *Epist.* 2, 3, 302 *sub verni temporis horam.*
17. **unde**: equivalent to *ex quo*, referring to **parens**. Cf. Verg. *A.* 1, 6 *genus unde Latinum.* This use of **unde**, referring to a person, is chiefly found in poetry, cf. 2, 12, 7 *unde = a quibus*, but occurs also in prose, e.g. Cic. *de Or.* 1, 67 *ille ipse, unde cognovit.*
18 f. **quicquam simile**: sc. *ei.* — **secundum . . . proximos**: the distinction between these words is clearly shown by Vergil in his account of the boat race, *A.* 5, 320 *proximus huic, longo sed proximus intervallo*, as earlier by Cicero, *Brut.* 173 *duobus summis (oratoribus) L. Philippus proximus accedebat, sed longo intervallo tamen proximus.* **Secundus** is used properly of that which is 'next,' closely connected, while **proximus** may be used of that which is

'nearest' although separated by a considerable distance.
21 f. **proeliis audax**: modifying **Pallas**. — **et**: continuing the negative **neque . . . silebo**. — **virgo**: Diana (Artemis), not simply as the huntress, but also as the destroyer of fierce monsters (**beluis**) and a benefactress of mankind. Cf. Callim. *Hymn to Artemis* 153 f. (Heracles speaks) βάλλε κακοὺς ἐπὶ θῆρας, ἵνα θνητοί σε βοηθόν | ὡς ἐμὲ κικλήσκωσιν.
23 f. **metuende certa Phoebe sagitta**: the list of beneficent divinities celebrated closes with Apollo, the slayer of the monster Python. He was the champion of Augustus at Actium, and afterward regarded by the emperor as his patron divinity. Cf Prop. 5, 6, 27 ff. *cum Phoebus linquens . . . Delon, adstitit Augusti puppim super, . . . qualis flexos solvit Pythona per orbis serpentem.* It should be also noticed

25 Dicam et Alciden puerosque Ledae,
hunc equis, illum superare pugnis
nobilem; quorum simul alba nautis
    stella refulsit,

defluit saxis agitatus umor,
30 concidunt venti fugiuntque nubes,
et minax, quod sic voluere, ponto
    unda recumbit.

Romulum post hos prius an quietum
Pompili regnum memorem an superbos

that the gods selected are those who had made the earth more tenable for man by freeing it of monsters, but none of the divinities especially connected with the Roman people, as Mars, or with the Julian line, as Venus, are included.

25–32. The demigods. — **Alciden**: *Hercules.* — **hunc equis, illum,** etc.: cf. *Il.* 3, 237 Κάστορά θ' ἱππόδαμον καὶ πὺξ ἀγαθὸν Πολυδεύκεα.

27 ff. **quorum simul,** etc.: cf. n. to 1, 3, 2 and the passages there quoted. This graphic passage, as well as 4, 8, 33, reflects Theoc. 22, 17 ff. ἀλλ' ἔμπας ὑμεῖς γε καὶ ἐκ βυθοῦ ἕλκετε νᾶας | αὐτοῖσιν ναύταισιν ὀιομ'νοις θανέεσθαι· | αἶψα δ' ἀπολήγοντ' ἄνεμοι, λιπαρὰ δὲ γαλάνα | ἀμπέλαγος· νεφ'λαι δὲ δι'-δραμον ἄλλυδις ἄλλαι. 'Yet even so do ye draw forth the ships from the abyss, with their sailors that looked immediately to die; and instantly the winds are still, and there is an oily calm along the sea, and the clouds flee apart, this way and that' (Lang). Cf. also Verg. *A.* 1, 1, 54 *sic cunctus pelagi cecidit fragor.* — **refulsit**: *i.e.* in answer to the sailors' prayers.

29 ff. **defluit ... concidunt ... fugiunt**: observe the effective emphasis given by position and rhythm.

33 f. Horace now turns to mortals — the noble Romans dead and gone. — **quietum Pompili regnum**: Numa's peaceful reign, during which tradition said religious observances were established, is contrasted with the warlike rule of Romulus. Livy describes the services of the two kings 1, 21 *duo deinceps reges, alius alia via, ille* (*Romulus*) *bello, hic* (*Numa*) *pace, civitatem auxerunt.* — **superbos Tarquini fascis**: the adjective belongs logically to **Tarquini**, who served the state by his conquests of the neighboring peoples. Although the remembrance of his haughtiness remained, his memory

35 Tarquini fascis dubito, an Catonis
       nobile letum.

Regulum et Scauros animaeque magnae
prodigum Paullum superante Poeno

was not stained with any baseness. Cic. *Phil.* 3, 9. *Tarquinius ... non crudelis, non impius, sed superbus habitus est et dictus ... nihil humile de Tarquinio, nihil sordidum accepimus.*

35 f. Catonis nobile letum: Horace passes in his examples of Roman *virtus* from the last of the kings to the last great republican. Cato's choice of suicide at Utica (46 B.C.) rather than of submission to the new order of things, is frequently referred to by his contemporaries and by writers of the following century in terms of the highest praise. Cf. Cic. *ad fam.* 9, 18 *Pompeius, Scipio, Afranius in bello civile foede perierunt,* '*at Cato praeclare.*' No question was raised as to Cato's honesty of purpose, and he became a kind of canonized hero. Augustus' policy of allowing praise of all that was noble in the champions of the republic made it possible for Horace to do honor to Cato even in an ode glorifying the emperor. Indeed Augustus wisely forestalled his opponents by praising Cato himself.

37 ff. Horace here returns to the heroes of an earlier time. — **Regulum**: Regulus was a traditional instance of that ancient Roman manhood (*virtus*) that preferred his country's honor to his own life. The fifth ode of the third book holds up his self-sacrifice as an example for the youth of Horace's own time. — **Scauros**: referring chiefly to M. Scaurus and his son. The father was called by Valerius Max. 5, 8, 4 *lumen et decus patriae*; the son was involved in the defeat on the Adige in 101 B.C. and shared the panic-stricken flight under Catulus. His father sent him a message saying that he should rather have found his dead body than see him alive after sharing in such a disgrace, whereupon the young man killed himself. Valer. Max. *l.c.*; Aur. Vict. 3, 72 *in conspectum suum vetuit accedere; ille ob hoc dedecus mortem sibi conscivit.* — **prodigum**: cf. Ovid. *Am.* 3, 9, 64 *sanguinis atque animae prodige Galle tuae.* — **Paullum**: L. Aemilius Paullus, who chose to die at the battle of Cannae (216 B.C.) rather than escape, as he might have done with honor, according to Livy's account (22, 49).

39. gratus: either of Horace's own feeling of gratitude toward so noble a character, or simply 'pleasing,' 'in verse pleasing **my readers.**'

gratus insigni referam camena
  Fabriciumque.

Hunc et intonsis Curium capillis
utilem bello tulit et Camillum
saeva paupertas et avitus apto
  cum lare fundus.

Crescit occulto velut arbor aevo
fama Marcelli; micat inter omnis
Iulium sidus velut inter ignis
  luna minores.

Cf. Mart. 4, 55, 10 *grato non pudeat referre versu.*—**insigni...camena**: 'with the Muse that gives men fame.'

40 ff. The following illustrations of ancient *virtus* and *continentia* are C. Fabricius Luscinus, whom Pyrrhus could neither frighten nor bribe; M'. Curius Dentatus, who was equally incorruptible; and M. Furius Camillus, who captured Veii (396 B.C.) and saved Rome from the Gauls (390 B.C.). All three, however, are chosen as examples, not of great deeds, but of great characters. Their natures were proverbial.

—**intonsis capillis**: barbers were not employed at Rome until about 300 B.C. (Plin. *N. H.* 7, 211); and the custom of shaving the beard and wearing the hair short became general much later.

43 f. saeva: *stern*, as training men to hardihood. All three worthies were men of small estate, but of great native worth.—**apto cum lare**: 'with humble house befitting their ancestral farms.'

45 ff. While the direct reference here is to the young Marcellus, Octavia's son, no doubt the name in this connection would call up to the Roman mind at once that M. Claudius Marcellus, who in 222 B.C. won the *spolia opima* for the third and last time, captured Syracuse in 212 B.C., and was the first successful general against Hannibal.—**occulto...aevo**: with **crescit**, *is growing with the unmarked lapse of time.* Cf. 2, 2, 5 *extento aevo.*

47 f. Iulium sidus: the star of the Julian house. This use of **sidus** ('fortune') would doubtless call to mind the comet that appeared shortly after Julius Caesar's murder (Suet. *Iul.* 88). Cf. Verg. *E.* 9, 47 *ecce Dionaei processit Caesaris astrum.*— **inter ignis luna minores**: a reminiscence of his earlier phrase,

Gentis humanae pater atque custos,
50 orte Saturno, tibi cura magni
Caesaris fatis data: tu secundo
    Caesare regnes.

Ille seu Parthos Latio imminentis
egerit iusto domitos triumpho
55 sive subiectos Orientis orae
    Seras et Indos,

te minor latum reget aequus orbem;
tu gravi curru quaties Olympum,
tu parum castis inimica mittes
60   fulmina lucis.

Epod. 15, 2 *caelo fulgebat luna sereno inter minora sidera.* In both he may have had in mind Sappho *Frg* 3, 1 f. ἄστερες μὲν ἀμφὶ κάλαν σελάνναν | ἂψ ἀποκρύπτοισι φάεννον εἶδος. 'The stars about the fair moon hide their bright face.'

49 ff. The climax of the ode. With the idea expressed, cf. Ovid's more extravagant laudation *Met.* 15, 858 ff. *Iuppiter arces | temperat aetherias et mundi regna triformis; | terra sub Augusto: pater est et rector uterque.*

51 f. secundo Caesare: logically part of the prayer, *and Caesar be second to thee only.*

53 f. The 'Eastern Question' was always an annoying one to the Romans. Cf. n. to 1, 2, 22. — **egerit**: *i.e.* as captives before his car. Cf. *Epod.* 7, 7 f. — **iusto . . .**

triumpho: a technical term, implying that all the conditions on which a triumph depended had been fulfilled.

55 f. The **Serae** ('Silk-people,' the Chinese) were known to the Romans only through trade. They and the Indians stand for the great remote East.

57 ff. te...tu...tu...: opposed to ille v. 53. Intr. 28c. — **te minor**: cf. 3, 6, 5 *Romane, quod dis minorem te geris, imperas.* — **reget aequus**: *rule in justice.* For the tense, see Intr. 102.

59 f. A stroke of lightning was a most important omen to the Romans; if a sacred grove was struck, that fact was proof that the grove had been polluted, and required purification. — **parum**: cf. n. to *minus* 1, 2, 27.

13

To contrast with the serious tone of the preceding ode, Horace placed here these impetuous verses to (an imaginary) Lydia. 'When thou praisest Telephus' beauty, Lydia, I swell with rage; my self-control all goes; pale and weeping I show my jealous love. The injuries done thy fair shoulders and sweet lips by that bold boy do not prove a lasting love. Happy they who love till death.' Metre, 71.

> Cum tu, Lydia, Telephi
>   cervicem roseam, cerea Telephi
> laudas bracchia, vae meum
>   fervens difficili bile tumet iecur.
> 5   Tum nec mens mihi nec color
>   certa sede manet, umor et in genas
> furtim labitur, arguens
>   quam lentis penitus macerer ignibus.
> Vror, seu tibi candidos
> 10   turparunt umeros immodicae mero

1 f. **Telephi ... Telephi**: reproducing in jealousy Lydia's fond repetition of her lover's name. Cf. the passionate delaration, Anacr. *Frg.* 3 Κλευβούλου μὲν ἔγωγ᾽ ἐρῶ, | Κλευβούλου δ᾽ ἐπιμαίνομαι, | Κλεύβουλον δὲ διοσκέω. Note the alliteration, **cervicem ... cerea**.

3 f. **vae**: *bah!* in angry disgust. — **tumet iecur**: *i.e.* in rage. iecur is to be taken literally as the seat of passion (*S.* 1, 9, 66 *meum iecur urere bilis*) that overflows with savage wrath. — **bilis**: equivalent to χόλος.

5 f. **mens ... color**, etc.: for his self-control is lost, and his color comes and goes. Cf. Apoll. Rhod. 3, 297 f. ἁπαλὰς δὲ μετετρωπᾶτο παρειὰς | ἐς χλόον, ἄλλοτ᾽ ἔρευθος, ἀκηδείῃσι νόοιο. 'Love turned her tender cheeks to pallor, again to blushing, for the weariness of her soul.' — **certa sede**: more closely connected with **color** than with **mens**, as its position shows. — **manēt**: Intr. 35. — **umor**: cf. Plat. *Tim.* 68 A. ὕδωρ ὃ δάκρυον καλοῦμεν.

8. **quam lentis**: modified by **penitus**; *slow, pervasive.* Cf. Verg. *A.* 5, 682 f. *lentusque carinas | est vapor.*

9 f. **uror**: the rudeness of my rival in his cups, and the passion of his love, alike inflame me. — **turparunt**: *harmed with blows.* — **immodicae**: modified by the causal abl. **mero**.

rixae, sive puer furens
 impressit memorem dente labris **notam.**
Non, si me satis audias,
 speres perpetuum dulcia barbare
15 laedentem oscula, quae Venus
 quinta parte sui nectaris imbuit.
Felices ter et amplius,
 quos inrupta tenet copula nec malis
divolsus querimoniis
20 suprema citius sólvet amor die.

13 f. non: emphatic, like the English 'No, you would not,' etc. — **dulcia barbare**: cf. n. to 1, 5, 9. Intr. 26.

16. quinta parte: simply 'the best part.' Cf. Meleager *Anth. Pal.* 12, 133 φίλημα τὸ νεκτάρεον Γανυμήδευς ... ψυχῆς ἡδὺ πέπωκα μέλι. In their efforts to determine the degree of sweetness that Horace means to indicate here, commentators have spent an amusing amount of energy without, however, succeeding in their attempts. We cannot be sure that Horace uses the phrase as equivalent to the Pythagorean ἡ πέμπτη οὐσία, τὸ πέμπτον ὄν, the mediaeval *quinta essentia* (quintessence), satisfactory as this explanation would be.

18 ff. inrupta: *unbreakable*, rather than 'unbroken'; used like *invictus*, etc., in the sense of an adj. in *-ilis, -bilis*. — **divolsus amor**: cf. 2, 4, 10 *ademptus Hector*. — **suprema die**: *life's last day*.

14

'O Ship of State, beware! avoid the open sea; thou art shattered by the storm just past. Put into port.' Quintilian 8, 6, 44 uses this ode as an illustration of an allegory — *at ἀλληγορία quam inversionem interpretantur, aut aliud verbis aliud sensu ostendit aut etiam interim contrarium. Prius fit genus plerumque continuatis translationibus: ut 'o navis ... portum.' totusque ille Horatii locus, quo navem pro re publica, fluctus et tempestates pro bellis civilibus, portum pro pace atque concordia dicit.'* This figure is as old as Theognis, and occurs frequently in Greek literature. Horace took as his model a poem of Alcaeus of which the following verses have been preserved, *Frg.* 18: —

CARMINA [1, 14, 4

ἀσυνέτημι τῶν ἀνέμων στάσιν · | τὸ μὲν γὰρ ἔνθεν κῦμα κυλίνδεται | τὸ δ' ἔνθεν ἄμμες δ' ἂν τὸ μέσσον | νᾶϊ φορήμεθα σὺν μελαίνᾳ, || χείμωνι μοχθεῦντες μεγάλῳ μάλα · | περ μὲν γὰρ ἄντλος ἰστοπέδαν ἔχει, | λαῖφος δὲ πᾶν ζάδηλον ἤδη | καὶ λάκιδες μεγάλαι κατ' αὐτο · | χάλαισι δ' ἄγκυλαι · 'I do not understand the winds' strife, for the wave rolls, now from this side, now from that, and we with our black ship are carried in the midst, struggling hard with the mighty storm. For the flood surrounds the mast step, the canvas is utterly destroyed, great rents are in it; and the yard-ropes are loosened.' The most familiar modern example of this allegory is Longfellow's *The Building of the Ship*. 'Thou, too, sail on, O Ship of State!' etc.

Apart from other considerations the poem is interesting as a sign that Horace's attitude toward the new government had changed from that of his student days when he served in Brutus' army (cf. v. 17 f.). The date of composition is most probably between the battle of Actium, 31 B.C., and the reorganization of the empire in 27 B.C.: in any case it was written at a time when civil war was lately past, but serious men still had reason to be anxious for the public peace; and we must remember that however lightly Horace treated many subjects, his attitude toward the state was that of earnest loyalty. See Sellar, pp. 29, 151 ff. Here Horace expresses his feeling that the state cannot endure another civil war, and that peace must be preserved. Cf. with this ode *Epod.* 7 and 16. Metre, 73.

O navis, referent in mare te novi
fluctus! O quid agis? Fortiter occupa
portum! Nonne vides ut
nudum remigio latus

1 f. **in mare**: in antiquity sailors kept near the shore. Cf. 2, 10, 1 ff. — **novi fluctus**: the new storms of (a possible) civil war. — **fortiter occupa**: *make a valiant effort and gain the port* before the storm breaks. — **occupare** is frequently used like the Greek φθάνειν; cf. *Epist.* 1. 6. 32 *cave ne portus occupet alter*.

4 ff. This passage is imitated by Claudian *de sexto cons. Honor.* 132 ff. *qualis piratica puppis . . . viduataque caesis | remigibus, scissis velorum debilis alis. | orba gubernaclis, antemnis saucia fractis | ludibrium pelagi vento iaculatur et unda.*

— **remigio**: *oars*, not 'rowers.' Cf. Ovid *A. A.* 2, 671 *mare re-*

5   et malus celeri saucius Africo
    antemnaeque gemant ac sine funibus
      vix durare carinae
        possint imperiosius

    aequor? Non tibi sunt integra lintea,
10 non di, quos iterum pressa voces malo.
      Quamvis Pontica pinus,
        silvae filia nobilis,

    iactes et genus et nomen inutile,
    nil pictis timidus navita puppibus
15   fidit. Tu nisi ventis
        debes ludibrium, cave.

migiis aut vomere findite terras. — **malus**: note the quantity; cf. v. 10 **malo**. For the rigging of an ancient ship see Torr *Ancient Ships*, p. 78-98. — **funibus**: ὑποζώματα; cables or girders passed about the ship horizontally to strengthen it against the force of the waves, or in the case of warships, the shock of ramming. Cf. *Acts* 27, 17; Torr *A. S.* p. 41-43.

7 f. **carinae**: plural, where we use the singular; cf. 1, 2. 15 f. *monumenta, templa*. — **imperiosius**: equivalent to *saevius, in its stern tyranny*.

10. **di**: i.e. the little images of the gods that were carried on the poop deck. Horace means that in the storm of civil war the ship of state lost her protecting divinities; cf. Ovid *Her*. 16, 114 *accipit et pictos puppis adunca deos*, and Pers. 6, 29 f. *iacet ipse in litore et una | ingentes de puppe dei.*

11 f. **Pontica pinus**: Pontus was famous for its ship timber. — **filia**: cf. Mart. 14, 90 *silvae filia Maurae* of a citrus table. For the arrangement of words, see Intr. 19.

13. **iactes**: *boastest*; emphatic by position. — **inutile**: added predicatively — *all in vain for thee*. — **pictis**: cf. the Homeric νῆες μιλτοπάρῃοι. — **timidus**: 'when he is frightened.'

15 f. **tu**: in direct address to the ship. — **debes**: cf. Greek ὀφλισκάνειν δίκην, *art bound, doomed to be* the sport of the winds.

Nuper sollicitum quae mihi taedium,
nunc desiderium curaque non levis,
   interfusa nitentis
      vites aequora Cycladas.

17 f. **nuper** . . . **nunc**: the time of the civil wars in contrast to the present moment. — **sollicitum . . . taedium**: *anxiety and heartsickness.* — **desiderium**: *object of my longing.*
19 f. **nitentis**: cf. 3, 28, 14

fulgentes Cycladas. The southern Aegean, dotted with frequent islands (Verg. *A.* 3, 126 *sparsasque per aequor Cycladas*) is subject to many squalls, but the particular sea has no significance in the allegory.

15

'When faithless Paris was carrying Helen home to Troy, Nereus becalmed the sea that he might foretell the doom that was to follow Paris' crime.' Porphyrio says that the motive was taken from Bacchylides, who made Cassandra prophesy the coming war and disaster, as Horace here has Nereus (Porphyrio read Proteus). If Porphyrio be right, Horace's model has been lost to us; the extant fragment 14 Blass, in which Menelaus warns the Trojans to remember the justice of Zeus, cannot be that to which Porphyrio refers. The theme is essentially epic and does not properly fall within the province of lyric poetry; and Horace has not been very successful in his treatment of it. While some dramatic skill is shown, the episode chosen has no natural limits and therefore offered him little opportunity for a climax; the length of the prophecy was determined solely by the poet's inclination. That Horace learned to handle narrative subjects later is proved by Book 3, Odes 11 and 27, with which this ode should be carefully compared. For Horace's view as to the proper field for lyric verse, see Book 2, Ode 12.

For the reasons given above and because of the technical defect of v. 36, we may regard this as one of Horace's earlier studies. Metre, 72.

Pastor cum traheret per freta navibus
Idaeis Helenen perfidus hospitam,

1. **pastor**: Paris, whom Verg. *A.* 7. 363 calls *Phrygius pastor.* Cf. also Bion 2, 10 ἅρπασε τὰν Ἑλέναν πόθ' ὁ βουκόλος, ἆγε δ'

ἐς Ἴδαν. — **traheret**: *was carrying away.*
2. **Idaeis**: *i.e.* their timber grew on Mt. Ida. — **perfidus hospitam**:

ingrato celeres obruit otio
ventos ut caneret fera

5   Nereus fata: 'Mala ducis avi domum
quam multo repetet Graecia milite,
coniurata tuas rumpere nuptias
et regnum Priami vetus.

Heu heu, quantus equis, quantus adest viris
10 sudor! Quanta moves funera Dardanae
genti! Iam galeam Pallas et aegida
currusque et rabiem parat.

cf. n. to 1, 5, 9. Intr. 26. No greater crime was known to antiquity than violation of the rights and privileges of hospitality. With this epithet of Paris, cf. 3, 3, 26 *famosus hospes*, and Prop. 2, 34, 7 *hospes in hospitium Menelao venit adulter*.

3 ff. ingrato . . . otio: as the winds favored the lovers in their flight. — **caneret**: the regular word of prophecy. Cf. *Epod.* 13, 11 *nobilis ut grandi cecinit centaurus alumno*.

5 ff. Note the dramatic force of the prophecy, and the many reminiscences of the *Iliad*. — **Nereus**: son of Pontus and Tellus, father of Thetis. Cf. Hesiod *Theog.* 233 ff. Νηρέα δ' ἀψευδέα καὶ ἀληθέα γείνατο Πόντος, | πρεσβύτατον παίδων · αὐτὰρ καλέουσι γέροντα, | οὕνεκα νημερτής τε καὶ ἤπιος. οὐδὲ θεμιστέων | λήθεται, ἀλλὰ δίκαια καὶ ἤπια δήνεα οἶδεν. — **mala . . . avi**: cf. 3, 3, 61 *alite lugubri*. Cf. Catull. 61, 20 *bona alite*.

7 f. coniurata: in solemn compact at Aulis. Cf. Verg. *A.* 4, 425 f. where Dido says, *non ego cum Danais Troianam exscindere gentem | Aulide iuravi*; Euripides, *Iph. in Aul.* 49 ff. makes Agamemnon tell of the earlier oath, by which the suitors bound themselves to protect and avenge the one who should win Helen. — **regnum**: with rumpere as Sen. *H. F.* 79 *Titanas ausos rumpere imperium Iovis*.

9 f. quantus equis . . . sudor: Horace had in mind *Il.* 2, 388 ff. ἱδρώσει μέν τευ τελαμὼν ἀμφὶ στήθεσφιν | ἀσπίδος ἀμφιβρότης, περὶ δ' ἔγχεϊ χεῖρα καμεῖται · | ἱδρώσει δέ τευ ἵππος ἐΰξοον ἅρμα τιταίνων. — **funera**: *disasters*.

11. galeam Pallas, etc.: a reminiscence of *Il.* 5, 738 ff. ἀμφὶ δ' ἄρ' ὤμοισιν βάλετ' αἰγίδα θυσσανόεσσαν | δεινήν. . . . κρατὶ δ' ἐπ' ἀμφίφαλον κυνέην θέτο τετραφάληρον | χρυσείην. — **aegida**: the breastplate of Athena, which

Nequiquam Veneris praesidio ferox
pectes caesariem grataque feminis
imbelli cithara carmina divides;
nequiquam thalamo gravis

hastas et calami spicula Cnosii
vitabis strepitumque et celerem sequi
Aiacem: tamen, heu, serus adulteros
crinis pulvere collines.

is represented on statues and paintings as a mail corselet, fringed with snakes and adorned with the Medusa's head in the center. See Baumeister, nos. 166-170. — **rabiem parat**: cf. Ovid *Met.* 13, 554 *se armat et instruit ira*.

13 ff. Cf. Hector's reproachful words *Il.* 3, 54 f. οὐκ ἄν τοι χραίσμῃ κίθαρις τά τε δῶρ' Ἀφροδίτης, | ἥ τε κόμη τό τε εἶδος, ὅτ' ἐν κονίῃσι μιγείης. — **nequiquam**: *all in vain*, emphatic. — **ferox**: in scorn, *made so bold by*. — **grata feminis . . . imbelli cithara . . . thalamo**: all said contemptuously.

15 f. **carmina divides**: apparently equivalent to μελίζειν, 'to sing rhythmically.' — **nequiquam**: Intr. 28 c — **thalamo**: cf. *Il.* 3, 380 ff. τὸν δ' ἐξήρπαξ' Ἀφροδίτη | ῥεῖα μάλ' ὥς τε θεός, ἐκάλυψε δ' ἄρ' ἠέρι πολλῇ, | κὰδ δ' εἷσ' ἐν θαλάμῳ εὐώδεϊ κηώεντι.

17. **calami spicula Cnosii**: light arrows in contrast to the heavy spears (**gravis**, equivalent to the Homeric epithets βριθύ, μέγα, στιβαρόν). The adj. Cnosii, referring to Cnosus, the chief city of Crete, is here employed, since the Cretans were famous archers. Cf. Verg. *A.* 5, 206 *Cnosia spicula*.

17 f. **vitabis**: *try to avoid* the din of battle (**strepitum**) and the forefighters of the Greeks. In the *Iliad* Paris is represented as shrinking from battle. only appearing occasionally on sudden impulse. Homer never opposes him to Ajax, son of Oileus, to whom Horace apparently gives the first place here simply as one of the foremost Greek heroes. — **celerem sequi Aiacem**: cf. *Il.* 2, 527 Ὀϊλῆος ταχὺς Αἴας. For the infinitive, see Intr. 108.

19 f. **tamen**: referring back to nequiquam, nequiquam; 'in spite of all thy own efforts and Aphrodite's aid.' — **serus**: an adj. where we employ an adverb. Cf. 1, 2, 45 *serus in caelum redeas*, and *Il.* 1, 424 χθιζὸς ἔβη Ζεύς. — **crinis . . . collines**: cf. Verg. *A.* 12, 99 *da . . . foedare in pulvere crines*.

I, 15, 21] HORATI

> Non Laertiaden, exitium tuae
> gentis, non Pylium Nestora respicis?
> Vrgent impavidi te Salaminius
> Teucer, te Sthenelus sciens
>
> 25 pugnae, sive opus est imperitare equis,
> non auriga piger. Merionen quoque
> nosces. Ecce furit te reperire atrox
> Tydides, melior patre,
>
> quem tu, cervus uti vallis in altera
> 30 visum parte lupum graminis immemor
> sublimi fugies mollis anhelitu,
> non hoc pollicitus tuae.

21-28. Laertiaden: Ulysses stole the Palladium and so sealed the fate of Troy. — **Nestora**: who kept the Greeks from abandoning the siege after Achilles' death. *Od.* 24, 51 ff. — **Teucer**: brother of Ajax and son of Telemon; cf. 1, 7, 21 ff. — **respicis**: 'as thou glancest backward in thy flight.' The prophetic god sees the future so vividly that he conceives of the pursuit of Paris as already begun.

24 f. Sthenelus: charioteer of Diomedes. For the description of him compare the account of the Cicones *Od.* 9, 49 f. ἐπιστάμενοι μὲν ἀφ' ἵππων | ἀνδράσι μάρνασθαι καὶ ὅθι χρὴ πεζὸν ἐόντα. — **pugnae**: objective gen. with **sciens**.

26 ff. Merionen: esquire of Idomeneus; cf. 1, 6, 15. — **Tydides**: Diomedes was one of the greatest heroes after Achilles. — **melior patre**: a reminiscence of *Il.* 4, 405, where Sthenelus says ἡμεῖς τοι πατέρων μέγ' ἀμείνονες εὐχόμεθ' εἶναι.

29 ff. Note the involved order; Intr. 21.

31. sublimi ... anhelitu: properly of the panting hind, who throws his head high in air (**sublimi**) as he flees; applied here to Paris through a confusion of the comparison and the thing compared. Cf. Stat. *Theb.* 11. 239 *nuntius exanimi suspensus pectora cursu.* — **mollis**: either *weak* with running, or *timid* by nature.

32. Cf. Helen's taunt to Paris *Il.* 3, 430 ἦ μὲν δὴ πρίν γ' εὔχε' ἀρηϊφίλου Μενελάου | σῇ τε βίῃ καὶ χερσὶ καὶ ἔγχεϊ φέρτερος εἶναι.

Iracunda diem proferet Ilio
matronisque Phrygum classis Achillei:
post certas hiemes uret Achaicus
ignis Iliacas domos.'

33-36. The climax of the prophecy. Up to this point only the disgraces and dangers of Paris have been foretold; these verses definitely announce the fall of Troy. The whole strophe is a reminiscence of Hector's prophecy *Il.* 6, 448 f. ἔσσεται ἦμαρ ὅτ᾽ ἄν ποτ᾽ ὀλώλῃ Ἴλιος ἱρὴ | καὶ Πρίαμος καὶ λαὸς ἐϋμμελέω Πριάμοιο. — **iracunda** ...

classis Achillei: as if the entire fleet shared Achilles' wrath. — **proferet**: *delay.* — **hiemes**: equivalent to *annos.* Cf. I, 11, 4 and n. — **ignis**: this use of the trochee where Horace ordinarily has an irrational spondee, as well as the repetition of **Iliacas** after Ilio (v. 33) are cited by critics as proof of the early date of this ode.

16

'Fair maid, do what thou wilt with my abusive verses. Passion shakes the mind more than that frenzy with which Dindymene, or Apollo, or Dionysus inspire their servants. Prometheus gave mankind the violence of the lion, and wild rage drove Thyestes to his end and has doomed cities. Beware and check thy wrath. I too have suffered madness, but now I would recant my cruel lines; forgive, and give me back thy heart.

A palinode which Porphyrio wished, without warrant, to connect with Tyndaris of the following ode. Neither can it be associated with any extant epode. Its very extravagance shows that the verses were not written with serious purpose. Cf. the mock palinode *Epod.* 17. It may be a study from the Greek, although Acron's statement, *imitatus est Stesichorum*, need mean nothing more than that Horace got the suggestion of a palinode from the Sicilian poet. The date is uncertain, although the prosody of v. 21 may indicate that it is one of the earlier poems. Metre, 68.

O matre pulchra filia pulchrior,
quem criminosis cumque voles modum

2. criminosis ... iambis: *abusive, slanderous.* Cf. Meleager *Anth. Pal.* 7, 352 ὑβριστῆρας ἰάμ-βους. The rapid movement of the iambus is suited to invective, and it was first employed for that purpose,

pones iambis, sive flamma
sive mari libet Hadriano.

5   Non Dindymene, non adytis quatit
mentem sacerdotum incola Pythius,
non Liber aeque, non acuta
sic geminant Corybantes aera

tristes ut irae, quas neque Noricus
10   deterret ensis nec mare naufragum
nec saevus ignis nec tremendo
Iuppiter ipse ruens tumultu.

according to tradition, by Archilochus, who was Horace's model in many of the Epodes. Cf. *Epist.* 2, 3, 79 *Archilochum proprio rabies armavit iambo.* — **quem... cumque**: cf. n. to 1, 6, 3.

3. **pones**: permissive; cf. 1, 7, 1 *laudabunt alii*, etc.

5 ff. Examples of the *furor divinus*. — **Dindymene**: Cybele or Rhea, identical with the *Magna Mater* of the Romans, named from the Phrygian mountain Dindymus. This was near Pessinus, where the chief shrine of the goddess was. Her orgiastic worship, in which her priests, the Corybantes, danced and cut themselves with knives, was introduced at Rome in 204 B.C.

6. The Pythia, priestess of Apollo, had her seat in the innermost shrine (*adyta*) of the temple, where, inspired with a divine ecstasy, as the ancients believed, she gave utterance to prophecy. For the ecstatic inspiration of the Cumaean Sibyl see Verg. *A.* 6, 77 ff. — **incola Pythius**: *he whose home is Pytho, i.e.* Apollo. Pytho was the ancient name of Delphi. With the phrase, cf. Catull. 64, 228 (of Athene), *incola Itoni*.

7. **Liber**: the orgiastic celebrations of the bacchanals were inspired by the god. — **non acuta**, etc.: the comparison is thus half interrupted, 'Neither the rites of Cybele, nor of Apollo, nor of Bacchus affect the mind so much (**aeque**)—no, nor do the Corybantes clash their shrill cymbals with so much effect (**sic**)—as bursts of passion distress the mind.' — **geminant... aera**: of the cymbals. Cf. Stat. *Theb.* 8, 221 *gemina aera sonant*.

9 ff. **Noricus**: the iron of Noricum was most esteemed. Cf. *Epod.* 17, 71. — **ensis,... mare,... ignis**: proverbial obstacles. Cf. *S.* 1, 1, 39 *ignis, mare, ferrum, nil obstet tibi*; and *Epist.* 1, 1, 46 *per mare, pauperiem fugiens, per saxa, per ignis.* — **mare naufragum**: *the wrecking sea*. Cf. Tibull. 2, 4, 10 *naufraga ...unda maris*.

Fertur Prometheus, addere principi
limo coactus particulam undique
    desectam, et insani leonis
        vim stomacho adposuisse nostro.

Irae Thyesten exitio gravi
stravere et altis urbibus ultimae
    stetere causae cur perirent
        funditus imprimeretque muris

hostile aratrum exercitus insolens.
Compesce mentem! Me quoque pectoris

13–16. While the belief that man possesses the characteristics of the lower animals is very ancient, the form of the myth which Horace gives here is not found in any earlier author. — **principi**: *principal, primordial;* 'primitive clay.' — **coactus**: for all the elements had been exhausted in making the other animals; therefore Prometheus was obliged to take a portion from each creature (**undique**) for man.

15 f. **et**: *even.* — **leonis vim**: *i.e. violentiam.* — **stomacho**: as the seat of passion. Cf. 1, 6, 6 *Pelidae stomachum cedere nescii.*

17. **irae**: resuming the irae of v. 9. — **Thyesten**: cf. 1.6.8 *saevam Pelopis domum,* and n. The special reference here is to the blind rage of Atreus, who served Thyestes' son to him at a banquet. The *Thyestes* of Varius had recently been published when Horace wrote. Cf. n. to 1, 6, 1.

18 f. **altis urbibus**: *e.g.* Thebes, which fell under the wrathful curse of Oedipus. — **ultimae . . . causae**: the causes farthest back, and so 'first.' — **stetere**: hardly stronger than *fuere.*

20. **imprimeret muris**, etc.: as the walls of a new city were marked out with a plow, so after the razing of a captured city, a plow was dragged across the ground as a sign that the spot was restored to its primitive condition. Propert. 4, 9, 41 f. *moenia cum Graio Neptunia pressit aratro* | *victor;* Isid. *Orig.* 15, 2 *urbs aratro conditur, aratro vertitur*; and *Jeremiah* 26, 18 'Zion shall be plowed like a field.'

21. **ex‖ercitus**: but two other cases of such caesura are found. 1. 37. 5; 2. 17. 21. Intr. 50. Both the poems belong to the year 30 B.C.

22. **me quoque**: the familiar personal illustration. Intr. 30.

temptavit in dulci iuventa
fervor et in celeres iambos

25 misit furentem: nunc ego mitibus
mutare quaero tristia, dum mihi
fias recantatis amica
opprobriis animumque reddas.

24. **fervor**: 'the fever of passion.'— **celeres iambos**: cf. n. to v. 2 above.— **mitibus ... tristia**: *kind ... cruel*. For the cases, see Intr. 98; for the number, cf.

1, 34, 12 *ima summis mutare*.— **dum ... fias**: the terms on which Horace recants; his offended lady-love is to give him back her heart.

17

An invitation to his mistress, Tyndaris. 'Faunus often leaves the Lycean Mount for Lucretilis and guards my goats from harm (1-4). When he is near, my flocks wander all in safety; when his pipe echoes, they fear not even the wolves of Mars (5-12). Not they alone are cared for: the gods care for me as well and for my Muse. Here, Tyndaris, is rustic plenty; here in quiet nook thou mayest sing the old-time songs; here quaff the innocent Lesbian wine and have no fear of quarrels or of harm from jealous Cyrus (13-28).'

On Horace's Sabine farm presented to him by Maecenas in 34 B.C., see Intr. 5. Sellar, p. 30 f. The date of composition is unknown. Metre, 68.

Velox amoenum saepe Lucretilem
mutat Lycaeo Faunus et igneam

1. **velox**: emphatic, *with all speed*. — **Lucretilem**: apparently Monte Gennaro, the highest mountain of the range between the Licenza valley in which Horace's farm was situated, and the Campagna. — **mutat**: note that the construction here is the reverse of

that in v. 26 of the preceding ode. Intr. 98.

2. **Lycaeo**: a mountain in southwestern Arcadia, where Pan had a shrine ($\mu\alpha\nu\tau\epsilon\hat{\iota}o\nu$). — **Faunus**: an old Italian divinity, of agriculture and of cattle (3, 18), sometimes prophetic (Verg. *A.* 7,

CARMINA [1, 17 14

defendit aestatem capellis
   usque meis pluviosque ventos.

5 Impune tutum per nemus arbutos
   quaerunt latentis et thyma deviae
      olentis uxores mariti,
         nec viridis metuunt colubras

   nec Martialis haediliae lupos,
10   utcumque dulci, Tyndari, fistula
         valles et Vsticae cubantis
            levia personuere saxa.

   Di me tuentur, dis pietas mea
      et musa cordi est. Hic tibi copia

48. 81), identified here with the
Arcadian god Pan, ὀρειβάτης,
montivagus. Cf. Ovid. *Fast.* 2,
285 f. *ipse deus velox discurrere
gaudet in altis | montibus.* He
was the inventor of the syrinx
(fistula v. 10). — igneam . . .
aestatem: *the fiery summer heat.*
 3 f. capellis: dative. Cf. Verg.
E. 7, 47 *solstitium pecori defendite.*
— usque: equivalent to *semper.*
 5 f. impune tutum: note the
force of the cumulation. — impune
is connected with deviae, which
implies a carelessness in their wandering search (quaerunt) for food.
— latentis: *i.e.* among the other
trees and shrubs.
 7. olentis uxores mariti: an
awkward phrase, made offensive
by translation, — *the wives of
the unsavory lord.* — mariti: cf.
Theoc. 8, 49 ὦ τράγε, τᾶν λευκᾶν

αἰγᾶν ἄνερ, and Verg. E. 7, 7 *vir
gregis ipse caper.* Mart. 14, 140, 1
imitates the phrase in his *olentis
barba mariti.*
 9. Martialis: a natural epithet
of the wolf as sacred to Mars.
Cf. Verg. *A.* 9, 566 *Martius lupus.*
Faunus as protector of cattle
guards them from the mountain
wolves. — haediliae: *my kidlets*
(sc. *metuunt*). This word is
found only here: it is formed from
haedus, as *porcilia* from *porcus.*
 10 f. utcumque: temporal. —
fistula: the god's pipes, the syrinx, not Tyndaris' flute, is meant.
— Vsticae: according to Porphyrio one of the Sabine mountains
with gently sloping (cubantis)
sides.
 14 ff. cordi: *dear*; originally
like *frugi,* a predicate dative. Note
the cumulative force of the follow-

15   manabit ad plenum benigno
   ruris honorum opulenta cornu;

  hic in reducta valle Caniculae
  vitabis aestus et fide Teia
  dices laborantis in uno
20   Penelopen vitreamque Circen;

  hic innocentis pocula Lesbii
  duces sub umbra, nec Semeleius
   cum Marte confundet Thyoneus
  proelia, nec metues protervum

ing epithets — **ad plenum, benigno** (*i.e. large, generous*), **opulenta.— copia**: here the contents of the horn. — **cornu**: the horn of Fortune, which Hercules wrenched from the river god Achelous and presented to the goddess. See Baumeister, nos. 605, 2037. — **ruris honorum**: fruits and flowers. Cf. *S.* 2, 5, 12 f. *dulcia poma | et quoscumque feret cultus tibi fundus honores.*

 17 f. **reducta valle**: cf. *Epod.* 2, 11 f. *aut in reducta valle mugientium | prospectat errantis greges.* — **Caniculae**: properly Procyon, but here not distinguished from Sirius. — **fide Teia**: Teos in Ionia was the native city of Anacreon, who sang of love and wine. — **dices**: *shalt sing.* Cf. 1, 6, 5. — **laborantis**: sc. *amore,* ἔρωτι πονοῦσαι. The object of their love is expressed by **in** with the abl. Cf. Catull. 64, 98 (of Ariadne) *in flavo saepe hospite suspirantem.*— **uno**: Odysseus.

 20. **vitream**: a natural epithet of Circe who was a sea nymph. Cf. Stat. *Silv.* 1, 3, 85 *vitreae iuga perfida Circes,* and *C.* 4, 2, 3 *vitreo ponto.* — **Penelopen** . . . **Circen**: the faithful wife and the treacherous sorceress contrasted.

 21 f. **innocentis**: explained by the following verses. 'no drunken quarrels shall result from its use.' — **duces**: *shalt quaff.* — **Semeleius** . . . **Thyoneus**: a combination of two metronymics imitated by a poet in the *Anth. Lat.* 1, 751 *Semeleie Bacche . . . laete Thyoneu.* — Thyōne (cf. θύω = 'to rush,' 'to be violently excited'). whom some legends make the mother of Dionysus, is identified with Semele in the older Homeric *Hymn to Dionysus* v. 21, and by Pindar *P.* 3, 176.

 23 f. **confundet . . . proelia**: a variation of the common *miscere, committere proelia.*

25 suspecta Cyrum, ne male dispari
    incontinentis iniciat manus
    et scindat haerentem coronam
    crinibus immeritamque vestem.

25. suspecta: for rude Cyrus is jealous.—**male dispari**: *a bad match*, i.e. *no match*, cf. 1, 9, 24 *male pertinaci* and n. to *minus* 1, 2, 27.

26 ff. Tyndaris is to be in festal dress, which Cyrus would injure if he should find her. Cf. Propert. 2, 5, 21 ff. *nec tibi periuro scindam de corpore vestem, | nec mea praeclusas fregerit ira fores, | nec tibi conexos iratus carpere crines | nec duris ausim laedere pollicibus.*—**immeritam**: the dress shares Tyndaris' innocence.

18

In praise of wine. 'Thou shouldst before all, Varus, plant the vine about Tibur, for total abstainers find life hard. Wine drives away cares; but immoderate use brings quarrels, boasting, and bad faith.'

The ode was suggested by a poem of Alcaeus, of which Horace has translated at least the beginning, *Frg.* 44 μηδὲν ἄλλο φυτεύσῃς πρότερον δένδριον ἀμπέλω. He has, however, after his usual manner given his verses an Italian setting. The date of composition is unknown. The Varus addressed was probably Quintilius Varus, whose death is lamented in 1, 24. Metre, 54.

Nullam, Vare, sacra vite prius severis arborem
circa mite solum Tiburis et moenia Catili.

1. sacra: as the vine is the gift of Bacchus. Cf. Ennius *Trag.* 107 f. R. *Bacchus pater | ... vitis inventor sacrae*. The position of **sacra** implies that this gift is not to be abused, but enjoyed in proper fashion as coming from the gods. —**severis**: *plant*. Cf. Caecilius apud Cic. *C. M.* 24 *serit arbores quae alteri saeclo prosint*.—**arborem**: a generic term of wider scope than our English 'tree.'

Plin. *N. H.* 14, 9 *vites iure apud priscos magnitudine quoque inter arbores numerabantur.*

2. circa: used in the same loose way as our English 'about'; with **solum** it denotes the place where, with **moenia** it means 'near', 'in the neighbourhood of.' —**mite**: *soft*, and hence *fertile*. Cf. Verg. *G.* 2, 226 ff. for an account of the best soil for vines. — **Tiburis**: for Horace's love of

Siccis omnia nam dura deus proposuit neque
mordaces aliter diffugiunt sollicitudines.
5 Quis post vina gravem militiam aut pauperiem crepat?
Quis non te potius, Bacche pater, teque, decens Venus?
Ac ne quis modici transiliat munera Liberi,
Centaurea monet cum Lapithis rixa super mero
debellata, monet Sithoniis non levis Euhius,

Tibur, see 1, 7, 11 ff. — **moenia Catili**: Cati(l)lus with his brothers Coras and Tiburnus from Arcadia founded Tibur, and gave his name to the mountain that overhangs the town. It is still Monte Catillo. Here the form with the short penult is chosen for the metre's sake.

3. **siccis**: *total abstainers*. For the opposite, *udus* or *uvidus*, cf. 1, 7, 22; 4, 5, 39. — **nam**: for the position, see Intr. 31. — **dura**: 'life's rough side.'

4. **mordaces**: *carking*. Cf. 2, 11, 18 *curae edaces*; and Verg. *A.* 1, 261 *quando haec te cura remordet.* — **aliter**: *i.e.* without the use of wine.

5. **gravem militiam**, etc.: *the hardships of war or of petty estate.* — **crepat**: *babbles, harps on.*

6. **pater**: in recognition of the god as giver of the vine and other blessings. Cf. 3, 3, 13; *Epist.* 2, 1, 5 *Liber pater*. Here he is named with Venus, as wine and love are boon companions. — **decens**: *comely*, 'fair in face and figure.' Cf. 1, 4, 6 *Gratiae decentes.*

7. **ne quis**, etc.: dependent on **monet** in the following verse. — **transiliat**: *lightly abuse.* — **modici**:

i.e. equivalent to *qui modum amat.* Cf. 1, 27, 3 *verecundus Bacchus.*

8 f. The first of the examples given to enforce the warning — the quarrel between the Centaurs and the Lapithae at the marriage of Peirithoos and Hippodamia — was a favorite subject of literary and plastic art. Cf. *e.g. Od.* 21, 294-304; Ovid. *Met.* 12, 210 ff. The contest was represented on the pediment of the temple of Zeus at Olympia, and on the metopes of the Parthenon. — **super mero**: local; *over their wine.*

9. **debellata**: note the force of the prefix; the brawl ended in the destruction of the Centaurs. — **Sithoniis**: a Thracian people dwelling on the peninsula Pallene. Tradition said that Dionysus destroyed the giants who once dwelt there. Whether the reference here is to some feature of the myth unknown to us or to the familiar impetuous character of the intemperate Thracians cannot be determined. Cf. 1, 27, 1 f. *natis in usum laetitiae scyphis | pugnare Thracum est.* — **non levis**: carrying the emphasis, — *the harshness of,* etc. — **Euhius**: a

10 cum fas atque nefas exiguo fine libidinum
discernunt avidi. Non ego te, candide Bassareu,
invitum quatiam nec variis obsita frondibus
sub divum rapiam. Saeva tene cum Berecynthio
cornu tympana, quae subsequitur caecus amor sui

name of Bacchus formed from the bacchanal cry εὐοῖ. Cf. 2, 19, 5. Notice that Horace employs here indiscriminately Latin and Greek names of the god — **Bacchus** 6, **Liber** 7, **Euhius** 9, **Bassareus** 11 — his purpose being simply to secure variety.

10. **exiguo fine**, etc.: *with appetite's narrow bound alone; i.e.* when men in their greed (**avidi**) make their passions the sole measure of right and wrong. In the following verses Horace expresses his thoughts, 'I will not abuse thy gift, fair Bacchus,' in the language of the Dionysiac mysteries.

11. **non ego**: the common personal note giving force and concreteness to the general statement. For the order of words, see Intr. 21. 30. — **candide**: used of brilliant youthful beauty, 'fair and young' (Wickham). Cf. Ovid *Fast.* 3, 771 ff. — **Bassareu**: an epithet formed from the Greek βασσάρα, a foxskin. This was worn by the bacchanals, who are themselves called in the Orphic hymn 44, 2 A. βασσάραι.

12. **quatiam**: *arouse*, κινήσω, properly applied to the thyrsus and other symbols of the god, as by Catull. 64, 256 *harum pars tecta quatiebant cuspide thyrsos.* — **variis obsita frondibus**: the sacred symbols (*orgia*) placed in baskets (*cistae*) and covered with ivy, grape, or fig leaves, etc. Cf. Catull. 64, 254 ff. and Theoc. 26, 3 ff.

13. **sub divum**: *into the light of day;* cf. 1, 1, 25 *manet sub Iove frigido venator.* — **saeva tene**, etc.: 'And we pray thee, Bacchus, do not excite our minds unduly lest we fall into excess.' — **saeva**: of the sound, 'the wild din of.' Cf. Verg. *A.* 9, 651 *saeva sonoribus arma,* and Catull. 64, 261 ff. *plangebant aliae proceris tympana palmis | aut tereti tenues tinnitus aere ciebant | multis raucisonos efflabant cornua bombos | barbaraque horribili stridebat tibia cantu.* — **Berecynthio cornu**: cf. 3, 19, 18 f. *cur Berecynthiae cessant flamina tibiae.* This is properly the horn used in the orgiastic cult of Cybele on Mt. Berecynthus in Phrygia; by extension applied to the horns employed in the worship of Bacchus.

14 f. **quae subsequitur**, etc.: *i.e.* in the train of mad ecstasy inspired by the god follow all too readily self-love (**amor sui**), boasting (**gloria**) and faithlessness (**arcani fides**

15   et tollens vacuum plus nimio gloria verticem
arcanique fides prodiga, perlucidior vitro.

prodiga). — **plus nimio**: *over much,* 'too high.' Cf. 1, 33, 1 *ne doleas plus nimio,* and *Epist.* 1, 10, 30 *res plus nimio delectavere secundae.*
16. Drunkenness causes men to babble secrets. Cf. 3, 21, 15 f. (to a wine jar) *tu . . . arcanum iocoso consilium retegis Lyaeo;* and the proverb in the scholia to Plato, p. 960 Or. τὸ ἐν καρδίᾳ νήφοντος, ἐπὶ τῇ γλώσσῃ τοῦ μεθύοντος. — **fides prodiga**: *the faith that is lavish.*

19

'I thought my days of love were over, but Venus and her allies will not let me go. Glycera inflames me; Venus forbids me sing of aught but love. Bring turf and let me build an altar to the goddess. The offer of a victim will soften her attack.'

This dainty poem should be compared with the thirtieth ode of this book. Possibly its place here was determined by the *decens Venus* v. 6 of the preceding ode. The date is wholly uncertain. Metre, 71.

    Mater saeva Cupidinum
        Thebanaeque iubet me Semeles puer
    et lasciva Licentia
        finitis animum reddere amoribus.
5   Vrit me Glycerae nitor
        splendentis Pario marmore purius;

1 f. **Mater saeva Cupidinum**: repeated years later in 4, 1, 5. Cf. Philod. *Anth. Pal.* 10, 21 Κύπρι, πόθων μῆτερ ἀελλοπόδων. — **Cupidinum**: the plural is not infrequent in Hellenistic and Roman literature. — **Semeles puer**: for Bacchus' association with Venus, see v. 6 of the preceding ode. Cf. also the Anacreontic fragment 2 to Dionysus ὦναξ, ᾧ δαμάλης Ἔρως . . . πορφυρέη τ' Ἀφροδίτη συμπαίζουσιν.

3 f. **lasciva**: *wanton,* as *lasciva puella,* Verg. *E.* 3, 64. — **Licentia**: Ὕβρις. — **finitis**: predicate to **amoribus** — *to loves I thought were past.* — **animum reddere**: here not as in 1, 16, 28, but almost equivalent to *me reddere.*

5 ff. **urit . . . urit**: Intr. 28 c. — **nitor**: *brilliant beauty;* so *niteo* in 2, 5, 18 f. *albo sic umero nitens.* — **Pario**: so Pindar celebrates the brilliancy of Parian marble *N.* 4, 81 εἰ δέ κελεύεις στάλαν θέμεν Παρίου λίθου λευκοτέραν.

urit grata protervitas
    et voltus nimium lubricus adspici.
In me tota ruens Venus
10   Cyprum deseruit, nec patitur Scythas
et versis animosum equis
    Parthum dicere nec quae nihil attinent.
Hic vivum mihi caespitem, hic
    verbenas, pueri, ponite turaque
15   bimi cum patera meri;
    mactata veniet lenior hostia.

7 f. grata protervitas: *her pretty, provoking ways*. Prudent. *praef.* 10 has a reminiscence of this ode in his repetition of the phrase *lasciva protervitas*. — lubricus aspici: ὑγρὸς βλέπεσθαι. Intr. 109.

9. tota: 'with all her power.' — Cyprum deseruit: Cyprus was one of the chief centers of the worship of Aphrodite; on its shores the goddess is said to have been born from the foam of the sea. Cf. Alcman *Frg.* 21 Κύπρον ἱμερτὰν λιποῖσα καὶ Πάφον περιρρύταν.

10 f. nec patitur Scythas, etc.: the goddess of love will not allow Horace to sing of serious subjects, the dangers that threaten the empire, or even of subjects to which she is wholly indifferent (quae nihil attinent). Love must be his only theme.

11 f. versis . . . Parthum: the famous maneuver of the Parthians, in which they pretended to flee and then, turning on their horses, shot at their pursuers, is frequently mentioned by the Romans. Cf. *e.g.* 2, 13, 18; Verg. *G.* 3, 31 *fidentemque fuga Parthum versisque sagittis*; also Ovid *A. A.* 3, 786 *ut celer aversis utere Parthus equis*. Plut. *Crass.* 24 ὑπέφευγον γὰρ ἅμα βάλλοντες οἱ Πάρθοι, καὶ τοῦτο κράτιστα ποιοῦσι μετὰ Σκύθας.

13 f. hic . . . hic: the anaphora expressed the poet's mock haste. He will build an altar on the spot, of fresh turf (vivum caespitem), and propitiate the goddess with sacrifice. — verbenas: defined by the ancients as anything green, whether branches of laurel, bay, or olive, or even grass, used for sacred purposes. Here branches to decorate the improvised altar. Cf. 4, 11, 6 f. *ara | castis vincta verbenis*. — pueri: the common address to slaves.

15. meri: pure wine unmixed with water was alone used in libation. — hostia: ordinarily only bloodless sacrifices were offered to Venus; but this is not to be taken too literally. — lenior: *with gentler sway;* in contrast to in me tota ruens above.

20

'Cheap Sabine wine in modest cups shall be thy drink with me, my dear Maecenas. I sealed the jar myself some years ago. Choice wines thou hast at home; but no Falernian nor Formian grape flavors my cups.'

These verses have the form of an answer to a letter from Maecenas announcing his intention to visit Horace on his Sabine farm. The event mentioned in v. 3 ff. fixes the date of composition as after 30 B.C. The ode shows a lack of finish, as if written in haste. Metre, 69.

> Vile potabis modicis Sabinum
> cantharis, Graeca quod ego ipse testa
> conditum levi, datus in theatro
>   cum tibi plausus,
>
> 5   care Maecenas eques, ut paterni
> fluminis ripae simul et iocosa

1. **vile** . . . **Sabinum**: just *vin ordinaire*. The Sabine was the lightest of the Italian wines, according to Galen *apud Athen.* 1, 27 B. who adds ἀπὸ ἐτῶν ἑπτὰ ἐπιτήδειος πίνεσθαι μέχρι πεντεκαίδεκα. — **modicis**: with reference to the material of which Horace's drinking cups (**canthari**) are made: plain earthen cups, not goblets of silver or of gold.

2. **Graeca . . . testa**: an amphora in which a Greek — and a superior — wine had been imported. The cheap Sabine would acquire a better taste from being stored in such a jar. Cf. Columella's instructions, 12, 28 *si vasa recentia ex quibus vinum exemptum sit habebis, in ea* (sc. *vinum*) *confundito*.

3. **conditum**: *stored away*, in the amphora. For the process of making wine, see *Dictionary of Antiquities*, s. v. *vinum*. — **levi**: equivalent to *oblevi*. The cork which stopped the amphora was sealed with pitch or plaster. Cf. 3, 8, 9 f. *hic dies . . . | corticem adstrictum pice dimovebit | amphorae*. — **datus in theatro**, etc.: the only permanent theater at this time was that built by Pompey on the Campus Martius in 55 B.C. The occasion referred to was in 30 B.C., when Maecenas was greeted with great applause on his first appearance after a severe illness. Cf. 2, 17, 25 f. *cum populus frequens | laetum theatris ter crepuit sonum*.

5 f. **care**: cf. 2, 20, 7 *dilecte Maecenas*. — **eques**: referring to Maecenas' modesty in remaining a member of the burgher class in

redderet laudes tibi Vaticani
   montis imago.
   Caecubum et prelo domitam Caleno
10   tu bibes uvam: mea nec Falernae
   temperant vites neque Formiani
   pocula colles.

spite of the opportunity his wealth and power gave him to rise from it. Intr. 5. — **paterni fluminis**: the Tiber is called by Horace *S.* 2, 2, 32 *amnis Tuscus*. Maecenas was of Etruscan stock; see n. to 1, 1, 1 and Propert. 4, 9, 1 *Maecenas eques Etrusco de sanguine regum*. — **iocosa ... imago**: as 1, 12, 3. — **redderet**: *answered back*.

7 f. **Vaticani montis**: the Vatican forms the northern spur of the range of hills of which the Janiculum is the highest.

9 ff. The four wines selected as representatives of the choicer brands were all grown on the coast of southern Latium and northern Campania. — **tu...mea**: contrasted. — **bibes**: *mayest drink at home*. For this use of the future, cf. 1, 7, 1 *laudabunt alii*. — **temperant**: *temper, flavor*; properly used of mixing wine with water in due proportion.

21

A hymn to Diana and Apollo as averters of ill. This may have been originally a study for a secular hymn, possibly for the celebration planned by Augustus for 23 B.C. Cf. Intr. to *C. S.* p. 388. The verses have a striking resemblance to Catull. 34, 1 ff. *Dianae sumus in fide | puellae et pueri integri; | Dianam pueri integri | puellaeque canamus*. Like Catullus' ode and the *Carmen Saeculare* this was written for a chorus of girls and boys. It should be compared also with 4, 6. Metre, 73.

   Dianam tenerae dicite virgines,
   intonsum, pueri, dicite Cynthium,

1 f. Note the parallelism, which is not unlike that in Catullus' verses quoted above. — **Dianam**: but *Dīana* 3, 4, 71. Intr. 34. — **dicite**: equivalent to *cantate*, as often. Cf. 1, 6, 5.

2. **intonsum**: Apollo, as a divinity ever young, is represented with flowing hair — ἀκερσεκόμης. Cf. *Epod.* 15, 9 *intonsos Apollinis capillos*; and Tibull. 1, 4, 37 f. *solis aeterna est Phoebo Bacchoque*

Latonamque supremo
   dilectam penitus Iovi.

5 Vos laetam fluviis et nemorum coma
   quaecumque aut gelido prominet Algido
      nigris aut Erymanthi
         silvis aut viridis Gragi;

   vos Tempe totidem tollite laudibus
10   natalemque, mares, Delon Apollinis
         insignemque pharetra
            fraternaque umerum lyra.

iuventa; | *nam decet intonsus crinis utrumque deum.* — **Cynthium**: so named from Mt. Cynthus in Delos, where he and his sister Diana were born.

3 f. **Latonam**: the mother also is included in the hymn. — **penitus**: 'deeply,' 'heartily,' κηρόθι.

5. **vos**: the half-chorus of girls; sc. *dicite*. — **laetam fluviis**: Diana was goddess of streams as well as of the woods. Cf. Catull. 34, 12 *domina ... amniumque sonantum*; Pind. *P.* 2, 6 Ὀρτυγίαν, ποταμίας ἕδος Ἀρτέμιδος. She is named Ἄρτεμις ποταμία also on Sicilian coins. — **coma**: not an uncommon figure, 'the tresses of the wood.' So e.g. *Od.* 23, 195 ἀπέκοψα κόμην τανυφύλλου ἐλαίης; Catull. 4, 11 *comata silva*. Milton *P. L.* 7 'bush with frizzled hair implicit.'

6. **Algido**: a ridge in the Alban Hills on a spur of which was a famous shrine of Diana, *dea Nemorensis*, near the present Lake Nemi. Its name was probably due to the fact that its woods and elevation made it a cool and pleasant contrast to the plain about it. Cf. 3, 23, 9 f. (*victima*) *quae nivali pascitur Algido* | *devota quercus inter et ilices.* 4, 4, 58 *nigrae feraci frondis in Algido.*

7. **Erymanthi**: a high mountain in north Acadia, a favorite hunting place of Diana. *Od.* 6, 102 οἵη δ' Ἄρτεμις εἶσι κατ' οὔρεος ἰοχέαιρα, | ἢ κατὰ Τηΰγετον περιμήκετον ἢ Ἐρύμανθον. The adjective **nigris** (*dark green*) is contrasted to **viridis** (*light green*). Cf. 4, 12, 11 *nigri colles Arcadiae.*
— **Gragi**: Gragus, a mountain in Lycia, and the home of Leto.

9 ff. **vos**: the boys. — **Tempe**: the valley of the Peneus between Olympus and Ossa. Cf. 1, 7, 4. — **natalem ... Delon**: cf. n. to v. 2 above, and Verg. *A* 4, 144 *Delum maternam.* — **totidem**: with **laudibus**.

12. **umerum**: a Greek accu. with **insignem** (sc. *deum*). — **fra-**

> Hic bellum lacrimosum, hic miseram famem
> pestemque a populo et principe Caesare in
>   Persas atque Britannos
>   vestra motus aget prece.

15

terna ... lyra: the story of the presentation of the lyre to Apollo by Mercury is told in the Homeric *Hymn to Hermes*, 490-502.

13 ff. hic ... hic: Apollo as the special protector of Augustus is invoked to avert the ills that threaten the state. Cf. the introductory note to 1, 2. — **bellum lacrimosum**: the Homeric πόλεμον δακρυόεντα (*Il.* 5, 737), Vergil's *lacrimabile bellum* (*A.* 7, 604). — **miseram famem**, etc.: with reference to the failure of the crops in 24 B.C. and Augustus' sickness, 24-23 B.C. The collocation **famem pestemque** may be simply a reproduction of the phrase λιμὸς καὶ λοιμός, Hes. *Op.* 243. — **principe**: 'the first citizen.' Cf. 1, 2, 50. — **Persas atque Britannos**: the remote East and West still unsubdued. Cf. 3, 5, 3 *adiectis Britannis | imperio gravibusque Persis*. Note the confidence expressed by the future **aget**.

22

'The upright man is safe, no matter where he roams. I know that this is true, friend Fuscus, for once in Sabine wood as I sang of Lalage, a monster wolf fled from me, though I was unarmed. Put me in chill northern gloom or beneath the torrid sun, still will I ever sing my Lalage.'

The affected solemnity of the first two strophes has often led commentators to interpret this ode too seriously, as if Horace were solemnly preaching a moral lesson. While an actual encounter with a wolf may have furnished the opportunity for the illustration, Horace was the last man to use such an event to point a moral, still less take himself for an example of the noblest virtue. He never preaches, and is always free from cant. As a matter of fact, the ode is a piece of humor which Horace knew his friend Aristius Fuscus would appreciate. No doubt Horace had had many proofs of Fuscus' fondness for joking; he tells of one occasion (*S.* 1, 9, 61-73) when his friend refused to rescue him from a bore. The relations between the two were the closest. Cf. *Epist.* 1, 10, 3 f. *paene gemelli fraternis animis*. Metre, 69.

Integer vitae scelerisque purus
non eget Mauris iaculis neque arcu
nec venenatis gravida sagittis,
    Fusce, pharetra,

sive per Syrtis iter aestuosas
sive facturus per inhospitalem
Caucasum vel quae loca fabulosus
    lambit Hydaspes.

Namque me silva lupus in Sabina,
dum meam canto Lalagen et ultra
terminum curis vagor expeditis,
    fugit inermem,

quale portentum neque militaris
Daunias latis alit aesculetis

1. **vitae ... sceleris**: genitives of reference; the first is not uncommon in Latin poetry, *e.g.* Verg. *A.* 9, 255 and Ovid *Met.* 9, 441 *integer aevi*. Intr. 93. The second is a Greek construction, καθαρὸς ἀδικίας, for which the Latin ordinarily preferred the abl. Cf. *S.* 2, 3, 213 *purum vitio cor*.

5. **Syrtis**: the desert coast on the north of Africa, opposite the whirlpools called by the same name; cf. Verg. *A.* 5, 51 *hunc* (sc. *diem*) *ego Gaetulis agerem si Syrtibus exsul*. Pliny *N. H.* 5, 26 speaks of this barren tract as the haunt of savage beasts and serpents.

6 ff. **facturus**: sc. *est*. — **fabulosus**: since the Hydaspes — the farthest river reached by Alexander in India — was famed to bear gems and gold, and the entire unknown eastern world for which the river stands was a land of marvels and wonders. — **lambit**: *lavos*.

9. **namque me**: introducing the special experience — shown by the emphatic **me** to be a personal one — to prove the general statement. Intr. 30. — **Lalagen**: λαλαγή, 'the prattler,' a name chosen to suit the character of the ode.

10 f. **ultra terminum**: *i.e.* of his own farm. — **curis expeditis**: cf. Catull. 31, 7 *o quid solutis est beatius curis*.

13. **quale portentum**: *such a monster as*, etc.

14. **Daunias**: the Greek Δαυνία, Apulia; named from Daunus, a mythical king of Northern Apulia.

15 nec Iubae tellus generat, leonum
       arida nutrix.

   Pone me pigris ubi nulla campis
   arbor aestiva recreatur aura,
   quod latus mundi nebulae malusque
20   Iuppiter urget;

   pone sub curru nimium propinqui
   solis, in terra domibus negata:
   dulce ridentem Lalagen amabo,
      dulce loquentem.

Cf. 3, 30, 11 f. *et qua pauper aquae | Daunus agrestium regnavit populorum.* Vergil introduced him into the *Aeneid* (12, 934) as the father of Turnus; another legend made him the father-in-law of Diomedes, who assisted him against the Messapians.

15. Iubae tellus: Mauretania. The reference is probably to the younger Iuba, son of the king Iuba who killed himself after the defeat at Thapsus in 46 B.C. The young prince received a Roman education and was established on the throne of Mauretania in 25 B.C. This barren country (**leonum arida nutrix**) was a poor return for the kingdom his father lost to the Romans.

16. arida nutrix: a weak oxymoron. Intr. 26a. Cf. Anon. *Anth. Pal.* 6, 51 μῆτερ ἐμή, γαίη Φρυγίων, θρέπτειρα λεόντων.

17-22. The same extremes as 3, 3, 54 ff. *visere gestiens | qua parte debacchentur ignes, | qua nebulae pluviique rores.* — **pigris**: *dull, barren.* Cf. Lucret. 5, 746 *bruma nives affert pigrumque rigorem,* and Ovid, *Am.* 3, 6, 94 *pigra hiems.*

19. quod latus: a parallel construction to *quale portentum*, v. 13. — **latus**: inasmuch as Horace here thinks of the world as flat. Cf. 3, 24, 38 *Boreae finitimum latus.* — **malus**: *a sullen.*

22. domibus negata: in contrast is Vergil's description of the temperate zones, *G.* 1, 237 f. *mortalibus aegris | munere concessae divom.*

23 f. Note the liquid sound of these verses. — **dulce ridentem . . . dulce loquentem**: like Sappho's ἆδυ φωνείσας . . . γελαίσας ἰμερόεν. Horace's second phrase reproduces the girl's name. Λαλαγή.

23

A study from a Greek original; possibly from Anacreon's verses, of which we have a fragment (51) ἀγανῶς οἷα τε νεβρὸν νεοθηλέα | γαλαθηνόν, ὅστ᾽ ἐν ὕλῃ κεροέσσης | ἀπολειφθεὶς ὑπὸ μητρὸς ἐπτοήθη. 'Gently as a new-born fawn unweaned, which quivers from terror, when left in the wood by its antlered mother.' The name Chloe (χλόη, 'a young shoot') was apparently chosen to suit the character of the girl, as was Lalage in the preceding ode and Lydia and Sybaris in 1, 8. Metre, 73.

Vitas inuleo me similis, Chloe,
quaerenti pavidam montibus aviis
matrem non sine vano
aurarum et siluae metu;

5   nam seu mobilibus veris inhorruit
adventus foliis, seu virides rubum
dimovere lacertae,
et corde et genibus tremit.

Atqui non ego te tigris ut aspera
10   Gaetulusve leo frangere persequor;

1 ff. **inuleo**: *a fawn.* — **quaerenti**: 'lost and seeking,' ἀπολειφθείς above. — **non sine**, etc.: a common form of litotes with Horace. Cf. 1, 25, 16 *non sine questu*; 3, 13, 2 *mero non sine floribus*. With the entire expression, cf. Lucan 8, 5 f. *pavet ille fragorem motorum ventis nemorum*.

4. **siluae**: trisyllabic, as *Epod.* 13, 2. Intr. 41.

5 f. **veris ... adventus**: *i.e.* the blowing of Favonius, the companion of the spring. Cf. 1, 4, 1 *solvitur acris hiems grata vice veris et Favoni*; 4, 12, 1 *veris comites*. — **foliis**: instrumental abl. with in-

horruit, *rustled.* Cf. Plato *Anth. Plan.* 16, 13 ὑψίκομον παρὰ τάνδε καθίζεο φωνήεσσαν | φρίσσουσαν πυκινοῖς κῶνον ὑπὸ Ζεφύροις. 'Sit thee down by this lofty pine tree which is vocal as it shivers and rustles under the frequent gusts of Zephyrus.'

7. **dimovere**: *have moved aside*, as they slip through the brambles. Cf. Verg. *E.* 2, 9 *nunc viridis etiam occultant spineta lacertos.* — **tremit**: the subject is the **inuleus** of the comparison, v. 1.

9 f. **atqui**: corrective — 'yet thy fear is vain, for.' — **frangere**: literally 'crush between the teeth.'

CARMINA [1, 24, 4

tandem desine matrem
tempestiva sequi viro.

Cf. *Il.* 11, 113 f. ὡς δέ λέων ἐλάφοιο ταχείης νήπια τέκνα | ῥηϊδίως συνέαξε, λαβὼν κρατεροῖσιν ὀδοῦσιν.

12. **tempestiva ... viro**: cf. Verg. *A.* 7, 53 *iam matura viro, iam plenis nubilis annis.*

24

A lament on the death of Quintilius Varus, the common friend of Horace and of Vergil. He was an accomplished and, according to Horace's words, *Epist.* 2, 3, 438 ff., an impartial critic, whose judgment was valued by his literary friends, *Quintilio siquid recitares, 'corrige sodes | hoc' aiebat 'et hoc.' melius te posse negares, | bis terque expertum frustra, delere iubebat | et male tornatos incudi reddere versus.* The year of his death is fixed by St. Jerome's entry against 24 B.C. *Quintilius Cremonensis Vergili et Horati familiaris moritur.* This ode must have been written within the next few months. The Varus of the eighteenth ode is probably identical with Quintilius. Metre, 72.

Quis desiderio sit pudor aut modus
tam cari capitis? Praecipe lugubris
cantus, Melpomene, cui liquidam pater
vocem cum cithara dedit.

1. **quis desiderio**, etc.: *i.e.* 'who can or would restrain his tears.' In prose we should have the genitive depending on **pudor**, while the dative is the natural case with **modus**; here the constructions are united because **modus** contains the predominant idea; so in Martial 8, 64, 15 *sit tandem pudor et modus rapinis.*

2. **tam cari capitis**: *for a soul so dear.* For this use of caput, cf. *Epod.* 5, 74 *o multa fleturum caput;* Verg. *A.* 4, 354 *puer Ascanius capitisque iniuria cari.* So in Greek, *e.g. Il.* 8, 281 Τεῦκρε, φίλη κεφαλή; and in English, Shelley, *Adonais,* 'Though our tears | Thaw not the frost which binds so dear a head.' — **praecipe**: *teach me.* — **lugubris**: indicating the character of the strains.

3 f. **Melpomene**: properly the muse of Tragedy; cf. n. to 1, 12, 2. — **liquidam ... vocem**: *clear toned;* cf. *Od.* 24, 62 Μοῦσα λίγεια.

Ergo Quintilium perpetuus sopor
urget! Cui Pudor et Iustitiae soror,
incorrupta Fides, nudaque Veritas
quando ullum inveniet parem?

Multis ille bonis flebilis occidit,
nulli flebilior quam tibi, Vergili;
tu frustra pius heu non ita creditum
poscis Quintilium deos.

Quid si Threicio blandius Orpheo
auditam moderere arboribus fidem?

5 f. **ergo**: emphatically introducing the θρῆνος, and expressing a reluctant conclusion, *so then*. Cf. Ovid, *Trist.* 3, 2, 1 *ergo erat in fatis Scythiam quoque visere nostris.*—**perpetuus**: *unbroken, forever.*—**urget**: *hold down.* Cf. *premet* 1, 4, 16, and Verg. *A.* 10, 745 f. *olli dura quies oculos et ferreus urget | somnus; in aeternam clauduntur lumina noctem.*—**cui**: emphatic, 'when shall we see his like again.'—**Iustitiae soror . . . Fides**: the personified virtues are those possessed by Quintilius; they are the basis of every high character and of all justice. Cf. Cic. *de Off.* 1, 23 *fundamentum autem est iustitiae fides, id est dictorum conventorumque constantia et veritas.*

7. **nuda Veritas**: cf. the unpersonified English 'naked truth.'

9 f. **multis . . . nulli**: depending on **flebilis . . . flebilior**. Adjectives in *-bilis* and *-ilis* are not infrequently used as equivalent to perfect pass. partic.; so **flebilis** is equivalent to *defletus*, as 1, 12, 36 *nobilis* to *notus*. Cf. *Epigr. Gr.* 215 Kaibel ἤλυθες εἰς Ἀΐδην ζητούμενος, οἷς ἀπέλειπες · | πᾶσι γὰρ ἀλγηδὼν ἐσθλὸς ἀπαχόμενος. 'Thou hast gone to Hades, missed by all thou hast left behind; for thy going is a goodly grief to all.'

11 f. **frustra**: with both **pius** and **poscis**. Intr. 100.—**pius**: *i.e.* in love for his friend.—**non ita creditum**: Vergil had commended his friend to the care of the gods, but not on the condition (ita) that they should bring him to death.

13 f. **quid si**: making the transition to the sole consolation Horace can offer at the end, 'All thy piety and prayers are vain; patience only can be thy consolation.'—**blandius Orpheo**: cf. the passages quoted on 1, 12, 8. Even Orpheus could not recall his beloved Eurydice from the lower world. For the story, read Vergil *G.* 4, 454–527.

15   Num vanae redeat sanguis imagini,
       quam virga semel horrida,

     non lenis precibus fata recludere,
       nigro compulerit Mercurius gregi?
     Durum: sed levius fit patientia
20   quicquid corrigere est nefas.

15. **vanae imagini**: the empty shade, εἴδωλον. Cf. *Od.* 11, 476 βρότων εἴδωλα καμόντων. Also Verg. *A.* 6, 293 *admoneat volitare cava sub imagine formae.*

16. **virga ... horrida**: the wand (*aurea* 1, 10, 19) which strikes the shades with terror (**horrida**), when Mercury gathers (**compulerit**) them once for all (**semel**) for the world below. Cf. Propert. 5, 11, 3 f. *cum semel infernas intrarunt funera leges, | non exorato stant adamante viae.*

17 f. **precibus**: dative with **recludere**; the same idea is expressed by Propert. 5, 11, 2 *panditur ad nullas ianua nigra preces.* — **recludere**: epexegetical inf. with **lenis**. Cf. 1, 10, 7 *callidus condere furto*, equivalent to *callide condit.* Intr. 108. — **nigro**: transferred from the gloomy nether world to the shades themselves; cf. 4, 2, 24 *nigro Orco.* Intr. 99.— **gregi**: the 'flock' of shades driven to their long home beneath the earth.

19 f. **durum**: summing up of the whole matter. The following precept is one of many ancient expressions of the truth. Cf. Soph. *Frg.* 526 ἀλγεινά, Πρόκνη, δῆλον · ἀλλ' ὅμως χρεὼν | τὰ θεῖα θνητοὺς ὄντας εὐπετῶς φέρειν, 'Aye, Procne, it is clearly hard, but still, as we are mortals, we must bear what the gods send.'

25

The old age of a faded courtesan, when lovers leave her for younger rivals. Metre, 69.

  Parcius iunctas quatiunt fenestras
    iactibus crebris iuvenes protervi,

1. **parcius**: in the emphatic position, marking her waning power. — **iunctas ... fenestras**: the *valvae* of the windows, which were fastened with a bar (*sera*) at night. Cf. Ovid *ex P.* 3, 3, 5 *bifores fenestras.* These windows were in the second, or a higher story;

nec tibi somnos adimunt, amatque
ianua limen,

5   quae prius multum facilis movebat
cardines; audis minus et minus iam
' Me tuo longas pereunte noctis,
Lydia, dormis?'

Invicem moechos anus arrogantis
10   flebis in solo levis angiportu,
Thracio bacchante magis sub inter-
lunia vento,

cum tibi flagrans amor et libido,
quae solet matres furiare equorum,
15   saeviet circa iecur ulcerosum,
non sine questu,

laeta quod pubes hedera virenti
gaudeat pulla magis atque myrto,

therefore the lovers must attract Lydia's attention by throwing sticks or stones (hence iactibus crebris) from below.

3. amatque limen: *hugs the threshold.* Cf. Verg. A. 5, 163 *litus ama*, 'hug the shore.'

5. prius: *in former days.* — **facilis**: modifying **quae**, 'with ready complaisance.' Cf. Tibull. 1, 2, 7 *ianua difficilis domini.* — **multum**: modifying **movebat**.

7 f. The words of the serenade, the παρακλαυσίθυρον. — **me tuo . . . pereunte**: temporal, *while I, who am thine, perish,* etc.

9. invicem: 'now thy turn has come.' — **anus . . . levis**: equivalent to *contempta*.

11 f. Thracio: the Tramontana of to-day. The verb **bacchari**, *hold revel*, is especially apt with a 'Thracian' wind. — **sub inter-lunia**: Intr. 69. The common belief that changes of the moon influence the weather is very ancient. Porphyrio remarks on this word *quia tunc fere concitantur tempestates.*

15. ulcerosum: *inflamed*, with love's wounds. Cf. Theoc. 11, 15 f. ἔχων ὑποκάρδιον ἕλκος | Κύπριδος ἐκ μεγάλας. 'With a sore in his heart inflicted by mighty Cypris.'

17 f. She bemoans the fact that youth is preferred to old age. — **pulla**: *dusky*, πόλιος. Cf. *Epod.* 16, 46 *pulla ficus.*

aridas frondes hiemis sodali
dedicet Euro.

20

19 f. aridas: note the asyndeton here, frequently employed in contrasts and antitheses. — **sodali**: cf. 1, 28, 22 *comes Orionis Notus.* —

Euro: a winter wind; cf. Verg. *G.* 2, 339 *et hibernis parcebant flatibus Euri.*

26

'Beloved by the Muses I can throw to the winds all fears of dangers from abroad. Sweet Muse, weave a chaplet for my Lamia, I pray. My verse is naught without thee. Celebrate him in Lesbian song.'

The Lamia here addressed has been identified with L. Aelius Lamia, one of the two sons of Cicero's friend and supporter, L. Aelius Lamia who was praetor 43 B.C. (Cic. *ad fam.* 11, 16, 2; *pro Sest.* 29). Lamia must have been young at the time this ode was written, for he was consul in 3 A.D. and praefectus urbi in 32 A.D. He died the following year. Tacitus, *Ann.* 6, 27, mentions him, *genus illi decorum vivida senectus;* Velleius Paterculus describes him (2, 116, 3), *vir antiquissimi moris, et priscam gravitatem semper humanitate temperans.* The most probable date of composition is that suggested by the references in vv. 3-5, as 30 B.C.; the words *fidibus novis,* v. 10, cause some critics to regard this as one of Horace's earliest attempts in Alcaic verse; a view that finds support from the somewhat harsh caesura in v. 11 *Lesbio* || *sacrare plectro.* Metre, 68.

Musis amicus tristitiam et metus
tradam protervis in mare Creticum
portare ventis, quis sub Arcto
rex gelidae metuatur orae,

1. amicus: in the sense of *gratus,* as 3, 4, 25 *vestris amicum fontibus et choris;* it gives the reason why Horace can consign his cares to the winds. — **tristitiam**: *gloom;* cf. 1, 7, 18.

2. protervis: *impetuous, rude.* Cf. *Epod.* 16, 22 *protervus Africus.* — **in mare Creticum**: particularizing. Cf. n. to 1, 1, 13.

3 f. portare: Intr. 107. — **quis**: nominative. The following questions depend on **securus,** v. 6. — **sub Arcto rex,** etc.: Cotiso, king of the Dacians, whose threatened invasion at the time of the battle of Actium, 31 B.C., the Romans greatly feared. Cf. 3, 6, 13 ff. *paene occupatam seditionibus | delevit urbem Dacus et Aethiops, | hic classe*

5   quid Tiridaten terreat, unice
       securus. O quae fontibus integris
          gaudes, apricos necte flores,
             necte meo Lamiae coronam,

       Pimplea dulcis. Nil sine te mei
10   prosunt honores. Hunc fidibus novis,
          hunc Lesbio sacrare plectro
             teque tuasque decet sorores.

formidatus, ille | missilibus melior sagittis; Verg. *G.* 2, 497 *coniurato descendens Dacus ab Histro.* He was finally crushed by P. Crassus in the campaigns of 30-28 B.C.

5. Tiridaten: not long before the battle of Actium, Tiridates successfully revolted against Phraates, king of the Parthians, and succeeded him on the throne. In 30 B.C. Phraates returned to the contest and forced his rival to flee for safety to Augustus, who was at that time in Egypt. Cf. *Mon. Anc.* 5, 54 ff. *ad me supp*[*li*]*ces confug*[*erunt*] *reges Parthorum Tirida*[*tes et postea*] *Phrat*[*es*] *regis Phrati*[*s filius*]. The accounts of Justin and Dio Cassius, our chief authorities for these points, are conflicting, but apparently Tiridates was again placed on the throne in 29 B.C. — cf. 3, 8, 19 f. *Medus infestus sibi luctuosis | dissidet armis* — only to be displaced again in 27 B.C. by Phraates, who had collected a large force of friendly Scythians to aid him. Tiridates then fled to Augustus, who was in Spain. — **unice securus**: *perfectly at ease.*

6. fontibus integris: fresh, pure fountains shall furnish the inspiration of his new song (**fidibus novis**). The same figure Lucret. 1, 927 *iuvat integros accedere fontis atque haurire.*

7. necte flores, etc.: *i.e.* exalt him in song. Cf. Pind. *O.* 6, 86 f. ἀνδράσιν αἰχματαῖσι πλέκων | ποικίλον ὕμνον.

9 f. Pimplea: *Muse of Pimplea*; named from a fountain of the Muses in Pieria near Mt. Olympus. Cf. Orph. 46 A. Πιμπληιάδες. — **mei honores**: *i.e.* conferred by my verse. Cf. Verg. *A.* 9, 446 *fortunati ambo! si quid mea carmina possunt.* — **hunc . . . hunc**: Lamia.

11. Lesbio . . . plectro: marking his new verse (*fidibus nobis*) as modelled on that of Alcaeus. Cf. 1, 1, 34 *Lesboum . . . barbiton.* The plectrum was a small ivory or metal instrument with which the strings of the lyre were struck. — **sacrare**: *consecrate*; 'canonize.' Cf. Stat. *Silv.* 4, 7, 7 f. *si tuas cantu Latio sacravi, | Pindare, Thebas.*

27

A dramatic picture of a *comissatio* at which the poet tries to check his hot companions; when they fill their cups and will make him drink, he parries their impetuosity by refusing, unless his neighbor tell him the name of his love. The whispered secret makes him exclaim in pity.

The ode is based on a similar one by Anacreon, according to Porphyrio; possibly the one of which Athenaeus (10, 42, 7) has preserved to us a fragment (*Frg.* 63) ἄγε δηὖτε μηκέτ' οὕτω | πατάγῳ τε κἀλαλητῷ | Σκυθικὴν πόσιν παρ' οἴνῳ | μελετῶμεν, ἀλλὰ καλοῖς | ὑποπίνοντες ἐν ὕμνοις. 'Come, now, let us no longer with din and shout practice Scythian drinking at our wine, but sip it while we blithely sing.' The exhortation to moderation in the use of wine (1-8) is similar to the theme of 1, 18. Metre, 68.

> Natis in usum laetitiae scyphis
> pugnare Thracum est: tollite barbarum
> morem, verecundumque Bacchum
> sanguineis prohibete rixis.
>
> 5   Vino et lucernis Medus acinaces
> immane quantum discrepat: impium

1. **natis**: a favorite figure; cf. 3, 21, 1 *nata mecum testa*; *Epist.* 2, 1, 233 *versus male nati*. Translate, *intended by nature.* — **scyphis**: large two-handled drinking cups used only by heavy drinkers. Macrobius 5, 21, 16 notes *scyphus Herculis poculum est ita ut Liberi patris cantharus.* Here they characterize the drinking bout as unrestrained. In *Epod.* 9, 33 the poet demands *capaciores . . . scyphos* with which to celebrate the victory over Sextus Pompey.

2. **Thracum**: predicate to pugnare; cf. the Σκυθικὴν πόσιν in the fragment quoted above. For the heavy drinking and quarrelsome character of the Thracians see n. to 1, 18, 9.

3 f. **verecundum . . . Bacchum**: the god who requires moderation in his devotees; *modicus Liber* 1, 18, 7. Hence the drunken shouting (**impium clamorem**, v. 6) is an offense against him. — **prohibete**: *save from.*

5 f. **Medus acinaces**: the short sword of the Medes; probably taken from the Greek original. The wearing of the sword at a banquet or drinking bout was a distinctly barbarian custom to the Roman, who was forbidden by law to carry weapons within the city. — **immane quantum**: *is a mon-*

lenite clamorem, sodales,
    et cubito remanete presso.

Voltis severi me quoque sumere
    partem Falerni? Dicat Opuntiae
frater Megillae quo beatus
    volnere, qua pereat sagitta.

Cessat voluntas? Non alia bibam
mercede. Quae te cumque domat Venus,
    non erubescendis adurit
        ignibus, ingenuoque semper

amore peccas. Quicquid habes, age
depone tutis auribus. — A miser,

strous anomaly amid (Smith). The phrase had become fixed and like *nescio quid* had lost its interrogative character before Horace's time. Cf. Sallust. *Frg.* 2, 44 M. *immane quantum animi exarsere:* so Liv. 2, 1, 11 *id mirum quantum profuit ad concordiam.*

8. **cubito . . . presso**: the Romans regularly reclined at table. With the phrase, cf. Petron. 27 *hic est apud quem cubitum ponetis.*

9 ff. 'Shall I too join you? Only on one condition.' — **severi**: *strong*, δριμύς. Cf. Catull. 27, 1 f. *minister vetuli puer Falerni | inger mi calices amariores.* Two kinds of Falernian are mentioned by Athen. 1, 26 C. εἴδη δύο, ὁ αὐστηρὸς καὶ ὁ γλυκάζων, three by Pliny *N. H.* 14, 8, 6 the *austerum* (equivalent to **severum**), *dulce,*

tenue. — **dicat**: *i.e.* that we may drink a toast; cf. Mart. 1, 71, 1 *Naevia sex cyathis, septem Iustina bibatur.* — **Opuntiae frater Megillae**: a similar designation, 3, 9, 14 *Thurini Calais filius Ornyti.* The mention of the presumably pretty Megilla is quite in keeping with the occasion and would direct the attention of all to the comrade addressed.

11 f. **beatus . . . pereat**: *dies a blessed death.*

13 f. **cessat voluntas**: *falters his will?* — **mercede**: *terms.* — **cumque**: cf. n. to 1, 6, 3. — **Venus**: in same sense as 1, 33, 13 *melior Venus*; also Verg. *E.* 3, 68 *parta meae Veneri sunt munera.*

16 f. **ingenuo . . . amore**: 'love for a freeborn girl,' *i.e.* not a *libertina* (1, 33, 15) or an *ancilla* (2, 4, 1). — **peccas**: *thy weak-*

quanta laborabas Charybdi,
20   digne puer meliore flamma!

Quae saga, quis te solvere Thessalis
magus venenis, quis poterit deus?
Vix inligatum te triformi
    Pegasus expediet Chimaera.

ness is for.—**quicquid habes,** etc.: Horace leans back to his friend reclining above him on the couch, who after a moment's hesitation whispers his loved one's name.—**tutis auribus**: abl. Intr. 95.—**a miser**: in pity for the youth's hard lot.

19 f. Charybdi: for the comparison of a mistress to Charybdis, cf. Anaxilas, *Frg.* 22 K. ἡ δὲ Φρύνη τὴν Χάρυβδιν οὐχὶ πόρρω του ποιεῖ, | τόν τε ναύκληρον λαβοῦσα καταπέπωκ' αὐτῷ σκάφει; 'But Phryne does not fall far behind Charybdis; she has caught the captain and engulfed him boat and all.'—**laborabas**: cf. 1, 17, 19 The imperfect expresses the state which has continued to the present moment. *You were struggling* (all the time). Cf. the Greek imperfect with ἄρα.

21 f. saga, . . . magus, . . . deus: a comic climax, *wise woman, . . . enchanter, . . . god.* — **Thessalis . . . venenis**: *potions*; instrum. abl. The mountains of southern Thessaly are the home of medicine in Homer; in Greek writers of the classical period the source of love philters and enchantments of all kinds.

23 f. inligatum: *entangled.* — **triformi**: cf. *Il.* 6, 181 πρόσθε λέων, ὄπιθεν δὲ δράκων, μέσση δὲ χίμαιρα, translated by Lucret. 5, 905 *prima leo, postrema draco, media ipsa Chimaera.* Bellerophon killed the chimaera with the aid of Pegasus, who was given him for this purpose by Hera.

28

This ode also is in dramatic form, but its interpretation has puzzled both ancient and modern critics. The best explanation is that it consists of two parts, probably studies based on Greek models, which Horace never worked into a unified whole, but hastily put together when arranging his odes for publication. The first 'fragment' comprises vv. 1-22. The scene is the Apulian seashore east of Venusia, by the grave of the philosopher Archytas. A spirit whose unburied body lies on the shore addresses Archytas (1-6), who in spite of all his wisdom, which enabled him to measure heaven and number the very sands, now lies under a little earth; this leads the shade to moralize on the universality of death, which comes to all without distinction (7-22). The last two verses of this part close the illustrations with the speaker's personal experience in the true Horatian manner. In the second part (23-36) the spirit appeals to a passing sailor to throw a little dust on its unburied body, that it may find rest in Hades.

Archytas was a statesman, general, and philosopher of Tarentum: according to tradition a friend of Plato. As a member of the Pythagorean school he tried to explain the physical universe by mathematics. Metre, 77.

> Te maris et terrae numeroque carentis harenae
> mensorem cohibent, Archyta,
> pulveris exigui prope litus parva Matinum
> munera, nec quicquam tibi prodest
> 5 aerias temptasse domos animoque rotundum
> percurrisse polum morituro.

1 ff. The opening verses are similar to Simias' epigram on Sophocles *Anth. Pal.* 7, 21 σὲ ... τὸν τραγικῆς Μούσης ἀστέρα ... τύμβος ἔχει καὶ γῆς ὀλίγον μέρος. — **numero carentis arenae mensorem**: note the slight oxymoron. Possibly there is a reminiscence of Archimedes' treatise ψαμμίτης, in which he maintained against his opponents that the sands could be counted; or this subject may have been treated in a philosophical work by Archytas himself. In any case there is a certain irony in this reference to the vanity of human effort, which the contrast in the succeeding **cohibent** (*hold fast*) emphasizes.

3. **pulveris...munera**: *the small gift of a little dust*; *i.e.* his narrow tomb. Cf. Verg. *G.* 4, 86 f. *hi motus animorum atque haec certamina tanta | pulveris exigui iactu compressa quiescunt.*—**Matinum**: explained by Porphyrio as a mountain or promontory of Apulia; it is uncertain which.

5. **aerias temptasse domos**, etc.: *i.e.* to have explored in his astronomical studies. The verb **temptasse** itself implies boldness on Archytas' part in venturing to extend his researches to the heavens. — **animo**: *in spirit;* to be taken with both infinitives.—**morituro**: agreeing with **tibi**. Its position at the end throws emphasis on the vanity of Archytas' wisdom.—'What availed it thee to practice all thy science? Thou wert destined to die none

Occidit et Pelopis genitor, conviva deorum,
   Tithonusque remotus in auras,
et Iovis arcanis Minos admissus, habentque
   Tartara Panthoiden iterum Orco
demissum, quamvis clipeo Troiana refixo
   tempora testatus nihil ultra

the less.' Cf. 2, 3, 4 *moriture Delli* and n. Intr. 23.

6 f. Examples to prove the general statement implied in **morituro**, 'all must die.'—**occidit**: emphatically presenting the main idea — *dead too is*, etc. Cf. *Il.* 21, 107 κάτθανε καὶ Πάτροκλος, ὅπερ σέο πολλὸν ἀμείνων.—**Pelopis genitor**: Tantalus, who shared the very table of the gods until their favor made him arrogant. Cf. Pind. *O.* 1, 54 f. εἰ δὲ δή τιν' ἄνδρα θνατὸν Ὀλύμπου σκοποὶ | ἐτίμασαν, ἦν Τάνταλος οὗτος. 'If the guardians of Olympus honored any mortal, that man was Tantalus.' Eurip. *Orest.* 8 ff. (Τάνταλος) ὡς μὲν λέγουσιν, ὅτι θεοῖς ἄνθρωπος ὢν | κοινῆς τραπέζης ἀξίωμ' ἔχων ἴσον, | ἀκόλαστον ἔσχε γλῶσσαν, αἰσχίστην νόσον. 'Men say that because Tantalus, though mortal, shared their table with the gods in equal honor, he had an unbridled tongue, most shameful plague.' And *Anth. Lat.* 931, 9 f. *Tantalus infelix, dicunt, conviva deorum | nunc quoque apud Manes victima sacra Iovi es.*

8. Tithonus: Laomedon's son and brother of Priam. He was loved by Eos, who obtained for him from Zeus the gift of immortality, but forgot to ask the boon of eternal youth; so Tithonus wasted away until he was a mere voice. Cf. 2, 16, 30 *longa Tithonum minuit senectus.* Mimnermus *Frg.* 4 Τιθωνῷ μὲν ἔδωκεν ἔχειν κακὸν ἄφθιτον ὁ Ζεὺς | γῆρας, ὃ καὶ θανάτου ῥίγιον ἀργαλέου. 'To Tithonus Zeus granted an eternal bane, old age, which is more painful than grievous death.'

9. Minos: *Od.* 19, 179 Διὸς μεγάλου ὀαριστής ('the friend'). He was instructed by Jove himself in the laws which he gave the Cretans.

10 ff. Tartara: here the place of the dead simply, equivalent to Hades, Orcus. So Verg. *G.* 1, 36, *nam te nec sperant Tartara regem.*—**Panthoiden**: Euphorbus, who was killed by Menelaus (*Il.* 17, 1-60). His shield was hung up in the temple of Hera at Argos. Now Pythagoras claimed that he was the reincarnated Trojan hero, and to prove his claim went to the temple and took down Euphorbus' shield, recognizing it as the one he had carried when formerly on earth. Yet his reincarnation could not save him from a second return to Orcus (**iterum Orco demissum**), although he yielded not his spirit, but only

nervos atque cutem morti concesserat atrae,
   iudice te non sordidus auctor
15 naturae verique.   Sed omnis una manet nox
   et calcanda semel via leti.
Dant alios Furiae torvo spectacula Marti,
   exitio est avidum mare nautis;
mixta senum ac iuvenum densentur funera; nullum
20   saeva caput Proserpina fugit.
Me quoque devexi rapidus comes Orionis
   Illyricis Notus obruit undis.
At tu, nauta, vagae ne parce malignus harenae
   ossibus et capiti inhumato

sinews and skin (**nervos atque cutem**) to death.   There is a certain irony in the patronymic as applied to Pythagoras.   For the dative **Orco**, see Intr. 88.

14. iudice te: Archytas was reckoned in later times the most distinguished Pythagorean, and hence most fit to judge. — **non sordidus auctor**: *no mean master*.

15. naturae: here 'nature of the universe.' — **sed**: the list ends with the general statement, 'but in spite of their wisdom and station all must die.' — **una nox**: cf. Catull. 5, 6 *nox perpetua una dormienda*.

17 ff. The various forms of death, closing with the speaker's personal experience (21 f.). — **alios**: the correlative *aliis* which we expect is represented by **nautis**. — **spectacula**: *as a show*; cf. *ludo* 1, 2, 37.

19. mixta ... densentur funera: *the funeral trains are crowded in confusion together*.   The verse was imitated nearly six centuries later by Corippus *B. Afr.* 1016 *mixti senibus densentur ephebi*.

20. fūgit: *lets pass*.   For the tense, see Intr. 103.   According to a common belief no one could die until a lock of hair had been cut from his head as an offering to Proserpina (cf. Verg. *A.* 4, 698). — **me quoque**: the personal experience.   Cf. 1, 5, 13. — **devexi**: cf. 3, 27, 18 *pronus Orion*. Orion began to set early in November, when severe storms were common. — **Ōrionis**: with this long initial vowel, cf. *Epod.* 15, 7 *Ŏrion*. Intr. 34.

23. At this point the address to the passing sailor begins. — **vagae**: emphasizing the cheapness of the boon asked. — **ne parce malignus**: *be not so churlish as to grudge the gift*, etc. — capiti | **inhumato**: for the hiatus, see Intr. 43.

25 particulam dare: sic, quodcumque minabitur Eurus
   fluctibus Hesperiis, Venusinae
plectantur silvae te sospite, multaque merces
   unde potest tibi defluat aequo
ab Iove Neptunoque sacri custode Tarenti.
30   Neglegis immeritis nocituram
postmodo te natis fraudem committere? Fors et
   debita iura vicesque superbae
te maneant ipsum: precibus non linquar inultis,
   teque piacula nulla resolvent.
35 Quamquam festinas, non est mora longa: licebit
   iniecto ter pulvere curras.

25 f. **sic**: 'if you grant my prayer.' See n. to 1, 3, 1. — **fluctibus Hesperiis**: apparently the Adriatic. Since Italy was called Hesperia, any waves that beat on its shore may be called by this name. — **Venusinae**: the woods near Horace's birthplace, about forty miles inland on the ridge of the Apennines, and so exposed to the winds.

27 f. **plectantur**, etc.: *i.e.* 'may the wind spend its fury on the woods, and thou be safe from harm.' The abl. abs., **te sospite**, is the important part of the prayer. — **merces**: *reward.* — **unde**: referring to **ab Iove**. Cf. 1, 12, 17.

29 f. **custode Tarenti**: Taras, the mythical founder of Tarentum, was said to be the son of Neptune and a local nymph. Some Tarentine coins bear the figure of the sea god seated on a dolphin. Next to Jove, Neptune is naturally the god who could confer most benefits on the sailor. — **neglegis committere**: *wilt thou carelessly commit?* The question is asked as the sailor starts to turn away.

32. f. **debita iura**, etc.: *thy just obligations; i.e.* the right of the dead to burial, withheld by the sailor in case he refuses the wraith's request. — **vices superbae**: *stern requital.* — **linquar**: sc. *a te.*

36. **ter**: the sacred number in offices due the dead. Cf. Verg. *A.* 6, 229 and 506 *magna Manis ter voce vocavi.* Likewise in other religious rites, cf. *C. S.* 23, *Epist.* 1, 1, 37.

29

'What, Iccius, now envious of the Arabs' wealth and ready for their conquest! Hast thou already chosen thy share of captured spoils? Upon my word, all Nature may go topsy-turvy, when thou dost barter all thy philosophic lore for a breastplate. I had thought better of thee.'

These bantering verses are addressed to Horace's friend Iccius, a philosophic dilettante, who suddenly showed an interest in the preparations for a campaign against Arabia Felix, under the direction of Aelius Gallus. The attempt terminated unsuccessfully in 24 B.C. The date of composition therefore may be approximately fixed as 26 B.C. or early 25 B.C. Five or six years later, in 20 B.C., *Epist.* I, 12 was addressed to the same friend, who then was manager of Agrippa's Sicilian estates. Metre, 68.

> Icci, beatis nunc Arabum invides
> gazis et acrem militiam paras
>   non ante devictis Sabaeae
>   regibus, horribilique Medo
>
> 5   nectis catenas? Quae tibi virginum
> sponso necato barbara serviet?
>   Puer quis ex aula capillis
>   ad cyathum statuetur unctis,

1. **Icci**: note the emphatic position, expressing Horace's surprise, 'Iccius! are you,' etc. — **beatis**: the adjective which expresses properly the condition of the person is here transferred to the cause of the Arabs' good fortune. **gazis**. Intr. 99. Arabia was the ancient El Dorado. Cf. 3, 24, 1 f. *intactis opulentior | thesauris Arabum*. — **nunc**: in contrast to his former philosophic interests.

3 f. **Sabaeae**: the Sheba of the Old Testament. *Kings* I, 10; Pliny *N. H.* 6, 16. — **horribilique Medo**: *i.e.* the Parthians; so 1, 2,

51 *neu sinas Medos equitare inultos*.

5. **nectis catenas**: as Florus (3, 7) says the elder Antony carried fetters ready made in his expedition against the Cretans, so confident was he of success. — **quae . . . virginum . . . barbara**: equivalent to *quae virgo barbara*; a favorite form of expression with Horace. Cf. *Epod.* 10, 13 *Graia victorum manus*.

7 f. **puer ex aula**: *page from royal court*. — **ad cyathum**: the 'cupbearer,' a page who drew the wine from the mixer (*crater*) with

CARMINA [1.30

doctus sagittas tendere Sericas
10   arcu paterno? Quis neget arduis
pronos relabi posse rivos
montibus et Tiberim reverti,

cum tu coemptos undique nobilis
libros Panaeti Socraticam et domum
15   mutare loricis Hiberis,
pollicitus meliora, tendis?

the *cyathus* into the cups. His title appears in inscriptions as *a cyatho*. For Iccius only a captured prince will do, when he is enriched with Arabian spoil.

9. **doctus**: the page's training has not been to menial service, but to speed (**tendere**) the arrow with his father's bow. — **Sericas**: with this adjective Horace pokes fun at his friend's extravagant expectations: the whole East to China is to be subdued.

10 ff. Proverbial; cf. *Epod.* 16, 25 ff.; Eurip. *Med.* 410 ἄνω ποταμῶν ἱερῶν χωροῦσι παγαί; Ovid. *Her.* 5, 29 f. *cum Paris Oenone poterit spirare relicta | ad fontem Xanthi versa recurret aqua.* —

pronos: *now gliding downward* — **arduis . . . montibus**: abl. of the way by which, *up the steep*, etc.

13 ff. **coemptos undique . . . libros**: hitherto Iccius' efforts have been solely to acquire a philosophical library. — **nobilis . . . Panaeti**: Panaetius of Rhodes, the leading Stoic philosopher of the second century B.C., was a friend of the younger Scipio and of Polybius and had a great influence at Rome. Cicero in his *de officiis* followed Panaetius' treatise on Duty. — **domum**: *school.* — **loricis Hiberis**: the iron and steel of Hispania Tarraconensis rivaled that of Noricum. Cf. 1, 16, 9.

30

A prayer to Venus to leave her home in Cyprus and take up her abode in Glycera's shrine. The motive is probably taken from a Greek ὕμνος κλητικός, hymn of invocation. Cf. Anacreon *Frg.* 2. ὦ 'ναξ, ᾧ δαμάλης Ἔρως | καὶ Νύμφαι κυανώπιδες | πορφυρέη τ' Ἀφροδίτη | συμπαίζουσιν, ἐπιστρέφεαι δ' | ὑψηλῶν κορυφὰς ὀρέων, | γουνοῦμαί σε· σὺ δ' εὐμενὴς | ἐλθ' ἡμῖν, κεχαρισμένης δ' | εὐχωλῆς ἐπακούειν. 'O prince

with whom sport Love the subduer, the dark-eyed nymphs, and rosy
Aphrodite, thou art wandering on the lofty mountain heights. I beseech thee, come in kindness to us, accept and listen to our prayer.'
Metre, 69.

> O Venus, regina Cnidi Paphique,
> sperne dilectam Cypron et vocantis
> ture te multo Glycerae decoram
>   transfer in aedem.
>
> 5 Fervidus tecum puer et solutis
> Gratiae zonis properentque Nymphae
> et parum comis sine te Iuventas
>   Mercuriusque.

1. **Cnidi**: a center of the worship of Aphrodite in Caria. In her shrine there was a statue of the goddess by Praxiteles, of which the Vatican Venus is a copy. — **Paphi**: Aphrodite's ancient home in Cyprus, where tradition said the goddess was born from the foam of the sea. Cf. *Od.* 8, 362 f. ἡ δ' ἄρα Κύπρον ἵκανε φιλομμειδὴς Ἀφροδίτη, | ἐς Πάφον, ἔνθα τέ οἱ τέμενος βωμός τε θυήεις, also Verg. *A.* 1, 415 f. *ipsa Paphum sublimis abit, sedesque revisit | laeta suas.*

2. **sperne**: *abandon.* Cf. Alcman *Frg.* 21 Κύπρον ἱμερτὰν λιποῖσα καὶ Πάφον περίρρυταν.

4. **aedem**: the private *shrine* that Glycera has established.

5. **fervidus ... puer**: Cupid who inflames men with love. — **solutis Gratiae zonis**: the Graces were in early art represented with flowing garments. Cf. Sen. *de Benef.* 1, 3 quoted on 1, 4, 6.

7. **Iuventas**: Ἥβη. Cf. Hom. hymn to Apollo quoted on 1, 4, 5. — **parum**: cf. 1, 12, 59 and n. to 1, 2, 27.

8. **Mercurius**: associated with Venus as god of persuasive eloquence.

31

'The poet's prayer to enshrined Apollo is not for wealth of land or store. He only asks for simple fare, for health of body and of mind; an old age not deprived of song.'

This ode is Horace's hymn to Apollo on the occasion of the dedication of his temple on the Palatine, Oct. 24, 28 B.C. The temple was vowed eight years before, and the belief that the victory at Actium was due to Apollo's aid gave his worship new significance. With the temple was

CARMINA [1, 31, 8

united a Greek and Latin public library. The decoration of its porticoes is described by Propertius 3, 29; the interior was adorned with busts and statues of famous writers. The statue of the god was a work of Scopas brought from Greece, described by Plin. *N. H.* 36, 28. See also Baumeister 1, 99. The motive of the ode may be compared with Pind. *N.* 8, 37 ff. χρυσὸν εὔχονται, πεδίον δ' ἕτεροι | ἀπέραντον · ἐγὼ δ' ἀστοῖς ἁδὼν καὶ χθονὶ γυῖα καλύψαιμ' | αἰνέων αἰνητά, μομφὰν δ' ἐπισπείρων ἀλιτροῖς. 'For gold some pray and some for land unlimited; but as for me I hope that I may shroud my frame in earth beloved by my townsmen, praising what is praiseworthy and sowing blame for evil-doers.' Metre, 68.

> Quid dedicatum poscit Apollinem
> vates? Quid orat de patera novum
> fundens liquorem? Non opimae
> Sardiniae segetes feracis,
>
> 5 non aestuosae grata Calabriae
> armenta, non aurum aut ebur Indicum,
> non rura quae Liris quieta
> mordet aqua taciturnus amnis.

1. **dedicatum**: *lately enshrined.* Cf. *Epod.* 7, 2 *enses conditi*, and n. The god and his temple are here confused as in Cic. *de D. N.* 2, 61 *ut Fides, ut Mens, quas in Capitolio dedicatas videmus.*

2. **vates**: *inspired bard.* Cf. n. to 1, 1, 35. — **novum**: new wine was regularly used in libations. Cf. Petron. 130 *spumabit pateris hornus liquor.*

3 f. **opimae**: with **segetes**. — **Sardiniae**: Sardinia, Sicily, and Africa, Cicero calls *pro leg. Man.* 34 *tria frumentaria subsidia rei publicae.*

5. **Calabriae**: Calabria was the best winter grazing ground in Italy; in summer the herds were driven into the mountains of Lucania and Samnium. Cf. *Epod.* 1, 27 f. *pecusve Calabris ante sidus fervidum* | *Lucana mutet pascuis.*

6. **ebur**: this expensive material was used for decoration in the houses of the wealthy. Cf. 2, 18, 1 f. *non ebur neque aureum* | *mea renidet in domo lacunar.*

7 f. The lower valley of the Liris produced fine wines. — **mordet**: the same figure as Lucret. 5, 256 *et ripas radentia flumina rodunt.* Note the doubling of epithets, quieta . . . taciturnus. Cf. Silius Ital. 4, 348 ff. *Liris . . . qui fonte quieto* | *dissimulat cursum ac nullo mutabilis imbri* | *perstringit tacitas gemmanti gurgite ripas.*

Premant Calena falce quibus dedit
Fortuna vitem, dives et aureis
mercator exsiccet culullis
vina Syra reparata merce,

dis carus ipsis, quippe ter et quater
anno revisens aequor Atlanticum
impune: me pascunt olivae,
me cichorea levesque malvae.

Frui paratis et valido mihi,
Latoe, dones et, precor, integra

9-16. The contrast between the luxury of the rich and Horace's simplicity is emphasized. — **premant**: *check, prune*; used by poets for the prose *putant*; e.g. Verg. G. 1, 157 *ruris opaci falce premes umbras.*—**Calena falce**: cf. 1, 20, 9. — **quibus dedit**: sc. *premere.*

11. **culullis**: according to Porphyrio, these were properly earthenware cups used by the pontifices and the Vestal Virgins in religious rites. But the merchant grown rich with trade uses cups of solid gold.

12. **Syra merce**: spices, unguents, and costly perfumes imported from the Orient.

13 f. **quippe . . . revisens**: *surely for he . . .*, giving the reason for the previous ironical statement **dis carus ipsis**. This participle with **quippe** is equivalent to the common '*quippe qui*' explanatory clause.—**aequor Atlanticum**: Gades (Cadiz), but a short distance outside the straits of Gibraltar, was practically the limit of navigation for the Romans; the Atlantic was an unknown and fearful ocean. With the thought, cf. Aristot. *apud Iamb. Protrep.* 6 οὐ δὲ δεῖ χρημάτων μὲν ἕνεκα πλεῖν ἐφ' Ἡρακλίους στήλας καὶ πολλάκις κινδυνεύειν, διὰ δὲ φρόνησιν μηδὲν πονεῖν μηδὲ δαπανᾶν. 'Nor for wealth need one sail to the pillars of Heracles and risk his life many times, but for prudence' sake he should not toil or spend (overmuch).' .

15 f. **me**: the position of the personal pronoun emphasizes the contrast. Cf. n. to 1, 1, 29. Intr. 30. — **leves**: *digestible.* Cf. *Epod.* 2, 57 f. *gravi | malvae salubres corpori.*

17 f. **paratis**: equivalent to *partis, my possessions.* — **valido . . . integra cum mente**: cf. the familiar words of Juvenal (10, 356) *orandum est ut sit mens sana in corpore sano.*

cum mente nec turpem senectam
                degere nec cithara carentem.

19 f. **nec turpem senectam**, etc.:
cf. Dobson's verses to Longfellow, 'Not to be tuneless in old age! Ah surely blest his pilgrimage, | Who, in his Winter's snow, | Still sings with note as sweet and clear | As in the morning of the year | When the first violets blow!' Also Eurip. *H. F.*
676 μὴ ζῴην μετ' ἀμουσίας, | αἰεὶ δ' ἐν στεφάνοισιν εἴ | ην · ἔτι τοι γέρων ἀοι | δὸς κελαδῶ Μναμοσύναν. 'Heaven grant that I may not live without the harmony of life, but among garlands ever spend my days; and still when I am old will I as bard celebrate the goddess Mnemosyne.'

32

'We are asked for a song. Come, my lyre, if ever we have sung light strains that shall live, now raise a true Latin song, like those Alcaeus sang of old. In war and shipwreck still he sang of wine and love. Sweet shell, beloved by Jove supreme, solace of toil, hear me when I duly call.'
   This ode may have been written as a prelude of some serious ode or collection such as the first six of the third book, to which '*Latinum carmen*' may refer. Horace quotes his great model to show that songs of love and wine are not inconsistent with serious poetry. Metre, 69.

Poscimur. Si quid vacui sub umbra
lusimus tecum, quod et hunc in annum
vivat et pluris, age dic Latinum,
        barbite, carmen,
    Lesbio primum modulate civi,

1. **poscimur.** Horace's friends may have asked him to write a thoroughly Roman ode and not simply studies from Greek models. — **vacui**: *with light heart*, free from care and anxieties.

2 f. **lusimus**: appropriate, with **vacui**, to light poetry. Cf. Verg. *E.* 1, 10 *ludere quae vellem calamo permisit agresti.* — **vivat**: *shall live.* Cf. *Epist.* 1, 19, 2 f. *nulla placere diu nec vivere carmina possunt | quae scribuntur aquae potoribus.* — **dic**: of instrumental music; cf. Cic. *de div.* 2, 122 *si velim canere vel voce vel fidibus.*

5. Not that Alcaeus (**Lesbio ... civi**) was the first to play the lyre, but the first to perfect lyric poetry. — **civi**: referring to Alcaeus' patri-

qui ferox bello tamen inter arma,
sive iactatam religarat udo
   litore navim,

Liberum et Musas Veneremque et illi
10 semper haerentem puerum canebat
et Lycum nigris oculis nigroque
   crine decorum.

O decus Phoebi et dapibus supremi
grata testudo Iovis, o laborum
15 dulce lenimen, mihi cumque salve
   rite vocanti!

otism that made him take a vigorous part in the politics of Mytilene, especially against the tyrants Myrtilus and Pittacus. His sentiments were expressed in political odes, στασιωτικά, of which we have a few fragments, 15-33 B. Cf. 4, 9, 7 *Alcaei minaces Camenae*.

6 ff. With these verses cf. 2, 13, 26 ff. *et, te sonantem plenius aureo,* | *Alcaee, plectro dura navis, dura fugae mala, dura belli.* — **ferox bello**: against the tyrants named in last note, and also against the Athenians in the Troad. The following **tamen** shows that the phrase is concessive. — **inter arma, sive**, etc.: 'in war or exile.'

7 f. religarat . . . litore: cf. Verg. *A.* 7, 106 *religarat ab aggere classem*. Intr. 95. — **udo**: *sea-beaten.*

9 ff. 'Wine and love were still the subjects of Alcaeus' song, as they must be of mine.'

11 f. Lycum: a favorite of Alcaeus. Cf. *Frg.* 58 written apparently in anger, οὐκέτ' ἐγὼ Λύκον ἐν Μοίσαις ἀλέγω. — **nigris oculis**, etc.: points of beauty. Note the shift of quantity **nīgris . . . nĭgro**. The description is repeated *Epist.* 2, 3, 37 *spectandum nigris oculis nigroque capillo*.

13 ff. A renewed invocation. — **dapibus supremi**, etc.: cf. *Il.* 1, 602 f. οὐδέ τι θυμὸς ἐδεύετο δαιτὸς ἐίσης | οὐ μὲν φόρμιγγος περικαλλέος ἣν ἔχ' Ἀπόλλων. — **testudo**: cf. Arnold's verses, quoted on 1, 10. 6.

15 f. cumque: temporal, modifying **vocanti** and equivalent to *quandocumque te vocabo*. No parallel can be adduced to this use of **cumque** as an independent word, but we can safely accept Porphyrio's explanation, who did not find the phrase unintelligible. — **mihi salve**: *accept my greeting.* Cf. Verg. *A.* 11, 97 f. *salve aeternum mihi, maxuma Palla,* | *aeternumque vale.*

33

'Albius, thou shouldst not grieve that Glycera prefers another, for Venus finds delight in binding together strange mates; I too have suffered from her whims.'

The Albius addressed is probably Tibullus, the elegiac poet, a contemporary and friend of Horace. The fact that the name Glycera is not found in Tibullus' poems does not make against the identification, which is as old as the first century A.D. There is no indication of the date of composition. Metre, 72.

>   Albi, ne doleas plus nimio memor
>   immitis Glycerae, neu miserabilis
>   decantes elegos, cur tibi iunior
>   laesa praeniteat fide,
>
> 5 insignem tenui fronte Lycorida
>   Cyri torret amor, Cyrus in asperam

1 ff. ne doleas... neu decantes: depending on the examples adduced in vv. 5 ff. Translate, *You should not grieve..., for.* — plus nimio: *over much*; connect with doleas. Cf. 1, 18, 15 *et tollens vacuum plus nimio gloria verticem.*

2. immitis: *unkind, unfaithful,* to thee. Note the contrast between the epithet and the name, Glycera. — decantes: *drone and drone.* The compound with de- acquired the meaning of continuously singing the same note or strain. Here it is especially appropriate with miserabilis, *gloomy.* — elegos: referring simply to the form, a couplet formed of a hexameter and a pentameter; the Alexandrian poets associated this form with sentiment and love. For the development of Roman elegy and its relation to its model, see Sellar, pp. 201-223.

3 f. cur, etc.: the complaint Albius repeats in his verses, and at the same time the reason for his sorrow. For the construction, cf. *Epist.* 1, 8, 9 f. *irascar amicis | cur me funesto properent arcere veterno.* — laesa fide: a second cause for Albius' grief.

5 ff. The following may have been suggested by Moschus 6, 1 ff. ἤρατο Πὰν Ἀχῶς τᾶς γείτονος, ἤρατο δ' Ἀχὼ | σκιρτητᾶ Σατύρω, Σάτυρος δ' ἐπεμήνατο Λύδᾳ· | ὡς Ἀχὼ τὸν Πᾶνα, τόσον Σάτυρος φλέγεν Ἀχώ, | καὶ Λύδα Σατυρίσκον· Ἔρως δ' ἐσμύχε τ' ἀμοιβά. 'Pan loved his neighbor Echo; Echo loved | A gamesome Satyr; he, by her unmoved, | Loved only

declinat Pholoen; sed prius Apulis
iungentur capreae lupis

quam turpi Pholoe peccet adultero.
Sic visum Veneri, cui placet imparis
formas atque animos sub iuga aenea
saevo mittere cum ioco.

Ipsum me melior cum peteret Venus,
grata detinuit compede Myrtale
libertina, fretis acrior Hadriae
curvantis Calabros sinus.

Lyde: thus through Echo, Pan, | Lyde, and Satyr, Love his circle ran' (Myers).
— tenui fronte; a point of beauty, as Lycus' black hair and eyes of the preceding ode. Cf. *Epist.* 1, 7, 26 *nigros angusta fronte capillos*; Petron. 126 *frons minima et quae apices capillorum retro flexerat.* — Lycorida: the name is apparently taken from the elegies of Gallus, as Pholoe from those of Tibullus (1, 8, 69).
7. declinat: sc. *a Lycoride.*
9. turpi ... adultero: *low-born lover.* — peccet: cf. 1, 27, 17 *ingenuo amore peccas.*

13 ff. ipsum me: the usual personal experience. Intr. 30. — melior Venus: in the same sense as 1, 27, 20 *meliore flamma.* The contrast is furnished by libertina v. 15.
15 f. fretis acrior Hadriae: concessive. The same figure is used 3, 9, 22 f. *improbo | iracundior Hadria.* The Adriatic was proverbially rough. Cf. 1, 3, 15; 2, 14, 14. — curvantis: *when it hollows out;* i.e. in time of storm. Cf. Ovid *Met.* 11, 229 *est sinus Haemoniae curvos falcatus in arcus.* — sinus: the accusative expresses the result of the verb's action.

34

'Careless of Heaven, devoted to a mad philosophy, I was forced by a bolt in the clear sky to change my course and to remind myself that God can put down the mighty and exalt the low.'

The ode tells its own story and must not be taken too seriously, for it may have been based on a Greek model. For Horace's religious views, see Sellar, p. 159 ff. Metre, 68.

Parcus deorum cultor et infrequens,
  insanientis dum sapientiae
    consultus erro, nunc retrorsum
      vela dare atque iterare cursus

5   cogor relictos. Namque Diespiter,
  igni corusco nubila dividens
    plerumque, per purum tonantis
      egit equos volucremque currum,

  quo bruta tellus et vaga flumina,
10 quo Styx et invisi horrida Taenari
    sedes Atlanteusque finis
      concutitur. Valet ima summis

2 ff. insanientis ... sapientiae: Epicurean philosophy, according to which the gods lived a life apart, undisturbed by interest in mortals. Note the oxymoron. — consultus: an extended use from such phrases as *iuris consultus*, 'skilled in the law.' — cursus ... relictos : the old national religion, faith in which was no longer held by men of Horace's education.
  5. Diespiter: the ancient name for Jupiter, according to Varro. Cf. our 'Father of light.'
  7. plerumque: with dividens. Note the emphasis given this by position, as 1, 31, 14 f. *revisens aequor Atlanticum | impune.* Intr. 23. — per purum tonantis: Lucretius closes his argument that thunder and lightning come from natural causes with the words (6, 400 f.) *denique cur numquam caelo iacit undique puro | Iuppiter in terras fulmen sonitusque profundit?*
  9 f. bruta: *inert;* contrasted with vaga. Cf. 3, 4, 45 *terra iners.* — Taenari: the southern promontory of Laconia, to-day Cape Matapan, where a cleft in the rocks was said to be the entrance to the lower world. Cf. Verg. *G.* 4, 467 *Taenarias etiam fauces, alta ostia Ditis.*
  11. Atlanteus finis: equivalent to Euripides' τέρμονες Ἀτλαντικοί (*Hippol.* 3), the western boundary of the world.
  12. valet ima summis, etc.: divinity's power to humble and exalt is a commonplace of Greek poetry. *E.g. Od.* 16, 211 f. ῥηίδιον δὲ θεοῖσι, τοὶ οὐρανὸν εὐρὺν ἔχουσιν, | ἠμὲν κυδῆναι θνητὸν βροτὸν ἠδὲ κακῶσαι, and Archil. *Frg.* 56 B. τοῖς θεοῖς τίθει τὰ πάντα· πολλάκις μὲν ἐκ

mutare et insignem attenuat deus,
obscura promens ; hinc apicem rapax
15   Fortuna cum stridore acuto
sustulit, hic posuisse gaudet.

κακῶν | ἄνδρας ὀρθοῦσιν μελαίνῃ κειμένους ἐπὶ χθονί, | πολλάκις δ' ἀνατρέπουσι καὶ μάλ' εὖ βεβηκότας | ὑπτίους κλίνουσ'. 'Intrust all things to the gods. Ofttimes from misfortune they set upright men who lie prostrate on the gloomy ground ; ofttimes too they overthrow and cast down even those who have prospered extremely.' Also from the Magnificat, *St. Luke* 1, 52 'He hath put down the mighty from their seats. and exalted them of low degree.'

14. apicem: properly the conical cap worn by the flamines, but used here as 3, 21, 20 *regum apices*, equivalent to *tiara*, the symbol of royal power.

15 f. stridore acuto: 'the shrill whir' of Fortune's wings. Cf. Verg. *A.* 1, 387 of the swans *stridentibus alis*. — **sustulit**: gnomic perfect. *has often before now.* Intr. 103.

35

'O Goddess, Queen of Antium, who canst exalt or humble. All court thy favor, the poor man and the prince, the wild Dacian and Scythian, the sturdy Latin stock, lest thou bring wild discord (1-16). Fierce Destiny goes before with wedge and clamp (17-20). but Hope and Faith are thy companions (21-24) ; yet at sign of thy disfavor the fickle crowd and false friend flee (25-28). Protect Caesar, we pray, in his campaign against the Britons ; guard our youth from dangers in the East (29-32). May we expiate the crimes of civil strife with swords new forged against our eastern foes (33-40).'

The motive of this prayer is probably taken from Pindar, *O.* 12, 1-6 λίσσομαι, παῖ Ζηνὸς Ἐλευθερίου, | Ἱμέραν εὐρυσθενέ' ἀμφιπόλει. Σώτειρα Τύχα. | τὶν γὰρ ἐν πόντῳ κυβερνῶνται θοαὶ | νᾶες. ἐν χέρσῳ τε λαιψηροὶ πόλεμοι | κἀγοραὶ βουλαφόροι. αἴ γε μὲν ἀνδρῶν | πόλλ' ἄνω. τὰ δ' αὖ κάτω, ψεύδη μεταμώνια τάμνοισαι. κυλίνδοντ' ἐλπίδες. 'I beseech thee, daughter of Zeus the Deliverer, Saving Fortune, guard wide-ruling Himera. For at thy beck the swift ships are piloted on the sea, and on the land fierce wars and council-giving assemblies. The hopes of men are tossed, often up, but again down, as they cut their way through the high waves of falsity.' Horace's ode forms the basis of Gray's *Ode to Adversity*, while Wordsworth used Gray's poem as a model for his *Ode to Duty*.

The expedition referred to in v. 29 f. was undertaken by Augustus in 27 B.C., when, according to Dio C. 53, 22, ἐξώρμησε μὲν ὡς καὶ ἐς τὴν Βριττανίαν στρατεύσων, ἐς δὲ δὴ τὰς Γαλατίας ἐλθὼν ἐνταῦθα. διέτριψεν. The following year he again laid plans for the invasion, but was kept back by an uprising in Spain. In this year, too, preparations were being made for the expedition of Aelius Gallus against the Arabians to which vv. 30-32 refer (cf. ode 29 of this book). 26 B.C. is therefore the most probable date of the ode. Metre, 68.

> O diva, gratum quae regis Antium,
> praesens vel imo tollere de gradu
> mortale corpus vel superbos
> vertere funeribus triumphos:
>
> 5   te pauper ambit sollicita prece
> ruris colonus, te dominam aequoris

1. **diva**: Fortune, the goddess who rules at will the vicissitudes of life, is here identified with the *Fortunae Antiates*, whose temple at Antium was a famous shrine until late times. With this shrine was associated a popular oracle; therefore the goddesses were called by Mart. 5, 1, 3 *veridicae sorores*. For representations of the goddesses on coins, see Baumeister nos. 606 and 607.
— **gratum**: probably equivalent to *dilectum*, 'beloved by thee'; cf. 1, 30, 2 *dilectam Cypron*. It may, however, refer to the beauty of the place, for Cicero speaking of it says (*ad. Att.* 4, 8 a, 1), *nihil quietius, nihil alsius, nihil amoenius*.

2. **praesens ... tollere**: *with power*, **praesens** being equivalent to *potens*. Intr. 108. — **imo tollere de gradu**: these words might suggest to the Roman reader the story of Servius Tullius, as the following **superbos ... triumphos** would surely call to his mind the case of Aemilius Paullus, the victor at Pydna, whose two sons died on the day of his triumph.

3 f. **mortale corpus**: *man's mortal clay*. — **vertere**: *change into*. Cf. *Epist.* 2, 3, 226 *vertere seria ludo*.

5 f. **te ... te**: note the frequent and emphatic anaphorae in this ode, by which the goddess addressed is constantly made prominent. Intr. 28 c. — **ambit**: *courts*. — **ruris colonus**: the farmer and the sailor (v. 7) are types of men especially dependent on the whims of Fortune, the former for his crops, the latter for his life as well as livelihood.

quicumque Bithyna lacessit
  Carpathium pelagus carina;
te Dacus asper, te profugi Scythae
  urbesque gentesque et Latium ferox
regumque matres barbarorum et
  purpurei metuunt tyranni,

iniurioso ne pede proruas
stantem columnam, neu populus frequens
  ad arma cessantis ad arma
concitet imperiumque frangat.

Te semper anteit saeva Necessitas,
clavos trabalis et cuneos manu
  gestans aena, nec severus
uncus abest liquidumque plumbum.

7 f. **Bithyna . . . Carpathium**: specializing, as 1, 1, 13 *trabe Cypria Myrtoum . . . secet mare.* — **lacessit**: *vexes.*

9 ff. The wild Dacian and the nomad (**profugi**) Scythian are contrasted with civilized peoples (**urbesque gentesque et Latium ferox**). — **profugi**: best explained by 3, 24. 9 f. *campestres . . . Scythae, | quorum plaustra vagas rite trahunt domos.* — **ferox**: *fearless.* Cf. 3, 3, 44 *Roma ferox.*

11 f. **regumque matres barbarorum**: as Atossa, the mother of Xerxes in Aeschylus' *Persians*; and the mother of Sisera in *Judges* 5, 28. — **purpurei . . . tyranni**: the color of the dress being the symbol of power: cf. Verg. *G.* 2, 495 *illum non populi fasces, non purpura regum | flexit.*

13 f. **iniurioso**: *insolent*, ὑβριστικῷ. — **columnam**: symbolical of stability. Cf. Sen. *Troad.* 6 f. *columen eversum occidit | pollentis Asiae.*

15. **ad arma . . . ad arma**: repeating dramatically the cry of the mob. Cf. Ovid *Met.* 12, 241 *certatimque omnes uno ore 'arma, arma' loquuntur.*

17 ff. **clavos, cuneos, uncus, plumbum**: these devices for fastening together building material — the *spikes, wedges* for loose joints, and *clamps* fastened with *lead* — are symbolical of the power of stern Necessity, who precedes Fortune, as the lictors go before the Roman consul. — **clavos**: *clavum figere* was used proverbially of that which was unalterably fixed by fate: cf. Cic. *Verr.* 2, 53

Te Spes et albo rara Fides colit
velata panno, nec comitem abnegat,
    utcumque mutata potentis
        veste domos inimica linquis;

25 at volgus infidum et meretrix retro
periura cedit, diffugiunt cadis
    cum faece siccatis amici
        ferre iugum pariter dolosi.

Serves iturum Caesarem in ultimos
30 orbis Britannos et iuvenum recens

ut hoc beneficium, quem admodum dicitur, trabali clavo figeret. — **manu . . . aena**: cf. the English 'iron hand.' — **severus**: *unyielding, harsh.*

21 ff. The constancy of Hope and Faith, even when Fortune denies her favor, is set over against the fickleness of the common crowd, the harlot, and false friends. — **Spes . . . Fides**: both had temples at Rome; tradition said that it was King Numa who established the festival to Fides (Livy 1, 21). — **rara**: since fidelity is seldom found. — **albo velata panno**: in offering sacrifices to Fides the priest wrapped his right hand in a white cloth. It is for this reason, according to Servius, that Vergil, *A.* 1, 292. calls Fides *cana.* — **nec comitem abnegat**: this is obscure. but the simplest interpretation is to supply *se:* 'even in adversity, Faith does not refuse to be man's companion.'

23 f. There were not simply *Fortunae* of places, cities, etc., but also *Fortunae* of private families. — **mutata . . . veste**: 'changed from festal to mourning garb.' — **inimica**: predicative.

25. volgus infidum: proverbial; cf. 1, 1, 7 *mobilium turba Quiritium.*

26 f. With the idea expressed, cf. the Greek proverb ζεῖ χύτρα, ζῇ φιλία. 'Friendship lives only so long as the pot boils.'

28. pariter: modifying **ferre**, which itself depends on **dolosi**, *too false to share.* The metaphor **ferre iugum** is a common one. Cf. Val. Max. 2, 1, 6 *impari iugo caritatis.*

29 f. ultimos orbis Britannos: cf. 4. 14, 47 *remoti . . . Britanni.* Catull. 11, 11 *ultimi Britanni.* Britain was practically a terra incognita to the Roman until the time of Claudius: the expeditions of Julius Caesar had had no permanent result except to arouse a desire for Britain's conquest

examen Eois timendum
partibus oceanoque rubro.

Eheu cicatricum et sceleris pudet
fratrumque. Quid nos dura refugimus
35   aetas? Quid intactum nefasti
liquimus? Vnde manum iuventus

metu deorum continuit? Quibus
pepercit aris? O utinam nova
incude diffingas retunsum in
40   Massagetas Arabasque ferrum.

— recens: *i.e.* newly recruited for the expedition of Aelius Gallus. — **timendum**: part of the prayer.

32 f. Cf. Verg. *A.* 8, 686 *victor ab Aurorae populis et litore rubro.* — **cicatricum et sceleris ... fratrumque**: note the cumulative force — 'the scars of civil strife are our shame, a crime, a crime against our brothers.' Cf. similar cumulations 1, 5, 11; 3, 5, 10.

34 ff. **quid nos dura**, etc.: reproducing the spirit of the first part of *Epod.* 16.

38 ff. **O utinam**, etc.: undoubtedly Horace expresses in this form his own deepest feeling, which was shared by his more earnest and wiser contemporaries. The disastrous effects of thirty years of civil war were everywhere apparent, and the new order introduced by Augustus was the only promise of a security that would enable the state to recover its prosperity. Deeper than all this were the horrors of the struggle just ended in which members of the same family had been set in armed opposition to each other. (Cf. the story of the two brothers in Livy *Per.* 79.) These did not fail to move even the insensitive Romans.

39 f. **retunsum**: *i.e.* in civil strife. — **in Massagetas**: dependent on **diffingas**, *forge anew against*. The *Massagetae* were an Oriental people east of the Caspian Sea.

36

A greeting to Numida, lately returned from the wars in Spain. Numida here appears as the warm friend and contemporary of Aelius Lamia; therefore considerably younger than Horace (cf. introductory n. to 1, 26).

The occasion for the ode may have been a dinner given by Lamia in honor of his friend; the date is unknown. Metre, 71.

>Et ture et fidibus iuvat
>>placare et vituli sanguine debito
>custodes Numidae deos,
>>qui nunc Hesperia sospes ab ultima
>5 caris multa sodalibus,
>>nulli plura tamen dividit oscula
>quam dulci Lamiae, memor
>>actae non alio rege puertiae
>mutataeque simul togae.
>10 Cressa ne careat pulchra dies nota,
>>neu promptae modus amphorae

1 f. ture et fidibus: the regular accompaniments of sacrifice. Cf. 4, 1, 21-24 *illic plurima naribus | duces tura, lyraeque et Berecynthiae | delectabere tibiae | mixtis carminibus non sine fistula.* — **debito**: *i.e.* vowed to the gods if Numida should have a safe return. Cf. 2, 7, 17 *obligatam redde Iovi dapem.*

4. Hesperia... ab ultima: from the Romans' point of view Spain was the 'farthest west land'; for the Greeks, Italy.

6. plura: *a larger share.* — **dividit**: properly used of allotting to each his portion.

8. rege: *captain, leader* in their sports. — **puertiae**: syncopated as 2, 2, 2 *laminae.*

9. mutatae... togae: the *toga praetexta* was usually given up for the *toga virilis* at the age of sixteen or seventeen years; the occasion was made a family festival. The phrase, therefore, is equivalent to our 'coming of age.' — **cressa**: *terra creta, chalk.* White was the color of joy, and happy days were given a white mark. Cf. Catull. 107, 6 *o lucem candidiore nota.* Cf. our 'red-letter day.' We are told that another way of marking the course of one's life was to drop each day a pebble in an urn — white for the happy, black for the sad. References in literature are not infrequent: *e.g.* Catull. 68, 148 *quem lapide illa diem candidiore notet*; Plin. *Epist.* 6, 11 *o diem laetum notandumque mihi candidissimo calculo.* Similar customs are reported as existing among the Thracians and Scythians. — **ne careat**, etc.: best regarded as a purpose clause dependent on the following verses, 11-16.

11. neu... neu: the repetition of the word six times marks the

neu morem in Salium sit requies pedum,
neu multi Damalis meri
Bassum Threicia vincat amystide,
neu desint epulis rosae
neu vivax apium neu breve lilium.
Omnes in Damalin putris
deponent oculos, nec Damalis novo
divelletur adultero,
lascivis hederis ambitiosior.

poet's eagerness. — **promptae**: proleptic: 'open the jar and let no bounds restrain.' — **amphorae**: dat., cf. 1, 24, 1.

12. **morem in Salium** (= *Saliarem*): the Salii were priests of Mars who danced in triple measure in worship of the god. Here the phrase means no more than 'in the dance.'

13. **multi Damalis meri**: πολύοινος. Cf. 3, 9, 7 *multi Lydia nominis*; S. 1, 1, 33 *magni formica laboris*; Cic *ad fam.*9, 26 *non multi cibi hospitem.* — **Damalis**: δάμαλις, a heifer. A common name for a libertina. In the columbarium of Livia's freedwomen were placed the ashes of a *Damalis Liviae sarcinatrix*.

14. 'Bassus shall drink deep today, deeper than the expert Damalis.' — **amystide**: ἀμυστὶ πίνειν. To drink a bowl of wine at a draught was a diversion learned from the intemperate Thracians. Cf. *Anacreont.* 8, 2 πιεῖν, πιεῖν ἀμυστί. Cf. intr. n. to 1, 27 above.

15 f. Flowers for garlands. — **vivax . . . breve**: chosen for the antithesis.

17 f. 'Damalis shall be the object of all eyes, but none shall win her from Numida.' — **putris**: *swimming*. Porphyrio says, *putres vino intellege.* — **nec**: 'yet Damalis will not.'

19 f. **adultero**: *lover*, i.e. Numida; abl. of separation. — **lascivis**: *wandering.* — **ambitiosior**: *more clinging than.* Cf. *Epod.* 15, 5 *artius atque hedera procera adstringitur ilex*. Catull. 61, 34 f. *ut tenax hedera huc et huc | arborem implicat errans.*

37

'Now is the time to drink, to dance, to render thanks unto the gods, my friends. Good cheer had no place with us so long as the mad queen with her base following threatened harm to Rome (1-12). But the flames of her ships checked her madness, and Caesar followed her in her flight as hawk pursues a dove (12-21). Yet she was no humble woman; she did not shudder at the sword nor shrink at serpent's bite. She scorned to grace a Roman triumph (21-32).'

The ode begins as a song of exultation on hearing the news of Cleopatra's death, which reached Rome in September, 30 B.C. But in v. 21, after applying the opprobrious *fatale monstrum* to the queen, Horace suddenly changes to a feeling of admiration for the heroic courage with which she faced death and cheated the Romans of half the glory of their triumph. With this ode should be compared *Epod.* 9, written in celebration of the victory at Actium. It is noteworthy that in neither is Antony mentioned, the poet forbearing to glory over a fellow Roman. The poem is probably modeled on Alcaeus' ode on the death of the tyrant Myrsilus; in any case the enthusiastic verses with which Horace opens were suggested by the verses of Alcaeus preserved by Athen. 10, 430 A. (*Frg.* 20) νῦν χρὴ μεθύσθην καί τινα πρὸς βίαν | πώνην, ἐπειδὴ κάτθανε Μύρσιλος. 'Now must we drink deep and riotously carouse, for Myrsilus is dead.' Metre, 68.

> Nunc est bibendum, nunc pede libero
> pulsanda tellus, nunc Saliaribus
>   ornare pulvinar deorum
>   tempus erat dapibus, sodales.

1. **nunc**: the triple repetition of this word strengthens the contrast with **antehac nefas** of the following strophe. — **libero**: *freed*, as if the dangers that threatened the state had fettered the very feet of its citizens.

2. **pulsanda**: the same expression, 3, 18, 15 f. *gaudet ... pepulisse fossor | ter pede terram.* Cf. 1, 4, 7 *terram quatiunt.* — **Saliaribus ... dapibus**: *feasts such as the Salii enjoy.* In the later republic and under the empire the chief sacred colleges were very wealthy and became in certain senses select clubs; the luxury of the banquets of the Salii and pontifices were proverbial. Cf. 2, 14, 28 *mero pontificum potiore cenis*; Porphyrio remarks on this verse, *in proverbio est Saliares cenas dicere opiparas et copiosas.*

3. **ornare pulvinar deorum**: in celebrating a *lectisternium* in thanksgiving to the gods, images of the divinities were placed on couches (*pulvinaria*), before which rich banquets were offered for a number of days; with this was associated a dinner for the priests.

4. **tempus erat**: the imperfect expresses surprise that this has not been done already, 'Why have we not ..., for it was time.' So Aristoph. *Eccl.* 877 τί ποθ' ἄνδρες οὐχ

> Antehac nefas depromere Caecubum
>   cellis avitis, dum Capitolio
>   regina dementis ruinas
>   funus et imperio parabat
>
> contaminato cum grege turpium
>   morbo virorum, quidlibet impotens
>   sperare fortunaque dulci
>   ebria. Sed minuit furorem

ἤκουσιν; ὥρα δ' ἦν πάλαι. Ovid *Am.* 3, 1, 23 f. *tempus erat thyrso pulsum graviore moveri,|cessatum satis est, incipe maius opus.* This interpretation is not inconsistent with the following **antehac nefas.**

5. **antehac**: dissyllabic. Intr. 38. This synizesis, as well as the neglect of the regular caesura in 5 and 14. probably marks this ode as one of Horace's earlier essays in Alcaic measure. — **Caecubum**: cf. *Epod.* 9, 1 ff. *quando repostum Caecubum ad festas dapes...tecum... Maecenas...bibam.*

6. **dum Capitolio**, etc.: there was genuine fear at Rome that Augustus would not be able to defend Italy against Antony and Cleopatra; cf. *Fast. Amit.* to Aug. 1, C.I.L. 1, p. 398, *feriae ex s(enatus) c(onsulto), q(uod) e(o) d(ie) imp. Caesar divi f(ilius) rem public(am) tristissimo periculo liberat.* It was even said that Cleopatra had vowed she would yet administer justice on the Capitol, and that Antony had promised her the Roman empire as a marriage portion. The Capitolium was the symbol of Rome's lasting power. So Horace, in declaring his fame shall be eternal, says, 3. 30, 8 ff. *dum Capitolium scandet...pontifex,...dicar... deduxisse modos,* etc.

7. **regina**: even more hateful than *rex*; cf. Prop. 4, 11, 47 ff. *quid nunc Tarquinii fractas iuvat esse secures | nomine quem simili vita superba notat, | si mulier patienda fuit;* and the scornful *emancipatus feminae, Epod.* 9, 12. — **dementis ruinas**: again the transferred adjective. Cf. 1, 3, 40 *iracunda fulmina.* Intr. 99.

9 f. **contaminato grege,** etc.: the *spadones rugosi* of *Epod.* 9, 13 and the roués of Cleopatra's court are meant. — **turpium morbo**, etc.: *defiled*, with lust. Catullus (57, 6) reviles Marmurra and Caesar for their dissolute lives with the words, *morbosi pariter.* — **virorum**: in this connection is ironical.

10. **impotens**: *weak enough to hope;* her passion had blinded her judgment.

12. **ebria**: cf. Demos. *Phil.* 1, 49 οἶμαι ἐκεῖνον μεθύειν τῷ μεγέθει τῶν πεπραγμένων.

vix una sospes navis ab ignibus,
mentemque lymphatam Mareotico
15 redegit in veros timores
    Caesar, ab Italia volantem

remis adurgens, accipiter velut
mollis columbas aut leporem citus
   venator in campis nivalis
20   Haemoniae, daret ut catenis

fatale monstrum. Quae generosius
perire quaerens nec muliebriter
   expavit ensem nec latentis
       classe cita reparavit oras;

13. **vix una sospes**: *the fact that hardly a single ship escaped.* As a matter of fact Cleopatra escaped with sixty ships, while Antony's fleet was burned. It may be that the first news of the battle reported the destruction of Cleopatra's ships as well.

14 ff. Her drunken madness was changed into genuine terror by Caesar's pursuit. — **lymphatam**: νυμφόληπτος, *distracted.* The word owes its origin to the belief that those who caught sight of water nymphs were bewitched and deprived of their senses. — **Mareotico**: sc. *vino*; the best wine produced near Alexandria.

16 f. **volantem**: sc. *eam.* — **remis adurgens**: an exaggeration, as Octavian did not pursue Antony and Cleopatra at once, but went in the autumn of 31 B.C. to Asia, wintered at Samos, and only reached Egypt in the summer of 30 B.C. — **accipiter velut**: a Homeric figure. Cf. *Il.* 22, 139 f. ἠύτε κίρκος ὀρεσφιν, ἐλαφρότατος πετεηνῶν, | ῥηιδίως οἴμησε μετὰ τρήρωνα πέλειαν.

19 f. **nivalis Haemoniae**: *i.e.* Thessaly in winter, the hunting season. — **monstrum quae**: construction according to sense. Cf. Cic. *ad fam.* 1, 9, 15 *illa furia muliebrium religionum qui,* etc.

21 f. At this point Horace suddenly changes to admiration for Cleopatra's courage, that made her prefer death to capture. — **generosius perire**: *to die a nobler death.* — **nec muliebriter expavit**: *nor like a woman did she fear.* Plutarch (*Ant.* 79) says that on the approach of Proculeius, Octavian's emissary, Cleopatra tried to stab herself.

23 f. **nec latentis**, etc.: there is a tradition (Dio C. 51, 6; Plut. *Ant.* 69) that Cleopatra thought of

25   ausa et iacentem visere regiam
    voltu sereno, fortis et asperas
      tractare serpentes, ut atrum
        corpore combiberet venenum,

    deliberata morte ferocior,
30 saevis Liburnis scilicet invidens
      privata deduci superbo
        non humilis mulier triumpho.

escaping through the Red Sea. Yet it may well be questioned whether Horace knew of such plans on the queen's part; he simply means to say that she had no fear of death, and did not run away. — **reparavit**: *exchange*; *i.e.* in return for the kingdom she had lost. Cf. 1, 31, 12 *vina reparata merce*.

25 f. Note the emphatic position of **ausa ... fortis.** — **iacentem**: *ruined*, razed to the ground. — **tractare**: dependent on **fortis**, *courageous enough to*. Intr. 108.

27 f. atrum: the 'deadly' color. Cf. 1, 28, 13 *morti...atrae*; 2, 14, 17 *ater... Cocytos*; 3, 4, 17 *atris viperis*. — **corpore**: *in her body*; abl. of instrument. — **combiberet**: the compound is intensive, 'drinking deep.' So Cicero (*de fin.* 3, 9) says figuratively, *quas (artes) si, dum est tener, combiberit, ad maiora veniet paratior*.

29. *The more courageous when once resolved to die.*

30 ff. The condensation of these verses makes translation especially difficult. — **Liburnis**: dat. with **invidens**. These were small swift ships, modeled after those of the Liburnian pirates, and proved successful against the unwieldy ships of the enemy at Actium. Cf. *Epod.* 1, 1 and n. — **scilicet**: *no doubt.* — **invidens**: cf. Shakespeare, *Ant. and Cleopatra*, 5, 2 'Shall they hoist me, | And show me to the shouting varletry | Of censuring Rome?' — **privata**: 'no longer a queen,' contrasted with *superbo triumpho*. — **deduci**: the object of **invidens**. — **non humilis mulier**: translate as parenthetical and in the predicate — *no humble woman she!* Cf. Tennyson's *Dream of Fair Women*, 'I died a Queen. The Roman soldier found | Me lying dead, my crown about my brows, | A name for ever!' It is said that Cleopatra frequently cried οὐ θριαμβεύσομαι. In Octavian's triumph in August, 29 B.C., an effigy of the queen appeared.

38

In contrast with the triumphant note of the preceding ode the book quietly closes with this little ode, in which Horace declares again his love of simplicity. 'Not orient display nor garlands rich please me, but simple myrtle crown and cup of wine beneath the arbor's shade.' Metre, 69.

> Persicos odi, puer, apparatus;
> displicent nexae philyra coronae;
> mitte sectari rosa quo locorum
>   sera moretur.
>
> 5 Simplici myrto nihil adlabores
> sedulus curo; neque te ministrum
> dedecet myrtus neque me sub arta
>   vite bibentem.

1. **Persicos**: the adjective suggests Oriental luxury. Probably Horace had in mind unguents and perfumes from the east. — **philyra**: strips of the inner bark of the linden were used to fasten together the flowers of elaborate chaplets. Cf. Ovid, *Fasti* 5, 335 ff. *tempora sutilibus cinguntur tota coronis | et latet iniecta splendida mensa rosa. | ebrius incinctis philyra conviva capillis | saltat.*

3 f. **mitte**: equivalent to *omitte*. — **sectari**: *hunting.* — **rosa sera**: *the rose out of season*, another symbol of luxury.

5 f. **myrto**: dat. with **adlabores**, which is equivalent to *laborando addas; embellish.* The subjunctive is independent, parallel to **curo**. — **nihil**: with **adlabores**. — **sedulus**: *with care*, predicate to **adlabores**.

7. **arta**: *thick grown.*

LIBER SECVNDVS

I

As the first three odes of the first book are given in order to Maecenas, Octavianus, and Vergil, so this book opens with odes addressed to three friends, Pollio, Sallustius Crispus, and Dellius. The place of honor is given to C. Asinius Pollio, who was one of the most distinguished men of his time; born in 76 B.C. he belonged in his youth to the literary circle of Catullus, Calvus, and Cinna. He had an honorable political and military career, attaining the consulship in 40 B.C.; his military services, in the course of which he served under Caesar and after Caesar's murder under Antony, culminated in a successful campaign against the Parthini, a tribe in Dalmatia, in 39 B.C. With the booty gained he founded the first public library in Rome.

From this time he gave himself up to literary and forensic pursuits, maintaining with honor a neutral position in the struggle between Octavianus and Antony. Quintilian, Seneca, and Tacitus praise his oratory (cf. 13 f.) in which he had hoped to rival Cicero; his tragedies (11-12) were celebrated in 39 B.C. by Vergil (*E.* 8, 10) as *sola Sophocleo tua carmina digna cothurno*. Horace refers to them in the verse (*S.* 1, 10, 42 f.) *Pollio regum | facta canit pede ter percusso*. Following possibly the example of Sallust, he undertook to write a history of the civil wars, with the first triumvirate, 60 B.C., as his starting point. We do not know to what date Pollio intended to bring his work — it undoubtedly included Pharsalus, Thapsus, and probably Philippi, — or whether he completed his plan, whatever it may have been; for while the work is referred to by Tacitus and Suetonius, it is to us entirely lost. Our knowledge of his literary ability is based solely on his letters to Cicero (*ad. fam.* 10, 31-33) which show a stiff and archaic style; an attempt in recent years to ascribe to him the *bellum Africum* and a portion of the *bellum Alexandrinum* has utterly failed. Pollio first introduced the practice of reading portions of one's works to a circle of friends (*recitationes*), which became a regular habit under the empire, and we may well believe that Horace had in this way heard portions of the work he praises, apparently the parts dealing with Pharsalus, Thapsus, and Cato's death (17-28).

The date of the ode is wholly uncertain, but it is noteworthy that vv. 29-36 express the same weariness of civil strife and bloodshed that we find *C.* 1, 2, and 14, *Epod.* 9 and 16. Metre, 68.

Motum ex Metello consule civicum
bellique causas et vitia et modos
ludumque Fortunae gravisque
principum amicitias et arma

5   nondum expiatis uncta cruoribus,
periculosae plenum opus aleae,

1 f. **motum**: *disturbance*, including all the troubles from the time of the first triumvirate. — **ex Metello consule**: L. Afranius and Q. Caecilius Metellus Celer, coss. 60 B.C. — **belli**: modifying the three following nouns. — **causas**: the defeat and death of Crassus at Carrhae (53 B.C.). Still, the death in 54 B.C. of Julia, Caesar's daughter and Pompey's wife, had already broken the last personal bond between these two members of the coalition. — **vitia**: *mistakes.* — **modos**: *phases.*

3 f. **ludum Fortunae**: here conceived as the goddess who delights in the arbitrary exercise of her power; she is so described 3, 29, 49 ff. *Fortuna saevo laeta negotio et ludum insolentem ludere pertinax | transmutat incertos honores, | nunc mihi, nunc alii benigna.* The varied fortunes and tragic deaths of Caesar, Crassus, and Pompey were eminent examples of Fortune's wanton sport. — **gravisque principum amicitias**: the first triumvirate, in which the compact and subsequent quarrels between the leading citizens (**principum**) were of serious import to the state. Cf. Caelius, *ad fam.* 8. 14. 2 *sic illi amores et invidiosa coniunctio* (sc. *inter Caesarem et Pompeium*) *non ad occultam recidit obtrectationem, sed ad bellum se erupit.* Also Lucan, 1, 84 ff. — **arma**: *i.e.* those used at Pharsalia, Thapsus. Philippi.

5. **nondum expiatis**: the sin of fraternal strife is still to be atoned for. Cf. 1, 2, 29; *Epod.* 7, 3. 19 f. — **cruoribus**: the plural emphasizes the different instances.

6 ff. **opus**: in apposition with the foregoing sentence. While Octavian was clearly victor after Actium, the struggles of the civil war were too recent to allow a

tractas et incedis per ignis
suppositos cineri doloso.

Paulum severae musa tragoediae
desit theatris; mox ubi publicas
res ordinaris, grande munus
Cecropio repetes coturno,

insigne maestis praesidium reis
et consulenti, Pollio, curiae,
cui laurus aeternos honores
Delmatico peperit triumpho.

frank historical treatment; old wounds would be torn open and old animosities revived. The expression **per ignis**, etc., is proverbial. Cf. Callim. *Epig.* 44. 2 πῦρ ὑπὸ τῇ σποδίῃ. Propert. 1, 5, 4 f. *infelix, properas ultima nosse mala | et miser ignotos vestigia ferre per ignes.* Macaulay, *Hist. Eng.* c. 6. 'When the historian of this troubled reign (that of James II) turns to Ireland, his task becomes peculiarly difficult and delicate. His steps — to borrow the fine image used on a similar occasion by a Roman poet — are on the thin crust of ashes beneath which the lava is still glowing.'

9 ff. Note how skillfully Horace introduces these complimentary allusions to Pollio's other literary attainments. — **paulum**: *for a little: i.e.* until the history shall be finished. — **severae**: *solemn.* — **desit**: the public will miss the tragedies. — **theatris**: with the plural, cf. 1, 2, 15 f. This is not proof that Pollio's plays were acted; they were probably intended to be read.

11 f. **ordinaris**: *set in order, i e.* have arranged the details of thy work. — **repetes**: *thou shalt resume thy glorious task* (**grande munus**). — Cecropio coturno : the high buskin (*cothurnus*) was worn by actors in tragedy, the low slipper (*soccus*) in comedy. The adjective **Cecropio** is appropriate, as Athens was the place where tragedy came to its highest perfection.

13 f. **praesidium . . . reis**: eight of the nine titles of Pollio's speeches are for the defense. This verse was probably in Ovid's mind when he wrote of Germanicus *Fasti* 1, 22 *civica pro trepidis cum tulit arma reis.* — **consulenti**: *in its deliberations.* The phrase **insigne praesidium** is still applicable here, as Pollio's advice was a defense to the welfare of the state.

16. Cf. introductory note to this ode.

Iam nunc minaci murmure cornuum
perstringis auris, iam litui strepunt,
 iam fulgor armorum fugacis
  terret equos equitumque voltus.

Audire magnos iam videor duces
non indecoro pulvere sordidos
 et cuncta terrarum subacta
  praeter atrocem animum Catonis.

Iuno et deorum quisquis amicior
Afris inulta cesserat impotens

17. **iam nunc**: Horace dramatically represents himself as actually listening to the reading of the history.

18 f. **perstringis**: *dinnest.* — **fulgor armorum**: cf. the Homeric χαλκοῦ στεροπή, and Quint. 10, 30 *fulgorem qui terreat, qualis est ferri, quo mens simul visusque praestringitur.* — **fugacis**: proleptic with **terret**, — 'throws the horses into terrified flight.' — **equos equitumque**: cf. Tennyson's similar assonance 'while horse and hero fell.' — **voltus**: by zeugma with **terret**, *daunts the rider's gaze*, etc. To make this refer to the story that Caesar ordered his soldiers at Pharsalus to strike at the faces of the young nobles in the opposing army is strained and unnatural. The phrase is intended simply to give us a vivid picture of the panic-stricken horsemen.

21 ff. **audire . . . videor**: 'as you read,' continuing the vividness of **iam nunc**, v. 17. — **duces . . .**

cuncta . . . subacta: both the objects of **audire** — *to hear the story of.*

23 f. **cuncta terrarum**: cf. 4, 12, 19 *amara curarum.* — **atrocem**: *stubborn*; in praise, as Sil. Ital. 13, 369 *atrox virtus.* — **Catonis**: the canonized object of praise by stoics and rhetoricians. Cf. n. to 1, 12, 35.

25 ff. The mention of Cato recalls Thapsus and the long history of wars in Africa. Juno was the patron goddess of Carthage, in the *Aeneid* the opponent of Aeneas, and so hostile to Italy. With this strophe Horace passes to expressions of regret for the civil struggles that form the subject of Pollio's history.

— **cesserat**: note the tense. 'Once the gods had been forced to withdraw from the doomed African cities, powerless (**impotens**) to help them; now they have had their revenge.' The Romans had a rite (*evocatio*) for

tellure victorum nepotes
rettulit inferias Iugurthae.

30 Quis non Latino sanguine pinguior
campus sepulcris impia proelia
testatur auditumque Medis
Hesperiae sonitum ruinae?

Qui gurges aut quae flumina lugubris
ignara belli? Quod mare Dauniae
35 non decoloravere caedes?
Quae caret ora cruore nostro?

calling forth from a beleaguered city of the enemy the local divinities, whose departure was necessary before the town could be captured. When the gods had gone, the city was doomed. Cf. Vergil *A*. 2, 351 f. (of Troy) *excessere omnes, adytis arisque relictis, | di, quibus imperium hoc steterat*, and Tac. *Hist.* 5, 13, of the capture of Jerusalem by Titus.

27. **victorum nepotes**, etc.: the commander of the Pompeian army at Thapsus was Metellus Scipio, grandson of the Metellus Numidicus who commanded (109-107 B.C.) in the war against Jugurtha. The Pompeians who fell at Thapsus, ten thousand in number, are here described as offerings at the tomb of the Numidian king. It is interesting to remember in this connection that Sallust had published his *Jugurtha* in recent years.

29. **Latino sanguine**: cf. *Epod.* 7, 3 f. *parumne campis atque Neptuno super | fusum est Latini sanguinis?* — **pinguior**: *fatter*. Cf Verg. *G*. 1, 491 f. *nec fuit indignum superis, bis sanguine nostro | Emathiam et latos Haemi pinguescere campos.*

30. **impia**: as *pietas* denotes the proper relation between relatives, the adjective *unholy* is especially applicable to the unnatural struggles of the civil war. Cf. *Epod.* 16, 9 *impia . . . aetas.*

31 f. **auditumque Medis**, etc.: the Parthians would naturally rejoice at the internal quarrels of Rome. Cf. *Epod.* 7, 9 f. *sed ut secundum vota Parthorum sua | urbs haec periret dextera.* — **Hesperiae**: *i.e.* the western world, Italy.

33 f. **gurges**: *flood*, but often nothing more than the poetic equivalent of *mare*. Cf. Verg. *G*. 4, 387 *in Carpathio Neptuni gurgite.* — **Dauniae**: Apulian, in the sense of Italian. Cf. n. to 1, 22, 14.

Sed ne relictis, musa procax, iocis
Ceae retractes munera neniae;
   mecum Dionaeo sub antro
      quaere modos leviore plectro.

37 ff. Horace suddenly checks himself; as the poet of love he must not allow his muse to raise a strain of grief. In a similar fashion he suddenly stops his serious verses 3, 3, 69 f. *non hoc iocosae conveniet lyrae; | quo, Musa, tendis?* — **ne ... retractes**: dependent on **quaere**, etc. *You must not, ... but rather*, etc. Cf. 1, 33, 1 ff. — **procax**: *bold*, here hardly to be distinguished in meaning from *lascivus*, applicable to the muse of love poetry. — **iocis**: παίγνια, songs of love and wine, as *e.g.* the fourth ode of this book. Cf. 3, 3, 69 *iocosa lyra*.

38. Ceae retractes munera neniae: *assume again the functions of the Cean dirge.* Simonides of Ceos (556-467 B.C.) was noted for the pathos of his elegies (θρῆνοι), such as he wrote on those who fell at Thermopylae and Salamis.

39 f. Dionaeo sub antro: Dione was the mother of Venus. The poet of love naturally seeks his inspiration in her grotto. — **leviore plectro**: cf. Ovid. *Met.* 10, 150 f. where Orpheus says *cecini plectro graviore gigantas, | nunc opus est leviore lyra.*

2

'Silver shines from use, Crispus, not when hidden in the earth. Proculeius has won eternal fame by his generosity. He who curbs his eager soul is more a ruler than the lord of Affica and Europe; avarice like dropsy grows by indulgence. True wisdom counts not happy even Phraates seated on the throne of Cyrus, but reckons king only him who has no lingering look for heaps of gold.'

The ode is addressed to C. Sallustius Crispus, the grandnephew and adopted son of Sallust the historian, whose great wealth he inherited in 36 B.C. At first he was a partisan of Antony, but later attached himself to Augustus and became his most trusted confidant next to Maecenas; like the latter he was content with equestrian rank, enjoying in reality greater power and position than senatorial dignity could have brought him. The moderation in expenditures here attributed to him is hardly consistent with the statement of Tacitus, whose full account (*Annal.* 3, 30) is as follows, *atque ille, quamquam prompto ad capessendos honores aditu, Maecenatem aemulatus, sine dignitate senatoria multos triumphalium consulariumque potentia anteiit, diversus a veterum instituto per cultum et munditias copiaque et affluentia luxu propior. Suberat tamen vigor animi ingentibus negotiis par, eo acrior, quo somnum et inertiam magis ostentabat.* His generosity is celebrated in an epigram of Crinagoras, *Anth. Pal.* 16, 40 γείτονες οὐ τρισσαὶ μοῦνον Τύχαι ἔπρεπον εἶναι, | Κρίσπε, βαθυπλούτου σῆς ἕνεκεν κραδίης, | ἀλλὰ καὶ αἱ πάντων πᾶσαι · τί γὰρ ἀνδρὶ τοσῷδε | ἀρκέσει εἰς ἑτάρων μυρίον εὐφροσύνην; | νῦν δέ σε καὶ τούτων κρέσσων ἐπὶ μεῖζον᾽ ἀέξοι | Καῖσαρ · τίς κείνου χωρὶς ἄρηρε τύχη. 'Not three goddesses of Fortune alone should be thy neighbors, Crispus, for thy rich and generous heart, but rather every kind of Fortune in every event should be thine. For what can be enough for such a man to reward his endless kindness toward his friends? Nay, now may Caesar who is mightier than these, exalt thee still more; what Fortune is pleasing without his favor?'

The ode is an expansion on the Stoic paradox, 'the wise alone is rich.' The date of composition is probably fixed by 17 ff. as soon after 27 B.C. Metre, 69.

> Nullus argento color est avaris
> abdito terris, inimice lamnae
> Crispe Sallusti, nisi temperato
>   splendeat usu.
>
> 5   Vivet extento Proculeius aevo,
> notus in fratres animi paterni;

1. An imitation of the verse quoted by Plutarch περὶ δυσωπίας 10, οὐκ ἔστ᾽ ἐν ἄντροις λευκὸς, ὦ ξέν᾽, ἄργυρος. — **color**: *luster*. — **avaris**: the adjective describing the greed of the miser is here applied to the earth, that hides the silver from the light. Intr. 99.

2. **terris**: abl. For the sentiment, cf. *S.* 1, 1, 41 f. *quid iuvat, inmensum te argenti pondus et auri | furtim defossa timidum deponere terra?* — **lamnae**: *bullion*. — **Crispe Sallusti**: the inversion of *nomen* and *cognomen* became common in the late republic when the *praenomen* was omitted: it possibly belonged to familiar address, but Cicero uses it in his speeches as well as in his letters.

3 f. **nisi . . . splendeat**: the protasis to **inimice lamnae**.

5 f. **extento aevo**: *with life prolonged beyond the grave*. Generosity secures immortality. — **Proculeius**: the brother-in-law of Maecenas and one of the closest friends of Augustus. He divided his property equally with his two brothers Caepio and Murena, who

illum aget penna metuente solvi
    fama superstes.

Latius regnes avidum domando
    spiritum quam si Libyam remotis
Gadibus iungas et uterque Poenus
    serviat uni.

Crescit indulgens sibi dirus hydrops,
    nec sitim pellit, nisi causa morbi
fugerit venis et aquosus albo
    corpore languor.

Redditum Cyri solio Phraaten
dissidens plebi numero beatorum
eximit Virtus populumque falsis
    dedocet uti

had lost their wealth in the civil wars. — **animi paterni**: genitive of specification, giving the reason for his fame (**notus**). Intr. 93.

7 f. **metuente solvi**: *i.e. indissolubili*; 'bear on wing that will not flag.' The idea of 'fearing' in **metuente** has in this phrase faded to that of 'shrinking,' 'hesitating.' Cf. 3, 11, 10 *metuit tangi = intacta*. — **superstes**: 'ever surviving' and so 'immortal.'

9. Cf. *Proverbs* 16, 32 'He that ruleth his spirit is mightier than he that taketh a city.'

11 f. **iungas**: *i.e.* as king and owner. — **uterque Poenus**: expanding the previous phrase. Horace means the Carthaginians of Africa and of Spain. — **uni**: sc. *tibi*.

13. **indulgens sibi**: the means by which avarice, like dropsy, grows. — **hydrops**: the disease is almost personified.

15 f. **fugerit**: *be driven from*; virtually the passive of *fugare*. — **aquosus . . . languor**: *weariness caused by the water*. — **albo**: *pallid*, from the disease.

17. **redditum**: probably in 27 B.C. Cf. n. to 1, 26, 5. Note the emphasis, 'for all his return.'

18 f. **beatorum**: 'the really fortunate and rich.' Note the hypermetric line. — **Virtus**: *right reasoning, i.e.* the opinion of the wise and good — the Stoics — opposed to the estimates of the vulgar herd (**dissidens plebi**).

20. **dedocet**: *teaches the people to give up the use of*, etc.

> vocibus, regnum et diadema tutum
> deferens uni propriamque laurum,
> quisquis ingentis oculo inretorto
> spectat acervos.

21 ff. falsis ... vocibus: 'to call a man *beatus* simply because he is rich or powerful is a misuse of the term. Wealth and power are the sure possession of him alone who is not moved by greed.' Cf. Sen. *Thy.* 389 f. *rex est, qui cupiet nihil; | hoc regnum sibi quisque dat.* — **regnum ... deferens**: the method by which *virtus* drives home her lesson. — **diadema**: properly the blue band that went around the Persian king's tiara.

22. uni: *to him and him alone, who*. — **propriam**: *as his sure possession*, repeating the idea expressed in **tutum**.

23 f. 'Whoever can look at great heaps of treasure (and pass on) without one backward glance.' — **inretorto**: a compound made by Horace with the negative prefix in- and the participle of *retorqueo*.

3

In the preceding ode Horace expanded a Stoic maxim; in this he gives us a similar treatment of a favorite Epicurean principle, 'enjoy life while you may, but never too extravagantly, for death is close at hand. Neither riches nor family can save us from the common doom.'

The Dellius addressed is undoubtedly Q. Dellius, whom Messala nicknamed *desultor bellorum civilium* because of his frequent changes of allegiance during the civil wars. In 31 B.C. he returned finally to Octavian's side, and later became one of his trusted courtiers. The place of the ode here was determined both by the similarity of its subject with that of 2, and especially by Horace's desire to give Dellius a place next Sallust. Cf. intr. n. to 2, 1.

The date of composition cannot be determined, but is clearly later than the reconciliation between Dellius and Octavianus. Metre, 68.

> Aequam memento rebus in arduis
> servare mentem, non secus in bonis

1 f. aequam ... mentem, etc.: 'a calm and even spirit is a defense against every change of life.' The sentiment is a commonplace. Cf. Archil. *Frg.* 66 μήτε νικῶν ἀμφάδην ἀγάλλεο | μήτε νικηθεὶς ἐν οἴκῳ καταπεσὼν ὀδύρεο. 'Rejoice not openly when victori-

ab insolenti temperatam
laetitia, moriture Delli,
5   seu maestus omni tempore vixeris,
seu te in remoto gramine per dies
festos reclinatum bearis
interiore nota Falerni.
Quo pinus ingens albaque populus
10   umbram hospitalem consociare amant

ous, nor when defeated lie down and weep within thy house.' — **arduis**: placed at the end of the verse to contrast with **aequam**, *an even mind, . . . a steep and toilsome path.* Intr. 27. — **non secus . . . temperatam**: *and no less to keep*, etc. — **in bonis**: in position as well as in thought contrasted with **in arduis**. Intr. 27.

3 f. insolenti: *unwonted*, and so *extravagant*. — **moriture**: equivalent to *cum moriturus sis*. The knell that gives the reason for the previous advice. Intr. 110.

5 f. seu . . . seu: following on **moriture**, not **memento**. With the sentiment of the strophe, cf. an anonymous epigram to Anacreon *Anth. Pal.* 7, 33 'πολλὰ πιὼν τέθνηκας, Ἀνάκρεον.' 'ἀλλὰ τρυφήσας· | καὶ σὺ δὲ μὴ πίνων ἵξεαι εἰς Ἀίδην.' 'Deep hast thou drunk and art dead, Anacreon.' 'Yet I enjoyed it. And thou, though thou drink not at all, wilt still come to Hades.' — **in remoto gramine**: *on some retired and grassy spot.* Cf. 1, 17, 17 *in reducta valle.* — **per dies festos**: the preposition is distributive, — *on every festal day.* Cf. 2, 14, 15 *per autumnos.*

8. interiore nota: *with an inner brand.* The wine after fermentation was drawn from the dolia into amphorae, which then were sealed with the name of the consuls of the year. Cf. 3, 21. 1 *o nata mecum consule Manlio* (sc. *testa*). The sealed amphorae were stowed away in the apotheca; and those in the farthest part of the storeroom (hence **interiore**) naturally contained the oldest and best wine. — **Falerni**: cf. n. to 1, 27, 9.

9-12. After vv. 6-8 Horace dramatically imagines that he and his friend are already lying on the grass with cups in hand, and puts the questions naturally suggested by the surroundings. 'Why do these things exist except for our enjoyment?'— **quo**: *why*. — **pinus . . . pŏpulus**: the tall Italian pine with its dark shade forms an artistic contrast to the white poplar with its trembling leaves. For the order, see Intr. 20. — **consociare**: *to entwine.* — **amant**: literally,

ramis? Quid obliquo laborat
    lympha fugax trepidare rivo?

Huc vina et unguenta et nimium brevis
    flores amoenae ferre iube rosae,
15   dum res et aetas et sororum
        fila trium patiuntur atra.

Cedes coemptis saltibus et domo
    villaque flavus quam Tiberis lavit,
    cedes et exstructis in altum
20   divitiis potietur heres.

not equivalent to *solent.* — **quid obliquo,** etc.: *why does the fleeting water fret its quivering way along the winding stream?* — **trepidare**: for the infin., see Intr. 107; for the order, 21.

13 f. **nimium brevis,** etc.: 'Gather ye rosebuds while ye may; | Old time is still a flying; | And this same flower that blooms to-day, | To-morrow will be dying.' With **brevis** cf. 1, 36, 16 *breve lilium.* The adjective emphasizes the fleeting character of life, expressed in the following **dum . . . patiuntur.**

15 f. **res**: *fortune, affairs,* in general. — **aetas**: *i.e.* before old age comes on us. Cf. 1, 9, 17 *donec virenti canities abest morosa.* — **sororum**: the Fates who spin the threads of life. Cf. Lowell *Villa Franca,* 'Spin, spin, Clotho, spin! Lachesis twist! and, Atropos, sever!'— **atra**: because the cutting of the thread brings death. Cf. n. to 1, 37, 27 *atrum venenum.*

17 ff. **cedes...cedes**: *thou shalt give up..., aye, give up.* Intr. 28 c. 'All thy riches cannot save thee.' — **saltibus**: *upland pastures,* in the mountain valleys between the hills, valuable for grazing. Cf. *Epist.* 2, 2, 177 ff. *quidve Calabris | saltibus adiecti Lucani* (sc. *prosunt*), *si metit Orcus | grandia cum parvis, non exorabilis auro?*—**domo villaque**: the city residence and country seat alike.

19 f. The dreaded specter of the heir who enters into the fruits of his predecessor's labors is common enough in Horace's moralizing. Cf. 2, 14, 25; 3, 24, 62; 4, 7, 19. So *Ecclesiastes,* 2, 19 'And who knoweth whether he shall be a wise man or a fool? yet shall he have rule over all my labour wherein I have laboured, and wherein I have shewed wisdom under the sun.' *Ecclesiasticus* 14, 4 'He that gathereth by defrauding his own soul gathereth for others, that shall spend his goods riotously.'

Divesne prisco natus ab Inacho
nil interest an pauper et infima
   de gente sub divo moreris,
      victima nil miserantis Orci.

25 Omnes eodem cogimur, omnium
versatur urna serius ocius
   sors exitura et nos in aeternum
      exsilium impositura cumbae.

21 f. **divesne**, etc.: predicate with **natus** and dependent on **nihil interest**; the verb is supplied by **moreris** below. — **Inacho**: Inachus, the mythical king of Argos, typical of antiquity. Cf. 3, 19, 1. 'An ancient noble line is of no more avail than a poor and humble one.'

23 f. **sub divo**: *beneath the light of day,* 'under the canopy.' Cf. 1, 1, 25 *sub Iove.* — **moreris**: 'this life is but an inn, no home.' Cf. Cic. *C.M.* 84 *commorandi enim natura devorsorium nobis, non habitandi dedit.* — **victima**, etc.: grammatically in apposition to the subject of **moreris**; but from its position at the end of the strophe it acquires an effective emphasis — *for none the less thou art,* etc.

25 f. **omnes . . ., omnium**: Intr.

28 c. — **cogimur**: the souls of the dead are driven by Mercury like cattle. Cf. 1, 24, 18 *nigro compulerit Mercurius gregi.* — **versatur urna**: in ancient determinations by lot small billets of wood or pebbles (*sortes*), each of which had a name written on it, were cast into a jar. This was then shaken until one of the lots leaped out. — **serius ocius**: *sooner or later;* in such combinations, asyndeton is common.

27 f. **aeternum**: with this hypermetric verse, cf. 2, 2, 18. — **exilium**: 'death is an exile from the joys of life; thence no man returns.' — **cumbae**: Charon's boat. Cf. Verg. *A.* 6, 303 *ferruginea subvectat corpora cumba,* and Prop. 4, 18, 24 *scandendast torvi publica cumba senis.*

4

Horace teases one of his friends who has fallen in love with a maidservant, and in mock-heroic style brings his victim precedents from the age of heroes. 'Achilles, Ajax, and even mighty Agamemnon have been smitten with captive hand-maidens before you. Be sure that your flame, like theirs, is the child of royal parents; she must be noble, she is so true. What, jealous! Bless you, I'm too old to play the part of rival.'

Who Horace's friend was is quite unknown. The name Xanthias of Phocis is an invention, like 'Cnidius Gyges' in v. 20 of the following ode. The date of composition is fixed by v. 23 f. as about 25 B.C. Metre, 69.

> Ne sit ancillae tibi amor pudori,
> Xanthia Phoceu, prius insolentem
> serva Briseis niveo colore
> movit Achillem,
>
> 5 movit Aiacem Telamone natum
> forma captivae dominum Tecmessae;
> arsit Atrides medio in triumpho
> virgine rapta,
>
> barbarae postquam cecidere turmae
> 10 Thessalo victore et ademptus Hector

1 ff. **ne sit**: a negative purpose clause, depending on the following illustrations. Cf. 1, 33, 1 ff.; 4, 9, 1. We may translate, *You need not be ashamed . . ., for Briseis*, etc. — **ancillae**: objective genitive with **amor**. — **prius**: used adverbially, belonging to all three examples; 'you are not the first.' — **insolentem**: *for all his haughtiness*. Cf. Horace's directions for the portrayal of Achilles, *Epist.* 2, 3, 120 ff. *scriptor si forte reponis Achillem, | impiger, iracundus, inexorabilis, acer | iura neget sibi nata, nihil non arroget armis*. — **niveo colore**: instrumental abl. with **movit**. So Helen's fair beauty was described by the Alexandrians, νιφόεσσα Ἑλένη.

4 ff. **movit . . . movit . . . arsit**: Intr. 28 c. — **Telamone natum**: the Homeric Τελαμώνιος Αἴας. —

forma: connect with **Tecmessae**. — **captivae dominum**: the contrast is emphasized by the juxtaposition. Intr. 26. — **Tecmessae**: for the quantity, cf. Intr. 34.

8. **virgine rapta**: Cassandra, who was torn from the altar of Athena by Ajax Oileus; in the division of the spoils after the capture of Troy she fell to Agamemnon's share.

9-12. The strophe fixes the time and gives the details of the triumph in the midst of which the victor was humbled by love for his captive. — **barbarae**: *i.e. Phrygiae*, a term frequently used by the Latin poets in imitation of the Greek. — **cecidere . . . Thessalo victore**: *i.e.* when Achilles returned to the battle after Patroclus' death, and drove the Trojans in flight before him. — **ademptus Hector**: *the loss of Hector*. Cf. 1, 3, 29 and n.

tradidit fessis leviora tolli
    Pergama Grais.

Nescias an te generum beati
Phyllidis flavae decorent parentes;
15 regium certe genus et penatis
    maeret iniquos.

Crede non illam tibi de scelesta
plebe dilectam, neque sic fidelem,
sic lucro aversam potuisse nasci
20   matre pudenda.

Bracchia et voltum teretisque suras
integer laudo : fuge suspicari
cuius octavum trepidavit aetas
    claudere lustrum.

11. **fessis**: *i.e.* with the ten years' war. — **leviora tolli**: *an easier prey.* Intr. 108. Horace seems to have had in mind *Il.* 24, 243 f. ῥηίτεροι γὰρ μᾶλλον Ἀχαιοῖσιν δὴ ἔσεσθε | κείνου τεθνηῶτος ἐναιρέμεν.

13 f. **nescias**: potential, *you cannot tell, it may well be that.* — **generum**: in bantering tone, 'you really will marry her.' — **beati**: cf. n. to 2, 2, 18. — **flavae**: a point of beauty. Cf. 1, 5, 4. — **decorent**: in contrast to the *ne . . . sit amor pudori* with which the ode opens.

15. **regium certe genus**: in the same construction as **Penatis iniquos**: *the unkindness of her Penates.* 'Phyllis will prove to be of no less royal birth than Briseis, Tecmessa, and Cassandra.'

17 ff. Another proof of noble lineage. — **scelesta plebe**: the *volgus infidum*, on whom doubtless Xanthias looked with scorn. — **sic . . . sic**: in mocking irony, *as she is.* — **lucro aversam**: likewise in mockery, for Phyllis' class was noted for its greed.

21 f. **teretis**, *shapely*. — **integer**: *heart-whole*, as 3, 7, 22 (*Gyges*) *adhuc integer.* — **fuge suspicari**: Intr. 104.

23 f. **trepidavit**: a favorite word with Horace. Cf. its use, 2, 3, 12. 11, 4 : 4, 11, 11. His life has hurried to the verge of forty years. Horace says this almost with a sigh, 'I am too old, or faith, I would have been your rival.' — **claudere**: Intr. 107.

5

'Lalage is too young to bear the yoke of love. Wait a bit, and she will follow you and outshine your former loves.'

The comparison of the young Lalage to the heifer and the unripe grape, as well as the bluntness of expression, did not offend the ancient as it does the modern taste. The ode lacks the unity of the better lyrics, for the last strophe distracts our attention from the central object. There is no hint of the date of composition. Metre, 68.

Nondum subacta ferre iugum valet
cervice, nondum munia comparis
aequare, nec tauri ruentis
in venerem tolerare pondus.

5 Circa virentis est animus tuae
campos iuvencae, nunc fluviis gravem
solantis aestum, nunc in udo
ludere cum vitulis salicto

praegestientis. Tolle cupidinem
10 immitis uvae; iam tibi lividos

1 f. The figure is as old as Homer, who uses παρθένος ἀδμής of a young girl; so δάμαλις and πόρτις in later writers.— **valet**: the indefinite subject is to be supplied from the context, either *puella*, *iuvenca*, or *Lalage*.— **munia**: continuing the figure of the first line,— 'to do her part in dragging the plow.'

5. **circa . . . est**: *is busy with*; an extension of the local use, first found in Horace; evidently in imitation of the Greek εἶναι περί τι.

6 f. **nunc ... nunc**: *now ... again.* — **fluviis**: instrumental abl. with **solantis**.

7 f. **udo . . . salicto**: *i.e.* which grows on the banks of the stream.

9 f. **praegestientis**: a doubly emphatic compound, in place of the simple *gestio*, expressing eager desire. Lalage's only thought is to gambol with her mates. — **cupidinem . . . uvae**: the figure of the heifer is abandoned for that of the unripe grape, made familiar by Alexandrian poetry. Cf. *Anth. Pal.* 5, 19, 3 f. εἴη μήτ' ὄμφαξ μήτ' ἀσταφίς· ἡ δὲ πέπειρος | ἐς Κύπριδος θαλάμους ὡρία καλλοσύνη. 'May she be neither a green nor an over-ripe grape; but let her beauty be

distinguet autumnus racemos
   purpureo varius colore.

Iam te sequetur; currit enim ferox
aetas, et illi quos tibi dempserit
   adponet annos; iam proterva
      fronte petet Lalage maritum,

dilecta quantum non Pholoe fugax,
non Chloris, albo sic umero nitens
   ut pura nocturno renidet
      luna mari, Cnidiusve Gyges,

quem si puellarum insereres choro,
mire sagacis falleret hospites
   discrimen obscurum solutis
      crinibus ambiguoque voltu.

ready, full grown for Cypris' bowers.'—**iam**: *presently*.

12. **purpureo...colore**: the color of the ripening, not the ripe, grape. Cf. Ovid. *Met.* 3, 484 f. *ut variis solet uva racemis | ducere purpureum, nondum matura, colorem.*—**varius**: *many-colored*, with almost active meaning.

13 f. **sequetur**: sc. *Lalage.*—**ferox aetas**: not Lalage's youth, but time in general, that unrelentingly hurries on.—**tibi dempserit**, etc.: as if time took from the lover's years, of which too many already have gone, to add to the child's small sum.

15 f. **proterva fronte**: half returning to the figure of the heifer. **Lalage**: the name is reserved to this point to avoid conflict with the comparisons that occupy the first three strophes.

17 ff. 'Then when she comes of her own accord, she will be dearer than any of thy former loves.'—**fugax**: *coquettish*.

19. **pura**: *unclouded*.

21 f. **si...insereres**: as Achilles was concealed by his mother among the daughters of Lycomedes, king of Scyros, that he might not go to Troy. Cf. n. to 1, 8, 13.—**mire**: with **falleret**.—**hospites**: *strangers*: with reference to Ulysses and Diomedes, who came in disguise to Lycomedes' court that they might find Achilles.

24. **crinibus...voltu**: ablative of means with **obscurum**, which is equivalent to *obscuratum*.

6

Addressed to the poet's devoted friend Septimius, probably the same whom he commends to Tiberius, *Epist.* 1, 9; he is also named in a letter by Augustus to Horace, of which a fragment has been preserved by Suetonius in his life of Horace (p. 297 R.). A melancholy strain runs through the ode: the poet is filled with thoughts of his old age and prays that Tivoli, or if that spot be refused, beautiful Tarentum, may be the home of his last years. There Septimius shall shed a tear over the ashes of his friend.

The exact date of composition cannot be determined, but it has been conjectured with good reason that the ode was written during an illness, or when Horace was oppressed with fears of early death; it was certainly at a time when he felt his position established so that he could speak of himself as '*vates*,' *i.e.* it was after the publication of the epodes. Possibly the reference in v. 2 may fix the date as between 27 and 25 B.C. See n. below. Metre, 69.

> Septimi, Gadis aditure mecum et
> Cantabrum indoctum iuga ferre nostra et
> barbaras Syrtis, ubi Maura semper
>   aestuat unda:
>
> 5   Tibur Argeo positum colono
> sit meae sedes utinam senectae,

1. **Gadis**: the modern Cadiz; 'to the limits of the world.' Cf. 2, 2, 11 *remotis Gadibus.* — **aditure**: *who wouldst go.* Intr. 110. So Catullus says ironically 11, 1 f. *Furi et Aureli, comites Catulli, | sive in extremos penetrabit Indos*, etc.

2. **iuga ferre**: dependent on **indoctum**. This figure taken from the breaking of cattle is a poetical commonplace. The Cantabri were a fierce people in northwestern Spain who successfully resisted the Romans for many years. Augustus conducted campaigns against them in person in 27-25 B.C., but they were not finally subjugated until 19 B.C. Cf. 3, 8, 22 *Cantaber sera domitus catena*, and 4, 14, 41 *Cantaber non ante domabilis*.

3. **barbaras Syrtis**: so called alike from their situation and cruel nature. Cf. 1, 22, 5 *per Syrtis . . . aestuosas* and Verg. *A.* 4, 41 *inhospita Syrtis*.

5. **Tibur**: for Horace's affection for Tivoli, cf. 1, 7, 1-21. — **Argeo positum**, etc.: *i.e.* Tiburtus

sit modus lasso maris et viarum
   militiaeque.

Vnde si Parcae prohibent iniquae,
dulce pellitis ovibus Galaesi
flumen et regnata petam Laconi
   rura Phalantho.

Ille terrarum mihi praeter omnis
angulus ridet, ubi non Hymetto

who with his brothers came from Greece and founded Tiber. Cf. n. to 1, 7, 13. — **colono**: dat. of agent.

6 ff. Cf. Mart. 4, 25, 7 *vos eritis nostrae requies portusque senectae.* — **sit . . . sit**: Intr. 29. — **utinam**: for the position, see Intr. 31. — **modus**: *bound.* Cf. Avien. *orb. terr.* 100 H. *hic modus est orbis Gadir.* — **lasso**: sc. *mihi.* — **maris et viarum**: cf. *Epist.* 1, 11, 6 *odio maris atque viarum;* the phrase was adopted by Tacitus *Ann.* 2, 14 *si taedio viarum ac maris finem cupiant.*

9 ff. Cf. *Epist.* 1, 7, 44 f. *parvum parva decent: mihi iam non regia Roma, | sed vacuum Tibur placet aut inbelle Tarentum.* — **prohibent**: sc. *me.* — **iniquae**: 'refusing their favor.'

10. **pellitis ovibus**: the sheep bred in the valley of the Galaesus near Tarentum had such fine fleeces that they were protected by skin blankets, according to Varro *R. R.* 2, 2. The river valley seems to have had an especial charm. It is praised by Archilochus *Frg.* 21 οὐ γάρ τι καλὸς χῶρος οὐδ' ἐφίμερος | οὐδ' ἐρατός, οἷος ἀμφὶ Σίριος ῥοάς. 'For no spot is fair or charming or lovely, as is that by Siris' streams.'

11 f. **regnata . . . rura Phalantho**: tradition said that Tarentum was founded by Phalanthus, who led hither a band of Lacedaemonian youth after the second Messenian war. — **Phalantho**: dat. of agent. Intr. 87.

13 f. **angulus**: *nook, corner*, a snug retreat for his old age. Cf. *Epist.* 1, 14, 23 *angulus iste feret piper*, of Horace's own farm, and Prop. 5, 9, 65 f. *angulus hic mundi . . . me . . . accipit.* — **ridet**: *has a charm for.* For the quantity, see Intr. 35. — **Hymetto**: equivalent to *melli Hymettio.* The honey of Mt. Hymettus was famous for its white color and its sweetness. With this use of the name of the place for the local product, cf. **Venafro** v. 16, **Aulon** v. 18, and 2, 14, 28 *mero . . . pontificum potiore cenis.*

15   mella decedunt viridique certat
            baca Venafro;

        ver ubi longum tepidasque praebet
        Iuppiter brumas et amicus Aulon
        fertili Baccho minimum Falernis
20   invidet uvis.

        Ille te mecum locus et beatae
        postulant arces, ibi tu calentem
        debita sparges lacrima favillam
            vatis amici.

15 f. decedunt: *yield to.* — **baca** *i.e.* the olive. — **Venafro**: Venafrum, in Campania near Minturnae, was famed for its olives.

17 ff. Ausonius four centuries later praises his native Burdigala in the same terms *ord. urb. nobil.* 20, 9 f. *ubi . . . ver longum brumaeque novo cum sole tepentes.* — **Aulon**: it is disputed whether this was a mountain or a valley near Tarentum, but in all probability it was a mountain side suited for sheep grazing and the production of grapes. Cf. Martial's description 13, 125 *nobilis et lanis et felix vitibus Aulon | det pretiosa tibi vellera, vina mihi.*

19. Baccho: dative with **amicus**. — **Falernis**: cf. n. to 1, 27. 9.

21 ff. te mecum . . . postulant: *invite*, returning to the sentiment of the first strophe. — **beatae**: because of their mild climate and productiveness. — **ibi tu . . . sparges**: the future is half prophetic and half appealing. Horace will die first, he cannot bear to lose his friend. Cf. the appeal *Anth. Pal.* 2, p. 855 J. μέμνεο κἦν ζωοῖς ἐμέθεν καὶ πολλάκι τύμβῳ σπεῖσον ἀπὸ βλεφάρων δάκρυ᾽ ἀπαχομένη. 'I pray thee remember me even among the living, and let fall ofttimes from thine eyelids tears on my grave as thou turnest away.'

— **calentem . . . favillam**: when the ashes of the dead were gathered from the pyre and placed in the funeral urn, wine and perfume were regularly sprinkled over them, but Horace asks Septimius for the tribute of the tear due their friendship. — **vatis amici**: effectively placed at the end, the last word emphasizing the relationship between them. Cf., however, 4, 6. 44 *vatis Horati*, where Horace reserves the mention of his name to the end for other reasons. See n. on the passage.

7

A welcome home to Pompeius, Horace's old companion in arms.

'Who has restored thee to thy home. Pompeius mine, with whom I once endured the dangers of the field and shared the joys of revelry (1-8)? The hurry of Philippi's rout we knew together. Yes, I ran away and saved myself—thanks be to Mercury. But thee war's tide swept off upon the sea of further trouble (9-16). Come then, make sacrifice and drain full cups of wine saved up against thy coming. Away with all restraint, for thou art home again (17-28)!'

We know nothing more of Pompeius than the ode tells us. Apparently Horace had not seen his friend from the year of Philippi (42 B.C.) to the time at which the ode was written; this was most probably 29 B.C., when Augustus' mild policy allowed those who had taken arms against him to return to Italy in safety. Metre, 68.

> O saepe mecum tempus in ultimum
> deducte Bruto militiae duce,
>   quis te redonavit Quiritem
>   dis patriis Italoque caelo,
>
> 5 Pompei, meorum prime sodalium,
> cum quo morantem saepe diem mero
>   fregi coronatus nitentis
>   malobathro Syrio capillos?

1. **saepe**: possibly somewhat of an exaggeration for the two years preceding Philippi. — **tempus in ultimum**: *i.e. into extremest peril.* So Catullus, 64, 151, and 169, uses *tempus supremum, tempus extremum*.

2 f. **deducte ... duce**: a play on words similar to that in v. 7 **fregi** and v. 11 **fracta**. — **redonavit**: found only here and 3, 3, 33, where the sense is different. Stronger than the common *reddere*. —

Quiritem: *i.e.* a citizen, with no loss of civic rights.

5 ff. **Pompei**: dissyllabic, Intr. 38. — **prime**: in point of time, *earliest.* — **morantem ... diem ... fregi**: cf. Tennyson *In Mem.* 79 'And break the livelong summer day | With banquet in the distant woods.' — **coronatus**: a middle participle. Intr. 84. — **malobathro Syrio**: connect with **nitentis**. *malobathrum* is the Latinized form of the Indian

[2, 7, 9]

Tecum Philippos et celerem fugam
sensi, relicta non bene parmula,
  cum fracta virtus et minaces
    turpe solum tetigere mento.

Sed me per hostis Mercurius celer
denso paventem sustulit aere;
  te rursus in bellum resorbens
    unda fretis tulit aestuosis.

'tamalapattram,' the leaf of the 'tamela' tree, identified with the fragrant laurel. Here of course the oil prepared from the leaf. The adjective **Syrius** was applied in general to all oriental goods, for which Antioch was the emporium.

9 f. tecum: emphatic. Cf. **me** 13, **te** 15. — **relicta . . . parmula**: no doubt Horace ran away with the others at Philippi, but only blind pedantry could take these words literally. If Horace had been very earnest he would not have used the diminutive **parmula**; he was 'reconstructed' and reconciled so that he was ready to joke at his own expense after the model of Archilochus *Frg.* 6 ἀσπίδι μὲν Σαίων τις ἀγάλλεται, ἣν παρὰ θάμνῳ | ἔντος ἀμώμητον κάλλιπον οὐκ ἐθέλων | αὐτὸς δ᾽ ἐξέφυγον θανάτου τελος · ἀσπὶς ἐκείνη | ἐρρέτω · ἐξαῦτις κτήσομαι οὐ κακίω. 'Some Saian glories in my shield which quite against my will I left beside a bush — a good shield too it was. Still I escaped death's end.

The shield may go; some other day I'll get one just as good.'

11 f. minaces: *for all their threats*. — **turpe**: the character of their action — we might expect *turpiter teligere* — is transferred to the dust. Intr. 99. — **solum tetigere mento**: in mock heroic imitation of the Homeric phrase, *Il.* 2, 418 πρηνέες ἐν κονίῃσιν ὀδὰξ λαζοίατο γαῖαν.

13 f. Horace was saved too like the Homeric heroes. Cf. *Il.* 3, 380 f. τὸν δ᾽ ἐξήρπαξ᾽ Ἀφροδίτη ῥεῖα μάλ᾽ ὥς τε θεός, ἐκάλυψε δ᾽ ἄρ᾽ ἠέρι πολλῇ. — **Mercurius**: the guardian of poets. Cf. 2, 17, 29 *viri Mercuriales* and n. — **paventem**: another hit at himself as *imbellis*.

15 f. te: emphatic contrast with **me** v. 13. — **rursus in bellum**: connect with both **resorbens** and **tulit**. The figure is that of the retreating billow that sweeps its victim out to sea. Horace says of his own entrance into war, *Epist.* 2, 2, 47 *civilisque rudem belli tulit aestus in arma.* — **fretis**: abl., *with its boiling flood.*

Ergo obligatam redde Iovi dapem,
longaque fessum militia latus
    depone sub lauru mea, nec
        parce cadis tibi destinatis.

Oblivioso levia Massico
ciboria exple, funde capacibus
    unguenta de conchis. Quis udo
        deproperare apio coronas
curatve myrto? Quem Venus arbitrum
dicet bibendi? Non ego sanius
    bacchabor Edonis; recepto
        dulce mihi furere est amico.

17. 'Enough of these reflections on the past. You are safe back once more, so then (ergo) we'll turn to revelry.' Horace is unwilling to awaken in his friend bitter memories of events during his long absence from Italy. — **obligatam**: *i.e.* the offering you vowed for your safe return; a technical word for obligations incurred by vows to the gods.

18 f. **longa . . . militia**: 44–29 B.C. See the introductory note above. — **latus**: *self*. — **lauru mea**: the scene of the welcome is Horace's own farm.

21 f. **oblivioso**: *that brings forgetfulness*. Alcaeus' οἶνον λαθικάδεα. — **ciboria**: cups made in imitation of the pods of the Egyptian bean. In the use of this foreign word some imagine that there is a reference to Pompeius' service with Antony in Egypt. — **exple**: *fill to the brim*. — **capacibus**: 'abundance shall prevail.'

23 f. **quis**, etc.: hurried questions that dramatically take us into the midst of the preparations. — **deproperare**: *have prepared with all speed;* the compound with de- is intensive as 1, 18, 9 *rixa . . . debellata*, 2, 1, 35 *decoloravere caedes*. — **apio**: the fragrant parsley was regularly used in chaplets. Cf. Verg. *E.* 6, 68 *floribus atque apio crinis ornatus amaro*.

25 f. **Venus**: *i.e.* the *iactus Veneris*, the best throw at dice in which each of the four *tali* fell on different sides. — **arbitrum . . . bibendi**: *i.e.* to preside over the drinking bout. Cf. 1. 4, 18 *nec regna vini sortiere talis* and the note.

27 f. **Edonis**: Thracians, notorious for their heavy drinking and riotous bouts. Cf. 1, 27, 1 f. — **furere**: cf. 3, 19, 18 *insanire iuvat*.

8

To Barine, a heartless coquette. 'All thy false oaths go unpunished, else I would believe thee. But with all thy perjuries thou growest still more beautiful, and the gods of love laugh in favor toward thee (1-16). The number of thy suitors grows from day to day (17-24).'

Horace must not be taken here too seriously. For the depth of his love poems, see Intr. 13. There is no hint of the date of composition. Metre, 69.

Vlla si iuris tibi peierati
poena, Barine, nocuisset umquam,
dente si nigro fieres vel uno
    turpior ungui,
5   crederem; sed tu simul obligasti
perfidum votis caput, enitescis
pulchrior multo, iuvenumque prodis
    publica cura.
Expedit matris cineres opertos
10   fallere et toto taciturna noctis

1. **iuris ... peierati**: formed after the analogy of *ius iurandum*; equivalent to *peiurii*.

3 f. **dente ... ungui**: both ablatives of degree with *turpior*. — **si fieres**: generalizing, *if ever*. — **nigro ... uno**: with both nouns. For the arrangement of words see Intr. 21. The ancients believed that perjury was punished by bodily blemish; and the Greeks had the same superstition which is current with us, that white spots on the nails are caused by lying.

5 f. **simul**: cf. n. to 1, 4, 17. — **obligasti**: for this technical word, see n. to 2, 7, 17. — **votis**: dative, equivalent to *devotionibus*, the punishments she has invoked on herself if she forswear. — **enitescis**: *i.e.* thy beauty is not diminished (cf. vv. 2-4), but becomes all the more brilliant.

7 f. **prodis**: *comest forth*, with thy admirers about thee. — **cura**: technically used of the object of one's love. Cf. Prop. 3, 25, 1 *unica nata meo pulcherrima cura dolori*, and Verg. *E.* 10, 22 *tua cura Lycoris*. Pindar *P.* 10, 92 says of Hippocleas νέαισίν τε παρθένοισι μέλημα.

9. **expedit**: sc. *te*. 'So far from perjury harming you, you actually profit by it.' — **matris fallere**, etc.: *to swear falsely by*, etc

signa cum caelo gelidaque divos
   morte carentis.

Ridet hoc, inquam, Venus ipsa, rident
simplices Nymphae ferus et Cupido,
semper ardentis acuens sagittas
   cote cruenta.

Adde quod pubes tibi crescit omnis,
servitus crescit nova, nec priores
impiae tectum dominae relinquunt,
   saepe minati.

So Propertius swears 3, 20, 15 *ossa tibi iuro per matris et ossa parentis | (si fallo, cinis heu sit mihi uterque gravis!) | me tibi ad extremas mansurum, vita, tenebras.* — **opertos**: *i.e. sepultos.* She prays her mother's shade may haunt her, if she be not true.

10 f. taciturna ... signa: 'the silent stars' that look down on the passionate loves of men. Cf. *Epod.* 15, 1 f. and n. — **gelida divos**, etc.: the advantage by which gods excel mankind.

13. ridet ... rident: Intr. 28 c. This gives the reason for Barine's escape. The idea that the gods laugh at lovers' perjuries is old as Plato, *Symp.* 183 B. Cf. Pseudo-Tibul. 3, 6, 49 *periuria ridet amantum | Iuppiter et ventos inrita ferre iubet.* Echoed by Shakespere, *Romeo and Juliet* 2, 2 'At lovers' perjuries | They say Jove laughs.'

14. simplices: *easy going.* εὐήθεις. Cf. Verg. *E.* 3, 9, *sed faciles Nymphae risere.* — **ferus ... Cupido**: since he pitilessly wounds and fires men's hearts. — **acuens sagittas**: Cupid is represented on ancient gems as sharpening his arrows on a grindstone. — **cruenta**: transferred from the arrows to the whetstone. Intr. 99.

17 f. adde quod, etc.: in place of the common prose *accedit quod.* Translate, — *to say nothing of the fact that.* It introduces with emphasis a new ground for the poet's distrust, — the number of her victims grows so that she has no need to be faithful. — **pubes ... omnis**: repeated in the predicate **servitus nova**, *to be a new band of devoted slaves*, thereby expressing the completeness of Barine's conquest. — **crescit**: *is growing up.* — **nec priores**, etc.: *i.e.* while Barine entraps the rising generation, she still keeps her hold on the former.

19 f. impiae: for her perjuries. — **saepe minati**: her lovers cannot carry out their threats to leave her.

Te suis matres metuunt iuvencis,
te senes parci miseraeque nuper
virgines nuptae, tua ne retardet
aura maritos.

So Horace once made determined vows, but still returned to his heartless Inachia, *Epod.* 11, 19-22. Cf. Tibul. 2, 6, 13 f. *iuravi quotiens rediturum ad limina numquam! | cum bene iuravi, pes tamen ipse redit.*

21 ff. te...te: Intr. 28 c. Three classes fear Barine: mothers for their sons, miserly old men for their money, and brides for their new husbands. — iuvencis: *their dear sons.* Cf. 2, 5, 6. — senes parci: who know she will squeeze their money bags if once she gets the chance. — miserae: proleptic. 'made wretched by their fear.' — virgines: like *puellae*, not infrequently used of newly married women. Cf. 3, 14, 11. — tua aura: *the breath of thy charm.* Cf. 1, 5. 11 *popularis aura*, and Propert. 3, 27, 15 *si modo clamantis revocaverit aura puellae.*

9

Horace exhorts his friend Valgius to give up mourning for his favorite Mystes.

'Winter rains and winds are not eternal, Valgius. It is not always the gloomy season. Yet you weep without ceasing (1-12). Not so did Nestor mourn for his Antilochus, nor Troilus' relatives for his loss. Give up your weak plaints, and rather sing the triumphs of Augustus Caesar (13-24).'

The reproof at the end runs into a celebration of the Emperor's deeds, and shows the court poet. The name Augustus (v. 19) proves that the date of composition is later than 27 B.C., but it cannot be more exactly fixed. See, however, notes to vv. 20 ff.

C. Valgius Rufus, consul suffectus in 12 B.C., was an elegiac poet belonging to Maecenas' circle. According to the Scholiast, Vergil alludes to his elegiac verses in *E.* 7, 22. An epic was apparently expected from him. Pseudo-Tibul. 4, 1, 179 f. *est tibi, qui possit magnis se accingere rebus, | Valgius: aeterno propior non alter Homero.* We hear also of his rhetorical and medical works, but none of his writings are preserved to us. His friendship with Horace is further attested by *S.* 1, 10, 81 f. *Plotius et Varius, Maecenas Vergiliusque, | Valgius et probet haec Octavius.* Metre, 68.

Non semper imbres nubibus hispidos
manant in agros aut mare Caspium
    vexant inaequales procellae
        usque, nec Armeniis in oris,

5   amice Valgi, stat glacies iners
    mensis per omnis aut Aquilonibus
        querceta Gargani laborant
            et foliis viduantur orni:

    tu semper urges flebilibus modis
10 Mysten ademptum, nec tibi Vespero

1 ff. For the careful arrangement of words, see Intr. 28 c. — **non semper**, etc.: cf. 2, 11, 9, and Herrick, 'Clouds will not ever poure down rain; | A sullen day will cleere again. | First, peales of thunder we must heare, | Then lutes and harpes shall stroke the eare.' — **hispidos**: *unkempt and dank; i.e.* covered with stubble (cf. 4, 10, 5) and drenched by the winter's rains. The comparison is between such fields and Valgius' countenance.

2. **mare Caspium**: the stormy character of this sea is mentioned by Mela 3, 5 *mare Caspium omne atrox, saevum, sine portubus, procellis undique expositum.* It is probable, however, that Horace's choice of this concrete example and of **Armeniis in oris** (cf. n. to 1, 1, 14) was determined by the coming reference to Augustus' successful diplomacy in the East (vv. 20-24).

3 f. **inaequales**: *gusty, squally.* — **usque**: temporal, as 1, 17, 4. —

Armeniis in oris: *i.e.* on Mount Taurus.

5. **stat**: expressive of the stability of the glacier. — **glacies iners**: cf. 4, 7, 12 *bruma iners.*

7 f. **Gargani**: with this Horace returns to Italy for his example. Garganus is a thickly wooded mountain in Apulia, especially exposed to storms. Cf. *Epist.* 2, 1, 202 *Garganum mugire putes nemus aut mare Tuscum.* — **querceta ... laborant**: cf. 1, 9, 3 *silvae laborantes.* — **viduantur**: *are widowed of*, the climax of his figures of desolation. The temporal idea, varied by **semper usque, mensis per omnis**, continues to the end of the second strophe.

9 f. **tu semper**: contrasted with Nature. — **urges**: *pursuest, dwellest on*; used by Propertius (5, 11, 1) as if the mourning distressed the dead, *desine, Paulle, meum lacrimis urgere sepulcrum.*

10 ff. **Vespero surgente**, etc.: so

surgente decedunt amores
nec rapidum fugiente solem.
At non ter aevo functus amabilem
ploravit omnis Antilochum senex
15   annos, nec impubem parentes
Troilon aut Phrygiae sorores
flevere semper: desine mollium
tandem querellarum, et potius nova

Orpheus mourned for his lost Euridice, Verg. *G.* 4, 466 *te veniente die, te decedente canebat.* Cf. Helvius Cinna's lines, *te matutinus flentem conspexit Eous | et flentem paulo vidit post Hesperus idem;* and Tennyson's *Mariana,* 'Her tears fell with the dews of even; | Her tears fell ere the dews were dried.'—**amores**: *i.e.* his elegies.—**rapidum**: placed in contrast with **fugiente**. It is a stock epithet of the sun. Cf. Mimn. 10, 5 ὠκέος Ἠελίοιο ἀκτῖνες, and Verg. *G.* 1, 92 *rapidive potentia solis.*

13 ff. **ter aevo functus**: Nestor, described *Il.* 1, 250 ff. τῷ δ' ἤδη δύο μὲν γενεαὶ μερόπων ἀνθρώπων | ἐφθίαθ', οἵ οἱ πρόσθεν ἅμα τράφεν ἠδ' ἐγένοντο | ἐν Πύλῳ ἠγαθέῃ, μετὰ δὲ τριτάτοισιν ἄνασσεν. Cf. Cic. *C.M.* 31 *tertiam enim aetatem hominum videbat.*—**amabilem**: placed here with adversative force, *in spite of all his loveliness.* Cf. **impubem** (v. 15), *a mere child.* The two adjectives doubtless are chosen as applying also to Mystes, whom Valgius has lost.—**non ploravit omnis an-** **nos**: when, in the *Odyssey,* Telemachus and his companion visit Nestor at his home in Pylus, they find him cheerful in spite of the loss of his son Antilochus, whom Memnon slew.—**Troilon**: Priam's young son, whom Achilles caught and slew near a spring. This was a favorite scene with vase painters of the early fifth century (Baum. p. 1901 f.). Troilus' sister Polyxena is frequently represented as witnessing his death. His fate was in poets the type of early death; cf. *e.g.* Verg. *A.* 1, 474 ff., where indeed Vergil is describing a wall painting, and Chaucer, *T. and C.* 5, 1806 'dispitously him slough the fiers Achille.'

17. **desine... querellarum**: this construction with the genitive of separation is in imitation of Greek usage with λήγω, παύομαι, etc. Cf. 3, 17, 16 *operum solutis;* 3, 27, 69 *abstineto irarum.*

18 f. **nova tropaea**: what successes are meant is uncertain. Some think of Augustus' campaigns against the Cantabri, 27–25 B.C.; others regard

cantemus Augusti tropaea
Caesaris et rigidum Niphaten

Medumque flumen gentibus additum
victis minores volvere vertices,
intraque praescriptum Gelonos
exiguis equitare campis.

tropaea as a general term, defined by what follows — **Niphaten, Medum flumen ... volvere, Gelonos ... equitare.** It is probable, however, that Horace had no definite victories in mind, but wished to say, 'Come, Valgius, let us turn to epic song; our subject is ready — Augustus' new successes (in general) and (in particular) the Niphates,' etc.

20 ff. These were victories of diplomacy rather than of arms. — **rigidum**: *ice-bound.* — **Niphaten**: according to Strabo and Dio Cassius, a mountain of Armenia. But Lucan 3, 245 and Sil. Ital. 13, 765 and Iuv. 6, 409 consider it a river. Verg. G. 3, 30 celebrates the same extension of the empire, *addam urbes Asiae domitas pulsumque Niphaten.* — **Medum flumen**: the Euphrates. The construction changes from the simple accusative to the accusative and infinitive, 'sing the Niphates, sing that,' etc. Propertius has a similar construction, 2, 1, 19 ff. *non ego Titanas canerem, non Ossan Olympo | inpositam, ut caeli Pelion esset iter | ... Xerxis et imperio bina coisse vada.* — **minores**: in token of its submission. Cf. Verg. A. 8, 726 *Euphrates ibat iam mollior undis.*

23. Gelonos: a nomad Scythian people on the river Don. The poets of this time, however, use their name for the Scythians in general. — **exiguis**: for they are now limited **intra praescriptum.** — **equitare**: *ride their raids.* Cf. 1, 2, 51. The reference in the last two verses is probably to an embassy from the Scythians which Augustus received at Tarraco in Spain. Cf. *Mon. Anc.* 5, 51 *nostram amicitiam petierunt per legatos Bastarnae Scythaeque et Sarmatarum qui sunt citra flumen Tanaim et ultra reges.*

10

A series of sententiae on the dangers of high and low estate and the advantages of the golden mean, which should be compared with 2, 2 and 3. The ode is an expansion of the Greek μηδὲν ἄγαν; more weight, however, is laid on the disadvantages of great position than on the wretchedness of extreme poverty.

Licinius Murena, to whom the ode is addressed, was apparently the son of the Murena whom Cicero defended; he was adopted by M.. Terentius Varro, and so became the brother-in-law of Proculeius (2, 2) and of Terentia, Maecenas' wife. In 23 B.C. he was consul with Augustus; during this year he entered into a conspiracy with Fannius Caepio against the emperor, but was detected and put to death. This is clear evidence that Horace's poem was published before that date. It is said that he was inordinately ambitious, so that the advice here given acquires a special significance in view of his later fate. Metre, 69.

> Rectius vives, Licini, neque altum
> semper urgendo neque, dum procellas
> cautus horrescis, nimium premendo
>   litus iniquum.

5
> Auream quisquis mediocritatem
> diligit, tutus caret obsoleti
> sordibus tecti, caret invidenda
>   sobrius aula.

> Saepius ventis agitatur ingens
10
> pinus et celsae graviore casu

1 ff. **rectius**: bearing the emphasis; *more fitly.* — **neque altum**, etc.: the common allegory of the voyage of life is a favorite with Horace. Cf. 1, 5, 13. 34, 3; 3, 2, 28. 29, 62; *Epist.* 2, 2, 202. — **urgendo**: *by pressing out to*, in contrast to hugging the shore (**premendo**). — **iniquum**: *unkind*, because of its dangerous reefs.

5 f. **auream mediocritatem**: *the golden mean*. A translation of the Greek μεσότης, τὸ μέτριον, which Cicero *de off.* 1, 89 defines *mediocritatem illam . . . quae est inter nimium et parum.* — **tutus caret**, etc.: *is safe and free from a squalid tumble-down house.*

7 f. **caret . . . caret**: Intr. 28 c. — **invidenda . . . aula**: cf. 3, 1, 45 f. *invidendis postibus.* — **sobrius**: *in his temperance*, the Greek σώφρων.

9-12. Three typical illustrations drawn from nature of the danger to too great prominence. Cf. Herod. 7, 10, 5. Seneca employs similar figures in a number of passages in his tragedies, *e.g. Oed.* 8-11 *ut alta ventos semper excipiunt iuga | rupemque saxis vasta dirimentem*

decidunt turres feriuntque summos
    fulgura montis.

Sperat infestis, metuit secundis
alteram sortem bene praeparatum
15   pectus. Informis hiemes reducit
    Iuppiter, idem

submovet; non, si male nunc, et olim
sic erit; quondam cithara tacentem
suscitat musam neque semper arcum
20   tendit Apollo.

Rebus angustis animosus atque
fortis appare; sapienter idem
contrahes vento nimium secundo
    turgida vela.

freta | quamvis quieti verberat fluctus maris, | imperia sic excelsa Fortunae obiacent. Notice that the emphasis is on **saepius, ingens, celsae graviore, summos.** Intr. 25.

13 f. 'A well-prepared breast can withstand all changes of fortune.' — **sperat... metuit**: emphatic, the subject being deferred to the end. — **infestis, secundis**: abstract neuters plural, dat. with the verbs. — **alteram sortem**: *the opposite lot.*

15. **informis**: *shapeless*, and so ugly. Cf. Verg. *G.* 3, 354 f. *sed iacet aggeribus niveis informis et alto | terra gelu.* — **reducit**: *brings back* (in their due season). For this force of **re-**, cf. 3, 8, 9 *anno redeunte.* — **idem**: *and yet he.* Cf. v. 22; 2, 19, 27.

17 f. **si male**: sc. *est.* — **olim**: *some day*, in contrast to **nunc.** — **quondam**: *sometimes*, in a general sense. — **cithara**: instrumental ablative.

19 f. Apollo does not always send war and pestilence (**arcum tendit**), but at times brings men song. The common application is to point the desirability of combining play with work. Reproduced in the *Laus Pis.* 142 f. *nec semper Gnosius arcum | destinat, exempto sed laxat cornua nervo.* — **rebus angustis**: *when times are hard.* — **sapienter idem**, etc.: *yet you will do wisely to take in*, etc. Horace closes, as he began, with a figure drawn from the sea. — **nimium**: connect with **secundo.**

II

Horace will teach his friend Hirpinus his own philosophy. 'Little is enough for life, enjoy the present fleeting moment with no thought of distant dangers, no greed for useless wealth. Youth quickly flies, and old age comes. All is change. How useless then to vex our souls with endless aims and efforts.'

Quinctius Hirpinus, apparently the friend to whom *Epist.* 1, 16 is addressed, is not further known. He seems to have been ambitious for wealth, but not averse to pleasures. The date of composition is probably fixed as 26-25 B.C. by the mention of the *bellicosus Cantaber* v. 1. Metre, 68.

> Quid bellicosus Cantaber et Scythes,
> Hirpine Quincti, cogitet Hadria
> divisus obiecto, remittas
> quaerere nec trepides in usum
>
> 5   poscentis aevi pauca. Fugit retro
> levis iuventas et decor, arida

1 ff. **Cantaber**: cf. n. to 2, 6, 2. — **Hirpine Quincti**: for the transposition of nomen and cognomen, see n. to 2, 2, 3. — **Hadria divisus obiecto**: as a matter of fact, not simply the Adriatic, but long tracts of land and sea separated the Scythians from Italy; but Quinctius was too anxious over these distant dangers, and Horace playfully exaggerates — 'set off from us only by,' etc. The danger of a barbarian invasion from the northeast was not sufficiently present to the Roman mind at this time to cause Horace to speak seriously of the barrier the Adriatic would afford. In later centuries, however, this sea often protected Italy. — **remittas quaerere**: cf. 1, 38, 3 *mitte sec-* *tari*; 3, 29, 11 *omitte mirari*. There is probably also the accessory idea of relaxing the anxious strain. We may translate, *give up thy anxious questioning.* Cf. Ter. *And.* 827 *remittas iam me onerare iniuriis.* — **trepides in usum**: *and do not fret about the needs*, etc. Cf. 1, 9, 14 f.; 3, 29, 32 f.

5-12. The thought is a commonplace. Cf. Theog. 985 f. αἶψα γὰρ ὥστε νόημα παρέρχεται ἀγλαὸς ἥβη· | οὐδ' ἵππων ὁρμὴ γίνεται ὠκυτέρη. 'For quick as thought bright youth passes; horses' speed is not swifter.' Auson. *Anth. Lat.* 646 *collige virgo rosas, dum flos novus et nova pubes,* | *et memor esto aevum sic properare tuum*; and, 'Gather ye rosebuds while ye may, | Old Time is still a-flying, | And

pellente lascivos amores
    canitie facilemque somnum.

Non semper idem floribus est honor
vernis, neque uno luna rubens nitet
    voltu. Quid aeternis minorem
    consiliis animum fatigas?

Cur non sub alta vel platano vel hac
pinu iacentes sic temere et rosa
    canos odorati capillos,
    dum licet, Assyriaque nardo

this same flower, that smiles today, | To-morrow will be dying.'
6 f. **lēvis**: *smooth cheeked, imberbis.* Cf. 4, 6, 28 *lēvis Agyieu.* — **arida . . . canitie**: *sapless, withered, and gray old age;* when 'the juice of life is gone.'
8. **facilem**: *gentle.* The same epithet 3, 21, 4; cf. 2, 16, 15 *lēvis somnos.*
9 f. **honor**: *beauty.* — **vernis**: corresponding to man's youth. — **rubens nitet**: *shines blushing.* Cf. Prop. 1, 10, 8 *quamvis . . . mediis caelo Luna ruberet equis;* Sen. *Phaedr.* 747 *exerit vultus rubicunda Phoebe.*
11 f. **aeternis . . . consiliis**: *endless schemings.* The ablative is dependent on both **minorem** and **fatigas**. Intr. 100. With the thought, cf. 4, 7, 7 f. *immortalia ne speres, monet annus et almum | quae rapit hora diem.*
13 ff. 'Far better give thyself up to pleasures here beneath the shade.' The following questions give the verses a vivid dramatic turn. — **platano . . . pinu**: the two most beautiful Italian shade trees; the plane (sycamore) came from the Orient and was cultivated in parks and gardens. — **hac**: 'this one close by.' — **sic temere**: *just as we are;* οὕτως εἰκῇ, Plat. *Gorg.* 506 D. 'No long elaborate preparation is necessary to gain life's pleasures; a garland, perfume, and the zither-playing Lyde are enough.'
15 f. **canos**: Horace describes himself *Epist.* 1, 20, 24 as *praecanus, prematurely gray;* he was at this time about forty. — **odorati**: a middle participle; so **uncti** v. 17 below. Intr. 84. — **dum licet**: 'our time is short.' Cf. 2, 3, 15. Ten years before Horace could say *Epod.* 13, 3 ff. *rapiamus, amici, | occasionem de die, dumque virent genua | et decet.* Now he has passed the line of middle age and knows that soon dry old age will steal from him his capacity for enjoyment. — **Assyria . . . nardo**:

potamus uncti? Dissipat Euhius
curas edacis. Quis puer ocius
   restinguet ardentis Falerni
20   pocula praetereunte lympha?

Quis devium scortum eliciet domo
Lyden? Eburna dic age cum lyra
   maturet, in comptum Lacaenae
      more comam religata nodum.

the same as the *malobathro Syrio* of 2, 7, 8. Cf. Tibull. 3, 6, 63 f. *Syrio madefactus tempora nardo | debueram sertis implicuisse comas.*
17 f. **dissipat**: cf. Cypria *Frg.* 10 K. οἶνόν τοι, Μενέλαε, θεοὶ ποίησαν ἄριστον | θνητοῖς ἀνθρώποισιν ἀποσκεδάσαι μελεδώνας. 'Wine, Menelaus, the gods made the best means to scatter the cares of mortal men.' — **Euhius**: formed from the cry of the Bacchanals, εὐοῖ. Cf. 1, 18, 9. — **edacis**: *gnawing, carking.* Cf. 1, 18, 4 *mordaces . . . sollicitudines.*
18 f. **puer**: cf. n. to *Epod.* 9, 33 and 1, 29, 7. — **restinguet**: *temper* (the fierceness of). — **ardentis Falerni**: cf. n. to 1, 27, 10.

21 ff. **devium scortum**: *the coy wench,* a zither player whose home, for the purpose of the ode, is supposed to be not far away. Yet the adjective **devium**, which apparently means here 'solitary,' 'apart,' as in Livy 3, 13, 10 *devio quodam tugurio* (hut) *vivere,* implies that Lyde is one who does not bestow her favors on all; this implication is emphasized by **eliciet**, *lure forth.* — **dic age,** etc.: *go bid her hasten.* Cf. 1, 32, 3 *age dic Latinum, barbite, carmen* ; and 3, 4, 1. — **maturet**: the subj. is independent, parallel to **dic**. — **in comptum nodum**: *in a neat simple knot.* No elaborate coiffure would be fitting for this extemporaneous carouse. — **religata**: cf. n. to 1, 5, 4.

12

Maecenas had apparently urged Horace to celebrate in verse Octavian's victory over Antony and his other successes in the East. This ode is the poet's reply.

'Not deeds of war long past (1-4), not ancient mythology (5-8), nor Caesar's present deeds and triumphs (9-12), but modest love, the charms of thy Licymnia, are alone fit subjects for my lyric muse (13-28).'

The ode should be compared with 1, 6, Horace's answer to a similar request from Agrippa. Metre, 72.

> Nolis longa ferae bella Numantiae
> nec durum Hannibalem nec Siculum mare
> Poeno purpureum sanguine mollibus
>   aptari citharae modis,
>
> nec saevos Lapithas et nimium mero
> Hylaeum domitosque Herculea manu
> Telluris iuvenes, unde periculum
>   fulgens contremuit domus

1. **nolis**: emphatic, *you certainly would not wish.* — **longa bella**: nine years, 141–133 B.C. — **ferae**: the war was ended with the suicide of the inhabitants and the burning of the city. Flor. 2, 18, 15 *deplorato exitu in ultimam rabiem furoremque conversi postremo mori hoc genere destinarunt: Rhoecogene duce se suos patriam ferro et veneno subiectoque undique igne peremerunt.*

2 ff. **durum**: since the defeat of Hannibal proved a hard task for the Romans. — **purpureum sanguine**: in 260 B.C. when C. Duilius won his famous naval victory at Mylae, and again in 242 B.C. at the battle of the Aegatian Islands. — **mollibus**: in sharp contrast to **ferae, durum,** and the savage picture called up by **mare ... purpureum sanguine.** Such fierce themes are not suited to the gentle strains of the lyre.

5 ff. The stock mythological themes of epic song. — **saevos Lapithas**, etc.: *i.e.* the quarrel between the Centaurs and the Lapithae at the marriage of Peirithous and Hippodamia. Cf. n. to 1, 18, 8. — **nimium mero**: *made insolent with wine.* Cf. Tac. *Hist.* 1, 35 *nimii verbis.* — **Hylaeum**: one of the Centaurs. Cf. Verg. *G.* 2, 457 *et magno Hylaeum Lapithis cratere minantem.* — **domitos ... iuvenes**: the giants who tried to storm the citadels of heaven. Cf. 3, 4, 42 ff. — **Herculea manu**: Hercules was summoned by the gods to aid them, for an oracle said that only a mortal could conquer the earth-born monsters. — **unde**: connect with **contremuit**: *from whom.* Cf. 1, 12, 7; 28, 28.

8. **fulgens ... domus**: because of its place in the bright upper air. Cf. 1, 3, 29 *aetheria domus*; 3, 3, 33 *lucidas sedes* and the Homeric δώματα μαρμαίροντα. — **contremuit**: transitive, as the simple verb, Verg. *A.* 3, 648 *sonitumque pedum vocemque tremesco.*

Saturni veteris; tuque pedestribus
dices historiis proelia Caesaris,
Maecenas, melius ductaque per vias
    regum colla minacium.

Me dulcis dominae Musa Licymniae
cantus, me voluit dicere lucidum
fulgentis oculos, et bene mutuis
    fidum pectus amoribus;

quam nec ferre pedem dedecuit choris
nec certare ioco nec dare bracchia

9 f. **tuque**: emphatically introducing the specific reason why Horace cannot celebrate Caesar's deeds, — 'And then *you* will tell,' etc. — **pedestribus . . . historiis**: *prose*, in contrast to poetry. Horace was the first to adopt this term, in imitation of the Greek πεζὸς λόγος. There is no evidence that Maecenas ever undertook such a work as Horace here suggests.

11 f. **ducta**: *i.e.* in the triumphal procession. — **colla**: 'with chains about their necks.' Cf. *Epod.* 7, 7 f. *intactus aut Britannus ut descenderet | sacra catenatus via*, and Prop. 2, 1, 33 f. with reference likewise to Augustus' triumphs (*canerem*) *regum auratis circumdata colla catenis | Actiaque in sacra currere rostra via.* —**minacium**: *but just now threatening.*

13. **me . . . me**: 'My task is this.' Intr. 30. — **dominae**: this became under the empire the regular title of address to a married woman, like our 'Mrs.,' 'Madam,' the Italian 'donna.' Translate, *my lady*. — **Licymniae**: ancient critics agreed that under this name Terentia, Maecenas' wife, is meant. The fact that the two names are metrically identical makes this very probable. So Catullus calls Clodia, Lesbia; Tibullus employs Delia for Plania, etc. That Licymnia in any case was a free-born Roman lady is proved by v. 19 f. See note. — **cantus**: modified by **dulcis**. — **bene**: connect with **fidum**. Cf. Cic. *Tusc.* 2, 44 *bene magnus*, and the French *bien*. The opposite is *male*: so 1, 17, 25 *male dispar*; Verg. *A.* 2, 23 *male fida*.

17 f. **ferre pedem**: *to move her feet in*, etc. Cf. Verg. *G.* 1, 11 *ferte simul Faunique pedem.* Dancing, except as part of a religious ceremony, was thought unbecoming a Roman woman although the severity of custom was

ludentem nitidis virginibus sacro
20   Dianae celebris die.

Num tu quae tenuit dives Achaemenes
aut pinguis Phrygiae Mygdonias opes
permutare velis crine Licymniae,
    plenas aut Arabum domos,

25   cum flagrantia detorquet ad oscula
cervicem, aut facili saevitia negat
quae poscente magis gaudeat eripi,
    interdum rapere occupet?

relaxed enough at this time to allow dancing within one's own house, and the reference here may be to such private amusement. Cf. 3, 6, 21 and n. — **nec . . . dedecuit**: cf. Ovid. *Am.* 1, 7, 12 *nec dominam motae dedecuere comae.* — **certare ioco**: *i.e.* in light conversation. — **dare bracchia**: rhythmical movements of the arms formed an important part of ancient dances, as they still do, *e.g.* in the Italian tarantella.

19 f. **nitidis**: *i.e.* in holiday dress. — **Dianae . . . die**: the chorus which sang and danced in honor of a divinity was composed of free-born youths and maidens, so that it is evident that Licymnia was in any case *ingenua.* — **celebris**: *thronged* with celebrants.

21 ff. 'Not all the riches of the East could purchase from you one lock of her hair.' — **Achaemenes**: the founder of the royal house of Persia. Cf. 3, 1, 44. — **Mygdonias**: Mygdon was an early king of Phrygia. The mention of Phrygia calls to mind Midas, whose touch turned all things to gold. — **crine**: *a lock* of hair. For the construction, see Intr. 98. — **plenas . . . Arabum domos**: cf. 3, 24, 1 f. *intacti . . . thesauri Arabum.*

25 ff. **detorquet**: for the caesura, see Intr. 53. — **facili**: because her sternness (**saevitia**) is easily overcome. — **poscente**: dependent on **magis**. 'Don't ask her for kisses, she would take more satisfaction in having them stolen from her than the one (*i.e.* you, Maecenas) who begs them would delight to get them; indeed she would sometimes begin by stealing them from you.' Cf. Tibul. 1, 4, 53 ff. *rapias tum cara licebit | oscula: pugnabit, sed tamen apta dabit; | rapta dabit primo, mox offeret ipse roganti, | post etiam collo se implicuisse volet.* — **rapere occupet**: equivalent to the Greek φθάνοι ἂν ἁρπάζουσα. Cf. 1, 14, 2.

13

Horace was nearly killed one day on his farm by a falling tree. The following ode was suggested by this event, which seems to have made a deep impression on him. (Cf. 2, 17, 27; 3, 4, 27.) Still here his very extravagance of earnestness gives the treatment a half jesting tone. After declaring that the man who planted the fatal tree could be guilty of any crime, Horace wanders into reflection on his favorite theme — the uncertainty of human life and the proximity of death. On the first anniversary of the event, he wrote 3, 8, which fixes the date of his narrow escape as March 1, 30 B.C. This ode then was probably written within that month. Metre, 68.

> Ille et nefasto te posuit die,
> quicumque primum, et sacrilega **manu**
> produxit, arbos, in nepotum
> perniciem opprobriumque **pagi**;
>
> 5   illum et parentis crediderim sui
> fregisse cervicem et penetralia

1 ff. Cf. Ovid's amusing diatribe against his writing tablets, *Am.* 1, 12, 15 ff. *illum etiam, qui vos* (sc. *tabellas*) *ex arbore vertit in usum, | convincam puras non habuisse manus, | praebuit illa arbor misero suspendia collo, | carnifici diras praebuit illa cruces: | illa dedit turpes ravis bubonibus umbras: | volturis in ramis et strigis ova tulit.* — **nefasto ... die**: technically the days on which the magistrates might not give judgment, *i.e.* utter the three words *do, dico, addico.* Cf. Ovid *Fasti* 1, 47 f. *ille nefastus erit, per quem tria verba silentur | fastus erit, per quem lege licebit agi.* Gradually extended, the word came to include all unlucky or ill-omened days.

2 ff. quicumque primum: parenthetical, sc. *te posuit* from the preceding verse. — **produxit in,** etc.: *reared to be.* — **pagi**: *district.*

5. illum: emphatically repeating the initial *ille* above; itself repeated by *ille* v. 8 below. Intr. 28 c. — **crediderim**: potential.

6 f. fregisse cervicem: *strangled.* Cf. *Epod.* 3, 2 *si quis . . . senile guttur fregerit.* — **penetralia**: the shrines of the household gods, the sacred hearthstone. Protection of one's guest was a holy obligation. — **nocturno**: giving an added touch of horror to the description, — *with blood of his guest slain by night.*

sparsisse nocturno cruore
   hospitis; ille venena Colcha

et quicquid usquam concipitur nefas
tractavit, agro qui statuit meo
   te triste lignum, te caducum
      in domini caput immerentis.

Quid quisque vitet, numquam homini satis
cautum est in horas. Navita Bosporum
   Poenus perhorrescit neque ultra
      caeca timet aliunde fata;

miles sagittas et celerem fugam
Parthi, catenas Parthus et Italum

---

8 f. Colcha: a standing epithet, as Medea, whose home was Colchis, was chief of sorceresses. Cf. *Epod.* 5, 24; 17, 35. — **tractavit**: *has had a finger in*; extended by a slight zeugma from **venena** to **quicquid nefas**. For this meaning, cf. *Epod.* 3, 8.

11 f. **triste lignum**: *fatal log.* Cf. 3, 4, 27 *devota arbor*; and Verg. *E.* 3, 80 *triste lupus stabulis.* Nearly the same meaning appears 2, 14, 8 *tristi unda*, said of the Styx. — **te . . . te**: the anaphora shows the poet's earnestness. — **caducum**: *ready to fall.* — **domini**: *owner*, showing that Horace's escape took place on his own farm.

13 ff. 'No one ever knows the particular danger he should avoid: with all the timid caution of sailor, soldier, or Parthian, death still comes in unexpected forms.' — **homini**: dat. of agent with **cautum est**. — **in horas**: *from hour to hour*, formed after the analogy of *in dies*. — **navita . . . Poenus**: of Sidon or Tyre. Cf. Soph. *Frg.* 823 N. Φοῖνιξ ἀνήρ, Σιδώνιος κάπηλος. — **Bosporum**: *i.e.* the Thracian Bosphorus, notorious for its storms. Cf. 3, 4, 30 *insanientem . . . Bosporum.* — **ultra . . . aliunde**: *from any other source besides.* — **timēt**: for the quantity, see Intr. 35.

17 ff. **miles**: *i.e.* the Italian, whose most dreaded foe was the Parthian. — **sagittas**, etc.: cf. n. to 1, 19, 11. The Parthian in his turn most fears subjection to the Romans (**catenas**) and the brave soldiers of Italy (**Italum robur**).

robur : sed improvisa leti
vis rapuit rapietque gentis.

Quam paene furvae regna Proserpinae
et iudicantem vidimus Aeacum
sedesque discriptas piorum et
Aeoliis fidibus querentem
Sappho puellis de popularibus,
et te sonantem plenius aureo,
Alcaee, plectro dura navis,
dura fugae mala, dura belli.

— **sed inprovisa**: emphatic, *still it is the unexpected*, etc.

21 ff. Horace returns to reflections on his own possible fate and to thoughts of the shades he would have seen in the lower world. As a poet he would desire to behold his great models, Sappho and Alcaeus; exactly as Socrates, in his cheerful anticipation of Hades (Plat. *Apol.* 40E-41C), wished to meet Palamedes, Ajax son of Telamon, and all others who had been victims of unjust judgments like himself. — **furvae**: *dusky*, the proper epithet for **regna**, here transferred to Queen Proserpina. Intr. 99. Seneca had the same thought in mind when he wrote *H. F.* 547 ff. *qua spe praecipites actus ad inferos | audax ire vias inremeabiles | vidisti Siculae regna Proserpinae?* — **Prŏserpinae**: here the first syllable is short, but ordinarily it is long. Cf. 1, 28, 20. — **Aeacum**: with Minos and Rhadamanthus, judge of the dead.

23 f. sedes discriptas: *homes set apart (separatas)*, *i.e.* from the place of punishment. So Vergil *A.* 8, 670 has *secretos pios*. Note the order of progress: the throne of Proserpina, the judgment seat, and after that the Elysian fields. — **Aeoliis**: the Aeolic dialect was the speech of Lesbos, the home of Horace's chief models, Sappho and Alcaeus, so that this adjective instantly suggested to the educated Roman these two poets. — **querentem**, etc.: because the maidens of her city were so cold in love.

25 ff. Sappho: accusative — **sonantem plenius**: *sounding a fuller strain*. Alcaeus sang of war and exile, as well as love.— **aureo . . . plectro**: instrumental abl. The adjective marks the splendor of Alcaeus' song. Cf. Quint. 10. 1, 63 *Alcaeus in parte operis aureo plectro merito donatur.* — **fugae**: *exile*. For the triple anaphora **dura, dura, dura**, see Intr. 28 c.

Vtrumque sacro digna silentio
mirantur umbrae dicere; sed magis
    pugnas et exactos tyrannos
        densum umeris bibit aure volgus.

Quid mirum, ubi illis carminibus stupens
demittit atras belua centiceps
    auris et intorti capillis
        Eumenidum recreantur angues?

Quin et Prometheus et Pelopis parens
dulci laborem decipitur sono,

29 ff. utrumque ... dicere: dependent on mirantur, *listen with wonder at.* — sacro ... silentio: such as was observed during prayers and religious rites. The very song is divine. The phrase is reproduced by Milton *P. L.* 5, 555 'Worthy of sacred silence to be heard.' — sed magis: *i.e.* the common crowd is stirred more by Alcaeus' songs of battles and civil strife than by Sappho's softer strains. — exactos tyrannos: *the expulsion of tyrants.* Cf. 2, 4, 10. Alcaeus took part in the struggles of his native island against the tyrants. One of the fragments of his poems (No. 37) is an invective against the tyrant Pittacus; another (No. 20) a triumphant ode over Myrsilus' death. Cf. introductory note to 1, 37.

32. densum umeris: *crowded shoulder to shoulder*, in desire to hear. — bibit aure: a common phrase for eager attention. Prop. 4, 6, 8 *suspensis auribus ista bibam*; Ovid. *Trist.* 3, 5, 14 *auribus illa bibi;* cf. Verg. *A.* 4, 359 *auribus hausi.*

33. quid mirum, ubi: *i.e.* 'what wonder that the shades listened, when even fierce Cerberus and the Furies relaxed their rage.' — stupens: *charmed, lulled by.* — demittit auris: *i.e.* under the spell of Alcaeus' music he gives up his fierceness. — centiceps: possibly Horace had in mind the snakes about Cerberus' head. — recreantur: *find rest*, with this strophe cf. Vergil's account, *G.* 4, 481-483, of the power of Orpheus' song *quin ipsae stupuere domus atque intima Leti | Tartara caeruleosque implexae crinibus anguis | Eumenides tenuitque inhians tria Cerberus ora.*

37. quin et: introducing a still greater marvel. Cf. 1, 10, 13. — Prometheus: only Horace places Prometheus' punishment in the lower world. Cf. 2, 18, 35; *Epod.* 17, 67. He is probably chosen simply as typical of those who

nec curat Orion leones
aut timidos agitare lyncas.

suffered the severest punishments; or was Horace following Maecenas' *Prometheus?* — **Pelopis parens**: *Tantalus*.

38 ff. **laborem decipitur**: *are beguiled to forget their toil.* In sense the phrase is like *laborem fallere* S. 2, 2, 12. Probably **decipitur** is to be regarded as a middle. For the meaning of **labor**, cf. n. to *Epod.* 17, 64. —

Orion: Odysseus on his visit to the lower world found Orion still engaged in his favorite sport. *Od.* 11, 572 f. τὸν δὲ μέτ' Ὠρίωνα πελώριον εἰσενόησα | θῆρας ὁμοῦ εἰλεῦντα κατ' ἀσφοδελὸν λειμῶνα. Milton seems to have had vv. 33–40 in mind, *P. L.* 2, 552 ff. 'Their song was partial, but the harmony | Suspended Hell and took with ravishment | The thronging audience.

14

A lament on the fleeting character of life. 'Alas, good friend, do what we will, old age and death come on apace. No sacrifice can stay the hand of the pitiless lord of death; rich and poor alike must come unto his realm, and all thy efforts to avoid war, the sea, or fell disease are vain. Thou must leave all behind that thou holdest now most dear. Then thy stored wine, thy heir, worthier than thou, will waste.' In the last strophe Horace in negative fashion returns to his philosophy of life, 'Seize the pleasure of the passing hour, and do not waste your time in gathering wealth you do not use yourself. To-morrow we all die and another wastes our savings.'

The Postumus to whom the ode is addressed was an imaginary personage; at least the name was so used by Martial 2, 23, 1 f. *non dicam, licet usque me rogetis, | quis sit Postumus in meo libello*, and 5, 58, 7 f. *cras vives? hodie iam vivere, Postume, serum est: | ille sapit, quisquis, Postume, vixit heri*. Horace's thoughts frequently turned to death; but this and 4, 7 are his finest treatments of the theme. There is no indication of the date of composition. Metre, 68.

Eheu fugaces, Postume, Postume,
labuntur anni, nec pietas moram

1–4. **eheu**: the opening word is a sigh, which indicates the gloomy nature of the entire ode. The second word emphasizes the fleeting character of life; and the repetition of the proper name shows the poet's earnestness. — **labuntur**: *slip by*, before we notice

CARMINA [2, 14, 10

rugis et instanti senectae
adferet indomitaeque morti,
5 non si trecenis quotquot eunt dies,
amice, places inlacrimabilem
Plutona tauris, qui ter amplum
Geryonen Tityonque tristi

compescit unda, scilicet omnibus,
10 quicumque terrae munere vescimur,

it. Cf. Ovid. *Fasti* 6, 771 *tempora labuntur tacitisque senescimus annis.* — **pietas**: *i.e.* toward the gods, expanded below in vv. 5-7. — **rugis ... senectae ... morti**: note the climax. — **instanti**: cf. Sen. *Q. N. praef.* 3 *premit a tergo senectus.* Mimner. 5, 4 γῆρας ὑπὲρ κεφαλῆς αὐτίχ᾽ ὑπερκρέμαται. — **indomitae ... morti**: *i.e. indomabili*, the Homeric Ἀίδης τοι ἀμείλιχος ἠδ᾽ ἀδάμαστος (*Il.* 9, 158). Cf. also Aeschylus *Frg.* 161 μόνος θεῶν γὰρ θάνατος οὐ δώρων ἐρᾷ, | οὐδ᾽ ἄν τι θύων οὐδ᾽ ἐπισπένδων ἄνοις, | οὐδ᾽ ἔστι βωμὸς οὐδὲ παιωνίζεται. 'For alone among the gods death cares not for gifts: thou canst not stay him a whit by sacrifice or libation; no altar has he nor is he praised in paean hymns.'
5 f. **non si**: *no, not even if.* — **trecenis ... tauris**: *three hecatombs every day.* — **amice**: for the short anacrusis, cf. 2, 9, 5. — **places**: conative. — **inlacrimabilem**: *tearless*, not moved to tears. Cf. n. to 1, 3, 22.

The same adjective is passive 4, 9, 26.
7 f. **ter amplum**: a translation of the Greek τρισώματον, which Euripides *H. F.* 423 applies to Geryones. Cf. Verg. *A.* 8, 202 *tergemini ... Geryonae.* — **Geryonen**: the monster with three bodies whom Hercules slew and then drove off his cattle. For a vase painting illustrating the fight, see Baumeister, p. 662. — **Tityon**: the son of earth, who offered violence to Leto. Cf. Verg. *A.* 6, 595-600. — **tristi**: cf. n. to *triste lignum* 3, 13, 11; Verg. *G.* 4, 478 ff. *quos circum limus niger et deformis arundo | Cocyti tardaque palus inamabilis unda | alligat, et noviens Styx interfusa coercet.*
9 f. **scilicet omnibus**, etc.: *which all of us in very truth*; dat. of agent with enaviganda. — **quicumque terrae**, etc.: imitated from the Homeric phrases *Il.* 6, 142 βροτοὶ οἳ ἀρούρης καρπὸν ἔδουσιν, and *Od.* 8, 222 ὅσσοι νῦν βροτοί εἰσιν ἐπὶ χθονὶ σῖτον ἔδοντες. — **munere**: *bounty.*

enaviganda, sive reges
sive inopes erimus coloni.

Frustra cruento Marte carebimus
fractisque rauci fluctibus Hadriae,
15   frustra per autumnos nocentem
corporibus metuemus Austrum.

Visendus ater flumine languido
Cocytos errans et Danai genus
infame damnatusque longi
20   Sisyphus Aeolides laboris.

Linquenda tellus et domus et placens
uxor, neque harum quas colis arborum

11 f. **enaviganda**: an intensive compound formed by Horace to express the idea of sailing completely across — to the further shore of — the gloomy stream. — **reges**: the rich in contrast to the poor farmers (coloni). Cf. our term 'merchant-princes.' See also 1, 4, 14.

13 f. Notice the alliteration and assonance in this and the following line. — **frustra . . . frustra**: emphatic anaphora; *it is all in vain that we . . . , in vain*. Intr. 28c. — **carebimus**: *try to avoid*. — **rauci**: *i.e.* as the waves break on the shore.

15 f. **per autumnos**, etc.: particularly the latter part of August and the month of September when the Sirocco (**Auster**) blows. — **corporibus**: with both *nocentem* and *metuemus*. Intr. 100.

17 f. **ater ... Cocytus**: cf. Verg. *G.* 4, 478-80 quoted on v. 8 above, and *A.* 6, 132 *Cocytosque sinu labens circumvenit atro*. — **genus infame**: because they all, save Hypermestra, killed their husbands on the wedding night. Cf. 3, 11, 23 ff. and notes.

19 f. **damnatus . . . laboris**: the genitive of the sentence inflicted is here used after the analogy of the objective genitive of the crime. — **longi**: in the sense of *aeterni*. Cf. 2, 16, 30; 3, 11, 38. For an archaic vase painting illustrating the punishment of the Danaids and Sisyphus, see Baum. p. 1924.

21 f. Possibly Horace had in mind here Lucretius' beautiful verses, 3, 894 ff. *iamiam non domus accipiet te laeta neque uxor | optima nec dulces occurrent*

te praeter invisas cupressos
ulla brevem dominum sequetur.

25 Absumet heres Caecuba dignior
servata centum clavibus et mero
tinguet pavimentum superbo,
pontificum potiore cenis.

oscula nati | praeripere et tacita pectus dulcedine tangent. Cf. also Gray's *Elegy* 21 ff. 'For them no more the blazing hearth shall burn, | Or busy housewife ply her evening care; | No children run to lisp their sire's return, | Or climb his knees the envied kiss to share.' — **placens**: *beloved.* — **quas colis**: *thou now prizest.*

23 f. invisas cupressos: because the cypress is the sign of mourning. Cf. *Epod.* 5, 18 *cupressos funebris*; Whittier, 'Alas for him who never sees the stars shine through his cypress trees.' — **brevem**: *short-lived.* 'Your very trees outlive you.' Cf. 1, 4, 15 *vitae summa brevis spem nos vetat incohare longam,* and Tennyson's 'little lives of men.'

25. heres: the dreaded heir.

Cf. n. to 2, 3, 19 f. — **Caecuba**: cf. n. to 1, 20, 9. — **dignior**: because he knows how to use wealth. 'You hoard it' With this taunt Horace drives home his lesson of the folly of treasuring one's possessions too highly.

26 f. centum: an indefinite number. — **mero . . . superbo**: the very wine is conscious of its excellence and proud that it outlives man. Cf. Petron. 34 *eheu! ergo diutius vivit vinum quam homuncio.* — **tinguet**: in his riotous *commissatio.*

28. pontificum: whose dinners were proverbial for their luxury and splendor. Cf. 1, 37, 2 *Saliaribus . . . dapibus* and n. — **potiore cenis**: *better than that drunk at the,* etc. A compendious expression. Cf. n. to 2, 6, 14.

15

A protest against the increasing luxury of the time. 'Palaces and fish ponds now leave little ground for cultivation; vineyards and orchards have given way to shade trees and flower beds. It was very different in the good old days, when private fortunes were small and men's first care was for the state; then private houses were not great; public buildings and temples only were of marble.'

Such protests are common to all times of wealth and luxury. Another example is 3, 6. Augustus tried to restrain the growth of private extravagance, and to restore the agricultural prosperity of Italy. Some editors have wished, therefore, to connect this ode with the date (28 B.C.) at which Octavian assumed the duties of censor, and indeed it is quite possible that it was written at the emperor's request. The verses are stiff, and bear the marks of being made to order. The position here after 14, from which in some manuscripts it is not separated, is a natural one, for it continues the attack on the folly of great wealth. The ode is, however, wholly impersonal, not even the indefinite second person being used, and lacks the poetical quality of 14. Metre, 68.

> Iam pauca aratro iugera regiae
> moles relinquent; undique latius
>   extenta visentur Lucrino
>   stagna lacu, platanusque caelebs
> 5   evincet ulmos; tum violaria et
> myrtus et omnis copia narium

1 ff. Cf. with the the general sentiment of the ode Seneca *Epist.* 89, 21 *quousque nullus erit lacus, cui non villarum vestrarum fastigia immineant, nullum flumen, cuius non ripas aedificia vestra praetexant? . . . ubicumque in aliquem sinum litus curvabitur vos protinus fundamenta facietis, nec contenti solo, nisi quod manu feceritis, mare agetis introrsus* (cf. *C.* 2, 18; 3, 24). — **regiae moles**: *i.e.* the palaces of the rich. Cf. n. to 2, 14, 11, also 3, 29, 10, where Maecenas' city house is called *molem propinquam nubibus arduis*.

3 f. **visentur**: *will be seen with wonder.* — **Lucrino . . . lacu**: near Baiae, famous for its oysters and fish. Cf. n. to *Epod.* 2, 49. — **stagna**: *piscinae*, in which the fish dear to Roman epicures were raised. — **platanus caelebs**: during the last century B.C. the plane tree became a favorite for parks and gardens. Cf. 2, 11, 13. The thick shade which its broad leaves cast made it unsuited as a support for the vine — therefore called **caelebs**. Cf. n. to *Epod.* 2, 10. Martial, 3, 58, 3, names it *vidua platanus*.

5. **evincet**: *shall drive out.* — **violaria**: *violet beds;* with the myrtle — a flowering shrub — and other sweet-smelling flowers, typical of luxury.

6 ff. **omnis copia narium**: *all the wealth* (of flowers) *that fills the nostrils;* an intentionally artificial expression for *odor*, used here to hint at Horace's dislike for such elaborate flower gardens. — **olivetis**: lo-

spargent olivetis odorem
    fertilibus domino priori;

tum spissa ramis laurea fervidos
10   excludet ictus.   Non ita Romuli
    praescriptum et intonsi Catonis
        auspiciis veterumque norma.

Privatus illis census erat brevis,
    commune magnum; nulla decempedis
15   metata privatis opacam
        porticus excipiebat Arcton,

nec fortuitum spernere caespitem
    leges sinebant, oppida publico

cative ablative. — **fertilibus**: predicate, *that were productive.* With the preceding, cf. Quintilian's question, 8, 3, 8 *an ego fundum cultiorem putem, in quo mihi quis ostenderit lilia et violas et anemonas, fontes surgentes, quam ubi plena messis aut graves fructu vites erunt? sterilem platanum tonsasque myrtos quam maritam ulmum et uberes oleas praeoptaverim?*

9 f. **ramis**: instrumental abl. The laurel was trimmed into fanciful shapes, and grew thick and close (**spissa**). — **laurea**: sc. *arbor.* — **ictus**: sc. *solis.* — **non ita**, etc.: 'it was different in the good old days.'—**Romuli**: like **Catonis**, modifying **auspiciis**.

11. **praescriptum**: sc. *est.* — **Catonis**: Cato the Censor, who died 149 B.C., devoted his best efforts to an attempt to stem the modern Hellenizing tendencies of his time; as a sign of his conservatism he is said to be bearded, like Curius in 1, 12, 41. He became typical of the stern, old-fashioned Roman. — **auspiciis**: *the example.* The *auspicia* could be taken only by high magistrates, so that the sentence means —'when men like a Romulus or a Cato ruled the state.'

13 f. **census**: *income.* — **brevis**: *i.e.* the record of their property was short. — **nulla**, etc.: *i.e.* as nowadays. — **decempedis**: surveyors' rods. *perticae*, used in measuring the new-fashioned porticoes of private citizens. — **privatis**: grammatically connected with **decempedis**, but emphasizing the fact that these are private buildings.

16. **excipiebat**: *caught, i.e.* opened to the cool north.

17 f. **fortuitum**: the first chance turf that came to hand, opposed

            sumptu iubentes et deorum
20   templa novo decorare saxo.

to novo saxo v. 20.—caespitem: for building a simple altar (cf. 1, 19, 13) or for thatching roofs. Verg. *E.* 1, 69 *congestum caespite culmen.*—leges: *i.e.* the prescriptions of ancient ritual.—oppida: *i.e.* the public buildings.—publico sumptu: in contrast to the private luxury typified in 14-16.

20. novo...saxo: undoubtedly marble is meant, which came into use for private dwellings only in the last half-century before the empire. Pliny *N. H.* 36, 48 says that Mamurra, in the time of Julius Caesar, was the first Roman to use marble slabs for lining the walls of his house, but marble columns had been used in private houses for half a century before this date. On the changes in the appearance of Rome during Augustus' reign, cf. his famous statement (Suet. *Aug.* 28) *marmoream se relinquere (urbem), quam latericiam accepisset.*

16

A collection of *sententiae* on Horace's favorite theme: 'a contented spirit is beyond all other possessions.'

'Peace is the prayer of all men—the sailor on the stormy sea, the warlike Thracian and Mede. Peace thou canst not buy. Neither wealth nor power will drive away men's wretched cares. He only lives well who lives on little, undistressed by fear or greed. Why should we move from land to land and put forth our weak efforts? Care follows hard upon us. No, life is mingled sweet and bitter, and all things have their compensation. Perhaps the flitting hour gives me something thou hast not. For thee an hundred herds low, thou hast thy stud and royal purple; yet I possess my little farm, a slight inspiration for Greek verse, and the power to scorn the envious.'

The Grosphus here addressed is probably the same Pompeius Grosphus recommended by Horace, *Epist.* 1, 12, 22-24, to his friend Iccius (cf. introduction to 1, 29), when the latter was managing Agrippa's estates in Sicily. That Grosphus also had large possessions there is evident from vv. 33-37, but that he was still a man who could appreciate Horace's expansion of his life's text may be a fair conclusion from the character given him in the epistle mentioned above, *nil nisi verum orabit et aequum.*

The exact date of composition cannot be determined, but the mention of Thrace and the Medes may point to a date before 27 B.C. In

July of that year M. Licinius Crassus enjoyed a triumph over the Thracians and Getae. In any case the verses came from the time when Horace felt his happiness secured and his position as lyric poet sure, so that he could scorn those who grudged him his position. Metre, 69.

> Otium divos rogat in patenti
> prensus Aegaeo, simul atra nubes
> condidit lunam neque certa fulgent
>   sidera nautis;
>
> 5   otium bello furiosa Thrace,
> otium Medi pharetra decori,
> Grosphe, non gemmis neque purpura ve-
>   nale neque auro.
>
> Non enim gazae neque consularis
> 10   submovet lictor miseros tumultus

1 f. **otium**: *peace*, in its widest meaning — escape from the dangers of the storm, relief from war, and freedom from the anxiety that ambition brings. — **patenti**: *the open*. — **prensus**: *caught*, for the more common *deprensus*. — **simul**: cf. n. to 1, 4, 17.

3 f. **certa**: predicate, *with sure and certain light*. The constellations by which the ancient sailor directed his vessel are meant by the general term, **sidera**.

5 f. For the emphatic anaphora, see Intr. 28c. — **bello furiosa**, etc.: Thrace is called by Vergil *A.* 3, 13 *Mavortia terra*.

7. **purpura**: calling to mind the stripe on the praetexta of the Roman magistrates, or the 'royal purple' of kings; in either case symbolizing power. — **ve-nale**: for close connection between the third and fourth verses, see n. to 1, 2, 19. Intr. 69.

9 f. **gazae ... lictor**: repeating the thought of the two preceding verses — 'neither wealth nor power can free the anxious mind.' This is a common moral sentiment; the most famous expression of it is by Lucretius 2, 37-52. Cf. also Tibull. 3. 3, 21 *non opibus mentes hominum curaeque levantur*; | *nam Fortuna sua tempora lege regit*. — **submovet**: a technical term for clearing the road before a magistrate. or making a crowd 'move on.' Cf. Liv. 3, 48, 3 *i. lictor, submove turbam*. The figure is continued in **tumultus**.

mentis et curas laqueata circum
    tecta volantis.

Vivitur parvo bene cui paternum
splendet in mensa tenui salinum
15   nec levis somnos timor aut cupido
    sordidus aufert.

Quid brevi fortes iaculamur aevo
multa? Quid terras alio calentis
sole mutamus? Patriae quis exsul
20   se quoque fugit?

11. **laqueata ... tecta**: *paneled ceilings*, of the rich man's house, round which cares batlike flit. 'Wealth brings anxiety with it.' Cf. Sen. *H. O.* 646 f. *aurea rumpunt tecta quietem | vigilesque trahit purpura noctes.*

13 f. **vivitur**, etc.: sc. *ab eo; he lives well on little*, etc. — **bene**: *well and happily*. — **paternum ... salinum**: the one piece of family plate on his modest board is the sacred saltcellar kept brightly polished. In the old days of Rome's greatness a saltcellar and a plate for offerings to the gods were all the silver that a Fabricius or an Aemilius possessed. Val. Max. 4, 4, 3 *in C. Fabricii et Q. Aemilii Papi, principum saeculi sui, domibus argentum fuisse confitear oportet: uterque enim patellam deorum et salinum habuit.* The saltcellar is used by Persius 3, 24 ff. as typical of 'little and enough,' *sed rure paterno | est tibi far modicum, purum et sine labe salinum: | quid metuas?* Notice that Horace is commending not poverty, but small estate as the proper environment for happiness. It is the desirable *aurea mediocritas* again.

15. **levis somnos**: cf. n. to 2, 11, 8 *facilem somnum*, and to *Epod.* 2, 28. — **cupido**: always masculine in Horace, in other writers generally feminine except when personified.

17 f. **brevi ... aevo**: the juxtaposition of **brevi** and the ironical **fortes**, *so brave*, lends a certain concessive force to this ablative, *despite our life's brief span*. — **multa**: emphatically placed. — **quid ... mutamus**: sc. *patria*. For the construction, see Intr. 98.

20. **fūgit**: perfect, *has ever*, etc. With the sentiment cf. *Epist.* 1, 11, 27 *caelum, non animum mutant, qui trans mare currunt.*

Scandit aeratas vitiosa navis
Cura nec turmas equitum relinquit,
ocior cervis et agente nimbos
    ocior Euro.

25 Laetus in praesens animus quod ultra est
oderit curare, et amara lento
temperet risu: nihil est ab omni
    parte beatum.

Abstulit clarum cita mors Achillem,
30 longa Tithonum minuit senectus,
et mihi forsan tibi quod negarit
    porriget hora.

Sen. *Epist.* 28, 2 *quaeris, quare te fuga ista non adiuvet? tecum fugis;* and Emerson *Self-Reliance,* 'I pack my trunk . . . and at last wake up in Naples, and there beside me is the stern fact, the sad self, unrelenting, identical, that I fled from.'

21-24. An amplification of the preceding two verses — 'neither ship nor horse is swift enough to escape pursuing care.' The same idea is better expressed 3, 1, 37 ff. — **aeratas**: *bronze-beaked.* — **vitiosa**: *carking, morbid.* — **ocior . . . ocior**: emphasizing the swiftness with which care moves. Intr. 28c.

25. 'Take with joy the present hour, do not be "careful" of tomorrow.' Cf. with the injunction contained in the subject **laetus . . . animus**, 3, 8, 27 f. *dona praesentis cape laetus horae ac | linque severa.* — **oderit**: subjunctive, *shrink from.* — **lento**: *quiet,* as befits a man who knows how to meet life's changes.

29 ff. Concrete illustration of the general statement in v. 27 f. — **clarum**: *glorious.* Notice its position next to **cita mors**, 'for all his glory death came quickly.'

30. The opposite fate of Tithonus. Cf. n. to 1, 28, 8. — **longa**: *i.e. aeterna,* as 2, 14. 19.

31 f. **et mihi**: Horace here, as frequently, drives home his statements by personal illustrations at the close. The following two strophes give the details of the bold comparison between himself and Grosphus. The contrast is modestly put, but the poet's pride rings in the last words, **malignum spernere volgus.** — **tibi**: with **negarit**. — **hora**: *the chance hour.*

> Te greges centum Siculaeque circum
> mugiunt vaccae, tibi tollit hinnitum
> 35 apta quadrigis equa, te bis Afro
> murice tinctae
>
> vestiunt lanae: mihi parva rura et
> spiritum Graiae tenuem Camenae
> Parca non mendax dedit et malignum
> 40 spernere volgus.

33–36. te ... tibi ... te : making Grosphus' wealth prominent in comparison with Horace's parva rura. — centum : like *mille* a round number. — hinnitum : *whinny.* For the hypermetric verse, see Intr. 69. — equa : cf. Verg. *G.* 1, 59 *Eliadum palmas ... equarum.* — bis ... tinctae : *twice dyed,* the Greek δίβαφι, a technical term. Cf. *Epod.* 12, 21 *muricibus Tyriis iteratae vellera lanae.* — Afro murice : the shellfish from which the scarlet dye was obtained was found on the coast of Africa as well as on the southern shore of the Peloponnesus.

37 f. Note the modest parva, tenuem. For the meaning of the latter here, cf. 1, 6, 9 *nec conamur tenues grandia.* — spiritum : *inspiration.* — Camenae : identified completely with the Greek Μοῦσα. Cf. 1, 12, 39.

39 f. non mendax : *who does not deceive, true.* A stock epithet. Cf. *C. S.* 25 *veraces cecinisse Parcae.* Pers. 5, 48 *Parca tenax veri.* — spernere : in the same construction as rura, spiritum. Horace's rise in the world aroused much envy and ill-natured comment among those of better birth but poorer talents. That he was sensitive to this is shown by his references here and elsewhere. and his pride is most natural. Cf. 2, 20, 4 *invidia maior,* and n.

17

The following ode seems to have been called forth by Maecenas' gloomy forebodings that his end was near. He was a great sufferer from insomnia and fever, but shrank from death. The verses open with a rebuke, but presently become an assurance of the deepest affection: the very gods have willed that the poet shall not outlive his friend. Moreover, the hour set by the Fates is not yet come, else Maecenas had not recovered from his last illness and Faunus had not saved Horace from the falling tree. So then they both must offer to the gods the sacrifices due.

Horace's prophecy was fulfilled, for he outlived Maecenas but a short time; both died in 8 B.C. The date of the occasions referred to in 25 ff. is 30 B.C. Cf. 1, 20, 3 ff.; 2, 13. The ode was probably written soon after. Metre, 68.

> Cur me querellis exanimas tuis?
> Nec dis amicum est nec mihi te prius
>   obire, Maecenas, mearum
>   grande decus columenque rerum.
>
> 5 A, te meae si partem animae rapit
> maturior vis, quid moror altera,
>   nec carus aeque nec superstes
>   integer? Ille dies utramque
>
>   ducet ruinam. Non ego perfidum
> 10 dixi sacramentum: ibimus, ibimus,

1 f. **exanimas**: *half kill me.* Cf. *Epod.* 14, 5 *occidis saepe rogando.* — **amicum est**: the Greek φίλον ἐστί, equivalent to *placet.*

3 f. **obire**: sc. *diem supremum.* — **grande decus columenque**: cf. 1, 1, 2 *o et praesidium et dulce decus meum.* The figure is old, *e.g.* Pindar *O.* 2, 89 calls Hector Τροίας κίονα, but Horace invented this phrase, which in his verse is no mere formal expression. It was adopted by the later poets, Ausonius, Prudentius, and Apollinaris Sidonius. Cf. *e.g.* the last's *C.* 23, 2 *Consenti columen decusque morum.* — **mearum . . . rerum**: τὰ ἐμά, *me and all I have.*

5 f. **partem animae**: sc. *alteram, i.e.* the half. Cf. the term of affection applied to Vergil 1, 3, 8 *animae dimidium meae.* — ma-turior: *too early, untimely.* — **vis**: the same as 2, 13, 19 *improvisa leti vis.* — **altera**: sc. *pars,* predicate to **moror**.

7 f. **carus**: *i.e. mihi.* — **aeque**: 'as before thou wert snatched away.' — **superstes**: modifying both **carus** and **integer**. — **integer**: for half his life will then be gone. — **utramque**: with possessive force, equivalent to *utramque nostrum ruinam.* Cf. the full form v. 21 below.

9. **ducet**: with a reminiscence of the figure in **columen**, *will drag down.* Cf. *traho* in the same sense Verg. *A.* 2, 465 (*turris*) *elapsa repente ruinam cum sonitu trahit.* — **non ego**: both emphatic. Cf. n. to 1, 18, 11. The negative affects **perfidum** alone.

10 f. **dixi sacramentum**: the technical term for the soldier's

utcumque praecedes, supremum
carpere iter comites parati.

Me nec Chimaerae spiritus igneae
nec, si resurgat, centimanus Gyas
15   divellet umquam; sic potenti
Iustitiae placitumque Parcis.

Seu Libra seu me Scorpios adspicit
formidulosus, pars violentior
natalis horae, seu tyrannus
20   Hesperiae Capricornus undae,

oath of allegiance to his commander, by which he bound himself to follow wherever he might lead. — **ibimus, ibimus**: the repetition marks Horace's earnestness. Intr. 28a. — **utcumque**: temporal, as always in Horace. Cf. 1, 17, 10.

13 f. **Chimaerae**: cf. n. to 1, 27, 23. — **igneae**: cf. Pindar *O*, 13, 90 χίμαιραν πῦρ πνέοισαν. — **si resurgat**: *i.e.* from beneath the earth to confront me. — **Gyas**: like Briareus (*Il.* 1, 401-405) a hundred-handed giant, son of Uranus and Earth.

15 f. **divellet**: sc. *a te.* — **Iustitiae**: the Greek Themis. — **placitumque**: for the position of the conjunction, see Intr. 31.

17 ff. 'It matters not what stars presided over my natal hour, our horoscopes agree in marvelous fashion.' This reference to astrology is an indulgence to Maecenas' belief in the art, for Horace had no faith in the *numeri* of the Babylonians (1, 11). — **Scorpios . . . formidulosus**: the adjective is apt, for under this sign warriors were born. Cf. Manil. 4, 220 f. *in bellum ardentis animos et Martia castra | efficit* (sc. *Scorpios*) *et multum gaudentem sanguine civem.* Libra, however, gave a more favorable destiny. Cf. Manil. 4, 548 *felix aequato genitus sub pondere Librae!* — **adspicit**: the present is used since astrologers taught that the constellation which presided over the child's birth affected him through life. — **pars violentior**: *the member* (any one of the three constellations named) *with greater power.* — **tyrannus**, etc.: the various quarters of the earth were assigned to the different signs of the zodiac; the system of astrology current in the early empire gave Capricornus the western part of the world. Cf. Manil. 4, 791 ff. *tu, Capricorne, regis, quicquid sub sole cadente | est positum, gelidamque Helicen quod tangit ab illo, | Hispanas gentes et quot fert Gallia dives*

utrumque nostrum incredibili modo
consentit astrum: te Iovis impio
   tutela Saturno refulgens
      eripuit volucrisque fati

25   tardavit alas, cum populus frequens
laetum theatris ter crepuit sonum;
   me truncus inlapsus cerebro
      sustulerat, nisi Faunus ictum

dextra levasset, Mercurialium
30   custos virorum.   Reddere victimas

21 f. utrumque, etc.: cf. n. to v. 8 above. — **consentit**: the passage is imitated by Persius 5, 45 f. *non equidem hoc dubites, amborum foedere certo | consentire dies et ab uno sidere duci.* — **te**: the contrasted **me** follows v. 27. 'Thou art under the protection of supreme Jove.' Possibly in Maecenas' horoscope Jupiter was in the ascendant. — **impio . . . Saturno**: connect with both **refulgens** and **eripuit**. According to the astrology of the time Saturn's influence was baneful. Cf. Prop. 5, 1, 84 *grave Saturni sidus in omne caput*; and our 'jovial' and 'saturnine.' — **refulgens**: *flashing out against.* Jupiter offsets Saturn's power to harm.

24. volucris: with **alas**. — **fati**: here equivalent to *mortis*. Cf. S. 2, 1, 58 *seu mors atris circumvolat alis.*

25 f. cum . . . crepuit: the date was 30 B.C. For the occasion, see n. to 1, 20, 4. — **theatris**: locative abl. — **ter**: a stock number. Cf. Prop. 4, 9, 4 *Camenae . . . manibus faustos ter crepuere sonos.*

27 f. me truncus, etc.: cf. 2, 13. — **sustulerat**: the indicative emphasizes the certainty of Horace's fate which was suddenly averted by Faunus. Cf. 3, 16, 3.

28 f. Faunus: the kindly woodland spirit, who loved to visit Horace's farm and to care for his flocks (1, 17), is named here as protector. The Muses hold this position 3, 4, 27; Liber 3, 8, 7. — **Mercurialium**, etc.: Mercury as god of speech and inventor of the lyre (3, 11, 1 ff.) is here made the guardian of poets. Ordinarily the phrase means the devotees of Mercury, the god of gain, as S. 2, 3, 24 f. *hortos egregiasque domos mercarier unus | cum lucro noram: unde frequentia Mercuriale | inposuere mihi cognomen compita.*

30. reddere: *to pay,* because the offering vowed is due the gods.

aedemque votivam memento;
nos humilem feriemus agnam.

Cf. 2, 7, 17 *ergo obligatam redde Iovi dapem*. — **victimas**: *i.e.* many large cattle.

32. **humilem ... agnam**: in playful reference to the difference in their estate. So Horace says (4, 2, 53 f.) to his rich friend Julius Antonius *te decem tauri totidemque vaccae, | me tener solvet vitulus*.

18

'No lordly pile or fortune great is mine, but a kind poetic gift, a little farm, are all that I possess. 'Tis quite enough for me. But you, though life is insecure, still build your palaces and grudge the very sea its shore; you drive your poor clients from their homes that you may satisfy your greed for land. Your sure home is the halls of Death; Earth's doors open for rich and poor alike. No bribes move the grim ferryman.'

This ode handles again Horace's favorite theme — the vanity of riches and ambition, the wisdom of the golden mean. The same sentiments are expressed 1, 31; 2, 16; 3, 1, 40-48. 24, 1 ff. As frequently elsewhere he takes his own case as an illustration of the ideal lot, in which man is content with his moderate estate, and contrasts it with that of the rich man whose greed defies the sacred laws of nature and of man. Horace has no individual in mind, but with his fondness for concrete statement gives his verses a dramatic turn by the direct form of address. His model may have been a poem of Bacchylides. *Frg.* 21 Bl. οὐ βοῶν πάρεστι σώματ', οὔτε χρυσός. | οὔτε πορφύρεοι τάπητες. | ἀλλὰ θυμὸς εὐμενής | Μοῦσά τε γλυκεῖα, καὶ βοιωτίοισιν | ἐν σκύφοισιν οἶνος ἡδύς. The date of composition is uncertain. Metre (only here), 82.

Non ebur neque aureum
mea renidet in domo lacunar,

1-5. Horace has in mind the splendid *atria* adorned with rare marbles which the rich had begun to build toward the end of the Republic. Cf. n. to 2, 15, 20. — **ebur**: equivalent to the prose *eburneum*; ivory and gold were used to adorn the panels (*lacunaria*) of the atrium. Cf. Lucr. 2, 27 f. *nec domus argento fulget auroque renidet | nec citharae reboant laqueata aurataque tecta*.

non trabes Hymettiae
    premunt columnas ultima recisas
5 Africa, neque Attali
    ignotus heres regiam occupavi,
nec Laconicas mihi
    trahunt honestae purpuras clientae;
at fides et ingeni
10   benigna vena est, pauperemque dives
me petit: nihil supra
    deos lacesso nec potentem amicum
largiora flagito,
    satis beatus unicis Sabinis.

3 f. The architraves of this splendid atrium are made of the bluish white marble from Mt. Hymettus; the columns of yellow *giallo antico* from Numidia.

5 f. neque Attali, etc.: the inheritance of great fortunes by persons not related to the testator was already known in Horace's day. In the following century inheritance hunting became a business. The ancient commentators believed that Horace here expressed his disapproval of the inheritance by the Romans of King Attalus' wealth in 133 B.C. Whether this be true or not, it is certain that many of the conservative Romans dated the introduction of luxury and the consequent degeneracy at Rome from this time. — **ignotus**: *i.e.* to the testator. The heir has no right to the fortune he greedily seizes. — **occupavi**: note the greed expressed in this word.

7 f. 'Nor am I so rich that I have high-born clients to spin me robes dyed with the purple.' — **Laconicas**: the murex from which the purple dye was obtained was found in great abundance on the shore of the island Cythera and along the Laconian coast.

9 f. at: marking the sharp transition to what the poet does possess. — **benigna**: *kindly*. — **pauperemque**, etc.: instead of going to the rich man's house to give him the morning greeting (*salutatio*), Horace is visited in his humble home by the rich who honor his poetic talent.

12. lacesso: *vex with my demands*; with two accusatives as a verb of asking. — **amicum**: Maecenas, as is shown by v. 14.

14. satis beatus: *enriched enough*; beatus has here an original participial sense. Cf. *Epod.* 1, 31 f. *satis superque me benignitas tua* |

15   Truditur dies die
          novaeque pergunt interire lunae:
      tu secunda marmora
          locas sub ipsum funus, et sepulcri
      immemor struis domos,
20   marisque Bais obstrepentis urges
      submovere litora,
          parum locuples continente ripa.
      Quid quod usque proximos
          revellis agri terminos et ultra
25   limites clientium
          salis avarus?   Pellitur paternos

ditavit. — **unicis Sabinis**: *my one dear Sabine farm.* For this meaning of unicus, cf. 3, 14, 5 *unico marito.*

15 ff. 'Time hurries on, and yet you are unmindful of your approaching end.' — **truditur**: cf. *Epod.* 17, 25 *urget diem nox et dies noctem*, and also Petron. 45 *quod hodie non est, cras erit: sic vita truditur.* — **interire**: Intr. 107.

17 f. tu: emphatic, *still you.* — **secanda ... locas**: a technical expression for letting out a contract; the work to be done being expressed by the gerundive. — **marmora**: *i.e.* slabs to adorn the walls. Cf. n. to 2, 15, 20. — **sub**: almost with concessive force, 'though you are on the very brink of.'

19. domos: in contrast to **sepulcri**, — 'you should be thinking of your tomb.'

20 ff. Bais: dat. with **obstrepentis**. The town, situated about ten miles northwest of Naples, was a favorite resort of the Romans of this time. — **urges submovere**: *strive to push out.* The rich man is not content with the natural shore line, but must push out his seaside villa into the very sea. Seneca, *de tranquil.* 3, 7, uses the same expression as typifying luxury, *incipiemus aedificia alia ponere, alia subvertere et mare summovere.* — **parum**: cf. n. to 1, 12, 59. — **continente ripa**: abl. abs., *so long as the shore restrains you.*

23 ff. quid quod: a rhetorical transition to a new point; **quid** directing the attention to the substantive clause that follows. Cf. *Epod.* 1, 5 *quid nos.* — **usque**: *still*, used to express the continuation and repetition of the action. — **revellis**: a strong word to express the man's unscrupulous greed. Cf. **salis** v. 26. The ordinary *movere, exarare* would be colorless here. To move

in sinu ferens deos
    et uxor et vir sordidosque natos.
Nulla certior tamen
30   rapacis Orci fine destinata
aula divitem manet
    erum. Quid ultra tendis? Aequa tellus
pauperi recluditur
    regumque pueris, nec satelles Orci
35 callidum Promethea
    revexit auro captus. Hic superbum

the boundary stone without warrant was an act of the greatest impiety. Cf. Paul. p. 368 *Numa Pompilius statuit eum qui terminum exarasset et ipsum et boves sacros (accursed) esse*; and *Deuteronomy*, 27, 17 'Cursed be he that removeth his neighbour's landmark.' — **ultra limites**, etc.: the sacred duty of patron toward client likewise has no weight with such a man. The laws of the Twelve Tables condemned the patron who should do his client wrong, PATRONVS SI CLIENTI FRAVDEM FECERIT, SACER ESTO.

26 ff. salis: cf. revellis v. 24 and 1, 3, 24 *transiliunt*. Horace may have seen an eviction like this in his own district. — **pellitur**: for the number, see Intr. 101. — **paternos ... deos**: the little images of his household gods are all that the evicted client now possesses. — **sordidos**: *ragged*.

29. tamen: 'in spite of all thy wealth and unrestrained greed, no palace is so sure for thee as Orcus' hall.' — **fine ... destinata**: to be taken together; ablative with certior. It is the end which Orcus fixes; the Greek θανάτοιο τελευτή. finis is feminine only here and *Epod.* 17, 36.

30. rapacis Orci: the adjective is emphatic — the rapacity of Orcus outdoes that of the greedy rich at last.

31 f. divitem ... erum: in sharp contrast to the position which he will presently hold. 'Now thou art rich and lord, but in Orcus' home thy riches will not help thee.' — **ultra**: *i.e.* 'strive to gain more than thou now possessest.' — **aequa**: *impartially, without distinction*. Cf. 1, 4. 13 f. *pallida mors aequo pulsat pede pauperum tabernas | regumque turris*.

34 ff. pueris: equivalent to *filiis*; for the metre, cf. Intr. 56. — **nec satelles Orci**, etc.: an attempt by Prometheus to bribe Charon to ferry him back is referred to only here. Cf. n. to 2, 13, 37. — **callidum**: predicate, *for all his clever-*

Tantalum atque Tantali
   genus coercet, hic levare functum
pauperem laboribus
40   vocatus atque non vocatus audit.

ness; imitated from the Greek αἰολόμητις, ἀγκυλομήτης, epithets applied to Prometheus.
37 ff. **Tantali genus**: Pelops, Atreus, Agamemnon, and Orestes. — **levare**: Intr. 107. — **functum... laboribus**: *done with life's toils.* Cf. the Greek θανόντα καὶ πόνων πεπαυμένον.

40. Cf. Aesop's fable, 'Death and the Old Man,' and Suidas *s.v.* καλούμενος· καλούμενος καὶ ἄκλητος ὁ θεὸς παρέσται. Horace gives the phrase a somewhat different turn in applying it to the poor. Note the oxymoron in **non vocatus audit**. Cf. the opposite 3, 7, 21 f. *scopulis surdior Icari voces audit.*

19

In dithyrambic strains Horace hymns the power of Bacchus. He pretends that he has unexpectedly discovered the god in a retired spot, and then filled with a divine frenzy bursts into song, celebrating the deeds and attributes of the divinity who has inspired him. Much of the ode was probably suggested by Euripides' *Bacchae.* It may be compared with the praise of Mercury 1, 10; cf. also the beginning of 3, 25. The date of composition is uncertain. Metre, 68.

Bacchum in remotis carmina rupibus
   vidi docentem, credite posteri,
      Nymphasque discentis et auris
         capripedum Satyrorum acutas.

1 f. **remotis...rupibus**: *i.e.* far from the busy paths of men. The lonely mountain tops are Bacchus' favorite haunt. Cf. Soph. *O. T.* 1105 ὁ Βακχεῖος θεὸς ναίων ἐπ' ἄκρων ὀρέων. — **carmina**: *hymns*, dithyrambic verses in his honor.
2 ff. Cf. 1, 1, 31. — **Nymphas**: who nursed the infant Bacchus. — **auris ...acutas**: *the pricked ears;* indicating the eagerness with which they listen, rather than calling attention to the shape of the satyrs' ears. — **capripedum**: the characteristics of Pan (τραγόπους, αἰγιπόδης, τραγοσκελής) and the Panisci are here transferred to the satyrs, as by Lucretius 4, 580 f. *haec loca capripedes satyros nymphasque tenere* | *finitimi fingunt.*

Euhoe, recenti mens trepidat metu
plenoque Bacchi pectore turbidum
   laetatur; euhoe, parce Liber,
      parce gravi metuende thyrso!

Fas pervicacis est mihi Thyiadas
vinique fontem lactis et uberes
   cantare rivos atque truncis
      lapsa cavis iterare mella;

5 f. The sight of the god has filled the poet with mingled fear and joy and raised him to ecstasy, in which he joins in the Bacchanal cry **euhoe, euhoe** (εὐοῖ). Cf. 2, 11, 17. — **trepidat**: the sight of a divinity was always fearful to mortals. Cf. *Il*. 20, 131 χαλεποὶ δὲ θεοὶ φαίνεσθαι ἐναργεῖς. — **pleno...pectore**: the god possesses him fully. Cf. 3, 25, 1 *quo me, Bacche, rapis tui plenum?* Iuv. 7, 62 *satur est cum dicit Horatius euoe*. — **turbidum**: accusative expressing the manner of his joy; cf. 2, 12, 14 *lucidum fulgentis oculos*.

7 f. **parce...parce**: in eager appeals to the god to spare him the maddening touch of the thyrsus. — **gravi metuende thyrso**: cf. 1, 12, 23 *metuende certa Phoebe sagitta*.

9. **fas...est**, etc.: without further warning the ecstatic poet begins his song, for the vision has given him certain inspiration. — **pervicacis**: *the never tiring, persistent*. Cf. *Epod*. 17, 14 where the adjective is applied to Achilles. — **Thyiadas**: properly the women who celebrated the ὄργια in honor of the god; from θύω, 'to rush wildly.'

10 ff. Wine, milk, and honey are the signs of Bacchus' fructifying power. The verses were probably suggested by Euripides' *Bacchae* 142 f. ῥεῖ δὲ γάλακτι πέδον, ῥεῖ δ' οἴνῳ, ῥεῖ δὲ μελισσᾶν | νέκταρι, also 706 ff. ἄλλη δὲ νάρθηκ' ἐς πέδον καθῆκε γῆς. | καὶ τῇδε κρήνην ἐξανῆκ' οἴνου θεός· | ὅσαις δὲ λευκοῦ πώματος πόθος παρῆν, | ἄκροισι δακτύλοισι διαμῶσαι χθόνα | γάλακτος ἑσμοὺς εἶχον· ἐκ δὲ κισσίνων | θύρσων γλυκεῖαι μέλιτος ἔσταζον ῥοαί. 'One in earth's bosom planted her reed-wand. | And up there-through the God a wine fount sent: | And whoso fain would drink white-foaming draughts, | Scarred with their finger-tips the breasts of earth, | And milk gushed forth unstinted: dripped the while | Sweet streams of honey from their ivy-staves.' (Way.) So the children of Israel were promised *Exod*. 3, 8 'a good land and a large — a land flowing with milk and honey.' — **truncis...mella**: cf. Horace's

fas et beatae coniugis additum
stellis honorem tectaque Penthei
    disiecta non leni ruina
        Thracis et exitium Lycurgi.

Tu flectis amnis, tu mare barbarum,
tu separatis uvidus in iugis
    nodo coerces viperino
        Bistonidum sine fraude crinis.

Tu, cum parentis regna per arduum
cohors Gigantum scanderet impia,

picture, *Epod.* 16, 47, of the Fortunate Isles, to which he exhorts his countrymen to flee, *mella cava manant ex ilice.* So Vergil says, *E.* 4, 30, in naming the blessings of the golden age that is about to come, *et durae quercus sudabunt roscida mella.* — **iterare**: a variant on *cantare,* equivalent to *narrare.*

13. **coniugis**: Ariadne, blessed (**beatae**) by becoming Bacchus' consort. — **additum . . . honorem**: her crown, the wedding gift of Venus, was set among the constellations. — **Penthei**: king of Thebes, who tried to hinder the Theban women in their worship, but was torn in pieces by them; and his palace was overthrown by an earthquake. His death and the attendant disasters form the subject of Euripides' *Bacchae.* — **Thracis . . . Lycurgi**: who drove from Thrace Bacchus and his nurse, but was punished with blindness and early death.

17. **tu . . . tu . . . tu**: the triple anaphora indicates the poet's rising ardor and forms a climax to **fas . . . fas . . .** above. The god's power extends over all nature. Horace probably refers to the story of Bacchus' Indian travels, for Nonnus 12, 123 ff. says that at the touch of his thyrsus the Hydaspes and Orontes retreated, and let him pass dry shod. — **flectis**: *i.e.* 'by thy command.' — **mare barbarum**: the Persian Gulf. Cf. Sen. *H. F.* 903 *adsit Lycurgi domitor et rubri maris.*

18 ff. **separatis**: equivalent to *remotis,* v. 1. — **uvidus**: *i.e. madidus,* βρεχθείς, with wine. Cf. 1, 7, 22 *uda Lyaeo tempora.* — **Bistonidum**: Thracian maenads who join in the bacchanal rout. — **sine fraude**: *without harming them,* archaic for *sine noxa.* Cf. *C. S.* 41 ff. *cui per ardentem sine fraude Troiam castus Aeneas . . . munivit iter.*

21 ff. **tu**: more effective than a conjunction. Intr. 29. — **cum parentis**, etc.: according to a post-

Rhoetum retorsisti leonis
   unguibus horribilique mala,

25 quamquam choreis aptior et iocis
   ludoque dictus non sat idoneus
     pugnae ferebaris; sed idem
        pacis eras mediusque belli.

   Te vidit insons Cerberus aureo
30   cornu decorum, leniter atterens
     caudam, et recedentis trilingui
        ore pedes tetigitque crura.

Hesiodic myth Bacchus, with Hercules, gave victory to the gods in their battle against the giants in the Phlegraean fields. The story of this attempt by the giants to storm heaven was confused with the older one of the Titans, if indeed it did not owe its origin to it. — **retorsisti**: alliterative with **Rhoetum**, expressing the force with which the giant was thrown back. — **leonis**: the god took on the lion's form, as when he was beset by pirates, who tried to make him captive. *Hom. Hymn* 7, 44.

25 ff. Bacchus' double nature often appears. — **quamquam**: corrective, *and yet*, with **ferebaris**. — **choreis... dictus**: sc. *a diis*, giving the reason for the gods' disbelief in his prowess. — **sed idem**: *still thou wast the same.* — **mediusque**: for the position of -que, see Intr. 31. — **belli**: with **medius**, the earliest example of this construction imitated from the Greek. It was employed by later poets, *e.g.* Ovid. *Met.* 6, 409 *qui locus est iuguli medius summique lacerti.*

29 ff. te vidit, etc.: when Bacchus descended to Hades to bring back his mother Semele. — **te**: cf. n. on tu v. 21. — **insons**: predicate, *and did no harm to thee.* — **aureo cornu**, etc.: the Greek χρυσόκερως, κερασφόρος. Here the golden drinking-horn is meant, rather than the horn as an emblem of power. — **atterens**: *wagging.* — **recedentis**: *as thou withdrewest;* opposed to the god's entrance, implied in **te vidit**. — **trilingui**: cf. 2, 13, 34 where Cerberus is *centiceps.* — **tetigitque**: Intr. 31.

20

In an allegory Horace prophesies his own immortality. He is not to die, but shall be transformed into a swan and fly from the Stygian wave to the confines of the world. His description of the change which he feels coming on him is given in such detail (9–12) as to rob the poem, for the modern reader at least, of much of the charm that it would otherwise possess. The identification of the poet's song with the flight of a bird was common in antiquity, as it is to-day. Cf. *e.g.* Theog. 237 ff., 1097 f.; Pind. *N.* 6, 47 ff.; Eurip. *Frg.* 911 N.; Theoc. 7. 47.

Apparently Horace wrote this ode after his collection in three books was practically complete, intending it as an epilogue to his lyric verse. Fortunately his second attempt, which now stands at the end of the third book, was far superior, so that he relegated these verses to their present position. Metre, 68.

> Non usitata nec tenui ferar
> penna biformis per liquidum aethera
>   vates, neque in terris morabor
>   longius, invidiaque maior
> 5 urbes relinquam. Non ego pauperum
> sanguis parentum, non ego quem vocas,

1 ff. non usitata, etc.: *no ordinary or weak;* for his verse was in new forms and his poetic gift was great. — **biformis**: in a literal sense, both bard and bird. The familiarity of the ancients with the idea of combining human forms with those of beasts, *e.g.* the centaur, minotaur (called *biformis* Verg. *A.* 6, 25) no doubt gave them a different feeling for Horace's concept than we can possibly have. Porphyrio too subtly interprets the adjective to mean writer in both hexameter and lyric measure. — **liquidum**: *clear*, as Verg. *G.* 1, 404 *apparet liquido sublimis in aere Nisus.* — **vates**: in its original sense of *inspired bard.* Cf. n. to 1, 1, 35.

4. invidia maior: the phrase may have been borrowed from the Greek. Cf. Callim. *Epigr.* 21, 4 ὁ δ' ἥεισεν κρέσσονα βασκανίης. In his earlier years, before his position as lyric poet was established, Horace suffered from the jibes of those who envied him Maecenas' favor. Cf. *S.* 1, 6, 46 f. *quem rodunt omnes libertino patre natum, | nunc quia sim tibi, Maecenas, convictor.* When his fame was certain he took no little satisfaction in scorning those who once scorned him. Cf. 2, 16, 39 f.

dilecte Maecenas, obibo,
  nec Stygia cohibebor unda.

Iam iam residunt cruribus asperae
10 pelles et album mutor in alitem
  superne nascunturque leves
  per digitos umerosque plumae.

Iam Daedaleo notior Icaro
visam gementis litora Bospori
15 Syrtisque Gaetulas canorus
  ales Hyperboreosque campos.

5 f. **urbis**: the plural is more effective than the simple *terram* would have been. — **non ego ... non ego**: intensive; Intr. 28c. — **pauperum sanguis parentum**: Horace never was ashamed of his low birth, but took a pardonable pride in his success in raising himself to an honored position by his own merits. — **vocas**: *invitest.*

9 ff. These — to us certainly — tasteless verses may have been suggested by Eurip. *Frg.* 911 N. χρύσεαι δή μοι πτέρυγες περὶ νώτῳ | καὶ τὰ σειρήνων πτερόεντα πέδιλα [ἁρμόζεται]. | βάσομαι τ' εἰς αἰθέριον πόλον ἀρθεὶς | Ζηνὶ προσμείξων. 'Golden wings are fastened on my back and I have on the Sirens' winged sandals. I shall go aloft to the aethereal sky to be with Zeus.' But Horace has gone far beyond his model. — **iam iam**: cf. *Epod.* 17, 1. — **cruribus**: abl. of place. — **asperae pelles**: the horny skin of the bird's legs and claws into which his human skin is settling. — **supernĕ**: with short ultima as in Lucretius and *Epist.* 2, 3, 4.

11. **lēves**: in contrast to *asperae.*

13 f. **iam**: *presently.* — **notior Icaro**: who gave his name to a sea. Cf. Ovid. *Fasti* 4, 283 f. (*mare*) *Icarium, lapsas ubi perdidit alas | Icarus et vastae nomina fecit aquae.* — **visam**, etc.: 'my fame will extend to the limits of the world.' — **gementis**: cf. Verg. *A.* 5, 806 *cum ... gemerent repleti amnes.* Soph. *Antig.* 592 στόνῳ βρέμουσι δ' ἀντιπλῆγες ἀκταί. Tennyson, *In Mem.* 35 'the moanings of the homeless sea.'

15 f. **canorus ales**: the swans are called by Callimachus *Hymn. in Del.* 252 Μουσάων ὄρνιθες, ἀοιδότατοι πετεηνῶν. Vergil *E.* 9, 29 says to his friend, *Vare, tuum nomen, ... cantantes sublime ferent ad sidera cycni.* — **Hyperboreos**: beyond the North Wind was a mythical folk said to live in unbroken peace and happiness. But Horace means only the distant North.

Me Colchus et qui dissimulat metum
Marsae cohortis Dacus et ultimi
  noscent Geloni, me peritus
    discet Hiber Rhodanique potor.

Absint inani funere neniae
luctusque turpes et querimoniae;
  compesce clamorem ac sepulcri
    mitte supervacuos honores.

17 f. 'The barbarous peoples in the East shall learn to know my works as well as the Romanized Spaniard and Gaul.' — **me**: cf. n. to 2, 19, 21. — **Marsae cohortis**: the Marsi were one of the bravest Italian peoples. Cf. n. to 1, 2, 39.

19 f. Geloni: cf. n. to 2, 9, 23. — **peritus Hiber**, etc.: that Spain and Gaul had made great advances in Roman civilization in Horace's day is shown by the fact that in the first century A.D. the former country furnished Rome with her most prominent writers — the two Senecas, Lucan, probably Valerius Flaccus, Columella, Mela, Quintilian, Martial, and others; the latter province with orators and rhetoricians. — **Rhodani potor**: cf. 3, 10, 1 *extremum Tanain si biberes, Lyce*, and *Il.* 2, 825 πίνοντες ὕδωρ μέλαν Αἰσήποιο, Τρῶες. The circumlocution is frequently employed by Apoll. Sid. *e.g. Epist.* 4, 17 *potor Mosellae*.

21 ff. Possibly suggested by Ennius' famous epitaph, *nemo me dacrumis decoret nec funera fletu | faxit. cur? volito vivos per ora virum*. — **inani**: for the poet will have flown away. — **neniae**: the mourning chants sung over the dead by women hired for that purpose (*praeficae*). — **luctus turpes**: *disfiguring grief*, such as tearing the hair, scratching the cheeks, and beating the breast.

23 f. clamorem: the *conclamatio*, the last call to the dead. It apparently consisted of a repetition of the dead man's name. — **supervacuos**: for the tomb will not contain the poet's body, and his verse will be his lasting memorial, a *monumentum aere perennius*.

LIBER TERTIVS

THE first six odes of this book, addressed to all patriotic citizens, are distinguished by a unity of purpose and a seriousness of tone not found elsewhere in Horace. The fact that all are in the Alcaic measure also contrasts them with other groups of his lyric poems, and proves that he has a particular purpose in mind: he wishes to show that mere riches and power are vain; that only by a return to the stern virtues and simple habits of an earlier day can Rome regain her greatness; and that the present disregard of religion and of domestic virtue is the gravest danger that threatens the future. It is remarkable that after expressing in the third and fourth odes confidence in Caesar's rule and the permanence of the Roman State, Horace closes his sixth ode with gloomy forebodings, — 'each generation is worse than the last, and our children will be baser than we.' The most probable explanation of this is that the sixth ode was written while Horace felt a certain despair for the future; in arranging his lyrics for publication he let these expressions stand, in the hope that they might rouse his audience by their very gloom.

The unity of the six is so marked that Porphyrio regarded them as a single ode — *multiplex* (ᾠδή) *per varios deducta est sensus.* Yet the entire collection was probably not written at the same time. The sixth ode is apparently the earliest, composed after Octavian's acceptance of the censorial power (28 B.C.); the third was written after January, 27 B.C., as the name Augustus (v. 11) shows; and the mention of the projected conquest of Britain in the fourth and fifth seems to refer them to 27-26 B.C.

I

The opening strophe of the first ode serves as introduction to the entire group. In exalted tone Horace announces that he, as sacred priest of the Muses, will sing to the rising generations the Muses' teachings in strains never heard before. He then shows that the powerful and the rich are alike subject to Necessity's impartial rule (5-16). 'Luxury will not bring gentle sleep; only they whose wants are few have easy spirits; the great owner cannot escape Fear, Threats, and black

Care (17-40). If then all that wealth can buy fails to ease the anxious spirit, why should I exchange my humble happy lot for one that brings only burdens with it (41-48).' Metre, 68.

> Odi profanum volgus et arceo.
> Favete linguis! Carmina non prius
>   audita Musarum sacerdos
>   virginibus puerisque canto.
>
> 5 Regum timendorum in proprios greges,
>   reges in ipsos imperium est Iovis,

1 f. Like a priest about to begin sacrifice, Horace bids the uninitiate, **profanum volgus**, withdraw. Cf. Callim. *Hymn. in Apoll.* 2 ἑκάς, ἑκάς, ὅστις ἀλιτρός (*profanus*); Verg. *A*. 6, 258 *procul o, procul este, profani*. By **profanum volgus** Horace means those who have not heard, and will not listen to, the teachings of the Muses, whose sacred priest he is. — **favete linguis**: the solemn call for holy silence, the Greek εὐφημεῖτε. Cf. Ovid. *Fasti* 1, 71 *linguis animisque favete*. — **carmina**, etc.: hymns of new and deeper meaning than have been sung before. Many commentators wish to see here a reference primarily to the new form, the Alcaic measure in didactic verse (cf. 2, 20, 1; 3, 30, 13 and nn.); but Horace has a more serious intention.

3 f. **Musarum sacerdos**: poets are the inspired interpreters of the Muses' will. Cf. Theoc. 16, 29 Μοισάων δὲ μάλιστα τίειν ἱεροὺς ὑποφήτας. 'To honor most of all the sacred interpreters of the Muses'; likewise Ovid. *Am*. 3, 8, 23 *ille ego Musarum purus Phoebique sacerdos*. Horace claims that his sacred office gives him a right to speak with authority. — **virginibus puerisque**: *i.e.* the rising generation, on whom the state's whole hope depends.

5 f. **regum timendorum**: modifying **imperium** of the next verse — 'Kings rule their peoples, but are themselves the subjects of Jove.' The expression seems almost proverbial. Cf. Philemon *Frg*. 31, 4. δοῦλοι βασιλέων εἰσίν. ὁ βασιλεῖς θεῶν. — **in**: *over*, showing the direction in which their rule is exercised. Cf. 4, 4, 2 f. *cui rex deorum regnum in avis vagas | permisit*. — **greges**: *herds*, a contemptuous word, fitting **regum timendorum**, which would call up to the Roman mind the thought of absolute tyrants, whose subjects were mere cattle. Notice the chiastic order in these and the two following verses Intr. 21.

clari Giganteo triumpho,
  cuncta supercilio moventis.

Est ut viro vir latius ordinet
  arbusta sulcis, hic generosior
    descendat in Campum petitor,
  moribus hic meliorque fama

contendat, illi turba clientium
sit maior: aequa lege Necessitas
  sortitur insignis et imos,
    omne capax movet urna nomen.

7 f. clari: *who is glorious for.* — **Giganteo**: cf. 2, 12, 7 f.; 19, 21 f. — **supercilio moventis**: a reminiscence of *Il.* 1, 528 ff. ἦ καὶ κυανέῃσιν ἐπ' ὀφρύσι νεῦσε Κρονίων · | ἀμβρόσιαι δ' ἄρα χαῖται ἐπερρώσαντο ἄνακτος | κρατὸς ἀπ' ἀθανάτοιο · μέγαν δ' ἐλέλιξεν Ὄλυμπον. Cf. Verg. *A.* 9, 106 *adnuit, et totum nutu tremefecit Olympum.*

9 ff. 'Men may differ in wealth, birth, reputation, and number of followers — Necessity levels all.' — **est ut**: *it is true that.* The subjects of **est** are the substantive clauses which follow, ut ... ordinet, ... descendat, ... contendat, ... sit. — **viro vir**: *one, another*; cf. Verg. *A.* 10, 361 *haeret pede pes densusque viro vir.* — **latius**: *i.e.* over a larger estate. — **arbusta**: trees on which vines could be trained. — **sulcis**: abl. with **ordinet**; *furrows*, made to mark the rows (*ordines*) of trees. — **generosior**: *nobler born.*

11 f. descendat: either literally, since the nobility lived on the hills (cf. Cic. *Phil.* 2, 6 *hodie non descendit Antonius*); or metaphorically of entering a contest, as Cic. *Tusc.* 2, 26 *descendere in certamen.* — **campum**: the Campus Martius, in which the elections were held. — **meliorque**: for the position of -que, see Intr. 31.

13 f. turba clientium: *i.e.* at the morning salutation and in his train when the great man walks abroad. The number of such attendants showed their patron's power. — **aequa lege**: emphatically placed — 'all in vain, for with impartial rule.' Cf. 1, 4, 13 *aequo pede;* 2, 18, 32 *aequa tellus.*

15 f. sortitur: *allots the fate of.* Cf. Verg. *A.* 3, 375 f. *sic fata deum rex | sortitur.* — **insignis**, etc.: cf. 1, 34, 12 f. *valet ima summis | mutare et insignem attenuat deus.* — **omne**, etc.: cf. 2, 3, 25 ff. *omnium | versatur urna serius ocius | sors exitura,* and the explanation there given of the ancient method of 'casting lots.' — **movet**: *shakes.*

Destrictus ensis cui super impia
cervice pendet, non Siculae dapes
dulcem elaborabunt saporem,
20   non avium citharaeque cantus

somnum reducent; somnus agrestium
lenis virorum non humilis domos
fastidit umbrosamque ripam,
non zephyris agitata tempe.

25 Desiderantem quod satis est neque
tumultuosum sollicitat mare

17 f. **destrictus ensis**, etc.: the reference is to the familiar story of the sword of Damocles, told by Cic. *Tusc.* 5, 61. It here typifies the uneasy conscience and ever-present fear of death that threaten the wicked; hence **impia cervice**. — **cui**: equivalent to *ei cui.* — **Siculae**: the Sicilians were proverbially luxurious, and the adjective is especially appropriate in connection with the reference to Damocles. Note that **dapes** is by its position contrasted with **impia** — 'No rich banquets can offset the tyrant's wickedness.'

19 f. **elaborabunt**: *produce*, when his natural appetite is gone. For the prepositional prefix, cf. n. to 1, 5, 8. — **avium**: aviaries were common in houses of the rich in Horace's day. — **citharaeque cantus**: we are told by Seneca, *De Prov.* 3, 10 that Maecenas, who suffered from insomnia, tried to allure sleep by soft and distant music, but naturally Horace is not here referring to his patron.

21 f. **reducent**: *bring back*, when it has fled. — **somnus**: note the effect of the repetition. — **agrestium ... virorum**: belonging grammatically to **somnus lenis**, but felt also with **domos**. The simple farmers with their lowly homes, the murmur of the breezes in pleasant valleys, are here contrasted with the rich man's palace, its aviaries and instrumental music. The sleep of the poor is proverbially sweet. Cf. *Epist.* 1, 7, 35 *somnum plebis laudo.* Also, *Ecclesiastes* 5, 12 'The sleep of a labouring man is sweet ...; but the abundance of the rich will not suffer him to sleep.'

23 f. Cf. *Epod.* 2, 25–28 *labuntur altis interim ripis aquae, | queruntur in silvis aves, | frondesque lymphis obstrepunt manantibus | somnos quod invitet levis.* — **tempe**: used here for any shady valley. Cf. n. to 1, 7, 4.

25 ff. **desiderantem**, etc.: 'the man who longs simply for enough to satisfy Nature's demands will

nec saevus Arcturi cadentis
    impetus aut orientis Haedi,

non verberatae grandine vineae
    fundusque mendax, arbore nunc aquas
    culpante, nunc torrentia agros
    sidera, nunc hiemes iniquas.

Contracta pisces aequora sentiunt
    iactis in altum molibus; huc frequens
    caementa demittit redemptor
    cum famulis dominusque terrae

fastidiosus: sed timor et minae
scandunt eodem quo dominus, neque

not be distressed by the chances of winds and floods.' Cf. 3, 16, 43 f. *bene est, cui deus obtulit | parca quod satis est manu.* — **neque tumultuosum**, etc.: cf. *Epod.* 2, 6 *neque horret iratum mare.*

27 f. **saevus ... impetus**: *the savage onset of Arcturus as he sets.* The time is the stormy month of October. — **Haedi**: regularly accompanied by rain. Cf. Verg. *A.* 9. 668 f. *quantus ab occasu veniens pluvialibus Haedis | verberat imber humum.*

29 ff. **non ... que**: continuing the **nec** of v. 27. — **verberatae grandine vineae**: *the lashing of his vineyards by the hail.* — **mendax**: the farm is personified, — it promised well, but has failed to keep its word. For similar personification, cf. 3. 16, 30 *segetis certa fides meae;* *Epist.* 1, 7, 87 *spem mentita seges.* — **arbore culpante**: continuing the personification. The (olive) tree excuses its failure by throwing the blame now on the excess of rain, now on the drought, and again on the cruel winters. — **sidera**: especially the Dog-star, which holds sway during the hottest season. Cf. 1, 17, 17.

33 f. **contracta pisces**: note the emphasis of position — 'the fish feel the narrowing of the main as the greedy rich man pushes his villa marina out into the very sea.' Cf. 2, 18, 19-22 and n.; 3, 24, 3 f. Also Apoll. Sid. *Carm.* 2, 57 *itur in aequor | molibus, et veteres tellus nova contrahit undas.* — **molibus**: masses of stone. — **huc**: *i.e. in altum.* — **frequens ... redemptor**: *many a contractor.*

36. **terrae**: obj. gen. with **fastidiosus**. Cf. 2, 18, 22 *parum locuples continente ripa.*

37 ff. 'No place is so secluded, no ship or horse so swift, that man

decedit aerata triremi et
post equitem sedet atra Cura.

Quod si dolentem nec Phrygius lapis
nec purpurarum sidere clarior
delenit usus nec Falerna
vitis Achaemeniumque costum,

cur invidendis postibus et novo
sublime ritu moliar atrium?
Cur valle permutem Sabina
divitias operosiores?

can escape his own self.' — **minae**: the threatening specters called up by the uneasy imagination of the rich, over whose heads (metaphorically) a drawn sword hangs; cf. 17 f. With this strophe, cf. 2, 16, 21-24 and n. Also *S*. 2, 7, 115 *frustra: nam comes atra premit sequiturque fugacem*. — **triremi**: here a private yacht. Cf. that of Verres, Cic. *Verr*. 5, 44, *navem vero cybaeam, maximam, triremis instar*.

41 ff. **quod si**: Horace sums up all that precedes, as frequently, with a personal application to himself, thus making the point he is urging more concrete and forceful. — **dolentem**: *a man distressed* (in mind or body). — **Phrygius lapis**: a costly marble with purple and violet workings, brought from Synnada, in Phrygia, and used for columns. — **purpurarum**, etc.: *nor the wearing of purple brighter than the stars*. Cf. *Il*. 6, 295 (of the robe to be offered to Athena) ἀστὴρ δ' ὣς ἀπέλαμπεν. — **clarior**: a 'transferred' epithet. Intr. 99.

44. **Achaemenium**: *i.e. Persian*, used for Oriental in general. Cf. n. to 2, 12, 21.

45 f. **invidendis**: *that rouse envy*. Cf. 2. 10, 7 f. *caret invidenda | sobrius aula*. — **novo ritu**: *in the new style*. Cf. n. to 2, 15, 20. — **moliar**: *laboriously build*, expressive of the size of the undertaking. Cf. *molibus* v. 34. So a palace is called (2, 15, 2; 3. 29. 10) *moles*, 'a pile.' — **sublime . . . atrium**: *i.e*. adorned with lofty columns. Cf. 2, 18, 4 and n.

47 f. **cur**: the anaphora marks Horace's impatience at the folly of such a proposal. — **valle . . . Sabina**: Horace's dearest possession. Intr. 5.

2

After showing in the first ode the vanity of power and riches, Horace here takes up a positive theme.

'Content with small estate the Roman youth should learn courage in the stern school of war, that he may fight for Rome and die for her if need be; death for one's native land is sweet and glorious; and the coward may not escape the common fate (1-16). True manhood is secure and independent of popular favor; it alone gives immortality (17-24). Fidelity and silence too have their secure reward. The wicked punishment sooner or later overtakes (25-32).' Metre, 68.

Angustam amice pauperiem pati
robustus acri militia puer
    condiscat, et Parthos ferocis
    vexet eques metuendus hasta,

5   vitamque sub divo et trepidis agat
in rebus; illum ex moenibus hosticis
    matrona bellantis tyranni
    prospiciens et adulta virgo

1. This verse forms the transition from the theme of the preceding ode. — **angustam**: *narrow, straitened*, as 2, 10, 21 f. *rebus angustis animosus atque | fortis appare.* — **amice . . . pati**: *to bear gladly, to welcome*, stronger than the common *lente, molliter ferre*.

2 ff. **robustus acri**, etc.: *hardened in war's fierce school*; predicate following **pati**, and like **metuendus** below logically part of the prayer 'may he be trained and learn. . . . be fearful and harass.'

5. **sub divo**: 'bivouacking beneath the open sky.' Cf. 1, 1, 25; 2, 3, 23. and *sub divum* 1, 18, 13. — **trepidis in rebus**: *amidst (war's) alarms.*

6 ff. The description may have been suggested by Briseis' lament *Il.* 19, 291 f. ἄνδρα μέν, ᾧ ἔδοσάν με πατὴρ καὶ πότνια μήτηρ, | εἶδον πρὸ πτόλιος δεδαϊγμένον ὀξέϊ χαλκῷ, or by book 22 where Hector is killed and dragged away before the eyes of his parents and wife. Cf. also *Il.* 3, 154 ff., and Verg. *A.* 11, 475 ff. — **illum**: emphatic — *such a Roman.* — **tyranni**: the lord of the besieged town. — **adulta**: *i.e. nubilis*, 'of a marriageable age.'

>   suspiret, eheu, ne rudis agminum
> 10   sponsus lacessat regius asperum
>   tactu leonem, quem cruenta
>   per medias rapit ira caedes.
>
>   Dulce et decorum est pro patria mori:
>   mors et fugacem persequitur virum
> 15   nec parcit imbellis iuventae
>   poplitibus timidoque tergo.

9 ff. suspiret, etc.: the verb belongs grammatically with both **matrona** and **virgo**, but its position makes it felt only with the latter. — **eheu**: the sigh which the maiden utters, skillfully placed between the verb and the following clause, **ne ... lacessat**, which expresses the fear that calls forth the sigh. — **ne**, etc.: *for fear that*. — **agminum**: *armed lines*; obj. gen. with **rudis**, equivalent to *rudis belli*. — **sponsus ... regius**: some allied prince to whom the maiden is betrothed, as Cassandra was to Coroebus (Verg. *A.* 2, 342 ff.). — **lacessat**: *vex, attack recklessly*. Cf. 1, 35. 7 *quicumque ... lacessit Carpathium pelagus*. — **asperum tactu leonem**: the comparison of a warrior to a lion is Homeric. *Il.* 5, 136 ff.; 20, 164 ff. — **cruenta**: 'transferred' to **ira** from **leonem**. Intr. 99.

13. dulce, etc.: emphasizing the preceding wish. 'Death may come, but how can the young Roman die better than for his country?' The expression is almost a commonplace. Cf. Tyrtaeus *Frg.* 10 τεθνάμεναι γὰρ καλὸν ἐνὶ προμάχοισι πεσόντα | ἄνδρ' ἀγαθὸν περὶ ᾗ πατρίδι μαρνάμενον. *Il.* 15, 496 f. οὔ οἱ ἀεικὲς ἀμυνομένῳ περὶ πάτρης | τεθνάμεν. Eurip. *Troad.* 386 f. Τρῶες δὲ πρῶτον μέν, τὸ κάλλιστον κλέος, | ὑπὲρ πάτρας ἔθνῃσκον, and Cic. *Phil.* 14, 31 *o fortunata mors, quae naturae debita pro patria est potissimum reddita*.

14 ff. 'Better die gloriously, for death overtakes the coward as well as the brave man.' — **mors**: emphatically continuing the idea of **mori**. Intr. 28 b. — **et**: *as well*. The verse is probably a reminiscence of Simonid. *Frg.* 65 ὁ δ' αὖ θάνατος κίχε καὶ τὸν φυγόμαχον. Cf. also Curt. 4, 14 *effugit mortem quisquis contempserit, timidissimum quemque consequitur*. — **fugacem**: not simply one who runs away, but also one who avoids battle. 'Death finds him as well.' Cf. Callinus *Frg.* 1. 14 ff. πολλάκι δηιοτῆτα φυγὼν καὶ δοῦπον ἀκόντων | ἔρχεται. ἐν δ' οἴκῳ μοῖρα κίχεν θανάτου. 'Often a man escapes safe from the strife of battle and din of

Virtus repulsae nescia sordidae
intaminatis fulget honoribus,
   nec sumit aut ponit securis
     arbitrio popularis aurae;

virtus recludens immeritis mori
caelum negata temptat iter via,
   coetusque volgaris et udam
     spernit humum fugiente penna.

   Est et fideli tuta silentio

(striking) spears — yet in his house death's doom finds him.' — **imbellis iuventae**: 'such as we see about us to-day' is implied. — **poplitibus**, etc.: the final disgrace of the coward — he is killed by a wound in the back.

17 ff. Horace here develops the Stoic paradox that the virtuous man, the man truly *sapiens*, is the only one who is really rich, free, and kingly. Cf. 2, 2, 9, and *Epist.* 1, 1, 106 f. *ad summam, sapiens uno minor est Iove, dives, | liber, honoratus, pulcher, rex denique regum.* — **virtus**: true manhood, ἡ ἀρετή. — **repulsae**: technical for defeat in an election; connect with **nescia**. — **intaminatis**: predicate — *still unsullied.*

19 f. **ponit**: *lays aside.* — **securis**: symbolical of power. — **aurae**: a common metaphor, marking here the fickleness of the people. Cf. 1, 5, 5; 2, 8. 24 and nn. Also Livy 22, 26 *aura favoris popularis.*

21 ff. 'True manhood secures immortality.' Cf. the epigram on those who fell at Thermopylae *Anth. Pal.* 7, 251 οὐδὲ τεθνᾶσι θανόντες, ἐπεί σφ' ἀρετὴ καθύπερθε | κυδαίνουσ' ἀνάγει δώματος ἐξ Ἀίδεω. 'Yet though they died they are not dead, for virtue by its power to glorify brings them up from the house of Hades.' Also Verg. *A.* 6, 130 *pauci, quos ... ardens evexit ad aethera virtus.* — **negata**: *i.e.* to all but her. 'Virtue alone can force a path.' Cf. Ovid. *Met.* 14, 113 *invia virtuti nulla est via.* Lowell, *Commemoration Ode,* 'Virtue treads paths that end not in the grave.' — **volgaris**: *of the common herd,* the *profanum volgus* of the preceding ode. — **udam**: *dank,* in contrast to the clear upper air (*liquidum aethera* 2, 20, 2) to which Virtue soars. — **spernit**: cf. 1, 30, 2.

25 ff. To the excellent quality of **virtus** is added **fidele silentium**, 'the ability to keep a secret.' — **est**, etc.: a translation of Simoni-

merces. Vetabo qui Cereris sacrum
volgarit arcanae sub isdem
sit trabibus fragilemque mecum

solvat phaselon: saepe Diespiter
30 neglectus incesto addidit integrum;
raro antecedentem scelestum
deseruit pede Poena claudo.

des, *Frg.* 6, 6 ἔστι καὶ σιγᾶς ἀκίνδυνον γέρας, which was a favorite quotation of Augustus. For the opposite, cf. 1, 18, 16 *arcani fides prodiga.* — **et**: *as well.* — **vetabo,** etc.: the common personal note, making the application vivid and concrete. — **Cereris sacrum**: the Eleusinian mysteries which could be disclosed only to the initiate; here used as a general illustration of what may not be told. Cf. 1, 18, 11 ff. — **sub isdem . . . trabibus**: cf. Callim. *Hymn. in Cerer.* 117 f. μὴ τῆνος ἐμὶν φίλος, ὅς τοι ἀπεχθής, εἴη μηδ᾽ ὁμότοιχος. 'May that man who has incurred thy displeasure, (goddess), be not my friend nor share the same house with me.' — **sit**: dependent on **vetabo.** Cf. the construction with *cave.* — **fragilem**: a conventional epithet (cf. 1, 3, 10), but here emphasizing the danger.

29 f. **saepe,** etc.: for the belief that the righteous run especial risks in embarking with the wicked, cf. Aesch. *Sept.* 601 ff. ὡς γὰρ ξυνεισβὰς πλοῖον εὐσεβὴς ἀνὴρ | ναύταισι θερμοῖς ἐν πανουργίᾳ τινὶ | ὄλωλεν ἀνδρῶν ξὺν θεοπτύστῳ γένει. 'For the pious man who has embarked with sailors hot in some rascality, has often perished with the god-detested lot.' Eurip. *Suppl.* 226 ff. κοινὰς γὰρ ὁ θεὸς τὰς τύχας ἡγούμενος | τοῖς τοῦ νοσοῦντος πήμασιν διώλεσε | τὸν οὐ νοσοῦντα κοὐδὲν ἠδικηκότα. — **neglectus**: *disregarded.* — **integrum**: cf. 1, 22, 1 *integer vitae.*

31 f. **raro**: emphatically stating the opposite of **saepe** above, — 'seldom does the wicked man escape.' — **deseruit**: *given up the pursuit of.* — **pede claudo**: concessive. The thought is a commonplace in all literature. Cf. Eurip. *Frg.* 979 ἡ Δίκη . . . βραδεῖ ποδὶ στείχουσα μάρψει τοὺς κακούς. ὅταν τύχῃ. Tibul. 1, 9, 4 *sera tamen tacitis Poena venit pedibus*; and Herbert, 'God's mill grinds slow, but sure.'

3

The theme of the third ode is similar to that of the second: the praise of two great virtues, *iustitia* and *constantia*, justice and steadfastness of purpose. The ode opens with the famous picture of the upright and constant man who is unmoved by the fury of the populace or by the raging elements; the fall of heaven itself would not shake him (1–8). Such were the qualities which secured immortality for Pollux, Hercules, Augustus, and Quirinus (9–16). Then with the mention of Romulus Horace seems to turn from the theme with which he began, and reports to us the speech of Juno before the council of the gods, in which she gives up in part her hatred toward the Trojans and their descendants, and prophesies for Rome an empire coterminous with the world, so long as her people shall keep themselves from avarice and not try to rebuild Ilium (17–68). Then he suddenly checks himself with a mock reproach to his lyre and muse for venturing on such mighty themes (69–72).

The introduction of Juno's long speech was apparently due to a desire to avoid the monotony of a long moral discourse; it further allowed Horace to drive home the lesson he wished to teach by making it part of Juno's prophecy. The protest against any attempt to rebuild Ilium has puzzled commentators. Some take it to refer to a design to move the capital to Ilium which rumor had attributed to Julius Caesar. Cf. Suet. *Div. Iul.* 79 *quin etiam varia fama percrebuit, migraturum Alexandream vel Ilium, translatis simul opibus imperii*. Others regard it as an allegorical condemnation of Asiatic vice and luxury, which Rome must avoid if she is to maintain her empire. Both views are improbable. Horace wished to represent Juno's fateful wrath toward Ilium as but partially appeased: she will allow the descendants of the Trojans to rule, but only in exile.

The name Augustus (v. 11) shows that the date of composition is after 27 B.C. Metre, 68.

Iustum et tenacem propositi virum
non civium ardor prava iubentium,

1 ff. Cf. Herrick's imitation. 'No wrath of Men or rage of Seas | Can shake a just man's purposes: | No threats of Tyrants, or the Grim | Visage of them can alter him; | But what he doth at first entend, | That he holds firmly to the end.' *Psalms* 46, 2 'Therefore will we not fear, though the earth do change, and though the moun-

non voltus instantis tyranni
   mente quatit solida, neque Auster,
5 dux inquieti turbidus Hadriae,
   nec fulminantis magna manus Iovis:
   si fractus inlabatur orbis,
   impavidum ferient ruinae.

   Hac arte Pollux et vagus Hercules
10   enisus arcis attigit igneas,

tains be moved in the heart of the seas'; and Tennyson's *Will.* The first two strophes were repeated by the great Cornelius de Witte while on the rack.

— **civium ardor, instantis tyranni**: 'neither the fury of the populace nor the insistant tyrant's look can shake him.' So Socrates was quite unmoved by the demands of the people, when presiding at the trial of the generals who had commanded at Arginusae. Plat. *Apol.* 32 B. Xen. *Mem.* 4, 4, 2. Cf. also Juvenal's exhortation 8, 81 ff. *Phalaris licet imperet ut sis | falsus et admoto dictet periuria tauro, | summum crede nefas, animam praeferre pudori | et propter vitam vivendi perdere causas.* — **mente**: locative abl. — **solida**: suggesting the simile which Seneca developed *de Consol. Sap.* 3 *quemadmodum proiecti in altum scopuli mare frangunt; . . . ita sapientis animus solidus est.*

5 ff. **dux . . . Hadriae**: cf. 1, 3, 15; 2, 17, 19. — **inquieti**: *rest-*less. — **nec fulminantis**, etc.: cf. 1, 16, 11 f. — **orbis**: (*the vault of*) *the sky.* — **impavidum**: *still undismayed.*

9 ff. Pollux, Hercules, Bacchus, and Quirinus are types of mortals who by their virtues attained immortality. Cf. 4, 5, 35 f. *Graecia Castoris | et magni memor Herculis.* Tacitus says (*Ann.* 4, 38) that when Tiberius refused divine honors the people murmured: *optimos quippe mortalium altissima cupere; sic Herculem et Liberum apud Graecos, Quirinum apud nos deum numero additos: . . . melius Augustum qui speraverit.* — **hac arte**: *i.e.* by means of the *iustitia* and *constantia* which form the theme of the ode. — **vagus**: a favorite epithet of Hercules. Cf. Verg. *A.* 6, 801 ff. where Augustus' travels in the East are compared to the wanderings of Hercules and Bacchus, *nec vero Alcides tantum telluris obivit,* etc. — **enisus**: *striving upward.* — **arcis igneas**: cf. Ovid. *Am.* 3, 10, 21 *siderea arx.*

quos inter Augustus recumbens
purpureo bibet ore nectar;

hac te merentem, Bacche pater, tuae
vexere tigres indocili iugum
15   collo trahentes; hac Quirinus
Martis equis Acheronta fugit,

gratum elocuta consiliantibus
Iunone divis: 'Ilion, Ilion
fatalis incestusque iudex
20   et mulier peregrina vertit

11 f. This prophecy marks the court poet. Cf. 1, 2, 41-52; Verg. G. 1, 24-42. — **recumbens**: at the banquet. — **purpureo**: *ruddy*, with the bloom of a divine youth. So Vergil says of Venus, *A.* 2, 593 *roseoque haec insuper addidit ore.*

13 ff. **hac**: sc. *arte*; connect with **merentem**, *winning* (heaven). Cf. Ovid. *Trist.* 5, 3, 19 (also of Bacchus) *ipse quoque aetherias meritis invectus es arces.* — **vexere**: *i.e. ad caelum.* — **tigres**: the tamed tigers symbolize the god's civilizing power. — **Quirinus**: for the story of Romulus' apotheosis, cf. Livy 1, 16; Ovid. *Fast.* 2, 481 ff. Note the contrast between **enisus** (v. 10), indicating the efforts of Pollux and Hercules, and **vexere** (v. 14), **Martis equis fugit** (v. 16), applied to Bacchus and the Roman Quirinus.

17 ff. Horace now represents the gods as debating whether Romulus shall be admitted to heaven and become one of them. Juno's speech affords him an opportunity to show the destiny of the Roman State if it be just, steadfast, and without greed.

— **gratum**: modifying **elocuta**. The gods were pleased that she abated her hatred toward Ilium. — **elocuta Iunone**: abl. abs., fixing the time. — **Ilion, Ilion**: the repetition marks the speaker's emotion. Cf. Eurip. *Orest.* 1381 ff. Ἴλιον, Ἴλιον, ὤμοί μοι . . . ὥς σ' ὀλόμενον στένω. Intr. 28 a.

19 f. **fatalis**: *fateful*. Cf. the epithets Δύσπαρις, Αἰνόπαρις. — **incestus**: *base, foul*, because his decision in awarding the prize for beauty was determined by a bribe. Cf. 3, 2, 30 *incesto.* — **peregrina**: the Greek βάρβαρος, scornfully applied to Helen. Cf. Eurip. *Andr.* 649, where Helen is called γυνὴ βάρβαρος. Notice that Juno in her wrath will not name either Paris or Helen.

in pulverem, ex quo destituit deos
    mercede pacta Laomedon mihi
        castaeque damnatum Minervae
            cum populo et duce fraudulento.

25 Iam nec Lacaenae splendet adulterae
    famosus hospes nec Priami domus
        periura pugnacis Achivos
            Hectoreis opibus refringit,

    nostrisque ductum seditionibus
30   bellum resedit: protinus et gravis
        iras et invisum nepotem,
            Troica quem peperit sacerdos,

21 ff. ex quo: fixing the time of **damnatum** v. 23. Troy was doomed from the day of Laomedon's default; *iudicium Paridis spretaeque iniuria formae* were then only one of the causes of Troy's fall. — **deos**: Apollo and Poseidon served Laomedon a year; according to the Homeric form of the story (*Il.* 21, 441 ff.), Poseidon built for him the walls of Troy while Apollo pastured his herds; but Laomedon refused to pay the price agreed on for the service. Other forms of the myth make Apollo Neptune's partner in building the walls. — **castae Minervae**: cf. 1, 7, 5 *intactae Palladis*. — **duce**: Laomedon.

25 ff. iam nec: *no longer now.* — **splendet**: reproducing the Homeric κάλλεί τε στίλβων καὶ εἵμασι *Il.* 3, 392. — **adulterae**: dat. with **splendet**, *in the eyes of*, etc. — **famosus**: Paris was the notorious example of such infamous action toward his host. — **periura**: referring to Laomedon's broken promise. — **refringit**: *breaks and drives back.*

29 ff. ductum: *prolonged.* The length of the war was due to division among the gods. — **resedit**: *has subsided*, like the waves of a stormy sea. — **protinus**: *from this moment.* — **nepotem**: Romulus, her descendant, hitherto hateful (**invisum**) to her because the child of a Trojan mother. — **Troica sacerdos**: Rhea Silvia. Horace here, as in 1, 2, 17 ff., follows the older tradition which made her the daughter of Aeneas. Notice that here, as in v. 25 f., Juno will not call the objects of her resentment by name.

Marti redonabo; illum ego lucidas
inire sedes, discere nectaris
35 sucos et adscribi quietis
ordinibus patiar deorum.

Dum longus inter saeviat Ilion
Romamque pontus, qualibet exsules
in parte regnanto beati;
40 dum Priami Paridisque busto

insultet armentum et catulos ferae
celent inultae, stet Capitolium

33 ff. redonabo: *resign as a free gift, condonabo*. Cf. *2, 7, 3, where the word is used in a different sense. — **illum**: emphatic and serving to connect the two sentences. Cf. 3, 2, 6. — **lucidas sedes**: cf. the Homeric αἰγλήεντος Ὀλύμπου. *Il.* 1, 532. — **discere**: *to learn* (the taste of). — **adscribi . . . ordinibus**: *to be enrolled in the ranks*; a technical expression taken from the enrollment of citizens in their proper orders. — **quietis**: for the gods live undistressed by cares that harass men. Cf. Verg. *A.* 4, 379 f. *ea cura quietos | sollicitat.*

37 ff. dum . . . dum: *so long as*, expressing the condition on which she yields. — **longus, saeviat**: emphasizing the separation. — **qualibet, etc.**: 'they may reign in good fortune wherever they will, provided they continue exiles.' — **busto**: loc. abl. Horace could picture Priam's tomb in his imagination, for Vergil's *A.* 2, 557 had not been published.

41 ff. The place where Troy once stood shall be utterly desolate. Cf. *Isaiah* 13, 20 f. 'It shall shall never be inhabited, neither shall it be dwelt in from generation to generation: neither shall the Arabian pitch tent there; neither shall shepherds make their flocks to lie down there. But wild beasts of the desert shall lie there: and their houses shall be full of doleful creatures: and ostriches shall dwell there, and satyrs shall dance there. And wolves shall cry in their castles, and jackals in the pleasant palaces.'

— **insultet**: *gambol on*, from which comes the connotation of insult. Cf. *Il.* 4, 176 f. καί κέ τις ὧδ' ἐρέει Τρώων ὑπερηνορεόντων | τύμβῳ ἐπιθρῴσκων Μενελάου κυδαλίμοιο. — **stet**: *may stand* (undisturbed); permissive like **regnanto** above. — **Capitolium**: the

fulgens triumphatisque possit
Roma ferox dare iura Medis;

45 horrenda late nomen in ultimas
extendat oras, qua medius liquor
secernit Europen ab Afro,
qua tumidus rigat arva Nilus.

Aurum inrepertum et sic melius situm,
50 cum terra celat, spernere fortior
quam cogere humanos in usus
omne sacrum rapiente dextra,

quicumque mundo terminus obstitit,
hunc tanget armis, visere gestiens

symbol of Rome's power. Cf. 1, 37, 6 and n. — **fulgens**: predicate with **stet**; contrasted with the desolation of Troy. — **triumphatis**: logically part of the permission, 'may conquer and impose her laws on.' — **Roma ferox**: *stern, warlike.* Cf. 1, 35, 10 *Latium ferox.*

45 ff. horrenda late: *feared afar.* Cf. Ovid. *Fasti* 1, 717 *horreat Aeneadas et primus et ultimus orbis.* — **nomen**: used almost technically — *i.e.* the remotest peoples are to come under the *nomen* (*Romanum*). Cf. *Latinum nomen* 4, 15, 13. — **qua medius liquor**, etc.: the straits of Gibraltar on the west, Egypt on the east. — **tumidus . . . rigat**: with its annual inundation. Cf. Verg. *G.* 4, 291 f. *et diversa ruens septem discurrit in ora | et viridem Aegyptum nigra fecundat arena.*

49 ff. The second condition on which Rome's future depends is that she show herself superior to lust for gold: if the Roman can resist that, he shall subdue the whole world. — **inrepertum**: *undiscovered,* because not sought for. — **spernere fortior**, etc.: *braver in scorning the gold than in,* etc.: epexegetical infinitives with *fortior.* Intr. 108. The expression is somewhat forced and the first part of the strophe is made obscure by the parenthetical et sic . . . celat. — **cogere**: a strong word — *forcibly gathering it.* — **humanos in usus**: with **rapiente**.—**sacrum**: with special reference to the gold hidden in the earth: it is **sacrum** since the gods have there concealed it.

53 ff. The goddess now passes from mere permission (**regnanto, stet, extendat**) to prophecy (**tan-**

qua parte debacchentur ignes,
    qua nebulae pluviique rores.

Sed bellicosis fata Quiritibus
hac lege dico, ne nimium pii
rebusque fidentes avitae
    tecta velint reparare Troiae.

Troiae renascens alite lugubri
fortuna tristi clade iterabitur,
    ducente victricis catervas
    coniuge me Iovis et sorore.

Ter si resurgat murus aeneus
auctore Phoebo, ter pereat meis

get). — **quicumque mundo,** etc.: *whatever bound has been set the world, that she shall touch,* etc. — **qua parte,** etc.: the torrid zone. — **debacchentur**: *keep wild revel.* — **qua nebulae,** etc.; the farthest north with which the Roman in Horace's day was actually acquainted was North Germany with its fogs and rains. Cf. 1, 22, 17-20.

57 ff. sed: Juno returns to the condition with which she began, v. 37 ff. — **bellicosis**: more than a mere ornamental epithet; it implies that the Romans will gain their empire by arms. — **hac lege ... ne**: *on this condition, that they shall not,* etc. — **pii**: *i.e.* toward their mother city, **avitae Troiae.** — **rebus fidentes**: with reference to the content of vv. 45-56.

61 ff. Troiae: echoing the preceding **Troiae.** Intr. 28 b. — **renascens**: transferred from **Troiae** to **fortuna,** a difficult hypallage in English. Intr. 99. — **alite**: cf. 1, 15, 5. — **ducente,** etc.: cf. Verg. *A.* 2, 612 ff. *hic Iuno Scaeas saevissima portas | prima tenet, sociumque furens a navibus agmen | ferro accincta vocat.* — **coniuge ... et sorore**: an Homeric phrase. κασιγνήτη ἄλοχός τε, adopted also by Verg. *A.* 1, 46 f. *ast ego, quae divom incedo regina, Iovisque | et soror et coniunx.*

65 ff. ter ... ter ... ter: Intr. 28 c. — **aeneus**: 'and be of bronze as well.' — **auctore Phoebo**: as they were before. Cf. v. 21 f. above and n. — **meis Argivis**: ablative of instrument rather than of agent.

excisus Argivis, ter uxor
capta virum puerosque ploret.'
Non hoc iocosae conveniet lyrae :
70   quo, musa, tendis ?   Desine pervicax
referre sermones deorum et
magna modis tenuare parvis.

69 ff. non hoc, etc.: Horace suddenly checks his muse with the warning that his lyre is **iocosa** and not suited to such serious themes. The strophe is a mere device to close the ode. Cf. 2, 1, 37 ff. — **conveniet**: the tense implies that all has not yet been said. — **pervicax** : *persistent*. — **tenuare**: *to lessen, dwarf*. Cf. 1, 6, 12 *deterere;* 1, 6, 9 *nec . . . conamur, tenues grandia*. Also Prop. 4, 1, 5 *dicite, quo pariter carmen tenuastis in antro?*

4

Horace begins this ode with a second invocation to the Muses and a renewed pledge of his loyalty and devotion to them. It was they who gave him safe escape at Philippi, protected him from the falling tree, and rescued him from drowning. Under their guardianship he may wander all unharmed among savage tribes on the very outskirts of the world (1-36). It is also they who protect mighty Caesar and aid him with gentle counsel (37-42). At this point in the ode Horace turns with apparent abruptness to the story of the giants' defeat in their battle with the gods, and closes with a warning against dependence on brute force and violence (42-80). No Roman, however, would fail to see that Horace wished to present Augustus here as the vice-regent of Jove, and that the powers of violence are those of rebellion against the emperor's moderate and beneficent rule. In the next ode the comparison is more outspoken.

The date of composition is approximately 26 B.C. ; cf. n. to v. 33. Metre, 68.

Descende caelo et dic age tibia
regina longum Calliope melos,

1 ff. descende caelo: for the Muses dwell on Olympus, *Il.* 2, 484 Μοῦσαι Ὀλύμπια δώματ' ἔχουσαι. The ancient commentators, however, understood it to mean: 'Come back to earth from the council of the gods (in the preceding ode).' This is possible,

CARMINA [3, 4, 9

seu voce nunc mavis acuta,
    seu fidibus citharave Phoebi.
Auditis, an me ludit amabilis
  insania? Audire et videor pios
    errare per lucos, amoenae
      quos et aquae subeunt et aurae.
Me fabulosae Volture in Apulo

but fanciful. — dic age: *come play upon thy pipe*, etc. Cf. 1, 32, 3; 2, 11, 22. — regina: thus addressed, since she rules the poet's song; cf. 1, 6, 10; 2, 12, 13 f. So Venus is called *regina* (3, 26, 11) 'queen of love.' — Calliope: with no reference to Calliope's special province as the muse of epic poetry. Cf. 1, 1, 32 and n. The invocation may have been suggested by Alcm. *Frg.* 45 Μῶσ' ἄγε, Καλλιόπα, θύγατερ Διός, ἄρχ' ἐρατῶν ἐπέων, or by Stesich. *Frg.* 45 δεῦρ' ἄγε, Καλλιόπεια λίγεια — seu voce, etc.: the expression is somewhat confused: Horace prays the Muse to sing either to the accompaniment of the pipe (tibia), or of the lyre (fidibus citharave) or with her clear, treble (acuta, equivalent to λίγεια above) voice alone. — fidibus citharave: the distinction between *cithara* and *lyra* was early confused (cf. the Hom. *Hymn. ad Merc.* 423 λύρῃ δ' ἐρατὸν κιθαρίζων), and Horace is obviously here thinking of a single instrument.

5 ff. auditis: in his imagination the poet hears already the voice of the Muse. — insania: the poetic ecstasy called by Plato (*Phaedr.* 245 A.) ἀπὸ Μουσῶν κατοκωχή (possession) τε καὶ μανία. — videor: sc. *mihi*. Cf. Verg. *E.* 10, 58 f. *iam mihi per rupes videor lucosque sonantis | ire.* — pios lucos: the haunts of the Muses, consecrated by their presence.

8. quos . . . subeunt: *beneath which glide.* subeunt is connected by a slight zeugma with aurae. Sappho, *Frg.* 4. describes in similar fashion the garden of the nymphs ἀμφὶ δ' ὕδωρ | ⟨ἴψοθεν⟩ ψῦχρον κελάδει δι' ὔσδων | μαλίνων, αἰθυσσομένων δὲ φύλλων | κῶμα καταρρεῖ. 'All around through branches of apple-orchards | Cool streams call, while down from the leaves a-tremble | Slumber distilleth'(Symonds).

9 ff. 'I have been favored by the Muses from my infant years'; explaining why he may be able to hear the Muses' song while duller ears cannot. Similar stories are told of Pindar, Stesichorus, Aeschylus, and others. Cf. Tennyson, *Eleanore* 2, 'Or the yellow-banded bees, | Thro' half open lattices |

243

[3, 4, 10]

10   nutricis extra limina Pulliae
         ludo fatigatumque somno
            fronde nova puerum palumbes

      texere, mirum quod foret omnibus,
         quicumque celsae nidum Acherontiae
15   saltusque Bantinos et arvum
            pingue tenent humilis Forenti,

      ut tuto ab atris corpore viperis
         dormirem et ursis, ut premerer sacra

Coming in the scented breeze, | Fed thee, a child, lying alone, | With whitest honey in fairy gardens cull'd — | A glorious child, dreaming alone, | In silk-soft folds, upon yielding down, | With the hum of swarming bees | Into dreamful slumber lull'd.'
— **fabulosae ... palumbes**: *the doves of story*. Some, however, connect **fabulosae** with **nutricis**. — **Volture**: Mt. Voltur, near the borders of Apulia and Lucania. — **extra limina**: the child had wandered away into the wood, where he at last fell asleep. — **Pulliae**: this is the reading of some of the best Mss., and the name is found in inscriptions. The other reading, *limen Apūliae*, is impossible. — **ludo**, etc.: possibly modelled after the Homeric (*Il.* 10, 98; *Od.* 12, 281) καμάτῳ ἀδηκότες ἠδὲ καὶ ὕπνῳ. For the position of -que, see Intr. 31. — **fronde nova**: *fresh* and fragrant.
13 ff. **mirum quod foret**: (a sight) *to be a marvel*; expanded v. 17 ff. **ut ... dormirem**, etc. — **nidum Ache-** **rontiae**: to-day, Acerenza, perched like a nest on the top of a hill. Many Italian towns were so placed for defense, and still retain the appearance graphically described by the word **nidus**. Cf. Cic. *de Or.* 1, 196 *Ithacam illam in asperrimis saxulis tamquam nidulum adfixam.* Macaulay, *Horatius*, 'From many a lonely hamlet, | Which, hid by beech and pine, | Like an eagle's nest, hangs on the crest | Of purple Apennine.' — **saltus Bantinos**: the modern Abbadia de' Banzi, on the side of the hill to the north of Acerenza. — **humilis Forenti**: the ancient town was in the lowlands; the modern Forenza, situated on a hill, preserves the name.
17 ff. **ut ... dormirem, ut ... premerer**: interrogative, the object of their wonder. Notice the effect of the interlocked order of the first line. — **atris**: the 'deadly' color. Cf. 1, 37, 27 and n. — **sacra**: the laurel was sacred to Apollo, the god of song, and the myrtle to Venus; therefore their use fore-

lauroque conlataque myrto,
    non sine dis animosus infans.

Vester, Camenae, vester in arduos
tollor Sabinos, seu mihi frigidum
    Praeneste seu Tibur supinum
        seu liquidae placuere Baiae.

Vestris amicum fontibus et choris
non me Philippis versa acies retro,
    devota non exstinxit arbor,
        nec Sicula Palinurus unda.

Vtcumque mecum vos eritis, libens
insanientem navita Bosporum
    temptabo et urentis harenas
        litoris Assyrii viator;

told that the child was to be a poet of love. — non sine dis: the Homeric οὔ τοι ἄνευ θεοῦ (*Od.* 2, 372), οὐκ ἀθεεί (*Od.* 18, 353). The child's spirit was divinely given.

21 ff. vester ... vester: the repetition emphasizes the poet's devotion to his task as *Musarum sacerdos.* — tollor: middle, *climb.* — Praeneste, Tibur, Baiae: three favorite resorts of the Romans. — frigidum: cf. Iuven. 3, 190 *gelida Praeneste.* — supinum: *sloping;* cf. Iuven. 3, 192 *proni Tiburis arce.* — liquidae: *clear,* of the air; cf. 2, 20, 2. But some commentators refer it to the water at Baiae.

25 ff. vestris: echoing vester of the preceding strophe. — amicum: giving the reason for his protection — 'because I am dear,' etc. — fontibus: cf. 1, 26, 6. — Philippis: cf. 2, 7, 9 ff.

28. We have no other reference to Horace's escape from shipwreck, and it is not impossible that he added this simply to round out his list of dangers and to show that the Muses protect him on land and sea. — Palinurus: a promontory of Lucania named from Aeneas' pilot; Verg. *A.* 6, 381 *aeternumque locus Palinuri nomen habebit.*

29 ff. utcumque: *whenever.* — insanientem ... Bosphorum: noted for its stormy character. Cf. 2, 13, 14, and with the adjective Verg. *E.* 9, 43 *insani feriant sine litore fluctus.* — urentis harenas, etc.: notice the contrast between Bosphorum, harenas, and navita, viator. — Assyrii: *i.e.* 'Syrian,' 'Eastern.' Cf. 2, 11, 16

visam Britannos hospitibus feros
et laetum equino sanguine Concanum,
  visam pharetratos Gelonos
   et Scythicum inviolatus amnem.

Vos Caesarem altum, militia simul
fessas cohortis abdidit oppidis,
  finire quaerentem labores
   Pierio recreatis antro.

Vos lene consilium et datis et dato
gaudetis, almae. Scimus ut impios

33 ff. Britannos: Augustus' projected expedition against the Britons may have occasioned their mention here (cf. introductory n. to 1, 35); or they may have been chosen as a type of the peoples living on the borders of the world. Cf. 1, 35, 30 *ultimos orbis Britannos*. — **hospitibus feros**: Tacitus, *Ann*. 14. 30, pictures them as savages. — **Concanum**: a Cantabrian tribe; cf. 2, 6, 2. Verg. *G*. 3, 463, says that the Geloni drink horses' blood mixed with milk. Statius. *Achil*. 1, 307, attributes a similar custom to the Massagetae. — **Gelonos**: cf. 2, 9, 23; 20, 19. — **Scythicum amnem**: the Tanais, Don. Cf. 3, 10, 1. — **inviolatus**: predicate, — *and still remain unharmed*.

37 ff. vos: connecting this strophe with the preceding, and bringing us back to the main theme of this part of the ode. — the Muses and their influence. — **altum**: *exalted*. — **militia simul**, etc.: after the battle of Actium Augustus settled 120,000 veterans on lands, spending enormous sums for this purpose. In spite of the vexation that the confiscations of land caused, this disposition of the troops was doubtless a great relief to many who feared that the victor might use his forces to secure tyrannical power. — **abdidit**: aptly expressing the disappearance of the troops. — **finire**, etc.: Augustus' great desire seems to have been for peace; the Roman world saw a warrant of this in the disbanding of his veterans just referred to. — **Pierio recreatis antro**: *i.e.* by literary pursuits in some quiet spot, as in a cave sacred to the Muses. Cf. 1, 12, 6. When Octavian was returning from the East in 29 B.C., he rested some time at Atella in Campania, where on four successive days the *Georgics*, which Vergil had just finished, were read to him by Vergil and Maecenas.

Titanas immanemque turbam
fulmine sustulerit caduco

45 qui terram inertem, qui mare temperat
ventosum et urbis regnaque tristia
divosque mortalisque turmas
imperio regit unus aequo.

Magnum illa terrorem intulerat Iovi
50 fidens iuventus horrida bracchiis,

41 ff. vos: cf. n. on 37 above. — lene consilium, etc.: with reference to Augustus' mild and beneficent policy after he had established his position (cf. *C. S.* 51 *iacentem lenis in hostem*). This policy of conciliation was in sharp contrast with the proscriptions of Marius, Sulla, and also of the second Triumvirate, consisting of Antony, Lepidus, and Octavian, to whose hatred many fell victims in 43 B.C., among them the orator Marcus Cicero. — consilium: trisyllabic. Intr. 39. — dato: sc. *consilio*; i.e. the Muses take delight in furthering the counsel that they have given. — scimus, etc.: emphatic, *we all know*. Horace thus suddenly turns to his contemporaries and reminds them that the lesson is intended for them; they must recognize that foolish rebellion against Caesar's kindly rule is as vain as the attack of the Titans on Jove's power. — fulmine . . . caduco: *the quick-falling bolt*. So in Aesch. *P. V.* 358 ff. it is said that the monster Typhon was consumed by the και-

αιβάτης κεραυνός ἐκπνέων φλόγα.
— sustulerit: *destroyed*. The subject is the antecedent of qui in the following verse.

45 ff. terram, mare, urbis, etc.: indicating the universality of Jove's rule. Observe also that the natural contrast of the nouns is heightened by the adjectives employed, — inertem, *brute*; ventosum, *gusty* (cf. 1, 34, 9 *bruta tellus et vaga flumina*); tristia, *gloomy*, contrasted with the cities of men. — temperat: *governs* (in harmony). Cf. 1, 12, 16. Its objects are terram and mare; the other nouns denoting animate creatures belong with regit. — unus: *alone*, emphasizing the unity of the world's order.

49 ff. The possibility that Jove should fear the giants is, strictly taken, inconsistent with his universal rule described in the preceding strophe; but Horace wished to exalt (57 f.) the position of Pallas, the embodiment of wisdom, in relation to the power of Jove.

50. fidens: absolutely, *presumptuous*. — iuventus horrida bracchiis:

fratresque tendentes opaco
Pelion imposuisse Olympo.

Sed quid Typhoeus et validus **Mimas,**
aut quid minaci Porphyrion statu,
55   quid Rhoetus evolsisque truncis
Enceladus iaculator audax

contra sonantem Palladis aegida
possent ruentes? Hinc avidus stetit

the Hecatoncheires, who in the common form of the myth guard for Jove the Titans whom he has hurled into Tartarus. But here Horace includes them among the monstrous, and therefore evil, powers that assail the majesty of right and wisdom. The violence done the old mythology would offend no one of Horace's audience, and the allegory would be evident to all. **horrida bracchiis**: *with their bristling arms.*

51 f. **fratres**: the Aloidae, Otus and Ephialtes.—**tendentes**, etc.: cf. *Od.* 11, 315 f. Ὄσσαν ἐπ' Οὐλύμπῳ μέμασαν θέμεν, αὐτὰρ ἐπ' Ὄσσῃ | Πήλιον εἰνοσίφυλλον. Verg. *G.* 1, 280 ff. *et coniuratos caelum rescindere fratres. | ter sunt conati imponere Pelio Ossam | scilicet, atque Ossae frondosum involvere Olympum;* Prop. 2, 1, 19 f. *non ego Titanas canerem, non Ossan Olympo | impositam, ut caeli Pelion esset iter.*—**imposuisse**: for the force of the tense, cf. 1, 1, 4.

53 ff. **Typhoeus**: according to Hesiod, *Theog.* 821, the youngest child of Earth, sent to punish Zeus for his destruction of the Giants; Pindar, *P.* 8, 21, makes him one of the Giants. — **Mimas**: also a Giant, Eurip. *Ion* 215.—**Porphyrion**: king of the Giants, Pind. *P.* 8, 15.—**minaci statu**: of threatening mien.—**Rhoetus**: cf. 2, 19, 23. — **truncis**: instrumental abl. with **iaculator.** Intr. 97. —**Enceladus**: buried under Aetna. Verg. *A.* 3, 578 ff. *fama est Enceladi semiustum fulmine corpus | urgueri mole hac, ingentemque insuper Aetnam | impositam ruptis flammam exspirare caminis.* Also Longfellow's *Enceladus.*

57 ff. **Palladis**: the embodiment of wisdom, and Jove's chief support. — **aegida**: represented in works of art as a breast-plate (cf. n. to 1, 15, 11), but apparently conceived of here as a shield, possibly after *Il.* 17, 593 ff. καὶ τότ' ἄρα Κρονίδης ἕλετ' αἰγίδα θυσσανόεσσαν (adorned with tassels) | μαρμαρέην (flashing), . . . τὴν δ' ἐτίναξε.— **ruentes**: *wildly rushing;* cf. n. to ruit, v. 65 below.—**hinc**: *i.e.* beside

Volcanus, hinc matrona Iuno et
numquam umeris positurus arcum,

qui rore puro Castaliae lavit
crinis solutos, qui Lyciae tenet
dumeta natalemque silvam,
Delius et Patareus Apollo.

Vis consili expers mole ruit sua:
vim temperatam di quoque provehunt
in maius; idem odere viris

Jove.—avidus: cf. the Homeric λιλαιόμενοι πολέμοιο *Il.* 3, 133. Verg. *A.* 9, 661 *avidus pugnae.*— numquam umeris, etc.: cf. 1, 21, 11 f. *(tollite laudibus) insignemque pharetra | fraternaque umerum lyra.* In Eurip. *Alc.* 40 Apollo says, in answer to the question why he has his bow and arrows with him, σύνηθες αἰεὶ ταῦτα βαστάζειν ἐμοί.
61 ff. Cf. Pind. *P.* 1, 39 Λύκιε καὶ Δάλοι᾿ ἀνάσσων Φοῖβε, Παρνασσοῦ τε κράναν Κασταλίαν φιλέων. Also Stat. *Theb.* 1, 696 ff. *Phoebe parens, seu te Lyciae Patarea nivosis | exercent dumeta iugis, seu rore pudico | Castaliae flavos amor est tibi mergere crines.*—Castaliae: a spring on Mt. Parnassus; for a variation of the place, cf. 4. 6, 26 *qui Xantho lavit amne crinis.*—solutos: *flowing*; cf. 1, 21, 2. and n.— Lyciae, etc.: according to the Delian legend of Apollo, the god spent the six summer months on the island, but withdrew for the other six to Patara, in Lycia.—natalem

silvam: in Delos, where he was born.
65 ff. vis consili expers, etc.: these words sum up what has preceded, —'mere force, blind rebellion, undirected by wisdom, is sure to fail; but when properly guided it enjoys the favor of the very gods, who yet abhor and punish reckless strength that urges men to wickedness. We have as a proof of this the cases of Gyas, Orion, and the rest, whose lawlessness brought on them the divine wrath.'
— mole ruit sua: *rushes to ruin of its own weight.* For this meaning of *ruo*, cf. n. to 1, 2, 25. With this sententia, cf. Eurip. *Frg.* 732 ῥώμη δέ τ᾿ ἀμαθὴς πολλάκις τίκτει βλάβην, and Pind. *P.* 8, 15 βίᾳ δὲ καὶ μεγάλαυχον (the boastful) ἔσφαλεν ἐν χρόνῳ.
66 ff. vim temperatam: contrasted both by position and meaning with the preceding. Intr. 28c.
— idem: *and yet they.* Cf. 2, 10, 16.— viris: here not distinguished in meaning from the singular.

omne nefas animo moventis.

Testis mearum centimanus Gyas
70   sententiarum, notus et integrae
temptator Orion Dianae,
virginea domitus sagitta.

Iniecta monstris Terra dolet suis,
maeretque partus fulmine luridum
75   missos ad Orcum; nec peredit
impositam celer ignis Aetnen,

Note the cumulative effect of vis, vim, viris.

69 ff. Examples of the punishment which overtakes those indicated in v. 68. — testis, etc.: with the expression and asyndeton, cf. Pind. *Frg.* 169 Schr. Νόμος ὁ πάντων βασιλεὺς | . . . ἄγει . . . τὸ βιαιότατον | ὑπερτάτᾳ χειρί. τεκμαίρομαι | ἔργοισιν Ἡρακλέος. 'Custom, lord of all, leads most forcibly with mightiest hand. My proof is from the deeds of Heracles.'— Gyas: cf. 2, 17, 14.

70 ff. notus: *i.e.* an example familiar to all; cf. scimus, v. 42. — temptator: *assailant*; only here in this sense. Cf. Stat. *Theb.* 11, 12 f. *quantus Apollineae temerator matris Averno | tenditur*. — virginea: *i.e.* shot by the chaste Diana.

73 ff. iniecta, etc.: one cause of Earth's sorrow is that she is forced to be the burial place of her own offspring (hence monstris suis). — monstris: dative with both iniecta and dolet. Intr. 100. — dolet maeretque: notice the tense, — *ever suffers and mourns for*. — partus: particularly the Titans. — fulmine: with missos. — luridum: *ghastly*; appropriate to the lower world. — nec peredit: the volcanic outbursts represent the struggles of the monster to escape, but his efforts are all in vain, for his punishment is eternal. With the gnomic perfect, cf. v. 78, reliquit. Intr. 103.

76. impositam . . . Aetnen: according to Aeschylus and Pindar, Typhoeus was buried beneath Aetna. *P. V.* 363 ff. καὶ νῦν ἀχρεῖον καὶ παράορον δέμας | κεῖται στενωποῦ πλησίον θαλασσίου | ἰπούμενος ῥίζαισιν Αἰτναίαις ὕπο. 'And now he lies a useless outstretched form hard by the sea strait, weighed down beneath the roots of Aetna.' Pind. *P.* 1, 32 ff. νῦν γε μὰν | ταί θ᾽ ὑπὲρ Κύμας ἁλιερκέες ὄχθαι | Σικελία τ᾽ αὐτοῦ πιέζει στέρνα λαχνάεντα· κίων δ᾽ οὐρανία συνέχει, | νιφόεσσ᾽ Αἴτνα. 'But now the sea-girt shores past Cumae and Sicily

incontinentis nec Tityi iecur
reliquit ales, nequitiae additus
    custos; amatorem trecentae
80   Pirithoum cohibent catenae.

likewise press down his shaggy breast; and snowy Aetna, a pillar of the sky, holds him in ward.' Other forms of the myth place Enceladus there (cf. n. to v. 56 above).—**celer**: *swift darting*, of the volcanic fires.

77 f. incontinentis: the position emphasizes Tityos' crime in offering violence to Latona.—**iecur**: the seat of passion, at which the punishment is appropriately directed.—**ales**: cf. Verg. *A.* 6, 597 ff. *rostroque inmanis voltur obunco | inmortale iecur tondens fecundaque poenis | viscera rimaturque epulis habitatque sub alto | pectore, nec fibris requies datur ulla renatis.*—**additus custos**: *set as warder;* implying that the vulture would never leave him. Cf. Verg. *A.* 6, 90 *nec Teucris addita Iuno usquam aberit.*

79 f. Pirithous, king of the Lapithae, and Theseus were chained to a rock in Hades for their impious attempt to carry off Proserpina. Theseus was rescued by Hercules, but Pirithous obtained no escape. Cf. 4, 7, 27 f.—**trecentae**: an indefinite number, 'countless.'

5

'While Jove is sovereign of the sky and Augustus rules on earth, can it be that Crassus' disgraceful defeat is yet unavenged! Has a Roman soldier so forgotten his birthright as to live under a Median King, married to a barbarian wife! It was this very thing that Regulus' wise mind foresaw when he opposed the ransoming of our soldiers captured by the Carthaginians, a precedent fraught with ill for later times (1-18). . . . "No," he said, " let those who yielded die; will they be braver when bought back? No, let them stay, for they have brought disgrace upon their native Italy (19-40)." So like one disgraced he put aside his wife and child, and stood with downcast eyes, until the Senate had agreed to his proposal; then he hurried back to torture and to death with heart as light as for a holiday (41-56).'

The ode thus treats of the degeneracy of the Roman arms and the loss of military prestige which Augustus was to remedy and revive. In the first strophe the allegory of the preceding ode gives way to plain speech. The date of composition is shown by v. 3 to be 27-26 B.C. Metre, 68.

[3, 5, 1]

> Caelo tonantem credidimus Iovem
> regnare: praesens divus habebitur
>   Augustus adiectis Britannis
>   imperio gravibusque Persis.
>
> 5 Milesne Crassi coniuge barbara
> turpis maritus vixit et hostium
>   (pro curia inversique mores!)
>   consenuit socerorum in armis,
>
> sub rege Medo Marsus et Apulus,
> 10   anciliorum et nominis et togae

1 ff. caelo: with **regnare**, in contrast to **praesens divus**. — **tonantem**: giving the reason for the belief; also a proper epithet of Jove. — **credidimus**: gnomic perfect. Intr. 103. — **praesens divus**: *a god in very presence*; *i.e.* on earth, visible to men. Cf. Ovid. *Trist.* 4, 4, 20 *superorum duorum, | quorum hic (Augustus) aspicitur, creditur ille (Iuppiter) deus.* 2, 54 *per te praesentem conspicuumque deum.* Verg. *G.* 1, 41 *nec tam praesentis alibi cognoscere divos (licebat).* — **adiectis**, etc.: *when they shall have been added.* — **gravibus**: *vexing*; cf. 1, 2, 22.

5 f. milesne: a sudden burst of indignation aroused by the mention of the Persians. Plutarch. *Crass.* 31, tells us that ten thousand Romans surrendered at Carrhae in 53 B.C. and settled among the Parthians; they were actually compelled by their victors to fight with them against the Romans. — **coniuge barbara**: abl. with **turpis**; cf. 1, 37, 9. — **maritus**: emphasizing the disgrace, for properly there could be no *conubium* between a Roman and a foreigner. The emphasis is continued in **hostium ... socerorum.** — **vixit**: *has actually lived.*

7 f. pro: an interjection. — **curia**: the senate house, or senate (cf. 2, 1, 14), typical of all that Rome held most ancient and sacred. — **consenuit**: almost a generation had passed since Carrhae. Aurel. Victor *Epit.* 32 says with exaggeration of the Prince Valerian in the third century A.D., *Valerianus ... in Mesopotamia bellum gerens a Sapore Persarum rege superatus, mox etiam captus, apud Parthos ignobili servitute consenuit.*

9 f. rege: a hateful word to a Roman; cf. 1, 37. 7. — **Medo Marsus et Apulus**: effective juxtaposition. The Marsi were among

oblitus aeternaeque Vestae,
   incolumi Iove et urbe Roma?

Hoc caverat mens provida Reguli
   dissentientis condicionibus
15   foedis et exemplo trahenti
   perniciem veniens in aevum,

si non periret immiserabilis
   captiva pubes. 'Signa ego Punicis
      adfixa delubris et arma
20   militibus sine caede' dixit

the bravest of the Italian peoples (cf. 2, 20, 18); here joined with the sturdy Apulians (cf. 1, 22, 14), Horace's fellow countrymen. — **anciliorum**: the ancilia were among the sacred *pignora imperii*, and were in charge of the Salii. See *Cl. Dict.* s.v. *Salii*. — **nominis**: sc. *Romani*. — **togae**: the distinctive dress of the Romans, the *gens togata*.

11 f. **aeternae Vestae**: the ever-burning fire on the hearth of Vesta was symbolical of the permanency of the state. — **incolumi Iove**: *i.e.* 'while Jove's temple stands.' With the three verses, cf. Florus 2, 21, 3 *patriae, nominis, togae, fascium oblitus (Antonius)*.

13 ff. **hoc**: emphatic, *it was this very thing.* — **Reguli**: M. Atilius Regulus, consul 256 B.C., was captured by the Carthaginians in Africa in 255 B.C. According to the common tradition he was sent to Rome in 250 B.C. to treat for peace or to obtain at least an exchange of prisoners, but persuaded the Senate to decline to consider either proposition. Polybius does not refer to this mission, so that the correctness of the tradition has been called into question, but in Cicero's time it had become a favorite commonplace. Cf. Cic. *de Off.* 1, 39; 3, 99; *de Orat.* 3, 109; Livy *per.* 18. — **condicionibus foedis**: *i.e.* those proposed by the Carthaginians. — **exemplo trahenti**: *a precedent destined to bring.*

17 f. **si non periret**: explaining **exemplo trahenti**. The subj. represents *peribit* of Regulus' speech. For the quantity **perirēt** see Intr. 35. — **signa**: this would recall to the Roman's mind Crassus' standards, still in the hands of the Parthians. — **ego**: 'with my own eyes.' — **militibus sine caede**, etc.; note the ironical contrast. 'soldiers who yielded up their arms — without a struggle'

'derepta vidi; vidi ego civium
retorta tergo bracchia libero
  portasque non clausas et arva
  Marte coli populata nostro.

25 Auro repensus scilicet acrior
    miles redibit. Flagitio additis
      damnum. Neque amissos colores
      lana refert medicata fuco,

    nec vera virtus, cum semel excidit,
30 curat reponi deterioribus.
      Si pugnat extricata densis
      cerva plagis, erit ille fortis

21 ff. vidi; vidi ego: Intr. 28 b.
— **civium**, etc.: *yes, citizens*; 'free citizens of Rome have given themselves up to become slaves.' — **libero**: *their free-born.* — **portas**, etc.; 'the Carthaginians have come to despise us so that they do not take the precaution to close their city gates, and cultivate again the fields our army devastated.'

25 ff. auro repensus, etc.: said in deepest scorn — 'a price forsooth (**scilicet**), will make them better soldiers.' — **flagitio**, etc.: impatiently disposing of the proposal, — 'besides suffering the present disgrace you will waste your money.' Cf. Ps.-Eurip. *Rhes.* 102 αἰσχρὸν γὰρ ἡμῖν καὶ πρὸς αἰσχύνῃ κακόν. — **neque** . . . **nec**: the simile is stated paratactically in place of the more common *ut . . . ita.* So in Greek, *e.g.* Aesch. *Sept.* 584 f. μητρός τε πληγὴν τίς κατασβέσει δίκη; | πατρίς τε γαῖα σῆς ὑπὸ σπουδῆς δορὸς | ἁλοῦσα πῶς σοι ξύμμαχος γενήσεται; 'What atonement can quench the sin of a mother's murder? How can thy native land, captured by thy incitement, ever be thy ally again.' That is — 'even as . . ., so . . .' — **colores**: the natural color of the wool (*simplex ille candor*, Quint. 1, 1, 5), lost when the wool is dyed. — **medicata**: a technical expression, containing the same figure as the Greek φαρμάσσειν. Four centuries later Paulin. Nol. *C.* 17, 23 repeated the phrase, *medicata vellera fuco.*

29 ff. semel: *once for all.* — **curat**: with infinitive, as 2, 13, 39 f. *nec curat . . . agitare.* — **deterioribus**: *i.e.* those made so by loss of **vera virtus**. The dative belongs with **reponi**. — **si pugnat**, etc.: an impossible supposition.

qui perfidis se credidit hostibus,
et Marte Poenos proteret altero
    qui lora restrictis lacertis
        sensit iners timuitque mortem.

Hic, unde vitam sumeret inscius,
pacem duello miscuit. O pudor!
    O magna Carthago, probrosis
        altior Italiae ruinis!'

Fertur pudicae coniugis osculum
parvosque natos ut capitis minor
    ab se removisse et virilem
        torvus humi posuisse voltum,

    donec labantis consilio patres
    firmaret auctor numquam alias dato,

33 ff. perfidis: contrasted with **credidit**, and emphasizing the cowardice of the soldier who actually trusted his life to an enemy whose faithlessness was well known. *Punica fides* was proverbial. Cf. also 4, 4, 49 *perfidus Hannibal* and n. — **altero**: *a second.* — **iners**: predicate, *tamely.*

37 f. hic: vividly continuing *ille* of v. 32. — **unde sumeret**: representing the anxious, *unde vitam sumam?* of the coward whose anxiety causes him to forget that he must fight, not bargain, for his life. — **duello**: this archaic form for *bello* is also found 3, 14, 18; 4, 15, 8. — **miscuit**: *has failed to distinguish between.*

40. ruinis: instrumental abl. with **altior** — *exalted over the*, etc.

41 ff. fertur: *and yet men say*, used to introduce a surprising statement. Cf. 1, 16, 13. This quiet account of Regulus' determination is in marked contrast with the vehement pathos of the preceding strophe. — **ut capitis minor**: *as one deprived of civil rights*, equivalent to the legal (prose) formula *capite deminutus.* The genitive is similar to the genitive in *integer vitae, militiae piger.* Regulus felt that as a captive of the Carthaginians he was no better than a slave, who of course possessed no civil rights, and was therefore unfit to enjoy the privileges of a Roman *pater familias.*

44. torvus: *grimly.*

45 ff. donec . . . firmaret, etc.: *while he established*; said with ref-

interque maerentis amicos
    egregius properaret exsul.

Atqui sciebat quae sibi barbarus
50   tortor pararet : non aliter tamen
    dimovit obstantis propinquos
    et populum reditus morantem

quam si clientum longa negotia
    diiudicata lite relinqueret,
55   tendens Venafranos in agros
    aut Lacedaemonium Tarentum.

erence to **removisse, posuisse**. — **consilio** : connect with **firmaret**. — **interque** : *and then through the midst of.* — **egregius** : cf. n. to 1, 6, 11. With the oxymoron, cf. 3, 3, 38 f. Notice that two points are brought out in this strophe : Regulus' moral courage in inducing the senate to accept his proposal, and the self-sacrifice which this involved.

49 ff. atqui : *and yet*, καί τοι. Cf. 1, 23, 9. — **sciebat** : *he knew all the while.* — **non aliter . . . quam si** : *as undisturbed . . . as if.* — **tortor**, etc. : the tortures to which Regulus was subjected, like the whole story of the embassy, may be inventions of a later time. Cf. n. to v. 13 ff. — **obstantis** : *who tried to hinder him.* — **reditus** : plural for euphony.

53 ff. longa : *wearisome.* — **diiudicata lite** : the Roman *patronus* of the Republic was bound to aid and protect his *clientes* ; whether the suit here is conceived of as one which Regulus decided as arbitrator or one in which he defended his client's interests in court is not clear. — **tendens** : *taking his way*, into the country for rest and refreshment. — **Venafranos agros . . . Tarentum** : cf. 2, 6, 12-16 and nn.

Note the contrast between the earlier part of the ode and this quiet close. The ode is one of Horace's noblest; its national characteristics are well summed up by Andrew Lang in his *Letters to Dead Authors*, p. 191 f. 'None but a patriot could have sung that ode on Regulus, who died, as our hero died on an evil day, for the honor of Rome, as Gordon for the honor of England. . . . We talk of the Greeks as your teachers. Your teachers they were, but that poem could only have been written by a Roman. The strength, the tenderness. the noble and monumental resolution and resignation — these are the gifts of the lords of human things, the masters of the world.'

6

In the last ode of the series Horace considers the reasons for the degeneracy of the times. These he finds to be the neglect of religion and the growth of immorality that is destroying the family and making each succeeding generation worse than the one which preceded it.

'The sins of thy fathers shall be visited on thee, Roman, until thou repairest the ruined temples of the gods and restorest the forgotten faith of an earlier time. Thy power depends on thy humility toward Heaven; it was in punishment for thy indifference that the Parthian, the allied Dacian and Ethiopian almost destroyed our city (1-16). But more dangerous than foreign foes is the flood of immorality that has swept over our state: all modesty and respect for marriage ties are gone; adultery is unabashed (17-32). It was not the offspring of such stock as this that saved the state from foreign foes in earlier days. There is no hope: we are worse than our forbears and our children will be more degenerate than we (33-48).'

By its reference to the loss of military prowess this ode is naturally connected with the preceding. In that, devotion to duty is the ideal; here, purity and simplicity of life, as exhibited by the Sabine stock. The pessimistic close is surprising and shows that the six odes were hardly composed originally to form a series. This ode was probably written soon after 28 B.C., the year in which Octavian, by virtue of his censorial power, tried to enforce ordinances intended to check the evil tendencies of the times. See also n. to v. 2 below. Metre, 68.

Delicta maiorum immeritus lues,
Romane, donec templa refeceris

1 ff. **delicta maiorum**: especially the civil wars, 88-31 B.C. — **immeritus**: concessive, 'although innocent of their sins.' With the idea, cf. Eurip. *Frg.* 980 τὰ τῶν τεκόντων σφάλματ' εἰς τοὺς ἐκγόνους | οἱ θεοὶ τρέπουσιν. *Ezek.* 18. 2 'The fathers have eaten sour grapes, and the children's teeth are set on edge.' — **Romane**: with this use of the singular, cf. Vergil's famous line (*A.* 6, 851) *tu regere imperio populos, Romane, memento*. — **refeceris**: one of Octavian's first acts after his return from the conquest of Egypt was to rebuild the temples that had fallen into decay. Cf. *Mon. Anc.* 4, 17 *duo et octoginta templa deum in urbe consul sextum* (28 B.C.) *ex decreto senatus refeci, nullo praetermisso quod eo tempore refici debebat*: and Suet. *Aug.* 30 *aedes sacras vetustate conlapsas aut in-*

aedisque labentis deorum et
foeda nigro simulacra fumo.

5 Dis te minorem quod geris, imperas:
hinc omne principium, huc refer exitum.
Di multa neglecti dederunt
Hesperiae mala luctuosae.

Iam bis Monaeses et Pacori manus
10 non auspicatos contudit impetus
nostros et adiecisse praedam
torquibus exiguis renidet.

cendio absumptas refecit. — **aedis**: here synonymous with *templa.* — **labentis**: *moldering.* — **foeda**: *defiled.*

5 ff. quod geris: *in that thou bearest thyself*; *i.e.* 'thy rule depends on thy humility toward the gods.' Cf. 1, 12, 57 *te minor latum reget aequus orbem.* — **hinc, huc**: *i.e.* the gods. Cf. Verg. *E.* 3, 60 *ab Iove principium.* Also Liv. 45, 39, 10 *maiores vestri omnium magnarum rerum et principia exorsi ab dis sunt et finem eum statuerunt.* — **principium**: for the scansion. cf. Intr. 39. — **di neglecti**: the cause of Rome's defeats and dangers, of which the concrete examples follow. — **Hesperiae**: Italy, cf. 2, 1, 32. — **luctuosae**: *i.e.* for those who have fallen in both civil and foreign wars.

9. iam bis, etc.: the Romans had actually suffered three defeats in the east: that of Crassus at Carrhae 53 B.C.; that of Decidius Saxa by Pacorus in Syria 40 B.C.; and that of Antony in Media 36 B.C. As the defeat of Saxa was avenged in 38 B.C. by Ventidius, Horace may refer to the first and third disasters only, but it is needless to demand historical accuracy of a poet in every case. The only Monaeses known to us was a Parthian noble who sought refuge from Phraates IV with Antonius in 37 B.C.; he afterwards became reconciled to Phraates and deserted Antony.

10 ff. non auspicatos: and therefore *infaustos*. We read in Vell. Pater. 2, 46 of Crassus' expedition *proficiscentem in Syriam diris cum ominibus tribuni plebis frustra retinere conati.* — **torquibus**: the necklaces. στρεπτοί, which with armlets, ψέλια. presented by the king, were the insignia most highly prized by the Persians. Cf. Xen. *Cyrop.* 8, 2, 8 ὥσπερ ἔνια (δῶρα) τῶν βασιλέως, ψέλια καὶ στρεπτοὶ καὶ ἵπποι χρυσοχάλινοι. — **exiguis**: in comparison with the rich booty

Paene occupatam seditionibus
delevit urbem Dacus et Aethiops,
15   hic classe formidatus, ille
missilibus melior sagittis.

Fecunda culpae saecula nuptias
primum inquinavere et genus et domos;
hoc fonte derivata clades
20   in patriam populumque fluxit.

Motus doceri gaudet Ionicos
matura virgo et fingitur artibus,

taken from the Romans.—**renidet**: *beams with delight*; hence used like *gaudet* (v. 21) with an infinitive.

13 ff. paene: with delevit.—**seditionibus**; it is important to remember that there was a strong party in Rome hostile to Octavian, so that the reference is not simply to the struggle between him and Antony, carried on outside of Italy. The point which Horace is emphasizing is that not only had the Romans failed in their attempts against foreign foes, but in the passion of civil strife had almost handed over the city to the mercies of the barbarian Dacian and Egyptian.—**Dacus et Aethiops**: Dacian bowmen served in Antony's land forces, while the Egyptian naval contingent was two hundred ships. That the Romans about this time had a lively fear of an invasion by the Dacians there can be no doubt. Cf. n to 1, 26, 3 f.

17 ff. Horace here turns to a new cause for the state's degeneracy — the decay of domestic virtue, the growth of immorality. With the following strophes, cf. 3, 24, 19-24; 4, 5, 21-24.—**fecunda**: *big with*. —**inquinavere**: cf. *Epod.* 16. 64.

21 ff. motus Ionicos: voluptuous dances introduced from Ionia. **motus** is the technical expression for a mimetic dance. The old-fashioned Romans did not look with favor on dancing, save in connection with worship; custom had, however, somewhat relaxed even in the time of the Gracchi. Macrobius 3, 14, 6 f. has preserved the complaint of Scipio Africanus, who bewailed the fact that boys and girls had come to associate with actors and learn songs and dances which a former generation would have considered disgraceful for a freeborn person to know.

22 ff. matura: *i.e. tempestiva viro* 1, 23, 12. 'Even if these dances and airs might be forgiven in a child, they cannot be overlooked in a full-grown maid.'—

iam nunc et incestos amores
    de tenero meditatur ungui;
25 mox iuniores quaerit adulteros
    inter mariti vina, neque eligit
        cui donet impermissa raptim
        gaudia luminibus remotis,

    sed iussa coram non sine conscio
30 surgit marito, seu vocat institor
        seu navis Hispanae magister,
        dedecorum pretiosus emptor.

    Non his iuventus orta parentibus
    infecit aequor sanguine Punico,

fingitur artibus: 'she learns artificial coquettish ways.' — iam nunc: *i.e.* while still unmarried; opposed to mox v. 25. — de tenero ... ungui: in imitation of the Greek ἐξ ἁπαλῶν ὀνύχων, 'from the very quick.' Translate, — *to her very finger tips.* Cf. Anth. Pal. 5, 129, 1 ff. τὴν ἀπὸ τῆς Ἀσίης ὀρχηστρίδα, τὴν κακοτέχνοις | σχήμασιν ἐξ ἁπαλῶν κινυμένην ὀνύχων, | αἰνέω ... 'The dancing girl from Asia, vibrating to her very finger tips in her shameless dancing figures, her I praise.'

25 ff. mox: *i.e.* when married. — iuniores: *i.e.* than her husband. — neque eligit: presently she falls so low that she can no longer choose the recipients of her favors, but must obey the orders of the lowest peddler or ship captain. Note the carefully planned contrasts between neque eligit and iussa, vocat; donet and emptor; impermissa gaudia and dedecorum; raptim and coram; luminibus remotis and conscio marito. — impermissa: coined by Horace.

29 ff. conscio ... marito: the corruption of the household is so complete that the husband consents to his wife's adulteries. — institor: while the peddler belonged to a despised class his trade naturally brought him into contact with the women of the household. Cf. Seneca's warning, *Frg.* 52 H. *institores gemmarum sericarumque vestium si intromiseris, periculum pudicitiae est.* — navis ... magister: also belonging to the lower classes, but like the peddler able to spend money freely (pretiosus emptor).

33 ff. non his: 'the Romans who made Rome great were sprung from different stock.' — infecit aequor,

35 Pyrrhumque et ingentem cecidit
        Antiochum Hannibalemque dirum,

    sed rusticorum mascula militum
    proles, Sabellis docta ligonibus
        versare glaebas et severae
40   matris ad arbitrium recisos

    portare fustis, sol ubi montium
    mutaret umbras et iuga demeret
        bobus fatigatis, amicum
            tempus agens abeunte curru.

45 Damnosa quid non imminuit dies?
    Aetas parentum, peior avis, tulit

etc.: in the first Punic war, 264–241 B.C., when Rome gained her naval supremacy. — **Pyrrhum**: Pyrrhus was defeated at Beneventum 275 B.C. — **ingentem... Antiochum**: Antiochus the Great, defeated at Magnesia, 190 B.C. — **dirum**: cf. 4, 4, 42 *dirus Afer*.

38 ff. Sabellis: the Sabines were proverbial for purity and uprightness. Cf. Liv. 1, 18, 4 *quo genere nullum quondam incorruptius fuit.* — **versare glaebas et**, etc.: 'when the field work is done, the sturdy youth must still cut and bring in a supply of wood to satisfy (**ad arbitrium**) his stern mother.'

41 ff. Observe the idyllic note in this description of the evening. Cf. *Epod.* 2, 61 ff. — **sol ubi mutaret**, etc.: 'as the day closes the mountain shadows shift and lengthen.' Cf. Verg. *E.* 1, 83 *maioresque cadunt altis de montibus umbrae*; 2, 66 f. *aspice, aratra iugo referunt suspensa iuvenci,* | *et sol crescentis decedens duplicat umbras.* — **iuga demeret**, etc.: so Hesiod, *Op.* 580 f. says of the morning, Ἠὼς ... ἐπὶ ζυγὰ βουσί τίθησιν. — **mutaret, demeret**: the subjunctives are probably due to the close connection between the relative clauses and the infinitive; they are possibly subjunctives of repeated action, but Horace has everywhere else the indicative with *ubi* in that sense. — **agens abeunte curru**: a slight oxymoron; with the phrase, cf. *Epist.* 1, 16, 6 *sol ... discedens fugiente curru*.

45 ff. The thought of the contrast between the Romans of an earlier time and those of his own day leads Horace to his hopeless conclusion. — **damnosa**: *damaging*; emphatically expressing the poet's despair. Notice the skillful com-

nos nequiores, mox daturos
progeniem vitiosiorem.

pression by which Horace has described the moral decay of four generations in three verses. Aratus, *Phaen.* 123 f. was less successful, οἵην χρυσείην πατέρες γενεήν ἐλίποντο | χειροτέρην, ὑμεῖς δὲ κακώτερα τεξείεσθε. — peior avis: *worse than that of our grandparents.* — mox daturos: *destined soon to produce.*

7

The unbroken serious strain of the national odes is relieved by these light verses addressed to Asterie, whose lover is kept from home by opposing winds. The names are Greek, but the setting is Roman.

'Why dost thou weep, Asterie, for thy lover, detained by winter winds across the sea? Be assured that he is faithful, and ever turns a deaf ear to the messages of his love-lorn hostess, who would tempt him to her. Fear not for him, but see that thou remain thyself as true. Yield not to the charms of thy handsome neighbor: do not listen to his serenade.'

There is no indication of the date. Metre, 73.

Quid fles, Asterie, quem tibi candidi
primo restituent vere Favonii
 Thyna merce beatum,
  constantis iuvenem fide,

5 Gygen? Ille Notis actus ad Oricum
post insana Caprae sidera frigidas
 noctis non sine multis
  insomnis lacrimis agit.

1 ff. Asterie: cf. the Greek names Ἀστερίς and Ἀστήρ. Also n. to 3, 9, 21 *sidere pulchrior.* — can.didi... Favonii: the breezes that bring in the bright spring weather. Cf. 1, 4. 1 and n. — Thyna: *i.e. Bithyna*; cf. 1. 35. 7. — beatum: *enriched*; cf. 1. 4. 14 — fide: genitive.

5 ff. Gygen: the name is found in Archil. *Frg.* 25 Γύγης ὁ πολύχρυσος. — ad Oricum: Gyges is detained at Oricum in Epirus, directly opposite Brundisium. — Caprae: this constellation sets about the middle of December, when the stormy winter season begins.

Atqui sollicitae nuntius hospitae,
   suspirare Chloen et miseram tuis
      dicens ignibus uri,
         temptat mille vafer modis.

Vt Proetum mulier perfida credulum
falsis impulerit criminibus nimis
   casto Bellerophontae
      maturare necem refert;

narrat paene datum Pelea Tartaro,
Magnessam Hippolyten dum fugit abstinens,
   et peccare docentis
      fallax historias movet.

Frustra: nam scopulis surdior Icari
voces audit adhuc integer.   At tibi

9 ff. **atqui**: corrective, 'Yet he might console himself, for,' etc. — **sollicitae**: sc. *amore*, *love-lorn*. — **tuis**: *like thine*. Naturally these are not the words of Chloe's messenger to Gyges, but Horace's to Asterie. — **mille vafer modis**: *skilled in countless wiles*.

12 ff. The classical parallels to the story of Joseph and Potiphar's wife. — **mulier**: Anteia in Homer (*Il.* 6, 160), Stheneboea in tragedy, wife of Proteus, king of Tiryns. — **perfida credulum**: cf. n. to 1, 6, 9. — **maturare necem**: *to bring an untimely death*. — **refert**: *i.e.* the nuntius of v. 9.

17 ff. **narrat**: repeating refert in sense, and thus connecting the two strophes. Intr. 29. — **datum . . . Tartaro**: a variation of the formula *leto datus*. — **Hippolyte**: wife of Acastus, king of Iolcus. — **abstinens**: *in his sobriety*. — **movet**: *sets a-going*.

21 ff. **frustra**: note the emphatic position, — *yet all in vain*, ' for the threats implied in the stories of Bellerophon and Peleus do not move thy Gyges.' — **scopulis surdior**: cf. Eurip. *Med.* 28 f. ὡς δὲ πέτρος ἢ θαλάσσιος κλύδων ἀκούει νουθετουμένη φίλων, ' But like a rock or billow of the sea she listens to her friends' advice.' Note the oxymoron in **surdior . . . audit**. — **Icari**: a rocky island near Samos. — **voces**, etc.: so Vergil says of Aeneas, *A.* 4. 438 f. *sed nullis ille movetur | fletibus, aut voces ullas tractabilis audit*. — **at tibi**: in sudden transition; cf. 2, 18, 9. —

> ne vicinus Enipeus
> plus iusto placeat cave,
>
> 25 quamvis non alius flectere equum sciens
> aeque conspicitur gramine Martio,
> nec quisquam citus aeque
> Tusco denatat alveo.
>
> Prima nocte domum claude, neque in vias
> 30 sub cantu querulae despice tibiae,
> et te saepe vocanti
> duram difficilis mane.

Enipeus: named after a river in Thessaly; cf. *Hebrus* 3, 12, 2.

25 ff. 'This dangerous rival excels in the athletic sports practiced by young nobles; Gyges is only a trader.' For riding and swimming, cf. 1, 8, 8; 3, 12, 3. — **flectere equum**: in elaborate evolutions. Cf. Ovid *A. A.* 3, 384 *in gyros ire coactus equus*. — **conspicitur**: *is the object of men's eyes.* — **gramine Martio**: *i.e.* on the Campus Martius.

29 ff. Cf. Ovid *Am.* 2, 19, 38 *incipe iam prima claudere nocte forem*. Also Shylock's warning, *Merchant of Venice* 2, 5 'Hear you me, Jessica: | Lock up my doors; and when you hear the drum | And the vile squealing of the wry-neck'd fife, | Clamber not you up to the casements then | Nor thrust your head into the public street.' — **querulae**: *the plaintive.* — **despice**: literally, *look down*, from an upper story. — **vocanti**: sc. *Enipeo*; the participle is concessive. — **duram**: *cruel*, predicate adjective with te. — **difficilis**: *unyielding*.

8

To Maecenas. 'You are puzzled then, my learned friend, over my bachelor's sacrifice on the matrons' Calends. This is the day the tree so nearly killed me: as each year comes round, I'll celebrate the season with a fresh jar of long-stored wine. So drink deep, Maecenas, for thy friend's escape. Let go the cares of state; our border foes are all subdued or vexed by their own quarrels. Become to-day a private citizen; dismiss your serious thoughts, and take what joys the passing hour now offers.'

In this strain Horace invites his patron to celebrate with him the anniversary of his escape from the falling tree (2, 13). The date is shown to be March 1, 29 B.C., by the references in vv. 17-23. Cotiso and the threatening Dacians were subdued in the campaigns of 30-28 B.C.: the news of the struggle between Phraates and Tiridates for the Parthian throne (cf. n. to 1, 26, 5) probably reached Rome in January, 29 B.C. Furthermore, at the time of composition Maecenas was clearly at the head of the state and Octavian absent; but the latter returned to the city in the summer of 29 B.C. All these facts tend to show that the occasion of the ode was March 1 of that year, and since this is evidently the first anniversary, that the date of Horace's escape was March 1, 30 B.C. Metre, 69.

> Martiis caelebs quid agam Kalendis,
> quid velint flores et acerra turis
> plena miraris, positusque carbo in
> caespite vivo,
>
> 5   docte sermones utriusque linguae?
> Voveram dulcis epulas et album
> Libero caprum prope funeratus
> arboris ictu.

1. **Martiis ... Kalendis**: the day of the *Matronalia*, a festival shared in by married women only. On this day the matrons carried their offerings to the temple of Juno Lucina on the Esquiline, not far from Maecenas' residence. The festival is called *femineae Kalendae* by Juvenal, 9, 53. Naturally Maecenas would be much puzzled over the preparations of his bachelor (**caelebs**) friend.

2. **velint**: *mean*.

4 f. **caespite vivo**: the material of his improvised altar. Cf. 1, 19, 13.—**docte**: given a bantering emphasis by its position,—*for all thy learning.*—**sermones**: *the lore, literature*. The accusative depends on **docte**; cf. 3, 9, 10 *dulcis docta modos.*—**utriusque linguae**: Greek and Latin, the two languages of the cultivated Roman. Cf. Suet. *Aug.* 89 *in evolvendis utriusque linguae auctoribus.*

6 ff. **voveram**: *i.e.* long ago, before all these preparations. The time is more exactly fixed by the participle. — **epulas**: the regular accompaniment of sacrifice. — **album**: as the sacrifice is to one of the *dii superi.*—**Libero**: the protector of poets. In 2, 17, 28, however, it was Faunus who saved him.

[3, 8, 9]   HORATI

      Hic dies, anno redeunte festus,
10   corticem adstrictum pice demovebit
      amphorae fumum bibere institutae
          consule Tullo.

      Sume, Maecenas, cyathos amici
      sospitis centum, et vigiles lucernas
15   perfer in lucem; procul omnis esto
         clamor et ira.

      Mitte civilis super urbe curas:
      occidit Daci Cotisonis agmen,
      Medus infestus sibi luctuosis
20   dissidet armis,

9 ff. **anno redeunte**: cf. the Homeric περιπλόμενος ἐνιαυτός, and *S.* 2, 2, 83 *sive diem festum rediens advexerit annus*. For **annus** in the sense of season, cf. *Epod.* 2, 29. — **corticem adstrictum**, etc.: cf. 1. 20, 3 and n. — **fumum bibere**: the *apotheca* was so placed in the upper part of the house that it could receive the smoke from the fire, which according to common belief aided the ripening of the wine. Cf. Colum. 1, 6, 20 *quoniam vina celerius vetustescunt, quae fumi quodam tenore praecocem maturitatem trahunt.* For the infinitive, see Intr. 107.

12. **consule Tullo**: Horace probably means the Tullus whose consulship fell in 33 B.C., hardly L. Volcacius Tullus, consul 66 B.C. Yet cf. 3, 21, 1, where the vintage is of 65 B.C.

13 ff. **cyathos . . . centum**: proverbial, not literal. — **amici sospitis**: *over the safe escape of.* The genitive of the toast; cf. 3, 19, 9 f. *da lunae . . . novae, da noctis mediae, da, puer, auguris Murenae.* Also Antiphan. ap. Athen. 10, 21 ἐγχεάμην ἄκρατον κυάθους θεῶν τε καὶ θεαινῶν μυρίους. — **perfer**: *endure.* — **in lucem**: *i.e.* of the dawn; the adjective **vigiles**, 'transferred' from the subject of **perfer**, emphasizes the exhortation to continue until morning. Cf. the Emperor Gallienus' words apud Trebell. Poll. 11 *sed vigiles nolite extinguere lychnos.* — **procul . . . esto**, etc.: *i.e.* the revel shall not degenerate into a brawl. Cf. 1, 27, 3 and n.

17 ff. During Octavian's absence Maecenas was in charge of affairs at Rome. — **super**: colloquial for the more common *de.* — **occidit**: cf. 1, 28, 7 and n. — **Cotisonis, Medus**: cf. introductory n. and nn. to

servit Hispanae vetus hostis orae
Cantaber sera domitus catena,
iam Scythae laxo meditantur arcu
   cedere campis.

25   Neglegens ne qua populus laboret,
parce privatus nimium cavere et
dona praesentis cape laetus horae;
   linque severa.

1, 26, 5; 3, 6, 14.—sibi: with both infestus and luctuosis. Intr. 100. —dissidet: used absolutely; cf. Theog. 763 f. πίνωμεν χαρίεντα μετ' ἀλλήλοισι λέγοντες, | μηδὲν τὸν Μήδων δειδιότες πόλεμον.
21 ff. servit: *a slave too is*. Cf. occidit above. The verses do not tell the whole truth; cf. n. to 2, 6, 2.—sera: in the predicate, *though late*; for he has been a vetus hostis. —domitus: probably with reference to the successes of Statilius Taurus and Calvisius Sabinus; the latter enjoyed a triumph over the Spaniards in 28 B.C.—Scythae, etc.: also exaggeration; cf. 2, 9,

23 f.—laxo ... arcu: recognizing the folly of further resistance.
25 f. neglegens: logically parallel to parce, linque, *be careless*, followed by ne ... laboret because of the anxiety, fear, which it implies. —parce: somewhat stronger than the common *noli*. Cf. Verg. *A.* 3, 42 *parce pias scelerare manus.* —privatus: also part of the exhortation,—'become for the nonce a private citizen once more.'
27 f. A favorite maxim repeated in many forms; cf. 1, 9, 13 ff.; 11, 8; 2, 16, 25 ff.; 3, 29, 41 ff.; 4, 12, 25 ff.

9

The Reconciliation. Lydia and her lover have fallen out, but are now ready to return to their former love. The ode dramatically tells the story. In the first strophe the lover's reproaches show his regret and hint that he is willing to be reconciled; Lydia answers in similar fashion, but without helping him on. Then each defiantly boasts of a new sweetheart; but in the last two strophes the lover yields, and proposes a reconciliation, to which Lydia joyfully agrees.

This exquisite ode is the only one of Horace's lyrics in dialogue. The amoebean form is perfectly preserved, not simply in the number of verses employed by each speaker, but in the exact parallelism of expression as well: Lydia always caps her lover's lines with stronger statements. The verses have been translated and imitated by almost countless writers since Horace's day. The best general comment on the ode is furnished by Terence's line, *Andria*, 555, *amantium irae amoris integratio est.* The date is unknown. Metre, 71.

 Donec gratus eram tibi
  nec quisquam potior bracchia candidae
 cervici iuvenis dabat,
  Persarum vigui rege beatior.
5 Donec non alia magis
  arsisti neque erat Lydia post **Chloen,**
 multi Lydia nominis,
  Romana vigui clarior Ilia.
 Me nunc Thressa Chloe regit,
10 dulcis docta modos et citharae **sciens,**
 pro qua non metuam mori,
  si parcent animae fata superstiti.
 Me torret face mutua
  Thurini Calais filius Ornyti,

1 ff. **gratus**: *in favor with.* — **potior**: *preferred;* cf. Tibul. 1, 5, 69 *at tu, qui potior nunc es, mea fata timeto.* — **dabat**: in place of the prose compound *circumdabat.* — **Persarum . . . rege**: proverbial for the height of happiness. Cf. 2, 2, 17. — **vigui**: *flourished.*

5 ff. **alia**: causal abl. with **arsisti.** — **arsisti**: note that this is much stronger than **gratus** of v. 1. The perfect expresses the same time as the imperfect **eram** above. — **post**: *second to.* — **multi Lydia nominis**: *a Lydia of mighty fame;* imitating the Greek adjectives πολυώνυμος, μεγαλώνυμος. — **Romana** . . . **Ilia**: mother of Romulus and Remus. Cf. n. to 1, 2, 17.

9 ff. **me**: emphasizing the lover's indifference. — **Thressa Chloe**: this name, like that in v. 14, is chosen for its pleasant sound. — **docta**: *versed in;* cf. *docte sermones,* v. 5 of the preceding ode. — **citharae**: objective gen. with **sciens.** Cf. 1, 15, 24 f. *Sthenelus sciens | pugnae.* — **animae**: *my life, i.e.* Chloe. — **superstiti**: proleptic, *and grant that she may live.*

13 ff. **torret**: this word far outbids **regit** of v. 9. — **Thurini**: *of Thurii,* the rich and luxurious city of southern Italy. Lydia's new

15 pro quo bis patiar mori,
       si parcent puero fata superstiti.
    Quid si prisca redit Venus,
       diductosque iugo cogit aeneo,
    si flava excutitur Chloe,
20   reiectaeque patet ianua Lydiae?
    Quamquam sidere pulchrior
       ille est, tu levior cortice et improbo
    iracundior Hadria,
       tecum vivere amem, tecum obeam libens.

lover is far superior in birth and fortune to Thracian Chloe. — **bis patiar**: again capping *non metuam* v. 11.

17 ff. redit: the present is colloquially used. — **diductos**: (*us*) *who are now separated.* — **iugo ... aeneo**: cf. 1, 33, 11. — **flava**: *fair-haired.* — **excutitur**: *i.e.* from her rule over me. — **Lydiae**: dative.

21 ff. Lydia teases her lover with a comparison unfavorable to him before she yields, and so has the last word in reproaches. — **sidere pulchrior**: cf. 3, 19, 26 *puro similem Vespero.* The comparison is very old; so Astyanax is said to be, *Il.* 6, 401 ἀλίγκιον ἀστέρι καλῷ. — **levior**: and so more fickle. — **iracundior Hadria**: cf. 1, 33, 15. — **libens**: *gladly.*

10

A παρακλαυσίθυρον, a lover's pleadings before his mistress' house, which is closed against him. Cf. 1, 25, 7 ff. Metre, 72.

Extremum Tanain si biberes, Lyce,
   saevo nupta viro, me tamen asperas

1 ff. extremum: *remotest*; cf. 2, 18, 4 *ultima Africa.* — **si biberes**: *i.e.* 'were dwelling by the Don.' Cf. 2, 20, 20 *Rhodani potor*; and 4, 15, 21 *qui profundum Danuvium bibunt.* — **saevo**: the adjective belongs to the supposition, and marks the contrast with the actual fact (v. 15). For the supposed virtues of the Sarmatian nomads, see 3, 24, 19 f. — **asperas**: *cruel*; cf. *Epod.* 11, 21 *non amicos postis.*

porrectum ante foris obicere incolis
  plorares Aquilonibus.

5 Audis quo strepitu ianua, quo nemus
inter pulchra satum tecta remugiat
ventis, et positas ut glaciet nivis
  puro numine Iuppiter?

Ingratam Veneri pone superbiam,
10 ne currente retro funis eat rota:
non te Penelopen difficilem procis
  Tyrrhenus genuit parens.

O quamvis neque te munera nec preces
nec tinctus viola pallor amantium

3 f. porrectum: *outstretched.* — **obicere**: object of **plorares**. — **incolis**: *native to that region.*

5 ff. The lover continues his appeal to Lyce's pity. — **nemus inter pulchra**, etc.: the second court, *peristylium*, in the houses of the rich was often large enough to contain trees. Cf. *Epist.* 1, 10, 22 *nempe inter varias nutritur silva columnas.* — **ventis**: abl. of cause. — **ut**, etc.: the question belongs by zeugma to **audis**, the exact force of which has been lost by distance. — **puro numine**: *in cloudless majesty* (Smith). Cf. 1, 34, 7. — **Iuppiter**: as god of the sky. Cf. n. to 1, 1, 25.

11 ff. ne currente, etc.: *lest the rope slip from thee as the wheel runs back; i.e.* thy present haughty virtue is sure to break. The figure is that of a wheel, possibly a windlass, which suddenly flies backward, carrying the rope with it. — **retro**: with both **currente** and **eat**. Intr. 100. — **non te**, etc.: with the order and expression, cf. Verg. *A.* 4, 227 f. *non illum nobis genetrix pulcherrima talem | promisit.* — **difficilem**: *unyielding*; cf. 3, 7, 32. — **Tyrrhenus**: far from being a stern Sarmatian, Lyce is of Etruscan birth; and the effeminacy and vices of the Etruscans were notorious.

13 ff. quamvis, etc.: the indic. is not common until later. — **tinctus viola pallor**: the lover's proper color according to Ovid *A. A.* 1, 729 *palleat omnis amans; hic est color aptus amanti.* The yellow, not the purple, violet is meant. — **paelice**: abl. of cause. — **saucius**: this bears the emphasis, 'thy hus-

15   nec vir Pieria paelice saucius
         curvat, supplicibus tuis

      parcas, nec rigida mollior aesculo
      nec Mauris animum mitior anguibus:
      non hoc semper erit liminis aut aquae
20   caelestis patiens latus.

band's infatuation for.' With this use of the adjective, cf. 1, 14, 5. —**curvat**: equivalent to *incurvat, flectit,* ἐπιγνάμπτει. — **supplicibus tuis parcas**: in irony, as if Lyce were some goddess at whose shrine her lovers pray.

18 ff. Mauris... anguibus: proverbially savage. — **non hoc.** etc.: the threat with which Horace closes is comic, like that in *Epod.* 11, 15-18, where he vows that if Inachia persists in smiling on his rich rival, he will give her up to him.

19 f. hoc: *i.e. meum*; cf. Greek ὅδε, οὗτος. — **aquae caelestis**: from which he has suffered on other occasions (cf. v. 8). — **latus**: equivalent to *corpus*; cf. 2, 7. 18.

11

'Mercury and my lyre, on you I call to raise a strain of music which shall make stubborn Lyde listen — for Lyde is as shy as an unbroken filly, and has no thought of love and wedlock (1-12). But thou, my lyre, canst charm wild beasts, the woods and rivers: aye, Cerberus gave up his fierceness before thee; even Ixion and Tityos smiled, forgetful of their pain; and Danaus' cruel daughters had respite from their endless toil (13-24). Ah! that is the tale to which Lyde must listen, that she may learn how punishment, though sometimes late, overtakes wrongdoers even in Hades. And I will sing of that sister, alone worthy of the marriage torch, who won eternal fame by her noble falsehood to her father, for she saved her husband's life, and feared not to pay forfeit for it with her own' (25-52).

The ode is arranged with no slight skill: the invocation of the lyre, and the celebration of the power of music in the first six strophes are merely a setting for the real theme, which seems first suggested by the apparently chance mention of the Danaids in v. 22 ff. From this point Lyde is forgotten, and the application of the rest of the ode is left to the reader's imagination. The Romans were familiar with the story of the daughters of Danaus, who, compelled to marry their cousins, Aegyptus' fifty sons, were forced by their father to promise to kill their husbands on their wedding night,—a crime for which they suffered eternal punishment. They had a constant reminder of the myth in the statues of Danaus and his daughters, which occupied the intercolumnary spaces of the portico to the temple of Apollo on the Palatine. Cf. introductory n. to 1, 31; Prop. 3, 29, 3; Ovid *Trist.* 3, 1, 61. The story is essentially narrative, and proper for epic treatment, but Horace wisely selected for his lyric form a single part of the myth—the story of Lycneus and Hypermestra, and from this chose the dramatic moment when Hypermestra rouses her husband and bids him flee for his life. The same good taste is shown in his treatment of the story of Europa 3, 27: but both odes are in marked contrast to 1, 15. Ovid followed Horace in handling the same theme in his *Heroides* 14. The treatment there should be carefully compared with this. Metre, 69.

> Mercuri, nam te docilis magistro
> movit Amphion lapides canendo,
> tuque testudo, resonare septem
>   callida nervis,
>
> 5   nec loquax olim neque grata, nunc et
> divitum mensis et amica templis,
> dic modos Lyde quibus obstinatas
>   adplicet auris,

1 ff. nam: giving the reason for the invocation. — **docilis**: equivalent to *doctus*; cf. 1, 24, 9 *flebilis* equivalent to *fletus*. — **Amphion**: the mythical singer to whose music the walls of Thebes rose. Cf. *Epist.* 2, 3, 394 ff. *dictus et Amphion, Thebanae conditor urbis, | saxa movere sono testudinis et prece blanda | ducere, quo vellet.* — **resonare**: dependent on **callida**. — **septem... nervis**: the lyre is called by Pindar *N.* 5, 24 φόρμιγξ ἑπτάγλωσσος.

5 ff. loquax: *vocal.* Sappho calls to her lyre *Frg.* 45 ἄγε δὴ χέλυ δῖα μοι | φωνάεσσα γένοιο. — **et**: used only here and 4, 13, 6 at the end of the verse without elision of the last syllable of the preceding word. — **mensis amica**, etc.: cf. *Od.* 8, 99 φόρμιγγός θ'. ἣ δαιτὶ συνήορός ἐστι θαλείῃ. and 17, 270 ἐν δέ τε φόρμιγξ ἠπύει, ἣν ἄρα δαιτὶ θεοὶ ποίησαν ἑταίρην. Also 1, 22, 13 f. — **dic modos**: cf. 1, 32, 3. — **obstinatas**: *stubborn.*

quae velut latis equa trima campis
ludit exsultim metuitque tangi,
nuptiarum expers et adhuc protervo
    cruda marito.

Tu potes tigris comitesque silvas
ducere et rivos celeris morari;
cessit immanis tibi blandienti
    ianitor aulae

Cerberus, quamvis furiale centum
muniant angues caput eius atque
spiritus taeter saniesque manet
    ore trilingui;

9 ff. For the comparison of a girl to a colt or heifer, cf. 1, 23. 1; 2, 5, 6. Also Anacr. *Frg.* 75 πῶλε Θρηκίη, τί δή με λοξὸν ὄμμασιν βλέπουσα | νηλεῶς φεύγεις, δοκέεις δέ μ' οὐδὲν εἰδέναι σοφόν; | ... νῦν δὲ λειμῶνάς τε βόσκεαι κοῦφά τε σκιρτῶσα παίζεις. 'Thracian filly, why now dost thou look distrustfully at me and flee without pity? Deemest thou me a witless fellow? Now thou grazest on the meadows and sportest, lightly gamboling.'

— **trima**: as yet unbroken, for colts were broken in their fourth year. Verg. *G.* 3, 190. — **tangi**: cf. 2. 2. 7 and n. — **cruda**: not yet *matura*; cf. Stat. *Th.* 7, 298 f. *expertem thalami crudumque maritis | ignibus.*

13 ff. The power of the lyre. Cf. the similar passage 1, 12, 9 ff. and n.

— **comites**: *in thy train*; predicate with both **tigris** and **silvas**. For the position of -**que**, see Intr. 31. — **cessit**: *gave way* before thy charms (**blandienti**). The reference is to the visit of Orpheus to Hades to bring back Eurydice. The story is told Verg. *G.* 4, 457 ff.; Ovid *Met.* 10. 8 ff. — **immanis**: with **aulae**. — **blandienti**: cf. 1, 12, 11; 24, 13.

17 ff. **furiale**: *fury-like*. — **eius**: some critics would reject this strophe as prosaic, and especially because **eius** here adds nothing to the sense. These are insufficient reasons for rejection, for Horace did not always maintain the highest level in his verse. — **spiritus**: belonging by a zeugma to **manet**. — **manet**: *drops from.* — **ore trilingui**: Cerberus is three-headed in 2, 19, 31 also, but hundred-headed 2, 13, 34.

quin et Ixion Tityosque voltu
risit invito; stetit urna paulum
sicca, dum grato Danai puellas
    carmine mulces.

25 Audiat Lyde scelus atque notas
virginum poenas et inane lymphae
dolium fundo pereuntis imo,
    seraque fata

quae manent culpas etiam sub Orco.
30 Impiae (nam quid potuere maius?),
impiae sponsos potuere duro
    perdere ferro.

Vna de multis face nuptiali
digna periurum fuit in parentem

21 ff. **quin et**: cf. n. to 1, 10, 13. — **voltu ... invito**: *i.e.* in spite of their pain. Ovid expands the scene *Met.* 10, 41 ff. *exsangues flebant animae: nec Tantalus undam | captavit refugam, stupuitque Ixionis orbis, | nec carpsere iecur volucres, urnisque vacarunt | Belides, inque tuo sedisti, Sisyphe, saxo. | Tunc primum lacrimis victarum carmine fama est | Eumenidum maduisse genas.* — **stetit urna**, etc.: thus Horace apparently chances on his theme.

25 f. **audiat**: the asyndeton is effective, — *yes, Lyde shall hear*, etc. — **notas**: with **scelus** as well as **poenas**. — **lymphae**: with **inane**. For the order of words, see Intr. 21.

28 f. **sera**: concessive, *though late.* — **culpas**: Lyde's sin is her failure to love.

30 f. **impiae ... impiae**: Intr. 28 c. — **potuere**: first of physical, secondly of moral courage — the Greek ἔτλησαν, *had the heart to.* — **duro ... ferro**: the Homeric νηλέι χαλκῷ.

Notice that Horace disposes of the general features of the story thus briefly, and quickly passes to his special theme.

33 f. **una de multis**: only Hypermestra of all the fifty failed to execute her father's orders. — **periurum**: because by betrothing his daughters to Aegyptus' sons he had pledged himself to do them no harm.

splendide mendax et in omne virgo
   nobilis aevum;

'Surge' quae dixit iuveni marito,
'surge, ne longus tibi somnus, unde
non times, detur; socerum et scelestas
   falle sorores,

quae, velut nanctae vitulos leaenae,
singulos eheu lacerant. Ego illis
mollior nec te feriam neque intra
   claustra tenebo:

me pater saevis oneret catenis,
quod viro clemens misero peperci;

35. **splendide mendax**: a striking oxymoron; cf. Tac. *Hist.* 4, 50 *egregio mendacio*. St. Ambrose uses the phrase *o beatum mendacium*. Cf. also Tennyson's 'His honour rooted in dishonour stood, | And faith unfaithful kept him falsely true.'
37 ff. **surge**, etc.: cf. Ovid *Her.* 14, 73 f. *surge age, Belide, de tot modo fratribus unus | nox tibi, ni properas, ista perennis erit.* Ausonius too, *Ephem.* 1, 17 ff., imitated Horace, *surge nugator lacerande virgis; | surge, ne longus tibi somnus, unde | non times, detur: rape membra molli, | Parmeno, lecto.* — **longus**: shown by the context here, as in 2, 14, 19 and 4, 9, 27, to be equivalent to *aeternus*. — **unde**: the antecedent is made clear by the following **socerum et**, etc.
40. **falle**: λάθε, *elude*. Cf. 1, 10, 16, and *Epist.* 1, 5, 31 *postico falle clientem.* — **sorores**: *cousins*. Cf. Ovid *Her.* 14, 123 where Hypermestra says *si qua piae, Lyncen, tibi cura sororis.*
41 ff. The comparison and the thing compared are here confused, as often by Horace: **singulos** designates the sons of Aegyptus, while **lacerant** belongs properly only to **leaenae**. 'Each destroys her husband, alas, as lionesses rend the bullocks they have made their prey.' The figure is Homeric, cf. *Il.* 5, 161 f. ὡς δὲ λέων ἐν βουσὶ θορὼν ἐξ αὐχένα ἄξῃ | πόρτιος ἠὲ βοός. With the statement, cf. Hypermestra's words, Ovid. *Her.* 14, 35 f. *circum me gemitus morientum audire videbar; | et tamen audibam, quodque verebar, erat.*
44. **tenebo**: for the more common compound *retinebo*.
45 f. **me**: in contrast with **te** — 'thou shalt suffer no harm, and as

me vel extremos Numidarum in agros
classe releget.

I pedes quo te rapiunt et aurae,
50   dum favet nox et Venus, i secundo
omine et nostri memorem sepulcro
sculpe querellam.'

for me, let my father do his worst.'
— **oneret catenis**: Ovid makes her write, *Her.* 14, 3 *clausa domo teneor gravibusque coercita vinclis.* — **clemens misero**: effective juxtaposition; cf. 1, 5, 9; 2, 4, 6.

47. **extremos**: cf. 3, 10, 1.

49 f. **i ... i**: the anaphora marks her eagerness. — **pedes ... aurae**: all inclusive, 'wherever on land and sea.' — **Venus**: it was she who prompted her to save her husband. In Aeschylus' lost *Danaids* (*Frg.* 44) it was Aphrodite who saved Hypermestra from condemnation.

51 ff. **nostri**: *of me*, dependent on **memorem. — sepulcro**: for the case, see Intr. 95. — **sculpe querellam**: in Ovid *Her.* 14, 128 ff. Hypermestra suggests her own epitaph, *sculptaque sint titulo nostra sepulchra brevi*: | '*Exul Hypermestra, pretium pietatis iniquum,* | *quam mortem fratri depulit, ipsa tulit.*' In Trajan's reign a woman touring in Egypt scratched this reminiscence of Horace's words on the pyramid at Gizeh. CIL. 3, 21. *Vidi pyramidas sine te, dulcissime frater,* | *et tibi quod potui, lacrimas hic maesta profudi* | *et nostri memorem luctus hanc sculpo querelam.*

12

Neobule, love-sick for her Hebrus, complains that she cannot give free rein to her love or wash away its pain in deep draughts of wine. All interest in her spinning is taken from her by the thought of the beauty of her lover, who excels as swimmer, horseman, boxer, runner, and hunter.

There has been some discussion among critics as to the nature of this ode, but it is best regarded as a monologue. It is the only experiment in pure Ionic measure that Horace has left us, and is an imitation of verses by Alcaeus, of which the opening line is preserved (*Frg.* 59) ἔμε δείλαν, ἔμε πασᾶν κακοτατῶν πεδέχοισαν. The details, however, as usual, are Roman. Metre. 83.

CARMINA [3, 12, 3

Miserarum est neque amori dare ludum neque dulci
  mala vino lavere, aut exanimari metuentis
  patruae verbera linguae.
2 Tibi qualum Cythereae puer ales, tibi telas
  operosaeque Minervae studium aufert, Neobule,
  Liparaei nitor Hebri,
3 simul unctos Tiberinis umeros lavit in undis,
  eques ipso melior Bellerophonte, neque pugno
  neque segni pede victus;

1. **miserarum est**, etc. : contrasting the narrow lot of girls with the freedom of young men. — **dare ludum** : *give free rein to.* Cf. Cic. *pro Cael.* 28 *datur ludus aetati.* — **lavere** : *wash away.* — **aut**: *or else.* Cf. 3, 24, 24 *et peccare nefas aut* ('or if one sin') *pretium est mori.* — **metuentis** : the accusative is natural following **exanimari**, but indicates the same unhappy girls as **miserarum**. — **patruae**, etc. : the uncle was proverbially harsh; cf. *S.* 2, 3, 88 *ne sis patruus mihi.* — **verbera** : *the scourgings.*

2. Cf. Sappho *Frg.* 90 γλύκεια μᾶτερ οὔτοι δύναμαι κρέκην τὸν ἴστον, πόθῳ δάμεισα παῖδος βραδίναν δι' Ἀφρόδιταν, 'Mother dear, I cannot mind my loom, for through soft Aphrodite's will, I am overcome with longing for that child,' and Landor's imitation, 'Mother, I cannot mind my wheel. | My fingers ache, my lips are dry.' Also Seneca *Phaed.* 103 f. *Palladis telae vacant et inter ipsas pensa labuntur manus.*

— **tibi** : in self-address, as Catul. 51, 13 *otium, Catulle, tibi molestum est.* — **qualum** : *wool basket*; with this **aufert** has its literal sense. — **operosae Minervae** : Ἀθηνᾶ ἐργάνη, the goddess of household industries, especially of spinning and weaving. — **Neobule** : the name seems to have been taken from Archilochus; *Frg.* 73 is supposed to have been written after the poet has lost his love, ἤμβλακον, καὶ πού τιν' ἄλλον ἤδ' ἄτη κιχήσατο. — **Liparaei** : *of Lipara*; the epithet simply individualizes. Cf. *Opuntiae Megillae* 1, 27, 10; also n. to 1, 1, 13. — **nitor**: *brilliant beauty*, as 1, 19, 5.

3. **simul . . . lavit**: connected closely with **nitor**. For the custom of swimming in the Tiber, cf. 1, 8. 8 and n.; 3, 7, 27 f. Also Ovid *Trist.* 3, 12, 21 *nunc ubi perfusa est oleo labente iuventus | defessos artus virgine tinguit aqua.* — **Bellerophontē**: abl. from nom. *Bellerophontes*: cf. 3, 7, 15. — **segni**: with both **pugno** and **pede**.

277

4   catus idem per apertum fugientis agitato
    grege cervos iaculari et celer arto latitantem
    fruticeto excipere aprum.

4. **catus**: cf. 1, 10, 3 and n. — **apertum**: substantive, *the open*. — **agitato grege**: with fugientis. — **arto latitantem fruticeto**, etc.: as in *Od.* 19, 439 ἔνθα δ' ἄρ' ἐν λόχμῃ πυκινῇ κατέκειτο μέγας σῦς. Cf. *Il.* 11, 415 ὁ δέ τ' εἶσι (*i.e.* ὁ κάπριος) βαθείης ἐκ ξυλόχοιο. — **excipere**: *to catch*.

13

To the spring Bandusia. These exquisite verses may have been occasioned by the festival of springs, the *Fontinalia*, which fell on October 13; but the situation of the spring thus immortalized — if indeed it ever existed outside Horace's fancy — is wholly unknown. A document of 1103 A.D. mentions a *fons Bandusinus* near Venusia, but it is very probable that this is an identification of the Middle Ages rather than an ancient name. Bandusia seems to be a corruption of Πανδοσία, and may have been given by Horace to the large spring on his Sabine farm, *fons etiam rivo dare nomen idoneus, Epist.* 1, 16, 12. We need be little concerned, however, with the situation, for the verses are sufficient in themselves. Metre, 73.

O fons Bandusiae, splendidior vitro,
    dulci digne mero non sine floribus,
        cras donaberis haedo,
            cui frons turgida cornibus

5   primis et venerem et proelia destinat;
        frustra: nam gelidos inficiet tibi

1 f. **vitro**: *crystal*. Cf. Apul. *Met.* 1, 19 *fluvius ibat argento vel vitro aemulus in colorem.* — **dulci digne**, etc.: note the effective alliteration and assonance here and elsewhere in the poem. The wine was poured and garlands thrown into the spring; cf. Varro *L. L.* 6, 22 (*Fontanalibus*) *et in fontes coronas iaciunt et puteos coronant.*

6 ff. **frustra**: the knell, *all in vain*. Cf. 3, 7, 21. — **gelidos**: *cool* (and clear), contrasted with rubro, *red* (and warm). — **inficiet**: *stain*. — **lascivi**: *sportive*.

CARMINA [3, 14

rubro sanguine rivos,
    lascivi suboles gregis.

Te flagrantis atrox hora Caniculae
10 nescit tangere, tu frigus amabile
    fessis vomere tauris
        praebes et pecori vago.

Fies nobilium tu quoque fontium,
me dicente cavis impositam ilicem
15   saxis unde loquaces
        lymphae desiliunt tuae.

9 ff. te . . . tu: Intr. 28 c. — **hora**: *season*; the 'dog days' of September. Cf. 1, 17, 17. — **nescit**: stronger than a colorless *nequit*. — **frigus**, etc.: the bullocks rest at midday, when cool draughts are most welcome.

13 ff. fies nobilium, etc.: *i.e.* the fountains celebrated in song, Castalia, Dirce, Hippocrene, etc. The prophecy has been fulfilled.

— **me dicente**: *from my song of.* — **impositam**: *perched upon.* — **loquaces lymphae desiliunt**: the Anacreontic λάλον ὕδωρ. The 'prattle' of these words Wordsworth reproduced by inserting a letter. 'Or when the prattle of Blandusia's spring | Haunted his ear, he only listening.' Cf. *Epod.* 16, 48 *levis crepante lympha desilit pede.*

14

The following ode was written in honor of Augustus' return to Rome in the spring of 24 B.C. after an absence in the West of nearly three years.

'Our Caesar, a second Hercules, comes home victorious from the Spanish shore. His faithful consort, his sister, all ye matrons with your children, should give thanks to the gods. For me this day puts all care to flight: so long as Caesar rules I have no fear of civil strife and violence. So, boy, bring unguent, flowers, and good old wine, that I may celebrate this festival. Fetch Neaera, too: yet if the surly porter hinders you — well, never mind; my hair is gray. When I was a hot-headed youth, I would not have stood it.'

While the first three strophes are somewhat stiff and formal, there can be no doubt that Horace's welcome was sincere and that the fourth strophe gives the basis of the poet's gratitude — the sense of security and peace under Augustus' rule. The light verses of the last three strophes simply expand *eximet curas* of v. 14 and show Horace's light-heartedness. Metre, 69.

> Herculis ritu modo dictus, o plebs,
> morte venalem petiisse laurum
> Caesar Hispana repetit penatis
>   victor ab ora.
>
> 5 Vnico gaudens mulier marito
> prodeat, iustis operata divis,
> et soror clari ducis et decorae
>   supplice vitta

1. **Herculis**: Augustus was frequently compared with Hercules; cf. 3, 3, 9; 4, 5, 36; Verg. *A.* 6, 802. The points of resemblance here are the danger of the undertaking and the victorious return — note the emphatic position of victor (v. 4). — **ritu**: *like, after the fashion of.* Cf. 3, 29, 34 *fluminis ritu*, 'like a river': and 3, 1, 45 f. — **modo dictus**: in the winter of 25-24 B.C. Augustus had been sick at Tarraco (Dio Cass. 53, 25), so that fears for his recovery may well have been entertained in Rome. — **plebs**: *ye people*: used here like *populus* in general addresses to the mass of the people, not restricted to the lowest class. Cf. 2, 2, 18.

2 ff. **morte venalem**, etc.: *which men buy with death*. Cf. Quint. 9, 3, 71 *emit morte immortalitatem*; Aeschin. *in Ctes.* 160 αἱματός ἐστιν ἡ ἀρετὴ ὠνία. — **petiisse**: *sought to win*. Note the play with **repetit**. — **Hispana . . . ora**: the northwestern coast of Spain. Cf. 3, 8, 21 and n.

5 f. **unico**: *her one dear;* cf. 2, 18, 14 *unicis Sabinis*. The word implies that her husband is the one source of all her happiness. — **mulier**: *Livia*. — **prodeat**: *i.e.* before the people to join with them in thanksgiving to the gods. — **operata**: in technical sense like *facere*, ῥέζειν, to sacrifice; cf. Verg. *G.* 1, 339 *sacra refer Cereri laetis operatus in herbis*. — **divis**: called **iustis** because, as Porphyrio says, they have granted Augustus victory and a safe return as he deserved.

7 ff. **soror**: Octavia. — **supplice vitta**: in place of the simple one

virginum matres iuvenumque nuper
sospitum; vos, o pueri et puellae
non virum expertae, male ominatis
   parcite verbis.

Hic dies vere mihi festus atras
eximet curas: ego nec tumultum
nec mori per vim metuam tenente
   Caesare terras.

I, pete unguentum, puer, et coronas
et cadum Marsi memorem duelli,
Spartacum si qua potuit vagantem
   fallere testa.

ordinarily worn. Augustus had declined the triumph which the senate proposed for his return, but there was probably a *supplicatio* in its stead. — **virginum**: the brides of the iuvenum. For this meaning of *virgo*, cf. 2, 8, 23. — **nuper sospitum**: *just now returned in safety*.

10 ff. **vos**: the last of the three classes here distinguished — the matrons, the young soldiers with their brides, and the unwedded boys and girls. — **non virum expertae**: i.e. *nondum nuptae*. — **male ominatis**: the hiatus is harsh, and can only be explained on the supposition that the two words were regarded as expressing a single idea. But the text of this entire line is very much in dispute. — **parcite verbis**: cf. *Epod.* 17, 6. The meaning is the same as 3, 1, 2 *favete linguis*.

13 ff. **vere**: modifying **festus**. — **curas**: *i.e.* for the welfare of Caesar and the state. — **tumultum**: *civil strife*; cf. 4, 4, 47 and n. — **mori per vim**: *violent death*. — **tenente Caesare**: temporal, *so long as*, etc. With this expression of confidence, cf. 4, 15, 17–20.

17 f. The requirements for his revel. Cf. 2, 3, 13–16; 11, 17; and *Anacreont.* 50, 10 f. βάλ' ὕδωρ, δὸς οἶνον, ὦ παῖ. | τὴν ψυχήν μου κάρωσον, 'Throw in water, give me wine, boy; dull my senses.' — **Marsi memorem duelli**: *i.e.* the Social War, 90–88 B.C. Cf. Iuv. 5, 31 *calcatamque tenet bellis socialibus uvam*.

19. The roving bands of gladiators under the lead of Spartacus harassed Italy 73–71 B.C. — **si qua**: *if by any chance*.

> Dic et argutae properet **Neaerae**
> murreum nodo cohibere crinem;
> si per invisum mora ianitorem
> fiet, abito.
>
> 25 Lenit albescens animos capillus
> litium et rixae cupidos protervae;
> non ego hoc ferrem calidus iuventa
> consule Planco.

21. With this summons of the music girl, cf. 2, 11, 21 ff. — **dic . . . properet**: *tell Neaera to hurry*. For the construction. cf. 2, 11, 22 f. — **argutae**: λιγεῖα, *clear-voiced*; cf. 4, 6, 25 *argutae Thaliae*. — **murreum**: *chestnut*. — **nodo**: *i.e.* in simple coiffure. — **ianitorem**: at the door of the apartment-building (*insula*) in which Neaera lives; he is called **invisum**, *churlish*, for refusing admittance to such messengers as Horace sends.

25 ff. lenit albescens, etc.: Horace is now forty-one, but gray before his time; so he describes himself, *Epist.* 1, 20, 24 f. *corporis exigui, praecanum, solibus aptum, | irasci celerem, tamen ut placabilis essem*. With the sentiment, cf. *Epist.* 2, 2, 211 *lenior et melior fis accedente senecta*. — **iuventa**: ablative. — **consule Planco**: 42 B.C., the year of Philippi. Eighteen years had cooled his ardor for amours as well as for political lost causes. The reminiscences here and in vv. 18 and 19 are intentional, calling up the contrast between those troubled times and the present peace.

15

This ode is similar in subject to 1, 25; *Epod.* 5 and 8. Chloris, the shameless wife of Ibycus, wishes in spite of her years to rival her own daughter. Metre, 71.

> Vxor pauperis Ibyci,
>   tandem nequitiae fige modum tuae

1 ff. uxor pauperis: her husband's poverty she makes an excuse for her infidelity. — **tandem**: impatiently — 'your day is long since past.' — **fige**: stronger than the common *pone*; cf. 1, 16, 3. — **famosis laboribus**: 'wool-working (v. 13) would be more fitting for you.'

       famosisque laboribus;
           maturo propior desine funeri
5   inter ludere virgines
           et stellis nebulam spargere candidis.
       Non, si quid Pholoen satis,
           et te, Chlori, decet: filia rectius
       expugnat iuvenum domos,
10   pulso Thyias uti concita tympano.
       Illam cogit amor Nothi
           lascivae similem ludere capreae:
       te lanae prope nobilem
           tonsae Luceriam, non citharae decent
15   nec flos purpureus rosae
           nec poti vetulam faece tenus cadi.

4 ff. **maturo**: *i.e.* for which you are old enough; your death would not be premature. — **propior**: 'now you are so near.' — **ludere**: παίζειν, *to wanton*. — **nebulam spargere**: *i.e.* 'to obscure.'

7 ff. **satis**: sc. *decet.* 'Pholoe is young, but you — !' — **expugnat**: may possibly be taken literally. Cf. Seneca. *Praef. ad N. Q.* 4, 6 *Crispus Passienus, saepe dicebat adulationibus nos non claudere ostium, sed aperire, et quidem sic, ut amicae opponi solet, quae si impulit, grata est, gratior, si effregit.* — **Thyias**: cf. n. to 2, 19, 9. — **tympano**: used in the orgiastic worship of Bacchus; cf. 1, 18, 14.

11. **illam**: *i.e.* the daughter, Pholoe. — **Nothi**: the name is known from inscriptions. Possibly chosen here as befitting the subject of the verses.

13 ff. **lanae**: nominative. Spinning was particularly the work of old women. Cf. Tibul. 1, 6, 77 f. *victa senecta | ducit inops tremula stamina torta manu.* — **nobilem ... Luceriam**: Apulian wool was famous for its excellence. — **non citharae**, etc.: 'It is not for you to play the music girl at revels.' — **poti**: passive. — **vetulam**: effectively reserved to this point. — **faece tenus**: cf. 1, 35, 27 *cadis cum faece siccatis.*

16

'Danae's lot, the ruin of Amphiraus' house, the overthrow of cities and defeat of rival princes by the Macedonian's bribes, all show the power of gold to harm (1-16). And gains when made but feed the greed for more. I have done well, Maecenas, to follow thy example, and to shun a high estate. The more each man denies himself, the more the gods bestow. My small farm with its clear stream, its little wood, and faithful crop, makes me more fortunate than the lord of fertile Africa, though he know it not (17-32). I have no luxuries, that is quite true; yet I escape the pangs of poverty. And thou wouldst give me more if I should wish. No, no; increase of income I shall best attain by lessening my desires. Happy is that man on whom God has bestowed little and enough (33-44).'

This ode thus treats Horace's favorite theme: the powerlessness of wealth to secure happiness, the value of a spirit content with little. It should be compared with 2, 2, and 16, and for Horace's personal desires with 1, 31; 2, 18. There is no indication of the date of composition. Metre, 72.

> Inclusam Danaen turris aenea
> robustaeque fores et vigilum canum
> tristes excubiae munierant satis
>   nocturnis ab adulteris,
>
> 5   si non Acrisium, virginis abditae
> custodem pavidum, Iuppiter et Venus

1. This cynical interpretation of the myth by which the golden shower in which Jupiter descended is made a bribe, is also found in Ovid *Am.* 3, 8, 29 ff. *Iuppiter, admonitus nihil est potentius auro, | corruptae pretium virginis ipse fuit,* etc. It occurs frequently in later writers, *e.g.* Petron. 137 B., *Anth. Pal.* 5, 216 — **inclusam**: the position emphasizes the fact of her imprisonment and its futility. — **turris aenea**: cf. 3, 3, 65.

2 ff. **robustae**: *oaken*; cf. 1, 3, 9. — **tristes excubiae**, *grim guard*. — **munierant**: cf. n. to 2, 17, 28. — **adulteris**: cf. 1, 33, 9.

6 ff. **pavidum**: for Acrisius had heard from an oracle that he was destined to die by the hand of his daughter's child. — **Venus**: naturally Jove's accomplice in this mat-

risissent: fore enim tutum iter et patens
    converso in pretium deo.

Aurum per medios ire satellites
    et perrumpere amat saxa potentius
    ictu fulmineo; concidit auguris
        Argivi domus, ob lucrum

demersa exitio; diffidit urbium
    portas vir Macedo et subruit aemulos

ter. — risissent : *laughed in scorn.*
— fore, etc.: in ind. disc. representing the thought of Jove and Venus. — converso ... deo: dative.

9. aurum : emphatically continuing pretium of the preceding verse. With the sentiment of the following, cf. the words Cicero attributes to Verres, *Verr.* 1, 2, 4 *nihil esse tam sanctum, quod non violari, nihil tam munitum, quod non expugnari pecunia possit.* Also Apul. *Met.* 9, 18 *cum ... auro soleant adamantinae etiam perfringi fores;* and Menand. *Monost.* 538 χρυσὸς δ' ἀνοίγει πάντα καὶ Ἅιδου πύλας. — per medios : *i.e.* openly, in broad daylight. — satellites: *guards;* cf. 2, 18, 34.

10. perrumpere : notice that this word, like concidit, diffidit, below, expresses the method by which gold attains its ends — it does not work subtly and in secret, but bluntly and directly, forcing its way against all opposition. — amat: *is wont.* — saxa: *i.e.* 'walls of,' etc.

11 ff. concidit ... diffidit : note the effect of position, —*fallen is*, etc. — auguris Argivi: Amphiaraus. When he was unwilling to join the expedition of the Seven against Thebes, for he foresaw it would end in disaster and cost him his own life, Polynices bribed Amphiaraus' wife, Eriphyle, with the necklace of Harmonia to induce her husband to go. Their son Alcmaeon slew his mother in anger at his father's death, and afterwards, like Orestes, was haunted by the Furies.

14 f. vir Macedo: Philip, father of Alexander the Great. It was said (Plut. *Aemil. Paul.* 12) that his conquests were made by means of bribes ὅτι τὰς πόλεις αἱρεῖ τῶν Ἑλλήνων οὐ Φίλιππος, ἀλλὰ τὸ Φιλίππου χρυσίον. The Delphic oracle has advised him to 'fight with silver spears.' Cicero, *ad Att.* 1, 16, 12, quotes a saying of his, *Philippus omnia castella expugnari posse dicebat in quae modo asellus onustus auro posset ascendere.* — aemulos reges: the rival claimants of the throne.

15   reges muneribus; munera navium
         saevos inlaqueant duces.

      Crescentem sequitur cura pecuniam
      maiorumque fames; iure perhorrui
      late conspicuum tollere verticem,
20   Maecenas, equitum decus.

      Quanto quisque sibi plura negaverit,
      ab dis plura feret. Nil cupientium
      nudus castra peto et transfuga divitum
         partis linquere gestio,

15 f. **muneribus; munera**: *with bribes; yes, bribes, I say.* Intr. 28 b. — **navium duces**: some see here a reference to Menas (or Menedorus), the freedman of Cn. Pompey and admiral of Sextus Pompey, who in 38 B.C. deserted to Octavianus; afterwards he returned to his earlier allegiance, only to desert again. — **saevos**: *stern though they be.* — **inlaqueant**: *ensnare.*

17 f. **crescentem**, etc.: a common sentiment. Cf. Theoc. 16, 64 f. ἀνήριθμος δέ οἱ εἴη ἄργυρος, αἰεὶ δὲ πλεόνων ἔχοι ἵμερος αὐτόν, 'His be unnumbered wealth, but may a longing for more ever possess him.' Iuv. 14, 139 *crescit amor nummi, quantum ipsa pecunia crevit.* — **fames**: cf. *Epist.* 1, 18, 23 *argenti sitis importuna famesque*; Verg. *A.* 3, 57 *auri sacra fames.*

19 f. **late conspicuum**: proleptic, *so that it could be seen afar.* — **equitum decus**: Maecenas was a good example of the moderation Horace is urging: although possessed of great wealth and influence, he modestly declined political preferment. Cf. n. to 1, 1, 1; 20, 5.

21 f. **plura, . . . plura**: the context in this paradox shows the meaning. By the first **plura** Horace means money and the unessential things which it procures, 'this world's goods'; by the second, the real goods which cannot be bought, but are gifts from heaven, — a contented mind and ability to find happiness in simple things. — **nil cupientium**: and so content. Cf. Maximian. 1, 54 *et rerum dominus nil cupiendo fui.*

23 f. **nudus**: *i.e.* leaving all encumbrances of wealth and luxury. — **transfuga**: continuing the figure of the soldier eager to leave the party (**partis**) to which he now belongs, and flee to the opposite camp. — **divitum**: and therefore discontent, contrasted with **nil cupientium.**

25   contemptae dominus splendidior rei,
      quam si quicquid arat impiger Apulus
      occultare meis dicerer horreis,
          magnas inter opes inops.

      Purae rivus aquae silvaque iugerum
30   paucorum et segetis certa fides meae
      fulgentem imperio fertilis Africae
          fallit sorte beatior.

      Quamquam nec Calabrae mella ferunt apes,
      nec Laestrygonia Bacchus in amphora

25 f. contemptae: *i.e.* by those who do not know the source of true happiness. — **splendidior**: in the sight of the wise. — **arāt**: put for the product of the field. Cf. the use *trahunt*, 2, 18, 8. For the quantity, see Intr. 35. — **impiger Apulus**: cf. *Epod.* 2, 42. Apulia was very productive according to Strabo 6, 284.

27 f. occultare: a poetic variant for *condere* 1, 1, 9. — **magnas**: used like **saevos**, v. 16 above. — **inter opes inops**: an oxymoron expressing the difference between the common view and the correct one. Cf. *Epist.* 1, 2, 56 *semper avarus eget*. Horace's phrase clung in men's minds: Paulinus of Nola at the end of the fourth century reproduced it exactly, 28, 292 *inter opes inopes*; Seneca with a slight variation, *Epist.* 74, 4 *in divitiis inopes*, a phrase St. Ambrose repeated three centuries later.

29 f. Horace describes his farm *Epist.* 1, 16. — **rivus**: cf. *Epist.* 1, 16, 12, quoted in introductory n. to 3, 13. — **segetis**: possessive gen. — **certa fides**: cf. 3, 1, 30 *fundus mendax* and n.

31 f. fulgentem imperio, etc.: the proconsul of Africa is probably meant, although it is possible that we should think rather of a great landed proprietor. The provinces of Asia and Africa were assigned each year to the two oldest men of consular rank eligible. — **fallit sorte beatior**: *happier in lot escapes the notice of*, i.e. *is a happier lot, although he does not know it, than that of*, etc. The Latin language having no present participle of *esse*, is unequal to the task of imitating the Greek idiom λανθάνει ὀλβιώτερον ὄν.

33 ff. Examples of the luxuries possessed by the rich. Cf. 1, 31, 5 ff.; 2, 16, 33 ff. — **Calabrae ... apes**: cf. 2. 6, 14 f. — **Laestrygonia**: Formian. See introductory

35 languescit mihi, nec pinguia Gallicis
　　crescunt vellera pascuis,

importuna tamen pauperies abest,
nec, si plura velim, tu dare deneges.
Contracto melius parva cupidine
40　　vectigalia porrigam

quam si Mygdoniis regnum Alyattei
campis continuem.　Multa petentibus
desunt multa ; bene est cui deus obtulit
　　parca quod satis est manu.

n. to 3, 17 for the name; for the wine, cf. n. to 1, 20, 10. — **languescit**: *grows mellow;* cf. 3, 21, 8 *languidiora vina.* — **Gallicis . . . pascuis**: Cisalpine Gaul produced a fine white wool according to Pliny *N. H.* 8, 190.

37. **importuna**: *the worry of.* Horace would have called himself *pauper*, a man of small estate; the point he is making here is that he is not so poor that he suffers from the worries of extreme poverty.

38. Cf. 2, 18, 12 f.; *Epod.* 1, 31 f.

39 f. **contracto . . . cupidine**, etc.: cf. 2, 2, 9 ff. — **vectigalia**: *income.* 'The less a man desires, the farther he can make his income go.' Cf. Cic. *Par.* 6, 49 *O di immortales! Non intelligunt homines quam magnum vectigal sit parsimonia.*

41 f. **Mygdoniis**: *Phrygian*; cf. n. to 2, 12, 22. — **Alyattei**: Alyattes was the father of Croesus and founder of the Lydian kingdom. — **campis**: dative with **continuem**: *join to* (so that I should be monarch of both realms).

43 f. **bene est**: colloquial; cf. Catul. 38, 1 *male est.* — **quod satis est**: *what is just enough.* With the sentiment, cf. Sen. *Epist.* 108, 11 *is minimo eget mortalis, qui minimum cupit, quod vult, habet, qui velle quod satis est potest.*

17

'Come, Aelius, child of the long Lamian line which sprang from ancient Lamus, that lord of Formiae and of Marica's strand, a storm is threatening. Before it breaks, lay in a stock of dry firewood; to-morrow shalt thou make merry with thy household.'

These verses are addressed to L. Aelius Lamia, apparently the friend named 1, 26, 8 (cf. 36, 8). The Lamian family was not prominent before Cicero's time and the name does not appear in the consular fasti until 2 A.D.; during the first century of our era, however, the house was one of the most distinguished. The Lamus to whom Horace playfully refers his friend's ancestry is none other than Homer's cannibal king of the Laestrygonians, *Od.* 10, 81. The scene is Lamia's country place: the occasion unknown. Metre, 68.

> Aeli vetusto nobilis ab Lamo,
> quando et priores hinc Lamias ferunt
> denominatos et nepotum
> per memores genus omne fastos,
>
> 5   auctore ab illo ducis originem
> qui Formiarum moenia dicitur
> princeps et innantem Maricae
> litoribus tenuisse Lirim

1. This verse of address is left hanging without a verb, but is resumed by v. 5 ff. — **nobilis**: almost 'ennobled by the descent from'; translate, *noble child of*.

2 ff. **quando**: with **ferunt**. These verses are inserted to support Aelius' relation to old Lamus — 'Since all Lamiae before thee trace their line back to Lamus, thou too must be one of his descendants.' — **hinc**: *i.e. ab Lamo*; cf. Verg. *A.* 1, 21 f. *hinc populum late regem belloque superbum | venturum*, and Hor. *C.* 1, 12, 17 *unde* equivalent *ab Iove*. — **nepotum**: *descendants*.

4. **memores . . . fastos**: family, not public, records are meant; see introductory n. The phrase is repeated 4. 14. 4 *per titulos memoresque fastos*.

5 ff. **auctore ab illo**: resuming v. 1. — **Formiarum moenia**: Formiae is identified with the capital of the Laestrygonians first perhaps by Cicero, *ad Att.* 2, 30; the Augustan poets adopted the identification, while the Greeks placed the city near Leontini in Sicily. — **Maricae**: *Marica's*. An Italian nymph; according to Verg. *A.* 7, 47 the mother of Latinus by Faunus. She was worshiped in the marshes near Minturnae, where the Liris loses itself in lagoons: hence **innantem**, *that overflows*. Cf. Mart. 13. 83, 1 f. *caeruleus nos Liris amat, quem silva Maricae | protegit*.

9 f. **late tyrannus**: the Homeric εὐρὺ κρείων, cleverly applied to the Homeric (cannibal) chief. Cf. Verg. *A.* 1, 21 *late regem* of

late tyrannus, cras foliis nemus
multis et alga litus inutili
demissa tempestas ab Euro
sternet, aquae nisi fallit augur

annosa cornix; dum potes, aridum
compone lignum; cras genium mero
curabis et porco bimenstri
cum famulis operum solutis.

the Roman people. — **alga . . . inutili**: proverbial; cf. *S.* 2, 5, 8 *vilior alga*.

12 f. **aquae . . . augur**: the Greek ὑετόμαντις. Cf. 3, 27, 10 *imbrium divina avis imminentum*. Also Arat. 1022 f. χειμῶνος μέγα σῆμα καὶ ἐννεάνειρα κορώνη | νύκτερον ἀείδουσα. — **annosa cornix**: the crow lives nine times as long as man according to Hesiod *Frg.* 193 ἐννέα τοι ζώει γενεὰς λακέρυζα κορώνη | ἀνδρῶν ἡβώντων, and cf. the quotation from Aratus above.

13 ff. Lamia's holiday is to be celebrated in simplicity, like one of Horace's own. — **cras**, etc.: notice that this verse has the same lilt as v. 9 above. — **genium**: the attendant self, a kind of guardian angel; the Greek δαίμων. The phrases *genio indulgere, genium placare*, etc., are common. Wine was the regular offering to the Genius as a pig was to the Lares. — **bimenstri**: the earliest age at which the animal might be sacrificed. — **operum**: for the construction, cf. 2, 9, 17 and n.

18

A hymn to Faunus as protector of the flocks and herds. The occasion, as the tenth verse shows, was not the great city festival of the Lupercalia on February 15, but the country celebration which fell on the 5th of December. The first two strophes contain the prayer for the god's favor; the remaining two describe the holiday. Metre, 69.

Faune, nympharum fugientum amator,
per meos finis et aprica rura

1. The character of the Greek Pan is given to his Italian counterpart, Faunus. Cf. 1, 17, 2 and n. — **fugientum amator**: juxtaposed in playful irony — 'they flee for all thy love.'

lenis incedas, abeasque parvis
    aequus alumnis,

5 si tener pleno cadit haedus anno,
larga nec desunt Veneris sodali
vina craterae, vetus ara multo
    fumat odore.

Ludit herboso pecus omne campo,
10 cum tibi nonae redeunt Decembres;
festus in pratis vacat otioso
    cum bove pagus;

inter audacis lupus errat agnos,
spargit agrestis tibi silva frondis,
15 gaudet invisam pepulisse fossor
    ter pede terram.

3 f. Notice the chiastic order. —**incedas abeasque**: not of a single occasion, but 'in thy revisitings.' — **aequus**: *in kindliness.* — **alumnis**: the young of herd and flock; cf. 3, 23, 7 *dulces alumni (non sentient) grave tempus.*

5 ff. si tener, etc.: the conditions on which the poet hopes for the god's favor. — **pleno anno**: ablative of time, *at the year's completion.* — **cadit**: *i.e.* as victim; sc. *tibi.* — **Veneris sodali . . . craterae**: Love and Wine are boon companions. Cf. the proverb Ἀφροδίτη καὶ Διόνυσος μετ' ἀλλήλων εἰσί. — **vina**: for the plural, cf. 1, 2, 15 f. — **vetus ara**, etc.: asyndeton.

9 ff. herboso . . . campo: in the Italian climate the fields are green in December. — **tibi**: dative of reference, *thy.* — **festus**: corresponding in emphasis to **ludit** above. — **otioso**: *free from work* (for the day). — **pagus**: *the country side.* 'Man and beast alike share in the holiday.'

13. audacis: *grown bold,* for Faunus protects the sheep against the wolves. Cf. Prud. *Cath.* 3, 158 f. *impavidas lupus inter oves tristis obambulat.* — **spargit**, etc.: in the poet's imagination the wood joins in honoring the god; cf. Verg. *E.* 5, 40 *spargite humum foliis (i.e.* in honor of Daphnis).

15 f. invisam . . . terram: hated as the source of all his toil. — **pepulisse**, etc.: *i.e.* in the dance, the *tripudium.* With the expression, cf. Ovid *Fast.* 6, 330 *et viridem celeri ter pede pulsat humum.* — **fossor**: *i.e.* the common peasant.

19

'You prate of ancient genealogies and wars, but never a word do you say on the real questions of the moment — how much we shall pay for a jar of wine, how, where, and when we shall drink. Come, a toast to the Moon, to the Night, to our friend Murena, the augur. The wine shall be mixed as your tastes demand; give music, scatter flowers, and let old Lycus hear our din and envy our light loves.'

Horace thus dramatically portrays a company which has fallen into serious conversation on mythological subjects, and forgotten the purpose of the gathering. In the first two strophes he recalls his companions from their soberer talk; then suddenly assuming the character of *magister bibendi*, he names the toasts, the strength of the wine that shall be used, and calls for flowers and music. The occasion for the ode may have been a symposium in Murena's honor (v. 10 f.), but it is more likely that the poet's imagination gave the impulse for the lines. They should be compared with C. 1, 27. The date of composition cannot be determined. Metre, 71.

> Quantum distet ab Inacho
> Codrus, pro patria non timidus mori,
> narras et genus Aeaci

1 ff. Such remote mythological questions were no doubt frequently discussed by littérateurs in Horace's day, as they were later. Iuv. 7, 233 ff. gives the kind of question the poor schoolmaster must be prepared to answer off-hand — *dicat | nutricem Anchisae, nomen patriamque novercae | Anchemoli, dicat quot Acestes vixerit annis*, etc. Cf. Mayor's note. Tiberius was fond of proposing similar questions: Suet. *Tib.* 70 *maxime tamen curavit notitiam historiae fabularis, usque ad ineptias atque derisum. Nam et grammaticos . . . eius modi fere quaestionibus experiebatur: 'quae mater Hecubae'? 'quod Achilli nomen inter virgines fuisset'? 'quid Sirenes cantare sint solitae'?* — **distet**: in point of time. — **Inacho**: the first mythological king of Argos. Cf. 2, 3, 21. — **Codrus**: the last king of Athens; he provoked his own death because of an oracle that the enemy would defeat the Athenians if they spared the life of the Athenian king. — **mori**: for this construction, see Intr. 108.

3 f. narras: *you babble*, colloquial. — **genus Aeaci**: Telamon and Peleus, with their descendants, Ajax, Teucer, Achilles, and Neoptolemus, all of whom engaged in

et pugnata sacro bella sub Ilio:
5   quo Chium pretio cadum
    mercemur, quis aquam temperet ignibus,
    quo praebente domum et quota
    Paelignis caream frigoribus, taces.
    Da lunae propere novae,
10   da noctis mediae, da, puer, auguris
    Murenae. Tribus aut novem
    miscentur cyathis pocula commodis.
    Qui Musas amat imparis,
        ternos ter cyathos attonitus petet

the war against Troy.—**pugnata...
bella**: cf. 4, 9, 19 *pugnavit proelia;
Epist.* 1, 16, 25 *bella tibi terra pugnata marique.*—**sacro... sub Ilio**:
the Homeric Ἴλιος ἱρή. Neuter
here as 1, 10, 14.

5 ff. The really important questions of the moment. The carouse
is a συμβολή, one to which each
participant makes a contribution.
—**Chium**: the Chian was a choice
wine.—**quis aquam**, etc.: to mix
with the wine, for the evening is
chill.—**quo praebente**, etc.: cf. *S.*
1, 5, 38 *Murena praebente domum,
Capitone culinam.*—**quota**: sc.
hora.—**Paelignis... frigoribus**:
old like that among, etc.—**taces**:
never a word do you say.

9 ff. Three toasts.—**da**: sc. *cyathos.*—**lunae... novae**: the Roman
month was originally lunar, so that
this is equivalent to a toast to the
New Month, as we drink a health
to the New Year. With the genitives **lunae, noctis, Murenae** giving
the subjects of the toasts, cf. 3, 8,

13. So in Greek, *e.g.* Marcus Argent. *Anth. Pal.* 5, 109, 1 f. ἔγχει
Λυσιδίκης κυάθους δέκα, τῆς δὲ ποθεινῆς | Εὐφράντης ἕνα μοι, λάτρι,
δίδου κύαθον. Theoc. 14, 18 f. ἔδοξ'
ἐπιχεῖσθαι ἄκρατον | ᾧ τινος ἤθελ'
ἕκαστος. 'We decided that each
should toast whom he wished in
unmixed wine.'

—**noctis mediae**: the carouse
shall last until morning.

11 f. **Murenae**: apparently the
Licinius Murena of 2, 10; but we
do not know from any other source
that he was ever augur.—**tribus
aut novem**, etc.: the *sextarius* was
divided into twelve *cyathi*. Here
the wine is to be mixed either three
parts wine to nine parts water for
the weaker brethren, or nine parts
wine to three parts water for the
stronger heads — **commodis**: *to
suit the taste.* Cf. 4, 8, 1 *commodus*
and n.

13 ff. 'The devotee of the nine
Muses will choose the stronger
mixture; those who honor the

15 vates; tris prohibet supra
       rixarum metuens tangere Gratia
    nudis iuncta sororibus.
       Insanire iuvat: cur Berecyntiae
    cessant flamina tibiae?
20   Cur pendet tacita fistula cum lyra?
    Parcentis ego dexteras
       odi: sparge rosas; audiat invidus
    dementem strepitum Lycus
       et vicina seni non habilis Lyco.
25 Spissa te nitidum coma,
       puro te similem, Telephe, Vespero
    tempestiva petit Rhode;
       me lentus Glycerae torret amor meae.

modest Graces, the weaker.'—**attonitus**: *inspired*, with a double meaning—by the Muses and the wine.—**tris...supra**: for the order, see Intr. 33.

16f. **rixarum**: objective genitive with **metuens**, as 3, 24, 22 *metuens alterius viri.*—**Gratia ... iuncta**: cf. 1, 4, 6 *iunctaeque Nymphis Gratiae decentes.*—**nudis**: so represented in Hellenistic and Roman art. Cf. n. to 1, 4, 7.

18 ff. **insanire**: *to revel, bacchari.* Cf. the Anacreontic θέλω, θέλω μανῆναι.—**Berecyntiae ... tibiae**: Mt. Berecyntus in Phrygia was the center of the wild orgiastic worship of the Great Mother.—**pendet**: *i.e.* on the wall unused.

21 ff. **parcentis**: *niggard;* bearing the emphasis.—**rosas**: here symbolical of luxury, for the season is winter (cf. v. 8), and the roses are to be scattered (**sparge**) with a generous hand. Cf. 1, 36, 15.—**audiat invidus**: parallel—*hear and envy.*—**Lycus ... Lyco**: scornful repetition, as 1, 13, 1 f.—**non habilis**: *not suited* (in years) as **tempestiva** (v. 27) shows.

25 f. **spissa**: *thick,* marking the contrast between young Telephus and old Lycus.—**te...te**: parallel to **Lycus...Lyco.**—**nitidum**: *sleek and spruce.*—**similem...Vespero**: the comparison is as old as Homer. Cf. *Il.* 22, 317 f. οἷος δ' ἀστὴρ εἶσι μετ' ἀστράσι νυκτὸς ἀμολγῷ | ἕσπερος, ὃς κάλλιστος ἐν οὐρανῷ ἵσταται ἀστήρ. Also, *C.* 3, 9, 21.—**tempestiva**: cf. 1, 23, 12.—**lentus**: cf. 1, 13, 8.—**Glycerae**: the same love 1, 19, 5; 30, 3. Cf. 1, 33, 2.—**torret**: cf. 1, 33, 6.

20

A warning to Pyrrhus, who attempts to steal the boy Nearchus from a girl who also loves him. 'She will fight like a lioness whose cubs are stolen; but the boy looks on unconcerned, as beautiful as Nereus or Ganymedes.'
The verses are evidently a study from the Greek. Metre, 69.

> Non vides quanto moveas periclo,
> Pyrrhe, Gaetulae catulos leaenae?
> Dura post paulo fugies inaudax
>   proelia raptor,
>
> 5   cum per obstantis iuvenum catervas
> ibit insignem repetens Nearchum:
> grande certamen, tibi praeda cedat,
>   maior an illa.
>
> Interim, dum tu celeres sagittas
> 10   promis, haec dentis acuit timendos,

1 ff. **moveas**: *disturb.*—**Gaetulae ... leaenae**: a similar comparison 1. 23. 10. — **post paulo**: in prose, ordinarily, *paulo post*. — **inaudax**: a compound coined by Horace, apparently to reproduce the Greek ἄτολμος.

5 ff. **per obstantis**, etc.: the conception is Homeric. Cf. *Il.* 18, 318 ff. The phrase represents the θαλεροὶ αἰζηοί of Homer; here it means the friends and supporters of Pyrrhus. The girl, enraged by the fear of losing Nearchus, will rush like a lioness through all opposition. The introduction of the name Nearchus disturbs the metaphor with which the ode begins,

and after v. 10 the figure is entirely dropped. For a similar confusion in comparisons, cf. 1, 15, 29 ff. — **insignem**: distinguished among all the rest, *peerless* (Smith). Cf. 1, 33, 5.

7 f. **grande certamen**: defined by the alternatives which follow. — **cedat**: *fall.* — **maior**: *superior, victorious.* — **illa**: sc. *sit*.

10 ff. **dentis acuit**: Homeric; cf. *Il.* 11, 416; 13, 474 of the wild boar. — **arbiter pugnae**: the boy is not only the prize of the contest, but is also its judge, since he may choose which he will follow. — **posuisse palmam**: quite indifferent as to the outcome, Nearchus places

arbiter pugnae posuisse nudo
   sub pede palmam

fertur et leni recreare vento
sparsum odoratis umerum capillis,
15   qualis aut Nireus fuit aut aquosa
   raptus ab Ida.

his foot on the emblem of victory. — **nudo**: added simply to help out the picture.

13 ff. fertur: 'you will hardly believe it, but this is the story.' Cf. 3, 5, 41 for a similar use of the verb. — **sparsum odoratis**, etc.: cf. Ovid *Fasti*. 2, 309 *ibat odoratis umeros perfusa capillis | Maeonis.* — **Nireus**: the fairest of the Greeks after Achilles, *Il.* 2, 673 f. Νιρεύς, ὃς κάλλιστος ἀνὴρ ὑπὸ Ἴλιον ἦλθε | τῶν ἄλλων Δαναῶν μετ' ἀμύμονα Πηλείωνα. Cf. *Epod.* 15, 22, *formaque vincas Nirea (licebit).* — **aquosa**: from its many springs; the Homeric Ἴδη πολυπίδαξ. — **raptus**: Ganymedes; cf. Verg. *A.* 5, 254 f. *quem praepes ab Ida | sublimen pedibus rapuit Iovis armiger uncis.*

21

An address to a jar of wine, which Horace will broach in honor of his friend Corvinus.

Marcus Valerius Messala Corvinus was a student in Athens with Horace, and like him served in Brutus' army in 42 B.C.; later he took part in the struggle against Antony. He was consul in 31 B.C., and in 27 B.C. enjoyed a triumph over the Aquitanians. After this he devoted himself to the practice of law and the pursuit and patronage of literature. His eloquence is praised by Cicero (*ad Brut.* 1, 15, 1); Quintilian (10. 1, 113) compared his oratory with that of Asinus Pollio. Messala's great wealth and high social position made it possible for him to gather about him a literary circle second only to that of Maecenas. Tibullus was the most distinguished of this company, and has left many references in his verses to his patron.

The ode is dramatically conceived: the poet stands before the jars stored in his apotheca and bids one contemporary with himself come down and yield up its store, whether it contain sport or contention. As the gossip of tradition credits Messala with being a connoisseur of wines, vv. 7-10 possibly refer to his ability. The date of composition may safely be put after 27 B.C., so that Horace and his wine were close to forty years. Metre, 68.

O nata mecum consule Manlio,
  seu tu querellas sive geris iocos
    seu rixam et insanos amores
      seu facilem, pia testa, somnum,
5 quocumque lectum nomine Massicum
    servas, moveri digna bono die,
      descende, Corvino iubente
        promere languidiora vina.

  Non ille, quamquam Socraticis madet
10 sermonibus, te negleget horridus:
    narratur et prisci Catonis
      saepe mero caluisse virtus.

1 ff. L. Manlius Torquatus was consul in 65 B.C. Cf. *Epod.* 13, 6 *tu vina Torquato move consule pressa meo.* Evenus addressed a measure of wine in similar fashion, *Anth. Pal.* 11, 49 Βάκχου μέ- τρον ἄριστον, ὃ μὴ πολὺ μήτ' ἐλάχιστον· | ἔστι γὰρ ἢ λύπης αἴτιος ἢ μανίης | . . . εἰ δὲ πολὺς πνεύσειεν, ἀπέστραπται μὲν ἔρωτας,| βαπτίζει δ' ὕπνῳ γείτονι τῷ θανάτου.
3 f. seu rixam, etc.: cf. 1, 13, 11 f.: 17, 22 ff. — facilem somnum: cf. 2, 11, 8; 3, 1, 20 f.; *Epod.* 2, 28. — pia: the amphora (testa) has been faithful to its charge.
5 ff. quocumque . . . nomine : a bookkeeping expression, *on whatever account.* — lectum: *vintage.* — moveri: *i.e.* from its place in the *apotheca*; cf. *Epod.* 13. 6 quoted above. For the infinitive, see Intr. 108. — bono die: 'a "red letter" day such as this in honor of Corvinus.' — descende: the *apotheca* was in the upper part of the house. See n. to 3, 8, 11. — promere: *to broach.* — languidiora: *mellower*; cf. 3, 16, 35 *languescit.*
9 f. non ille: emphatic as non ego 1, 18, 11. — Socraticis . . . sermonibus: *the arguments of the Socratic school.* — madet: *is steeped;* used as by us in a double sense. Cf. Mart. 6, 44 1 f. *credis te . . . solum multo permaduisse sale (wit).* — horridus: *rude, boorish.*
11 f. prisci Catonis . . . virtus: *honest old Cato.* With the expression, cf. 1, 3, 36 *Herculeus labor,* and Iuv. 4, 81 *Crispi iucunda senectus,* 'cheery old Crispus.' — saepe mero, etc.: Cicero

Tu lene tormentum ingenio admoves
plerumque duro; tu sapientium
    curas et arcanum iocoso
        consilium retegis Lyaeo;
tu spem reducis mentibus anxiis
virisque et addis cornua pauperi,
    post te neque iratos trementi
        regum apices neque militum arma.

in his essay *de Senectute* makes old Cato say that he is fond of *modica convivia*; cf. also Sen. *de Tranq. Animi* 17, 4 *Cato vino laxabat animum curis publicis fatigatum*.

13 ff. For similar praise of wine. see 1, 18, 3 ff.; 4, 12, 19 f. (*cadus*) *spes donare novas largus amaraque | curarum eluere efficax*. Also Bacchyl. *Frg.* 20 Bl. (ὅταν) γλυκεῖ' ἀνάγκα | σευομενᾶν κυλίκων θάλπῃσι θυμόν, | Κύπριδος δ' ἐλπὶς διαιθύσσῃ φρένας, | ἀμμειγνυμένα Διονυσίοισι δώροις, | ἀνδράσι δ' ὑψοτάτω πέμπει μερίμνας· | αὐτίκα μὲν πολίων κράδεμνα λύει, | πᾶσι δ' ἀνθρώποις μοναρχήσειν δοκεῖ· | χρυσῷ δ' ἐλέφαντί τε μαρμαίρουσιν οἶκοι· | πυροφόροι δὲ κατ' αἰγλάεντα ⟨πόντον⟩ | νᾶες ἄγουσιν ἀπ' Αἰγύπτου μέγιστον | πλοῦτον· ὣς πίνοντος ὁρμαίνει κέαρ. 'When sweet constraint warms the soul as the cups hurry round, and Cypris' hope commingled with the gifts of Dionysus rushes through the heart, men's thoughts are raised most high. This straightway breaks down the battlements of cities, and seems sole lord of all; with gold and ivory gleam the houses; the grain ships bring greatest riches from Egypt over the glimmering sea. So is the heart moved of the man who drinks.'

— **tu ... tu ... tu**: resuming the address to the jar and serving as connectives. — **tormentum**: *spur.* — **plerumque**: cf. 1, 34, 7 and n. — **curas**: *serious thoughts.* — **et arcanum**, etc.: cf. Vitalis *Anth. Lat.* 633, 6 R. *arcanum demens detegit ebrietas.* — **Lyaeo**: *the releaser;* cf. 1, 7, 22 and n.

18 f. virisque: object of **addis**. For the position, see Intr. 31. Cf. Ovid *A. A.* 1, 239 *tunc* (*i.e. post vina*) *veniunt risus, tum pauper cornua sumit,* | *tum dolor et curae rugaque frontis abit.* On **cornua** as the symbols of power, cf. n. to 2, 19, 30; Ovid *Am.* 3, 11, 6 *venerunt capiti cornua sera meo*, and 1 *Sam.* 2, 1 'Mine horn is exalted in the Lord.'

19 f. post te: cf. 1, 18, 5. — **iratos apices**: for the transferred

Te Liber et, si laeta aderit, Venus
segnesque nodum solvere Gratiae
   vivaeque producent lucernae
      dum rediens fugat astra Phoebus.

adjective, see Intr. 99. — **apices**: see n. to 1, 34, 14. — **trementi**: transitive here.

21 ff. Love and wine are companions, cf. 3, 18, 6 f. — **nodum**: of intertwined arms; cf. 3, 19, 16 f. — **solvere**: with *segnes*. — **Gratiae**: to the pleasures of wine and love the Graces add the charm of wit and courteous society. — **vivae**: cf. 3. 8, 14 *vigiles lucernae*. — **producent**: *carry on, prolong*; cf. *S.* 1, 5, 70 *prorsus iucunde cenam producimus illam*, Mart. 2, 89 *nimio gaudes noctem producere vino*.

22

A hymn dedicating to Diana of the woods, a pine tree that rises above the poet's country house. Metre, 69.

   Montium custos nemorumque virgo,
   quae laborantis utero puellas
   ter vocata audis adimisque leto,
      diva triformis,

5   imminens villae tua pinus esto,
   quam per exactos ego laetus annos

1 ff. This strophe is very similar to Catull. 34, 9 ff. *montium domina ut fores | silvarumque virentium | saltuumque reconditorum | amniumque sonantum. | Tu Lucina dolentibus | Iuno dicta puerperis, | tu potens Trivia et notho es | dicta lumine Luna*. — **custos**: cf. Verg. *A.* 9, 405 *nemorum Latonia custos*. On Diana Nemorensis, cf. 1, 21, 6 and n.

2 ff. quae. etc.: as the goddess of child-birth, Ilithyia. Cf. *C. S.*

13 ff. — **puellas**: used of young married women. Cf. Ovid *Am.* 2, 13, 19 *tuque laborantes utero miserata puellas*. — **ter**: the sacred number; cf. 1, 28, 36. — **triformis**: Luna, Diana, and Hecate. Cf. Verg. *A.* 4, 511 *tergeminamque Hecaten, tria virginis ora Dianae*.

5 ff. The Italian pine grows to a large size; its lower trunk is free from branches, but above it spreads into a broad 'umbrella' head. — **quam ... donem**: *that I may*, defin-

verris obliquum meditantis ictum
sanguine donem.

ing the purpose of the dedication. — **per exactos ... annos**: *as the years close.* Cf. 3, 18, 5. — **laetus**: *rejoicing* (in the service). corresponding to the *libens merito* of inscriptions. — **verris obliquum**, etc.: the regular stroke of the boar, due to the way his tusks grow. Cf. *Od.* 19, 451 λικριφὶς ἀίξας, of the wild boar that wounded Odysseus. Also Ovid. *Her.* 4, 104 *obliquo dente timendus aper.* The description of the victim fixes his age, as also in 3, 13, 4 f.

23

'Thy small but faithful offerings, Phidyle, will save thy crops and flocks; thou needest not be anxious that thou hast no great victim. Pure hands, a little salt and meal, is all thy guardian gods require.'

Thus Horace reassures a country housewife, and shows that, for all his lack of faith in the state religion, he was not without sympathy with the beliefs of the common folk. Read Lang, *Letters to Dead Authors,* p. 210; Sellar, p. 162 f. Metre, 68.

Caelo supinas si tuleris manus
nascente luna, rustica Phidyle,
si ture placaris et horna
fruge Laris avidaque porca,

5   nec pestilentem sentiet Africum
fecunda vitis nec sterilem seges

1 f. **caelo**: dative. Intr. 88. — **supinas**: with palms upturned (ὕπτιος), the regular attitude of prayer. Cf. Verg. *A.* 3, 176 f. *tendoque supinas | ad caelum cum voce manus.*

nascente luna: on the first day of the month, the Kalends. Cf. 3, 19 9 and n. On this day sacrifice was regularly made to the household gods. — **Phidyle**: Φειδύλη, the 'Sparer' (φείδομαι), well chosen to suit the subject of the ode. — **horna**: *i.e.* with the first fruits of the harvest. — **porca**: cf. 3, 17, 15, and n.

5 ff. **pestilentem ... Africum**: the Sirocco, whose parching heat burned up the grapes. — **fecunda**: *big-clustered.* — **sterilem**: active as *palma nobilis* 1, 1, 5. — **robiginem**:

robiginem aut dulces alumni
pomifero grave tempus anno.

10 Nam quae nivali pascitur Algido
devota quercus inter et ilices
aut crescit Albanis in herbis
victima pontificum securis

cervice tinguet: te nihil attinet
temptare multa caede bidentium
15 parvos coronantem marino
rore deos fragilique myrto.

the rust which injured the grain in a wet spring. The festival to the divinity Robigo fell on April 25.—**alumni**: as 3, 18, 4.—**pomifero... anno**: a similar circumlocution *Epod.* 2, 29 *annus hibernus.*—**grave tempus**: cf. Livy 3, 6 *grave tempus et... annus pestilens.* The careful arrangement of this second strophe should be noted: each of the three subjects, **vitis, seges, alumni**, has a position different from the other two with reference to its object.

9 ff. **nam quae**, etc.: Mt. Algidus, a ridge of the Alban hills, belonged to the pontifices, and was used by them as pasturage for their intended victims (*devotae victimae*). Cf. n. to 1, 21, 6.—**inter**: for the position, see Intr. 32.—**Albanis in herbis**: a part of the ancient Alban territory which tradition said (Dionys. Hal. 3, 29) King Numa assigned to the pontifices.

13 ff. **tinguet**: concessive, *may stain*; cf. 1, 7, 1 *laudabunt alii*,

etc.—**te nihil attinet,** etc.: 'the great and powerful may offer rich sacrifice, but for thee there is no need,' etc. With this emphatic contrast, cf. *e.g.* 1, 7, 10.—**temptare**: *to beset, importune*; its object is **deos**, which also serves as object of **coronantem.**—**bidentium**: *i.e.* of the age when they might be sacrificed. The meaning of the technical term *bidens* was uncertain in antiquity: in one place the epitome of Festus (p. 4) says that it means sheep with both rows of teeth, in another (p. 33) it offers the commoner explanation which refers it to the two prominent teeth in the sheep's lower jaw which replace the milk teeth. Translate, *full-grown.*—**parvos**: intentionally contrasted with **multa caede**, thus suggesting the folly of great sacrifice to the little images of the household gods kept by the hearth. —**coronantem**: on the Kalends, Nones, and Ides of each month and at

Immunis aram si tetigit manus,
non sumptuosa blandior hostia,
mollivit aversos Penatis
farre pio et saliente mica.

other special festivals honor was paid to the Lares. So Cato *de Agr.* 143 directs (*vilica*) *kalendis idibus nonis, festus dies cum erit, coronam in focum indat, per eosdemque dies Lari familiari pro copia supplicet.* — **marino rore** : the aromatic rosemary used by those who could not afford the costly imported incense. — **fragili**: *brittle.*

17 f. **immunis**: here *innocent, guiltless*; elsewhere in Horace it means 'without bringing a gift,' 4, 12, 23; *Epist.* 1, 14, 33. In this passage, however, the point which Horace wishes to emphasize is the acceptability of innocence over great offerings, so that *immunis* is used absolutely in the sense of *immunis sceleris.* The idea is commonplace. Cf. Eurip. *Frg.* 327 ἐγὼ δὲ πολλάκις σοφωτέρους | πένητας ἄνδρας εἰσορῶ τῶν πλουσίων, | καὶ ⟨τοὺς⟩ θεοῖσι μικρὰ θύοντας τέλη | τῶν βουθυτούντων ὄντας εὐσεβεστέρους. 'I ofttimes see poor men are wiser than the rich, and they who make small offerings to the gods more pious than men who sacrifice great victims;' also *Frg.* 946 εὖ ἴσθ', ὅταν τις εὐσεβῶν θύῃ θεοῖς, | κἂν μικρὰ θύῃ, τυγχάνει σωτηρίας. 'Be sure that when a pious man makes offering to the gods, even though his offering be small, he gains their saving aid.'

— **non sumptuosa**, etc. : the verse somewhat awkwardly adds a new idea to the preceding statement — (thy hand) *not made the more persuasive by any costly victim.*

19 f. **mollivit**: the gnomic perfect in conclusion — *it has* (and always will), etc. — **aversos**: not 'hostile,' but *disinclined, indifferent*; cf. *Epod.* 10, 18. — **Penatis**: not distinguished from the Lares. — **farre pio**, etc.: a circumlocution for the *mola salsa*, the sacrificial cake, made of spelt and salt. The phrase is used by Tibullus 3, 4, 10 *farre pio placant et saliente sale*: also by Ovid *Fast.* 4, 409 f. *farra deae micaeque licet salientis honorem detis.* — **saliente**: *i.e.* when the salt was thrown on the fire.

24

'Not all the wealth of the Orient nor villas by the sea shall set thee free from fear of death. The nomad Scythians live better far, for among them virtue and chastity have their true place; there the price

CARMINA [3, 24, 5

of sin is death (1-24). He who will be known as father of the state, must check the current license, trusting to posterity for his reward (25-32). Our sin must be cut out, laws without the support of character are vain. The source of our sin is greed for gain, so that neither torrid heat nor northern cold check the eager trader; for gold men do and suffer all. Poverty alone is great disgrace. Then let us dedicate to Jove or cast into the sea our gems and gold if we are really penitent (33-50). Present luxury is too great. Our boys must be trained in a sterner school. To-day no freeborn youth can ride his horse; yet he is well skilled in weaker sports and dice. Honor and fidelity are gone. Riches will still grow to harm, but never satisfy (51-64).'

This moralizing on riches as the source of evil is similar to much in the opening odes of this book, especially to 3, 1, 14-44. Cf. also 2, 15; 16; 18; *Epod.* 16. The savior invoked in vv. 25 ff. is clearly Augustus, who endeavored by legislation and example to check the growing license of his time. His success was only slight and temporary in spite of his words *Mon. Anc.* 2, 12-14 *legibus novis latis complura exempla maiorum exolentia iam ex nostro usu reduxi et ipse multarum rerum exempla imitanda posteris tradidi.* The date of composition cannot be determined, but probably the ode was written at about the same time as 3, 1-6. Metre, 71.

>   Intactis opulentior
>   thesauris Arabum et divitis Indiae
>   caementis licet occupes
>   Tyrrhenum omne tuis et mare Apulicum,
> 5   si figit adamantinos

1 f. **intactis**: *unrifled*, and therefore the greater. Probably the word contains a covert reproach also, for by Horace's time the Romans had looted Asia Minor and might be thought to be longing for the treasures of the East. Cf. Prop. 2, 10, 16 *et domus intactae te tremit Arabiae.* On the wealth of Arabia, cf. 1, 29, 1 and n. Trade with India by way of Asia Minor had existed from an early date, and the nature of the merchandise — ivory, precious stones, and costly stuffs — had impressed the Romans with the wealth of the Indies.

3 f. **caementis**: *rubble*, for foundations; cf. 3, 1, 35 and n. — **Tyrrhenum . . . et mare Apulicum**: *i.e.* every part of the seacoast from North to South.

5 f. **figit**: for the quantity, see Intr. 35. — **adamantinos**: cf. 1,

303

summis verticibus dira Necessitas
clavos, non animum metu,
   non mortis laqueis expedies caput.
Campestres melius Scythae,
10   quorum plaustra vagas rite trahunt domos,
vivunt et rigidi Getae,
   immetata quibus iugera liberas
fruges et Cererem ferunt,
   nec cultura placet longior annua,
15 defunctumque laboribus
   aequali recreat sorte vicarius.
Illic matre carentibus

6, 13. — **summis verticibus** : *i.e.* in the roof tree of your palaces. 'Man may plan and build but the completion is in the hands of Fate.' In 1, 35, 18 *clavi trabales* are the instruments of Necessitas. With the general concept, cf. 2, 18, 29–32.

8. **mortis laqueis** : the figure is old; cf. *Psalms* 18, 5 ' The snares of death prevented me.'

9 f. **campestres** : *of the steppes* ; cf. 3, 8, 24. The position of the word emphasizes the patent contrast between these nomads and the Romans with their magnificent palaces. With this description of the Scythians, cf. Aesch. *P. V.* 709 f. Σκύθας δ᾽ ἀφίξῃ νόμαδας, οἳ πλεκτὰς στέγας | πεδάρσιοι ναίουσ᾽ ἐπ᾽ εὐκύκλοις ὄχοις. ' And thou shalt reach the Scythian nomads, who dwell in wattled homes raised in the air on fair wheeled cars.' Sall. *Hist.* 3, 76 M. *Scythae no-mades tenent quibus plaustra sedes sunt.* — **rite** : *as is their custom*.

11 f. **rigidi Getae** : *stern* ; cf. *Epist.* 1, 1, 17 *virtutis verae custos rigidusque satelles* ; and *Anth. Lat.* 899, 7 B. *qui potuit rigidas Gothorum subdere mentes.* — **immetata quibus**, etc. : the land is not held in severalty and the products are common (**liberas**) property.

14 ff. Caesar *B. G.* 4, 1 attributes the same customs to the Suevi. Cf. Tac. *Germ.* 26. — **annua** : ablative. — **defunctum laboribus** : cf. 2, 18, 38 *functum laboribus*, used in a different sense. — **aequali . . . sorte** : ablative of manner. — **vicarius** : *substitute*.

17 f. Examples of the virtues that flourish among these simple peoples, as pictured by Horace's imagination. In similar fashion Tacitus extols the excellences of the Germans. Notice that here

> privignis mulier temperat innocens,
> nec dotata regit virum
> coniunx, nec nitido fidit adultero;
> dos est magna parentium
> virtus et metuens alterius viri
> certo foedere castitas,
> et peccare nefas aut pretium est mori.
> O quisquis volet impias
> caedis et rabiem tollere civicam,
> si quaeret pater urbium
> subscribi statuis, indomitam audeat
> refrenare licentiam,

the comparison is to the disadvantage of the women alone; the appeal to the Roman men is made somewhat differently, v. 25 ff. — **matre carentibus**: *motherless.* With the periphrasis, cf. 1, 28, 1. — **temperat**: *treats kindly.* The cruelty of the stepmother was proverbial. Cf. *Epod.* 5. 9. — **innocens**: *and does them no harm,* logically parallel to **temperat**.

19 f. On the proverbial arrogance of richly dowered wives, cf. Plaut. *Men.* 766 *ita istaec solent quae viros subservire | sibi postulant dote fretae, feroces.* Also Martial's clever answer 8. 12 *uxorem quare locupletem ducere nolim | quaeritis? uxori nubere nolo meae.* — **nitido**: cf. 3, 19, 25 and n.

21 f. **dos est**, etc.: cf. Plaut. *Amph.* 839 f. *non ego illam mihi dotem esse dico, quae dos dicitur, | sed pudicitiam et pudorem et sedatum cupidinem.* — **metuens**: *that shrinks from;* cf. 3, 19, 16. Notice that the second half of this verse is contrasted by position as well as by thought with the corresponding part of v. 20.

23 f. **certo foedere**: descriptive ablative, loosely attached to **castitas**. — **peccare**: in the restricted sense of infidelity; cf. 3, 7, 19. — **nefas**: sc. *est.* — **aut**: cf. 3, 12, 1 and n.

25 ff. **quisquis volet**: equivalent to *si quis volet.* — **impias**: because the strife had been between kinsmen. Cf. n. to 2, 1, 30. — **pater urbium**: a title of honor similar to *pater patriae.* The colony of Jadera in Illyria called Augustus *parens coloniae* CIL. 3. 2907; he was also called CIL. 11, 3083 *pater patriae et municip(ii)*: and Statius *Silv.* 3. 4, 48 names Domitian *pater inclitus urbis.* — **refrenare**, etc.: cf. 4, 15, 10 *frena licentiae iniecit.*

30   clarus post genitis, — quatenus, heu nefas!
       virtutem incolumem odimus,
          sublatam ex oculis quaerimus invidi.
       Quid tristes querimoniae,
          si non supplicio culpa reciditur,
35   quid leges sine moribus
       vanae proficiunt, si neque fervidis
       pars inclusa caloribus

30 ff. **post genitis**: found only here. — **quatenus**: *since*, introducing an explanation of the preceding words. The sentiment is a commonplace. Cf. Menander (?) δεινοὶ γὰρ ἀνδρὶ πάντες ἐσμὲν εὐκλεεῖ | ζῶντι φθονῆσαι, κατθανόντα δ' αἰνέσαι, 'For we all are quick to envy the man of good repute while he is alive, but when he is dead to praise him.' Horace himself has developed the thought *Epist.* 2. 1. 10 ff., 26 ff. Modern poets too have many echoes of the strain. Herrick declares with mock resignation, 'I make no haste to have my numbers read: | Seldome comes Glorie till a man be dead.' Pope's line also is familiar, 'These suns of glory please not till they set.'

— **incolumem**: *in the living*. — **quaerimus**: ποθοῦμεν. *long for, miss*. As soon as one generation is dead, its virtues are extolled by the surviving to disparage the generation that succeeds.

33 f. **quid**, etc.: *i.e.* 'to bring about a genuine reform we must cut at the root of the civic corruption; mere dismal (**tristes**) complainings are of no avail without bold action.' — **reciditur**: a metaphor taken from pruning; cf. *S.* 1. 3. 122 *et magnis parva mineris (delicta)* | *falce recisurum simili te.*

35 f. The inefficiency of laws unless supported by public sentiment and character (**mores**) is recognised by Aristotle *Pol.* 2. 5. 14 ὁ ... νόμος ἰσχὺν οὐδεμίαν ἔχει πρὸς τὸ πείθεσθαι παρὰ τὸ ἔθος. and present day conditions supply many examples. Some years later Horace extolled Augustus' reign with the words *mos et lex maculosum edomuit nefas* (4. 5. 22); Tacitus glorifies his Germans *plus ibi boni mores valent quam alibi bonae leges* (*Germ.* 19).

36 ff. **si neque**, etc.: the special cases to illustrate the general truth contained in the preceding question: 'if the greed for gain has grown so great that men dare everything save the crowning disgrace of poverty, what can mere statutes do?' Cf. Petron. 14 *quid faciant leges, ubi sola pecunia regnat?* — **pars**: cf. 3, 3, 55. —

mundi nec Boreae finitimum latus
duratacque solo nives
40   mercatorem abigunt, horrida callidi
vincunt aequora navitae,
magnum pauperies opprobrium iubet
quidvis et facere et pati,
virtutisque viam deserit arduae?
45   Vel nos in Capitolium,
quo clamor vocat et turba faventium,

inclusa: *fenced in, intrenched* (against man). The same idea 1, 22. 22 *terra domibus negata.* — latus: cf. 1, 22, 19. — solo: locative ablative. Intr. 95.

40. mercatorem: Horace's type of the man restless and reckless for gain. Cf. 1, 1, 16; 1, 3 entire; *Epist.* 1, 1, 45 f. *impiger extremos currit mercator ad Indos,* | *per mare pauperiem fugiens, per saxa, per ignes.* — horrida callidi: juxtaposed to strengthen the contrast between man's skill and nature's savagery.

42 f. magnum . . . opprobrium: cf. *S.* 2, 3, 91 f. *credidit ingens pauperiem vitium.* With the sentiment, cf. Theogn. 649 ff. ἆ δειλὴ πενίη, τί ἐμοῖς ἐπικειμένη ὤμοις σῶμα καταισχύνεις καὶ νόον ἡμέτερον; | αἰσχρὰ δέ μ' οὐκ ἐθέλοντα βίῃ καὶ πολλὰ διδάσκεις, 'Ah, wretched poverty, why dost thou weigh on my shoulders and degrade my body and my mind? And though I would not, thou dost teach me perforce much that is shameful.' Lucian *Apol.* 10 πενίαν πάντα ποιεῖν καὶ πάσχειν ἀναπείθουσαν, ὡς ἐκφύγοι τις αὐτήν, 'Poverty who persuades a man to do and suffer all things that he may escape her.'

44. 'The path of virtue steep' is proverbial; cf. Hes. *Op.* 289 ff. τῆς δ' ἀρετῆς ἱδρῶτα θεοὶ προπάροιθεν ἔθηκαν | ἀθάνατοι· μακρὸς δὲ καὶ ὄρθιος οἶμος ἐπ' αὐτήν, and Hamlet's 'steep and thorny way to Heaven.' — deserit: the abstract pauperies suggests a concrete subject *pauper*.

45 ff. Horace here expresses himself with the fire of a religious reformer. Sacrifice of jewels and gold will prove the people's sincerity. *Epod.* 16 is written in the same strain. — in Capitolium: as an offering to Jove. There is no verb until we reach mittamus v. 50. but the Roman reader would hardly be conscious of the lack. — clamor et turba: *the shouting crowd.* — faventium: Horace pictures the common people applauding the rich as they march to the Capitol to dedicate their wealth

vel nos in mare proximum
  gemmas et lapides aurum et inutile
summi materiem mali,
50   mittamus, scelerum si bene paenitet.
Eradenda cupidinis
  pravi sunt elementa et tenerae nimis
mentes asperioribus
  formandae studiis.   Nescit equo rudis
55 haerere ingenuus puer
  venarique timet, ludere doctior,
seu Graeco iubeas trocho,
  seu malis vetita legibus alea,
cum periura patris fides
60   consortem socium fallat et hospites,

48 ff. gemmas et lapides: no distinct classes are meant any more than in our parallel expression 'gems and precious stones.' — **aurum et**: on the position, see Intr. 31. — **inutile**: *that is good for naught*. — **materiem**: *the source;* the 'stuff' of which anything is made. Cf. Sall. *Catil.* 10 *primo imperi, deinde pecuniae cupido crevit; ea quasi materies omnium malorum fuere.* — **bene**: *truly, sincerely.*

51 f. eradenda, etc.: practical measures of reform — the Roman youth must be trained in a sturdier school, and taught to give up his present luxury. Similar expressions are found 3, 2, 1 ff.; 6, 37 ff. — **elementa**: *the seeds.* — **tenerae nimis**: *i.e.* beyond nature's limit.

54 ff. rudis: supporting **nescit**, *ignorant and untaught*, and contrasted with **doctior**. — **ingenuus**: emphasizing the disgrace, for riding and hunting were distinctly the exercises of a Roman gentleman. — **ludere**: Intr. 108.

57 f. trocho: trundling a hoop was a favorite amusement of Greek children, but to the conservative Roman mind it stood in marked contrast to the sturdier native sports. — **mālis**: notice the quantity. — **vetita legibus alea**: gambling with dice was much practiced among the Romans; although forbidden by law, the vice was but slightly checked.

59 ff. cum, etc.: *while*, etc. The clause adds another characteristic of the time. — **periura ... fides**: cf. 1, 5, 5 and n. — **consor-**

indignoque pecuniam
 heredi properet. Scilicet improbae
crescunt divitiae: tamen
 curtae nescio quid semper abest rei.

tem socium: *his partner. Sors* is the word for capital invested. — **indigno . . . heredi**: the dreaded heir, called ironically *dignior* 2, 14, 25. — **properet**: cf. *deproperare* 2, 7, 24.

62 ff. **scilicet**: *yes, of course.* Summing up the whole sad matter. — 'with all man's getting, he will never get enough.' — **im-probae** : *shameless,* for they have no regard for right and honor. — **curtae** : proleptic, 'the greedy man's wealth cannot keep pace with his desires.' Cf. *Epist.* 1, 2, 56 *semper avarus eget*; Apul. *de Mag.* 20 *nec montibus auri satiabitur (avarus), sed semper aliquid, ante parta ut augeat, mendicabit.*

25

In dithyrambic strains Horace celebrates 'the eternal glory of Caesar.' The poet imagines himself carried away by the power of Bacchus to the wild haunts of the Naiads and Nymphs, where he will sing his new and loftier theme. The ode has the form of an introduction to a larger work; the mention of the Emperor is apparently merely incidental, but forms the real subject of the verses. The occasion is unknown. Metre, 71.

Quo me, Bacche, rapis tui
 plenum? Quae nemora aut quos agor in specus
velox mente nova? Quibus
 antris egregii Caesaris audiar
5 aeternum meditans decus

1 ff. **tui plenum**: cf. 2, 19, 6. — **quae nemora**: in the same construction as **quos . . . specus.** — **mente nova**: *i.e.* being possessed by the god, the poet has become a new being.

4. **antris**: dative. Intr. 87. — **egregii**: see n. to 1, 6, 11. — **meditans**: *practicing, planning,* μελετῶν, used here of composing aloud, as by Verg. *E.* 6, 82 t. *omnia quae Phoebo quondam medi-*

stellis inserere et consilio Iovis?
Dicam insigne, recens, adhuc
    indictum ore alio. Non secus in iugis
exsomnis stupet Euhias,
10   Hebrum prospiciens et nive candidam
Thracen ac pede barbaro
    lustratam Rhodopen, ut mihi devio
ripas et vacuum nemus
    mirari libet. O Naiadum potens
15   Baccharumque valentium
proceras manibus vertere fraxinos,

tante beatus | audiit Eurotas. — **et consilio Iovis**: the deification of Augustus was early accomplished by the poets of his court. Cf. Verg. *G.* 1, 24 f. *tuque adeo, quem mox quae sunt habitura deorum | concilia, incertum est.* Also introductory n. to 1, 2, p. 56 f.

7. **insigne**: cf. 1, 12, 39 and n. The context makes it unnecessary to supply the obvious *carmen.* Cf. n. to 1, 6, 5.

8 f. **non secus**, etc.: the poet is possessed by the divine influence as fully as ever Maenad, who in her ecstasy has wandered unawares far from her home to some height where, suddenly coming to herself, she sees before her the valley of the Hebrus and Rhodope beyond. — **exsomnis**: the revels of the bacchantes were carried on by night. Sleeplessness is a characteristic of the orgiastic state. — **stupet**: *is amazed*; cf. Ovid. *Trist.* 4. 1. 42 (Bacche) *dum stupet Idaeis cindulata iugis.*

10 ff. **nive candidam**: a traditional epithet of Thrace. Cf. *Il.* 14, 227 Θρῃκῶν ὄρεα νιφόεντα. — **pede barbaro lustratam**: *traced by stranger feet; i.e.* she has passed out of her own country. — **ut**: with **non secus** in place of the more common *ac* to avoid collision with *ac* in the preceding verse.

13. **ripas**: used absolutely as 3, 1, 23. — **vacuum**: the sacred grove (cf. 1, 1, 30) is untenanted by mortals, so that the poet may wander there at will (**devio**).

14 ff. **Naiadum potens**: cf. 1. 3, 1 and n. Also 2, 19, 3; and Orph. *Hymn* 53. 6 Ναΐσι καὶ Βάκχαις ἡγούμενε. — **valentium**, etc.: the bacchantes were supposed to possess superhuman strength. The special allusion is to the murder of Pentheus at the hands of the Maenads, who pulled up by the roots the tree from which he had overlooked their orgies, and then in their frenzy tore him limb from limb. — **vertere**: equivalent

nil parvum aut humili modo,
    nil mortale loquar. Dulce periculum est,
O Lenaee, sequi deum
20   cingentem viridi tempora pampino.

to *evertere*. For the mood, see Intr. 108.

18 ff. **dulce periculum**: an oxymoron. The danger consists in the near presence of the god; cf. 2, 19, 5 ff. — **Lenaee**: 'god of the wine press' (ληνός).— **cingentem**: best taken with the subject of sequi, — the poet crowns his brow with fresh grape leaves in honor of the god and follows in his train.

26

'Not without honor have I served in Cupid's cause; now I'll give up my arms and dedicate them in Venus' temple. Goddess Queen, I pray thee, punish with a single blow Chloe so disdainful.'

The last verse betrays the lover and the cause of his determination to be done with love. A similar turn will be found 4, 1, 33 ff. Metre, 68.

Vixi puellis nuper idoneus
    et militavi non sine gloria:
        nunc arma defunctumque bello
            barbiton hic paries habebit,

5   laevum marinae qui Veneris latus
            custodit. Hic, hic ponite lucida

1 f. **vixi**: the definite perfect shows that all is over. — **idoneus**: *i.e.* a fit companion, *aptus*. — **militavi**: for this common figure, cf. 4, 1, 1 f. *intermissa, Venus, diu | rursus bella moves*; Ovid. *Am.* 1, 9, 1 *militat omnis amans et habet sua castra Cupido*.

4. **hic paries**, etc.: the dedication of weapons, implements, as a sign of completed service was customary. Cf. *Epist.* 1, 1, 4 *Veianius armis Herculis ad postem fixis*, as a sign that his service as gladiator was ended; Terent. *Maur.* 2633 f. *opima adposui senex Amori arma Feretrio.* So here Horace will hang the implements he has used while in Love's service on the right wall of Venus' shrine. — **marinae . . . Veneris**: protectress of sailors; cf. 1, 3, 1.

6 ff. **hic, hic**: marking his haste to be done with his service. Cf.

funalia et vectis et arcus
oppositis foribus minacis.

O quae beatam diva tenes Cyprum et
Memphin carentem Sithonia nive,
regina, sublimi flagello
tange Chloen semel arrogantem.

2, 17, 10; *Epod.* 4, 20. — **lucida**: expressing the general characteristics; the links are not lighted at the time of dedication. — **funalia**: to light the lover on his nocturnal raids. — **vectis**: to pry open doors where the lover is excluded. — **arcus**: if this be the correct reading, the instrument thus designated is unknown to us, unless we may conceive that the lover is armed with Cupid's bow and arrows.

9 f. **o quae**, etc.: cf. 1, 3, 1; 30, 1. — **Memphin**: here was a shrine of Ἀφροδίτη ξείνη, according to Herod. 2, 112. — **carentem**, etc.: cf. Bacchyl. *Frg.* 39 τὰν ἀχείμαντόν τε Μέμφιν. With the periphrasis cf. 1, 28, 1; 31, 20. etc. — **Sithonia**: cf. 1, 18, 9.

11 f. **regina**: cf. 1, 30, 1 and n. — **sublimi flagello tange**: *raise thy whip and touch.* Cf. Mart. 6, 21, 9 *arcano percussit (Venus) pectora loro.* — **semel**: *once and once only.* — **arrogantem**: the last word betrays the cause of all the lover's distress.

27

'May the wicked be attended by all bad omens; but only good signs be thy companions, Galatea; live happily and ever remember me. Yet beware of storms. I know the tricks of the Adriatic and of the West Wind. May our foes, their wives and children, tremble before them, as Europa once trembled (1-28). That maid, who so lately gathered flowers in the meadow, broke into bitter self-reproaches when she reached Crete with its hundred cities (29-66). But Venus came, laughed her to scorn, and told her the honors that awaited her (67-76).'

The structure of this ode is similar to that of 3, 11 with which and with 1, 15 it should be carefully compared. The first six strophes are designed solely to introduce the real subject of the poem. This introduction, however, is less skillfully managed than the opening strophes of 3, 11. The story of Europa was as well known as that of Hypermestra; the familiar portions of it are passed quickly over in vv. 25-32; and touched on again at the end (66-76). The scene chosen for fuller treatment is the moment when Europa, having reached Crete, realizes her position. Metre, 69.

> Impios parrae recinentis omen
> ducat et praegnans canis aut ab agro
> rava decurrens lupa Lanuvino
>   fetaque volpes;
>
> 5 rumpat et serpens iter institutum,
> si per obliquum similis sagittae
> terruit mannos: ego cui timebo
>   providus auspex,
>
> antequam stantis repetat paludes
> 10 imbrium divina avis imminentum,

1-12. 'May the wicked only be exposed to the evil powers; but for thee I will secure a good omen.' All the omens mentioned vv. 1-7 are ἐνόδιοι σύμβολοι, 'signs by the way,' Aesch. *P. V.* 487. — **parrae**: mentioned with other prophetic birds by Plautus, *Asin.* 260 *picus et cornix ab laeva, córvos parra a déxtera | cónsuadent*, and also by Festus s.v. *oscines* (cf. v. 11) — *cum cecinit corvus cornix noctua parra picus*. The bird, however, is not identified. *Owl* may be used in translation. — **recinentis**: *droning*.

2 ff. ducat: *escort* (on their way). — **agro . . . Lanuvino**: Lanuvium was situated on one of the southwestern spurs (hence *decurrens*) of the Alban Hills, on the right of the Appian Way as one traveled from Rome. It is evident from vv. 17 ff. that Horace has in mind for his Galatea a long journey across the Adriatic to Greece. — **rava**: *tawny*; cf. *Epod.* 16, 33 *ravos leones*.

5 f. rumpat: *break off*. If such unfavorable omens as are mentioned here appeared, the traveler would feel obliged to turn back and begin his journey anew. — **per obliquum**: logically modifying **similis sagittae**; translate, *darting across*.

7 f. mannos: *ponies*, bred in Gaul. Cf. *Epod.* 4, 14. — **ego**: bearing the emphasis, but giving the logical contrast — 'but for my friends.' — **cui**, etc.: *i.e. ei cui timebo . . . suscitabo*.

9 ff. 'I will anticipate bad omens by securing good.' — **stantis**: *stagnant*. — **divina**: *prophetic of*; cf. *Epist.* 2, 3, 218 *divina futuri*. — **avis**: the crow: cf. 3, 17, 12. Also Verg. *G.* 1, 388 *tum cornix*

oscinem corvum prece suscitabo
solis ab ortu.

Sis licet felix, ubicumque mavis,
et memor nostri, Galatea, vivas,
15   teque nec laevus vetet ire picus
nec vaga cornix.

Sed vides quanto trepidet tumultu
pronus Orion? Ego quid sit ater
Hadriae novi sinus et quid albus
20   peccet Iapyx.

plena pluviam vocat improba voce.
— **oscinem**: a technical term in augury for birds that give omens by their cries; to this class belong all the birds named in this ode (cf. Festus quoted above); those whose flight was significant, such as the eagle and vulture, were called *alites.* — **solis ab ortu**: a favorable quarter.

13 f. **sis**: optative subjunctive. — **licet**: added paratactically in the sense of *per me licet,* to show that he will not hinder. Cf. Plaut. *Rud.* 139 *mea quidem hercle causa salvos sis licet.* — **memor nostri**: cf. 3. 11, 51. The phrase is a formula of farewell.

15 f. **laevus**: when observing the omens the Roman *auspex* sat facing the south so that the east — the quarter in which good omens appeared — was on his left, therefore *laevus* and *sinister* in the technical usage may mean favorable; the Augustan poets, however, influenced by the Greek usage, employ both words in the sense of 'unlucky,' so that confusion frequently follows. Here **laevus** is unfavorable. — **vaga**: *flitting.*

17 ff. **sed vides**, etc.: suddenly the poet remembers the dangers to which Galatea will be exposed, and exclaims thus in anxious warning. The abruptness of this strophe after the smoothness of the preceding corresponds to the change in mood. — **trepidet**: as if the constellation were trembling at the storm it caused. — **pronus**: *as he sets;* cf. 1, 28, 21 *devexus Orion.* — **ater**: *i.e.* with the storm, but the word has also by association the meaning 'gloomy,' 'fatal.' Cf. 1. 28, 13; 37. 27; 2. 14. 17. — **albus . . . Iapyx**: cf. 1. 7, 15 *albus Notus* and n. — **peccet**: *how treacherous he is.* — **Iapyx**: the last two verses show that Horace has in mind a voyage to Greece.

Hostium uxores puerique caecos
sentiant motus orientis Austri et
aequoris nigri fremitum et trementis
    verbere ripas.

25   Sic et Europe niveum doloso
credidit tauro latus et scatentem
beluis pontum mediasque fraudes
    palluit audax.

   Nuper in pratis studiosa florum et
30   debitae Nymphis opifex coronae,
nocte sublustri nihil astra praeter
    vidit et undas.

21 ff. 'May the storms smite our enemies,' a common execration; cf. Verg. *G.* 3, 513 *di meliora piis erroremque hostibus illum*; Ovid *A. A.* 3, 247 *hostibus eveniat tam foedi causa pudoris.* — **caecos ... motus**: such as squalls and sudden storms. — **sentiant**: cf. 2, 7, 9 *fugam sensi.* — **orientis**: ordinarily *surgentis* is used of a wind.

23 f. Notice the recurrence of the r-sounds. — **nigri**: cf. n. to 1, 5, 7. — **verbere**: *the lash* (of the surf).

25 ff. **sic**: *i.e.* 'as confidently as thou dost prepare to face the dangers of the sea.' — **doloso credidit**: for the juxtaposition, cf. 1, 6, 9 and n.; also 3, 5, 33 *perfidis se credidit.* — **latus**: *self*; cf. 2, 7, 18. — **scatentem beluis**: cf. 1, 3, 18. — **medias**: *around her.* — **palluit audax**: *grew pale at . . . in her boldness*; cf. the oxymoron with 3, 20, 3 f. *inaudax raptor.* With this transitive use of *pallere*, cf. Pers. 5, 184 *sabbata palles.*

29 ff. **nuper**: *but just now*; emphatically contrasting Europa's position as described in vv. 29-30 with that indicated in 30-31. — **debitae**: *i.e.* as vowed; cf. 1, 36, 2 *sanguine debito.* — **nocte sublustri**: *the glimmering night.* — **nihil astra praeter**, etc.: so Mosch. 2, 127 ff. ἡ δ' ὅτε δὴ γαίης ἀπὸ πατρίδος ἦεν ἄνευθεν, | φαίνετο δ' οὔτ' ἀκτή τις ἁλίρροθος οὔτ' ὄρος αἰπύ, | ἀλλ' ἀὴρ μὲν ὕπερθεν, ἔνερθε δὲ πόντος ἀπείρων. . . . 'But when she now was far off from her own country, and neither sea-beat headland nor steep hill could now be seen, but above, the air, and beneath, the limitless deep . . . (Lang). For the position of **praeter**, see Intr. 32.

Quae simul centum tetigit potentem
oppidis Creten, ' Pater, — o relictum
filiae nomen, pietasque ' dixit
   ' victa furore!

Vnde quo veni?   Levis una mors est
virginum culpae.   Vigilansne ploro
turpe commissum, an vitiis carentem
   ludit imago

vana, quae porta fugiens eburna
somnium ducit?   Meliusne fluctus
ire per longos fuit, an recentis
   carpere flores?

---

33 ff. Horace adopted that form of the story according to which the bull vanished on reaching Crete, and Europa was left alone for a short time until Zeus reappeared in his proper form. While alone she comes to herself and breaks out in self-reproaches. — **centum ... potentem oppidis**: the Homeric Κρήτη ἑκατόμπολις.

34 ff. pater: her first word reminds her that by her folly she has lost a daughter's right to appeal to her father for protection. — **filiae**: genitive defining **nomen**. — **furore**: *folly*.

37 ff. unde quo: the compressed double question marks her excitement. Cf. the Homeric τίς πόθεν εἰς ἀνδρῶν; also Verg. *A.* 10, 670 *quo feror, unde abii, quae me fuga quemve reducit?* — **levis una mors**: imitated by Seneca *H. O.* 866 *levis una mors est: levis, at extendi potest.* — **virginum**: the generalizing plural, *a maiden's.* — **culpae**: *dative*; for the meaning of the word, see 3, 6, 17. — **vigilans**, etc.: she can hardly believe that it is not all a delusion. — **ludit imago**: cf. Verg. *A.* 1, 407 f. *quid natum totiens crudelis tu quoque falsis | ludis imaginibus?*

41. porta ... eburna: whence false dreams issued. Cf. Vergil's imitation, *A.* 6, 893 ff., of *Od.* 19, 562 ff. *sunt geminae somni portae, quarum altera fertur | cornea, qua veris facilis datur exitus umbris, | altera candenti perfecta nitens elephanto, | sed falsa ad caelum mittunt insomnia manes.*

42 f. meliusne, etc.: in ironical self-reproach. — **fluctus ... longos**: of the distance she has come. Cf. 3, 3, 37 *longus pontus*.

45 Si quis infamem mihi nunc iuvencum
dedat iratae, lacerare ferro et
frangere enitar modo multum amati
cornua monstri.

Impudens liqui patrios penatis,
50 impudens Orcum moror. O deorum
si quis haec audis, utinam inter errem
nuda leones!

Antequam turpis macies decentis
occupet malas teneraeque sucus

45 ff. si quis ... dedat: a virtual wish. — **nunc**: in contrast to the time when she yielded to his approaches. — **lacerare**: with cornua; cf. v. 71 f. below. — **enitar**: even in her rage she is conscious of her own weakness. — **modo ... amati**, etc.: in the meadow she had wreathed his horns with flowers.

49 f. impudens: she now feels the shame of her position and fears possible starvation or slavery — for her, a princess. Therefore she prays for death. — **liqui patrios penatis**: so Europa exclaims in Moschus' poem 142 ff. οἴμοι, ἐγὼ μέγα δή τι δυσάμμορος. ἦ ῥα τε δῶμα | πατρὸς ἀποπρολιποῦσα καὶ ἑσπομένη βοῒ τῷδε | ξείνην ναυτιλίην ἐφέπω καὶ πλάζομαι οἴη, 'Alas for me, and alas again, for mine exceeding evil fortune, alas for me that have left my father's house, and following this bull, on a strange sea-faring I go, and wander lonely' (Lang). — **Orcum moror**: *I keep death waiting*, (when I ought to seek him).

51 f. si quis: equivalent to *quisquis*. Cf. 3, 24, 25 and n. — **inter**: Intr. 33. — **nuda**: defenseless.

53 ff. With the ancient concept of life after death as a continuation of the present, it was natural to believe that in the other world the body appeared in the same form in which it left this. The cases of Dido and Deiphobus, *A.* 6, 450 and 494, are familiar illustrations. Also Stat. *Silv.* 2, 1, 154 ff. says of the death of a favorite boy *gratum est, fata, tamen, quod non mors lenta iacentis | exedit puerile decus manesque subivit | integer et nullo temeratus corpora damno*. It was natural then that Europa should pray for death before her beauty had faded.

53 ff. decentis: *comely*; cf. 1, 4, 6. — **sucus**: cf. Ter. *Eun.* 318 of a girl, *color verus, corpus soli-*

55   defluat praedae, speciosa quaero
          pascere tigris.

      Vilis Europe, pater urget absens.
      Quid mori cessas? Potes hac ab orno
      pendulum zona bene te secuta
60   laedere collum;

      sive te rupes et acuta leto
      saxa delectant, age te procellae
      crede veloci, nisi erile mavis
          carpere pensum

65   regius sanguis, dominaeque tradi
      barbarae paelex.'   Aderat querenti

dum et suci plenum. — **praedae**: said in self-pity, which is heightened by the adjective **tenerae**. — **speciosa**: *while still fair*.

57 f. **vilis**: she recognizes that she has cheapened herself by her folly. — **pater urget**: the thought of her father spurs her on to suicide. — **potes hac ab orno**, etc.: so Helen cries, Eurip. *Hel.* 298 ff. θανεῖν κράτιστον· πῶς θάνοιμ' ἂν οὖν καλῶς; | ἀσχήμονες μὲν ἀγχόναι μετάρσιοι | . . . σφαγαὶ δ' ἔχουσίν εὐγενές τι καὶ καλόν, 'To die is best. How then can I die nobly? Unseemly is choking by the noose in mid-air, . . . but the sword's blows have something fair and noble in them.'

59 f. **zona bene te secuta**: *which fortunately you have with you*. Spoken in irony: her girdle, emblem of maidenhood, will be a fit instrument of her death. — **laedere**: in place of the harsher *elidere*.

61 ff. **sive**: *or if*, cf. 1, 15, 25. — **leto**: dative. The rocks below the cliffs (**rupes**) are sharpened for her death. — **procellae**: which blow off the cliffs and will carry her out as she leaps to her doom. — **erile**: *set by a mistress.* — **carpere pensum**: the duty of enslaved women was to card and spin the wool assigned them by their mistress. Cf. Hector's fear for Andromache, *Il.* 6, 456 καί κεν ἐν Ἄργει ἐοῦσα πρὸς ἄλλης ἱστὸν ὑφαίνοις, and Prop. 4, 6, 15 f. *tristis erat domus, et tristes sua pensa ministrae | carpebant, medio nebat et ipsa loco.*

65 f. **regius sanguis**: spoken with proud indignation, which prompts the adjective **barbarae**

perfidum ridens Venus et remisso
    filius arcu;

    mox, ubi lusit satis, 'Abstineto'
70 dixit 'irarum calidaeque rixae,
    cum tibi invisus laceranda reddet
    cornua taurus.

    Vxor invicti Iovis esse nescis.
    Mitte singultus, bene ferre magnam
75 disce fortunam : tua sectus orbis
    nomina ducet.'

also. Cf. Creusa's speech Verg. *A.* 2, 785 ff. *non ego Myrmidonum sedes Dolopumve superbas | aspiciam, aut Graiis servitum matribus ibo, | Dardanis, et divae Veneris nurus.* — **aderat querenti**: the goddess comes and interrupts the maiden's self-reproaches.

67 f. **perfidum**: cf. 1, 22, 23 *dulce ridentem.*—**remisso...arcu**: *with bow unstrung*, for his task is ended. So Tennyson says, *Eleanore,* 'His bowstring slackened, languid Love.'

69 ff. **lusit**: sc. *Venus.* — **irarum . . . rixae**: genitive of separation. Intr. 94. — **laceranda**, etc.: referring in mockery to Europa's wish v. 45 ff.

73 ff. **uxor esse**: a Greek construction for the more common *te uxorem esse.*—**invicti**: 'so it is useless for thee to struggle against thy fate.' — **mitte**: cf. 3, 8, 17. — **sectus orbis**: *half the world.* Cf. Varro *L. L.* 5, 31 *divisa est caeli regionibus terra in Asiam et Europam;* and Plin. *N. H.* 3, 5 *Europam plerique merito non tertiam portionem fecere, verum aequam, in duas partes ab amne Tanai ad Gaditanum fretum universo orbe diviso.* — **nomina**: cf. 1, 2, 15. — **ducet**: *shall take*; cf. *S.* 2, 1, 66 *Laelius aut qui | duxit ab oppressa meritum Carthagine nomen.*

28

'Come, Lyde, bring out some good old wine, relax your fortified sobriety. 'Tis now past noon; we must be quick to celebrate with cup and song Neptune's great holiday. We'll sing in amoebean strains until Night claims a parting song.'

The festival which occasioned this ode was the *Neptunalia*, which fell on July 23. The people celebrated it in open air festival, erecting booths of boughs, called *umbrae*, along the banks of the Tiber or on the seashore, for protection from the sun. Horace, however, represents himself as on his farm, where he bids his severe housekeeper join him in a carouse. Metre, 71.

> Festo quid potius die
>   Neptuni faciam? Prome reconditum,
> Lyde, strenua Caecubum,
>   munitaeque adhibe vim sapientiae.
> 5 Inclinare meridiem
>   sentis et, veluti stet volucris dies,
> parcis deripere horreo
>   cessantem Bibuli consulis amphoram.
> Nos cantabimus invicem

1 ff. It suddenly occurs to Horace that it is the day of Neptune's festival, which furnishes him an excuse for some relaxation. — **prome**: cf. 1, 36, 11. — **reconditum**: hoarded away in the back of the *apotheca*; cf. *Epod.* 9, 1 *repostum Caecubum*. — **strenua**: to be taken with **prome**, *hurry and broach*. — **munitae ... sapientiae**: *your well fortified (and stern) philosophy*. Lyde is evidently not given to carouses, but Horace begs her for once to do violence to her strenuous principles. Some critics have wished to believe that Lyde — who probably lived only in Horace's imagination — was a flute girl, yet music girls possessed no *munitam sapientiam* to hinder a carouse, and the whole wit of Horace's verses lies in the absurdity of this proposal to his severe and probably old housekeeper to join him in a drinking bout and song.

5 f. 'It is already late and we must hurry.'— **inclinare meridiem**: a common belief was that the sun and stars were fixed in the vaulted sky, which revolved, carrying them with it. Cf. Cic. *Tusc.* 3, 3, 7 *inclinato iam in postmeridianum tempus die*. — **et**: *and yet*. — **stet**: *were standing still*.

7 f. **deripere**: *to hurry down*. Cf. 3, 21, 7, *descende* and n. With the infin., cf. *Epist.* 1, 3, 16 *ut tangere vitet*. — **horreo**: *i.e.* the apotheca. — **cessantem**: as if the jar were reluctant.—**Bibuli**: M. Calpurnius Bibulus, consul in 59 B.C.

9 f. **nos**: *I*, as *tu*, v. 11 shows; cf. 1, 6, 5 and n.—**invicem**: *in my turn*. — **viridis**: the tradi-

Neptunum et viridis Nereidum comas;
tu curva recines lyra
    Latonam et celeris spicula Cynthiae;
summo carmine quae Cnidon
    fulgentisque tenet Cycladas, et Paphum
iunctis visit oloribus;
    dicetur merita Nox quoque nenia.

tional color of the sea-nymphs. In general the colors and appearance of the sea are attributed to the divinities whose home is in it; hence Thetis is *mater caerula*, *Epod.* 13, 16. Cf. also Stat. *Silv.* 1, 5, 16 f. *ite deae virides liquidosque advertite vultus | et vitreum teneris crinem redimite corymbis.*

11 f. **recines**: *sing in answering strains.* — **Latonam ... spicula**: note the correspondence with v. 10. With the theme, cf. Eurip. *Hec.* 462 f. σὺν Δηλιάσιν τε κούραις Ἀρτέμιδός τε θεᾶς χρυσέαν ἄμπυκα τόξα τ' εὐλογήσω. 'And with the Delian maidens I will praise the golden head-band and the weapons of the goddess Artemis '

13 f. **summo carmine**: *at the end of*; cf. *Epist.* 1, 1, 1 *summa dicende camena*; and Iuv. 1, 5 *summi libri.* — **quae**: *i.e. eam quae;* cf. 3, 26, 9. The verb **cantabimus** still continues. With this paraphrase for Venus, cf. the address of Posidippus *Anth. Pal.* 12, 131, 1 f. ἃ Κύπρον ἅ τε Κύθηρα καὶ ἃ Μίλητον ἐποιχνεῖς | καὶ τὸ καλὸν Συρίης ἱπποκρότου δάπεδον. — **fulgentis**: cf. 1, 14, 19 *nitentes Cycladas.* The worship of Aphrodite was widespread among the islands of the Aegean, and was especially cultivated at Naxos.

15 f. **iunctis ... oloribus**: *drawn by,* etc. The swan was sacred to the goddess and in poetry frequently draws her car. For the construction, cf. 3, 3, 16. — **dicetur**: cf. 1, 6, 5 and n. — **Nox**: 'we will continue until nightfall.' — **nenia**: *a good-night song;* not here a 'dirge' as in 2, 1, 38.

29

'Maecenas, child of Tuscan kings, long have the wine and roses waited for thee on my Sabine farm. Do not delay; leave thy lofty city pile, and all that thou canst see from it of Tivoli and Tusculum, the smoke and din of Rome, and soothe thy cares with grateful, simple feasts (1-16). Now rages dog-day heat and drought; the shepherd and his flock seek the shade and cool, and every breeze is stilled. Yet thou art anxious for our state and fear our furthest border foes (17-28). All that is wrong. God has hidden the future from man's sight and laughs at mortals' anxious care. Deal with the present and be satisfied; for all besides goes like a stream, now quiet, now wild (29-41). He shall be master of himself who lives the present hour; that single gift Heaven cannot take back (41-48). Dame Fortune plays with man, but I will not be her sport. If she be kind, 'tis well; but if she fly away, I am unchanged with honor still. No timid trader I to bargain with the gods to save my goods when the southwester blows. Nay, from the storm my little boat and the Twin Gods will keep me still unharmed (49-64).'

The last place before the epilogue in his collected lyrics Horace thus gives to the friend and patron to whom he had dedicated the three books. See Introductory n. to 1, 1. Maecenas' care for the well-being of the state and anxiety over possible foreign foes furnish Horace an opportunity to urge again the wisdom of thinking solely of the present hour; that only that which we already have is surely ours. He then goes to develop in his own manner a kindred theme — independence of the whims of fortune.

The allusions in vv. 26-28 seem to fix the date as **26-25 B.C.**, when Augustus was absent in the West. Metre, 68.

> Tyrrhena regum progenies, tibi
> non ante verso lene merum cado
>   cum flore, Maecenas, rosarum et
>   pressa tuis balanus capillis
>
> 5   iamdudum apud me est: **eripe te morae,**
>   ne semper udum Tibur et Aefulae

1 ff. Tyrrhena, etc.: see 1, 1, 1 and n. — **verso**: 'tipped' to pour the wine into the mixer; hence *broached.* — **lene**: *mellow*; cf. 3, 21, 8 *languidiora vina.* — **flore** ... **rosarum**: cf. 2, 3, 14 *flores amoenae rosae*; 3, 15, 15. — **balanus**: properly the *myrobalanus*, 'ben nut,' grown in Egypt and Arabia; here the oil pressed from the nut for unguent; translate, *nut oil.* — **iamdudum,** etc.: 'I have waited long; come.' Cf. *Epist.* 1, 5, 7 *iamdudum splendet focus et tibi munda supellex.*

5 ff. morae: *hesitancy.* — **ne,** etc.: a purpose clause following *eripe.* Translate, however, as a

declive contempleris arvum et
Telegoni iuga parricidae.

Fastidiosam desere copiam et
molem propinquam nubibus arduis;
omitte mirari beatae
fumum et opes strepitumque Romae.

Plerumque gratae divitibus vices,
mundaeque parvo sub lare pauperum

negative exhortation, *do not always*, etc. — **udum Tibur**: *well watered Tivoli*. For the applicability of the adjective cf. 1, 7, 13 and n. — **Aefulae**, etc.: a town among the hills between Tibur and Praeneste.

8. Telegoni, etc.: Tusculum, founded by Telegonus, the son of Ulysses and Circe. When his mother sent him in quest of his father he came to Ithaca and there unwittingly slew Ulysses. With the preceding verses cf. Ovid. *Fast.* 4, 71 f. *et iam Telegoni, iam moenia Tiburis udi | stabant.*

9 f. fastidiosam: *cloying*. — **molem propinquam**, etc.: *thy pile, near neighbor*, etc. Cf. 2, 15, 2. The palace called *alta domus Epod.* 9, 3 which Maecenas built on the Esquiline. It had a lofty tower which commanded a view of the Campagna and surrounding hills. From this *turris Maecenatiana*, as it was later called, Nero is said (Suet. *Nero* 38) to have watched the burning of Rome.

11 f. omitte: cf. the simple *mitte* 1, 38, 3; 3, 27, 74. — **beatae**: cf. 1, 4, 14; 3, 26, 9. — **fumum et opes**, etc.: this graphic line is famous; Tennyson's verse, *In Mem.* 89, is a reminiscence of it, 'The dust and din and steam of town.'

13. A general statement — 'the rich suffer from ennui and are eager for a change simply for a change's sake, and not because it brings them any real advantage.' Cf. Lucretius' description of the uneasy 3, 1057 ff. *haud ita (i.e.* if men could know the cause of their uneasiness) *vitam agerent ut nunc plerumque videmus | quid sibi quisque velit nescire et quaerere semper | commutare locum, quasi onus deponere possit; | exit saepe foras magnis ex aedibus ille, | esse domi quem pertaesumst, subitoque revertit | quippe foris nilo melius qui sentiat esse. | currit agens mannos ad villam praecipitanter.*

— **plerumque**: cf. 1, 34, 7 and n. — **gratae**: sc. *sunt*. — **vices**: *a change*.

14 ff. mundae: *simple*, striking

15   cenae sine aulaeis et ostro
           sollicitam explicuere frontem.

        Iam clarus occultum Andromedae pater
        ostendit ignem, iam Procyon furit
           et stella vesani Leonis,
20   sole dies referente siccos;

        iam pastor umbras cum grege languido
        rivumque fessus quaerit et horridi
           dumeta Silvani, caretque
              ripa vagis taciturna ventis:

25   tu civitatem quis deceat status
        curas et urbi sollicitus times

the mean between pretentiousness and cheap squalor, as Horace himself defines the word, *S.* 2, 2, 65 f. *mundus erit, qui non offendet sordibus atque | in neutram partem cultus miser.* Cf. n. on *munditiis* 1, 5, 5. — **lare**: *roof*; cf. 1, 12, 44. — **pauperum**: cf. n. on *pauperiem* 1, 1, 18. — **aulaeis**: *tapestries.* — **ostro**: used in the *aulaea* and upholstery. — **explicuere**: gnomic perfect. Intr. 103.

17 ff. 'The dog days are come; it is the time for rest.' — **clarus occultum**: with this antithesis, cf. 1, 6, 9 and n. — **Andromedae pater**: Cepheus, once king of Egypt, husband of Cassiopea and united with her in the sky in the constellation that bears her name. It rose July 9. — **Procyon**: the lesser dog-star, rising July 15. — **Leonis**: now called Regulus, rising July 30.

21 ff. **iam pastor**, etc.: cf. the anonymous Greek epigram χώ ποιμὰν ἐν ὄρεσσι μεσαμβρινῶ ἀγχόθι παγᾶς | συρίσδων, λασίαις θάμνῳ ὑπὸ πλατάνου | καύματ' ὀπωρινοῖο φυγὼν Κυνός. 'And the shepherd on the mountains at midday, piping by a spring and shunning the heat of the summer dog-star in a copse under a thick plane tree;' and Theognis' impatience, 1039 f., at those who do not fortify themselves in hot weather ἄφρονες ἄνθρωποι καὶ νήπιοι, οἵτινες οἶνον | μὴ πίνουσ' ἄστρου καὶ κυνὸς ἀρχομένου. 'Silly senseless men, who drink not wine while the Dog-star is supreme!'

— **rivum**: cf. 2, 5, 6 and 3, 13, 9–12. — **horridi**: *rough*, as becomes the dweller in the thickets: cf. n. to *Epod.* 2, 22.

25 ff. **tu**: 'The shepherd and his sheep rest, but you,' etc. Cf. 2, 9, 9. — **status**: *policy*. The

quid Seres et regnata Cyro
    Bactra parent Tanaisque discors.

    Prudens futuri temporis exitum
30 caliginosa nocte premit deus,
    ridetque si mortalis ultra
        fas trepidat. Quod adest memento

    componere aequus: cetera fluminis
    ritu feruntur, nunc medio alveo

reference is apparently to Maecenas' position as Augustus' chief adviser in the settlement of the empire, and as the Emperor's representative during his absence in 26-25 B.C. — **urbi**: with both sollicitus and times. — **Seres**, etc.: Horace ironically chooses remote peoples to show how needless Maecenas' fears are. — **regnata Cyro**: cf. 2, 6, 11. — **Bactra**: the farthest part of the Parthian Empire. — **Tanais**: *i.e.* the Scythians. With this use of the river for the people who dwell by it, cf. 2, 9, 21; 20, 20. — **discors**: and so not to be feared by us.

29 ff. The uncertainty of tomorrow and the folly of being anxious for it. Cf. Theog. 1075 ff. πρήγματος ἀπρήκτου χαλεπώτατόν ἐστι τελευτὴν | γνῶναι, ὅπως μέλλει τοῦτο θεὸς τελέσαι. | ὀρφνὴ γὰρ τέταται. 'Of that which is yet unaccomplished it is most difficult to recognize the end and know how God will complete it. A mist is stretched before us.'

— **prudens . . . deus**: cf. 1, 3,

21. — **caliginosa**: cf. ὀρφνή in the passage of Theognis just quoted, and Iuv. 6, 556 *et genus humanum damnat caligo futuri*.

31 f. ridet: *laughs in scorn*; cf. 3, 27, 67 *ridens Venus*. — **mortalis ultra**, etc.: 'mortal should have mortal's thoughts;' cf. 2, 16, 17. — **trepidat**: *frets himself*; cf. 2, 11, 4. — **quod adest**, etc.: one of Horace's favorite rules for a wise life. So Pind. P. 3, 21 ff. ἔστι δὲ φῦλον ἀνθρώποισι ματαιότατον, | ὅστις αἰσχύνων ἐπιχώρια παπταίνει τὰ πόρσω, | μεταμώνια θηρεύων ἀκράντοις ἐλπίσιν. 'There is a tribe most foolish among men, of such as scorn the things of home and gaze at that which is far off, chasing vain objects with hopes that shall never be fulfilled.'

33 ff. aequus: *i.e.* 'keep thyself unruffled whether the hour bring good or ill.' — **cetera**: *i.e.* all the future. — **ritu**: *like*; cf. 3, 14, 1 and n. — **feruntur**: *are swept along*: marking the impossibility of directing the future. Cf. Sen.

35   cum pace delabentis Etruscum
               in mare, nunc lapides adesos

            stirpisque raptas et pecus et domos
            volventis una, non sine montium
               clamore vicinaeque silvae,
40   cum fera diluvies quietos

            inritat amnis. Ille potens sui
            laetusque deget, cui licet in diem
               dixisse 'Vixi; cras uel atra
               nube polum pater occupato,

Epist. 23 *celeri, eorum more quae fluminibus innatant, non eunt sed feruntur.* — nunc **medio alveo**, etc.: most of the rivers known to Horace were mountain streams, which in dry seasons are small and quiet, but after a rainfall become swollen torrents quickly. — **Etruscum**: the verse is hypermetric. Intr. 68. — **lapides adesos**, etc.: cf. *Il.* 11, 492 ff. ὡς δ' ὁπότε πλήθων ποταμὸς πεδίονδε κάτεισιν | χειμάρρους κατ' ὄρεσφιν, ὀπαζόμενος Διὸς ὄμβρῳ. | πολλὰς δὲ δρῦς ἀζαλέας, πολλὰς δέ τε πεύκας | ἐσφέρεται, and Lucret 1, 281 ff. *et cum mollis aquae fertur natura repente | flumine abundanti, quam largis imbribus auget | montibus ex altis magnus decursus aquai, | fragmina coniciens silvarum arbustaque tota. | . . . ita magno turbidus imbri . . . amnis | dat sonitu magno stragem volvitque sub undis | grandia saxa.*

37 ff. **raptas**: with all three nouns. — **clamore**: personifying the mountains and woods.

41. **potens sui**: *independent;* i.e. not enslaved by his thoughts of the morrow, by 'hope to rise or fear to fall.' The dependent man is described *Epist.* 1, 16, 65 *nam qui cupiet, metuet quoque; porro | qui metuens vivet, liber mihi non erit umquam.*

43 ff. 'To-day is mine; let to-morrow be what it will, it cannot take from me that which I have once enjoyed.' A common sentiment. Cf. Sen. *Epist.* 12 *in somnum ituri laeti hilaresque dicamus: 'vixi et quem dederat cursum Fortuna, peregi.'* Mart. 1, 15, 11 f. *non est, crede mihi, sapientis dicere: 'vivam.' | sera nimis vita est crastina. vive hodie;* 5, 58, 7 f. *cras vives? hodie iam vivere, Postume, serum est. | ille sapit quisquis, Postume, vixit heri.* — **dixisse**: with the tense, cf. 3, 4, 51, — **pater**: cf. 1, 2, 2.

vel sole puro: non tamen inritum
quodcumque retro est efficiet, neque
   diffinget infectumque reddet
      quod fugiens semel hora vexit.'

Fortuna, saevo laeta negotio et
ludum insolentem ludere pertinax,
   transmutat incertos honores,
      nunc mihi, nunc alii benigna.

Laudo manentem: si celeris quatit
pennas, resigno quae dedit et mea
   virtute me involvo probamque
      pauperiem sine dote quaero.

Non est meum, si mugiat Africis
malus procellis, ad miseras preces

45 ff. inritum: *void.* — **diffinget:** *change.* — **infectum reddet:** *destroy.* — **fugiens:** *in its flight.*

49 ff. cf. Dryden's famous paraphrase, 'Fortune that with malicious joy | Does Man, her slave, oppress, | Proud of her office to destroy, | Is seldom pleased to bless: | Still various, and inconstant still, | But with an inclination to be ill, | Promotes, degrades, delights in strife, | And makes a lottery of life. | I can enjoy her while she's kind; | But when she dances in the wind, | And shakes her wings and will not stay, | I puff the prostitute away: | The little or the much she gave, is quickly resigned, | Content with poverty my soul I arm, | And virtue, though in rags, will keep me warm.'

49 ff. laeta: *rejoicing in.* — **ludum:** cf. 2, 1, 3. — **ludere:** Intr. 108. — **transmutat honores:** cf. 1, 34, 14 ff.

52. mihi: Horace here lapses into his common habit of using himself as a concrete illustration of the principle (here of independence) he has been urging.

54 ff. pennas: Fortune is always winged: cf. 1, 34, 15. — **resigno:** *I yield back*; apparently a book-keeping term 'to carry to the other side of the account,' 'to credit back.' — **me involvo:** his honor is his only cloak. Cf. Plato's proposal for his ideal state *Rep.* 5, 457 A. ἀρετὴν ἀντὶ ἱματίων ἀμφι᾽σονται (αἱ γυναῖκες). — **quaero:** as a lover his bride.

57. non est meum: colloquial, *it's not my way.* Cf. Plaut. *Asin.*

>   decurrere et votis pacisci,
> 60   ne Cypriae Tyriaeque merces
>   addant avaro divitias mari:
>   tunc me biremis praesidio scaphae
>   tutum per Aegaeos tumultus
>   aura feret geminusque Pollux.

190 AR. *non meum est.* CL. *nec meum quidem edepol.* — **mugiat**: cf. 1, 14, 5.

59 f. **votis pacisci**: ironically said of the common 'bargain' prayer. — **Cypriae Tyriaeque**: concrete for 'Oriental.'

61 ff. **avaro . . . mari**: a common personification; cf. 1, 28, 18. — **biremis**: *two-oared skiff*. The point is that a tiny boat will save a man from the storms of life if only he possess a soul content within itself. — **aura**: *the breeze*, contrasted with **Africis procellis**. — **geminus Pollux**: Castor and Pollux, who will secure him the favoring breeze and a safe voyage. For the Dioscuri as protectors of sailors, see 1, 3, 2 and n.

30

In the prologue to the three books of odes Horace expresses the modest hope that Maecenas will count him a lyric poet; in the epilogue he triumphantly declares that he has built a monument of verse that will outlast bronze and unnumbered time itself. He boasts that his fame shall grow when he is dead, and that so long as Rome shall last, men shall say that he was the first to transplant Aeolian verse to Italy. So let the Muse place the laurel crown upon his brow.

It is little wonder that when Horace surveyed the substantial body of lyric verse which he was about to intrust to the world, he felt a natural pride in his accomplishment. This feeling was undoubtedly increased by the thought of his humble origin and by the memory of his early struggles for recognition and of the envious scorn he had aroused among the noble poetasters of his day. Of this last, however, there is no hint in this ode. Horace now knew that his fame was secure. He was the first Roman to write a large amount of lyric poetry, and his odes had already received the favorable judgment of the best critics in Rome. If to our modern taste he seems too frank in expression, we must remember that antiquity apparently took no such offense, for he had many predecessors, and later poets did not hesitate to speak with equal boldness. Metre, only 1, 1 and here, 53.

Exegi monumentum aere perennius
regalique situ pyramidum altius,
quod non imber edax, non Aquilo impotens
possit diruere aut innumerabilis
5   annorum series et fuga temporum.
Non omnis moriar, multaque pars mei
vitabit Libitinam; usque ego postera
crescam laude recens; dum Capitolium

1 ff. **exegi**: emphasizing the completion of the work. Horace may have had in mind Pindar's boast, *P.* 6, 7 ff. ἑτοῖμος ὕμνων θησαυρὸς ... τετείχισται ... | τὸν οὔτε χειμέριος ὄμβρος ἐπακτὸς ἐλθὼν ἐριβρόμου νεφέλας,|στρατὸς ἀμείλιχος, οὔτ' ἄνεμος ἐς μυχοὺς ἁλὸς ἄξοισι παμφύρῳ χεράδει | τυπτόμενον. 'A ready treasury of song has now been built. ... neither winter storm, coming fiercely from the thunder cloud, a grim host, nor wind-blast shall carry it to the secret recesses of the sea, beaten by the sweeping rubble.' Cf. also Ovid's imitation of Horace in the epilogue to the *Metamorphoses*, *iamque opus exegi quod nec Iovis ira nec ignis | nec poterit ferrum nec edax abolere vetustas*, etc.
2 ff. **situ**: *pile.* — **pyramidum**: the lofty pyramids have naturally been a measure of man's supremest accomplishment in both ancient and more modern times. — **quod**: *such that*, etc. — **edax**: frequently applied to time. *e.g. Anth. Lat.* 1167, 46 M. *quae non tempus edax, non rapit ira Iovis.* Claud. *Carm.*

min. 34, 5 *aetatis spatium non tenuavit edax.* — **impotens**: *powerless to harm*, not 'weak,' as in 1, 37, 10. — **fuga**: cf. 2, 14, 1 *fugaces anni;* 3, 29, 48.
6 f. **non omnis moriar**, etc.: cf. Ovid's imitations *Am.* 1, 15, 42 *parsque mei multa superstes erit:* Met. 15, 875 f. *parte tamen meliore mei super alta perennis | astra ferar.* — **Libitina**: the goddess at whose temple all the requirements for funerals were rented out and where the registry of deaths was kept. Therefore by metonymy, 'the rites of death.'
7. **usque**: *still, on and on.* — **crescam**: *i.e.* 'my glory.' — **recens**: *ever new.* — **dum Capitolium**, etc.: in the last half of the first century before our era the vast extent of the Roman empire and the fixity of Roman institutions made a strong appeal to the imaginations of men; the permanence of Rome became the measure of all permanence; it is at this time that we find the phrase *urbs aeterna* first applied to the city. Horace and others chose

scandet cum tacita virgine pontifex,
10 dicar, qua violens obstrepit Aufidus
et qua pauper aquae Daunus agrestium
regnavit populorum ex humili potens,
princeps Aeolium carmen ad Italos
deduxisse modos. Sume superbiam
15 quaesitam meritis et mihi Delphica
lauro cinge volens, Melpomene, comam.

the Capitol as the most significant center of Roman institutions. Cf. Verg. *A.* 9, 446 ff. *fortunati ambo! si quid mea carmina possunt, | nulla dies umquam memori vos eximet aevo, | dum domus Aeneae Capitoli inmobile saxum | accolet.* Ovid *Trist.* 3, 7, 50 ff. *me tamen extincto fama superstes erit, | dumque suis victrix omnem de montibus orbem | prospiciet domitum Martia Roma, legar.* Also Mart. 9, 1, 5 ff.

9. **scandet**, etc.: we do not know whether Horace refers to any regular procession; it is most probable that he mentions the Vestal Virgin and Pontifex simply as representatives of two ancient institutions.

10 ff. **dicar**: *men shall say.* — **qua**, etc.: *i.e.* ' I shall be honored in the district where I was born.' — **obstrepit** : the Aufidus is a mountain stream in its upper course.— **pauper aquae** : cf. *Epod.* 3, 16 *siticulosae Apuliae;* Ovid *Met.* 14, 510 *arida Dauni arva.* — **Daunus**: cf. n. to 1, 22, 14. — **populorum** : object of **regnavit**; a Greek construction. — **ex humili potens**: with **Daunus**, *a ruler sprung from low estate.*

13 f. **princeps**: Horace ignores Catullus. — **Aeolium** : cf. 1, 1, 34 and n.; 2, 13, 24. — **Italos** : since the conquest of Italy, equivalent to *Latinos.* — **deduxisse** : *composed;* apparently a metaphor taken from spinning. Cf. *Epist* 2, 1, 225 *tenui deducta poemata filo,* and our common ' spin,' ' to run on at length,' ' to relate.' — **modos**: *strains.* Horace's claim to eminence is that he has been the pioneer in writing lyric poetry after the manner of the best of the Greeks.

14 ff. **sume superbiam** : *i.e.* 'as is thy right, for thou, goddess, hast inspired all my song.' Cf. the acknowledgment 4, 3, 24 *quod spiro et placeo, si placeo tuum (Pieri) est.* — **Delphica** : cf. 4, 2, 9, *laurea Apollinari.* — **volens**: *graciously;* with *propitius* a common formula in prayers. So Livy 1. 16, 3 *precibus exposcunt uti volens propitius suam semper sospitet progeniem.* — **Melpomene** : cf. n. to 1, 1, 33.

LIBER QVARTVS

I

Ten years after the publication of what he had regarded as the definitive edition of his lyric poems, Horace gathered into a fourth book some occasional odes written at the request of Augustus, and certain other poems. See Intr. 9. At the head of the collection he placed some light verses reminiscent of his earlier service as a poet of love, and intended to remind the reader that this was still his proper field. In these verses he protests that at fifty his days of love are over, and that Venus should spare him. Young Paulus Maximus, the noble, comely, and eloquent, will do the goddess larger service and pay her greater honor. For himself, he no longer finds delight in maid or boy, in hope for love returned, in sport with wine and flowers. And yet, what means this tear!

The unexpected turn at v. 33 is similar to that in 3, 26, 11 f. Paulus Maximus is introduced by Horace, partly to compliment his young friend, and partly to secure a foil for himself and his ten lustra. The ode was probably written but a short time before the publication of the book, *i.e.* about 14-13 B.C. Metre, 71.

> Intermissa, Venus, diu
>   rursus bella moves? Parce, precor, precor.
> Non sum qualis eram bonae
>   sub regno Cinarae. Desine, dulcium

1 f. **intermissa**: naturally placed first, referring to the ten years in which his lyre had not sung of love. — **bella**: cf. v. 16 below, and 3, 26, 2 and n. — **parce**, etc.: frequently imitated by later poets; cf. *e.g.* Ovid *Trist.* 2, 179 *parce precor fulmenque tuum, fera tela,* *reconde;* 5, 2, 53; Mart. 7, 68, 2 *parce precor socero.*

4 f. **sub regno**: *sway*; cf. 3, 9, 9 *me nunc Thessa Chloe regit.* — **Cinarae**: apparently the only one among all of Horace's loves who had a real existence. Between her and the poet there seems to

5   mater saeva Cupidinum,
            circa lustra decem flectere mollibus
       iam durum imperiis; abi
            quo blandae iuvenum te revocant preces.
       Tempestivius in domum
10   Pauli purpureis ales oloribus
       comissabere Maximi,
            si torrere iecur quaeris idoneum.
       Namque et nobilis et decens
            et pro sollicitis non tacitus reis
15   et centum puer artium
            late signa feret militiae tuae,
       et quandoque potentior

have been a genuine bond of affection; the reference to her in 4, 13, 22 ff. shows that at this time she was dead. — **dulcium . . . saeva**: the two sides to love. Cf. Catull. 68, 17 *dea . . . quae dulcem curis miscet amaritiem.* — **mater**: an echo of 1, 19, 1 *mater saeva Cupidinum.*

6 ff. **circa lustra decem**: sc. *me.* The lack of a present participle in Latin (Greek ὄντα) makes the expression awkward. Horace was 50 in 15 B.C. — **flectere**: conative. — **imperiis**: dative with **durum**, as the interlocked order and the contrast between **mollibus** and **durum** show. — **revocant**: *call* (with greater right); cf. n. on *reponens* 1, 9, 6.

9. **tempestivius**: for he is young; cf. *tempestiva* 3, 19, 27. — **Pauli**: Paulus Maximus, cos. 11 B.C., was a member of one of the noblest Roman families, the friend of Ovid, and a confidant of Augustus. He was about twenty-two years Horace's junior. — **purpureis**: the rosy hue of divinity; cf. 3, 3, 12 and n. — **ales**: *winged by;* cf. 3, 28, 15. — **comissabere**: *carry thy revelry.* — **torrere**: cf. 1, 33, 6 *Lycorida Cyri torret amor.* — **iecur**: 1, 13, 4.

13 f. **et . . . et . . . et**, etc.: the repetition has a cumulative force; cf. **nec . . . nec**, etc. v. 29 ff. — **pro sollicitis**, etc.: cf. similar compliment to Pollio 2, 1, 13: Ovid *ex Pont.* 1, 2, 118 addressing this same Maximus. (*vox tua*) *auxilio trepidis quae solet esse reis.*

16. **signa**, etc.: cf. **bella**, v. 2 above. On the order of words see Intr. 21.

17 ff. **quandoque**: *whenever.* — **potentior**: *i.e.* through the

largi muneribus riserit aemuli,
   Albanos prope te lacus
20   ponet marmoream sub trabe citrea.
   Illic plurima naribus
      duces tura, lyraeque et Berecyntiae
   delectabere tibiae
      mixtis carminibus non sine fistula;
25 illic bis pueri die
      numen cum teneris virginibus tuum
   laudantes pede candido
      in morem Salium ter quatient humum.
   Me nec femina nec puer
30   iam nec spes animi credula mutui
   nec certare iuvat mero
      nec vincire novis tempora floribus.

favor of Venus. — **muneribus**: ablative with **potentior**, although it also expresses that at which he laughs in scorn. — **Albanos prope lacus**: the *lacus Albanus* and *lacus Nemorensis* in the Alban Hills. Near the latter was the famous shrine of Diana. Probably Horace had no definite spot in mind but simply means, 'Paulus will build a new shrine to thee near (or like) that of Diana Nemorensis.'

20. **marmoream**: *in marble.* — **trabe**: collectively, *the rafters.* — **citrea**: *of African cedar*; an expensive wood. Cross sections of large trunks were used for the tops of tables, and were extremely costly.

21 f. **plurima**: *abundant.* — **Berecyntiae**: cf. 1, 18, 13; 3, 19, 18.

24. **non sine**: cf. n. to 1, 23. 3.

25 ff. **bis**: *i.e.* morning and evening. — **pueri . . . cum teneris virginibus**: a choral band similar to that for which 1, 21 was written, and which sang the *Carmen Saeculare*. See introductory notes to 1, 21 and *C. S.*; also cf. 4, 6, 31 ff.

28. **Salium**: cf. 1, 36, 12 and n. — **ter quatient**: cf. 3, 18, 16.

29 ff. **me**: returning to the personal experience. — **nec . . . nec**, etc.: cf. n. to v. 13. — **animi . . . mutui**: *of a heart that returns my love.* Cf. 3, 9, 13 *face mutua.* — **credula**: observe the effect of its position, although it is not grammatically connected with the inclosing words. Intr. 20. — **mero**: *i.e.* in a drinking contest. — **vincire**: in preparation for a

        Sed cur heu, Ligurine, cur
           manat rara meas lacrima per **genas**?
35   Cur facunda parum decoro
           inter verba cadit lingua **silentio**?
        Nocturnis ego somniis
           iam captum teneo, iam volucrem **sequor**
        te per gramina Martii
40   campi, te per aquas, dure, **volubilis**.

comissatio. — **novis**: of the spring, when the young man (but not the man of fifty years) lightly turns to thoughts of love.

33 ff. sed: the unexpected turn. — **cur ... cur**: Intr. 28 c. — **Ligurine**: the same name occurs again 4, 10, 5. We need not suppose that he existed outside Horace's fancy. — **rara**: a single tear, which he unexpectedly finds on his cheek. Cf. 1, 13, 6 *umor et in genas furtim labitur.* — **facunda lingua**: *i.e.* ordinarily. — **parum**: cf. n. to *minus* 1, 2.

27. — **decoro**: hypermetric. Intr. 71. With the signs of love, cf. Sappho, *Frg.* 2, 7 ff. ὡς γὰρ εἶδον βροχέως σε, φώνας | οὐδὲν ἔτ' εἴκει· | ἀλλὰ καμ μὲν γλῶσσα ἔαγε. Imitated by Catullus 51, 6 ff. *nam simul te, Lesbia, adspexi, nihil est super mi ... lingua sed torpet.* Also *Epod.* 11, 9.

38 ff. iam ... iam: cf. *nunc ... nunc* above. — **aquas**: of the Tiber. — **volubilis**: cf. *Epist.* 1, 2, 43 *at ille (amnis) labitur et labetur in omne volubilis aevum.*

2

'Whoever tries a flight in rivalry with Pindar, will surely fall like Icarus. That mighty poet pours forth his verse like mountain flood and is supreme in every field (1-24). He soars aloft, a swan of Dirce, while I am but a Matine bee that gathers sweets with toil (25-32). But thou, Antonius, art a poet, and canst sing in fuller strain the triumphs of our supreme Caesar and hymn his glad return. Then I too will add my voice to swell the greeting (33-52). Thou shalt make large thanksgiving sacrifice of ten bulls and heifers, while I offer a young calf, as fits my humble station (53-60).'

This ode is evidently composed in anticipation of the return of Augustus to Rome from the German frontier, to which he went in 16 B.C. after the defeat of M. Lollius. The Iullus Antonius addressed was the son of Mark Antony and Fulvia. He was educated in Augustus' household by his stepmother, Octavia; every honor was shown him until the discovery of his liaison with the infamous Julia, when he was put to death (2 B.C.). It is said that he was the author of an epic, *Diomedea*, in twelve books, and of some prose works besides.

The occasion and date of the ode are both uncertain. It was probably written in the winter of 16-15 B.C. or early in the following spring, with the expectation that the Emperor would soon return; many, however, prefer to place its composition in 14-13 B.C. But why should Horace, if writing at that date, mention only Augustus' comparatively unimportant success over the Sygambri and their allies in 16 B.C., and have nothing to say of the brilliant Alpine campaigns of Tiberius and Drusus in 15 B.C.? The fact that these are celebrated in odes 4 and 14 will hardly account for silence here, if the later date of composition be accepted. The occasion which prompted the verses may have been a request from Antonius for a Pindaric ode, which Horace turns aside in a manner similar to that of 1, 6. Or we may suppose that Horace chose this way to express his own eager anticipation of Augustus.' return and to pay Antonius a (possibly) extravagant compliment. Whatever its date, the position of the ode gives it the effect of a deprecatory preface to odes 4 and 14. Metre, 69.

> Pindarum quisquis studet aemulari,
> Iulle, ceratis ope Daedalea
> nititur pennis, vitreo daturus
>   nomina ponto.
>
> 5   Monte decurrens velut amnis, imbres
>   quem super notas aluere ripas,

1 f. **Pindarum**: (522-448 B C.) a native of Thebes, the greatest of the nine lyric poets of Greece. His odes for victory ('Ἐπινίκια) became the model for such poems. Pindar had no slight influence on Horace. — **aemulari**: *to vie with*. — **Iulle**: dissyllabic here, but used by Vergil as a trisyllable and spelled with a single *l*. It was the name of a mythical ancestor of the Julian gens, but employed by the members as a *praenomen*. — **ceratis**: *wax-joined.* — **ope Daedalea**: *by the art of Daedalus.*

3 f. **nititur**: *soars.* — **vitreo**: *glassy, crystal.* Cf. n. to 3, 13, 1. — **daturus**: *destined to give.* Cf. 2, 3, 27.

5. **velut amnis**, etc.: a common comparison, *e.g.* Cic. *Acad.*

fervet immensusque ruit profundo
  Pindarus ore,

  laurea donandus Apollinari,
10 seu per audacis nova dithyrambos
  verba devolvit numerisque fertur
   lege solutis,

  seu deos regesve canit, deorum
  sanguinem, per quos cecidere iusta
15 morte Centauri, cecidit tremendae
   flamma Chimaerae,

2, 119 *flumen orationis aureum.* Cf. also our (uncomplimentary) 'flood of words.'

7 f. **fervet**, etc.: *seethes and rushes along in boundless flood.* The poet is confused with the river to which he is compared. Cf. 1, 15, 29 ff. and n. For the feminine caesura here and elsewhere in this book, see Intr. 51.— **profundo . . . ore**: *with deep and mighty speech.* — **ore**: with reference to Pindar alone. The description refers to Pindar's richness of language, his 'grand style.' So Horace says *S.* 1. 4. 43 f. that you can give the name poet only to a man, *cui mens divinior atque os magna sonaturum.*

9 ff. **laurea . . . Apollinari**: cf. 3, 30, 16. — **donandus**: forming the conclusion to the following conditions. *i.e.* 'Pindar deserves to be crowned with the sacred laurel for each and every kind of poetry he essayed.' — **audacis**: *i.e.* in compounds and metaphors. — **nova**: *fresh compounds.* — **dithyrambos**: choral songs in honor of Dionysus. — **devolvit, fertur**: keeping up the figure of the torrent. — **lege solutis**: *i.e.* not composed in strict symmetry, with strophe and antistrophe; or Horace may mean nothing more than 'free.' The phrase with the addition of a word was applied by St. Jerome to rhythmical prose, *Praef. in Iob, interdum quoque rhythmus ipse dulcis et tinnulus fertur numeris lege metri solutis.* The common expression for prose is *soluta oratio.*

13 ff. **seu deos**, etc.: in his Hymns and Paeans. — **reges**: *heroes,* as **deorum sanguinem** shows. — **per quos**: *i.e.* Theseus and Pirithous, who overcame the Centaurs (cf. 1, 18, 8), and Bellerophon, slayer of the Chimaera. — **iusta**: *deserved,* as the Centaurs began the quarrel that ended in their death. — **flamma Chimaerae**: with

sive quos Elea domum reducit
palma caelestis pugilemve equumve
dicit et centum potiore signis
20   munere donat,

flebili sponsae iuvenemve raptum
plorat et viris animumque moresque
aureos educit in astra nigroque
invidet Orco.

25 Multa Dircaeum levat aura cycnum,
tendit, Antoni, quotiens in altos
nubium tractus: ego apis Matinae
more modoque

the form of expression, cf. 1, 3, 36; 3, 21, 11.

17 ff. His extant Olympian, Pythian, Nemean, and Isthmian odes. — **Elea**: the Olympian games; the most important of the four being taken as typical of all. — **caelestis**: cf. 1, 1, 5 and Sil. Ital. 15, 100 *me cinctus lauro producit ad astra triumphus.* — **pugilemve equumve**: in partitive apposition to **quos**. With this passage, cf. *Epist.* 2, 3, 83 *musa dedit fidibus divos puerosque deorum | et pugilem victorem et equum certamine primum | ... referre.* — **dicit**: cf. n. to 1, 6, 5. — **signis**: *statues.*

21 ff. His lost Eulogies, Θρῆνοι. — **flebili**: active, *weeping.* Cf. 1, 24, 9. — **ve**: for the position, see Intr. 31. — **viris animumque**, etc.: telling over in detail the youth's virtues. This and the following verse are hypermetric. — **aureos**:

cf. n. on 1, 5, 9. — **invidet**: *begrudges* (and saves from).

25 ff. After reviewing in the last three strophes the various forms of Pindar's poetry, Horace now returns to his preëminence. — **multa**: *a mighty.* — **Dircaeum**: the fountain of Dirce was near Thebes. — **cycnum**: a common comparison; cf. 2, 20 and introductory n. — **tractus**: *stretches.*

27. **apis**, etc.: also a stock figure; cf. Plat. *Ion* 534 A. λέγουσι γὰρ ... πρὸς ἡμᾶς οἱ ποιηταί, ὅτι ἀπὸ κρηνῶν μελιρρύτων ἐκ Μουσῶν κήπων τινῶν καὶ ναπῶν δρεπόμενοι τὰ μέλη ἡμῖν φέρουσιν ὥσπερ αἱ μέλιτται. With the comparison which Horace makes between himself and Pindar, cf. Lucretius' words in regard to his relation to Epicurus 3, 6 ff. *quid enim contendat hirundo cycnis? ... tuisque ex, inclute, chartis |*

grata carpentis thyma per laborem
plurimum circa nemus uvidique
Tiburis ripas operosa parvus
    carmina fingo.

Concines maiore poeta plectro
Caesarem, quandoque trahet ferocis
per sacrum clivum merita decorus
    fronde Sygambros;

quo nihil maius meliusve terris
fata donavere bonique divi
nec dabunt, quamvis redeant in aurum
    tempora priscum.

floriferis ut apes in saltibus omnia libant, | omnia nos itidem depascimur aurea dicta.
— **Matinae**: with reference to the district in which he was born. Cf. 1, 28, 3.

30 f. plurimum: with **laborem**. — **circa nemus**, etc.: his favorite Tivoli; cf. 2, 6, 5 ff. — **Tiburis**: modifying both **nemus** and **ripas**. — **operosa parvus**: Intr. 26.

33 f. concines: with **Caesarem** in the following verse, bearing the emphasis. 'Caesar shall be sung, but in a different strain than that of which I am master.' — **maiore . . . plectro**: *i.e.* 'of a grander style'; cf. 2, 1, 40 *leviore plectro*. The ablative is descriptive, modifying **poeta**. Augustus' deeds were better themes for an epic poet like Antonius than for a lyricist. — **quandoque**: 'whenever the day of his triumph shall come.' —

ferocis: a decorative epithet (yet cf. 4, 14, 51 *caede gaudentes*) which secures a contrast with **trahet**.

35 f. per sacrum clivum: the Sacra Via from the arch of Titus down to the Forum. The expression is found elsewhere only twice, Mart. 1, 70, 5; 4, 78, 7. — **decorus**: *adorned with.* — **fronde**: the laurel wreath of the triumphing general. — **Sygambros**: they defeated Lollius' army (cf. introductory n.), but withdrew before the Emperor's approach and hastened to make peace with him.

37 ff. These verses show the court poet. A similar expression is found in *Epist.* 2, 1, 16 f. *iurandasque tuom per numen ponimus aras, | nil oriturum alias, nil ortum tale fatentes.* — **quamvis**, etc.: 'though the Golden Age should return.' — **priscum**: cf. *Epod.* 2, 2.

Concines laetosque dies et urbis
publicum ludum super impetrato
fortis Augusti reditu forumque
    litibus orbum.

45 Tum meae, si quid loquar audiendum,
vocis accedet bona pars, et 'O sol
pulcher, o laudande!' canam, recepto
    Caesare felix.

Teque dum procedis, 'Io Triumphe!'
50 non semel dicemus 'Io Triumphe!'
civitas omnis, dabimusque divis
    tura benignis.

Te decem tauri totidemque vaccae,
me tener solvet vitulus, relicta

41 f. concines: Intr. 28 c. — **laetos**: *i.e. festos*, when Augustus returns. — **ludum**: *joy;* cf. *Epist.* 2, 3, 226 *ita vertere seria ludo.* — **super**: with the construction, cf. 3, 8, 17 *super urbe curas.* — **impetrato**: *granted* (to our prayers). There are extant coins of 16 B.C. with the inscription S. P. Q. R. V(*ota*) S(*uscepta*) PRO S(*alute*) ET RED(*itu*) AUG(*usti*).

44. litibus orbum: the courts would be closed when the Emperor returned in triumph. The technical term is *iustitium*. As a matter of fact, when Augustus did return in 13 B.C., he declined a triumph and entered the city by night to avoid any public demonstration.

45 ff. 'I too will swell the acclaim with the best of my weak powers.'— **loquar**: less common than *dico* for the poet's work; repeated 4, 15, 1 *Phoebus volentem proelia me loqui . . . increpuit.* **audiendum**: *worth hearing.* — **sol pulcher**: the very day of Augustus' return will be glorified by his presence. — **laudande**: the future passive participle is very frequently used in the fourth book. In this ode it occurs vv. 9, 45, 47. Also 4. 68; 9, 4. 21; 11, 3. 14. 34; 14, 17.

49 ff. teque: personifying the Triumph itself; object of **dicemus**. — **Io Triumphe**: the cry of greeting to the triumphal procession as it moved along. Cf. n. to *Epod.* 9, 21 f. — **non semel**: *not once alone*, but many times. — **civitas**:

55   matre qui largis iuvenescit herbis
            in mea vota,
        fronte curvatos imitatus ignis
        tertium lunae referentis ortum,
        qua notam duxit niveus videri,
60   cetera fulvus.

in opposition to the subject of dicemus. Cf. 1, 35, 35 *nos, aetas*.
53 f. te ... me: cf. 2, 17, 30 ff. This te, referring to Antonius, is awkward after te in v. 49.—solvet: from the obligation of our vows.
55 ff. The detailed description of the young bullock furnishes the ode with a quiet idyllic ending similar to that in 3, 5, 53–56. At the same time it emphasizes the contrast between the wealthy Antonius, who must sacrifice twenty head of cattle off hand, and the simple Horace who loves to linger on the charms of his single victim.

— relicta matre: *weaned.*—largis: *luxuriant.*—in: *against, in anticipation of.*
57 ff. curvatos: *the crescent.* With the description, cf. Claud. *Rapt. Pros.* 1, 129 *nec nova lunatae curvavit germina frontis.* Moschus 2, 88 describes the horns of Europa's bull as curved ἅτε κύκλα σελήνης. — referentis: cf. 3, 29, 20. — qua: referring to fronte and defining niveus videri. (Cf. λευκὸς ἰδέσθαι.) Intr. 109.—duxit: *has got, taken on.* Cf. Verg. E. 9, 49 (*astrum*) *quo duceret apricis in collibus uva colorem.*

3

The poet's grateful acknowledgment to his Muse.

'He on whom thou dost look with kindly eye in his natal hour, Melpomene, is set apart from the pursuit of common glories. He shall not win renown as athlete or as general. But the quiet groves and streams shall be his haunts and he shall gain his fame through poesy (1–12). So through thy gift am I counted to-day a lyric bard and Envy's tooth is dulled. All my fame, my inspiration, and my power to please are thine, sweet Muse (13–24).'

The publication of his three books of odes in 23 B.C. had established Horace's name as a lyric poet, and his appointment in 17 B.C. to write the *Carmen Saeculare* had officially fixed his position. The petty critics who had carped at him in earlier years and the noble poetasters who had shown a snobbish envy of his skill were now silenced; the

Romans gladly gave him the recognition he deserved. He had indeed obtained the object of his ambitions expressed in *C.* 1, 1. In the present ode he shows his gratitude to the Muse for his success; and this feeling is expressed, not in boasting, but with a humility which shows that Horace felt his skill to be due to some power beyond himself. The ode has evident reminiscences of 1, 1 in the contrast between the aims of ordinary men and the quiet life of the poet. Metre, 71.

> Quem tu, Melpomene, semel
>   nascentem placido lumine videris,
> illum non labor Isthmius
>   clarabit pugilem, non equus impiger
> 5 curru ducet Achaico
>   victorem, neque res bellica Deliis
> ornatum foliis ducem,
>   quod regum tumidas contuderit minas,
> ostendet Capitolio;
> 10 sed quae Tibur aquae fertile praefluunt

1 ff. The same idea is expressed in Greek poetry, *e.g.* by Hesiod *Theog.* 81 ff. ὅντινα τιμήσωσι Διὸς κοῦραι μεγάλοιο | γεινόμενόν τε ἴδωσι διοτρεφέων βασιλήων, | τῷ μὲν ἐπὶ γλώσσῃ γλυκερὴν χείουσιν ἐέρσην (*dew*), τοῦ δ᾽ ἔπε᾽ ἐκ στόματος ῥεῖ μείλιχα.
— **Melpomene**: cf. 3, 30, 16. — semel: *but once.* — placido lumine: cf. Alciphr. 3, 44 εὐμενεστέροις ὄμμασιν ἐκεῖνον εἶδον οἱ Χάριτες.

3 ff. **labor**: the Greek πόνος. — **Isthmius**: cf. 4, 2, 17 and n. — **pugilem, equus**: the same types 4, 2, 18. — **Achaico**: *i.e. Greek*; contrasted with the Roman triumph which follows. — res bellica: *deeds in war.* Cf. *res ludicra,* 'comedy,' *Epist* 2, 1, 180. — **Deliis . . .**

foliis: the laurel, a crown of which was worn by the triumphing general. Cf. 3, 30, 15 *Delphica lauro,* 4, 2, 9 *laurea Apollinari.*

8 f. **tumidas**: contrasted with **contuderit,** *crushed down.* The adjective was adopted by Seneca, *H. O.* 927 *depone tumidas pectoris laesi minas.* — **minas**: cf. 2, 12, 12 *regum minacium.* — **Capitolio**: the end of the triumphal procession.

10 f. Horace uses the streams and groves of his beloved Tivoli as typical of the haunts of the Muses and their devotees; he also secures through their associations with himself an easy transition to his own case. — **quae Tibur aquae,** etc.: cf. 1, 7, 12 ff. — **prae-**

et spissae nemorum comae
fingent Aeolio carmine nobilem.
Romae, principis urbium,
dignatur suboles inter amabilis
15   vatum ponere me choros,
et iam dente minus mordeor invido.
O testudinis aureae
dulcem quae strepitum, Pieri, temperas,
o mutis quoque piscibus
20   donatura cycni, si libeat, sonum,
totum muneris hoc tui est,
quod monstror digito praetereuntium

fluunt: *flow past*, a variant of the more common *praeterfluunt*. — **spissae . . . comae**: cf. 1, 21, 5, and the verse from Milton there quoted.

12. **Aeolio carmine**: cf. 3, 30, 13 and n. The adjective also serves to aid the transition, as Horace's chief models were Alcaeus and Sappho.

13 ff. **Romae, principis,** etc.: Horace's pride in Rome, queen of cities (cf. *Epist.* 1, 7, 44 *regia Roma*), adds to his satisfaction in the recognition he receives from her children (**suboles**). — **vatum**: cf. n. to 1, 1, 35. — **ponere**: 1, 1, 35 *inserere*.

16. **dente . . . invido**: cf. *Epod.* 6, 15: Ovid *ex Pont.* 3, 4, 73 f. *laedere vivos livor et iniusto carpere dente | solet.*

17 f. **testudinis aureae**: Pindar's χρυσέα φόρμιγξ, *P.* 1, 1. Cf. C. 2, 13, 26 *aureo . . . plectro.* —

dulcem . . . strepitum: cf. Milton's 'melodious noise.' — **temperas**: *modulate.*

19 f. **mutis**: a stock epithet; the Hesiodic ἔλλοπας ἰχθῦς *Scut. Her.* 212. — **donatura**: *thou who couldst give.* — **cycni**: but *cycni* 4, 2, 25.

21. **muneris**: predicate. Cf. Ovid *Trist.* 1, 6, 6 (to his wife) *si si quid adhuc ego sum, muneris omne tui est.*— **quod monstror**: defining the preceding. This form of complimentary recognition is frequently mentioned. Cf. 4, 9; Lucian *Herod.* 2 εἴ πού γε φανείη μόνον, ἐδείκνυτο ἂν τῷ δακτύλῳ, οὗτος ἐκεῖνος Ἡρόδοτός ἐστιν . . . ὁ τὰς νίκας ἡμῶν ὑμνήσας. St. Jerome, *ad Eustoch.* 22, urged *ne ad te obviam praetereuntium turba consistat et digito monstreris.* Stevenson wrote after a visit to Sydney (Vailima Letters, XXVIII, April, 1893), 'I found my fame

Romanae fidicen lyrae;
quod spiro et placeo, si placeo, tuum est.

much grown on this return to civilization. *Digito monstrari* is a new experience; people all looked at me in the streets of Sydney; and it was very queer.'

23 f. **fidicen**: cf. Horace's claim, *Epist.* 1, 19, 32 *hunc (Alcaeum) ego Latinus volgavi fidicen.* — **quod spiro et placeo**: *my inspiration and my power to please.*

4 '

'Like a young eagle swooping on his prey or a lion just weaned tearing its first victim, so the Vindelici saw the young Drusus fight under the shadow of the Raetian Alps. Now through defeat they have come to feel what the noble young Neros, piously reared beneath Augustus' roof, can do (1-28). Brave and noble are those who spring from noble sires. Training is powerless when character fails (29-36). Thy debt, O Rome, to Nero's line is witnessed by the Metaurus, the defeat of Hasdrubal, and that glorious day when the fearful leader was forced by the renewed strength of Rome to say " We are but deer. This people, tossed to this land from Troy destroyed by fire, gains strength through loss, grows Hydra-like more strong. No more proud messages shall I send to Carthage. All hope was lost when Hasdrubal was killed (37-72)." Such noble deeds have the Claudii done; no bound is there to what they yet shall do, with the aid of Jove's favor and man's wise counsel (73-76).'

This and the fourteenth ode celebrate the victories in 15 B.C. of the young Neros, Drusus and Tiberius, stepsons of Augustus. In the spring of that year Drusus, then but twenty-three years old, led his troops up the river Atagis (Adige) and defeated the Vindelician forces not far from Tridentum (Trent). He then pushed northward across the Brenner pass and defeated the Breuni and Genauni in the valley of the river Inn. Tiberius approached from the west by the upper Rhine and Lake Constance, and the armies under the two brothers scoured the valleys in which the Rhine and Inn have their sources so successfully that in a single campaign the district of the Grisons and Tirol was completely subjugated and made into the province Raetia.

The occasion of this and the fourteenth ode, as Suetonius tells us (*vita Hor.*), was the 'command' of Augustus — *scripta quidem eius usque adeo probavit mansuraque perpetua opinatus est, ut non modo seculare carmen componendum iniuxerit sed et Vindelicam victoriam*

4, 4, 1]   HORATI

Tiberii Drusique, privignorum suorum. It was a task for which Horace had often declared himself unfit, but he could hardly disregard the Emperor's command, even had he been so inclined. In spite of his protestations in the second ode of this book, he adopted here the Pindaric form which allowed him to pass over the exploits of Drusus very briefly and to devote the greater part of the ode to the deeds of the house of Nero in the almost mythical past. Metre, 68.

> Qualem ministrum fulminis alitem,
> cui rex deorum regnum in avis vagas
>   permisit expertus fidelem
>   Iuppiter in Ganymede flavo,
>
> 5 olim iuventas et patrius vigor
> nido laborum propulit inscium,
>   vernique iam nimbis remotis
>   insolitos docuere nisus
>
> venti paventem, mox in ovilia
> 10   demisit hostem vividus impetus,

1–16. The young eagle illustrates the impetuosity with which Drusus attacked his foes, the young lion the terror his attack aroused.

1 ff. **ministrum**: in opposition with **alitem**, which is object of **permisit**. We may translate, however, *the winged messenger*. Cf. Verg. *A.* 5, 255 *Iovis armiger*. — **rex, regnum**: intentional antithesis. The concept of the eagle as king of birds, οἰωνῶν βασιλεύς, is Pindaric. — **in**: cf. 3, 1, 5. — **expertus fidelem**: *having proved him faithful in the case of*. — **Ganymede**: cf. 3, 20, 15 f. — **flavo**: *fair-haired*. ξανθός, a decorative epithet. Cf. 1, 5, 4.

5 ff. **olim**: *once*. The reference to the eagle which carried off Ganymedes is confined to the first strophe; that which follows is said of the bird in general. — **nido**: with **propulit**. — **laborum**: *of strife and toil*. — **propulit**: gnomic perfect. Intr. 103. The object of this, as of the following verbs, is easily brought over from v. 1. — **verni**: *i.e.* 'gentle.' The fact that young eagles do not fly until late summer need not disturb us. — **iam**: with **docuere**.

9 ff. **paventem**: *in his timidity*. — **mox**: *presently*; marking the second stage in the eaglet's development — first he timidly learns to fly, presently he swoops on his

nunc in reluctantis dracones
   egit amor dapis atque pugnae;

qualemve laetis caprea pascuis
intenta fulvae matris ab ubere
15   iam lacte depulsum leonem
   dente novo peritura vidit:

videre Raetis bella sub Alpibus
Drusum gerentem Vindelici (quibus
   mos unde deductus per omne
20   tempus Amazonia securi

prey, and at last engages in battle with snakes (**dracones**) that fight back. Horace may have had in mind the description of the struggle between the eagle and snake, *Il.* 12, 200 ff. imitated by Verg. *A.* 11, 751 ff.

13 ff. laetis: *luxuriant.* — **matris ab ubere:** editors are not agreed whether these words refer to **caprea** or **leonem**. It is probable that the second alternative is right, and that **lacte depulsum** is to be considered as expressing a single idea, *weaned.* Vergil has *G.* 3, 187 *depulsus ab ubere* and *E.* 7, 15 *depulsos a lacte . . . agnos.* Horace's expression is then tautological but not unnatural. We may render, *lately weaned from his tawny mother's dugs.*

16. peritura vidit: notice the force of the juxtaposition — the fawn sees the lion and recognizes its own fate at the same moment.

17 f. videre: the anadiplosis makes *talem* unnecessary. Intr. 28 b. — **Raetis:** equivalent to *Raeticis.* — **quibus:** the relative; translate, *their.* The indirect question is introduced by **unde**. The reference here to an archæological discussion is most inopportune, and some have wished to regard the verses as the invention of a later writer. It is more probable that Horace's usual good taste deserted him. The passage may be an attempt to imitate a Pindaric digression. In any case we must remember that the ode was made to order, and that such a task was not inspiring to Horace's muse.

19 f. deductus: the participle, as frequently, contains the main idea. — **per omne tempus:** *i.e.* from the mythological period to the present time. — **Amazonia securi:** see Baumeister 1, pp. 60, 63 for illustrations of this form

dextras obarmet, quaerere distuli,
nec scire fas est omnia), sed diu
    lateque victrices catervae
        consiliis iuvenis revictae

25 sensere quid mens rite, quid indoles
    nutrita faustis sub penetralibus
        posset, quid Augusti paternus
            in pueros animus Nerones.

    Fortes creantur fortibus et bonis;
30   est in iuvencis, est in equis patrum
        virtus, neque imbellem feroces ·
            progenerant aquilae columbam:

of axe. — **obarmet**: coined by Horace.

22 f. nec scire fas, etc.: said almost with impatience. — 'don't ask me how this custom has been handed down. Man should not try to know everything.' — **diu lateque**: modifying **victrices**. The reference is to the successes of the Vindelici before they were checked by Drusus.

24. consiliis: *wise strategy.* — **revictae**: *defeated in their turn.*

25 f. rite... nutrita: with both **mens** and **indoles**, *intelligence and character.* — **faustis ... penetralibus**: the phrase is chosen, like **rite** above, to suggest the sacred character of the training the young princes received in the Emperor's house. So Velleius 2, 94, 1 says of the training of Tiberius under Augustus, *innutritus caelestium praeceptorum disciplinis.*

28. Nerones: Tiberius and Drusus — the latter was born after his mother was divorced from Ti. Claudius Nero and married to Octavianus — were both treated by their stepfather as his own sons (cf. **paternus animus**).

29 ff. fortes, etc.: good birth is the first essential. The sentiment of the verse is a commonplace. Cf. *e.g.* Eurip. *Frg.* 75, 2 ἐσθλῶν ἀπ' ἀνδρῶν ἐσθλὰ γίγνεσθαι τέκνα, κακῶν δ' ὅμοια τῇ φύσει τῇ τοῦ πατρός. — **fortibus et bonis**: a frequent commendatory expression. Cf. *Epist.* 1, 9, 13 *scribe tui gregis hunc et fortem crede bonumque.* — **est ... est**: emphatic, *no doubt there is.* At the same time the sentence is logically concessive with reference to the following strophe. — **imbellem feroces**: juxtaposed as 1, 6, 9 *tenues grandia.* Intr. 26.

doctrina sed vim promovet insitam,
rectique cultus pectora roborant;
    utcumque defecere mores,
        indecorant bene nata culpae.

Quid debeas, o Roma, Neronibus,
testis Metaurum flumen et Hasdrubal
    devictus et pulcher fugatis
        ille dies Latio tenebris,

qui primus alma risit adorea,
dirus per urbis Afer ut Italas

33 ff. 'Yet correct training is essential.' Notice the emphasis on doctrina, recti cultus, indecorant. — sed : *and yet.* — cultus : *nurture*. With the sentiment of the two verses cf. *Epist.* 2, 3, 408 ff.: Cic. *pro Arch.* 15 *idem ego contendo, cum ad naturam eximiam atque inlustrem accesserit ratio quaedam conformatioque doctrinae, tum illud nescio quid praeclarum ac singulare solere exsistere.* Quint. *Inst.* 12, 2, 1 *virtus etiamsi quosdam impetus ex natura sumit, tamen perficienda doctrina est.*

35 f. utcumque: *as soon as.* Cf. 1, 17, 10. — defecere: definite perfect. — bene nata: the generalizing plural; translate, *that which is naturally good.*

37 ff. The chief theme of the ode — 'the glorious ancestry of Drusus.' In 207 B.C. Hannibal was waiting at Canusium in Apulia for the arrival of his brother Hasdrubal with a large army. Hasdrubal had already crossed the Alps when the consul M. Claudius Nero, who was watching Hannibal, took 7000 picked men and without the enemy's knowledge marched rapidly to the north to reënforce his colleague, M. Livius, from whom also Drusus was descended by his mother's side. The two consuls defeated the enemy at the river Metaurus, and Claudius Nero returned quickly south, bringing Hasdrubal's head as a grim messenger to Hannibal of his brother's defeat. The story is told by Livy 27, 43 ff. — Hasdrubal devictus: *the victory over*, etc. ; cf. mos deductus v. 19 above. — pulcher: cf. n. to *sol pulcher* 4, 2, 47. — Latio: abl. with fugatis.

41 ff. adorea : *victory*, apparently an archaic word which Horace called back into use. — dirus . . . Afer: cf. 3, 6, 36 *Hannibalem dirum.* — ut: temporal, *since.* Cf. *Epod.* 7, 19. — ceu: only here

ceu flamma per taedas vel Eurus
    per Siculas equitavit undas.

45 Post hoc secundis usque laboribus
    Romana pubes crevit, et impio
        vastata Poenorum tumultu
    fana deos habuere rectos,

    dixitque tandem perfidus Hannibal:
50 'Cervi, luporum praeda rapacium,
        sectamur ultro quos opimus
    fallere et effugere est triumphus.

    Gens quae cremato fortis ab Ilio
    iactata Tuscis aequoribus sacra

in Horace. — **Eurus per Siculas,** etc.: cf. Eurip. *Phoen.* 209 ff. περιρρύτων | ὑπὲρ ἀκαρπίστων πεδίων | Σικελίας Ζεφύρου πνοαῖς | ἱππεύσαντος ἐν οὐρανῷ. 'On the blasts of Zephyrus as he drives in the sky over the barren (sea-)plains that encompass Sicily.'

44. equitavit: this verb does double duty for **Afer** and for **flamma, Eurus**.

45 ff. post hoc: *i.e.* after Hasdrubal's defeat. — **usque**: *ever, constantly*; cf. 3, 30, 7. — **crevit**: *grew strong*; cf. Eurip. *Suppl.* 323 (σὴ πατρὶς) ἐν . . . τοῖς πόνοισιν αὔξεται. — **tumultu**: *rout*. The word properly denotes war within or on the Roman borders, and it is here disparagingly applied to Hannibal's campaign.

48. rectos: *upright* (again).

49. perfidus: a stock Roman epithet for the Carthaginians. Cf. Livy 21, 4, 9 (describing Hannibal) *inhumana crudelitas, perfidia plus quam Punica, nihil veri, nihil sancti, nullus deum metus, nullum ius iurandum, nulla religio.*

49 ff. Livy, 27, 51, 12 gives a similar account of Hannibal's dejection, *Hannibal . . . agnoscere se fortunam Carthaginis fertur dixisse.* — **cervi**: *mere hinds*, emphatic. — **praeda**: *the (natural) prey*. — **ultro**: beyond what is usual, *actually*. — **opimus . . . triumphus**: calling to mind the *spolia opima*. — **effugere est triumphus**: note the slight oxymoron.

53 ff. gens quae, etc.: the *Aeneid* had been published two years when this was written. Cf. n. to *C. S.* 41 ff. — **fortis**: *still brave*, in contrast to **cremato**, which pictures the complete destruction of the city. — **iactata**:

55 natosque maturosque patres
        pertulit Ausonias ad urbis,

    duris ut ilex tonsa bipennibus
    nigrae feraci frondis in Algido,
        per damna, per caedis, ab ipso
60   ducit opes animumque ferro.

    Non hydra secto corpore firmior
    vinci dolentem crevit in Herculem,
        monstrumve submisere Colchi
            maius Echioniaeve Thebae.

65   Merses profundo, pulchrior evenit;

with **gens**; cf. Verg. *A.* 1, 3 (of Aeneas) *multum ille et terris iactatus et alto.* — **Tuscis aequoribus,** etc.: cf. Juno's speech. Verg. *A.* 1, 67 f. *gens inimica mihi Tyrrhenum navigat aequor | Ilium in Italiam portans victosque Penatis.*

58. **nigrae**: cf. 1, 21, 7. — **Algido**: cf. n. to 1, 21, 6.

61 f. **non**: with **firmior**. — **hydra**: the simile is attributed by Plutarch to Cineas, Pyrrhus' adviser. But cf. Florus *Epit.* 1, 18, 19 *cum Pyrrhus 'video me' inquit 'plane procreatum Herculis semine, cui quasi ab angue Lernaeo tot caesa hostium capita quasi de sanguine suo renascuntur.'* — **vinci**: Intr. 108.

63. **monstrumve**: the negative **non** continues, modifying **maius**. The allusion in **monstrum,** *marvel,* is to the troops of armed men that sprang up from the dragon teeth sown by Jason in Colchis and by Cadmus at Thebes. — **submisere**: cf. Lucret. 1, 7 *daedala tellus submittit flores.*

64. **Echioniae**: Echion was one of the five survivors of the struggle among the warriors sprung from the Theban dragon's teeth; by marriage with Agave, Cadmus' daughter, he became an ancestor of the Theban royal line.

65 ff. **merses, luctere**: *you may,* etc., sc. *eam (gentem).* The subjunctive is jussive, but the two verbs are virtually protases to **evenit, proruet, geretque.** These verses were paraphrased four centuries and a quarter later by Rutilius Namatianus 1, 128 ff. *flevit successus Annibal ipse suos: | quae mergi nequeunt, nisu maiore resurgunt | exiliuntque imis altius icta vadis.*

— **evenit**: in its rare literal meaning. — **proruet, geret**: these futures differ from the present

>   luctere, multa proruet integrum
>   cum laude victorem geretque
>   proelia coniugibus loquenda.
>
>   Carthagini iam non ego nuntios
> 70   mittam superbos; occidit, occidit
>   spes omnis et fortuna nostri
>   nominis Hasdrubale interempto.'
>
>   Nil Claudiae non perficient manus,
>   quas et benigno numine Iuppiter
> 75   defendit et curae sagaces
>   expediunt per acuta belli.

evenit only in showing what will happen in each case, while evenit expresses what always does happen. — **integrum** : (hitherto) *unharmed*. — **laude** : *glory*. — **coniugibus loquenda** : 'for old wives' tales.'

70. **occidit, occidit** : Intr. 28 a. Cf. Dryden's well-known lines from *Alexander's Feast*, 'He sang Darius great and good | By too severe a fate | Fallen, fallen, fallen, | Fallen from his high estate.'

73 ff. After the Pindaric fashion the closing verses are given to reflections on the great merits of the Claudii and the expectations that may be cherished of them. Some modern commentators make these verses also a part of Hannibal's speech, but not so Porphyrio.

75 f. **curae sagaces** : probably on the part of Augustus, who cares on earth for them, as Jupiter protects them from the sky. — **expediunt** : *bring through* ; cf. Verg. A. 2, 632 f. *ducente deo flammam inter et hostis | expedior*.

5

The blessings of Augustus' rule. 'Guardian of the Roman race, thou art too long away. Grant us again the light of thy countenance that makes the very sun shine brighter. As a mother suffers for her son detained across the sea by winter winds, so longs thy land for thee (1-16). Safe are our cattle, bounteous our crops, no pirates vex the sea. Faith, chastity, and justice sure, no fear of foreign foe — these are the blessings which thy rule has brought (17-28). After a peaceful day of toil, the farmer at his evening meal makes libation and offers prayer to thee among his household gods, even as Greece remembers her great benefactors. At morning and at eventide we pray that thou wilt give thy country peace (29-40).'

For the military events that called Augustus from Rome in 16 B.C. see the introductory n. to 4, 2. It was also said (Dio Cass. 55, 19), that the Emperor wished to withdraw from the city for a time, as Solon once had done from Athens, until the unpopularity of his reform measures should have somewhat abated. His return at an early date, however, was confidently expected; when it was put off from time to time — he did not come back until 13 B.C. — the feelings of the great body of citizens were expressed by Horace in this ode. Peace had been so long reëstablished that its blessings were evident on every hand; it was natural that those who remembered the horrors of the civil wars should have a lively feeling of gratitude to the Emperor who had brought order out of chaos and had revived the weakened and impoverished state. To this class Horace belonged; in these verses he shows a genuine warmth of feeling which is not found in his earlier odes to the Emperor, and which his official position as laureate did not call forth. The sense of security here expressed is in marked contrast to the hopeless tone of 3, 6.

The ode is carefully polished; the frequent cases of assonance and alliteration should be noted. Its date cannot be absolutely determined, but may be approximately fixed as 14 B.C. It forms a pendant to 4, as Ode 15 to 14. Metre, 72.

> Divis orte bonis, optume Romulae
> custos gentis, abes iam nimium diu;
> maturum reditum pollicitus patrum
>   sancto concilio, redi.
>
> 5   Lucem redde tuae, dux bone, patriae;

1 f. **divis . . . bonis** : ablative absolute, *when the gods were kind*. Augustus is said to be the gift to men of the *boni divi* 4, 2, 38. — **Romulae . . . gentis** : cf. Verg. *A.* 6, 876 *Romula . . . tellus*. — **custos**: cf. 4, 15, 17 *custode rerum Caesare*.

4. **sancto**: *august*; so Cic. *in Catil.* 1, 4, 9 *in hoc orbis terrae sanctissimo gravissimoque consilio*.

5. **lucem**: *i.e. tuam;* cf. Amphitryon's exclamation, Eurip. *H. F.* 531 f. ὦ φίλτατ' ἀνδρῶν, ὦ φάος μολὼν πατρὶ | ἥκεις. Horace's strophe was probably in the mind of the Christian Prudentius when he wrote *Cath.* 5, 1, 4 *inventor rutili, dux bone, luminis . . . lucem redde tuis, Christe, fidelibus*.

instar veris enim voltus ubi tuus
adfulsit populo, gratior it dies
    et soles melius nitent.

10   Vt mater iuvenem, quem Notus invido
flatu Carpathii trans maris aequora
cunctantem spatio longius annuo
    dulci distinet a domo,

votis ominibusque et precibus vocat,
curvo nec faciem litore demovet,
15   sic desideriis icta fidelibus
    quaerit patria Caesarem.

Tutus bos etenim rura perambulat,
nutrit rura Ceres almaque Faustitas,

6 ff. **instar**: here of quality; usually of quantity, size, as Verg. A. 2, 15 *instar montis equum.* — **veris**: cf. Theoc. 12, 3 ff. ὅσσον ἔαρ χειμῶνος ... ἥδιον ... τόσσον ἔμ᾽ εὔφρηνας σὺ φανείς. 'As spring is sweeter than winter, even so hast thou cheered me by thy appearing.'
— **it dies**: cf. 2, 14, 5 *quotquot eunt dies.* — **soles**, etc.: see n. on *pulcher* 4, 2, 47.

9 ff. **mater iuvenem**: note the juxtaposition which gives at once the members of the comparison. — **Notus, Carpathii**: cf. n. to 1, 1, 13. — **invido**: the mother's epithet for the wind that detains her son. — **spatio longius annuo**: he must spend the winter away, as Gyges at Oricum 3, 7, 1 ff.

13 f. **votis**, etc.: the mother employs every means to call him home. The verse was employed by Ausonius, *Epist.* 25, 120 f. *votis ominibusque bonis precibusque vocatus | adpropera.* — **vocat**: literally. — **curvo**: a stock epithet; cf. *Epod.* 10, 21. There is a reminiscence of these two verses in St. Jerome, *ad Ruf.* 1 *non sic curvo adsidens litori anxia filium mater expectat.*

15. **icta**: *smitten by*, ἱμέρῳ πεπληγμένος, Aesch. *Ag.* 544. Cf. Lucret. 2, 360 *desiderio perfixa iuvenci.*

17 ff. Notice that the emphasis falls on **tutus, nutrit, pacatum**. — **etenim**: '(we cannot spare thee from us), for under thy protection the kine,' etc. — **perambulat**: as it grazes.

18. **rura**: the repetition is not emphatic, but causes us to linger on the picture. — **Faustitas**: this

pacatum volitant per mare navitae,
   culpari metuit fides,

nullis polluitur casta domus stupris,
mos et lex maculosum edomuit nefas,
laudantur simili prole puerperae,
   culpam poena premit comes.

Quis Parthum paveat, quis gelidum Scythen,
quis Germania quos horrida parturit
fetus, incolumi Caesare? Quis ferae
   bellum curet Hiberiae?

Condit quisque diem collibus in suis

abstract divinity is named only here, but is evidently the same as *Fausta Felicitas*, 'Fertility.'

19 f. **pacatum**: *i.e.* of pirates. Cf. *Epod.* 4, 19. *Mon. Anc.* 5, 1 *mare pacavi a praedonibus.*—**volitant**: *flit.*—**culpari**: *unfair action.*

21-24. This strophe refers to Augustus' attempt by means of the *lex Iulia de adulteriis* passed in 18 B.C. to check the growth of immorality and to restore the purity of domestic life. (Cf. *C. S.* 17 ff.) Unfortunately the picture here given of his success is too rose-colored. — **casta**: proleptic, *now pure, is,* etc. — **mos et lex**: *sentiment and law;* without the support of the first the second is of little service. Cf. 3, 24, 35 and n. — **edomuit**: *has completely,* etc.

23 f. **simili prole**: *for children that resemble (their fathers).* Cf. Hesiod *Op.* 235 τίκτουσιν δὲ γυναῖ-κες (the wives of the righteous) ἐοικότα τέκνα τοκεῦσι. Also Catul. 61, 221 *sit suo similis patri | Manlio et facile insciis | noscitetur ab omnibus | et pudicitiam suae | matris indicet ore.* — **premit comes**: *i.e.* no longer limps far behind; cf. 3, 2, 32. With the phrase, cf. *S.* 2, 7, 115 (*Cura*) *comes atra premit sequiturque fugacem.*

25 ff. Peace on the borders. — **Parthum**: in 20 B.C. the Parthians had given back the Roman standards. Cf. 3, 14, 15 and n. — **Scythen**: cf. 3, 8, 23 f. and n. — **parturit**: *breeds.* — **fetus**: *swarms.* — **incolumi Caesare**: *so long as,* etc. Cf. 3, 5, 12. — **bellum Hiberiae**: *i.e.* the long-continued resistance of the Cantabrians, finally overcome in 19 B.C. Cf. 2, 6, 2.

29 f. **condit**: *brings to rest, i.e.* spends peacefully. Cf. Verg. *E.* 9, 51 f. *saepe ego longos | cantando puerum memini me condere soles.*

30   et vitem viduas ducit ad arbores;
       hinc ad vina redit laetus et alteris
          te mensis adhibet deum;

       te multa prece, te prosequitur mero
       defuso pateris, et Laribus tuum
35   miscet numen, uti Graecia Castoris
          et magni memor Herculis.

       'Longas o utinam, dux bone, ferias
       praestes Hesperiae!' dicimus integro
       sicci mane die, dicimus uvidi,
40   cum sol Oceano subest.

—collibus: cf. 1, 20, 12. — suis: *his own*, emphasizing the possession of lands by small holders. One of Augustus' most cherished plans was the restoration of agriculture in Italy. — viduas : *unwedded.* — ducit : cf. *Epod.* 2, 10 and the passage from Milton there quoted. 'They led the vine to wed her elm,' etc.

31. redit : sc. *domum.* — alteris mensis : before the dessert, *mensae secundae*, was brought, libations and offerings of food were made to the household gods ; with these divinities Augustus was early associated by the sentiment of the people. Later a decree of the Senate required this worship. Cf. Ovid. *Fast.* 2, 633 ff. *et libate dapes ut. grati pignus honoris, | nutriat incinctos missa patella Lares; | iamque ubi suadebit pla-* *cidos nox umida somnos, | larga precaturi sumite vina manu, | et 'bene vos, bene te, patriae pater, optime Caesar' | dicite suffuso ter bona verba mero.*

32. adhibet : *invites*, in his prayer.

33 f. te . . . te: Intr. 28 c. — Laribus: dative. Intr. 89. — uti Graecia, etc.: 'the honor which Greece pays her mythical benefactors, thou receivest in thy lifetime.' — Castoris, Herculis : belonging to both numen and memor. Intr. 100.

37 ff. o utinam, etc.: *i.e.* 'long may'st thou live, and may thy life secure thy land continued peace.' — ferias : 'vacations,' *i.e. days of peace.* — Hesperiae: cf. 2, 1, 32. — integro: *untouched*, and entire before us. — sicci: cf. 1, 18, 3. — uvidi : βεβρεγμένοι. Cf. 1, 7, 22 ; 2, 19, 18.

6

A prelude to the *Carmen Saeculare.*

'Apollo, thou who didst punish Niobe and Tityos, and didst lay low Achilles for all his prowess; he who but for thee and Venus would have slain ruthlessly every Trojan child, so that none would have remained to found another state with better auspices (1-24). Thou divine minstrel, guard, I pray, the glory of the Daunian Muse (25-28). Phoebus it is who gives me my power and name. Ye noble maids and boys, mark well the measure. Sing Apollo and Diana. Proud shall be thy boast when matron that at the great festival thou didst render the song of the poet Horace (29-44).'

The poem thus falls into two divisions — the prayer to Apollo (1-28), and the address to the chorus of boys and girls that is to sing the Secular Hymn (31-44). The two parts are connected by vv. 29-30, in which Horace acknowledges that he owes his inspiration, skill, and even name of poet to the god. The date of composition is evidently not far from that of the *Carmen Saeculare,* 17 B.C. Metre, 69.

Dive, quem proles Niobea magnae
vindicem linguae Tityosque raptor
sensit et Troiae prope victor altae
Phthius Achilles,

1. **dive**: Apollo, as the following verses clearly show. The invocation is resumed v. 25 and the verb, **defende**, is not found until v. 27. — **proles Niobea**: the seven sons and seven daughters whom Apollo and Diana shot down to punish Niobe for her boast that, while Leto bore but two children, she had many. In Horace's day a group representing the slaying was to be seen in the portico of Apollo's temple, built by C. Sosius. The group was thought to be the work of Praxiteles or Scopas. Fragments of a similar group are now in the Uffizi in Florence. Certain figures are reproduced in Baumeister 3, pp. 1673 ff.

2 f. **magnae ... linguae**: boasting — μεγάλῃ γλώσσῃ — the gods will not brook. Cf. Soph. *Ant.* 127 f. Ζεὺς γὰρ μεγάλης γλώσσης κόμπους ὑπερεχθαίρει. — **Tityosque raptor**: cf. n. to 2, 14, 8. — **sensit**: cf. 4, 4, 25. — **prope victor**: *i.e.* after killing Hector, Troy's chief bulwark of defense. When dying, Hector foretold the death of his slayer. *Il.* 22, 359 f. ἤματι τῷ ὅτε κίν σε Πάρις καὶ Φοῖβος Ἀπόλλων | ἐσθλὸν ἐόντ' ὀλέσωσιν ἐνὶ Σκαιῇσι πύλῃσιν. — **Troiae ... altae**: the Homeric Ἴλιος αἰπεινή.

ceteris maior, tibi miles impar,
filius quamvis Thetidis marinae
Dardanas turris quateret tremenda
    cuspide pugnax,

(ille, mordaci velut icta ferro
pinus aut impulsa cupressus Euro,
procidit late posuitque collum in
    pulvere Teucro;

ille non inclusus equo Minervae
sacra mentito male feriatos
Troas et laetam Priami choreis
    falleret aulam,

sed palam captis gravis, heu nefas heu,
nescios fari pueros Achivis

5 ff. tibi: *to thee alone.* — **filius**, etc.: *though he was the son of Thetis and shook*, etc. — **quateret**: cf. Verg. *A.* 9, 608 *quatit oppida bello.* — **tremenda cuspide**: Achilles' mighty spear is described *Il.* 16, 141 ff. and 19, 387 ff. πατρώιον ἐσπάσατ' ἔγχος | βριθύ, μέγα, στιβαρόν· τὸ μὲν οὐ δύνατ' ἄλλος Ἀχαιῶν | πάλλειν, ἀλλά μιν οἶος ἐπίστατο πῆλαι Ἀχιλλεύς, | Πηλιάδα μελίην, τὴν πατρὶ φίλῳ πόρε Χείρων | Πηλίου ἐκ κορυφῆς, φόνον ἔμμεναι ἡρώεσσιν. — **pugnax**: with participial force, as Livy 22, 37, 8 *pugnacesque missili telo gentes.*

9 ff. mordaci: the same personification as Eurip. *Cyc.* 395 πελέκεων γνάθοις. — **procidit late**: the metaphor of the tree is still remembered, but cf. *Il.* 18, 26 f. αὐτὸς δ' ἐν κονίῃσι μέγας μεγαλωστὶ τανυσθεὶς | κεῖτο. — The story of the wooden horse had been revived in the minds of Roman readers by the *Aeneid*, which had been recently published.

13 ff. Minervae: with both **equo** and **sacra**. — **mentito**: *that pretended to be.* — **male feriatos**: their holiday was ill-fated. — **falleret**: a past apodosis as the context requires. The formal protasis appears v. 21 f. — **aulam**: *the court.*

17 ff. sed palam: modifying **captis**; in contrast with **falleret** — 'he would not have resorted to secret devices, but would have taken his captives in open warfare,' etc. — **gravis**: βαρύς, *cruel, merciless.* — **nescios fari**: a periphrasis for *infantes*, νήπια τέκνα. — **Achivis**: *i.e. set by the Greeks.* —

ureret flammis, etiam latentem
matris in alvo,

ni tuis victus Venerisque gratae
vocibus divum pater adnuisset
rebus Aeneae potiore ductos
alite muros;)

doctor argutae fidicen Thaliae,
Phoebe, qui Xantho lavis amne crinis,
Dauniae defende decus Camenae,
levis Agyieu.

Spiritum Phoebus mihi, Phoebus artem
carminis nomenque dedit poetae.
Virginum primae puerique claris
patribus orti,

etiam latentem, etc.: cf. *Il.* 6, 57 ff. τῶν (Τρώων) μή τις ὑπεκφύγοι αἰπὺν ὄλεθρον | χεῖράς θ' ἡμετέρας· μηδ' ὅν τινα γαστέρι μήτηρ | κοῦρον ἐόντα φέροι, μηδ' ὃς φύγοι.

21 ff. 'If it had not been for thy prayers and those of Venus, there would have been none left to found Rome.'—ni: found nowhere else in the Odes, but common in the Satires.—adnuisset: transitive.—potiore ... alite: cf. 1, 15. 5 *mala avi* and n.—ductos: *traced.*

25 f. Resuming the address to Apollo.—doctor, etc.: Ἀπόλλων Μουσαγέτης.—argutae: λιγείας. Cf. 3, 14. 21.—fidicen: cf. Horace's description of his own function. 4, 3, 23.—Xantho: in Lycia. —lavis, etc.: cf. 3, 4, 61 ff.

27 f. Dauniae: equivalent to 'Italian,' 'Roman'; but selected with reference to Horace's birthplace. Cf. n. to 3, 30, 10; also 2, 1, 34. —lēvis: *smooth-cheeked.*—Agyieu: as guardian of streets. The epithet is found only here in Roman poetry, but is common in Greek. Cf. Eurip. *Phoen.* 631 καὶ σὺ, Φοῖβ' ἄναξ Ἀγυιεῦ.

29 f. The poet's warrant for his charge.—spiritum: cf. 2, 16. 38. — artem: 'technical skill'; the contrast with spiritum is strengthened by the chiasmus.—poetae: only here applied by Horace to himself; elsewhere he prefers vates. Cf. n. to 1, 1, 35.

31. primae, etc.: the boys and girls of the chorus which sang the *Carmen Saeculare* were of gentle

Deliae tutela deae, fugacis
lyncas et cervos cohibentis **arcu**,
35   Lesbium servate pedem meique
     pollicis ictum,

rite Latonae puerum canentes,
rite crescentem face Noctilucam,
prosperam frugum celeremque pronos
40   volvere mensis.

Nupta iam dices 'Ego dis amicum,
saeculo festas referente luces,

birth and *patrimi et matrimi, i.e.* 'with both parents living.'

33 ff. **tutela**: in passive sense, *wards.* Diana, the virgin goddess, was the especial protectress of innocent youth. Cf. Catull. 34, 1 *Dianae sumus in fide* | *puellae et pueri integri.* By the mention of this function Horace is enabled to give the goddess a place in his hymn beside her brother Apollo. — **lyncas et cervos**: possibly imitated from Callim. *Hymn. in Dian.* 16 f. ὁππότε μηκέτι λύγκας | μήτ' ἐλάφους βάλλοιμι. — **cohibentis**: *who checks.* — **Lesbium pedem**: *i.e.* Sappho's measure. Cf. 1, 1, 34 *Lesboum barbiton.* — **pollicis ictum**: in his imagination Horace pictures himself as χοροδιδάσκαλος, striking the lyre to direct the song.

37 f. **rite**: *duly; i.e.* performing the solemn function in the prescribed form. — **Latonae puerum canentes**: the boys; while the girls praise *Noctiluca.* — **crescentem**: *with growing light* (face). — **Noctiluca**: an archaic name of *Luna*, who under this designation was worshiped on the Palatine.

39 f. **prosperam**: with objective genitive. Cf. *C. S.* 29 *fertilis frugum.* Intr. 92. — **celerem** . . . **volvere**: Intr. 108. — **pronos**: *the gliding, hurrying.* Cf. 1, 29, 11 *pronos rivos.* For this function of the goddess, cf. Catull. 34, 17 ff. *tu cursu, dea, menstruo* | *metiens iter annuum,* | *rustica agricolae bonis* | *tecta frugibus exples.*

41 f. **nupta**: the address is confined to the girls who would remember their participation in the *ludi saeculares* as one of the greatest events in their lives. The singular number is used after the Greek fashion. — **iam**: *presently,* when married. — **amicum**: agreeing with carmen. For the meaning, cf. 1, 26, 1. — **saeculo**: cf. introductory note to *C. S.* p. 388 f. — **luces**: cf. 4, 11, 19; 15, 25.

CARMINA [4, 7, 7

reddidi carmen docilis modorum
vatis Horati.'

43 f. **reddidi**: *rendered;* regularly used of repeating what has been committed to memory. Cf. 4, 11, 34 *modos . . . quos reddas.* — **modorum**: obj. genitive with

docilis, *trained in.* Intr. 92. — **vatis Horati**: thus at the end Horace casually mentions his office and his name to secure the emphasis he desired.

7

'Spring is here again; hand in hand the Nymphs and Graces dance. The seasons change and wane, but come again. But we, when we are gone, come not back. So give thyself good cheer while yet thou mayst; thou canst not buy escape from nether gloom.'

The ode is a close parallel to 1, 4, with which it should be carefully compared. The Torquatus addressed was an intimate of Horace and an advocate of considerable prominence. See *Epist.* 1, 5. There is no hint of the date of composition. Metre, 78.

Diffugere nives, redeunt iam gramina campis
  arboribusque comae;
mutat terra vices et decrescentia ripas
  flumina praetereunt;
5 Gratia cum Nymphis geminisque sororibus audet
  ducere nuda choros.
Immortalia ne speres, monet annus et almum

2. **comae**: cf. 1, 21, 5 and n.; 4, 3, 11.

3 f. **mutat terra vices**: the expression was frequently imitated by later writers — *e.g. Anth. Lat.* 676, 3 *R. alternant elementa vices et tempora mutant.* — **vices**: the 'inner object' of **mutat.** Cf. 1, 4, 1. — **decrescentia**: since the winter floods are over. — **praetereunt**: *i.e.* no longer overflow.

5 f. Cf. 3, 19, 16 *Gratia nudis*

iuncta sororibus; 1, 4, 6 *iunctaeque Nymphis Gratiae decentes.*

7. **immortalia**: *immortality.* — **ne speres**: dependent on **monet**; cf. 1, 18, 7 f. With the sentiment, cf. Eurip. *Frg.* 1075 θνητὸς γὰρ ὢν καὶ θνητὰ πείσεσθαι δόκει· | ⟨ἢ⟩ θεοῦ βίον ζῆν ἀξιοῖς ἄνθρωπος ὤν; 'For as thou art mortal, expect to bear a mortal's lot, or dost thou ask to live a god's life, when thou art but a man?'

quae rapit hora diem:
frigora mitescunt Zephyris, ver proterit aestas,
10   interitura simul
pomifer autumnus fruges effuderit, et mox
bruma recurrit iners.
Damna tamen celeres reparant caelestia lunae:
nos ubi decidimus
15   quo pius Aeneas, quo Tullus dives et Ancus,
pulvis et umbra sumus.

—annus: *the changing year*, περιπλόμενος ἐνιαυτός. — quae rapit: *that hurries on*, etc.; snatching away from man the time of his enjoyment. Cf. 3, 29, 48 *quod fugiens semel hora vexit.*

9-12. The progress of the seasons. Cf. Lucretius' description 5, 737 ff. *it Ver et Venus et Veris praenuntius ante | pennatus graditur Zephyrus. . . . inde loci sequitur calor aridus . . . inde autumnus adit . . . tandem bruma nives adfert pigrumque rigorem.* — Zephyris: cf. n. to 1, 4, 1. — proterit: 'treads on the heels of.' — interitura: *destined to die.* Intr. 110. — pomifer: cf. 3, 23, 8; Epod. 2, 17. — effuderit: as it were from a horn of plenty. Cf. *Epist.* 1, 12, 28 *aurea fruges Italiae pleno defundit Copia cornu.* — iners: contrasting winter with the other seasons.

13. damna . . . caelestia: *the losses of the heavens, i.e.* the seasons. The contrast is furnished by the following verse. With the sentiment cf. Catull. 5, 4 ff. *soles occidere et redire possunt: | nobis cum semel occidit brevis lux, | nox est perpetua una dormienda.*

14 f. decidimus: cf. *Epist.* 2, 1, 36 *scriptor abhinc annos centum qui decidit.* — pius: established by the *Aeneid* as the epithet of its hero. — Tullus: the mythical king famed for his wealth. — Ancus: whose goodness was immortalized by Ennius' line *lumina sis* (i.e. *suis*) *oculis etiam bonus Ancus reliquit.*

16. pulvis et umbra: in the grave and the lower world. Cf. Soph. *Elec.* 1158 f. ἀντὶ φιλτάτης μορφῆς σποδόν τε καὶ σκιὰν ἀνωφελῆ. Also Asclepiades' warning to a maiden, *Anth. Pal.* 5, 84 φείδῃ παρθενίης· καὶ τί πλέον; οὐ γὰρ ἐς ᾅδην | ἐλθοῦσ' εὑρήσεις τὸν φιλέοντα, κορή. | ἐν ζωοῖσι τὰ τερπνὰ τὰ Κύπριδος· ἐν δ' Ἀχέροντι | ὀστέα καὶ σποδιή. παρθένε, κεισόμεθα. 'Thou sparest thy maidenhood, and what advantage? For when thou goest to Hades, maid, thou wilt not there find thy lover. Among the living only are the delights of

Quis scit an adiciant hodiernae crastina summae
    tempora di superi?
Cuncta manus avidas fugient heredis, amico
20   quae dederis animo.
Cum semel occideris et de te splendida Minos
    fecerit arbitria,
non, Torquate, genus, non te facundia, non te
    restituet pietas.
25 Infernis neque enim tenebris Diana pudicum
    liberat Hippolytum,
nec Lethaea valet Theseus abrumpere caro
    vincula Pirithoo.

Cypris; in Acheron, maiden, we shall be only bones and ashes.'

17 f. Cf. 1, 9, 13 ff.; *Epist.* 1, 4, 12 ff. *inter spem curamque, timores inter et iras | omnem crede diem tibi diluxisse supremum; | grata superveniet quae non sperabitur hora.* Also *Anac.* 15, 9 f. τὸ σήμερον μέλει μοι, τὸ δ' αὔριον τίς οἶδεν. — **summae**: cf. 1, 4, 15.

19 ff. The lesson of the preceding. — **heredis**: the dreaded heir, the thought of whom haunts every man who gathers riches. Cf. n. to 2, 3, 19; also 2, 14, 25; 3, 24, 62. — **dederis animo**: essentially the same as *genium curare* 3, 17, 14. The adjective **amico** is added in imitation of the Homeric φίλον ἦτορ.

21. **semel**: cf. n. to 1, 24, 16.
— **splendida**: *stately*; properly the characteristic of Minos' court, transferred to his decrees. Intr. 99.

23 f. **genus, facundia, pietas**: the first two at least applied to Torquatus, for he was a member of the noble Manlian gens and was an advocate of some eminence. Note the cadence of the verse.

25 ff. Two mythological illustrations. Observe that **pudicum** and **caro** are set over against each other, and express the qualities for which Hippolytus and Pirithous were famous — the first for his chastity in refusing the advances of Phaedra, his step-mother, the second for his friendship with Theseus. Horace follows the Greek legend according to which Artemis could not save her devotee from death; but the myth among the Romans made Diana restore Hippolytus to life and transfer him under the name of Virbius to her grove by Lake Nemi (Verg. *A.* 7, 768 ff.; Ovid. *Met.* 15, 548 ff.). — **Pirithoo**: cf. n. to 3, 4, 80.

8

The two following odes treat a single theme—the immortality of song.

' Bronzes, marbles, pictures I have none to give, good friend Censorinus, nor wouldst thou desire them. Song is thy delight, and song I can bestow. The chiseled record of men's deeds is weaker than the Muse. Through her gift the great ones of the past escaped oblivion, and have their place in heaven.'

C. Marcius Censorinus, cos. 8 B.C., is known only from these verses and a single reference in Velleius. It has been conjectured not without reason that this ode was Horace's gift to his friend on the Calends of March or on the Saturnalia, when presents were exchanged as at our Christmas. Metre, 53.

> Donarem pateras grataque commodus,
> Censorine, meis aera sodalibus,
> donarem tripodas, praemia fortium
> Graiorum, neque tu pessima munerum
> 5 ferres, divite me scilicet artium
> quas aut Parrhasius protulit aut Scopas,
> hic saxo, liquidis ille coloribus
> sollers nunc hominem ponere, nunc deum.
> Sed non haec mihi vis, non tibi talium
> 10 res est aut animus deliciarum egens:

1. **donarem**: the protasis is expressed in a general way by **divite me** v. 5, which, however, is closely joined with the words that follow it. — **commodus**: *consulting their taste*, so that the gifts would be **grata**. — **aera**: *bronzes*, especially vases.

3. **donarem**: *yes, I should*, etc. Intr. 28 c. — **praemia**: in apposition with **tripodas**, which were used as early as Homer's day for prizes. Cf. *Il.* 23, 259 νηῶν δ' ἔκφερ' ἄεθλα, λέβητάς τε τρίποδάς τε ('Αχιλλεύς).

5 f. **ferres**: equivalent to *auferres*: cf. 3, 16, 22. — **scilicet**: *that is, of course*. — **artium**: *works of art*. — **Parrhasius**: a famous painter born at Ephesus, a contemporary in Athens of Socrates. — **Scopas**: of Paros, a distinguished sculptor in the first half of the fourth century B.C.

8. **ponere**: *at representing*. For the mood, see Intr. 108.

9 f. **non haec**, etc.: *I have not the power* (to give such presents). Cf. *Epod.* 5, 94. — **res ... aut animus**: *estate or tastes*. That is,

gaudes carminibus; carmina possumus
donare et pretium dicere muneri.
Non incisa notis marmora publicis,
per quae spiritus et vita redit bonis
15   post mortem ducibus, non celeres fugae
reiectaeque retrorsum Hannibalis minae,
non incendia Carthaginis impiae

Censorinus is rich enough to buy these rare things if he desired, but is too simple in his tastes to wish them. — deliciarum: *curios*, with disparaging force.

11. Horace will bring a gift which will please his friend, but such as money cannot buy.

12. pretium dicere muneri: *tell the worth of, set a price on*. The common expression is *pretium statuere, ponere*. The following verses state the worth. The thought is the same as in *Epist.* 2, 1, 248 ff.

13 ff. 'Neither inscribed statues nor great deeds in war have secured Scipio the fame which he has gained from Ennius' poem.' — notis . . . publicis: *inscriptions cut at the state's orders*; instrumental abl. — marmora: the following clause shows that this includes both the statues and their bases on which the inscriptions are engraved. Translate simply, *marbles*. — spiritus et vita: a double expression of a single idea, yet somewhat more comprehensive than either word would be alone; cf. 4, 2, 28 *more modoque*. Also with the general sentiment, cf. Verg. *A.* 6, 847 f. *excudent alii spirantia mollius aera,* | *credo equidem, vivos ducent de marmore voltus.* — non fugae, reiectae minae, incendia: all these confer fame, and might secure the memory of the leader under whom they were accomplished; yet all are inferior to song. — fugae: from Italy or after the battle of Zama, or both. — reiectae . . . minae: Hannibal's threats against Rome were hurled back by the reduction of Carthage. — incendia, etc.: this verse has troubled critics, both because it has no diaeresis and because the burning of Carthage was not accomplished until 146 B.C., when the Scipio who brought the Second Punic war to an end had been dead for seventeen, and Ennius, who celebrated his fame, for five years. It was the younger Scipio Aemilianus who razed Carthage. However, Horace may have consciously taken the name Scipio Africanus — inherited by the younger — simply as typical of one who had won great fame in war. Yet vv. 18 f. can strictly only apply to the elder Scipio.

— impiae: cf. n. to 4, 4, 46.

eius, qui domita nomen ab Africa
lucratus rediit, clarius indicant
20   laudes quam Calabrae Pierides; neque
si chartae sileant quod bene feceris,
mercedem tuleris. Quid foret Iliae
Mavortisque puer, si taciturnitas
obstaret meritis invida Romuli?
25   Ereptum Stygiis fluctibus Aeacum
virtus et favor et lingua potentium

19. **lucratus**: *enriched by*; the word is intentionally used for its commercial connotation, but without the unpleasant connotation which **lucrum** has 3, 16, 12. Scipio boasted that his name was all the profit he made in Africa. Val. Max. 3. 8, 1 *cum Africam totam potestati vestrae subiecerim, nihil ex ea quod meum diceretur praeter cognomen rettuli.*

20 f. **Calabrae Pierides**: *i.e.* the poetry of Ennius whose birthplace was Rudiae in Calabria. He celebrated Scipio's deeds in his *Annales* as well as in a special poem. — **chartae**: *books*, papyrus rolls. — **sileant**: transitive.

22 ff. **quid foret**, etc.: without song men's deeds die with them. Cf. Pind. *O.* 10, 91 ff. καὶ ὅταν κ.ιλὰ ἔρξαις ἀοιδᾶς ἄτερ Ἀγησίδαμ' εἰς Ἀΐδα σταθμὸν | ἀνὴρ ἵκηται, κενεὰ πνεύσαις ἔπορε μόχθῳ βραχύ τι τερ | πνόν. τὶν δ' ἁδυεπής τε λύρα | γλυκύς τ' αὐλὸς ἀναπάσσει χάριν. | τρέφοντι δ' εὐρὺ κλέος | κόραι Πιερίδες Διός. 'Even so, Agesidemus, when a man hath done noble deeds and goeth unsung to the house of Hades, his breath hath been spent in vain and he hath gained but brief delight by his toil. But on thee the sweet-toned lyre and pleasant pipe shed their grace; and the Pierian daughters of Zeus foster thy widespread fame,' also Ovid to Germanicus. *Ex Pont.* 4, 8, 31 ff. *nec tibi de Pario statuam, Germanice, templum marmore . . . Naso suis opibus, carmine, gratus erit . . . carmine fit vivax virtus expersque sepulchri notitiam serae posteritatis habet . . . quis Thebas septemque duces sine carmine nosset, et quidquid post haec, quidquid et ante fuit?*

— **Iliae**: cf. 1, 2, 17 and n. — **Mavortis**: *Mavors* is an archaic name of Mars preserved in ritual and adopted by poets. — **invida**: cf. 4, 5, 9, and 4, 9, 33 *lividas obliviones.*

25 f. **Aeacum**: cf. 2, 13. 22. Pindar celebrates him in *I.* 1, 8. — **virtus**: *his excellence.* — **favor**: *popular acclaim.* — **potentium vi-**

vatum divitibus consecrat insulis.
Dignum laude virum Musa vetat mori;
caelo Musa beat. Sic Iovis interest
30   optatis epulis impiger Hercules,
clarum Tyndaridae sidus ab infimis
quassas eripiunt aequoribus ratis,
ornatus viridi tempora pampino
Liber vota bonos ducit ad exitus.

tum: *i.e.* able to confer immortality. — divitibus ... insulis: cf. *Epod.* 16, 42 and n. The case is loc. abl. Intr. 95.

29 ff. 'Song confers not simply immortality; it actually raises mortals to the rank of gods.' Horace makes no distinction between mere subjective immortality, which can be given by poetry, and an actual existence after death. Cf. 3, 3, 9 ff. — sic: *i.e.* by song. Even the gods would be unknown, if poets did not make them known to men. Cf. Ovid. *Ex Pont.* 4, 8, 55 *di quoque carminibus, si fas est dicere, fiunt, | tantaque maiestas ore canentis eget.*

30. optatis: *for which he had longed.*

31. clarum ... sidus: in apposition with Tyndaridae: cf. n. to 1, 3, 2.

33. ornatus: middle participle. Intr. 84. The remainder of the verse repeats 3, 25, 20.

9

The first half of this ode continues the theme of the preceding but with a somewhat different turn. The remainder is in praise of M. Lollius.

'Do not despise my lyric Muse. Though Homer with his epic verse holds the supreme place, the verses of the lyric bards of Greece are not thereby obscured. Homer's Helen was not the first to love; nor his Troy the only city vexed; his heroes not the only ones to fight for wives and children dear, yet the others are unwept because unsung (1–28). My verse shall save thy deeds from oblivion's doom. For thou art wise, firm, upright; not consul for a single year, but victor, ruler over all (29–44). Truly fortunate is that man who wisely uses what the gods bestow, fears not small estate, and does not shrink from death for friend or native land (45–52).'

The M. Lollius addressed was consul 21 B.C.; in 16 B.C. he was defeated by the Sygambri while governor of Belgian Gaul. In 2 B.C. he was appointed governor of Syria and adviser and tutor of the young Gaius Caesar, who was then on a mission to Armenia. He died suddenly, gossip said by suicide, in the following year. Horace's ode was probably written soon after Lollius' defeat in 16 B.C., as an apology for his friend. Strangely enough the very virtues attributed to him here — honesty and rectitude — are the ones denied him by Velleius (2, 97; cf. Plin. *N. H.* 9, 58), who charges him with avarice and venality in the East. Which account is nearer the truth we cannot determine. Metre, 68.

> Ne forte credas interitura quae
> longe sonantem natus ad Aufidum
> non ante volgatas per artis
> verba loquor socianda chordis:
>
> 5   non, si priores Maeonius tenet
> sedes Homerus, Pindaricae latent
> Ceaeque et Alcaei minaces
> Stesichorique graves camenae,

1 ff. **ne ... credas**: not prohibitive, but giving the purpose of the statements in the two following strophes. Cf. nn. to 1, 33, 1; 2, 4, 1. Translate, 'You should not think ... for,' etc. — **longe sonantem**: with this epithet of the Aufidus, cf. *violens* 3, 30, 10. — **natus ad Aufidum**: said with a certain pride, 'I, a rustic born.' — **non ante volgatas**: cf. his more sweeping claim 3, 30, 13. — **verba ... socianda chordis**: *i.e.* lyric poetry distinguished from epic, which was recited, not sung to the accompaniment of the lyre. With the expression, cf. Ovid. *Met.* 11, 4 *cernunt Orphea percussis soci-antem carmina nervis.* — **loquor**: of the poet, in place of the more common *dico.* Cf. 3, 25, 18; 4, 2, 45.

5-12. In spite of Homer's preeminence, the Greek lyric poets are not unknown.

5 ff. **Maeonius**: cf. 1, 6, 2. — **Pindaricae (camenae)**: described 4, 2, 5-24. — **latent**: *are not hid.* — **Ceae**: of Simonides; cf. 2, 1, 38. — **minaces**: *i.e.* in his poems against the tyrants of Mitylene. Cf. n. to 1, 32, 5; 2, 13, 30 ff. — **Stesichori**: a poet of Himera in Sicily (ca. 640-555 B.C.), who treated heroic myths in lyric form. Quintilian 10, 1, 62, characterizes

nec, si quid olim lusit Anacreon,
10   delevit aetas; spirat adhuc amor
vivuntque commissi calores
Aeoliae fidibus puellae.

Non sola comptos arsit adulteri
crinis et aurum vestibus inlitum
15   mirata regalisque cultus
et comites Helene Lacaena,

him thus: *Stesichorus quam sit ingenio validus materiae quoque ostendunt, maxima bella et clarissimos canentem duces et epici carminis onera lyra sustinentem.* The last clause explains Horace's adjective **graves.**

9. lusit: of light themes, in contrast to the seriousness of Stesichorus and the passion of Sappho. With this use of the word, cf. 1, 32, 2.—**Anacreon**: a native of Teos, who flourished in the second half of the sixth century B.C. He resided at the court of Polycrates, tyrant of Samos, and later at that of Hipparchus in Athens. The extant collection of poems called *Anacreontea* are, however, of Alexandrian origin.

10 ff. spirat . . . vivunt: cf. n. to 4, 8, 14.—**commissi**: with **amor** and **calores** alike. The secrets of her love she intrusted to her lyre. Cf. S. 2, 1, 30 *ille (Lucilius) velut fidis arcana sodalibus olim | credebat libris.*—**Aeoliae**: cf. 2, 13, 24 and n.

13 ff. Horace now takes up the more general aspect of his theme. All his illustrations are from Homer. Notice the variety of expression and the cadence of the rhythm. — **comptos . . . crines**: *smooth locks;* the common object of **arsit,** *blazed with love's fire,* and **mirata,** *looked on with wondering admiration.* The latter continues with the three following accusatives, while **arsit** is forgotten. With this description of Paris, cf. 1, 15, 13 ff. and n.— **inlitum** : 'smeared on,' the word is chosen to emphasize the barbaric magnificence of Paris and his train. — **cultus**: *dress;* cf. 1, 8, 16. — **Lacaena**: the epithet is added in the epic fashion. Horace found models in the Greek writers for this account of the effect produced on Helen's mind by the appearance of Paris. Cf. *e.g.* Eurip. *Troad.* 991 f. ὃν εἰσιδοῦσα βαρβάροις ἐσθήμασι | χρυσῷ τε λαμπρὸν ἐξεμαργώθης φρένας. 'At sight of whom, brilliant in his barbarian dress and gold, thou lost thy senses.'

primusve Teucer tela Cydonio
direxit arcu; non semel Ilios
vexata; non pugnavit ingens
20   Idomeneus Sthenelusve solus

dicenda Musis proelia; non ferox
Hector vel acer Deiphobus gravis
excepit ictus pro pudicis
coniugibus puerisque primus.

25   Vixere fortes ante Agamemnona
multi; sed omnes inlacrimabiles
urgentur ignotique longa
nocte, carent quia vate sacro.

17 f. primusve : the negative continues. — Teucer : cf. 1, 7, 21. According to *Il.* 13, 313 he was the best bowman among the Greeks. — Cydonio : *i.e.* Cretan. Cydonia was a town in Crete; cf. 1, 15, 17. — Ilios : *an Ilium*. The siege of Troy is taken as typical of great sieges.
20. Idomeneus : captain of the Cretans. — Sthenelus : cf. 1, 15, 24 and n.
21 ff. dicenda Musis proelia : cf. 4, 4, 68. — non : with primus. — Hector, Deiphobus : two examples chosen from the Trojan side.
25. vixere fortes, etc.: often quoted. The line sums up all that has gone before.
26 ff. inlacrimabiles : passive; cf. 2, 14, 6. Translate, *and none can weep for them.* — urgentur ... longa nocte : cf. 1, 24, 5 f. *ergo*

Quintilium perpetuus sopor | urget!
— vate sacro : because consecrated to the service of the Muses; cf. 3, 1, 3 f. *Musarum sacerdos|virginibus puerisque canto.* With the preceding, cf. Pind. *N.* 7, 12 f. ταὶ μεγάλαι γὰρ ἀλκαί | σκότον πολὺν ὕμνων ἔχοντι δεόμεναι. | ἔργοις δὲ καλοῖς ἔσοπτρον ἴσαμεν ἐνὶ σὺν τρόπῳ, | εἰ Μναμοσύνας ἕκατι λιπαράμπυκος | εὕρηται ἄποινα μόχθων, κλυταῖς ἐπέων ἀοιδαῖς. 'For mighty feats of strength suffer deep darkness if they lack song; yet for glorious actions we know a mirror in one single way, if by the favor of Mnemosyne of the shining fillet a man find recompense for toil through glorifying strains of verse.' Also Boeth. *Phil. Cons.* 2, 7 *sed quam multos clarissimos suis temporibus viros scriptorum inops delevit opinio.*

Paulum sepultae distat inertiae
  celata virtus. Non ego te meis
    chartis inornatum silebo
      totve tuos patiar labores

impune, Lolli, carpere lividas
  obliviones. Est animus tibi
    rerumque prudens et secundis
      temporibus dubiisque rectus,

vindex avarae fraudis et abstinens
  ducentis ad se cuncta pecuniae,
    consulque non unius anni,
      sed quotiens bonus atque fidus

29 f. 'The hero, if posterity does not know his bravery, has but little advantage over the coward.' Thus Horace sums up the force of the preceding illustrations and passes on to assure Lollius that his excellence shall not go unsung. With the sentiment, cf. Claudian. *Cons. Hon.* 4, 225 f. *vile latens virtus. quid enim submersa tenebris | proderit obscuris?*

30 ff. non ego te: cf. 1, 18, 11. — chartis: cf. n. to 4, 8, 21. — inornatum: proleptic. — labores: *thy toils and struggles.*

33 ff. impune: *i.e.* without an effort to prevent. — carpere: *to prey;* suggesting Envy's biting tooth. — lividas: *malicious;* cf. 4, 8, 23. — est animus: cf. Verg. *A.* 9, 205 *est animus lucis contemptor.* — rerum prudens: *wise in affairs* (through experience). Cf. Verg. *G.* 1, 416 *ingenium* ('natural endowment') *aut rerum prudentia.* — secundis temporibus dubiisque: some see here a reference to Lollius' defeat in 16 B.C. — rectus: *steadfast.*

37 f. vindex, etc.: *i.e.* ready to punish cupidity in others and himself free from that sin. — abstinens pecuniae: for the genitive, cf. sceleris purus 1, 22, 1. Also 3, 27, 69 f. Cf. Intr. 94.

39 f. consul: in a figurative sense, suggested by the Stoic tenet that only the wise, *sapiens,* is the true consul or king. Cf. n. to 3, 2, 17. Superiority to the temptations of ordinary men makes a man supreme not for a single year, but so long as he maintains his integrity. There is a certain confusion here and in the following lines, as Horace seems to shift his

iudex honestum praetulit utili,
reiecit alto dona nocentium
   voltu, per obstantis catervas
      explicuit sua victor arma.

45 Non possidentem multa vocaveris
recte beatum; rectius occupat
   nomen beati, qui deorum
      muneribus sapienter uti

duramque callet pauperiem pati
50 peiusque leto flagitium timet,
   non ille pro caris amicis
      aut patria timidus perire.

thought from **animus** with which **vindex, consul,** and **iudex** are in apposition, to Lollius, the possessor of this incorruptible spirit. In translation we follow this shift, *whenever as a judge he*, etc.

41. **honestum**: τὸ καλόν, *virtue*. — **utili**: τὸ συμφέρον, *expediency*.

42 ff. **reiecit**: following **quotiens** by asyndeton. — **nocentium**: *the wicked*. — **per obstantis**, etc.: Porphyrio's explanation of this as an apodosis to **quotiens . . . praetulit, reiecit**, seems the simplest. — **catervas**: *i.e.* of those who would block his righteous course,

the *nocentium*. — **explicuit**: *has carried*, etc.

45 ff. The ideal man. — **non possidentem multa**, etc.: *it is not the man who*, etc. Cf. 2, 2, 17 ff. — **recte . . . rectius**: Intr. 28 c. — **occupat**: *claims as his own*. — **qui deorum**, etc.: cf. Claudian. *in Ruf.* 1, 215 f. *natura beatis omnibus esse dedit, siquis cognoverit uti.*

49 f. **callet**: cf. *callidus* 1, 10, 7. — **pauperiem pati**: repeated from 1, 1, 18. — **peius**: cf. *Epist.* 1, 17, 30 *cane peius et angue vitabit chlamydem.* — **non ille**: cf. 3, 21, 9.

52. **timidus perire**: Intr. 108.

10

The following four odes treat of love and good cheer in contrast to the serious tone of most of the other odes of the book.

These eight verses addressed to a beautiful boy, Ligurinus (4, 1, 33), warn him that beauty fades and soon he will repent his present haughtiness. The subject may have been suggested to Horace by certain Greek epigrams. Cf. *Anth. Pal.* 12, 35, 186. Metre, 54.

CARMINA [4, 11

O crudelis adhuc et Veneris muneribus potens,
insperata tuae cum veniet pluma superbiae
et quae nunc umeris involitant deciderint comae,
nunc et qui color est puniceae flore prior rosae
5 mutatus, Ligurine, in faciem verterit hispidam,
dices ' Heu,' quotiens te speculo videris alterum,
'quae mens est hodie, cur eadem non puero fuit,
vel cur his animis incolumes non redeunt genae?'

1 ff. Cf. Theoc. 23, 33 f. ἥξει καιρὸς ἐκεῖνος, ὁπανίκα καὶ τὺ φιλάσεις, | ἀνίκα τὰν κραδίαν ὁπτεύμενος ἁλμυρὰ κλαύσεις.—Veneris muneribus: cf. Il. 3, 54 f. οὐκ ἄν τοι χραίσμῃ κίθαρις τά τε δῶρ' Ἀφροδίτης, | ἥ τε κόμη τό τε εἶδος, ὅτ' ἐν κονίῃσι μιγείης. — insperata: predicate with veniet, unexpectedly. — pluma: down (of thy first beard), not found elsewhere in this sense. — deciderint comae : i.e. as a sign of man's estate.

4 f. flore . . . rosae: cf. 3, 29, 3. — verterit: intransitive. — hispidam: i.e. with thy new beard.
6 ff. speculo: instrumental ablative. — alterum: 'changed into another self.' Cf. Anth. Pal. 11, 77 ἢν δ' ἐθέλῃς τὸ πρόσωπον ἰδεῖν ἐς ἐσόπτρον ἑαυτοῦ | 'οὐκ εἰμὶ Στρατοφῶν,' αὐτὸς ἐρεῖς ὀμόσας. 'But if thou wilt look at thy face in the mirror, thou wilt say on thy oath, "I am not Stratophon."'

II

An invitation to Phyllis to join in celebrating the birthday of Maecenas.

'Come, Phyllis, here is plenty, and my house is all abustle with our preparations (1-12). We must keep the birthday of Maecenas, dearer to me almost than my own (13-20). Telephus is not for thee, but for a maid of richer station. Remember it was ambition that brought low Phaethon and Bellerophon. Come then, last of my flames, and learn a song to lessen thy love cares (21-36).'

In theme and treatment this ode is not unlike 3, 28. It is interesting to note that it contains the only reference to Maecenas in this book, which is so largely devoted to the praise of Augustus and his stepsons: but the warmth of vv. 17-20 shows that no shadow had fallen on the friendship between Horace and his patron. The year of composition is unknown. Metre, 69.

[4, 11, 1]

Est mihi nonum superantis annum
plenus Albani cadus; est in horto,
Phylli, nectendis apium coronis;
    est hederae vis

5   multa, qua crinis religata fulges;
ridet argento domus; ara castis
vincta verbenis avet immolato
    spargier agno;

    cuncta festinat manus, huc et illuc
10   cursitant mixtae pueris puellae;
sordidum flammae trepidant rotantes
    vertice fumum.

1 ff. **est**: the triple anaphora shows the poet's earnestness — 'yes, everything we need is here in abundance.' Cf. Theoc. 11 45 ff. ἐντὶ δάφναι τηνεῖ, ἐντὶ ῥαδιναὶ κυπάρισσοι, | ἔστι μέλας κισσός, ἔστ' ἄμπελος ἁ γλυκύκαρπος, | ἔστι ψυχρὸν ὕδωρ. 'There are laurels thereby, there are slender cypresses, there is dark ivy, and the vine with its sweet clusters, there is cool water.' — **Albani**: in quality next after the Caecuban and Falernian, according to Pliny *N. H.* 14. 64. — **nectendis . . . coronis**: dative of purpose. — **apium**: cf. 1, 36, 16; 2, 7, 24.

4. **vis**: *supply, copia*.

5 ff. **religata**: *middle*; cf. 2, 11, 24. — **fulges**: gnomic present: somewhat stronger in meaning than the common *niteo*, 1, 5, 13. — **ridet**: cf. Hesiod. *Theog.* 40 γελᾷ δέ τε δώματα πατρός. The silver has been polished up for the occasion. Cf. Juvenal's description of preparations for guests 14, 59 ff. *hospite venturo cessabit nemo tuorum*; | '*Verre pavimentum, nitidas ostende columnas,* | *arida cum tota descendat aranea tela;* | *hic leve argentum, vasa aspera tergeat alter*' | *vox domini furit.* — **ara . . . vincta**, etc.: cf. 1, 19, 13 f. and nn.

— **avet**: used only here in the lyric poems and the Epistles. — **spargier**: the archaic passive pres. inf. is not found elsewhere in the lyrics, but is employed five times in the Satires and Epistles.

9 ff. **manus**: *the household, familia*. — **puellae**: rare in this meaning of *famulae*. — **sordidum**: *murky, smoky.* — **trepidant**: *quiver;* cf. 2, 3, 11; 3, 27, 17. The word

Vt tamen noris quibus advoceris
gaudiis, Idus tibi sunt agendae,
15   qui dies mensem Veneris marinae
findit Aprilem,

iure sollemnis mihi sanctiorque
paene natali proprio, quod ex hac
luce Maecenas meus adfluentis
20   ordinat annos.

Telephum, quem tu petis, occupavit
non tuae sortis iuvenem puella
dives et lasciva, tenetque grata
compede vinctum.

has a certain personifying force like avet above, and pictures the fire as sharing in the excitement of preparation. — vertice: *i.e.* 'in eddying column.'

13 f. ut noris: the purpose of the explanation Idus tibi, etc. Cf. 4, 9, 1 ff. and n.

15 f. Veneris marinae: cf. 1, 4, 5; 3, 26, 5. In explanation of the fact that April was sacred to Venus, it was said that in this month the goddess ('Αφροδίτη ἀναδυομένη) was born from the sea, and in fact the name Aprilis was falsely derived from ἀφρός, 'sea-foam.' — findit: hinting at the derivation of idus from the Etruscan *iduare*, to divide (Macrob. 1, 15, 17).

17. sollemnis: *festal.* — sanctior: cf. Tib. 4, 5. 1 f. *qui mihi te, Cerinthe, dies dedit, hic mihi sanctus | atque inter festos semper habendus erit.* Also Iuv. 12, 1 ff. *natali, Corvine, die mihi dulcior haec lux, | qua festus promissa deis animalia caespes | expectat.*

19 f. luce: cf. 4, 6, 42. — adfluentis . . . annos: *the years in their onward flow.* The phrase does not necessarily imply that Maecenas was already old. — ordinat: *reckons*, adds to the tale of those already passed.

21 ff. 'Do not let your love for Telephus delay you, he is not for thee.' — Telephum: the name is found 1, 13, 1 f.; 3, 19, 26. — petis: frequent in this sense; cf. 1, 33. 13. — occupavit: cf. 1, 14, 2 and n. — sortis: *station.* — lasciva: *coquettish.* — tenet grata compede: cf. 1, 33, 14. — Also Tibul. 1, 1, 55 *me retinent vinctum formosae vincla puellae.*

25   Terret ambustus Phaethon avaras
     spes, et exemplum grave praebet ales
     Pegasus terrenum equitem gravatus
         Bellerophontem,

     semper ut te digna sequare et ultra
30   quam licet sperare nefas putando
     disparem vites. Age iam, meorum
         finis amorum,

     (non enim posthac alia calebo
     femina,) condisce modos, amanda
35   voce quos reddas; minuentur atrae
         carmine curae.

25 ff. terret: cf. the position of *monet* 1, 18, 8. — **ambustus Phaethon**: cf. 2, 4, 10 *ademptus Hector*. — **ales**: *winged*; cf. 1, 2, 42. — **terrenum**: *earth-born*, and hence unfit for the heavens to which he attempted to fly on Pegasus. — **gravatus**: transitive. — **Bellerophontem**: used by Pindar *I.* 6, 44 ff. and later writers as an example of the punishment which falls on overvaulting ambition.

29 ff. ut sequare, etc.: following on **exemplum**. — **te**: with **digna**. — **putando**: the ablative of the gerund here approaches the meaning of the present participle.

— **disparem**: euphemistic in place of *superiorem*. — **age iam**, etc.: 'come, do not waste thought on what is hopeless.'

32. finis amorum: Horace never loved very deeply and could not declare with Propertius 1, 12, 19 f. *mi neque amare aliam neque ab hac discedere fas est; | Cynthia prima fuit, Cynthia finis erit.*

33 ff. calebo: cf. 1, 4, 19. — **condisce**: *i.e.* under my teaching. — **reddas**: cf. n. to 4, 6, 43. — **minuentur**, etc.: cf. the prescription Nemesian. 4, 19 *cantet amat quod quisque: levant et carmina curas.*

12

On the return of Spring. 'The breezes of the Spring are here again; the mourning swallow builds her nest; the shepherds pipe their songs once more (1-12). It is the thirsty season, Vergil. If thou wouldst drink a cup of choice wine at my house, bring a box of precious nard with thee. Let go thy cares and give thyself up to our revel (13-28).'

This is the third of Horace's poems on this theme; but whereas in the others (1, 4 and 4, 7) he employs the changes of the year to remind us of the fleeting character of life, here he gives the matter a more cheerful turn with only a glance (v. 26) at the gloomy world below. The invitation is not unlike that of Catullus (*C.* 13) to his friend Fabullus to dine with him and provide all the entertainment save the unguent only.

The Vergil addressed cannot be the poet, who died in 19 B.C.; but we know nothing more of him than the ode tells us. Some critics think that the similarity of v. 21 to v. 13 f. of the preceding ode shows that they were written at about the same time. Metre, 72.

> Iam veris comites, quae mare temperant,
> impellunt animae lintea Thraciae;
> iam nec prata rigent nec fluvii strepunt
>   hiberna nive turgidi.
>
> 5   Nidum ponit, Ityn flebiliter gemens,
> infelix avis et Cecropiae domus

1 f. Cf. Meleager *Anth. Pal.* 9, 363, 9 f. ἤδη δὲ πλώουσιν ἐπ' εὐρέα κύματα ναῦται | πνοιῇ ἀπημάντῳ Ζεφύρου λίνα κολπώσαντες. — **veris comites**: in apposition with **animae ... Thraciae**. — **temperant**: *quiet*; cf. 3, 19, 6. — **animae**: only here in Horace for *venti.* Cf. Vergil *A.* 8, 403 *quantum ignes animaeque valent.* — **Thraciae**: apparently the Zephyrus. The epithet is purely conventional, adopted from Homer. Some editors take it to be the north winds. Cf. Colum. 11, 2 *venti septentrionales, qui vocantur Ornitheae, per dies XXX* (i.e. from about Feb. 20) *esse solent, tum et hirundo advenit.*

5. **Ityn**: the son of Procne and Tereus. The mother slew her son and served him up at table to his father to avenge the latter's outrage of Philomela, Procne's sister. When Tereus discovered the horrible deceit that had been practiced on him, he and the two sisters were changed into birds; Procne became a swallow, and Philomela a nightingale, according to the form of the myth which Horace seems to follow here. The swallow is the proverbial messenger of spring with both Greeks and Romans, so there seems little doubt that this bird is meant by **infelix avis**. — **flebiliter**: *piteously.*

6 ff. **Cecropiae**: Procne was the daughter of Pandion, king of

aeternum opprobrium, quod male barbaras
regum est ulta libidines.

Dicunt in tenero gramine pinguium
10   custodes ovium carmina fistula
delectantque deum cui pecus et nigri
colles Arcadiae placent.

Adduxere sitim tempora, Vergili;
sed pressum Calibus ducere Liberum
15   si gestis, iuvenum nobilium cliens,
nardo vina merebere.

Nardi parvus onyx eliciet cadum,
qui nunc Sulpiciis accubat horreis,
spes donare novas largus amaraque
20   curarum eluere efficax.

Athens. — **male**: with **ulta**, *took an unnatural revenge on*, etc. — **regum**: generalizing plural, as *virginum* 3, 27, 38.

9 ff. **dicunt**: cf. 1, 6, 5. — **tenero**: as it is early spring. — **fistula**: instrumental abl.; cf. 3, 4, 1 f. *dic age tibia . . . longum melos*. — **deum**: Pan, the Arcadian god. — **nigri colles**: cf. 1, 21, 7 *nigris Erymanthi silvis*.

14 ff. **pressum Calibus**; cf. 1, 20, 9 and n. — **ducere**: *quaff*; 1, 17, 22. — **iuvenum nobilium cliens**: who the *iuvenes nobiles* were we have no means of knowing; but the purpose of introducing this phrase is to imply, 'At the tables of your noble patrons you are entertained scot-free, but at mine you must pay.' — **nardo**: cf. n. to 2, 11, 16. — **vina**: plural as 4, 5,

31 and frequently. — **merebere**: the future of mild command.

17. **onyx**: usually masculine, as here; a small flask to hold ointment, so named since such receptacles were originally made of alabaster. Cf. *St. Mark* 14. 3 'As he sat at meat, there came a woman having an alabaster cruse of ointment of spikenard very costly; and she brake the cruse and poured it on his head.' The adjective **parvus** emphasizes the cost of the ointment. — **eliciet**: personifying the **cadus**; cf. 3, 21, 1 ff

18 ff. **Sulpiciis . . . horreis**: storehouses on the river at the foot of the Aventine. — **donare** . . . **largus**: *generous in giving*. Intr. 108. — **amara curarum**: cf. 2, 1, 23 *cuncta terrarum*. — **eluere efficax**: Intr. 108.

Ad quae si properas gaudia, cum tua
velox merce veni; non ego te meis
immunem meditor tinguere poculis,
    plena dives ut in domo.

25 Verum pone moras et studium lucri,
nigrorumque memor, dum licet, ignium
misce stultitiam consiliis brevem:
    dulce est desipere in loco.

21 ff. **properas**: *art eager*, not of physical hurry. — **merce**: *i.e.* the nard. — **immunem**: the Greek ἀσύμβολον, *scot-free, without bringing your share.*—**tinguere**: colloquial; cf. Alcaeus *Frg.* 39 τέγγε πνεύμονα οἴνῳ. — **plena...domo**: cf. 2, 12, 24.

25 ff. **verum**: dropping his jocose manner. The word is found only here in the lyrical poems. — **nigrorum**: cf. 1, 24, 18 and n. — **misce stultitiam**, etc.: cf Menander's precept οὐ πανταχοῦ τὸ φρόνιμον ἁρμόττει παρόν, καὶ συμμανῆναι δ' ἔνια δεῖ. — **in loco**: *on occasion*; ἐν καιρῷ. Cf. Ter. *Adelphi* 216 *pecúniam in locó neclegere máximum interdúmst lucrum.*

13

In mockery to a faded courtesan. The subject of the ode is similar to that of 1, 25 and 3, 15. This Lyce can hardly be the same as the Lyce of 3, 10; and we can only guess how much of the ode represents any real experience. Metre, 73.

    Audivere, Lyce, di mea vota, di
    audivere, Lyce: fis anus; et tamen
        vis formosa videri,
            ludisque et bibis impudens

5   et cantu tremulo pota Cupidinem
    lentum sollicitas. Ille virentis et

1 f. **audivere ... audivere**: exultant repetition. — **vota**: *i.e. devotiones*; cf. n. to 2, 8, 6.

4 f. **ludis**: cf. 3, 15, 5. — **tremulo**: with old age and wine.

— **pota**: cf. 3, 15, 16. — **lentum**: *slow in coming, unresponsive.* — **ille virentis**, etc.: cf. Aristaenet. 2, 1 ἀπηνθηκότι σώματι οὐ πέφυκε προσιζάνειν ὁ Ἔρως·

doctae psallere Chiae
  pulchris excubat in genis;

importunus enim transvolat aridas
10 quercus et refugit te quia luridi
  dentes, te quia rugae
    turpant et capitis nives;

nec Coae referunt iam tibi purpurae
nec cari lapides tempora quae semel
15   notis condita fastis
    inclusit volucris dies.

Quo fugit venus, heu, quove color, decens
quo motus? Quid habes illius, illius,
  quae spirabat amores,
20   quae me surpuerat mihi,

οὗ δ᾽ ἂν εὐανθές τε καὶ εὐῶδες ᾖ, ἐνταῦθα καὶ ἐνιζάνει καὶ μένει. 'Love is not wont to rest upon a form from which the flower of beauty has already fled; but where fair bloom and fragrance sweet exist, there he lights and ever stays.' — **Chiae**: this name is found on inscriptions of freedwomen. — **excubat**: *keeps vigil on*.

9 ff. **importunus**: *rude, ruthless*. — **aridas**: in contrast with virentis v. 6. Cf. also n. on *sucus* 3, 27, 54. — **quercus**: typical of long life. — **te**: object alike of refugit and turpant, as the repeated te makes clear. — **capitis nives**: if this metaphor was not invented by Horace, it certainly is not much older. Quintilian 8, 6, 17 condemns the figure as far fetched; *sunt et durae (translationes), id est a longinqua similitudine ductae ut capitis nives*. To us it is common as snow itself, which Romans saw much less often.

13 ff. **Coae**: the famous semi-transparent silk of Cos was a favorite stuff with women of Lyce's class. — **notis condita fastis**: *i.e.* 'your years are safely stored away and all can read the record; you cannot hope to hide them.' — **volucris dies**: cf. 3, 28, 6 and 4, 7, 8 *rapit hora diem*.

18 ff. **illius, illius**: *of her, of her*; partitive with **quid**. — **spirabat amores**: cf. *Epist.* 2, 1, 166 *nam spirat tragicum satis*. Intr. 86. — **surpuerat**: by syncope for the common *surripuerat*

felix post Cinaram notaque et artium
gratarum facies? Sed Cinarae brevis
   annos fata dederunt,
      servatura diu parem

25 cornicis vetulae temporibus Lycen,
possent ut iuvenes visere fervidi
   multo non sine risu
      dilapsam in cineres facem.

21 f. felix post: *happy and fortunate next to*, etc. — Cinaram: cf. 4, 1, 4 and n. — nota: with facies, *a vision known* (to all). — artium gratarum: genitive of quality. Cf. 4, 1, 15 *centum puer artium.*

24 f. servatura: almost adversative, *yet bound to keep.* — parem: proleptic, *to match.* — cornicis vetulae: cf. 3, 17, 13 *annosa cornix* and n. — temporibus: *the years.*

26 ff. fervidi: youths in whom the fire of passion burns fiercely, contrasted with Lyce, whose fire has become ashes. — non sine: cf. n. to 1, 23, 3. — dilapsam: crumbled; cf. Meleager *Anth. Pal.* 12, 41, 1 f. πυραυγὴς πρίν ποτε, νῦν δ' ἤδη δαλός Ἀπολλόδοτος. 'Once bright as flame, but now at last a burned-out torch is Apollodotus.'

14

The following ode is written ostensibly to celebrate the exploits of Tiberius in his campaign of 15 B.C. against the Tirolese tribes. (See intr. n. to 4, 4). In reality the greater part of the ode is occupied with the glorification of Augustus' service to the state.

'How can the senate and the people honor thee enough or worthily transmit thy memory to posterity, Augustus? Under thy auspices Drusus overcame the savage Alpine peoples, and Tiberius drove the Raeti before him, even as Auster drives the stormy waters, or Aufidus pours its torrent on the fertile plain (1-34). It was on the day of Alexandria's fall that fortune bestowed this new honor (35-40). Thou art recognized as lord by all the world, the peoples of the farthest West and East, the South and North alike (41-52).'

It should be noted that while Tiberius was only alluded to in the fourth ode, here Drusus is distinctly mentioned, although Tiberius is given the greater prominence. This partiality toward the younger of the brothers may have been intended to please Augustus, with whom Drusus was more of a favorite than his brother. The position of the ode in the book is thought by many to be due to the same cause; but it is more probable that Horace placed it and its companion ode, the fifteenth, at the end, that he might close the book with the Emperor's praise. The date of composition must be about the same as that of the fourth ode, *i.e.* 14 B.C. Metre, 68.

> Quae cura patrum quaeve Quiritium
> plenis honorum muneribus tuas,
>   Auguste, virtutes in aevum
>   per titulos memoresque fastos
>
> 5   aeternet, o qua sol habitabilis
> inlustrat oras maxime principum?
>   Quem legis expertes Latinae
>   Vindelici didicere nuper
>
>   quid Marte posses. Milite nam tuo
> 10   Drusus Genaunos, implacidum genus,
>   Breunosque velocis et arcis
>   Alpibus impositas tremendis

1 f. **patrum . . . Quiritium**: a poetic turn for the official *senatus populusque Romanus*. — **plenis**: *adequate*.

4. **titulos**: inscriptions on statues, honorary decrees, etc. — **memoresque fastos**: repeated from 3, 17, 4.

5. **o qua sol**, etc.: the whole inhabitable world.

7 f. **quem didicere . . . quid posses**: this Greek construction is found in the lyrics only here and v. 17 **spectandus . . . quantis**, etc. — **legis expertes**: *i.e.* not yet brought under our rule. — **Vindelici**: cf. introductory n. to 4, 4. — **nuper**: referring to Drusus' victory near Tridentum. The adverb helps fix the date of composition.

9 ff. **Marte**: cf. 3, 5, 24. 34. — **milite**: cf. 1, 15, 6 and v. 33 below. — **Genaunos, Breunos**: two Raetian tribes living in the valley of the river Inn. The latter tribe gave its name to the Brenner Pass. — **implacidum**: first found here. — **velocis**: *quick, agile;* a characteristic of mountaineers. — **arcis . . . impositas**: repeated by Horace *Epist.* 2, 1, 252.

deiecit acer plus vice simplici;
maior Neronum mox grave proelium
   commisit immanisque Raetos
auspiciis pepulit secundis,

spectandus in certamine Martio,
devota morti pectora liberae
   quantis fatigaret ruinis,
      indomitas prope qualis undas

exercet Auster Pleiadum choro
scindente nubis, impiger hostium
   vexare turmas et frementem
mittere equum medios per ignis.

Sic tauriformis volvitur Aufidus,

13. **deiecit**: especially applicable to the mountain citadels, but belonging by a slight zeugma to Genaunos, Breunos also. — **vice**: *requital; i.e.* they suffered greater losses than they had themselves caused.

14 ff. **maior Neronum**: cf. n. to 4, 4, 28. The name Tiberius cannot be employed in Alcaic verse. — **mox**: Tiberius' attack from the north followed Drusus' successes. — **immanis**: *monstrous* (in their cruelty). The savagery of the Alpine tribesmen is described by Strabo 4, 6, 8.

17. **spectandus**: cf. n. to v. 7 above. The gerundive is equivalent to *dignus qui spectaretur*; cf. 4, 2, 9 *donandus*. Observe that the verse lacks the caesura. Intr. 50.

18 ff. **morti . . . liberae**: *a freeman's death*. — **ruinis**; *shocks, blows*. — **indomitas prope qualis**, etc.: the comparison is twofold — Tiberius is likened to the *Auster*, his foes to the invincible waves. Strictly speaking, of course, the Raeti were not *indomiti*. — **prope**: prosaically qualifying the simile; cf. *S.* 2, 3, 268 *tempestatis prope ritu.*

21 ff. **exercet**: *vexes*. — **Pleiadum choro**: the constellation set in November, a stormy month. — **nubis**: *i.e. the (drifting) stormclouds.* — **vexare**: for the mood, see Intr. 108. — **medios per ignes**: may be taken literally of the burning villages, or metaphorically of extreme danger. Cf. Sil. Ital. 14, 175 f. *si tibi per medios ignis mediosque per ensis | non dederit mea dextra viam.*

25 ff. **sic . . . ut**: an unusual inversion by which the subject of the comparison occupies the relative clause. — **tauriformis**: the Greek

qui regna Dauni praefluit Apuli,
  cum saevit horrendamque cultis
    diluviem meditatur agris,

ut barbarorum Claudius agmina
  ferrata vasto diruit impetu,
    primosque et extremos metendo
      stravit humum, sine clade victor,

te copias, te consilium et tuos
  praebente divos. Nam tibi, quo die
    portus Alexandrea supplex
      et vacuam patefecit aulam,

Fortuna lustro prospera tertio
  belli secundos reddidit exitus,

ταυρόμορφος. Such compounds are very rare in Horace.—**Aufidus**: a favorite illustration. Cf. 3, 30, 10; 4, 9, 2.

26. **Dauni**: cf. n. to 1, 22, 14. —**praefluit**: cf. 4, 3, 10 and n.— **diluviem**: *flood*; cf. 3, 29, 40.

29 ff. **Claudius**: *i.e.* Tiberius. —**ferrata**: *mail clad.* The use of mail by the Germanic and Gallic tribes is not stated before Tacitus *Ann.* 3, 43, 3 (he is speaking of Gauls) *quibus more gentico continuum ferri tegimen.*— **diruit**: properly of razing buildings; here the mailed ranks of the enemy are likened to a fortress.— **primos et extremos**: *i.e.* the entire army.— **metendo**: see n. to 4, 11, 30 for this use of gerund; for the figurative use, cf. Verg. *A.* 10, 513 *proxuma quaeque metit gladio.*

32. **stravit humum**: *i.e.* with their corpses. — **sine clade victor**: Velleius 1, 95 says that the victory was won *maiore cum periculo quam damno Romani exercitus.*

33. **te . . . te . . . tuos**: Intr. 28 c.

34 ff. **nam**, etc.: explaining **tuos . . . divos**; *i.e.* 'since the day, when Alexandria fell, the gods have smiled on all thy undertakings and have granted this last success.' —**quo die**: we need not suppose that the victory in the Alps fell exactly on Aug. 1, the probable date of Alexandria's surrender. — **vacuam**: made so by the death of Cleopatra.

37 ff. **lustro . . . tertio**: abl. of time completed. —**reddidit**: *gave as thy due.*— **laudem**: in the recognition of Rome's power by the

laudemque et optatum peractis
imperiis decus adrogavit.

Te Cantaber non ante domabilis
Medusque et Indus, te profugus Scythes
   miratur, o tutela praesens
      Italiae dominaeque Romae;

te fontium qui celat origines
Nilusque et Hister, te rapidus Tigris,
   te beluosus qui remotis
      obstrepit Oceanus Britannis,

te non paventis funera Galliae
duraeque tellus audit Hiberiae,

remote peoples named below. — **adrogavit**: *has bestowed.*

41 ff. Augustus' world-wide dominion. — **te, te,** etc.: the multifold repetition keeps the subject constantly before us. Cf. n. to 1, 10, 17. — **Cantaber**: cf. n. to 2, 6, 2. — **Medus**: cf. n. to 1, 2, 22. — **Indus**: cf. 1, 12, 56. — **tutela**: here active, *protector;* cf. its use 4, 6, 33. — **praesens**: cf. 3, 5, 2. — **dominae**: *imperial;* cf. 4, 3, 13 *Romae principis urbium.*

45. qui celat origines: the sources of the Nile were not discovered until the nineteenth century, so that they were long a synonym for unknown and remotest regions. Cf. Lucan 10, 189 ff. where Caesar says *nihil est quod noscere malim | quam fluvii causas per saecula tanta latentis | ignotumque caput; spes sit mihi certa videndi | Nili-*

acos fontes, bellum civile relinquam. In 20 B.C., when Augustus was in Samos, an embassy of Ethiopians visited him. For the use of the river to designate the people living by it, cf. n. to 2, 20, 20.

46 ff. Hister: the Dacians. — **Tigris**: the Armenians. — **beluosus**: *teeming with monsters.* The word is not found after Horace until Avienus in the 4th century. It reproduces the Homeric μεγακήτεα πόντον. — **obstrepit**: *that roars against.* Cf. 2, 18, 20. — **Britannis**: some of the chiefs of Britain had sought protection from Augustus (Strabo 4, 5, 3).

49. non paventis funera: the Gallic indifference to death was attributed by the Romans to Druidical teachings as to the immortality of the soul. Cf. Caes. *B. G.* 6, 14. 5 *in primis hoc volunt per-*

[4, 14, 51]   HORATI

    te caede gaudentes Sygambri
    compositis venerantur armis.

suadere, non interire animas....   51. **Sygambri**: the list closes
atque hoc maxime ad virtutem exci-   with a people lately subdued. See
tare putant, metu mortis neglecto.   intr. n. to 4, 2.

15

The closing ode of the book is appropriately given to the praise of Augustus alone. It stands in the same close relation to 14 that 5 does to 4. (See the introductions to these odes.)

'When I would sing the deeds of war, Apollo checked my course. My song shall rather be of thy age, Caesar, which has brought back peace and its blessings, and recalled the ancient virtues which built our empire from the rising to the setting sun (1-16). So long as Caesar guards our state, no fear of civil strife or foreign foe shall vex our peace (17-24). And every day over our wine, with wives and children by, we'll pray the gods in forms prescribed, and hymn the great ones of our past, kindly Venus' line (25-32).'

It should be noted that this ode like 5 extols Augustus as the restorer of peace and morality, while 4 and 14 glorify his success in war. In date of composition it is probably the latest of all; the fact that no mention is made of Augustus' return to Rome on July 4, 13 B.C., or of the honors planned for his return, makes it very probable that it was written before that date, approximately toward the end of 14 B.C. Metre, 68.

    Phoebus volentem proelia me loqui
    victas et urbis increpuit lyra,

1 f. **Phoebus**, etc.: possibly in imitation of Verg. *E.* 6. 3 f. *cum canerem reges et proelia, Cynthius aurem | vellit et admonuit.* Ovid makes a similar apology for his *Amores,* 1, 1, 1 ff. *arma gravi numero violentaque bella parabam | edere, materia conveniente modis ; | par erat inferior versus ; risisse Cupido | dicitur atque unum surripuisse pedem.* — **proelia ... loqui,** etc.: *i.e.* sing of epic themes, for which Horace had again and again declared his unfitness. On the use of *loqui,* cf. n. to 4, 2, 45. — **increpuit**: *checked and warned me,* etc. — **lyra**: Porphyrio connected this with **loqui,** which then means 'handle epic themes in lyric verse'; but it is more natural to read it with **increpuit.** both from its position and because the lyre is Apollo's

>   ne parva Tyrrhenum per aequor
>   vela darem. Tua, Caesar, aetas
> 5   fruges et agris rettulit uberes
>   et signa nostro restituit Iovi
>   derepta Parthorum superbis
>   postibus et vacuum duellis
>
>   Ianum Quirini clausit et ordinem
> 10   rectum evaganti frena licentiae

natural instrument for arousing and directing his subjects. Cf. 2, 10, 18 *quondam cithara tacentem suscitat musam ... Apollo.* Also Ovid. *A. A.* 2, 493 f. *haec ego cum canerem subito manifestus Apollo | movit inauratae pollice fila lyrae.*

3 f. The metaphor is common for bold undertakings; cf. *e.g.* Prop. 4, 9, 3 f. *quid me scribendi tam vastum mittis in aequor? | non sunt apta meae grandia vela rati.* — **parva**: as befitting his lyric verse. Cf. 1, 6, 9 *tenues grandia,* etc. — **tua aetas**: the abruptness of the transition brings these words into special prominence as the theme which Apollo assigns.

5. **fruges**, etc.: cf. n. to 4, 5, 18. — **et ... et**, etc.; the polysyndeton in the following three strophes gives a cumulative force to this recital of the blessings of Augustus' rule.

6 ff. **signa**: restored in 20 B.C., when the Parthian king was distressed by domestic troubles and overawed by Augustus' preparations for an expedition against him. — **nostro ... Iovi**: *i.e.* Capitoline Jove. It is conjectured from this passage that the standards were deposited in the temple on the Capitol until transferred to the temple of Mars Ultor, dedicated in 2 B.C. Horace's words, however, do not necessitate this conclusion. — **derepta**: poetic exaggeration. — **postibus**: of their temples. — **duellis**: cf. 3, 5, 38 and n.

9 f. **Ianum Quirini**: a variation of the common *Ianum Quirinum*, the name given the temple as well as the god. The shrine stood near the north end of the Forum. — **clausit**: in 29 and 25 B.C. The gates had then not been closed since the end of the First Punic War. They were shut a third time during Augustus' rule, but the exact year is not known. When Horace wrote the gates were open. — **evaganti**: transitive. Intr. 86. — **frena**, etc.: Horace's hope expressed 3, 24, 28 f. is fulfilled. With the expression, cf. Val. Max. 2, 9. 5 *freni sunt iniecti vobis, Quirites: lex enim lata est, quae vos esse frugi iubet.*

iniecit emovitque culpas
et veteres revocavit artes,

per quas Latinum nomen et Italae
crevere vires famaque et imperi
porrecta maiestas ad ortus
solis ab Hesperio cubili.

Custode rerum Caesare non furor
civilis aut vis exiget otium,
non ira, quae procudit ensis
et miseras inimicat urbis.

Non qui profundum Danuvium bibunt
edicta rumpent Iulia, non Getae,
non Seres infidive Persae,
non Tanain prope flumen orti.

12. artes: *the virtues*; cf. 3, 3, 9. With these statements, cf. Augustus' claims *Mon. Anc.* 2, 12 *legibus novis latis multa revocavi exempla maiorum exolescentia.*

13 ff. Latinum nomen, Italae vires, imperi maiestas: the three steps of Roman dominion. — **nomen**: cf. 3, 3, 45. — **fama**: modified by **imperi**. — **porrecta**: participle, *which has been*, etc. — **ad ortus**, etc.: cf. *e.g.* Tib. 2, 5, 57 *Roma, tuum nomen terris fatale regendis, | qua sua de caelo prospicit arva Ceres, | quaque patent ortus et qua fluitantibus undis | sous anhelantes abluit amnis equos.*

17 ff. A similar passage to 3, 14, 14 ff. — **non . . . non**, etc.: the effect of the anaphora in the two following strophes is like that secured by the polysyndeton in the three preceding. — **furor**: *madness*; cf. *Epist.* 2, 2, 47 *civilis aestus*. — **ira**: cf. 1, 16, 9 ff. — **inimicat**: a compound coined by Horace.

21 ff. qui profundum Danuvium bibunt: the peoples living by the Danube had not been reduced to complete submission at the time Horace wrote; that was accomplished later. All Horace means is that they were at peace with Rome. — **edicta . . . Iulia**: not in a technical, but a general sense. — *the terms set by Augustus*. — **Getae**: cf. 3, 24, 11. — **Seres**: cf. n. to 1, 12, 56. — **infidi**: cf. *Epist.* 2, 1, 112 *Parthis mendacior.* — **Persae**: 1, 2, 22. — **Tanain prope flumen orti**: cf. 3, 29, 28. This

Nosque et profestis lucibus et sacris
inter iocosi munera Liberi,
    cum prole matronisque nostris
    rite deos prius adprecati,

virtute functos more patrum duces
Lydis remixto carmine tibiis
    Troiamque et Anchisen et almae
    progeniem Veneris canemus.

list of peoples should be compared with that in 4, 14, 41–52. It will be noted that none of the peoples here named were actually subject to Rome; but as remote nations which had more or less dealings with Rome, they appealed to the Roman imagination.

25 ff. nos: marking the shift to the Romans' own happy lot. — **et profestis . . . et sacris**: *i.e.* every day alike. — **lucibus**: cf. 4, 6, 42; 11, 19. — **iocosi munera Liberi**: the Hesiodic δῶρα Διωνύσου πολυγηθέος. Cf. 1, 18, 7. — **cum prole**, etc.: each in his own home. — **rite**: in prescribed fashion.

29. virtute functos: varying the common *vita functos*; cf. 2, 18, 38 *laboribus functos*. Translate, *who have done their noble work*. — **more patrum**: modifying *canemus*. The custom of extolling the virtues of their ancestors in song at banquets was an ancient one among the Romans, according to Cato. Cf. Cic. *Tusc.* 4, 3 *in Originibus dixit Cato morem apud maiores hunc epularum fuisse, ut deinceps qui accubarent canerent ad tibiam clarorum virorum laudes atque virtutes.*

30 ff. Lydis: apparently a purely ornamental epithet. — **remixto**: an unusual word. — **tibiis**: dative. — **Anchisen et . . . progeniem Veneris**: *i.e.* the long line descended from Anchises and Venus; but the special reference is obviously to Augustus, as in *C. S.* 50 *clarus Anchisae Venerisque sanguis.*

CARMEN SAECVLARE

Horace's preëminent art was officially recognized in 17 B.C. by his appointment to write the hymn for the celebration of the *ludi saeculares*. This festival originated in a worship of the gods of the lower world by the *gens Valeria* at a spot in the Campus Martius called Terentum (or Tarentum), near the bend in the river not far below the present Ponte San Angelo. In 249 B.C., after the defeat at Drepanum, some fearful portents prompted a consultation of the Sibylline Books: these ordered a celebration of the *ludi Terentini*, and further directed that the festival should be repeated every hundred years. Thus the gentile cult became a national one. The second celebration was not in 149 but 146 B.C.; the confusion of 49 B.C. must have prevented any thought of the *ludi* in that year. Apparently Augustus thought of a similar festival in honor of Apollo and Diana for 23 B.C.; this undoubtedly would have taken the form of an appeal to these divinities to avert the misfortune which then threatened the state and the emperor — the bad harvest with its attendant hardship and Augustus' sickness (cf. Intr. n. to I, 21 and n. to I, 21, 6). For some unknown reason the celebration was deferred. The year 17, however, marked the close of the decade for which Augustus in January, 27 B.C., had undertaken the direction of the state. In this ten years the Roman world had revived under the blessings of peace and had seemed to enter on a new era. Augustus proposed to celebrate the close of this period by a revival of the *ludi saeculares* in new and magnificent form.

To obtain religious sanction for his plan he applied to the *quindecimviri*, the college in charge of the Sibylline Books, who took 110 years as the length of the *saeculum*, — antiquarians differed as to whether 100 or 110 years was the correct number, — and on this basis pointed to four previous dates for celebrations beginning with 456 B.C.; the one proposed by Augustus was then the fifth, and fell in the last year of the *saeculum* instead of at its close. Claudius celebrated the festival in 47 A.D., taking the traditional date of the founding of the city as his starting point and reckoning a *saeculum* as 100 years; Domitian's celebration was in 88 A.D.; that of Antoninus Pius, in 147, marked the close of the city's ninth century. Later celebrations were by Septimius Severus in 204; by Philip in 248 in honor of the completion of the first millennium of the state. Whether there were celebrations by Gallienus in 257 or by Maximian in 304 is uncertain. They were revived by Pope Boniface as papal jubilees in 1300.

Augustus, however, made important changes in the nature of the festival. Hitherto it had been a propitiatory offering to the gods of the lower world; now it became rather a festival of thanksgiving for present blessings and of prayer for the continuance of them forever. Pluto and Proserpina were not mentioned, but Apollo and Diana had the most prominent place. Jupiter and Juno were also honored. Zosimus (2, 5) has preserved for us an account of the celebration and the oracle which contains directions for it. This oracle in its present detailed form was unquestionably written for the festival or after it, but is probably based on an earlier production. After the celebration was past, two pillars, one marble, the other bronze, inscribed with a complete record, were erected at the spot Terentum; in 1890 some fragments of the marble pillar were recovered and are now preserved in the Museo delle Therme which occupies a portion of the remains of the baths of Diocletian.[1] These fragments and literary notices, especially Zosimus, enable us to trace the course of the festival clearly. The celebration proper began on the evening before June 1; but on May 26-28 the magistrates distributed to all citizens who applied *suffimenta*, pitchpine, sulphur, and bitumen, for purposes of purification; May 29-31 the citizens brought contributions of grain to the officials to be used by them in paying the musicians and actors.

The festival itself lasted three nights and days: the nocturnal sacrifices were at Terentum; the ceremonies by day were at the temples of the several divinities. Augustus, assisted by Agrippa, conducted the entire celebration. On the first night nine black ewe lambs and nine she-goats were burnt whole in sacrifice to the *Parcae* (*C. S.* 25 ff.); on the following night consecrated cakes were offered to the *Ilithyiae*

---

[1] The inscription is best edited by Mommsen in the *Ephemeris Epigraphica*, 1891, pp. 225-274. For accounts of the festival see also Lanciani in the *Atlantic Monthly*, February, 1892; Slaughter, *Transactions of the Am. Phil. Association*, 1895, pp. 69-78; and *Harper's Classical Dictionary*, p. 974 f.

(*C. S.* 13 ff.) ; and on the third night a sow big with young was sacrificed to *Tellus* (*C. S.* 29 ff.).[1]

After the sacrifice of the first night, scenic representations were begun on a stage without seats for the audience, and continued uninterruptedly throughout the festival; beginning with the first day, however, they were given in a theater erected for the occasion (*ludi Latini in theatro ligneo quod erat constitutum in campo secundum Tiberim*).

On the first day Augustus and Agrippa each sacrificed a white bull to Jupiter on the Capitol, and the following day each a white cow to Juno in the same place; on the third day, when the festival reached its climax, Augustus and Agrippa offered consecrated cakes to Apollo and Diana at the temple of Apollo on the Palatine (cf. introductory n. to 1. 31); and then twenty-seven boys and a like number of girls, especially chosen for this service, sang the hymn which Horace had written for the occasion, and repeated it on the Capitol (*sacrificioque perfecto pueri XXVII quibus denuntiatum et puellae totidem carmen cecinerunt; eodemque modo in Capitolio. Carmen composuit Q. Horatius Flaccus*). In addition to these ceremonies 110 matrons conducted *sellesternia* to Juno and Diana on each day; and *ludi circenses* and *ludi honorarii* were continued seven days (June 4–11) after the close of the festival.[2]

The ode itself lacks the grace and ease of most of Horace's lyric verse; its formal phrases when read seem stiff and rigid. Doubtless

---

[1] The verses of the oracle ordering these ceremonies are as follows: —

μεμνῆσθαι, Ῥωμαῖε, . . .
ῥέζειν ἐν πεδίῳ παρὰ Θύβριδος ἄπλετον ὕδωρ,
ὅππη στεινότατον, νὺξ ἡνίκα γαῖαν ἐπέλθῃ,
ἠελίου κρύψαντος ἑὸν φάος· ἔνθα σὺ ῥέζειν
ἱερὰ παντογόνοις Μοίραις ἄρνας τε καὶ αἶγας
κυανέας, ἐπὶ ταῖς δ' Εἰλειθυίας ἀρέσασθαι
παιδοτόκους θυέεσσιν, ὅπη θέμις· αὖθι δὲ Γαίῃ
πληθομένῃ χοίροις ὗς ἱρεύοιτο μέλαινα.

[2] The oracle prescribes these rites also in detail: —

πάνλευκοι ταῦροι δὲ Διὸς παρὰ βωμὸν ἀγέσθων
ἤματι μηδ' ἐπὶ νυκτί· . . .
. . . δαμάλης δὲ βοὸς δέμας ἀγλαὸν Ἥρης
δεξάσθω νηὸς παρὰ σεῦ. καὶ Φοῖβος Ἀπόλλων,
ὅστε καὶ ἠέλιος κικλήσκεται, ἴσα δεδέχθω
θύματα Λητοΐδης. καὶ ἀειδόμενοί τε Λατῖνοι
παιᾶνες κούροισι κόρησί τε νηὸν ἔχοιεν
ἀθανάτων. χωρὶς δὲ κόραι χορὸν αὐταὶ ἔχοιεν,
καὶ χωρὶς παίδων ἄρσην στάχυς, ἀλλὰ γονήων
πάντες ζωόντων, οἷς ἀμφιθαλὴς ἔτι φύτλη,
αἱ δὲ γάμου ζεύγλαισι δεδμημέναι ἤματι κείνῳ
γνὺξ Ἥρης παρὰ βωμὸν ἀοίδιμον ἱδρυόωσαι
δαίμονα λισσέσθωσαν.

this was intentional and marked no falling off in Horace's skill as a versifier. He saw that for this ceremonial occasion simplicity and dignity were of chief importance. Any just appreciation of the poem on our part must start with the consideration that it was written to be sung to musical accompaniment by a trained chorus in the open air before a large body of people. Thus performed it must have been beautiful and impressive. The ode is carefully polished; the number of feminine caesuras is striking. It is impossible to determine to-day with accuracy the way in which the strophes were assigned; it is probable that the first, second, and last were sung by the full chorus, and it is clear that vv. 33-34 belong to the boys, 35-36 to the girls. Beyond this all is mere conjecture. For the influence of the *Aeneid* in this ode, cf. n. to vv. 37 ff. Metre, 69.

> Phoebe silvarumque potens Diana,
> lucidum caeli decus, o colendi
> semper et culti, date quae precamur
> tempore sacro,
>
> 5   quo Sibyllini monuere versus
> virgines lectas puerosque castos
> dis quibus septem placuere colles
> dicere carmen.

1 ff. Phoebe ... Diana: the opening verse shows that these are the chief divinities of the festival. — **silvarum potens**: cf. 1, 3, 1 *diva potens Cypri, i.e.* Venus, and n. On Diana, goddess of the woods, cf. 1, 21, 5; 3, 22, 1. — **caeli decus**: *i.e.* as sun and moon; in apposition with both **Phoebe** and **Diana**. The phrase is repeated by Seneca *Oed.* 409; cf. also Verg. *A.* 9, 405 *astrorum decus et nemorum Latonia custos.* — **colendi ... culti**: almost a ritual expression, *ye, who are ever to be, and have ever been, worshipped.* Cf. Ovid *Met.* 8, 350 *Phoebe ... si te coluique coloque;* and Horace's own phrase, *Epist.* 1, 1, 1 *prima dicte mihi, summa dicende Camena (Maecenas).* — **semper**: with both colendi and culti.

5 ff. quo: with dicere. — **Sibyllini ... versus**: the older collections of Sibylline oracles were destroyed at the burning of the Capitol, 83 B.C. A new collection was made which was added to from time to time. The oracle preserved by Zosimus, as said above, was compiled after the details of the festival had been determined, or after the celebration itself. — **lectas, castos**: both ad-

Alme Sol, curru nitido diem qui
promis et celas, aliusque et idem
nasceris, possis nihil urbe Roma
    visere maius.

Rite maturos aperire partus
lenis, Ilithyia, tuere matres,
sive tu Lucina probas vocari
    seu Genitalis.

Diva, producas subolem patrumque
prosperes decreta super iugandis

jectives belong to each noun. Cf.
4, 6, 31 f. — **dis quibus**, etc. : the
guardian gods in general, not
limited to Apollo and Diana. —
placuere : *have found favor*; cf. 3,
4, 24.
    9 ff. Apollo as the sun god.
Cf. v. 16 f. of the oracle καὶ Φοῖβος
'Απόλλων | ὅστε καὶ ἠέλιος κικλή-
σκεται. — **alme**: cf. 4, 7, 7 *almum
diem*. — **alius et idem** : *another
and yet the same*. — **possis**: optative subj. — **nihil urbe**, etc. : cf.
Verg. *A*. 7, 602 f. *maxima rerum
Roma*, and Pausanias 8, 33, 3 with
reference to Babylon, Βαβυλῶνος
. . . ἥν τινα εἶδε πόλεων τῶν τότε
μεγίστην ἥλιος.
    12 ff. The goddess of child-
birth, Ilithyia (tacitly identified
with Diana). — **maturos**: *in due
season*. — **aperire** : with **lenis**,
which is a part of the prayer — *be
thou gentle*, etc. — **Ilithyia** : among
the Greeks we find now one, now
many, goddesses so called. In

the inscription we read *deis Ilithyis*
and in the oracle Εἰλειθυίας, but
the inscription gives the prayer
Ilithyia, uti tibei, etc. There can
be little question that the goddess
was identified with Diana, although
the adjective **Lucina** properly belongs to Juno ; **Genitalis** is apparently Horace's invention, possibly
to represent the Greek Γενετυλλίς.
    15 f. sive . . . seu : in early
Roman religion the divinities were
not clearly conceived : hence arose
the habit of addressing them in
prayers by various appellations
that they might not be offended,
*e.g. sive deus sive dea ; sive quo alio
nomine te appellari volueris*; etc.
    17 ff. producas : *rear*. — **de-
creta** : with reference to the *lex
Iulia de maritandis ordinibus*
passed the preceding year. This
was a law to discourage celibacy
and to encourage marriage and
raising of children (cf. 4, 5, 22 and
n.). — **super**: *in regard to*; cf.

     feminis prolisque novae feraci
20   lege marita,

     certus undenos deciens per annos
     orbis ut cantus referatque ludos,
     ter die claro totiensque grata
        nocte frequentis.

25   Vosque veraces cecinisse, Parcae,
     quod semel dictum est stabilisque rerum
     terminus servet, bona iam peractis
        iungite fata.

     Fertilis frugum pecorisque Tellus
30   spicea donet Cererem corona;

1, 9, 5. — **feraci**: part of the prayer — *which we pray may be productive of.*

21 ff. The purpose of the prayer in the preceding strophe, — 'grant us an abundant posterity that the festival may surely (**certus**) be repeated at the close of each *saeculum* by great throngs (**frequentis**) of citizens.' — **certus** : this with the last word of the strophe, **frequentis**, bears the emphasis. — **undenos**, etc. : a paraphrase for 110 years. — **per** : *extending through.* — **orbis** : *cycle.* — **ut** : for its position, see Intr. 31. — **frequentis** : modifying **ludos**.

25 ff. **veraces cecinisse** : *true in your past prophecies.* For the infinitive, see Intr. 108. Cf. 2, 16, 39 *Parca non mendax.* — **Parcae** : Μοῖραι in the inscription and oracle, to whom offerings were made on the first night. — **quod semel dictum est** : equivalent to *fatum*; **quod** does double duty as subject of **dictum est** and object of **servet**. We may translate, *as has been ordained once for all, and as we pray the fixed bound of events may keep it.* — **stabilis rerum terminus** is a paraphrase for 'destiny.' Cf. Verg. A. 4. 614 *et sic fata Iovis poscunt, hic terminus haeret.* — **servet** : optative subj. — **iam peractis** : *to those already passed; i.e.* in the *saeculum* just closed.

29 ff. **fertilis**, etc. : a part of the prayer. With the expression. cf. Sall. *Iug.* 17, 5 *ager frugum fertilis.* — **Tellus** : *Terra Mater* in the inscription. Sacrifice was made to her on the third night. — **spicea donet**. etc. : *i.e.* may the crops of grain be abundant. Cf.

nutriant fetus et aquae salubres
et Iovis aurae.

Condito mitis placidusque telo
supplices audi pueros, Apollo;
35   siderum regina bicornis audi,
Luna, puellas.

Roma si vestrum est opus Iliaeque
litus Etruscum tenuere turmae,
iussa pars mutare laris et urbem
40   sospite cursu,

cui per ardentem sine fraude Troiam
castus Aeneas patriae superstes

the prayer of Tibullus 1, 1, 15 *flava Ceres, tibi sit nostro de rure corona | spicea.* — **fetus**: restricted to the **fruges**, as the context clearly shows.

33 ff. In the previous strophes the divinities worshipped by night have been invoked; the hymn is now directed to the gods of light. This strophe forms the transition. — **condito mitis**, etc.: logically parallel to **audi**, — *replace thy weapon, be kind*, etc. — **telo**: *i.e.* his arrow. Apollo was represented in his temple on the Palatine (cf. 1, 29) as a gracious and kindly god, not armed but playing on the lyre. See Baumeister, no. 104.

35 f. siderum regina: cf. 1, 12, 47 f. — **bicornis**: *i.e.* of the crescent moon.

37 ff. The *Aeneid*, which had recently been published, supplied the theme of this and the following strophe. Horace appeals to the gods to protect their own creation. — **si**: the condition expresses no doubt, but has rather a causal force, — *if Rome is your work* (and it surely is); *i.e.* 'since Rome, etc.' — **vestrum**: not referring to Apollo and Diana of the preceding strophe, but meaning the great gods who cared for the destinies of the state. The vagueness of the adjective must be counted a defect. — **tenuere**: *gained.* — **pars**: *the remnant*; in apposition with **turmae**. — **laris**: 'their hearths and homes.'

41 f. fraude: harm. Cf. 2, 19, 20. — **castus**: and therefore saved while the wicked perished. Cf. with the epithet, Vergil's *pius*. — **patriae**: dative; cf. *Ep.* 5, 10.

liberum munivit iter, daturus
    plura relictis,

45 di, probos mores docili iuventae,
    di, senectuti placidae quietem,
    Romulae genti date remque prolemque
        et decus omne;

    quaeque vos bobus veneratur albis
50 clarus Anchisae Venerisque sanguis,
    impetret, bellante prior, iacentem
        lenis in hostem.

    Iam mari terraque manus potentis
    Medus Albanasque timet securis,
55 iam Scythae responsa petunt, superbi
        nuper, et Indi.

43 f. daturus: *destined to give.* — **plura relictis**: *i.e.* a city (Rome) greater than the one they had left.

45 ff. probos mores, etc.: one of Augustus' chief desires was to restore a healthy moral life. Cf. 3, 24, 25 ff.; 4, 5, 22 and nn. — **docili, placidae**: proleptic, belonging to the prayer. — **remque**, etc.: cf. Ovid *Fast.* 3, 86 *arma ferae genti remque decusque dabant.* — **prolemque**: hypermetric. Intr. 69.

49 ff. quae: with **veneratur**, *prays for with sacrifice of*, etc. — **bobus . . . albis**: offered to Jupiter on the first day, on the second to Juno. The prayer, preserved in the inscription, was for the safety and exaltation of the Roman state and its arms. — **clarus Anchisae**, etc. The phrase is a solemn paraphrase for Augustus, but at the same time it emphasized the connection of the present with the beginnings of the state (cf. **Romulae genti**). — **bellante prior**: continuing the prayer in **impetret**. With the sentiment, cf. Vergil *A.* 6, 853 *parcere subiectis et debellare superbos.*

53 ff. iam: marking the following as victories already secure. — **Medus, Scythae, Indi**: cf. 4, 15, 21 ff. and n. Also Ovid *Trist.* 2, 227 f. *nunc petit Armenius pacem, nunc porrigit arcus | Parthus eques timida captaque signa manu.* — **Albanas**: having the same connotation as **Romulae** v. 47, **Anchisae Venerisque** v. 50. — **responsa petunt**: as from a god. Cf.

Iam Fides et Pax et Honor Pudorque
priscus et neglecta redire Virtus
audet, adparetque beata pleno
60   Copia cornu.

Augur et fulgente decorus arcu
Phoebus acceptusque novem Camenis,
qui salutari levat arte fessos
   corporis artus,

65   si Palatinas videt aequus aras,
remque Romanam Latiumque felix
alterum in lustrum meliusque semper
   prorogat aevum;

quaeque Aventinum tenet Algidumque
70   quindecim Diana preces virorum

Apoll. Sid. *Epist.* 8, 9, 20 *dum responsa petit subactus orbis.*

57 ff. Peace and her companions. — **Fides**: cf. 1, 35, 21. — **Pax**: Peace had an altar on the Campus Martius, built at Augustus' direction. — **Honor**: to whom with *Virtus* Marcellus dedicated a temple in 205 B.C. — **Pudor**: cf. 1, 24, 6 f. — **Copia**: cf. 1, 17, 14.

61–72. The closing prayer is to Apollo, the augur, god of the silver bow, leader of the Muses, and god of healing. — **fulgente . . . arcu**: of silver; the Homeric ἀργυρότοξος. — **Camenis**: cf. 1, 12, 39.

63 f. qui salutari, etc.: Ἀπόλλων Παιών. Cf. 1, 21, 13 f.

65 ff. si: expressing the same confidence as in v. 37. — **Palatinas . . . aras**: where the hymn was sung. — **aequus**: *with favor*; cf. *iniquus* 1, 2, 47. — **remque Romanam Latiumque**: calling to mind Ennius' verse 478 M. *qui rem Romanam Latiumque augescere voltis.* — **felix**: proleptic with **Latium**, — *in prosperity.* — **que . . . que**: observe the archaic usage: the first -que does not connect **videt** and **prorogat**, but is correlative with the second. — **alterum**: *a new.* Augustus' imperium was renewed for five years in 17 B.C.: but the idea is rather, 'from lustrum to lustrum'; as **semper** clearly shows.

69 ff. Diana's chief temple at Rome was built on the Aventine at an early period — later tradition ascribed its founding to Servius Tullus — to be a common

curat et votis puerorum amicas
    adplicat auris.

Haec Iovem sentire deosque cunctos
spem bonam certamque domum reporto,
75   doctus et Phoebi chorus et Dianae
    dicere laudes.

sanctuary for the Latin tribes. — **Algidum**: the shrine of Diana Nemorensis was on the slopes of this ridge. Cf. n. to 1, 21, 6. — **quindecim ... virorum**: the sacred college in charge of the Sibylline Books: the members led by Augustus and Agrippa, had charge of all the ceremonies of the festival. — **puerorum**: the children, including both boys and girls, as in ancient usage. Cf. Naev. 30 M. *Cereris puer, Proserpina*.

73 ff. The hymn closes with an expression of confident belief that all the prayers and hopes expressed will be fulfilled. — **haec**: referring to the last three strophes. — **sentire**: depending on **spem**. — **reporto**: the singular is used after the manner of a Greek chorus. Cf. 4, 6, 41. — **doctus**: cf. *docilis* 4, 6, 43. — **Phoebi ... Dianae**: modifying both **chorus** and **laudes**. Note that the hymn closes with the mention of the two divinities named in the opening verse.

EPODON LIBER

For a general account of the Epodes and the conditions under which they were written, see Intr. 4.

I

Addressed to Maecenas in the spring of 31 B.C., when he was about to leave Rome. Antony and Cleopatra had spent the winter of 32-31 B.C. at Patrae, while their fleet of five hundred vessels had remained on guard at Actium. When the spring opened, Octavian summoned the most influential senators and knights to meet him at Brundisium, before he crossed to Epirus to engage in the final struggle. Maecenas naturally was to go with the rest. Dio Cassius, 51, 3, tells us that Maecenas was left in charge of Italy during Octavian's absence, so that it is generally assumed that he was not present at the battle of Actium. On the other hand, an anonymous elegy, regarded by Bücheler as contemporary, speaks of him as actually present *cum freta Niliacae texerunt laeta carinae | fortis erat circum, fortis et ante ducem. PLM.* 1, 122 ff. However, the evidence is inconclusive; yet it seems clear from Horace's words that at the time he wrote this epode he expected Maecenas to share in the dangers of the coming struggle. He remonstrates with his patron for his readiness to run all risks (1-4); assures him of his own devotion and willingness to share every danger, and of his anxiety, if he be forced to stay behind (5-22); and closes with the protestation that it is not selfish hope of gain that moves him: Maecenas has given him all he can desire (23-34). The last verses bear the emphasis of the epode. Horace's devotion is unselfish.

This epode serves as a dedication of the collection to Maecenas. There is a warmth of expression in it that Horace does not employ elsewhere. Metre, 74.

Ibis Liburnis inter alta navium,
    amice, propugnacula,
paratus omne Caesaris periculum
    subire, Maecenas, tuo.
5   Quid nos, quibus te vita si superstite
    iucunda, si contra, gravis?

1. **ibis**: *you are then really going*. Emphatic as *feremus* v. 11. So Tibullus 1, 3, 1 says in his address to Messala, who left him behind in Corcyra when traveling to the East in 30 B.C., *ibitis Aegaeas sine me, Messala, per undas.* — **Liburnis**: in contrast with the **alta navium propugnacula** — *lofty battlemented ships* — of Antony and Cleopatra. These huge galleons, some of which had as many as nine banks of oars, proved no match for the small swift two-banked *Liburnae* of Octavian's fleet; the latter, modeled after the vessels used by the Liburnian pirates, in the imperial period formed the chief part of the Roman navy. Antony had felt his ships invincible. According to Dio Cassius 50, 18, he called to his troops, ὁρᾶτε γάρ που καὶ αὐτοὶ καὶ τὸ μέγεθος καὶ τὸ πάχος τῶν ἡμετέρων σκαφῶν. Cf. also Vergil's description of the battle, *A.* 8, 691-693 *pelago credas innare revolsas | Cycladas, aut montis concurrere montibus altos: | tanta mole viri turritis puppibus instant.*

4. **tuo**: sc. *periculo*.

5 f. **nos**: i.e. *I and such as I*. The plural of modesty, which Horace uses in his lyrics only here and *C.* 1, 6, 5. 17; 2, 17, 32; 3, 28, 9. While we employ a verb in translating, it is improbable that the Romans were conscious of any ellipsis in such phrases as this. — **si superstite**, etc.: the apparent use of **si** with the abl. abs. is anomalous. **te superstite** alone would form a protasis to **vita . . . iucunda**, and we should expect as the alternative, *te mortuo (vita) gravis*. To avoid the ominous *te mortuo*, Horace euphemistically says *si contra*, with which some such verb as *vivitur*, or, as Porphyrio suggests, *sit*, is necessary; this construction has its influence on the preceding clause, so that we must regard the entire relative sentence as a condensed form for *quibus vita si te superstite (sit), iucunda, si contra (sit), gravis.* The ellipsis is somewhat similar to that in v. 8 below, **ni tecum simul (persequemur)**, etc. — **superstite**: **superstes** here means 'living on,' elsewhere in the epodes and odes 'out-living,' 'surviving another's death.'

utrumne iussi persequemur otium,
  non dulce, ni tecum simul,
an hunc laborem, mente laturi decet
10   qua ferre non mollis viros?
Feremus, et te vel per Alpium iuga
  inhospitalem et Caucasum,
vel Occidentis usque ad ultimum sinum
  forti sequemur pectore.
15 Roges tuum labore quid iuvem meo,
  imbellis ac firmus parum?
Comes minore sum futurus in metu,
  qui maior absentis habet,

7. utrumne: a combination of two interrogatives introduced by Horace, who uses it only here and in *S.* 2, 3, 251; 6, 73. It is employed by Curtius, Pliny, and other later prose writers. — **iussi**: sc. *a te, at thy bidding.* Horace's request to be allowed to accompany Maecenas had already been refused. — **persequemur otium**: *give ourselves up to a life of ease.*

8. ni tecum: cf. n. on v. 5.

9 f. laborem: in contrast to **otium** v. 7. By a slight zeugma connected with **persequemur**, whereas the more natural verb with it is *fero*, which is used in the relative clause immediately following. — **laturi**: *ready to bear.* Intr. 110.

11 f. feremus: the position and form show Horace's emphatic resolve. — **Alpium, Caucasum**: the Alps and the Caucasus were stock examples of hardships. — **inhospitalem Caucasum**: repeated *C.* 1, 22, 6 and adopted by Seneca, *Thyest.* 1052 *quis inhospitalis Caucasi rupem asperam Heniochus habitans* ' For the position of **et**, see Intr. 31.

13. sinum: *recess*, expressing the remoteness of the western sea Cf. Verg. *G.* 2, 122 *India . . . extremi sinus orbis.*

15. roges: equivalent to *si roges.* — **tuum . . . meo**: parallel in form to *Caesaris periculum subire, Maecenas, tuo* 3 f.

16. imbellis ac firmus parum: cf. the Homeric ἀπτόλεμος καὶ ἄναλκις. Horace laughs at himself for running away at Philippi *C.* 2, 7, 8 ff. (Intr. p. 11); the second half of his description here probably refers to his poor health — **parum**: cf. *C.* 1, 12, 59 and n. to 1, 2, 27.

17 f. An appeal to Maecenas' friendship, 'I do not claim that I can help you, but I beg you, save

ut adsidens implumibus pullis avis
   serpentium adlapsus timet
magis relictis, non, ut adsit, auxili
   latura plus praesentibus.
Libenter hoc et omne militabitur
   bellum in tuae spem gratiae,
non ut iuvencis inligata pluribus
   aratra nitantur meis
pecusve Calabris ante sidus fervidum

me from the fears that absence and anxiety bring.'—**maior habet**: *has a stronger hold.*

19–22. The comparison of the mother bird who fears for her chicks is old and familiar in literature. Cf. Aesch. Sept. 291 ff. δράκοντας δ' ὥς τις τέκνων | ὑπερδέδοικεν λεχαίων δυσευνάτορας | πάντρομος πελειάς. 'As a fostering dove fears the snakes, ill mates for her nestlings.' Cf. also Mosch. 4. 21 ff. and especially Claudian *Rapt. Proserp.* 3, 141 ff. *sic aestuat ales, | quae teneros humili fetus commiserit orno | allatura cibos et plurima cogitat absens, | ne gracilem ventus discusserit arbore nidum, | ne furtum pateat homini neu praeda colubris.*

— **pullis**: dative, more closely connects with **timet** than with **adsidens**; (Intr. 100) the latter may be translated attributively with **avis**, *the brooding mother bird,* thus expressing the condition rather than the act.

21 f. **ut adsit**: *even if she were with them.* — **non latura**: conces-

sive, *though she could not give.* — **praesentibus**: repeating **adsit** in sense, but added in contrast to **relictis**. This use of repetition to express the reciprocal relation is common in Latin, and is most clearly seen in such examples as Plaut. *Pseud.* 1142 *tute praesens praesentem vides,* or Verg. *A.* 4, 83 *illum absens absentem auditque videtque.*

24. **in spem**: *to further my hope.* Cf. *C.* 1, 7, 8 *in Iunonis honorem.* — **tuae . . . gratiae**: *favor in thy sight.*

25 f. **non ut**, etc.: emphatically placed to deny the possible charge of selfishness. — **nitantur**: the oxen's efforts in dragging the plow,—suggesting a heavy, fertile soil,—is transferred to the plow itself. Intr. 99.

27 f. Cf. *C.* 1, 31, 5 *non aestuosae grata Calabriae armenta.* In the heat of summer the flocks were driven from the rich pastures of low Calabria to the higher lands of Lucania and Samnium. Cf. Varro *R. R.* 2, 1, 6

Lucana mutet pascuis,
neque ut superni villa candens Tusculi
30   Circaea tangat moenia.
Satis superque me benignitas tua
ditavit ; haud paravero
quod aut avarus ut Chremes terra premam,
discinctus aut perdam nepos.

greges ovium longe abiguntur ex Apulia in Samnium aestivatum.
— **mutet**: for the varying constructions with *mutare*, see Intr. 98.

29 f. The lofty ridge of Tusculum, on the northeast side of the Alban Hills, about fifteen miles from Rome, was a favorite resort in antiquity, as it has been in modern times. The northern slope was then as now occupied by villas; Cicero, Julius Caesar, Lucullus, and others possessed country homes there. The buildings had stucco, or possibly in some cases marble, walls, whose gleam (**villa candens**) could be seen from Rome, as the present villas can to-day.

— **Circaea moenia**: so named because tradition said that Telegonus, the son of Circe by Ulysses, founded Tusculum. So the town is called *C.* 3, 29, 8 *Telegoni iuga parricidae.* — **tangat**: *border on*. Cf. Cic. *pro Mil.* 51 *villam quae viam tangeret.*

31. satis superque: note the emphasis. With the sentiment, cf. *C.* 2, 18, 12 *nec potentem amicum largiora flagito*, and *C.* 3, 16, 38 *nec, si plura velim, tu dare deneges.*

32 f. haud paravero: also emphatic; *I will never try to amass wealth*, etc. — **avarus ut Chremes**: *like a greedy Chremes,* — a typical miser, probably from some drama now lost. No miser Chremes appears in our extant plays, although the name is common enough. On the position of ut, cf. v. 12 above. Intr. 31.

34. discinctus . . . nepos: *loose spendthrift*, in the same construction as **avarus Chremes**.

2

In praise of country life.

' " Free from the busy rush of town, how fortunate is he who can till his ancestral fields, care for his vines, his orchards, flocks, and bees (1-16). His are the delights of autumn, summer, and winter (17-36). These make one forget the pains of love (37-38) ; and if there be beside a sturdy, honest housewife to do her part, care for the children, milk the ewes, prepare the evening meal, what life more joyful ! Not all the dainties of a city table can compare with the country's simple meal, which I enjoy, watching the sheep and cattle come at evening's fall, while round the bright hearth sit the slaves (39-66)." So spoke the broker Alfius, who straightway planned to foreclose his mortgages — and to put his money out again' (67-70).

The sudden turn in the last four verses is very characteristic of Horace, but it gives us no reason for doubting the sincerity of his praise of rural life. He was a man of real simplicity and of great sensitiveness; but like every conventional man of the world, shrank from too great enthusiasms: he will never preach, and when he feels himself approaching the danger line, he pulls himself up suddenly, as here, with a whimsical, half cynical turn. Another famous example, in which the serious note is not so long continued, is the *Integer vitae*, C. 1, 22. There is no hint of the date of composition. Metre, 74.

Beatus ille qui procul negotiis,
   ut prisca gens mortalium,
paterna rura bobus exercet suis,
   solutus omni faenore,
5   neque excitatur classico miles truci,
   neque horret iratum mare,

1 ff. This is similar to a fragment of Aristophanes in praise of peace 387 K. ὦ μῶρε, μῶρε πάντα ταῦτ' ἐν τῇδ' (sc. εἰρήνῃ) ἔνι | οἰκεῖν μὲν ἀργὸν αὐτὸν ἐν τῷ γῃδίῳ | ἀπαλλαγέντα τῶν κατ' ἀγορὰν πραγμάτων | κεκτημένον ζευγάριον οἰκεῖον βοοῖν, | ἔπειτ' ἀκούειν προβατίων βληχωμένων. 'Foolish, foolish man, peace has everything — living without hard work on one's bit of land, free from the troubles of the market-place, with one's own little yoke of oxen; and besides, the hearing of the bleating sheep.' — **negotiis**: in a narrow sense, like our 'business.'

2 f. prisca gens: the ancient folk of the Golden Age. — **paterna ... suis**: the fortunate farmer is he who has inherited his lands, which he works (**exercet**) with his own oxen; such is a *dominus*, not a mere *colonus*. No mortgage vexes him; secure in his own estate he can enjoy the freedom of his country life.

4. faenore: the double meaning — 'money borrowing,' 'money lending' — of the word is not apparent until v. 67.

5-8. The farmer escapes the stress of war, the danger of the sea, the worry of courts, and the haughtiness of patrons. Cf. the reminiscence of these verses in

forumque vitat et superba civium
    potentiorum limina.
Ergo aut adulta vitium propagine
    altas maritat populos,
aut in reducta valle mugientium
    prospectat errantis greges,
inutilisve falce ramos amputans
    feliciores inserit,
aut pressa puris mella condit amphoris,
    aut tondet infirmas ovis;

Claudian *Carm. min.* 52, 7 f. *non freta mercator tremuit, non classica miles; | non rauci lites pertulit ille fori.* — **superba . . . limina**: referring to the morning call, *salutatio*, and the humiliations to which clients were exposed from their patrons. Imitated by Seneca, *Epist.* 68, 10 *pulsare superbas potentiorum fores.*

9. **ergo**: *and so*, being free from such cares. — **adulta**: according to Columella, when three years old. In this word lurks the figurative sense — 'old enough for marriage.' — **propagine**: *shoot*, properly the 'layer' by which new vines were obtained. See *Class. Dict.* s.v. *vitis.*

10. **maritat populos**: the black poplar was considered second only to the elm as a support for grape vines. The 'wedding' of the vine and tree seems to have been a farmer's expression that established itself early in literature; so Cato says *R. R.* 32 *arbores facito ut bene maritae sint.* Milton adopts the figure *P. L.* 5 ' or they led the vine | To wed her elm; she, spoused, about him twines | Her marriageable arms.' The plane tree which has a thick foliage was unfitted for this purpose; so *C.* 2, 15, 4 *platanus caelebs.*

11 f. **in reducta valle**: repeated *C.* 1, 17, 17. Connect with **errantis**. — **mugientium**: used substantively like Vergil's *balantum gregem, G.* 1, 272, for sheep.

13 f. **ramos**: of fruit trees. — **feliciores**: *more fruitful.* The root appears in *fē-mina, fē-cundus.* — **inserit**: *grafts*, a technical term. Cf. **insitiva**, v. 19.

15 f. Note the alliteration. — **pressa . . . mella**: after as much honey had drained out as naturally would, the comb was pressed to extract the remainder. Cf. Verg. *G.* 4, 140 f. *spumantia cogere pressis mella favis.* — **infirmas**: *weak,* and so unresisting. A stock epithet; cf. Ovid. *Ib.* 44 *pecus infirmum.*

vel, cum decorum mitibus pomis caput
    autumnus agris extulit,
ut gaudet insitiva decerpens pira,
20   certantem et uvam purpurae,
qua muneretur te, Priape, et te, pater
    Silvane, tutor finium.
Libet iacere modo sub antiqua ilice,
    modo in tenaci gramine;
25   labuntur altis interim ripis aquae,
    queruntur in silvis aves,

17 f. decorum: *decked.* — **autumnus**: personified as *C.* 4, 7, 11 *pomifer autumnus.* Cf. Colum. *R. R.* 10, 43 *autumnus quassans sua tempora pomis.* — **agris**: probably dative.

19 f. insitiva: implying a better sort. — **decerpens**: with **gaudet**, ἥδεται δρέπων. This Greek construction of a participle agreeing with the subject after a verb of emotion is rare and poetical. Cf. *Epist.* 2, 2, 107 *gaudent scribentes.* — **purpurae**: poetic usage allows the dative with **certare**, while in prose we find the ablative. The grape as it ripens takes on a color that rivals the 'royal purple.' Cf. n. to *C.* 2, 5, 12.

21 f. muneretur: potential, expressing suitability. — **Priape**: a Hellespontic divinity, peculiarly the genius of the garden, who was represented by a rude wooden statue that also served the useful purpose of scaring away the birds. Cf. *S.* 1, 8, 1 ff. (Priapus speaks) *Olim truncus eram ficulnus, inutile lignum, | cum faber, incertus scamnum faceretne Priapum, | maluit esse deum. deus inde ego, furum aviumque | maxima formido.* — **Silvane**: an ancient Italian divinity of the wood and field, protector of flocks (Verg. *A.* 8, 601 *arvorum pecorisque deus*), and guardian of the farm boundaries. Cf. Gromat. 1, p. 302 *primus in terram lapidem finalem posuit* (sc. *Silvanus*).

24. tenaci: *i.e.* with firm hold on the rich soil, not easily pulled up like grass that grows where the soil is thin; hence *luxuriant, deep.*

25. interim: *i.e.* while we lie in the deep grass. — **ripis**: instrumental abl. denoting the route taken, *between the banks;* cf. Lucret. 2, 362 *flumina summis labentia ripis.*

26 f. queruntur: the low sad notes of the birds are heard in the distance, while the rustle of the

frondesque lymphis obstrepunt manantibus,
  somnos quod invitet levis.
At cum tonantis annus hibernus Iovis
30 imbris nivisque comparat,
aut trudit acris hinc et hinc multa cane
  apros in obstantis plagas,
aut amite levi rara tendit retia,
  turdis edacibus dolos,
35 pavidumque leporem et advenam laqueo gruem
  iucunda captat praemia.
Quis non malarum quas amor curas habet
  haec inter obliviscitur?
Quod si pudica mulier in partem iuvet
40 domum atque dulcis liberos,

leaves vies and mingles with the murmuring waters. Cf. Prop. 5, 4, 4 *multaque nativis obstrepit arbor aquis*.

28. quod invitet: *a sound to woo*. — **levis**: *gentle*, not the heavy sleep of exhaustion.

29 ff. Horace now turns to the delights of winter. In contrast to the fair and quiet weather, we now have **tonantis ... Iovis**. — **annus**: *season*, as C. 3, 23, 8 *pomifer ... annus*, i.e. *autumnus*.

31–36. Three winter sports — hunting the wild boar, catching thrushes, and snaring the hare and the crane. These are followed 39–48 by three typical occupations of the good housewife.

31. cane: the singular represents the class. Cf. Verg. *A.* 1, 334 *multa tibi ... cadet hostia*.

32 ff. obstantis plagas: the toils into which the boar was driven by the beaters and the dogs. — **amite lĕvi**: the smooth pole of the wide-meshed (**rara**) spring-net. For the scansion, see Intr. 58. — **turdis edacibus**: cf. Mart. 3, 58, 26 *sed tendit avidis rete subdolum turdis*.

35. For the scansion, see Intr. 58. — **advenam** : *wandering, the stranger*.

37. curas: the substantive common to both antecedent and relative clauses. — **amor**: *passion*. Horace is thinking of city intrigues in contrast to the domestic happiness implied in the following lines.

39. in partem: *for her part*; i.e. 'does her share in caring for,' etc.

Sabina qualis aut perusta solibus
    pernicis uxor Apuli,
sacrum vetustis exstruat lignis focum
    lassi sub adventum viri,
45 claudensque textis cratibus laetum pecus
    distenta siccet ubera,
et horna dulci vina promens dolio
    dapes inemptas adparet;
non me Lucrina iuverint conchylia
50   magisve rhombus aut scari,
si quos Eois intonata fluctibus
    hiems ad hoc vertat mare;
non Afra avis descendat in ventrem meum,

41. The Sabine women were the ideal farmers' wives (*C.* 3, 6, 37 ff.); the Apulians were noted for their industry (*C.* 3. 16, 26).

43 f. sacrum ... focum: made sacred by being the shrine of the household gods. — **vetustis**: therefore 'dry,' 'seasoned.' — **sub**: *against*. Cf. Gray's *Elegy* 'For them no more the blazing hearth shall burn, | Or busy housewife ply her evening care.'

45. textis cratibus: *in wattled folds.* — **laetum**: *sturdy, lusty.*

47 f. horna ... vina: the common folk drank the wine the same year it was pressed, without fermenting it; hence the adjective **dulci**. The finer wines were fermented in *dolia* and then drawn off into *amphorae*, which were sealed and put away. — **inemptas**: therefore simple and doubly sweet. Cf. Verg. *G.* 4, 133 *dapibus mensas onerabat inemptis*.

49 ff. The apodosis begins here. Five dainties of the luxurious city table are set off against five articles of country diet. — **Lucrina ... conchylia**: the Lucrine lake near Baiae produced the best oysters, which are meant here. — **scari**: so highly esteemed that it was called by Ennius, *Heduphag.* 8, *cerebrum Iovis*. Cf. also Suidas s.v. Διὸς ἐγκέφαλος· τὸ κάλλιστον βρῶμα.

51 f. si quos: the scar was most common in the eastern half of the Mediterranean sea, the coast of Sicily being the western limit of its range. It was believed that storms in the east drove the fish westward. — **intonata**: with active meaning.

53 f. Afra avis: *guinea-hen.* According to Varro, in Horace's

non attagen Ionicus
iucundior quam lecta de pinguissimis
oliva ramis arborum,
aut herba lapathi prata amantis et gravi
malvae salubres corpori,
vel agna festis caesa Terminalibus,
vel haedus ereptus lupo.
Has inter epulas ut iuvat pastas ovis
videre properantis domum,
videre fessos vomerem inversum boves
collo trahentis languido,

day a new and costly delicacy from Numidia. — **attagen** : a. kind of grouse ; another dainty from the East. St. Jerome warns his friend against luxury of the table, using this bird as a typical article, *ad Salvin.* 79 *procul sint a conviviis tuis Phasides aves, crassi turtures, attagen Ionicus.*

55. **iucundior** : predicate, *giving greater satisfaction.* — **pinguissimis** : the epithet is transferred from the fruit to the branches on which it grows. Intr. 99.

57 f. For the scansion, see Intr.
58. — **herba lapathi** : *sorrel,* for salad. — **gravi . . . corpori** : from the indigestion caused by overeating.

59 f. The simple country diet is relieved by fresh meat only on some holyday when sacrifice is made, or when some chance offers. It was a proverb that the wolf selected the choicest of the flock. Plut. *Sympos.* 2. 9 τὰ λυκόβρωτα λέγεται τὸ μὲν κρέας γλυκύτατον

παρέχειν. At the present time also fresh meat is a great rarity to the Italian peasant. — **Terminalibus** : this festival to Terminus, the god of boundaries, fell on February 23. It is described by Ovid. *Fasti* 2. 639 ff. The blood offering was either a lamb or sucking pig ; cf. *Fast.* 655 f. *spargitur et caeso communis Terminus agno | nec queritur lactans cum sibi porca datur.* — **lupo** : dative with **ereptus**.

61-66. This picture with its expression of quiet joy forms a fitting close to the preceding description. Notice that the rapid movement of 61-62 is followed by the slow verses 63-64, expressing the quiet return of the weary cattle at the close of day. Cf. Gray's *Elegy,* ' The curfew tolls the knell of parting day, | The lowing herd winds slowly o'er the lea.' | etc.

62 f. **videre . . . videre** : the anaphora is expressive of the farmer's satisfaction. Intr. 28 c.

positosque vernas, ditis examen domus,
　　circum renidentis Laris.
Haec ubi locutus faenerator Alfius,
　　iam iam futurus rusticus,
omnem redegit Idibus pecuniam ;
　　quaerit Kalendis ponere.

65. positosque vernas : *the home-born slaves in their places* (at supper). *Vernae* were slaves born within the house, not bought from abroad. Such were highly prized, sold only from necessity, and formed an important part of a well-to-do house. Cf. Tibul. 2, 1, 23 *turbaque vernarum, saturi bona signa coloni*. On the scansion of **positos**, see Intr. 58.

66. renidentis : the polished images of the household gods, placed about the hearth, reflect the firelight and seem to share in the satisfaction of the scene.

67 ff. Horace breaks off with this unexpected turn which is not fully understood until the last line is reached, as if he would say : 'But I am getting too serious. Any man, even an Alfius, can talk this way, and yet have no real feeling for the country; his enthusiasm will not last a fortnight.' It is a favorite method with Horace to hide a deeper purpose behind an apparently light expression.

— **locutus** : sc. *est*. — **Alfius** : a well known *faenerator* of Cicero's day, whom Horace takes as typical.
— **iam iam** : intensive, *in hot haste to*. Cf. Tac. *Ann*. 1, 47, 5 *iam iamque iturus*. — **idibus** . . . **kalendis** : settlements were made and new arrangements entered into regularly on the Calends, Nones, or Ides. Alfius called in (**redegit**) his money on the Ides, but before the Calends of the next month came, repented of his enthusiasm for country life, and tried to invest (**ponere**) his wealth again.

3

With comic pathos and extravagance Horace inveighs against garlic, declaring that it is worse than all the drugs and poisons known. The occasion of Horace's indignation seems to have been a fit of indigestion caused by a salad, of which garlic had been an ingredient, offered him at Maecenas' table. In his distress he calls down vengeance on his friend. This epode was written after Horace had acquired an intimate footing with his patron. The date of composition cannot be more exactly fixed. Metre, 74.

[3, 1]

    Parentis olim si quis impia manu
        senile guttur fregerit,
    edit cicutis alium nocentius.
        O dura messorum ilia!
5   Quid hoc veneni saevit in praecordiis?
        Num viperinus his cruor
    incoctus herbis me fefellit, an malas
        Canidia tractavit dapes?
    Vt Argonautas praeter omnis candidum
10   Medea mirata est ducem,
    ignota tauris inligaturum iuga
        perunxit hoc Iasonem;
    hoc delibutis ulta donis paelicem

1 ff. The parricide shall henceforth be punished by a dose of garlic, surer in its results than the hemlock (**cicutis**) that carried off Socrates. — **olim**: *ever*. — **guttur fregerit**: *strangle*, as *C.* 2, 13. 6 *fregisse cervicem*. — **edit**: the old and colloquial form of the subjunctive *edat*. Cf. Plaut. *Trin.* 339 *dé mendico mále meretur qui eí dat quod edit aút bibat*.

4. o dura: as if caught by a fresh spasm of pain, Horace cries out in amazement that reapers (here typical of all classes of toilers) can be so fond of garlic as they are. Porphyrio quotes Verg. *E.* 2, 10 f. *Thestylis et rapido fessis messoribus aestu | alia serpullumque herbas contundit olentis*.

5. quid veneni: comically graphic, like Terence's *quid mulieris uxorem habes? Hec.* 643.

8. Canidia: for an account of Canidia, probably a dealer in unguents and perfumes, to whom the practice of poisoning was attributed, see *Epod.* 5. From Canidia Horace passes to the queen of poisoners, Medea. — **tractavit**: *had a finger in*. Cf. *C.* 2, 13, 8 *ille venena Colcha ... tractavit*.

9 f. praeter omnis: connect with *mirata est*. — **candidum**: used of youthful beauty as in *C.* 1, 18, 11 *candide Bassareu*.

11. tauris: connected with **ignota** and **inligaturum** alike. Intr. 100.

13 f. When Jason deserted Medea at Corinth for King Creon's daughter Glauce, Medea avenged herself by sending the bride, here opprobriously called **paelicem**, a poisoned robe and diadem, which burst into flames and caused her death. Cf. 5, 63 ff. Medea es-

serpente fugit alite.
15 Nec tantus umquam siderum insedit vapor
siticulosae Apuliae,
nec munus umeris efficacis Herculis
inarsit aestuosius.
At si quid umquam tale concupiveris,
20 iocose Maecenas, precor
manum puella savio opponat tuo,
extrema et in sponda cubet.

caped on a chariot drawn by winged snakes.
— hoc : emphatic anaphora. Intr. 28 c.
15 f. vapor: *heat.* Cf. Sen. Oed. 47 *gravis et ater incubat terris vapor.* — siticulosae Apuliae : cf. the Homeric πολυδίψιον Ἄργος. The heat of Apulia is frequently mentioned by Horace ; cf. 2, 41 f. ; C. 3, 30, 11 ; S. 1, 5, 77 ff., 91 f.
17 f. The robe dipped in the blood of the Centaur, Nessus, which Deianira sent to Hercules, hoping to win back his love from Iole. Cf. 17, 31. — efficacis : with reference to the successful accomplishment of his labors.
19 ff. The close of the epode is a comic imprecation against the author of Horace's distress.
— at : regular in curses. Cf. 5, 1 ; Catull. 3, 13 *at vobis male sit, malae tenebrae Orci,* and Verg. A. 2, 535 ff. *at tibi pro scelere, exclamat, pro talibus ausis, | di, si qua est caelo pietas, quae talia curet, | persolvant grates dignas et praemia reddant | debita.* Cf. the Greek ἀλλά in address.

4

The rich parvenu became common in Rome during the last years of the Republic. The increase of this class, chiefly made up of freedmen, was fostered by the disorders and confiscations of the civil wars ; so that society was contaminated by those vulgar rich who wished to establish themselves in it. They were not satisfied with enrollment in the equestrian order, but pressed even into the senate, which Octavian purged in the winter of 29-28 B.C. Cf. Suet. *Aug.* 35 *senatorum affluentem numerum deformi et incondita turba (erant enim super mille, et quidam indignissimi et post necem Caesaris per gratiam et praemium adlecti, quos orcinos vulgus vocabat*) *ad modum pristinum et splendorem redegit duabus lectionibus.*

Horace was himself the son of a freedman, but nothing could be more offensive to him than the straining and display of such parvenus. His own attitude is clearly seen in *S.* 1, 6, where his calm tone shows that he is discussing a general question. The fierceness of this epode seems to warrant the belief that he has some definite individual in mind, who probably was easily recognized by his contemporaries. All efforts to identify him are useless. Many of the Mss. have the inscription: *ad Sextum Menam Libertinum. Vedium Rufum ex servitute miratur usurpasse equestrem dignitatem usque ad tribunatum militum.* The first part refers to Menas, or Menodorus, a freedman of Sextus Pompey who twice deserted to Octavian. The name Vedius was probably suggested to the earlier commentators by a passage in Cicero's letter to Atticus (*ad Att.* 6, 1, 25) which was written at Laodicea in 54 B.C., but not published until some time in the first century A.D. *hoc ego ex P. Vedio, magno nebulone* (*rascal*), *sed Pompeii tamen familiari, audivi: hic Vedius venit mihi obviam cum duobus essedis* (*English gigs*) *et raeda* (*carryall*) *equis iuncta et lectica et familia magna, pro qua, si Curio legem pertulerit, HS centenos pendat necesse est; erat praeterea cynocephalus* (*a dog-headed ape*) *in essedo nec deerant onagri* (*wild asses*): *numquam vidi hominem nequiorem.* The possibility remains, however, that this epode is nothing more than an exercise after Archilochus (Intr. 4). The date of composition is probably 36 B.C. See n. to 17–19. Metre, 74.

> Lupis et agnis quanta sortito obtigit,
> tecum mihi discordia est,

1 f. The enmity of wolves and sheep has been proverbial in literature from the Homeric poems down. Cf. *Il.* 22, 262 ff. ὡς οὐκ ἔστι λέουσι καὶ ἀνδράσιν ὅρκια πιστά. | οὐδὲ λύκοι τε καὶ ἄρνες ὁμόφρονα θυμὸν ἔχουσιν | ἀλλὰ κακὰ φρονέουσι διαμπερὲς ἀλλήλοισιν, | ὣς οὐκ ἔστ' ἐμὲ καὶ σὲ φιλήμεναι, and Ovid. *Ib.* 43 *pax erit haec nobis, donec mihi vita manebit, | cum pecore infirmo quae solet esse lupis.* — **sortito**: in origin an ablative absolute, it is equivalent to *sorte, lege naturae*, i.e. 'the allotment made by nature'; this meaning clearly appears in *S.* 2, 6, 93 *terrestria quando mortalis animas vivunt sortita*, also Plaut. *Merc.* 136 *at tibi sortito id optigit*, said in answer to the cry *perimus.*

Hibericis peruste funibus latus
   et crura dura compede.
5 Licet superbus ambules pecunia,
   fortuna non mutat genus.
Videsne, Sacram metiente te viam
   cum bis trium ulnarum toga,
ut ora vertat huc et huc euntium
10   liberrima indignatio?
'Sectus flagellis hic triumviralibus

3. Hibericis ... funibus: made of *spartum*, the tough Spanish broom, used in antiquity for the best ropes and cables (Plin. *N. H.* 19, 26). — **peruste**: *scarred*; with latus, *body*, and crura. For the use of the word, cf. *Epist.* 1, 16, 47 *Iris non ureris.*

4 ff. compede: fetters were used only on the lowest slaves. — **ambules**: *strut abroad*. Cf. 8, 14; Claudian, *in Eutrop.* 1, 306 f. *erecto pectore dives | ambulat.* — **fortuna**: in the restricted sense of our 'fortune,' as the previous line shows.

7 f. sacram viam: the fashionable promenade at Rome, running down from the Velia along the foot of the Palatine through the Forum. — **metiente**: *pacing*, as if he pompously would measure the street's length. — **bis trium ulnarum**: the *ulna* was about half a yard; this rich man's toga was then three yards wide, which made it possible for him to arrange it in elaborate folds. Such a toga was in marked contrast to the *exigua toga* such as simple Cato would wear, which Horace mentions, *Epist.* 1, 19, 13.

9 f. vertat: 'causes their color to change with indignation.' Cf. *S.* 2, 8, 35 f. *vertere pallor tum parochi faciem.* — **huc et huc**: *up and down*, with euntium. — **liberrima**: *free spoken*; cf. 11, 16. The following lines give the words of the indignant passers-by.

11. sectus: stronger than the ordinary *caesus.* — **triumviralibus**: the *tresviri capitales* were police commissioners whose chief duty was the safe custody of condemned persons and the execution of the punishment inflicted by the court. And under the Republic they were responsible for good order in the city. They had the power of executing summary punishment on disorderly persons and slaves. Cf. Schol. Cic. *Div. in Caecil.* 16, 50 *fures et servos nequam qui apud IIIviros capitales apud columnam Maeniam* (where the *IIIviri capitales* had their headquarters) *puniri solent.*

praeconis ad fastidium
arat Falerni mille fundi iugera
et Appiam mannis terit
15 sedilibusque magnus in primis eques
Othone contempto sedet.
Quid attinet tot ora navium gravi
rostrata duci pondere

12. **praeconis**: the crier who proclaimed the reason for the punishment while the flogging was going on. This particular upstart has in his time been flogged so often and so much that even the *praeco* is sick and tired of it; and yet to-day, **arat Falerni mille fundi iugera**.

13. **arat**: equivalent to *possidet*. Cf. Verg. *A*. 3, 13 f. *terra procul vastis colitur Mavortia campis | Thraces arant*. — **Falerni**: the *ager Falernus*, in the south of Campania, was famous for its vineyards. — **iugera**: the *iugerum* was the Roman unit of measure for land, containing about five-eighths of an acre.

14. **Appiam**: sc. *viam*, the great road leading to the south of Rome, called by Statius *longarum regina viarum*. This the parvenu wears out (**terit**) as he drives, either to exhibit his fine turnout to the throng of travelers, who continually pass along the road, or to visit his country estates. On this use of **tero**, cf. Ovid. *ex Ponto* 2, 7, 44 *nec magis est curvis Appia trita rotis*. — **mannis**: Gallic ponies, fashionable for pleasure driving.

15 f. L. Roscius Otho, tribune of the people, in 67 B.C. had a law passed by which the knights were assigned fourteen rows in the theater back of the orchestra, which belonged to the senators. This upstart, regardless of his low birth, takes his seat as knight, swollen with pride (**magnus**) over his great wealth. Worse than that, as *tribunus militum* he sits in the first of the fourteen rows. **magnus** is used in the same ironical sense *S*. 1, 6, 72 *magni quo pueri magnis e centurionibus orti*.

17-19. The allusions here give us reason to believe that this epode was written soon after the completion of the large ships referred to. In 38 B.C. Octavian was badly defeated by Sextus Pompey; in the following winter 37-36 B.C. he had a new fleet built, consisting of very large and heavy vessels. The date at which this epode was composed is then probably 36 B.C. — **ora rostrata**: an artificial expression similar to the Greek πρόσωπον νεώς, Achil. Tat. 3, 1;

contra latrones atque servilem manum,
20   hoc, hoc tribuno militum?'

Diod. Sic. 13, 40 has τὰ στόματα τῶν ἐμβόλων. — **latrones ... servilem manum**: such as Sextus Pompey welcomed to his standards. Augustus says in the *Mon. Anc.* 5, 1 that he captured and returned to their former owners some thirty thousand runaway slaves that had joined Sextus Pompey's army.

20. hoc, hoc: emphatic Intr. 28 a. Cf. Sen. *H. F.* 99 *hoc, hoc ministro noster utatur dolor.*

5

The Romans were extremely superstitious, and during the last century of the Republic especially, there was a rapid increase in the number of people among them who professed to practice the magic arts. The efficacy of witchcraft and love potions was not doubted by the mass of the people. In this epode Horace pictures four hags, of whom Canidia is the chief, in the act of preparing one of their most potent charms by which Canidia hopes to win back the affections of her aged lover. The quartette have captured a boy whom they propose to bury to the chin in the atrium of Canidia's house, that he may starve. His death is to be made the more painful by the sight of food frequently renewed, that his longing for it may sink into his liver and very marrow, which then shall be used for the irresistible philter. It is not impossible that children were occasionally murdered for such purposes; at any rate there was a current belief that such atrocities were practiced, as the Chinese are said to believe to-day that the missionaries kill young children to obtain the ingredients for certain charms. Cicero charges Vatinius, *in Vatin.* 14 *cum inaudita ac nefaria sacra susceperis, cum inferorum animas elicere, cum puerorum extis deos manes mactare soleas,* etc. The following inscription, found in a columbarium on the Esquiline, is also important testimony. CIL. 6, 19. 747 *Iucundus Liviae Drusi Caesaris f(ilius) Gryphi et Vitalis. In quartum surgens comprensus deprimor annum, | cum possem matri dulcis et esse patri. | eripuit me saga manus crudelis ubique, | cum manet in terris et nocit arte sua. | vos vestros natos concustodite parentes, | ni dolor in toto pectore fixsus eat.*

Commentators have been much puzzled as to the identity of this Canidia, whom Horace mentions in two other epodes (3 and 17) and in *S.* 1, 8. Porphyrio says that she was a certain Gratidia from Naples, whose business was the manufacture of perfumes. There is also the tradition that Horace was once in love with her, and that the *celeres iambi* which he recants in the sixteenth ode of the first book, are this epode and the seventeenth, a mock palinode. But Porphyrio's identification is probably only a clever guess, based on verses 43 and 59, and *Epode* 17, 23, which give after all very insufficient basis for his statement; and the rest of the tradition has no foundation whatever.

It may be true that Horace attacked under the name Canidia some *unguentaria*, well known at the time, who was ready to furnish potions and poisons to her customers, but it is equally probable that Horace had a purely literary motive in depicting a scene similar to that in Vergil's eighth eclogue, the *Pharmaceutria*, which is based on Theocritus' second Idyll.

The epode is dramatically constructed. It opens with the cries and prayers of the boy as he is hurried into the house (1-10). Canidia orders the various materials for her infernal rites (11-24), while Sagana sprinkles the house with water from Avernus (25-28); Veia digs the pit in which the boy is to be buried (29-40). A fourth hag. Folia, who can call down the very moon and stars, is also present (41-46). Canidia then prays that the charm she has already used may bring her aged lover to her doors; but suddenly the fear comes on her that some more skillful rival may detain him (47-72). At this thought she breaks out with the threat that she will use an irresistible charm (73-82). The boy, seeing that his prayers are of no avail, calls down curses on his murderesses and threatens that his shade shall haunt them (82-102). The date of composition cannot be exactly fixed, but is later than that of *S.* 1, 8 and probably earlier than that of *Epod.* 17. Metre, 74.

'At o deorum quicquid in caelo regit
  terras et humanum genus,

1. **at**: used regularly at the beginning of entreaties, prayers, and curses; here it marks the sudden outburst of the kidnapped boy. Cf. n. to 3, 19. — **o deorum quicquid**: cf. Livy, 23, 9, 3 *iurantes per quidquid deorum est*, and *S.* 1, 6, 1 *Lydorum quicquid ... involuit.* — **in caelo**: apparently added pleonastically, but Horace may have wished to make the contrast between *dii superi* and *dii inferi* under whose protection the boy's tormentors were. If so, he betrays a lack of skill, for a frightened child would hardly think of so subtle a taunt as this. Cf. n. to v. 5.

quid iste fert tumultus, et quid omnium
　　voltus in unum me truces?
5　Per liberos te, si vocata partubus
　　Lucina veris adfuit,
per hoc inane purpurae decus precor,
　　per improbaturum haec Iovem,
quid ut noverca me intueris aut uti
10　　petita ferro belua?'
Vt haec trementi questus ore constitit
　　insignibus raptis puer,
impube corpus quale posset impia
　　mollire Thracum pectora,
15　Canidia, brevibus implicata viperis

3 f. fert: *means*. This supplies the verb for the following verse. — **omnium**: in contrast to **unum**. — **in me**: connect with **truces**. Cf. C. 1, 2, 39 *acer . . . voltus in hostem*.

5 f. te: the boy now turns to Canidia as the leader of the four. — **si vocata**, etc.: the addition of **veris** makes the clause carry an implication that Canidia has never had a child, although she has tried to palm one off as her own. This is plainly expressed in 17, 50. Such an insinuation is, however, quite too clever for a child in this situation. — **Lucina**: Juno as goddess of childbirth. Cf. *C. S.* 15 and n.

7 f. purpurae decus: the *toga praetexta*, worn by boys until they reached the age of manhood, is here the badge of innocence and should protect the child, but it is of no avail (**inane**). — **improbaturum**: a mild word for *vindicaturum*.

9 f. ut noverca: typical of savage hatred. Cf. Sen. *Cont.* 4, 6 *hic tuus est; quid alterum novercalibus oculis intueris?* and Tac. *Ann.* 12, 2 (*coniunx*) *novercalibus odiis visura Britannicum et Octaviam*. — **petita**: equivalent to *saucia*.

12 f. insignibus raptis: the *toga praetexta* and the *bulla*, the amulet which the Roman boy wore about his neck. These symbols of his innocent youth are ruthlessly stripped from him, so that he stands naked before them: but the helplessness of his childish figure (**impube corpus**), a sight to touch even barbarian hearts, makes no appeal to Canidia and her crew.

15 f. Notice the effect produced by the succession of short syllables. Canidia is pictured as a fury

crinis et incomptum caput,
iubet sepulcris caprificos erutas,
iubet cupressos funebris
et uncta turpis ova ranae sanguine
20   plumamque nocturnae strigis
herbasque quas Iolcos atque Hiberia
mittit venenorum ferax,
et ossa ab ore rapta ieiunae canis

with snakes intertwined in her disheveled hair. Indeed she is called *furia* in *S.* 1, 8, 45. Cf. Ovid. *Her.* 2, 119 *Alecto brevibus torquata colubris.* — crinis . . . caput: Intr. 84.

17-24. These verses name the materials for the witches' infernal sacrifice. — caprificos: the first ingredient shall be from the barren wild fig tree, naturally associated with the dead, for it grew most often in the crevices of tombs. Cf. Mart. 10. 2, 9 *marmora Messalae findit caprificus*, and Iuv. 10, 143 ff. *laudis titulique cupido | haesuri saxis cinerum custodibus, ad quae | discutienda valent sterilis mala robora fici*.

18 f. cupressos funebris: cypress from some house of mourning. Cf. *C.* 2, 14, 23 *invisas cupressos.* — ranae: the *rana rubeta*, a poisonous toad described by Plin. *N. H.* 8, 110 *ranae rubetae, quarum et in terra et in umore vita, plurimis refertae medicaminibus deponere ea cotidie ac resumere pastu dicuntur, venena tantum semper sibi reservantes*. This creature was regularly used in potions. Cf. Iuv. 1. 69 *matrona potens, quae molle Calenum | porrectura viro miscet sitiente rubetam*.

20. strigis: modifying both ova and plumam. The *strix* was probably the ordinary screech-owl, which frequented tombs and deserted places. Popular superstition still magnifies it into a bugaboo. It is described by Ovid. *Fasti* 6, 133 *grande caput, stantes oculi, rostra apta rapinis; | canities pinnis, unguibus hamus inest*. On the use of these ingredients in potions, cf. Prop. 4, 6, 27 ff. *illum turgentis ranae portenta rubetae | et lecta exsectis anguibus ossa trahunt | et strigis inventae per busta iacentia plumae*, reminding one of the witches' brew in *Macbeth*, 4, 1.

21. Iolcos: in Thessaly, famous for witchcraft. Cf. *C.* 1, 27, 21 *Thessalis magus.* — Hiberia: in Pontus, near Colchis, the home of Medea. Cf. *Colchicis*, v. 24.

23 f. Bones snatched from a hungry dog are efficacious as communicating the craving of the baffled animal to the one bewitched.

flammis aduri Colchicis.
25 At expedita Sagana, per totam domum
spargens Avernalis aquas,
horret capillis ut marinus asperis
echinus aut currens aper.
Abacta nulla Veia conscientia
30 ligonibus duris humum
exhauriebat ingemens laboribus,
quo posset infossus puer
longo die bis terque mutatae dapis
inemori spectaculo,
35 cum promineret ore quantum exstant aqua
suspensa mento corpora,

25–28. Saganá is mentioned also *S.* 1, 8, 25 as Canidia's assistant. With dress tucked up (**expedita** = *succinta*) she hurries like a wild creature through the house, sprinkling it with water from Avernus in lustral preparation for the infernal rites. The waters of Lake Avernus, being near, as was supposed, to an entrance to the lower world, were especially appropriate for such purposes as these. So Vergil says of Dido, *A.* 4, 512 *sparserat et latices simulatos fontis Averni*.

29 f. Veia: her function is to dig in the floor of the atrium the pit in which the boy is to be buried. — **ligonibus**: plural, magnifying the difficulty and intensity of her toil; so **laboribus** in the following line. — **duris**: *pitiless*, with **ligonibus**. Cf. *C.* 3, 11, 31 *duro perdere ferro*.

31. ingemens: showing the difficulty of her task. Cf. Verg. *G.* 1, 45 f. *depresso incipiat iam tum mihi taurus aratro | ingemere*.

33. The food is to be changed again and again (**bis terque**) to increase the boy's longing, a refinement of torture whereby the day is to be made interminably long for him.

34. inemori: a compound found only here: *pine to death at (sight of,* etc.). The **in-** has the same force as in **ingemens** v. 31, or in the simpler compound *immori*, *Epist.* 1, 7, 85. — **spectaculo**: dative like *laboribus*, v. 31.

36 f. suspensa, etc.: an artificial expression for *natantes*.— **exsecta, aridum**: modifying both substantives. His marrow, his innermost part, and his liver, the seat of the passions, shall be cut out and dried to form the basis of the philter.

exsecta uti medulla et aridum **iecur**
    amoris esset poculum,
interminato cum semel fixae **cibo**
40   intabuissent pupulae.
Non defuisse masculae libidinis
    Ariminensem Foliam
et otiosa credidit Neapolis
    et omne vicinum oppidum,
45 quae sidera excantata voce Thessala
    lunamque caelo deripit.
Hic inresectum saeva dente livido
    Canidia rodens pollicem

38 ff. amoris poculum: cf. 17, 80 *desiderique temperare pocula*. — **interminato**: *forbidden*, in passive sense. — **semel**: connect with **intabuissent**. — **cibo**: dative with **fixae** and **intabuissent** alike. Intr. 100.

41–46. Horace skillfully says that he has only heard from Neapolitan gossip that Folia was present, thus implying that his statements in regard to the other three are based on certain knowledge. — **masculae libidinis**: descriptive genitive with **Foliam**.

43. **otiosa . . . Neapolis**: cf. Ovid. *Met*. 15, 711 *in otia natam Parthenopen*. This Greek city was given to gossip; according to the ancient commentator it was called *fabulosa*. Gossip and curiosity are characteristic of the Greek people. Cf. Demost. *Philip*. 1, 10 (to the Athenians) ἢ βούλεσθε. εἰπέ μοι, περιιόντες αὑτῶν πυνθά-

νεσθαι "λέγεταί τι καινόν;" and *Acts* 17, 21. Livy represents the Roman point of view when he says of the Neapolitans. 8, 22 *gens lingua magis strenua quam factis*.

44. **omne vicinum oppidum**: especially the luxurious watering-place Baiae, whose characteristics in the following century are so well depicted in Petronius' *Cena Trimalchionis*.

45 f. The power regularly assigned to incantations. Cf. Verg. *E*. 8, 69 *carmina vel caelo possunt deducere lunam*.

47 f. **hic**: *then*, marking a point in the preparations. — **inresectum**: *with untrimmed nail*. Long nails are marks of witches; with them they tear their victims, since the use of iron is impossible in magic Canidia gnaws her nail in frenzied impatience. Cf. Mart. 4, 27, 5 *ecce iterum nigros conrodit lividus ungues*. — **livido**: her very teeth

quid dixit aut quid tacuit? 'o rebus meis
    non infideles arbitrae,
Nox et Diana, quae silentium regis,
    arcana cum fiunt sacra,
nunc, nunc adeste, nunc in hostilis domos
    iram atque numen vertite.
Formidolosis dum latent silvis ferae
    dulci sopore languidae,
senem, quod omnes rideant, adulterum
    latrent Suburanae canes,

show her envy and rage. Cf. 6, 15 *atro dente*.

49. tacuit: *thought*, i.e. left unexpressed in words. The following lines represent both what she thought and what she said. — **rebus meis**: with **adeste**, v. 53.

51 f. Cf. Medea's prayer, Ovid. *Met.* 7, 192 ff. *nox, ait, arcanis fidissima . . . tuque, triceps Hecate, quae coeptis conscia nostris adiutrixque venis . . . adeste;* also Verg. *A.* 3, 112 *fida silentia sacris,* and 2, 255 *tacitae per amica silentia lunae.*

53 f. nunc, nunc: cf. *hoc, hoc* 4, 20. Intr. 28a. — **hostilis domos**: a common formula in prayers; here used to include the homes of her rivals. Cf. 3, 27, 21 ff. — **iram atque numen**: *the power of your divine wrath.*

55 f. This with v. 51 shows that the time is night, when all creatures are lulled in sleep save unhappy lovers. Cf. Verg. *A.* 4, 522 ff. *nox erat, et placidum carpebant fessa soporem | corpora per terras, silvaeque et saeva quierant | aequora, cum medio volvuntur sidera lapsu, | cum tacet omnis ager, pecudes pictaeque volucres, | . . . at non infelix animi Phoenissa.*

57. In spite of her preparations, Canidia still hopes that the unguent she has already used may prove effective. — **senem**: her aged lover, the Varus of v. 73, whose foppish appearance excites the mirth of the passers-by. Cf. Plaut. *Casin.* 240 *senectan aetate unguentatus per vias, ignave, incedis?*

58. latrent: transitive. She trusts that the barking of the dogs may announce his approach. So Vergil's enchantress hears Daphnis' coming, *E.* 8, 107 *Hylas in limine latrat.* — **Suburanae**: Canidia's house is in the Subura, the Roman slums, situated east of the fora between the Esquiline, Quirinal, and Viminal hills. It was crowded with small shops, cafés, and brothels.

nardo perunctum quale non perfectius
    meae laborarint manus.
Quid accidit? Cur dira barbarae minus
    venena Medeae valent,
quibus superbam fugit ulta paelicem,
    magni Creontis filiam,
cum palla, tabo munus imbutum, novam
    incendio nuptam abstulit?
Atqui nec herba nec latens in asperis
    radix fefellit me locis.
Indormit unctis omnium cubilibus
    oblivione paelicum.
A, a, solutus ambulat veneficae
    scientioris carmine.
Non usitatis, Vare, potionibus,
    o multa fleturum caput,

59 f. quale . . . laborarint: *tale* is implied in **quale**, in place of which we might expect *quo non*, 'none more perfect will my hands ever make.' The future perfect expresses Canidia's confidence.

61 ff. At v. 60 Canidia listens, but to no purpose — her lover does not come. She fears that the potent unguent, prepared from Medea's own recipe, has lost its power. — **minus**: equivalent here to *parum*.

63. quibus: connect with **ulta**, which contains the main idea. — **superbam**: as exultant over Medea, Jason's lawful wife. — **paelicem**: the opprobrious term applied by Medea to Creusa.

65. tabo . . . imbutum: *death-dyed*. The robe burst into flames as soon as the princess put it on.

67 ff. 'Yet I made no mistake. Still he must be sleeping over all my magic unguents, forgetful of every mistress.' She has smeared his very bed with her potent ointment.

71 ff. A, a: suddenly the fear strikes her that a clever rival may have some more powerful charm, and in fury she threatens Varus with her irresistible philter. — **solutus**: *set free*; cf. C. 1, 27, 21. — **ambulat**: *walks abroad*.

74. fleturum: *doomed to weep*; like the Greek κλαίω. Intr. 110. — **caput**: in the sense of 'person,' most common in addresses expressing either love or, as here,

75   ad me recurres, nec vocata mens tua
       Marsis redibit vocibus:
     maius parabo, maius infundam tibi
       fastidienti poculum,
     priusque caelum sidet inferius mari,
80   tellure porrecta super,
     quam non amore sic meo flagres·uti
       bitumen atris ignibus.'
     Sub haec puer iam non, ut ante, mollibus
       lenire verbis impias,
85   sed dubius unde rumperet silentium,
       misit Thyesteas preces:
     venena magnum fas nefasque non valent

hate. Cf. *C.* 1, 24, 1 *desiderium . . . tam cari captis.* So κεφαλή, κάρα in Greek, *e.g. Il.* 8, 281 Τεῦκρε, φίλη κεφαλή. Soph. *Antig.* 1 ὦ κοινὸν αὐτάδελφον Ἰσμήνης κάρα.

76. **Marsis . . . vocibus**: 'no home-made spells shall avail you to call back your mind when once it has fallen under this new charm.' For Marsic spells, cf. 17, 29 and Verg. *A.* 7, 750.

78 f. **fastidienti**: 'in spite of all your disregard for me.' — **inferius**: for the metre, see Intr. 58.

82. **uti bitumen**: she draws the comparison from her own rites. Cf. Verg. *E.* 8, 82 *fragilis incende bitumine laurus.* — **atris**: the actual color of the flame.

83 f. **sub haec**: *thereupon.* The boy now sees that there is no hope of escape and turns to threats. — **lenire**: the only case of the his-

torical infinitive in the odes and epodes.

85 f. **unde**: 'with what words.' — **Thyesteas preces**: such curses as Thyestes uttered when betrayed into eating the flesh of his own son. The words Horace had in mind are probably those in Ennius' famous Thyestes, which Cicero, *Tusc.* 1, 107, has preserved to us *ipse summis saxis fixus asperis, evisceratus, | latere pendens, saxa spargens tabo, sanie et sanguine atro, | neque sepulcrum, quo recipiat, habeat portum corporis, | ubi remissa humana uita corpus requiescat malis.* Cf. also *in Pis.* 43. — **preces**: *curses*, as Caes. *B. G.* 6, 31 *omnibus precibus detestatus Ambiorigem.*

87 f. The passage is corrupt, but the sense is: 'Sorceries cannot overturn the mighty law of

        convertere humanam vicem.
      diris agam vos ; dira detestatio
90   nulla expiatur victima.
     Quin ubi perire iussus exspiravero,
        nocturnus occurram furor,
     petamque voltus umbra curvis unguibus,
        quae vis deorum est manium,
95   et inquietis adsidens praecordiis
        pavore somnos auferam.
     Vos turba vicatim hinc et hinc saxis petens
        contundet obscaenas anus ;
     post insepulta membra different lupi

right and wrong after the manner of men (**humanam vicem**).' That is, 'neither your evil practices nor offerings of victims are powerful enough to save you from the vengeance of the gods.' — **humanam vicem**: adverbial accus. Cf. Sall. *Hist. Frg.* 4. 67 M. *ceteri vicem pecorum obtruncabantur.*

89 f. **diris**: substantively, *curses*, repeated in the formal **dira destatio** that follows. — **nulla**, etc.: It was commonly believed that there was no escape from a solemn curse of this kind. Cf. *C.* 1, 28. 34 *teque piacula nulla resolvent,* and Plin. *N. H.* 28. 19 *defigi quidem diris precationibus nemo non potuit.* Cf. Dido's threat, *A.* 4. 384 ff. *sequar atris ignibus absens, | et, cum frigida mors anima seduxerit artus, | omnibus umbra locis adero.*

92. **furor**: *an avenging spirit*; the masculine of *furia*.

94. 'Such is the power of the spirits of the dead (to return and harm).' Cf. Livy 3, 58, 11 *manesque Verginiae . . . per tot domos ad petendas poenas vagati nullo relicto sonte tandem quieverunt.*

95. **inquietis**: proleptic. — **assidens**: like the incubus in a nightmare.

97 f. **hinc et hinc**: 'on every side.' Cf. 2, 31 n. — **obscaenas**: 'foul hags,' giving the cause of their punishment. Stoning to death in Rome was rare. Livy 4, 50. 5 f. speaks of a case in which a military tribune was killed in this fashion by a mob of soldiers.

99 f. The Esquiline outside the walls was a common burial place for the poor until Maecenas redeemed it by buying it up and laying it out into beautiful gardens. Cf. *S.* 1, 8. Here the hags' bodies are to be cast unburied, for the

100   et Esquilinae alites;
        neque hoc parentes, heu mihi superstites,
        effugerit spectaculum.'

wolves and birds to prey on. — **post**: adverb. — **Esquilinae** ‖ **alites**: for the hiatus, see Intr. 43.

101 f. **neque hoc . . . effugerit**: 'my parents will not fail to see your mangled corpses and gloat over them.' — **heu mihi superstites**: The boy turns from his own fate to pity for his parents. His death will deprive them of the joy and support which their old age should have known. The sadness of such bereavement oppressed the ancients, whose religious ideas gave no consolation for early death.

Horace here breaks off, observing the rules he laid down himself for the drama, *Epist.* 2, 3, 182 ff. *non tamen intus | digna geri promes in scaenam, multaque tolles | ex oculis, quae mox narret facundia praesens, | ne pueros coram populo Medea trucidet, | aut humana palam coquat exta nefarius Atreus, | aut in avem Procne vertatur, Cadmus in anguem.* He thus leaves us impressed with the pathos of the situation, not the manner of the boy's horrible death.

6

An attack on a scurrilous defamer, who like a cowardly cur dared to assail only those who could not fight in return. 'Attack me,' says Horace, 'and you will find I am ready to bite back. You bark nobly and then sniff the bone thrown to you (1-10). I shall prove a bull with horns as sharp as the iambi of Archilochus or Hipponax; I am no boy to cry and not strike back (11-16).' The metaphors are only apparently mixed, for at v. 11 Horace definitely abandons the figure of the dog.

Who the object of this attack was must remain uncertain. A number of Mss. have the inscription *in Cassium Severum*, by which the early commentators probably meant the orator Cassius Severus, banished by Augustus on account of his defamatory writings (Tac. *Dial.* 19; *Ann.* 1, 27; 4, 21). But this Cassius belonged to Ovid's generation, so that he can hardly be the person meant. All other guesses are equally futile. The verses may be only an exercise in *iambi* (Intr. 4). Metre, 74.

Quid immerentis hospites vexas canis
    ignavus adversum lupos?
Quin huc inanis, si potes, vertis minas
    et me remorsurum petis?
5   Nam qualis aut Molossus aut fulvus Lacon,
    amica vis pastoribus,
agam per altas aure sublata nivis
    quaecumque praecedet fera.
Tu cum timenda voce complesti nemus,
10   proiectum odoraris cibum.
Cave, cave: namque in malos asperrimus
    parata tollo cornua,
qualis Lycambae spretus infido gener
    aut acer hostis Bupalo.

1. **hospites**: *passers-by*. The word frequently has this sense in epitaphs. Cf. Cicero's translation of the inscription over the Spartans who fell at Thermopylae, *Tusc.* 1, 42, 101 *dic, hospes, Spartae nos te hic vidisse iacentes.* Also Catullus' verse 4, 1 *Phasellus ille quem videtis hospites.* — **canis**: a shepherd dog, as the following verse shows.

3 f. **inanis**: a barking dog, you have no bite. — **remorsurum**: equivalent to a relative clause. — **petis**: *fly at.*

5. **Molossus ... Lacon**: adjectives used substantively like our 'St. Bernard,' 'bull,' etc. These were the choice breeds of watchdogs, mentioned together by Vergil *G.* 3, 405 *velocis Spartae catulos acremque Molossum.* Cf. Shakespere, *Midsummer Night's Dream* 4, 1, 124 'My hounds are bred out of the Spartan kind.'

6 f. **vis**: cf. Lucret. 6, 1220 *fida canum vis;* Verg. *A.* 4, 132 *odora canum vis.* — **aure sublata**: *i.e. arrecta.* Cf. the opposite *demittit auris* C. 2, 13, 34.

9 f. 'A scrap of meat flung to you is quite enough to stop your noise; you are a blackmailer.' — **proiectum**: more contemptuous than the ordinary *obiectum.* — **cave, cave**: cf. *nunc, nunc* 5, 53; *hoc, hoc* 4, 20. Intr. 28 a.

12. **parata tollo cornua**: the same figure as in the proverbial *S.* 1, 4, 34 *faenum habet in cornu.*

13 f. Lycambes promised his daughter Neobule in marriage to Archilochus, the great master of iambic poetry, but later refused

15   An, si quis atro dente me petiverit,
           inultus ut flebo puer?

him (**infido**); tradition says that Archilochus by his bitter verses drove both father and daughter to suicide. The dative depends on **spretus**. — **acer hostis Bupalo**: Hipponax, who retaliated with bitter verses on Bupalus and Athenis, two sculptors who in sport had made a bust of the homely poet with which they amused their friends. The story is told by Pliny *N. H.* 26, 12.

15 f. **an**: introducing an interrogative conclusion. Cf. 17, 76. — **atro dente**: *i.e.* 'with envious malice.' Cf. *Epist.* 1, 19, 30 *versibus atris*; *C.* 4, 3, 16 *iam dente minus mordeor invido*. — **inultus**: connect with the subject rather than with the predicate **puer**.

7

An appeal to the Romans not to renew civil war, written probably in 38 B.C. on the eve of the outbreak of hostilities between the triumvirs and Sextus Pompey. In August, 39 B.C., a treaty between the opposing parties signed at Misenum had raised the hope that the exhausted Roman world might have an opportunity to recover itself in peace; but within a year these hopes were disappointed. It was most natural then that Horace should express himself in this gloomy way; later he was more hopeful of the state. Notice the dramatic form of which Horace is fond. He makes a personal appeal to the opposing lines. Metre, 74.

    Quo, quo scelesti ruitis? aut cur dexteris
        aptantur enses conditi?
    Parumne campis atque Neptuno super
        fusum est Latini sanguinis, —
5   non ut superbas invidae Carthaginis

1 f. **quo, quo**: cf. *hoc, hoc* 4, 20. Intr. 28 a. — **scelesti**: *i.e.* with fratricide. — **ruitis**: literally, *rushing down to ruin*. Cf. 16, 2 *ipsa Roma ... ruit*; *C.* 1, 3, 26 *gens humana ruit per vetitum nefas*. — **conditi**: 'that were so lately sheathed.' Cf. *C.* 1, 31, 1 *dedicatum Apollinem* and n.

3. **campis atque Neptuno**: with **super**. Intr. 32.

5. **non ut**: *shed not that*, etc. The Roman youth are no longer wasted to punish a proud enemy

Romanus arcis ureret,
intactus aut Britannus ut descenderet
Sacra catenatus via,
sed ut secundum vota Parthorum sua
urbs haec periret dextera.
neque hic lupis mos nec fuit leonibus,
numquam nisi in dispar feris.
Furorne caecus an rapit vis acrior
an culpa? Responsum date!

or to extend the Roman empire, but solely to compass the destruction of their own state. — **invidae**: cf. Sall. *Cat.* 10, 1 *Carthago aemula imperi Romani ab stirpe interiit*.

7 f. **intactus Britannus**: practically true, as Caesar's expeditions to Britain had had no practical results. Cf. Tac. *Agric.* 13 *igitur primus omnium Romanorum divus Iulius cum exercitu Britanniam ingressus, quamquam prospera pugna terruerit incolas ac litore potitus sit, potest videri ostendisse posteris, non tradidisse*. It is not improbable that Octavian planned an expedition against the Britons after the peace of Misenum, as he certainly did in 34 B.C. Dio Cass. 49, 38. — **descenderet Sacra . . . via**: the *Sacra via* made a descent of some fifty feet from the Velia to the forum and then ascended the Capitol. The descent into the forum and passage through it formed the most brilliant part of the triumphal procession. — **catenatus**: *a chained captive*, before the car of triumph. Cf. 4, 2, 34 ff.

9 f. **secundum vota**: the Parthians at this time had overrun Syria and Asia Minor and were the most powerful opponents of the Romans. Finally when driven back and overawed, in 20 B.C., they gave up the standards they had captured from Crassus in 53 and from Antony in 36 B.C. Cf. *C.* 3, 5, 5 ff.; 6, 9 ff.: 4, 15. 6 ff., and the notes on these passages. — **sua**: emphatic. With the expression in these two verses, cf. 16, 1-10.

11 f. **hic . . . mos**: *i.e.* of destroying their own kind. — **dispar**: used substantively, equivalent to *dispar animal*. — **feris**: here an adjective, agreeing with **lupis** and **leonibus**. — *who are never fierce save*, etc.

13 f. **vis acrior**: some external force, more powerful than your own strength, *i.e.* Fate. — **culpa**: defined below by **scelus fraternae necis**.

Tacent, et albus ora pallor inficit,
  mentesque perculsae stupent.
Sic est: acerba fata Romanos agunt
  scelusque fraternae necis,
ut immerentis fluxit in terram Remi
  sacer nepotibus cruor.

15 f. Horace dramatically turns to the spectators, 'They have no answer,' etc. — **albus**: *deathly.* — **perculsae**: *i.e.* with horror at their own situation.

17. sic est: 'this is the sum of the whole matter.' — **acerba fata**: the vis acrior of v. 13.

19 f. ut: temporal, *ever since.* Cf. *C.* 4. 4. 42. — **sacer**: *that brought a curse on.* **sacer** means 'consecrated,' 'set apart for the gods,' then 'devoted to a god for destruction'; hence 'accursed.' 'polluting,' the Greek ἐναγής. Cf. Verg. *A.* 3. 56 *quid non mortalia pectora cogis,* | *auri sacra fames?* Lucan echoes the idea that the curse of the first fratricide hung over the whole Roman people. *Phars.* 1, 95 *fraterno primi maduerunt sanguine muri.*

8

Rogare longo putidam te saeculo
  viris quid enervet meas,
cum sit tibi dens ater et rugis vetus
  frontem senectus exaret,
hietque turpis inter aridas natis
  podex velut crudae bovis!
Sed incitat me pectus et mammae putres,
  equina quales ubera,
venterque mollis et femur tumentibus
  exile suris additum.
Esto beata, funus atque imagines
  ducant triumphales tuum,
nec sit marita quae rotundioribus
  onusta bacis ambulet.

15 Quid quod libelli Stoici inter sericos
      iacere pulvillos amant?
    Inlitterati num minus nervi rigent?
      minusve languet fascinum,
    quod ut superbo provoces ab inguine,
20   ore adlaborandum est tibi?

9

Addressed to Maecenas in September, 31 B.C., on hearing of Octavian's success at Actium. In eager enthusiasm Horace asks his patron when they can hope to celebrate together this glorious victory, as they had celebrated a few years before the defeat of Sextus Pompey. The evidence seems to show that Maecenas was in Rome at the time this was written (see introduction to *Epod.* 1), but those who believe that Maecenas was present at Actium regard the opening lines as additional evidence that he took part in the battle. Some even hold that the graphic details mentioned prove that Horace also was there.

After the address to Maecenas (1–10), Horace reflects on the disgrace Antony has brought on the Romans by enslaving himself to an oriental queen (11–16), a sight that made the Gauls desert to Caesar, and the queen's own fleet withdraw (17–20). 'Hail, Triumph, dost thou delay the great procession for the mightiest leader thou hast ever yet brought home (21–26). The enemy has changed his purple robe for mourning and flees to farthest lands (27–32). Come, boy, bring larger cups and stronger wine; I will forget my care and fear for Caesar (33–38).' With this epode compare *C.* 1, 37 written a year later in joy at the news of Cleopatra's death. Metre, 74.

Quando repostum Caecubum ad festas dapes
  victore laetus Caesare
tecum sub alta (sic Iovi gratum) domo,

1. **repostum**: for the syncope, see Intr. 40. — **Caecubum**: one of the choicer wines. Cf. *C.* 1, 20, 9; 37, 5.

3 f. **sub alta ... domo**: Maecenas' palace on the Esquiline: Horace calls it *C.* 3, 29, 10 *molem propinquam nubibus arduis*, with

beate Maecenas, bibam,
sonante mixtum tibiis carmen lyra,
hac Dorium, illis barbarum?
ut nuper, actus cum freto Neptunius
dux fugit ustis navibus,
minatus urbi vincla quae detraxerat
servis amicus perfidis.
Romanus eheu (posteri negabitis)
emancipatus feminae
fert vallum et arma, miles et spadonibus
servire rugosis potest,

reference no doubt to its lofty tower which commanded a view of the city and surrounding country.—**beate**: *fortunate, blest and happy.* Cf. 2, 1 *beatus ille.*

5 f. **tibiis**: Intr. 89. — **carmen**: *strain.* The lyre shall raise a Dorian strain of victory, the music of a Pindaric epinicion; the pipes a Phrygian (**barbarum**) dithyrambic tune, suitable for reveling. Cf. the *Berecyntiae tibiae* of C. 3, 19, 18; 4, 1, 22.

7 f. **nuper**: in 36 B.C. after the battle of Naulochus. — **freto**: sc. *Siculo.* — **Neptunius dux**: said in scornful mockery. Pompey had styled himself the son of Neptune, according to Appian *B. C.* 5, 100 ἔθυε (ὁ Πομπήιος) μόνον θαλάσσῃ καὶ Ποσειδῶνι, καὶ υἱὸς αὐτῶν ὑφίστατο καλεῖσθαι.

9 f. **vincla**: Intr. 40. —**servis**: cf. n. to 4, 19. It is dependent on both **detraxerat** and **amicus.** Intr. 100. — **perfidis**: for they had run away from their owners to fight with Pompey against them.

11 f. **Romanus**: emphatic, Antony and his soldiers. 'To think that a Roman could fall so low! Future generations will say it was impossible!' — **emancipatus**: *in slavery to.*

13. **fert**, etc.: 'Romans actually serve as common soldiers and carry on the march the *valli* and their arms, subject to a woman's orders!'— **miles**: contrasted with **spadonibus rugosis**, as **fert vallum et arma** is set over against **feminae.** According to the Schol. Verg. *A.* 7, 696 the Roman contingent was commanded by Cleopatra and her eunuchs, *Augustus in commemoratione vitae suae refert Antonium iussisse, ut legiones suae apud Cleopatram excubarent, eiusque nutu et iussu parerent.*

14. **servire**: emphatic by position.—**potest**: *can bring himself to.*

15 interque signa turpe militaria
sol adspicit conopium.
Ad hoc frementis verterunt bis mille equos
Galli canentes Caesarem,
hostiliumque navium portu latent
20 puppes sinistrorsum citae.
Io Triumphe, tu moraris aureos
currus et intactas boves?

15 f. **turpe**: *a shameful sight*, with **conopium**. — **sol adspicit**: the all-seeing sun is regularly invoked as the witness of shameful deeds. So by Aeschylus' Prometheus in his suffering, *P. V.* 91 καὶ τὸν πανόπτην κύκλον ἡλίου καλῶ. Likewise by Shelley's, 'I ask you, Heaven, the all-beholding sun, | Has it not seen?' — **conopium**: 'a mosquito bar,' then a 'canopied couch.' Symbolical of the abomination of oriental luxury. Cf. the similar passage in Propertius, who is speaking of Cleopatra, 3, 9, 45 *foedaque Tarpeio conopia tendere saxo (ausa).*

17 f. **ad hoc**: (*in disgust*) *at this.* — **Galli**: Galatians, led by Amyntas and Deiotarus, who went over to Octavian before the battle. **vertērunt**: Intr. 36. — **canentes Caesarem**: cf. Verg. *A.* 7, 698 *ibant aequati numero regemque canebant.*

19 f. The naval maneuver here spoken of is not clearly understood. Horace evidently refers to a defection or at least a withdrawal from active battle by a part of the fleet, similar to the action of the Galatian cavalry. The ships seemed to have abandoned the rest of the fleet by making a turn to the left (**sinistrorsum citae**). — **citae**: apparently a real participle, equivalent to the Greek κινηθεῖσαι.

21 f. **io Triumphe**: the shout of the people to the personified Triumph, as the procession advanced towards the Capitol. Cf. *C.* 4, 2, 49. Horace already in imagination sees Octavian in the triumphal car. The triumph did not actually take place until Aug. 13-15, 29 B.C. Cf. Verg. *A.* 8, 714-728. — **aureos currus**: the gilded car of triumph, to be used in the triumphal procession. With the plural, cf. 1, 2, 15 f. — **intactas**: sc. *iugo*. Only cattle that had not been broken to the service of man could be used in sacrifice to the gods. Cf. Verg. *A.* 6, 38 *grege de intacto . . . mactare iuvencos.* The reference here is to the white bulls (the gender of **boves** is due to custom) which were driven in the triumphal procession and sacrificed to Jupiter on the Capitol.

Io Triumphe, nec Iugurthino parem
    bello reportasti ducem,
neque Africanum, cui super Carthaginem
    virtus sepulcrum condidit.
Terra marique victus hostis punico
    lugubre mutavit sagum;
aut ille centum nobilem Cretam urbibus,
    ventis iturus non suis,
exercitatas aut petit Syrtis Noto,
    aut fertur incerto mari.
Capaciores adfer huc, puer, scyphos
    et Chia vina aut Lesbia,

23 f. **parem** . . . **ducem** : *i.e. parem Caesari.* Marius is meant. The mention of his service in the war against Iugurtha rather than of his greater exploits in repulsing the Teutons and Cimbri, is probably due to the recent appearance of Sallust's *Bellum Iugurthinum.*

25 f. The younger Scipio Africanus, who destroyed Carthage in 146 B.C. — **Africanum** : in the same construction as **ducem**. — **cui** . . . **virtus sepulcrum condidit** : *i.e.* his valor has raised over the ruins of Carthage an eternal memorial. Cf. Vell. Pater. 1, 12 *Carthaginem magis invidia imperii, quam ullius eius temporis noxiae invisam Romano nomini funditus sustulit fecitque suae virtutis monumentum, quod fuerat avi eius clementiae.*

27 f. Horace now returns to the present. — **hostis** : Antony. — **punico lugubre**, etc. : a general in battle wore either a purple or a white cloak (*sagum purpureum*). This Antony has put aside for that of the common soldier, as Pompey did after the battle at Pharsalia. Caesar *B. C.* 3, 96. For the order, see Intr. 21.

29 f. **centum** . . . **urbibus** : ἑκατόμπολις. Cf. *C.* 3, 27, 33 *centum . . . potentem oppidis Creten.* — **Cretam** : paralleled in construction with **Syrtis**. — **non suis** : *i.e. adversis.* Cf. Mart. 10, 104, 3 f. *et cursu facili tuisque ventis | Hispanae pete Tarraconis arces.*

32. **incerto** : in doubt whither to turn his course. Intr. 99. Cf. Stat. *Silv.* 3, 2, 6 *dubio committitur alto.*

33 f. **capaciores** . . . **scyphos** : ordinary cups are quite too small. Seneca adapted the expression *de Ira* 3, 14, 2 *bibit deinde liberalius quam alias capacioribus scyphis.* — **puer** : the universal address to

35 vel quod fluentem nauseam coerceat
    metire nobis Caecubum.
    Curam metumque Caesaris rerum iuvat
    dulci Lyaeo solvere.

a slave. So the Greek παῖ. — Chia ... Lesbia: sweet Greek wines which used in excess might well produce the 'rising qualms' mentioned in the next verse. The frankness with which this result of overdrinking is mentioned was less offensive to the ancient than to us. There is no reason for saying as some have done that Horace is on the sea off Actium and beginning to suffer from sea-sickness.

36 ff. Caecubum: the Caecuban was strong and dry. — rerum: obj. gen. — Lyaeo: the 'Releaser': cf. C. 1, 7, 22; 3, 21, 16, as if from the Greek λύω, so that there may be a play between the name and solvere.

10

A propempticon to the poet Mevius, hated by Horace and the circle to which he belonged. Vergil has secured immortality for Mevius and his associate Bavius by his verses *E.* 3, 90 f. *qui Bavium non odit, amet tua carmina, Mevi; | atque idem iungat vulpes et mulgeat hircos.* The ill-nature of Horace's poem should be compared with the good wishes in the propempticon addressed to Vergil *C.* 1, 3.

That this epode also is modeled on a poem by Archilochus is shown by a fragment recovered from a papyrus sheet in 1899.[1] The beginning, which probably contained the name of the poet's false friend, is lost; the fragment, as restored, is as follows:

> κύμ⟨ατι⟩ πλα⟨ζόμ⟩ενος.
> κἀν Σαλμυδ⟨ησσ⟩ῷ γυμνὸν εὐφρονέσ⟨τατα⟩
> Θρήϊκες ἀκρό⟨κο⟩μοι
> λάβοιεν ⟨ἔνθα πολλ᾽ ἀναπλήσει κακὰ
> δούλιον ἄρτον ἔδων⟩
> ῥίγει πεπηγότ᾽ αὐτόν· ἐκ δὲ τοῦ ⟨ῥό⟩θου
> φυκία πόλλ᾽ ἐπ⟨έ⟩χοι.
> κροτέοι δ᾽ ὀδόντας, ὡς ⟨κύ⟩ων ἐπὶ στόμα
> κείμενος ἀκρασίῃ

[1] First published by Reitzenstein, *Sitzungsb. d. Akad. d. Wissenschaften zu Berlin*, 1899, p. 857 ff.

ἄκρον παρὰ ῥηγμῖνα κυμάτω⟨ν ὁ⟩μοῦ·
ταῦτ' ἐθέλοιμ' ἂν ἰδεῖν,
ὅς μ' ἠδίκησε λ⟨ὰ⟩ξ δ' ἐφ' ὁρκίοις ἔβη
τὸ πρὶν ἑταῖρος ⟨ἐ⟩ών.

'... driven by the wave, and in Salmydessus may the tufted Thracians give him kindest welcome, naked, stiffened with cold, — there shall he suffer many woes to the full, eating the bread of slavery. And I pray that he may have over him (for his covering) deep weed from the surge, that his teeth may chatter as those of a dog that in its weakness lies on its belly on the edge of the strand near the waves. This is what I could wish to see (the man suffer) who has done me injustice and trampled on his pledges, though he was once my friend.' Metre, 74.

>Mala soluta navis exit alite,
>   ferens olentem Mevium :
>ut horridis utrumque verberes latus,
>   Auster, memento, fluctibus ;
>5 niger rudentis Eurus inverso mari
>   fractosque remos differat ;
>insurgat Aquilo, quantus altis montibus
>   frangit trementis ilices,
>nec sidus atra nocte amicum adpareat,
>10   qua tristis Orion cadit,
>quietiore nec feratur aequore

1 f. **mala ... alite**: modifying **soluta**. Cf. *C.* 1, 15, 5 *mala ducis avi domum.* — **olentem**: *rank*, for Horace will have it that he, like Gargonius. *S.* 1, 2, 27, *olet hircum.*

3 f. All the winds of Heaven unfavorable for a voyage to Greece shall compass Mevius' ruin. — **ut verberes**: optative subjunctive. — **memento**: parenthetical.

5. **niger ... Eurus**: as it gathers dark clouds. Cf. *C.* 1, 5, 6 *aspera nigris aequora ventis.*

The opposite, *C,* 1, 7, 15, is *albus Notus* and 3, 7, 1 *candidus Favonius.* — **inverso mari**: cf. Verg. *A.* 1, 43 *evertitque aequora ventis.*

7. **quantus**: *with the power it has when*, etc. — **montibus**: locative abl. Intr. 95.

9 f. **amicum**: predicate, *with kindly light.* — **Orion**, etc.: Orion's setting is accompanied with heavy winds and storms. Cf. *C.* 1, 3, 14. Hence he, like the Hyades, is **tristis**.

>   quam Graia victorum manus,
>   cum Pallas usto vertit iram ab Ilio
>   in impiam Aiacis ratem.
> 15 O quantus instat navitis sudor tuis
>   tibique pallor luteus
>   et illa non virilis eiulatio
>   preces et aversum ad Iovem,
>   Ionius udo cum remugiens sinus
> 20   Noto carinam ruperit.
>   Opima quod si praeda curvo litore
>   porrecta mergos iuverit,

12. **Graia victorum manus**: the adjective is equivalent to the genitive *Graecorum*, and so is modified by **victorum**.

13 f. After the fall of Troy, Pallas transferred her wrath against the city to the Greeks because Ajax Oileus had torn from the altar Cassandra, Pallas' priestess. This act polluted the entire fleet. Cf. Verg. *A.* 1, 39 ff. *Pallasne exurere classem | Argivom atque ipsos potuit submergere ponto, | unius ob noxam et furias Aiacis Oilei?*

15 f. **O quantus sudor**: a reminiscence of *Il.* 2, 388 ff. quoted in n. to *C.* 1, 15, 9 f. *heu heu, quantus equis, quantus adest viris sudor!* — **luteus**: Greek ὠχρός. The dark skins of Italians and Greeks take on this greenish yellow tint when pale. Cf. Tibul. 1, 8, 52 *nimius luto corpora tingit amor*.

17 f. **illa**: almost equivalent to 'your common.' — **non virilis**: cf. Cic. *Tusc.* 2, 55 *ingemescere nonnumquam viro concessum est idque raro, eiulatus ne mulieri quidem.* — **et**: for the position, see Intr. 31. — **aversum**: cf. *C.* 3, 23, 19 *aversos Penatis.*

19 f. **udo ... Noto**: *i.e.* 'rain-bringing.' — **remugiens**: cf. *C.* 3, 10, 6.

21. **opima praeda**: *a fat prize.* — **quod si**: introducing a conclusion. Cf. *C.* 1, 1, 35. Notice that Horace here makes no mention of Mevius by name, and euphemistically avoids ill-omened expressions such as *tuum corpus*, which is implied, however, in **porrecta**. In this way he makes his wish for Mevius' harm all the harsher. Porphyrio saw a special point in **opima**, for he remarks *apparet et pinguem fuisse* (*Mevium*).

22. **mergos**: the voracious coots are, however, not given to eating carrion.

libidinosus immolabitur caper
et agna Tempestatibus.

23 f. Horace mockingly closes with the promise of a solemn sacrifice of thanksgiving for the storm that shall drown Mevius. The **libidinosus caper** is clearly chosen as a fit offering for relief from an *olens Mevius*. With the sacrifice of a lamb to the storms, cf. Verg. *A.* 5, 772 *Tempestatibus agnam caedere deinde iubet*.

I I

Horace no longer finds any pleasure in writing verses, for love once more has him in his meshes (1-4). Two years have passed since he freed himself from Inachia, who long charmed and tortured him (5-22); now he is ensnared by the fair Lyciscus (23-28). The Pettius to whom these verses are addressed is otherwise unknown to us. The names Inachia and Lyciscus are borrowed from the Greek. Metre, 80.

> Petti, nihil me sicut antea iuvat
>   scribere versiculos amore percussum gravi,
> amore qui me praeter omnis expetit
>   mollibus in pueris aut in puellis urere.
> 5   Hic tertius December, ex quo destiti
>   Inachia furere, silvis honorem decutit.
> Heu me, per urbem (nam pudet tanti mali)

1 f. nihil: cognate object of *iuvat*. — **versiculos**: the diminutive in disparagement of the epodic measure, unsuited for love verses. — **amore**: not fully personified.

3 f. amore: for the anaphora, see Intr. 28 c. — **praeter omnis**: the lover's inevitable extravagance. 'No one ever suffered as he does.' — **in puellis urere**: cf. *C.* 1, 17. 19 f. *dices laborantis in uno | Penelopen vitreamque Circen.* For the infinitive, see Intr. 107.

5 f. hic tertius December, etc.: *this December which is stripping, is the third since*, etc. Horace measures the years by the month in which his birthday fell. — **Inachiā furere**: like the Greek μαίνεσθαι ἐπί τινι. — **honorem**: *splendor*. Cf. Verg. *G.* 2, 404 *frigidus et silvis aquilo decussit honorem*.

7 f. nam: in apology for his sigh, *heu me*. Notice that the broken order also expresses Horace's feeling of shame.

fabula quanta fui! Conviviorum et paenitet,
in quis amantem languor et silentium
10   arguit et latere petitus imo spiritus!
'Contrane lucrum nil valere candidum
pauperis ingenium!' querebar adplorans tibi,
simul calentis inverecundus deus
fervidiore mero arcana promorat loco.
15   'Quod si meis inaestuet praecordiis
libera bilis, ut haec ingrata ventis dividat
fomenta volnus nil malum levantia,
desinet imparibus certare submotus pudor.'
Vbi haec severus te palam laudaveram,
20   iussus abire domum ferebar incerto pede

8. **fabula**: *subject of gossip*. So Ovid. *Am.* 3, 1, 21 *fabula, nec sentis, tota iactaris in urbe.* — **et**: Intr. 31.

9. **quis**: this form is found only here in the lyric poems. — **amantem**: sc. *me*. — **languor**: *lack of interest, indifference*, which showed itself in his silence.

11 f. The poet's indignant outburst against his richer rivals. For the construction, see Intr. 106. — **adplorans**: *i.e.* 'accompanying my plaints with tears.'

13 f. **simul**: regularly used by Horace equivalent to *simul ac.* — **calentis**: genitive agreeing with the genitive implied in the possessive pronoun that is naturally understood here, *i.e. mea arcana.* Cf. Cic. *in Pis.* 3, 6 *iuravi hanc urbem mea unius opera esse salvam.* — **inverecundus deus**: the god who destroys all *verecundia*, when taken in excess. The god and his gift are identified. Cf. the opposite *C.* 1, 27, 3 *verecundum Bacchum.* — **mero**: with **calentis**. — **loco**: *i.e.* 'their proper place' — my own mind.

15 ff. **quod si**, etc.: resuming the quotation of his former confidences. — **libera bilis**: 'my anger find free speech,' etc. Cf. 4, 10 *liberrima indignatio*. Propertius desired the same relief, 1, 1, 28 *sit modo libertas quae velit ira loqui*. — **ingrata**: *vain, inrita.* Cf. Verg. *A.* 9, 312 f. *sed aurae | omnia discerpunt et nubibus inrita donant.* — **fomenta**: figuratively used of his plaintive outpourings to Pettius. — **pudor**: the false pride that still urged him to the contest.

19 f. **ubi haec severus**, etc.: *when I determined grown had spoken thus so nobly.* — **iussus**: sc. *a te*. Pettius approved his praise-

ad non amicos heu mihi postis et heu
   limina dura, quibus lumbos et infregi latus.
Nunc gloriantis quamlibet mulierculam
   vincere mollitia amor Lycisci me tenet;
25   unde expedire non amicorum queant
   libera consilia nec contumeliae graves,
sed alius ardor aut puellae candidae
   aut teretis pueri longam renodantis comam.

worthy resolution. — **ferebar**: note the tense. He wished to carry out his determination to break with his love, but still with irresolute steps (**incerto pede**) he wandered to his mistress' home. Tibullus acknowledges the same weakness, 2, 6, 13 *iuravi quotiens rediturum ad limina numquam:* | *cum bene iuravi, pes tamen ipse redit.*

21 f. **heu . . . heu**: he sighs over his weak will; the exclamations are to be taken with the entire sentence rather than with any particular words. — **dura**: literally, as the relative clause shows.

23. **mulierculam**: Lyciscus uses the diminutive disparagingly.

25 f. **expedire**: *set free* (from these toils). Cf. *C.* I, 27, 23 f. *vix inligatum te . . . Pegasus expediet.* — **libera consilia**: *frank advice.* Cf. v. 16. — **contumeliae**: on the part of Lyciscus.

28. **teretis**: *shapely.* Cf. *C.* 2, 4, 21 *teretis suras.* — **renodantis comam**: *binding his long hair into a knot. renodo* has here the same sense as *religare C.* 1, 5, 4 *cui flavam religas comam?* For the custom of such boys to wear the hair long, see *C.* 2, 5, 23 f.; 3, 20, 14; 4, 10, 3.

12

Quid tibi vis, mulier nigris dignissima barris?
   Munera cur mihi quidve tabellas
mittis, nec firmo iuveni neque naris obesae?
   Namque sagacius unus odoror,
5   polypus an gravis hirsutis cubet hircus in alis,
   quam canis acer ubi lateat sus.
Qui sudor vietis et quam malus undique membris
   crescit odor, cum pene soluto

indomitam properat rabiem sedare, neque illi
    iam manet umida creta colorque
stercore fucatus crocodili, iamque subando
    tenta cubilia tectaque rumpit!
Vel mea cum saevis agitat fastidia verbis:
    'Inachia langues minus ac me;
Inachiam ter nocte potes, mihi semper ad unum
    mollis opus. Pereat male quae te
Lesbia quaerenti taurum monstravit inertem,
    cum mihi Cous adesset Amyntas,
cuius in indomito constantior inguine nervus
    quam nova collibus arbor inhaeret.
Muricibus Tyriis iteratae vellera lanae
    cui properabantur? Tibi nempe,
ne foret aequalis inter conviva, magis quem
    diligeret mulier sua quam te.
O ego non felix, quam tu fugis ut pavet acris
    agna lupos capreaeque leones.'

13

A study from the Greek. The motive is taken from the same poem of Alcaeus that Horace imitated later in *C.* 1. 9. While snow and rain fall outside, the poet calls his friends to celebrate the day with a jar of old wine, so long as youth yet is theirs. As warrant for this he quotes Chiron's advice to his pupil Achilles. Metre, 79.

Horrida tempestas caelum contraxit, et imbres
    nivesque deducunt Iovem; nunc mare, nunc siluae

1 f. **caelum contraxit**: the heavy clouds have covered the sky and brought it nearer to the earth. — **deducunt Iovem**: the identification of the sky and the supreme divinity of the heavens was a common- place of Hellenistic and Roman literature. Cf. *C.* 1. 1. 25 *sub Iove frigido* (= *sub caelo*). Verg. *E.* 7. 60 *Iuppiter et laeto descendet plurimus imbri*, and *G.* 2. 325 ff. *tum pater omnipotens fecundis imbri-*

EPODON LIBER [13, 10

Threicio Aquilone sonant: rapiamus, amici,
  occasionem de die, dumque virent genua
5 et decet, obducta solvatur fronte senectus.
  Tu vina Torquato move consule pressa meo.
  Cetera mitte loqui; deus haec fortasse benigna
    reducet in sedem vice. Nunc et Achaemenio
  perfundi nardo iuvat et fide Cyllenea
10   levare diris pectora sollicitudinibus,

bus aether | coniugis in gremium laetae descendit, et omnis | magnus alit magno commixtus corpore, fetus. — **siluae**: trisyllabic as *C.* 1, 23, 4.

3. **Threicio ‖ Aquilone**: for the hiatus, see Intr. 43. Thrace is the home of the North wind. Cf. *C.* 1, 25, 11 *Thracio . . . vento.* — **rapiamus**: an intensive expression, *eagerly seize.* Plutarch's ἁρπάσας τὸν καιρόν. Cf. Publil. Syr. p. 129 W. *occasiones non modo accipe, arripe.*

4. **de die**: 'offered by the day,' with the suggestion of beginning early. Cf. the expressions *de die bibere; de die convivia facere.* — **virent genua**: cf. *C.* 1, 9, 17 *donec virenti canities abest.* Theoc. 14, 70 ποιεῖν τι δεῖ ἇς (*i.e.* ἕως) γόνυ χλωρόν.

5. **et decet**: 'youth is the time for drinking'; some ten years later, Horace called his friend to a carouse *dum licet, C.* 2, 11, 16. — **obducta**: *clouded.*

6. **tu**: with this abrupt address Horace invests one of his imaginary company with the duties of host. Cf. *C.* 1, 9. — **vina . . . move**, *broach.* Cf. *C.* 3, 21, 6 (*testa*) *moveri digna bono die.* — **Torquato . . . consule . . . meo**: L. Manlius Torquatus, cos. 65 B.C., the year of Horace's birth. Cf. *C.* 3, 21, 1 *o nata mecum consule Manlio* (*testa*).

7 f. **cetera**: *all else,* save words of cheer. It is possible that Horace means, 'do not discuss politics or refer to our present state, the losses we have suffered in the civil wars (**haec**).' — **benigna vice**: *with kindly compensation.* Cf. *C.* 4, 14, 13 *plus vice simplici,* 'with more than equal return.' — **sedem**: sc. *suam*; cf. Suet. *Aug.* 28 *ita mihi salvam ac sospitem rem publicam sistere in sua sede liceat.*

8 f. **Achaemenio . . . nardo**: oriental perfume; cf. *C.* 3, 1, 44 *Achaemenium costum.* Achaemenes was the mythical founder of the Persian dynasty. — **fide Cyllenea**: the lyre was invented by Hermes, who was born on Mt. Cyllene in Arcadia.

10. Cf. *C.* 4, 11, 35 *minuentur atrae carmine curae.*

nobilis ut grandi cecinit centaurus alumno:
'Invicte, mortalis dea nate puer Thetide,
te manet Assaraci tellus, quam frigida parvi
   findunt Scamandri flumina lubricus et Simois,
15 unde tibi reditum certo subtemine Parcae
   rupere, nec mater domum caerula te revehet.
Illic omne malum vino cantuque levato,
   deformis aegrimoniae dulcibus adloquiis.'

11 ff. Horace supports his exhortation by quoting the example of Chiron, as he introduces Teucer later (C. 1, 7) for a similar purpose. — grandi: *full grown*. Cf. Iuv. 7, 210 *metuens virgae iam grandis Achilles*. — invicte: used substantively, as Verg. *A.* 6, 365 *eripe me his, invicte, malis.* — mortalis: predicate with nate. For the order, see Intr. 21.

13. Assaraci tellus: Assaracus was king of Troy, great-grandfather of Aeneas. — frigida: probably with reference to one of the Scamander's sources. Cf. *Il.* 22, 151 f. ἡ δ' ἑτέρη (sc. πηγή) θέρει προρέει ἐικυῖα χαλάζῃ | ἢ χιόνι ψυχρῇ ἢ ἐξ ὕδατος κρυστάλλῳ. — parvi: in Homer it is μέγας ποταμός.

14. lubricus: of the swift smooth current. Cf. Ovid. *Am.* 3, 6, 81 *supposuisse manus ad pectora lubricus amnis dicitur*. The Scamander and Simois are to be the witnesses of Achilles' mighty deeds.

So the Fates prophesy, Catull. 64, 357 ff. *testis erit magnis virtutibus unda Scamandri,|quae passim rapido diffunditur Hellesponto.| cuius iter caesis angustans corporum acervis | alta tepefaciet permixta flumina caede.*

15 f. unde: connect with reditum. — certo subtemine: instrumental ablative with rupere. The web of the Fates determines man's destiny. Cf. Catull. 64, 327 *currite ducentes subtegmina, currite, fusi*. Also Verg. *A.* 10, 814 f. *extremaque Lauso | Parcae fila legunt.* — caerula: for her home is in the sea. Cf. n. to *C.* 3, 28, 10, and Ovid. *Her.* 9, 14 *Nereus caerulus*.

17 f. illic: *i.e.* before Troy. When Agamemnon's envoys came to Achilles (*Il.* 9, 186) they found him cheering himself before his tent, τὸν δ' εὗρον φρένα τερπόμενον φόρμιγγι λιγείῃ. — adloquiis: equivalent to *solaciis*. Cf. Catull. 38, 4 *quem tu . . . qua solatus es allocutione?*

14

Maecenas had urged Horace again and again to finish up some collection of verses, probably the book of epodes. Horace answers that he cannot now, for he is in love, and even Anacreon could not write polished verses when smitten with Bathyllus. The poem closes with the retort: 'You too are in love, Maecenas, and should understand; thank Heaven that your flame is not like mine.' The colloquial and familiar tone of the epode should be noticed. Metre, 75.

Mollis inertia cur tantam diffuderit imis
    oblivionem sensibus,
pocula Lethaeos ut si ducentia somnos
    arente fauce traxerim,
5   candide Maecenas, occidis saepe rogando:

1–4. Maecenas' constant question, given here in indirect form, dependent on **rogando**, v. 5. — **mollis**: the opening word gives the keynote of the reproach. Horace has grown 'soft,' and has forgotten all his promises. — **imis ... sensibus**: dative, equivalent to *penitus*. Cf. Verg. *E.* 3, 54 *sensibus haec imis reponas*.

3. **Lethaeos ... somnos**: the sleep of complete forgetfulness. Cf. Verg. *A.* 6, 714 f. *Lethaei ad fluminis undam | securos latices et longa oblivia potant.* — **ut si**: not to be connected with **tantam** only, but rather with **imis ... sensibus**, showing how completely forgetfulness has taken possession of him. — **ducentia**: cf. *C.* 3, 1, 20 f. *non avium citharaeque cantus | somnum reducent*, also *Epist.*

1, 2, 31 *ad strepitum citharae cessantem ducere somnum.*

4. **traxerim**: like the Greek ἕλκειν; stronger than the ordinary *bibere* or *ducere*, which is used *C.* 1, 17, 21 *pocula ... duces sub umbra.* The latter word, however, would be impossible here, as it has just been used in v. 3.

5. **candide Maecenas**: with general reference to Maecenas' upright character; here used because Horace recognizes the justice of his patron's reproaches. Cf. 11, 11 *candidum ingenium.* In similar fashion he addresses Tibullus *Epist.* 1, 4, 1 *Albi, nostrorum sermonum candide iudex.* Cf. the English 'candid.' — **occidis**: colloquially extravagant. Cf. *C.* 2, 17, 1: also Plaut. *Pseud.* 931 *occidis me, quom istuc rogas.*

deus, deus nam me vetat
inceptos, olim promissum carmen, iambos
ad umbilicum adducere.
Non aliter Samio dicunt arsisse Bathyllo
10   Anacreonta Teium,
qui persaepe cava testudine flevit amorem
non elaboratum ad pedem.

6 f. deus, deus: 'for it is the god, the god, I tell you, who.' Emphatically stating the cause of his delay. Intr. 28 a. — **carmen**: used here apparently of the entire collection for which his friends have so long waited (**olim promissum**). For the order cf. *Epist.* 2, 1, 234 *acceptos, regale nomisma, Philippos*; and Verg. *E.* 2, 3 *inter densas, umbrosa cacumina, fagos.* — **iambos**: this word seems to show that the poems in epodic form are meant, for this is the term Horace applies to them, *Epist.* 1, 19, 23; 2, 2, 59. Intr. 4.

8. ad umbilicum adducere: a stick was fastened to the last sheet of the strip of papyrus paper on which the book was written; when the book was finished the strip was rolled on this stick, which was called the umbilicus because it was in the center of the roll. See Schreiber's *Atlas*, pl. 90 ff. Therefore the phrase means, 'to finish the book.' So Martial opens the last epigram of his fourth book *ohe iam satis est, ohe libelle, | iam pervenimus usque ad umbilicos.*

9–12. None of Anacreon's poems to his favorite Bathyllus are preserved, so that we cannot determine the correctness of this statement. — **non aliter**: generally used to return to the main theme after an illustration, not as here to introduce the illustration itself. — **cava testudine**: the sounding box of the lyre. Cf. *C.* 1, 32. 13 f. *o decus Phoebi et dapibus supremi | grata testudo Iovis.* — **flevit amorem**: *gave sad expression to his love.* Domitius Marsus says in his elegy on Tibullus *te quoque Vergilio comitem non aequa, Tibulle, | mors iuvenem campos misit ad Elysios, | ne foret, aut elegis molles qui fleret amores, | aut caneret forti regia bella pede.* Dioscorides, a writer of the Hellenistic period, testifies that Anacreon often became lachrymose over his love and cups. *Anth. Pal.* 7, 31, 3 f. τερπνότατε Μούσῃσιν Ἀνάκρεον, ὣ 'πὶ Βαθύλλῳ | χλωρὸν ὑπὲρ κυλίκων πολλάκι δάκρυ χέας.

12. non elaboratum. etc.: probably meaning that Anacreon employed only simple measures for his love poems.

Vreris ipse miser; quod si non pulchrior ignis
   accendit obsessam Ilion,
15 gaude sorte tua: me libertina nec uno
   contenta Phryne macerat.

13. **ipse**: 'you know how it is from your own experience, Maecenas.' — **quod si**: *now if;* introducing a supposition recognized as true. Cf. *C.* 3, 1, 41. — **ignis**: *flame*, with the same double meaning that the English word has. Cf. 3, 7, 10 f. Helen was the 'flame' that fired besieged Ilion. The early commentators think Maecenas' 'flame' was Terentia, whom he later married. Cf. *C.* 2, 12.

15 f. **me**: emphatic, *as for me.* Horace frequently thus concentrates attention on himself at the end of his verses. Cf. *e.g. C.* 1, 1, 29, when after enumerating the interests of other men, he suddenly says, *me doctarum hederae praemia frontium | dis miscent superis; me gelidum nemus*, etc. — **nec**: adding a second characteristic, — 'she is not only a libertina, but she is not even,' etc. Catullus complains of his Lesbia 68, 135 *uno non est contenta Catullo.* — **macerat**: cf. *C.* 1, 13, 6 *umor et in genas furtim labitur, arguens | quam lentis penitus macerer ignibus.*

15

Horace's reproach to faithless Neaera.

'In the depth of night thou didst swear thy constancy to me (1-10). Now thou art no longer true. I tell thee I am man enough to seek another love (11-16). Thy present lover may have all riches, wisdom, and the beauty of a Nereus, his triumph will be short, for presently he shall weep over thy broken faith. And I shall laugh last (17-24).'
Metre, 75.

Nox erat et caelo fulgebat luna sereno
   inter minora sidera,
cum tu, magnorum numen laesura deorum,

1 f. Night is the time for lovers' vows; the moon and stars their proper witnesses. Cf. Catull. 7, 7 f. *sidera . . . cum tacet nox, | furtivos hominum vident amores.* — **inter minora sidera**: repeated *C.* 1, 12, 47.

3 f. **laesura**: *ready to outrage.* Intr. 110. — **in verba . . . mea**: *i.e.* repeating the oath after me. The

in verba iurabas mea,
5   artius atque hedera procera adstringitur ilex
      lentis adhaerens bracchiis,
    dum pecori lupus et nautis infestus Orion
      turbaret hibernum mare
    intonsosque agitaret Apollinis aura capillos,
10   fore hunc amorem mutuum.
    O dolitura mea multum virtute Neaera!
    nam si quid in Flacco viri est,
    non feret adsiduas potiori te dare noctis,
      et quaeret iratus parem;

phrase *in verba alicuius iurare* was originally a technical expression for taking the military oath of fidelity to the general; then extended to include any oath of allegiance. Cf. *Epist.* 1, 1, 14 *iurare in verba magistri.*

5. **artius atque**: cf. 12, 14 *minus ac.* For the figure, cf. *C.* 1, 36, 20 *lascivis hederis ambitiosior.*

7. **dum**, etc.: giving the oath in indirect form. In the form in which the sentence was first conceived v. 7 was a complete idea **dum pecori lupus et nautis infestus Orion** (*esset*). The following verse contains an attribute of Orion which would naturally be expressed by *qui turbaret*, etc. This was, however, made the predicate of **infestus Orion** to parallel v. 9, so that **dum pecori lupus** is left without a verb. In translating supply *esset* with **lupus**. For the comparison of the wolf and the lamb, cf. 4, 1 and n. On Orion as a storm-bringing constellation, cf. 10, 10 *tristis Orion*, and *C.* 1, 28, 21 f. *devexi rapidus comes Orionis | Notus.*

9 f. 'So long as Apollo's youth shall last,' *i.e.* 'forever.' Cf. Tibul. 1, 4, 57 *solis aeterna est Phoebo Bacchoque iuventas, | nam decet intonsus crinis utrumque deum.* — **hunc**: *this love of ours.* — **mutuum**: *requited.* Catullus says of Septumius and Acme 45, 20 *mutuis animis amant amantur.*

11 f. **virtute**: literally, 'spirit that becomes a man': the idea is repeated in *si quid ... viri est.* — **Flacco**: use of the proper name instead of *me* gives the same dignity to the expression that is lent to Teucer's words *C.* 1, 7, 27 *nil desperandum Teucro duce et auspice Teucro.*

13 f. **potiori**: *more favored rival*, as *C.* 3, 9, 2 *nec quisquam potior.* — **parem**: *i.e.* one who will return true love with like; in sense equivalent to *se dignam.*

15   nec semel offensi cedet constantia formae,
         si certus intrarit dolor.
     Et tu, quicumque es felicior atque meo nunc
         superbus incedis malo,
     sis pecore et multa dives tellure licebit
20   tibique Pactolus fluat,
     nec te Pythagorae fallant arcana renati,
         formaque vincas Nirea,
     heu heu, translatos alio maerebis amores;
         ast ego vicissim risero.

15 f. offensi: sc. *Flacci*, modifying **constantia**. Cf. n. to *calentis*, 11, 13. — formae : dative. — si ... dolor: Horace has not yet completely shut the door of his heart ; Neaera can still return. But if once his painful jealousy be confirmed (certus ... dolor), then beware! Cf. 11, 15 ff.

17 f. et tu, etc.: the successful rival. Cf. Tibul. 1, 5, 69 *at tu, qui potior nunc es, mea fata timeto*. — superbus incedis: *struttest in thy pride*. Cf. 4, 5.

19 ff. Wealth, wisdom, beauty cannot oppose her fickleness. — licebit: future to conform to maerebis v. 23. — tibique Pactolus fluat: 'though you have Midas' riches.'

21 f. Pythagorae ... renati: cf. n. to *C.* 1, 28, 10. — arcana : *i.e.* his esoteric teachings, reserved for his closest disciples. — Nirea : cf. *Il.* 2, 673 f. Νιρεύς, ὃς κάλλιστος ἀνὴρ ὑπὸ Ἴλιον ἦλθεν | τῶν ἄλλων Δαναῶν μετ' ἀμύμονα Πηλείωνα, and *C.* 3, 20, 15.

23 f. heu heu: in mocking pity for his rival. — ast : an archaic form, favored by Vergil, but used by Horace only here and *S.* 1, 6, 125 ; 8, 6. — risero : the fut. perf. expresses Horace's confidence. 'I shall certainly have my time to laugh.'

16

This epode was probably written at the outbreak of the Perusine War between Octavian and Antony, 41 B.C. At this time Horace had just returned broken in fortune after the defeat at Philippi, and had not yet met Maecenas, whose favor later relieved his personal necessities, or been reconciled to the new order of government. In this poem, however, he shows no thought for his personal needs, but is anxious solely for tne state, which doubtless seemed to many to be sinking into ruin. The difference between his feelings now and a few years later can be seen from the words C. 1, 14, 17 f. *nuper sollicitum quae* (sc. *navis* = *civitas*) *mihi taedium,* | *nunc desiderium curaque non levis.* Sellar (p. 122) has acutely observed that Horace seems to express the feelings of the losing side before the peace of Brundisium; Vergil, in his fourth eclogue, those of the winning side after its conclusion. The poem is not only the earliest, but the best of Horace's political verses. There is an intensity of feeling and a patriotic enthusiasm that did not appear later when the poet's anxieties had been calmed and somewhat blunted. In form also it is the most perfect of the epodes. Elision is wholly avoided in the hexameters — a new effect in Latin verse — and there are only three cases in the iambics. Furthermore there is a careful regard for assonance and a skillful use of alliteration that combine with other excellencies to make this one of the most remarkable productions of the Latin poets. The epode has been a favorite with many.

The mention of the Fortunate Isles may be due to the belief that Sertorius, after his defeat, wished to settle there. Cf. Plut. *Sert.* 9. The Scholiast says on v. 42 *ad quas* (*insulas fortunas*) *Sallustius in historia dicit victum voluisse ire Sertorium.* Probably the Canaries were meant. It is not impossible that some of the party defeated at Philippi had conceived the same plan. The thought running through the entire epode is that the state is hopelessly distracted by internal strife; it cannot escape ruin. Therefore all who are earnest and strenuous should settle in a new land where life can begin anew. The poem should be compared with *Epod.* 7 and with Vergil's *E.* 4. Metre, 76.

Altera iam teritur bellis civilibus aetas,
suis et ipsa Roma viribus ruit.

1 ff. Solon had similar forebodings for the Athenian state, 4, 1 ff. ἡμετέρα δὲ πόλις κατὰ μὲν Διὸς οὔποτ' ὀλεῖται | αἶσαν καὶ μακάρων θεῶν φρένας ἀθανάτων | ... αὐτοὶ δὲ φθείρειν μεγάλην πόλιν ἀφραδίῃσιν | ἀστοὶ βούλονται χρήμασι πειθόμενοι. | δήμου θ' ἡγεμόνων ἄδικος νόος, οἷσιν ἑτοῖμον | ὕβριος ἐκ μεγάλης ἄλγεα πολλὰ παθεῖν.

— altera . . . aetas: a second generation from that of Marius and Sulla, in whose time civil war began. — teritur: *is being wasted.*

2. suis et ipsa, etc.: cf. Livy *Praef. res ... ut iam magnitudine laboret sua,* and Aug. *Civ. Dei* 18, 45 *Roma late orbi terrarum imperans tamquam se ipsa ferre non valens sua se quodammodo magnitudine fregerat.* In these

Quam neque finitimi valuerunt perdere Marsi
   minacis aut Etrusca Porsenae manus,
5 aemula nec virtus Capuae nec Spartacus acer
   novisque rebus infidelis Allobrox,
nec fera caerulea domuit Germania pube

passages, however, the idea is that Rome has grown too great, whereas Horace feels that the state is rushing to suicidal ruin.

3-8. An enumeration of the great dangers that have threatened Rome from without, arranged according to distance rather than time. — **quam**: *that city which.* — **Marsi**: who led in the Social War in 91 B.C.; they proposed to reduce Rome and to establish a new capital of Italy at Corfinium. — **Porsenae manus**: 'Lars Porsena of Clusium,' who adopted the cause of the banished Tarquins and accordingly brought the city to surrender. Tacitus in writing of the burning of the Capitol in the year of anarchy 69 A.D. employs a similar expression, *Hist.* 3, 72 *nullo externo hoste . . . sedem Iovis . . . , quam non Porsena dedita urbe neque Galli capta temerare potuissent, furore principum exscindi!*

5. **aemula nec virtus Capuae**: cf. the reminiscence in Auson. *Ord. Urb. Nobil.* 49 f. *de Capua: nunc subdita Romae | aemula.* After the battle of Cannae in 216 B.C. the Capuans went over to Hannibal, and openly aimed to become the leaders in Italy. The Romans never forgot this perfidy. Cf. Cic. *Leg. Agr.* 2, 87 *quo in oppido maiores nostri nullam omnino rem publicam esse voluerunt ; qui tres solum urbes in terris omnibus, Karthaginem, Corinthum, Capuam, statuerunt posse imperii gravitatem ac nomen sustinere.* — **Spartacus acer**: the gladiator who carried on the war against the Romans 73-71 B.C. Cf. *C.* 3, 14, 19.

6. **novis rebus**: abl. of time. — **Allobrox**: with reference to the conspiracy of Catiline in 63 B.C., when an attempt was made to win over to the side of the conspiracy the Allobrogian envoys then in Rome. They hesitated, but finally decided it was for their interests to betray the plot. Cf. Sall. *Cat.* 40 ff., Cic. *in Cat.* 3, 4. In 54 B.C., however, they revolted but were subdued by C. Pomptinus, and this revolt was thought to be due to the conspiracy. Cf. Cic. *Prov. Cons.* 32 *C. Pomptinus . . . ortum repente bellum Allobrogum atque hac scelerata coniuratione* (sc. *Catilinaria*) *excitatum proeliis fregit eosque domuit, qui lacessierant.*

7. The greatest danger to Rome since its capture by the Gauls in 390 B.C. was the invasion of the

parentibusque abominatus Hannibal,
impia perdemus devoti sanguinis aetas,
10   ferisque rursus occupabitur solum.
Barbarus heu cineres insistet victor et urbem
eques sonante verberabit ungula,
quaeque carent ventis et solibus ossa Quirini
(nefas videre) dissipabit insolens.

Teutones and Cimbri, who were defeated and cut to pieces by Marius at Aquae Sextiae in 102 B.C., and at Versellae in the following year. — **caerulea**: *blue-eyed*. The blue eyes and fair hair of the Germans excited the wonder of the dark Italians. Cf. Iuv. 13, 164 f. *caerula quis stupuit Germani lumina, flavam | caesariem?*

8. **parentibus abominatus**: cf. *C.* 1, 1, 24 *bella matribus detestata.*

9 f. **impia ... aetas**: in opposition with the subject of **perdemus**. Cf. *C.* 1, 35, 34 *quid nos dura refugimus aetas?* — **devoti sanguinis**: *with a taint in the blood*, caused by the *scelus fraternae necis* 7, 18. — **rursus**: as before the founding of Rome.

11 f. **barbarus**: the Parthian particularly was in Horace's mind, as **eques** in the following verse shows. Cf. 7, 9. — **cineres**: *i.e.* of fallen Rome. Accus. with insistet. — **sonante**: 'and the hoofs of the victor's horse will clatter and echo through the empty streets.' Cf. Ezek. 26, 11 'with the hoofs of his horses shall he tread down all thy streets.'

13. **carent**: *now are safe from.* Tradition placed the tomb of Romulus — in spite of his apotheosis — behind the *rostra.* So Porph. *Varro post rostra fuisse sepultum Romulum dicit.* Whether it was at the spot marked by a slab of black stone was uncertain, according to Festus. p. 177 M. *niger lapis in Comitio locum funestum significat, ut alii, Romuli morti destinatum.* In 1899–1900 the spot beneath this *niger lapis* was excavated, but nothing that could be regarded as a tomb of a hero was discovered; yet the place was clearly hallowed, as the remains of sacrifices show. The most important discovery was a fragmentary ancient inscription, which can hardly be later than 500 B.C.

14. **nefas videre**: sc. *est.* Said with reference to the entire act of desecration. — **insolens**: *all unwittingly.* Cf. *C.* 1, 5, 8. With the expression in the last two verses, cf. Jeremiah 8, 1 'At that time, saith the Lord, they shall bring out the bones of the kings of Judah, and the bones of his princes, and the bones of the

15 Forte quid expediat communiter aut melior pars
    malis carere quaeritis laboribus.
Nulla sit hac potior sententia: Phocaeorum
    velut profugit exsecrata civitas
agros atque laris patrios habitandaque fana
20 apris reliquit et rapacibus lupis,
ire pedes quocumque ferent, quocumque per undas
    Notus vocabit aut protervus Africus.
Sic placet, an melius quis habet suadere? Secunda

priests, and the bones of the prophets, and the bones of the inhabitants of Jerusalem, out of their graves: ... they shall be for dung upon the face of the earth.'

15 ff. The poet dramatically appeals to his audience as if it were assembled in council.— **forte**: equivalent to *forsitan*. Instead of putting the clause in the form of a condition, *si . . . quaeritis*, a direct statement is used. — **communiter**: equivalent to *omnes*, in contrast to **melior pars**. — **aut**: *or at least*. — **carere**: *to escape*. An infinitive of purpose, dependent on **quid expediat**. Intr. 107. Cf. *C.* 1, 26, 1 *metus tradam . . . portare ventis.*

17 f. nulla sit, etc.: 'no proposal shall prevail over this.' The proposal proper begins v. 21 ire, etc.— **Phocaeorum**: in 534 B.C. the Phocaeans left their home rather than submit to the Persian yoke. The story is told by Herodotus I, 165. — **exsecrata**: *having bound themselves by a curse* (if any should try to return). Herod. *l.c.* ἐποιή-σαντο ἰσχυρὰς κατάρας τῷ ὑπολειπο-μένῳ ἑαυτῶν τοῦ στόλου. They furthermore sunk a mass of iron in the sea and swore they would not return to Phocaea until the iron should come to the surface again. This act became proverbial. Cf. Callim. *Frg.* 209 Φωκαέων μέχρις κε μένῃ μέγας εἰν ἁλὶ μύδρος.

19. laris patrios . . . fana: 'their hearths and temples.'— **habitanda**, etc.: marking the desolation of their city. Cf. n. to v. 10 above.

21 f. pedes . . . per undas: 'by land and sea.' — **quocumque . . . quocumque**: the anaphora marks the poet's feeling. Intr. 28 c. — **vocabit**: of a favorable wind. Cf. Catull. 4, 19 f. *laeva sive dextera | vocaret aura.*

23 f. sic placet: the language of the Roman senate, where the form of putting the question was *placetne?* Thus Horace continues the dramatic figure of a deliberative assembly. — **suadere**: with *habeo*, like the Gr. ἔχω πείθειν — **secunda . . . alite**: cf. n. to 10, 1.

ratem occupare quid moramur alite?
25 Sed iuremus in haec: 'Simul imis saxa renarint
vadis levata, ne redire sit nefas;
neu conversa domum pigeat dare lintea quando
Padus Matina laverit cacumina,
in mare seu celsus procurrerit Appenninus,
30 novaque monstra iunxerit libidine
mirus amor, iuvet ut tigris subsidere cervis
adulteretur et columba miluo,
credula nec ravos timeant armenta leones,
ametque salsa levis hircus aequora.'
35 Haec et quae poterunt reditus abscindere dulcis
eamus omnis exsecrata civitas,
aut pars indocili melior grege; mollis et exspes
inominata perprimat cubilia.

25. sed: 'but before we set sail, we must bind ourselves by an oath as the Phocaeans did.' — **in haec**: sc. *verba*. Cf. n. to 15, 4. — **simul**, etc.: the simple 'never' which we might expect is expanded into four ἀδύνατα, a favorite figure with the Romans. Cf. *C.* 1, 29, 10 ff.; 33, 7 f. Verg. *E.* 1, 59 ff. — **vadis**: abl. of separation.

28. Matina . . . cacumina: in Apulia. Cf. 1, 28, 3. 'The river shall climb the mountain heights.' Then follows the opposite figure of the Apennines running into the sea.

30. nova: *strange, unnatural.* — **monstra**: proleptic, changed to unnatural monsters by their strange passion (**mirus amor**).

31 f. subsidere: *mate with.* The reversal of nature is the more complete as the tiger and the lion become gentle, the deer and cattle bold; the dove too is to be wanton, whereas it was typical of fidelity. Cf. Prop. 3, 7, 27 *exemplo iunctae tibi sint in amore columbae.* — **miluo**: trisyllabic.

33 f. credula: proleptic, *trustful.* — **lēvis**: also proleptic, *become smooth*, like a sea animal.

35 f. haec: resuming the preceding oath; object of **exsecrata**. — **et quae**: *and whatever else.* — **civitas**: for the construction, cf. v. 9 *aetas*.

37 f. aut pars . . . melior: cf. n. to v. 15. The dull crowd, the inactive (**mollis**), and the fainthearted (**exspes**) may remain behind. — **inominata**: equivalent to *male ominata*; found only here.

Vos, quibus est virtus, muliebrem tollite luctum,
    Etrusca praeter et volate litora.
Nos manet Oceanus circumvagus; arva beata
    petamus, arva divites et insulas,
reddit ubi Cererem tellus inarata quotannis
    et imputata floret usque vinea,
germinat et numquam fallentis termes olivae
    suamque pulla ficus ornat arborem,
mella cava manant ex ilice, montibus altis

39 f. vos: *i.e.* the melior pars. — virtus: *manly courage*, in contrast to muliebrem ... luctum. — Etrusca ... litora: on the voyage to the West. — et: for the position, see Intr. 31.

41 f. nos, etc.: the decision is now made, and the poet returns to the glories of their new home in the Fortunate Isles.—circumvagus: apparently coined by Horace to reproduce the Homeric ἀψόρροος, the stream that circles around the world. Ovid. *Met.* 1, 30 uses *circumfluus* for the same purpose. Cf. Aesch. *P. V.* 138 ff. τοῦ περὶ πᾶσάν θ' εἱλισσομένου | χθόν' ἀκοιμήτῳ ῥεύματι παῖδες πατρὸς Ὠκεανοῦ. 'Children of father Ocean, who circles round the entire earth with stream unwearied.' — arva ... arva: Intr. 28 c. — divites insulas: *i.e.* the Fortunate Isles in the Western sea; Homer's Elysian Plain (*Od.* 4. 563 ff.). Hesiod's Islands of the Blest (*Op.* 170 ff.), where the heroes dwell. Cf. also Tenn. *Ulysses*, 'It may be that the gulfs will wash us down: | It may be we shall touch the Happy Isles, | And see the great Achilles, whom we knew.' The 'Fortunate Isles' of later times are probably to be identified with the Madeiras or the Canaries, which were visited by the traders. In this distant western land poets thought that nature supplied all man's needs without effort on his part.

43. reddit: *i.e.* as man's due.

45 f. numquam fallentis: cf. *C.* 3, 1, 30 *fundus mendax*. This, like *imputata* and *inarata* above, emphasizes man's ease and confidence there. — suam: emphatic. The better varieties of figs can be obtained only by grafting. Cf. 2, 19 *insitiva pira* and n. So Vergil says of a grafted tree, *G.* 2, 82 *miraturque novas frondes et non sua poma.* — pulla: *i.e.* 'ripe.'

47. mella: typical of abundance, like the Biblical 'land flowing with milk and honey.' Cf. *C.* 2. 19. 10–12, and Tibul. 1. 3. 45 f. *ipsae mella dabant quercus, ultroque ferebant* | *obvia securis ubera lactis oves.* — montibus: Intr. 95.

  levis crepante lympha desilit pede.
  Illic iniussae veniunt ad mulctra capellae,
50 refertque tenta grex amicus ubera,
  nec vespertinus circum gemit ursus ovile,
  neque intumescit alta viperis humus;
61 nulla nocent pecori contagia, nullius astri
  gregem aestuosa torret impotentia.
53 Pluraque felices mirabimur, ut neque largis
  aquosus Eurus arva radat imbribus,

48. The music of this verse has been noted by commentators ever since Porphyrio's day. Cf. *C.* 3, 13, 15 f. *unde loquaces lymphae desiliunt tuae.* In this verse the *p*-sound is added to that of the liquid. This new home will also have an abundant supply of water, which is far more important in such countries as Italy, especially in the *siticulosa Apulia*, or in our California, where there is a long dry season, than in the middle and eastern part of the United States. — **pede**: carrying the figure in **desilit** to its extreme. Anticipated by Lucretius 5. 272 *qua via secta semel liquido pede detulit undas.*

49 ff. The cattle need no herdsman to bring them home, no protection against wild beasts. A little later Vergil used the same description to picture the golden age that was approaching. *E.* 4. 21 f. *ipsae lacte domum referent distenta capellae | ubera.* In Vergil's verse *ipsae* is equivalent to Horace's *iniussae*, and *distenta* replaces the simple *tenta*.

51. vespertinus: in effect an adverb. Cf. Verg. *G.* 3, 537 f. *non lupus insidias explorat ovilia circum | nec gregibus nocturnus obambulat.* — **circum gemit**: Intr. 33.

52. intumescit: the action of the angry snake is transferred to the ground. Cf. Intr. 99. — **alta**: proleptic with **intumescit**, *swells and rises with.*

61 f. These verses stand in all the Mss. after v. 60, but are obviously out of place; by transferring them to this position the continuity of thought is maintained. — **nulla ... nullius**: Intr. 28 c. — **astri**: especially such as Sirius: cf. *C.* 3, 29, 17 ff. — **aestuosa ... impotentia**: the dog-star's furious heat, which brings disease on the flocks and herds. With this meaning of **impotentia**, cf. *impotens C.* 1. 37, 10; 3. 30, 3.

53-56. 'They shall be oppressed neither by too abundant rains as in the Italian winter, nor by too great drought as in the Italian summer.' — **ut**: *how.* — **radat**: cf.

55 pinguia nec siccis urantur semina glaebis,
       utrumque rege temperante caelitum.
    Non huc Argoo contendit remige pinus,
       neque impudica Colchis intulit pedem;
    non huc Sidonii torserunt cornua nautae,
60   laboriosa nec cohors Ulixei:
63 Iuppiter illa piae secrevit litora genti,
       ut inquinavit aere tempus aureum;
65 aere, dehinc ferro duravit saecula, quorum
       piis secunda vate me datur fuga.

Lucret. 5, 256 *ripas radentia flumina rodunt.* — **siccis**: proleptic.

57–60. 'That land is yet uncontaminated by man; no adventurers or traders have ever reached its shores.' — **Argoo remige**: collectively, an instrumental abl. With the use of the adjective, cf. *Etrusca* v. 4 above and n. to 10, 12. — **pinus**: *i.e.* the ship made from the pines of Pelion. Cf. Eurip. *Med.* 3 f. μηδ' ἐν νάπαισι Πηλίου πεσεῖν ποτε | τμηθεῖσα πεύκη. 'Would that the pine had ne'er fallen under the ax in the vale of Pelion.' And Catull. 64, 1 f. *Peliaco quondam prognatae vertice pinus | dicuntur liquidas Neptuni nasse per undas.* — **impudica Colchis**: Medea, queen of sorceresses, who helped Jason win the golden fleece, and then fled with him in the Argo, murdering her brother Apsyrtus to delay her father's pursuit.

59 f. Sidonii: the great traders of antiquity — **torserunt cornua**: swung their yards, *i.e.* directed their ships. — **laboriosa**: the epithet proper to Ulysses — Homeric πολύτλας, πολυτλήμων — is transferred to his companions. Cf. 17, 16. Intr. 99.

63 f. secrevit: *set apart for an upright people* (**piae genti**), *i.e.* the *melior pars,* comprising Horace and his friends. — **ut**: temporal. — **inquinavit**: *alloyed.*

65. aere: in the same construction as **ferro**. For the anaphora, cf. *arva, arva* v. 42. Intr. 28 c. The present age is the age of iron. — **quorum**: *from which,* objective gen. with **fuga**. — **vate me**: *according to my prophecy; vates,* 'inspired bard.' was the earliest word for poet among the Romans, but had been displaced by *poeta* until the poets of the Augustan Age restored it to its former dignity. Cf. Verg. *A.* 6, 662 *quique pii vates et Phoebo digna locuti.* Cf. *C.* 1, 1, 35.

17

A mock palinode addressed to Canidia; in pretended terror at the sorceress' power Horace pleads for mercy. Yet in his very prayer (1-52), as also in Canidia's reply (53-81), he makes his sharpest attack by rehearsing again all the charges he has ever made against her. Cf. *Epod.* 5 and *S.* 1, 8. With the palinodic form, cf. *C.* 1, 16. The date of composition naturally falls after these other two poems; it cannot be more accurately fixed. Metre, 58.

> Iam iam efficaci do manus scientiae,
> supplex et oro regna per Proserpinae,
> per et Dianae non movenda numina,
> per atque libros carminum valentium
> 5 refixa caelo devocare sidera,
> Canidia, parce vocibus tandem sacris
> citumque retro solve, solve turbinem.

1. **iam iam**: cf. 2, 68, where the meaning, however, differs, owing to the tense of the verb. So Catullus says 63, 73 *iam iam dolet quod egi.* Intr. 28 c. — **efficaci ... scientiae**: for it has accomplished its end, and Horace is forced to recognize its power. — **do manus**: yield like a captive who extends his hands for fetters.

2 ff. Horace adjures her by the divinities and powers under whose protection she stands. — **et**, etc.: for the position of the conjunctions, see Intr. 31. — **Dianae**: *i.e.* Hecate. Cf. n. to 5, 51. — **non movenda**: according to Porphyrio, equivalent to *non lacessenda — not to be disturbed with impunity, inviolable.*

4 f. **libros**, etc.: books containing formulae for incantations and magic. Cf. *Acts* 19, 19 'And not a few of them that practiced curious arts brought their books together, and burned them in the sight of all.' — **valentium ... devocare**: cf. v. 78 and n. to 5, 45. — **refixa**: proleptic — *unfix and*, as if the stars were fastened to the vault of heaven. Cf. Verg. *A.* 5, 527 f. *caelo ceu saepe refixa | transcurrunt crinemque volantia sidera ducunt.*

6. **parce**: *refrain from.* Cf. *C.* 3, 14, 12 *male ominatis parcite verbis.* — **sacris**: intentionally ambiguous, meaning both 'holy' and 'accursed.' Cf. n. to 7, 20.

7. **citum**: a participle (*ciere*), proleptically used with **retro**, *whirl swiftly backward, and*, etc. — **solve, solve**: Intr. 28 b. — **turbinem**: a rhombus, or 'bull roarer,' employed in magic rites. It was a smooth

Movit nepotem Telephus Nereium,
in quem superbus ordinarat agmina
10 Mysorum et in quem tela acuta torserat.
Unxere matres Iliae addictum feris
alitibus atque canibus homicidam Hectorem,
postquam relictis moenibus rex procidit
heu pervicacis ad pedes Achillei.

board which, when whirled at the end of a string, made a whirring noise, and was supposed to exercise a charm over the intended victim. To loose the spell it was whirled in the opposite direction (retro). It is still in use among some uncivilized peoples. See Andrew Lang, *Custom and Myth*, p. 29 ff. Cf. Theoc. *Id.* 2, 30 f. χὼς δινεῖθ᾽ ὅδε ῥόμβος ὁ χάλκεος, ἐξ Ἀφροδίτας | ὣς κεῖνος δινοῖτο ποθ᾽ ἀμετέρῃσι θύρῃσι. 'And as whirls this brazen wheel, so restless, under Aphrodite's spell, may he turn and turn about my doors,' (Lang). Lucian, *Dial. Meretr.* 4, 5 describes its use.

8-18. Three mythical examples of the effect of supplication. Telephus, King of the Mysians, was wounded by Achilles when the Greeks landed at Troy. His wound would not heal, and he was finally forced to come as a suppliant to his enemy, in accordance with an oracle which said he could be cured only by the rust of the spear that had struck him. Aged Priam's prayers made Achilles relent and give back Hector's body. Circe allowed Odysseus' companions to regain their human form. — **nepotem . . . Nereium**: Achilles' mother Thetis was the daughter of Nereus.

11. **unxere**: *i.e.* prepared for burial Hector's body. — **addictum**: *i.e. destined to be the food of*, etc., as a consolation to Patroclus' shade. Cf. *Il.* 23, 179 ff. χαῖρέ μοι, ὦ Πάτροκλε, καὶ εἰν Ἀΐδαο δόμοισι· πάντα γὰρ ἤδη τοι τελέω, τὰ πάροιθεν ὑπέστην. | δώδεκα μὲν Τρώων μεγαθύμων υἱέας ἐσθλοὺς | τοὺς ἅμα σοὶ πάντας πῦρ ἐσθίει· Ἕκτορα δ᾽ οὔ τι | δώσω Πριαμίδην πυρὶ δαπτέμεν, ἀλλὰ κύνεσσιν.

12. **homicidam**: reproducing the Homeric Ἕκτωρ ἀνδροφόνος.

13 f. **rex**: Priam. For the Romans the pathos of the situation lay not in Priam's loss of his son, but in the fact that this mighty king was forced to humiliate himself and weep for his son before Achilles. Cf. *Il.* 24, 509 f. ὁ μὲν Ἕκτορος ἀνδροφόνοιο | κλαῖ᾽ ἁδινά· προπάροιθε ποδῶν Ἀχιλῆος ἐλυσθείς. It is said this passage moved Macaulay to tears. — **pervicacis**: *obstinate*, but yielding in the end.

15   Saetosa duris exuere pellibus
     laboriosi remiges Ulixei
     volente Circa membra; tunc mens et sonus
     relapsus atque notus in voltus honor.
     Dedi satis superque poenarum tibi,
20   amata nautis multum et institoribus.
     Fugit iuventas et verecundus color,
     reliquit ossa pelle amicta lurida,
     tuis capillus albus est odoribus;
     nullum a labore me reclinat otium,
25   urget diem nox et dies noctem, neque est

15 f. The example of Circe is well chosen. The poet prays that Canidia like the early sorceress will reverse her spell. — **saetosa**: *i.e.* with swinish bristles. — **duris pellibus**: abl. with **exuere**. — **laboriosi**: Homeric πολύτλας, πολυτλήμων; best taken with **Ulixei**. Still, cf. 16, 60.

17 f. **mens**: Horace supposes that Circe's victims lost their minds as well as shapes, but in the Homeric account their fate is made the more pathetic because their wits remain. — **sonus**: *voice*. — **honor**: in contrast to the ugly swinish faces they had just put off.

20. **amata**, etc.: in this ironical compliment Horace gives Canidia the best thrust. — **nautis . . . et institoribus**: the lowest classes; cf. n. to 3, 6, 30.

21–36. With mocking extravagance Horace describes his sufferings. — **fugit, reliquit**, etc.: note the animated asyndeton. — **iuventas et . . . color**: *modest youth's fresh color*.

22. Horace is reduced to skin and bones. He may have derived his description from Theoc. 2, 88 ff. καί μευ | χρὼς μὲν ὁμοῖος ἐγίνετο πολλάκι θάψῳ, | ἔρρευν δ' ἐκ κεφαλᾶς πᾶσαι τρίχες· αὐτὰ δὲ λοιπὰ | ὀστί' ἔτ' ἦς καὶ δέρμα. 'And oftentimes my skin waxed wan as the color of boxwood, and all my hair was falling from my head, and what was left of me was but skin and bones' (Lang). Cf. also Sil. Ital. 2, 466 ff. *iam lurida sola | tecta cute et venis male iuncta trementibus ossa | extant, consumptis visu deformia membris*.

23. **albus**: *whitened*. — **odoribus**: *sweet smelling* (magic) *unguents*. Cf. 5, 59.

24 f. **labore**: *distress*. — **urget**: *presses close*. Cf. C. 2, 18, 15 *truditur dies die*. Note the effective order of the following. — **neque est levare**: a Greek construction.

levare tenta spiritu praecordia.
Ergo negatum vincor ut credam miser,
Sabella pectus increpare carmina
caputque Marsa dissilire nenia.
30 Quid amplius vis? O mare et terra, ardeo
quantum neque atro delibutus Hercules
Nessi cruore nec Sicana fervida
virens in Aetna flamma: tu, donec cinis
iniuriosis aridus ventis ferar,
35 cales venenis officina Colchicis.
Quae finis aut quod me manet stipendium?
Effare! Iussas cum fide poenas luam,
paratus expiare seu poposceris

26 f. tenta spiritu: *gasping, strained.* — negatum: sc. *a me*, equivalent to *quod negaveram*.

28 f. In apposition with negatum. — Sabella ... Marsa: the Sabines, Marsi, and (v. 60) Paeligni, all mountain folk, were skilled in magic. — increpare: *distress, assail.* — dissilire: *split in two.* Popular belief held that incantations literally had this power over snakes. Cf. Verg. *E.* 8, 71 *frigidus in pratis cantando rumpitur anguis,* and Ovid. *Am.* 2, 1, 25 *carmine dissiliunt abruptis faucibus angues.*

30. o mare et terra: a common expression like our 'great heavens.' Cf. Plaut. *Trin.* 1070 *mare terra caelum, di vostram fidem!* and Ter. *Ad.* 790 *o caelum, o terra, o maria Neptuni!*

31 f. atro: *deadly.* Cf. *C.* 1, 28, 13. — delibutus Hercules: cf. n. to 3, 17. — Sicana: with *flamma.*

33 f. virens: *ever burning.* — cinis: *a cinder.* — iniuriosis: *relentless.* Cf. *C.* 1, 35, 13 f. *iniurioso ne pede proruas | stantem columnam.*

35. cales: *art hot,* Canidia being identified with officina, — she is a very 'still-house' of poisons. Cf. Plaut. *Truc.* 581 *stabulum flagiti,* 'a very stall of sin.' — Colchicis: cf. n. to 5, 21; also *C.* 2, 2, 13, 8.

36. stipendium: *service, penalty.* The figure of the defeated foe (*do manus* v. 1, *vincor* v. 27) is continued in this word.

37 f. Horace is willing to do most extravagant penance (poenas luam), whether she require a hundred bullocks or even ask that he proclaim her brilliant purity.

— seu ... sive: the same variation *C.* 1, 4, 12.

centum iuvencis, sive mendaci lyra
voles, sonare 'Tu pudica, tu proba
perambulabis astra sidus aureum.'
Infamis Helenae Castor offensus vicem
fraterque magni Castoris, victi prece
adempta vati reddidere lumina:
et tu (potes nam) solve me dementia,
o nec paternis obsoleta sordibus,
nec in sepulcris pauperum prudens anus
novendialis dissipare pulveres!
Tibi hospitale pectus et purae manus,

39. **mendaci**: a telling thrust. This word like *sacris* v. 6, has a double meaning. His lyre may be **mendax** in what it has already said or in what it will proclaim.

40 f. **sonare**: *sound abroad*. Cf. *C.* 2, 13, 26. — **tu pudica, tu proba**: so Catullus in mockery 42, 24 *pudica et proba, redde codicillos*. — **perambulabis**: for her virtues Canidia shall be raised to heaven and wander among the other stars.

42-44. Helen's brothers, Castor and Pollux, punished her defamer Stesichorus with blindness (cf. *C.* 4, 9, 8); his recantation is preserved by Plato, *Phaedr.* 243 A. οὐκ ἔστ' ἔτυμος λόγος οὗτος | οὐδ' ἔβας ἐν νηυσὶν εὐσέλμοις, οὐδ' ἵκεο Πέργαμα Τροίας.
— **vicem**: *lot.* — **vati**: *a bard.* Cf. n. to 16, 66.

45. **et tu**: 'you too have divine power.' For the complimentary **potes nam**, cf. *S.* 2, 3, 283 f., '*unum me surpite morti! dis etenim facile est*' *orabat*.

46-52. At the very climax of the appeal Horace repeats the worst slanders current against Canidia. — **o nec paternis**, etc.: 'unsullied by disgraceful parents,' implying that Canidia's parentage was dubious. With the phrase, cf. *C.* 2, 10, 6 *obseleti sordes tecti*, and Cic. *pro Sest.* 60 (*virtus*) *neque alienis unquam sordibus obsolescit*.

47 f. **prudens anus**: *nor art thou a hag skilled to scatter*, etc. The ashes of the poor whose relatives could not protect their tombs were stolen by such witches for their magic rites — **novendialis**: *i.e.* just put away. According to Apul. *Met.* 9, 31 the funeral rites were not ended until the ninth day (*nono die completis apud tumulum sollemnibus*). They closed apparently with a sacrifice and banquet in honor of the dead. — **pulveres**: plural, to match **sepulcris**.

50   tuusque venter Pactumeius, et tuo
      cruore rubros obstetrix pannos lavit,
      utcumque fortis exsilis puerpera.
      Quid obseratis auribus fundis preces?
      Non saxa nudis surdiora navitis
55   Neptunus alto tundit hibernus salo.
      Inultus ut tu riseris Cotyttia
      volgata, sacrum liberi Cupidinis,
      et Esquilini pontifex venefici
      impune ut urbem nomine impleris meo?
60   Quid proderit ditasse Paelignas anus

49. **tibi**: sc. *est.* — **hospitale pectus**, etc.: some wish to see here a reference to *Ep.* 5, but perhaps the sneer should be taken in a general sense.

50–52. **tuusque ... tuo**: Intr. 28 c. The charge implied in 5, 5. — **venter**: cf. Livy 1, 34. 3 *ignorans nurum ventrem ferre.* — **Pactumeius**: a genuine Roman name. — **utcumque**, etc: *as often as*, implying that Canidia has practiced this deceit more than once; her recovery is so rapid and complete (**fortis exsilis**) that all the world knows her children are supposititious.

53. Canidia's answer. The poet skillfully makes his victim condemn herself by her threats of vengeance on him, her accuser.

54 f. **non saxa**, etc.: this line continues the figure, and we may translate, — *rocks are not ... when Neptune.* Cf. *C.* 3, 7, 21 *scopulis surdior Icari.* — **nudis**: shipwrecked and stripped of all they owned.

56. **inultus**: emphatic, expressing the gist of her exclamation. — **ut**: with the subj. in exclamation, — 'What, shall you,' etc. — **Cotyttia**: this reference to the sensual orgiastic worship of the Thracian Cotytto is only literary; there is no evidence that it was practiced at Rome. — **sacrum**, etc.: added in explanation of the foregoing. The rites are those of unrestrained passion (**liberi Cupidinis**).

58. **Esquilini**, etc.: the interpretation of this is doubtful. It probably means that Canidia in scorn calls him **pontifex**, *i.e.* censor and judge of her magic rites, for the part he had presumed to play in representing her and Sagana (*S.* 1, 8) busy with their foul work among the burial places of the poor on the Esquiline. The *pontifices* had oversight over all *sacra*.

velociusve miscuisse toxicum?
Sed tardiora fata te votis manent:
ingrata misero vita ducenda est in hoc,
novis ut usque suppetas laboribus.
65 Optat quietem Pelopis infidi pater,
egens benignae Tantalus semper dapis,
optat Prometheus obligatus aliti,
optat supremo conlocare Sisyphus
in monte saxum : sed vetant leges Iovis.
70 Voles modo altis desilire turribus,
modo ense pectus Norico recludere,
frustraque vincla gutturi nectes tuo
fastidiosa tristis aegrimonia.

60 f. quid proderit: 'if I fail now to punish you, what will be the gain?' etc. — **Paelignas anus**: from whom she had learned sorcery. — **velociusve**: *i.e.* in its effect; connect with **toxicum**.

62. sed tardiora: 'do not imagine that you will quickly meet your doom, as you pray you may; I will bring on you a lingering death with all the pangs a Tantalus ever suffered.'

63. misero: for the metre, see Intr. 58. — **in hoc**: *to this end;* defined in the following verses.

64. usque: temporal, *ever, constantly*. — **laboribus**: the regular expression for the torments of the damned. Cf. v. 24 and *C.* 2, 13, 38; 14, 19 f. *damnatusque longi | Sisyphus Aeolides laboris.*

65 ff. Three examples of long continued punishment such as Canidia will inflict on Horace. — **optat . . . optat . . . optat**: for a similar anaphora, cf. *C.* 2, 16, 1. 5. 6. Intr. 28 c. — **infidi**: because he treacherously threw into the sea his charioteer Myrtilus, through whose aid he had won Hippodamia as bride. Sophocles says this was the beginning of the curse that rested on all of Pelops' line. — **egens . . . semper**: *ever longing for*. — **benignae**: *abundant*. and so increasing his suffering.

67 f. obligatus aliti: the vulture that continually fed on his vitals. — **supremo**: equivalent to the more common *summo monte*.

70 ff. 'Thou wilt try all means of suicide in vain.' — **ense . . . Norico**: cf. n. to *C.* 1, 16, 9. — **pectus . . . recludere**: cf. Verg. *A.* 10, 601 *tum, latebras animae, pectus mucrone recludit.* — **vincla**:

Vectabor umeris tunc ego inimicis eques,
75   meaeque terra cedet insolentiae.
An quae movere cereas imagines,
ut ipse nosti curiosus, et polo
deripere lunam vocibus possim meis,
possim crematos excitare mortuos
80   desiderique temperare pocula,
plorem artis in te nil agentis exitus?

i.e. a noose. — **fastidiosa**: *with loathing weariness.* Cf. *C.* 3, 29, 9.

74. She will tame him and ride in triumph on his shoulders. In certain children's games the one defeated had to carry the victor about on his back. Cf. Plaut. *Asin.* 699 *vehes pol hodie me.* Such scenes were represented in certain terra-cotta groups and in vase paintings. See Schreiber's *Atlas*, pl. 79, 8; Baumeister no. 836.

75. She will spurn the earth in her pride and mount to the very stars. Cf. v. 41.

76 ff. **an**: introducing an interrogative conclusion. Cf. 6, 15

'or shall I with all my power have to weep over the failures of my art.' Canidia's claims here repeat the account of her practices given in *S.* 1, 8, 30–41. — **cereas imagines**: *i.e.* puppets representing the person to be affected. They are mentioned in Theoc. 2, 28 and Verg. *E.* 8, 80; similar images are still used in hoodoo charms.

78. **deripere lunam**: cf. 5, 45 f. and n.

80 f. **desiderique poculum**: love philters. Cf. 5, 38 *amoris poculum*, and n. — **plorem**: deliberative subjunc. — **artis . . . nil agentis**: proleptic with **exitus**, giving the cause of her grief. — **in te**: abl. *in thy case.* — **exitus**: accusative.

INDEX TO FIRST LINES

Aeli vetusto, 3, 17.
Aequam memento, 2, 3.
Albi, ne doleas, 1, 33.
Altera iam teritur, *Epod.* 16.
Angustam amice pauperiem, 3, 2.
At, o deorum, *Epod.* 5.
Audivere, Lyce, 4, 13.

Bacchum in remotis, 2, 19.
Beatus ille, qui procul, *Epod.* 2.

Caelo supinas, 3, 23.
Caelo tonantem, 3, 5.
Cum tu, Lydia, Telephi, 1, 13.
Cur me querellis, 2, 17.

Delicta maiorum, 3, 6.
Descende caelo, 3, 4.
Dianam tenerae dicite, 1, 21.
Diffugere nives, 4, 7.
Dive, quem proles Niobea, 4, 6.
Divis orte bonis, 4, 5.
Donarem pateras, 4, 8.
Donec gratus eram tibi, 3, 9.

Eheu fugaces, 2, 14.
Est mihi nonum superantis, 4, 11.
Et ture et fidibus iuvat, 1, 36.
Exegi monumentum, 3, 30.
Extremem Tanain si biberes, 3, 10.

Faune Nympharum, 3, 18.
Festo quid potius die, 3, 28.

Herculis ritu modo dictus, 3, 14.
Horrida tempestas, *Epod.* 13.

Iam iam efficaci, *Epod.* 17.
Iam pauca aratro, 2, 15.
Iam satis terris, 1, 2.
Iam veris comites, 4, 12.
Ibis liburnis inter alter navium, *Epod.* 1.
Icci, beatis nunc Arabum, 1, 29.
Ille et nefasto te posuit die, 2, 13.
Impios parrae recinentis, 3, 27.
Inclusam Danaen, 3, 16.
Intactis oppulentior, 3, 24.
Integer vitae, 1, 22.
Intermissa, Venus, diu, 4, 1.
Iustum et tenacem, 3, 3.

Laudabunt alii claram Rhodon, 1, 7.
Lupis et agnis, *Epod.* 4.
Lydia, dic, per omnes, 1, 8.

Maecenas atavis, 1, 1.
Mala soluta navis, *Epod.* 10.
Martiis caelebs, 3, 8.
Mater saeva Cupidinum, 1, 19.
Mercuri, facunde nepos, 1, 10.
Mercuri, nam te docilis, 3, 11.
Miserarum est neque amori, 3, 12.
Mollis inertia cur, *Epod.* 14.
Montium custos, 3, 22.
Motum ex Metello, 2, 1.
Musis amicus tristitiam, 1, 26.

Natis in usum laetitiae, 1, 27.
Ne forte credas, 4, 9.
Ne sit ancillae tibi amor, 2, 4.
Nolis longa ferae bella, 2, 12.
Nondum subacta ferre, 2, 5.
Non ebur neque aureum, 2, 18.

INDEX TO FIRST LINES

Non semper imbres, 2, 9.
Non usitata nec tenui ferar, 2, 20.
Non vides quanto, 3, 20.
Nox erat et caelo, *Epod.* 15.
Nullam, Vare, sacra vite, 1, 18.
Nullus argento color, 2, 2.
Nunc est bibendum, 1, 37.

O crudelis adhuc, 4, 10.
O diva, gratum quae regis, 1, 35.
O fons Bandusiae, 3, 13.
O matre pulchra filia, 1, 16.
O nata mecum consule, 3, 21.
O navis, referent in mare, 1, 14.
O saepe mecum, 2, 7.
O Venus, regina Cnidi, 1, 30.
Odi profanum vulgus, 3, 1.
Otium divos rogat, 2, 16.

Parcius iunctas, 1, 25.
Parcus deorum cultor, 1, 34.
Parentis olim siquis, *Epod.* 3.
Pastor cum traheret, 1, 15.
Persicos odi, puer, 1, 38.
Petti, nihil me sicut antea iuvat, *Epod.* 11.
Phoebe silvarumque potens, *C. S.*
Phoebus volentem, 4, 15.
Pindarum quisquis, 4, 2.
Poscimur, siquid, 1, 32.

Quae cura patrum, 4, 14.
Qualem ministrum, 4, 4.
Quando repostum Caecubum, *Epod.* 9.

Quantum distet ab Inacho, 3, 19.
Quem tu, Melpomene, semel, 4, 3.
Quem virum aut heroa, 1, 12.
Quid bellicosus Cantaber, 2, 11.
Quid dedicatum poscit, 1, 31.
Quid fles, Asterie, 3, 7.
Quid immerentis hospites, *Epod.* 6.
Quid tibi vis, mulier, *Epod.* 12.
Quis desiderio sit pudor, 1, 24.
Quis multa gracilis te puer, 1, 5.
Quo me, Bacche, rapis, 3, 25.
Quo, quo scelesti ruitis, *Epod.* 7.

Rectius vives, Licini, 2, 10.
Rogare longo putidam te, *Epod.* 8.

Scriberis Vario, 1, 6.
Septime, Gadis aditure, 2, 6.
Sic te diva potens Cypri, 1, 3.
Solvitur acris hiems, 1, 4.

Te maris et terrae, 1, 28.
Tu ne quaesieris, 1, 11.
Tyrrhena regum progenies, 3, 29.

Vlla si iuris tibi, 2, 8.
Vxor pauperis Ibyci, 3, 15.

Velox amoenum, 1, 17.
Vides, ut alta, 1, 9.
Vile potabis modicis, 1, 20.
Vitas inuleo me similis, 1, 23.
Vixi puellis nuper idoneus, 3, 26.

Morris and Morgan's Latin Series

EDITED FOR USE IN SCHOOLS AND COLLEGES

UNDER THE SUPERVISION OF

EDWARD P. MORRIS, L.H.D.,
PROFESSOR OF LATIN IN YALE UNIVERSITY

AND

MORRIS H. MORGAN, PH.D.,
PROFESSOR OF CLASSICAL PHILOLOGY IN HARVARD UNIVERSITY

VOLUMES OF THE SERIES

Essentials of Latin for Beginners. Henry C. Pearson, Teachers College, New York. 90 cents.

A School Latin Grammar. Morris H. Morgan, Harvard University. $1.00.

A First Latin Writer. M. A. Abbott, Groton School. 60 cents.

Connected Passages for Latin Prose Writing. Maurice W. Mather, formerly of Harvard University, and Arthur L. Wheeler, Bryn Mawr College. $1.00.

Caesar. Episodes from the Gallic and Civil Wars. Maurice W. Mather, formerly of Harvard University. $1.25.

Cicero. Ten Orations and Selected Letters. J. Remsen Bishop, Eastern High School, Detroit, Frederick A. King, Hughes High School, Cincinnati, and Nathan W. Helm, Evanston Academy of Northwestern University. $1.25.
Six Orations. $1.00.

Selections from Latin Prose Authors for Sight Reading. Susan Braley Franklin and Ella Catherine Greene, Miss Baldwin's School, Bryn Mawr. 40 cents.

Cicero. Cato Maior. Frank G. Moore, Columbia University. 80 cents.

Cicero. Laelius de Amicitia. Clifton Price, University of California. 75 cents.

Selections from Livy. Harry E. Burton, Dartmouth College. $1.50.

Horace. Odes and Epodes. Clifford H. Moore, Harvard University. $1.50.

Horace. Satires. Edward P. Morris, Yale University. $1.00.

Horace. Satires and Epistles. Edward P Morris, Yale University. $1.25.

Horace. Odes, Epodes, and Carmen Saeculare, Moore. **Satires and Epistles,** Morris. In one volume. $2.00.

Pliny's Letters. Albert A. Howard, Harvard University.

Tibullus. Kirby F. Smith, Johns Hopkins University.

Lucretius. William A. Merrill, University of California. $2.25.

Latin Literature of the Empire. Alfred Gudeman, University of Pennsylvania.
   Vol. I. Prose: Velleius to Boethius $1.80
   Vol. II. Poetry: Pseudo-Vergiliana to Claudianus. $1.80

Selections from the Public and Private Law of the Romans. James J. Robinson, Hotchkiss School. $1.25.

Others to be announced later.

HORACE
THE SATIRES

WITH INTRODUCTION AND NOTES

BY

EDWARD P. MORRIS

PROFESSOR OF LATIN IN YALE COLLEGE

NEW YORK ·:· CINCINNATI ·:· CHICAGO
AMERICAN BOOK COMPANY

Copyright, 1909, by
EDWARD P. MORRIS and MORRIS H. MORGAN.

Entered at Stationers' Hall, London.

MORRIS. HORACE SATIRES.

PREFACE

THIS book will be found to differ from the many excellent editions of the Satires accessible to American students chiefly in the emphasis which I have desired to place upon the thought of Horace, as distinguished from the language or the verse or the allusions. That is, without denying that Horace may be made useful as the basis for a study of Roman life, and without forgetting that it is absurd to talk of studying the thought, if the language is only imperfectly understood, I have nevertheless believed that of all the Latin writers read in college Horace was the one in whose writings literary form could be most interestingly studied. In the Satires, too, the connection of thought is peculiar and, at first, difficult to follow. To meet this difficulty and to facilitate the understanding of each satire as a whole, the introductions have been made somewhat fuller than is usual.

E. P. MORRIS.

INTRODUCTION

THE events in the life of Horace are known to us from two sources: first, from an extract from Suetonius, preserved in the manuscripts of Horace and printed below; and, second, from the many personal allusions in his works.

Quintus Horatius Flaccus was born in Venusia, a Roman colony in the borderland between Lucania and Apulia, on the 8th of December, 65 B.C. His father was a freedman, that is, he had been a slave, but had bought his freedom or had been manumitted, and was engaged in some small business in or near Venusia. He was apparently of Italian stock, and in character and circumstances he was a man of the older Roman type, energetic, prudent, ambitious. The ambition took, in particular, the form of a determination to give to his son the best possible education and opportunities, — one of many modern touches in the life of Horace, — and in furtherance of this determination he brought the son to Rome and placed him in one of the best schools of the city. Somewhere about 45 B.C. Horace went to Athens — as young men now go to a university — to carry on studies and hear lectures on rhetoric, philosophy, and mathematics; this was the ordinary culmination of a Roman higher education, and Horace at this time, as probably also in the school in Rome, formed associations and friendships with young men of intellectual tastes and of social position somewhat higher than his own. While he was still a student at Athens, not yet quite twenty-one, the death of Caesar in March, 44, divided the Roman world into two hostile camps, and when

INTRODUCTION

Brutus came to Athens in the late summer of 44, on his way to assume the governorship of Macedonia and Asia Minor, Horace abandoned his studies and accompanied him with the nominal title of *tribunus militum*. Of the two years that intervened between the death of Caesar and the battle of Philippi, in 42, there is no record except the rather juvenile seventh satire of the First Book. It is probable that his father had died and that the property had been lost, perhaps confiscated; for when Horace returned to Rome in 41, he was obliged to support himself by taking a clerkship in the treasury department; here he began his career as a writer.

Behind these bare facts of his early life the temperament and character of Horace were taking shape. The story has in it so much that is modern that we are perhaps in danger of forcing the analogies, yet the outlines of the process are clear. Horace was a country boy, trained in the prudent traditions of a quiet life; his father desired for him the rise in station which he had himself only partially achieved, and sought it by means of a higher education and more stimulating associations than a remote village could afford. From the studies of the university the young man was plunged into the floods of civil war, following the leadership of the half-mystical and wholly romantic Brutus. He returned to Rome a pardoned rebel; the cause which he still believed to have been the cause of liberty was lost; his hopes of advancement in public life were at an end; his father was dead, his friends scattered, his property gone. Obscure, disappointed, perhaps a little embittered, he was to begin life over again. If this young man seems a different person from the Horace whom we associate with graceful love poems and the doctrine of the golden mean, it is only because we accept the result without following the process which led to it. For the two are identical; there is no break in the development; indeed, it is out of precisely such material that the mellow and penetrating commentator upon life is made, when success and recogni-

INTRODUCTION

tion, as well as disenchantment and difficulty, have done their part in shaping his character.

It was in the decade between 41, when he returned after Philippi, and 30, when at the age of thirty-five he published the Epodes and the Second Book of Satires, that his character and his life philosophy were matured. Few events are known to us out of these years. In 39 or 38 he was introduced by Vergil and Varius to Maecenas, and in 33 he received from Maecenas the gift of the Sabine farm, which was in a special sense his home for the rest of his life. But the intimacy with the circle of poets and critics who were gathered about Maecenas, greatly as it stimulated him, and the lasting friendship with Maecenas himself, with all the resulting benefits, were only important incidents in his development; his real life was in his writings. He began with a group of three satires, 2, 7, and 8 of Book I, and it was these which, with some of the Epodes, brought him to the notice of Vergil, and ultimately of Maecenas. They are plainly the work of a young writer. The seventh, though it is well written, is trivial; the eighth is a kind of burlesque Priapus-poem, without wit or real humor, unpleasantly personal and with no marked attractiveness of style. Of the second it must be said plainly that it is an attempt to draw attention by jesting indecency; there is no other possible interpretation of the choice of subject. On the other hand, the style of the seventh is good, the eighth is better than most poems of its kind, and the second, except in the choice of subject, is the real Horace, easy in style and handling, humorous and yet in a certain way serious. There is enough of sharpness and even of bitterness in it to explain the criticisms that it brought upon the writer, and the tone of the next satire, 4 of Book I, shows that Horace was himself aware that the earlier satires needed defense, if not apology. But a clear-sighted critic, on the lookout, as the members of the circle of Maecenas were, for young men of promise, would certainly have seen that the writer of these poems was a man not to be

INTRODUCTION

neglected. The satires which followed the admission of Horace to the friendship of Vergil and Varius and Maecenas need no specific comment beyond that which will be found in the special introductions; they are not the work of an obscure beginner, but of a man tempered by association with men of taste, mellowed by friendly recognition, and already master of an easy style and a sane and humorous philosophy of life.

His choice of satire as a means of expression is explained by Horace in *Sat.* 1, 10, 40-47; he says that other fields — comedy, tragedy, the epic, the bucolic — were already occupied, and that satire alone seemed open to him. But this explanation is not to be taken seriously; the causes which determined his choice were deeper, partly in his own temperament, partly in the conditions of his time. He was by nature an observer of men; he found in the interplay of character and circumstance a spectacle of constant interest, and the account which he gives (*Sat.* 1, 4, 105-143) of the teachings of his father and of his own habitual attitude, however humorous the application which he makes of it, is essentially true. To a man of such a habit of mind satire, in the sense which Horace gave to the word, as a good-natured commentary, that is, upon the follies and upon the virtues, too, of the men with whom he lived, was the most natural vehicle of expression. In so far as he was inclined toward more serious and emotional expression, he used at first the half-lyrical form of the Epodes, and the absence of the more profound feelings from the Satires is to be explained in part by the fact that they found another outlet in such poems as Epodes 4, 7, 9, and 16. But these strongly emotional verses look backward to the tempestuous past; they express the attitude of the obscure and defeated republican, struggling with circumstances and not yet in harmony with himself, and their subjects belong rather to the period of strife than to the new era upon which Rome was entering. The Augustan Age, precisely because it checked the vigorous public activities of the preceding period and turned

INTRODUCTION

men back upon science and philosophy and law and literature, was of all periods in Roman history the one which offered the most inviting material for humorous commentary. As on the crowded streets of the city men of every country and of all stations met and passed on, — a peasant from the mountains, a deposed Eastern king, a Greek philosopher, a Roman noble, — so in the complex social structure motives of every possible form and color were at work. Though public activities were checked, the office-holding and office-seeking politician flourished as he always flourishes under a one-man power, and his ambitions, selfish enough, yet not wholly unworthy, were an open invitation to discriminating satire. The immense business interests, too, which centered at Rome, presented then, as now, their puzzling mixture of motives and of influences, and it was to the man of business that Horace addressed the satire which was the preface to his first collected publication, as if the business man was to him the most marked figure of the age. Intermingled with these ambitions as a kind of common reward for every form of success was the prize of social recognition and prominence, which seems to have had for a Roman, with his outspoken personal conceits and vanities, an attractiveness even greater and more general than it has in modern societies; and certainly no spectacle offers itself more invitingly to the genial satirist than the spectacle of the social struggle. Horace played his part in society, as Thackeray did, and gathered material for his Book of Snobs. Somewhat apart from all these rivalries, but with rivalries no less keen in their own sphere, were the two schools of philosophy, the Epicurean and the Stoic. Horace is often, in a vague way, regarded as an Epicurean, but he was, in fact, of no school or of a school of his own, and it is not as an Epicurean that he occasionally strikes a sudden blow at a Stoic, or, more often, burlesques the paradoxes of the school with ironical solemnity. He recognized the underlying truth of the Stoics; he was by no means unconscious of the seriousness of life; he was, indeed, himself a preacher; but he was also a discriminating humorist, and the formal Stoic, apparently more concerned about the growth of his beard than about his growth in grace, and more insistent upon the phraseology of his doctrines than upon their intelligibility, appealed to both sides of his mind. In the long picture gallery of the Satires no figure is more frequently recurrent. Nor did Horace neglect the men of his own craft. The Augustan Age, which is often called the golden age of Latin literature, was, at any rate, a period most prolific in skillful writers. Through chance allusions, serious or satirical, we are able to see, behind the figures of the greater poets whose writings have survived to our times, a long array of men of lesser rank, not undistinguished among their contemporaries, and undoubtedly writers of merit. And below them was the crowd of poets and historians and critics and essayists whose names even have been lost. Here was rich material for the satirist, and material especially for such a satirist as Horace, who was always as much critic as poet and interested alike in the practice and in the theory of his art. Somewhat less prominent in the life of the city, yet marked enough to give occasional color to the scene, were various minor caprices or eccentricities, each with its little circle of devotees. There were the collectors of old bronzes and tableware, indifferent to the artistic imperfections of their rare pieces, but credulous of their antiquity. The professional musicians formed, then as now, a class by themselves, with their own standards and judgments. Petty officials rejoiced in opportunities to display themselves in elaborate costume. It is in part the notice which Horace has bestowed upon them that makes the so-called legacy hunters seem to have been so numerous in Rome, but the brilliant satire in which their arts are burlesqued was the product of observation, not of invention. The proper arrangement of a *menu* and the doctrines of gastronomy were quite certainly matters of serious concern to many persons in Roman society, though it is possible that the humorously detailed descriptions and travesties in the Second Book make the followers of this particular mania more prominent than they actually were in Roman life. But certainly the society to which Horace's friendship with Maecenas gave him access was a highly complex society, one which brought before his observant eye a most interesting variety of types and of individuals, and invited good-humored comment and even caustic remark. The Satires are not the result of so mechanical a choice as Horace jokingly implies, but the inevitable expression of the reflections of such a man as Horace was upon such a society as that of the Augustan Age.

The form which Horace's commentary on life was to take was already determined for him. In this respect ancient literature was to a high degree conventional and traditional; when once the type was fixed by the influence of some great originator, the range of subsequent deviation from the type was small. Didactic poetry was written in hexameters from Hesiod to Ovid; innovator as Euripides was, his variations from the norm of tragedy are in reality slight. Form and content are identified under one name in the *iambi* of Archilochus. The form of Roman satire, or at least the prevalent form, was fixed by C. Lucilius. He was an *eques* of the period of the Gracchi and the younger Scipio Africanus, a man of education and rank, a conservative in politics, and a writer of force and courage. His range of subjects was not very different from that of Horace, — literary criticism, ethical discussion, social comment, — but a large place was occupied by political satire, which was almost inevitable in that stormy period and in the writings of a friend of Scipio. In tone he was, so far as can be judged from the extant fragments and from the statements of his successors, extremely personal and harsh. The fact that the fragments of his writings have come down largely in quotations by the grammarians, who were interested chiefly in unusual words or phrases, makes it difficult to form an independent judgment of his style. The longest quotation, a definition of *virtus* in thirteen verses, is not without dignity of thought and expression, but in general the criticism of Horace, that Lucilius wrote too freely and with too little attention to finish of style, seems to be justified. The loss of his writings is a loss to linguistic and literary history, rather than to literature itself. But he performed the great service of determining both the tone and the form of satire. He gave to it for all time that critical and censorious tone which is still associated with the name and, after considerable experiment with other verse forms which had been used by Ennius, he settled upon the hexameter as the most suitable meter. In selecting satire as his field, Horace therefore felt himself bound by all the force of strong tradition to a certain tone and a certain verse.

But the force of tradition and convention in ancient literature, strong as it was, did not preclude originality; it merely set the bounds within which originality might work. Of imitation, in any proper sense of the word, that is, of attempt to copy as closely as possible the work of an older writer, there is very little evidence in Greek or Latin literature, and Horace, setting himself to write *Lucili ritu*, as he says, accepting as his starting point the definition which Lucilius had given to satire, was also acutely conscious of the imperfections of his predecessor, and fully determined to avoid them in his own work. The most evident of these imperfections was in the matter of style. The fragments of the satires of Lucilius are bold and crude in expression; they say what was to be said, but they say it without charm. There is no evidence of care for workmanship, of pleasure in attractive expression. But between Lucilius and Horace was the great Ciceronian period, in which the whole subject of Latin style in prose and in verse was most warmly debated by men who were daily practicing the art of writing. Two generations had contributed to raise the standard of good style, and Horace and the friends with whom he lived were desirous of raising it still further. Horace was, besides, by nature a literary artist, to whom the shaping of phrases into effective and pleasing form was an end in itself. It is, indeed, surprising to a modern reader that the justice of his guarded and moderate criticisms of the style of Lucilius should have been questioned by any intelligent student of Latin literature in the Augustan Age. That he was entirely successful in his attempt to improve in respect to style upon the work of his predecessor has never been doubted.

The other direction in which Horace endeavored to surpass Lucilius, without deviating too widely from the type, led him into greater difficulties. The satire of Lucilius was undoubtedly pungent and bitter in its attacks upon persons and upon parties, and this savageness of tone, which in various forms was familiar and agreeable to the Romans, was, in fact, an essential element in satire of the Lucilian type. But it was in every way impossible in the Augustan Age; the political situation between 42 and 31 B.C. would not have borne rough handling, and the softening of manners had put a check upon personalities. The problem, therefore, which presented itself to Horace was to retain the pungency of individual criticism without violation of the canons of good taste and without offense to public men. A part of the problem he made no attempt to solve; he left politics out of his satire entirely, even at the time when his patriotic feeling was expressing itself in the Epode *quo, quo scelesti ruitis?* and in Epode 16. But to the problem of giving to his satire the appearance without the reality of personal attack, he addressed himself with much ingenuity. The Satires seem to bristle with proper names, but examination shows that only a very few of the allusions are in fact personal attacks. Many of the names are taken from Lucilius and had long since ceased to be anything but types in literature. Others are from the Ciceronian period, the names of men who were then notorious.

Still others, men of Horace's day, were in their lifetime already so much the subject of open gossip and comment that an allusion to them was no more properly offensive or, indeed, personal, than an allusion in a modern newspaper to the men whose names are upon everybody's lips. Many names are fictitious, some pure inventions like the names in a novel, others disguising an allusion to a real person. The residuum of actual personality, such as would be offensive to modern feeling, is extremely small. Direct attack upon an individual was, in fact, as little to Horace's taste as to our own, and was incompatible with the lightness of touch which he was endeavoring to attain. Even the semblance of severity, which the Lucilian tradition obliged him to maintain in his earlier work, grows less distinct as he becomes conscious of his peculiar powers. The Second Book has less of it than the First; indeed, the first satire of that book is a kind of travesty of the severely personal satire and, by implication, a renunciation of it. The place of Horace in the history of Roman satire is, it is true, in the line of succession from Lucilius, but his own contribution to that history amounts almost to the creation of a new literary *genre*, a new variety of satire.

The events in the life of Horace after the publication of the Epodes and the Second Book in 30 B.C. are of interest to the reader of the Satires only in so far as they interpret his earlier period. He turned at once from satire to lyric poetry, following still further the path upon which he had entered in the Epodes, and published in 23 B.C. the first three books of the Odes, to which he gave the best of his powers and the best years of his life. Aside from other and more determining motives,— the inner impulse and the fact that the lyric is a higher form of art than satire,— the choice doubtless indicates also a feeling that he had for the time exhausted the field of satire, that he had carried his modifications of the Lucilian type as far as it was possible for him to carry them. But the habit of observation was still strong in him, and after the publication of the Odes he resumed his commentary on life and society in the form of epistles in hexameter. By the choice of a new and different form he freed himself from the limitations of satire; at the same time, as the tradition of the epistle in verse was less definitely fixed, the new form did not hamper him. The interval that separates such a satire as 2, 6 from such an epistle as 1, 7 is very slight; by addressing the satire to Maecenas, he could easily have made it an epistle in form, and with a few modifications the epistle might have been published with the Satires. It might be said that the three collections of hexameter poetry represent three steps in a continuous process; the First Book of the Satires is, in the main, satire after the manner of Lucilius, the Second Book is an experiment with the dialogue form, and the First Book of the Epistles marks the complete breaking away from the Lucilian tradition. They are three stages in the working out of a literary form within which the temperament of Horace could express itself with the least possible sense of restriction.

Before his death, which occurred on the 27th of November, 8 B.C., Horace was already recognized as the greatest of Roman lyric poets and as the most conspicuous figure, next to Vergil, in the literature of his time. This position his poems retained after his death; they were universally read and were used as text-books in schools. Critical and learned commentary began to gather about them in the first century of the Empire, and, before the fall of Roman power in the West, copies of his works were in wide circulation, often prefaced by the account of his life from Suetonius and annotated with *scholia*. During the Middle Ages, when knowledge of the ancient world was at its lowest, his poems were still read in schools and frequently copied in the monastery libraries, and with the Revival of Learning many editions were issued from the early printing presses. In modern times they have formed a part of the

INTRODUCTION

school or university curriculum in all countries; they have been translated more often than the works of any other ancient writer, and have deeply influenced modern literature. All this is evidence of the high esteem in which his poetry has been held by scholars and men of letters; the estimate of men of affairs, of men outside of academic life, is somewhat similar. For it is probably true that of all the writers of Greek and Latin poetry — many of them greater than Horace — no one has so frequently been carried away from the university life and become a part of the familiar intellectual furniture of educated men in active life. The explanation of an interest so widespread and so long-continued is not, of course, to be sought in those qualities or characteristics which Horace shares with other writers. He reflects, it is true, a highly interesting period in history, but the letters of Cicero are an even more vivid reflection of a more critical period. His poetic form, as it is worked out in the lyrics, is most admirable, and poetic form is one of the main reasons for our continued study of the two classic literatures, but the range of its attractive power is limited. That which has differentiated Horace from other writers and made him permanently attractive to men of widely varied taste is independent of his circumstances and, to a considerable degree, of his artistic form; it lies partly in the personal character which his writings disclose and partly in the permanent worth of his comments upon life.

The character of a writer or an artist as it shows itself in his work must be learned by indirection, by impressions repeated and deepened into familiarity. For this kind of personal acquaintance Horace gives abundant material. Enough has been said above to correct the notion that he was a *dilettante*, playing with life. He was, it is true, fundamentally an observer rather than an actor, and he was by temperament genial and tolerant; these are the qualities upon which the charm of his personality rests; but a merely temperamental tolerance is, like temperamental optimism, a very superficial and uninteresting quality. Horace was a man of warm feeling and of strong convictions, though his convictions are in part alien to our thought, and the lightness with which he sometimes touches serious things is not the lightness of carelessness. He had learned early, not without struggle and pain, the lesson of adjustment to the limitations of life, had learned that the secret of a composed and dignified life lies in the acceptance of the inevitable. Even in his less cheerful moods he faced his heaviest losses with steadiness : —

> durum : sed levius fit patientia,
> quidquid corrigere est nefas.

But his ordinary mood was not tragic ; he preferred to meet life with a smile, not underestimating the possibilities of loss and trouble, but also not overestimating them. And it is the fact that his genial acceptance of life rests upon a foundation of cool judgment and shrewd comprehension that gives it meaning. It is this combination that makes him the philosopher for men of the world. For the man of affairs, if he is conscious of life at all, is seeking for a formula which will include all the follies and weaknesses of men and will teach him how to accept them with a smile. The real meaning of Horace's philosophy is poorly expressed by *nil admirari*, as the words are commonly understood, and not very well by *aurea mediocritas;* it is a philosophy of comprehension and tolerance, and the charm of his personality is that he so perfectly embodies his own doctrine.

The value of his comments upon men and society lies partly in the application of his philosophy to life, partly in the peculiar forms in which he expresses it. His satires, and, to a less degree, his epistles, are a picture gallery. He does not describe individuals or, if he does, it is in terms so general as to make them types ; his little pictures are done in few lines, but in lines so expressive that they tell the essential truth about a man. Such a characterization as that of Tigellius in *Sat.* 1, 3 or that of Damasippus in *Sat.* 2, 3, or the longer description by suggestion in *Sat.* 1, 9, is as true and as recognizable now as it was when it was written, because it presents the essential qualities which are of no single period or race. The power to draw such pictures is not, it is true, the highest kind of artistic power, and it does not necessarily carry with it either a profound philosophy or great breadth of view. Great artists have lacked it, and some caricaturists have had it. The most obvious modern illustrations are in fiction; George Eliot had not a trace of it; Anthony Trollope had it in a high degree. Such little pictures do not teach us the meaning of life, in its larger aspects and relations. They teach us in a nearer way about people; they show us how to analyze and classify; they stimulate our intelligent comprehension of the men we meet. The reader of Horace, if he gets his lesson truly, understands better the man who sits in the seat next to him, and, if he becomes a true disciple, he understands himself better, too.

INTRODUCTION

VITA HORATII

From Suetonius, *De Viris Illustribus*

Q. Horatius Flaccus Venusinus, patre, ut ipse tradit, libertino et exactionum coactore, ut vero creditum est, salsamentario, cum illi quidam in altercatione exprobrasset: 'quotiens ego vidi patrem tuum brachio se emungentem!' Bello Philippensi excitus a M. Bruto imperatore tribunus militum meruit, victisque partibus venia impetrata scriptum quaestorium comparavit. Ac primo Maecenati, mox Augusto insinuatus non mediocrem in amborum amicitia locum tenuit. Maecenas quantopere eum dilexerit satis testatur illo epigrammate: —

> ni te visceribus meis, Horati,
> plus iam diligo, tu tuum sodalem
> Ninnio videas strigosiorem;

sed multo magis extremis iudiciis tali ad Augustum elogio: 'Horati Flacci ut mei esto memor.' Augustus epistularum quoque ei officium obtulit, ut 'hoc ad Maecenatem scripto significat: 'ante ipse sufficiebam scribendis epistulis amicorum, nunc occupatissimus et infirmus Horatium nostrum a te cupio abducere. Veniet ergo ab ista parasitica mensa ad hanc regiam et nos in epistulis scribendis adiuvabit.' Ac ne recusanti quidem aut succensuit quicquam aut amicitiam suam ingerere desiit. Extant epistulae, e quibus argumenti gratia pauca subieci: 'sume tibi aliquid iuris apud me, tamquam si convictor mihi fueris; recte enim et non temere feceris, quoniam id usus mihi tecum esse volui, si per valitudinem tuam fieri possit.' Et rursus: 'tui qualem habeam memoriam poteris ex Septimio quoque nostro audire; nam incidit ut illo coram fieret a me tui mentio. Neque enim si tu superbus amicitiam nostram sprevisti, ideo nos quoque ἀνθυπερηφανοῦμεν.' Praeterea saepe eum inter alios iocos purissimum penem et homuncionem lepidissimum appellat unaque et altera liberalitate locupletavit. Scripta quidem eius usque adeo probavit mansuraque perpetuo opinatus est, ut non modo Saeculare carmen componendum iniunxerit, sed et Vindelicam victoriam Tiberii Drusique privignorum suorum, eumque coegerit propter hoc tribus carminum libris ex longo intervallo quartum addere; post sermones vero quosdam lectos nullam sui mentionem habitam ita sit questus: 'irasci me tibi scito, quod non in plerisque eius modi scriptis mecum potissimum loquaris. An vereris ne apud posteros infame tibi sit, quod videaris familiaris nobis esse?' expresseritque eclogam ad se cuius initium est:—

> cum tot sustineas et tanta negotia solus,
> res Italas armis tuteris, moribus ornes,
> legibus emendes, in publica commoda peccem,
> si longo sermone morer tua tempora, Caesar.

Habitu corporis fuit brevis atque obesus, qualis et a semet ipso in satiris describitur et ab Augusto hac epistula: 'pertulit ad me Oniscus libellum tuum, quem ego, ut excusantem, quantuluscumque est, boni consulo. Vereri autem mihi videris ne maiores libelli tui sint quam ipse es, sed tibi statura deest, corpusculum non deest. Itaque licebit in sextariolo scribas, quo circuitus voluminis tui sit ὀγκωδέστατος, sicut est ventriculi tui.' Vixit plurimum in secessu ruris sui Sabini aut Tiburtini domusque eius ostenditur circa Tiburni luculum. Venerunt in manus meas et elegi sub titulo eius et epistula prosa oratione quasi commendantis se Maecenati, sed utraque falsa puto; nam elegi vulgares, epistula etiam obscura, quo vitio minime tenebatur. Natus est vi. Idus Decembris L. Cotta et L. Torquato consulibus, decessit v. kal. Decembris C. Marcio Censorino et C. Asinio Gallo consulibus septimo et quinquagesimo anno, herede Augusto palam nuncupato, cum urgente vi valetudinis non sufficeret ad obsignandas testamenti tabulas. Humatus et conditus est extremis Esquiliis iuxta Maecenatis tumulum.

Q. HORATI FLACCI

SERMONES

LIBER PRIMVS

I

There is no reference to current events sufficiently definite to fix the date of this Satire by internal evidence. It was written after Horace's introduction to Maecenas in 38, and the maturity of style and treatment show a great advance upon the early Satires of this book, 2, 7, and 8. Obviously, it is introductory to the whole book, published in 35, and it was probably written shortly before that date.

'What is the source of the social discontent of our times? Not, certainly, as is sometimes said, in the peculiar hardships of this or that occupation. The very men who offer this explanation disprove it by their conduct. Nor can the persistent devotion of men to business be justified, as some of them appear to think, by the praiseworthy desire to provide against future needs. It is something deeper than this and less worthy — the mere desire to get rich, to be richer than others.

'A life given up to this pursuit is no better than the life of the miser of fiction. Such a man dares not spend anything, lest he spend all, and does not see that, to one who lives a natural life, the possession of what is never to be used is not a gain, but a burden.

'To say that social standing depends upon money is to say what is perhaps true, but is not to the point. For the result is the same; the man with such an ambition merely gathers wealth to tantalize himself, purchasing only terrors and unhappiness with it. He kills the natural affections, and spends his life in providing against contingencies that will, in all probability, never arise. I am not arguing that one should waste his money; that is only another extreme of folly; between the two lies the safe middle course.

'The source of our unhappiness, to answer the question with which I began, is the desire to be rich, to be a little richer. We forget the many who are poorer than we, and see only the few who are ahead of us. We spend our lives in an ignoble struggle, and we come still unsatisfied to the end.

'Enough of sermonizing. I'm no Crispinus.'

The subject of this introductory satire is the race for wealth. In the universal peace which followed the civil wars, the financial affairs of the world centered at Rome as an imperial clearing house, and great fortunes were rapidly made by men of the capitalist class. In general, the old nobility and the philosophers and writers kept aloof from business, which consequently fell into the hands of the *equites*, who had had only a slight part in public affairs, or of the freedmen, who were ill-fitted by character and experience to make a large-minded or even a rational use of their money. Some of them burst out into ridiculous display, and furnished easy material for the satirist; others, with less obvious folly, knew no better use of their acquired wealth than to make it the means of acquiring still more. It is to men of the latter class that this discourse is addressed. For this is not pure satire, holding up the peculiarities of certain men to the scorn of others; it is, in part, a discourse, a sermon, addressed directly to the over-eager man of business, and intended to show to him, for his possible betterment, the intrinsic littleness of the occupation to which he was so ardently devoting himself.

Horace frequently employs in other places the thoughts and sometimes the figures and expressions of this satire. Compare especially the end of Epode 1, the main thought of Epode 2, and the whole of Epode 4. The similarity between the social structure of the Augustan Age and our own times could scarcely be made more vivid than it is by the fact that the satirist of that society chose for the theme of his opening satire the race for wealth.

> Qui fit, Maecenas, ut nemo, quam sibi sortem
> seu ratio dederit seu fors obiecerit, illa

1. Qui fit: *how does it happen?* But the interrogative form is merely a rhetorical way of introducing the general subject — the discontent of men — by beginning with its source. — **Maecenas**: the direct address serves to dedicate the first book of Satires to Horace's patron and friend. The dedication of the Odes is like this, a little formal and unconnected with the subject of the poem. The address to Maecenas in the first Epode is more natural and graceful. — **quam sortem . . . illa**: = *illa sorte . . . quam*. The word *sors* is used without thought of its original sense, as 'lot' is in English.

2. ratio and **fors** are often used together to cover the whole field of human life; everything is due either to deliberate *choice* or to

contentus vivat, laudet diversa sequentis?
'O fortunati mercatores!' gravis annis
5 miles ait, multo iam fractus membra labore.
Contra mercator, navem iactantibus Austris,
'Militia est potior. Quid enim? Concurritur; horae

mere *chance*. The same contrast is implied in *Sat.* 1, 6, 54, though *ratio* is not actually used. The two verbs, *dederit*, *obiecerit*, carry on the contrast between the deliberate and the accidental.

3. laudet: the full expression of the thought would seem to require *sed unus quisque laudet*, but the negative of *nemo* goes only with *contentus*, not with *vivat*, so that the thought is 'every one is discontented with his own life and envious of the lives of others.' Cf. vs. 109, where the phrases *nemo se probet* (= *contentus vivat*) and *laudet* are connected by *ac potius*. The meaning of *laudare* is not precisely *to praise*, but 'to speak of with admiration,' as in Plaut. *Rud.* 523, *laudo fortunas tuas*, and in combination with *diversa sequentis* it suggests the idea of envy.

4-12. The two pairs of contrasted examples — soldier and sailor, lawyer and farmer — and indeed the whole scene which is half described, half suggested in vss. 15-22, come from the conventional popular philosophy, perhaps from some Greek burlesque drama. Horace uses them frequently with slight variations.

4-5. The first illustration is barely suggested, without specific details. *gravis annis* means, in ordinary usage, *weighed down with years*, not distinguishing between years of life and years of service, and the thought is repeated and amplified in the next phrase. — **fractus membra**: *broken in health*. The soldier, feeling old and worn, says, 'I wish I had gone into business.'

6-8. mercator: a merchant who sails his own vessel on a business venture, as the merchants in the China trade did a hundred years ago. He is therefore called, indifferently, either *mercator* or *nauta* (vs. 29), and the following lines deal only with the hardships of the sailor's life. — **iactantibus**: the tense is important; he is in the midst of a gale. — **Austris**: the southerly winds are heavy and squally in the Mediterranean, and Horace generally uses *Auster* with an implication of storm, as 'northeaster' is used in English. — **Quid enim?** simply *why?* or *why then? enim* was originally a strengthening particle, and before it had acquired the meaning *for*, it formed compound phrases with conjunctions and particles (*at enim, non*

[1, 1, 8]

    momento cita mors venit aut victoria laeta.'
    Agricolam laudat iuris legumque peritus,
10 sub galli cantum consultor ubi ostia pulsat.
    Ille, datis vadibus qui rure extractus in urbem est,
    solos felices viventis clamat in urbe.

enim, quia enim) in which the earlier meaning is preserved. There is no ellipsis here. — **Concurritur**: impersonal, expressing the brevity of the crisis in a soldier's life. — **horae momento**: the Romans did not measure short spaces of time with precision, and there is no Latin word for 'minute' or 'second.' *hora* is therefore somewhat vague, like the English 'the hour of victory'; cf. *puncto mobilis horae, Epist.* 2, 2, 172. — The second illustration is more detailed than the first, and the folly of the momentary desire to exchange occupations is more clearly suggested. The sailor's endurance is broken down by the long-continued storm, and he wishes for the short crisis of the soldier's life, forgetting alike the greater profits of a business career and the wearisome routine of garrison life.

  9-10. **Agricolam laudat**: scarcely more than ' wishes he were a farmer.' — **ius** and **leges** are sometimes contrasted, — *e.g.*, as the general body of law and the special legislative enactments, — but here the two contrasting terms are used together to express one general idea. — **peritus**: the *patronus*, to whom friends and clients came at the early morning *salutatio* to ask advice on business and legal matters. There is a personal touch in this illustration, for Horace did not like to get up early (*ad quartam iaceo, Sat.* 1, 6, 122).

  11-12. **Ille**: *the other*, the farmer, of the class whose unembarrassed life the lawyer has just been praising. He is not quite identified with the *consultor*. — **datis vadibus**: not necessarily bail in a criminal action, but surety for his appearance as defendant in any legal case. In this second pair of illustrations Horace allows the absurdity of the discontent to appear plainly and comically. The lawyer, in his momentary annoyance at being called early in the morning, wishes he were a farmer, forgetting that the farmer is habitually an early riser. The lack of serious consideration on the part of the countryman is shown by the suddenness of his conversion: he has been dragged (*extractus*) against his will into the city, but once there he loudly proclaims (*clamat*) not only that the city is better than the country, but even that city people are the only persons who are happy.

Cetera de genere hoc, adeo sunt multa, loquacem
delassare valent Fabium. Ne te morer, audi
15 quo rem deducam. Si quis deus, 'En ego,' dicat,
'iam faciam quod voltis: eris tu, qui modo miles,
mercator; tu, consultus modo, rusticus: hinc vos,
vos hinc mutatis discedite partibus. — Heia!
quid statis?' — nolint. Atqui licet esse beatis.
20 Quid causae est, merito quin illis Iuppiter ambas

13. **Cetera de genere hoc**: Horace was familiar with Lucretius (see notes on 23, 117–119) and uses this common Lucretian phrase to give to the passage a burlesque air of philosophizing.

14. **Fabium**: the scholiast says that he was a man in public life who had written some volumes on Stoic philosophy. It is characteristic of Horace to put his personal satire, which is not very frequent or very severe, into such light touches as this, given in passing and merely by way of illustration. Cf. the allusion to Crispinus below, vs. 120. And these humorous attentions are often bestowed upon the Stoics, whose formalism and austerity were repugnant to a man of Horace's temperament, and led him to overlook their good qualities. With all their superficial defects, they were the most serious religious teachers in Roman life. — **Ne te morer**: *not to delay you*, 'not to be too long about it'; a parenthetic clause of purpose.

15 f. **quo rem deducam**: 'what my point is going to be,' 'what conclusion I am going to reach.' — **Si quis deus ... dicat**: the apodosis is in *nolint*, 19. The god is at this point indefinite, but, as the scene becomes clearer, he is definitely named, vs. 20. — **En ego**: *here I am*; to be taken closely with *faciam*. Both *ego* and *iam* are emphatic; 'here I am, *I* will do your business for you on the spot.'

18. **mutatis ... partibus**: exactly like the English *parts* in a drama; cf. *partes* of a political party. — **Heia**: a colloquial exclamation of surprise and dissatisfaction, as if the god was annoyed that his friendly offices were not acceptable.

19. **beatis**: dat. after *esse*, as if *eis* had been expressed after *licet*.

20. **causae**: partitive gen. with a neut. pron.; very common in colloquial Latin, Plautus, Terence, Cicero's Letters, Catullus.

iratus buccas inflet, neque se fore posthac
tam facilem dicat, votis ut praebeat aurem?
Praeterea, ne sic, ut qui iocularia, ridens
percurram, (quamquam ridentem dicere verum
25 quid vetat? ut pueris olim dant crustula blandi
doctores, elementa velint ut discere prima;
sed tamen amoto quaeramus seria ludo;)
ille gravem duro terram qui vertit aratro,
perfidus hic caupo, miles, nautaeque per omne

21. **buccas inflet**: cf. Plaut. *Stichus*, 767, *age, iam infla buccas*, addressed to a flute player. *bucca* is a Low Latin word (French *bouche*), and the phrase is an intentional vulgarism to depict the burlesque expression of anger. — **illis**: dat. of disadvantage. The whole passage, 15-22, reads like a description of a *mimus*, in which a god suddenly appears upon the stage between the pairs of discontented men and, with bustling good nature, grants their wishes; then, as it appears at once from their looks that they do not really desire the change, his good nature changes to comic anger. From vss. 4 f., which are serious in expression and thought, to the final burlesque there is a gradual and skillful uncovering of the underlying absurdity of ascribing the discontent of men to their occupations or their lot in life.

23. **Praeterea**: a Lucretian word for passing to a new point. — **ut qui iocularia**: supply *percurrit*; 'like a writer for the comic papers.'

24. **quamquam**: *and yet*; corrective, not subordinating.

25. The kindergarten method of teaching children their letters by turning the work into play is alluded to by Quintilian (1, 1, 26), and Jerome advises a father to reward his daughter's efforts to learn to read by giving her *crustula, cookies*. and *mulsa, sweet drinks*. — **olim**: *sometimes;* a not uncommon meaning.

27. **sed tamen**: not exactly correlative to *quamquam*. The thought is twice reversed: "I will treat this matter seriously, not jokingly; and yet I might properly treat it jokingly, for a joke may sugar-coat a serious purpose, like the candies that teachers sometimes give to children; but, all the same (*tamen*), I prefer now to keep to my original plan and treat the matter seriously."

28. **ille**: demonstrative, to pair with *hic* below. — **gravem duro**: by way of emphasizing the severity of the labor.

29. **perfidus ... caupo**: from

30 audaces mare qui currunt, hac mente laborem
    sese ferre, senes ut in otia tuta recedant,
    aiunt, cum sibi sint congesta cibaria : sicut
    parvola (nam exemplo est) magni formica laboris
    ore trahit quodcumque potest atque addit acervo,
35 quem struit, haud ignara ac non incauta futuri.

this point the thought turns more directly toward the main subject of the satire — money-making — and, in the review of the four types of discontented men from this point of view, the *iuris consultus*, who serves for honor rather than fees, is omitted, and the *caupo, huckster, innkeeper*, is substituted; as a man of the town, he makes a good contrast to the farmer. For variety, the order also is changed. — **perfidus** : people of the better classes seldom used inns in traveling (compare *Sat.* 1, 5), and the poor taverns frequented by slaves and laborers had a bad reputation for cheating and robbery.

30. currunt : this verb is used of sailing also in *Epist.* 1, 1, 45; 1, 11, 27 and perhaps in *Carm.* 1, 28, 36. Cf. 'run before the wind.' — **hac mente** : *this is their object*, emphatic by position and explained in the clause *ut . . . recedant*.

31-35. These lines contain the explanation which men give of their apparent inconsistency in continuing in occupations which they themselves complain of as dangerous or wearisome, and the words are carefully selected: *senes*, 'only when they are old'; *otia tuta*, 'freedom from labor and danger'; *recedant*, 'retire'; *congesta*, 'scraped together'; *cibaria*, *rations*, 'just enough to live on.' It is a reminder of the modernness of the Augustan Age that all these expressions find easy counterparts in the talk of men who are carrying the loads of life in our time.

32. cum . . . sint : subjunctive because it was a part of the indirectly quoted speech.

33. parvola : colloquial diminutive of *parvus*, to contrast with *magni*. — **exemplo** : dat.; 'for this is the pattern which they choose to follow.' — **magni . . . laboris** : *hard-working*. This genitive usually has a noun of general meaning with it (*animal, vir*), but the omission is not infrequent. The ant is occasionally referred to elsewhere in Latin literature as a model of industry (*e.g.* Verg. *Georg.* 1, 186), but the frequency of the comparison in modern literature is doubtless due to *Proverbs* 6, 6.

Quae, simul inversum contristat Aquarius annum,
non usquam prorepit et illis utitur ante
quaesitis sapiens; cum te neque fervidus aestus
demoveat lucro, neque hiems, ignis, mare, ferrum,
40 nil obstet tibi, dum ne sit te ditior alter.
    Quid iuvat immensum te argenti pondus et auri
furtim defossa timidum deponere terra?

36. **Quae**: not exactly = *at ea*. The reply rather accepts the ant as a model, and criticises those who have chosen it as a model for not following their pattern closely enough. 'Yes, the ant is a good model, for it provides against a time of want and, when the time of want comes, it uses . . .' *sapiens*, 38, is thus an emphatic repetition of *haud ignara . . . futuri*. — **inversum**: the year is thought of as a circle, which turns back into itself, and this figure finds expression in many forms, περιτελλόμενος, *vertens*, *volvitur*. — **Aquarius**: the sign of the Zodiac which the sun enters in January, the severest part of the Italian winter.

37. **utitur**: the important word; it not merely gathers, but also *uses*.

38. **sapiens**: emphatic by its position at the end, where it is placed to make a strong contrast with *te* at the beginning of the next clause; 'like the philosopher it is; while *you* haven't even ordinary sense.'

39. **hiems . . . ferrum**: conventional obstacles. Cf. the variation in *Sat.* 2, 3, 54 ff., and the English 'to go through fire and water.'

40. **dum . . . alter**: 'as long as any other man is richer than you are.' Lit., *provided that no other*. With these words the true subject of the satire is reached, the foolish complaints and false pleas of discontented men having been pushed aside. At this point, too, the dialogue form and the direct address (*te, tibi, te*) become more distinct. Vss. 28–35, which contain the plea in defence, begin descriptively, then fall into informal indirect quotation, and close (*sicut parvola*) with what is in effect a direct quotation. And the reply, 36–40, in which the plea is shown to be false, continues and accentuates the directness of dialogue, and thus emphasizes the point toward which the discussion has been tending. The whole introduction, 1–40, is a good example of the manner of Horace.

41–42. These lines depict, with a heaping-up of epithets (*immensum, furtim, defossa, timidum*), the conventional figure of the miser, already familiar to Latin lit-

'Quod si comminuas, vilem redigatur ad assem.'
At ni id fit, quid habet pulchri constructus acervus?
45 Milia frumenti tua triverit area centum,

erature in the *Aulularia* of Plautus. The man of business in the Augustan Age had his investments and his varied money interests and no more buried his coin in a hole in the ground than the cautious investor of our time keeps his money in an old stocking. The verses really constitute an argument in the form of a suggested comparison: 'What is the good of it all to you? You're no better than a regular miser.'

43. Quod: usually taken to be the pron., = *at id*, as *quae*, 36, is taken. But it is, I think, the ordinary adversative *quod si*, which is freely used by Horace; cf. *Epist.* I, 3, 25, *Epod.* 2, 39, and see examples in Kühner, II, 872. In this usage *quod* conj. has diverged only slightly from *quod* pron., and when a possible antecedent can be found before it (here *pondus*), it may easily be mistaken for the pron. But the thought is really general: 'but if you once begin the breaking-up process, your money is soon gone.' These words are not the reply of a real miser, but a perfectly sound maxim of prudence—'if you once begin to dip into your capital, it will soon be gone'; but it is misused by the man of acquisitive temperament to disguise to himself and to others his innate love of money. In answering (44 –51) Horace does not stop to discriminate between the truth and the error, but strikes at the heart of the matter: 'the ultimate value of money is in its use, not in its acquisition.'

44. At ni id fit: *but if you don't do it*, that is, begin to use it.— **quid . . . pulchri**: the neut. gen. of the adj. with a neut. pron. instead of the abstract noun. Very common in colloquial Latin.— **acervus**: with a reminiscence of the ant, 34.

45-46. The figure is from Lucilius, 555 f. (Marx):—

milia ducentum frumenti tollis medimnum,
vini mille cadum.

— **triverit**: this should be called a fut. perf., to correspond to the fut. *capiet*, but in many uses of these forms the Latin did not make the sharp distinction between indic. and subj. which we make in our systematic grammar. The phrase is in paratactic relation to *capiet*, expressing a hypothetical concession; cf. 1, 3, 15; 1, 10, 64; 2, 6, 48, and many places in the Satires and Epistles.— **area**: so *teret area*, Verg. *Georg.* 1, 192, with a slight personification of the threshing floor.

non tuus hoc capiet venter plus ac meus; ut si
reticulum panis venalis inter onusto
forte vehas umero, nihilo plus accipias quam
qui nil portarit.   Vel dic, quid referat intra
50 naturae finis viventi, iugera centum an
mille aret? 'At suave est ex magno tollere acervo.'
Dum ex parvo nobis tantundem haurire relinquas,
cur tua plus laudes cumeris granaria nostris?

46. hoc: *on this account*; so 1, 3, 93; 1, 6, 110, and often, especially with comparatives. — ut, si: to be taken separately; *just as, if you should carry . . . you would receive.* . . .

47. inter: prepositions of two syllables are often placed after the noun in Horace.

48. accipias: pres.; when the train of slaves halts for the noon-day lunch. — portavit: perf.; on the march, now past.

49. intra naturae finis: this limitation, a doctrine of Stoic philosophy, is necessary to the argument, which is directed, not against great fortunes in themselves, but against the accumulation of unused wealth.

50. viventi: with *refert* the person interested is expressed by the gen. and no good parallel to this dat. is known. Yet the general sense is such that the dat. is perfectly intelligible.

51. At suave . . . acervo: the reply is not very effective and it is, in fact, scarcely more than an interjected remark: 'it's rather nice to have a large bank account to draw upon.' The argument in 52 ff. continues the thought of *intra naturae finis viventi*, with a side reference to *ex magno acervo*.

52. tantundem: 'as much as one would take from the great heap.' — haurire: properly of drawing off a liquid, used here in anticipation of the next illustration. — relinquas contains both the suggestion of 'leave to me in spite of your desire to get everything' and the meaning *concede*, *permit*, and in the latter sense takes the infin. *haurire*.

53. cumeris granaria: *cumerae* are described by the scholiast as small bins of wickerwork or large earthenware jars, used for storing small quantities of grain. The word is somewhat rare, but is used again by Horace (*Epist.* 1, 7, 30) and was perhaps familiar to him from the management of his own small farm. It is, of course, set in contrast to the *granaria* of the large estate, and the sentence really repeats the idea of 45-46 and of 49-51.

ut tibi si sit opus liquidi non amplius urna,
55 vel cyatho, et dicas, ' Magno de flumine mallem
quam ex hoc fonticulo tantundem sumere.' Eo fit,
plenior ut'si quos delectet copia iusto,
cum ripa simul avolsos ferat Aufidus acer;
at qui tantuli eget quanto est opus, is neque limo
60 turbatam haurit aquam, neque vitam amittit in undis.
At bona pars hominum, decepta cupidine falso,

54. ut . . . si: *just as if*, 'that is as if'; to be taken together, not like *ut si*, 46, where *ut* has its own verb. — liquidi: here, as in so many cases, Horace begins with the general and advances to the specific; *liquidi*, instead of *aquae*, gives a sense like 'something to drink.' So *magno de flumine* is general, *Aufidus*, 58, is specific. — urna: *a pitcher*, cyatho, *a glass*, the precise measurements not being in mind here.

55. mallem: *I should have preferred*. The man is thought of as standing near the little spring (notice *hoc*) and wishing, contrary to the fact, that he were near a river.

56. fonticulo: diminutive of contempt, to contrast with *magno*.

57. plenior . . . iusto: *more than he ought to have*; the whole sentence must be rendered freely. — ut: with *ferat*.

58. cum ripa simul: *bank and all*. The Aufidus, a rapid river in Horace's native Apulia, would undermine its banks in flood time and be turbid with mud.

59. The distinction here made between eget, *wants, desires*, and opus est, *needs*, is fundamental to the whole argument; it repeats *intra naturae finis*, 49 f., and is the opposite of *plenior si quos delectet*, 57.

60. turbatam, vitam amittit: these ideas merely carry the thought on into vivid details which make the folly of the device more evident, as, in the triumph of using a successful comparison in argument, one is easily tempted to carry it beyond the likeness. Horace does not mean that the money of the rich man was muddy or 'tainted'; that thought was not Roman; nor is he at this point thinking of the loss of real life in over-absorption in business.

61. At: to introduce the reply or counter-argument contained in vs. 62. — bona pars: like the English 'a good many.' — cupidine: masc., as always in Horace and sometimes in other writers.

'Nil satis est,' inquit, 'quia tanti quantum habeas sis.'
Quid facias illi? Iubeas miserum esse, libenter
quatenus id facit; ut quidam memoratur Athenis
65 sordidus ac dives, populi contemnere voces
sic solitus: 'Populus me sibilat, at mihi plaudo
ipse domi, simul ac nummos contemplor in arca.'
Tantalus a labris sitiens fugientia captat
flumina. . . . Quid rides? Mutato nomine, de te
70 fabula narratur; congestis undique saccis

62. From Lucilius, 1119 f. (Marx): —

aurum atque ambitio specimen virtutis utrique est:
tantum habeas, tantum ipse sies tantique habearis.

— **Nil satis est**: 'there is no such thing as the *enough* of which you speak.' This is a denial of the foundation of the preceding argument as expressed in vss. 49-51 and 59 f. — **sis**: subjv. of the indef. 2d pers.

63 f. **illi**: *for such a man*, individualizing the subject of *inquit*. — **Iubeas miserum esse**: *iubeo* is used to represent the impv. of the direct *miser esto*; so *iubeo valere* for the direct *vale*. — **quatenus**: always *since* in Horace. — ʻThe only thing one can do for a man so wrong-headed is to let him go his own way, since he will have it so (*libenter . . . facit*), though one may know that it leads to misery. He is as fixed in his error as the man in the Greek story, who, when he looked at his money bags, was indifferent to public opinion.'

65-66. **voces, sibilat**: the people on the streets hooted at him and hissed him. — **plaudo**: for the contrast with *sibilat*.

68. **Tantalus**: Horace follows here the Homeric version of the Tantalus story.

69 ff. **Quid rides?** he laughed because he did not think the old story had any bearing upon his own case. The reply is that the picture tallies exactly, that, with a change of name, it corresponds even in details. — **undique**: with *congestis*; ʻwhich you have got together by raking and scraping everywhere.' — **indormis**: *sleep upon*; because he cannot be parted from them. Cf. Lucilius, 243-246 (Marx): —

cui neque iumentum est nec servus nec comes ullus:
bulgam, et quidquid habet nummorum, secum habet ipse,
cum bulga cenat, dormit, lavit, omnia in una
sunt homini bulga: bulga haec devincta lacerto est.

indormis inhians, et tamquam parcere sacris
cogeris, aut pictis tamquam gaudere tabellis.
Nescis quo valeat nummus, quem praebeat usum?
Panis ematur, holus, vini sextarius, adde
75 quis humana sibi doleat natura negatis.
An vigilare metu exanimem, noctesque diesque
formidare malos fures, incendia, servos,
ne te compilent fugientes, hoc iuvat? Horum
semper ego optarem pauperrimus esse bonorum.

— inhians: the involuntary physical sign of ardent desire. Such expressions sound exaggerated to us because in modern life we repress the signs of strong emotion. — tamquam ... sacris: he can make no more use of them than if they were put out of his reach by being consecrated to the gods. — pictis ... tabellis: 'the only pleasure you get from them is the pleasure of looking at them,' and that pleasure could be just as well enjoyed by looking at a picture of a pile of money as by looking at the money itself. These details, like those above, 41 f., must not be supposed to be descriptive; they are intended to make the complete devotion to business contemptible by dwelling upon the inherent likeness between the money-maker and the conventional figure of the miser.

73 ff. quo valeat: *what money is good for*; repeated in another form in *quem praebeat usum*. In harmony with the preceding thought the question here implied is answered both positively and negatively: 'money will buy the simple necessities of life (74–75), but you, by making it an object of pursuit in itself, are buying for yourself a life of constant anxiety and trouble' (76–78). — quis: *quibus*; with *negatis*. The comment of Porphyrio gives the sense correctly: 'non autem ea vult intellegi, quae ad delicias vitae pertinent, sed quae ad utilitatem, ut quae frigori aut fami repellendae et commodiori mansioni sunt necessaria aliaque similia.'

76 ff. The dangers of life in Rome are often alluded to; cf., *e.g.*, *Epist.* 2, 1, 121 f. and Catullus, 23, 8–10, on the freedom of the poor man from such terrors: —

nihil timetis,
non incendia, non graves ruinas,
non furta inpia, non dolos veneni.

— compilent fugientes: *plunder you and run away*. The *fugitivus* is a frequent figure in the pictures of ancient society, and the difficulty of recovering a runaway

80   At si condoluit temptatum frigore corpus,
      aut alius casus lecto te adflixit, habes qui
      adsideat, fomenta paret, medicum roget, ut te
      suscitet ac gnatis reddat carisque propinquis.
      Non uxor salvum te volt, non filius; omnes
85   vicini oderunt, noti, pueri atque puellae.
      Miraris, cum tu argento post omnia ponas,

slave, in a population so miscellaneous, was very great. — **Horum**: emphatic, with *bonorum*; 'if these are what you call the good things of life, I wish I might always remain a poor man.'

80 ff. These lines are all addressed by Horace to his imagined interlocutor, the over-anxious man of business, the direct dialogue form being resumed only in vs. 101. But vss. 80-83 (beginning with *at*, the usual introduction to a counter-argument) contain in substance a reply to vss. 76-78. The thought is, 'You are dwelling too much upon the anxieties which my money brings and are forgetting its real benefits; for instance, its value in a time of illness.' — **temptatum**: almost a technical term of the attack of illness; *Epist.* 1, 6, 28. — **frigore**: the *chill* of malaria. — **corpus**: not *body*, but *health, strength*. Cf. *fractus membra*, vs. 5. — **adflixit**: *has dashed one down upon his bed*. — **adsideat, roget**: *sit by your bedside, call in*; ordinary, almost technical terms.

84 ff. The defence closes with a note of false pathos, — 'My money protects my life, which is precious to my family.' The reply of Horace, vss. 84-91, takes up this suggested point, passing by vss. 80-83 as, in reality, unimportant. 'Your life precious to your family! On the contrary, you are an object of universal dislike. Your pursuit of money not only makes no friends for you, but even checks the natural affections of your relatives.' — **non uxor**: the reply begins without an adversative particle; cf. 36, 52, and below, 102.

85. vicini, noti (*acquaintances*), **pueri atque puellae**: specific expansions of the general term *omnes*. Cf., on the last, *Sat.* 2, 3, 130, *insanum te omnes pueri clamentque puellae*. 'Without distinction of age or sex' (Greenough).

86. post . . . ponas: cf. *Sat.* 1, 3, 92, *positum ante*; 1, 6, 58, *circum . . . vectari*. — **omnia**: obj. of *ponas*. — **ponas, praestet, merearis**: the subj. all hang together. They are not dependent upon *si*, for *miror si* takes the indic., but are more vaguely hypo-

si nemo praestet, quem non merearis, amorem?
At si cognatos, nullo natura labore
quos tibi dat, retinere velis servareque amicos,
90 infelix operam perdas, ut si quis asellum
in campo doceat parentem currere frenis.
  Denique sit finis quaerendi, cumque habeas plus,
pauperiem metuas minus, et finire laborem
incipias, parto quod avebas, ne facias quod

thetical, — 'do you wonder that no one should wish to give you . . . ? — **merearis**: not exactly *deserve*, but *earn*, *buy* (by giving love in return), an old sense of *mereor*.

88-91. Vss. 84-85 contain a bare statement of fact, without argument, and vss. 86-87 are an interjected remark ('it is quite just and natural'); the essence of the reply is in vss. 88-91, and *at*, the particle of retort, is therefore postponed to this point. The reply is, 'Why, on the contrary, instead of winning affection, you have so distorted your character that you would be incapable of retaining the love of your nearest relatives, if you should now choose to attempt it. You have made yourself a beast of burden, unfitted for the finer uses of life.' [A good summary of the arguments on this disputed passage may be found in Palmer's edition. The decisive reason, in my judgment, for rejecting *an* is that it is incompatible with the emphasis laid upon *operam perdas* by the comparison which follows.]

89. **retinere velis**: an expansion of *retineas*, to express more clearly the idea of choice. So *ponas*, 86, might have been *ponere velis*. — **amicos**: predicate.

91. **in campo**: in the Campus Martius, on the race track. — **parentem . . . frenis**: the heavier draught animals were driven with a goad; bits and reins were used only for racing or in driving for pleasure.

92 ff. A conclusion, driving home the lesson of the preceding arguments. — **plus**: the standard of comparison is left vague ('more than you once had,' 'more than most people') to balance *minus*, to which a standard ('less than you have done') is easily supplied.

94. **incipias**: ironically understating the case: 'take just one step toward reasonable moderation.' — **parto**: abl. abs. with the antecedent of *quod*. — **facias**: neutral, *fare*.

95 Vmmidius quidam.   Non longa est fabula: dives,
ut metiretur nummos, ita sordidus, ut se
non umquam servo melius vestiret, ad usque
supremum tempus, ne se penuria victus
opprimeret, metuebat.   At hunc liberta securi
100   divisit medium, fortissima Tyndaridarum.
' Quid mi igitur suades ? ut vivam Naevius ? aut sic

95. **Vmmidius**: the name does not occur in the extant fragments of Lucilius, but the story may well have been Lucilian. — **Non longa**: the details are therefore given with an appearance of haste; this motive leads also to the use of *dives* with an *ut*-clause of degree without *tam* (or *ita*, as with *sordidus*). Other instances occur in Horace, *Sat.* 1, 5, 33 ; 1, 7, 13 ; 2, 7, 10, etc.

96. **metiretur**: instead of counting them; proverbial of great wealth.

98. **supremum tempus**: *to the very last*, to the end of his life. — **victus**: gen.

99. **At**: *but* matters turned out very differently; after spending his life in providing against one danger, he met with a wholly unexpected end and had, as it were, wasted his life in misdirected prudence.

100. **divisit medium**: *chopped him in two*, an intentionally short and brutal way of putting it, followed, in order to brighten the sordidness of the story, by a burlesque allusion to a great tragic legend. — **fortissima Tyndarida-**rum: *i.e.* as brave as any of the line of Tyndareus; with special reference to Clytemnestra, who killed Agamemnon with an ax.

101 f. The man of business has still one line of defence left, — 'Your reasoning, carried to its legimate conclusion, leads to sheer waste and the dissipation of property.' To which the answer is obvious, — 'Do not carry it so far; do not rush from one extreme to the other, but keep the wise middle course.' — **Naevius, Nomentanus**: these names are used as well-known representatives of a class — the spendthrifts. A Naevius is mentioned in *Sat.* 2, 2, 68 as a man who was too easy-going in his housekeeping, and this characteristic would fit well enough with carelessness in money matters. Of a L. Cassius Nomentanus, a contemporary of Sallust and notorious for his prodigality, Porphyrio gives a circumstantial account. Nomentanus is also a Lucilian character, and a Nomentanus, apparently a different one, is mentioned in *Sat.* 2, 8, 23, 25, 60. Precise identification is impossible.

ut Nomentanus?' Pergis pugnantia secum
frontibus adversis componere? Non ego, avarum
cum veto te fieri, vappam iubeo ac nebulonem.
105 Est inter Tanain quiddam socerumque Viselli.
Est modus in rebus, sunt certi denique fines,
quos ultra citraque nequit consistere rectum.
Illuc, unde abii, redeo, qui nemo ut avarus

102-104. Pergis: often used without an interrogative particle in half-exclamatory sentences. — **pugnantia secum, frontibus adversis, componere**: these three expressions combine to suggest from different sides the figure of two gladiators, matched (*componere* is the technical word) against one another. So the argument of vss. 101 f. sets up the figure of the *vappa ac nebulo* to destroy the effect of the figure of the *avarus*, as described in the body of the satire.

105. The reference is probably to some Greek saying, then well enough known to make a mere allusion intelligible; at any rate, the names represent two widely separated extremes.

107. ultra citraque: the safe 'middle ground' is the only place where the right (ὀρθόν) can find a sure standing place.

108 f. Illuc, unde abii, redeo: this is not perfectly accurate. To return precisely to the opening question, 'What is the source of our discontent?' would be absurd, since the whole satire has been spent in setting forth the answer to that question. But a repetition of the text is a very suitable way of bringing the sermon to its conclusion. Horace therefore repeats the opening words (*qui nemo se probet = qui fit ut nemo contentus vivat*), attaching them somewhat forcedly to the leading clause *illuc redeo* and inserting the substance of the answer in the brief phrase *ut avarus*, which is taken up more fully in vss. 110 ff. The obscurity produced by using *qui nemo* instead of *qui fit ut nemo* and by making it depend upon *illuc redeo* is increased by the use of *ut avarus* (= 'because of the love of money'; cf. *ut male sanos*, *Epist.* 1, 19, 3; *ut capitis minor*, *Odes* 3, 5, 42), which is easily mistaken for a repetition of the *ut* in *qui fit ut*. The obscurity of the passage has led copyists into making various changes in the text, *nemo ut*, *nemon ut*. The true reading was found only in a single manuscript. 'I come back to my starting point, the discontent of men, which comes from their love of money and their envy.'

se probet ac potius laudet diversa sequentis,
110 quodque aliena capella gerat distentius uber,
tabescat, neque se maiori pauperiorum
turbae comparet, hunc atque hunc superare laboret.
Sic festinanti semper locupletior obstat,
ut, cum carceribus missos rapit ungula currus,
115 instat equis auriga suos vincentibus, illum
praeteritum temnens extremos inter euntem.
Inde fit, ut raro, qui se vixisse beatum
dicat, et, exacto contentus tempore, vita
cedat uti conviva satur, reperire queamus.

110. A mean and petty illustration is chosen intentionally.

112. **hunc atque hunc**: 'first one and then another.' The adversative idea, as often in Latin, is left unexpressed.

113. **Sic**: with *festinanti*; 'one who is in such haste to be rich.'

114 ff. The figure of the chariot race is used with a serious effect which suits the tone of vss. 111-119. It is a natural comparison, often used in Latin literature, and it is not necessary to suppose that this passage is either copied from or imitated in Vergil, *Georg.* 1, 512 ff. : —

Vt cum carceribus sese effudere quadrigae,
addunt in spatia et frustra retinacula tendens
fertur equis auriga, neque audit currus habenas.

The only similarity is in the use of technical terms. — **carceribus**: the stalls in which the chariots stood ready to be started (*missos*) by the raising of the barrier. — **rapit ungula**: so *quatit ungula*, Ennius, *Ann.* 224 Vahl., Verg. *Aen.* 8, 596, in the same place in the verse. — **illum**: *the one*. — **extremos inter**: cf. *venalis inter*, 47, n.

117-119. **Inde fit**: this also, like vs. 108, is a return to the beginning of the satire, *qui fit*, but with a more sober restraint (*raro* instead of *nemo*) and with an effective use of the figure of the satisfied feaster. This is another reminiscence of Lucretius, 3, 938 : —

Cur non ut plenus vitae conviva recedis,
aequo animoque capis securam, stulte, quietem?

Compare also the **closing lines** of Bryant's *Thanatopsis*.

120   Iam satis est.   Ne me Crispini scrinia lippi
      compilasse putes, verbum non amplius addam.

120–121. It is thoroughly characteristic of Horace to turn abruptly from grave to gay, — *ridentem dicere verum,* — and the very abruptness of the change is often an effective enforcement of the moral. Several of the *Satires* will be found to close with a jest. Cf. also the close of some of the *Odes*; 1, 6: 2. 1; and especially 3, 3, *quo, musa, tendis.* — **Crispini**: said by Porphyrio to be Plotius Crispinus, a writer of much verse (cf. *Sat.* 1, 4, 14) and a teacher of Stoic doctrines (*Sat.* 1, 3, 139; 2, 7, 45). — **scrinia**: cylindrical boxes in which the papyrus rolls were kept. — **lippi**: personal peculiarities or defects, of which we should think it discourteous to speak, were frequently matter for ridicule to the ancients.

2

This satire was written before 3, since the death of Tigellius, which is there (vs. 3 ff.) referred to as having occurred some time before, is here spoken of as a quite recent event, and before 4, where (in vs. 91) a line of this satire (vs. 27) is quoted. It is therefore to be placed in the group of early satires, with 7 and 8, written before the introduction to Maecenas in 39 or 38 B.C.

The announced subject of the satire is the tendency of men to run to extremes, their inability to keep to the golden mean. Of this tendency the first part, down to vs. 28, gives various illustrations, not lacking in humor and unobjectionable in tone. But the particular illustration which is treated in detail, and which occupies the rest of the satire, is excess in sensual indulgence, and especially the vice of adultery, which had become rife in the Ciceronian period and was still increasing in Roman society.

The satire betrays in various ways the immaturity of the writer. It is the most personal of Horace's writings; it is coarse in expression, and it is intentionally sensational in manner. These characteristics are in part the result of a too close adherence to the manner of Lucilius, in part of a desire to attract attention, in part of the bitter and rebellious feeling of the writer. Yet it is not difficult to find in it, as undoubtedly Vergil and Varius did, the indications of what the writer was later to become.

Ambubaiarum conlegia, pharmacopolae,
mendici, mimae, balatrones, hoc genus omne
maestum ac sollicitum est cantoris morte Tigelli:
quippe benignus erat.   Contra hic, ne prodigus esse
5 dicatur metuens, inopi dare nolit amico,
frigus quo duramque famem propellere possit.
Hunc si perconteris, avi cur atque parentis
praeclaram ingrata stringat malus ingluvie rem,
omnia conductis coëmens obsonia nummis,
10 sordidus atque animi quod parvi nolit haberi,
respondet.   Laudatur ab his, culpatur ab illis.
Fufidius vappae famam timet ac nebulonis,

1. **Ambubaiarum**: *flute-girls*, like the *copa Syrisca* of Vergil's poem, whose associations are called *conlegia, guilds*, with a touch of derision.

2. **mendici**: the organizations of begging priests. — **mimae**: women were not allowed to act in the more respectable dramas, but only in the farces called *mimi*. — **balatrones**: cf. the use of this name for a parasite as a proper name in *Sat.* 2, 8, 21 and 40.

3. **Tigelli**: see note on *Sat.* 1, 3, 4.

4. **benignus**: *kind, generous;* the word is used as if in quotation. — **hic**: *this other man*, the meaning being made plainer by *contra*.

7. **Hunc**: a third person, not the same as *hic*, 4. Whatever slight confusion is caused by the use of the same pronoun is dispelled by the next line, which shows that this man was a spendthrift.

8. **ingrata**: *unprofitable*, that gives no adequate return for the money spent upon it. — **stringat**: *strips*, as leaves from a tree.

9. **omnia ... obsonia**: *all kinds of dainties*, everything that his appetite suggested. — **conductis**: *hired*, i.e. *borrowed* at interest.

10. **animi ... parvi**: *mean;* the opposite of *benignus*, 4.

11. **his, illis**: *one side, the other side*, people who are of the same or of the opposite opinion.

12. **Fufidius**: a well-known family name, but the individual here referred to is unknown. He is a money-lender who combines in himself the extreme of great wealth — which he gets by discreditable methods — with the extreme of stinginess in the spending of money upon himself.

[dives agris, dives positis in faenore nummis];
quinas hic capiti mercedes exsecat, atque
15 quanto perditior quisque est, tanto acrius urget;
nomina sectatur modo sumpta veste virili
sub patribus duris tironum.   'Maxime' quis non
'Iuppiter!' exclamat, simul atque audivit?   'At in se
pro quaestu sumptum facit hic.'   Vix credere possis
20 quam sibi non sit amicus, ita ut pater ille, Terenti
fabula quem miserum gnato vixisse fugato
inducit, non se peius cruciaverit atque hic.
   Si quis nunc quaerat, 'Quo res haec pertinet?' illuc:

14. quinas ... mercedes: the usual rate of interest was one per cent a month, but Fufidius collected five times this rate. — **capiti**: *from the principal*. — **exsecat**: 'the verb is chosen to express the severity of the demand; *cuts off* beforehand, as in discounting. In all such matters the methods of Roman business were less systematized than the banking of modern times.

15. perditior: *nearer to ruin*.

16 f. nomina: *names*, but with a suggestion of 'accounts,' as in English. — **tironum**: young men who had just put on the *toga virilis* and whose fathers still kept them on small allowances would be the natural prey of the unscrupulous money-lender.

19. pro quaestu: *in proportion to his gains*; the supposed exclamation of some one who hears of his great income. This suggests at once the strangeness of the contrast between his wealth and his meanness, which is carried out in the next phrase, *vix credere possis*.

20. quam ... non ... amicus: not exactly the same as *quam inimicus*, but 'how far he is from being kind to himself.' — **pater ille**: a father in the play of Terence, the *Heautontimorumenos* (*Self-tormentor*), who, because he thinks that his harshness has driven his son away from home, refuses himself all comforts until the son returns.

22. inducit: 'brings on the stage,' but used like a verb of saying with the infin. *vixisse; represents as having lived*. — **cruciaverit**: a repetition of the word *timorumenos*, in the title of the play.

23. Quo ... pertinet: *what's the point of all this?* Cf. *Sat.* 1, 1, 15 f., *quo rem deducam*, and *Sat.* 2, 7, 21. — **illuc**: the answer to the question, which is then explained in the next line.

dum vitant stulti vitia, in contraria currunt.
25 Malthinus tunicis demissis ambulat; est qui
inguen ad obscenum subductis usque facetus.
Pastillos Rufillus olet, Gargonius hircum.
Nil medium est. Sunt qui nolint tetigisse nisi illas,
quarum subsuta talos tegat instita veste;
30 contra alius nullam nisi olenti in fornice stantem.
Quidam notus homo cum exiret fornice, 'Macte
virtute esto,' inquit sententia dia Catonis.
'Nam simul ac venas inflavit taetra libido,
huc iuvenes aequum est descendere, non alienas
35 permolere uxores.' 'Nolim laudarier,' inquit,
'sic me,' mirator cunni Cupiennius albi.
Audire est operae pretium, procedere recte
qui moechos non voltis, ut omni parte laborent;
utque illis multo corrupta dolore voluptas

25-27. Two illustrations of excess, each described in a line, followed by two other extremes condensed into a single line. Vs. 27 is quoted in *Sat.* 1, 4, 92 as an example of jesting that is really harmless and in fact it is not likely that any of the names was meant to designate an individual.

29. **instita**: a border sewed on to the *stola* of the married woman, so that the garment came down to the ankles.

30. **contra alius**: cf. *contra hic*, 4.

31 f. **Macte virtute esto**: a colloquial phrase of approval; *well done! that's right.* — **sententia dia Catonis**: formal and epic; Lucilius, 1316 (Marx), has *Valeri sententia dia*, and Horace frequently uses this kind of periphrasis in parody of the heroic style, *e.g. Sat.* 2, 1, 72.

35. **laudarier**: the old form of the infin. pass., used also in 78 and 104 with intentional archaism.

36. **Cupiennius**: identified by the scholiast with a certain C. Cupiennius Libo, a friend of Augustus. But it is much more likely that the name is selected for its suggestion of *cupio*. — **albi**: of the white dress of married women, in contrast to the dark toga worn by prostitutes.

37 f. A parody of a line of Ennius (454 Vahl.), *audire est operae pretium, procedere recte | qui rem Romanam . . . voltis*, with emphatic insertion of *non*.

40 atque haec rara cadat dura inter saepe pericla.
　Hic se praecipitem tecto dedit; ille flagellis
　ad mortem caesus; fugiens hic decidit acrem
　praedonum in turbam; dedit hic pro corpore nummos;
　hunc perminxerunt calones; quin etiam illud
45 accidit, ut quidam testes caudamque salacem
　demeteret ferro. 'Iure,' omnes; Galba negabat.
　Tutior at quanto merx est in classe secunda,
　libertinarum dico, Sallustius in quas
　non minus insanit, quam qui moechatur. At hic si,
50 qua res, qua ratio suaderet quaque modeste
　munifico esse licet, vellet bonus atque benignus
　esse, daret quantum satis esset nec sibi damno
　dedecorique foret. Verum hoc se amplectitur uno,
　hoc amat et laudat, 'Matronam nullam ego tango.'
55 Vt quondam Marsaeus, amator Originis ille,

40. rara: with *haec (voluptas)* in a predicate use, contrasting with *saepe*. — **dura**: with *pericla*.

43. pro corpore: paid a ransom to save himself from the penalty which might have been inflicted on him.

46. Galba: this may be a reference to a known person, a jurist who is said by the scholiast to have been himself caught in adultery. This would explain the point of *negabat*; as a jurist he dissented from the general judgment. But the story of the scholiast may have started with *negabat*.

48. Sallustius: not the historian. It may have been his nephew and heir, but this is not easily reconciled with the fact that Horace addressed a friendly ode (*Carm.* 2, 2) to him.

50. res, ratio: the two leading motives for self-restraint, care for his property and good sense.

51. licet: the verb itself expresses by its meaning the shading which in *suaderet* is expressed by the mode. — **bonus atque benignus**: as if quoted from those who would receive the money. Cf. *benignus*, vs. 4.

53. hoc . . . uno: explained in the words *matronam . . . tango*.

55. Originis: said by the scholiast to have been a *mima* (cf. vs. 2) of Cicero's time. Marsaeus is unknown and this is therefore an apparent personality, which in reality refers to a long-past scandal.

qui patrium mimae donat fundumque laremque,
' Nil fuerit mi,' inquit, 'cum uxoribus unquam alienis.'
Verum est cum mimis, est cum meretricibus, unde
fama malum gravius quam res trahit.   An tibi abunde
60 personam satis est, non illud, quidquid ubique
officit, evitare ?   Bonam deperdere famam,
rem patris oblimare, malum est ubicunque.   Quid interest in matrona, ancilla peccesne togata?
Villius in Fausta Sullae gener, hoc miser uno
65 nomine deceptus, poenas dedit usque superque
quam satis est, pugnis caesus ferroque petitus,
exclusus fore, cum Longarenus foret intus.
Huic si mutonis verbis mala tanta videntis
diceret haec animus 'Quid vis tibi? Numquid ego a te
70 magno prognatum deposco consule cunnum
velatumque stola, mea cum conferbuit ira ? '
quid responderet?   ' Magno patre nata puella est.'
At quanto meliora monet pugnantiaque istis

59. fama, res: the same combination (in reversed order) that is used in *damno dedecorique*, vs. 52 f., to express from both sides the consequences of excess.

60. personam: the character, the rôle, of a *moechus*, contrasted with *illud . . . officit*, the results of excess, which come in any case (*ubique*).

62. ubicunque: repeating *ubique*; 'whatever *persona* you may assume.'

63. togata: cf. note on *albi*, 36.

64-67. This is also a reference to a scandal of Cicero's time. Fausta was the daughter of Sulla and the wife of Milo. Villius was one of her lovers, called *Sullae gener* in derision, and Longarenus was another lover. — **in Fausta**: *in the case of Fausta*, with the verbal phrase *poenas dedit*. — **hoc . . . uno**: abl. with *miser deceptus*, with *nomine* (*i.e.* the noble name Fausta) in apposition. — **fore**: abl. with *exclusus*.

68-72. si . . . diceret: the conclusion is *responderet*, 72.

73. meliora . . . pugnantia: after *monet*, the subject of which is *natura*. — **pugnantia istis**: 'opposite to what you have said,' *i.e.*

dives opis natura suae, tu si modo recte
75 dispensare velis ac non fugienda petendis
immiscere. Tuo vitio rerumne labores,
nil referre putas? Quare, ne paeniteat te,
desine matronas sectarier, unde laboris
plus haurire mali est quam ex re decerpere fructus.
80 Nec magis huic inter niveos viridisque lapillos,
sit licet hoc, Cerinthe, tuum, tenerum est femur aut crus
rectius, atque etiam melius persaepe togatae est.
Adde huc, quod mercem sine fucis gestat, aperte
quod venale habet ostendit, nec, si quid honesti est,
85 iactat habetque palam, quaerit quo turpia celet.
Regibus hic mos est: ubi equos mercantur, opertos
inspiciunt, ne, si facies, ut saepe, decora
molli fulta pede est, emptorem inducat hiantem,
quod pulchrae clunes, breve quod caput, ardua cervix.

to *magno patre . . . est.* Cf. *pugnantia secum, Sat.* 1, 1, 102.

74. **dives opis natura suae**: a doctrine of Epicurean philosophy, stated by Cicero, *de Fin.* 1, 13, 45 . . . 'ipsa natura divitias, quibus contenta sit, et parabiles et terminatas habet.' The figure is carried on in *dispensare*, 'to deal out' like a careful steward.

75. **fugienda petendis**: used again in *Sat.* 1, 3, 114, as equivalent to *bona diversis*.

76. **Tuo vitio rerumne**: cf. *Sat.* 1, 10, 57 f., *num illius, num rerum . . . natura.*

80-82. **huic**: the *matrona*; contrasted with *togatae*, 82. —

sit . . . tuum: *although this may be your judgment, i.e.* that the adornment of the married woman adds to her attractions. Cerinthus is unknown.

84. **honesti**: used of physical charms for the contrast with *turpia.*

86-89. **opertos**: *i.e.* they cover those parts of the horse which by their beauty might attract the purchaser — *emptorem inducat* — the parts specified in vs. 89, in order to examine with the more coolness of judgment the parts which might be unsound, *molli . . . pede.* The custom, if there ever was such a custom, is not elsewhere alluded to.

90 Hoc illi recte : ne corporis optima Lyncei
    contemplere oculis, Hypsaea caecior illa,
    quae mala sunt, spectes. O crus! O brachia! Verum
    depygis, nasuta, brevi latere ac pede longo est.
    Matronae praeter faciem nil cernere possis,
95 cetera, ni Catia est, demissa veste tegentis.
    Si interdicta petes, vallo circumdata, nam te
    hoc facit insanum, multae tibi tum officient res,
    custodes, lectica, ciniflones, parasitae,
    ad talos stola demissa et circumdata palla,
100 plurima, quae invideant pure apparere tibi rem.
    Altera, nil obstat : Cois tibi paene videre est
    ut nudam, ne crure malo, ne sit pede turpi ;
    metiri possis oculo latus. An tibi mavis
    insidias fieri pretiumque avellier ante
105 quam mercem ostendi? 'Leporem venator ut alta
    in nive sectetur, positum sic tangere nolit,'

90 f. **Lyncei**: famous for his power of sight; cf. *Epist.* 1, 1, 28, *non pos is oculo quantum contendere Lynceus.* — **ne . . . contemplere**: a parenthetic clause of purpose. — **Hypsaea**: unknown except by a note in the scholia, which does not really explain the allusion.

96 f. **vallo circumdata**: figurative, as an amplification of *interdicta*, and itself further amplified in vs. 98-100. — **facit insanum**: the fact that there are difficulties in the way.

98. The attendants of a great lady, either in the streets (*custodes, lectica* — with the bearers) or in her house (*ciniflones*, hairdressers. *parasitae*, at the table), which made it difficult to find her alone.

100. **invideant . . . apparere**: the construction is unusual, but it is found in Plautus, *e.g. Bacch.* 543. Cf. the infin. after *prohibere.*

101. **Altera**: without a verb, to give a conversational tone; the thought is easily filled out from *pure apparere* and from the rest of vs. 101. — **Cois**: abl. neuter. A transparent kind of silk made originally in the island of Cos.

105-108. **ut**: *how;* the clause depends upon *cantat.* These verses give the substance of an epigram of Callimachus (*Anth. Pal.,* xii.

cantat et apponit: 'Meus est amor huic similis; nam
transvolat in medio posita et fugientia captat.'
Hiscine versiculis speras tibi posse dolores
110 atque aestus curasque gravis e pectore pelli?
Nonne, cupidinibus statuat natura modum quem,
quid latura sibi, quid sit dolitura negatum,
quaerere plus prodest et inane abscindere soldo?
Num, tibi cum fauces urit sitis, aurea quaeris
115 pocula? Num esuriens fastidis omnia praeter
pavonem rhombumque? Tument tibi cum inguina, num, si
ancilla aut verna est praesto puer, impetus in quem
continuo fiat, malis tentigine rumpi?
Non ego: namque parabilem amo venerem facilemque.
120 Illam, 'Post paulo,' 'Sed pluris,' 'Si exierit vir,'
Gallis, hanc Philodemus ait sibi, quae neque magno
stet pretio neque cunctetur, cum est iussa venire.

102) in which the lover is compared to a hunter; the game that he prefers is that which costs him trouble in the pursuit and capture.
— **apponit**: the point of the epigram is here added in direct quotation and in a very close paraphrase, almost a translation of the original. The comparison was probably common enough. Ovid (*Amor.* 2, 9, 9) has compressed the whole into a single line.

109-110. versiculis: 'do you think that such verses are a healing charm which will cure your troubles?'

111. natura modum: the same thought is in *Sat.* 1, 1, 49 f., 59, 73.

112. dolitura negatum: cf. *Sat.* 1, 1, 75.

113. inane: the *void* or *space* of Epicurean physics, in which the *atoms* or *matter* (*solidum*) moved. But here figuratively, like the English *substance* and *shadow*; 'to distinguish the mere appearance from the reality.'

116. pavonem rhombumque: the fashion which dictated the use of certain fish or fowls as a part of every formal dinner is directly ridiculed in other satires, esp. *Sat.* 2, 2, 23 ff., and 48 ff.

120-122. A reference to an epigram of Philodemus, an Epicurean of Cicero's time. This particular

Candida rectaque sit, munda hactenus, ut neque longa
nec magis alba velit, quam dat natura, videri.
125 Haec ubi supposuit dextro corpus mihi laevum,
Ilia et Egeria est: do nomen quodlibet illi,
nec vereor, ne, dum futuo, vir rure recurrat,
ianua frangatur, latret canis, undique magno
pulsa domus strepitu resonet, vepallida lecto
130 desiliat mulier, miseram se conscia clamet,
cruribus haec metuat, doti deprensa, egomet mi.
Discincta tunica fugiendum est ac pede nudo,
ne nummi pereant aut puga aut denique fama.
Deprendi miserum est; Fabio vel iudice vincam.

epigram is not extant, but the construction reflects the colloquial tone; '"that one (the *matrona*) for the *Galli*, this one (the *libertina*) for me," says Philodemus.'

123. **munda**: *neat*, but with the suggestion that adornment may be carried too far. — **hactenus**: *only so far*.

129. **vepallida**: the prefix is here intensive, *very pale*; elsewhere it is negative, as in *vesanus = insanus*.

130. **conscia**: the slave-woman who was the accomplice.

134. **Fabio**: probably the Stoic philosopher referred to in *Sat.* 1, 1, 14. The Stoic doctrine was that no evil could befall the true philosopher. The point therefore is that the misfortune of being caught is so great that not even a Stoic, in spite of his doctrine, could deny that it was *miserum*.

3

The only indication of the date of this satire is the allusion in vs. 64, which implies a considerable degree of intimacy with Maecenas, to whom Horace was introduced in the year 38. In style and thought it is one of the more mature satires of the First Book.

'Musical people are odd. Look at Tigellius, a bundle of inconsistent absurdities. "Very fine," says some one, "but how about you, who criticize others with so much penetration? Are you faultless yourself?" "Not at all," answers the critic, "but, frankly, I don't think my faults are as bad as his." No, you do not, and your self-satisfied attitude is a proper subject for a satire.

'Your habit of criticism brings its natural result, that others criticize you, and both you and they, seizing upon some trifling fault, fail to see the finer and nobler qualities and, still worse, make no effort to correct your own faults.

'I wish that we might rather be as blind to the faults of a friend as a lover is to the defects in the face of his mistress or, if see them we must, might treat them with the indulgent tenderness of a father toward his child, interpreting bluntness as frankness and a hot temper as only an excess of high spirit.

'But we follow just the opposite course and turn good qualities into faults, modesty into stupidity, prudence into trickiness. A fairer judgment would show us that virtues are more common than vices and would teach us to exchange pardon rather than censure.

'A reasonable philosophy for a world of faulty men should not be over-strict. To break a friendship for some trifling breach of good manners is to lose all sense of proportion between crime and penalty.

'The Stoics, to be sure, teach in their paradoxical way that all faults are sins and deserve the heaviest penalty. But this doctrine is repugnant to our best feelings and opposed to all that we know of the gradual evolution of the moral code. A real understanding of the source of our moral sense makes it unreasonable to punish the slightest error with death, as the Stoic says he would do, if he were king. "And how now, my Stoic friend? Wishing that you were king? I thought another of your Paradoxes proved that you are a king already." "No, no, you don't understand. That means a potential king, not a king *de facto*." "Potential? What's that?" "Why, like Hermogenes, who doesn't need to be singing all the time to prove that he's a singer. Even when he isn't singing, he's a potential singer. In the same way I'm a king, potentially." "Very well, I won't argue with you, but I don't think much of Your Majesty, hustled by street boys on your way to the cheap baths. I will remain a private citizen and forgive as I hope to be forgiven."'

It is not probable that the subject of this satire was suggested by any particular set of circumstances. Roman society was censorious, and Horace was himself an object of criticism, but this is neither a satire, in the proper sense, nor an argument in self-defence. It is a broadly human plea for generosity toward one's friends. The treatment of the Stoics is not to be taken seriously, and it would not be fair to press too far the obvious modern analogies.

Thackeray's Roundabout Paper called *On a Chalk-mark on the Door* is an excellent companion piece to this satire in its general tone and especially in the manner in which the subject is introduced.

> Omnibus hoc vitium est cantoribus, inter amicos
> ut numquam inducant animum cantare rogati,
> iniussi numquam desistant. Sardus habebat
> ille Tigellius hoc. Caesar, qui cogere posset,
> 5 si peteret per amicitiam patris atque suam, non
> quicquam proficeret; si collibuisset, ab ovo

1–2. vitium: not *vice*, but *defect, fault*. — **rogati**: contrasted with *iniussi*, both predicate.

3. Sardus: with contemptuous emphasis. The Sardinians were in bad repute at Rome; cf. the saying, *Sardi venales, alter altero nequior*.

4. Tigellius: a musician of the Ciceronian period, several times alluded to in Cicero's letters and in the scholiasts. Cicero speaks of him always as Sardus Tigellius, but his name was Hermogenes Tigellius, and it is unlikely that Sardus was accepted by him as a cognomen. He was an acquaintance of many persons of prominence, Julius Caesar, Cleopatra, Cicero, and the younger Caesar, but not, apparently, on terms of equality. He had died shortly before the second satire was written. He is to be distinguished from another Hermogenes Tigellius, still alive, also a musician and probably a freedman or adopted son of the former. The tone of Horace toward the elder Tigellius is not hostile, though not respectful; toward the younger he is distinctly hostile (*Sat.* 1, 4, 72; 1, 10, 18, 80, 90). There are two places where the reference might be to either (1, 3, 129; 1, 9, 25). — **habebat ... hoc**: *had this way, habit*; *hoc* does not refer grammatically to *vitium*. — **Caesar**: the young Octavius took this name immediately after the death of his great-uncle, in 44. The title Augustus was not given to him till 27. He is always referred to by Horace as Caesar, never as Octavianus, which could not be used in hexameter. — **qui cogere posset**: the words are not meant literally, but as a complimentary recognition of his position and influence.

5. patris: Julius Caesar, his adoptive father. — **si peteret**: a future condition, put into past time.

6. collibuisset: an impf. in force.

usque ad mala citaret 'Io Bacche!' modo summa
voce, modo hac resonat quae chordis quattuor ima.
Nil aequale homini fuit illi; saepe velut qui
10 currebat fugiens hostem, persaepe velut qui
Iunonis sacra ferret; habebat saepe ducentos,
saepe decem servos; modo reges atque tetrarchas,
omnia magna loquens, modo, 'Sit mihi mensa tripes et
concha salis puri et toga, quae defendere frigus,

6-7. **ab ovo usque ad mala**: eggs were a usual part of the preliminary *gustatio* (cf. *Sat.* 2, 4, 12), and fruit was served as a dessert at the end of the dinner.

7-8. **Io Bacche**: the opening words or the refrain of a drinking song. The final *e* should be short, but may be explained as having been lengthened in the song by its position at the end of a musical phrase. — **summa, ima**: the accompanying reference to the lyre shows that these words are used of the position of the strings, not of the tone. As the lyre was held, the bass string was uppermost. The Romans used *summus* and *imus* also of the tones of the voice in the same sense as the English *high* and *low*.

9. **aequale**: *consistent*.

10. The expression is somewhat condensed; in full it would be *saepe currebat velut qui fugiens hostem (curreret), persaepe (incedebat* or some similar verb) *velut qui . . . ferret*.

11. **Iunonis sacra**: the κανηφόροι, who in religious processions carried the offerings and sacred vessels in baskets on their heads and would naturally walk with dignity.

11-12. **ducentos . . . decem**: one number suggests domestic profusion, the other a quiet dignity; neither is to be interpreted literally. Horace himself, in speaking of the easy simplicity of his own life, says that he was waited on at supper by three slaves (*Sat.* 1, 6, 116).

12. **reges atque tetrarchas**: that is, at one time he talked of court life and Oriental monarchs, at another time his attitude was that of a true philosopher who had reduced his desires to the bare necessities.

13-14. **tripes, concha**: the Roman gentleman regarded a handsome dining table, supported upon a central pedestal, as necessary to a properly furnished dining room, and even poor people had a silver salt cellar; cf. *Carm.* 2, 16, 13 f., *Vivitur parvo bene cui paternum | splendet in mensa tenui salinum.* — **puri**: salt was sometimes perfumed or flavored.

15 quamvis crassa, queat.' Deciens centena dedisses
huic parco, paucis contento, quinque diebus
nil erat in loculis. Noctes vigilabat ad ipsum
mane, diem totum stertebat. Nil fuit umquam
sic impar sibi. — Nunc aliquis dicat mihi : ' Quid tu?
20 nullane habes vitia?' Immo alia et fortasse minora.
Maenius absentem Novium cum carperet, ' Heus tu,'
quidam ait, ' ignoras te, an ut ignotum dare nobis
verba putas?' 'Egomet mi ignosco,' Maenius inquit.

15. **Deciens centena**: sc. *millia sestertium, a million sesterces.* — **dedisses**: a paratactic condition, without *si*. Cf. *Sat.* 1, 1, 45.

16. **parco, paucis contento**: these words summarize the professions of Tigellius in 13-15. The substance of the passage therefore is: 'But if you had taken this ascetic philosopher at his word and given him a million or two, he would have turned spendthrift in a week.'

17. **erat**: the whole passage is a description of a man who had been dead some years, and all the tenses are past, impf., perf., plupf.; in present time it would have been *dederis . . . erit:* 'Suppose you gave him a million; a week afterward you look in his pocketbook — nothing there!'

18. **Nil**: the neuter is colloquial and more sweeping than the more exact masculine. Cf. Catullus, 9, 11, *quid me laetius est beatiusve?*

19. **impar sibi**: = *(in)aequale,* 9. — **Nunc**: *at this point* in the talk. — **aliquis, mihi**: merely the two conventional figures that Horace often employs to enliven his Satires with bits of dialogue. — **Quid tu?** *how about yourself?*

21-23. These verses repeat in brief, with the added point of a double pun, the essence of 1-20. Maenius corresponds to the critic, Novius to Tigellius, *heus tu* to *quid tu? ignoras . . . putas?* is a slight expansion of *nullane habes vitia?* and *egomet mi ignosco* is a neater variation upon *immo . . . minora.* The pun upon *ignotas, ignotum, ignosco* gains force from the double question: 'Which is it, Maenius, *igno-ras* or *ignotum?*' 'Neither,' says Maenius: 'it's *igno-sco.*' The scholiast gives a long account of a Maenius, but it has no point here, nor is it important to identify Novius with one of the persons mentioned in *Sat.* 1, 6, 121; the names are only more vivid substitutes for *aliquis* and *mihi,* vs. 19.

Stultus et improbus hic amor est, dignusque notari.
25 Cum tua pervideas oculis mala lippus inunctis,
    cur in amicorum vitiis tam cernis acutum
    quam aut aquila aut serpens Epidaurius? At tibi contra

24. hic amor: *such satisfaction as this*, that is, as has been exhibited in the preceding verses. — **dignusque notari**: 'a proper subject for a satire.'

Verses 1-24 introduce the subject of the satire with an easy skill which Horace has nowhere surpassed. The passage reads like the talk of a group of men sitting about the fire at a club. There is no attempt to reproduce the exact form of dialogue, and the suggestion of dialogue in the introduction is intended only as an interpretation of the spirit of the passage. Some chance has brought up the oddities of musical people, of which Tigellius affords an excellent illustration. The mention of his name leads easily to the amusing and not ill-natured analysis of the character of this much-flattered and extravagant musical artist. But the characterization, though not really ill-natured, illustrates the inconsistency of censuring others for failings which we excuse in ourselves, an inconsistency which is even more clearly apparent in the Maenius–Novius anecdote, and which furnishes a subject for the satirist.

25-27. mala: stronger than *vitiis*, in the next line. — **lippus, inunctis**: there are frequent references to this inflammation of the eyelids and to the use of eye-salve (*Sat.* 1, 5, 30; *Epist.* 1, 1, 29); both 'the disease and the remedy obscured for the time the power of vision. — **aquila, serpens**: the eagle is still used in literature as a symbol of acuteness of sight; the attributing of the same quality to the serpent, common in Greek literature, was due to a supposed connection between δράκων and the stem of δέρκομαι, *to see*. — **Epidaurius** refers to the story of the bringing of a sacred serpent from the temple of Aesculapius in Epidaurus to Rome. This is the use, frequent in Horace, of the definite and particular for the general. — **pervideas**: taken by many editors to mean *examine sharply*, making an intentional oxymoron with *lippus*. But *pervidere* usually means only *to look at*, and is here contrasted with *cernis acutum*, as *mala* is with *vitiis* and *lippus inunctis* with *aquila* and *serpens*.

27-28. contra, rursus: *i.e.* when their turn comes. — **illi**: not referring precisely to *amicorum*, but more general, — 'when the criticized turn critics.'

evenit, inquirant vitia ut tua rursus et illi.
'Iracundior est paulo, minus aptus acutis
30 naribus horum hominum; rideri possit eo, quod
rusticius tonso toga defluit, et male laxus
in pede calceus haeret.' At est bonus, ut melior vir
non alius quisquam, at tibi amicus, at ingenium ingens
inculto latet hoc sub corpore. Denique te ipsum
35 concute, num qua tibi vitiorum inseverit olim
natura aut etiam consuetudo mala; namque
neglectis urenda filix innascitur agris.

29-30. A single fault in two forms, *iracundior, quick-tempered,* and *minus aptus . . ., impatient of criticism,* the general followed by the particular. — **acutis naribus**: from the instinctive turning up of the nostrils at a disagreeable odor. The phrase is a slightly inaccurate combination of the descriptive (*acutis*) with the figurative (*naribus*). — **horum**: *nowadays*, with a side-reference to literary criticism; cf. *Sat.* 1, 10, 67-71.

30-32. **rideri possit**: 'people may laugh at him,' *i.e.* he exposes himself to possible ridicule. — **tonso**: dat.; *sc. ei*. The two distinct criticisms are better expressed in English by two verbs: 'because his hair is cut by a country barber and his toga isn't properly creased.' — **defluit**: *hangs loose,* instead of being creased in folds across the chest. — **male**: with both *laxus* and *haeret*; *is loose and ill-fitting.* On these lines cf. *Epist.* 1, 1, 94 ff., and Quint. 11, 3, 137, 'et toga et calceus et capillus tam nimia cura quam neglegentia sunt reprendenda.'

34. **inculto . . . corpore**: *is hidden beneath this careless exterior.*

35. **concute**: from shaking the loose folds of the garments to see whether anything was concealed in them. Cf. Plaut. *Aul.* 646 f., *agedum, excutedum pallium . . . ne inter tunicas habeas.* The implied notion of searching governs the indirect question, *num . . . inseverit.* — **olim**: *once, i.e.* at your birth, with reference to *natura* only.

36-37. **consuetudo**: added as an after-thought, to remind the overcritical censor that he has not only faults which were inborn, but also faults which are due to his own carelessness. — **neglectis**: almost 'for if you are careless.' — **filix**: a common pest to the Italian farmer, which he got rid of by burning over the fields.

Illuc praevertamur: amatorem quod amicae
turpia decipiunt caecum vitia, aut etiam ipsa haec
40 delectant, veluti Balbinum polypus Hagnae:
vellem in amicitia sic erraremus, et isti
errori nomen virtus posuisset honestum.
At pater ut gnati, sic nos debemus amici
si quod sit vitium non fastidire; strabonem

38-54. 'As the lover finds in the defects of his mistress only added beauties, and as the father calls his boy by a pet name which minimizes his physical weaknesses, so we should try to see the better side of our friends' qualities.'

Horace is here strengthening his argument by appealing to two well-recognized traits. The blindness of the lover was a commonplace of philosophy (Plato, *Rep.* 5, 474 d; Lucretius, 4, 1160-1169; Ovid, *Ars Am.* 2, 657 ff.) and the giving of nicknames based upon physical peculiarities was so common among the Romans that most of their family names, including those used in this passage (*Paetus, Pullus, Varus, Scaurus*), are derived from this custom.

38. Illuc praevertamur, quod: *let us turn rather to this fact, that* . . . ; *i.e.* 'let us prefer to imitate the lover's blindness.'

39. decipiunt: *are unnoticed by.* Cf. *fallere, latere,* with acc. of the person.

40. Balbinum: unknown. — **Hagnae:** (Ἅγνη) a common *libertina* name.

41. vellem . . . erraremus: *I wish that we made the same mistake;* the unfulfilled form of *velim . . . erremus;* there is no implied condition.

42. virtus: *ethics, ethical philosophy.* Cf. *Carm.* 2, 2, 17 ff., *Phraaten . . . numero beatorum eximit virtus.* — **honestum:** *creditable, honorable.* Though such blindness to obvious facts may be an error, yet it is so generous an error that philosophers, especially the Stoics, should have given it a name which would recognize its nobler side.

43-48. This passage cannot be exactly translated; modern English, in which physical deformities are ignored or relegated to the scientific vocabulary of surgeons, has no equivalents for *paetus, pullus, varus, scaurus.* Each of these words designates in an extenuating way deformities which are more broadly described by the corresponding words *strabo, male parvus* and *abortivus, distortis cruribus, pravis . . . talis.*

43. At: adversative to the main thought of 29 ff., not exclusively

45 appellat paetum pater, et pullum, male parvus
    si cui filius est, ut abortivus fuit olim
    Sisyphus; hunc varum distortis cruribus; illum
    balbutit scaurum pravis fultum male talis.
    Parcius hic vivit: frugi dicatur. Ineptus
50 et iactantior hic paulo est: concinnus amicis
    postulat ut videatur. At est truculentior atque
    plus aequo liber: simplex fortisque habeatur.
    Caldior est: acris inter numeretur. Opinor
    haec res et iungit, iunctos et servat amicos.

to what immediately precedes. The expression is somewhat condensed, for *ut pater gnati vitium non fastidit, sic nos debemus amici vitium non fastidire*.

47. Sisyphus: a dwarf kept by Antony.

48. balbutit: properly *lisps*, *i.e.* the father speaks the word *scaurus* in gentle tones, in a kind of baby talk, so that it is a pleasant nickname to the child.

49-54. These lines contain the application of the foregoing illustrations. Each of the four qualities mentioned may be regarded as a fault, but each has its good side, so that it may, upon a generous interpretation, be considered a virtue. The words which express the overcritical interpretation are in the comparative degree, as if to suggest that the faults are only exaggerations of good qualities.

49. Parcius: *too stingy.*—**frugi**: *economical*, ' careful in money matters.'

49-51. ' He sometimes thrusts himself forward too much (*iactantior*) and really makes an ass of himself (*ineptus*), but it is in the effort (*postulat*) to be entertaining.' The best commentary on these qualities is in Cicero, *de Orat.* 2, 4, 17, 'qui aut tempus quid postulet non videt aut plura (*too much*) loquitur aut se ostentat (= *iactantior*) . . . aut denique in aliquo genere aut inconcinnus aut multus est, is ineptus dicitur.' This sense of *postulare, to expect, desire*, almost = *velle*, is common in Plautus and should have fuller treatment in the Lexicons.

51-52. 'Too much inclined to be overbearing, and more free in speech than he ought to be.' On its good side this quality should be regarded as merely frankness and fearlessness.

53. Caldior: = *calidior*; cf. *soldum, Sat.* 2, 5, 65; *hot-tempered.* — **acris**: *high-spirited.*

54. haec res: *i.e.* this way of treating the qualities of our friends, this generous interpretation.

55   At nos virtutes ipsas invertimus, atque
sincerum cupimus vas incrustare. Probus quis
nobiscum vivit, multum demissus homo: illi
tardo cognomen, pingui damus. Hic fugit omnis
insidias nullique malo latus obdit apertum,
60 cum genus hoc inter vitae versetur, ubi acris
invidia atque vigent ubi crimina: pro bene sano
ac non incauto, fictum astutumque vocamus.
Simplicior quis et est, qualem me saepe libenter
obtulerim tibi, Maecenas, ut forte legentem

55-56. 'But we follow a course exactly the opposite of this; instead of looking for the virtues which underlie faults, we seek for the faults that accompany virtues.' Of the two figures by which this is expressed, the first, *invertimus*, is quite general; the second is derived from the soiling of a clean (*sincerum*) jar by the incrustation deposited from sour wine. — **cupimus**: *i.e.* we find pleasure in it.

56-58. The opposed interpretations are expressed by pairs of adjectives, put together without a connective. — **Probus**: *honest*; **demissus**: *modest, quiet*. Cicero uses the two words together (*de Orat.* 2, 43, 182), contrasting them with *acres, pertinaces*. — **pingui**: somewhat stronger than *tardo*.

58-62. The *virtus* of these lines is less obvious than the preceding, and is therefore described more at length, before the point is reached in the pairs of contrasting adjectives. — **nulli malo**: masc. — **latus**: *flank*, the figure being from the military vocabulary. — **inter**: see note on 1, 1, 47. — **invidia, crimina**: many allusions in the *Satires* show that Horace was himself exposed to envy and criticism by reason of his friendship with Maecenas. — **sano, non incauto**: *a man of sense and not without prudence*. — **fictum**: *insincere*; cf. Cic. *Lael.* 8, 26, where *simulatus* is used as a parallel.

63-66. The quality here described, perhaps suggested by contrast with the 'prudence' of 58-62, is that single-mindedness and absence of self-consciousness which is at times a most engaging characteristic, but at other times may become annoying thoughtlessness. — **et**: connecting *simplicior* with *talis*, implied by *qualem*. — **libenter**: *in my eagerness*; it is essentially the same as *simplicior*, 'with my thoughts fixed too intently upon some one idea.' — **quovis sermone**: *with some unimportant remark*, not referring to *molestus...caret*. — **Molestus**: *he's*

65 aut tacitum impellat quovis sermone : ' Molestus ;
communi sensu plane caret,' inquimus. Eheu,
quam temere in nosmet legem sancimus iniquam !
Nam vitiis nemo sine nascitur ; optimus ille est
qui minimis urgetur. Amicus dulcis, ut aequum est,
70 cum mea compenset vitiis bona ; pluribus hisce
(si modo plura mihi bona sunt) inclinet, amari
si volet ; hac lege in trutina ponetur eadem.
Qui ne tuberibus propriis offendat amicum
postulat, ignoscet verrucis illius ; aequum est
75 peccatis veniam poscentem reddere rursus.
Denique, quatenus excidi penitus vitium irae,

a nuisance. — **communi sensu**: not ' common sense,' but *ordinary tact*, almost *common politeness*; cf. Seneca, *de Ben.* 1, 12, 3, *sit in beneficio sensus communis*; *tempus, locum observet*.

67. temere: *hastily, thoughtlessly*, not seeing that the law condemns ourselves also (*in nosmet*) and is unjust besides.

69. urgetur: *i.e.* has the smallest load of faults to carry. The thought suggests the figure of weights balanced in the scales, which is more elaborately worked out in the following lines ; so *insenerit*, 35, suggests vs. 37.

70. cum: prep. governing *vitiis*; *will set my good qualities over against my faults.* Cf. Cic. *de Fin.* 2, 30, 97, *compensabatur cum summis doloribus laetitia.* — **hisce**: *i.e.* the *bona*.

71. inclinet: as if he were himself the scales.

72. hac lege: *on this condition.*

73-74. tuberibus: *wens;* larger than *verrucae, warts.* On the Roman freedom of speech about such defects, cf. 44 ff. and notes. — **postulat**: as in vs. 51.

75. poscentem: with the subj. of *reddere.* — **veniam**: obj. of *poscentem*, but to be supplied also with *reddere.*

76 ff. 'In short, since we are born with faults (68) which no philosophy can wholly eradicate, it is reasonable that we should recognize the difference between the lighter and the heavier, and should not condemn all with an equal severity.'

The figure of the scales (70-72), in which faults may be weighed against virtues, suggests the weighing of one fault against another, and this recalls the Stoic doctrine that all faults are alike in heinousness. Against this doc

cetera item nequeunt stultis haerentia, cur non
ponderibus modulisque suis ratio utitur, ac res
ut quaeque est, ita suppliciis delicta coercet?
80 Si quis eum servum, patinam qui tollere iussus
semesos piscis tepidumque ligurrierit ius
in cruce suffigat, Labeone insanior inter
sanos dicatur.   Quanto hoc furiosius atque
maius peccatum est: paulum deliquit amicus,

trine the rest of the satire is directed, at first with an assumed humility and an ironical seriousness, but finally with open parody and humor.

76. **vitium**: subj. of *nequit*, to be supplied from the next line. — **irae**: this particular fault, already mentioned in vss. 29 and 53, is singled out because Horace was conscious of the failings of his own temper.

77. **item**: this supplies the place of a connective between *vitium irae* and *cetera (vitia)*. — **stultis**: the technical Stoic word for all men except the ideal *sapiens*; its use at this point gives a double meaning to *ratio* (78) — either 'the logical deductions of the Stoics' or 'the common sense of mankind' — and prepares the way for the more open attack in 96 ff.

79. **ut ... ita**: do not try to render literally; 'make the penalty fit the crime.'

80-81. **tollere**: *remove* from the table at the end of the course. — **semesos**: the fragments left on the platter. — **tepidum**: already growing cold and unpalatable. These details are added to lighten the offense.

82. **in cruce**: the extreme penalty. But it is to be remembered that it had none of the associations now connected with it; it was oftener threatened than carried out, and is frequently alluded to in the humorous slang of Latin comedy. — **Labeone**: it is not clear whether this was a Labeo who was tribune in the year 131 or the Labeo who fought in the army of Brutus, or his son, a free-spoken opponent of Augustus. It is clear, however, that the allusion is not at all to some act of extreme cruelty or of serious misjudgment, but to some notorious extravagance of conduct which would be recalled with humorous appreciation by readers familiar with the gossip of Rome.

83. **Quanto ... furiosius**: not, of course, to be taken seriously. — **hoc**: subj. of *est*, referring to what follows.

85 quod nisi concedas, habeare insuavis, acerbus:
    odisti, et fugis, ut Rusonem debitor aeris,
    qui nisi, cum tristes misero venere Kalendae,
    mercedem aut nummos undeunde extricat, amaras
    porrecto iugulo historias captivus ut audit.
90 Comminxit lectum potus, mensave catillum
    Evandri manibus tritum deiecit; ob hanc rem,
    aut positum ante mea quia pullum in parte catini
    sustulit esuriens, minus hoc iucundus amicus

85. quod nisi concedas: *i.e.* a fault so trifling that only a man of the most irritable temper would take offense at it.

86–89. odisti: the construction is intentionally abrupt; in full it would be, 'but you, instead of pardoning the slight fault, turn your friendship into dislike and avoidance.' — **fugis, ut**: the natural conclusion would be 'as hard as you can,' but for this general comparison Horace substitutes a special allusion which has a point of its own. Ruso, unknown except from this reference, is a money-lender, keen in collecting his interest, but with a weakness for writing histories. His clever debtor, unable to meet his notes, pretends an interest in Ruso's writings and so gets easy terms from the flattered author. But the histories are so dull that to listen to them is as painful as to stand with outstretched neck awaiting the blow of the executioner, and Ruso's debtors therefore avoid him even more persistently than other debtors avoid their creditors. — **Kalendae**: the first of the month was one of the dates for collecting money. Cf. *Epod.* 2, 69 f. — **mercedem**: the interest; **nummos**: the principal. — **undeunde**: the duplication makes it indefinite; cf. *quisquis, utut,* etc. — **captivus ut**: *like a prisoner of war*, about to be executed.

91. Evandri: a king in the mythical time before the coming of Aeneas to Latium. — **manibus tritum**: the owner would point to the handle and remark that it had been worn smooth by the hands of the good king. The craze for collecting old pottery and bronzes and claiming for them a fabulous antiquity is ridiculed again in *Sat.* 2, 3. 20 ff.

92. positum ante: = *antepositum, served.* — **mea in parte**: the food was served in a platter placed in the middle of the table and each guest helped himself, taking naturally that portion which was nearest to him.

93. esuriens: his hunger being

sit mihi? Quid faciam si furtum fecerit, aut si
95 prodiderit commissa fide sponsumve negarit?
    Quis paria esse fere placuit peccata, laborant
    cum ventum ad verum est; sensus moresque repugnant
    atque ipsa utilitas, iusti prope mater et aequi.
    Cum prorepserunt primis animalia terris,

a partial excuse for the breach of etiquette. — **minus . . . mihi**: the same as *odisti et fugis*, 86.

94. furtum fecerit: as in the Twelve Tables, *furtum factum sit*.

95. fide: the old dative form. — **sponsum**: a promise made by the formal *sponsio*. As many business transactions were ratified only by oral formulas, without written evidence, the failure to keep a verbal promise in such matters was regarded as an especially serious crime.

96 ff. The Paradoxes of the Stoics were doctrines which, though they transcended ordinary experience, were held to express essential truths. There is a brief review of them in Cicero, *pro Mur.* 29, 60 ff., where the particular Paradox here discussed is stated thus: 'omnia peccata esse paria; omne delictum scelus esse nefarium, nec minus delinquere eum qui gallum gallinaceum, cum opus non fuerit, quam eum qui patrem suffocaverit.' Against this Horace sets the results of actual observation, enforced by a condensed history, from Epicurean philosophy, of the development of the ideas of right and wrong. The Stoic teaching is not unlike the Calvinistic doctrine of sin — that the sinfulness of an act lies in the violation of the law of God, the particular details or consequences being immaterial — while the attitude of Horace is that of the believers in evolutionary ethics.

96. Quis: the old dat. form for *quibus*. — **fere**: with *paria*. — **placuit**: technical; ἀρέσκει; transl. *those who hold*.

97. ad verum: 'to the test of actual experience.' — **sensus moresque**: so Cicero, *de Fin.* 4, 19, 55, arguing against this doctrine, says that *sensus cuiusque et natura rerum atque ipsa veritas* cry out against it.

98. utilitas: in the broader sense, 'the common good,' not individual advantage. The utilitarian philosophy has a prominent place in modern thought. — **prope**: qualifies the figurative *mater*; 'which may almost be called the mother of the sense of justice.'

99. The following account of the evolution of society is Epi-

100 mutum et turpe pecus, glandem atque cubilia propter
unguibus et pugnis, dein fustibus, atque ita porro
pugnabant armis, quae post fabricaverat usus,
donec verba, quibus voces sensusque notarent,
nominaque invenere; dehinc absistere bello,
105 oppida coeperunt munire et ponere leges,
ne quis fur esset, neu latro, neu quis adulter.
Nam fuit ante Helenam cunnus taeterrima belli
causa; sed ignotis perierunt mortibus illi,
quos venerem incertam rapientis more ferarum
110 viribus editior caedebat, ut in grege taurus.
Iura inventa metu iniusti fateare necesse est,
tempora si fastosque velis evolvere mundi.

curean; compare Lucretius, 5, 780-1457. — **prorepserunt**: from the earth which gave them birth. — **animalia**: living creatures, but not yet men.

100. **mutum**: lacking the power of articulate speech. — **turpe**: still, shapeless, not of human form. — **glandem atque cubilia**: food and shelter no better than that of animals.

101-102. **unguibus et pugnis, fustibus, armis**: various steps in a civilization to which we are still engaged in making contributions.

103-104. **verba**: ῥήματα, *verbs*: **nomina**: ὀνόματα, *nouns*; technical terms of grammar, somewhat less precise than the corresponding English words, together standing for the whole of speech. — **voces sensusque notarent**: 'might give meaning to their cries (*voces*) and express their feelings.'

106. **adulter**: it is a touch of sensationalism that leads Horace to select this particular sin for detailed illustration in the next four verses.

107. **ante Helenam**: cf. *Carm.* 4. 9. 25. *vixere fortes ante Agamemnona*. Recorded history is thought of as beginning with the Trojan war.

108. **sed ignotis**: emphatic by position at the beginning and in caesura; 'but we know nothing of all that went before.'

109. **incertam**: *promiscuous*, before the recognition of the institution of marriage.

110. **viribus editior**: *a stronger*: a very rare figurative use of *editus*.

111-112. A restatement of the point to be proved (*iura inventa*

Nec natura potest iusto secernere iniquum,
dividit ut bona diversis, fugienda petendis;
115 nec vincet ratio hoc, tantundem ut peccet idemque
qui teneros caules alieni fregerit horti,
et qui nocturnus sacra divom legerit. Adsit
regula, peccatis quae poenas irroget aequas,
ne scutica dignum horribili sectere flagello.
120 Nam, ut ferula caedas meritum maiora subire
verbera, non vereor, cum dicas esse pares res

metu iniusti = utilitas iusti mater), which is now regarded as demonstrated to one who will read the history of the race (*si fastos velis evolvere*).

113-114. A conclusion from the preceding argument, which in a logical form would be introduced by *ergo*: 'there is therefore no natural instinct which distinguishes between right and wrong.' — **bona**: not in the moral sense, for that would contradict the whole argument, but *agreeable, pleasant*, further defined by *petendis*, as *diversis (their opposites)* is by *fugienda*.

115-117. A further conclusion: 'Therefore — since the distinction between right and wrong is neither innate nor absolute — there is no such thing as sin *per se*, but each error or fault must be judged separately, according to its effect upon the common advantage.' — **nec vincet ratio**: *nor will philosophy* (*i.e.* the Stoics) *succeed in proving*. — **tantundem**: quantitative; **idem**: qualitative; *in the same degree and kind* (Greenough). The two kinds of theft here named are said to have been specifically mentioned in the laws of Draco as deserving the same punishment. — **sacra legerit**: an old legal formula, preserved in the compound *sacrilegus*.

118. **regula**: *a scale.* — **aequas**: *just, fair*, proportioned to the offense.

119. **scutica**: *the whip.* — **flagello**: *the scourge*, a knout or cat-of-nine-tails, a much more dreadful instrument of punishment than the *scutica*.

120-124. **Nam**: 'we need a scale of sins which shall prevent you from inflicting too severe a penalty; for that you, a Stoic, with your overstrict laws, should inflict too light a penalty is highly improbable.' — **ferula**: *a cane*, such as was used by schoolmasters: substituted for *scutica* for variety. — **ut caedas . . . , non vereor**: the regular construction would be *ne caedas . . . , non vereor*, but the underlying thought

furta latrociniis, et magnis parva mineris
falce recisurum simili te, si tibi regnum
permittant homines.   Si dives qui sapiens est,
125 et sutor bonus et solus formosus et est rex,
cur optas quod habes?   'Non nosti quid pater,' inquit,
'Chrysippus dicat: sapiens crepidas sibi numquam
nec soleas fecit, sutor tamen est sapiens.'   Qui?

here does not call for a verb of fearing. Expressed without irony the verb would be *non verisimile est* or something like that, and the *ut*-clause conforms to the underlying thought and all the more easily because the *ut*-clause comes first. But Horace has substituted for the simple expression the ironical *vereor*, which in this connection ceases to be really a verb of fearing. — **pares res** : = *paria*, 96. — **magnis**: after *simili*; a condensed construction for *falce simili qua falce magna*. — **recisurum**: as a farmer prunes the vines. — **si tibi regnum** . . . : with *dicas*, 121, begins a quotation in indirect form of the purpose of the Stoic philosopher: 'I would do thus and so, if I had the power.' But the last thought is carelessly expressed in the common phrase, 'if I were king,' and Horace seizes upon this phrase to turn the rest of the satire into a humorous flouting of Stoic doctrine.

124-126. This Paradox is thus stated by Cicero, *pro Mur.* 29, 61 : 'solos sapientes esse, si dis- tortissimi, formosos, si mendicissimi, divites, si servitutem serviant, reges ; and is referred to by Lucilius, 1225 f. (Marx). The fundamental truth which underlies the Paradox is that character makes the man, that character is the essential and circumstances are the accidents, a truth which Horace in other places (*e.g. Carm.* 2, 2, 17 ff.) fully recognizes ; here it suits his purpose to ridicule the exaggerated form in which the doctrine was expressed.

127. Chrysippus: next to Zeno the chief of Stoic philosophers, called *pater* as a term of honor.

128. sutor: this particular illustration, which tends to make the whole doctrine ridiculous, was selected partly with reference to the story of Alfenus, 130, partly to illustrate the dogged persistence with which the Stoics defended their Paradox, even in its most extreme applications. — **Qui?** an exclamation of bewilderment · 'how is that? I don't see it.'

'Vt, quamvis tacet Hermogenes, cantor tamen atque
130 optimus est modulator ; ut Alfenus vafer, omni
abiecto instrumento artis clausaque taberna,
sutor erat ; sapiens operis sic optimus omnis
est opifex solus, sic rex.' Vellunt tibi barbam
lascivi pueri ; quos tu nisi fuste coerces,
135 urgeris turba circum te stante miserque
rumperis et latras, magnorum maxime regum!

129-133. 'The ideal man, the *sapiens*, is potentially master of all arts and crafts, though he may not actually practice them, just as Hermogenes is a singer even when he is not singing.'—**Hermogenes**: see on vs. 4.—**modulator**: a more technical word than *cantor*.—**Alfenus**: apparently, as the scholiast says, the famous jurist (*vafer* is used of the law in *Sat.* 2, 2, 131) Alfenus Varus, consul in 39. He is said to have been in early life a cobbler at Cremona, and the argument of the Stoic is that he remained potentially a cobbler even after he became a great man.—**instrumento**: collectively; 'the tools of his trade.'—**sic**: '*in this sense*,' as Alfenus was potentially a shoemaker; not = *ergo, therefore*.—**solus**: the Stoic's argument, even if it be accepted at its best, does not prove that only the *sapiens* is an ideal craftsman; in fact, it proves just the contrary. But *solus* was used in the Paradox, and is therefore added by the Stoic in a triumphant tone, as if he had now proved his whole point.

133 ff. As often, Horace makes no direct answer to the argument, but turns to other matters which form in the end a most conclusive, though indirect, reply. 'Very well, you seem to have proved that you are a king, but appearances are against you, and certainly you are a very odd kind of king.'—**barbam, fuste**: philosophers of the stricter sect sometimes chose to distinguish themselves from other men by wearing a long beard (cf. *Sat.* 2, 3, 35, *iussit sapientem pascere barbam*) and by carrying an old-fashioned staff.—**rumperis et latras**: *i.e.* 'make yourself hoarse with howling.'—This exaggerated use of *rumpere* was colloquial; cf. *Epist.* 1, 19, 15 and Plaut. *Capt.* 14. *latras* suggests the Cynic school (from κύων, *dog*), with which the Stoics were connected. —**magnorum maxime regum**: as if it were a formal title of respect. 'Your Most Gracious Majesty.'

Ne longum faciam, dum tu quadrante lavatum
rex ibis, neque te quisquam stipator ineptum
praeter Crispinum sectabitur, et mihi dulces
140 ignoscent, si quid peccaro stultus, amici,
inque vicem illorum patiar delicta libenter,
privatusque magis vivam te rege beatus.

137. Ne longum faciam: cf. *ne te morer*, *Sat.* 1, 1, 14, and the more abrupt *iam satis*, 1, 1, 120. — **quadrante**: one fourth of an *as*, the price of admission to the public baths.

138–139. stipator: *as an escort*. — **ineptum**: with *Crispinum*, who is called *lippus* and otherwise derided in 1, 1,

120 f. — **et**: correlated with -*que*, 141.

140. stultus: in the Stoic use of the word. — With these verses Horace returns to the serious thought of the earlier part of the satire, which is in fact latent in his mind even while he is ridiculing the Stoic solemnity and Pharisaism.

4

There is no reference in this satire which fixes the date precisely, and we are obliged to fall back upon general indications. The criticisms to which it is a reply were called forth by the sensational and personal tone of the early seventh and eighth satires, and especially of the second; in particular, vss. 91 ff. show that this was written after the second and, probably, very soon after it. Maecenas is not mentioned in this satire, as he is not referred to in the other earlier ones, though a personal mention would have been natural in 8, 8 and 14. Nor is there any reference to the group of distinguished friends whose approval is in the tenth satire the final answer to the critics. This satire may therefore with probability be placed with 2, 7 and 8 of this book and with some of the *Epodes*, all written before Horace's introduction to Maecenas in 38.

The reference to Tigellius (vs. 72) is too vague to give any indication of the date (cf. note on 1, 3, 4).

'The great Athenian writers of comedy were the founders of satire. After them came Lucilius, not less keen than they, but too careless and too profuse. His faults I desire to avoid, for mere quantity is not a merit; but the spirit of his satire I shall attempt to preserve. I am aware, however, that exposure of the weaknesses of men makes my writings unpopular, and I desire to say a word in self-defence.

'In the first place, I do not think that satire is poetry or should be judged by the standards of poetry. It lacks the imaginative inspiration and the lofty expression of poetry, and is, in this respect, like comedy, a mere reproduction in verse-form of ordinary talk on everyday subjects.

'The main question, however, is whether the satirist deserves to be regarded with dislike and suspicion. You compare him to a detective, not noticing that you thereby compare yourself to a criminal, but the comparison fails because my notes are not taken for use in a court or for publication. You say that the satirist is a man of meanly critical spirit, who finds pleasure in exhibiting the failings of others. But this also is untrue; my satire is no more personal or serious than the raillery of a good talker at a dinner table. It is in fact only the exercise of a habit of observation taught me by my good father, who without knowing the philosophy of books instructed me in a practical philosophy founded on observation. The only fault you can find with me is that I write down my observations. But everybody nowadays writes; if you object to that, we'll unite to condemn you and the penalty shall be that you shall turn writer yourself.'

The connection of thought is less clearly indicated in this satire than in the first or third; there is occasional sharpness of retort and there is little of the mellow humor of the later work. These are the marks of immaturity. The sensitiveness to criticism, also, is of the kind that decreases with experience.

Eupolis atque Cratinus Aristophanesque poetae,
atque alii, quorum comoedia prisca virorum est,
si quis erat dignus describi, quod malus ac fur,

1-2. The three most important writers of the Old Comedy (*prisca comoedia*), of whose works only the eleven plays of Aristophanes (444-388 B.C.) are extant. The names make a sonorous opening of the speech for the defendant. — **poetae**: to close the verse with emphasis; 'true poets, all of them.' — **virorum**: attracted into the relative clause and the genitive; cf. the corresponding verse, *Sat.* 1, 10, 16.

3. **dignus describi**: *deserved to be satirized*; cf. vs. 25, *culpari dignos*, and *Sat.* 1, 3, 24, *dignus . . . notari*. These are all various ways of saying, 'a suitable subject for satire.' — **malus ac fur**: the same as *malos fures, Sat.* 1,

quod moechus foret aut sicarius aut alioqui
famosus, multa cum libertate notabant.
Hinc omnis pendet Lucilius, hosce secutus
mutatis tantum pedibus numerisque, facetus,
emunctae naris, durus componere versus.
Nam fuit hoc vitiosus: in hora saepe ducentos,
ut magnum, versus dictabat stans pede in uno;

1, 77, with no more difference than there is between 'rascals and thieves' and 'rascally thieves.'

5. **famosus**: in a bad sense, the common meaning in early Latin. — **libertate**: *with the utmost freedom of speech*. The extant plays of Aristophanes, in which public men are ridiculed with great license, abundantly support this statement.

6. **Hinc ... pendet**: *upon them Lucilius is entirely dependent*, i.e. as the context shows, they were his predecessors and models in the open ridicule of individuals, his warrant for the use of personal satire. It does not mean that Roman satire, as a form of literature, was derived from or an imitation of Greek comedy. — **C. Lucilius**: see Introd. — **hosce**: = *hos*. In Plautus the forms in *-ce* are used only before vowels.

7. **mutatis ... numeris**: Lucilius wrote partly in iambics and trochaics, but the verse which he used most frequently and which became the traditional verse for satire was the dactylic hexameter, which is not employed in the drama. — **tantum**: not to be taken too strictly, for Lucilius of course did not use the dramatic form. The emphasis here is upon the satirical spirit. — **facetus**: originally 'brilliant or polished in speech' (from *fa-ri, to speak*), and this is the meaning always in Plautus; cf. also *Sat.* 1, 10, 44, *molle atque facetum*, of Vergil's bucolic poetry. The meaning 'humorous,' 'facetious,' comes over into the adj. from the noun *facetiae*. It combines with *emunctae naris* to express the single idea 'keen in words and in thought,' 'sarcastic.' The same idea is expressed in *Sat.* 1, 10, 3 f., *sale multo urbem defricuit*.

9. **hoc**: *in this*, referring to what follows, which is at the same time an expansion of *durus componere versus*.

10. **ut magnum**: 'considering it a great feat.' — **stans ... uno**: apparently a proverbial expression for doing something without effort, but it does not occur elsewhere; Quintilian, 12, 9, 18, *in his actionibus omni, ut agricolae dicunt, pede standum est*, seems to be a reference to the opposite idea.

cum flueret lutulentus, erat quod tollere velles;
garrulus atque piger scribendi ferre laborem,
scribendi recte; nam ut multum, nil moror. — Ecce,
Crispinus minimo me provocat: 'Accipe, si vis,
15 accipiam tabulas; detur nobis locus, hora,
custodes; videamus uter plus scribere possit.'

11. **tollere**: *take out*, before using the water for drinking. The figure is that of a muddy stream; cf. the repetition in *Sat.* 1, 10, 50 f., *at dixi fluere hunc lutulentum, saepe ferentem plura quidem tollenda relinquendis*, and the comment in Quintilian, 10, 1, 94, 'ego ab Horatio dissentio, qui Lucilium fluere lutulentum et esse aliquid quod tollere possis putat.' The scholiast thinks that *quod tollere velles = quod sumere optares*, but this is quite wrong.

12-13. **garrulus**: this must go back in agreement to 9-10, in spite of the verse between. It is a loose construction, but the whole passage is loosely hung together; *secutus* without *est, facetus, durus, vitiosus* with its own verb, *garrulus*, form a series of half-connected appendages to the noun, *Lucilius*. — **scribendi recte**: a corrective; 'of writing properly, I mean.' — **ut multum**: *sc. scripserit*. — **nil moror**: a common colloquialism, which usually means 'I don't care,' 'I don't bother about it.' The construction is properly acc. and infin., and the only way of explaining the *ut*-clause is to say that *nil moror* has here the meaning and construction of *concedo*; 'for that he wrote much, I grant with indifference.' — **Ecce**: the mere mention of writing much brings forward Crispinus at once with a boast.

14. **minimo**: this must mean *offers me heavy odds*, i.e. will accept a bet in which Horace puts up the smallest possible pledge. There is no precise parallel to this use of *minimo*, but cf. Sueton. *Iul.* 50, *amplissima praedia . . . minimo addixit*; Catull. 44, 4, *quovis Sabinum pignore esse contendunt*; Verg. *Ecl.* 3, 31, *tu dic, mecum quo pignore certes*. The scholiasts appear to know the expression: 'minimo provocare dicuntur hi qui in sponsione plus ipsi promittunt quam exigant ab adversario,' but the explanation that it is *minimo digito*, with a gesture, is a mere guess. — **Accipe**: *sc. tabulas*. — **si vis**: less formal than 'if you please'; often used in colloquial language of comedy in the shortened form *sis* to lessen the abruptness of the bare impv. Cf. *sodes*, *Sat.* 1, 9, 41 n., and the enclitic -*dum*.

15 f. **detur custodes**: arrangements for a formal contest, with supervisors.

Di bene fecerunt, inopis me quodque pusilli
finxerunt animi, raro et perpauca loquentis;
at tu conclusas hircinis follibus auras,
20 usque laborantis dum ferrum molliat ignis,
ut mavis, imitare. Beatus Fannius, ultro
delatis capsis et imagine, cum mea nemo
scripta legat, volgo recitare timentis ob hanc rem,
quod sunt quos genus hoc minime iuvat, utpote pluris

17. Di bene fecerunt: not merely a statement, but a colloquial expression of gratitude; *Thank Heaven*. Cf. *bene facis, you're very kind;* Plaut. *Amph.* 937, *iam nunc irata non es?* ‖ *non sum.* ‖ *bene facis.* — **quodque**: *quod* introduces the whole clause, after the verb of emotion; *-que* connects *inopis* and *pusilli,* but is attached to a word between them; so 115, below, *vitatu quidque petitu*; *Sat.* 1, 6, 44, *cornua ... vincatque tubas,* and often in Horace.

18. loquentis: agreeing grammatically with *animi*, but in sense with *me*. The transfer of epithets is common in the *Odes* (*e.g.* 1, 4, 6 f., *aspera nigris aequora ventis*), and the attraction of *loquentis* from *me* to *animi* is made easier by the frequent use of *animus* for the whole man (1, 2, 69, *diceret haec animus*).

19 ff. 'Go and be a pair of bellows, a mere wind-bag, as is evidently your preference.' — **ut mavis**: *as you in fact prefer*, not 'since you so choose.'

21 ff. Fannius: mentioned also in 1, 10, 80, with the adj. *ineptus*, as a follower of Hermogenes Tigellius, but otherwise unknown. There are five *scholia* attempting to explain the reference and the words *ultro ... imagine,* but they are confused and only partially intelligible. The clause *cum ... legat* contrasts the good fortune of Fannius with the unpopularity of Horace; *beatus* must therefore mean 'happy in his popularity' and *ultro ... imagine* must contain a satirical reason for calling Fannius popular. The sense would then be 'The truly fortunate poet is neither Crispinus with his facile versification nor I with my satire, but Fannius; he *must* be popular, for he has of his own accord set up (in a public place, at the bookseller's?) his bookcases and portrait-bust, while, as to my writings, no one reads them.' But in addition to the obscurity of the allusions, the whole sentence is too condensed for clearness.

23 f. timentis: agreeing with the gen. implied in *mea*. — **genus hoc**: satire — **pluris**: acc., with *quos*.

25 culpari dignos. Quemvis media elige turba:
aut ob avaritiam aut misera ambitione laborat;
hic nuptarum insanit amoribus, hic puerorum;
hunc capit argenti splendor; stupet Albius aere;
hic mutat merces surgente a sole ad eum quo
30 vespertina tepet regio; quin per mala praeceps
fertur, uti pulvis collectus turbine, ne quid
summa deperdat metuens aut ampliet ut rem.
Omnes hi metuunt versus, odere poetas.
'Faenum habet in cornu, longe fuge; dummodo risum

26 f. ob avaritiam ... ambitione: the variation in construction is intentional and is carried still further in the following lines — *hic ... insanit, hunc capit, stupet* — until the last craze, the absorption in business, is reached; this, as a most conspicuous and widespread folly, is given fuller description in 29-32. — **laborat**: a technical word, used of *suffering from* a chronic ailment.

28. argenti splendor: the craze for collecting silver plate was a common one in Rome, but Albius is a person of independent judgment who has a little special craze for bronzes. There are many references (*e.g. Epist.* 1, 6, 17) to both of these 'fads.' — **Albius**: unknown. He cannot well be the man whose son was used by Horace's father (below, vs. 109) to illustrate the folly of wastefulness. — **stupet**: so *torpes, Sat.* 2, 7, 95, in a colloquial slang, like the Engl. nouns 'fad,' 'craze,' 'rage.'

29-32. The idea of passionate absorption in some single interest, which is expressed above by the verbs *laborat, insanit, capit, stupet*, is in these lines suggested by the elaborate detail of the description. — **surgente, vespertina**: 'from the East to the West'; the Romans felt a kind of wonder at the extent of their business enterprises. — **praeceps fertur**: as if by a force stronger than his own will. — **ne ... deperdat, ampliet ut**: in the proper sense of *ut* and *ne* after a verb of fearing.

33. versus, poetas: an intentional exaggeration; the dread of being satirized leads them to fear all poetry.

34. *quando feriunt boves, horum in cornibus ligatur faenum.* Schol. The saying happens not to occur elsewhere, but is given in Greek form by Plutarch, *Crass.* 7, Χόρτον ἔχειν φησὶν ἐπὶ τοῦ κέρατος. Cf. also *Epod.* 6, 11, *cave, cave; namque in malos asperrimus parata tollo cornua.*

35   excutiat sibi, non hic cuiquam parcet amico;
     et quodcumque semel chartis illeverit, omnis
     gestiet a furno redeuntis scire lacuque
     et pueros et anus.'   Agedum, pauca accipe contra.
     Primum ego me illorum, dederim quibus esse poetas,
40   excerpam numero ; neque enim concludere versum

34–38. Two indictments against the satirist, that he finds pleasure in inflicting pain (cf. *laedere gaudes*, 78) and that he violates the decent reserves of social intercourse by publishing his strictures upon individuals (repeated in 82-85). — **risum excutiat**: *raise a laugh;* *excutere* is used of causing tears (Plaut. *Capt.* 419, Ter. *Heaut.* 167) and disgust (Plaut. *Merc.* 576). — **illeverit** : *has smeared, scrawled.* — **furno**: the poorer classes had their baking done in public ovens and got their water from the public pools (*lacu*). At these places crowds of slaves (*pueros*) and old women (*anus*) would be gathered. The whole involves a comparison: the satirist is no better than a scandalmonger, who retails his gossip to the meanest of the public.

39–62. In these lines Horace gives the earliest indication of that interest in the theory of poetry which appears more plainly in *Sat.* 1, 10 and 2, 1 and in the Epistles, and which culminated in the *Ars Poetica*. For various reasons the passage deserves special attention. It contains the observations of a conscious artist upon the art which he was practicing with success, and such observations are always interesting. At this period of his life Horace was writing both Satires and Epodes, and this passage reveals the effort that he was making to distinguish between the two forms and to assign to the Epodes those lyrical thoughts and emotions which he found incompatible with the conventional limitations placed upon satire by Lucilius. And, in themselves, the lines are an admirable illustration of the somewhat elusive and colloquial form of argument which Horace habitually employs. The sense, in brief, is this : 'Satire is verse, but not poetry, since it lacks the imaginative thought and the lofty expression which characterize true poetry and which remain even when the verse-form is destroyed.'

39. poetas: not attracted into the dative ; cf. 1, 1, 19, *licet esse beatis*.

40. concludere versum: *to round out a verse.* Verse is conceived of as bound, as shut in within the limits of the metrical feet (cf. 1, 10, 59, *pedibus . . . claudere senis*), while prose is thought of as relaxed (*oratio soluta* is the technical term; cf. *dissolvas*, 55; *solvas*, 60, below).

dixeris esse satis, neque si quis scribat, uti nos,
sermoni propiora, putes hunc esse poetam.
Ingenium cui sit, cui mens divinior atque os
magna sonaturum, des nominis huius honorem.
45 Idcirco quidam comoedia necne poema
esset quaesivere, quod acer spiritus ac vis
nec verbis nec rebus inest, nisi quod pede certo
differt sermoni, sermo merus. 'At pater ardens
saevit, quod meretrice nepos insanus amica
50 filius uxorem grandi cum dote recuset,
ebrius et, magnum quod dedecus, ambulet ante

42. **sermoni propiora**: *things more truly like conversation.* *Sermo* here and below, 48, is clearly defined by *Auct. ad Herenn.* 3, 13, 23, *sermo est oratio remissa et finitima (= propiora) cottidianae locutioni.*

43-44. **Ingenium, mens divinior**: not two distinct characteristics, but two ways of describing a single characteristic, *an inspired imagination.* — **os magna sonaturum**: *a noble style;* expressed in a figure retained from the time when the poet sang his own verses.

45. **quidam**: the students of literary form, like the Alexandrian grammarians. Cicero, *Orat.* 20, 67, also refers to this discussion. — **comoedia**: the Attic New Comedy or the comedy of Plautus and Terence ; the rule would not apply to *Midsummer Night's Dream.*— **necne**: the prose order would be *quaesivere (utrum) comoedia poema esset necne;* cf. 63.

46. **acer spiritus ac vis**: *lively and vigorous inspiration;* the same thing as *mens divinior* and *os magna sonaturum,* but the expression is intentionally ambiguous, to give an opening for the objection which follows.

48-52. 'But there is certainly *acer spiritus ac vis* in the angry reproaches which a father in the comedies frequently addresses to a wayward son.' — **nepos**: *prodigal;* used as an adjective. — **meretrice . . . insanus amica**: *mad with passion for a harlot mistress; meretrice* also is used as an adj. with *amica.* — **ambulet ante noctem**: a reference to the *comissatio,* a wild procession through the streets after a drinking bout. To indulge in such a revel before night would be particularly disgraceful. The whole situation here is Greek.

noctem cum facibus.' Numquid Pomponius istis
audiret leviora, pater si viveret? Ergo
non satis est puris versum perscribere verbis,
55 quem si dissolvas, quivis stomachetur eodem
quo personatus pacto pater. His, ego quae nunc,
olim quae scripsit Lucilius, eripias si
tempora certa modosque, et quod prius ordine verbum est
posterius facias, praeponens ultima primis,
60 non, ut si solvas ' Postquam Discordia taetra
belli ferratos postis portasque refregit,'
invenias etiam disiecti membra poetae.

52. Pomponius: a name is used to point the retort, but it is quite unlikely that it refers to any definite person. — **istis**: 'the kind of talk you have just been describing.' — The argument is that the *acer spiritus ac vis* of comedy is merely the anger that any father in real life might express and is wholly different from the inspired imagination of the poet.

54. puris . . . verbis: *in plain everyday language*; the same as *sermo merus* and the opposite of *os magna sonaturum*.

56. personatus . . . pater: *the father on the stage*, the *pater ardens* of vs. 48. Masks (*personae*) were worn by actors in comedy in the time of Cicero. — **his**: neut., dat. after *eripias*.

58-59. tempora certa modosque: *the fixed quantities and rhythms* which make the hexameter. — **quod prius . . . primis**: i.e. change the words from the order demanded by the versification to the order of prose.

60-62. non: with *invenias*. — **etiam**: with *disiecti*. The true poet would be a poet still, even though torn limb from limb. There is a side reference to the story of Orpheus. — **Postquam . . . refregit**: a quotation from the *Annales* of Ennius; cf. Verg. *Aen.* 7, 622, *belli ferratos rupit Saturnia postis*. The thought might have been expressed in plain prose by *postquam bellum coortum est*; for this unadorned statement the poet has substituted the imaginative figure of Discord bursting open the gates of Janus and in the brief description has used, almost to excess, words charged with poetic suggestion, *taetra, ferratos, postis portasque*. The two essential qualities of poetry, *mens divinior* and *os magna sonaturum*,

Hactenus haec : alias iustum sit necne poema,
nunc illud tantum quaeram, meritone tibi sit
suspectum genus hoc scribendi. Sulcius acer
ambulat et Caprius, rauci male cumque libellis,
magnus uterque timor latronibus; at bene si quis
et vivat puris manibus, contemnat utrumque.
Vt sis tu similis Caeli Birrique latronum,
non ego sim Capri neque Sulci; cur metuas me?
Nulla taberna meos habeat neque pila libellos,
quis manus insudet volgi Hermogenisque Tigelli :

would still remain, even though the verse-form were destroyed by changing the order of the words.

63. alias: *sc. quaeram.* This vague intention was never carried out, for the interest which Horace felt in satire came to an end with the publication of the Second Book in 30, and his later literary discussions deal with other forms of poetry. — **sit**: the subject is to be supplied from *genus hoc scribendi.*

64-65. merito ... suspectum: *justly disliked, i.e.* 'whether your dislike (cf. vs. 33) is just.' — **tibi**: the satire had begun impersonally and the critics of satire are vaguely thought of (*sunt quos*, 24; *omnes hi.* 33), but from this point the critic is addressed directly and replies for himself; the monologue becomes dialogue.

55-66. Sulcius, Caprius: detectives, who got their living out of the fines collected on evidence furnished by them. Such men were a necessary part of the Roman police system, but, like the *publicani*, they were held in ill repute and the implied comparison of the satirist to a detective was intentionally offensive. — **libellis**: *notebooks* in which the evidence was recorded.

69. Vt sis tu: *however true it may be that you are like a highwayman.* The honest citizen does not fear a detective, and the man who says that he dreads a satirist as he would a detective forgets that he is thereby comparing himself to a criminal.

70 ff. sim, habeat: 'I should not be like the detective, for my notes would not be published.' But the faint hypothetical shading passes over into the indic. *recito.* — **taberna**: *bookshop*, where books were apparently hung upon the posts (*pilae*, cf. *columnae*, *A. P.* 373) to be examined by purchasers, as second-hand books are now exposed for sale outside the bookshops. — **quis**: *quibus.* — **Tigelli**: cf. *Sat.* 1, 3,

nec recito cuiquam nisi amicis, idque coactus,
non ubivis coramve quibuslibet. In medio qui
75 scripta foro recitent sunt multi, quique lavantes:
suave locus voci resonat conclusus. Inanis
hoc iuvat, haud illud quaerentis, num sine sensu,
tempore num faciant alieno. 'Laedere gaudes,'
inquis, 'et hoc studio pravus facis.' Vnde petitum
80 hoc in me iacis? Est auctor quis denique eorum
vixi cum quibus? 'Absentem qui rodit, amicum

4 n. — The declaration that the Satires were not written for publication seems at first sight irreconcilable with the fact that this satire is itself a reply to criticisms based upon a knowledge of the earlier Satires, especially the second. But the method of multiplying copies by hand made it possible to limit the circulation of a poem, so that it might be somewhat widely read without being offered for sale or put into general circulation. The collection and publication of the whole book was evidently a later decision.

73. recito: the habit of giving private readings from one's own works became later so common as to be ridiculous, and Horace here recognizes its possible exaggerations. But Vergil read parts of the *Aeneid* to Augustus and others, and Ovid (*Tristia*, 4, 10, 49) was present at a reading given by Horace.

75 f. lavantes: in the public baths, where men were at leisure; but Horace attributes the choice of the location to the pleasure the reader had in hearing his voice reverberating from the arched ceiling (*locus . . . conclusus*).

76. Inanis: emphatic; men are fools to find pleasure in that.

78 f. Laedere gaudes, studio: the emphasis of this second accusation is upon the mean pleasure that the satirist finds in wounding the feelings of others. — studio: *intentionally*.

79–80. Vnde . . . iacis? *What is the source of this accusation that you are hurling at me?* This demand for his authority the critic meets indirectly by saying, in effect, 'I do not need to quote the testimony of others, for your own conduct — your criticism of your friends, your lack of decent reticence — proves that you are a deliberate defamer.'

81. Absentem qui rodit: *he who slanders a man behind his back.* — amicum goes with the following clause, as in all the other clauses a word or two precedes the relative.

qui non defendit, alio culpante, solutós
qui captat risus hominum famamque dicacis,
fingere qui non visa potest, commissa tacere
85 qui nequit, hic niger est, hunc tu, Romane, caveto.'
Saepe tribus lectis videas cenare quaternos,
e quibus unus amet quavis aspergere cunctos
praeter eum qui praebet aquam; post hunc quoque potus,
condita cum verax aperit praecordia Liber.
90 Hic tibi comis et urbanus liberque videtur,
infesto nigris; ego si risi, quod ineptus

82. **defendit**: the final syllable is long under the ictus. Both Horace and Vergil frequently preserve the original long vowel in perf. forms like *figīt, subiīt*, but the vowel of the pres. 3d sing., 3d conj., was not originally long, and this instance and *agīt* (*Sat.* 2, 3, 260) must be explained by false analogy. The few instances quoted from Plautus are doubtful.

84. **commissa tacere**: the Romans placed a peculiarly high valuation upon the ability to keep a secret; cf. *Epist.* 1, 18, 70, *nec retinent patulae commissa fideliter aures.*

85. **niger**: *black at heart.* So Catullus, 93, 2, says of Caesar, *nec (studeo) scire atrum sis albus an ater homo.* — **Romane**: *true Roman*, i.e. an honest gentleman. Such expressions of national pride are common; *echt Deutsch*, and, for the opposite, *un-English, un-American.* — **caveto**: formal in style, like an oracular utterance.

86. **tribus, quaternos**: the usual number was nine, three on each couch, and the motive for specifying an unusual number is not clear. Perhaps it is connected with the emphasis upon *unus*; 'if you go a little beyond the usual number of guests, you will find that you have included one, at least, who is witty at the expense of the rest.'

87 f. **aspergere**: *besprinkle* with personal jokes. The figure leads to the selection of the phrase *qui praebet aquam* (water for washing the hands) to designate the host.

88. **post**: adv. — **hunc**: sc. *aspergit.* — **potus**: absolute; cf. *Sat.* 1, 3, 90.

89. An intentionally elaborate expression of the common idea *in vino veritas.*

90-93. 'Such conduct you consider, and rightly, mere friendly raillery; my little jokes, however, you are very ready to condemn.' — **infesto nigris**: *i.e.* 'you who call me *niger* in so hostile a tone.'

pastillos Rufillus olet, Gargonius hircum,
lividus et mordax videor tibi ? Mentio si qua
de Capitolini furtis iniecta Petilli
95 te coram fuerit, defendas, ut tuus est mos :
'Me Capitolinus convictore usus amicoque
a puero est, causaque mea permulta rogatus
fecit, et incolumis laetor quod vivit in urbe ;
sed tamen admiror, quo pacto iudicium illud
100 fugerit.' Hic nigrae sucus loliginis, haec est
aerugo mera. Quod vitium procul afore chartis,

92. Quoted from *Sat.* 1, 2, 27. But it is quite unlikely that either of these persons, who were used to illustrate the extremes of foppishness and of neglect of cleanliness, is more than a mere name.

93 ff. An example of really malicious slander, to be distinguished from friendly banter, *comitas* and *libertas*. — **Mentio . . . iniecta**: *if some one happens to mention.* — **Petilli**: a Petillius was quaestor about 43 B.C. and was acquitted, apparently against the evidence, on a charge of peculation. The name Petillius Capitolinus is also found on coins. That the trial was well known and that the accused owed much to the skill of his lawyers is implied by the reference in *Sat.* 1, 10, 26 to the *dura causa Petilli*. But the further statement of the scholiast that Petillius had stolen the crown from the head of the Capitoline Jupiter is a mere confusion with a popular saying which is as old as Plautus (*Men.* 941, *Trin.* 83).

96. convictore usus : *I have been a frequent guest of Capitolinus;* cf. 1, 6, 47, where Horace calls himself a *convictor* of Maecenas. — This verse is hypermetric like 1, 6, 102, which also ends in an enclitic.

98. incolumis . . . in urbe: acquitted and not exiled.

99. admiror: in English the corresponding phrase would be 'but I can't help wondering how he managed to keep out of jail.'

100. nigrae . . . loliginis: *the black ink of the cuttlefish,* with transference of the adj. and a reference back to vs. 85. — **aerugo**: *verdigris,* copper rust, which was thought of as an eating poison. Together the two figures express the same quality as *lividus et mordax,* 93, and *niger,* 85, and the opposite of *comis et urbanus,* 90, just as in the preceding paragraph, 39-62, the qualities of poetry and prose are repeatedly defined and contrasted.

atque animo prius, ut si quid promittere de me
possum aliud vere, promitto. Liberius si
dixero quid, si forte iocosius, hoc mihi iuris
105 cum venia dabis: insuevit pater optimus hoc me,
ut fugerem exemplis vitiorum quaeque notando.
Cum me hortaretur, parce frugaliter atque
viverem uti contentus eo quod mi ipse parasset:
'Nonne vides Albi ut male vivat filius utque
110 Baius inops? Magnum documentum ne patriam rem
perdere quis velit.' A turpi meretricis amore

102. **animo prius**: *i.e.* he will first of all keep malice out of his heart, and then it will certainly not appear in his writings. — **ut si quid ...promitto**: a colloquial confusion of *ut . . . promittere possum* and *si quid promittere possum*; 'I promise this as surely as I can promise anything.'

103-106. 'Malice I promise to avoid, but a considerable freedom of speech and jest (*liberius, iocosius*, with a reference back to vs. 90) you must permit (*hoc iuris dabis*) and pardon (*cum venia*).' — **hoc me**: double acc. after *insuevit*, which is here a verb of teaching. *hoc* is not precisely *liberius dicere*, but the humorously observant attitude of mind of which a habit of friendly bantering may be the expression. The structure of 106 is somewhat involved; *notando* is the leading word, *vitiorum quaeque* depends upon it, *exemplis* is an abl. of means with it, and *ut fugerem* expresses its purpose. 'I owe my habit of observing the follies of men to my father; he used to point out all sorts of errors in concrete cases — in the conduct of individuals — in order to teach me to avoid them.'

107-108. The order is *uti parce atque frugaliter viverem*; the whole passage, 101-108, is somewhat confusedly written.

109. **Albi**: not the Albius of vs. 28. The point of the illustration — *ne patriam rem perdere quis velit* — would be spoiled if the father had wasted the property: *Albi filius* is the spendthrift son of a prosperous father, and so an excellent illustration (*magnum documentum*) of the conduct which Horace's prosperous father wished his own son to avoid. All these instances are reminiscences of Horace's boyhood (cf. 121) and the persons mentioned are unknown. — **male vivat**: *i.e.* in wretched poverty.

cum deterreret: 'Scetani dissimilis sis.'
Ne sequerer moechas, concessa cum venere uti
possem : ' Deprensi non bella est fama Treboni,'
115 aiebat. 'Sapiens, vitatu quidque petitu
sit melius, causas reddet tibi ; mi· satis est, si
traditum ab antiquis morem servare tuamque,
dum custodis eges, vitam famamque tueri
incolumem possum; simul ac duraverit aetas
120 membra animumque tuum, nabis sine cortice.' Sic me
formabat puerum dictis; et sive iubebat
ut facerem quid : ' Habes auctorem, quo facias hoc,'
unum ex iudicibus selectis obiciebat;

115. Sapiens: *a philosopher*, a teacher of the theory of ethics, in contrast with *mi*, 116, the practical instructor of youth. — **quidque**: *quid vitatu petituque*; cf. vs. 17 n. The two words express the *malum* and *bonum* of philosophy, as these ideas are expressed in *Sat.* 1, 3, 114, by *bona diversis, fugienda petendis*.

116. causas reddet: *will explain*, as a matter of theory.

118. custodis, vitam famamque: not only the character (*vitam*) but also the good name (*famam*) of a Roman boy of respectable family was carefully guarded up to the time when he assumed the *toga virilis*. Cf. *Sat.* 1, 6, 82 ff., *pudicum . . . servavit ab omni non solum facto, verum opprobrio quoque turpi*, where *facto* corresponds to *vitam* and *opprobrio* to *famam*.

121 f. sive: the apodosis is, grammatically, *obiciebat*, but this verb, preceded by the direct quotation, implies a verb of saying; 'when he advised a particular course of conduct, he used to say, " There is your example," pointing out . . . ' — **ut facerem**: depending on *iubebat*. Horace elsewhere uses the infin. with *iubeo*, but the construction with *ut* is perfectly good Latin (Plautus, Cicero, Livy). [To supply *aliquid*, duplicating *quid*, and to make *ut facerem* depend on *obiciebat* or the supplied verb of saying, is to resort to an artificial construction in order to avoid supposing that Horace in a single instance uses a good Latin construction which he elsewhere avoids.]

123. iudicibus selectis: the panel of *special jurymen* selected by the *praetor urbanus* to act in criminal cases. They were likely to be citizens of character and standing.

sive vetabat: 'An hoc inhonestum et inutile factu
125 necne sit addubites, flagret rumore malo cum
hic atque ille?' Avidos vicinum funus ut aegros
exanimat, mortisque metu sibi parcere cogit,
sic teneros animos aliena opprobria saepe
absterrent vitiis. Ex hoc ego, sanus ab illis
130 perniciem quaecumque ferunt, mediocribus et quis
ignoscas vitiis teneor; fortassis et istinc
largiter abstulerit longa aetas, liber amicus,
consilium proprium: neque enim, cum lectulus aut me
porticus excepit, desum mihi. 'Rectius hoc est.'
135 'Hoc faciens vivam melius.' 'Sic dulcis amicis
occurram.' 'Hoc quidam non belle; numquid ego illi

124 f. An: introducing the main question, *addubites*. The indirect question is (*utrum*) *inhonestum sit necne*; cf. 45 and 60, notes. — **hoc**: some forbidden act.

126 f. Avidos: *gluttons*, in the literal sense, whom the sight of death reminds of the consequences of self-indulgence. — **sibi parcere**: 'to take some care of their own health.'

129. Ex hoc: *as a result of this*, of such training by his father.

130 ff. quis ignoscas: *pardonable*; there was no adj. *ignoscibilis* in use in the time of Horace. *quis* is a dative. — **et istinc**: *even from these*, i.e. the slight and pardonable faults. — **liber**: *frank*; cf. *Sat.* 1, 3, 52.

133 ff. consilium proprium: 'my own reflections' (Palmer), based upon such observations as those which follow. — **neque enim**: takes up *consilium proprium* and expands it, thus providing for the return of the thought to the subject of satire. — **lectulus**: *reading couch.* — **porticus**: *the public colonnade*, a place which would give opportunity to observe the conduct of others who were strolling there. — **hoc, hoc, sic, hoc**: each refers to some act of another person which attracts his attention and serves as an example to be followed or a warning. — **quidam**: *so and so.* — **belle**: a colloquial word; 'not pretty conduct of so and so.' — **numquid**: suggesting a negative; 'I hope I shall not sometime (*olim*) when I am off my guard (*imprudens*) do anything like that.'

> imprudens olim faciam simile?' Haec ego mecum
> compressis agito labris; ubi quid datur oti,
> illudo chartis. Hoc est mediocribus illis
> 140 ex vitiis unum; cui si concedere nolis,
> multa poetarum veniet manus auxilio quae
> sit mihi (nam multo plures sumus), ac veluti te
> Iudaei cogemus in hanc concedere turbam.

137 f. Haec agito: *so I think to myself*, recurring to the thought of *neque . . . desum mihi* and *consilium proprium*. — **compressis . . . labris**: *i.e.* 'I say nothing at the time, but wait till I get home and then write it down.'

139. illudo chartis: cf. *chartis illeverit*, vs. 36. A jokingly apologetic way of describing the writing of satire. — **mediocribus**: referring back to vs. 130.

140. concedere: *pardon*; cf. 1, 3, 85.

141 f. multa . . . manus, multo plures: with joking exaggeration he says that the poets are in the majority and can compel the critics to join their party, as it is sometimes said now 'everybody writes novels.' But it was a fact that light verse writing was a frequent amusement of educated Romans — Pliny gives a long list of famous names — and that it was especially characteristic of the Augustan Age, when politics no longer offered a career.

143. Iudaei: the best commentary on this allusion is chap. 28 of Cicero's speech *pro Flacco*, in which he refers to the number and influence of the Jews in Rome (scis quanta sit manus, quanta concordia, quantum valeat in contionibus), to their religion (huic barbarae superstitioni) and their obstinate resistance to Roman ideals (istorum religio sacrorum a splendore huius imperii, gravitate nominis nostri, maiorum institutis abhorrebat). To a Roman, who admitted the gods of foreigners easily to his Pantheon, the desire of the Jew to make converts was wholly unintelligible.

5

The evidence for the date of this satire is found in vs. 27-29; Maecenas and Cocceius (L. Cocceius Nerva) were making the journey to Brundisium on an important mission, to reconcile friends who were at variance, a mission which they had performed before. The *aversi amici* (29) can be only the younger Caesar, and Antonius, whose relations were never clearly defined and were in constant need of readjustment. In the year 40 B.C. an arrangement called the Treaty of Brundisium was made by Maecenas, representing Caesar, Asinius Pollio, representing Antonius, and Cocceius, as the friend of both sides. This explains *soliti componere* (29). In the following years, 39-38 B.C., Caesar was twice defeated by the fleet of Sextus Pompeius and was obliged to call upon Antonius for aid. Antonius came to Brundisium in the spring of 39, but Caesar did not meet him at that time, or, so far as is known, send representatives to a conference. But in the autumn of 38, the difficulties with Sextus Pompeius increasing, Maecenas was sent to Athens to confer with Antonius. With him went Fonteius Capito, as a friend of Antonius, and Cocceius, presumably to be a referee, as on the previous occasion, and the three ambassadors were accompanied on the overland journey to the port of Brundisium by a party of literary friends, Horace, Vergil, Plotius Tucca and Varius (the two friends to whom the publication of the *Aeneid* was intrusted after the death of Vergil), and a Greek rhetorician, Heliodorus. The satire was probably written soon after the date of the journey, late in 38 or early in 37.

The connection of thought is simple; the satire is a rather bare recital of the events of the journey, with some description of humorous episodes and adventures. The route can be easily followed on a map and the daily stages are for the most part indicated. But Horace was not writing a guidebook of the well-known route, and he has intentionally paraphrased the names of some places (24, 37, 45, 79 f., 87) and has used phrases which leave it uncertain whether the party spent a night at Anxur, at Capua, or at Beneventum. The journey was made partly on foot (though this is not certain), partly in a canal boat, but chiefly by riding or driving. The distance was about 340 English miles, the time from twelve to fifteen days.

The satire has a certain accidental interest from the glimpses it gives of the manner of traveling in the year 38 B.C., and it contains a few interesting personal allusions (27-29, 32-33, and especially 39-44), but it is for the most part made up of trivialities. It falls short to a surprising degree of the account which we should expect Horace to give of a fortnight's association with a group of men so cultivated and so eminent. There are two explanations of the limitations of the satire. In the first place, personal biography and reminiscence are modern; they had not made a place in ancient literature. The nearest approach to them would be in books like Caesar's Commentaries or Cicero's account of his consulship — both in reality political pamphlets — or in the collection of Cicero's letters and of his witticisms. There are no true parallels in Latin literature to the many books of personal reminiscence which enrich modern literature. In the second place, Horace was deliberately attempting a very different task; he was writing a satire which was intended to be a close parallel to the similar description of a journey in the Third Book of Lucilius, and he has therefore been more closely bound by tradition in this satire than in any other. He was deliberately following a particular model and setting himself and his art in the closest possible comparison with the work of Lucilius. Unfortunately, the fragments of the satire of Lucilius are too scanty — about 50 verses, 98-147 in Marx — to enable us to follow the correspondence into details.

Egressum magna me accepit Aricia Roma
hospitio modico; rhetor comes Heliodorus,
Graecorum longe doctissimus; inde Forum Appi,
differtum nautis cauponibus atque malignis.
5   Hoc iter ignavi divisimus, altius ac nos
praecinctis unum; minus est gravis Appia tardis.

1. **magna**: in contrast with the small town of Aricia and its modest inn.

2. **hospitio**: the well-to-do Roman had friends or connections in many places by whom he was received as a guest (cf. 38, 50), so that he was rarely obliged to depend upon the public inns, and the inns were in consequence rather humble places of entertainment (cf. 71 ff.).

3. **longe doctissimus**: a humorous and not unfriendly superlative; cf. vss. 39 and 50. A considerable part of the humor of the satire is in the form of obvious exaggerations of discomforts (4, 7, 80, 88, 91, 95).

4. **nautis**: *boatmen*, employed upon the canal which ran through the Pomptine marshes from Forum Appi to Feronia. — **cauponibus ... malignis**: cf. *Sat.* 1, 1, 29. A propensity to dishonesty and stinginess is a traditional attribute of innkeepers.

5. **Hoc iter**: the stretch of nearly 40 English miles from Rome to Forum Appi. — **divisimus**: *i.e.* we made two day's journeys of it, stopping halfway at Aricia. — **altius ... praecinctis**: cf. εὔζωνος and the scriptural phrase 'to gird up the loins'; the opposite of *ignavi* and *tardis*. The words, however, might be used figuratively of any energetic traveler and do not quite prove that this part of the journey was made on foot.

6. **tardis**: *to those who travel slowly*. But the point of the remark is not quite clear. As the

Hic ego propter aquam, quod erat deterrima, ventri
indico bellum, cenantis haud animo aequo
exspectans comites. Iam nox inducere terris
10 umbras et caelo diffundere signa parabat;
tum pueri nautis, pueris convicia nautae
ingerere: 'Huc appelle!' 'Trecentos inseris!' 'Ohe,
iam satis est!' Dum aes exigitur, dum mula ligatur,
tota abit hora; mali culices ranaeque palustres
15 avertunt somnos; absentem cantat amicam
multa prolutus vappa nauta atque viator
certatim; tandem fessus dormire viator

via Appia was one of the best of Roman roads, it seems necessary to take it as a general observation, carrying on the humorous confession of laziness in *ignavi*; 'traveling isn't so bad if you are not too energetic about it.'

8. indico bellum: parody of serious style. As the poor water had affected his digestion, he cut off the supplies, and his annoyance (*haud aequo animo*) at having to go without his dinner was increased by his being obliged to wait while Heliodorus and the slaves dined.

9-10. Iam nox . . . parabat: parody of the epic style; cf. 2, 6, 100 f., *iamque tenebat nox medium caeli spatium*, in the story of the Town Mouse and the Country Mouse.

11. pueri: the slaves of the embarking travelers.

12. Huc appelle: a cry from some slave on the bank, as the boat was picking up passengers from the various inns. The other shouts are complaints of overcrowding from the passengers already on board. — **Trecentos**: of a round number, like *sescenti, ducenti*, 1, 4, 9.

14 ff. The experiences of the night are told in a series of unconnected sentences, without comment, as things that speak for themselves. [I have omitted the indefensible *ut* in 15, which was inserted by a copyist who did not understand the *asyndeta*.]

16 ff. nauta, viator: 'nauta in navi, viator vero qui mulam ducebat.' Acro. This is certainly the correct explanation, since a canal boat requires a steersman (*nauta*), as well as a driver on the towpath (*viator*). The driver is the first to get tired; he stops for a nap and the steersman jumps ashore, ties up the mule, and lies down with him. [The note of Porphyrio, in which *viatores* refers to the passengers on the boat,

incipit, ac missae pastum retinacula mulae
nauta piger saxo religat stertitque supinus.
20 Iamque dies aderat, nil cum procedere lintrem
sentimus, donec cerebrosus prosilit unus
ac mulae nautaeque caput lumbosque saligno
fuste dolat; quarta vix demum exponimur hora.
Ora manusque tua lavimus, Feronia, lympha.
25 Milia tum pransi tria repimus, atque subimus
impositum saxis late candentibus Anxur.
Huc venturus erat Maecenas, optimus atque
Cocceius, missi magnis de rebus uterque

is usually taken as the starting point of the explanation of this passage; wrongly, I think.] — **retinacula**: occurs only in plur.; *the halter*.

20 ff. Iam ... aderat ... cum ... sentimus: a good example of *cum inversum*, in parody of the epic style (Rolfe). — The meter of vs. 22 is jokingly suggestive of the repeated blows. — **saligno fuste**: *i.e.* with a cudgel which he gets from the willows along the bank. — **dolat**: slang, like 'polishes off,' 'trims up.' *dolare* is a slang term in Plaut. (*M. G.*, 938, *Men.* 859), though in a slightly different sense. — **quarta ... hora**: about ten o'clock. — **vix demum**: an expression of annoyance at the discomforts of travel, as the modern traveler recalls the lateness of his train; while vs. 24 is a reminiscence of the comfort of a bath and breakfast after a wretched night.

24. Feronia: a goddess whose temple and fountain were near the end of the canal.

25 f. subimus: the regular verb for going toward a high place; Anxur was an old city on the hill, Tarracina the newer town at the foot of the hill. — **late candentibus**: cf. *Epod.* 1, 29, *superni villa candens Tusculi* and Martial, 5, 1, 6, *candidus Anxur*. The cliffs are of white limestone.

27. Huc venturus erat: the official members of the party had perhaps been in conference with the younger Caesar at some country house in the neighborhood. The tense of *venturus erat* means 'it had been arranged that he should come.'

28. Cocceius: L. Cocceius Nerva, consul in 36 B.C., the great-grandfather of the emperor Nerva. See also the introduction to this satire.

legati, aversos soliti componere amicos.
30   Hic oculis ego nigra meis collyria lippus
illinere. Interea Maecenas advenit atque
Cocceius, Capitoque simul Fonteius, ad unguem
factus homo, Antoni, non ut magis alter, amicus.
Fundos Aufidio Lusco praetore libenter
35   linquimus, insani ridentes praemia scribae,
praetextam et latum clavum prunaeque vatillum.
In Mamurrarum lassi deinde urbe manemus,

30 f. Cf. *Sat.* 1, 3, 25 n. The mention of this personal trifle, like the allusions to other details, gives the effect of a diary, and this is heightened by the use of the 'historical' infinitive. Cf. *Sat.* 1, 9, 9-10, and 66.

32 f. **Capito**: C. Fonteius Capito, consul in 33 B.C., the representative of Antonius in the conference. — **ad unguem factus homo**: the figure is said to be taken from the habit of testing the smoothness of a surface by passing the edge of the thumb nail over it. The expression was proverbial, like the English 'a polished gentleman' or 'a man, every inch of him,' and there is an intentional courtesy in the compliment to the representative of Antonius. — **non ut magis alter**: so Nepos, *Epam.* 2, *eruditus sic ut nemo Thebanus magis.*

34-36. As the distinguished travelers passed through Fundi, they were met by the mayor of the town in his robes of office. — **Aufidio ... praetore**: a formal expression, like *Caesare et Bibulo consulibus*, as if it fixed a date. It is not certain whether the chief magistrate of Fundi was properly called *praetor* or the word is used in derision. — **libenter**: the formal reception bored them. — **insani ... scribae**: *i.e.* he had formerly been a clerk (cf. 66, below) and was too much elated by his rise in station. — **praetextam**: the toga with a purple border. — **latum clavum**: the purple stripe down the front of the tunic. — **prunae vatillum**: a pan or shovel of coals, for burning incense. The severity of this satirical allusion seems at first sight scarcely justifiable. Horace was, in fact, only a humble retainer of the great men to whom the honors were paid, and he was himself a *scriba*. But, like Thackeray, he had a keen eye for a snob.

37. **Mamurrarum urbe**: Formiae. Only one Mamurra is known to us, a knight of Formiae, who was *praefectus fabrum* (chief of engineers) under Julius Caesar, was enriched by him and

Murena praebente domum, Capitone culinam.
Postera lux oritur multo gratissima ; namque
40 Plotius et Varius Sinuessae Vergiliusque
occurrunt, animae, qualis neque candidiores
terra tulit, neque quis me sit devinctior alter.
O qui complexus et gaudia quanta fuerunt!
Nil ego contulerim iucundo sanus amico.
45 Proxima Campano ponti quae villula tectum
praebuit, et parochi quae debent ligna salemque.

made an offensive display of his ill-gotten money. He was attacked with especial bitterness by Catullus and, apparently, on good grounds. Nothing is known of his family (the scholia describe a later condition of things), and it seems likely that the calling of Formiae by his name and the use of the plural, as if there were many distinguished persons of the family, are satirical touches.

38. Murena: L. Licinius Terentius Varro Murena, brother of Terentia, the wife of Maecenas. *Carm.* 2, 10 is addressed to him. He was put to death in 22 B.C. for conspiracy. — **praebente domum**: the implication is that he was not himself occupying the villa at this time.

40. Plotius Tucca and L. Varius Rufus were Vergil's literary executors, and Varius and Vergil were the friends who had introduced Horace to Maecenas (*Sat.* 1, 6, 53). Varius was very highly esteemed, perhaps beyond his merits, by his contemporaries as a writer of epic and of tragedy; he is mentioned by Horace more frequently than any other of his literary friends.

41. qualis ... candidiores: the expression is perfectly logical — 'of which kind the earth has borne none fairer (than they)' — and it is used again in *Epod.* 5, 59 f.: *nardo ... , quale non perfectius meae laborarint manus;* there is no similar idiom in English.

42. tulit: *brought forth.* — **quis**: dative.

44. sanus: *while I am in my senses;* so *Sat.* 1, 6, 89, *nil me paeniteat sanum patris huius.*

45 f. quae villula: *sc. est.* This was a public house, maintained by the government for the use of officials traveling on state business. The *parochi* (παρέχω) furnished the necessary supplies (*ligna salemque* are not to be taken quite literally, for Cicero, *ad Att.* 5, 16, 3, mentions also fodder), which were at this time designated by law; hence *quae debent.*

Hinc muli Capuae clitellas tempore ponunt.
Lusum it Maecenas, dormitum ego Vergiliusque;
namque pila lippis inimicum et ludere crudis.
50 Hinc nos Coccei recipit plenissima villa,
quae super est Caudi cauponas. Nunc mihi paucis
Sarmenti scurrae pugnam Messique Cicirri,
Musa, velim memores, et quo patre natus uterque

47. Hinc: *i.e.* starting from this point. — **tempore:** *in good season*, so that there was time for exercise before supper.

49. lippis: Horace; cf. vs. 30. — **crudis:** Vergil, of whom Donatus says, 'plerumque a stomacho et a faucibus ac dolore capitis laborabat.'

50. plenissima: *well-stocked*. So Cicero, *Cat. Maior*, 56, says 'semper enim boni assiduique domini referta cella vinaria, olearia, etiam penaria est, villaque tota locuples est, abundat porco, haedo, agno, gallina, lacte, caseo, melle.' — **Caudi:** where the Romans were defeated by the Samnites in 321 B.C.

51–70. The custom of inviting semi-professional jesters to enliven the conversation of the dinner table, a custom which has prevailed more or less in all societies, is alluded to in many Roman writers from Plautus down. The jesters were of all degrees, from the buffoon or the mere butt of practical jokes to the more refined wit and story-teller. Examples of both kinds are mentioned in *Sat.* 2, 8, Porcius, who could eat whole cakes at a gulp, and Vibidius and Balatro, hangers-on of Maecenas and leaders of the joking, but not buffoons.

This passage is the record of a contest of wits between two such parasites. Sarmentus is described at some length in a scholium to Juvenal, 5, 3, and was evidently a well-known person; he had been a slave, was perhaps at this time a freedman, had become a *scriba*, and was small and somewhat effeminate in appearance. He represents the type of *scurra*, the more polished wit. Messius Cicirrus (κίκιρρος, a fighting-cock) is the clown, an Oscan, large and clumsy, with his face disfigured by a scar. He is a countryman, brought in for the occasion to be pitted against the city-bred Sarmentus, who was in the train of Maecenas, perhaps as a secretary.

53–55. Musa: in epic style. — **quo patre natus:** as in Homer, before two heroes engage in fight, the genealogy of each is recited. But in this case the heroic demand (*quo patre natus*) cannot be met: 'of Messius the glorious lineage is — Oscan; of the family

contulerit lites. Messi clarum genus Osci;
55 Sarmenti domina exstat: ab his maioribus orti
ad pugnam venere. Prior Sarmentus: 'Equi te
esse feri similem dico.' Ridemus, et ipse
Messius 'Accipio,' caput et movet. 'O, tua cornu
ni foret exsecto frons,' inquit, 'quid faceres, cum
60 sic mutilus minitaris?' At illi foeda cicatrix
saetosam laevi frontem turpaverat oris.
Campanum in morbum, in faciem permulta iocatus,
pastorem saltaret uti Cyclopa rogabat;
nil illi larva aut tragicis opus esse cothurnis.
65 Multa Cicirrus ad haec: Donasset iamne catenam

of Sarmentus there survives only — his owner.' The Oscans were regarded by the Romans with special contempt, and a slave had, legally, no family.

56 f. Equi . . . feri: *a unicorn*. The comparison is suggested by the scar mentioned below, 60. This is clearly a variation on the verse of Lucilius, *dente adverso eminulo hic est | rinoceros* (Marx 117 f.), 'This is a rhinoceros with a tooth sticking out in front.'

58. Accipio: 'all right; so I am, and you will find me dangerous.' with a threatening shake of the head.

60. sic: both with *mutilus* and with *minitaris;* 'when, hornless as you are, you threaten so.' — **At**: explanatory, not adversative; *and, in fact*.

61. laevi: 'on the left side of his face.' [But the expression is awkward and the comparison to a unicorn and, below, to the Cyclops requires that the scar should have been in the middle; the text must be regarded as quite doubtful.]

62. Campanum in morbum: some disease, not understood even by the scholiasts, which was thought to be the cause of the scar. *Campanus* contains the same kind of slur as *Osci*, 54.

63. saltaret . . Cyclopa: *should play the Cyclops* in a pantomimic dance; accus. of the inner object.

64. larva: because he was so ugly and the scar would represent the one eye of the Cyclops. — **cothurnis**: because he was so big and clumsy.

65 ff. The account is shortened by giving the substance of the retorts of Cicirrus without comment. They turn upon the fact that Sarmentus had been a slave and upon his small size and effeminate ap-

ex voto Laribus, quaerebat; scriba quod esset,
nilo deterius dominae ius esse : rogabat
denique, cur umquam fugisset, cui satis una
farris libra foret, gracili sic tamque pusillo.
70 Prorsus iucunde cenam producimus illam.
Tendimus hinc recta Beneventum, ubi sedulus hospes
paene macros arsit dum turdos versat in igni;
nam vaga per veterem dilapso flamma culinam
Volcano summum properabat lambere tectum.
75 Convivas avidos cenam servosque timentis
tum rapere, atque omnis restinguere velle videres.
Incipit ex illo montis Apulia notos
ostentare mihi, quos torret Atabulus, et quos

pearance. — **ex voto**: as gladiators at the end of their professional career dedicated their arms (*Epist.* 1. 1, 4 f.) or as men who had escaped from shipwreck hung up their dripping garments in a temple (*Carm.* 1, 5, 13-16), so a slave who had escaped from slavery — perhaps by running away — might dedicate his chains to the gods who had helped him. — **scriba**: the emphatic position shows what the point is; 'even though you have attained to the lofty position of a clerk, still . . . ' — **una farris libra**: the ordinary ration was four or five pounds and such a puny little man might have lived on a quarter of his allowance and bought his freedom with his savings, instead of running away.

70. **Prorsus** : with *iucunde*; 'certainly it was a jolly supper . . . So *prorsus vehementer*,

Cic. *ad Att.* 16, 15, 2; *prorsus valde*, *ad Fam.* 6, 20, 2.

72. **paene . . . arsit**: *almost set his house afire.* So Verg. *Aen.* 2, 311 f., *ardet Vcalegon.* — **macros**: with *turdos* and *dum* with *versat.* It is possible that the confused order is meant to represent the confused efforts of the anxious landlord.

73-74. **vaga . . . veterem . . . Volcano**: parody of the alliteration in the epic style of Ennius. — **dilapso . . . Volcano**: the logs which were piled together on the raised hearth fell apart and were scattered on the floor.

76. **videres**: 'then there was a pretty spectacle for you to see, of hungry guests and frightened slaves.'

78. **mihi**: they were approaching the region of Venusia, where Horace had passed his boyhood,

[1, 5, 79]

numquam erepsemus, nisi nos vicina Trivici
80 villa recepisset, lacrimoso non sine fumo,
udos cum foliis ramos urente camino.
86 Quattuor hinc rapimur viginti et milia raedis,
mansuri oppidulo quod versu dicere non est,
signis perfacile est: venit vilissima rerum
hic aqua; sed panis longe pulcherrimus, ultra

and he began to recognize well-known landmarks. — **Atabulus**: a name for the *sirocco*, peculiar to Apulia and recalled by Horace as he approaches his old home. Gellius (2, 22, 25) calls it *Horatianus ille Atabulus*.

79. **erepsemus**: *erepsissemus*; such colloquial forms are used freely in the Satires, *e.g.*, *surrexe* for *surrexisse*, 1, 9, 73. — **nisi**: the expression is somewhat condensed, perhaps with humorous intention; 'we should never have crawled out, if we hadn't stopped,' meaning 'we should never have had the strength to crawl out, if we had not refreshed ourselves by a night's rest.'

81. **udos**: the emphatic word; 'because of the dampness of the fuel.' — **urente camino**: so *triverit area*, 1, 1, 45. The *caminus* (cf. *Epist.* 1, 11, 19) was an arrangement, other than the open hearth, for heating a room, but the details of its construction are unknown.

86. **raedis**: both *raeda* (or *reda*) and *petorritum* (or *petoritum*) are Gallic words (Quint. 1. 5, 57), and this fact accounts for the variation in spelling. The mention of carriages at this stage of the journey and the contrast between *rapimur* and *erepsemus* must certainly imply a change in the mode of traveling, from riding to driving.

87. **quod versu dicere non est**: so Lucilius (228 f., Marx) has ' servorum festus dies hic, | quem plane hexametro versu non dicere possis' of the feast of the *Sigillaria*, and Ovid (*ex Ponto*, 4, 12) jokes about the impossibility of bringing the name of his friend *Tūtīcānus* into elegiac verse. The name of the town is unknown, in spite of statements by the scholiasts.

88 ff. **signis**: by the indications which follow, the lack of good water and the excellence of the bread. — **venit**: from *veneo*; emphatic by position and by contrast with *vilissima*; 'they ask here for what can elsewhere be had for nothing — water.' — **ultra**: *i.e.* the traveler who knows what he is about (*callidus*) lays in a supply for the next stage of the journey. — **soleāt**: an early long

90　callidus ut soleat umeris portare viator:
　　nam Canusi lapidosus, aquae non ditior urna
　　qui locus a forti Diomede est conditus olim.
　　Flentibus hinc Varius discedit maestus amicis.
　　Inde Rubos fessi pervenimus, utpote longum
95　carpentes iter et factum corruptius imbri.
　　Postera tempestas melior, via peior ad usque
　　Bari moenia piscosi; dein Gnatia lymphis
　　iratis exstructa dedit risusque iocosque,
　　dum flamma sine tura liquescere limine sacro
100　persuadere cupit. Credat Iudaeus Apella,
　　non ego; namque deos didici securum agere aevum,

quantity preserved here, as occasionally elsewhere in Horace and in Vergil and frequently in Plautus. — **umeris portare**: a general term, for most travelers would have slaves to carry their provisions.

91 f. Canusi: gen., not locative: *sc. panis.*—**lapidosus**: *gritty.* — **aquae**: gen. with *ditior*; so *dives artium*, *Carm.* 4, 8, 5; *dives opis*, *Sat.* 1, 2, 74. — **urna**: abl. of degree of difference. — The narrative hurries on here through uninteresting scenes and events and three distinct statements ('the bread of Canusium is gritty; water there is scarce; the town was founded by Diomed') are condensed into a single sentence. The intentional awkwardness expresses the haste of the story.

93. Flentibus ... amicis: 'leaving his friends in tears'; a dative of separation. The exaggeration is intentionally humorous.

96. tempestas: *weather*, as frequently in early and classical Latin.

97 f. piscosi: Barium was on the coast.—**dein**: monosyllabic. — **lymphis iratis exstructa**: 'built under the frown of the water nymphs,' *i.e.* lacking in good water.

99. The 'miracle' was exhibited to the distinguished visitors. As described by Pliny, *H.N.* 2, 107, 240, it was the wood on the altar which took fire of itself.

100. Credat Iudaeus Apella: there were many Jews in Rome at this time and Horace had evidently some knowledge of their beliefs (*Sat.* 1, 4, 143; 1, 9, 66 f.; perhaps also 2, 3, 288 ff.), possibly even of their belief in this particular kind of miracle (*Levit.* 9, 24; *I Kings* 18, 38).

101. securum: 'Careless of mankind,' Tennyson, *The Lotus*

nec, si quid miri faciat natura, deos id
tristis ex alto caeli demittere tecto.
Brundisium longae finis chartaeque viaeque est.

Eaters. The verse is a quotation of Lucretius, 5, 82 — *nam bene qui didicere deos securum agere aevom* — and an expression of Horace's Epicurean skepticism.

102 f. **natura**: the working force which in the Epicurean philosophy is sufficient to explain all phenomena, however strange. — **tristis**: *in their anger.* Early religions are, in general, rather a means of propitiating the wrath of the gods than an expression of gratitude or trust.

6

The date of this satire cannot be precisely fixed, but it was written between 38 and 33 B.C. The upper limit is fixed by the allusion in vss. 54 ff. to Horace's introduction to Maecenas, which was probably not earlier than 38 B.C. On the other hand, the second half of the satire would certainly have contained some allusion to the Sabine form, which came into Horace's possession in 33, if the satire had been written after that date.

'Your high position, my dear Maecenas, as a man of noble family, evidently does not seem to you to justify you in looking down upon other men, upon me, for instance, a freedman's son. On the contrary, your admission of all freeborn citizens to social equality seems to express your belief that character, not birth, is the proper basis of a claim to public recognition. And, in fact, even the ordinary voter, prone as he is to be dazzled by noble birth, sees this truth and acts upon it. But we, whose vision is clearer, ought to see still deeper and to distinguish between social recognition and political advancement. A political ambition, like that of Tillius, not improperly raises questions of family and of inherited fitness for public office. But, for me, I have no political ambition and the office which I once held in the army of Brutus came to me by mere chance; I will not even take the trouble to defend myself against the criticisms which it excited. But my friendship with you is no chance; two sponsors whom I am proud to name, Vergil and Varius, introduced me to you and after careful deliberation you accepted me as a friend, judging me not by my father's rank, but by my own character.

'And yet that very character which has won your esteem was my father's gift to me He was a poor man, a freedman, yet he gave me such an education as a knight or a senator might have given to his son, attending me himself to guard me against the dangers of the city, not deterred by the fear of educating me above my station. I should be mad to wish that I had had a different father. I will not even say, as some do, that I was not responsible for my humble parentage. On the contrary, I would not exchange my father for any other, not even for one who had sat in the curule chair and worn the purple.

'For, after all, I prefer my quiet life. No bother about money, no formal calls to make, no swarm of servants, no fuss. I stroll about town as I please and watch the sights of the streets; I go home to a plain dinner and a good night's sleep, untroubled by the thought of early business engagements in the morning. I read or write, I take a little exercise, I have a light lunch and an afternoon of leisure. That's a great deal more comfortable than the life of the people who think they have a position to maintain.'

This satire belongs in subject and treatment with the third, the fourth, and the tenth. It springs directly out of the circumstances of Horace's life at the time it was written and marks another step in his progress from the earlier years of rebellious obscurity to the assured position of the Second Book. His friendship with men of rank, his acceptance by Maecenas, and, in particular, the publication of the account of the journey to Brundisium had revived the old criticisms which his position in the army of Brutus had aroused and had given new grounds for suspecting him of social and political ambitions. The satire is in form a disclaimer of such ambitions, while in substance it is a defence of the friends who had accorded him social recognition and a very manly and dignified declaration of pride in his father's wisdom and of contentment with his own quiet life.

> Non quia, Maecenas, Lydorum quicquid Etruscos
> incoluit finis, nemo generosior est te,

1. **Non**: with *suspendis*, vs. 5, not with *quia*. The sentence is best translated by changing its structure: 'although no one..., and although your ancestors..., you do not, for that reason, treat with contempt...'—**quia**: not different in sense from *quod*, vs. 3, though *quia* is, in general, the more colloquial. — **Maecenas**: the fact that Maecenas had publicly recognized Horace as a friend is the natural starting point of the argument. — **Lydorum**: there was a tradition that the Etruscan nobility was descended from Lydian colonists (Herod. 1, 94), as the Roman aristocracy claimed de-

nec quod avus tibi maternus fuit atque paternus,
olim qui magnis legionibus imperitarent,
5   ut plerique solent, naso suspendis adunco
ignotos, ut me libertino patre natum.
Cum referre negas quali sit quisque parente
natus, dum ingenuus, persuades hoc tibi vere,
ante potestatem Tulli atque ignobile regnum

scent from Troy, and as many Italian cities were supposed to have been founded by Greek heroes; cf. *Sat.* 1, 5, 92. The gen. plur. is a partitive gen. with *quicquid* (Catull. 3, 2, *quantum est hominum venustiorum*; 31, 14, *quicquid est domi cachinnorum*), but by its position it is made to serve also as a gen. for *nemo*.

2. **generosior**: *more nobly born*. There are various general references, like *Carm.* 1, 1, 1, *Maecenas, atavis edite regibus*, to the nobility of the Cilnii, but it does not appear that the family had taken a conspicuous place in Roman public life.

3-4. **avus maternus . . .** : the reference is general, as the subjv. *imperitarent* shows, though the use of *maternus* may be an allusion to the Etruscan custom of reckoning descent through the mother's side. — **legionibus**: also general; *great armies*.

5. **naso suspendis adunco**: such phrases as this, which express an emotion by describing the instinctive distortion of the features which accompanies it, are common in Latin, and are found even in serious passages, as here; they are doubtless colloquial in origin, but they are much less undignified than the corresponding English phrases like 'turn up your nose at.'

6. **ignotos**: *men of humble birth*. Cf. vss. 24, 36, below; *notus* and *nobilis* are only partially differentiated in meaning.

7. **Cum referre negas**: *in refusing to consider*; the explicative use of *cum*; 'your refusal to consider . . . is, in reality, a declaration of your belief that . . .'

8. **ingenuus**: *freeborn*. Maecenas, like Augustus (Sueton. *Aug.* 74), admitted to social equality any man who was born in freedom, but did not extend such recognition to freedmen (*libertini*). Horace is here dwelling upon the liberality of the admission; the exclusion of freedmen seemed to him, as, indeed, it well might, a natural limitation, to be mentioned only incidentally. — **persuades . . . tibi**: *you express your conviction*.

9-17. In this somewhat difficult passage two distinct ideas are fused into one statement, and a third is appended which strictly

10 multos saepe viros nullis maioribus ortos
et vixisse probos, amplis et honoribus auctos;
contra Laevinum, Valeri genus, unde superbus
Tarquinius regno pulsus fugit, unius assis
non umquam pretio pluris licuisse, notante
15 iudice, quo nosti, populo, qui stultus honores

belongs with the next sentence: (1) 'Your belief is that men of humble birth often deserve honor, and men of noble birth sometimes deserve to be obscure'; (2) 'this principle has often been illustrated in Roman history—plebeians have been elected to the consulship, and patricians have been nobodies'; (3) 'if the common voter can judge so correctly, then you and I should certainly not be misled by the accident of birth.' If Horace had been trying to use the forms of precise reasoning, only the first of these statements would have been subordinated to *persuades hoc tibi vere*; the second would have been put into an independent sentence, and the third would have been connected with vss. 17-18, to which it is a kind of protasis.

9. ante ... regnum: *i.e.* even before the reign of Servius Tullius, who was traditionally held to be the son of a slave woman, and before the Servian reform of the constitution, which was regarded as the beginning of democracy in Rome.

11. et ... probos ... et ... auctos: predicate with *vixisse*.

The sentence is paratactic; translate, 'because they lived upright lives, were honored with high offices.'

12. Laevinum: unknown. The statement of the scholiast adds nothing to what is implied in the context. — **Valeri genus:** *of the Valerian gens*, one of the great Roman families. — **unde:** = *a quo*, to be taken with *pulsus*. M. Valerius Poplicola aided Brutus in expelling Tarquinius Superbus, and was one of the consuls of the first year.

14. licuisse: *sold for*, i.e. *was worth*; from *liceo*. — **pluris:** gen. of indefinite value. — **pretio:** abl. after the comparative, with *unius assis* depending upon it.

14 f. notante iudice: abl. absolute; *iudice* is defined by *quo nosti* (by attraction from *quem nosti*) and by the appositive, *populo*. The defeat at the polls is like the judgment of the censors; either excludes from the Senate.

15 ff. The indic. in this clause emphasizes its detachment from the indirect discourse. — **famae servit:** *i.e.* the judgment of the common people is, too often, taken captive by family reputation. —

saepe dat indignis et famae servit ineptus,
qui stupet in titulis et imaginibus.   Quid oportet
nos facere, a volgo longe longeque remotos?
Namque esto populus Laevino mallet honorem
20   quam Decio mandare novo, censorque moveret
Appius, ingenuo si non essem patre natus:
vel merito, quoniam in propria non pelle quiessem.
   Sed fulgente trahit constrictos Gloria curru
non minus ignotos generosis.   Quo tibi, Tilli,

imaginibus: the waxen masks of ancestors who had held curule office. — **titulis**: the inscription under each mask enumerating the offices held by the original. The masks were hung in the *atrium*, and the possession of them indicated that the family was *nobilis*.

17-22. 'If the people, prone as they are to be dazzled by appearances, can sometimes see below the surface, then we, the intelligent classes, should be able to see still more deeply into the truth. For, whether the machinery of government favors the patrician or the plebeian, it is certainly true that, for such a man as I am, political ambition is folly. — **esto**: used frequently by Horace (*Sat.* 2, 1, 83; 2, 2, 30) to express a concession; here, in parataxis with *mallet*, it becomes almost a concessive conjunction, as in the English, 'granted the people might prefer . . . . yet . . .' — **Decio . . . novo**: P. Decius Mus, a plebeian and *novus homo*, the first of his family to hold a curule office. He de-voted himself to death in order to secure victory in the battle of Mt. Vesuvius in 340 B.C., and is frequently referred to as a type of heroic patriotism. — **censor** . . . **Appius**: Appius Claudius Pulcher, the brother of Clodius, censor in 50 B.C. He scrutinized the senatorial lists with great severity, excluding many nobles and all sons of freedmen.

22. vel merito: *and rightly, too*; *i.e.* 'I should deserve it for being such a fool as to be tempted by political ambition.' — **propria . . . pelle**: an allusion to Aesop's fable of the Ass in the Lion's Skin; cf. *Sat.* 2, 3, 314-320: 2. 5, 56.

23 f. 'But most men do not see this deeper truth: Ambition drags them after her, chained to her chariot.' The same figure is used in *Epist.* 2, 1, 177. *ventosa gloria curru.* — **ignotos**: = *ignobiles*, as in vs. 6.

24 f. Quo tibi: regularly followed by an infin., as here: lit., 'to what end is it for you to . . . ?'

25 sumere depositum clavum fierique tribuno?
   Invidia adcrevit, privato quae minor esset.
   Nam ut quisque insanus nigris medium impediit crus
   pellibus, et latum demisit pectore clavum,
   audit continuo 'Quis homo hic?' et 'quo patre natus?'
30 Vt, si qui aegrotet quo morbo Barrus haberi
   et cupiat formosus, eat quacumque, puellis
   iniciat curam quaerendi singula, quali
   sit facie, sura, quali pede, dente, capillo;
   sic qui promittit civis, urbem sibi curae,
35 imperium fore et Italiam, delubra deorum,
   quo patre sit natus, num ignota matre inhonestus,
   omnis mortalis curare et quaerere cogit.

what good does it do you . . . ? — Tilli: he had had the *latus clavus*, the broad purple stripe which was worn by senators on the tunic, had for some reason lost it (*depositum*), and was now proposing to win it again (*sumere*) by being elected *tribunus plebis* as a first step toward a curule office. To these inferences from the text the scholiast (*recepit post Caesarum occisum; nam pulsus ante senatu fuerat*) adds little. The reference may be to a brother of L. Tillius Cimber. — **tribuno**: dat.; cf. 1, 1, 19.

27 f. **nigris . . . pellibus**: senators wore a shoe which was tied by four black leather bands wound crosswise about the ankle and up the calf (*medium crus*).

29. **continuo**: *immediately*; corresponding to *ut*, *as soon as*.

30 f. **aegrotet, morbo**: figurative, as in *Sat.* 2, 3, 306 f., *quo me aegrotare putes animi vitio?* The following clause, *et cupiat*, explains the nature of the disease. — **Barrus**: the name occurs again in *Sat.* 1, 7, 8, but identification with any known person is uncertain. — **haberi**: depends on *cupiat*.

32. **iniciat**: *i.e.* his evident belief that he is handsome leads the girls to consider his features in detail (*singula*) to see whether he really is all that he claims to be.

34 f. The promises of the candidate are intentionally exaggerated. No single official had so wide a range of duties.

36. **ignota, inhonestus**: with reference to birth, as elsewhere in this satire, vss. 6, 24, 96.

37. **curare, quaerere**: repeating *curam quaerendi*, 32. The bit of

'Tune, Syri, Damae, aut Dionysi filius, audes
deicere e saxo civis aut tradere Cadmo?'
40 'At Novius collega gradu post me sedet uno;
namque est ille, pater quod erat meus.' 'Hoc tibi Paulus
et Messalla videris? At hic, si plostra ducenta
concurrantque foro tria funera magna, sonabit
cornua quod vincatque tubas; saltem tenet hoc nos.

dialogue which follows expands the idea and makes it vivid.

38. These are ordinary foreign slave names; Syrus is used in the plays of Terence and Dama occurs in *Sat.* 2, 5, 18.

39. **deicere**: in three syllables. — **e saxo**: from the Tarpeian Rock. This old form of punishment was carried into execution by the tribunes, but it had fallen into disuse except as a figure of speech for an extreme penalty; cf. Cic. *ad Att.* 14, 15, 1. — **Cadmo**: *Cadmus carnifex illo tempore fuisse dicitur.* Schol.

40 f. **Novius**: this name is selected to suggest a derivation from *novus*, like Thackeray's *Newcome* or Henry James's *Newman.* — **gradu . . . uno**: not literally, for there was no assignment of special seats to freedmen; but figuratively, with an allusion to the law of Otho, 67 B.C., assigning to the knights fourteen rows of seats behind the senators. The law had made much talk and the distinction had passed into a kind of proverb. — **est ille, . . . meus**: *i.e.* 'he is himself a freedman, while I am the son of a freedman.'

41 f. **Hoc**: abl., *for this reason* as in vs. 52, below. — **Paulus et Messalla**: the *cognomina* of two of the most distinguished noble families in Rome. The absurdity of the claim is heightened by the use of *et*, as if the man could suppose himself to be both at once.

42–44. **hic**: = *Novius collega.* 'Your claim to superiority is based upon an advantage so petty that it is more than counterbalanced by his having a big voice.' — **plostra**: the plebian form of *plaustra* (cf. *Claudius* and *Clodius*), employed here because the argument represents the view of the common people (*saltem tenet hoc nos*). — **magna**: with *funera*. [Neither *Sat.* 1, 4, 44, *os magna sonaturum,* nor Juv. 7, 108, *ipsi magna sonant,* justifies the taking of *magna sonare* as a standing phrase, *to shout loudly*. In neither passage is the plural force quite lost and the quality designated is loftiness of style, not mere loudness of voice.] — **quod**: the antecedent is the internal object of

Nunc ad me redeo libertino patre natum,
quem rodunt omnes libertino patre natum,
nunc, quia sim tibi, Maecenas, convictor, at olim,
quod mihi pareret legio Romana tribuno.
Dissimile hoc illi est; quia non, ut forsit honorem
iure mihi invideat quivis, ita te quoque amicum,
praesertim cautum dignos assumere, prava

sonabit. — **-que**: connecting *cornua* and *tubas*; cf. *Sat.* 1, 4, 17. — This incidental picture of the Roman Forum, though it is intentionally exaggerated, is in harmony with what Juvenal says in his third satire of the dangerously crowded Roman streets. The Forum was the official center of all political and public life, the place where the funeral processions of great men, with their horns and trumpets, paused to listen to the *laudatio*, and it was at the same time the principal business center of the city. At this period great public works also were under construction, which necessitated the hauling of blocks of stone in heavy wagons.

45. Nunc ad me redeo: *i.e.* to vs. 6, as the repetition here of the last words of that line shows. The intervening verses are not altogether a digression; they meet the suspicion that Horace was ambitious of political influence, and thus enable him to pass lightly over that criticism (vss. 48–50) and to come to the main theme of the satire, the dignity and comfort of a quiet life.

47 f. **sim, pareret**: subjv., giving the reasons of the critics as expressed by themselves. — **convictor**: cf. *Sat.* 1, 4, 95, *convictore ... amicoque.* — **tribuno**: sc. *militum*. This curious episode in his life is briefly mentioned in the *Vita Horati* of Suetonius: *bello Philippensi excitus a M. Bruto imperatore tribunus militum meruit.*

49. honorem: *office*, as in the phrase *cursus honorum*, and often.

50. iure: it is, however, unlikely that the office was given to him without reason. Probably he had shown, even in his student years at Athens, those qualities of sanity and good judgment which made him in later life the valued friend of men of affairs. — **te**: obj. of *invideat*.

51 f. **cautum dignos assumere**: the friends whom Maecenas had already gathered about him were men of high standing and character, and, especially, men interested in literature rather than in politics. Admission to this circle was, of itself, evidence that Horace was not cherishing a political ambition. — **prava ambitione procul**:

ambitione procul. Felicem dicere non hoc
me possim, casu quod te sortitus amicum;
nulla etenim mihi te fors obtulit: optimus olim
55 Vergilius, post hunc Varius dixere quid essem.
Vt veni coram, singultim pauca locutus
(infans namque pudor prohibebat plura profari),
non ego me claro natum patre, non ego circum
me Satureiano vectari rura caballo,

men free from distorted ambition; an amplification of *dignos*. The expression is lacking in clearness, but cf. *Carm.* 4, 1, 4–6, *desine . . . circa lustra decem flectere, a man of ten lustra*. The word *inambitiosus*, which is used once by Ovid, would not have expressed the thought, especially the effect of *prava*, and, in the lack of an article or a present participle of *esse*, some such periphrasis as this is necessary.

52-54. Felicem: the gossip which attributed the friendship of Maecenas to mere chance (cf. *Sat.* 2, 6, 49, '*Fortunae filius*,' *omnes*) is emphatically denied by the position of *felicem* and by *casu, sortitus, fors*. 'My acceptance by you is not due at all to luck, but to the kindness of my friends and to your deliberate choice.'

54 f. optimus: cf. *candida anima, Sat.* 1, 5, 42; *animae dimidium meae, Carm.* 1, 3, 8; *pius, Carm.* 1, 24, 11. These terms of respect and admiration are quite in accord with the account of Vergil's life and character in the *Vita* of Donatus. — **olim**: *some time ago*; but the contrast with *post hunc* (cf. *olim . . . mox*) gives it a meaning like *first*.

57. infans: in the original sense, *speechless, i.e.* 'which made me tongue-tied.' The embarrassment is further indicated by the alliteration *p-udor p-rohibebat p-lura p-rofari*.

58 ff. non ego . . . narro: Horace's birth and circumstances were, of course, known to Maecenas, and his character had already been described by his friends (*dixere quid essem*). This sentence, therefore, does not mean that he did not attempt to deceive Maecenas, — which would have been absurd, — but that he spoke of himself frankly, with the modesty which befitted the son of a freedman and a poor man, and with a recognition of his own limitations of character (*quod eram*). — **Satureiano**: = *Tarentino* ('quia Satureia dicta est Tarentina civitas.' Schol.); the neighborhood of Tarentum was a particularly pleasant part of Italy

60 sed, quod eram, narro. Respondes, ut tuus est mos,
    pauca; abeo, et revocas nono post mense iubesque
    esse in amicorum numero. Magnum hoc ego duco,
    quod placui tibi, qui turpi secernis honestum,
    non patre praeclaro, sed vita et pectore puro.
65   Atqui si vitiis mediocribus ac mea paucis
    mendosa est natura, alioqui recta, — velut si
    egregio inspersos reprehendas corpore naevos, —
    si neque avaritiam neque sordes nec mala lustra
    obiciet vere quisquam mihi, purus et insons
70 (ut me collaudem) si et vivo carus amicis,
    causa fuit pater his, qui, macro pauper agello,
    noluit in Flavi ludum me mittere, magni
    quo pueri magnis e centurionibus orti,

(cf. *Carm.* 2, 6, 9 ff.) and was occupied by large estates (*rura*). — **caballo**: the low Latin word (for *equus*), from which the Romance words *cavallo*, *cheval*, are derived.

63. turpi secernis honestum: cf. *honestum* as a philosophical term, *Sat.* 1, 3, 42, and *iusto secernere iniquum*, *Sat.* 1, 3, 113. The adj. is in all these cases neuter and general; 'you who distinguish worth from unworthiness, not by the position of one's father, but by his own uprightness of character.'

65 ff. 'And yet that very uprightness of life and character, upon which my claim is based, is my father's legacy to me; it is to his training that I owe all that I am.' — **mediocribus, paucis**: these express the modesty which is implied in *quod eram*, vs. 60; cf. also 1, 4, 139.

67. reprehendas: strictly, the comparison would be 'which are merely like slight defects in an otherwise handsome person,' but the idea of *reprehendas* expands the suggestion implied in *mendosa*; 'spotted by few faults, no more to be made a matter of censure than . . .'

68. sordes: *low tastes and habits.* — **mala lustra**: *haunts of vice.*

69 f. The order is *si purus et insons et carus amicis vivo*.

72 f. Flavi: the schoolmaster in Venusia. — **magni, magnis**: the families of veteran soldiers, to whom land had been assigned near Venusia, constituted a local aristocracy.

laevo suspensi loculos tabulamque lacerto,
75 ibant octonos referentes Idibus aeris,
sed puerum est ausus Romam portare, docendum
artis quas doceat quivis eques atque senator
semet prognatos. Vestem servosque sequentis,
in magno ut populo, si qui vidisset, avita
80 ex re praeberi sumptus mihi crederet illos.

74. **loculos, tabulam**: the 'Greek' accus. with passive verb, like *inutile ferrum cingitur, Aen.* 2, 510 f. *loculi* (in the plur. only, in this sense), *satchel*; *tabula*, *slate* made of wood and covered with wax.

75. The general sense is clear; the boys carried their tuition money to the school at regular times. But the text is uncertain and the customs alluded to are not clearly known. Translate 'carrying their eight asses (*nummos* to be supplied) of money on the monthly pay-day.'

The amount would be small (ten or twelve cents) and the petty details — the limited curriculum, the carrying of slates and satchels by the children, the promptness in paying the tuition — are set in ironical contrast with the pretensions of the village magnates.

76. **est ausus**: a very pleasant recognition of the courage and independence shown by his father.

77. **artis**: the higher studies, which were not taught at Venusia; the study of early Latin poetry is alluded to in *Epist.* 2, 1, 69 f. and the reading of the Iliad in *Epist.* 2, 2, 41 f.

79–80. **in magno ut populo**: *in the midst of the crowd.* [This is *ut* restrictive. Ordinarily it restricts an adj., as in the familiar passage in Cic. *Cato Maior*, 12, *multae etiam, ut in homine Romano, litterae*; so in Cic. *Brit.* 102, *scriptor fuit, ut temporibus illis, luculentus*, and in the passages quoted by Schütz. Here it restricts *vidisset*, which is not simply *had seen*, but *had noticed*; this use is perfectly supported by two passages quoted by Orelli from Ovid, *Trist.* 1, 1, 17 f., *si quis, ut in populo, nostri non immemor . . . erit*, and *ex Ponto*, 4, 5, 11, *si quis, ut in populo, qui sitis et unde, requiret.*] — This passage does not mean that Horace's father encouraged him in an unsuitable display; the context forbids that understanding. The lines continue the thought of 76 ff.; as the father's foresight led him to give his son the best possible education, so it led him also to provide proper dress and attendance.

Ipse mihi custos incorruptissimus omnis
circum doctores aderat. Quid multa? Pudicum,
qui primus virtutis honos, servavit ab omni
non solum facto, verum opprobrio quoque turpi;
85 nec timuit sibi ne vitio quis verteret, olim
si praeco parvas aut, ut fuit ipse, coactor
mercedes sequerer; neque ego essem questus; at hoc nunc
laus illi debetur et a me gratia maior.
Nil me paeniteat sanum patris huius, eoque
90 non, ut magna dolo factum negat esse suo pars,
quod non ingenuos habeat clarosque parentes,

81. custos: *i.e.* as *paedagogus*, the slave 'who accompanied a properly cared-for boy in the streets. — **incorruptissimus:** *who could not be bribed.*

82 ff. 'In short, he kept me clean — and that is beginning and foundation of manliness — not only from vice itself, but also from the touch of scandal.'

85. nec timuit: the same thought as that in *est ausus*, vs. 76. He risked the possibility that he might sometime be reproached with having educated his son above the son's actual station in life. — **vitio verteret:** a standing phrase; 'should consider it an error on his part,' 'should reproach him.' — **olim:** of the future, as not infrequently.

86. coactor: the *Vita* of Suetonius says that Horace's father was *exactionum coactor* (a subordinate official in the collecting of taxes) or, according to some Mss., *auctionum coactor*, a collector of money at auctions. The latter is consistent with *praeco, an auctioneer*, and with *parvas mercedes*. Either was a respectable and useful business, but one which did not require much education.

87. hoc: *on this account*, as in 41, 52. — **nunc:** 'as things have turned out.'

89. Cf. 1, 5, 44, *nil ego contulerim iucundo sanus amico.* — **huius:** qualitative; *such a father.*

90 ff. ut ... negat ..., sic ... defendam: a condensed form of comparison; 'I will not defend myself as many do by saying that it wasn't my fault.' — **dolo:** a legal term, in full *dolus malus*. Technical definitions are quoted in the lexicon.

sic me defendam.   Longe mea discrepat istis
et vox et ratio: nam si natura iuberet
a certis annis aevum remeare peractum,
95 atque alios legere ad fastum quoscumque parentes
optaret sibi quisque, meis contentus, honestos
fascibus et sellis nollem mihi sumere, demens
iudicio volgi, sanus fortasse tuo, quod
nollem onus haud umquam solitus portare molestum.
100 Nam mihi continuo maior quaerenda foret res,
atque salutandi plures; ducendus et unus
et comes alter, uti ne solus rusve peregreve
exirem; plures calones atque caballi
pascendi, ducenda petorrita.   Nunc mihi curto
105 ire licet mulo vel si libet usque Tarentum,

92 ff. istis: dat. masculine, referring to *magna pars*, with some suggestion of contempt. — **et vox et ratio**: *both my way of speaking and my way of thinking.* — **a certis annis**: *i.e.* if there were some natural law which obliged all men, upon reaching a certain fixed age, say twenty-one, to go back and start life again, with a free choice as to their parentage. The apodosis is *nollem*, 97.

96. honestos: *honored;* cf. 36; not as in vs. 63.

97. fascibus et sellis: with *honestos;* the insignia of curule office.

98. iudicio . . . tuo: the judgment referred to in the beginning of this satire, but with a reference also to the unwillingness of Maecenas to hold office; 'hoc ad Maecenatem recte dicitur, qui, abhorrens senatoriam dignitatem, in equestris ordinis gradu se continuit.' Schol.

101. salutandi plures: the burden of making and receiving the formal morning calls became very oppressive and is frequently alluded to by later writers. — **ducendus et**: for *et ducendus.* The social proprieties required that a man of rank should take with him on a journey a retinue of servants and friends, as Maecenas did on the journey to Brundisium.

104. petorrita: a Gallic name for a four-wheeled traveling wagon; cf. *Sat.* 1, 5, 86 n. — **Nunc**: cf. vs. 87. — **curto**: apparently in a general sense, like *curta res, Carm.* 3, 24, 64; *humble, plain, little.*

mantica cui lumbos onere ulceret atque eques armos;
obiciet nemo sordes mihi quas tibi, Tilli,
cum Tiburte via praetorem quinque sequuntur
te pueri, lasanum portantes oenophorumque.
110 Hoc ego commodius quam tu, praeclare senator,
milibus atque aliis vivo.   Quacumque libido est,
incedo solus; percontor quanti olus ac far;
fallacem circum vespertinumque pererro
saepe forum; adsisto divinis; inde domum me

106. A reminiscence of Lucilius, 1027 (Marx), *mantica cantheri costas gravitate premebat.* — **ulceret**: subjv., because the whole situation is hypothetical (*si libet*).

107 ff. Horace may travel the whole length of Italy alone, riding his mule and carrying his baggage behind the saddle, but a praetor must have a retinue to go only to Tibur and even then may be accused of meanness because his attendants are so few in number. — **Tilli**: the same man who is mentioned in vs. 24. — **quinque . . . pueri**: a number great enough to be an incumbrance, but not sufficient for real dignity according to Roman standards.

109. lasanum . . . oenophorumque: *camp kettle and wine basket.* But the exact uses of these utensils are not made clear and we can only guess whether the carrying of them is mentioned as evidence of a desire for display or as proof of *sordes,* because he wished to avoid the expense of an inn.

111. milibus atque aliis: *and in a thousand other ways*; corresponding to *hoc.* — **libido est**: = *libet,* as often in early Latin. — The picture of a day's round of interests and occupations, which occupies the rest of the satire, begins with the middle of the afternoon and closes (vs. 128) with lunch and the afternoon *siesta.*

112. solus: without a troublesome retinue, such as a senator would feel obliged to have. — **percontor**: not with the intention of buying, but in order to get into conversation with the hucksters.

113. fallacem circum: the Circus Maximus was a gathering-place for all sorts of swindlers and street fakirs. — **vespertinum**: by the middle of the afternoon the courts had adjourned (cf. *Epist.* 1, 7, 46–48, where the lawyer goes home *octavam circiter horam*), the main business of the day was over and the Forum was given up to idlers.

114. adsisto divinis: *I stop and watch the fortune tellers.* —

115 ad porri et ciceris refero laganique catinum.
Cena ministratur pueris tribus, et lapis albus
pocula cum cyatho duo sustinet; adstat echinus
vilis, cum patera guttus, Campana supellex.
Deinde eo dormitum, non sollicitus, mihi quod cras
120 surgendum sit mane, obeundus Marsya, qui se
voltum ferre negat Noviorum posse minoris.
Ad quartam iaceo; post hanc vagor; aut ego, lecto
aut scripto quod me tacitum iuvet, unguor olivo,

These details are given to illustrate Horace's freedom from the embarrassment of social position; they illustrate also his humorous interest in all sides of life.

115. The Romans were not vegetarians, but they ate meat less often than the more northern races and regarded it as a luxury. Cf. *Carm.* 1, 31, 15 f., where the 'simple life' is suggested by saying *me pascunt olivae, me cichorea levesque malvae.*

116-118. The details are further evidence of the unostentatious simplicity of his life. — **pueris tribus**: a moderate number for a Roman gentleman; cf. *Sat.* 1, 3, 11 f., where an establishment of ten slaves is contrasted with one of two hundred to illustrate the extremes of simplicity and extravagance. — **lapis albus**: a slab of marble on three legs; cf. *Sat.* 1, 3, 13 n. — **pocula . . . duo**: perhaps for two kinds of wine or two different mixtures of wine and water. — **cyatho**: the ladle for dipping the wine out of the mixing bowl. — **echinus**: the scholiasts make various guesses as to the use of this unknown utensil. — **cum patera guttus**: *an oil bottle with its saucer.* — **Campana**: ordinary earthenware.

120 f. **obeundus Marsya**: *must go to meet Marsyas, i.e.* must go to the part of the Forum where the statue of Marsyas stood, to meet some early business obligation. The statement of Servius (on *Aen.* 4, 58) that statues of Marsyas with uplifted hand were erected in market places points to a Silenus figure and excludes a reference to the flaying of Marsyas by Apollo. The gesture is here humorously interpreted as an expression of dislike to the looks of the younger Novius, a banker whose stall stood in the neighborhood of the statue.

122. **Ad quartam**: somewhere about ten o'clock. A senator was expected to receive clients early in the morning; cf. 1, 1, 10 n.

123. **tacitum iuvet**: *i.e.* he finds pleasure in his reading or writing, without needing any com-

non quo fraudatis immundus Natta lucernis.
125 Ast ubi me fessum sol acrior ire lavatum
admonuit, fugio campum lusumque trigonem.
Pransus non avide, quantum interpellet inani
ventre diem durare, domesticus otior. Haec est
vita solutorum misera ambitione gravique;
130 his me consolor victurum suavius ac si
quaestor avus pater atque meus patruusque fuisset.

panion to express it to. — **unguor**: he is rubbed down with olive oil, preparatory to his regular exercise.

124. Natta: unknown. The oil which he stole from the lamps would be of poor quality.

126. trigonem: in appos. to *lusum*. The game was played by three persons (hence τρίγωνος), who stood at the corners of a triangle and 'passed' the ball, not using a bat.

127 f. Pransus: the *prandium*, *lunch*, was usually about one o'clock. — **domesticus otior**: a humorous expression; *domesticus* is not precisely the same as *domi*, and *otior*, of which the scholiast says 'verbum finxit quod significat *otium ago*,' is used only once before this, in a joking quotation by Cicero (*de Off.* 3, 14, 58).

130. his: abl. neut., like *hoc*, 110, and *milibus aliis*, 111.

131. quaestor: the lowest office in the *cursus honorum*, election to which gave admission to the Senate. To have reached this office, however, without going beyond it, was not a great distinction, and the line therefore means 'than if my ancestors had barely squeezed into the Senate,' with a little good-humored scorn of men who prided themselves upon mere senatorial rank.

7

The event which is the subject of this satire occurred at Clazomenae in Asia Minor, while Brutus was acting as governor of Macedonia and Asia, either in 43 B.C. or in the first half of 42, before the battle of Philippi.

But the date of composition is less certain; the satire may have been written immediately after the incident or it may be a reminiscence of the campaign written out at any time between 41, when Horace returned to Rome, and 35 B.C., when the first book of satires was published. As the satire itself contains no specific allusions to fix the date of composition, there is left only the rather uncertain method of adjusting its general tone to what may be supposed to have been Horace's attitude of mind at one date or another. These indications point to the earliest date; the tone toward Rupilius is different from his general attitude of loyalty toward his companions in that ill-fated campaign; the allusion in vs. 3 to the widespread circulation of the story would be pointless five years after the occurrence; the reference to Brutus in vss. 33 ff., which in any case seems flippant, is easier to understand if the lines were written before the battle of Philippi and left standing as a part of the record, than if we suppose them to have been written with deliberation after the tragic death of Brutus. And, in general, the tone of the satire is distinctly less mature and thoughtful than the tone of Satires 3, 4, 6. There is a certain crudeness and harshness in it, a certain sensationalism, a failure to reach the principles of conduct which underlie particular events; in these respects it is like Satires 2 and 8 and is to be classed with them as belonging to the earliest period of Horace's work. It is as an example of the work of that period — a better example than either Satire 2 or 8 — that it is here provided with a commentary.

The course of the thought is so simple as to need no paraphrase.

Proscripti Regis Rupili pus atque venenum
hybrida quo pacto sit Persius ultus, opinor
omnibus et lippis notum et tonsoribus esse.

1. P. Rupilius Rex of Praeneste had been an adherent of Pompey's party and was praetor at the time of Caesar's death. He was proscribed by Antony and Octavius and took refuge with Brutus, who gave him, as a man of some prominence, a place on his staff (vs. 25). The cognomen Rex was common in his family. — **Proscripti**: in contrast with *Regis*.

Rupili pus atque venenum: a parody of the epic phrases like ἱερὸν μένος Ἀλκινόοιο; cf. *virtus Scipiadae et mitis sapientia Laeli*,

Sat. 2, 1, 72; *the abusive and venomous Rupilius*.

2. **hybrida . . . Persius**: *the half-breed Persius*. He is said by the scholiasts to have been the son of a Greek father and a Roman mother: if this is correct, he had taken a Roman name. — **sit . . . ultus**: *punished, castigated*. The idea of *vengeance* in this word is much less prominent than the ordinary definitions make it.

3. **lippis, tonsoribus**: the shops of apothecaries and barbers were lounging places and centers of

Persius hic permagna negotia dives habebat
5 Clazomenis, etiam litis cum Rege molestas,
durus homo, atque odio qui posset vincere Regem,
confidens tumidusque, adeo sermonis amari,
Sisennas, Barros ut equis praecurreret albis.
Ad Regem redeo. Postquam nihil inter utrumque
10 convenit (hoc etenim sunt omnes iure molesti,
quo fortes, quibus adversum bellum incidit; inter
Hectora Priamiden animosum atque inter Achillem

gossip. The obvious words would have been *et medicis et tonsoribus*, but inflammation of the eyes was a frequent subject of ridicule and Horace substitutes the name of this one class of patients for the commoner phrase.

5. etiam litis: *and likewise lawsuits*, as if the lawsuits were an inevitable consequence of the large business interests. Rupilius had been the head of a syndicate of contractors for the taxes (*magister in ea societate* [*publicanorum*], Cic. *ad Fam.* 13, 9, 2), a position which would easily give rise to lawsuits.

6. odio ... vincere: *surpass Rex in making a nuisance of himself.* So Plaut. *Asin.* 446, *iam hic me abegerit suo odio*; Ter. *Phorm.* 849, *numquam tu odio tuo me vinces*.

8. Sisennas, Barros: unknown; the plural indicates the class; *men like Sisenna.* — **equis ... albis**: white horses were proverbial for speed, so that the sense is 'with perfect ease,' 'he could give odds to.'

9. Ad Regem redeo: this is a common formula for returning to the main point after a digression (cf. vs. 45 of the preceding Satire), but here there is no real digression and certainly no returning to Rex. The stock phrase is used partly with humorous intent, but chiefly to keep the name *Rex*, upon which the pun is to be made, before the reader's mind.

10 f. convenit: *i.e.* no compromise out of court could be made. The parenthesis, 10–18, explains, again in parody of epic style, why they would not compromise. — **hoc ... incidit**: 'all nuisances (*molesti*) have just the same rights that mighty heroes (*fortes*) have, who meet in deadly fray.' *hoc iure* is the pred. of *sunt, omnes molesti* the subject; *hoc* is the antecedent of *quo* (sc. *iure*). — **adversum**: *battle face to face*; of the matching of two warriors against each other.

ira fuit capitalis, ut ultima divideret mors,
non aliam ob causam nisi quod virtus in utroque
15 summa fuit: duo si discordia vexet inertis,
aut si disparibus bellum incidat, ut Diomedi
cum Lycio Glauco, discedat pigrior, ultro
muneribus missis): Bruto praetore tenente
ditem Asiam, Rupili et Persi par pugnat, uti non
20 compositum melius cum Bitho Bacchius. In ius
acres procurrunt, magnum spectaculum uterque.
Persius exponit causam; ridetur ab omni

13. **capitalis**: *deadly*; expanded in the following clause. — **ultima**: *i.e.* death alone, death at the end.

14. **non aliam ob causam**: the higher motives, like Hector's patriotism, are intentionally ignored and, in parody of the heroic spirit, the heroes fight simply because they are fighters (*virtus . . . summa*).

15 f. **inertis**: *cowards*; contrasted with *fortes*, vs. 11. — **disparibus**: contrasted with *adversum*, vs. 11, which implies equality.

16 ff. Cf. *Il.* 6, 119 ff., where Glaucus refuses to fight Diomed because of the old friendship between them, and they part with an exchange of armor and gifts. This pleasing incident in the war is here, in continuation of the parody of heroic motives, intentionally misinterpreted into cowardice and the payment of a ransom.

18. **praetore**: Brutus was *praetor urbanus* in 44 and in 43-42 was holding Macedonia and Asia Minor in a partially legalized way as *propraetor*. But the title *praetor* is especially suitable to him when he was holding court, as here.

19 f. **par**: *the pair*; a technical term, of two gladiators. — **pugnat**: grammatically the leading verb of *postquam . . . convenit*, 9-10. — **compositum**: also a technical word, of the matching of two gladiators; cf. *Sat.* 1, 1, 103 n. — **cum Bitho Bacchius**: two well-known gladiators of the time of Augustus. The combined phrase (= *Bithus et Bacchius*) is the subject of *sit* to be supplied and *compositum* (sc. *par*) *melius* is the predicate, drawn into the subordinate clause as *candidiores* is drawn into the *qualis-*clause in *Sat.* 1, 5, 41 f. 'So matched that Bithus and Bacchius are not a better matched pair.'

21. **procurrunt, spectaculum**: these words carry on the metaphor from the arena.

22. **ridetur**: impers.; *laughter from the whole court.*

conventu; laudat Brutum laudatque cohortem:
solem Asiae Brutum appellat, stellasque salubris
25 appellat comites, excepto Rege; canem illum,
invisum agricolis sidus, venisse. Ruebat,
flumen ut hibernum, fertur quo rara securis.
Tum Praenestinus salso multoquo fluenti
expressa arbusto regerit convicia, durus
30 vindemiator et invictus, cui saepe viator
cessisset, magna compellans voce cuculum.

23. **conventu**: the regular term for the officials gathered to meet the praetor at the places in his circuit where he held court. — **cohortem**: the *staff* of a provincial governor; also called *comites*, as in vs. 25.

25. **canem**: Sirius, the Dog-star, which brought the heat and drought. The whole series of comparisons, which were meant to prejudice the court in favor of the speaker, are to be thought of as made from the standpoint of the native farmers.

27. **fertur quo rara securis**: *whither the ax of the woodcutter is seldom carried*, *i.e.* in the depths of the forest, as the snow of winter melts. The figure of a rushing torrent is common enough, but this phrase is too poetic for the context and sounds like parody.

28. **multo**: adj., but to be joined closely with *fluenti*; the two together are the dat. of the ptc. of *multus fluo* (cf. *Sat.* 1, 4, 11, *cum flueret lutulentus*); *salso* and *multo fluenti* agree with a dat. to be supplied after *regerit*.

29. **expressa arbusto**: lit., 'squeezed from the vineyard,' *i.e.* drawn from the vocabulary of the vinedresser, redolent of the vineyard, as the English 'billingsgate' is language from the fishmarket. The general idea is more specifically expressed in vss. 30-31. — **regerit**: *hurled back*.

30. **vindemiator**: in four syllables, *vindēmiātor*. *Like a tough and invincible vinedresser;* without *ut*, as often in Horace.

31. **cessisset**: *i.e.* had been obliged to admit himself beaten in fluency of insult. — **cuculum**: the tradition given by the elder Pliny (*H. N.* 18, 66, 249) is that, since the pruning ought to have been finished in the early spring, before the cuckoo came, the passer-by would imitate the cry of the cuckoo to a vinedresser as an intimation that he was behindhand in his work. But this sounds like the forced explanation of a grammarian; *compellans cuculum*

At Graecus, postquam est Italo perfusus aceto,
Persius exclamat : ' Per magnos, Brute, deos te
oro, qui reges consueris tollere, cur non
35   hunc Regem iugulas? Operum hoc, mihi crede,
tuorum est.'

means simply *calling him a cuckoo*. [The Plautine passages are *Asin*. 923, 934, *Pers*. 282, *Ps*. 96, *Trin*. 245. They all antedate the explanation given by Pliny.]

32. **Graecus, Italo** : in contrast.

34. **qui . . . consueris**: *since you have the habit of removing Kings*, with reference to his ancestor, who had driven out the Tarquins, and to Brutus himself as one of the *liberatores* who had killed Caesar.

35. **Regem**: the same pun upon the name of Q. Marcius Rex was made by Cicero (*ad Att*. 1, 16, 10). — **Operum . . . tuorum**: pred. gen.; 'this is just in your line,' 'just the proper kind of business for you.'

8

There is no allusion in this satire definite enough to fix the date. The plot of ground which is the scene had been a burial-place, and was afterward acquired by Maecenas and used as the site for his palace and gardens. But the date when he acquired the land is not known. Nor is it clear that the land is in the possession of Maecenas either at the time when the events are represented as occurring or at the later time when the garden god tells the story. The spot cannot be thought of as still in use for burial, since the figure of Priapus stands there, and, on the other hand, the gathering of bones (vs. 22) and the selection of the spot by two witches as a place for incantations is scarcely compatible with its being a private garden. Apparently the events are thought of as having occurred while the transformation from burial-place to garden was still incomplete. Verses 14-16 allude to a later stage, but it is strange that there should be no direct allusion to Maecenas, to whom in later satires Horace refers with such evident pride and pleasure, if he already owned the land and had built his great house there.

The satire evidently belongs in the same period as Epodes 5 and 17, and seems to be referred to in vss. 47, 55 and 77 of the latter Epode. But neither of these poems can be dated with certainty. In the absence of *data*, on the general grounds of tone and manner — the lack of real humor, the coarseness, the cynicism — the satire may be placed with 2 and 7 of this book in the group of earlier writings.

The fact that the speaker is the figure of the garden god Priapus gives to the satire a certain resemblance to the *Priapea*, of which we have a collection, but in substance this is a satire upon the kind of incantations described by Vergil in Eclogue 8. On the personal side it is an attack upon a certain Canidia, who is also savagely attacked in Epode 5 and ironically ridiculed in Epode 17, and who is mentioned in several places in the Satires and Epistles. The scholiast says that her real name was Gratidia, that she was a seller of drugs, a witch and a poisoner. How much of this is fact we do not know, but undoubtedly a real person is referred to under the name. The hostility with which Horace pursues her is distinctly unpleasant, and this poem and Epodes 5 and 17 reveal him on his least admirable side.

> Olim truncus eram ficulnus, inutile lignum,
> cum faber, incertus scamnum faceretne Priapum,
> maluit esse deum. Deus inde ego, furum aviumque
> maxima formido; nam fures dextra coercet
> 5 obscaenoque ruber porrectus ab inguine palus;
> ast importunas volucres in vertice arundo
> terret fixa vetatque novis considere in hortis.
> Huc prius angustis eiecta cadavera cellis
> conservus vili portanda locabat in arca;

1. **Olim truncus eram**: the contrast between roughness of the figure and the fact that it was supposed to represent a god is not infrequently alluded to in Priapus poems. — **inutile**: the wood of the fig-tree splits easily.

2. **Priapum**: the statue was set up originally to represent the god of fertility, but was generally interpreted as a kind of scarecrow, who frightened away thieves and birds.

3. **Deus inde ego**: humorously emphasizing his claim to divinity, immediately after the acknowledgment that he owed it to a workman.

4. **dextra**: the right hand held a club or a sickle.

6. **arundo**: the reed was moved by the wind.

8-9. **angustis ... cellis**: the small chambers which they had occupied while alive. — **conservus**: the master paid no attention to

10 hoc miserae plebi stabat commune sepulchrum,
Pantolabo scurrae Nomentanoque nepoti:
mille pedes in fronte, trecentos cippus in agrum
hic dabat, heredes monumentum ne sequeretur.
Nunc licet Esquiliis habitare salubribus atque
15 aggere in aprico spatiari, quo modo tristes
albis informem spectabant ossibus agrum;
cum mihi non tantum furesque feraeque, suetae
hunc vexare locum, curae sunt atque labori,
quantum carminibus quae versant atque venenis

the death of a slave. — **locabat**: not *placed*, but *contracted for* the burial with the undertakers. — **arca**: the box in which the body was carried to the burial-place. — These details are pathetic to the modern reader, but it is not likely that Horace felt the pathos or intended to express it. His tone is rather hard and cynical.

11. This verse is probably Lucilian, though the scholiast gives an account of the man who was called by the nickname Pantolabus.

12-13. **in fronte, in agrum**: technical terms in surveying, like the English ' 1000 feet front, 300 feet deep ' ; usage varies between the acc. and the abl. and Horace has used both cases. — **cippus**: a stone pillar on which the dimensions of the plot of ground were inscribed, followed often by the letters H. M. H. N. S., *hoc monumentum heredes ne sequatur* (or *non sequitur*), meaning that the lot and tombstone shall not be considered a part of the estate and shall therefore not pass to the heirs, but shall remain perpetually a burial-place.

14. **salubribus**: predicate; it had been before especially unhealthy.

15. **aggere**: the Mound of Servius Tullius, the old wall of earth that surrounded the smaller early city. — **quo**: the absence of a preposition is perhaps to be explained by the nearness of *in aprico*; there seems to be no good parallel for *quo* in the sense of *ubi*. — **tristes**: predicate; *depressed* by the sight.

17. **cum**: *while* I, in contrast to their leisurely strolling (*spatiari*), have only care and trouble. — **ferae**: the wolves and vultures (*Epod.* 5, 99 f.) that fed upon the unburied bodies. — **suetae**: in three syllables.

19. **quae**: the antecedent is the subj. of *sunt curae*, to be supplied. — **versant**: *affect, move.*

20 humanos animos. Has nullo perdere possum
nec prohibere modo, simul ac vaga luna decorum
protulit os, quin ossa legant herbasque nocentis.
Vidi egomet nigra succinctam vadere palla
Canidiam pedibus nudis passoque capillo,
25 cum Sagana maiore ululantem. Pallor utrasque
fecerat horrendas aspectu. Scalpere terram
unguibus et pullam divellere mordicus agnam
coeperunt; cruor in fossam confusus, ut inde
manis elicerent, animas responsa daturas.
30 Lanea et effigies erat, altera cerea: maior
lanea, quae poenis compesceret inferiorem;
cerea suppliciter stabat servilibus, ut quae
iam peritura, modis. Hecaten vocat altera, saevam

21. **simul ac**: at the time of full moon; the phases of the moon have always been considered potent in the working of spells.

22. **ossa, herbas**: for use in the magic rites.

23 f. **Vidi egomet**: with these words Priapus begins the story which is the real subject of the satire. The details of Canidia's dress and appearance are conventional, the gown girded up, the black robe, the bare feet and flowing hair. They are repeated in Ovid's description of Medea, *Metam.* 7, 182 f.

25. **Sagana**: mentioned again in *Epod.* 5, 25. — **maiore**: *the elder* of two sisters. — **ululantem**: regularly of the cries of women; *Aen.* 2, 488. — **Pallor**: the witches shared the horror of the scene.

26. **Scalpere terram**: to make the *fossa* into which the blood of the victim was allowed to flow.

27. **unguibus, mordicus**: these details are added to heighten the horrors of the rites.

29. **responsa**: in the scene in the lower world, Hom. *Od.* 11, 36 ff., the shades come to drink of the blood, and the Theban seer, Tiresias, prophesies to Odysseus. Cf. also the Introd. to *Sat.* 2, 5.

30–33. **effigies**: in Verg. *Ecl.* 8, 80 f., one of the figures is of clay, the other of wax. The one which is not affected by heat represents the person for whose benefit the rites are performed; the waxen image represents the person who is to be subdued and melted with love. The dominion of the one is expressed in *poenis compesceret,*

altera Tisiphonen ; serpentis atque videres
35 infernas errare canes, Lunamque rubentem,
ne foret his testis, post magna latere sepulchra.
Mentior at si quid, merdis caput inquiner albis
corvorum, atque in me veniat mictum atque cacatum
Iulius et fragilis Pediatia furque Voranus.
40 Singula quid memorem? quo pacto alterna loquentes
umbrae cum Sagana resonarent triste et acutum,
utque lupi barbam variae cum dente colubrae
abdiderint furtim terris, et imagine cerea
largior arserit ignis, et ut non testis inultus
45 horruerim voces Furiarum et facta duarum :
nam, displosa sonat quantum vesica, pepedi
diffissa nate ficus : at illae currere in urbem ;
Canidiae dentes, altum Saganae caliendrum
excidere atque herbas atque incantata lacertis
50 vincula cum magno risuque iocoque videres.

the submission of the other in *inferiorem, suppliciter, servilibus modis* (like a slave), *iam peritura*.

35. **infernas**: of the lower world, such as followed Hecate.

36. **magna . . . sepulchra**: such great tombs as stood, and in part still stand in ruins, along the Appian Way, south of the city.

40 f. **alterna**: Sagana asked questions and the shades answered. — **acutum**: in the thin voice of the dead. *Aen.* 6, 492 f.

42. **lupi barbam**: cf. *Macbeth*, IV. 1, 'Fillet of a fenny snake,' and 'Scale of dragon, tooth of wolf,' which were put into the witches' cauldron.

44. **largior**: the fire burned brighter as the waxen image melted into the flame.

48. **dentes**: *i.e.* false teeth. — **caliendrum**: a wig or structure of false hair. The witches are represented as hags who tried to conceal the ravages of age.

49. **incantata**: tied on with magic rites; a formula had been uttered as the bands were fastened about their arms. This had not been alluded to before, but *licia, threads*, were used in Verg. *Ecl.* 8, 73.

50. **risuque iocoque**: cf. *Sat.* 1, 5, 98. *dedit risusque iocosque.* — **videres**: indefinite second person, especially frequent with this verb, *e.g. Sat.* 1, 5, 76.

9

This satire was written between 38 and 35 B.C., later than the first group, Satires 2, 7, and 8, but before Satire 1 and probably before 10. There is no allusion which makes a more precise dating possible and, as is usually the case where distinct allusions are lacking, there is nothing in the satire which would gain in interpretation if a more precise date could be fixed.

In form the satire is an account of a morning walk in which Horace was joined by a mere acquaintance, who desired to cultivate a closer intimacy with him, in order, as finally appeared, to secure through him an introduction to Maecenas. Various attempts to shake him off were unsuccessful and an appeal to a passing friend was without effect, until chance intervened to save the poet. In grace and lightness of tone the satire is equaled only by some of the odes. The struggle between politeness and the desire to be free, the humorous consciousness of the joke upon himself, the happily conceived dramatic form, reaching a climax in the encounter with Fuscus — all these make it unnecessary to look for an underlying purpose. But a secondary motive was doubtless the opportunity which the story afforded of returning to the theme of the sixth satire and of showing again how ill-founded was the suspicion that Horace was seeking social advancement through his acquaintance with Maecenas.

> Ibam forte Via Sacra, sicut meus est mos,
> nescio quid meditans nugarum, totus in illis:
> accurrit quidam notus mihi nomine tantum,

1. **Via Sacra**: the principal street of the city, running from the Esquiline past the Palatine, along one side of the Forum. It was the street which Horace would naturally take in going from the residence part of the city to the Tiber. — **sicut ... mos**: cf. 1, 6, 112, 122; with *ibam*, not with *meditans*.

2. **nugarum**: *verses*; almost a technical term for light lyric poems, *e.g.* Catull. 1, 4. — **totus**: so *omnis in hoc sum*, *Epist.* 1, 1, 11.

3. **notus ... tantum**: *i.e.* a mere acquaintance. The person cannot be identified, nor is it at all likely that Horace had in mind a definite individual or was recounting the events of an actual experience. His purpose was rather to draw a typical picture of the Social Struggler, without direct reference to any individual.

arreptaque manu, 'Quid agis, dulcissime rerum?'
5 'Suaviter, ut nunc est,' inquam, 'et cupio omnia quae
vis.'
Cum adsectaretur, 'Numquid vis?' occupo. At ille
'Noris nos' inquit; 'docti sumus.' Hic ego 'Pluris
hoc' inquam 'mihi eris.' Misere discedere quaerens,

4. **arrepta**: *seizing my hand*, with a show of cordiality and intimacy. — **dulcissime rerum**: *my dearest fellow*; a very familiar form of greeting. *rerum* is frequently used as a generalizing addition, especially with a superlative. It is of the same nature as the use of a gen. plur. with a neut. sing. pron., *quidquid hominum*.

5. The reply is made up of polite phrases which, from the frequency of their use, are mere formulas with no more meaning than the English 'Very well, thank you; I hope you are well.' — **ut nunc est**: *all things considered, as times go*. — **cupio ... vis**: a common phrase of politeness, which appears in various forms in dialogue.

6. **adsectaretur**: after speaking the words of vs. 5, Horace started to walk on. — **Numquid vis**: a common phrase used in taking leave of another person; *formula abeundi*, Donatus calls it. It is very frequently used in Plautus and Terence. — **occupo**: *i.e.* he got in the words *numquid vis?* before the other could reply, as a hint that he wished to go on.

7. **Noris**: = *noveris*. Ordinarily the phrase *numquid vis?* expects no reply, but occasionally (*Trin.* 192, *Capt.* 191, *M. G.* 575) the person addressed takes the question literally, as here, and replies with a verb in the subjv., as if with *volo*; 'yes, there is; I should like to have you make my acquaintance.' — **docti sumus**: I'm a literary man,' 'I'm a man of culture.' *doctus* was used especially of the newer school of poets, those who followed the Alexandrian models; it became a kind of party cry, employed by the new school as a term of honor and by their opponents as a term of ridicule. Horace was distinctly of the opposite school (cf. *Sat.* 1, 10, 19) and the person is therefore represented as offering, as an inducement to further acquaintance, a reason which would, in fact, lead Horace to avoid him.

7 f. **Pluris hoc ... eris**: *I shall value you all the more for that*, i.e. 'because you are *doctus*'; politeness struggles with irony.

8. **Misere**: *awfully*; so below, 14; a colloquialism, very frequent in Plautus and Terence.

ire modo ocius, interdum consistere, in aurem
10 dicere nescio quid puero, cum sudor ad imos
manaret talos. ' O te, Bolane, cerebri
felicem!' aiebam tacitus; cum quidlibet ille
garriret, vicos, urbem laudaret. Vt illi
nil respondebam, ' Misere cupis' inquit ' abire;
15 iamdudum video; sed nil agis; usque tenebo;
persequar. Hinc quo nunc iter est tibi?' ' Nil opus est te
circumagi; quendam volo visere non tibi notum;
trans Tiberim longe cubat is, prope Caesaris hortos.'
' Nil habeo quod agam, et non sum piger; usque sequar te.'
20 Demitto auriculas, ut iniquae mentis asellus,

10. **puero**: his attendant, *pedisequus*, to whom he pretends to give some private orders. — **dicere**: historical infin., as are *ire* and *consistere*. — **sudor**: as all his efforts to escape fail.

11. **Bolane**: a man of hot temper, who would not have been long restrained by a sense of courtesy. — **cerebri**: for the gen., cf. *integer vitae*; for the meaning, cf. *cerebrosus, Sat.* 1, 5, 21.

13. **vicos, urbem laudaret**: *i.e.* talked cheerfully about trifles, endeavoring to lead Horace into conversation.

14 ff. As Horace's lack of cordiality is too obvious to be ignored, the persistent man attempts to joke about it, hoping in this way to extract a disclaimer. — **nil agis**: colloquial; *it's no use.*

17 f. **circumagi**: *of your being dragged around.* — **visere**: *to call upon.* This is, of course, an invention of the moment, elaborated in the following words, in which the details are given in the order in which they occur to him: 'across the Tiber — a long way off — he's sick in bed, too — way over by Caesar's Gardens.' Cf. the similar embarrassed search for an excuse in Catull. 10, 28 ff. — **Caesaris hortos**: an estate on the Janiculum, left by Caesar's will to the Roman people, to be a public park.

20 f. **Demitto auriculas**: a condensed way of saying ' I felt like an ill-treated donkey, whose ears drop down when he is overloaded.' **dorso**: abl. with *subiit*, as in *Aen.* 2, 708, *subito umeris.* — **subiit**: the subj. is *asellus*; *onus* is the object.

cum gravius dorso subiit onus. Incipit ille :
' Si bene me novi, non Viscum pluris amicum,
non Varium facies ; nam quis me scribere pluris
aut citius possit versus ? quis membra movere
25 mollius? invideat quod et Hermogenes, ego canto.'
Interpellandi locus hic erat : ' Est tibi mater,

The final syllable is long, as frequently in the perf. indic. in Plautus.

22. Si bene me novi: a condition in form only; *as sure as I know myself.* — **Viscum**: there were two brothers of this name, both literary men and friends of Horace and Maecenas. They are mentioned with honor in *Sat.* 1, 10, 83 and one of them was a guest at the dinner described in *Sat.* 2, 8. — **Varium**: see note on 1, 5, 40.

23 ff. To any one who knew Horace well — and this satire is intended especially for the amusement of his intimate friends — it would be plain that the selection of these three accomplishments as recommendations to his favor was, like the mention of *doctus* in vs. 7, a most comical blunder. He particularly disliked rapid and profuse verse writing (cf. 1, 4, 11 ff., 17 f.); he regarded dancing as scarcely decent (*Sat.* 2, 1, 24 f.); and his opinion of singing in general and of Hermogenes in particular is plainly implied in *Sat.* 1, 3, 1 ff. — The prose order of the last phrase would be *ego canto quod et Hermogenes invideat.*

26 ff. Interpellandi locus: *here was my chance to break in.* The context shows that Horace had invented, as he hoped, a new expedient for getting rid of his persevering friend, but the exact nature of the plan is not at first sight apparent. The use of *interpellandi* shows that it was not connected with the remarks in vs. 22-25; the words *quis* [=*quibus*] *te salvo est opus* must mean that he was going to point out some serious danger which would be incurred in accompanying him, and the mention of dependent relatives is an elaborate provision to anticipate a possible declaration from the other that he did not fear danger. All these combine to indicate that Horace was preparing to say that the friend on whom he was going to call had a contagious disease, exposure to which would be almost certainly fatal. It is an added touch of humor that Horace represents himself as so discouraged by the first slight failure — for the dependent relatives were not essential to the plan — that he surrendered in despair.

cognati, quis te salvo est opus?' 'Haud mihi quisquam;
omnis composui.' 'Felices! Nunc ego resto;
confice; namque instat fatum mihi triste, Sabella
30 quod puero cecinit divina mota anus urna:
"Hunc neque dira venena, nec hosticus auferet ensis
nec laterum dolor aut tussis, nec tarda podagra;
garrulus hunc quando consumet cumque; loquaces,
si sapiat, vitet, simul atque adoleverit aetas."'
35 Ventum erat ad Vestae, quarta iam parte diei
praeterita, et casu tunc respondere vadato
debebat; quod ni fecisset, perdere litem.
'Si me amas,' inquit, 'paulum hic ades.' 'Inteream, si

28-34. These lines express his emotions, but were of course not spoken aloud.

28. Nunc ego resto: *i.e.* 'my turn next; finish me off, too.'

29. Sabella: with *anus*. There are various references to the superstitions of the peasants in the mountains away from the influence of the city.

30. divina mota ... urna: abl. abs.; *shaking the lots in her urn*, until one of them fell out.

31-34. The epic-oracular style is parodied in *dira*, the plur. *venena, hosticus, ensis*, in the transferred epithet *tarda*. — **laterum dolor**: *pleurisy*. — **quando ... cumque**: tmesis; *some time or other*.

35 f. Ventum erat: the plupf. implies *by this time*,' while all this was going on.' — **ad Vestae**; *sc. templum.* as in English *St. Paul's, St. Mary's.* The temple of Vesta was at the lower end of the Forum and the law courts were near it. — **quarta ... praeterita**: *i.e.* about nine o'clock. This has been held to be inconsistent with 1, 6, 122, *ad quartam iaceo; post hanc vagor,* but it is obvious that neither statement is meant to be taken precisely. The only reason for mentioning the hour here is to show that the courts were open for business and so to introduce the next scene in the little drama. — **respondere**: a technical term of law; *to appear in court.* — **vadato**: apparently an impersonal abl. abs. like *sortito, auspicato; under bonds, having given a bond.*

38. Si mĕ amas: monosyllabic hiatus with shortening of the long vowel; this is very common in Plautus, but only under the ictus. The words are a mere phrase of politeness to soften the urgency of the imperative; ' will you be so

aut valeo stare aut novi civilia iura ;
40 et propero quo scis.' 'Dubius sum quid faciam,' inquit,
'tene relinquam an rem.' 'Me, sodes.' 'Non faciam,' ille,
et praecedere coepit. Ego, ut contendere durum est
cum victore, sequor. 'Maecenas quomodo tecum?'
hinc repetit; 'paucorum hominum et mentis bene sanae.
45 Nemo dexterius fortuna est usus ; haberes

kind as to . . .'—**ades**: in the technical sense, to be present in court as a supporting friend and adviser, *advocatus*. The same request is made to Horace in *Sat.* 2, 6, 34 f.—**Interveam**: *I'll be hanged*. So Catull. 92, 4, *dispeream nisi amo*.

39. valeo stare: *am strong enough to stand*, as was customary in the praetor's court. The excuse is of course quite inconsistent with *propero quo scis*, but Horace represents himself as having reached a point where he was careless of either consistency or truth.

41. rem: *my case*, which would go by default, if he failed to appear. — **sodes**: = *si audes, please, if you please*, used like *sis* (=*si vis*, *Sat.* 1, 4, 14 n.) to soften an imperative. *Audeo* (from *aveo, avidus, avideo*) regularly means *to wish, desire*, in Plautus; the meaning *to venture, dare*, is later.

43. Maecenas quomodo tecum: *how do you and Maecenas get on together?* The pride which Horace felt in the friendship of Maecenas and the strength of his determination that the friendship should remain disinterested render this question peculiarly offensive.

44. hinc repetit: *with this he begins again*, after the slight pause. — **paucorum . . . sanae**: *a man of few friends and of very sound judgment* (cf. Ter. *Eun.* 408 f., *sic homost; perpaucorum hominum*); there are various references to the care with which Maecenas selected the limited number of friends whom he admitted to intimacy; but the best commentaries on these words are *Sat.* 1, 6, 51 f., *praesertim cautum dignos assumere, prava ambitione procul*, with the account, which follows, of Horace's introduction, and the general remarks in *Sat.* 1, 3, 58 ff., summarized in *pro bene sano ac non incauto fictum astutumque vocamus*.

45. Nemo . . . usus: *i.e.* 'you've been very lucky and very skillful, too, in the way you have used your chances to get into the circle of his friends.' This is the same

magnum adiutorem, posset qui ferre secundas,
hunc hominem velles si tradere; dispeream, ni
summosses omnis.' 'Non isto vivimus illic
quo tu rere modo; domus hac nec purior ulla est
50 nec magis his aliena malis; nil mi officit, inquam,
ditior hic aut est quia doctior; est locus uni
cuique suus.' 'Magnum narras, vix credibile!' 'Atqui

suggestion that Horace vehemently repudiates in *Sat.* 1, 6, 52 ff.; *fortuna* here expresses briefly what is there emphasized in *felicem, casu, sortitus, fors*. But the idea in *dexterius usus* is an addition which prepares the way for the proposal in the next sentence: 'you have shown yourself a skillful wire-puller; now bring me into the game to help you and you'll complete your victory.'

[The difficulty which all commentators, beginning with the scholiasts, have felt in interpreting these lines and in assigning them to the speakers is due, I think, to the fact that Horace is not reporting the whole conversation, but is giving only the main points, omitting, especially in 44 f., the connecting links of the thought. This is a favorite method with him (*e.g. Sat.* 1, 4, 52 ff., 85 ff., 1, 6, 17-25) and it suits perfectly the informal style of the *Sermones*, but it sometimes leaves the thought insufficiently expressed. In this passage, between the desire to suggest the subject of the remarks and the desire to suppress the details, with their low estimate of Maecenas and of himself, he has suppressed too much.]

46. secundas: *sc. partes*; the second actor on the stage should support the leading actor.

47. hunc hominem: colloquial for *me*; with jocular purpose like 'your humble servant,' 'the undersigned.' — **dispeream, ni**: cf. the line of Catullus, quoted above.

48. summosses: = *summovisses*; cf. *surrexe*, 73. The plupf. looks forward to the completion of the process.

48-52. This is the longest speech that Horace makes in the whole conversation, as though he felt the insinuations in 44-48 to be unbearable without the most earnest and explicit denial. — **aliena**: *free from*; but *malis* is, grammatically, a dative. — **inquam**: *I tell you*; the insertion of this in the midst of his words adds to the earnestness.

52 f. Magnum . . . credibile: the offensive incredulity betrays the character of the speaker. — **Atqui sic habet**: *it's so, anyhow*.

sic habet.' 'Accendis, quare cupiam magis illi
proximus esse.' 'Velis tantummodo: quae tua virtus,
55 expugnabis; et est qui vinci possit, eoque
difficilis aditus primos habet.' 'Haud mihi dero:
muneribus servos corrumpam; non, hodie si
exclusus fuero, desistam; tempora quaeram,
occurram in triviis, deducam. Nil sine magno
60 vita labore dedit mortalibus.' Haec dum agit ecce
Fuscus Aristius occurrit, mihi carus et illum
qui pulchre nosset. Consistimus. 'Vnde venis et
quo tendis?' rogat et respondet. Vellere coepi
et prensare manu lentissima brachia, nutans,

After permitting himself some warmth of expression, Horace falls back upon short answers.

54-56. Velis tantummodo: *you have only to wish it.* — **virtus**: with the underlying sense of 'impudence,' 'pushing determination.' Horace represents himself as returning from the earnestness of 48 ff. and the curtness of 52 f. to the ironical attitude, with a pleasant anticipation of seeing Maecenas attacked next. To further the joke he adds the encouraging words of 55 f.: 'if you find that he makes it a little hard at first, that will be only because he is conscious of his weakness.'

56. dero: = deero.

59 f. deducam: *escort him* from his house to the Forum, a mark of respect to men of eminence. Cicero mentions *deduci, reduci* among the attentions paid to old men. — **Nil . . . mortalibus**: a maxim of proverbial philosophy, by which the social struggler encourages himself to renewed efforts.

61. Fuscus Aristius: *Carm.* 1, 22, *Integer vitae* and *Epist.* 1, 10, are addressed to him. He is mentioned in *Sat.* 1, 10, 83, among Horace's most valued friends. The varying tradition of the scholiasts calls him *grammaticus* (*i.e.* a literary critic) and a writer of plays.

62 f. pulchre: colloquial, like *belle, valide, misere*. — **qui . . . nosset**: a characterizing clause, parallel to the adj. *carus*; 'and perfectly well acquainted with my companion.' — **Vnde . . . tendis**: *i.e.* the usual questions are asked and answered. So *Sat.* 2, 4, 1, *unde et quo Catius?*

63 f. vellere: *to pull his toga*. — **lentissima**: *unfeeling*; *i.e.* Fuscus gave no sign that he understood what Horace wanted.

65 distorquens oculos, ut me eriperet.   Male salsus
ridens dissimulare , meum iecur urere bilis.
'Certe nescio quid secreto velle loqui te
aiebas mecum.'   ' Memini bene, sed meliore
tempore dicam ; hodie tricesima sabbata : vin tu
70 curtis Iudaeis oppedere ? '   ' Nulla mihi,' inquam,
' religio est.'   ' At mi ; sum paulo infirmior, unus
multorum.   Ignosces ; alias loquar.'   Huncine solem
tam nigrum surrexe mihi !   Fugit improbus ac me
sub cultro linquit.   Casu venit obvius illi
75 adversarius, et, ' Quo tu, turpissime ? ' magna

65. Male salsus: *the wretched joker*. The *Integer vitae* is evidence that he loved a joke.

66. ridens: *i.e.* with the exasperating smile of a friend who perceived nothing unusual in the situation. The rest of the line points the contrast; ' but I, for my part, was in a perfect fury.' — **iecur . . . bilis**: the supposed seat of the emotions, as the heart in modern times.

68. Memini bene: the reply is intended to show that Fuscus understood perfectly that Horace was inventing the engagement.

69. tricesima sabbata: this and the illusion to circumcision (*curtis*) show a surprising knowledge on Horace's part of Jewish customs, but it is not possible to identify this with any known Jewish feast. Indeed, it would increase the humor of the solemn scruples of Fuscus, if we suppose the *tricesima sabbata* to be an invention of the moment.

70 f. oppedere: *insult*. — **Nulla . . . religio**: in the eagerness of desperation Horace is willing to declare that he hasn't a single religious scruple.

73. surrexe = *surrexisse*; the infin. in exclamation, either with or without *-ne*, is colloquial and is very common in Terence.

74. sub cultro: like a helpless victim under the uplifted knife of the priest.

75 ff. adversarius: his opponent in the suit which he had abandoned, vs. 41. If a party to a suit failed to appear, his opponent could summon him and, calling upon a bystander to act as witness, could take him by force into court. The law of the XII Tables was ' si in ius vocat, ito, ni it (if he does not come), antestamino (call a witness) ; igitur, em (= eum) capito.' The question *licet antestari?*

inclamat voce, et ' Licet antestari ? '   Ego vero
oppono auriculam.   Rapit in ius ; clamor utrimque,
undique concursus.   Sic me servavit Apollo.

is addressed to Horace and his assent was expressed, according to the legal procedure, by allowing the other person to touch his ear. The short sentences hurry the scene to its conclusion.

78. **Apollo**, as the guardian of poetry and poets. The satire thus closes with a reminiscence of its opening lines, *nescio quid meditans nugarum*.

10

There are many allusions in this satire to persons and events, but none sufficiently definite to fix the date of composition. Evidently it was written after *Sat.* 4 and therefore after 2, 7, and 8, somewhere between 38 B.C. and 35. The large circle of friends whose names are mentioned in the closing lines would indicate a late date, and the general tone is that of an epilogue to the whole collection, as the first satire is an introduction to the whole. This interpretation also harmonizes with the last line of the satire (see notes).

'It is quite true that I said that Lucilius was a rough verse writer. His power as a satirist I acknowledge, but that alone does not make a poet. Many other qualities are necessary to a poetic style, brevity, variety, wit, such polished wit as is found in the Old Comedy, of which, indeed, some of my critics seem never to have heard. The mingling of Greek with Latin in Lucilius is not a merit, but a defect; no serious Roman writer mixes the two languages or writes in Greek at all.

'The grand style I leave to others to attempt, successfully or not. My aim is less ambitious. The fields of comedy and tragedy, of epic and bucolic poetry, are well occupied and I have turned to satire, not, however, to be the rival of Lucilius or to lessen his glory. But it is true that I have mentioned his defects, as he had noticed the defects of Ennius and Accius. The copiousness of Lucilius and his lack of finish are real defects, which, if he were writing now, he would himself perceive and correct.

'For finish of style appeals to the only public worth considering. Hermogenes may not like my work, but if Plotius and Varius, Maecenas and Vergil, approve, I need no other defence and can publish this book of satires without misgivings.'

In the fourth satire Horace had defended himself against the charge that he was malicious and was seeking notoriety. The reply was in general direct and convincing, but in the course of his argument he happened to say (vss. 6–13) that his prototype, Lucilius, had written too profusely and with too little attention to finish. This chance remark — which is abundantly justified by the extant fragments of Lucilius — had brought upon him some censure from that school of literary critics in Rome whose cardinal doctrine was the excellence of the early Latin poetry, and had at the same time exposed him to the less sincere attacks of others who seized the opportunity to renew their personal and unfriendly criticisms. This satire is a reply to both classes. To the serious admirers of early Latin poetry he replies with a serious discussion of the nature and causes of the defects of Lucilius and with candid praise of his merits. To the little clique of personal enemies he scarcely replies at all, brushing them aside with contemptuous brevity and twitting them (17–19) with their ignorance of the very poetry about which they were pretending to be solicitous.

Prefixed to the text of this satire in some Mss. are eight verses: —

> Lucili, quam sis mendosus, teste Catone,
> defensore tuo, pervincam, qui male factos
> emendare parat versos; hoc lenius ille,
> quo vir est melior, longe subtilior illo,
> qui multum puer et loris et funibus udis
> exhortatus, ut esset opem qui ferre poetis
> antiquis posset contra fastidia nostra,
> grammaticorum equitum doctissimus. Vt redeam illuc:

These lines contain Horatian phrases (cf. *loris et funibus* with *Epod.* 4, 3, *Epist.* 1, 16, 47) and opinions (cf. vs. 7 with *Epist.* 2, 1, 18 ff.); the reference to P. Valerius Cato, though not exactly identical with the statement in Sueton. *de Gram.* 2, is a similar bit of grammatical tradition; the satirical allusion in vss. 5 ff. is obscure and contradictory, but comes evidently from the same school of literary and personal gossip; the phrasing is stiff (*hoc lenius ille, ille* and *illo* referring to different persons, the apposition of *doctissimus* to *qui*), and the joining of the lines to vs. 1 of the satire by the words *ut redeam illuc* is very awkward. These facts all point to one conclusion, that the verses were written by a grammarian who saw in the abruptness of *nempe dixi* an opportunity to perpetuate a bit of his own learned satire by prefixing it to the text of Horace.

Nempe incomposito dixi pede currere versus
Lucili. Quis tam Lucili fautor inepte est
ut non hoc fateatur? At idem, quod sale multo
urbem defricuit, charta laudatur eadem.
Nec tamen, hoc tribuens, dederim quoque cetera;
5   nam sic
et Laberi mimos ut pulchra poemata mirer.
Ergo non satis est risu diducere rictum

1. **Nempe**: *yes, I did say*, with intentional abruptness, as if in immediate reply to a critic. — **incomposito . . . pede currere**: the exact words are *durus componere versus*, *Sat.* 1, 4, 8, and *cum flueret lutulentus*, 1, 4, 11.

2. **fautor**: with a tinge of the meaning that it has in Plautus, *Amph.* 67, 78, *claqueur*, a man hired to applaud in the theater, so *partisan*. As a verbal noun in combination with *est* it takes the adv. *inepte*. — **tam**: with *inepte*.

3 f. **idem . . . eadem**: emphasizing the adversative connection expressed in *at;* so in English *but at the same time*. — **sale multo defricuit . . . *scoured down the city with strong brine*.** Individually the words are to be taken in their literal sense, but the phrase as a whole implies the common comparison of wit to salt. — **charta**: *i.e.* in the same satire; cf. *Sat.* 1, 5, 104 and *membrana*, *Sat.* 2, 3, 2.

5. **sic**: *on that principle, by such reasoning. i.e.* if it were granted that wit alone made poetry.

6. **Laberi**: Decimus Laberius was a knight, who had died some ten years before the date of this satire. He was one of two or three successful writers of mimes, popular farces which were put into literary form in the Ciceronian period. About 150 lines or fragments from Laberius are preserved (see Ribbeck. *Com. Rom. Fragm.*², pp. 279 ff.), including a large part of the prologue spoken by Laberius when he was compelled by Caesar to act in one of his own farces. Some of the lines of this are well known: —

Ego bis tricenis ánnis actis sine nota
Equés Romanus é Lare egressús
   meo
Domúm revertar mímus.

Necésse est multos tímeat quem multí
   timent.

But such farces were of course not *pulchra poemata*.

7. **Ergo**: the mere mention of Laberius is enough to prove that witty verse is not necessarily poetry. — **diducere rictum**: a slightly contemptuous colloquialism; *to make your hearer grin*.

auditoris — et est quaedam tamen hic quoque virtus;
est brevitate opus, ut currat sententia neu se
10 impediat verbis lassas onerantibus auris;
et sermone opus est modo tristi, saepe iocoso,
defendente vicem modo rhetoris atque poetae,
interdum urbani, parcentis viribus atque
extenuantis eas consulto.   Ridiculum acri

8. et ... virtus: a concession in the form of a parenthetic statement.

9 ff. In these lines Horace again discusses the nature of satire, as he had already done in *Sat.* 1, 4, 39-61. This argument, however, since its main purpose is to justify the criticism of Lucilius, is less general and only those qualities are mentioned in which it is implied that Lucilius was lacking. These are specifications under the general statement *durus componere versus* and are, in form, two in number — brevity and variety. But the idea of variety is expressed by contrasting two styles, the serious and the light, and the contrast is carried on through vs. 15; in a very general way *tristi, rhetoris atque poetae* and *acri* express one side, and *iocoso, urbani,* and *ridiculum* the other. The implication, however, is not merely that Lucilius was monotonous, but also and especially that he lacked the lighter and more polished forms of wit. The quality of *urbanitas* is therefore brought into greater promi-nence both by the definition *parcentis, extenuantis,* and by the carrying over of the thought into the next sentence. The reference to the Old Comedy, as a standard of polished wit, is then used to clinch the argument, as in *Sat.* 1, 4 it had been used to open it.

9. brevitate: that condensation of style which is secured by the selection of words that carry the meaning adequately (*ut currat sententia*) and by the avoidance of commonplace and meaningless phrases. The quality is admirably exemplified by Horace in the *Odes, e.g.* 1, 5; 1, 24; 1, 31.

12. defendente vicem: *playing the part,* using the dignified and serious style of the orator or poet. Horace has also *partes defendere, A. P.* 193 f., and *vice fungi, A. P.* 304. Strictly *defendente* should agree, not with *sermone* but with some word like *scriptore*.

13. urbani: first used as a technical term of rhetoric by Cicero. - **parcentis viribus**: expressed in *Epist.* 1, 9, 9 by *dissimulator opis propriae*.

15 fortius et melius magnas plerumque secat res.
    Illi, scripta quibus comoedia prisca viris est,
    hoc stabant, hoc sunt imitandi ; quos neque pulcher
    Hermogenes umquam legit, neque simius iste
    nil praeter Calvum et doctus cantare Catullum.
20 'At magnum fecit, quod verbis Graeca Latinis
    miscuit.'   O seri studiorum! quine putetis
    difficile et mirum, Rhodio quod Pitholeonti

15. secat: *decides, settles.* Cicero, expressing the same thought (*de Orat.* 2, 58, 236), uses *dissolvit*.

16. An intentional repetition of 1, 4, 2, in order to remind the reader that Horace is maintaining the opinion there expressed.

17 ff. 'But the men who are pretending to be so disturbed by my criticism of Lucilius know nothing of the best standards or even of the earlier Latin writers.' — pulcher: the point of applying this adj. to Hermogenes is not known, but it is meant to contrast with *simius*. — simius: the scholiast says that this is Demetrius, mentioned also in vs. 90.

19. Calvum: C. Licinius Calvus, the orator and poet, an intimate friend of Catullus. He had a high, perhaps an exaggerated, reputation with his contemporaries. — Catullum: C. Valerius Catullus, one of the four great Roman poets, inferior to Horace in sanity and judgment, but superior in spontaneity and brilliancy. This is the only allusion to him in Horace, and, while the contempt is directed against *simius iste*, it cannot be denied that the allusion is slighting in tone.

20. Graeca Latinis: to judge by the extant fragments the Greek words are sometimes technical terms, sometimes quotations, and only occasionally used for comic effect. Lucilius himself ridicules the use of Greek words in common conversation (vss. 88-94, Marx).

21. seri studiorum: a translation of ὀψιμαθεῖς, men who have just learned something that everybody else has known before and who parade their new knowledge. — qui-ne: nom. plur. The appending of *-ne* to a relative is not unfrequent. Translate *oh, pedants, to think* . . . [I will not add to the mass of commentary on this passage, but will refer to *A.J.P.* XI, 1 (41), pp. 17-19, and Schmalz, *B. Ph. W.*, 1907, Sp. 1292.]

22. Pitholeonti: probably Pitholaus, a barely known writer of epigrams. The context supplies all that is necessary to understand the point ; he used Greek words in his verse and yet was so poor a

contigit? 'At sermo lingua concinnus utraque
suavior, ut Chio nota si commixta Falerni est.'
25 Cum versus facias, te ipsum percontor, an et cum
dura tibi peragenda rei sit causa Petilli?
scilicet oblitus patriaeque patrisque Latini
cum Pedius causas exsudet Poplicola atque
Corvinus, patriis intermiscere petita

poet that the mere mention of his name is an argument. Cf. the similar condensed argument in vs. 6.

23 f. **concinnus**: *blended*; the word anticipates the following comparison. — **nota**: *label, brand*; the mark attached to the *amphora* to tell the vintage. — **Chio, Falerni**: a slight flavor of the sweet Greek wines was thought to improve the native Falernian; cf. *Carm.* 1, 20, 2 f., where Horace speaks of putting his wine into a jug that had held Greek wine.

25 f. 'Are you not thinking too exclusively of verse writing? Would you mix Greek with Latin if you were arguing a difficult case at law?' That is, the use of an occasional Greek word is an artifice of style which no one would employ in serious speech; cf. *vicem rhetoris*, vs. 12. — **versus facias**: *in your verse making*, with a slight tone of depreciation. The subjv. is used because the omitted main clause would be subjv., — *num sermo . . . suavior sit*. — **causa Petilli**: see note on *Sat.* 1, 4. 94.

27. **patrisque Latini**: *Father Latinus*, from whom our language gets its name. Cf. the reference to Quirinus, vs. 32.

28. **Pedius Poplicola**: perhaps a brother of Messalla (vs. 85), who had been adopted by Q. Pedius, a nephew of Julius Caesar. Almost nothing is known of him, but Horace uses him here as a type of the great lawyer.

29. **Corvinus**: M. Valerius Messalla Corvinus, the friend of Tibullus and one of the important personages of the Augustus period, distinguished as an orator. It is known that he took special pains (*exsudet*) to preserve a pure Latin style, excluding Greek derivatives. — **intermiscere**; *to thrust in among*. This is the proper meaning of *intermiscere* with the dative, not merely *to mix together*; cf. Verg. *Ecl.* 10, 5, *sic tibi, . . . Doris amara suam non intermisceat undam*, 'not intermingle her waters with yours'; Livy, 4, 56, 3; 10, 20, 8. The sense is, 'would you actually be so forgetful of the very name of your country that, when Pedius and Corvinus are working

30 verba foris malis, Canusini more bilinguis?
    atque ego cum Graecos facerem, natus mare citra,
    versiculos, vetuit me tali voce Quirinus,
    post mediam noctem visus, cum somnia vera:
    'In silvam non ligna feras insanius, ac si
35 magnas Graecorum malis implere catervas.'
    Turgidus Alpinus iugulat dum Memnona, dumque
    defingit Rheni luteum caput, haec ego ludo,
    quae neque in aede sonent certantia iudice Tarpa,

out a speech in pure Latin, you would wish to thrust in among their native words (*patriis*) your imported Greek phrases (*petita verba foris*)?' [This gives the sense which Bentley, interpreting the passage correctly, but not distinguishing *intermisceo* with the dat. from *misceo*, sought to get by supplying *eos*.]

30. foris: *from abroad*, from the Greek. — Canusini bilinguis: at Canusium and in Apulia generally both Greek and Latin (or, earlier, Oscan) were native languages, as both German and French are native in parts of Switzerland. This seemed odd to a Roman, who was obliged to learn Greek in school; probably, also, neither language was spoken in strict purity.

31. atque ego: 'I too once thought of making Greek verses, but Quirinus forbade it.' — Quirinus: the deified Romulus, as head of the Roman race. Cf. *Latini*, vs. 27.

33. cum somnia vera: this superstition is often referred to.

34. In silvam ... ligna: proverbial, like γλαῦκ' ἐς Ἀθήνας, 'carrying coals to Newcastle.' — ac si: *than if*.

36 ff. The connection of thought is somewhat elliptical; 'giving up Greek, therefore, and leaving to others their high and mighty epics, I turn to a humbler style.' — Alpinus: this satirical side-stroke would have been immediately intelligible to Horace's contemporaries. Probably Alpinus is a nickname for M. Furius Bibaculus, the author of a poem on Gaul from which the bombastic line [*Iuppiter*], *hibernas cana nive conspuit Alpis* is quoted, *Sat.* 2, 5, 41. He wrote also an epic which included the killing of Memnon by Achilles, here alluded to with a play upon the double meaning of *iugulat*, 'murders.' The phrase *defingit ... caput*, 'misshapes the muddy head of the Rhine,' contains a similar play upon some passage in the poem on Gaul, but the point is lost to us.

38. aede: called by the scholiasts *aedes Musarum*, a temple in

nec redeant iterum atque iterum spectanda theatris.
40 Arguta meretrice potes Davoque Chremeta
eludente senem comis garrire libellos
unus vivorum, Fundani; Pollio regum
facta canit pede ter percusso; forte epos acer,
ut nemo, Varius ducit; molle atque facetum
45 Vergilio adnuerunt gaudentes rure Camenae.

which Sp. Maecius Tarpa, perhaps as public censor of plays and as head of the *collegium poetarum*, passed judgment upon new poetry. Tarpa is referred to with respect in *Ars Poet.* 387. — **sonent**: *resound*, as the poets read aloud their own verses; cf. 1, 4, 76.

40 ff. 'Other fields were already occupied, but satire was open to me.'

40 f. **meretrice, Davo, Chremeta**: typical figures in comedy; the commonest plot in Plautus and Terence is one in which a young man's confidential slave (*Davus*) with the help of his mistress (*meretrix*) deceives the father (*Chremeta senem*). The ablatives go with *eludente*, of which *Chremeta* is the object. — **comis libellos**: acc. of the inner object after *garrire*.

42. **Fundani**: unknown except by the references to him in *Sat.* 2, 8. — **Pollio**: C. Asinius Pollio, statesman, orator, and poet, one of the most distinguished men of his time. Vergil dedicated the Fourth Eclogue to him, and Horace addressed to him one of his finest odes (*Carm.* 2, 1). His writings are all lost, but his history of the Civil Wars was famous, and the tragedies here alluded to were highly esteemed.

43. **pede ter percusso**: iambic trimeter, the ordinary verse of tragedy, which has the heavy ictus on the first, third and fifth feet. — **forte, acer**: the two adjectives express the same quality from two sides, the *power* of epic poetry and the *lofty spirit* of the epic writer.

44. **ducit**: *shapes, fashions*, used of the work of the artist or poet. The three verbs, *garrire, canit, ducit*, are carefully selected. — **molle atque facetum**: *tenderness and elegance*. On *facetum* cf. *Sat.* 1, 4, 7 n. Vergil had not yet written the *Aeneid* nor published the *Georgics;* he was the poet of the *Eclogues* and of the still lighter poems, which, with more or less doubt of their authenticity, have come down to us under his name.

45. **adnŭĕrunt**: with short penult, as in a few places in Vergil.

Hoc erat, experto frustra Varrone Atacino
atque quibusdam aliis, melius quod scribere possem,
inventore minor; neque ego illi detrahere ausim
haerentem capiti cum multa laude coronam.
50   At dixi fluere hunc lutulentum, saepe ferentem
plura quidem tollenda relinquendis. Age, quaeso,
tu nihil in magno doctus reprehendis Homero?
nil comis tragici mutat Lucilius Acci?

46. Hoc: satire. — **Varrone**: M. Terentius Varro, called Atacinus from the river Atax, in southern Gaul, where he was born, to distinguish him from the great antiquarian and scholar of the same name. He wrote in several styles, but without marked success in any.

47. quibusdam aliis: it is not to be supposed that Horace stood alone in writing satire in the Augustan period; the names of some of the *alii* are known, but all knowledge of their writings is lost.

48 f. inventore minor: concessive; 'even though I fall short of Lucilius.' It was an accepted doctrine of literary history that Lucilius was the inventor of satire, that is, was the first to put it into hexameter and give it the distinct form which it thereafter retained. — The thought of these verses, 48-49, is connected with the preceding, *hoc erat . . . possem*, as if it was a natural consequence of his choice of satire. If it had been put into a separate sentence, it would have been strongly adversative; 'but I do not claim to be his equal nor desire to lessen his credit.'

50 f. At dixi: repeating with emphasis *dixi* of vs. 1. — **fluere**: the figure used in 1, 4, 11, as *tollenda* repeats *erat quod tollere velles*. — **relinquendis**: abl. after the compar. *plura*. The rubbish seemed often more in amount than the water which swept it along. But the figure is not very clearly conceived.

52. doctus: *with all your learning*; the word frequently implies a slur. The Alexandrians and their followers (the *docti*) criticized Homer freely.

53. comis: *genial, kindly*. The word is used as if it were quoted from the admirers of Lucilius, as below, vs. 65, and is selected for the partial contrast with *tragici*. — **mutat**: not actually, but by implication. — **Acci**: L. Accius, the greatest of the early writers of tragedy. Only fragments of his works are extant.

SERMONES [1, 10, 64

  non ridet versus Enni gravitate minores,
55 cum de se loquitur non ut maiore reprensis?
  Quid vetat et nosmet Lucili scripta legentis
  quaerere, num illius, num rerum dura negarit
  versiculos natura magis factos et euntis
  mollius, ac si quis, pedibus quid claudere senis,
60 hoc tantum contentus, amet scripsisse ducentos
  ante cibum versus, totidem cenatus; Etrusci
  quale fuit Cassi rapido ferventius amni
  ingenium, capsis quem fama est esse librisque
  ambustum propriis. Fuerit Lucilius, inquam,

54 f. gravitate minores: *as inferior in dignity*, less dignified than the subject-matter demanded. The unrhythmical verse *sparsis hastis longis campus splendet et horret* Lucilius proposed to change to *horret et alget*. — **cum ... loquitur**: *while at the same time* he claims no superiority for himself. — **reprensis**: *than those whom he criticized*, Accius and Ennius.

57. quaerere: the simplest conclusion of the argument would have been something like *Lucilium reprehendere*, but that is expanded and at the same time made milder by substituting *quaerere* with its dependent questions. — **num ... num**: parallel questions, not alternative. — **rerum**: in the most general meaning, *circumstances*, including his difficult subject-matter and the imperfection of his times in verse-writing.

58. magis factos: *more polished*; *factus* is used in this sense by Cicero (*de Orat.* 3, 48, 184; *Brut.* 30) with a slight apology for the novelty of the use.

59 f. ac si quis ... contentus: 'than a man would write if, content with merely getting what he had to say within six feet, he was in a hurry to ...' — **pedibus senis**: a hexameter, *i.e.* merely making a verse that would scan. So in 1, 4, 40, *concludere versum*. — **claudere**: appos. of *hoc*.

61. ante cibum ... cenatus: a humorous variant upon *stans pede in uno*, 1, 4, 10.

62 f. Cassi: nothing is known of him except what is implied here, that he was so prolific that his books and their cases (*capsis*) were sufficient for his funeral pile.

64. Fuerit: *suppose that Lucilius was*, *i.e.* 'granting, for the moment, that Lucilius was all you claim, genial and witty.'

65 comis et urbanus, fuerit limatior idem
quam rudis et Graecis intacti carminis auctor,
quamque poetarum seniorum turba; sed ille,
si foret hoc nostrum fato dilatus in aevum,
detereret sibi multa, recideret omne quod ultra
70 perfectum traheretur, et in versu faciendo
saepe caput scaberet, vivos et roderet unguis.
Saepe stilum vertas, iterum quae digna legi sint

65. comis et urbanus: these words describe one quality from two sides and are, like *comis* in vs. 53, a quotation; they are admitted with reserve, having been already denied by implication (vs. 13), in order to show that they would not disprove Horace's criticism.

66. quam ... auctor: the thought is altogether general; *carmen* is not satire and the *auctor* is not Lucilius or Ennius. The statement of Quintilian (10, 1, 93), *satira tota nostra est*, is, in a way, correct, but it represents an entirely different literary tradition from that which Horace is following. His doctrine, expressed with an even exaggerated emphasis in 1, 4, 1–6, was that satire came directly from the Greeks of the Old Comedy; in fact, the error of underestimating the force and value of the purely Italic influences runs through all his literary criticism. With the opening words of 1, 4 in mind — and they are distinctly in his mind all through this satire — he could not have called satire *rude et Graecis intactum carmen*. The thought is quite different: 'Lucilius did not invent satire out of nothing; the way had been already prepared by the Greeks and he learned from them. I grant, therefore, that he had a certain degree of polish, more, of course, than a writer composing some entirely new (*rude*) kind of poetry, some poetry untouched by the Greeks, would have had, more even than the early poets generally, but if he had lived ...'

67. seniorum: *senex* is frequently used of the early Latin writers. — **ille**: emphatic.

68. nostrum dilatus in aevum: *prolonged in life down to our time*. So Ovid, *M*. 12, 76, *decimum dilatus in annum Hector erat*.

69. detereret: *would file off many roughnesses;* the same figure as that in *limatior*. — **omne quod ultra**: *i.e.* the *plura tollenda* of vs. 51.

72 ff. From the completed argument in support of his criticism of Lucilius, Horace turns first to a general truth and then to his

scripturus, neque te ut miretur turba labores,
contentus paucis lectoribus. An tua demens
75 vilibus in ludis dictari carmina malis?
non ego; nam satis est equitem mihi plaudere, ut audax,
contemptis aliis, explosa Arbuscula dixit.
Men' moveat cimex Pantilius, aut cruciet quod
vellicet absentem Demetrius, aut quod ineptus

less worthy assailants, Hermogenes and his friends.

72. stilum vertas: the blunt upper end of the *stilus* was used to smooth out the marks made in the wax of a tablet, as a lead-pencil is reversed to use the eraser.

73. scripturus: with the effect of a condition; *if you hope to write.*

74. contentus: continuing the advice; *but be content with.*

75. vilibus ... dictari: poetry to be learned was dictated by the teacher and taken down by the pupils. So Orbilius dictated Livius Andronicus to Horace, *Epist.* 2, 1, 70 f. and Vergil and Horace were in the curriculum of schools in the time of Juvenal (7, 226 f.). Horace, of course, did not, as is sometimes said, 'dread this fate'; he is merely saying in a humorous way, 'do not aim at popularity; don't try to be one of the "best sellers."'

76. equitem: the educated class; so *Epist.* 2, 1, 187. It is quite possible, too, that the word would be taken as a complimentary reference to Maecenas. — **audax**: *undismayed* by the disapproval expressed by the crowd.

77. Arbuscula: an actress in mimes like those of Laberius (vs. 6). Cicero wrote to Atticus in 54 B.C., *quaeris nunc de Arbuscula; valde placuit* (4, 15, 6).

78. cimex: as this is not used by us as a term of reproach, a modern equivalent, *beast, reptile,* may be substituted. — **Pantilius**: unknown; but the name actually occurs and there is no good reason for connecting it with πᾶν τίλλειν or supposing it to be fictitious. — **cruciet**: the subj. is *quod vellicet.*

79 ff. Demetrius is unknown; cf. vs. 18. Most of the other names in this list have been mentioned before: Fannius, 1, 4, 21; Hermogenes, 1, 3, 4; Plotius, 1, 5, 40; Varius, 1, 5, 40; Fuscus, 1, 9, 61; Viscus, 1, 9, 22; Pollio, vs. 42; Messalla, vs. 29. Of the others, C. Valgius Rufus was an elegiac poet and a friend to whom Horace addressed *Carm.* 2, 9. Octavius Musa (the emperor is called by Horace either Caesar or

80   Fannius Hermogenis laedat conviva Tigelli?
     Plotius et Varius, Maecenas Vergiliusque,
     Valgius, et probet haec Octavius, optimus atque
     Fuscus, et haec utinam Viscorum laudet uterque!
     Ambitione relegata te dicere possum,
85   Pollio, te, Messalla, tuo cum fratre, simulque
     vos, Bibule et Servi, simul his te, candide Furni,
     compluris alios, doctos ego quos et amicos
     prudens praetereo; quibus haec, sint qualiacumque,
     arridere velim, doliturus si placeant spe
90   deterius nostra. Demetri, teque, Tigelli,
     discipularum inter iubeo plorare cathedras.
     I, puer, atque meo citus haec subscribe libello.

Augustus) was a poet and historian, mentioned in the *Catalecta*, 14, 1. Bibulus is probably L. Calpurnius Bibulus, a son of Caesar's colleague in the consulship and a fellow-student with Horace in Athens. Servius may be a son of Servius Sulpicius Rufus, referred to several times by Cicero. C. Furnius is mentioned by Plutarch as an orator.

It is worthy of note that, with scarcely an exception, all the men here named as friends are of sufficient importance to be referred to by other writers than Horace.

84. ambitione relegata: *without flattery*, without fear that he may be suspected of boasting; the phrase is put in here because the men whose names follow were all of high rank and social standing.

86. simul: here used as a preposition governing *his*.

87. doctos: *good critics*, without the slur which *doctus* often implies.

88. prudens: *intentionally*, to avoid too long a list. — **sint qualiacumque**: perhaps a reminiscence of Catull. 1, 8 f., *quidquid hoc libelli, qualecumque*.

89. arridere: *be pleasing*; cf. Carm. 2, 6, 13 f., *ille terrarum mihi . . . angulus ridet*.

91. discipularum . . . cathedras: *the easy-chairs of the women to whom you give lessons.* — **iubeo plorare**: with double meaning, first with reference to their singing and also as a humorous substitute for *valere iubeo*.

92. meo . . . libello: this can mean nothing else than the whole book of satires and indicates that this satire was a kind of epilogue to the collection. — **puer**: the slave who was acting as his secretary.

LIBER SECVNDVS

The Second Book of the Satires was published in 30 B.C., five years after the First Book, and the changes which the interval had produced in the temper and in the art of Horace are quite evident; his tone is less personal and more mellow and he has adopted the dialogue form instead of the monologue. In both respects the change is an advance. The earlier satires, with all their geniality, are touched here and there with sensationalism, and even the later work betrays at times a certain uneasiness about his own position and success. But by the year 30 B.C. Horace, now about thirty-five years of age, had won recognition as a writer. He was secure in the esteem of a circle of friends; he had accommodated himself, not indeed without difficulty, but quite sincerely, to the great political changes which he had at first opposed, and he writes like a man at peace with himself and with his world. He is not less serious; in his treatment of philosophy he is more serious; but he is less insistent, less urgent, and his touch is lighter. With this change in tone the change in form, from monologue to dialogue, and especially to a dialogue in which Horace himself plays only a subordinate part, is quite in harmony. A tendency toward informal dialogue is evident in some of the satires of the First Book (*e.g.*, 1, 1, 30 ff.; 1, 4, 38 ff.), but the step from this to the formal dialogue of 2, 1 and 2, 5 is a long one, and the change was undoubtedly regarded by Horace as a distinct advance in the form of satire.

I

There are no allusions in this satire which fix the date of composition. The reference to the Parthians (vs. 15) is entirely general and might have been made before the battle of Actium, while Antonius was still master of the East. But it is probable that this satire was written after the rest of the book was completed, in accordance with the custom which Horace had begun in *Sat.* 1, 1 and which he afterward followed in *Epod.* 1, 1, *Carm.* 1, 1, and *Epist.* 1, 1. This would fix the date about 30 B.C., after the battle of Actium, to which *Caesaris invicti* (vs. 11) may be an allusion.

'Trebatius, people say that my satire is worthless. What shall I do about it? — Keep still! — What, not write at all? — Yes. — By Jove, you may be right. But I can't go to sleep. — Can't sleep? Take some exercise and drink a bottle of wine just before bed-time and you will sleep perfectly well. Or, if what you mean is that you can't stop writing, then write about Caesar; that is work that will pay you. — I wish I could, my dear sir, but I am not equal to describing battles. — Then write about his justice and his energy. — Some other time, perhaps; just now I don't think I will try it. — It would be a great deal better than the things you do write, which make enemies on all sides. — I can't help myself. Writing is my hobby. I have fighting blood in my veins, as Lucilius had in his. But I never attack; I simply defend myself with my natural weapon, as a bull does with his horns. I can't help myself; write I must. — You won't live long if you stick to that course. Some of your great friends will turn a cold shoulder to you. — What, did Lucilius's friends desert him? I am not as great a man as he was, but if any man attacks me, he will find that I am no easy prey — unless, of course, you advise differently. — No, I don't think I can say anything against that. But there are libel laws for the writers of bad verses. — Bad verses! Yes, but mine are not bad; they are very good. Can I be sued for writing good verses? — Certainly not. Good poetry is above all law.'

In issuing a second collection of writings in the same style as that by which he had already won both friends and enemies, Horace thought it well to preface it with a further defence of satire, continuing the subject of 1, 4 and 1, 10. But as 1, 10 is at once less serious and more assured than 1, 4, so this satire is less obviously argumentative than 1, 10. Its underlying purpose is self-defence and explanation, but under the cover of pure burlesque. It represents a consultation between Horace and his legal adviser, C. Trebatius Testa. The latter is well known to us through the group of letters addressed to him by Cicero (*ad Fam.* 7, 6-22); he was a distinguished jurisconsult and a man of much humor, and therefore a suitable figure for a burlesque consultation. The dialogue is managed with great skill; Trebatius, in a dry, legal manner, gives prudent advice, which Horace rejects as fast as it is given, arguing with much heat in favor of the course that he had already determined upon before he went through the form of consulting the lawyer. The arguments, too, by which Horace defends his course are all farcical: Milonius gets drunk and dances, therefore I may write satire: the bull gores, the wolf bites, and Scaeva poisons his mother, therefore I may use my satire to wound and poison. From beginning to end there is not an argument that is meant to be taken seriously and the satire becomes thus a kind of proclamation by Horace of his assurance that his writings need no serious defence.

Horatius. Sunt quibus in satira videor nimis acer et ultra
legem tendere opus; sine nervis altera, quicquid
composui, pars esse putat, similisque meorum
mille die versus deduci posse. Trebati,
5 quid faciam praescribe. *Trebatius.* Quiescas. *Hor.* Ne faciam, inquis,
omnino versus? *Treb.* Aio. *Hor.* Peream male, si non
optimum erat; verum nequeo dormire. *Treb.* Ter uncti

1. **satira**: here used for the first time by Horace and in a general, not a concrete, sense; *in the writing of satire.*

2. **legem**: *i.e.* the artistic law which should govern this kind of writing; cf. vs. 63 and *operis lex; Ars Poet.* 135. — **tendere**: *bend, force,* of bending a bow. — **sine nervis**: *without vigor;* cf. the adj. *enervis. Nervus* is usually *sinew, muscle,* not *nerve.* The two criticisms, *nimis acer* and *sine nervis,* are direct opposites and, therefore, mutually destructive.

4. **deduci**: *spun out, reeled off.*

5. **praescribe**: a rather formal word, used especially in legal language. — **Quiescas**: with sententious brevity, as befits an eminent legal authority, and with a humorous double meaning, since it may be either 'never mind your critics,' or 'stop your writing.'

6. **Peream male, si**: cf. 1, 9, 38 and 47.

7. **optimum erat**: *would not be best.* The impf. indic. of neglected duty or opportunity, especially common with impersonals; see any grammar. — **dormire**: *go to sleep, i.e.* give up writing and, it is implied, all activity.

7-9. Trebatius is represented as pretending to understand *dormire* literally (*somno quibus est opus alto*) and as giving a favorite remedy for insomnia, in which Horace touches two hobbies or foibles of the great lawyer. He was very fond of swimming (Cicero, *ad Fam.* 7, 10, 2, calls him *studiosissimus homo natandi*) and was not disinclined to the bottle (cf.

transnanto Tiberim, somno quibus est opus alto,
irriguumque mero sub noctem corpus habento.
10 Aut, si tantus amor scribendi te rapit, aude
Caesaris invicti res dicere, multa laborum
praemia laturus. *Hor.* Cupidum, pater optime, vires
deficiunt; neque enim quivis horrentia pilis
agmina nec fracta pereuntis cuspide Gallos
15 aut labentis equo describat volnera Parthi.

ad Fam. 7, 22, written after a night with Trebatius, *inluseras heri inter scyphos*, and *domum bene potus seroque redieram*). — **Ter**: a sacred number, used to give formality to the prescription. — **uncti**: oil was used by athletes to soften the skin. — **transnanto, habento**: old forms used in laws and in medical recipes. — **irriguum**: one of many euphemisms (*madidus, uvidus*, etc.), like the Engl. 'full,' 'tight.'

10. **tantus amor**: Trebatius now recognizes the real meaning of *dormire*, which he had pretended to take literally. — **aude**: it would require some courage to write an epic.

11. **Caesaris**: the nephew, not the uncle, as below, vs. 19, and everywhere in the Satires except 1, 9, 18. — **invicti**: this may be a reference to the battle of Actium, but the word might fairly have been used before that event with reference to the earlier victories in the civil war.

12. **praemia**: it may perhaps be a little hit at the legal profession to represent Trebatius as thinking first of the payment which epic poetry might bring. — Both *laturus* and *cupidum* should be rendered in English by clauses, as Greenough remarks. — **pater**: a term of respect from a younger man to an older. Cf. *puer*, vs. 60.

31-15. Here, as in *Carm.* 1, 6, and elsewhere, in professing his inability to write of warlike scenes, Horace cannot refrain from a few phrases of description which suggest that his real reason for refusing is not so much conscious inability as disinclination. — **pilis**: the Roman weapon. — **fracta . . . cuspide, pereuntis**: the signs of defeat; the broken spear is merely one of the evidences of rout and disaster, not a reference to the detached head of the *pilum*, to which *fracta* would not be applicable. So *labentis equo* indicates the defeat of the Parthian cavalry. The Gauls and the Parthians are selected merely as conspicuous among the enemies of Rome, without reference to particular campaigns.

Treb. Attamen et iustum poteras et scribere fortem,
Scipiadam ut sapiens Lucilius. *Hor.* Haud mihi dero,
cum res ipsa feret. Nisi dextro tempore, Flacci
verba per attentam non ibunt Caesaris aurem,
20 cui male si palpere, recalcitrat undique tutus.
Treb. Quanto rectius hoc, quam tristi laedere versu
Pantolabum scurram Nomentanumque nepotem,

16. **poteras**: *you might*; cf. *optimum erat*, vs. 7. — **iustum, fortem**: *i.e.* in his capacity as law-giver (*iustum*) and administrator (*fortem*).

17. **Scipiadam**: for *Scīpīŏnem*, which could not be used in hexameter; there is no patronymic force in the ending. The younger Scipio was a contemporary and friend of Lucilius; cf. vss. 65 f. — **sapiens**: pred., 'like a man of sense,' with an indirect reflection upon Horace's lack of worldly wisdom. — **Lucilius**: the mention of Horace's model in satire of course implies that Trebatius is no longer advising him to give up satire for epic, but only to turn his satire to more profitable uses. — **Haud mihi dero**: cf. 1, 9, 56, where the context shows that *cum res ipsa feret* means the same thing as *dextro tempore*, 'when a proper opportunity shall present itself.'

18. **Flacci**: *a Flaccus*; a man of so humble a name as Flaccus, in contrast with *Caesaris*.

19 f. **attentam ... aurem**: the comparison of Caesar to a high-spirited horse is suggested in these words, to be expressed more fully in the next line. — **non**: with the whole phrase, not with *attentam* alone or *ibunt* alone. — **ibunt**: the future implies intention. As there is no English phrase corresponding to *ire per aurem*, the construction must be shifted in translation; 'the words of a Flaccus shall not try to reach the ear of a Caesar.' — **tutus**: *to protect himself.*

22. Quoted, with change of case, from *Sat.* 1, 8, 11. The effect is therefore as if he had said, 'than to write such a savage verse as that in the Eighth Satire.' Cf. 1, 4, 92, where a line of similar character is quoted from 1, 2, 27. That quotation is introduced by *ego si risi* and the argument, there seriously made, is that the line is a harmless jest. It is almost a necessary inference that here also the verse quoted by Trebatius was regarded by Horace as in fact quite harmless. This could be true only if the persons referred to were either fictitious, as the name Pantolabus certainly is, or already notorious, as was probably the case with Nomentanus (cf. 1, 1, 102 note).

cum sibi quisque timet, quamquam est intactus, et odit !
Hor. Quid faciam ? Saltat Milonius, ut semel icto
25　accessit fervor capiti numerusque lucernis;
Castor gaudet equis, ovo prognatus eodem
pugnis ; quot capitum vivunt, totidem studiorum
milia : me pedibus delectat claudere verba
Lucili ritu, nostrum melioris utroque.
30　Ille velut fidis arcana sodalibus olim
credebat libris, neque, si male cesserat, usquam

23. **timet . . . et odit**: a repetition of the charge made in 1, 4, 33. The purely farcical character of the reply here shows how secure Horace felt himself to be.

24-29. 'I can't help writing, any more than Milonius can help getting drunk and dancing. Everybody has his little weakness; mine is satire.'

24. **icto**: with *capiti;* a euphemism for intoxication, like *irriguum*, vs. 9.

25. **accessit**: in a double sense with *fervor* and *numerus*. — **lucernis**: *i.e.* when he has drunk so much that he begins to see double.

26. 'Even twin brothers differ in their interests.' The contrast is emphasized by using *ovo prognatus eodem* for Pollux, and, in accordance with the general character of the argument, two of the lower gods with lower interests are selected instead of, *e.g.*, Apollo and Mercury.

27. **quot capitum**: proverbial and better expressed by Terence,

Phorm. 454, *quot homines, tot sententiae;* 'many men of many minds.'

28. **pedibus . . . claudere verba**: a repetition of the phrase *pedibus quid claudere senis*, used in *Sat.* 1, 10, 59 to describe the merely mechanical construction of hexameters. Here also, with a different purpose, it puts the matter in its lowest terms, 'I amuse myself by stringing together verses that will scan.'

29. **melioris**: not in the moral or social sense, but a better judge, a better authority. — **utroque**: as if the thought began very modestly — 'a better authority than I am' — and then went on to a little hit at his advisor — 'or than you, either.'

30-34. The Scholiasts note that this is a bit of traditional literary criticism, going back to Aristoxenus, who had said that Alcaeus and Sappho *volumina sua loco sodalium habuisse*. — **arcana**: his deepest and most intimate thoughts about the events (*si male cesse-*

decurrens alio, neque si bene; quo fit ut omnis
votiva pateat veluti descripta tabella
vita senis.   Sequor hunc, Lucanus an Apulus anceps:
35 nam Venusinus arat finem sub utrumque colonus,
missus ad hoc, pulsis, vetus est ut fama, Sabellis,
quo ne per vacuum Romano incurreret hostis,
sive quod Apula gens seu quod Lucania bellum
incuteret violenta.   Sed hic stilus haud petet ultro
40 quemquam animantem, et me veluti custodiet ensis
vagina tectus; quem cur destringere coner,
tutus ab infestis latronibus?   O pater et rex

rat, si bene) of life; not *secrets*.— **votiva ... tabella**: such a picture as is referred to in *Carm.* 1, 5, 13 f., where the successive scenes of some event like an escape from shipwreck were represented in a single picture. Cf. the scenes from the Trojan War in *Aen.* 1, 456 ff. — **senis**: the word *senex* was sometimes applied to writers of the early period as a synonym for *vetus, antiquus*, without reference to the age of the individual. [The opposite opinion may be found in Müller, *Lucil.* p. 288.]

34-39. The expression is elliptical: 'I take Lucilius for my leader, for I too come of fighting stock. But I fight only in self-defence.' The digression upon the question whether Venusia is properly Lucanian or Apulian is subordinate to the main line of reasoning. — **anceps**: nom. masc., with the subj. of *sequor*; the phrase should be rendered freely. — **ad hoc**: antec. of the clause *quo ne .. incurreret*. — **Sabellis**: *the Samnites*. Venusia was founded in 291 B.C., in the Third Samnite War. — **quo ne**: for *ut ne* or *ut eo ne*; but this use of *quo* is without a parallel. — **quod**: after *si-ve* and with *bellum*.

39. **Sed**: adversative to the underlying thought of the preceding sentence. — **hic stilus**: *this pen of mine*, but with some reference to the fact that the sharp metal *stilus* could be actually used as a weapon.

40. **animantem**: *living being*, to generalize the thought.

41. **vagina tectus**: these are the important words in the comparison; 'as a sword is a defence, even though it is not drawn from its scabbard.'

42. **tutus**: *i.e.* 'as long as I am not attacked.'

Iuppiter, ut pereat positum robigine telum,
nec quisquam noceat cupido mihi pacis! At ille
45 qui me commorit ('melius non tangere!' clamo),
flebit, et insignis tota cantabitur urbe.
Cervius iratus leges minitatur et urnam,

43. ut pereat: a wish introduced by *ut* exactly as wishes are introduced by *utinam*, which is nothing but a strengthened form of *uti* (cf. *quis, quisnam*); instances are not infrequent. The verse is in form, though not in sentiment, a reminiscence of Catull. 66, 48, *Iuppiter, ut Chalybon omne genus pereat.* — **positum**: a part of the wish; 'may I be able to put it away and let it rust;' almost the same as *vagina tectus*.

44-46. In these lines the humorous exaggeration and affected solemnity of the satire reach a climax. Whatever Horace may have been in his earlier years, he was at this time as far removed as possible from a bragging swashbuckler, whose war-cry (*clamo*) was 'Better not touch me!' He is, in fact, setting up here the figure of himself which his earlier critics had constructed, exaggerating it and making it ridiculous by a burlesque defence, in the confident assurance that his real purpose in satire was by this time fully recognized.

45. commorit: = *commoverit*. There is a kind of progress in pretended touchiness from *infestis latronibus* to *commorit* (*stir me up*) and *tangere* (*lay a finger on me*).

46. cantabitur: *i.e.* the whole town shall be repeating the satirical verses that I will write about him.

47-56. These lines serve a double purpose. As a part of the ironical argument they pretend to justify the determination (44-46) to continue the writing of satire ('Canidia poisons her enemies and I will poison mine: the wolf bites and therefore I will write biting satire'), and they illustrate the general principle (vss. 24-28) that men are not to be blamed for yielding to their special weaknesses ('and satire is my weakness,' vs. 28). At the same time, these allusions, which a reader of Horace's time would at once understand, show how harmless and impersonal his satire really was. For no one of the five persons named was really an enemy of Horace. Cervius, Albucius, and Scaeva are names which occur elsewhere (*Sat.* 2, 6, 77; 2, 2, 67; *Epist.* 1, 17, 1), but with quite different characteristics; they are merely Roman names which do not refer to individuals. Canidia is frequently mentioned (*Sat.* 1, 8, 2, 8, 95; *Epod.* 3, 8; 5, 17) in

Canidia Albuci quibus est inimica venenum,
grande malum Turius, si quid se iudice certes.
50 Vt quo quisque valet suspectos terreat, utque
imperet hoc natura potens, sic collige mecum :
dente lupus, cornu taurus petit : unde nisi intus
monstratum ? Scaevae vivacem crede nepoti
matrem ; nil faciet sceleris pia dextera: mirum,
55 ut neque calce lupus quemquam neque dente petit bos:
sed mala tollet anum vitiato melle cicuta.

a way which shows that she was already notorious. Turius appears to have been a character of the Ciceronian period, long since dead, whose abuse of his judicial office was a matter of common knowledge. The whole passage, therefore, savage as the personal allusions are made to appear, is in reality, like the quotation in vs. 22, a reminder of Horace's moderation in satire and of his avoidance of personal attacks upon contemporaries.

47. **Cervius**: an informer; cf. *Sat.* 1, 4, 65 n. — **urnam**: the vase from which the names of jurymen were drawn and in which their votes were deposited.

48. **Albuci**: with *venenum*. — **quibus**: the antec. is the obj. of *minitatur* to be supplied from vs. 47.

49. **grande malum**: *i.e. a heavy penalty* without regard to the justice of the case.

50. **Vt**: *how*, introducing *terreat* and *imperet*.

51. **sic**: from the following, vs. 52. — **collige**: *you may judge*; the potential use of the impv., like *scito*. — **mecum**: *as I do*, *i.e.* by following the line of argument which I now present.

52. **dente, cornu**: the emphatic words. — **intus**: *from within*, the usual Plautine and colloquial meaning.

53. **vivacem**: *too long-lived*, so that the son's inheritance of his property is delayed.

54 f. **sceleris**: crime of violence. — **pia**: *filial*. He would not cut her throat or strangle her; his little weakness is poisoning, not bloodshed. — **mirum, ut**: *as astonishing as it is that*, *i.e.* no more astonishing. — **calce**: suggesting the contrast of the wolf to a kicking horse (cf. vs. 20) as a slight variation from vs. 52.

56. **mala**: a standing epithet with poisons. — **tollet**: euphemistic, as the whole line is; the matter will be managed quietly, without publicity.

Ne longum faciam, seu me tranquilla senectus
exspectat seu Mors atris circumvolat alis,
dives, inops, Romae, seu fors ita iusserit, exul,
60 quisquis erit vitae, scribam, color. *Treb.* O puer, ut sis
vitalis metuo, et maiorum ne quis amicus
frigore te feriat. *Hor.* Quid, cum est Lucilius ausus
primus in hunc operis componere carmina morem,
detrahere et pellem, nitidus qua quisque per ora
65 cederet, introrsum turpis, num Laelius aut qui
duxit ab oppressa meritum Carthagine nomen
ingenio offensi aut laeso doluere Metello

57. Ne longum faciam: the same words in 1, 3, 137, and cf. *ne te morer*, 1, 1, 14.

60. vitae ... color: this figurative use of *color* is especially common in rhetorical writings, *e.g. Ars Poet.* 86, 236.

61 f. vitalis: *long-lived;* Trebatius goes back to 58. *Mors ... circumvolat;* 'I am afraid that you won't live long, if that's your spirit.' — **maiorum:** with *amicus.* The reference is to the friends of high station mentioned by Horace with pride in *Sat.* 1, 10, 81 ff., Maecenas, Pollio, Messalla. — **frigore ... feriat:** a little more forcible than *strike you with a chill; ferire* is used of striking an enemy dead, 'striking down' and *frigus* suggests the dangerous fever and chill.

63. primus: *i.e.* Lucilius began this kind of writing; I am merely a follower and therefore less liable to suffer for it.

64 f. pellem: an allusion to the fable of the Ass in the Lion's Skin; cf. *Sat.* 1, 6, 22 and *Epist.* 1, 16, 45, *introrsum turpem, speciosum pelle decora.* — **per ora:** *among men;* the phrase occurs only a few times, but the meaning is clear. — **cederet:** colloquial for *incederet.* — **introrsum turpis:** *i.e.* under the skin is an ugly ass.

65. Laelius: C. Laelius, consul in 140 B.C., a friend of Terence, used by Cicero as a speaker in the two dialogues *de Senectute* and *de Amicitia.*

66. The younger Scipio Africanus, whose friendship with Laelius was historic.

67. offensi: *sc. sunt.* — **laeso ... Metello:** Q. Caecilius Metellus Macedonicus, consul in 143 B.C., a political opponent of Scipio.

famosisque Lupo cooperto versibus? Atqui
primores populi arripuit populumque tributim,
70 scilicet uni aequus virtuti atque eius amicis.
Quin ubi se a volgo et scaena in secreta remorant
virtus Scipiadae et mitis sapientia Laeli,
nugari cum illo et discincti ludere, donec
decoqueretur olus, soliti. Quicquid sum ego, quamvis

68. **Lupo**: L. Cornelius Lentulus Lupus, consul in 156 B.C., also an enemy of Scipio and attacked by Lucilius apparently with special bitterness. — **famosis**: *which made them notorious.* — **cooperto**: *overwhelmed*; the verses fell upon him like a volley of javelins.

The argument of vss. 62–68 is ironical, though less broadly so than that of 47–56; 'do you suppose that Scipio and Laelius were greatly disturbed when Lucilius turned his satire upon their political opponents?' — **Atqui**: *and yet* Lucilius was much more daring and more sweeping in his satire than I am.

69. **arripuit**: a technical term of law; *summoned to court*. — **tributim**: *a tribe at a time.* This is a reference to a political satire in which Lucilius *tribus omnes XXXV laceravit* (Schol. to Pers. 1, 114); of this two fragments remain, containing the names of two of the tribes attacked, *Papiria* and *Oufentina*.

70. **scilicet**: *of course.* The line is a humorous afterthought, really in direct contradiction of the preceding statement, just as in vss. 43 ff. and below in vss. 77 f. an exaggerated pugnacity and a regard for the proprieties are set in contrast; 'he attacked everybody, high and low, and the whole people, tribe by tribe, but of course, you understand, he attacked only bad people (cf. vs. 85) and never satirized the virtuous — any more than I do.'

71. **Quin**: *why*; corrective of the insufficient expression in *offensi*, *doluere*. — **scaena**: the stage of public life.

72. **virtus Scipiadae**: Homeric circumlocutions; 'the virtuous Scipio and the wise and gentle Laelius.'

73. **discincti**: *i.e.* laying aside all the formalities of city life. There are other references (Schol. and Cic. *de Orat.* 2, 6, 22) to this distinct tradition that Scipio and Laelius enjoyed the opportunities of relaxation in the country.

74. **olus**: *i.e.* a simple country meal, 'a dinner of herbs.' — **soliti**: *sc. sunt*, as with *offensi* in vs. 67.

75 infra Lucili censum ingeniumque, tamen me
cum magnis vixisse invita fatebitur usque
invidia, et, fragili quaerens illidere dentem,
offendet solido, — nisi quid tu, docte Trebati,
dissentis. *Treb.* Equidem nihil hinc diffindere possum.
80 Sed tamen ut monitus caveas, ne forte negoti
incutiat tibi quid sanctarum inscitia legum:
si mala condiderit in quem quis carmina, ius est
iudiciumque. *Hor.* Esto, si quis mala; sed bona si quis

75. **censum**: *rank*. Lucilius was an *eques* and therefore naturally connected with men of station.

76. **invita**: *i.e.* even against its will, in spite of itself.

77 f. **fragili, solido**: dat. neut.; alluding to the fable of the Viper and the File. — **illidere**: *to dash in*, expressing the eagerness of the bite.

78. **nisi . . . dissentis**: cf. 70 note. Horace represents himself as suddenly remembering, at the very climax of his bragging, that he is supposed to be asking advice.

79. **hinc diffindere**: lit., 'to cut off anything from this,' with the figure of *fragili . . . solido* still in mind; translate, 'I can't find anything in this to take exception to.' [But the text is not sure.]

80. **ut . . . caveas**: not a final clause and not to be explained by supplying a main clause. This is the use of *ut* (more often *uti*) in sentences of command, parallel to the use of *uti-nam* in wishes; it is not infrequent in Plautus (*Bacch.* 739, *proin tu ab eo ut caveas tibi*; *Capt.* 115, etc.) and Terence (*Ad.* 280, *Phorm.* 212), but survives especially in legal formulas (C.I.L. 1, 196, 23 and in quotations in Livy) and is used here to give a formal tone to the injunctions of the lawyer; cf. vs. 8 f. *transnanto, habento*, and vs. 82. — **negoti**: *trouble*, a common colloquial meaning; gen. partitive with *quid*.

81. **sanctarum**: *sacred*, as a lawyer would naturally think them.

82. **si mala . . . carmina**: this is almost the phraseology of the law of the XII Tables as quoted by Pliny, *H. N.* 28, 4, 18, *qui malum carmen incantassit*, and by Cicero *de Rep.* 4, 10, 12, *sive (quis) carmen condidisset.* — **ius est iudiciumque**: *there is right of action and a legal remedy*; the offended party has a legal right to sue.

83. **mala**: Horace represents himself as understanding this word, which in the law means

iudice condiderit laudatus Caesare? si quis
85 opprobriis dignum latraverit, integer ipse?
Treb. Solventur risu tabulae, tu missus abibis.

injurious, abusive, in the esthetic sense, *bad poetry.*

84. **Caesare**: Caesar is named rather than some recognized critic like Quintilius Varus because he would be accepted by a lawyer as the highest authority.

86. The sense of this line is perfectly clear, 'the case will be laughed out of court and you will go free,' and the figure in *solventur* is used elsewhere (Quint. 5, 10, 67, *cum risu tota res solvitur*; Cic. *de Orat.* 2, 58, 236, *res . . . ioco risuque dissolvit*), but the exact meaning of *tabulae* (the indictment, the voting tablets, the benches of the jury-men) cannot be determined.

2

There is no internal evidence to fix the date of this satire; it was written between 35 and 30 B.C.

'The advantages of plain living — I am repeating what I once heard from a wise old farmer — cannot be properly set forth in an after-dinner conversation; only a hungry man can know how good plain food may be. At a dinner party your judgment is confused by the elaborate cookery and — still worse — by the rarity or the novelty of the viands. Indeed, the very over-abundance sometimes drives you back in disgust to simple flavors. For it is only lately that you have learned, in obedience to fashion, to like stork; roast sea-gull will be the next whim, I suppose.

'But you must not think — says my old farmer — that simplicity means stinginess. Do not rush to the other extreme; keep to the middle course of a plain neatness.

'Consider, now, the advantages of such a way of living: health, vigor, the pleasure of occasional indulgence, hospitality, good repute, money left in your purse, and, chief of all, readiness to meet the buffets of fortune. I used to hear the old farmer, then a hired laborer on the farm he had once owned, discoursing about this to his sons: "I have lived a temperate life and my wants are few. Let Fortune do her worst; he that is down need fear no fall."'

In form, this satire, like 3, 4, 7, 8 of this book, consists of a main body of didactic discourse set in an introductory framework. In the other satires, however, the framework is in dialogue, generally very skilfully adapted to its special purpose, while here the setting is not clearly conceived (cf. vs. 7 note), the introduction is too brief (vss. 2 f.), and the quotation passes from indirect to direct without sufficient motive and with a second and superfluous introduction (vss. 112-115). In the main discourse also there is a similar lack of clearness of outline. The change from the plural (vss. 1-7) to the vague *tu* breaks the continuity. The reference to Ofellus in vs. 53 is not distinct enough to preserve the illusion of quotation. The knowledge of places, fashions, and persons in Rome is quite inconsistent with the circumstances of an Apulian peasant; this is in part to be explained by the fact that the whole satire is a parody of a Stoic sermon, in which allusions to Roman affairs would be quite in place, but the inconsistency remains and adds nothing to the humor. The explanation of these incongruities in structure is that Horace is here experimenting with a form of satire which is a compromise between the dialogue form of Satires 3, 4, 7, and 8 and the frankly personal monologue of Satire 6, and is inferior to either.

There is a similar compromise or combination in the subject-matter; on the one hand, the satire contrasts country life with the life of the city, as is done in greater fulness and with greater effectiveness in Satire 6; on the other hand, the luxuries and fashions of the table, which are ridiculed here, are treated more fully and more humorously in Satires 4 and 8. But the two subjects harmonize more easily than the two forms The combination, however, is marked enough to suggest the hypothesis that this satire is the earliest of the book in date of composition, and that both form and subject were worked out to greater perfection in the later satires.

Quae virtus et quanta, boni, sit vivere parvo
(nec meus hic sermo est, sed quae praecepit Ofellus
rusticus, abnormis sapiens, crassaque Minerva),

1. **boni**: ἀγαθοί, as a friendly form of address.

2. **nec meus ... est**: the same phrase, κοὐκ ἐμὸς ὁ μῦθος, occurs in a fragment of Euripides and is quoted by Plato, *Symp.* 177 A.

3. **abnormis**: *unschooled*, not bound by the doctrines of any sect. So Cicero, *de Amic.* 5, 18, says that certain Roman worthies were not philosophers, *ad istorum normam*. — **crassa Minerva**: *of a rough-and-ready wit*. Cf. *pingui Minerva*, Cic. *de Amic.* 5, 19. Minerva is the goddess of intelligence.

discite, non inter lances mensasque nitentis,
5 cum stupet insanis acies fulgoribus et cum
acclinis falsis animus meliora recusat,
verum hic impransi mecum disquirite. 'Cur hoc?'
Dicam, si potero. Male verum examinat omnis
corruptus iudex. Leporem sectatus equove
10 lassus ab indomito, vel, si Romana fatigat
militia adsuetum graecari, seu pila velox,
molliter austerum studio fallente laborem,

4 f. **nitentis, fulgoribus**: the gleaming of silver plate, which the Romans used very freely, is often alluded to in descriptions of the tables at a banquet, *e.g.* Catull. 64. 44 ff. — **stupet acies**: *the eyes are dazzled*, of course in a figurative sense, 'the judgment is distracted.'

7. **hic impransi**: *here*, not at a table, and *fasting, hungry*, not after an elaborate dinner. The two words seem to suggest a particular scene and certain definite circumstances — a group of friends or neighbors waiting for their lunch, — but if such a setting for the discourse was in Horace's mind, it is lost sight of at once and not again alluded to in the satire. Cf. note on vs. 17. — **Cur hoc**: *i.e.* 'why *impransi?*'

8. **si potero**: this gives the air of a lecturer: 'I will endeavor to tell you.' — **Male**: with *examinat*. The sentence can be best translated by turning it into the negative form; 'no judge who has been bribed . . .'

9-16. The outline of this loosely constructed sentence is simple; 'get an appetite by hard exercise, and then see whether you are disposed to refuse plain food.' But after mentioning two kinds of Roman exercise, hunting (cf. *Epod.* 2. 29 ff.; *Carm.* 1, 1, 25 ff.) and riding (*Carm.* 1. 8. 5 ff.), he introduces as an alternative two kinds of Greek athletics, ball-playing and the throwing of the *discus*, each in a conditional clause, *seu pila* (*te agit*), *seu discus te agit*; the first is left without a formal apodosis, but *pete* is the apodosis to the second. Then as the formal structure of the sentence has been disturbed, the substance of 9-13 is condensed into *cum . . . extuderit* and repeated in *siccus, inanis*. — **militia**: with special reference to riding. — **graecari**: there is a suggestion of effeminacy in this verb. — **velox**: the game consisted in rapid passing of the ball from one player to another. — **molliter . . . laborem**: *i.e.* 'in which the interest in the game makes the

seu te discus agit, pete cedentem aera disco;
cum labor extuderit fastidia, siccus, inanis
15 sperne cibum vilem; nisi Hymettia mella Falerno
ne biberis diluta. Foris est promus, et atrum
defendens piscis hiemat mare: cum sale panis
latrantem stomachum bene leniet. Vnde putas aut
qui partum? Non in caro nidore voluptas
20 summa, sed in te ipso est. Tu pulmentaria quaere
sudando; pinguem vitiis albumque neque ostrea
nec scarus aut poterit peregrina iuvare lagois.
Vix tamen eripiam, posito pavone, velis quin

player enjoy the exercise, forgetting how severe it is.' This abl. abs. clause takes the place of an apodosis to *seu pila*. — **discus**: a large flat quoit, thrown for distance, not for accuracy. — **agit**: *stirs, rouses, attracts*. A rare use, but exactly paralleled in Cic. *Arch.* 7, 16, *haec studia adulescentiam agunt, senectutem oblectant.* — **pete**: *strike*. — **disco**: abl. — **extuderit**: *i.e.* 'has knocked the nonsense out of you'; a colloquial use. — **Hymettia, Falerno**: the finest honey and wine. — **promus**: the *butler* or *steward*, who keeps the keys of the storeroom.

17. **hiemat mare**: this has been taken to indicate that the scene of the discourse was a villa on the seashore, where Horace repeats the precepts of Ofellus to a group of friends. But the reference is too general for that; fish are mentioned here, as in 31 ff., 48 f., 95,

merely as other kinds of food are specified.

18. **leniet**: the future implies 'you will find that it will soothe.'

19. **qui partum**: *whence or how do you suppose that this comes about*, that you are glad to get the plainest food?

20. **Tu**: emphatic, with reference to *te ipso*. — **pulmentaria**: the Scholiasts refer to the story that Socrates, being asked why he was taking such a long walk, replied ὄψον συνάγω, which is almost *pulmentarium quaero*. Cf. also the saying *fames optimum condimentum*.

21 f. **vitiis**: *excesses* in eating and drinking. — **ostrea, scarus, lagois**: three expensive delicacies. But neither the *scarus*, a kind of fish, nor the *lagois*, a game bird, can be precisely identified. — **iuvare**: *to give you pleasure*.

23. **eripiam**: with prohibitive force and therefore followed by

hoc potius quam gallina tergere palatum,
25 corruptus vanis rerum, quia veneat auro
rara avis, et picta pandat spectacula cauda;
tamquam ad rem attineat quicquam. Num vesceris ista
quam laudas pluma? Cocto num adest honor idem?
carne tamen quamvis distat nihil, hanc magis illa
30 imparibus formis deceptum te petere esto,
unde datum sentis, lupus hic Tiberinus an alto
captus hiet, pontisne inter iactatus an amnis

quin. — **posito**: on the table, as in *Sat.* 1, 3, 92. — **pavone**: the peacock was first used as an article of food by Hortensius the orator and was afterward regarded as a necessary part of a banquet. Cf. Cic. *ad Fam.* 9, 20, 2, *sed vide audaciam; etiam Hirtio cenam dedi sine pavone.*

24. **tergere**: almost exactly like the English *to tickle the palate.*

25. **corruptus**: cf. vs. 9. — **vanis rerum**: = *vanis rebus;* so *fictus rerum, Sat.* 2, 8, 83. — **veneat**: the subjv. suggests the real, though unexpressed, motive for the preference.

28. **Cocto . . . idem**: the peacock was cooked with its plumage, but the brilliancy of the feathers would be lost. — **num adest**: monosyllabic hiatus with a word ending in *-m* or a long vowel; cf. *si me amas, Sat.* 1, 9, 38.

29-32. 'You pretend to prefer peacock to fowl, but it is a mere pretence; you could not tell them apart if it were not for the difference in size. Let me try you with two pike of the same size and see if you can distinguish the one caught in the Tiber — which you epicures consider so much better — from one caught in the sea.' — **quamvis**: frequently with the indic. in Horace, *e.g. Sat.* 1, 3, 129. — **hanc illa**: *sc. carnem, carne.* — **imparibus . . . deceptum**: this does not mean that the epicure could not distinguish fowl from peacock, but that he allowed the fact that the peacock was bigger to delude him into thinking that it was also better. It is the same as *corruptus vanis rerum,* vs. 25; *misled by the false standard of size.* — **esto**: *grant that.* — **unde datum sentis**: *whence do you get the power to distinguish;* i.e. 'when there is no difference in size, there is no way in which you can distinguish, as you pretend to do.' Cf. vs. 18 and *unde petitum hoc in me iacis? Sat.* 1, 4, 79. — **hiet**: this should be made subordinate in the translation; 'whether this pike with its mouth open was caught . . .' — **pontis inter**: *between the*

ostia sub Tusci? Laudas, insane, trilibrem
mullum, in singula quem minuas pulmenta necesse est.
35 Ducit te species, video: quo pertinet ergo
proceros odisse lupos? Quia scilicet illis
maiorem natura modum dedit, his breve pondus.
Ieiunus raro stomachus volgaria temnit.
'Porrectum magno magnum spectare catino
40 vellem,' ait Harpyiis gula digna rapacibus. At vos,
praesentes Austri, coquite horum obsonia! Quamquam

bridges, *i.e.* from the shore of the island which was connected by bridges with the two banks. The fish caught in the swift current here (*iactatus*) were thought to have a finer flavor. This passage is reminiscent of Lucilius, 1176 (Marx), *pontes Tiberinus duo inter captus catillo* (*scavenger*, *i.e.* a pike).

33. **insane**: a Stoic form of address; cf. *Sat.* 2, 3, 81, and 326. — **trilibrem**: the mullet was usually a small fish, rarely weighing as much as two pounds, and enormous sums were paid for those of abnormal size.

34. **pulmenta**: *helps, portions.* — **minuas . . . necesse est**: parataxis, as often with *necesse est*. The argument is that there is no real reason for preferring the large mullet, since it must be divided into portions to be served.

35 ff. The sententious brevity of the clauses is in parody of the Stoic manner. — **Quia scilicet**: giving the real reason in an ironical form; 'it is mere fashion without taste which leads you to prefer the rare and unnatural — small pike and large mullets.' The modern parallel to this is serving fruits out of season.

38. **raro**: with *ieiunus*; 'it is because you seldom feel real appetite that you seek for such varieties.'

39. **magno magnum**: a sort of outcry as if from some one who feels himself free from the whims of fashion; 'but I should really like to see a big fish in a big dish.' The answer is, 'your gluttony is no more natural than the caprices of fashion.'

40. **At**: not adversative, but, as frequently in curses, a particle of transition.

41. **praesentes**: *i.e.* 'come yourselves and cook (taint) the food of such people.' — **Austri**: the warm south winds. — **Quamquam**: '*and yet* I need scarcely say this, for those whose appetites are spoiled with an over-abundance of rich viands cannot distinguish fresh food from tainted.'

putet aper rhombusque recens, mala copia quando
aegrum sollicitat stomachum, cum rapula plenus
atque acidas mavolt inulas.   Necdum omnis abacta
45 pauperies epulis regum; nam vilibus ovis
nigrisque est oleis hodie locus.   Haud ita pridem
Galloni praeconis erat acipensere mensa
infamis.   Quid? tum rhombos minus aequor alebat?
Tutus erat rhombus, tutoque ciconia nido,
50 donec vos auctor docuit praetorius.   Ergo
si quis nunc mergos suavis edixerit assos,
parebit pravi docilis Romana iuventus.
　　Sordidus a tenui victu distabit, Ofello
iudice; nam frustra vitium vitaveris illud,

42. **quando**: *since;* the more common use in Horace.
43 f. **sollicitat**: *disturbs, troubles.* — **rapula, inulas**: *radishes and pickles.* The root of the elecampane (*inula*) is no longer used as a food. — **Necdum**: *not even yet; i.e.* 'we still use some simple kinds of food, for it is not so very long ago that these absurd fashions were introduced.'
45. **pauperies**: plain food, the food of a poor man; contrasted with *regum, the rich.*
46–52. 'It is not long since the introduction of the sturgeon made Gallonius notorious. Now a turbot or a stork is the proper thing for a fine dinner. Such fashions have not even the excuse of a love of good food; they are nothing but silly caprices.' — **Galloni**: Publius Gallonius, satirized by Lucilius for having set the fashion of serving a large sturgeon at dinner. — **Quid?** . . . **alebat**: the exclamation of a person to whom the present fashion of having turbot for a fish-course seems like a law of nature. — **auctor . . . praetorius**: his name is variously given by the Scholiasts, who quote an anonymous epigram upon him, alluding to his setting the fashion of eating storks and to his defeat for the praetorship. *Praetorius* would then be ironical. — **mergos**: some sea bird whose flesh was not fit for eating. — **edixerit**: *issue an edict,* as a praetor did; another hit at the *auctor praetorius.* — **pravi docilis**: *quick to learn corruption.*
53 f. 'But Ofellus did not rush to the other extreme; it was simplicity, not stinginess, that he recommended.' The mention of Ofellus is a reminder of vss. 2 f.

55   si te alio pravum detorseris. Avidienus
     cui Canis ex vero ductum cognomen adhaeret,
     quinquennis oleas est et silvestria corna,
     ac nisi mutatum parcit defundere vinum, et
     cuius odorem olei nequeas perferre, licebit
60   ille repotia, natalis, aliosve dierum
     festos albatus celebret, cornu ipse bilibri
     caulibus instillat, veteris non parcus aceti.
     Quali igitur victu sapiens utetur, et horum
     utrum imitabitur ?   Hac urget lupus, hac canis, aiunt.

55. alio: adverb. — pravum: with *te*, but to be rendered freely. — Avidienus: a coined name, probably with a vague suggestion of *ávidus*, in spite of the difference in quantity.

56. Canis: *i.e.* Κύων; a depreciatory reference to the rival sect of the Cynics, in the manner of a Stoic preacher. — ex vero ductum: *deservedly applied*, based on the actual facts of his temper and habits. The phrase occurs elsewhere; Plautus, *Stich.* 242, *nunc Miccotrogus nomine e vero vocor*; Ovid, *Fast.* 2, 859.

57. est: from *edo*. — silvestria corna: *i.e.* such poor food as primitive man used before the cultivation of grain; cf. Verg. *Georg.* 1, 1, 147 ff.

58. mutatum: *turned*, soured.

59. olei: attracted from the acc. after *instillat* into the relative clause. — licebit: paratactically with *celebret*; there are many cases where the pres. *licet* is felt as a verb rather than as a conjunction.

60. repotia: *wedding feasts*, occasions when the best of food would be served.

61. albatus: wearing the white toga of ceremony; he would observe the proprieties where the observance cost nothing. — cornu . . . bilibri: *i.e.* the oil was served in a large vessel of the cheapest material, instead of a *guttus* (*Sat.* 1, 6, 118), and the host poured it with his own hand (*ipse*) drop by drop (*instillat*) that there might be no waste.

62. veteris . . . aceti: the point of this is not quite clear. Old vinegar is better than new; the implication may be that he was generous only with vinegar, which was cheaper than oil, or this may be, as the Scholiast says, a joke of the kind called παρὰ προσδοκίαν, the substitution of *aceti* for an expected *vini*.

64. aiunt: *as the saying is*. The

65 Mundus erit, qua non offendat sordibus, atque
in neutram partem cultus miser. Hic neque servis,
Albuci senis exemplo, dum munia didit,
saevus erit, nec sic ut simplex Naevius unctam
convivis praebebit aquam; vitium hoc quoque magnum.
70 Accipe nunc victus tenuis quae quantaque secum
adferat. In primis valeas bene: nam variae res
ut noceant homini credas, memor illius escae
quae simplex olim tibi sederit; at simul assis
miscueris elixa, simul conchylia turdis,
75 dulcia se in bilem vertent, stomachoque tumultum
lenta feret pituita. Vides ut pallidus omnis
cena desurgat dubia? Quin corpus onustum

verb *aiunt* is often used parenthetically in the quotation of a proverb.

65. Mundus erit, qua: 'the philosopher will be refined in his way of living, but will not carry refinement to such an extreme that it will seem to be mere stinginess.' The meaning of *mundus* (*munditia*) is limited in the same way in *Sat.* 1, 2, 123 and in Cic. *de Off.* 1, 36, 130; cf. also *Carm.* 2, 10, 5 ff.

66. cultus: with *miser, anxious about his way of living.*

67-69. Albucius (not to be connected with the Albucius of *Sat.* 2, 1, 48) is so overanxious to have all the service at dinner perfect that he scolds his servants even when he is assigning their duties; Naevius (a mere name) is so careless that he allows his slaves to be slovenly. — **unctam . . . aquam**: *greasy water* for rinsing the hands after the meal.

— **vitium . . . magnum**: this solemn condemnation of a rather trifling fault (cf. *Sat.* 1, 3, 80 f. and *Sat.* 2, 8) comes with burlesque effect from the lips of an old farmer.

71. valeas: potential, as is *credas* in the next line, with protases implied in the general sense and in *memor, if you recall.*

73. sederit: like the colloquial English 'to set well on the stomach.'

75 f. dulcia, bilem, lenta pituita: phrases of popular physiology, to describe indigestion. *Pituita* is in three syllables.

77. cena . . . dubia: a quotation from Terence, *Phorm.* 342. 'cena dubia adponitur. | quid istuc verbi est? :| ubi tu dubites quid sumas potissumum,' *i.e.* a dinner

hesternis vitiis animum quoque praegravat una,
atque affigit humo divinae particulam aurae.
80 Alter, ubi dicto citius curata sopori
membra dedit, vegetus praescripta ad munia surgit.
Hic tamen ad melius poterit transcurrere quondam,
sive diem festum rediens advexerit annus,
seu recreare volet tenuatum corpus, ubique
85 accedent anni et tractari mollius aetas
imbecilla volet; tibi quidnam accedet ad istam
quam puer et validus praesumis mollitiem, seu
dura valetudo inciderit seu tarda senectus?

so good that you don't know what to take first. — **Quin**: corrective, as often, of the inadequacy of the previous sentence; *nay more*.

78 f. **vitiis**: *excesses* in eating, as in vs. 21. — The conception of the soul as a part of the divine spirit imprisoned within the body is often expressed in Latin literature; it was a fundamental doctrine of Stoic philosophy and is introduced here, in words that are intentionally too elevated for the context and the speaker, to give a burlesque of the Stoic preacher.

80 f. **Alter**: the philosopher, the man of simple habits. — **dicto citius**: a colloquialism, with the exaggeration common in the language of conversation. — **curata membra**: *i.e.* he refreshes himself with supper; cf. *corpora curare, cibo se curare* and the frequent use of *membra* of health or strength, *e.g. Sat.* 1, 1, 5. The whole phrase *curata . . . dedit* goes together, as the order suggests, and *dicto citius* goes with the whole; 'in less time than it takes me to tell it he has had his supper and fallen asleep.'

82-88. 'A man who lives ordinarily on plain fare can indulge himself on occasion, but the man who is always self-indulgent has exhausted his possibilities of pleasure.'

82. **Hic**: referring to *alter*. — **tamen**: in spite of his habitual self-restraint.

83-84. **sive . . . seu . . . ubique**: three reasons for relaxation, a feast-day, illness, old age. To avoid a too elaborate accuracy in expression, a different conjunction, *ubi-que* for *si-ve*, is used to introduce the third clause.

87. **praesumis**: 'take before the time, allow yourself prematurely.'

Rancidum aprum antiqui laudabant, non quia nasus
90 illis nullus erat, sed, credo, hac mente, quod hospes
tardius adveniens vitiatum commodius quam
integrum edax dominus consumeret. Hos utinam inter
heroas natum tellus me prima tulisset!
Das aliquid famae, quae carmine gratior aurem
95 occupat humanam? Grandes rhombi patinaeque
grande ferunt una cum damno dedecus; adde
iratum patruum, vicinos, te tibi iniquum
et frustra mortis cupidum, cum derit egenti
as, laquei pretium. 'Iure,' inquit, 'Trausius istis

89-93. 'The economical farmer will always have a reserve of food — even though it may not be of the freshest — for a chance guest.'

89 f. Rancidum ... laudabant: intentionally put in a paradoxical form in order to burlesque the seriousness of the speaker. — **non quia ... sed quod:** there is no difference between *quia* and *quod* in this form of sentence, but the subjv. is used in the second clause because it gives the motive of the *antiqui*.

91 f. vitiatum: = *rancidum.* — **integrum:** with double meaning, 'the whole of it while it was still fresh.' — **commodius:** *i.e.* they thought it more suitable, they praised such conduct more.

93. The wish is, of course, comic, though the Stoic is represented as uttering it in all seriousness. Cf. *vitium ... magnum,* vs. 69.

94-99. 'A display of luxury brings notoriety and, in the end, ruin.' — **Das aliquid:** *i.e.* 'Do you consider that a good name is of some account?' — **patruum:** the uncle is in Latin literature a type of severity, so that *patruus* in *Sat.* 2, 3, 88, *ne sis patruus mihi,* becomes almost equal to *iniquus.* — **iniquum:** *hateful.* — **derit:** = *de-erit.* — **laquei pretium:** a standing comic situation (*e.g.* Plaut. *Pseud.* 88 f.), in which a bankrupt tries to borrow a penny to buy rope enough to hang himself.

99-111. 'You may think that your income is sufficient for any expenses, but — if you do not care to bestow any of it upon others — all men suffer losses and your course of life is a poor preparation for meeting misfortune.'

99. Trausius: unknown; a mere name to represent a man who lives beyond his income. For the form of argument, which is a favorite one with Horace, cf. *Sat.* 1, 4, 52;

100 iurgatur verbis; ego vectigalia magna
divitiasque habeo tribus amplas regibus.' Ergo
quod superat non est melius quo insumere possis?
Cur eget indignus quisquam te divite? Quare
templa ruunt antiqua deum? Cur, improbe, carae
105 non aliquid patriae tanto emetiris acervo?
Vni nimirum recte tibi semper erunt res,
o magnus posthac inimicis risus! Vterne
ad casus dubios fidet sibi certius, hic qui
pluribus adsuerit mentem corpusque superbum,
110 an qui contentus parvo metuensque futuri
in pace, ut sapiens, aptarit idonea bello?
Quo magis his credas, puer hunc ego parvus Ofellum

1, 10, 5; 1, 10, 21–23. It consists in the mere mention of a name which suggests circumstances that refute the previous statement.

102. quod superat: *your surplus.* — **non ... possis**: construe *non est quo melius*, etc.

103–105. Exhortations to charity or to the giving of money to public objects are less common in classic literature than in modern times (cf., however, *Carm.* 2, 15, 18 ff.; 3, 6, 2 ff.; Cic. *de Off.* 3, 15, 63), but such donations to individuals and to communities were not uncommon. Cf., e.g., *Sat.* 1, 9, 18 note; and Pliny's endowment of a library (*Epist.* 1, 8, 2) and of a school (4, 13, 5).

106. Vni: with emphatic irony; 'Do you expect to be the only exception to the general law of change in human fortunes?'

107. Vterne: the interrogative *-ne* is occasionally appended even to interrogative pronouns; so 2, 3, 295, 317.

109. pluribus: 'to superfluities, to a variety of luxuries.' — **superbum**: with predicate force; 'and thereby have made them his masters.'

111. This is a reference to a proverbial saying, 'in time of peace prepare for war,' which appears in Latin in various forms (*si vis pacem, para bellum*) and, like other proverbs, is still accepted by the unsophisticated as the essence of wisdom.

112–115. At this point Horace assumes, more distinctly than in vss. 2 f. and 53, the person of the narrator, adding to the effectiveness of the closing argument (*quo magis his credas*) by personal reminiscence (*puer ego parvus*) and specific details (*nunc accisis, metato, mercede*). The skill of the

integris opibus novi non latius usum
quam nunc accisis. Videas metato in agello
115 cum pecore et gnatis fortem mercede colonum,
'Non ego,' narrantem, 'temere edi luce profesta
quicquam praeter olus fumosae cum pede pernae.
Ac mihi seu longum post tempus venerat hospes,
sive operum vacuo gratus conviva per imbrem
120 vicinus, bene erat non piscibus urbe petitis,
sed pullo atque haedo; tum pensilis uva secundas
et nux ornabat mensas cum duplice ficu.
Post hoc ludus erat culpa potare magistra,
ac venerata Ceres, ita culmo surgeret alto,

artifice is so great that many commentators have taken it for reality, but cf. *Sat.* 2, 6, 11 f. for a similar, though less detailed, reference. — **latius**: so Juv. 14, 234, *indulgent sibi latius*; *angustus* is frequently used of the opposite. — **metato**: *i.e.* measured by the land-commissioners appointed to survey and apportion confiscated land; as in ordinary circumstances farms were marked by boundary stones and not surveyed, the verb *metari* came to be used especially of the surveys preliminary to confiscation and allotment. — **mercede**: *i.e.* the new proprietor hired the former owner to carry on the farm.

116. **Non...temere**: *not without reason*, only when there was some special reason; the ordinary sense of *non* (*haud*) *temere*.

118 ff. 'Even on the rare occasions our food was still simple.' — **hospes**: a guest from a distance, who came infrequently (*longum post tempus*). — **vicinus**: the celebrating of a neighbor's visit is excused by the additional circumstances, *operum vacuo, per imbrem.* — **pensilis uva**: *raisins.* — **duplice ficu**: split for drying. The point is that only the products of the farm were used, even for special occasions; cf. *dapes inemptas, Epod.* 2, 48.

123. **Post hoc**: the wine was served according to the country custom after the dessert (*secundae mensae*), and was drunk without the formal etiquette of elaborate dinners (cf. *Sat.* 2, 6, 67 ff.); instead of selecting a *magister bibendi* to regulate their drinking, they were governed only by their own sense of propriety (*culpa*).

124. **ita...surgeret**: the indirect form of the prayer *ita Ceres surgat* or *ita tu surgas*, often followed by a statement of some evi-

125 explicuit vino contractae seria frontis.
Saeviat atque novos moveat Fortuna tumultus,
quantum hinc imminuet? Quanto aut ego parcius aut
    vos,
o pueri, nituistis, ut huc novus incola venit?
Nam propriae telluris erum natura neque illum
130 nec me nec quemquam statuit: nos expulit ille,
illum aut nequities aut vafri inscitia iuris,
postremum expellet certe vivacior heres.
Nunc ager Vmbreni sub nomine, nuper Ofelli
dictus, erit nulli proprius, sed cedet in usum
135 nunc mihi, nunc alii. Quocirca vivite fortes,
fortiaque adversis opponite pectora rebus.'

dent truth in an *ut*-clause. Cf. *Sat.* 2, 3, 300; *Carm.* 1, 3, 1 ff. 'And the wine that we drank as we prayed to Ceres, "so may you rise on the high stalk," smoothed the wrinkles from our brows.'

126. **tumultus**: like the dissensions that preceded Philippi and resulted in the confiscation of the farm of Vergil's father.

128. **pueri**: his sons, gathered about him as he watches the herds (vs. 115). — **novus incola**: Umbrenus, the veteran to whom the farm had been allotted.

129. **propriae**: predicate; *to hold it as his own.*

131. **nequities, inscitia iuris**: there is abundant evidence that the veterans who were suddenly changed from soldiers to farmers often made but poor use of their property, managing it badly, falling into debt, and suffering, perhaps unfairly, from their ignorance of civil life.

132. **postremum**: acc. masc. with *illum*; but translate, *at last.*

134. **proprius**: contrasted with *cedet in usum*; we merely use our possessions, we do not really own them.

135 f. These lines return to the thought of vss. 107-111, as if to prove by an example the general statement made there.

3

The allusion in vs. 185, *plausus quos fert Agrippa*, shows that the satire was written as late as the year 33 B.C., when Agrippa, as aedile, gave the games with unusual splendor. The reference to the Saturnalia (vs. 5) fixes the time of year when the dialogue is supposed to take place, but indicates nothing in regard to the time when it was composed.

In structure this is the most carefully arranged of all the satires. The main body is a sermon by the philosopher Stertinius (alluded to in *Epist.* 1. 12, 20, but otherwise unknown to us) upon the Stoic Paradox πᾶς ἄφρων μαίνεται, that all men except the Stoic philosopher are mad. The discourse is carefully divided into four parts, taking up in turn the avaricious (82-157), the ambitious (158-223), the self-indulgent (224-246, with a special subdivision, 247-280, for the amorous), and the superstitious (281-295). There is a brief introduction (77-81) and a corresponding conclusion (296-299). This discourse is repeated to Horace by Damasippus, a recent convert to Stoicism, whose character and circumstances are admirably adapted to his part. He had been a collector of antique bronzes and a dealer in real estate and is alluded to by Cicero (*ad Fam.* 7, 23, 2; *ad Att.* 12, 29, 2; 12, 33, 1) in connection with the purchase of statuary and of land for gardens. But he had afterward failed in business and in his despair was about to throw himself into the Tiber, when he was saved by the intervention of Stertinius. The logical reasoning by which Stertinius convinced him that his motive for suicide was insufficient is an excellent bit of philosophical fooling and serves as an introduction to the main sermon.

The circumstances which brought Damasippus into contact with Horace are disclosed in a brief introductory dialogue (1-31). Horace represents himself as having gone out to his quiet Sabine farm at the time of the Saturnalia to escape the Christmas festivities and to do some work. But the work had been postponed and he was sitting in his study dozing after a good dinner (*vini somnique benignus*), when Damasippus burst in upon him, uninvited, having come out from the city full of zeal to rouse him from his laziness. To his exhortations Horace replies with good-natured irony in a rather superior tone and finally submits to a recital of the long sermon. When it is over (300-326), he rouses himself to make further ironical remarks, to which Damasippus replies with such point that Horace for a moment loses his temper and then surrenders, acknowledging himself to be as great a madman — almost — as his visitor. The opening and the closing bits of dialogue thus form a framework for the main body of the satire.

To the carefulness in construction an equal care in expression has been added. There are few passages where the thought is not clearly expressed and there are many of special excellence, like the farcical scene from the camp before Troy (187-207), a forerunner of *Sat.* 2. 5, or the brilliant paraphrase of the first lines of the *Eunuchus* (262-271).

The synonyms for *insanus* collected by Teuffel (*furiosus, excors, delirus, amens, amentia versatus, demens, cerritus, commotus, commotae mentis, mentem concussus, male tutae mentis, putidi cerebri*) are evidence of the pains taken to avoid monotony.

As to the underlying motive of the satire, it seems probable that the accusations of idleness in the opening lines were not without foundation. After the publication of the First Book there was probably a period in which Horace was disinclined to go on with precisely the same kind of writing and was perhaps turning toward lyric poetry. During this time of hesitation he may well have seemed to be occupied with his farm (307 f.) and to have abandoned his literary ambitions. To the doubts of his friends and the criticisms of his enemies this long and carefully constructed satire was intended to be a reply. At the same time it is, even more distinctly than *Sat.* 2, 2, an attempt to touch the follies of mankind with a lighter touch. The burlesque of Stoic formalism and solemnity runs through the whole and is in many places worked out in detail, so that the satire might well be taken to be a satire upon that sect. On the other hand, however, the absurdities and follies which are the subject-matter are equally the objects of attack, but they are made ridiculous by exaggeration rather than reproved. If the first part of the sermon of Stertinius (vss. 82-157) be compared with *Sat.* 1, 1, which deals with the same subject, the difference in manner will be apparent. There is in this satire none of the direct argument which gives a serious tone to *Sat.* 1, 1; the sermon of Stertinius is a series of absurd illustrations, — Staberius, Aristippus, the senseless miser, Orestes, Opimius, — which ridicule avarice by presenting it in its extremest forms. In short, the genial raillery of Horace is here directed by turns upon the preacher, upon the congregation, and upon the satirist himself.

Damasippus. Sic raro scribis, ut toto non quater anno
membranam poscas, scriptorum quaeque retexens,
iratus tibi, quod, vini somnique benignus,
nil dignum sermone canas. Quid fiet? At ipsis

1. **scribis**: the final long syllable before the caesura occurs in a few other places; *e.g. Sat.* 1, 4, 82.

2. **membranam**: the parchment upon which the rough draft was written out; writing upon this material could be erased and corrections made. — **retexens**: *unraveling*, with a change in the figure to weaving. — **scriptorum**: neut., partitive gen.

4. **dignum sermone**: *worth talk-*

5   Saturnalibus huc fugisti. Sobrius ergo
dic aliquid dignum promissis! Incipe! Nil est.
Culpantur frustra calami, immeritusque laborat
iratis natus paries dis atque poetis.
Atqui voltus erat multa et praeclara minantis,
10 si vacuum tepido cepisset villula tecto.
Quorsum pertinuit stipare Platona Menandro,
Eupolin, Archilochum, comites educere tantos?
Invidiam placare paras virtue relicta?
Contemnere, miser! Vitanda est improba Siren
15 desidia, aut quicquid vita meliore parasti

ing about; likely to increase your reputation. — **Quid fiet**: *what is to be the outcome?*

5. Saturnalibus: this feast began on Dec. 17 and was prolonged for several days. It was a time of feasting, of the giving of presents, and of special freedom for slaves. — **huc**: to his farm. — **Sobrius ergo**: 'well then, since you have chosen to keep out of the festivities.'

6-8. To the absurd exhortation to sit down at once and begin a poem Horace of course makes no response and Damasippus hastens to forestall his excuses: 'There is no use in blaming the pens or in pounding the wall, which doesn't deserve to bear the responsibility.' — **iratis natus dis**: *i.e.* under unfortunate auspices; cf. *Sat.* 1, 5, 97 f., *Gnatia lymphis iratis exstructa*.

9 f. 'And yet just recall your determination to do some work if you could only escape to the quiet of your farm.'

11 f. The Greek writers here named are poets; Eupolis, Plato, and Menander as representatives respectively of the Old, the Middle, and the New Comedy, and Archilochus as a writer of iambics like the Epodes. The selection of these writers is meant to indicate that Horace was turning from satire, in the traditional Roman form, toward satirical iambics. — **stipare**: of packing closely in his traveling-bags.

13. 'Are you preparing to pacify your enemies by abandoning satire?' To the Stoic reformer the earnest satirist seemed a kindred spirit and his attacks upon the follies of men seemed a *virtus*, almost as good as a Stoic sermon.

15 f. quicquid ... parasti: not exactly his fame as a poet, for which the Stoic cared nothing, but his standing as a hortatory

ponendum aequo animo. *Hor.* Di te, Damasippe, deaeque
verum ob consilium donent — tonsore. Sed unde tam bene me nosti? *Dam.* Postquam omnis res mea Ianum
ad medium fracta est, aliena negotia curo,
20 excussus propriis. Olim nam quaerere amabam,
quo vafer ille pedes lavisset Sisyphus aere,
quid sculptum infabre, quid fusum durius esset;

reformer, which he would lose if he turned aside to the mere prettinesses of lyric poetry. — **aequo animo**: *i.e.* 'with such composure as you can muster.'

16 f. Di ... deaeque ... donent: a solemn formula in wishes and curses, though *dent* or *duint* is the more common verb. — **tonsore**: *i.e.* with that which the philosopher, with his long beard, seemed to need most. The reply is, of course, an expression of lazy irony, in the utmost possible contrast to the intense earnestness of Damasippus.

17 f. unde ... nosti: with the implication, under the form of a polite question, that Damasippus was entirely mistaken.

18-20. Ianum ad medium: the same words are used by Cicero (*de Off.* 2, 24, 87) of a part of the Forum given up to the banking business, near the middle one of three arches. Such arches were frequently consecrated to Janus as the god of openings (cf. *ianua*). The expression would then be like the phrase 'in Wall Street.' — **aliena negotia curo**: a hit at the reforming philosophers, who were thought of as busybodies in other men's matters. The phrase must be supposed to be used by the Stoic without consciousness of its double meaning, though Horace in some other places (cf. vss. 28-30 and note) puts into the mouth of Damasippus words that he would hardly have used. — **excussus**: the figure is that of a man knocked overboard from a shipwrecked vessel, a figure already suggested by *fracta*. — **quaerere**: *to investigate*, as a skilled expert in antiquities.

21. Cf. *Sat.* 1, 3, 90 f. Both passages touch with humorous exaggeration the inclination of collectors to claim a fabulous antiquity for their artistic treasures. Sisyphus was king of Corinth, the center of artistic work in bronze.

22. sculptum infabre, fusum durius: the unskilful carving and hard (*i.e.* stiff and formal) casting, though they were defects in

callidus huic signo ponebam milia centum;
hortos egregiasque domos mercarier unus
25 cum lucro noram; unde frequentia Mercuriale
imposuere mihi cognomen compita. *Hor.* Novi,
et miror morbi purgatum te illius. *Dam.* Atqui
emovit veterem mire novus, ut solet, in cor
traiecto lateris miseri capitisve dolere,
30 ut lethargicus hic cum fit pugil et medicum urget.

23. huic signo: *such a statue.* —**milia centum**: *i.e.* the large price which its age would command in the market.

24–26. unus cum lucro: in spite of his bankruptcy and his adoption of the life of a philosopher, Damasippus cannot refrain from speaking with pride of his earlier successes in business. — **frequentia ... compita**: the crowds that gathered at the street-corners, where statuary and bronzes were sold at auction. — **Mercuriale ... cognomen**: *favorite of Mercury*, the god of trade (*merx*). But *Mercuriales viri* (*Carm.* 2, 17, 29 f.) means the favorites of Mercury as the god of speech.

27. morbi: Horace jokingly uses the technical term *morbus*, a translation of πάθος, which was used to describe any form of passion or any departure from calm philosophic reason.

28–30. mire: this repeats *miror* in a kind of unintentional pun. Horace had used *miror* with irony — 'a surprising cure'; Damasippus in his well-meaning eagerness overlooks the irony and uses *mire* in the better sense: 'Oh, but the wonderful thing is not the cure; it is this new interest, which effected the cure, that is so wonderful.' But it is scarcely possible to explain in the same way, as due to the blundering eagerness of Damasippus, the comparison of Stoicism to a *morbus*, even to a kind of frenzy. Though Horace has not actually put the word into the mouth of Damasippus, the expression is still quite clearly inconsistent with his character, and we must say that Horace has here, as perhaps in vss. 19 and 33, failed to make the speech quite consistent with the character of the speaker. — The illustration in vs. 30 — 'as some man (*hic*) in a lethargy suddenly turns boxer and assaults his doctor' — is chosen in order to give an opening for the remark in vs. 31 and to lead up to the subject of madness.

Hor. Dum ne quid simile huic, esto ut libet. *Dam.*
O bone, ne te
frustrere; insanis et tu stultique prope omnes,
si quid Stertinius veri crepat, unde ego mira
descripsi docilis praecepta haec, tempore quo me
35 solatus iussit sapientem pascere barbam
atque a Fabricio non tristem ponte reverti.
Nam, male re gesta, cum vellem mittere operto
me capite in flumen, dexter stetit et 'Cave faxis
te quicquam indignum! Pudor' inquit 'te malus angit,
40 insanos qui inter vereare insanus haberi.

31. **huic**: neut., referring to *fit pugil et urget*. 'I bar such conduct as that; otherwise, have it your own way.' The implication of course is that Damasippus is liable to an attack of frenzy.

32. **ne te frustrere**: *don't make a mistake*; the common phrase is *ne sis frustra*. — **insanis . . . omnes**: this is the Stoic Paradox which forms the text of the sermon.

33. **crepat**: *prates*. The word is contemptuous, and inconsistent with 296, *sapientium octavus*, as with the general attitude of Damasippus. It is another slip on Horace's part, like 19 and 28. — **unde**: *a quo*.

35. **sapientem pascere barbam**: put first, as if this external sign were more important than the thing signified. Cf. *Sat.* 1, 3, 133.

36. The *pons Fabricius* is still standing, with an inscription recording the fact that it was rebuilt by L. Fabricius, in the year 62 B.C. — **non tristem**: not as he had come, but reconciled to life.

37 f. **operto capite**: one who devoted himself to the gods of the lower world covered his face; so Decius, giving up his life to win victory, covered his head, and (Livy, 4, 12, 11) *multi . . . capitibus obvolutis se in Tiberim praecipitaverunt.* — **dexter**: the side of good omen. — **faxis**: an old form (an optative of the sigmatic aorist) preserved in this colloquial combination with *cave*; 'don't do anything unworthy.' Horace uses a great variety of forms of prohibition.

39. **Pudor . . . malus**: not exactly what we call *false shame*, but a sense of humiliation which is really based upon a mistake *Malus* is the emphatic word.

Primum nam inquiram quid sit furere : hoc si erit in te
solo, nil verbi pereas quin fortiter addam.
Quem mala stultitia et quemcumque inscitia veri
caecum agit, insanum Chrysippi porticus et grex
45   autumat.   Haec populos, haec magnos formula reges,
excepto sapiente, tenet.   Nunc accipe quare
desipiant omnes aeque ac tu, qui tibi nomen
insano posuere.   Velut silvis, ubi passim
palantis error certo de tramite pellit,
50   ille sinistrorsum, hic dextrorsum abit, unus utrique

41 ff. These lines illustrate the double humor of the whole satire; they analyze the universal folly of men and at the same time they exhibit the folly of the Stoic himself, who addresses an elaborate argument to a man about to commit suicide and, in particular, an argument which does not prove the hearer sane, but only no more insane than his fellow-men.

41. Primum: in proper Stoic style, the argument begins with a definition. — **furere**: a synonym for *insanum esse*.

42. fortiter: Stoic teaching did not forbid suicide and Stertinius treats the question as one of pure logic.

43 f. Quem: add *-cumque* from the following *quemcumque.* — **stultitia, inscitia**: these are not two distinct qualities, but *stultitia* is the general term of which *inscitia veri* is a particular definition, still further defined by *caecum agit:* 'madness consists in being moved by blind and ignorant impulse, instead of being guided by wisdom' (the opposite of *stultitia*). — **Chrysippi**: Zeno was the founder of the school, which took its name from the στοά, the Porch, where he taught. Chrysippus was the greatest of Zeno's successors and was often spoken of as the head of the school. — **grex**: not infrequently used, as here, of a *sect* of philosophy, usually with a slighting tone. It is hardly a word which a Stoic would have used of his school. Cf. 19, 28, 33 and notes.

45 f. formula: the definition just given. — **tenet**: *covers, includes*. — **Nunc**: introducing the argument based on the definition and corresponding somewhat loosely to *primum*, 41.

50 f. unus, variis: *i.e.* the fundamental error is the same, *inscitia veri caecum agit*, though the particular manifestations are different

error, sed variis illudit partibus : hoc te
crede modo insanum, nihilo ut sapientior ille,
qui te deridet, caudam trahat. Est genus unum
stultitiae nihilum metuenda timentis, ut ignis,
55 ut rupis fluviosque in campo obstare queratur ;
alterum et huic varum et nihilo sapientius ignis
per medios fluviosque ruentis : clamet amica
mater, honesta soror cum cognatis, pater, uxor,
'Hic fossa est ingens, hic rupes maxima, serva!'
60 non magis audierit quam Fufius ebrius olim,
cum Ilionam edormit, Catienis mille ducentis

51 f. **hoc . . . modo**: referring back to *velut* and also forward to *ut*; 'just as in the woods men stray from the path in one direction or another, — it makes no difference which side, — so you must understand your own madness, realizing that it is no greater than that of others.'

53. **caudam trahat**: the explanation of the Scholiast is 'solent enim pueri deridentes nescientibus a tergo caudam suspendere, ut velut pecus caudam trahant.' The conservatism of boys still preserves this form of humor.

54. **nihilum**: with *metuenda*, as a mere negative. Kiessling refers to the statement of this thought in Xenophon. *Mem.* 1, 1, 14. — **timentis**: agreeing with *stultitiae*, but the concrete *stultus* is so plainly implied that no subject is expressed for *queratur* and in the next sentence the abstract is forgotten and *ruentis* is masc., as if agreeing with *stulti*.

55. **in campo**: *i.e.* on perfectly clear and level ground, where there are no fires or cliffs or rivers.

56. **huic varum**: *different from this; varus* seems to be very rare in this sense and perhaps has some humorous effect.

57. **amica**: with *mater* ('the mother who loves him'), to balance *honesta* ('whom he respects') with *soror*.

59. **fossa, rupes**: substituted for *ignis, fluvios*, merely for variety.

60–62. **audierit**: apodosis to the protasis expressed without *si* in *clamet*. — **Fufius, Ilionam, Catienis**: in the play of Pacuvius there was a scene in which the mother, Iliona, is roused from sleep by the spirit of her murdered son, who addresses her with the words *mater, te adpello, tu, quae curam somno suspensam levas;*

'Mater, te appello' clamantibus. Huic ego volgus
errori similem cunctum insanire docebo.
Insanit veteres statuas Damasippus emendo:
65 integer est mentis Damasippi creditor? Esto.
'Accipe quod numquam reddas mihi' si tibi dicam,
tune insanus eris si acceperis? an magis excors

the mother should reply *age, adsta, mane, audi.* But, on one occasion, an actor named Fufius, who was playing the part of Iliona, had been drinking (*ebrius*) and actually fell asleep, so that the appeal of the son (played by Catienus) did not waken him, and the audience, seeing the situation, joined in repeating the first words *mater, te appello.* — **Ilionam edormit**: a cognate acc., like *Cyclopa saltare* (*Sat.* 1, 5, 63), but with a humorous effect; *was sleeping the part of Iliona.* — **mille ducentis**: twice the usual round number, *sescenti.*

62 f. Huic . . . errori: refers back to 49 and 51; the *error* is *inscitia veri* (43), the failure to see things as they really are. — **similem**: sc. *errorem*, which would be a cognate acc. after *insanire.*

65. integer mentis: = *sanus.* — **esto**: *i.e.* 'grant it for the moment and then see what absurdities it leads to.' The argument is that if Damasippus had proved himself a madman, as his creditors declared, by losing money in speculation, then the creditors had still more proved themselves madmen by loaning him the money that he had lost. The *error* was the same, though the manifestations of it were different.

67 f. excors: = *insanus.* — **praesens Mercurius**: a creditor who offered money with the full understanding that it was never to be repaid would be to the debtor like the very god of riches in person.

67–71. These words are addressed to the lender of the money and the general sense is plain: 'take all the precautions you can, ten notes or, if ten are not enough, a hundred, a thousand; yet you must certainly know that your debtor can slip through them all, as Proteus slips through all bonds.' Nerius is the banker who pays over the money on an order from the créditor. With *decem* some general word like *scripta* was in Horace's mind, but the sentence is interrupted by the hasty words *non est satis* and when the thought is resumed, *tabulas* takes the place of the object; ten copies of the entry or order are not enough. Cicuta is a money-lender (referred to only here and in vs. 175) who is especially skilful in drawing up

reiecta praeda, quam praesens Mercurius fert?
Scribe decem a Nerio; non est satis : adde Cicutae
70 nodosi tabulas centum, mille adde catenas:
effugiet tamen haec sceleratus vincula Proteus.
Cum rapies in ius malis ridentem alienis,
fiet aper, modo avis, modo saxum, et, cum volet, arbor.
Si male rem gerere insani est, contra bene sani,
75 putidius multo cerebrum est, mihi crede, Perelli
dictantis quod tu numquam rescribere possis.
Audire atque togam iubeo componere, quisquis
ambitione mala aut argenti pallet amore,

legally binding forms of obligation; *nodosi* and *catenas* express the same figure. The creditor is not named here, though, as the thought becomes more definite (cf. *Sat.* 1, 1, 15, and 20), he is called Perellius. Proteus is the sea-god who prophesies only when he is caught and held and who changes himself into many forms (vs. 73) to escape his captor. [The difficulty of this passage centers in *scribe decem a Nerio*, and it is the desire to make the sense of the whole passage square with our really insufficient knowledge of the technical terms and the method of procedure that has led Bentley and Kiessling into forced interpretations.]

72. **malis ridentem alienis**: a parody of the Homeric οἱ δ' ἤδη γναθμοῖσι γελώων ἀλλοτρίοισιν (*Od.* 20. 347). But the phrase, which is perhaps proverbial, occurs only once in Homer, and the situation there is highly tragic and dramatic; the suitors laughed because Athene had taken away their judgment, but woe was in their hearts. Some such sense as *unnatural, hysterical laughter* would perhaps fit both passages, but it is possible that Horace merely translated the phrase literally, without attaching a definite meaning to it.

75 f. **putidius**: another synonym for *insanius*. — **dictantis**: *i.e.* attending carefully to the exact wording of the document. — **rescribere**: *repay* by another written document; cf. *scribe*, vs. 69.

77–81. The introduction to the formal sermon. Both in the elaborate manner and in the matter it is a parody of Stoic teaching. It is addressed to other hearers than Damasippus, but it is not necessary to suppose that Horace meant to represent Stertinius as still standing on the *pons Fabri-*

quisquis luxuria tristive superstitione
80 aut alio mentis morbo calet; huc propius me,
dum doceo insanire omnis vos ordine, adite.
   Danda est ellebori multo pars maxima avaris;
nescio an Anticyram ratio illis destinet omnem.
Heredes Staberi summam incidere sepulchro,
85 ni sic fecissent, gladiatorum dare centum
damnati populo paria atque epulum arbitrio Arri,

cius; rather, this is some discourse noted down at a later time by the new convert. — **togam componere**: to intimate that the sermon was to be a long one. — **ambitione**: this is taken up second in the discourse, though here named first. — **pallet**: pale with the chill of fear, while *calet* refers to the fever of passion. — **omnis vos ordine**: *all from first to last*; this use of *ordine* with *omnis* is colloquial and common in Plautus; *Amph.* 599, *Capt.* 377, *Most.* 552, etc. [*M. G.* 875, which is sometimes referred to as evidence that *ordine* goes with *doceo*, has been misunderstood; it is like the other Plautine passages.]

82 f. **ellebori**: *hellebore* was the recognized medicine for cases of insanity. It grew especially about Anticyra, in Phocis. — **nescio an**: with an implication of the affirmative, *I don't know but*. — **ratio**: *reason*, i.e. philosophy, as in *Sat.* 1. 3. 78. 115; here with special thought of philosophy as a cure of souls.

84. **Staberi**: unknown. He need not have been a real person, but one such inscription is extant and the rich man in Petronius (71) expresses his desire to have the amount of his fortune put on his tombstone.

85 f. **fecissent**: in indirect quotation from the will. — **damnati**: the technical word to express the penalty for failure to carry out the provisions of a will; the formula was *heres meus dare damnas* (= *damnatus*) *esto*. — **centum**: one hundred pairs of gladiators would be a very large number. — **arbitrio Arri**: a public feast that would be extravagant enough to suit even Q. Arrius, who had himself given a notoriously extravagant funeral feast. — **frumenti**: a third penalty, a distribution of grain, as much as would be produced in a season from Egypt, the grain-producing center for Italy. The three penalties are made excessive in order to express the anxiety of Staberius that the requirement of his will should not be neglected.

frumenti quantum metit Africa. 'Sive ego prave
seu recte hoc volui, ne sis patruus mihi;' credo
hoc Staberi prudentem animum vidisse. Quid ergo
90 sensit, cum summam patrimoni insculpere saxo
heredes voluit? Quoad vixit, credidit ingens
pauperiem vitium et cavit nihil acrius, ut, si
forte minus locuples uno quadrante perisset,
ipse videretur sibi nequior; omnis enim res,
95 virtus, fama, decus, divina humanaque pulchris
divitiis parent; quas qui construxerit, ille
clarus erit, fortis, iustus. Sapiensne? Etiam, et rex,
et quicquid volet. Hoc, veluti virtute paratum,
speravit magnae laudi fore. Quid simile isti

87 f. Sive ego: a direct quotation from the will. — **ne sis patruus**: *don't refuse me*; cf. *Sat.* 2, 2, 77 note.

89 f. hoc: the hesitation of his heirs and their probable desire to avoid a requirement which they might think foolish; *sive prave, seu recte*. — **vidisse**: gets from *prudentem* the sense of *providisse; foresaw in his wisdom*. — **Quid ergo sensit**: *well, then, what was his idea?*

92. ut: a clause of result, without antecedent, as in *Sat.* 1, 1, 96.

94. nequior: *i.e.* just so much the worse man; he measured himself by his success in business.

95 f. pulchris divitiis: cf. *Sat.* 1, 1, 44. *quid habet pulchri constructus acervus.*

97. Sapiensne: this question is interjected by the speaker to forestall the thought of a hearer: 'ah, but will he be a Stoic philosopher?' and the question is answered in the affirmative as the strongest possible expression of the value that men put upon money. The best commentary on the curt questions and answers here and below, 158 ff., 187 ff., is the remark of Cicero (*Parad.* 1, 2). 'Cato . . ., perfectus mea sententia Stoicus, . . . minutis interrogatiunculis, quasi punctis, quod proposuit efficit.' — On the Stoic Paradox here alluded to cf. *Sat.* 1, 3, 124 and note. — **Etiam**: *yes*; often in colloquial Latin.

99. Quid simile isti: *i.e.* 'what is the likeness (or difference) between Staberius and Aristippus?' The question is repeated in more definite form in vs. 102, *uter . . . insanior?*

100 Graecus Aristippus? qui servos proicere aurum
in media iussit Libya, quia tardius irent
propter onus segnes.   Vter est insanior horum?
Nil agit exemplum, litem quod lite resolvit.
Si quis emat citharas, emptas comportet in unum,
105 nec studio citharae nec musae deditus ulli,
si scalpra et formas non sutor, nautica vela
aversus mercaturis, delirus et amens
undique dicatur merito.   Qui discrepat istis
qui nummos aurumque recondit, nescius uti
110 compositis, metuensque velut contingere sacrum?
Si quis ad ingentem frumenti semper acervum

100. **Aristippus**: of the town of Cyrene, the founder of the Cyrenaic (or Hedonic) school of philosophy, whose fundamental doctrine is stated by Horace, *Epist.* 1, 1, 19, *et mihi res, non me rebus, subiungere conor*, 'things were made for man, not man for things.'

103. 'There is no force in an illustration which proposes to answer one question by asking another.' The introduction of Aristippus serves the same purpose in the argument as the mention of Naevius and Nomentanus in *Sat.* 1, 1, 101 f., and the reply there, *pergis pugnantia secum . . . componere*, means essentially the same thing as this line.

104. **emptas comportet in unum**: 'and, as soon as he has bought them, piles them up together,' as a miser stores his money. Cf. Livy, 1, 5, 3, *latrones . . . Remum cepisse, captum regi Aemulio tradidisse.*

105. **musae . . . ulli**: *to any kind of music.*

106. **non sutor**: *though he was not a shoemaker.*

107. **aversus mercaturis**: merely a variation in phrase for *non nauta*. The *mercator* was a trader by sea (*Sat.* 1, 1, 6).

108. **undique**: *on all sides, i.e.* by everybody. — **Qui discrepat istis**: exactly the same in effect as *quid simile isti* (99).

109 f. **nummos aurumque**: since the coined money was chiefly silver, this double phrase is like 'silver and gold,' a double expression for a single idea. — **nescius uti**: like *nescis quo valeat nummus* (*Sat.* 1, 1, 73), as *metuens . . . sacrum* repeats *tamquam parcere sacris* (*Sat.* 1, 1, 71).

111 ff. The thought of this passage — that mere accumulation

porrectus vigilet cum longo fuste, neque illinc
audeat esuriens dominus contingere granum,
ac potius foliis parcus vescatur amaris ;
115 si positis intus Chii veterisque Falerni
mille cadis — nihil est, tercentum milibus — acre
potet acetum ; age, si et stramentis incubet, unde-
octoginta annos natus, cui stragula vestis,
blattarum ac tinearum epulae, putrescat in arca :
120 nimirum insanus paucis videatur, eo quod
maxima pars hominum morbo iactatur eodem.
Filius aut etiam haec libertus ut ebibat heres,
dis inimice senex, custodis ? Ne tibi desit ?
Quantulum enim summae curtabit quisque dierum,

is folly — is much like parts of *Sat.* 1, 1. In order to maintain the Stoic tone, the details are carried out to the point of extravagance (114, 116, 125), but the underlying idea is so distinctly Horace's own that the fiction of the Stoic preacher is almost forgotten.

112. **porrectus vigilet**: cf. *indormis inhians*, *Sat.* 1, 1, 71.

117 f. **acetum**: cf. *veteris non parcus aceti*, *Sat.* 2, 2, 62. — **age**: as if a new and still more striking illustration had suddenly occurred to him. — **unde-octoginta**: a little more emphatic than the round number would be: 'just short of eighty,' 'all but eighty years old.'

120. **paucis**: used unexpectedly instead of *multis* or *omnibus*, to preserve the Stoic doctrine that only the *sapiens* is sane.

121. **iactatur**: of the tossing about of a fever-stricken man.

122. **libertus**: the wretched condition of the old miser is increased by the suggestion (more fully expressed in *Sat.* 1, 1, 80 ff.) that he has alienated his natural heirs. — **ebibat**: with special reference to the preceding illustration, vss. 115–117, though of course with general application to 111 ff. and 117 ff. The same thought was afterward more effectively expressed by Horace in *Carm.* 2, 14, 25 ff.

123. **dis inimice**: *God-forsaken*.

124. **enim** : not *for*, but like the English use of *now* or *why* to strengthen an argumentative question. — **summae**: dat.; for the sense cf. vs. 84. — **quisque dierum** : *i.e.* each of the few days still left to a man of your age.

126 f. These details of per-

125 unguere si caules oleo meliore caputque
coeperis impexa foedum porrigine? Quare,
si quidvis satis est, periuras, surripis, aufers
undique? Tun' sanus? Populum si caedere saxis
incipias servosve tuos quos aere pararis,
130 insanum te omnes pueri clamentque puellae:
cum laqueo uxorem interimis matremque veneno,
incolumi capite es? Quid enim? Neque tu hoc facis
Argis,

sonal untidiness and moral obliquity are part of the conventional picture of the miser. They are used occasionally in *Sat.* 1, 1 (*e.g.* vss. 96 ff.), but always with a humorous recognition of their extravagance; here the fanatical Stoic attributes the sins of the individual (a malefactor of great wealth) to the whole class, as if he were using a serious argument. — **si quidvis satis est** : *i.e.* 'if you accept the doctrine of philosophy that enough is as good as a feast.' Cf. Turpil. 144 R., *ut philosophi aiunt isti quibus quidvis sat est*, and *Sat.* 1, 1, 59, *qui tantuli eget quanto est opus.*

128–141. 'You in your senses? Most certainly not. To be sure, the common judgment is that madness shows itself in violence, but when you poison your mother, do you think that the absence of violence proves you sane? What, you think it does? You are no Orestes, you say, the madman who went to Argos and killed his mother with a sword, for you did the deed without bloodshed and not in Argos either. But it is the crime, not the manner or the place of it, that proves a man mad. As to Orestes, his madness began before his violent outbreak and in fact, after the act that is commonly considered evidence of his madness, his conduct was most normal and exemplary — except a little harmless cursing.'

129. **servos tuos**: a little hit at the lover of money, who would be quite unlikely to injure the money-value of his own slaves.

130. **pueri . . . puellae**: proverbial, as in *Sat.* 1, 1, 85.

131. **cum... interimis**: *i.e.* 'when you are engaged in some quiet crime, all in the family.' There is, of course, no implication that any such crime has been committed; much less, as is generally said, that the miser had murdered his mother for her money. That motive is suggested in the parallel passage, *Sat.* 2, 1, 53 ff., but not here.

132. **Argis**: locat. from *Argi.* The point is to show that the

nec ferro ut demens genetricem occidis Orestes.
An tu reris eum occisa insanisse parente,
135 ac non ante malis dementem actum Furiis quam
in matris iugulo ferrum tepefecit acutum?
Quin, ex quo est habitus male tutae mentis Orestes,
nil sane fecit quod tu reprehendere possis:
non Pyladen ferro violare aususve sororem
140 Electram, tantum maledicit utrique, vocando
hanc Furiam, hunc aliud, iussit quod splendida bilis.
Pauper Opimius argenti positi intus et auri,
qui Veientanum festis potare diebus
Campana solitus trulla vappamque profestis,

manner of the crime is wholly unessential, as unessential as the place where it was committed.

134. **occisa insanisse**: 'that his madness began *after* he had killed his mother.'

135. **dementem actum**: *driven mad.*

137. **Quin**: '*why, on the contrary.*' — **male tutae**: *non tutae*; one of the synonyms for *insanus*.

138. **sane**: strengthening *nil; he certainly did nothing.*

139 ff. **Pyladen, Electram**: the friend and the sister who had helped him to carry out his purpose. The passage in which he calls his sister a Fury is in Euripides, *Orest.* 264, but there is no place in an extant play in which he uses hard words of Pylades. The whole reference in 140 f. has nothing to do with the argument; it may be introduced as a bit of Stoic precision in trifles or it may be mere burlesque of a tragic situation. — **splendida bilis**: bile was considered to be the cause of madness and *splendida* is apparently used literally, *shining*, from the descriptions in medical books. — It is entirely in the manner of Horace to drop the argument here, without drawing a conclusion, and to go on without preface to a new illustration. Cf., *e.g.*, *Sat.* 1, 1, 67 f. and below, vss. 186 f.

142. **Opimius**: coined from *opimus*, as *Novius*, in *Sat.* 1, 6, 40, from *novus*, and contrasted with *pauper*. — **argenti**: gen. with *pauper*.

143 f. **Veientanum**: a poor wine, but better than *vappa*, mere lees of wine. — **Campana**: cheap ware, which Horace himself used for ordinary purposes (*Sat.* 1, 6, 118), though perhaps not for drinking. — **trulla**: the ladle, so that he

145 quondam lethargo grandi est oppressus, ut heres
    iam circum loculos et clavis laetus ovansque
    curreret. Hunc medicus multum celer atque fidelis
    excitat hoc pacto: mensam poni iubet atque
    effundi saccos nummorum, accedere pluris
150 ad numerandum; hominem sic erigit. Addit et illud,
    'Ni tua custodis, avidus iam haec auferet heres.'
    'Men' vivo?' 'Vt vivas, igitur, vigila, hoc age.'
        'Quid vis?'
    'Deficient inopem venae te, ni cibus atque
    ingens accedit stomacho fultura ruenti.
155 Tu cessas? Agedum, sume hoc ptisanarium oryzae.'
    'Quanti emptae?' 'Parvo.' 'Quanti, ergo?' 'Octus-
        sibus.' 'Eheu!
    quid refert, morbo an furtis pereamque rapinis?'
        Quisnam igitur sanus? Qui non stultus. Quid
        avarus?

did not need to have a drinking-cup.

147. multum: with *celer* and *fidelis*; cf. *Sat.* 1, 3, 57.

148. hoc pacto: *i.e.* in the way which is described in the next verses.

149 ff. The details (*pluris* to make a little confusion, *iam, immediately, this very moment*) are added to show the directness of the appeal to the tenderest sensibilities of Opimius.

152. vigila: both in the literal sense and in the freer meaning. — **hoc age**: a general form of exhortation to pay attention; *attend to business!*

154. ingens: *immense*, with intentional exaggeration. — **fultura ruenti**: *fulcire* and its derivatives are used in a half-technical sense of food and stimulants, and the figure is carried on in *ruenti*.

155. Tu cessas: he hesitated at the thought of the expense. — **ptisanarium oryzae**: *rice-gruel*.

157. furtis . . . rapinis: *i.e.* the cost, which seemed to him so great, of the gruel which the doctor was trying to get him to take. — With this exclamation he falls back in despair.

158-160. On the short questions and answers cf. vs. 97 and note. They are all spoken by

Stultus et insanus. Quid, si quis non sit avarus,
160 continuo sanus? Minime. Cur, Stoice? Dicam.
Non est cardiacus (Craterum dixisse putato)
hic aeger. Recte est igitur surgetque? Negabit,
quod latus aut renes morbo temptentur acuto.
Non est periurus neque sordidus: immolet aequis
165 hic porcum Laribus; verum ambitiosus et audax:
naviget Anticyram. Quid enim differt, barathrone
dones quicquid habes, an numquam utare paratis?
Servius Oppidius Canusi duo praedia, dives

Stertinius, but the questions express the supposed attitude of a listener. The use of *Stoice*, however, with its suggestion of some slight scorn (cf. vs. 300), is not dramatically correct; cf. *crepat*, vs. 33 and note. — **continuo**: *i.e.* 'may we *at once* conclude that he is sane?'

161 f. **cardiacus**: *dyspeptic*. — **Craterum**: a physician of the Ciceronian time, referred to in *ad Att.* 12, 13, 1; 12, 14, 4, as worthy of confidence. — **Recte est**: sc. *ei*, but translate personally.

163. **temptentur**: a half-technical word of illness. The subjv. is used to imply that this is the reason given by Craterus for his refusal to let the patient get up.

164-167. The application of the story and the transition from the folly of avarice to the folly of ambition. — **periurus, sordidus**: these adjectives go back in particular to vss. 125 ff., but with a general reference to the avaricious man. — **immolet ... porcum**: *i.e.* 'let him thank the gods for his sanity — so far.' In Plautus, *Men.* 289 ff., a pig is to be offered to the gods to bring about a recovery from insanity; here it is in gratitude for exemption from insanity; the two ideas are essentially the same. — **ambitiosus et audax**: *recklessly ambitious*. — **naviget**: 'he may as well engage passage for the land of hellebore;' *i.e.* he is beyond question a mad-man. — **barathro dones**: the emphasis through vs. 186 is upon the heavy expense of a political career, so that this paragraph serves as a transition from avarice, through its opposite, to ambition. — **numquam utare**: cf. *nescius uti compositis*, vss. 109 f.

168. **Canusi**: Canusium was not far from Venusia and this story of Servius Oppidius (*oppidum*?) belongs in the same class as the Ofellus satire (2, 2) and the story told by Cervius (*Sat.*

antiquo censu, gnatis divisse duobus
170 fertur, et hoc moriens pueris dixisse vocatis
ad lectum: 'Postquam te talos, Aule, nucesque
ferre sinu laxo, donare et ludere vidi,
te, Tiberi, numerare, cavis abscondere tristem,
extimui ne vos ageret vesania discors,
175 tu Nomentanum, tu ne sequerere Cicutam.
Quare per divos oratus uterque Penatis,
tu cave ne minuas, tu ne maius facias id
quod satis esse putat pater et natura coercet.
Praeterea ne vos titillet gloria, iure

2, 6, 77 ff.). They are bits of practical philosophy which are most appropriately clothed in the guise of homely tales from the country.

169 f. antiquo censu: *according to old-fashioned standards.* — pueris: they were still young enough for boyish games.

171. talos, nuces: for games like jack-stones and marbles. So Augustus (Suet. *Oct.* 83): *animi laxandi causa . . . talis aut ocellatis nucibusque ludebat cum pueris minutis.*

172 f. sinu laxo: the fold of the toga served as a pocket; in this case a pocket with a hole in it. — donare: with careless generosity. — ludere: *i.e.* to gamble and, occasionally, to lose. — tristem: *with anxious look.*

174. ageret: cf. *agit*, vs. 44. — vesania discors: *two different kinds of madness.* There is no suggestion of discord between the brothers.

175. Nomentanum: *Sat.* 1, 1, 102. — Cicutam: above, vs. 69.

176. oratus: agreeing with *uterque*, but the words must be freely rendered; 'wherefore I beseech you both.'

177. minuas, maius facias: the same idea of frugal contentment with a modest patrimony was urged upon Horace by his father (*Sat.* 1, 4, 107 f.) and, he says, became his rule of life (*Sat.* 2, 6, 7 f.).

178. natura coercet: *i.e.* within the limits set by natural desires; cf. *Sat.* 1, 1, 50. Strictly, *quod* is the obj. of *coercet*; 'the patrimony which nature limits.'

179 ff. The warning against political ambition is apparently addressed to both sons, but it has little meaning in its application to Tiberius and, indeed, no connection at all with the first part of the story, the point of which is the *vesania discors*, the

180 iurando obstringam ambo: uter aedilis fueritve
vestrum praetor, is intestabilis et sacer esto.
In cicere atque faba bona tu perdasque lupinis,
latus ut in Circo spatiere et aeneus ut stes,
nudus agris, nudus nummis, insane, paternis?
185 Scilicet ut plausus, quos fert Agrippa, feras tu,
astuta ingenuum volpes imitata leonem!'
'Ne quis humasse velit Aiacem, Atrida, vetas cur?'
'Rex sum.' 'Nil ultra quaero plebeius.' 'Et aequam

contrast between the different dispositions of the two boys.

181. intestabilis: 'shall forfeit his legacy.' — **sacer esto**: the common legal formula for one who violates a law; here a part of the oath which the sons were to take.

182. cicere, faba, lupinis: gifts of food to the common people to win favor and votes. The reference is to customs in Rome, as the other local and personal allusions show (175, 183, esp. 185).

183. latus . . . spatiere: such a man is described in *Epod.* 4, 7 f.: *Sacram metiente te viam | cum bis trium ulnarum toga.* — **aeneus**: *i.e.* may have a bronze statue of you erected in some public place.

185 f. Agrippa: see introd. to this satire. Agrippa was one of the really influential men of the period. — The next line cannot be an allusion to the fable of the Ass in the Lion's Skin (*Sat.* 2, 1, 64 f.), and there is apparently no fable which quite corresponds to this; it may very well be general, 'like a fox who tries to act a lion's part.'

187–207. A scene in the camp before Troy. Ajax, having been defeated in the contest for the arms of Achilles and becoming insane from disappointment, attacks the flocks of sheep under the delusion that they are his rivals and finally takes his own life. Agamemnon forbids the burial of the body and a common soldier comes to remonstrate. There is no attempt to avoid anachronisms; on the contrary, the humor consists largely in the introduction into a Homeric situation of modern words, like *plebeius, consulere*, and of Stoic forms of sentence and methods of argument.

187. Ne quis . . . velit: legal phraseology, in which the perf. infin. is often used.

188 f. Et aequam: the pretended humility of the soldier obliges the king to add a further

rem imperito; ac si cui videor non iustus, inulto
190 dicere quod sentit permitto.' 'Maxime regum,
di tibi dent capta classem reducere Troia !
Ergo consulere et mox respondere licebit?'
'Consule.' 'Cur Aiax, heros ab Achille secundus,
putescit, totiens servatis clarus Achivis?
195 Gaudeat ut populus Priami Priamusque inhumato,
per quem tot iuvenes patrio caruere sepulchro?'
'Mille ovium insanus morti dedit, inclutum Vlixen
et Menelaum una mecum se occidere clamans.'
'Tu, cum pro vitula statuis dulcem Aulide gnatam
200 ante aras, spargisque mola caput, improbe, salsa,
rectum animi servas?' 'Quorsum?' 'Insanus quid
enim Aiax

justification; 'and, besides, what I am ordering is just.' The rest of the sentence is a still more rapid descent from *rex sum.* — inulto : *with impunity*.

191. A complimentary wish, to introduce the request with a courteous formula; translated from the Iliad, 1, 18 f.

192. consulere : the technical term for consulting a jurist. — mox respondere : the jurist then gave his formal 'opinion' upon the case. Strictly, the thought would require *tibi libebit* instead of *licebit* with *respondere*.

194. putescit : *i.e.* lie unburied.

195. Gaudeat : from the Iliad, 1, 255.

197. Mille : a subst. with the gen. This construction is common in early Latin, but is retained in the classical period only rarely in the singular. — insanus : this turns the dialogue in the desired direction.

199. pro vitula : the important words and the basis of the argument that follows; 'of course Ajax was mad when he mistook a sheep for a man, but so also were you when you mistook your daughter for a heifer.'

200. mola . . . salsa : the sprinkling of salted meal on the head of the victim was a part of the ordinary ceremonial, but its mention here serves to make the scene more vivid.

201. rectum animi servas : another periphrasis for the frequently recurring idea of sanity. — Quorsum : *the point?* Short for *quorsum haec tendunt?* Cf. *Sat.* 2, 7, 21.

fecit, cum stravit ferro pecus? Abstinuit vim
uxore et gnato; mala multa precatus Atridis,
non ille aut Teucrum aut ipsum violavit Vlixen.'
205 'Verum ego, ut haerentis adverso litore navis
eriperem, prudens placavi sanguine divos.'
'Nempe tuo, furiose.' 'Meo, sed non furiosus.'
Qui species alias veris scelerisque tumultu
permixtas capiet, commotus habebitur, atque
210 stultitiane erret nihilum distabit an ira.
Aiax immeritos cum occidit desipit agnos:
cum prudens scelus ob titulos admittis inanis,

203. **mala . . . precatus**: as the violent language of Orestes to his sister and his friend was not inconsistent with sanity (vss. 140 f.).

204. **ipsum**: Ulysses was his successful rival in the contest for the arms.

205 f. **adverso**: *hostile,* 'on a lee-shore.' — **prudens**: *intentionally,* after careful deliberation, not on a mad impulse. 'And the act was a pious one; I pacified the gods.'

207. **furiose**: a much stronger word than *insanus.* — At this point the dialogue ends as abruptly as it had begun and the following lines (208-213) are the comment of Stertinius.

208 f. The terms here used are colored with Stoic meanings. *Species* are the impressions received through the senses; if they do not correspond to the reality (*alias veris*), that fact is evidence of illusion, as in vss. 53-58. If they are still further distorted by passion (*tumultu permixtas*), the evidence of insanity is complete (*commotus habebitur*). The sense of *scelus* also is technical, for the Stoic refused to distinguish crime from madness (cf. vss. 278 ff.); *sceleris tumultu* is hardly more than *insano tumultu.*

210. **stultitia**: the fault of Agamemnon, who claimed *prudentia.*
— **ira**: the cause of the madness of Ajax.

212. **titulos**: the inscriptions under the masks in the atrium of a Roman house. They recited the public offices held by each person represented and constituted the claim of the owner of the house to nobility. — **admittis**: the contrast with vs. 211 suggests that this is addressed to Agamemnon, as if he were present, but it is also addressed to the hearer, the ambitious man; 'when you

stas animo, et purum est vitio tibi, cum tumidum est,
   cor?
Si quis lectica nitidam gestare amet agnam,
215 huic vestem, ut gnatae, paret, ancillas paret, aurum,
Rufam aut Pusillam appellet, fortique marito
destinet uxorem, interdicto huic omne adimat ius
praetor, et ad sanos abeat tutela propinquos.
Quid? si quis gnatam pro muta devovet agna,
220 integer est animi? Ne dixeris. Ergo ubi prava
stultitia, hic summa est insania; qui sceleratus,
et furiosus erit; quem cepit vitrea fama,
hunc circumtonuit gaudens Bellona cruentis.
   Nunc age, luxuriam et Nomentanum arripe mecum;
225 vincet enim stultos ratio insanire nepotes.

commit such a crime for empty honors ...'

213. stas animo: the same figure as that in *commotus*, 219. — **tumidum**: absolute; 'when it is in the tumult of passion.' For this contrast with philosophic calm see Cic. *Tusc.* 3, 9, 19, where *in tumore, tumidus*, and *tumens* are all used absolutely, and esp. *sapientis autem animus semper vocat vitio, numquam turgescit, numquam tumet.*

214 ff. gestare: *i.e.* to have it carried. — **Rufam, Pusillam**: ordinary feminine names, taken at random. — **interdicto**: to be translated as a verb: 'the praetor would lay his interdict upon him and ...' This was a regular proceeding under Roman law and this is only an elaborate way of saying that he would be adjudged insane.

221. sceleratus: cf. *sceleris tumultu*, vs. 208; the same contrast as that between *stultitia* and *ira*, vs. 210.

222. vitrea: not infrequent in this general sense, *glittering, dazzling*. — **fama**: = *gloria*, 179.

223. Bellona: an eastern goddess whose rites were celebrated with crazy orgies and self-inflicted wounds (*gaudens cruentis*).

224-280. The third head of the discourse, the folly of luxury.

224. Nomentanum: cf. vs. 175. — **arripe mecum**: = *arripiamus*, 'let us attack.' The verb is suited either to the Stoic preacher or to the satirist, 2, 1, 69.

225. vincet ... ratio: cf. vs. 83 and *Sat.* 1, 3, 115. — **stultos**: with *insanire*; are *fools and madmen*.

Hic simul accepit patrimoni mille talenta,
edicit, piscator uti, pomarius, auceps,
unguentarius, ac Tusci turba impia vici,
cum scurris fartor, cum Velabro omne macellum,
230 mane domum veniant. Quid tum? Venere frequentes.
Verba facit leno: ' Quicquid mihi, quicquid et horum
cuique domi est, id crede tuum, et vel nunc pete vel
cras.'
Accipe quid contra iuvenis responderit aequus:
' In nive Lucana dormis ocreatus, ut aprum
235 cenem ego; tu piscis hiberno ex aequore verris;
segnis ego, indignus qui tantum possideam: aufer!

226-238. A picture of the Rake's Progress, not inferior in its irony and its real moral power to Hogarth's engravings. The effectiveness of it lies in the artifice of representing the essentials of a spendthrift's career as if the events had actually occurred in this bare form. For Horace does not mean that such a gathering as this took place or that these words were uttered, but that this is what the whole story really amounts to, if we go below the surface. There is a grave irony in the lines and the burlesque of the Stoic manner is dropped.

227 ff. edicit: *proclaims* by his attitude and conduct. Cf. *Sat.* 2, 2, 51 for a similar, ironical use of this formal word — piscator, pomarius. . . . : purveyors of various luxuries. — Tusci . . . vici: a street leading from the Forum toward the river, one of the disreputable quarters of the city. — scurris: a *scurra* was a hanger-on of some richer man, a professional diner-out who lived by his wits. — fartor: perhaps *the sausage-maker*. — Velabro: a street opening from the *Tuscus vicus*, a center of the trade in various kinds of provisions. — Quid tum: *what next?*

231. leno: the procurer is the suitable spokesman.

233. aequus: *fair-minded*; for their valuable services he proposes to make a fair return.

234. Lucana: the boars of Lucania were especially esteemed for food. — ocreatus: greaves were worn to protect the hunter from the tusks of the boar. These details of hardship and danger carry on the irony of *aequus*.

235. hiberno: cf. *Sat.* 2, 2, 16 f.

237. deciens: sc. *centena milia sestertium*, *a million*, of course an absurd sum.

sume tibi deciens; tibi tantundem; tibi triplex,
unde uxor media currit de nocte vocata.'
Filius Aesopi detractam ex aure Metellae,
240 scilicet ut deciens solidum absorberet, aceto
diluit insignem bacam : qui sanior ac si
illud idem in rapidum flumen iaceretve cloacam?
Quinti progenies Arri, par nobile fratrum,
nequitia et nugis pravorum et amore gemellum,
245 luscinias soliti impenso prandere coemptas,
quorsum abeant? Sanin' creta, an carbone notandi?
Aedificare casas, plostello adiungere mures,

238. unde: = *a quo*. — Notice again the abrupt ending of one story and beginning of another.

239. Aesopi: a distinguished actor of Cicero's time, of whose follies some reports have come down to us. He left to his son, however, a large fortune and a taste for extravagance. — **Metellae**: probably the wife of Cornelius Lentulus Spinther, several times referred to in Cicero's letters.

240. solidum: agreeing with *deciens* as a substantive; 'a whole million,' somewhat as we say 'a lump sum.' — This story is also connected with Antony and Cleopatra. But pearls do not dissolve in wine or vinegar.

243. Arri: cf. vs. 86 and note. — **par nobile fratrum**: often quoted as if *nobile* meant *noble* and were used here ironically. It is the not infrequent use of *nobilis* in precisely the sense of *notus*, with either a good or a bad sense; here *notorious*.

244 f. pravorum: with *amore*. — **gemellum**: agreeing with *par*, but to be rendered freely. — **impenso**: *at vast expense*. Stories quite incredible have come down to us of the cost of a single nightingale.

246. quorsum abeant: *into which class shall they be put?* — **creta, carbone**: so *albus et ater*, *Epist.* 2, 2, 189, and *albus an ater homo*, Catull. 93, 2. All these are merely expressions of the natural association of black with evil and white with good. For completeness *insani* would be used with *carbone*, but it is unnecessary to supply it.

247-280. The madness of lovers. This subject is not announced in the introduction (vss. 77-81), but may be considered to be included under the third heading, the passion for luxury.

ludere par impar, equitare in arundine longa,
si quem delectet barbatum, amentia verset.
250 Si puerilius his ratio esse evincet amare,
nec quicquam differre utrumne in pulvere, trimus
quale prius, ludas opus, an meretricis amore
sollicitus plores, quaero, faciasne quod olim
mutatus Polemon, ponas insignia morbi,
255 fasciolas, cubital, focalia, potus ut ille
dicitur ex collo furtim carpsisse coronas,
postquam est impransi correptus voce magistri?
Porrigis irato puero cum poma, recusat:
'Sume, catelle!' negat; si non des, optet: amator

247-249. The children's games here mentioned are still in vogue. — **barbatum**: *i.e.* after he had come to manhood. — **amentia verset**: synonym for *insanus sit*.

250. **amare**: subj. of *esse*, of which *puerilius* is predicate.

251 f. **in pulvere**: *in the sand*, with a suggestion of the waste of labor which is again expressed in *ludas opus*, 'fool away your labor.' — **prius**: agreeing with *opus* to be supplied and referring back to vss. 247 ff.

254. **Polemon**: an example of the reforming power of philosophy, often referred to by Greek and Latin writers. He was a young clubman in Athens who, as he was returning from a drinking-bout, heard the voice of Xenocrates expounding the philosophy of the Academic school. He entered the room, was immediately converted (*mutatus*) by the doctrine, and afterward became the successor of Xenocrates as head of the school.

255. **fasciolas**: bindings about the ankle, a kind of decorative garter. — **cubital**: an *elbow-cushion*, apparently carried about for use at any time. — **focalia**: wrappings for the throat, *neckcloths*. These are all signs of that effeminacy an affectation of which was fashionable in the Augustan period; it is difficult to tell in regard to Maecenas, for example, how far it was real and how far assumed.

256. **furtim**: as he began to realize how the signs of dissipation looked to serious people. — **coronas**: he was still wearing flowers from the banquet.

257. **impransi**: cf. *Sat.* 2, 2, 7.

259. **catelle**: a humorous term of mingled reproval and endearment, without any of the suggestions of the English 'puppy' or 'whelp'; *little scamp, little rogue*.

260 exclusus qui distat, agit ubi secum eat an non,
   quo rediturus erat non arcessitus, et haeret
   invisis foribus? 'Nec nunc, cum me vocat ultro,
   accedam, an potius mediter finire dolores?
   Exclusit; revocat: redeam? Non, si obsecret.' Ecce
265 servus, non paulo sapientior: 'O ere, quae res
   nec modum habet neque consilium, ratione modoque
   tractari non volt. In amore haec sunt mala, bellum,
   pax rursum: haec si quis tempestatis prope ritu
   mobilia et caeca fluitantia sorte laboret
270 reddere certa sibi, nihilo plus explicet ac si

260. qui distat: cf. *quid simile*, vs. 99; *qui discrepat istis*, vs. 108. The endeavor to prove all men equally mad leads to the frequent use of this kind of phrase. — **agit:** *considers, argues.*

262 ff. This passage is a transposition of the first lines of Terence's *Eunuchus* from iambic senarii into hexameters. The corresponding verses of the *Eunuchus* (46 ff.) are as follows: —

Phaedria, the lover, speaks: —

   Quid ígitur faciam? nón eam ne núnc quidem
   quam accérsor ultro? an pótius ita me cómparem,
   non pérpeti meretrícum contumélias?
   exclúsit; revocat: rédeam? non, si me óbsecret.

Parmeno, the slave, replies (vss. 57 ff.): —

   ere, quaé, res in se néque consilium néque modum
   habet úllum, eam consílio regere nón potes.
   in amóre haec omnia ínsunt vitia: iniúriae,
   suspíciones, ínimicitiae, indútiae,
   bellúm, pax rursum; incérta haec si tu póstules
   ratióne certa fácere, nihilo plús agas
   quam sí des operam ut cúm ratione insánias.

265. sapientior: the confidential slave in the comedies is usually in the position of advisor to his young master.

267. non volt: *i.e. cannot*, does not submit to such treatment.

268 f. tempestatis . . . ritu: *changeable as the weather.* In this use *ritu* is no more than *modo*. — **caeca . . . sorte:** the direct opposite of *certa ratione*.

270. explicet: *untangle, straighten out, i.e.* reduce the matter to system and certainty.

insanire paret certa ratione modoque.'
Quid? cum, Picenis excerpens semina pomis,
gaudes si cameram percusti forte, penes te es?
Quid? cum balba feris annoso verba palato,
275 aedificante casas qui sanior? Adde cruorem
stultitiae, atque ignem gladio scrutare. Modo, inquam,
Hellade percussa Marius cum praecipitat se,
cerritus fuit? An commotae crimine mentis
absolves hominem, et sceleris damnabis eundem,
280 ex more imponens cognata vocabula rebus?

272 f. **Picenis**: specified merely for vividness. Picenum was a region of good orchards. — The moist appleseeds were pinched out between the thumb and the forefinger; if one could be made to strike the ceiling (*cameram*), it was an omen of success in love.

274 f. **feris**: the words of love are stammering because the organs of speech (*palato*) are those of an old man and the sounds stumble over them. For the rather forced *feris* Persius, imitating this passage (in 1, 35), uses *tenero supplantat* ('trips up') *verba palato*. — **aedificante**: this refers back to vs. 247.

275. **cruorem**: *i.e.* the violent crimes into which men are led by love.

276 f. **ignem . . . scrutare**: a reference to the Pythagorean saying πῦρ μαχαίρᾳ μὴ σκαλεύειν, but with a different sense, like *oleum adde camino*, vs. 321. — **Modo**: *just lately*; the murder and suicide had occurred just before this and had been much talked about, so that a bare allusion is enough. For the same reason *praecipitat* is used alone without *in Tiberim* or *de rupe*. The persons mentioned are unknown to us.

278. **cerritus**: *mad*; an old word of uncertain origin, used several times in Plautus.

278-280. 'Or will you acquit him of insanity and in the same breath call him a murderer, giving, as people do, different names to things which are really identical?' The interpretation is not quite easy, the difficulty being in *cognata, related, kindred*. The general sense is clear. The Stoic doctrine was that crime and madness were the same thing — *qui sceleratus, et furiosus erit*, 221 f. — and should be called by the same name; but the common way was to give them different names (*insania, scelus*) which are nevertheless alike (*cognata*) in meaning.

Libertinus erat, qui circum compita siccus
lautis mane senex manibus currebat et ' Vnum '
(' quid tam magnum?' addens), 'unum me surpite morti,
dis etenim facile est!' orabat ; sanus utrisque
285 auribus atque oculis ; mentem, nisi litigiosus,
exciperet dominus cum venderet.   Hoc quoque volgus
Chrysippus ponit fecunda in gente Meneni.
' Iuppiter, ingentis qui das adimisque dolores,'
mater ait pueri mensis iam quinque cubantis,
290 ' frigida si puerum quartana reliquerit, illo
mane die, quo tu indicis ieiunia, nudus

281–295. Fourth head, the folly of superstition. This is a subject in which Horace felt little interest; he scarcely touches it elsewhere in the satires, and the brief treatment of it here is rather lifeless.

281 f. The details are not insignificant. The man was old, so that death was not far away ; he was a freedman, probably a foreigner, and therefore more inclined to superstition; he observed the foreign (perhaps Jewish) customs of fasting (*siccus*) and of ceremonial washings (*lautis manibus*) and one shrine was to him as good as another (*circum compita*).

282 f. Vnum: not *me only*, in preference to others, but 'exercise your power just once — such a little thing to do.'—**surpite**: *surripite*; the shortened forms are colloquial.

286 f. exciperet: 'would have made a distinct exception' in giving a guaranty of soundness. The tense refers back to the time when he was still a slave. — **hoc . . . volgus**: the superstitious, as exemplified in the case just described, with the implication that there are many of them. — **fecunda . . . Meneni**: the general sense is plain, that the superstitious are to be reckoned among the insane, but no contemporary Menenius is known, to whom the allusion would apply.

288 ff. As so frequently, the next illustration begins abruptly, without explanation.

289. cubantis: *lying ill*; cf. *Sat.* 1, 9, 18.

290 f. quartana: one of the forms of recurrent malaria, *quartan chills*. — **illo . . . die**: there was no Roman week, but there are traces of the eastern week here and there in Latin literature. Tibullus (1, 3, 18) refers to *Saturni dies* (Sat-

in Tiberi stabit.' Casus medicusve levarit
aegrum ex praecipiti : mater delira necabit
in gelida fixum ripa febrimque reducet,
295 quone malo mentem concussa ? Timore deorum.'
    Haec mihi Stertinius, sapientum octavus, amico
arma dedit, posthac ne compellarer inultus.
Dixerit insanum qui me, totidem audiet, atque
respicere ignoto discet pendentia tergo.
300   *Hor.* Stoice, post damnum sic vendas omnia pluris,
qua me stultitia, quoniam non est genus unum,

urday) and the *dies Iovis* was Thursday, *i.e.* Thor's day. On this day the stricter sects of the Jews fasted (*ieiunia*) and ceremonial bathing in the early morning (*mane*) was an Oriental observance. All this indicates that this instance, like the preceding, was regarded by Horace as foreign. Our native superstitions do not attract our notice.

292. Casus medicusve : not the god.

293 f. ex praecipiti : *from the crisis* of the illness. — **necabit . . . febrimque reducet :** *i.e.* 'will kill him by bringing back the fever.' — **fixum :** cf. *stabit* ; the child is to stand still, perhaps during prayer.

295. quone : cf. *uterne, Sat.* 2, 2, 107. — **Timore deorum :** the Greek δεισιδαιμονία, quite different from the Roman *pietas* or from that 'fear of God' which is the beginning of wisdom.

296-299. An epilogue, spoken by Damasippus in his own person

and corresponding to the introduction by Stertinius, vss. 77-81. — **octavus :** as Sappho was sometimes called the Tenth Muse. — **amico :** spoken with pride that the great man calls him a friend. — **inultus :** amplified in the next two lines. — **totidem :** *i.e.* shall be called a madman himself. — **pendentia :** with reference to the fable of the two sacks ; the one in front contains the faults of other people, but each man puts his own faults into the sack that hangs behind him, where he will not see them.

300-326. The concluding conversation. Horace rouses himself after the long sermon and inquires with no expectation of a reply, whether it applies to him. Damasippus, with Stoic directness, points out various applications.

300. sic vendas : the introductory wish ; cf. vs. 16 note, vs. 191. — **pluris :** *at a profit*, so that he may, if he chooses, resume his life as a business man.

insanire putas? Ego nam videor mihi sanus.
Dam. Quid? caput abscissum manibus cum portat Agaue
gnati infelicis, sibi tum furiosa videtur?
305 *Hor.* Stultum me fateor (liceat concedere veris),
atque etiam insanum; tantum hoc edissere, quo me
aegrotare putes animi vitio? *Dam.* Accipe: primum
aedificas, hoc est, longos imitaris, ab imo
ad summum totus moduli bipedalis; et idem
310 corpore maiorem rides Turbonis in armis

302. **videor mihi sanus**: *i.e.* under the cover of asking for his particular form of insanity Horace is really implying that he is not insane at all. Damasippus goes straight to the point.

303 f. The story is told in the *Bacchae* of Euripides, where Agave, the mother of Pentheus, appears, carrying the head of her son, whom she and the other Bacchantes have torn to pieces, mistaking him in their frenzy for an animal. The argument is that, as no madman recognizes his condition, such a statement as *videor mihi sanus* proves nothing.

305 f. Horace represents himself as yielding to the Stoic's argument, as indeed he must, but he does it grudgingly, at first admitting only the milder *stultus* and then at last making full submission in *atque etiam insanum.* — **liceat**: *let me yield to facts, i.e.* 'permit me to yield as gracefully as I can.'

306. **edissere**: a rather formal word, *Tell me fully.* The question *quo ... vitio?* repeats *qua ne stultitia ... putas?* in different words and with much less confidence that the Stoic will find it a difficult question to answer.

307 ff. **primum**: as if there was to be a series of charges. — **aedificas**: this must be a reference to some building operations on Horace's farm. See introd. to this satire. — **longos**: *big people, i.e.* the rich; but the word is selected for its double meaning. The *Vita* of Suetonius says 'Horatius ... habitu corporis fuit brevis atque obesus' and he speaks of himself as *corporis exigui* (*Epist.* 1, 20, 24). — **bipedalis**: of course ironical, as if he had said 'you who are little better than a dwarf in comparison with really big people like Maecenas.' — **idem**: with restrictive or adversative force, as often; cf. vs. 279. Translate, *in spite of that* or *and yet you.* — **Turbonis**: a gladiator of small size, but great spirit.

spiritum et incessum : qui ridiculus minus illo?
An quodcumque facit Maecenas, te quoque verum est,
tantum dissimilem, et tanto certare minorem?
Absentis ranae pullis vituli pede pressis,
315 unus ubi effugit, matri denarrat, ut ingens
belua cognatos eliserit.   Illa rogare:
'Quantane, num tantum,' sufflans se, 'magna fuisset?'
'Maior dimidio.'   'Num tantum?'   Cum magis atque
se magis inflaret, 'Non, si te ruperis,' inquit,
320 'par eris.'   Haec a te non multum abludit imago.
Adde poemata nunc, hoc est, oleum adde camino;
quae si quis sanus fecit, sanus facis et tu.
Non dico horrendam rabiem — *Hor.* Iam desine!
Dam. Cultum
maiorem censu — *Hor.* Teneas, Damasippe, tuis te.

312. Maecenas had laid out gardens and built a splendid palace on the Esquiline, to which Horace refers in *Sat.* 1, 8, 7 as if it were not yet completed. In *Epod.* 9, 3 and *Carm.* 3, 29, 10, Maecenas was living in it. Other passages (*Sat.* 2, 6, 31; 2, 7, 32 ff.) show that Horace was not unwilling to joke about his relation to his great friend. — **verum** : *proper, suitable.*

314 ff. The Fable of the Ox and the Frogs. Horace took the story from some Greek source, different from that of Phaedrus (1. 24).

317. **Quantane** : cf. *quone*, vs. 295.

320 ff. **non multum abludit** : *hits pretty near.* — **poemata** : the epodes and lyrics which Horace was beginning to write; cf. vss.

11 ff. There is a similar reference to the divine inspiration of poets in *Sat.* 2, 7, 117, *aut insanit homo aut versus facit.* — **si quis ... et tu** : *i.e.* you can no more be free from the insanity of the poet than others have been.

323. **rabiem** : cf. *Epist.* 1, 20, 25, *irasci celerem, tamen ut placabilis essem*; but cf. also *Sat.* 1, 9, 11 f., where he wishes he had a temper. The expression here is a humorous exaggeration. — **Iam desine** : it is, of course, a very neat touch to represent himself as made angry by the charge of having a hot temper. For the outbreak cf. *Sat.* 2, 7, 116 ff.

323 f. **Cultum** : *way of living.* — **censu** : here no more than *income,* not as in *Sat.* 2, 1, 75.

325 *Dam.* Mille puellarum, puerorum mille furores —
Hor. O maior tandem parcas, insane, minori!

326. This turns the teaching of Damasippus (vss. 298 f.) back upon himself.

4

The date of this satire cannot be fixed, but its character is such that the precise date is of no importance. It was probably written after *Sat.* 2, 2.

In form it is, like the preceding satire, a main body of discourse enclosed in a framework of dialogue. Horace meets upon the street an acquaintance who is hurrying home to commit to writing certain precepts of gastronomy which he had just heard. At Horace's request he consents to repeat them and after he has done so, in the main body of the satire (vss. 12-87), Horace, deeply impressed, begs that he may himself be allowed to attend the next lecture on the important subject and hear with his own ears. The introductory dialogue and the concluding request are less dramatic than the corresponding parts of the preceding satire, but they contrast in a somewhat similar way the enthusiasm of the believer with the attitude of Horace and they are admirable specimens of ironical deference.

The main discourse consists of a series of precepts for the selection and serving of the courses of a dinner. They follow in general the order of the Roman dinner, the *gustatio*, the main course, wines and sauces, and the dessert, with advice about the service of the table. Each precept is given separately, as if it were an oracle which needs no explanation or logical connection. The style is serious and almost epic, as befits the seriousness of the speaker, but there is no such parody of the manner of the philosopher as in Satires 2 and 3. The irony which is easily felt in the dialogue is here less apparent, especially to the modern reader, to whom many of the details of Roman cookery must remain unknown. The reader of Horace's time, however, would feel at once the absurdity of the precepts, both in general and in details, and would therefore be conscious of the humor of lines which to the modern reader are rather dull.

The speaker is called Catius and he is represented (vs. 11) as quoting from the discourse of an authority on gastronomy whose name he avoids giving. This is, in form, the same device that is used in *Sat.* 2, 3, where Damasippus quotes from Stertinius, and in *Sat.* 2, 7, in which the slave repeats the teachings which he had learned from the door-keeper of Crispinus (vs. 45). Such machinery of the satirical form is not to be taken seriously; in *Sat.* 2, 7 it is plainly a mere joke and the Damasippus-Stertinius relation in *Sat.* 2, 3 serves only to give a background for the parody of Stoic preaching. Of the various identifications of Catius the only one which has both plausibility and point is the one proposed by Manso and revived by Palmer, that the name is a disguise of Matius, the friend of Cicero, Caesar, Trebatius and Augustus. But, in fact, the precise identification of either Catius or the mysterious *auctor* is of no more importance than the precise determination of the date of composition. The satire contains in itself its own best commentary. It is a bit of humorous and not unfriendly irony, directed primarily against some person whose name is ostentatiously withheld and, more broadly, against the science and art of gastronomy. So far as there is any personality in it, it is of a kind which would be especially understood and appreciated by Horace's intimate friends, and the satire belongs, in this respect, to the same class as *Sat.* 1, 9 and *Sat.* 2, 8. In all three there is the note of intimacy and it is not at all impossible that the learning of this satire is a parody of gastronomic conversations which Horace had heard at the table of Maecenas.

Hor. Vnde et quo Catius ? *Cat.* Non est mihi tempus aventi
ponere signa novis praeceptis, qualia vincant
Pythagoran Anytique reum doctumque Platona.
Hor. Peccatum fateor, cum te sic tempore laevo
5   interpellarim; sed des veniam bonus, oro.
Quod si interciderit tibi nunc aliquid, repetes mox,
sive est naturae hoc sive artis, mirus utroque.

1. **Vnde et quo**: two questions condensed into one: cf. *Sat.* 1, 9, 62.

2. **ponere signa**: to set down or fix upon his mind, as he went along, the mnemonic signs which would assist him in recalling the whole discourse and putting it into writing.

3. **Anyti reum**: Socrates. In his trial Anytus was the chief accuser.

7. **naturae, artis**: the distinction between natural and artificial memory, by the aid of mnemonic signs (*imagines, signa*), was traditional in rhetoric, and is briefly discussed in *ad Heren.* 3, 16-17, 28-30.

Cat. Quin id erat curae, quo pacto cuncta tenerem,
utpote res tenuis, tenui sermone peractas.
10 *Hor.* Ede hominis nomen, simul et Romanus an
   hospes.
Cat. Ipsa memor praecepta canam, celabitur auctor.
   Longa quibus facies ovis erit, illa memento,
ut suci melioris et ut magis alba rotundis,
ponere ; namque marem cohibent callosa vitellum.
15 Cole suburbano qui siccis crevit in agris
dulcior ; irriguo nihil est elutius horto.
Si vespertinus subito te oppresserit hospes,
ne gallina malum responset dura palato,
doctus eris vivam mixto mersare Falerno ;
20 hoc teneram faciet. Pratensibus optima fungis
natura est ; aliis male creditur. Ille salubris
aestates peraget, qui nigris prandia moris
finiet, ante gravem quae legerit arbore solem.

8. **id**: with a reference back to vs. 6; the idea is then amplified in *quo . . . tenerem*.

10–11. These lines suggest a joking reference to some friend, whose name would be known to the inner circle of readers. — **canam**: with a certain formality.

12. **facies**: *shape*.

14. **callosa**: *compact, solid*. — **vitellum**: *chick*; this is merely an elaborate way of saying that male fowls are hatched from long eggs.

15–16. **Cole**: *cabbage*. — **suburbano**: in a garden near the city water for irrigation would be more abundant. — **elutius**: *more insipid*; literally, *washed out*.

18. **malum responset**: *defy, resist*, as in Sal. 2, 7, 85, 103. — **dura**: *tough*, because the fowl was killed after the unexpected guest had appeared.

19. **doctus**: 'you will show yourself learned in the art of cookery by smothering it.'

20. **Pratensibus . . . fungis**: 'mushrooms that grow in the meadows.'

22. **moris**: *mulberries*. This advice about lunch and the preceding lines on the preparation of a fowl for supper show that there is no intention of following precisely the order of the courses of a dinner.

Aufidius forti miscebat mella Falerno,
25 mendose, quoniam vacuis committere venis
nil nisi lene decet; leni praecordia mulso
prolueris melius.   Si dura morabitur alvus,
mitulus et viles pellent obstantia conchae
et lapathi brevis herba, sed albo non sine Coo.
30 Lubrica nascentes implent conchylia lunae;
sed non omne mare est generosae fertile testae;
murice Baiano melior Lucrina peloris,
ostrea Circeiis, Miseno oriuntur echini,
pectinibus patulis iactat se molle Tarentum.
35   Nec sibi cenarum quivis temere arroget artem,
non prius exacta tenui ratione saporum;
nec satis est cara piscis averrere mensa
ignarum quibus est ius aptius et quibus assis
languidus in cubitum iam se conviva reponet.

24-26. **Aufidius**: unknown. He is quoted with formality as a rival authority, to be refuted in the single word *mendose*. The *mulsum*, a mixture of wine and honey, was drunk at the beginning of the meal. The error of Aufidius was in using a strong wine, *forti Falerno*; the emphasis of the correction is upon *lene, leni*.

27-29. **Si . . . alvus**: *i.e.* for constipation. — **mitulus**: *mussel.* — **conchae**: a general term for shell-fish. — **lapathi**: *sorrel.* — **brevis**: *small-leaved,* or perhaps *low-growing.* — **Coo**: a Greek wine.

30. **conchylia**: another general term for shell-fish. The meaning of the line is that they should be gathered when the moon is increasing, during the first half of the lunar month.

32-34. **murice**: *cockle.* — **peloris**: *giant mussel.* — **echini**: *sea-urchins.* — **pectinibus**: *scallops.* These lines give the proper places for getting the best shell-fish of each kind, like Little Neck clams, Blue Point oysters.

36. **non prius**: *i.e.* 'until he shall have learned thoroughly.' — **tenui**: *fine, subtle,* as in vs. 9.

37. **averrere**: *to sweep up* from the table of the fish-dealer, but with a reference also to the use of nets in catching the fish.

38 f. **assis**: *broiled.* — **langui-**

40 Vmber et iligna nutritus glande rotundas
curvat aper lances carnem vitantis inertem;
nam Laurens malus est, ulvis et arundine pinguis.
Vinea submittit capreas non semper edulis.
Fecundae leporis sapiens sectabitur armos.
45 Piscibus atque avibus quae natura et foret aetas,
ante meum nulli patuit quaesita palatum.
Sunt quorum ingenium nova tantum crustula promit.
Nequaquam satis in re una consumere curam,
ut si quis solum hoc, mala ne sint vina, laboret,
50 quali perfundat piscis securus olivo.
Massica si caelo supponas vina sereno,
nocturna, si quid crassi est, tenuabitur aura,
et decedet odor nervis inimicus; at illa
integrum perdunt lino vitiata saporem.
55 Surrentina vafer qui miscet faece Falerna

dus: *i.e.* even a sated guest will raise himself again on his elbow at the sight of the appetizing dish.

40-42. iligna glande: *acorns.* — **curvat:** *bends;* the platters were of silver. — **vitantis inertem:** the important words; 'the epicure, the man who avoids tasteless meat, will get an Umbrian boar that has lived on acorns.' — **ulvis:** *sedge.*

44. fecundae: *prolific,* in general; but the use of the feminine appears to be intentional. The emphasis is upon *armos;* the true epicure will select for his guests the forelegs of the female hare. Cf. *Sat.* 2, 8, 89.

46. ante meum: cf. the claim to originality in vs. 73 and the similar claim in *Sat.* 2, 8, 51.

47. promit: *produces, i.e.* invents. The line seems to be a veiled reference to some particular person.

50. securus: *careless,* governing the clause *quali . . . olivo;* 'as if one should take great pains to get good wine, but be careless about the quality of the olive oil.'

51-54. crassi: *roughness, harshness* of taste. — **tenuabitur:** *will be refined out of it.* — **lino:** 'the straining of wine through a piece of linen spoils the flavor.'

55-57. vafer: cf. *doctus,* vs. 19, *sapiens,* vs. 44. — **faece:** a slight mixture of the lees of Falernian

vina, columbino limum bene colligit ovo,
quatenus ima petit volvens aliena vitellus.
Tostis marcentem squillis recreabis et Afra
potorem cochlea: nam lactuca innatat acri
60 post vinum stomacho; perna magis ac magis hillis
flagitat immorsus refici; quin omnia malit,
quaecumque immundis fervent allata popinis.
Est operae pretium duplicis pernoscere iuris
naturam.   Simplex e dulci constat olivo,
65 quod pingui miscere mero muriaque decebit,
non alia quam qua Byzantia putuit orca.
Hoc ubi confusum sectis inferbuit herbis
Corycioque croco sparsum stetit, insuper addes
pressa Venafranae quod baca remisit olivae.
70 Picenis cedunt pomis Tiburtia suco;
nam facie praestant.   Venucula convenit ollis;
rectius Albanam fumo duraveris uvam.
Hanc ego cum malis, ego faecem primus et allec,
primus et invenior piper album cum sale nigro

gives body to the light Surrentine wine. — **limum**: *the sediment.* — **volvens aliena**: *gathering the foreign matter.* — **vitellus**: *the yolk.*

58–63. Various kinds of food which will tempt the appetite of one who has taken much wine (*marcentem potorem*). — **Tostis . . . squillis**: *fried shrimps.* — **cochlea**: *snails.* — **lactuca**: *lettuce.* — **perna**: *ham.* — **hillis**: *sausages.* — **immorsus**: *bitten, i.e. stimulated* to fresh appetite.

63. **Est operae pretium**: an epic phrase.

64–69. The simple sauce consists of olive oil mixed with thick wine and brine (*muria*) from a jar in which fish from Byzantium had been pickled. This is called *duplex* when it has been poured over chopped herbs and boiled, then sprinkled with saffron and allowed to stand, and finally mixed with Venafran oil.

71. **Venucula**: *sc. uva*; grapes for preserving.

72. **duraveris**: *dry* into raisins.

73–75. **cum malis**: *i.e.* he first used raisins with fruit. — **allec**:

75 incretum puris circumposuisse catillis.
   Immane est vitium dare milia terna macello
   angustoque vagos piscis urgere catino.
   Magna movet stomacho fastidia, seu puer unctis
   tractavit calicem manibus, dum furta ligurrit,
80 sive gravis veteri craterae limus adhaesit.
   Vilibus in scopis, in mappis, in scobe quantus
   consistit sumptus? Neglectis, flagitium ingens.
   Ten' lapides varios lutulenta radere palma
   et Tyrias dare circum inluta toralia vestis,
85 oblitum, quanto curam sumptumque minorem
   haec habeant, tanto reprehendi iustius illis
   quae nisi divitibus nequeant contingere mensis?
       Hor. Docte Cati, per amicitiam divosque rogatus,
   ducere me auditum, perges quocumque, memento.
90 Nam quamvis memori referas mihi pectore cuncta,
   non tamen interpres tantundem iuveris. Adde

something like caviare. — **incretum**: *sifted on*. — **puris . . . catillis**: on plates which held nothing else.

76–77. **milia . . . macello**: this is the same thing that is said in *vs.* 37, that mere spending of money is not enough. — **vagos**: the line expresses in high-flown language the rule that fish should not be crowded together on too small a platter.

79. **furta ligurrit**: cf. *Sat.* 1, 3, 80 f.

80. **limus**: *sediment* left in the mixing bowl because it had not been properly washed.

81. **scopis**: *brooms*. — **scobe**: *sawdust* sprinkled upon the floor before sweeping.

83 f. The emphasis is upon *lutulenta* and *inluta*. — **palma**: a broom of palm leaves.

86 f. **illis quae**: in general, the things which only the rich can have; neatness requires only care, not money.

88. **Docte**: this is an ironical acceptance of the attitude of Catius, that such knowledge is true learning.

91. **interpres**: Catius can give only second-hand reports. — **Adde**: *and, besides, think of the look and bearing*. All this has especial point, if Horace was really refer-

voltum habitumque hominis, quem tu vidisse beatus
non magni pendis, quia contigit ; at mihi cura
non mediocris inest, fontis ut adire remotos
95 atque haurire queam vitae praecepta beatae.

ring to some friend who was at times earnest in laying down the gastronomic law.

94 f. A parody of Lucret. 1, 927 and 4. 2, *iuvat integros accedere fontis atque haurire*.

5

The date of this satire is fixed by vss. 62 ff. The phrase *tellure marique magnus* would not have been used in the years just before Actium, when it was increasingly apparent that the supremacy by sea was still to be decided. After Actium there was a general expectation that Octavius would carry out the project of his uncle for a war of conquest in the East and it is to such expectations that *Parthis horrendus* refers. The satire was written soon after the battle of Actium, late in 31 or early in 30.

The subject-matter is the practice of seeking legacies. To treat this as a profession, however, is to take satire too seriously ; it was a social evil, like free divorce or political bribery, which the satirist ridicules by assuming an ironical seriousness. The custom of leaving legacies, often small, but not infrequently of substantial amount, to many friends was already common in the Ciceronian period. It was to be expected that the custom would lead to the cultivation of friendships in the hope of a legacy and the tendency was strengthened by the large increase of wealth in the hands of men who did not know how to use it. Such men, often of the freedman class, sometimes without family connections, would be especially open to the flattering approaches of persons of higher position.

The satire is a continuation, in burlesque, of a scene in the Odyssey, 11. 90 ff. The shade of the Theban seer, Tiresias, meets Odysseus in the lower world and at his request tells him how he may secure his return to Ithaca and how he may summon the shade of his mother. After this interview the seer returns (vss. 150 f.) to the home of Hades. At this point Horace interjects the conversation which forms this satire. The selection of the venerable prophet of Thebes to give advice such as this is as happy as the selection of Trebatius in *Sat.* 2, 1, and Odysseus, with the mingling of the crafty and the heroic in his traditional character, is admirably suited to receive the doctrine.

Travesty of heroic legends had a considerable place in Greek literature, especially in comedy; Plautus has one example in the *Amphitruo* and Varro had used it in his *Saturae Menippeae*. It has been frequently used in modern literature; Thackeray's *Rebecca and Rowena* and Mark Twain's *A Yankee in King Arthur's Court* are familiar examples. Horace has combined the humor of travesty with the humor of pretended seriousness in the treatment of his subject-matter, like the seriousness of De Quincey in *Murder as a Fine Art*.

> *Vlixes.* Hoc quoque, Tiresia, praeter narrata petenti
> responde, quibus amissas reparare queam res
> artibus atque modis. Quid rides? *Tiresias.* Iamne doloso
> non satis est Ithacam revehi patriosque penatis
> 5 aspicere? *Vlix.* O nulli quicquam mentite, vides ut
> nudus inopsque domum redeam, te vate; neque illic
> aut apotheca procis intacta est aut pecus; atqui
> et genus et virtus, nisi cum re, vilior alga est.

1. **praeter narrata**: *i.e.* the prophecy as to his safe return to Ithaca. *Narrare* in its colloquial sense, *tell, speak*.

2. **amissas ... res**: the seer had told him of the havoc that the suitors were making of his property at home.

3. **Quid rides**: the seer smiled at the desire of Ulysses for a little more, after he had received so much. — **doloso**: a translation of the standing epithets πολύτροπος, πολυμήχανος, but with a touch of sarcasm.

4. **penatis**: the anachronism of the Roman idea is intentional.

5. **nulli ... mentite**: so Tiresias says of himself (*Od.* 11, 96), νημερτέα εἴπω.

6. **nudus inopsque**: this had been distinctly said (*Od.* 11, 114 ff.). — **te vate**: *according to your prophecy*; not quite as if he doubted the seer, but as if he accepted it unwillingly. — **neque illic**: *nor, when I get there.*

7. **procis**: the suitors of Penelope, ἄνδρας ὑπερφιάλους, οἵ τοι βίοτον κατέδουσιν. — **apotheca, pecus**: the anxiety of Odysseus and of his son Telemachus about the consumption of provisions by the suitors, natural as it is to the Homeric simplicity, seemed to the Roman, as it seems to the modern reader, a little comic.

8. **vilior alga**: proverbial for worthlessness; the expression is perhaps selected with special ref-

Tir. Quando pauperiem, missis ambagibus, horres,
10 accipe qua ratione queas ditescere. Turdus
sive aliud privum dabitur tibi, devolet illuc
res ubi magna nitet domino sene; dulcia poma
et quoscumque feret cultus tibi fundus honores,
ante larem gustet venerabilior lare dives;
15 qui quamvis periurus erit, sine gente, cruentus
sanguine fraterno, fugitivus, ne tamen illi
tu comes exterior, si postulet, ire recuses.
    Vlix. Vtne tegam spurco Damae latus? Haud ita
    Troiae .

erence to the sea-beaten Odysseus. — The sentiment of the line is, of course, intentionally unheroic.

9. missis ambagibus: *without any pretence*, in plain words.

10 ff. Turdus: cf. *Sat.* 1. 5, 72. — **privum**: *for your own*; pred. with *dabitur*. The fact that it was the special property of the giver will add to its value in the eyes of the receiver. — **devolet**: with humorous effect, in both literal and figurative meaning. — **nitet**: *flourishes*; i.e. be sure that the property is large and unincumbered. — The abrupt beginning and the rather obscure expression is a parody of the ordinary style of prophecy. *obscuris vera involvens* (*Aen.* 6. 100).

13. honores: fruits and flowers, as in *Carm.* 1. 17. 16.

14. ante larem: the first-fruits were properly offered to the *Lar Familiaris*.

15. sine gente: *of no family*; a freedman or a slave had no legal claim to be *gentilis*. There is no necessary connection with *fugitivus*, since no definite person is in mind; the various discreditable attributes are piled together, as in *Carm.* 2, 13. 5 ff.; *Epod.* 3, 1 f.

17. comes exterior: 'to escort him, walking on his left side'; this is expressed in the next line by *tegam . . . latus*. It was the Greek and the Roman custom for the inferior, as escort, to walk on the left side. The explanation given was that the left side was more open to attack, the right being protected by the drawn sword. — **si postulet**: in the colloquial sense of *postulare, to expect, desire*.

18. Vtne tegam: a common form of repudiating exclamation. — **Damae**: a common name of a slave; cf. *Sat.* 1, 6, 38.

SERMONES [2, 5, 27

 me gessi, certans semper melioribus. *Tir.* Ergo
20 pauper eris. *Vlix.* Fortem hoc animum tolerare iubebo;
 et quondam maiora tuli. Tu protinus, unde
 divitias aerisque ruam dic, augur, acervos.
 Tir. Dixi equidem et dico: captes astutus ubique
 testamenta senum, neu, si vafer unus et alter
25 insidiatorem praeroso fugerit hamo,
 aut spem deponas aut artem illusus omittas.
 Magna minorve foro si res certabitur olim,

19. melioribus: dat.; the phrase appears to be a reminiscence of *Il.* 21, 486, κρείσσοσιν μάχεσθαι and means 'with men of the better class,' Achilles and Ajax. — **Ergo**: *well, then.*

20 f. A translation of the words with which Odysseus encourages himself before the slaughter of the suitors, *Od.* 20, 18: τέτλαθι δή, κραδίη· καὶ κύντερον ἄλλο ποτ' ἔτλης. The point of the quotation here is that the hero is encouraging himself to endure a humiliation (*hoc* means *comes ... ire*) in order to make money. Cf. the similar remark in *Sat.* 1, 9, 59 f., *nil sine magno vita labore dedit mortalibus.*

21. protinus: *go ahead and tell me.* The completeness of the surrender of the heroic pose is emphasized by the moment of indignant repudiation.

22. ruam: transitive, in a vaguely poetic use: *rush together, quickly collect.*—**augur**: with intentional Roman coloring.

23. Dixi ... et dico: he had not, in fact, said anything that was really intelligible. vss. 10-17 being obscure and having no apparent bearing on the getting of money. But it all seemed plain to the prophet, and he therefore speaks here with some impatience and then goes on to put it in words as plain as a prophet can use; *captes ... testamenta.*

25. praeroso: *i.e.* nibbles off the bait and gets away. The figure is suggested in *captes* and carried on to greater distinctness in *praeroso hamo.*

26. artem: *i.e.* the *ars captandi, ars piscandi*. In so far as this hints at a profession of legacy-hunting, it is like our speaking of the profession of burglary or wire-pulling. — **illusus**: 'because you have failed once.'

27. minorve: added as an afterthought; 'an important case — or even one that is not so important,' for the diligent man allows nothing to escape him. — **olim**: *sometime;* of the future, as often.

    vivet uter locuples sine gnatis, improbus, ultro
    qui meliorem audax vocet in ius, illius esto
30 defensor; fama civem causaque priorem
    sperne, domi si gnatus erit fecundave coniunx.
    'Quinte,' puta, aut ' Publi '(gaudent praenomine molles
    auriculae) 'tibi me virtus tua fecit amicum;
    ius anceps novi, causas defendere possum;
35 eripiet quivis oculos citius mihi, quam te
    contemptum cassa nuce pauperet; haec mea cura est,
    ne quid tu perdas, neu sis iocus.' Ire domum atque
    pelliculam curare iube; fi cognitor ipse.
    Persta atque obdura, seu ' rubra Canicula findet

28 ff. uter: *whichever of the two* parties to the suit. — **improbus**: coördinate with *locuples* and defined by the following clause. — **ultro**: *actually;* going so far in his impudence (*audax*) as to bring a suit without justification. — **illius**: emphatic; *'that's* the man for you to back.' — **fama . . . causaque priorem**: a fuller expression of the idea in *meliorem*; the dignified *civem* adds to the contrast, the other being *sine gente*, a freedman. — **fecunda**: with the possibility of natural heirs.

32. Quinte: as a sign of familiarity and affection. The genuine Roman *praenomen* Quintus or Publius would be agreeable to the freedman, who during his slavery had had some foreign name like Dama or Syrus. — **puta**: *for instance.* As an impv. this has regularly a long *a*, but the final vowel of iambic impv. forms is often shortened in comedy, and as this word passed over into semi-adverbial uses, it retained the colloquial quantity.

34. ius anceps: *the uncertainties of the law*, with a suggestion of the tricks of the unscrupulous lawyer.

36. contemptum: with the force of a verb; *bring you into contempt*. — **cassa nuce**: a proverbial phrase (Plaut. *Pseud.* 371; *Rud.* 1324).

38. pelliculam: so *cutem curare*, *Epist.* 1, 2, 29; other objects (*membra, Sat.* 2, 2, 80 f., *corpora, se suamque aetatem*) are used with *curare* in the same general sense, 'to take care of one's health.' *Pelliculam* is used with special effect, *his precious health*. — **cognitor**: in the legal sense, *attorney*.

39. Persta atque obdura: a colloquialism; Plaut. *Asin.* 322. *pernegabo atque obdurabo;* Catull. 8,

40 infantis statuas,' seu pingui tentus omaso
Furius 'hibernas cana nive conspuet Alpis.'
'Nonne vides,' aliquis cubito stantem prope tangens
inquit, 'ut patiens! ut amicis aptus! ut acer!'
plures adnabunt thynni et cetaria crescent.
45 Si cui praeterea validus male filius in re
praeclara sublatus aletur, ne manifestum
caelibis obsequium nudet te, leniter in spem
adrepe officiosus, ut et scribare secundus
heres, et, si quis casus puerum egerit Orco,
50 in vacuum venias: perraro haec alea fallit.
Qui testamentum tradet tibi cumque legendum,

11, *perfer, obdura*; Ovid, *Trist.* 5, 11, 7, *perfer et obdura*.

39 ff. The quotations are from a lost poem of M. Furius Bibaculus, of Cremona, a contemporary of Cicero, still living at the time this was written and already alluded to in *Sat.* 1, 10, 36. The first phrase, *rubra ... statuas*, meaning 'in extreme heat,' is turgid in conception and in single words, especially *infantis*, 'speechless.' The second is quoted also by Quintil. 8, 6, 17 as an example of poor rhetoric, with *Iuppiter* as the first word; Horace has substituted the poet's own name. The personal allusion in *pingui ... omaso*, 'stuffed with fat tripe,' is offensive to modern taste and the particular justification for it is not known.

42. prope: with *stantem*; *standing next to him* in the law-court.

44. cetaria: this must mean a fish-pond or weir, which is at the same time a trap and a place for keeping fish alive until they are wanted for the table. The figure is not exactly the same as that in vs. 25.

45. praeterea: *furthermore*, introducing the special precepts of vss. 45-50. — **validus male**: = *invalidus*.

46. sublatus: *recognized*, lit., *taken up*; the new-born child was placed before the father, who recognized it as his by taking it up.

47. caelibis: objective gen. with *obsequium*. — **nudet te**: *expose you*, betray your plans to your victims.

48 f. ut: the clause is explicative of *spem*. — **secundus heres**: *i.e.* to inherit in case of the death of the first-named heir. — **Orco**: the seer uses epic language.

51-69. A warning against being taken in by the testator.

abnuere et tabulas a te removere memento,
sic tamen, ut limis rapias, quid prima secundo
cera velit versu; solus multisne coheres,
55 veloci percurre oculo.   Plerumque recoctus
scriba ex quinqueviro corvum deludet hiantem,
captatorque dabit risus Nasica Corano.
Vlix. Num furis? an prudens ludis me obscura canendo?
Tir. O Laertiade, quicquid dicam aut erit aut non:

51 ff. **Qui . . . cumque**: cf. *quando . . . cumque, Sat.* 1, 9, 33. — **memento**: *be sure, don't forget*. The point is to make a show of indifference to the question of money. — **sic tamen**: *in such a way, however*. — **limis**: sc. *oculis*; the noun is so frequently omitted that in late Latin *limis* was mistaken for a nom. sing.; *with a side glance*. — **prima . . . cera**: the will was written on wax tablets with raised edges, which could be tied together and sealed. On the inside of the first leaf the name of the testator was written in the first line and the name of the heir in the second (*secundo versu*). The fixed position of the names made it easy to read them at a glance. — **quid . . . velit**: *what the first page says*; the sense is different when *sibi* is added, as in vs. 61.

55 ff. This instance of the unhappy result of a neglect of the precautions just mentioned is put in the form of a reference to an event of Horace's time, which the seer relates as a prophecy (*deludet, dabit*) and in the ambiguous language of an oracle. Of course all the Roman words and names (*scriba, quinquevir, Nasica, Coranus*) are unintelligible to Ulysses, and the fable of the Fox and the Raven was unknown to him. — **recoctus**: *boiled over*, with a reference to the Medea legend. — **quinqueviro**: a subordinate police official — Coranus — who had risen to the unimportant office of *scriba*. The details increase the perplexity of Ulysses and help to make the whole incident ridiculous.

59 f. **aut erit aut non**: as Tiresias is supposed to mean it, this would be 'what I say will happen, will, and what I say will not happen, will not,' but the possible double meaning makes it a burlesque of the solemn claims of sooth-sayers. The verse is quoted by Boethius (*de Cons.* 5, 3) as *vaticinium illud ridiculum Tiresiae.* The absurdity is heightened

divinare etenim magnus mihi donat Apollo.
Vlix. Quid tamen ista velit sibi fabula, si licet, ede.
Tir. Tempore quo iuvenis Parthis horrendus, ab alto
demissum genus Aenea, tellure marique
magnus erit, forti nubet procera Corano
filia Nasicae, metuentis reddere soldum.
Tum gener hoc faciet: tabulas socero dabit atque
ut legat orabit; multum Nasica negatas
accipiet tandem et tacitus leget, invenietque
nil sibi legatum praeter plorare suisque.

by the next verse in Homeric style. — **donat**: present, as if he felt the gift of the god at that moment.

61. The reply of Ulysses is more humble (*si licet*) than vs. 58, as if he had been impressed by the lofty tone of vss. 59–60. — **tamen**: *i.e.* '*but nevertheless* I should like to understand the story, if I may.' — **Quid . . . velit sibi**: *what it means*.

62 ff. The seer re-tells the story in plain language, with an introduction in the heroic style. On the date see introd. to this satire.

62 f. iuvenis: Octavius was a little over thirty. — **demissum**: cf. *Aen.* 1, 288, *a magno demissum nomen Iulo*. — **genus**: cf. *Sat.* 1, 6, 12, *Valeri genus*, in apposition with a proper noun, as here with *iuvenis*.

64. forti, procera: stock epithets (cf. *Sat.* 2, 3, 216) used in derision in this case, where the inducement to the marriage was neither courage nor beauty, but the payment of a debt.

65. metuentis: the sense of *metuo* is frequently weakened, especially when it takes an infin., to meanings like *hesitate, be unwilling*; cf. *Carm.* 2, 2, 7, *penna metuente solvi.* — **soldum**: the syncopated colloquial form for *solidum, the principal* of the debt. The point is that as Nasica was unwilling to pay a debt (presumably to Coranus), he gave Coranus his daughter instead, hoping that the son-in-law would leave to him or to his daughter a sum which would more than counterbalance the debt. The relative age of father-in-law and son-in-law is left out of account, or the case is like the marriage of Pompey to Caesar's daughter.

66 ff. tabulas: the will, as in vs. 52. — **multum . . . negatas**: *i.e.* having made a great show of refusing, as advised in vs. 52. — **praeter plorare**: the prepos. gov-

70   Illud ad haec iubeo: mulier si forte dolosa
libertusve senem delirum temperet, illis
accedas socius; laudes, lauderis ut absens;
adiuvat hoc quoque, sed vincit longe prius ipsum
expugnare caput. Scribet mala carmina vecors:
75   laudato. Scortator erit: cave te roget; ultro
Penelopam facilis potiori trade. *Vlix.* Putasne
perduci poterit tam frugi tamque pudica,
quam nequiere proci recto depellere cursu?
    Tir. Venit enim magnum donandi parca iuventus
80   nec tantum Veneris, quantum studiosa culinae.
Sic tibi Penelope frugi est, quae si semel uno

erns the infin. as a noun. *Plorare* means *to lament* and, as used in the will, it would mean that Coranus left to Nasica the legacy of grief which his death would cause, but with an ironical suggestion of the grief that he would feel at receiving no legacy in money. Cf. *Sat.* 1, 10. 91.

70–74. 'Do not disdain to play a second part as a helper to others who may be managing an old man.' — **ad haec**: cf. *praeterea*, vs. 45. — **mulier . . . libertusve**: *i.e.* under the most discreditable and humiliating influences. — **delirum**: *childish*; cf. Cic. *de Sen.* 11, 36, *senilis stultitia quae deliratio appellari solet.* — **ipsum . . . caput**: the old man himself.

74. **Scribet**: a condition expressed without *si*, in parataxis. — **vecors**: cf. *excors, Sat.* 2, 3, 67.

76 f. **potiori**: so in *Epod.* 15, 13. — **Putasne . . . poterit**: parataxis like the English, *do you think she can . . . ?* This is very common in colloquial Latin, *e.g.* Plaut. *Rud.* 1269, *censen hodie despondebit eam mihi?*

78. **nequiere proci**: the faithfulness of Penelope had become in Horace's time the main element in the story of the suitors, and it is alluded to here as a well-known fact, but it had in truth been barely hinted at by Tiresias (*Od.* 11, 117) and would not be known to Ulysses.

79. **enim**: *of course, for.* — **magnum**: obj. of *donandi*, which depends upon *parca*. They gave gifts, but not big enough gifts; this adds a touch to the travesty of the heroic, to which, indeed, this part of the story is particularly exposed; cf. *Od.* 18, 275-280.

81. **Sic . . . quae si**: *under such conditions* (with stingy suitors) *. . . , but if she . . .* — **semel**

de sene gustarit tecum partita lucellum,
ut canis a corio numquam absterrebitur uncto.
  Me sene quod dicam factum est: anus improba Thebis
85 ex testamento sic est elata: cadaver
unctum oleo largo nudis umeris tulit heres,
scilicet elabi si posset mortua; credo,
quod nimium institerat viventi.   Cautus adito,
neu desis operae, neve immoderatus abundes.
90 Difficilem et morosum offendet garrulus; ultra
non etiam sileas; Davus sis comicus, atque

uno: *just once from one old man.*

83. The line is a condensed comparison; 'it will be as hard to get her away as to . . .' — **a corio . . . uncto**: a Greek saying, like the English 'to drive a dog away from his bone.'

84–88. A story to enforce the need of caution in one's attentions. — **Me sene**: Tiresias had long been dead, and he refers back to the time when he was an old man, as an old man refers to his youth with *me puero* or *me iuvene*. Cf. *Sat.* 2, 2, 112 f., *puer . . . ego . . . Ofellum . . . novi*. — **sic est elata**: *i.e.* was to be carried out for burial, if the heir could fulfil the condition. — **scilicet . . . si**: *to see, you understand, whether*; this use of *si* is explained in the grammars. — **nimium institerat**: *i.e.* she had never been able to slip away from him while she was alive.

88. Cautus: the moral of the story, expanded in the following lines.

89. operae: dat., as in *haud mihi dero*, *Sat.* 1, 9, 56.

90 f. Difficilem, morosum: these words are used of old men by Cicero (*de Sen.* 18, 65). — **ultra**: 'don't even be *too* silent.' Cf. the rebuke of the impatient judge to the talkative lawyer: 'The Court wants nothing from you but silence — and not very much of *that*.' — **non**: there are occasional uses of *non* with a subjv. like this scattered through Latin writers [Schmalz, *Lat. Synt.*[3] § 205], especially in poetry and in Low Latin. Such instances are usually explained by connecting *non* with some single idea in the sentence, other than the verb, or by twisting the subjv. into a potential meaning. — **comicus**: *be like Davus in the comedy*. Davus was a stock name for the confidential slave.

stes capite obstipo, multum similis metuenti.
Obsequio grassare ; mone, si increbuit aura,
cautus uti velet carum caput ; extrahe turba
95 oppositis umeris ; aurem substringe loquaci.
Importunus amat laudari ; donec ' Ohe iam!'
ad caelum manibus sublatis dixerit, urge,
crescentem tumidis infla sermonibus utrem.
Cum te servitio longo curaque levarit,
100 et certum vigilans, ' Quartae sit partis Vlixes '
audieris ' heres ' : ' Ergo nunc Dama sodalis
nusquam est ? Vnde mihi tam fortem tamque fidelem?'

92. **capite obstipo**: this is the attitude of extreme deference, represented in vase-paintings and in the illustrated Ms. of Terence. — **multum** : with *metuenti;* 'like a man deeply respectful.' [Usually taken with *similis*, on the basis of *Epist.* 1, 10, 3 ; in that passage, however, the contrast demands an emphasis upon *dissimiles*, which is quite out of place here. There are parallels enough to the use of *multum* (as well as *multa*) with such a verb as *metuo*.]

93. **Obsequio**: the emphatic word ; it makes a slight intentional contrast with *grassare*, which carries the suggestion of approach with an unfriendly purpose : *get at him by flattery*.

95. **substringe** : *i.e. gather up your ear with your hand, as if anxious not to lose a word*.

96. **Importunus** : *insatiate, exacting*, as in *Epist.* 2, 2, 185. — **amat** : a paratactic condition, like

scribet, 74. — **Ohe iam**: the full form, *ohe iam satis est*, is used in *Sat.* 1, 5, 12 f. and *ohe iam satis* in Plaut. *Stich.* 734. The phrase was so fixed that the meaning was suggested without *satis*.

98. **tumidis**: *swelling*, in the active sense : cf. Verg. *Aen.* 3, 357. *tumido inflatur . . . Austro.* A similar figure is used in *Sat.* 1, 4, 19.

99. **levarit** : *shall release you by his death*.

100. **certum vigilans** : ' be perfectly sure that you are wide awake, that it is no dream.' — **Quartae sit** : as if quoted from the will, though the exact formula would be *Vlixes heres ex quadrante esto*.

101 f. **Ergo** : *so then* ; the conventional word to introduce an expression of grief. Cf. *Carm.* 1, 24, 5 ; Ovid, *Trist.* 3, 2, 1. — **sodalis**: cf. vs. 18, *spurco Damae*. — **nusquam est** : one of the many periphrases for death.

sparge subinde, et, si paulum potes, illacrimare : est
gaudia prodentem voltum celare. Sepulchrum
105 permissum arbitrio sine sordibus exstrue; funus
egregie factum laudet vicinia. Si quis
forte coheredum senior male tussiet, huic tu
dic, ex parte tua seu fundi sive domus sit
emptor, gaudentem nummo te addicere. — Sed me
110 imperiosa trahit Proserpina : vive valeque!

103 f. **sparge**: the object is the preceding remark. — **paulum**: in sense with *illacrimare* as well as with *potes*. — **est**: *it is your part, it is for you to.* — **gaudia**: obj. of *prodentem*.

105 f. **permissum arbitrio**: *i.e.* when no specific directions are given. The emphatic words are *sine sordibus* and (in 106) *egregie factum*.

108 f. **sive sit emptor**: *if he should wish to buy.* — **nummo**: our formula is, 'for one dollar and other considerations'; the form of legal sale is gone through in order to make the gift valid.

110. **imperiosa**: so *saeva Proserpina*, *Carm.* 1, 28, 20; she is the mistress of the dreaded underworld. But there is a bit of travesty in the abruptness of the farewell, which is quite different from the dignified withdrawal of Tiresias in the Homeric scene, *Od.* 11, 150 f. The common formula of farewell, *vive valeque*, is also used with humorous effect.

6

This satire was written at about the same time as the preceding (2. 5), late in 31 B.C. or early in 30. The 'chilling rumor about the Dacians' (vss. 50, 53) refers to the popular fear of an invasion of Italy by the Daci after the battle of Actium, and the uncertainty in regard to the allotment of land to the veterans (vss. 55 f.) was terminated by the brief visit of Octavius to Brundisium early in 30. Other indications (38) point to the same date.

The connection of thought is simple: 'I now have in my Sabine farm more than I had dared to hope for, and my only desire is that my present happiness may continue without change. No better subject than this could offer itself to my humble Muse, as I begin the day here. For at Rome the day begins quite differently, with one engagement after another, and even though a visit to Maecenas may be one of them, yet the pleasure is half spoiled by the requests of my acquaintances that I should use my influence with Maecenas on their behalf. They do not understand that my friendship with him has nothing to do with public affairs; in fact, we never speak of such things, and I am glad to escape from it all and get back into the country, and to hear the simple talk of my good neighbors, like Cervius' story of the Town Mouse and the Country Mouse.'

This satire is a partial return to the forms used in the First Book. The main body of the discourse (vss. 77-117) is, it is true, formally separated from the rest and put into the mouth of another speaker; in so far Horace uses the newer form with which he had been experimenting in *Sat.* 2, 2; 2, 3. The main body, however, is not enclosed in a framework of formal dialogue, but is introduced by an expression of personal opinion and feeling, like that with which *Sat.* 1, 6 concludes. It was, undoubtedly, the strength of personal feeling to be expressed that led Horace to return to his earlier method of treatment instead of using the form of *Sat.* 2, 2 and 2, 3, which is better suited to burlesque and *persiflage* than to serious discussion.

In general tone, also, this satire — which has in it little of the satirical element — is a return to the manner of the First Book. It is not, however, a mere turning back. The intervening years had left their healthful mark upon Horace, and in his personal attitude he shows the good effect that success in honest endeavor has upon all men of large nature; he is not less modest, perhaps he is more modest (vss. 40-58), but he no longer needs to explain himself or to defend his conduct. The sense of easy security centered about his closest friend, Maecenas, and about the farm which was the gift of that friend, and he felt the impulse to express his contentment. It is to be remembered, also, that Horace was, as Kiessling reminds us, a 'country boy.' It was in Rome that he had done his work, and there he had made himself a place, but his profoundest interest was not in the life of clubs and dinners. He never ceased to feel the desire for the quieter life of the country, as this satire and *Epod.* 2 sufficiently testify.

Meanwhile, a change had come over public affairs, not unlike the change in his own circumstances. The rule of Octavius had justified itself, so far as such rule can ever be justified, and the security which Horace had received from Maecenas, Rome had had as a gift from Maecenas' chief. Between Octavius and Antony no sane man could hesitate, and beneath the personal contentment which this satire expresses it is easy to hear the note of political repose and contentment which followed the decision at Actium. This satire was not written by the young republican who fought at Philippi, or by the satirical follower of the more satirical Lucilius, but by a contented friend and citizen.

> Hoc erat in votis: modus agri non ita magnus,
> hortus ubi et tecto vicinus iugis aquae fons
> et paulum silvae super his foret. Auctius atque
> di melius fecere. Bene est. Nil amplius oro,
> 5   Maia nate, nisi ut propria haec mihi munera faxis.
> Si neque maiorem feci ratione mala rem,

1. **Hoc**: elaborated in the rest of the sentence, but with reference also to the scene that lay before him, as he looked out from his farm-house in the morning. — **in votis**: 'was one of the things for which I made my vows.'

2. **iugis**: in form either gen. or nom., but the balance — *vicinus -fons, iugis-aquae* — requires a genitive.

3. **super his**: the acc. is more common, but the abl. is freely used by Horace (*super foco, Carm.* 1, 9, 5; *super Pindo, Carm.* 1, 12, 6). His usage favors the local meaning *above these* (not *in addition to these things*), *i.e.* on the overhanging ridge of the hill. This little wood-land is referred to also in *Carm.* 3, 16, 29 f., *silva iugerum paucorum* and in *Epist.* 1, 14, 1, and there is a fuller description in *Epist.* 1, 16, 5 ff. — **Auctius**: *more liberally*.

5. **Maia nate**: cf. Vergil's *nate dea*. Mercury, as the god of gain (*e.g. Sat.* 2, 3, 25), was the god to whom the prayer for *amplius* would be addressed. — **haec ... munera**: even more distinctly than *hoc*, vs. 1, a reference to the scene before him. — **faxis**: the archaic form (*fac-s-is*, a sigmatic aorist optative), still used in prayers and curses.

6 f. Cf. the advice of the father to his two sons, *Sat.* 2, 3, 177 f., and the note there. The thought here is the same, but it is expressed somewhat elliptically and with a careful contrast of phrasing which covers up the thought. The real emphasis is upon Horace's contentment with what he has and his determination to avoid in the future, as he has in the past, either of the extremes against which so much of his preaching is directed, either the extreme of money-loving or the opposite extreme of wastefulness. There is no contrast between *ratione mala* and some *ratio bona* nor between *vitio culpave* and some creditable way of lessening one's property, *e.g.* by charity; the contrast is between the *avarus* with his usual *ratio mala* and the *nepos* with his *vitium culpave*.

nec sum facturus vitio culpave minorem;
si veneror stultus nihil horum: 'O si angulus ille
proximus accedat, qui nunc denormat agellum!
10 O si urnam argenti fors quae mihi monstret, ut illi,
thesauro invento qui mercennarius agrum
illum ipsum mercatus aravit, dives amico
Hercule!' si quod adest gratum iuvat, hac prece te
oro:

The sense of the whole is, 'I am content with what I have. I have not tried (and shall not try) to increase it as men usually do and I (have not been tempted and) shall not be tempted into the common fault of wastefulness.'

8. veneror: a rather infrequent use, with cognate acc. or acc. of the thing asked for, without the acc. of the person. Cf. *Carm. Saec.* 49. 'If I utter no such prayer as these.' — **O si**: this expression of a wish is explained in the grammars and is familiar to us from the corresponding English; 'oh, if only . . .'

9. accedat: *were added* to his farm. — **denormat**: a technical term in surveying; expressive of the natural and common desire to have a farm marked by straight border-lines.

10. urnam argenti: almost exactly the English *a pot of money*, in its original sense.

11 f. mercennarius: this would naturally be in the main clause, but is put into the relative clause in order to bring it into closer contrast with *mercatus*. The whole should be very freely rendered into English: 'the man who found a buried treasure and with it bought and cultivated the very farm on which he had been before a hired laborer.'

13. Hercule: there are a few references, not perfectly clear, to Hercules as the god of hidden treasures, but the explanation of the reference to him here is to be found in the folk-story that Horace is alluding to, which is given by Porphyrio: 'traditur fabula, fuisse quendam mercennarium qui semper Herculem deprecatus sit, ut sibi boni aliquid praestaret. Quem Hercules ad Mercurium duxit et obsecratum thesaurum fecit ostendi. Quo effosso ille eundem agrum, in quo operam mercennarium faciebat, comparavit et labori solito operam dedit; sique probavit Mercurius, quod de eo praedixerat Herculi, nulla re illum posse beatum vivere, cum in eadem opera post inventionem thesauri perseveravit.' In his allusion Horace has omitted Mercury, who is the real god of gain, and has dropped the

pingue pecus domino facias et cetera praeter
15 ingenium, utque soles, custos mihi maximus adsis!
   Ergo ubi me in montis et in arcem ex urbe removi,
quid prius illustrem saturis Musaque pedestri?
Nec mala me ambitio perdit nec plumbeus Auster
autumnusque gravis, Libitinae quaestus acerbae.
20 Matutine pater, seu Iane libentius audis,

moral. — **si ... iuvat**: this repeats the substance of the conditions *si ... feci, si veneror*, after the long interruption, in order to bring them near the apodosis *oro*.

14 f. pingue pecus, ingenium: a pun upon the literal meaning of *pinguis, fat*, and the derived sense, *heavy*, as in the English *fat-witted*. — **ut soles**: other references to Mercury as his guardian divinity are *Carm.* 2, 7, 13 (at Philippi); 2, 17, 29 ff.

16 f. in montis: Horace says of the site of his farm *continui montes* (*Epist.* 1, 16, 5). — **in arcem ex urbe**: the play upon the similar sound of the words is intentional (cf. Enn. *et arce et urbe* and Livy's famous *hostis pro hospite*) and may be rendered by *citadel* and *city*. — **prius**: like the English *rather*, *i.e. sooner*, in preference to my farm. — **Musa pedestri**: cf. *Sat.* 1, 4, 39 f., *ego me illorum dederim quibus esse poetas excerpam numero*, with the argument which follows. The ambition to be a true lyric poet lies behind this estimate of the work he had already done.

18 f. ambitio: something of the original meaning (*amb-ire*, *to go about*, canvassing for votes) is still left in this word, though here the reference is to the social struggle (23 ff.), rather than to the political. — **plumbeus**: the sirocco, *Auster*, brings a peculiar sense of oppression, like a weight. — **Libitinae quaestus**: at the temple of Venus Libitina funerals were registered and fees paid, and the things necessary for a funeral were obtained by undertakers. A season of ill-health, like the autumn (*Epist.* 1, 7, 1–9), was therefore a time of gain (*quaestus*) for the goddess.

20 ff. As the references to the farm, especially vss. 16 f., are meant to indicate the place where this satire was written, so these lines are meant to indicate the time of day, the early morning. And the peaceful beginning of the day in his place of refuge suggests to Horace both the invocation to the god of morning and of all beginnings and also, by contrast, the hurried and senseless round of duties to which the morning sum-

unde homines operum primos vitaeque labores
instituunt (sic dis placitum), tu carminis esto
principium. Romae sponsorem me rapis. 'Heia,
ne prior officio quisquam respondeat, urge!'
25 Sive Aquilo radit terras seu bruma nivalem
interiore diem gyro trahit, ire necesse est.
Postmodo quod mi obsit clare certumque locuto,

mons him at Rome. — **seu Iane**: it was customary in ritual to address the divinity by several different names, leaving it to him to select, as it were, the most acceptable (*libentius*); cf. *Carm. Saec.* 15 f., *sive tu Lucina probas vocari* (= *libentius audis*) *seu Genitalis*. The vocative is used as a direct quotation from the prayer. — **audis**: *art called*; so *rexque paterque audisti, Epist.* 1, 7, 37 f., and often. — **unde**: = *a quo*, 'with an invocation to whom.' — In the rather heavy phrases — *operum vitaeque labores, instituunt, sic dis placitum* — there is a playful formality, as if in his cheerful morning mood Horace amused himself by adopting the formal ritualistic style.

23 ff. These half-humorous lamentations over the so-called social duties which waste the time in Rome are quite in the vein of *Sat.* 1, 9. He is struggling between a sense of what courtesy demands and an impatient desire to be rid of the annoyances. It is annoying to have to go to court on a cold day, but it would be still more annoying to feel that he had failed to meet the claims of friendship; it is highly unpleasant to him to push his way through the crowd and give just cause for remonstrance, and his consciousness of being in the wrong only makes it the harder to bear the impudent remonstrance of the man whom he has jostled.

23 f. Romae: emphatic; 'at Rome how differently the day begins!' — **sponsorem**: 'to be security for a friend'; to be asked to perform this office would be evidence that one was regarded as an intimate friend and would often be an honor. — **rapis**: addressed to the god; the morning brings the demand and expresses it in the words which follow, *heia . . . urge*.

25 f. The details — the cold wind, mid-winter, snow, the short day — picture from different sides the discomfort of going out of the house. — **interiore . . . gyro**: as the sun sinks lower in approaching the winter solstice, each daily circle seems to be within that of the preceding day.

27. Postmodo: *hereafter*, at some future time. This is the

luctandum in turba et facienda iniuria tardis.
'Quid tibi vis, insane, et quam rem agis?' improbus
    urget
30 iratis precibus; 'tu pulses omne quod obstat,
ad Maecenatem memori si mente recurras.'
Hoc iuvat et melli est, non mentiar. At simul atras
ventum est Esquilias, aliena negotia centum
per caput et circa saliunt latus. 'Ante secundam

regular meaning of *postmodo* and it is usually joined with some expression of futurity, as in *Carm.* I, 28, 31 with *nocituram*; it is to be taken here with *obsit*, not with *luctandum* in the sense of *next, afterwards*. — **quod obsit**: if the friend should fail to meet his obligation. The hazards of such *sponsiones* are often alluded to in classical literature, as the dangers of financial endorsements are in modern literature. — **clare certumque**: *i.e.* having had the disagreeable experience of being told to 'speak out, so that the Court can hear.'

28. **facienda**: it seems worse to him to be forced to be rude than it would be to suffer rudeness.

29. **Quid tibi vis, insane**: a common phrase of colloquial speech. — **quam rem agis**: scarcely less frequent in Plautus than *quid agis?* [The text of this line is taken from Bentley's convincing note.] — **improbus**: *some impudent fellow*; though the remonstrance is justified, the manner of it and the reference to Maecenas are impertinent.

30 f. **precibus**: *curses*, like *di te perduint*, which in form are prayers. This sense of *preces* is usually marked by some distinguishing word in the context (*hostilis, Thyesteus*), as here by *iratis*. — **tu**: as the speaker turns and recognizes Horace, he goes on from general curses to a direct and individual taunt: 'oh, it's you, is it? you would of course be in a hurry, on your way to see your great friend!' — **memori ... mente**: *i.e.* 'your mind is so full of him that you can't remember to be decently polite to the rest of us.'

32. **Hoc**: the thought of his friendship with Maecenas. — **non mentiar**: *i.e.* 'I acknowledge it, though it is inconsistent with my argument that Rome isn't a pleasant place to live in.' — **At**: *but* even this pleasure is half-spoiled. — **atras**: the Esquiline, where the palace and gardens of Maecenas were, had been the site of a large burial-place.

34. **per caput, circa latus**: the

35 Roscius orabat sibi adesses ad Puteal cras.'
'De re communi scribae magna atque nova te
orabant hodie meminisses, Quinte, reverti.'
'Imprimat his cura Maecenas signa tabellis.'
Dixeris, 'Experiar:' 'Si vis, potes,' addit et instat.
40 Septimus octavo proprior iam fugerit annus,

figures are slightly different from ours, but we say 'it runs through my head,' 'it springs into my mind'— **Ante secundam**: *before seven o'clock;* Roman business began at an early hour.

35. **orabat**: like the epistolary imperfect. — **adesses**: on banking or court business. The *Puteal* was a stone curbing around a spot in the Forum where lightning had struck; the praetor's tribunal was not far from it.

36 f. These lines afford an interesting little glimpse into the professional relations of Horace as a member still of the *ordo* of minor government officials, the *scribae*. It is, in effect, a notice of a meeting of the organization ('important business'), given orally to Horace, who is addressed familiarly by his 'first' name.— **orabant meminisses**: parataxis. — **reverti**: *i.e.* 'to *come back* to the meeting-place to which he used to come when he was an active member of the organization.'

38. **Imprimat . . . cura**: parataxis, like *cura valeas, fac sis fidelis*. — **signa**: *i.e.* he wished Horace to ask Maecenas to set his seal and signature on the document. This would be like putting 'OK' and initials on a paper. As it is known that, during the months within which the composition of this satire must fall, Maecenas was the representative of Octavius in Rome and had authority to use his seal, the document was probably one that had to do with public business.

39. **Dixeris**: as if putting the reader into Horace's position, to make the situation more vivid.

40 ff. The form of expression is apparently intended to suggest increasingly definite reminiscence: 'it's seven years — almost eight — since . . .' — **iam fugerit**: *will soon have passed.* — For the story of the introduction, see *Sat.* 1, 6, 54 ff. The expression here is almost the same as the one used there, *iubes esse in amicorum numero*, with the evident intention of recalling that satire, as the next words recall the journey to Brundisium, *Sat.* 1, 5. The earlier claims to friendship are here qualified, to guard against the interpretations which had been put upon them. The friendship has nothing to do with public affairs.

ex quo Maecenas me coepit habere suorum
in numero, dumtaxat ad hoc, quem tollere reda
vellet iter faciens, et cui concredere nugas
hoc genus: 'Hora quota est?'— 'Thraex est Gallina
    Syro par?'—
45 'Matutina parum cautos iam frigora mordent;'—
et quae rimosa bene deponuntur in aure.
Per totum hoc tempus subiectior in diem et horam
invidiae noster. Ludos spectaverat una,
luserat in Campo: 'Fortunae filius!' omnes.
50   Frigidus a Rostris manat per compita rumor:
quicumque obvius est, me consulit: 'O bone (nam te
scire, deos quoniam propius contingis, oportet),
numquid de Dacis audisti?' 'Nil equidem.' 'Vt tu

44 f. Humorous under-statements. The things about which Horace and Maecenas talked were, to people who were thinking of political influence, no more important than remarks about athletics or the weather. — **Thraex**: a particular kind of gladiator armed like a Thracian. — **Gallina**: *the Chicken*, the name given to him in sporting circles. — **Syro**: a slave name, here borne by the gladiator who was to be matched against *Gallina*.

46. deponuntur: used of placing valuables or money 'on deposit' in safe hands. — **rimosa**: *i.e.* 'Maecenas tells me none of the state secrets' like those mentioned below.

48 ff. noster: *our friend*, as if holding himself up as an object of sympathy. This use is colloquial and the following illustrations are told in colloquial manner.— **spectaverat**: paratactic with the verb of *omnes*. The plupf. tense makes the relation of the clauses plainer: 'he had been to the shows with Maecenas; then everybody said . . .'—**luserat**: *Sat.* 1, 5, 48; 1, 6, 126.

50. a Rostris: the platform in the Forum decorated with the beaks of ships was the center of public discussion and announcement. — **per compita**: *i.e.* through the city, wherever men were gathered; *Sat.* 2, 3, 25 f.

52. deos: a slang word for the prominent men in the state: 'the bosses,' 'The Big Four.'

53 f. numquid: frequently used in colloquial Latin, as here, with-

semper eris derisor!' 'At omnes di exagitent me,
55 si quicquam.' 'Quid, militibus promissa Triquetra
praedia Caesar, an est Itala tellure daturus?'
Iurantem me scire nihil mirantur, ut unum
scilicet egregii mortalem altique silenti.
    Perditur haec inter misero lux non sine votis:
60 O rus, quando ego te aspiciam? quandoque licebit
nunc veterum libris, nunc somno et inertibus horis
ducere sollicitae iucunda oblivia vitae?

out the expectation of a negative answer; 'have you heard anything about the Dacians?' Cf. introd. to this satire and *Carm*. 3, 6, 13 ff., *paene... delevit urbem Dacus.* — **Vt... eris**: 'how determined you are to prove yourself a mere jester!'—**At**: very common in such asseverations. For the general form of the sentence cf. *di me perdant, si bibi*, Plaut. *M. G.* 833.

55 f. The allotment of land to the soldiers of Octavius (*Caesar*) after the battle of Actium was expected and there was great desire among those who were likely to be affected by confiscations or forced sales to know where the lands were to be taken and especially whether they were to be in Italy or perhaps in Sicily.

57 f. **unum**: *the one man*. This is not very different from *unus* with the superlative, *egregii altique* supplying the standard of comparison; cf. *Sat*. 2. 3. 24. — **scilicet**: ironical; he was credited with great power of keeping a secret which was, in fact, not known to him.

59. **Perditur**: the only occurrence of a passive form of *perdo* in classical Latin, the forms of *pereo* being elsewhere used. Acro glosses it with *consumitur*. — **misero**: it is hardly necessary to supply *mihi*; the thought is still somewhat impersonal, as in vs. 48. — **votis**: such as follow. But the wishes pass over easily and imperceptibly into a description of an evening in the country and so to the story of Cervius.

61. **veterum libris**: like those Greek books which he had taken with him for his Christmas vacation, *Sat*. 2, 3, 11 f. Horace did not care much for the early Latin literature, though he speaks with respect of Ennius. — **somno**: an undisturbed *siesta*.

62. **ducere... oblivia**: *drink in forgetfulness;* so souls about to be born again *longa oblivia potant* (*Aen*. 6, 715) at the water of Lethe.

O quando faba Pythagorae cognata simulque
uncta satis pingui ponentur holuscula lardo?
65 O noctes cenaeque deum! quibus ipse meique
ante larem proprium vescor vernasque procacis
pasco libatis dapibus.   Prout cuique libido est,
siccat inaequalis calices conviva, solutus
legibus insanis, seu quis capit acria fortis
70 pocula, seu modicis uvescit laetius.   Ergo

63 f. The simple fare of the country. — **Pythagorae cognata** : *the relative of Pythagoras*; a little fling at the Pythagorean philosophy. Pythagoras forbade the eating of the flesh of animals because the soul of a human being might be inhabiting the body of the animal. He also forbade the eating of beans; whatever may have been the reason for this prohibition (and many different explanations are given), it was attributed to the same motive, to the belief that the soul of a man, even of a relative, might be dwelling in the bean, and the doctrine in this probably perverted form was made a matter of derision. — **uncta satis**: the fat bacon took the place of olive oil in the salad.

65 ff. This is an ideal picture of the cheerful supper with its pleasant details (*ipse*, the host; *mei*, the intimate friends; *larem*, the sacred hearth; *proprium*, at home; *vernas*, the old family servants; *procacis*, on easy terms with the master; *libatis dapibus*, there is enough for all). A similar scene is suggested, though with less detail, in Cic. *Cat. mai.* 14, 46. — **libatis dapibus**: abl. with *pasco*. the food which the guests have left is enough for the slaves. Cf. *Sat.* 1, 3, 80 f.

67. **Prout . . . libido** : '*each guest, according to his own taste. . . .*'

68 ff. **inaequalis**: defined in the following clauses, *seu . . . seu.* The etiquette of a formal dinner (*legibus insanis*) obliged the guests to drink their wine and water mixed in the same proportion, without regard to the taste of the individual. — **capit**: *holds, carries.* — **acria**: *strong.* — **fortis**: *strong-headed.* — **uvescit**: *grows mellow.* These are all words of half-specialized meaning, in use as a kind of slang in regard to drinking. There is a considerable vocabulary of such words in English, euphemistic and half-humorous.

70. **Ergo** : *so then*, in consequence of all that has been said of the character of the gathering.

sermo oritur, non de villis domibusve alienis,
nec male necne Lepos saltet; sed quod magis ad nos
pertinet et nescire malum est agitamus: utrumne
divitiis homines an sint virtute beati;
75 quidve ad amicitias, usus rectumne, trahat nos;
et quae sit natura boni, summumque quid eius.
  Cervius haec inter vicinus garrit anilis
ex re fabellas. Si quis nam laudat Arelli
sollicitas ignarus opes, sic incipit: 'Olim
80 rusticus urbanum murem mus paupere fertur

71 f. **non de villis**: not the envious or silly gossip that one may hear at more ambitious city dinners. — **Lepos**: *Charm, the Charmer*, a nickname of some dancer on the stage; a real person, admired by Caesar, the Scholiast says.

73 ff. **nescire malum est**: these fundamental doctrines of ethical philosophy cannot be ignored without loss and discredit. — **divitiis ... an virtute**: *i.e.* whether happiness comes from within, from character, or from external advantages, like wealth. — **usus rectumne**: whether friendship is the result of need and of a sense of its advantages (*usus*) or comes from the attractive power of high character. This is one of the questions on which Epicureans and Stoics held opposite views. It is discussed by Cicero in the *de Amicitia*. — **natura boni**: the nature and essence of the Good and the Highest Good — *summum bonum* — the fundamental question in all ancient philosophy, of which Cicero wrote in the *de Finibus Bonorum et Malorum*.

77 ff. **garrit anilis ... fabellas**: there is a touch of modesty in these words — 'he recounts some little story that he had heard from some old woman' — not the tone of contempt that is in 'old-wives' fables,' but enough to disarm criticism. — **ex re**: *to the point*, connected with the talk, perhaps with the question *divitiis an virtute*. — **Arelli**: Greenough's note on this is thoroughly Horatian: 'so that, after all, human nature was too much for them, and they did talk "de villis domibusve alienis."' — **ignarus**: not knowing that money brings anxiety (*sollicitas*). — **Olim**: *once upon a time*.

80 ff. The old story of the Town Mouse and the Country Mouse is retold and put into the mouth of a Sabine farmer with a purpose — like so much of Horace — at once serious and humorous.

accepisse cavo, veterem vetus hospes amicum,
asper et attentus quaesitis, ut tamen artum
solveret hospitiis animum.   Quid multa? neque ille
sepositi ciceris nec longae invidit avenae,
85 aridum et ore ferens acinum semesaque lardi
frusta dedit, cupiens varia fastidia cena
vincere tangentis male singula dente superbo;
cum pater ipse domus palea porrectus in horna
esset ador loliumque, dapis meliora relinquens.
90   Tandem urbanus ad hunc: 'Quid te iuvat,' inquit,
'amice,

It enforces in general terms the lesson of Horace's own preference, and it is at the same time an *anilis fabella*, at which one smiles while he recognizes its underlying truth. The actors are Lilliputian, but their action embodies a large truth. This double purpose is reflected in the style, which has a kind of old-fashioned formality. The tone is carefully set in the elaborate structure of the first sentence: the four words *rusticus . . . mus* balance *veterem . . . amicum* —adj.-adj., noun-noun; nom-acc., acc.-nom; *rusticus-urbanum, murem-mus*. This is the manner of the serious teller of an old story, conscious of his moral purpose and not quite conscious of the incongruity between the purpose and the vehicle by which he conveys the lesson.

82. **asper, attentus**: like the ideal Sabine or New England farmer. — **ut tamen**: *but yet such that he could . . . Ita* is commonly used in this kind of sentence.

83. **solveret**: to balance *artum*; he could *relax* his *closeness*.— Quid multa: the same phrase is used in *Sat.* 1, 6, 82 and cf. *ne te morer, Sat.* 1, 1, 14.

84. **ciceris**: the gen. after *invidit* is a Greek construction. — **sepositi**: *set aside* as too good for ordinary days. The kinds of food — peas, oats, seeds, bits of bacon — are specified in order to heighten the contrast between the solemn moral tone and the littleness of the actions and objects.

86. **fastidia**: *the dainty appetite.*

87. **male**: with ' *tangentis*; *scarcely touching.*

88. **pater . . . domus**: *the master of the house*; an intentionally fine phrase.

89. **esset**: from *edo*. — **ador loliumque**: *spelt and darnel*, sup-

praerupti nemoris patientem vivere dorso?
Vis tu homines urbemque feris praeponere silvis?
Carpe viam, mihi crede, comes, terrestria quando
mortalis animas vivunt sortita, neque ulla est
95 aut magno aut parvo leti fuga: quo, bone, circa,
dum licet, in rebus iucundis vive beatus,
vive memor quam sis aevi brevis.' Haec ubi dicta
agrestem pepulere, domo levis exsilit; inde
ambo propositum peragunt iter, urbis aventes
100 moenia nocturni subrepere. Iamque tenebat
nox medium caeli spatium, cum ponit uterque
in locuplete domo vestigia, rubro ubi cocco
tincta super lectos canderet vestis eburnos,

posedly easy for a mouse to collect and therefore standing for ordinary food.

91 f. These lines drop back into the purely human attitude; to a mouse *praerupti, nemoris, dorso* are not hardships nor *homines urbemque* advantages. — **patientem**: 'enduring a hard life.' — **Vis tui**: *why don't you* . . . ? with hortatory effect. [Bentley's note on the difference between *vis tu* and *vin tu* is repeated in substance by most editors, with a reference to *Sat.* 1, 9, 69 as a true interrogation. But *vin tu . . . oppedere?* is, not a simple question and Bentley's dictum, though fairly correct for *vis tu*, is entirely fanciful for *vin tu*, many examples of which in Plaut. and Ter. are parallel to his *vis tu*. The evidence is collected in A. J. P., X. 4 (40), p. 415.]

93 f. **mihi crede**: a parenthetic exhortation, to add force to *carpe viam*. — **terrestria** . . .: the Epicurean doctrine, put into fine phrases. — **sortita**: the idea of getting by *lot* is almost lost or resolved into a vague sense of destiny.

95. **aut magno aut parvo**: as commonly used, this means 'even the greatest of us cannot escape': spoken by the mouse, the meaning is comically reversed. — **quo . . . circa**: an unusual tmesis.

98. **pepulere**: *struck*, influenced his decision. — **levis**: *light-heartedly*.

100 f. In the epic style; cf. *Sat.* 1, 5, 9 f. Cf. also *Sat.* 1. 5, 20 for *iam tenebat . . . cum*.

102 f. **cocco . . . eburnos**: the contrast of the red covering with the ivory couch is used also in Catull. 64. 47 ff. in a description of a splendidly furnished palace.

multaque de magna superessent fercula cena,
105 quae procul extructis inerant hesterna canistris.
Ergo, ubi purpurea porrectum in veste locavit
agrestem, veluti succinctus cursitat hospes
continuatque dapes, nec non verniliter ipsis
fungitur officiis, praelambens omne quod affert.
110 Ille cubans gaudet mutata sorte bonisque
rebus agit laetum convivam, cum subito ingens
valvarum strepitus lectis excussit utrumque.
Currere per totum pavidi conclave, magisque
exanimes trepidare, simul domus alta Molossis
115 personuit canibus. Tum rusticus ' Haud mihi vita

104 f. **fercula**: trays, and then the *courses* served on them. — **procul**: *set aside*, removed from the table to a sideboard. — **hesterna**: *i.e.* of the evening before, it being now after midnight.

106 ff. All the appointments of the feast are in contrast to the entertainment in the country (vss. 83 ff.) and the host hurries about like a slave girt up (*succinctus*) for waiting on the table. — **continuat**: *i.e.* brings on the courses in quick succession. — **verniliter**: *in true servant-fashion;* defined by *praelambens*. He took stealthily a taste of the food before he brought it to his guest — again in contrast with the true hospitality of the country mouse, vss. 88 f.

110 ff. **bonis rebus**: with *agit ... convivam*, not with *laetum* alone. — **agit**: *he plays the joyous guest;* this use of *agere* is technical of actors, *e.g. egit* in the Didascaliae to the plays of Terence. — **strepitus**: made by the servants coming in the early morning to put the dining-room in order. — **excussit**: a very graphic word.

113 f. **Currere**: the name which Lane gives to this, the infinitive of intimation, is here very apt, while the ordinary name, historical infinitive, is particularly inappropriate. — **trepidare**: often used in connection with *cursare, discursu, concursare,* as here with *currere,* of aimless and terrified running about. — **simul**: *when*. — **Molossis**: large hounds kept as watch-dogs.

115 ff. **Haud ... est**: 'I do not care for such a life as this.' For this slightly weakened colloquial sense of *opus est* cf. *Sat.* 1. 9, 27 and the common phrase *nil moror*. It appears to be

' est opus hac,' ait, 'et valeas; me silva cavusque
  tutus ab insidiis tenui solabitur ervo.'

most marked in negative sentences. — **solabitur**: *i.e.* for the loss of the splendors of a city life.

7

The precise date of this satire cannot be fixed. The allusion in vs. 23 may be either to *Sat.* 2, 2 or to the second half of *Sat.* 2, 6, and vs. 28, *Romae rus optas*, may also refer to *Sat.* 2, 6, 59 ff. These indications point in a general way to a late date.

The form is the characteristic form of this book, which is used also in Satires 3, 4, and 8. The main body of the satire is a discourse addressed to Horace himself, which is introduced and then brought to a close by bits of dialogue suited to the subject and to speaker and listener. The resemblance to the third satire is particularly close; both are on the feast of the Saturnalia, in both Horace is interrupted by the intrusion of the speaker and in turn interrupts the speaker before the main discourse is reached (3, 26 and 31; 7, 21 f.), and both close with an outbreak of anger on Horace's part.

In substance also this satire is much like the third. That is a discourse upon the Stoic Paradox that all men except the philosopher are insane; this has for its text the other Paradox that all men but the philosopher are slaves, ὅτι μόνος ὁ σοφὸς ἐλεύθερος, καὶ πᾶς ἄφρων δοῦλος. This is the subject of Cicero's *Parad.* V. and Horace follows in part the same line of reasoning, using in vss. 89 ff. the illustration of the lover enslaved by a woman and in vss. 95 ff. the illustration of the infatuated admirer of works of art, almost precisely as they are used by Cicero. As in the third satire the preacher upon the insanity of men is the half-crazy Damasippus, so here the person who discourses upon the slavery of men is Horace's own slave, Davus, and as Damasippus gets his wisdom from Stertinius (and Catius, in the fourth satire, from an unnamed *auctor*), so in this satire, with a clever parody, Davus has learned his philosophy from the door-keeper of the philosopher Crispinus. The form of Stoic discourse is less distinctly parodied than in *Sat.* 3, perhaps only in vs. 83, and it is evident that Horace was less inclined to burlesque this Paradox than he had been to flout the doctrine that all men are insane. The truth that men are the slaves of their follies and vices is so familiar to us, that we are, in fact, obliged to remind ourselves that slavery was an ever-present reality in the Roman world, in order to understand how the doctrine could have been called a paradox at all. This satire is, therefore, even more than the third, and more, indeed, than any other in the Second Book, a direct attack upon the follies of mankind. But the sharpness which shows itself in some of the satires of the First Book is entirely avoided by the humorous expedient of representing the satire as directed against Horace himself, as in the close of the third. That Horace is not drawing a picture of himself, however, is plain from such passages as vs. 53, vss. 89 ff., 102 ff., 110 f.: the faults there attacked are not those to which Horace was prone. But there is enough caricature of himself (vss. 23 ff., 29 ff.) to add a pleasant humor to the whole. It must be said also that there is some return to the intentional coarseness of *Sat.* 1, 2.

Davus. Iamdudum ausculto, et cupiens tibi dicere servus
pauca, reformido. *Horat.* Davusne? *D.* Ita, Davus,
amicum
mancipium domino et frugi, quod sit satis, hoc est,
ut vitale putes. *H.* Age, libertate Decembri,
5   quando ita maiores voluerunt, utere; narra.
D. Pars hominum vitiis gaudet constanter et urget

1. **ausculto**: the slave has listened at the door to see whether Horace has a caller with him; finding that his master is alone, he ventures to speak. The hesitation and humility (*servus*) of the first words are meant to contrast with his boldness later.

2. **Davusne**: Horace is preoccupied and only half recognizes the slave's voice. The name is a traditional name for a slave.

3. **frugi**: the ordinary adjective in comedy for a good slave, as *nequam* is the adjective for the opposite. — **quod sit satis**: a humorous modification of the claim to goodness; 'honest, or at least honest enough.'

4. **vitale**: cf. *Sat.* 2, 1, 60 f., *ut sis vitalis metuo*; he is good, but not so good as to be in danger of dying young. — **Decembri**: at the feast of the Saturnalia slaves were given a considerable liberty of speech and action, in memory of the Golden Age when there were no masters and no slaves.

5. **narra**: *speak*; this is the early meaning, not *tell, narrate*.

6–20. 'Men are not governed by reason even in their vices. Priscus swings from one extreme to the other, as if he were the very

propositum; pars multa natat, modo recta capessens,
interdum pravis obnoxia. Saepe notatus
cum tribus anellis, modo laeva Priscus inani,
10 vixit inaequalis, clavum ut mutaret in horas,
aedibus ex magnis subito se conderet, unde
mundior exiret vix libertinus honeste;
iam moechus Romae, iam mallet doctus Athenis
vivere, Vertumnis quotquot sunt natus iniquis.
15 Scurra Volanerius, postquam illi iusta cheragra
contudit articulos, qui pro se tolleret atque
mitteret in phimum talos, mercede diurna
conductum pavit; quanto constantior isdem
in vitiis, tanto levius miser ac prior illo,

god of change himself, while Volanerius hangs on to his follies with as much determination as if they were virtues.'

7. **propositum**: cf. *iustum et tenacem propositi virum*, Carm. 3, 3, 1. — **natat**: figurative of hesitation and uncertainty; *float, drift*.

8. **obnoxia**: *submissive to*, agreeing with *pars*.

9. **tribus**: one ring was usual, two were conspicuous, three would be effeminate. — **laeva ... inani**: *i.e.* without any ring, as they were worn only on the left hand.

10. **inaequalis**: cf. *nil aequale homini fuit illi*, in the description of Tigellius at the beginning of Sat. 1, 3. — **clavum**: he changed within an hour from the broad stripe of the senator to the narrow stripe of a knight.

12. **mundior**: *more respectable*, a freedman of self-respecting habits. — **honeste**: *decently*. But the contrast is between the refinements of his palace and the dirt and squalor of a hut — *obsoleti sordibus tecti*, Carm. 2, 10, 6.

13. **doctus Athenis**: like Cicero's friend, T. Pomponius Atticus.

14. **Vertumnis**: the god of the changing year and so of all change. — **quotquot sunt**: a colloquialism, a little more emphatic than *omnibus*. — **natus iniquis**: cf. Sat. 1, 5, 97 f.; 2, 3, 8.

15. **Volanerius**: unknown. — **iusta**: *deserved* by his habits.

17. **in phimum talos**: *put the dice into the box*. — **diurna**: he was too poor to own a slave, but hired a man by the day.

18. **pavit**: from *pasco*; *kept*.

19. **levius**: equal to *minus*; cf. vs. 78.

20 qui iam contento, iam laxo fune laborat.
H. Non dices hodie quorsum haec tam putida tendant,
furcifer? *D.* Ad te, inquam. *H.* Quo pacto, pessime?
   D. Laudas
fortunam et mores antiquae plebis, et idem,
si quis ad illa deus subito te agat, usque recuses,
25 aut quia non sentis, quod clamas, rectius esse,
aut quia non firmus rectum defendis, et haeres
nequiquam caeno cupiens evellere plantam.
Romae rus optas; absentem rusticus urbem
tollis ad astra levis. Si nusquam es forte vocatus
30 ad cenam, laudas securum olus, ac, velut usquam
vinctus eas, ita te felicem dicis amasque
quod nusquam tibi sit potandum. Iusserit ad se
Maecenas serum sub lumina prima venire
convivam: 'Nemon' oleum fert ocius? Ecquis

20. contento, laxo: the sense of this figure is plain, but the precise comparison is not clear.

21. hodie: in the weakened colloquial sense, as often in comedy; 'aren't you ever going to tell me . . . ?' There is no reference to the Saturnalia.

24. illa: the old ways. — **deus subito:** as in *Sat.* I, I, 15 ff., a god is represented as suddenly fulfilling wishes that were not sincere.

28. absentem: not often used, as here, of things.

29. levis: *fickle.* This is the point of the criticism; the accusation of affectation (vs. 25) is aside from the main course of thought.

30 f. securum olus: the 'dinner of herbs where love is.' — **usquam:** *i.e.* 'as if you never went out anywhere except on compulsion (*vinctus*).' — **amas:** the nearest English phrase is 'you hug yourself'; cf. *Sat.* I, 2, 54.

33. serum: the invitation comes so late that Horace had already himself invited some unimportant guests, whom he is represented as abandoning in order to accept the invitation of Maecenas.

34. Nemon'. Ecquis: these are colloquial forms of question used in Plautus and Terence with imperative force: 'won't some one bring the oil? Won't some one listen?'

35 audit?' cum magno blateras clamore fugisque.
    Mulvius et scurrae, tibi non referenda precati,
    discedunt. 'Etenim fateor me,' dixerit ille,
    'duci ventre levem, nasum nidore supinor,
    imbecillus, iners, si quid vis, adde, popino.
40 Tu, cum sis quod ego et fortassis nequior, ultro
    insectere velut melior, verbisque decoris
    obvolvas vitium?' Quid, si me stultior ipso
    quingentis empto drachmis deprenderis? Aufer
    me voltu terrere; manum stomachumque teneto,
45 dum quae Crispini docuit me ianitor edo.
        Te coniunx aliena capit, meretricula Davum.
    Peccat uter nostrum cruce dignius? Acris ubi me
    natura intendit, sub clara nuda lucerna
    quaecumque excepit turgentis verbera caudae,
50 clunibus aut agitavit equum lasciva supinum,
    dimittet neque famosum neque sollicitum ne
    ditior aut formae melioris meiat eodem.
        Tu cum proiectis insignibus, anulo equestri

35. **fugis**: *and off you go.*
36. **non referenda**: *things that I must not repeat.* — **precati**: cf. *Sat.* 2, 6, 30, *iratis precibus.*
37. **ille**: Mulvius.
39. **si quid vis**: *if you choose.* — **popino**: a haunter of cheap taverns.
40 f. **Tu ... insectere**: a repudiating question or exclamation. — **verbis decoris**: with fine words about his obligations to Maecenas, when in fact he is, Mulvius implies, going simply to get a good dinner.
42 f. **me**: Davus. — **quingentis**: a rather low price, to emphasize the point; 'you are proved to be a worse fool than I, and I am a cheap slave, too.' — **aufer**: like *noli*; cf. *mitte sectari*, *Carm.* 1, 38, 3.
44. **manum**: as if Horace, annoyed by vs. 42 f., had started up to strike the slave.
45. **Crispini**: *Sat.* 1, 1, 120, note. The absurdity of quoting him to Horace as an authority is heightened by the fact that the wisdom had trickled down to Davus through the philosopher's door-keeper.
53. **insignibus**: especially the tunic with the narrow purple stripe.

Romanoque habitu, prodis ex iudice Dama
55 turpis, odoratum caput obscurante lacerna,
non es quod simulas? Metuens induceris, atque
altercante libidinibus tremis ossa pavore.
Quid refert, uri virgis ferroque necari
auctoratus eas, an turpi clausus in arca,
60 quo te demisit peccati conscia erilis,
contractum genibus tangas caput? Estne marito
matronae peccantis in ambo iusta potestas?
In corruptorem vel iustior. Illa tamen se
non habitu mutatve loco peccatve superne,
65 cum te formidet mulier neque credat amanti.
Ibis sub furcam prudens, dominoque furenti
committes rem omnem et vitam et cum corpore famam.
Evasti: credo metues doctusque cavebis:
quaeres quando iterum paveas, iterumque perire

—anulo: the gold ring which was one of the signs of equestrian rank.
—equestri: there is no other passage in Horace which suggests that he was an *eques*, and such a supposition is quite inconsistent with the tenor of *Sat.* 1, 6. The reference is general and *tu* is the imaginary person to whom Horace so frequently addresses his remarks; the Davus-Crispinus machinery is for the moment ignored.

54 f. prodis: *i.e.* 'when you come out, you are no longer a citizen of good standing (*iudex*), but a miserable slave.' Cf. *Sat.* 2, 5, 18, *spurco Damae*. — lacerna: a coarse cloak with a hood for concealing the face.

59. auctoratus: *bound over*, as a gladiator was.
60. conscia: cf. *Sat.* 1, 2, 130.
61 f. Estne: with the force of *nonne*, as often in comedy. — iusta potestas: this leads directly toward the point, that in such a case the man is no more than a slave.
66. sub furcam: a common punishment for a slave; his wrists were bound to the ends of a forked beam, which rested upon his neck.
68 f. Evasti: *i.e.* 'suppose you have got off once safely.' — quaeres: an adversative conjunction would be used, if the thought were fully expressed; 'on the contrary, you will seek.'

70 possis, o totiens servus! Quae belua ruptis,
cum semel effugit, reddit se prava catenis?
'Non sum moechus,' ais. Neque ego, hercule, fur, ubi vasa
praetereo sapiens argentea. Tolle periclum,
iam vaga prosiliet frenis natura remotis.
75 Tune mihi dominus, rerum imperiis hominumque
tot tantisque minor, quem ter vindicta quaterque
imposita haud umquam misera formidine privet?
Adde super, dictis quod non levius valeat: nam,
sive vicarius est qui servo paret, uti mos
80 vester ait, seu conservus, tibi quid sum ego? Nempe
tu, mihi qui imperitas, alii servis miser, atque
duceris, ut nervis alienis mobile lignum.
    Quisnam igitur liber? Sapiens, sibi qui imperiosus,
    quem neque pauperies, neque mors, neque vincula terrent,

70. **totiens servus**: this approaches still nearer to the point of the argument. Cf. *iusta potestas*, vs. 62.

75 f. **Tune mihi**: repudiating exclamation. — **imperiis**: abl. after *minor;* 'subject to so many and so severe commands.' — **vindicta**: the rod which the lictor laid upon (*imposita*) the slave in going through the old ceremony of manumission.

77. **privet**: *deliver, set free.*

78-82. 'And there is another argument, not less forcible than these. For the fact that you are my master proves nothing; according to your own customs a slave may be himself the owner of a slave and they are then simply fellow-slaves, like you and me.' — **vicarius**: a slave bought or hired by another slave to do his work for him. — **servis**: the verb. — **nervis**: puppets were made of wood and jointed so that their arms and legs could be moved by strings. — **alienis**: controlled by another person.

83. **Quisnam**: the Stoic form of argument, by brief questions and answers. — **Sapiens**: the Stoic philosopher.

85. **responsare**: *defy;* cf. *Sat.* 2, 4, 18. The infin. depends upon *fortis.*

85 responsare cupidinibus, contemnere honores
fortis, et in se ipso totus, teres atque rotundus,
externi ne quid valeat per leve morari,
in quem manca ruit semper fortuna. Potesne
ex his ut proprium quid noscere? Quinque talenta
90 poscit te mulier, vexat foribusque repulsum
perfundit gelida, rursus vocat: eripe turpi
colla iugo. 'Liber, liber sum,' dic age! Non quis;
urget enim dominus mentem non lenis, et acris
subiectat lasso stimulos, versatque negantum.
95 Vel cum Pausiaca torpes, insane, tabella,
qui peccas minus atque ego, cum Fulvi Rutubaeque
aut Pacideiani contento poplite miror
proelia rubrica picta aut carbone, velut si
re vera pugnent, feriant, vitentque moventes
100 arma viri? Nequam et cessator Davus; at ipse
subtilis veterum iudex et callidus audis.

86 f. in se ipso: with *totus* only; *self-contained*, independent of all else. The phrase is usually quoted wrongly, as if *totus* by itself were an adjective like *teres*. — **externi ... morari**: 'so that nothing foreign may be able to rest upon (*morari*) its smooth surface (*leve*).'

88. manca: *powerless*.

89. ex his: of the qualities just mentioned. The answer to the question is given in the following lines; he cannot be *sibi imperiosus* who is infatuated with a woman or a picture.

91. rursus vocat: cf. *Sat.* 2, 3, 260 ff. The picture of the lover is traditional; cf. Ter. *Eun.* 46-49.

94. stimulos, versat: as a rider subdues a horse by wearying him.

95. Pausiaca: a picture by the famous Greek painter Pausias of the fourth century. — **torpes**: cf. *stupet, Sat.* 1, 4, 28, of unbounded admiration for works of art.

96. Fulvi: names of gladiators, whose performance was advertised by pictures in black and red drawn on the walls.

100. cessator: *i.e.* 'you blame me for having stopped to look at the posters when you had sent me on an errand.'

Nil ego, si ducor libo fumante: tibi ingens
virtus atque animus cenis responsat opimis?
Obsequium ventris mihi perniciosius est cur?
105 Tergo plector enim. Qui tu impunitior illa,
quae parvo sumi nequeunt, obsonia captas?
Nempe inamarescunt epulae sine fine petitae,
illusique pedes vitiosum ferre recusant
corpus. An hic peccat, sub noctem qui puer uvam
110 furtiva mutat strigili; qui praedia vendit,
nil servile, gulae parens, habet? Adde, quod idem
non horam tecum esse potes, non otia recte
ponere, teque ipsum vitas, fugitivus et erro,
iam vino quaerens, iam somno fallere curam:
115 frustra: nam comes atra premit sequiturque fugacem.
  H. Vnde mihi lapidem? *D.* Quorsum est opus?
    H. Vnde sagittas?
  D. Aut insanit homo, aut versus facit. *H.* Ocius hinc te
ni rapis, accedes opera agro nona Sabino!

102. **Nil ego**: sc. *sum*. — **libo**: *pancake*.

105 f. **plector enim**: 'I get a thrashing, to be sure, but that proves nothing, for you suffer worse penalties.'

107. **inamarescunt**: *turn sour*. — **sine fine**: with *petitae*.

110. **mutat**: 'gets a bunch of grapes in exchange for a scraper that he has stolen.'

111. **nil servile ... habet**: *has nothing of the slave about him.* — **parens**: with the subject of *vendit*.

111-115. These lines, which are rather more serious and penetrating than any other part of the satire, seem to be a condensation of Lucr. 3, 1053-1070.

116. **lapidem**: cf. *Sat.* 2, 3, 128 f., where a master throws stones at his slaves. — **sagittas**: these unusual weapons of attack are named in order to give an opening for the final remark of Davus, *versus facit*; that is, *unde sagittas?* sounds as if it might be taken from a play.

118. **opera ... nona**: 'You shall be the ninth slave.' The threat to send a slave from the city to the harder work of the farm is frequent in comedy.

SERMONES

8

Nothing in this satire fixes the date of composition. It can only be said that it was written between 35 and 30 B.C., and that in subject and general treatment it is like the other satires of this book.

In form it most closely resembles *Sat.* 2, 4; the main part of it is an account of certain sayings and doings related by another person to Horace at his request, with a brief introductory dialogue. The subject-matter connects it both with *Sat.* 2, 2, as a contrast to simple living, and with 2, 4, as a satire in a different vein upon the serious-minded epicure.

The main body of it is a description of a dinner, given in much detail. The names of the guests are mentioned and their places at the table and there are elaborate descriptions of the food and cookery. After the dinner had advanced a little and the host had shown a disposition to brag of his food and wines, some of the guests proposed heavy drinking. The host turned their attention again to the food, but while he was describing one of the dishes, a canopy over the table fell and covered the whole company with dust. The host at this mishap burst into tears and was with difficulty induced by the encouragements of some of his guests, which he did not perceive to be ironical, to proceed with the feast. When he did go on, he continued to talk so much about the food, that the guests, in revenge, declined to eat it. The satire ends abruptly, without the concluding dialogue or comment which is generally found in the satires of this book.

This is not a description of some actual dinner at the house of an individual who might be identified. All attempts to connect the host, Nasidienus Rufus, with some person known to us, — for example, with Salvidienus Rufus, — fail in details and are mistaken in their purpose. It is quite inconceivable that Horace should have made public the story of such a dinner, at which Maecenas and Varius were guests, and should have represented a well-known man like Fundanius as guilty of the extreme discourtesy of ridiculing the host whose invitation he had accepted. To readers of Horace's time the mere fact that the story is told by Fundanius, the writer of humorous plays, would at once have given the clew to the burlesque character of the whole. It is no more to be taken as serious narrative than the legal consultation in *Sat.* 2, 1, the discourse of Ofellus in 2, 2, the sermon of Damasippus in 2, 3, or in fact any satire of this book except the earlier half of the sixth.

But though the setting and the details are pure burlesque, there is a certain amount of serious purpose underneath, as in *Sat.* 2, 3, for example, where the Stoic is burlesqued, but the follies of mankind are also satirized. The host at the banquet, who is here ridiculed on his lighter side, is a type of the same man who is attacked with savage directness in *Epod.* 4, the man of low station and no culture, whose suddenly acquired wealth has not changed his nature. He is represented here as an aspiring epicure, proud of his knowledge of the art of cookery and seeking to advance his acquaintance with Maecenas by giving him a particularly fine dinner. But the ridicule is directed quite as much, perhaps even more, against the absurd solemnities of the epicure. There are passages (vss. 6 ff., 43 ff., especially 85 ff.) which are indistinguishable in tone and manner from parts of *Sat.* 2, 4, and which have no point at all unless we understand them as we do that satire, — as ironical parodies of the precepts of fine cookery.

This is not one of the best of the satires. The humor is not always in good taste; there is too close an approach to horse-play and, though Maecenas and the literary men are kept in the background, with the evident purpose of guarding their dignity, the rest of the guests are not superior in good-breeding to the host whom they ridicule. The scene is, with some differences, not unlike the supper described in *Sat.* 1, 5, 51 ff. and, in general, this satire has many of the characteristics, both positive and negative, of *Sat.* 1, 5. The explanation is that Horace is here also, as in 1, 5, following a satire of Lucilius (Charis. in *Gr. Lat.* p. 100 K., *Lucilius . . . deridens rusticam cenam*; the fragments are in Marx, 193 ff.), doubtless improving upon the form, but hampered by his model. The grave and sustained irony of *Sat.* 2, 4, when no Lucilian influence is discernible, is much superior to this.

Horatius. Vt Nasidieni iuvit te cena beati?
Nam mihi quaerenti convivam dictus heri illic

1. **Vt . . . iuvit te**: change the construction in translating; 'how did you enjoy yourself at the dinner of —— ?' — **Nasidieni**: in four syllables, the second *i* being consonantal and lengthening the preceding syllable; this is probably a plebeian pronunciation, intentionally used in the first line. — **beati**: *rich, the millionaire*, with a touch of irony.

2. **quaerenti convivam**: sc. *te*; 'when I tried to get you to come and dine with me.' — **dictus**: sc. *es*; the omission is not at all infrequent in colloquial Latin, as in

de medio potare die. *Fundanius.* Sic, ut mihi numquam
  in vita fuerit melius. *Hor.* Da, si grave non est,
5 quae prima iratum ventrem placaverit esca.
  Fund. In primis Lucanus aper leni fuit Austro
  captus, ut aiebat cenae pater; acria circum
  rapula, lactucae, radices, qualia lassum

comedy. — **heri**: the pronunciation of the last letter was so indistinct that the word was written sometimes *heri*, sometimes *here*.

3. de medio die: the dinner began before the usual hour, which was three o'clock or later, as it was to be a formal affair. The Roman custom in this respect was the opposite of ours.

4. fuerit melius: *mihi bene est*, 'I am enjoying myself,' is a common colloquialism; cf. *Sat.* 2, 2, 120.

5. iratum ventrem: cf. *latrantem stomachum, Sat.* 2, 2. 18. The question is ironical, as if the object of a formal dinner was to satisfy a natural hunger.

6-9. Our knowledge of Roman dinner customs is imperfect, the fashions changed from time to time, and this description is meant to be only a series of allusions. It is therefore quite impossible to arrange the *menu* or even to decide whether this course constituted the *gustatio* (*promulsis*); the relishes served with the boar would indicate that it did; the fact that no drink (*mulsum*) is mentioned would, however, be a strange omission.

6 f. leni . . . Austro captus: not predicate with *fuit*; 'one of the first things was a Lucanian boar, killed, as the host said, when a mild southerly wind was blowing.' The Lucanian boar was especially prized and the state of the weather at the time the animal was killed was supposed to affect the flavor of the meat; cf. *Sat.* 2, 2, 32 ff. and the modern superstitions about the 'dark of the moon.' — **cenae pater**: he is called also *erus* (vss. 16, 43), *ipse* (23), *parochus* (36), and *convivator* (73), as well as *Nasidienus* (1, 75, 84) and *Rufus* (58).

7 f. acria: introducing the whole list and repeated in *qualia . . . stomachum*. The relishes are only partly in use now nor is the precise identification of them at all important: 'rape, lettuce, radishes, skirret, fish-pickle, and burnt tartar from Coan wine.' These were arranged around (*circum*) the boar, perhaps on the same platter.

pervellunt stomachum, siser, allec, faecula Coa.
10 His ubi sublatis puer alte cinctus acernam
gausape purpureo mensam pertersit et alter
sublegit quodcumque iaceret inutile quodque
posset cenantis offendere, ut Attica virgo
cum sacris Cereris procedit fuscus Hydaspes
15 Caecuba vina ferens, Alcon Chium maris expers.

10. **ubi**: introduces *pertersit et sublegit*; 'when these had been removed and after a slave had wiped . . .'— **alte cinctus**: the same as *succinctus*, 2, 6, 107; the slave was in the proper dress for waiting at the table. — **acernam**: *maple*, one of the more valuable woods for dining-tables; as one might speak of 'the mahogany table,' not as a rarity, but as the 'proper thing.'

11. **gausape purpureo**: abl.; this was a bit of unnecessary display. Lucilius, in a corresponding passage (Marx, 568), has *purpureo tersit tunc latas gausape mensas*.

12. **sublegit**: this is mentioned merely as a part of the ordinary table service in order to prepare for the formality of the next event; 'a slave in proper dress wiped the table — with a purple cloth, to be sure — and the crumbs were gathered up, when in came . . .'

13 f. **ut**: with *virgo*: 'like a girl at Athens in a religious procession.' The κανηφόρος (cf. *Sat.* 1, 3, 10 f.) carried the sacred symbols in a basket on her head and walked with slow step and upright carriage. — **Hydaspes**: an Eastern slave-boy, named after the river of his native land.

15 f. **Alcon**: another slave. The fact that his name is given would seem to indicate that there was some point in it, as in *Hydaspes*, but we do not know what it was. — **Caecuba**: one of the best of the Italian wines, as were also the Alban, in the time of Horace, and Falernian. The Chian was a fine Greek wine, with which sea-water was sometimes sparingly mixed to give it a tang. Horace frequently mentions these and other special kinds of wine, contrasting them with the ordinary Sabine wine, as we might contrast special French or German wines with Californian claret, but he does not make sharp distinctions between them. The preference for Caecuban came later, when the vineyards were dying out and the wine was becoming rare. The many attempts of commentators to find hidden meanings in these lines are all misleading. The slaves brought in the best of wine,

SERMONES [2, 8, 20

Hic erus: 'Albanum, Maecenas, sive Falernum
te magis appositis delectat, habemus utrumque.'
Hor. Divitias miseras! Sed quis cenantibus una,
Fundani, pulchre fuerit tibi, nosse laboro.
20 *Fund.* Summus ego, et prope me Viscus Thurinus, et
infra,

with a trifle more ceremony than was necessary, and the host, also with unnecessary display, said 'if you prefer, I can give you some Alban or Falernian.' The wines are all right, — the very best, — but why such a fuss about them? — **maris expers**: *i.e.* not mixed with sea-water. This was a proper, if less usual, way of serving Chian wine, but it might have been left to the guests to discover it, instead of making a formal announcement, as it is implied that the slave did.

18 f. **Divitias miseras**: 'oh, the curse of being so rich!' or perhaps like saying, 'oh, poor millionaire!' This exclamation interprets to us the point of the preceding lines. The unfortunate host thinks that the wines and cookery which his money can buy are the things that make a successful dinner. But Horace goes to the root of the matter by asking who the other guests were. — **quis**: *quibus*, interrogative. The English structure would make *cenantibus* the leading verb: 'but who were dining there with you, that you should have such a good time? That's what I want to know.'

20 ff. The guests reclined on couches on three sides of the table. The arrangement can be understood from the following diagram: —

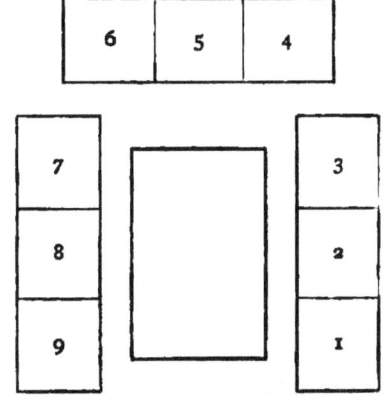

1. Fundanius; 2. Viscus; 3. Varius; 4. Servilius Balatro; 5. Vibidius; 6. Maecenas; 7. Nomentanus; 8. Nasidienus Rufus; 9. Porcius.

20. **Summus**: the three places numbered 1, 4, and 7 were the *summi loci*, in position, not in honor, and *infra* and *super* refer to this designation. — **Viscus**: one of the brothers mentioned in *Sat.* 1, 10, 83, here distinguished by the addition of *Thurinus*.

247

si memini, Varius; cum Servilio Balatrone
Vibidius, quas Maecenas adduxerat umbras;
Nomentanus erat super ipsum, Porcius infra,
ridiculus totas simul absorbere placentas;
25 Nomentanus ad hoc, qui, si quid forte lateret,
indice monstraret digito: nam cetera turba,
nos, inquam, cenamus avis, conchylia, piscis,
longe dissimilem noto celantia sucum,
ut vel continuo patuit, cum passeris atque

21. **Varius**: cf. *Sat.* 1, 5, 40; 1, 10, 44. and often; one of Horace's and Vergil's closest friends. There is probably some little joke in *si memini*.

22. **Maecenas**: he was in the place of honor, the *locus consularis*, numbered 6 in the diagram. — **umbras**: persons whom the chief guest might bring with him, without special invitation from the host. So Horace, inviting a friend, says (*Epist.* 1, 5, 28), *locus est et pluribus umbris*. Men who came in such a way would ordinarily be of lower rank, and Servilius and Vibidius were evidently *scurrae* (see note on *Sat.* 2, 3, 229), who were expected to furnish entertainment for the others. In fact all the conversation reported (vss. 34, 65 ff., 80 ff.) comes from them or from the host and his own *scurrae*.

23. **Nomentanus, Porcius**: two parasites of the host. Nomentanus is not the spendthrift mentioned in other satires (1, 1, 102; 1, 8, 11: 2, 1, 22: 2, 3, 175. 224).

The name Porcius is coined from *porcus*; cf. the next verse. — **super ipsum**: *i.e.* Nasidienus had given the host's place (no. 7) to his more fluent parasite, for the reason given in vs. 25.

24. **totas simul**: *all at once*. Various kinds of buffoonery like this are alluded to in Plautus as practiced by parasites.

25 f. **ad hoc**: also in *Sat.* 2, 1, 36, to introduce a clause of purpose. — **lateret**: *pass unnoticed* by the guests. — **indice digito**: *i.e.* he should not only speak of it, but also point to it. — **cetera turba**: the instruction was obviously given to Maecenas and the others were a mere *turba*, left for the most part uninstructed as to the nature of the food before them.

27. **inquam**: not strengthening the previous statement, but explaining it; *we, I mean*.

28 ff. **celantia**: neut., agreeing with the three nouns of different gender. — **noto**: sc. *suco*; dat. after *dissimilem*. — **vel**: *in fact*. — **passeris**: *flat-fish*; the name

30 ingustata mihi porrexerat ilia rhombi.
    Post hoc me docuit melimela rubere minorem
    ad lunam delecta. Quid hoc intersit, ab ipso
    audieris melius. Tum Vibidius Balatroni,
    'Nos nisi damnose bibimus, moriemur inulti;'
35 et calices poscit maiores. Vertere pallor
    tum parochi faciem, nil sic metuentis ut acris

of a bird transferred to a fish, as in 'sea-robin.' — **ingustata**: apparently found only here; it can mean either *untasted*, *i.e.* 'which I did not taste,' or *untasted hitherto*, 'of such a flavor as I had never known before.' — **prorrexerat**: the subject is Nasidienus. — **ilia**: *the roe.* — The sense is: 'Nomentanus explained the excellence of the dishes to Maecenas only, for the rest of us were of no importance (*turba*) and ate all sorts of things without knowing what was fish, flesh, or fowl; for the ordinary taste was covered up by some extraordinary sauce. I in fact made a mistake at the outset by failing to recognize some fish-roe which my host had passed to me and which had a taste that I had never known before.'

31. **melimela rubere**: 'that the honey-apples were red because they were picked . . .' — **minorem**: the waning moon. This verse has nothing to do with the preceding, but is a bit of esoteric wisdom which the epicure obligingly imparted (*docuit*) to his ignorant guest. Cf. vs. 6 f. This is exactly in the ironical manner of *Sat.* 2, 4.

32 f. **ab ipso**: *i.e.* 'you will have to ask him; *I* don't pretend to know.' — **audieris**: the potential with a comparative, as often.

34. **damnose**: *i.e.* to the ruin of the host; 'drink him bankrupt.' — **moriemur inulti**: this is the cry of the epic hero facing death; so Hector, *Il.* 22, 304 f., μὴ μὰν ἀσπουδί γε καὶ ἀκλειῶς ἀπολοίμην, | ἀλλὰ μέγα ῥέξαστι, and Aeneas, *Aen.* 2. 670, *numquam omnes hodie moriemur inulti.*

35 ff. **Vertere pallor . . . faciem**: *i.e.* 'he turned pale,' but the expression is somewhat odd; not the same as *Epod.* 4, 9 ff. — **parochi**: *our steward, our caterer*; with some contempt. Cf. for the use of the word in its ordinary sense, *Sat.* 1, 5, 46. — **vel quod . . . vel quod**: there is no reason whatever for looking behind these perfectly good explanations to discover some discreditable motive, like stinginess. Vss. 41 and 81 are perfectly consistent with these lines taken in their simple sense. —

potores, vel quod male dicunt liberius vel
fervida quod subtile exsurdant vina palatum.
Invertunt Allifanis vinaria tota
40 Vibidius Balatroque, secutis omnibus; imi
convivae lecti nihilum nocuere lagenis.
　　Affertur squillas inter murena natantis
in patina porrecta. Sub hoc erus 'Haec gravida,' inquit,
'capta est, deterior post partum carne futura.
45 His mixtum ius est: oleo quod prima Venafri
pressit cella; garo de sucis piscis Hiberi;
vino quinquenni, verum citra mare nato,
dum coquitur — cocto Chium sic convenit, ut non
hoc magis ullum aliud; — pipere albo, non sine aceto,

male dicunt: as in *Sat.* 1, 4, 86 ff.
— exsurdant: the real epicure is especially anxious that his fine cookery should be properly appreciated.

39. Allifanis: large cups, named from the town of Allifae. — vinaria: *jugs;* we should say 'bottles,' 'decanters.'

40 f. imi . . . lecti: the three couches were called *summus* (nos. 1, 2, 3 on the diagram), *medius* (nos. 4, 5, 6), and *imus.* The two parasites of the host of course followed his wish and drank little. — nihilum nocuere: the same idea is in the English 'to spare the bottle.'

42 f. The Roman cooks sought to produce odd or realistic effects in the arrangement of the food on the platter. — Sub hoc: *at this,* as this appeared.

44. futura: *for it would be.* This piece of epicure's wisdom is accepted by commentators as sound and a matter of common knowledge; it may be so.

45 ff. His: 'the following ingredients.' The other ablatives — *oleo, garo, vino, pipere* — are appositives of *his.* — Venafri: the olives of Venafrum were considered especially good and the oil which came from the first pressing was better than that extracted later. — garo: something like *caviare.* — piscis Hiberi: *mackerel.* — citra mare: Italian; the phrase is a little too fine to be used of wine. Cf. *Sat.* 1, 10, 31. — dum coquitur: *while it is cooking.* — cocto: *after it is cooked* Chian wine is exactly the right thing to pour in; here also the wisdom is clothed in fine language.

50 quod Methymnaeam vitio mutaverit uvam.
    Erucas viridis, inulas ego primus amaras
    monstravi incoquere; inlutos Curtillus echinos,
    ut melius muria quod testa marina remittat.'
    Interea suspensa gravis aulaea ruinas
55 in patinam fecere, trahentia pulveris atri
    quantum non Aquilo Campanis excitat agris.
    Nos maius veriti, postquam nihil esse pericli
    sensimus, erigimur: Rufus posito capite, ut si
    filius immaturus obisset, flere. Quis esset
60 finis, ni sapiens sic Nomentanus amicum
    tolleret: 'Heu, Fortuna, quis est crudelior in nos
    te deus? Vt semper gaudes illudere rebus

50. The sense is almost hidden under the poetic expression; 'vinegar made by fermentation (*vitio*) of the Methymnaean cluster,' *i.e.* from Lesbian wine.

51 ff. A little claim to original research by Nasidienus—he had discovered the good effect of boiling green rockets and bitter elecampane into the sauce—with a generous acknowledgment of the investigations of a certain Curtillus, who had observed that if sea-urchins are not washed in fresh water before boiling, the brine from their shells is better than the ordinary brine. The construction in vs. 53 is *ut* (*id*) *quod marina testa* (the shell of the sea-urchin) *remittat melius* (*est*) *muria*. Cf. 89, note.

54 ff. While Nasidienus was speaking, the canopy which hung from the ceiling suddenly fell upon the table, destroying the valuable sauce and covering the guests with dust. — **Campanis**: the level lands of Campania were especially dusty in the dry season.

57. **maius**: the fall of the ceiling itself. — **veriti**: make this a leading verb in the translation.

58. **erigimur**: like a middle voice and in a literal sense, 'we lifted up our heads,' to contrast with *posito capite*. — **Rufus**: *i.e.* Nasidienus. — **posito capite**: this also should be a leading verb in the English; 'put down his head and wept.'

59 f. **Quis ... finis**: 'what would have ended it?' *i.e.* 'he would be crying still, had not Nomentanus ...' — **sapiens**: *like a philosopher*, with the philosophic remarks which follow.

humanis!' Varius mappa compescere risum
vix poterat. Balatro suspendens omnia naso,
65 'Haec est condicio vivendi,' aiebat, 'eoque
responsura tuo numquam est par fama labori.
Tene, ut ego accipiar laute, torquerier omni
sollicitudine districtum, ne panis adustus,
ne male conditum ius apponatur, ut omnes
70 praecincti recte pueri comptique ministrent!
Adde hos praeterea casus, aulaea ruant si,
ut modo, si patinam pede lapsus frangat agaso.
Sed convivatoris, uti ducis, ingenium res
adversae nudare solent, celare secundae.'
75 Nasidienus ad haec: 'Tibi di quaecumque preceris
commoda dent! Ita vir bonus es convivaque comis:'

63. **Varius**: a little joke at the expense of a good friend, possibly with some special point to it which their common friends would see.

64. **suspendens . . . naso**: cf. *Sat.* 1, 6, 5, *naso suspendis adunco*, and note. Greenough translates, *always a scornful cynic*. He felt himself to be a great man's attendant.

65. **eo**: *for that reason*, because we are all subject to the chances of life.

67 ff. A distinct reminiscence, both in structure and in substance, of the parasite's speech in Terence, *Phorm.* 339 ff., to which there is a reference also in *cena dubia, Sat.* 2, 2, 77. — **ego**: ironical, since Balatro had come merely as Maecenas' *umbra*. — **laute**: colloquial; *handsomely*. — **male conditum ius**: with reference to the sauce which Nasidienus had just been describing. — **compti**: the dressing of the hair of the young slaves who waited on the table was attended to as carefully as their attire.

71 f. **Adde . . . praeterea**: 'and on the top of it all come such misfortunes as these.' — **ut modo**: *as happened just now*, to distinguish the actual occurrence from the imagined mishap of a fallen platter. — **agaso**: *i.e.* some clumsy slave, no better than a stable-boy.

73 f. **uti ducis**: a flattering comparison; 'the giver of a dinner is like a general.' — **nudare**: *disclose, reveal* his powers.

75 f. **Tibi di . . . dent**: a common kind of wish, often used in greetings; Plaut. *M. G.* 1038, *di tibi dent quaequomque optes*, and cf.

et soleas poscit. Tum in lecto quoque videres
stridere secreta divisos aure susurros.
   Hor. Nullos his mallem ludos spectasse; sed illa
80 redde, age, quae deinceps risisti. *Fund.* Vibidius dum
quaerit de pueris, num sit quoque fracta lagena,
quod sibi poscenti non dantur pocula, dumque
ridetur fictis rerum Balatrone secundo,
Nasidiene, redis mutatae frontis, ut arte
85 emendaturus fortunam; deinde secuti

Sat. 1, 9, 5, *cupio omnia quae vis*. It is like 'God bless you!' Nasidienus takes the ill-bred irony of Balatro quite seriously and simply, showing in fact better manners than some of his guests.

77. soleas poscit: the light shoes ordinarily worn in the house were removed when the guests took their places, and to ask for them was to express a desire to rise from the table. Nasidienus, encouraged by what the two parasites had said, prepares to go on with the feast and gets up in order to have the damage repaired and the other dishes brought in. — **Tum**: when he had gone out to give his orders. — **quoque**: from *quisque*. — **videres**: *you might see*; indefinite 2d pers. with potential meaning, as often; cf. *Sat.* 1, 5, 76.

78. divisos: first to one side, then to the other. The alliteration with *s* imitates the sound of whispering.

79 f. The interruption by Horace marks the end of the main story and introduces the conclusion, giving the effect of dialogue. Cf. the similar and rather more skilful dialogue in *Sat.* 2, 3, 300-307, followed by the speech of Damasippus, 307-323. — **Nullos . . . ludos**: 'I'd rather have seen this than any games.' Greenough compares the English 'as good as a play.' — **quae deinceps**: 'what you found next to laugh at.'

81 f. quoque: with *sit fracta*; he asked whether there was another breakage, of the wine-jugs as well as of the *aulaea*. — **quod**: *that*. — **pocula**: the wine, not the cups. In the confusion the slaves had forgotten to keep the cups filled.

83. fictis rerum: they invented jokes to cover their laughter at the fall of the canopy and the simplicity of the host. Cf. *vanis rerum, Sat.* 2, 2, 25. — **secundo**: playing second to Vibidius, who led the pretended jesting.

84 f. Nasidiene: the vocative and the phrase *arte emendaturus* are parodies of the epic style.

mazonomo pueri magno discerpta ferentes
membra gruis sparsi sale multo, non sine farre,
pinguibus et ficis pastum iecur anseris albae,
et leporum avolsos, ut multo suavius, armos,
90 quam si cum lumbis quis edit. Tum pectore adusto
vidimus et merulas poni et sine clune palumbes,
suavis res, si non causas narraret earum et
naturas dominus; quem nos sic fugimus ulti,
ut nihil omnino gustaremus, velut illis
95 Canidia afflasset peior serpentibus Afris.

86. **mazonomo**: properly a platter for bread, here put to a different use as a novelty in table-service. — **discerpta**: already carved; the custom was to serve fowls and game whole and have them carved on the table by a specially trained slave.

87 f. **gruis**: here masc., though commonly fem., as *anser*, commonly masc., is here made fem. The gender of such words is grammatical and somewhat shifting, but apparently the unusual gender is chosen to indicate sex, as though the epicure could tell the sex by the taste. — **albae**: used in the same way, to ridicule the epicure's claim to delicacy of palate. — **iecur**: a kind of *pâté de foie gras*. And the white goose must have been fed upon ripe figs.

89. **avolsos, ut suavius**: an exact parallel to *inlutos ut melius*, vss. 52 f.; but the order here expresses the sense better. The doctrine that in this case the shoulders should be torn off, not cut, is like the notion that a pear should never be cut, a pure fantasy.

90 ff. **edit**: pres. subjv., the older optative form, for the most part displaced by the regular subjv. *edat*. — The peculiarity of the dishes is in *pectore adusto* 'with the breasts broiled' and *sine clune*, 'without the rump.' — **suavis res**: 'very good eating, if only . . .' — **causas . . . et naturas**: philosophical terms; Nasidienus discoursed about his dishes as a philosopher might *de rerum natura*.

93. **sic**: with *ulti*, anticipating *ut*; 'taking our revenge for his talk by not eating any more of his food.'

95. **Canidia**: often mentioned as a sorceress and poisoner and directly attacked in *Sat.* 1, 8 and *Epod.* 5 and 17. This personal stroke at the end is like *Sat.* 1, 1, 120 f.; 1, 2, 134.

HORACE

THE EPISTLES

WITH INTRODUCTION AND NOTES

BY

EDWARD P. MORRIS
PROFESSOR OF LATIN IN YALE COLLEGE

NEW YORK ∴ CINCINNATI ∴ CHICAGO
AMERICAN BOOK COMPANY

COPYRIGHT, 1911, BY
EDWARD P. MORRIS AND MORRIS H. MORGAN.

ENTERED AT STATIONERS' HALL, LONDON.

MORRIS. HORACE, EPISTLES

PREFACE

IT has been taken for granted in the preparation of this edition that the Epistles are not read until after the Satires and perhaps after the Odes, and parallels in the earlier poems have been rather freely used for illustration. In other respects the commentary is like that upon the Satires, and is intended to direct the attention of the reader both to the artistic structure of the Epistles and to the body of ideas which Horace was endeavoring to express in them. I have tried to remember that the student, learning his lessons, is in reality a reader.

E. P. MORRIS.

INTRODUCTION

THE Epistles were written, with perhaps a single exception, between 23 B.C. and 17. No event of Horace's life during this period is on record, but from occasional references in his writings it is to be seen that he was at this time living a quiet life, partly in Rome, more often on his farm, and sometimes in the winter months at Baiae or in Southern Italy. His circle of friends was large and included many men of high character and position, both in literature and in public life. But it was already a narrowing circle. Men of the earlier generation, whom he had known when he was a young man, were passing off the stage and, of his contemporaries, Quintilius Varus had died in 23, Vergil died in 19, and Varius not long after. He was already, at a little more than forty, feeling himself to be a representative of an older generation. On the other hand, as the letters show, he was on terms of friendly intercourse with the younger men of all sets, and he seems, indeed, to have made a deliberate effort to cultivate and maintain such relations. His own position in literature was assured. There is evidence, it is true, that he was not beyond the reach of criticism; the tone of *Epist.* 1, 19 shows that; and it is possible that the first reception of the Odes had been less favorable than he had hoped it would be. Undoubtedly, also, the school of the *docti*, the poets and critics who preferred the more ornate manner of the Alexandrian literature, was at this time strong in popular favor. But, with all allowance for the difference between contemporary judgments and the judgment of posterity, it is quite

INTRODUCTION

certain that Horace was, at the time when the Epistles were written, a leader, perhaps a sort of dean of letters, among Roman writers.

The course of his life as an artist up to the year 23 B.C. is clearly revealed in his writings. He had begun by writing satires in the general form set by Lucilius, but finding this in several ways unsuited to his temperament and recognizing its artistic limitations, he had made such modifications in it as to amount to the creation, or perhaps the crystallization, of a new literary form, the *sermo*, the 'talk' on life and art. These modifications were carried still further in the Second Book of the Satires; the dialogue, which in the earlier book is only half recognized, becomes in the Second Book the framework of the *sermo*, and is worked out in the different satires with very great care. During the same period, before 30 B.C., Horace was also making his first attempts in lyric poetry. For this he chose the somewhat restricted field of *iambi*, that is, of the form that had been fixed by Archilochus, in which the iambic couplet was used to express a more emotional satire than could be expressed in hexameters. He did not, however, remain long content with this simple form; it was only the bridge that carried him over from satire to the more complex lyric.

The Odes, of which three books were published as a completed whole in 23, represent a second and quite distinct stage in Horace's artistic development. In them he did not consider that he was creating a new art form, but only that he was introducing into Latin literature a form which had not before been used there, the lyric form of Alcaeus and Sappho. We have too little of the Greek lyric poetry to be able to judge in detail of the closeness with which he followed his models, and it would perhaps not be correct to claim for him more than he claimed for himself. Yet it is probable enough that, as he became master of this new form and learned to use it freely for his own purposes, he did with it what Vergil had done with

INTRODUCTION

the idylls of Theocritus, that is, employed it for purposes different from those for which it was used by its originators. The connected group of Alcaic odes which stand at the beginning of the Third Book would then represent a modification in use like that which is represented in Vergil's Fourth Eclogue. Such an adaptation of the Alcaic stanza to new uses is in fact a modification and development of the artistic form, less in amount than Horace had undertaken in the development of the Lucilian satire, but similar in kind and revealing the same underlying artistic purpose.

Horace's career, then, as an artist, had been, up to the year 23 B.C., that of a man whose interest had been in the shaping of given poetic forms to new uses. In satire the modifications had been deliberate and of considerable effect, so that he was in this field almost a creator; in lyric poetry the adaptations had been of narrower scope, yet not without influence upon the poetic form. He was now to take up a third form of literature, the Epistle.

The history of the epistle as a literary form is not yet wholly clear. In early Latin literature it was used chiefly for practical ends. Cato published letters addressed to his son, probably of a didactic character, and there existed in Cicero's time a collection of letters by Cornelia to her sons, the Gracchi. Cicero's own letters have come down to us, a most interesting collection, but they are real letters and can have been only in an incidental way models for Horace. In verse the historical sequence is even less clear. The custom of dedicating a poem to an individual by a direct address, as Horace inscribes his first satire to Maecenas, is an approach to the epistolary form; no distinct line can be seen between the manner in which Lucretius addresses Memmius at intervals in the *de Rerum Natura* and the occasional address to the Pisones in the *Ars Poetica*. Some of the poems of Catullus are epistolary in form and even in substance. But from these scattered approximations to the

INTRODUCTION

epistolary type we are not able to form an accurate conception of any models that Horace may have had before him or even to be sure that he had such models at all.

The artistic problem, however, is clear. It was to unite two elements, the personal and the public, into a harmonious whole, that is, to preserve a measure of personality and individuality and a certain degree of spontaneity, and at the same time to introduce a considerable element of a kind that would be interesting to the general reader. The two are to some extent antagonistic. The easy confidence which characterizes the best private letters is so delicate that it almost surely disappears if it is known to the writer that the letter is to be read by others than the person addressed. Yet if this disappears entirely, the epistle is a letter only in form. In the solution of this problem, Horace has gone from one side to the other, as circumstances led him, allowing first one, then the other, element to predominate. The invitation to dinner (1, 5) addressed to Torquatus is so personal and natural that this may well have been a real letter for a real purpose, put into verse form for the mere pleasure of the writer and for the compliment which it paid to the recipient. The same thing is true of 1, 9, introducing Septimius to Tiberius. One of the three Epistles to Maecenas (1, 7) is extremely personal, both to the writer and to the recipient, so much so that it seems almost too confidential for publication, yet it contains some of Horace's best stories and is in parts not distinguishable from *Sat.* 2, 6. In others, 1, 3; 1, 11; 1, 12; 1, 15, the situation of the recipient or the writer is made the occasion for comments equally interesting to the general public; in 1, 3 this has been done with special success, and the two elements are so harmoniously blended that it is impossible to tell whether this is really a letter, sent as is implied, or an Epistle written on the model of a personal letter. At the other extreme, 1, 16 opens with a description of the farm, but runs off into a poem which has nothing of the tone of a letter in it,

INTRODUCTION

while 1, 2 is a letter chiefly by virtue of the address and the closing lines, and 1, 6 is not a letter at all, but a *sermo* on philosophy addressed to an individual. To the skillful mingling of these two elements, the personal and the public, Horace has plainly devoted much thought, shaping the Epistle into a literary form, as he had shaped the dialogue-satire, and perhaps extending its range, as he had extended the range of the Alcaic stanza.

All this, however, applies chiefly to the First Book. In the Second Book there is less attempt to preserve the epistolary form. The *Ars Poetica* has scarcely anything but the address to remind the reader that it is an Epistle. In 2, 2 the fiction of excusing himself from further writing of lyrics is used by Horace to furnish a framework for the thought through the first half, but the latter part is quite impersonal. The letter to Augustus (2, 1) is inevitably formal, but the consciousness that it is addressed to one who had it in his power to influence the trend of literary taste is present through the whole and influences the thought.

It is not to be thought, however, that Horace's attention was given wholly to the form of his writings. He was primarily an artist in words and phrases and forms of expression, but he had also something to say. In the First Epistle he announces the subject of the new collection; he has given up lyric poetry and is to devote himself hereafter to philosophy, not, indeed, the philosophy of a sect, but the philosophy of life. This announcement fairly describes the subject-matter or the point of view of the book. A few of the Epistles (1, 5; 1, 9; 1, 13) make no reference to it; in others (1, 2; 1, 4; 1, 6; 1, 16) it is the staple of the Epistle; in several, including some of the best (1, 3; 1, 8; 1, 11; 1, 12; 1, 15), it is not quite the subject, but is the conclusion, as if to show how in the writer's mind all things lead back to the large philosophy of life. But Horace was not by temper or habit a student or what is called a pro-

INTRODUCTION

found thinker. He was a man who had seen much of life on various sides, had observed many men and had given serious thought to their conduct and his own. Out of this experience and consideration, he had come to certain conclusions which he had formulated into what we call, loosely, a philosophy of life. It was not, of course, a philosophy of the schools; it did not concern itself with questions of natural or physical science or with the nature of knowledge, and, though it was ethical, it did not involve the fundamental problems of ethics. But it had this in common with ethical philosophy, that it was based upon a real comprehension of vital interests and that it was to Horace a true and determining principle of life. In this sense he was justified in regarding himself as a philosopher and in feeling it to be his right and his duty to summon other men to accept his doctrine. He is thus, as indeed he had been in the earlier days of the Satires, a preacher, uttering his doctrine with conviction and seriousness. Perhaps it should rather be said that he was at once preacher and artist. The variety of setting and of personalities which a collection of letters involves afforded him an opportunity to set forth his philosophy with variety, as a climax and a final answer to all troubles and queries and situations.

The subject of the Second Book is literature; the three long letters consist of comments on the prevailing tendencies of literature in Rome. In this comment some two or three elements are combined. Horace had read, though perhaps not very deeply or widely, the treatises on rhetoric and on the history of literature, and he made considerable use of the knowledge thus acquired. Much of this, however, must be recognized as conventional and traditional, without any very real connection with the condition of things in Rome. Especially the history of literature, of the drama or the *satura*, or the origins of certain poetic forms, which was once accepted as authoritative, must not be taken seriously. Horace had no access to real sources,

INTRODUCTION

for example, of the early Latin literature; no such sources existed. This element in his writings has no great value or interest. A second element has more life in it; in so far as his comments reveal the tendencies of contemporary literature, they have real value. The extant remains of the literature of the Augustan Age, even though they include so much, are but scanty in amount compared with the writings of all kinds that were published in that period, and all the glimpses that we get in Horace of the work of younger men or of minor writers enable us to understand better the literature that has survived. A third element is the most important of all; it is the personal judgment which Horace expresses. For the work of the critic he was all the better qualified because his own work was not inspired, but was the result of a conscious process. He had thought much of the choice of words, of the combination of phrases, of the enlargement of vocabulary, and all that he says on such things is weighty with authority. One of the most interesting of experiences is to hear a good craftsman speak of the art that he practices. It is this which makes Cicero's *Brutus* and *Orator* interesting; Horace's presentation is more indirect than Cicero's and less systematic, but it has the same essential quality of authority.

It is not always possible to distinguish these three elements, the traditional, the contemporary, and the personal, but so far as it is possible it throws much light upon the meaning of these Epistles. Thus it is probable that the great space given to the drama has nothing to do with Horace's own interest; it may be due to some transient public interest, but it is probably a tradition from the books of rhetoric. On the other hand, it is not unlikely that the discussion of the satyric drama is to be explained by a revived interest in mimes and farces. But much of the general discussion of poetry, the injunctions to frequent revision, the constant reference to Greek models, comes from Horace himself and constitutes the most attractive element in these writings. For behind the artist and critic the Epistles reveal to us a man of most human temper and judgment, at once shrewd and mellow, by turns an observer of men and a lover of retirement. To turn back after reading the latest of these letters, *Epist.* 2, 1, and reread *Sat.* 1, 7 and 1, 8, is to see what some twenty years of life had done for Horace.

Q. HORATI FLACCI

EPISTVLAE

LIBER PRIMVS

I

The date of this Epistle is not fixed by any definite allusion in the text. It is, however, clearly introductory to the book and was therefore written after the others, at about the same date as Epist. 20, in the year 20 B.C. This was three years after the publication of the first three books of the Odes : the writer was nearly forty-five years old.

'My dear Maecenas, you are proposing that I should go back to my verse writing. I must decline the invitation ; I have won my discharge and am through with the follies of youth. Philosophy is now my only interest. "What school ?" you ask. My own school ; sometimes I rise to Stoic heights, and then, before I know it, I am a follower of Aristippus. But, school or no school, I am impatient of delay. For even the rudiments of philosophy have their value ; they will cure our avarice, our ambition, our laziness. And to get rid of our faults is the beginning of wisdom. See what pains men take to satisfy their desires, when half the labor would rid them of the desire itself. But all the Roman world is money-mad and careless, in its madness, of the higher claim of character.

'I know that I am setting myself against the common judgment, but the common judgment is both inconsistent and inconstant. It is, in fact, a ludicrous exhibition of whims and contradictions. You laugh at it yourself, as you laugh, rightly enough, at my carelessness in dress. But don't you see that carelessness in regard to the principles of life is much worse ? This is the very thing that I am trying to cure by the study of philosophy. I tell you, philosophy is a cure for everything — except influenza.'

This introductory epistle has two objects, which are not distinctly stated, but are left to be inferred from the general tone. The first is to explain the writer's change from lyric poetry back to the social comments with which he began his career in the Satires. This is accomplished by the device of a supposed request from Maecenas — which may or may not have been real — that Horace would continue his writing of lyrics. In answering this request the writer is able to give, without the appearance of egotism, his reasons for following a different course. The second purpose is to announce the fact that this collection of writings contains, more distinctly than the Satires, a kind of life philosophy, not systematic and not too serious, yet by no means wholly humorous.

Of the change of form, from the satire to the epistle, nothing is said. It is evident and is left to explain itself.

> Prima dicte mihi, summa dicende Camena,
> spectatum satis et donatum iam rude quaeris,
> Maecenas, iterum antiquo me includere ludo.
> Non eadem est aetas, non mens. Veianius, armis

1. This verse, like the first two verses of the first Ode, is distinct in thought from the rest of the poem and constitutes therefore a more formal dedication than that with which the first Satire and the first Epode begin. — The thought is entirely general; cf. Verg. *Ecl.* 8, 11, *a te* (Pollio) *principium, tibi desinam*; Horace is not thinking of the precise chronology of his writings nor, in using *Camena* (the Latin equivalent of *Musa*), is he distinguishing between satire and lyric poetry.

2. **spectatum**: a technical term applied to a gladiator who had fought with credit. The letters *sp.* or *spect.*, on medals (*tesserae*) presented to such gladiators, seem to be an abbreviation of this word. — **rude**: the *wooden sword* was given to a gladiator when he was finally discharged from service; he was thereafter *rudiarius* (= *donatus rude*). The implied comparison of one who had completed his term of service to a discharged gladiator occurs in other writers also.

3. **antiquo ... ludo**: 'in the old gladiatorial school where I used to serve.' But there is also a suggestion of the other meaning of *ludus*, which is taken up again in vs. 10. — **includere**: this word is selected to contrast the discipline of the gladiator's life with the freedom of the *rudiarius*.

4–6. **Veianius**: the context implies that he had been successful and had retired. — **Herculis**: so Horace, *Carm.* 3. 26, 3 f, proposes to dedicate to Venus the lyre with which he had accompanied his love songs and in *Carm.*

5   Herculis ad postem fixis, latet abditus agro,
    ne populum extrema totiens exoret arena.
    Est mihi purgatam crebro qui personet aurem:
    'Solve senescentem mature sanus equum, ne
    peccet ad extremum ridendus et ilia ducat.'
10 Nunc itaque et versus et cetera ludicra pono;
    quid verum atque decens curo et rogo et omnis in hoc
        sum;

1, 5, 13 ff., the shipwrecked sailor hangs his dripping garments in the temple of Neptune. — **latet abditus**: to be taken together; 'goes and buries himself in the country.' — **ne ... exoret**: *i.e.*, lest he should be tempted again into his old life, with its inevitable consequences. — **extrema ... arena**: the defeated gladiator laid down his arms and went toward the barrier between the seats and the arena to ask for favor and pardon. This would be granted by the giver of the games when the spectators (*populus*) indicated that they were satisfied with the fight. — **totiens**: *so many times*, as he would probably be obliged to, if he went back into the profession. — This line suggests what is put more clearly in vss. 8-9, that Horace felt himself to be too old for resuming the writing of poetry.

7. **est qui**: render freely; 'I hear a voice that warns me. . . .' — **purgatam, crebro, personet**: these emphasize in different ways the idea that the warning is clear and unmistakable. Cf. *Sat.* 1, 3, 25, *pervideas ... lippus*, *see dimly*.

· 8-9. The figure of the old racehorse repeats more distinctly the whole thought of vss. 2-7. — **sanus**: 'if you are wise,' as in *Sat.* 1, 5, 44, *nil ego contulerim iucundo sanus amico*, and *Sat.* 1, 6, 89. — **ilia ducat**: *strain his flanks*, become broken-winded.

10. **itaque**: acknowledging the force of the argument which underlies the preceding comparisons. — **cetera ludicra**: *i.e.*, 'as I lay aside all the other light pursuits, amusements, in order to devote myself to serious philosophy.' The implication is that verse writing is also *ludicrum*; cf. *Sat.* 1, 10, 37, *haec ego ludo*, of the Satires.

11. **verum**: the general term. — **decens**: more specific, translating the technical term τὸ πρέπον, which Cicero translates also by *honestum; true and right.* — **omnis in hoc**: cf. *Sat.* 1, 9, 2, *totus in illis.*

condo et compono quae mox depromere possim.
Ac ne forte roges quo me duce, quo lare tuter,
nullius addictus iurare in verba magistri,
15　quo me cumque rapit tempestas, deferor hospes.
Nunc agilis fio et mersor civilibus undis,
virtutis verae custos rigidusque satelles;
nunc in Aristippi furtim praecepta relabor,
et mihi res, non me rebus, subiungere conor.

12. **condo, depromere**: regularly used of *laying in* and, later, *drawing out* a stock of provisions at a country house. — **compono**: *arrange* in order.

13. **ne ... roges**: cf. *ne te morer*, *Sat.* 1, 1, 14. A leading clause may be expressed (*audi, scito*), but is not necessary. — The question to what school of formal philosophy Horace proposed to attach himself is one which, in fact, would not have been asked by Maecenas or by any reader of the Satires and Odes, since Horace has made it abundantly clear that he did not belong to any school. But the question with the humorous answer, vss. 14-19, leads on to the illustrations of a practical social philosophy, which make up the main body of the epistle. — **lare**: a school of philosophy was sometimes called *familia* or *domus* (*Carm.* 1, 29, 14) and might therefore be supposed to have a hearth and a *Lar familiaris*.

14. **addictus**: property of a debtor, *bound over* or assigned to the creditor, but also used of a gladiator; the line is thus a reminiscence of vss. 2-6 and the figure is continued in *iurare* and *magistri*, which may be either master of a gladiatorial school or of a philosophical sect.

15. **tempestas**: the figure was a common one; cf. Cic. *Acad.* 2, 3, 8, *ad quamcumque sunt disciplinam quasi tempestate delati*, and *Ephes.* 4, 14, 'carried about with every wind of doctrine.'

16-17. The sense is 'I become for a time a Stoic.' — **agilis**: πρακτικός. The Stoic doctrine was that intelligent action was a necessary part of the philosopher's life and that he should therefore take his part in public matters. — There is humorous irony in almost every word of vs. 17, especially *verae, custos, rigidus*.

18-19. 'Then again I slip quietly back into the school of Aristippus.' Cf. the story referred to in *Sat.* 2, 3, 100 ff., which illustrates the way in which Aristippus released himself from the bondage of things. — There is irony also in these lines, in *furtim, relabor, conor*.

20 Vt nox longa quibus mentitur amica, diesque
longa videtur opus debentibus, ut piger annus
pupillis quos dura premit custodia matrum,
sic mihi tarda fluunt ingrataque tempora, quae spem
consiliumque morantur agendi gnaviter id quod
25 aeque pauperibus prodest, locupletibus aeque,
aeque neglectum pueris senibusque nocebit.
Restat ut his ego me ipse regam solerque elementis.
Non possis oculo quantum contendere Lynceus,
non tamen idcirco contemnas lippus inungi;

21. **opus debentibus**: 'to those who are obliged to work by the day,' servants and day laborers.

21–22. A year seems an endless time to a boy eagerly anticipating the day when he shall be his own master and chafing under restraint. To him any control seems harsh and oppressive (*dura*, *premit*), especially control by a woman, even by his mother. Strictly, a fatherless boy would be under the guardianship (*tutela*) of a man; *custodia* is used only in a general sense.

23–24. **spem consiliumque**: the intention already announced in vss. 11–12. — **morantur**: it is not precisely the time which causes the delay, but the obstacles in the form of other occupations, like the writing of poetry. — **agendi ... id quod**: *i.e.*, 'of devoting myself wholly to philosophy.'

25–26. Instead of using some single word for philosophy (*vir-tus, sapientia*, vs. 41) or some phrase like *verum atque decens* (vs. 11) which would emphasize the theoretical side, Horace here lays stress upon philosophy as a guide in the practical affairs of life. There is a half-humorous earnestness in the sweeping phrases; not only *prodest*, but also (*si neglectum fuerit*) *nocebit*, and it applies to all ages and conditions.

27. **restat**: *i.e.*, 'in spite of delays (20–24) and of my inability to attain to perfection (24–29), I can at least get a rudimentary knowledge that will meet my practical needs.' — **his**: without definite reference either backward or forward; 'such rudiments as I have.' — **ipse regam solerque**: since he has no *dux* or *lar* (vs. 13) to guide or protect him.

28–31. The same idea is expressed twice in the two comparisons, with slight variation in the construction. *Non possis* is repeated in *desperes*, both being

30 nec, quia desperes invicti membra Glyconis,
nodosa corpus nolis prohibere cheragra.
Est quadam prodire tenus, si non datur ultra.
Fervet avaritia miseroque cupidine pectus:
sunt verba et voces, quibus hunc lenire dolorem
35 possis et magnam morbi deponere partem.

potentials of the indefinite second person, and the two clauses are at the same time concessive, as is implied by *tamen*, and causal; the causal meaning is expressed by *idcirco* in the first main clause and by *quia* in the second subordinate clause. — **oculo . . . contendere**: so *quantum potero voce contendam*, Cic. *pro Lig.* 3, 6. — **Lynceus**: the far-sighted Argonautic hero, referred to also in *Sat.* 1, 2, 90. — **Glyconis**: a famous athlete, to whom a Greek epigram (*Anth. Pal.* 7, 692) is addressed; he is called ὁ παμμάχων and the adj. ἀνίκατος (*invictus*) is applied to him. — **prohibere cheragra**: for the construction cf. *Epist.* 1, 8, 10, *me arcere veterno*. The other construction, *prohibere cheragram a corpore*, is more frequent. Gout in the hand or in the foot (*podagra*) was called *nodosa* because of the chalk stones that it produces in the joints.

32. **est**: almost the same as *potest*, but with the implication that it is also worth while, since it is possible. This is the main thought of the whole passage, 27–

40, expressed in *possis*. 28, *possis*, 35, *poterunt*, 37, and *possit*, 39. — **quadam . . . tenus**: like *quatenus, hactenus*.

33. **avaritia**: the vice which Horace everywhere puts at the head of his list; cf. *Sat.* 1, 1. *Epod.* 1, 33 f., and often. — **cupidine**: the general term, *passion*, following the particular; they mean only one thing, as *hunc dolorem* shows.

34. **verba et voces**: *words and sayings*, i.e., teachings of philosophy which will be as effectual as the magic formulas by which disease is cured. This does not imply a real belief in charms, any more than the English phrase 'it acts like magic.' The line is a paraphrase of a well-known line of Euripides, *Hippol.* 478.

35. **morbi**: a translation of πάθος, the technical term for a disturbing passion, used here with literal meaning also; cf. *fervet, lenire, dolorem, tumes, recreare*, all words from the medical vocabulary. — **partem**: the same idea already expressed in *elementis, est quadam prodire tenus*, and in vss. 28–31.

EPISTVLAE [I, I, 44

    Laudis amore tumes: sunt certa piacula, quae te
ter pure lecto poterunt recreare libello.
Invidus, iracundus, iners, vinosus, amator,
nemo adeo ferus est ut non mitescere possit,
40 si modo culturae patientem commodet aurem.
Virtus est vitium fugere, et sapientia prima
stultitia caruisse. Vides quae maxima credis
esse mala, exiguum censum turpemque repulsam,
quanto devites animi capitisque labore;

36. **laudis amore**: *ambition*; cf. *Sat*. 2, 3, 164 ff., esp. *tumidum*, 213. — **piacula**: = *verba et voces*.

37. **ter**: the sacred number, carrying on the thought of *piacula*; cf. *Sat*. 2, 1, 7 f., *ter uncti transnanto Tiberim*. — **pure**: after religious purification. — **libello**: the little book of magic verses and also the book of philosophic teaching.

38-40. The list of sins — not unlike the seven deadly sins of early Christian teaching — is summed up in *nemo*, by a kind of apposition. — **amator**: cf. *Sat*. 2, 3, 247-280. — **ferus**: a change of figure; the cure of envy or hot temper by philosophy is like the taming (*mitescere*) of a wild animal. — **culturae**: properly of the cultivation of land, but in this line the figurative meaning is almost lost sight of and *patientem commodet aurem* is used simply of the listener to philosophic teaching.

41. **prima**: with *virtus* as well as with *sapientia*. The sentence is used in a condensed form (*prima virtus est vitio carere*) by Quintilian, 8, 3, 41, and was probably a current maxim of philosophy. It summarizes and enforces the thought of vss. 28-40; 'it is worth while to take the first steps by listening to the teachings of wisdom, by which our faults may be cured. For to get rid of our follies is the beginning of wisdom.' At the same time it introduces the argument of 42-52; 'take the first steps, which are not difficult; for half the labor you spend in the pursuit of your foolish ends would suffice to rid you of your folly.'

43. **exiguum censum**: referring to *avaritia*. — **turpem repulsam**: referring to ambition, *laudis amor*.

44. **animi capitisque labore**: this cannot be simply 'labor of mind and body.' — *animi labor* is 'trouble of spirit,' *capitis labor* is 'risk of life'; *labor* is used in a vague sense for which there is no exact English equivalent and must therefore be translated twice, 'anxiety of spirit and peril of life.'

45 impiger extremos curris mercator ad Indos,
per mare pauperiem fugiens, per saxa, per ignis:
ne cures ea, quae stulte miraris et optas,
discere, et audire, et meliori credere non vis?
Quis circum pagos et circum compita pugnax
50 magna coronari contemnat Olympia, cui spes,
cui sit condicio dulcis sine pulvere palmae?
Vilius argentum est auro, virtutibus aurum.
'O cives, cives, quaerenda pecunia primum est,

45-46. The thought is often expressed by Horace, in substantially this form; cf. *Sat.* 1, 1, 30; 1, 4, 29 ff.; *Carm.* 1, 31, 10 ff. It was undoubtedly proverbial.

47-48. 'Are you not willing to attain the same end, freedom from anxieties, by the easier method of learning from philosophy to be indifferent to your foolish ambitions?'— **ne cures**: a clause of purpose, depending on the whole of the next line; 'in order to attain to indifference.'— **meliori**: the wise philosopher, whose superiority the learner acknowledges by the act of seeking instruction from him.

49. circum ... pugnax: an allusion to the wrestlers and boxers who gave street shows to the crowds gathered for feast days like the Paganalia and Compitalia. They are alluded to in other places (Suet. *Oct.* 45, *catervarii oppidani, inter angustias vicorum pugnantes*). — **circum compita**: also in *Sat.* 2, 3, 281.

50. Olympia: a cognate accus., like *vicit Olympia*, Cic. *Cat. M.* 14, both from the Greek στεφανοῦσθαι Ὀλύμπια.

51. sine pulvere: ἀκονιτί. The expression was proverbial and was extended beyond its strict meaning, so that it came to be used of prizes awarded to athletes whose fame was so great that no one dared to contend with them. It suggests therefore the ease with which the benefits of philosophy may be obtained, in contrast to the struggles necessary to get money or satisfy ambition (44-46).

52. The conclusion of the argument; 'just so character, the product of philosophy, is better than the rewards which men rate so high.' But, as often, the conclusion is put in the form of a general assertion, without indication of its connection (*Sat.* 1, 1, 59 f., 78 f., 105; 1, 3, 24; 1, 6, 23, and often), and in a form which leaves its real force intentionally in the background.

53-69. 'But this conclusion, we must acknowledge, runs counter to

EPISTVLAE [I, I, 60

virtus post nummos.' Haec Ianus summus ab imo
55 prodocet, haec recinunt iuvenes dictata senesque,
laevo suspensi loculos tabulamque lacerto.
Est animus tibi, sunt mores et lingua fidesque,
sed quadringentis sex septem milia desunt:
plebs eris. At pueri ludentes, ' Rex eris,' aiunt,
60 ' si recte facies.' Hic murus aeneus esto,

the opinion of Rome, which places money above character.'
54. summus ab imo: *from top to bottom*; cf. *A. P.* 254, *primus ad extremum, from beginning to end*. But the precise meaning of the phrase as applied to *Ianus* is not clear, because our knowledge of the topography of the Forum in the Augustan period is very limited. The same spot is referred to in *Sat.* 2, 3, 18 (*medius Ianus*) and by Cicero as the center of the banking business in Rome; it was in the lower corner of the Forum. Translate 'Janus, from top to bottom,' like 'all Wall Street,' 'the whole Stock Exchange.'
55. prodocet: only in this passage; *proclaims loudly*. — **recinunt**: the pupils repeated in a kind of chant the words pronounced slowly (*dictata*) by the teacher. — **senesque**: a humorous addition to the picture of the school children.
56. Repeated without change from *Sat.* I, 6, 74. There are a few other repetitions of lines in Horace, some of which are mere errors in the Mss. In this case, however, the point of the comparison of business men to school children is heightened by the quotation; ' like the children I described once, with their satchels and slates hanging from their arms.' — **loculos tabulamque**: accus. of the part with *suspensi*.
57. The four nouns are carefully chosen and arranged, *animus*, *ability*, is balanced by *mores*, *character*, and then each is repeated in a more specific way in *eloquence and loyalty*.
58. quadringentis: sc. *milibus sestertium*. This sum, 400,000 sesterces, was the rating necessary to enrollment among the *equites*. — **sex septem**: used in this way, without connective, in several other places (Ter. *Eun.* 331, Cic. *Att.* 10, 8, 6). apparently for phonetic reasons. No other cardinal numbers are so used.
59-60. The full verse is given by the Scholiast: 'réx erit qui récte faciet, qui non faciet non erit,' a trochaic septenarius, sung by boys in some game.
60-61. The underlying thought is, ' in this song of children at play

nil conscire sibi, nulla pallescere culpa.
Roscia, dic sodes, melior lex, an puerorum est
nenia, quae regnum recte facientibus offert,
et maribus Curiis et decantata Camillis?
65 Isne tibi melius suadet qui rem facias, rem,
si possis, recte, si non, quocumque modo rem,
ut propius spectes lacrimosa poemata Pupi,
an qui Fortunae te responsare superbae
liberum et erectum praesens hortatur et aptat?

one may find a rule of life; upright conduct gives secure happiness.' *Murus aeneus* is a common figure to express security and stability, here in contrast to the troubles of a life spent in the pursuit of money or position (43-46). The whole of vs. 61 is nothing but an expansion of *recte facere.* — conscire: absolute, as the noun *conscientia* is occasionally. — sibi: not *tibi*, because the words are a maxim of general application. The line should be paraphrased, rather than rendered literally.

62. **Roscia . . . lex**: the law which reserved the first fourteen rows behind the *orchestra* for the knights. As the *equites* were in general the capitalists, the law is taken as an embodiment of the public opinion which gave undue honor to wealth (vs. 53).

63. **nenia**: used of any rhyme or jingle in rhythm, like charms and proverbs, in distinction from formal poetry. Here with intention, to contrast the song of boys at play with the law of the Roman people.

64. **maribus**: *manly*. As these heroes of the good old times sang the verse when they were boys, so they acted upon the principle when they became men. Curius and Camillus are named together in *Carm.* 1, 12, 41 f. as products of *saeva paupertas*.

65-66. **rem . . . rem . . . rem**: the repetition is made more emphatic by the position of the monosyllable at the end of the hexameter. — **facias**: in parataxis with *suadet* to be supplied as the verb for *qui*; it represents an independent *fac*.

67. **propius**: *i.e.*, 'become a knight by reason of your money and sit in one of the front rows.' — **Pupi**: unknown. The Scholiast quotes a couplet in which Pupius is supposed to pride himself upon his success in moving his audience to tears. But *lacrimosa* is of course ironical, like all the rest of the line.

68. **responsare**: *defy*, as in *Sat.* 2, 7, 85, 103.

69. **praesens**: most frequently used of a god who is present in

EPISTVLAE

I, 1, 77

70 Quod si me populus Romanus forte roget, cur
non, ut porticibus, sic iudiciis fruar isdem,
nec sequar aut fugiam quae diligit ipse vel odit,
olim quod vulpes aegroto cauta leoni
respondit referam: 'Quia me vestigia terrent,
75 omnia te adversum spectantia, nulla retrorsum.'
Belua multorum est capitum. Nam quid sequar aut quem?
Pars hominum gestit conducere publica; sunt qui

person to give help. The use here suggests that the help of the moral philosopher is like that of a divinity.

70–93. 'If I am asked why I advocate views so opposed to the popular standards, my answer is that there is no common standard; men are utterly at variance with each other and inconsistent with themselves.'

70. **Romanus**: not in contrast to the Greek, but 'the great Roman people, my countrymen, with whom I might be expected to agree.' Cf. *cives*, 53, and *Roscia lex*, 62.

71. **porticibus**: the public colonnades, where men met for talk; cf. *Sat.* 1, 4, 133, *cum lectulus aut me porticus excepit*. This is a figurative way of saying 'since I live in the same city, in the same society.'

72. An expansion of *iudiciis fruar isdem*. — **sequar**: = *diligit*. — **fugiam**: = *odit*. The variety of expression prepares the way for vs. 76.

73. **olim**: *once, once upon a time*, as often (*e.g., Sat.* 2, 6, 79) to introduce a fable. The story which follows is not in Phaedrus, but was one of Aesop's fables and had been used by Lucilius (30, 80 ff. M.). The moral is that one who gives up his own judgment and adopts the popular views surrenders his independence beyond recovery.

76. **belua ... capitum**: the figure was proverbial and has passed over through Horace into modern literature. There is a change of argument here, from the danger of losing one's independence to the new argument drawn from the confusing variety in public opinion (76–80), but the figure of the beast of many heads is suggested by the previous comparison of the people to a lion.

77. **conducere publica**: *to take government contracts*. This was one of the chief uses of large capital in Rome, but it was looked upon with some contempt, as is shown by its association here with legacy hunting and usury.

crustis et pomis viduas venentur avaras,
excipiantque senes quos in vivaria mittent;
80 multis occulto crescit res faenore. Verum
esto aliis alios rebus studiisque teneri:
idem eadem possunt horam durare probantes?
' Nullus in orbe sinus Bais praelucet amoenis'
si dixit dives, lacus et mare sentit amorem
85 festinantis heri; cui si vitiosa libido
fecerit auspicium, ' Cras ferramenta Teanum
tolletis, fabri.' Lectus genialis in aula est:
nil ait esse prius, melius nil caelibe vita:
si non est, iurat bene solis esse maritis.

78-79. The practice of seeking for legacies from rich and childless old people is the subject of *Sat.* 2, 5. where illustrations of these lines can be found: *crustis et pomis*, vs. 12; *viduas*, 84-88; *vivaria*, 44.

80. occulto: the context requires that this should mean *secret* and therefore discreditable, because the loan was in some sense illegal or improper.

81. esto ... teneri: *i.e.*, 'passing over this point without further argument'; a frequent use of *esto*, *Sat.* 1, 6, 19; 2. 2. 30.

82. idem: nom. plur. 'Can these same persons, who are so at variance with each other, be consistent with themselves?'

83. Bais: a fashionable resort on the shore of Campania.

84. lacus et mare: houses were built out into the sea or into the shallow salt water pools, like the Lucrine lake. Cf. esp. *Carm.* 3, 1, 33 ff.

85. vitiosa libido: *morbid fancy*, carrying on to an extreme the figure suggested in *amorem*.

86. auspicium: *gives the signal*. Properly *auspicium* is a sign sent by the gods, but to the capricious and self-indulgent man his own whim is as good as a sign from heaven. — Teanum: an inland resort in Campania; he changes in a day from the seashore to the mountains. The order is given by the master to'the workmen who are still engaged upon the unfinished villa at Baiae.

87. lectus genialis: the *marriage couch* which stood in the *atrium* in honor of the *Genius* of the family, the god of fruitfulness.

88. prius, melius: *better, more desirable*. The same idea is also expressed by *antiquius*.

90 Quo teneam voltus mutantem Protea nodo?
    Quid pauper? Ride: mutat cenacula, lectos,
    balnea, tonsores, conducto navigio aeque
    nauseat ac locuples quem ducit priva triremis.
    Si curatus inaequali tonsore capillos
95 occurri, rides; si forte subucula pexae
    trita subest tunicae vel si toga dissidet impar,
    rides: quid, mea cum pugnat sententia secum,
    quod petiit spernit, repetit quod nuper omisit,
    aestuat et vitae disconvenit ordine toto,
100 diruit, aedificat, mutat quadrata rotundis?

90. **Protea**: cf. *Sat.* 2, 3, 71 ff.

91-93. 'And as the rich man (84) is subject to his whims, so the poor man in his small way indulges his caprices.' All the details are intentionally petty; *cenacula, lodgings*, is a parody upon vss. 83-87, the *lectos, balnea, tonsores* are the cheap luxuries of the poor, and the poor man, seasick in his hired boat, is an especially keen hit. There is in these lines a tone of sharpness not usual in Horace and more like the bitterness of Juvenal's satire.

94-108. 'These and other like inconsistencies, ridiculous as they are, are small compared to the inconsistencies of judgment from which I hope to save myself by philosophy.'

94. **curatus**: almost a technical term of attention to health or the toilet. Cf. *Sat.* 2, 5, 38, *pelliculam curare*. — **inaequali**: *uneven*, a humorous transfer of the adj. from the work to the workman.

95-96. **subucula**: *undertunic*. The inconsistency is between the well-worn undergarment, from which the nap has been rubbed off (*trita*), and the new tunic with long and fresh nap (*pexae*). — **dissidet impar**: *sets badly, hangs unevenly*; cf. *Sat.* 1, 3, 31, *rusticius tonso toga defluit*. The careful creasing of that part of the toga which hung across the chest was a matter of importance to a Roman who wished to be well dressed.

98-100. The list of moral inconsistencies is given rapidly, as if they had only to be named in order to be recognized and acknowledged. — **aestuat**: *ebbs and flows* like the tide. — **diruit, aedificat**: *i.e.*, is guilty of the same foolish vacillation that was described in vss. 83-87. — **quadrata rotundis**: a proverbial figure, used of making a meaningless change.

Insanire putas sollemnia me neque rides,
nec medici credis nec curatoris egere
a praetore dati, rerum tutela mearum
cum sis et prave sectum stomacheris ob unguem
105 de te pendentis, te respicientis amici.
Ad summam: sapiens uno minor est Iove, dives,
liber, honoratus, pulcher, rex denique regum,
praecipue sanus, nisi cum pituita molesta est.

101. 'You think that my madness is merely the usual thing — not remarkable at all — and do not laugh.' — **neque rides**: recalling *ride* 91, *rides* 95 and 97. All the laughter that external incongruities excite comes to an end when the inconsistency is in the moral sphere.

102. **medici, curatoris**: *i.e.*, 'you do not see that this is real insanity which calls for the care of a physician and the appointment of a guardian.'

103. **tutela**: this is an intentional reminder of *Carm.* 1, 1, 2, *o et praesidium et dulce decus meum.* — **prave sectum**: cf. *Epist.* 1, 7, 51. — **stomacheris**: not of serious anger, but humorously and with recognition of the friendly concern which causes the annoyance of Maecenas. 'Though you are so anxious to have me avoid even the most trifling carelessness.'

105. The line is an explicit and intentional profession of friendship, to guard against the possibility that the preceding reproaches (94-104) addressed directly to Maecenas might be taken too seriously by any reader.

106-108. Cf. the abrupt and humorous conclusion of *Sat.* 1, 1; 1, 3; 1, 4; 1, 6. On the Stoic paradox which is here ridiculed cf. *Sat.* 1, 3, 124 ff. — **sanus**: this, in contrast to the *insania* of all other men, was the quality which the Stoic philosopher especially claimed as his own. It is the subject of the longest of the Satires, 2, 3. But Horace, accepting its correctness on the philosophical side, turns it into a joke by taking it in a physical sense; 'healthy — except for an occasional cold' in the head.'

2

This letter is addressed to a certain Lollius Maximus, who is also addressed in *Epist.* 1, 18. From the latter, written in 20 B.C., it appears that he had served as a soldier in the war against the Cantabri,

25-24. This letter was therefore written somewhere between 24 and 20.

Beyond this nothing is known of the young man, but he may well have been a relative of the distinguished M. Lollius to whom *Carm.* 4, 9, is addressed.

' My dear young friend, I have just been re-reading Homer and am struck with the wealth of illustration of philosophic doctrines in his poems. He is really better than the philosophers themselves. Just consider the debate between Antenor and Paris or the quarrel between the two chiefs of the Greeks. The follies of kings could not be better shown. And Ulysses, in the Odyssey, is as good as a Stoic ; recall the description of him in the opening of the poem. And you and I are there, too, in the picture of the easy-going Phaeacians.

' But don't be too easy-going ; don't postpone too long the beginning of serious philosophic living. There are temptations everywhere. Do not be like the men who hope to find happiness in their possessions, instead of cleansing their own hearts. Avoid pleasure, love of money, envy, anger ; especially anger. Begin early to train yourself. But don't expect me to be your companion in the path of reform ; I am middle-aged and I go my own sober way.'

The tone of the letter is half serious, half light, as suits an older man's advice to a younger friend. It is probable that the advice has some personal applications which can no longer be understood, but the general tenor is impersonal ; begin in youth to train yourself to virtue.

> Troiani belli scriptorem, Maxime Lolli,
> dum tu declamas Romae, Praeneste relegi ;

1. **Maxime**: the family name is not infrequently put before the gentile name, *e.g.*, *Carm.* 2, 2, 3, *Crispe Sallusti.*

2. **declamas**: with *scriptorem* as a cognate accus., meaning to write and deliver declamations based upon situations in the Homeric poems, *e.g.*, the prayer of Priam to Achilles for the return of the body of Hector. This was a very common practice in the schools of rhetoric. The sense therefore is 'while you at Rome are studying Homer from the rhetorical point of view, I at Praeneste have been re-reading him and find him a philosopher.'
— **Praeneste**: a summer resort among the mountains. The mention of the two towns where the writer and the recipient were gives the epistle a more distinct letter form.

[1, 2, 3] HORATI

qui quid sit pulchrum, quid turpe, quid utile, quid
non,
planius ac melius Chrysippo et Crantore dicit.
5 Cur ita crediderim, nisi quid te detinet, audi.
Fabula, qua Paridis propter narratur amorem
Graecia barbariae lento collisa duello,
stultorum regum et populorum continet aestus.
Antenor censet belli praecidere causam :
10 quid Paris? Vt salvus regnet vivatque beatus
cogi posse negat. Nestor componere litis

3. **pulchrum, turpe, utile** : the technical terms of ethical philosophy, which taken together define the *summum bonum*.

4. **planius**: *more clearly*, and therefore better, than any philosopher. — **Chrysippo** : the Stoic, mentioned several times by Horace. — **Crantore** : a leader of the Academy.

5. **detinet**: *draws you away, distracts you* from giving me your undivided attention.

6-31. 'The Iliad gives us pictures of the follies of mankind, the Odyssey a picture of a practical philosopher; and we may even find our own portraits there.'

7. **Graecia . . . collisa** : the frequent construction of noun with participle instead of a gen. with an abstract noun. — **barbariae** : Phrygians, who did not speak Greek, but with a suggestion of the modern meaning. — **lento** : the ten years' war. — **duello** : this old form for *bello* is used several times

by Horace, perhaps with some epic tone.

8. **stultorum** : *i.e.*, not philosophers. — **aestus** : *passions* ; not from the ebb and flow of the tide, as in *Epist.* 1, 1, 99, but from the irregular tossing of waves, making a slight contrast with the literal meaning of *continet*.

9. **Antenor**: *Il.* 7, 347 ff. — **censet**: in the formal sense, almost like the English *moves*. — This line is merely preliminary to vs. 10, which gives the example of *stultitia*; 'when Antenor gives good advice, Paris refuses to consider it, and when Nestor tries to heal the breach between Achilles and Agamemnon, their foolish passions prevent.'

10. **salvus . . . beatus** : this is what the giving up of Helen would really bring about. But Paris cannot even be compelled, much less persuaded, to take the sensible course.

11. **Nestor**: *Il.* 1, 247 ff. and 9, 96 ff.

inter Peliden festinat et inter Atriden;
hunc amor, ira quidem communiter urit utrumque.
Quicquid delirant reges, plectuntur Achivi.
15 Seditione, dolis, scelere, atque libidine et ira,
Iliacos intra muros peccatur et extra.
Rursus, quid virtus et quid sapientia possit,
utile proposuit nobis exemplar Vlixen;
qui, domitor Troiae, multorum providus urbes
20 et mores hominum inspexit, latumque per aequor,
dum sibi, dum sociis reditum parat, aspera multa
pertulit, adversis rerum immersabilis undis.
Sirenum voces et Circae pocula nosti;
quae si cum sociis stultus cupidusque bibisset,
25 sub domina meretrice fuisset turpis et excors

12. **inter ... et inter:** so in *Sat.* 1, 7, 11; an example of slightly illogical colloquialism.

13. **hunc**: Agamemnon, who in *Il.* 1, 113 speaks of his love for Chryseis. In fact, both were moved by the same motives, *amor* and *ira*, but as the wrath of Achilles is the announced subject of the Iliad, only this passion is attributed to him.

14-16. 'Every folly of the chiefs involves the people, too, and it is all a mad world, within Troy and without.' A concise summary of the meaning of vss. 9-13, repeating the statement of vs. 8.

17. **rursus**: *on the other hand*, as vs. 3 had spoken of *quid pulchrum, quid utile*, as well as the opposite.

19-22. A paraphrase of the first lines of the Odyssey. — **domitor Troiae**: this is the standing Roman tradition from Plautus down. — **providus ... inspexit**: ἴδεν καὶ νόον ἔγνω. — **immersabilis**: an addition to the Homeric description; the Stoic phrase (cf. *Epist.* 1, 1, 16, *mersor civilibus undis*) suggests 'like a true Stoic philosopher.'

23. **Sirenum**: *Od.* 11, 39 ff. — **Circae pocula**: *Od.* 10, 136 ff.

24. **stultus cupidusque**: *with foolish eagerness*; he did in fact drink, but not until he had taken the antidote and not, therefore, *stultus*.

25. **turpis**: in the form of an animal, losing his human form. Cf. *Sat.* 1, 3, 100. *mutum et turpe pecus.* — **et**: connects the verbs; *turpis* goes with *fuisset*, and *excors* with *vixisset*.

vixisset canis immundus vel amica luto sus.
Nos numerus sumus et fruges consumere nati,
sponsi Penelopae nebulones, Alcinoique
in cute curanda plus aequo operata iuventus,
30 cui pulchrum fuit in medios dormire dies et
ad strepitum citharae cessantem ducere somnum.
Vt iugulent hominem, surgunt de nocte latrones;
ut te ipsum serves, non expergisceris? Atqui
si noles sanus, curres hydropicus; et ni

26. canis: not in the Homeric story. But the legend easily took various forms.

27–31. 'We too may find our prototypes there, among the common people, of course, and the easy-going.'

27. numerus: *mere ciphers.* ἀριθμός is used in this sense, but *numerus* apparently only here. The rest of the line is also Greek, οἳ ἀρούρης καρπὸν ἔδουσιν, 'mere consumers of the fruits of the earth.'

28. sponsi: *suitors.* Strictly, they were *proci*, but all these words of relation, *sponsus, sponsa, gener, socer*, are loosely used. — nebulones: here as an adj., *wasteful*. — Alcinoi: king of the Phaeacians, *Od.* 8, 11 and 249 f.

29. cute curanda: cf. esp. *pelliculam curare, Sat.* 2, 5, 38 and *membra, corpora curare*. — operata: with intentional irony; their only labors are the labors of the toilet.

30–31. pulchrum: the philosophical term; they found their *summum bonum* in sleeping late.

— These details are not in Homer nor is the character of the Phaeacians so entirely self-indulgent. But on the basis of a few lines, esp. *Od.* 8, 248 f., they had become types of ease and luxury in philosophical writings, and Horace is here following the later interpretation, rather than the pure Homeric description.

32 ff. The following lines, almost to the end of the epistle, contain a series of exhortations in philosophical form. There is no real relation between them and the Homeric allusions, but the two parts are connected by the exhortation to energetic living which is itself suggested by the slothfulness of the Phaeacians.

33. serves: *i.e.*, 'if robbers will get up early to take life, will you not do it to save your own soul?' — expergisceris: with a literal reference backward, but also in the figurative sense.

34. noles: sc. *currere*. This is one of the forms of exercise prescribed for dropsy.

35 posces ante diem librum cum lumine, si non
 intendes animum studiis et rebus honestis,
 invidia vel amore vigil torquebere. Nam cur
 quae laedunt oculum festinas demere; si quid
 est animum, differs curandi tempus in annum?
40 Dimidium facti qui coepit habet: sapere aude:
 incipe. Qui recte vivendi prorogat horam,
 rusticus exspectat dum defluat amnis; at ille
 labitur et labetur in omne volubilis aevum.
 Quaeritur argentum puerisque beata creandis

35-36. The two meanings, literal and figurative, are intentionally run together: 'unless you waken early to work, you will find yourself sleepless as a result of your self-indulgence, and unless you study philosophy, you will suffer from the passions that philosophy would have cured.' — **posces**: so *Epist.* 2, 1, 112 f., *prius orto sole vigil calamum et chartas et scrinia posco*. The habit of reading or writing in the early morning, reclining on a couch, was general. — **rebus honestis**: *i.e.*, philosophy, which is alluded to with increasing distinctness in *curandi* 39, *sapere* 40, and *recte vivendi* 41.

37. cur: with both verbs, *festinas* and *differs;* 'why is it that you hasten . . . and yet postpone . . . ?'

39. est: from *edo.*

40. dimidium . . . habet: a familiar proverb; 'well begun is half done.'

42. rusticus: *i.e.*, 'is like the countryman who . . . ,' with the condensed comparison so frequent in Horace. The story is not otherwise known to us, but the brief form of the allusion presupposes a knowledge of it on the part of the readers. — **ille**: *amnis.*

43. The repetition of the letter *l*, the feminine caesura, and the rapid movement of the line are intentional. Cf. *Epod.* 16, 48. *levis crepante lympha desilit pede.*

44. From this point the exhortations become more specific, beginning, as always in Horace, with exhortations addressed to men of wealth (44-54). — **quaeritur**: emphatic; 'men are always seeking.' — **beata**: *rich; dotata.* — **creandis**: the formula of marriage contract contained the words *liberorum quaerundorum causa* as expressing the legitimate object of marriage, the founding of a family. The insertion of *beata* into the phrase is intentional irony.

45 uxor et incultae pacantur vomere silvae;
   quod satis est cui contingit, nihil amplius optet.
   Non domus et fundus, non aeris acervus et auri
   aegroto domini deduxit corpore febris,
   non animo curas; valeat possessor oportet,
50 si comportatis rebus bene cogitat uti.
   Qui cupit aut metuit, iuvat illum sic domus et res,
   ut lippum pictae tabulae, fomenta podagram,
   auriculas citharae collecta sorde dolentes.
   Sincerum est nisi vas, quodcumque infundis acescit.

45. **incultae ... silvae**: merely a vivid mention of one form of wealth, like *domus et fundus*, 47. Cf. also *Carm.* 1, 31, 7-10.

46. The apodosis of 44-45, in paratactic form. For the thought cf. *Sat.* 1, 1, 50, 62 ff., 92 ff.

48. **deduxit**: perfect tense of "an action often done, or [with a negative, as here] never done"; Lane, § 1611. 'has never removed the fevers from the body.' The two parts of this sentence also, like 44-46, are in paratactic relation. The thought is, 'as they have never cured bodily ills, so they have never cured the soul.'

49-50. 'The owner of all this wealth must first be well, must first cure himself of his passions, if he hopes to enjoy his property.'
— **valeat ... oportet**: parataxis.
— **bene**: with *uti*. — The thought is expressed at greater length in *Sat.* 2, 3, 104-120.

51. **cupit aut metuit**: *i.e.*, is under the dominion of the passions. — **sic ut**: *no more ... than*.

52. **lippum**: this disease, frequently referred to in Horace, would not actually blind the victim, but would render the use of his eyes so painful that he could not enjoy the finest painting. — **fomenta**: not poultices to cure the gout, but warm wrappings or foot muffs used by the luxurious (Sen. *de Provid.* 4, 9; *de Vita Beat.* 11). But a sufferer from the acute pains of gout would get no pleasure from them.

53. **collecta sorde**: with *dolentes*.

54. This summarizes the arguments of 44 ff., esp. that of 49-50, in a single condensed comparison; 'the man, I say, must first be sound himself in order to find his possessions sweet to him, as a jar must be clean if it is to keep sweet the wine that is poured into it.' It will be seen that this treatment of the familiar theme is more

55 Sperne voluptates; nocet empta dolore voluptas.
Semper avarus eget; certum voto pete finem.
Invidus alterius macrescit rebus opimis;
invidia Siculi non invenere tyranni
maius tormentum. Qui non moderabitur irae,
60 infectum volet esse dolor quod suaserit et mens,
dum poenas odio per vim festinat inulto.
Ira furor brevis est: animum rege, qui nisi paret,
imperat; hunc frenis, hunc tu compesce catena.
Fingit equum tenera docilem cervice magister
65 ire viam qua monstret eques; venaticus ex quo
tempore cervinam pellem latravit in aula,
militat in silvis catulus. Nunc adbibe puro
pectore verba puer, nunc te melioribus offer.

mature and more profound than the earlier treatment in *Sat.* 1, 1 or 2, 3.

55-63. Brief apothegms on pleasure, avarice, envy, and anger.

56. certum: *definite, fixed*, since the great danger is that the *avarus* will never know *quod satis est.* — **voto**: to the desires, which are expressed as solemnly as a vow.

58. Siculi ... tyranni: their cruelty and their ingenuity in inventing tortures had become proverbial.

60. infectum volet: *i.e.*, 'shall often have occasion to wish that he could undo ...' — **dolor et mens**: 'anger (*mens*) roused by a sense of injury (*dolor*).' — **odio ... inulto**: 'for his unsatisfied hatred.'

62. brevis: *while it lasts;* the emphasis is upon *furor, a raging madness.*

63. frenis: anticipating the figure of the horse. — **catena**: anticipating the comparison with the hound.

64. tenera docilem: the emphatic words. Training should begin early.

65-66. ex quo tempore: *i.e.*, his training is begun in the courtyard, as in a school. The hound was trained by means of a stuffed figure of a deer, which he was taught to bark at.

67-68. nunc, puer, nunc: emphasizing in its direct application to Lollius the truth which had been set forth in figures, that youth is the time to learn. — **melioribus**: cf. *Epist.* 1, 1, 48, *meliori credere,*

Quo semel est imbuta recens servabit odorem
70　testa diu. Quodsi cessas aut strenuus anteis,
nec tardum opperior nec praecedentibus insto.

of acknowledging the authority of the philosopher.

69. recens: continuing the idea of *tenera, catulus, puer*. For the general thought cf. *Carm.* 1, 20, 2, *Graeca quod ego ipse testa conditum levi*, which refers to the fact that the jar kept the flavor of the Greek wine.

70–71. The frequent jesting close, with humorous abruptness. 'Such is my advice. Take it and go your way. But, as for me, I am middle-aged and shall neither wait for you, if you are slow, nor press after you, if you hurry on...'

3

The date is fixed by the first lines. In the year 20 Tiberius went to the East as the personal representative of Augustus, taking with him, as was usual on such occasions, a considerable retinue. Among those who accompanied him were several young men interested in literature, as was Tiberius himself.

Julius Florus, to whom the letter is addressed, is the same person to whom *Epist.* 2, 2 is dedicated. Both letters are evidence of his friendship with Tiberius, as of his interest in literature, but beyond this nothing is known with certainty of him.

'I am anxious to know, my dear Florus, where you and your companions are. In Thrace? Or on the Hellespont? Or already in Asia? And what are you doing? Who has undertaken the epic on Augustus? How is Titius, my Pindaric hero? Or has he turned tragic poet? And how is Celsus? Remind him again of that fable of Aesop. And what are you undertaking? I expect great things of you, whatever line you choose to follow. If only you would drop some of your ambitions and turn to philosophy! This — as I am telling everybody nowadays — is the duty of us all. And, speaking of duty, have you made up your quarrel with Munatius? I hope so, for I think too well of you both to be satisfied with anything less than a complete reconciliation.'

This Epistle deserves careful study. It is, on the one hand, a perfectly natural letter, expressing the interest of the writer in his correspondent, revealing the personality of both and the friendly relation between them. It reads like a letter dashed off in high spirits, full of friendly banter, and yet at bottom serious enough. On the other hand, it is a most carefully written piece of literature, artistic in expression and in the transition from one topic to another. The combination of spontaneity of feeling with artistic expression, which is one of the charms of the lyric poetry of Catullus, is rarely to be found in the Odes. In the Satires there is a nearer approach to it. In this letter it is attained.

> Iuli Flore, quibus terrarum militet oris
> Claudius, Augusti privignus, scire laboro.
> Thracane vos Hebrusque nivali compede vinctus,
> an freta vicinas inter currentia turres,
> 5   an pingues Asiae campi collesque morantur?
> Quid studiosa cohors operum struit? Hoc quoque curo.
> Quis sibi res gestas Augusti scribere sumit?

1. **terrarum**: the plural makes the question more general; cf. *ubi terrarum*. — **militet**: he was in command of troops, though the mission was not in reality a campaign. — **oris**: *distant lands*; *ora* is not necessarily a seashore, but any edge; cf. 'ends of the earth.'

2. **Claudius**: Tiberius Claudius Nero, the stepson and successor of Augustus, not yet adopted as a son. — **laboro**: so *Sat.* 2, 8, 19. *nosse laboro*; repeated in *curo*, vs. 6.

3. **Thraca**: the form *Thracia* is later. In the Odes Horace uses the Greek form *Thrace*. — **nivali ... vinctus**: this fixes the time of the year. But *compede vinctus* is not to be taken quite literally; the cold of Thrace was proverbial.

4. **freta**: the Hellespont, on opposite sides of which stood, in poetic tradition, the towers of Hero and Leander, near Sestos and Abydos. The Hellespont is here less than a mile wide (*vicinas*) and the current runs swiftly.

6. **studiosa cohors**: the suite of young men who accompanied Tiberius, as Catullus went on the staff of Memmius to Bithynia. Tiberius was himself in early life interested in literature and was doubtless inclined to follow the example of Maecenas and Messala and Augustus in the patronage of men of letters. — **operum**: with *quid*; in this context necessarily works of literature.

7. **sumit**: *chooses, takes upon himself*. This is the task which had more than once been suggested to Horace (cf. *Sat.* 2, 1, 10 ff.), but which he had always declined to undertake. There is a little irony in *sumit*.

Bella quis et paces longum diffundit in aevum?
Quid Titius, Romana brevi venturus in ora,
10   Pindarici fontis qui non expalluit haustus,
fastidire lacus et rivos ausus apertos?
Vt valet? Vt meminit nostri? Fidibusne Latinis
Thebanos aptare modos studet auspice musa,
an tragica desaevit et ampullatur in arte?

8. **diffundit**: of the extensive circulation that an epic poem on Augustus ought to merit. — **in aevum**: such a poem should be good enough to endure for all time.

9. **Titius**: unknown. The accounts in the Scholiasts are made up from the text. — **in ora**: so in the epitaph attributed to Ennius, *volito per ora virum*; 'soon to be famous in Rome.'

10-11. **non expalluit**: it required a certain audacity to attempt a Pindaric ode (cf. *Carm.* 4. 2. 1, *Pindarum quisquis studet aemulari*). The thought is repeated in positive form in *ausus*, vs. 11. For the accus. *haustus* cf. *Carm.* 3. 27, 27, *fraudes palluit*. — The contrast between the draughts from the fountain of the Muses on Helicon and the waters of the public pool (*lacus*) or the stream, easy of access to all (*apertos*), is used by Quintilian, 10, 1, 109, *non enim pluvias, ut ait Pindarus, aquas colligit, sed vivo gurgite exundat*, with a slightly different sense.

13. **Thebanos**: i.e., Pindaric. — **auspice musa**: 'with the help of the Muses'; the sense is affected by the proximity of *studet*, so that it means 'hoping for the blessing of the Muses.'

14. **desaevit**: only here in Horace. The word is coined to go with *ampullatur* and to express humorously, because it is coined, the high emotions of tragedy. — **ampullatur**: a translation of ληκυθίζει (cf. *A. P.* 97). This word, from ληκύθος, *ampulla*, a *flask*, was used in derision of the tendency of tragedy to run into bombast. The figure seems to be taken from the hollow humming sound made by the wind in the neck of a jar. — It is certainly impossible to take these lines, which are in effect a message to Titius, quite seriously; the phrasing (*non expalluit, ausus, auspice, musa, desaevit, ampullatur*) forbids that interpretation. But neither can they be taken, in so friendly a letter meant for publication, as mere irony. They are the friendly banterings of an older man addressed to a young friend of high ambitions and they are at the same time a reminder of the writer's disinclination to attempt either tragedy or the Pindaric ode.

EPISTVLAE [I, 3, 25

15 Quid mihi Celsus agit? Monitus multumque monen-
    dus,
    privatas ut quaerat opes et tangere vitet
    scripta, Palatinus quaecumque recepit Apollo;
    ne, si forte suas repetitum venerit olim
    grex avium plumas, moveat cornicula risum
20 furtivis nudata coloribus. Ipse quid audes?
    Quae circumvolitas agilis thyma? Non tibi parvum
    ingenium, non incultum est et turpiter hirtum:
    seu linguam causis acuis seu civica iura
    respondere paras seu condis amabile carmen,
25 prima feres hederae victricis praemia. Quodsi

15. mihi: an excellent example of the ethical dative. — Celsus: this must be Celsus Albinovanus, addressed in *Epist.* 1, 8 as *comes scribaque Neronis*. — monitus: already, when he was with me in Rome.

16–17. privatas: explained by the rest of the line; he should not imitate the great and well-known writers, whose works were already in the library of the temple of Apollo, but should seek after some originality.

18–20. The fable of the bird that dressed itself out in the feathers of other birds, Phaedrus 1, 3. Horace has slightly changed the story to fit his purpose here. — olim: *sometime*. — cornicula: the diminutive form is apparently derisive, *the poor crow;* but in all fables the birds and animals are changed about without much regard to tradition or natural history, and *cornicula* may be some smaller bird of the crow family. — The bantering tone of 9–14 is continued in these lines.

20. audes: *attempt;* used absolutely the word suggests more of encouragement and less of raillery than is implied in *fastidire . . . ausus*, vs. 11.

21. thyma: *i.e.*, 'from what flowers do you gather honey?'

22. turpiter hirtum: the figure is of a field left uncultivated and therefore ugly with rough-growing bushes.

23–24. causis: as pleader in court, as orator. — iura respondere: as *iuris consultus*, like Trebatius in *Sat.* 2, 1. — carmen: lyric poetry.

25. hederae: cf. *Carm.* 1, 1, 29, *doctarum hederae praemia frontium*. This is applicable only to the last of the three forms of literary activity, but is somewhat

frigida curarum fomenta relinquere posses,
quo te caelestis sapientia duceret, ires.
Hoc opus, hoc studium parvi properemus et ampli,
si patriae volumus, si nobis vivere cari.
30 Debes hoc etiam rescribere, sit tibi curae,
quantae conveniat, Munatius. An male sarta
gratia nequicquam coit et rescinditur? At vos

generalized by *prima feres;* 'you will reach the first rank, you will get the reward of the ivy wreath.'

26-27. **fomenta**: not like the *fomenta* of *Epist.* 1, 2, 52, but bandages to be kept wet with cold water. This kind of water cure was used by Augustus on the advice of his physician (Sueton. *Aug.* 81) and was at this time in fashion. — **curarum**: gen. of definition (Lane, § 1255) or material, like *hederae praemia,* vs. 25. Cf. Cic. *de Fin.* 2, 29, 95, *patientiae, fortitudinis fomentis dolor mitigari solet.* The sense is, 'if you could bring yourself to give up the practice of treating your soul with the cold-water bandages that your anxieties wrap around you, you would follow where philosophy would lead.' — **sapientia**: this single reference, with the two vss. which follow, is the only connection between the epistle and the social philosophy which is the general theme of this Book.

28. **parvi**: not necessarily a reference to the circumstances of either Florus or Horace; cf. *Epist.* 1, 1, 25 f.

29. **nobis ... cari**: not different, in spite of Lachmann's dictum, from *nobis amici (Epist.* 1, 18, 101); the sense is 'to be in harmony with others and with ourselves.'

30-31. **debes**: *i.e.,* 'I especially urge you,' 'you are especially bound to tell me.' — **etiam**: the earlier part of the letter contains many questions, direct and indirect, which call for a reply to the epistle. — **sit tibi curae**: indirect question after *rescribere,* the second member being expressed in the direct form *an . . . rescinditur?* The sense is 'whether Munatius is as dear to you (*curae* dat.) as he ought to be.' — **Munatius**: another of the young men in the retinue of Tiberius, with whom Florus had quarreled. The quarrel had been partly made up, and Horace is asking whether the reconciliation was proving permanent. — **sarta**: transferred figuratively from the sewing up of a rent in cloth or a wound; cf. Engl. 'patch up a quarrel.'

32. **coit**: also a surgical term, used of the healing of a wound.

seu calidus sanguis seu rerum inscitia vexat
indomita cervice feros, ubicumque locorum
35 vivitis indigni fraternum rumpere foedus,
pascitur in vestrum reditum votiva iuvenca.

33. rerum inscitia: *i.e.*, 'inexperience in life, in affairs.' As *calidus sanguis* would be to a young man a grateful excuse, so *rerum inscitia* is just the form of reproach which would be most efficacious in bringing him back to good sense.

34. cervice: like young cattle or horses that have not yet felt the yoke.

35. vivitis indigni: to be taken together; *indigni* is the important word; 'you ought not, wherever you may be (cf. vs. 1), to break so close a friendship.'

36. 'Nor shall I permit it; for I feel affection for you both, and you must dine together at my house when you return.'

Vss. 30-36 are a kind of postscript containing the only wholly serious thoughts of the epistle. The opening word, *debes*, connects them directly with the preceding exhortation to philosophy, and the closing invitation to both to dine with him is a most graceful expression of his determination to see their friendship renewed. The lines are scrupulously neutral and yet there is not a word that could give offense to Florus. It would not be possible to express such thoughts as these with greater tact.

4

The date of this Epistle cannot be definitely fixed. The absence of any allusion to the Odes in vs. 1 seems to require a date before 23 B.C., when the Odes were published, and the reference to a favorable judgment expressed by Tibullus in regard to the Satires points to a still earlier date. Tibullus returned to Rome from a campaign in Aquitania in 27 and may then for the first time have read the Satires.

Albius Tibullus, addressed in this epistle and in *Carm.* 1, 33, the elegiac poet, was a younger friend of Horace and a man of attractive character. He was, however, of a somewhat melancholy temperament, and this note of general invitation and inquiry is intended to cheer him.

'What are you doing at your home in Pedum, my dear Albius? Writing or philosophizing in silence? The gods have given you much; be grateful for what you have. If you will make me a visit, you will find me fat and cheerful, as an Epicurean ought to be.'

Albi, nostrorum sermonum candide iudex,
quid nunc te dicam facere in regione Pedana?
Scribere quod Cassi Parmensis opuscula vincat,
an tacitum silvas inter reptare salubris,
5   curantem quicquid dignum sapiente bonoque est?
Non tu corpus eras sine pectore: di tibi formam,
di tibi divitias dederunt artemque fruendi.
Quid voveat dulci nutricula maius alumno,
qui sapere et fari possit quae sentiat, et cui

1. **sermonum**: the Satires. — **candide**: the opposite, *niger*, is used in *Sat.* 1, 4. 85, 91, and *candidae animae* of Plotius and Varius and Vergil, *Sat.* 1, 5, 41. It means *fair* or *friendly*, rather than 'candid.'

2. **dicam**: often inserted into a question in colloquial style (*quo te dicam ego ire?* Plaut. *Curc.* 12, *unde id futurum dicam?* Ps. 106) to increase the effect of uncertainty. Cf. Engl. 'what am I to suppose that you are doing?' — **Pedana**: Tibullus had an estate near Pedum, which was not far from Horace's Sabine farm.

3. **scribere**: sc. *dicam te*. — **Cassi**: one of the assassins of Caesar, called *Parmensis* here to distinguish him from Cassius Longinus. He was put to death after the battle of Actium by the order of Augustus. Of his literary activity almost nothing is known, but the comparison here is entirely respectful. — **opuscula**: the word could properly be used of elegies, which would afford a natural standard of comparison for the poems of Tibullus.

4. **tacitum ... reptare**: this coincides well with the character of Tibullus, as it is revealed in his elegies.

5. **curantem**: *i.e.*, intent upon philosophy.

6–7. **eras**: the tense refers back to the time in the past when they were together, in contrast to Horace's present state (*nunc*, vs. 2) of ignorance. 'You were not, when I knew you.' — **formam, divitias, artem**: the blessings of the fortunate, expressed in somewhat conventional terms, and made more individual and specific in vss. 9–11.

8. **voveat**: *wish, pray for*. — **maius**: *i.e.*, *what more, what besides*; the standard of comparison is implied in vss. 6–7.

9–10. **qui**: *i.e.*, 'if he have the power....' — Tibullus had all the gifts of fortune here specified — intelligence, power of expression, attractiveness, a good name — except perhaps *valetudo*; he was

10   gratia, fama, valetudo contingat abunde,
     et mundus victus non deficiente crumina?
     Inter spem curamque, timores inter et iras
     omnem crede diem tibi diluxisse supremum:
     grata superveniet quae non sperabitur hora.
15   Me pinguem et nitidum bene curata cute vises,
     cum ridere voles, Epicuri de grege porcum.

of a somewhat melancholy temperament, and *valetudo* is added to the list as an encouragement to him in his depression. — Vs. 10 is a more accurate statement than *divitias* (7); Tibullus had an estate and money enough for his moderate needs.

12. 'In the ordinary experiences of life, which is a succession of varying emotions.' This description, not quite in Horace's usual vein, is in reality meant to be encouraging to Tibullus by reminding him that there is nothing unusual in his experience.

13-14. The doctrine of the Odes (1. 9, 9-16; 1, 11; 2, 3; 2, 10). — The two lines are in paratactic relation; 'accept each day as your last; (then) you will be grateful when a new day dawns.'

15-16. The allusions to Horace's own cheerful state of mind are humorously clothed in allusions to his physical well-being. It is said of him in the *Vita* of Suetonius, *habitu corporis brevis fuit atque obesus.* — **cute**: cf., *Epist.* 1, 2, 29. note. — **vises**: *i.e.*, 'you shall find me in the best of condition, when you come to see me, as I hope you will.' — **grege**: in a double sense, as the usual word for a school of philosophy, and with reference to *porcum*. — **porcum**: often used as a term of reproach of Epicureanism, which the Romans generally understood only in its less elevated form.

5

The year in which this Epistle was written is left entirely uncertain, as is natural in an invitation to dinner. The day of the month was Sept. 22d (vs. 7).

Torquatus was probably of the family of the Manlii Torquati, a lawyer and orator, but otherwise unknown. He is addressed in *Carm.* 4, 7, where his *genus, facundia*, and *pietas* are mentioned.

The letter has all the appearance of being a real invitation to a dinner that actually took place on a special occasion. Two things make it worthy of preservation in this collection of letters. It is, in the first place, a very successful illustration, in concrete form, of a fundamental principle of Horace's social philosophy. He is here in the position of the host of no wealth or social position approaching a man of high standing and of importance in the world of affairs. The merit of the invitation is that it recognizes these differences, but with such openness and humor as to show that the writer did not overestimate their importance and was confident that his guest also did not give them undue weight. As host, Horace is humorously profuse in saying that he is making anxious preparations for the dinner ; as a friend, he takes for granted the absolute equality which is the only foundation for friendship, without either servility or self-assertion. To this subject his relation to Maecenas had led Horace to give careful attention, and it is the theme of *Sat.* 1, 6 and of two Epistles, 7 and 18, of this Book.

In the second place, the occasion gave an opportunity for the recommendation of that philosophy of moderate enjoyment of pleasure to which Horace so frequently recurs. The praise of wine was a standing theme of Greek and Roman lyric ; an invitation to dinner furnished an appropriate motive for introducing it again.

Si potes Archiacis conviva recumbere lectis
nec modica cenare times olus omne patella,
supremo te sole domi, Torquate, manebo.
Vina bibes iterum Tauro diffusa palustris

1. **Archiacis**: the implication is that this was some modest kind of couch, not quite fitted for use at a dining table. The Scholiast says *Archias breves lectos fecit*, which may be a genuine tradition. — **conviva**: to be taken with *recumbere*; 'to recline as one does at the table.' Horace does not use the ordinary verb, *accumbere*; but it is possible that there is some special point in *recumbere*; ' if you are able to stretch yourself out in the usual way on a short couch.'

2. **olus omne**: *i.e.*, 'nothing but the plainest food.' — **patella**: the diminutive form is expressive of the pretended humility.

3. **supremo sole**: 'at the end of the day.' The more usual hour was in the middle of the afternoon, but this dinner was to be prolonged into the night, 10-11.

4. **iterum Tauro**: sc. *consule*. Taurus was consul for the second time, with Augustus, in 26 B.C. The wine was of a respectable age, though not at all remarkable. —

5   inter Minturnas Sinuessanumque Petrinum.
    Si melius quid habes, arcesse, vel imperium fer.
    Iamdudum splendet focus et tibi munda supellex.
    Mitte levis spes et certamina divitiarum
    et Moschi causam : cras nato Caesare festus
10 dat veniam somnumque dies ; impune licebit
    aestivam sermone benigno tendere noctem.
    Quo mihi fortunam, si non conceditur uti ?

diffusa: *bottled, i.e.*, poured from the single large jar in which it had fermented into the many smaller *amphorae* (hence *dis-fusa*) in which it was sealed up to ripen.

5. These places were all in the better wine-producing district, though not in the best part of it; the wine was neither Falernian nor Massic, but still pretty good, as the careful description shows.

6. **arcesse**: *send it.*—**imperium fer**: 'or put yourself under my command,' *i.e.*, 'take what I give you,' but with a secondary reference to the office of *magister bibendi*, which Horace pretends to assume for himself. — The line is to be taken humorously, as a sort of climax to the description of the dinner.

8-9. **mitte**: a natural and perhaps also a conventional part of an invitation to a banquet; cf. *Carm.* 3, 8, 17, *mitte civilis super urbe curas*; *Carm.* 1, 26, 1-6. — **spes**: a very general reference to all kinds of ambition. — **certamina divitiarum**: a more definite reference to the struggle for wealth which, in Horace's judgment, was far too common at Rome; *divitiarum* is an objective gen.—**Moschi causam**: a direct allusion to a case which was then occupying the attention of Torquatus. Moschus was a rhetorician, accused of poisoning, and defended by Torquatus and Asinius Pollio.

9. **nato Caesare**: to a reader of Horace's time this bare phrase would have been perfectly intelligible; to us, knowing little of the circumstances, it is not clear whether the reference is to Julius Caesar or to Augustus. But we know of no custom of celebrating the birthday of Julius Caesar so long after his death and, on the other hand, the birthday of Augustus was an occasion for festivities (Sueton. *Oct.* 62). This fell on September 23, and we must therefore take *aestivam* (vs. 11) in a general sense. The weather would still be summer-like at that date. — **festus**: there would be no session of courts and no public business.

12. **fortunam**: the accus. is regular in this exclamation; cf. *Sat.*

Parcus ob heredis curam nimiumque severus
adsidet insano; potare et spargere flores
15 incipiam, patiarque vel inconsultus haberi.
Quid non ebrietas designat? Operta recludit,
spes iubet esse ratas, ad proelia trudit inertem,
sollicitis animis onus eximit, addocet artes.
Fecundi calices quem non fecere disertum,
20 contracta quem non in paupertate solutum?
Haec ego procurare et idoneus imperor et non
invitus: ne turpe toral, ne sordida mappa

2, 5, 102; 2, 7, 116; with slight variations the phrase occurs half a dozen times, followed by a *si-* clause. It is not necessary to supply any definite verb. 'What is fortune for if not for use?' Cf. the same thought more fully expressed in *Carm.* 2, 3, 9 ff.

13. **parcus ... curam**: 'the man who starves himself in order to provide for his heir.' Cf. *Carm.* 2, 14, 25, *absumet heres.*

14. **adsidet**: Engl. 'is next door to.' Cf. 'sitteth in the seat of the scornful.' Those who are alike will naturally sit together. — **flores**: a usual accompaniment of a feast.

15. **inconsultus**: Horace's best phrase for this is *dulce est desipere in loco* (*Carm.* 4, 12, 28); here, however, the word is selected with reference to his guest, who is *iuris consultus* and would regard *in-consultus* as a synonym of *in-sanus* or *in-sipiens*.

16-18. **ebrietas**: not, of course, intoxication, but the exhilaration produced by wine. The best commentary on this passage is *Carm.* 3, 21, 13-20; *designat* (*effect, accomplish*) is the same as *tu lene tormentum* (*i.e., stimulus*) *ingenio admoves | plerumque duro; operta recludit* is a short phrase for *tu sapientium | curas et arcanum iocoso | consilium retegis Lyaeo*; *spes iubet esse ratas* is equivalent to *tu spem reducis mentibus anxiis*, and *ad proelia trudit inertem* to *virisque et addis cornua pauperi.* The following phrases, however, have no precise parallel in the Ode.

19-20. **fecundi**: *frequent, frequently refilled*; in effect the same as *ebrietas*. — **contracta**: contrasted with *solutum* at the end of the verse; 'freed from the limitations of poverty.'

21. **haec**: the details of arrangement and preparation which follow in *ne* and *ut* clauses. — **imperor**: *I am bound,* as host, 'I take it upon myself.'

22-25. Cf. in general, *Sat.* 2, 4.

corruget nares; ne non et cantharus et lanx
ostendat tibi te; ne fidos inter amicos
sit qui dicta foras eliminet; ut coeat par
iungaturque pari. Butram tibi Septiciumque
et nisi cena prior potiorque puella Sabinum
detinet adsumam. Locus est et pluribus umbris;
sed nimis arta premunt olidae convivia caprae.
   Tu quotus esse velis rescribe et rebus omissis
atria servantem postico falle clientem.

81–87, where some emphasis is laid upon the fact that these matters demand only attention, not expense, and are therefore within the reach of persons of moderate means, as Horace represents himself to be. — **ostendat**: *i.e.*, 'be brightly polished.' — **eliminet**: 'carry beyond the threshold of the dining room.'

26–27. The three men named are all unknown to us. — **prior**: *earlier*, one to which he has already been invited.

28–29. **umbris**: persons whom the chief guest might bring with him. Cf. *Sat.* 2, 8, 22, *quas Maecenas adduxerat umbras.* — But not so many as to make it necessary to sit close together.

30–31. **quotus**: *i.e.*, 'name your number,' and I will provide accordingly. — **rescribe**: the note was sent by a slave, who would wait for an answer. — **rebus omissis**: 'drop your business'; a renewal of the exhortation in vs. 8. — The humorous suggestion of vs. 31 is also an indirect compliment to the busy lawyer.

6

There is no evidence to determine the date of this Epistle, and Numicius, whose name stands in the first line, is entirely unknown.

'The steady composure of philosophy is the only source of happiness, Numicius. If men can look without superstitious dread upon the wonders of the universe, they must surely be able to look without passion upon the petty attractions of ambition and wealth, neither desiring their rewards nor fearing their loss. For they are all a passing show, here to-day and gone to-morrow. But the rewards of philosophy are permanent.

'You think otherwise? Very well; follow your own course. Hurry and labor to get rich and then to get richer, until you are so rich that your money is a mere superfluity to you and a temptation to thieves. Or is it office that is to make you happy? Then crawl in the dirt to get votes. Or are you going to be a lover of good dinners? That is a simple ambition, and certainly a low one. Or is it to be love and jests? You know where that ends.

'If this statement of your views does not suit you, make a better one or else accept my ideals.'

This Epistle is not a letter. In its general form it is not essentially different from the Satires of the First Book. The only indications of that personal tone which distinguishes a letter from a short essay are the purely formal address in vs. 1, the two closing lines, and the possible allusion to the opinions of Numicius in vs. 31, *virtutem verba putas*. These, however, are too slight to produce the impression of a letter. For this reason it may be surmised that this is one of the earlier of the Epistles, in which Horace is endeavoring to shape a new form for his social comments, different from the Lucilian form of the First Book and from the dialogue form of the Second Book.

In the substance of the Epistle, however, in the handling of the familiar thoughts about wealth and ambition, there is a decided change. Horace here writes as one to whom philosophy is a reality, an actual and accepted guide in the affairs of life. In this respect the Epistle is quite unlike the earlier work and this element brings it into harmony with the other writings in this collection.

Nil admirari prope res est una, Numici,
solaque, quae possit facere et servare beatum.
Hunc solem et stellas et decedentia certis
tempora momentis sunt qui formidine nulla

1. **nil admirari**: *to be undisturbed in spirit*, ' to be free from the distractions of fear and desire.' No words in Horace or perhaps in Latin literature have been more completely misunderstood than these. Horace is not preaching indifferentism; the words stand for that self-control and inward composure which, under various names (ἀταραξία, ἀπάθεια), was the end sought after in all Greek systems of philosophy. To express this he translates τὸ μηδὲν θαυμάζειν, a phrase used by Pythagoras and often repeated in later philosophical writings. The same thought is expressed in vs. 14. below.

3–5. **hunc**: as if pointing to it. — **tempora**: *the seasons*. — **momentis**: not *times*, but *changes*,

5 imbuti spectent; quid censes munera terrae,
   quid maris extremos Arabas ditantis et Indos,
   ludicra quid plausus et amici dona Quiritis,
   quo spectanda modo, quo sensu credis et ore?
   Qui timet his adversa, fere miratur eodem
10 quo cupiens pacto; pavor est utrobique molestus,
   improvisa simul species exterret utrumque.
   Gaudeat an doleat, cupiat metuatne, quid ad rem,
   si quidquid vidit melius peiusque sua spe
   defixis oculis animoque et corpore torpet?

alternations (movi-mentis). — The machinery of the universe is looked upon by the savage as something awful, something to be feared, but some men (especially the Epicurean philosophers like Lucretius) can gaze upon its wonders without superstitious dread. The whole sentence is a paratactic protasis to the thought of vss. 5-8; 'if men can look upon the wonders of nature without undue excitement, can we not remain unmoved by trifles like wealth or office?'

5-8. **quid censes**: the question is put in its most general form and then taken up at the end in the more definite form in vs. 8. This is a colloquialism, like the use of *quid ais?* to introduce a question. Cf. Cic. *pro Rosc.* 17, 49, 'quid censes hunc ipsum Sex. Roscium, quo studio et qua intellegentia esse in rusticis rebus?' and often. — **maris**: with *munera*; the reference is to pearls from the eastern seas. — **ludicra . . . plausus**: *the absurd applause*; *plausus* is appositional gen. with *ludicra*. [The line is, however, by no means clear in sense.] — **dona**: *i.e.*, offices. — **ore**: *expression*; *i.e.*, 'with what kind of looks.'

9. **his . . . adversa**: the opposites of wealth (vs. 6) and honors (vs. 7). — **miratur**: his fear of poverty is in effect the same kind of emotion as love of money; either is an unworthy passion.

11. **simul**: = *simul ac*, as often. — **species**: *i.e.*, the unexpected appearance of either success or defeat.

12. **quid ad rem**: *i.e.*, what difference does it make whether it is pleasure or pain? — The argument of these lines is enforced by being repeated in different forms. *miratur = pavor = torpet*; *improvisa species = melius peiusque sua spe*; but the variation is produced by the use of slightly changed figures, so that there is no impression of useless repetition.

15 Insani nomen sapiens ferat, aequus iniqui,
ultra quam satis est virtutem si petat ipsam.
I nunc, argentum et marmor vetus aeraque et artes
suspice, cum gemmis Tyrios mirare colores ;
gaude quod spectant oculi te mille loquentem ;
20 navus mane forum et vespertinus pete tectum,
ne plus frumenti dotalibus emetat agris
Mutus et — indignum, quod sit peioribus ortus, —
hic tibi sit potius quam tu mirabilis illi.
Quicquid sub terra est in apricum proferet aetas,

15-16. This is a summary of the argument in an extreme, almost paradoxical, form ; ' even the pursuit of the philosophic coolness may be too ardent.' — **insani nomen . . . ferat** : cf., with the same meaning, *adsidet insano, Epist.* 1, 5, 14. — **aequus** : this particular virtue is selected for specification, after the general word *sapiens*, because this is precisely the virtue which should prevent *ultra quam satis est*.

17-18. **i nunc** : *i.e.*, 'in view of these facts go on, if you can, and surrender yourself to the passion for art or honors or wealth.' — The objects named in these lines have not been mentioned above ; they are the signs of a life of luxury and, self-indulgence, silver plate, statues, and other artistic objects. Cf. the reference in *Sat.* 2, 7, 95 to excessive devotion to the enjoyment of art, which is there satirized as a form of slavery.

19. The gratified ambition of the orator.

20-23. The seeker after money. — **forum** : as the market place, the Exchange, not the place of public business. — **vespertinus** : only the especially eager man of business would stay so late. — **frumenti** : one form of wealth, as in *Sat.* 1, 1, 49 ff. and often. — **dotalibus** : this is parenthetic in sense, like the formal parenthesis in the next line ; 'lest Mutus should have a larger income than you — his money came from his wife, by the way, and he is a man of very humble origin.' — **emetat** : *reap, harvest*; only here in classical Latin. — **Mutus** : unknown. He is of the same class as the man who is attacked in *Epod.* 4.

24-25. The emphasis is on the second part of the sentence, *defodiet condetque*, and the first part is in sense a clause of comparison ; 'as time has brought all this to light, so time will bury it all.' —

25 defodiet condetque nitentia. Cum bene notum
porticus Agrippae et via te conspexerit Appi,
ire tamen restat Numa quo devenit et Ancus.
Si latus aut renes morbo tentantur acuto,
quaere fugam morbi. Vis recte vivere: (quis non?)
30 si virtus hoc una potest dare, fortis omissis
hoc age deliciis. Virtutem verba putas et

in apricum: *i.e.*, into the light of day, into our range of vision. This particular expression for a thought which is more frequently expressed by birth and death or growth and decay is chosen in order to continue the figure of seeing, gazing upon, which is prominent in the earlier lines (*spectent* 5, *spectanda* 8, *species* 11, *vidit* 13, *oculis* 14, *suspice* 18).

25. bene notum: *i.e.*, when you win the fame you are seeking.

26. porticus Agrippae: a new portico opened in the year 25. Cf. also *Epist.* 1, 1, 71. — via . . . Appi: the same form (for *Appia via*) in *Epist.* 1, 18, 20. This was a favorite place for driving; cf. *Epod.* 4, 14, *Appiam mannis terit.*

28-68. 'Since philosophy is, as I have proved, the only source of happiness, give up all else — money making, ambition, pleasure — and seek this.' The thought is clear, but its connection with the earlier part of the Epistle is somewhat obscured by the detailed description of the three pursuits which are to be abandoned.

28. This line, with *quod* instead of *si*, is repeated from *Sat.* 2, 3, 163; cf. *Epist.* 1, 1, 56. In this case there is no point in the repetition, which seems to be merely an accidental reminiscence.

29. vis: a condition in the form of a statement, in order to avoid the awkwardness of two conditions with one main clause, *hoc age*.

30. virtus . . . una: referring back to vs. 1. — omissis: this is the real verb, corresponding to *quaere fugam*; 'if you have a disease of the body, go to a doctor and be cured; if you have a disease of the soul and wish to be freed from it (*recte vivere*), then give up the follies that have caused it and — if my argument has convinced you that philosophy is the only cure — go to philosophy.'

31. The opposite of vs. 30; 'but if you think that philosophy is nonsense, then go your own way.' The rest of the Epistle is an amplification of this thought, expressed in words which reveal the unsoundness of the hope of finding happiness in such ways and therefore, by indirection, re-

lucum ligna : cave ne portus occupet alter,
ne Cibyratica, ne Bithyna negotia perdas;
mille talenta rotundentur, totidem altera, porro et
35   tertia succedant, et quae pars quadret acervum.
Scilicet uxorem cum dote fidemque et amicos
et genus et formam regina pecunia donat,
ac bene nummatum decorat Suadela Venusque.
Mancipiis locuples eget aeris Cappadocum rex :
40   ne fueris hic tu.   Chlamydes Lucullus, ut aiunt,
si posset centum scaenae praebere rogatus,
'Qui possum tot?' ait, 'Tamen et quaeram et quot
    habebo

mind the reader of the doctrine of vs. 1 and vs. 30.

32. **lucum ligna**: *i.e.*, to think that philosophy is mere words is as foolish as to think that a sacred grove is nothing but so much firewood. — **portus occupet**: not as in *Carm*. 1, 14, 2, where the port is a harbor of refuge from storm ; the *portus* is here the harbor where the cargo is to be sold and the first comer will get the best prices.

33. **Cibyratica**: business with Cibyra, a city in Asia Minor. — **negotia**: *ventures* was the word used in the China trade.

35. **quadret**: 'make the pile four-square,' add still a fourth thousand talents.

36. **scilicet**: *of course, you know,* often as here with irony. — **fidem**: *credit,* in the business sense.

37. **regina**: another ironical suggestion of the absurdity of this ideal.

38. **Suadela**: goddess of persuasive eloquence. — The terms used here are in part the same used in stating the Stoic Paradox that the *sapiens* possesses everything ; cf. *Sat*. 1, 3, 123 ff.

39. **mancipiis**: with *locuples*. — **aeris**: after *eget*. — Cappadocia furnished many slaves to Roman masters, but the kingdom was hard pressed for cash (*aeris*). Of the previous king Cicero says, 'nullum aerarium, nullum vectigal habet . . . nihil illo regno spoliatius, nihil rege egentius.' *ad Att*. 6, 1, 3.

40. **ne fueris**: *i.e.* 'do not be content unless you have wealth of every kind,' of course ironically. — The following story of Lucullus is repeated also by Plutarch, *Lucull*. 39, with a reference to Horace's comment in vs. 45.

41. **scaenae**: the cloaks were needed to dress a large chorus, who were to appear in rich dress.

mittam.' Post paullo scribit sibi milia quinque
esse domi chlamydum; partem vel tolleret omnes.
45 Exilis domus est, ubi non et multa supersunt
et dominum fallunt et prosunt furibus. Ergo
si res sola potest facere et servare beatum,
hoc primus repetas opus, hoc postremus omittas.
Si fortunatum species et gratia praestat,
50 mercemur servum qui dictet nomina, laevum
qui fodicet latus et cogat trans pondera dextram
porrigere. 'Hic multum in Fabia valet, ille Velina;
cui libet hic fasces dabit, eripietque curule

43. **milia quinque**: Plutarch, with the sobriety of a biographer, puts the number at two hundred.

44. **tolleret**: the subject is the praetor who was giving the games; in the note it would be *tolle*.

45-46. The application of the story. 'Don't be like the king of Cappadocia, but be really rich, like Lucullus, who had more things than he could possibly use — mere plunder for thieves.'

47. A reminder of vss. 1-2 and therefore of the ironical meaning of all this exhortation.

48. This also repeats vs. 20, in a slightly different form, and the repetition has the effect of saying, ' we are back where we were before.'

49-55. 'If office holding is your ideal, then use the unpleasant methods of the politician.'

49. **species**: the state and splendor of high office. — **gratia**: the personal influence that wins votes.

50. **servum**: the *nomenclator*, whose business it was to know the names of citizens and remind his master, so that the master might greet them as if he remembered them.

51. **fodicet**: a colloquial word, *nudge*. — The rest of the verse contains an allusion to some action of a candidate soliciting votes, some act which would not be agreeable to a self-respecting man, but which his desire to propitiate a voter compels him to perform. But there are many details of Roman life about which we know so little that an allusion to them must remain unintelligible. It is not worth while to repeat here the attempts that have been made by scholars to explain *trans pondera*; the data are not sufficient to make the allusion clear.

52. **Fabia, Velina**: sc. *tribu*. These are voting districts, frequently mentioned.

53-55. **curule . . . ebur**: the

cui volet importunus ebur.' 'Frater,' 'pater' adde;
55 ut cuique est aetas, ita quemque facetus adopta.
Si, bene qui cenat, bene vivit, lucet; eamus
quo ducet gula : piscemur, venemur, ut olim
Gargilius, qui mane plagas, venabula, servos,
differtum transire forum populumque iubebat,
60 unus ut e multis populo spectante referret
emptum mulus aprum ; crudi tumidique lavemur,
quid deceat, quid non, obliti, Caerite cera

ivory chair of the curule magistrate. — **importunus**: 'when he is in a bad temper.' It is an added humiliation that the candidate must keep surly voters in good humor. — **pater**: Horace represents himself as addressing Trebatius as *pater optime, Sat.* 2, 1, 12. — **facetus**: not *jokingly* but *with ready speech*, suiting the address to the age of the voter.

56–64. 'If the pleasures of the table seem to you the highest good, then follow where appetite leads.' The new thought is introduced abruptly, as in vs. 49.

56. lucet: 'it's morning' and the time to provide food for the day's feasting.

57. piscemur, venemur: not literally, but in the market; 'let us look for fish and game as earnestly as Gargilius did.'

58–60. The comparison is carried out into ludicrous details which have nothing to do with the argument. Cf. the allusion to Ruso, *Sat.* 1, 3, 86 ff. — **differtum . . . populumque**: for *differtum populo*. The repetition in the next line is intentional. — **ut**: grammatically a clause of purpose, but in content an expression of the very small results of so much preparation. — **emptum**: this joke is still in circulation.

61. crudi: so in *Sat.* 1, 5, 49, of one who began to take exercise too soon after a meal. The three words go together; 'let us go at once from a gluttonous meal to a hot bath, from one indulgence to another.' The verb *lavemur* resumes the construction of *piscemur, venemur*, vs. 57, after the long comparison, *ut . . . aprum.*

62. Caerite cera: the wax-covered tablets on which were the lists of citizens who had not the right of suffrage. These were called *tabulae Caeritum*, and *Caerite cera digni* therefore means 'unworthy of the rights of Roman citizens.'

digni, remigium vitiosum Ithacensis Vlixi,
cui potior patria fuit interdicta voluptas.
65 Si, Mimnermus uti censet, sine amore iocisque
nil est iucundum, vivas in amore iocisque.
Vive, vale: si quid novisti rectius istis,
candidus imperti; si non, his utere mecum.

63. **remigium**: collective, for *remiges*, *the crew*. The words contain, of course, a condensed comparison.

65-66. A fourth object in life, which, however, is regarded as scarcely distinct from the one which has just preceded and is therefore barely mentioned. Cf. *Sat.* 2, 3, where the main heads of the sermon are given in vss. 78-79 and amorousness is treated as a subdivision of *luxuria*, 247-280. —

Mimnermus: a writer of erotic elegy, a contemporary of Solon.

67-68. **vive, vale**: so *Sat.* 2, 5, 110. — **istis**: 'than these ideas of yours,' with the proper force of the second person. Cf. the words which introduce these ideals of life, *virtutem verba putas*. — **his**: 'my views,' as set forth in the first part, 1-27.

The abruptness of the close is characteristic of Horace, *e.g.*, *Sat.* 1, 1; 1, 2; 1, 3.

7

In spite of the personal allusions in the early part of this Epistle, it is impossible to determine with certainty the year in which it was written. Nor is it clear where Horace was when he wrote; he was in the country, and it may be inferred from the fact that there is no reference to his Sabine farm that he was at some other place in the mountains. Maecenas was in Rome.

'I have changed my mind, my dear Maecenas, and am not coming to Rome now nor even soon. I shall go down to the coast for the winter and shall not see you, my dear friend, until spring comes. My debt to you is great, but I count with confidence upon your consideration for me : I am not as young as I was once. Perhaps my refusal to return seems to you ungrateful : you are reminded, perhaps, of the fable of the fox in the corn bin. I admit the justice of the application and stand ready to submit. I can return your gifts without any change in the esteem I have long felt for you. Telemachus, you remember, returned the gift of Menelaus, saying that he could not use horses and a chariot on his little island. So it is with me ; Rome is too big for me, and I am too small for Rome. Let me tell you a story. Philippus, the lawyer, once made acquaintance with a small tradesman and, partly for his own amusement, induced him to give up his life in Rome and turn farmer. The natural result followed ; the amateur farmer came to utter grief. As he looked at the ruins, he saw his mistake, galloped back to Philippus and begged to be allowed to return the gift. The moral is that every man must go his own way.'

This Epistle was written late in August or early in September. Horace had left Rome in midsummer, promising to return after a short stay in the mountains. He had, however, stayed for a month, and Maecenas, detained in Rome, had written him, asking him to come back and reminding him of his promise and probably of his obligation to his benefactor. To that letter Horace replies in this Epistle. The personal tone is strong in vss. 1-13, 24-28, 34-39, but the greater part of the Epistle consists of the four stories which are woven into it, the story of the Calabrian, vss. 14-19, of the fox, 29-33, of Telemachus, 40-43, and the long story of Philippus, 46-95. The effect of the introduction of this large amount of impersonal material is to make the Epistle read like a Satire. And a comparison with *Sat.* 1, 6 and *Sat.* 2, 6 will show that Horace has here, in treating a serious subject, returned in part to his earlier form. The fusion, however, of the two elements is carried out with great skill, and this Epistle is justly regarded as one of the poet's most finished productions.

But the personal aspect of it is even more interesting than the artistic form. The position was one of real difficulty. It is handled with admirable independence and candor and with most friendly consideration for the feelings of Maecenas. Undoubtedly, as the fact of publication shows, it was received by him with appreciation and with generous cordiality.

> Quinque dies tibi pollicitus me rure futurum
> Sextilem totum mendax desideror. Atqui
> si me vivere vis sanum recteque valentem,

1. **quinque dies**: a 'round' number, as in *Sat.* 1, 3, 16; 2, 3, 289, and often ; 'a week.'

2. **Sextilem**: not at this time named after Augustus. — **mendax**: the blunt confession is meant to take off the edge of Maecenas' annoyance.

3. **sanum ... valentem**: such expressions are frequently doubled,

quam mihi das aegro, dabis aegrotare timenti,
5 Maecenas, veniam, dum ficus prima calorque
dissignatorem decorat lictoribus atris ;
dum pueris omnis pater et matercula pallet,
officiosaque sedulitas et opella forensis
adducit febris et testamenta resignat.
10 Quodsi bruma nives Albanis illinet agris,
ad mare descendet vates tuus et sibi parcet
contractusque leget ; te, dulcis amice, reviset

without any real difference in the meaning of the two words; so *valere et vivere, vive vale.*

4. aegrotare timenti: the next lines amplify this thought. — Verbs of fearing are occasionally followed by an infin. ; Lane, 1959.

5. ficus prima: *i.e.*, late August, the time when the first figs ripen, but with reference also to the belief that early-ripening figs were injurious to the health.

6. dissignatorem: *the undertaker;* he directed the funeral procession, with attendants (*lictores*) dressed in black to clear the way.

7. dum: the thought is better expressed in Engl. by an independent sentence; 'and meanwhile,' 'and all the time.' — **matercula**: cf. *nutricula, Epist.* 1, 4, 8.

8. officiosa: not with reference to public duties, but to those social obligations which Horace himself found so oppressive when he was in the city; cf. *Sat.* 2, 6, 23 ff. — **opella**: the diminutive form expresses the writer's feeling of the pettiness of all such things.

9. resignat: *i.e.*, brings fatal disease and therefore causes the opening of wills.

10. quodsi: temporal, not conditional; *but when*. This is regularly the meaning of *si* when the fact stated in the *si*-clause is certain to occur.

11. ad mare: to some place on the southern seacoast, perhaps not yet definitely selected, or perhaps Tarentum ; cf. vs. 45.— **vates**: this old word had fallen into disuse, but was restored to good usage by the Augustan writers as a substitute for the Greek *poeta*. Here it is probably a quotation from the letter of Maecenas, to which this is a reply.

12. contractus: 'huddled together,' as if drawn up by the chill of cold. — **leget**: *read*. The expression here is rather brief, but is made easier by the plainer phrase *sibi parcet.*

cum zephyris, si concedes, et hirundine prima.
Non quo more piris vesci Calaber iubet hospes,
15 tu me fecisti locupletem. 'Vescere sodes!'
'Iam satis est.' 'At tu quantum vis tolle.' 'Benigne.'
'Non invisa feres pueris munuscula parvis.'
'Tam teneor dono quam si dimittar onustus.'
'Vt libet; haec porcis hodie comedenda relinques.'
20 Prodigus et stultus donat quae spernit et odit;
haec seges ingratos tulit et feret omnibus annis.
Vir bonus et sapiens dignis ait esse paratus;
nec tamen ignorat, quid distent aera lupinis.

13. **si concedes**: *if you will permit*. This friendly formula, like the address *dulcis amice*, is inserted with real delicacy of feeling into the sentence which conveys to Maecenas the full extent of Horace's purpose, to remain away from Rome not only through August and September, but all winter, until the signs of spring come. — **hirundine**: the poetic herald of spring.

14. There is both firmness and delicacy in the immediate turning to the story, without argument or excuse. — **Calaber**: merely to make the story seem real, as names are often used in the Satires, *e.g.*, 1, 1, 6; 20, 58.

15. **locupletem**: it is only in this connection, where it emphasizes his gratitude, that Horace speaks of himself as rich.

16. **benigne**: a courteous formula of refusal; so *tam gratia*. Used again in vs. 62.

20. **quae spernit**: *i.e.*, things that are of no value to him, *porcis comedenda*. The thought is expressed with a slight difference by Seneca, *Epist.* 120, 8, *multi sunt, qui non donant, sed proiciunt*; cf. the whole section.

21. **seges**: the use of this figure is suggested by a proverb like that quoted by Cicero, *de Or.* 64, 261, *ut sementem feceris, ita metes.*

22. **vir bonus**: the adversative connection is merely suggested, as often in Horace, by the contrast between these words and *prodigus et stultus*. — **dignis . . . paratus**: 'is ready to give to men of worthy character.' Cf. the similar thought in *Sat.* 1, 6, 51, *praesertim cautus dignos adsumere*, used also of Maecenas, as if that was a principle definitely laid down by him in bestowing his friendship. Cf. also *Sat.* 1, 6, 7 f.

23. **lupinis**: *lupines*, a kind of bean used as stage money; Plaut. *Poen.* 597. — This line amplifies

Dignum praestabo me etiam pro laude merentis.
25 Quodsi me noles usquam discedere, reddes
forte latus, nigros angusta fronte capillos;
reddes dulce loqui, reddes ridere decorum et
inter vina fugam Cinarae maerere protervae.
Forte per angustam tenuis vulpecula rimam
30 repserat in cumeram frumenti, pastaque rursus
ire foras pleno tendebat corpore frustra.
Cui mustela procul: ' Si vis,' ait, ' effugere istinc,
macra cavum repetes artum, quem macra subisti.'
Hac ego si compellor imagine, cuncta resigno;

sapiens; he knows the value of his gifts.

24. dignum: as you, *bonus et sapiens*, are ready for the worthy, so I am ready to show myself *dignum* by my gratitude, *pro laude merentis*.

25-26. 'I am indeed grateful, but I must have my freedom too; I am no longer young, and you must not expect from me a constant attendance. If you expected that, I should have to remind you of the story of the fox in the corn bin and act according to the moral of the tale.'

26. latus: *lungs, chest*; but we do not know that Horace suffered from any disease of the kind this would suggest. — **nigros**: he says that he was *praecanus*, 'gray before his time'; *Epist.* 1. 20, 24. — **angusta fronte**: *i.e.*, not yet beginning to get bald.

27-28. 'Give me again the power to enjoy the pleasures of youth.' The details are not meant to be personal, but general; 'the pleasant voice and laughter of youth.' — **Cinarae**: cf. *Carm.* 4. 1, 3-4, *non sum qualis eram bonae | sub regno Cinarae.* She is the only one of the girls mentioned by Horace who seems to have had a real existence.

29. vulpecula: the fox is the hero of many of the Fables, as of many of the tales of Uncle Remus. In such stories almost no attention is paid to the real habits of the animals; indeed, it is common to find that in different versions the animals are changed about freely, as, for example, this fable is also told with a mouse for the chief actor.

30. cumeram: *bin* or *jar* for storing grain; cf. *Sat.* 1, 1, 53.

32. procul: *at a little distance*; this is a common meaning; cf. *Sat.* 2, 6, 105.

34. ego: emphatic. — **compellor**: not as in *Sat.* 2, 3, 297, but in the legal sense: 'I too, if I

35 nec somnum plebis laudo satur altilium, nec
otia divitiis Arabum liberrima muto.
Saepe verecundum laudasti, rexque paterque
audisti coram, nec verbo parcius absens;
inspice si possum donata reponere laetus.
40 Haud male Telemachus, proles patientis Vlixi:
'Non est aptus equis Ithace locus, ut neque planis
porrectus spatiis nec multae prodigus herbae;
Atride, magis apta tibi tua dona relinquam.'
Parvum parva decent: mihi iam non regia Roma,
45 sed vacuum Tibur placet aut imbelle Tarentum.

am summoned on the analogy of this fable, . . .' — resigno: also formal; *restore*, 'transfer back to you under my hand and seal.' The word is used in a similar context in *Carm.* 3, 29, 54, *resigno quae [Fortuna] dedit*.

35-36. altilium: with *satur*; it means, properly, fowls fattened for eating, then any specially fine food. The meaning is, 'I am in earnest in saying *cuncta resigno*; I am not so inconsistent as to be praising a simple life while I live in luxury; I do not wish to give up my freedom for all the wealth of Arabia.'

37. verecundum: *for my modesty*; cf. *Carm.* 2, 18, 12, *nec potentem amicum largiora flagito, satis beatus unicis Sabinis*. — rex: = *patronus*. — pater: Maecenas was only a few years older than Horace, but the difference was enough to justify the use of this term of respect.

38. audisti: *you have been called*; so *Sat.* 2, 6, 20 and often. — absens: with no reference to his separation at this time, but in contrast to *coram*.

39. 'Try me and see whether I cannot do as I say, and without repining, too.' *laetus* at the end of the line is emphatic.

40-43. Menelaus presented horses and a chariot to Telemachus as an expression of friendship for him and his father. The reply of Telemachus, of which vss. 41-43 are a paraphrase, is in *Odys.* 4, 601 ff. — patientis: an ornamental epithet, translating the Homeric πολύτλας.

44-45. parvum parva: *i.e.*, 'so it is with me; I can accept only gifts that are suitable to my tastes, not gifts that require a change of life.' — regia, vacuum, imbelle: *royal, quiet, peaceful*; the adjectives are carefully chosen to carry on the modesty of *parvum*. — There is a change of emphasis

Strenuus et fortis causisque Philippus agendis
clarus, ab officiis octavam circiter horam
dum redit atque foro nimium distare Carinas
iam grandis natu queritur, conspexit, ut aiunt,
50   adrasum quendam vacua tonsoris in umbra
cultello proprios purgantem leniter ungues.
' Demetri,' (puer hic non laeve iussa Philippi
accipiebat,) 'abi; quaere et refer, unde domo, quis,

at this point. Hitherto the stress has been upon Horace's inability to stay in Rome, upon the sincerity of his gratitude to Maecenas, and upon his unwillingness to be bound by the gifts he had received. From vs. 44 the emphasis is rather upon his unfitness for such a life as he must lead if he were to be constantly in attendance upon his patron.

46–95. The story of Philippus and Volteius Mena is a companion piece to the story of the Town Mouse and the Country Mouse, which enforces the moral of *Sat.* 2, 6.

46. **Philippus**: one of the famous Roman orators, consul in the year 91. The description of him in Cic. *de Orat.* 3, 1, 4, *et vehementi et diserto et imprimis forti ad resistendum*, agrees with the description given here.

47. **octavam**: the courts opened early, by nine o'clock (*Sat.* 1, 9, 35 f.), and all public business was over early in the afternoon. This bit of detail, with others below (vss. 50 f., 71, 76, 80, 90), is intended to give vividness to this traditional (*ut aiunt*, vs. 49) tale.

48. **Carinas**: a part of the city in which it is known that various persons of importance (Pompey, Q. Cicero) resided. It was not, in fact, far from the Forum, but it seemed so to an old man, tired with his day's work.

50. **adrasum**: *i.e.*, he was already shaved and therefore at leisure. — **vacua ... in umbra**: the barber's shop was a booth, open toward the street, at this time empty and, in contrast with the hot street, cool and shaded.

51. **proprios**: this was sometimes done by the barber; the only reason for representing the man as doing it for himself is that the leisurely (*leniter*) occupation adds to the picture of ease and independence, which attracted the attention of the tired old lawyer as he passed.

52. **puer hic**: the *pedisequus* who accompanied any respectable man in the streets, *e.g.*, Horace himself (*Sat.* 1, 9, 10).

53. **unde domo**: this colloquial

cuius fortunae, quo sit patre quove patrono.'
55 It, redit et narrat Volteium nomine Menam,
praeconem, tenui censu, sine crimine, notum
et properare loco et cessare, et quaerere et uti,
gaudentem parvisque sodalibus et lare certo
et ludis et post decisa negotia campo.
60 'Scitari libet ex ipso quodcumque refers; dic
ad cenam veniat.' Non sane credere Mena;
mirari secum tacitus. Quid multa? 'Benigne,'
respondet. 'Negat ille mihi?' 'Negat improbus,
et te

doubling of expression is frequent in Plaut. and Ter., and *unde* is often used for *a quo* (*Sat.* 1, 6, 12) or *a qua*.

54. **patrono**: *i.e.*, if, in answer to the question *cuius fortunae*, he should say that he was a freedman.

55. **Volteium ... Menam**: the names show that he was a Greek, freedman of some patron named Volteius.

56–59. These details answer the question *cuius fortunae*. — **praeconem**: *an auctioneer*, but in a small way, cf. vs. 65. This was one of the occupations which Horace mentions (*Sat.* 1, 6, 86) as a possible one for himself, had matters not turned out otherwise. — **loco**: 'in the proper place,' as occasion might demand; cf. the well-known *dulce est desipere in loco* (*Carm.* 4, 12, 28). The two verbs are further defined by *et quaerere et uti* and form a combination of qualities which Horace often recommends to the man of business. — **lare certo**: *i.e.*, a respectable householder. — **post ... negotia**: further evidence of good character; he did not neglect his business for amusements. — The description gives an interesting picture of a kind of person who does not often find a place in Latin literature.

61–62. The historical infinitives, the short sentences, and the phrase *quid multa?* are characteristic of the story teller, hurrying over unimportant details. — **benigne**: cf. vs. 16.

63. **negat ille**: 'does he refuse me?' A repudiating exclamation. [There are many instances of this kind of exclamation in Plaut. with the indic., but none parallel to this with the subjv. *neget* and answered by an indic. *negat*.] — **improbus**: the slave shares his master's indignation.

neglegit aut horret.' Volteium mane Philippus
65 vilia vendentem tunicato scruta popello
occupat et salvere iubet prior. Ille Philippo
excusare laborem et mercennaria vincla,
quod non mane domum venisset, denique quod non
providisset eum. 'Sic ignovisse putato
70 me tibi, si cenas hodie mecum.' 'Vt libet.' 'Ergo
post nonam venies : nunc i, rem strenuus auge.'
Vt ventum ad cenam est, dicenda tacenda locutus
tandem dormitum dimittitur. Hic ubi saepe
occultum visus decurrere piscis ad hamum,
75 mane cliens et iam certus conviva, iubetur

64. mane : *i.e.*, the next morning. The story again hurries over details.

65. tunicato : the toga was an inconvenient dress for persons engaged in active work, and was, therefore, worn by the common people only on formal occasions. — popello : the diminutive carries on the suggestion of disparagement in *tunicato*. — scruta : *trash*, second-hand stuff; a rather rare Lucilian word.

66. occupat : 'gets ahead of him,' explained in the following words, *salvere iubet prior*. Cf. *Sat.* 1, 9, 6.

67. laborem : an accus. of the 'inner object,' the 'object effected'; 'he gives his occupation as his excuse.'

68. mane : for the morning *salutatio*; he was aware that politeness required that he should acknowledge the invitation, though he had declined it, by the Roman equivalent for a dinner call.

68-69. non providisset : this is implied by vs. 66. — sic : correlative with *si*; *on this condition, that* . . .

70. ut libet : '*as you please*'; a formula of assent (cf. vs. 19), which would take its tone from the manner of the speaker.

72. dicenda tacenda : the corresponding phrases (ῥητὰ ἄρρητα, *fanda nefanda, honesta inhonesta*) usually imply blame, but here it is merely that he was talkative, spoke of whatever came into his head; *i.e.*, he was at his ease with his patron, as he had been in the barber's shop.

73. hic : nomin. masc. ; 'the man whom I have described'; the story now passes on to the climax.

75. mane : now accustomed to the *salutatio*, which he had at first neglected. — certus conviva : =

rura suburbana indictis comes ire Latinis.
Impositus mannis arvum caelumque Sabinum
non cessat laudare. Videt ridetque Philippus,
et sibi dum requiem, dum risus undique quaerit,
80 dum septem donat sestertia, mutua septem
promittit, persuadet uti mercetur agellum.
Mercatur. Ne te longis ambagibus, ultra
quam satis est, morer, ex nitido fit rusticus atque
sulcos et vineta crepat mera, praeparat ulmos,
85 immoritur studiis et amore senescit habendi.
Verum ubi oves furto, morbo periere capellae,
spem mentita seges, bos est enectus arando,

convictor, a regular guest, as Horace was a guest at the table of Maecenas, *Sat.* 1, 6, 47.

76. **indictis . . . Latinis**: the great Latin festival in April or May, when all public business was suspended.

77. **impositus mannis**: 'in a carriage.' In Homer ἵπποι is used for the chariot, and the same usage is found occasionally in Latin. *manni* were Gallic ponies used for driving, *Epod.* 4, 14.

79–81. **requiem, risus**: *relief* from the burden of work, which he expected to get from the *amusement* afforded by the experiment. — **dum . . . dum . . . dum**: the second clause, *dum donat*, is quite different in sense from the first, *dum quaerit*; 'seeking relief and amusement, by giving . . . and lending . . .'; the use of the same construction for the two different thoughts is intended to give the effect of hurrying the story forward.

83. **nitido**: as he had been when he was sitting in the barber's booth.

85. **immoritur, senescit**: with intentional exaggeration of the severity of a farmer's labor. Cf. also the description of his former life in vs. 57.

86–87. These details also are intentionally exaggerated and are mentioned as if they were the ordinary incidents of a farmer's life, in order to make the point of the story more effective. They are, of course, in humorous contrast to the idyllic pictures of country life which Horace had so often drawn, *e.g.*, in *Epod.* 2. — **periere**: *are lost.* — **mentita**: this figure is often used; cf. *Carm.* 3, 1, 30, and the opposite in *Carm.* 3, 16, 30, *segetis certa fides.*

offensus damnis media de nocte caballum
arripit iratusque Philippi tendit ad aedes.
90 Quem simul adspexit scabrum intonsumque Philippus,
'Durus,' ait, 'Voltei, nimis attentusque videris
esse mihi.' 'Pol me miserum, patrone, vocares,
si velles,' inquit, 'verum mihi ponere nomen.
Quod te per genium dextramque deosque Penates
95 obsecro et obtestor, vitae me redde priori.'
Qui semel adspexit, quantum dimissa petitis
praestent, mature redeat repetatque relicta.
Metiri se quemque suo modulo ac pede verum est.

88. media de nocte: in order to get to town in time for the *salutatio*. And the early hour expresses also his hasty determination. Cf. *arripit* and *iratus*.

90. scabrum intonsumque: again in contrast to the first picture, vs. 50, *adrasum*.

91. durus ... attentus: so the country mouse, *Sat.* 2, 6, 82, *asper et attentus quaesitis*.

92. miserum: *i.e.*, '*durus attentusque* do not half express my condition; you must call me *miserum*.'

94. quod: *wherefore;* formulaic in such sentences as this, with *oro, obsecro;* cf. Verg. *Aen.* 2, 141, Ter. *Andr.* 289. — per genium: the guardian spirit which attends each man through life. A modern parallel would be 'by your own soul.' — dextram: *your honor.*

96-97. This is at bottom the same moral as that of *Sat.* 2, 6, and the same situation as that depicted in *Sat.* 1, 1, 4 ff.

98. modulo: the general word, followed by the more specific, *pede,* which at the same time suggests that each man has his own natural standard in himself.— verum: *right.*
— As at the end of *Sat.* 2, 6, the personal application of the universal rule is left to the reader.

8

This Epistle was written, either in the summer of the year 20 or in the next summer, to a young friend who was in the suite of Tiberius on his mission to the East. It goes, therefore, with *Epist.* 1, 3, in which also Celsus is mentioned.

'My greetings, O Muse, to Celsus! If he asks of me, tell him that I am well in body, but not in spirit, that I am idle and hesitating and unsatisfied with myself. Ask, too, how it is with him and give him from me a friendly warning not to misuse his fortunes.'

In this note the personal and the artistic motives are successfully combined. Both must be kept in mind in the interpretation of it. The fact that it was deliberately selected for publication is a warning against taking the personal element too seriously ; doubtless the bit of advice at the end had a real meaning, but neither that nor the expressions of discontent which skillfully pave the way for the advice should be over-interpreted. The warning is a very general one, such as might be addressed to many young men, and the sense of dissatisfaction with himself and his work is more than once expressed by Horace.

> Celso gaudere et bene rem gerere Albinovano
> Musa rogata refer, comiti scribaeque Neronis.
> Si quaeret quid agam, dic multa et pulchra minantem
> vivere nec recte nec suaviter ; haud quia grando
> 5 contuderit vitis oleamque momorderit aestus,

1. **Celso**: mentioned, with a message, in the letter to Florus, *Epist.* 1, 3, 15 ff. — The change in the order of the names is common, *e.g., Epist.* 1, 2, 1. — **gaudere, gerere**: *i.e.*, χαίρειν καὶ εὖ πράττειν. The phrase is treated as a whole and put after *refer* ('take my greeting and good wishes'), so that the need of the ordinary *iube* is not felt.

2. **Musa**: as if she were a letter carrier, who was to deliver the message orally. In form, the whole letter is therefore addressed to the Muse. — **rogata**: by Horace; *at my request*. — **scribae**: *private secretary*, an office of trust and honor. Augustus had asked Horace to be his secretary. — **Neronis**: Tiberius.

3. **minantem**: cf. *Sat.* 2, 3, 9, *atqui voltus erat multa et praeclara minantis*, used, as here, of one who is trying to work, but not succeeding. Horace felt at times very strongly the self-reproach of a man who was conscious of yielding to the temptation to postpone his work.

4. **nec recte**: *i.e.*, not as his sense of right, his philosophy, requires of him. — **nec suaviter**: a consequence of *nec recte*; 'and therefore not happily.'

5–6. These are merely typical of external discomforts and misfortunes. They are referred to or suggested in other places as perils to which the wealthy are exposed. — **longinquis**: *i.e.*, in the distant mountain pastures to which cattle

nec quia longinquis armentum aegrotet in agris;
sed quia mente minus validus quam corpore toto
nil audire velim, nil discere, quod levet aegrum;
fidis offendar medicis, irascar amicis,
10 cur me funesto properent arcere veterno;
quae nocuere sequar, fugiam quae profore credam;
Romae Tibur amem ventosus, Tibure Romam.
Post haec ut valeat, quo pacto rem gerat et se,
ut placeat iuveni percontare utque cohorti.
15 Si dicet recte, primum gaudere, subinde

were driven in the heat of summer; cf. *Carm.* 1, 31, 5.

7. minus . . . quam: the comparison is aside from the main thought and might have been put into a parenthesis; 'because in weariness of mind — my bodily health is good enough — I am unwilling. . . .' The words *corpore toto* of course serve as an assurance to Celsus.

8. 'I am unwilling (cannot bring myself) to listen to the teachings of philosophy.' Almost a repetition of *Epist.* 1, 1, 48.

9. medicis: the philosophers, whose writings would minister to a mind diseased.

10. cur: an indirect question used instead of a causal clause; cf. *Carm.* 1, 33, 3, *ne doleas . . . neu . . . decantes elegos, cur tibi iunior . . . praeniteat.* It is the causal meaning of *cur* that makes the substitution possible. — **veterno**: the many references to lethargy as a disease seem to point to something more definite than the nervous breakdown which is the modern counterpart. The abl. is after *arcere*, as after *prohibere*, *Epist.* 1, 1, 31.

11. sequar: after *quia*, like *offendar*, *irascar*. — The tenses of *nocuere* and *profore* are significant and should not be neglected in translation. — For the general sense cf. Ovid's phrase (*Met.* 7, 21), *video meliora proboque; deteriora sequor.*

12. ventosus: *fickle as the wind.* Cf. the same reproach, put into the mouth of his slave, in *Sat.* 2, 7, 28, *Romae rus optas; absentem rusticus urbem tollis ad astra levis* (= *ventosus*).

14. iuveni: Tiberius, who was at this time about twenty-two years old. — **percontare**: imperative, addressed to the Muse as messenger. — **cohorti**: especially the young men mentioned in *Epist.* 1, 3.

15 gaudere: grammatically de-

praeceptum auriculis hoc instillare memento:
ut tu fortunam, sic nos te, Celse, feremus.

pendent upon *memento*; 'remember to say *gaudeo*, as a polite messenger should.'

17. The friendly little admonition to self-control in prosperity is all the more friendly and the less likely to give offense because of the confessions of weakness which form the body of the letter and because of the lightness of tone in vss. 15-16.

9

It is altogether probable, though it is not definitely stated, that this Epistle was written in the year 20, when Tiberius was making preparations for his trip into Asia Minor. Of the Septimius whom the letter introduces nothing is known with certainty; but one of the Odes (*Carm.* 2, 6) is addressed to a Septimius, and a man of this name is mentioned in a letter of Augustus to Horace, quoted in the *Vita* of Suetonius.

Some other letters of introduction have come down to us (Cic. *ad Fam.* 2, 14; 7, 5; Pliny, 4, 4), but none so skillful and so charming as this. Tiberius, even as a young man, was both scornful and suspicious of the attentions paid to him on account of his relation to Augustus, but he was not incapable of perceiving the mingled frankness and deference of such a letter as this. And he was also a lover of literature, to whom the delicate art of expression and thought would appeal strongly. The publication of the Epistle is evidence that it was successful.

Septimius, Claudi, nimirum intellegit unus,
quanti me facias: nam cum rogat et prece cogit,
scilicet ut tibi se laudare et tradere coner,

1. **Claudi**: more formal than *Nero*. — **nimirum**: *no doubt*, with a little touch of irony. In this compound *ni* has no conditional force, but is the old negative, a form of *ne*. — **unus**: *i.e.*, 'he and he alone.'

3. **scilicet**: continuing the ironical tone; to be taken with the *ut*-clause, as in *Sat.* 2, 3. 185; 2, 3, 240; 2, 6, 58; *Epist.* 1, 15, 36; 1, 18, 16; 1, 20, 2; 2, 2, 44. It is not, as is commonly said, a compound of *scire* and *licet*, but a paratactic combination of the impv. *sci* with *licet*. So *vide-licet*. — **tradere**: *introduce*, as in *Sat.* 1, 9, 47.

dignum mente domoque legentis honesta Neronis,
munere cum fungi propioris censet amici;
quid possim videt ac novit me valdius ipso.
Multa quidem dixi, cur excusatus abirem;
sed timui, mea ne finxisse minora putarer,
dissimulator opis propriae, mihi commodus uni.
Sic ego maioris fugiens opprobria culpae
frontis ad urbanae descendi praemia. Quodsi
depositum laudas ob amici iussa pudorem,
scribe tui gregis hunc et fortem crede bonumque.

4. **legentis:** *gathering about him*, with special reference to his Eastern journey. — **honesta:** the neuter is more general than *honestos* would have been. — **Neronis:** *i.e.*, of one who bears an honorable name. With the rise of Tiberius into prominence through his mother's marriage to Augustus there was an inclination to magnify the past of his family, which had not, in fact, been especially prominent in Roman history. Cf. *Carm.* 4, 4, 28 and 37 ff.

5. **munere fungi:** *i.e.*, 'That I am in the position of an intimate friend'; the tense is significant. — **cum:** here and in vs. 2 in the explicative use, not temporal.

6. **valdius:** stronger than *melius*; 'puts a higher estimate upon my powers.'

7. **cur:** cf. *Epist.* 1, 8, 10, note.

8–9. **mea ... minora:** the rather vague expression is made more definite in the next line. — **dissimulator:** cf. *Sat.* 1, 10, 13 f., *parcentis viribus atque extenuantis eas consulto.* — **mihi ... uni:** *i.e.*, 'thinking only of my own convenience.'

11. **frontis ... praemia:** 'desiring to avoid the reproach of selfishness, I have chosen to incur the reproach — and, if you choose, to receive the reward also — of putting on a bold front and asking a favor.' — **urbanae:** 'of a man of the world,' a city man, less modest than the rustic. — **descendi:** the other course would have shown a loftier virtue. — **praemia:** this is a suggestion of the hope that Tiberius may be inclined to grant the favor.

12. **depositum ... pudorem:** the same in sense as *frontis urbanae*.

13. **fortem ... bonumque:** the only words of praise of Septimius in the letter, and all the more effective because they are so simple.

10

There is no definite indication of the date of this Epistle; it may have been written about the same time as *Epist.* 1, 7.

Fuscus Aristius is the friend who figures in a humorous way in *Sat.* 1, 9, 61 ff. and to whom the *Integer Vitae* (*Carm.* 1, 22) is addressed. He is named also in *Sat.* 1, 10, 83 in the list of friends whose approval Horace regards with satisfaction.

'Greetings, my dear Fuscus, to the lover of town from the lover of the country. This is an old dispute between us, but I stand by my opinion; country air and sleep and grass for me! You are all wrong: that life in town is enslaving you. Suit your life to your needs, as I mean to do, and be content. I am the picture of contentment at this moment, writing in the shade of that old shrine of Vacuna on my farm — or I should be content if only you were here.'

The thought of this epistle has been so often expressed by Horace that he can scarcely find novel form for it. But the fact that he was writing to a friend whose general attitude toward life was harmonious with his own gives to the familiar thoughts an easy simplicity and an air of true contentment.

> Vrbis amatorem Fuscum salvere iubemus
> ruris amatores.   Hac in re scilicet una
> multum dissimiles, at cetera paene gemelli,
> fraternis animis (quicquid negat alter, et alter)
> 5 adnuimus pariter vetuli notique columbi.
> Tu nidum servas; ego laudo ruris amoeni
> rivos et musco circumlita saxa nemusque.

1. **salvere iubemus**: a common formula of greeting, which here gives a humorous formality to the opening phrase. The first person plural is often used in Latin, *e.g.*, in the letters of Cicero, for the singular, apparently without difference of meaning.

2. **ruris amatores**: the position in the line is intentional, to contrast with *urbis amatorem*. — **scilicet**: *you know*, without irony.

5. **adnuimus**: like two doves 'billing and cooing.' — **vetuli notique**: though these adjectives agree with *columbi*, they are meant to apply especially to Fuscus and Horace, whose friendship was intimate and of long standing.

7. **circumlita**: an unusual and

EPISTVLAE [1, 10, 16

Quid quaeris? Vivo et regno, simul ista reliqui,
quae vos ad caelum effertis rumore secundo,
10 utque sacerdotis fugitivus liba recuso;
pane egeo iam mellitis potiore placentis.
Vivere naturae si convenienter oportet
ponendaeque domo quaerenda est area primum,
novistine locum potiorem rure beato?
15 .Est ubi plus tepeant hiemes, ubi gratior aura
leniat et rabiem Canis et momenta Leonis,

poetic word, as if the moss were a color spread over the rock.

8. quid quaeris? a common phrase in Terence and in Cicero's letters, to cut short further details; lit., 'what do you ask (want further)?' 'in short,' 'what more need I say?' Such phrases are rather characteristic of Horace; cf. *ne te morer, quid multa? ne longum faciam.* — **vivo et regno**: with emphasis; 'I really live and am a king.' — **ista**: in the proper second person sense.

9. A free quotation of an epic phrase; Ennius, *Ann.* 260, *mox efferre domos populi rumore secundo*; Verg. *Aen.* 8, 90, closes the line with *rumore secundo*; it is in sense the same as *summis laudibus ad caelum extulerunt*.

10-11. liba: *cakes* offered in sacrifice, and therefore very abundant in a priest's house, so that the slave had become tired of them and had run away to get plain food. The condensed comparison is made clearer in the next line; in which *pane egeo* explains *recuso*, and *mellitis placentis* amplifies *liba*. There is perhaps an allusion in these lines to some comic story or play popular at the time.

12. vivere: this is the Stoic doctrine, used somewhat humorously, since neither Fuscus nor Horace was a Stoic.

13. domo: dative, a rarer form for *domui*. The whole expression is condensed; 'if we ought to live naturally, and if we are seeking a place for natural living — as one seeks a site for his house — then the country is best.'

15. tepeant hiemes: *i.e.*, the winters in southern Italy; cf. *Carm.* 2, 6, 17. *ver ubi longum tepidasque praebet Iuppiter brumas*, of Tarentum. All of Italy outside of Rome was *rus*.

16. momenta Leonis: with poetic personification: 'the quick movements,' 'the rushing of the Lion,' further carried out in *furibundus*.

cum semel accepit Solem furibundus acutum?
Est ubi divellat somnos minus invida cura?
Deterius Libycis olet aut nitet herba lapillis?
20 Purior in vicis aqua tendit rumpere plumbum,
quam quae per pronum trepidat cum murmure rivum?
Nempe inter varias nutritur silva columnas,
laudaturque domus longos quae prospicit agros.
Naturam expelles furca, tamen usque recurret
25 et mala perrumpet furtim fastidia victrix.
Non, qui Sidonio contendere callidus ostro
nescit Aquinatem potantia vellera fucum,

17. **accepit . . . acutum**: the rays of the sun are like sharp arrows that wound (*accepit*) the Lion and rouse him to fury.

18. **somnos**: this is one of the traditional advantages of country life, often alluded to by Horace.

19. **Libycis . . . lapillis**: Lybian marbles set to make mosaic patterns in the floor. — **olet**: perfumed water was sprinkled over the floor.

20. **rumpere plumbum**: *i.e.*, 'rushes out of the lead pipes.' The distribution of water under pressure in pipes was well understood by Roman engineers, though it was somewhat less elaborately carried out than it is in modern houses.

22-23. **nempe**: *in fact, you know*; cf. *Sat.* 1, 10, 1. — **varias**: of the colored patterns of marble. — **silva**: trees were planted in the open court of a city house, within the colonnades. — **prospicit**: the hills of the city afforded sites from which a wide view could be had. Maecenas' house on the Esquiline commanded a view of the mountains toward the north and east.

24. **expelles**: a paratactic condition, with *recurret* as apodosis. The line has become proverbial; it is usually quoted with the older reading *expellas*, which, however, has no good support from the Mss.

25. **furtim**: 'in unexpected fashion,' 'when you least expect it.' — **victrix**: at the end of the line, with emphasis; 'and finally win the victory.'

26-29. 'But, though nature conquers in the end, the process of learning to distinguish the real from the imitation involves losses and mistakes, like those which a man suffers in buying artistic objects without real knowledge of the things he is purchasing.' — **Sidonio**: the genuine Tyrian purple was very expensive. — **callidus**:

certius accipiet damnum propiusve medullis,
quam qui non poterit vero distinguere falsum.
30 Quem res plus nimio delectavere secundae,
mutatae quatient. Si quid mirabere, pones
invitus. Fuge magna ; licet sub paupere tecto
reges et regum vita praecurrere amicos.
Cervus equum pugna melior communibus herbis
35 pellebat, donec minor in certamine longo
imploravit opes hominis frenumque recepit.
Sed postquam victor violens discessit ab hoste,
non equitem dorso, non frenum depulit ore.
Sic qui pauperiem veritus potiore metallis
40 libertate caret, dominum vehet improbus atque

i.e., one who believes, mistakenly, that he knows how to compare (*contendere*) and distinguish; cf. *Sat.* 2, 3, 23, and the whole description of such a connoisseur, vss. 20–25. — **Aquinatem . . . fucum** : after *potantia*; a dye made from lichens which produced a color like the true Sidonian purple. — **medullis** : *to his heart.* — **vero, falsum** : this is a slight reference to the standards of philosophy.

30–31. The same thought that is expressed more fully in *Epist.* 1, 6, 9 ff., and, with more personal reference, in the letter to Maecenas, *Epist.* 1, 7. It was a familiar thought to Horace. — **mirabere** : cf. *Epist.* 1, 6, 1, *nil admirari.* — **pones** : almost technical in this sense; *Epist.* 1, 1, 10; *Sat.* 2, 3, 16, etc.

34–38. This fable was often used to teach a serious lesson; it is found in Phaedrus, 4, 4. — **pugna melior** : cf. note on *Epist.* 1, 7, 29. — **imploravit** : the subject is *minor*, to be taken as a substantive ; but the omission of a more definite subject is in the manner of fables.

37. **violens** : *i.e.*, 'after a fierce contest'; to be joined with *discessit*, not directly with *victor*.

39. **metallis** : one of the various ways of expressing the general idea of riches; cf. Engl. 'a gold mine.' Horace uses the word only here.

40. **improbus** : *i.e.*, 'because of his immoderate desire for wealth'; cf. *Carm.* 3, 24, 62, *improbae crescunt divitiae*, in a context similar to this.

serviet aeternum, quia parvo nesciet uti.
Cui non conveniet sua res, ut calceus olim,
si pede maior erit, subvertet, si minor, uret.
Laetus sorte tua vives sapienter, Aristi,
45 nec me dimittes incastigatum, ubi plura
cogere quam satis est, ac non cessare videbor.
Imperat aut servit collecta pecunia cuique,
tortum digna sequi potius quam ducere funem.
Haec tibi dictabam post fanum putre Vacunae,
50 excepto quod non simul esses, cetera laetus.

41. **serviet**: this is the theme of *Sat.* 2, 7. — **uti**: as in *Sat.* 1, 1, 37; 2, 3, 109, 167, and often.
42. **conveniet**: cf. vs. 12. — **olim**, *sometimes*.
44-46. 'Live content, therefore, and remind me of this admonition, if I seem to you to need it.' — **cessare**: as in *Epist.* 1, 7, 57.
47-48. The thought is expressed more diffusely by Seneca, *de Vita Beat.* 26, 1, 'divitiae enim apud sapientem virum in servitute sunt, apud stultum in imperio.' — **tortum ... funem**: the line repeats in a figurative form the thought of *imperat* (= *ducere*) *aut servit* (= *sequi*), but the allusion is to some custom or some story which is unknown to us; it may be the figure of an animal led by a rope, or of a machine of which a rope forms part. Cf. note on *Epist.* 1, 6, 51, *trans pondera*, and *Sat.* 2, 7, 20. — **tortum**: an ornamental epithet.
49-50. As the letter begins with a formal greeting, so it closes with a formal giving of the exact place of writing. In Cicero's letters the place is usually named at the end of the letter, if at all. — **dictabam**: the epistolary imperfect; see grammar. — **putre**: 'falling into decay.' — **Vacunae**: a local goddess. The meaning of the name is quite unknown. — **laetus**: with reference back to vs. 44.

II

There is nothing to fix the date of this Epistle nor is Bullatius, to whom it was addressed, mentioned elsewhere.

'And how do you like the famous cities of Asia, my friend? Are you thinking of home or of settling down there, far from the world? But one doesn't settle down for life in some inn, just because one is tired of travel. Pleasant scenery will not make you happy. It is better to stay at home and sing the joys of travel at your ease. For happiness is not in some distant future or in some far-off country; it is here and now, in our own hearts, if we are wise enough to take it.'

Horace was not a traveler. He went to Athens in early life for study, but after his return his life was spent in the neighborhood of Rome or about Tarentum. He was free from that form of restlessness which seeks excitement in novelty and was perhaps not quite just to those who find stimulus in sight seeing. In this Epistle he has used the fact that Bullatius was abroad as an occasion for restating the doctrine which he often preaches, that the sources of happiness are within, setting it in contrast to the pleasures of travel.

> Quid tibi visa Chios, Bullati, notaque Lesbos,
> quid concinna Samos, quid Croesi regia Sardis,
> Smyrna quid et Colophon? Maiora minorane fama?
> Cunctane prae campo et Tiberino flumine sordent?
> 5 An venit in votum Attalicis ex urbibus una?
> An Lebedum laudas odio maris atque viarum?
> Scis Lebedus quid sit; Gabiis desertior atque
> Fidenis vicus: tamen illic vivere vellem,

1-3. These are the names of cities in Asia Minor, known in history and in literary tradition to all Romans, even those who had not visited them, as European cities are known to Americans. Cf. Catull. 46, 6, *ad claras Asiae volemus urbes.* — **nota**: = *nobilis*; Lesbos was the home of Alcaeus and Sappho. — **concinna**: *handsome*, with reference apparently to the regularity of the streets. — **Sardis**: the Greek nom. plur. Σάρδεις. — **fama**: *i.e.*, 'than you had expected from what you had heard of them.'

4. **campo**: the Campus Martius, standing for all the familiar spots in Rome. — **sordent**: *i.e.*, 'do they all seem poor in comparison . . . ?' This implies the answer *minora* to the previous question.

5. **venit in votum**: *suit your desires;* this is an expansion of *maiora*. For the expression cf. *Sat.* 2, 6, 1, *hoc erat in votis.* — Pergamum was the most famous of the cities of Attalus.

6-10. 'Or are you so weary of travel that a deserted village seems good enough to you? I can understand that feeling easily.' — **Lebedum**: a small town on the coast near Smyrna. — **odio maris**: Horace was not a traveler; cf. *Carm.*

oblitusque meorum obliviscendus et illis
10 Neptunum procul e terra spectare furentem.
Sed neque qui Capua Romam petit, imbre lutoque
adspersus volet in caupona vivere; nec qui
frigus collegit, furnos et balnea laudat
ut fortunatam plene praestantia vitam;
15 nec, si te validus iactaverit Auster in alto,
idcirco navem trans Aegaeum mare vendas.
Incolumi Rhodos et Mitylene pulchra facit, quod
paenula solstitio, campestre nivalibus auris,

2, 6, 7, *lasso maris et viarum.* — Gabii and Fidenae, which were towns of importance in earlier history, were in Horace's time only villages. — **vellem**: the tense implies that it is a mere expression of emotion, without expectation of fulfilment. — 'The world forgetting, by the world forgot' (Pope). — The comparison of a peaceful life to the contentment of one who looks from shore at the wild sea is frequent in literature. The best expression of it is in Lucr. 2, 1-2, 'suave, mari magno turbantibus aequora ventis, e terra magnum alterius spectare laborem.'

11. 'But such a life would not be truly satisfying.' — **Capua Romam**: *i.e.*, to one who is going toward the great city, which is his home. — **imbre lutoque**: this corresponds to *odio maris atque viarum*, vs. 6: these things are the temporary discomforts of travel, from which we get only a temporary refuge in an inn.

12. **caupona vivere**: the figure of an inn as a temporary resting place, but not a home to live in (*vivere* is emphatic), is used frequently in classic as well as in Christian writings.

13. **frigus collegit**: 'has become chilled,' not 'caught cold.' — **furnos**: *bakers' shops*, where one could get warm.

16. **vendas**: *i.e.*, give up the plan of completing the journey and settle in Asia Minor. This brings the thought back to the main theme.

17. **incolumi**: 'a man of sound mind'; cf. *Sat.* 2, 3, 132, *incolumi capite* (=*sanus*). The dat. is to be taken with *facit*, as in *Sat.* 1, 1, 63, *quid facias illi?* and often in Plautus. — **pulchra**: 'in spite of its beauty.' — **facit quod**: *i.e.*, 'is the same as,' 'has the same effect as.'

18-19. Four illustrations of things that are, in the special circumstances, particularly useless.—

per brumam Tiberis, Sextili mense caminus.
20 Dum licet ac vultum servat Fortuna benignum,
Romae laudetur Samos et Chios et Rhodos absens.
Tu quamcumque deus tibi fortunaverit horam
grata sume manu, neu dulcia differ in annum ;
ut quocumque loco fueris vixisse libenter
25 te dicas. Nam si ratio et prudentia curas,
non locus effusi late maris arbiter aufert,
caelum, non animum, mutant qui trans mare currunt;
strenua nos exercet inertia ; navibus atque
quadrigis petimus bene vivere ; quod petis, hic est,
30 est Vlubris, animus si te non deficit aequus.

paenula: a heavy cloak for cold weather. — **campestre**: a very light garment worn about the loins in taking vigorous exercise.

20. The line is an expansion of *incolumi*; 'so long as I am not driven to foreign travel.'

21. Romae: the emphatic word; 'I will stay at home and sing the praises of foreign cities without seeing them (*absens*).'

22-24. The mistake of overlooking present happiness in the anticipation of some other happiness in the future is, at bottom, the same as the mistake of looking for contentment in change of place. The two thoughts are really identified here, though in form the second is treated as the purpose of the first; 'just as you should gratefully enjoy the present, so you should live happily in the place where you may happen to be.' The thought of vss. 22-23 is often expressed by Horace, *e.g. Carm.* 1, 9; 1, 11.

25. ratio: as in *Sat.* 1, 1, 2. — **curas**: after *auferunt*, to be supplied from *aufert*.

26. arbiter: in the early meaning *witness*, *i.e.*, 'having a wide outlook over the sea,' with reference back to vss. 7-10.

27. One of the lines of Horace that has become proverbial, because it expresses so concisely a truth of universal experience.

28-30. strenua inertia: an intentional putting together of two contradictory words, like *splendide mendax*, to characterize the idle activity of the pleasure seeker. — **navibus, quadrigis**: cf. *Carm.* 3, 1, 37-40, *post equitem sedet atra cura*. — **hic**: 'where we are now.' — **Vlubris**: *i.e.*, in any little village; there is no implication that Horace was in Ulubrae. — **animus ... aequus**: the same as *incolumi*, vs. 17.

12

This Epistle was written in the summer of the year 20 B.C., as the closing lines show. The person addressed, Iccius, is the same young man to whom, some five or six years before, Horace had written an ode, *Carm.* I, 29. He is otherwise unknown, but some traits of character are clearly revealed by the tone in which Horace addresses him. He was one of the circle of younger men whom Horace knew well, a student of philosophy, though probably not a serious scholar. He was not rich and was looking for an opportunity to make his way in the world. This he had sought to find by joining the expedition of Gallus against the Persians and after the failure of this campaign he had become the agent of Agrippa, taking charge of his estates in Sicily. This Epistle was written in reply to a letter from Iccius, in which there was some expression of dissatisfaction with his position and of regret that business interfered with philosophy.

'The trusted agent of Agrippa, my dear young friend, should not call himself a poor man. If one has plenty to eat and health to enjoy it, he is as rich as a king. Or if you have turned vegetarian, no amount of money will make any difference to such a philosopher. You are a greater wonder than Democritus, to be so active in business and at the same time so deep in philosophy. But, whether you are living high or have become an ascetic, don't neglect my friend and your neighbor, Pompeius Grosphus; he is a man you can trust.

'The news at Rome is all cheerful; victories everywhere and a fine harvest in Italy.'

This is, in form, one of the most successful of the Epistles. It is precisely such a letter as might have been written in prose, commenting upon the letter to which it is a reply, recommending a friend to the notice of the recipient and giving in brief the news of the day. Its tone, too, is entirely personal, as if it were meant to be read only by the person addressed, and that tendency to fall into the essay manner, which in some of the letters is out of harmony with the epistolary form, is here the more easily avoided, because the interest of Iccius in philosophy makes the introduction of that subject quite natural. At the same time, the personal matters are so treated as to be of general interest, and the revelation of the character of both writer and recipient is most attractive. In lightness of touch and in humorous irony this letter resembles *Epist.* I, 3, also addressed to a younger friend.

Fructibus Agrippae Siculis, quos colligis, Icci,
si recte frueris, non est ut copia maior
ab Iove donari possit tibi. Tolle querellas,
pauper enim non est, cui rerum suppetit usus.
5 Si ventri bene, si lateri est pedibusque tuis, nil
divitiae poterunt regales addere maius.
Si forte in medio positorum abstemius herbis
vivis et urtica, sic vives protinus, ut te

1. **fructibus**; *revenues*, but with special reference to revenue derived from an estate.

2. **recte**: not in the philosophical sense, but *properly*, 'as you have a a right to do.' The general meaning of the word is specialized by its connection with *frueris*.

3. **querellas**: *laments* over his poverty; the exhortation does not imply that Iccius was over-anxious to be rich, but only that he was inclined to regret the necessity of earning his living as a business man in Sicily.

4. **rerum ... usus**: no more than *quod satis est*, that sufficient supply of the necessaries of life to which men should limit their desires.

5. **ventri, lateri, pedibus**: *i.e.* 'if your wants are supplied and your health is good.' The form in which the general thought is expressed is taken from a Greek proverb (Theognis. 719), but Horace uses the same words often, putting specific illnesses in the place of some general term; cf. *latus aut renes*, Epist. 1, 6, 28; *laterum dolor*, Sat. 1, 9, 32; *podagram*, Epist. 1, 2, 52.

6. The same as *non est ut copia maior*; cf. also *Epist.* 1, 4, 7-8.

7. **forte**: the addition of this word prevents the condition, *si vivis*, from assuming that he is actually living an ascetic life. The two conditions, *si ventri bene est* and *si vivis herbis*, thus present the two possible alternations, without choosing between them; 'whether you are living on the fat of the land or are, perhaps, a vegetarian, in either case you are independent of money and have no right to call yourself pauper.'— in **medio positorum**: the gen. depends on *abstemius*, which takes the abl. or the gen. without distinction of meaning. For *in medio posita*, 'things that are within the reach of everybody,' cf. *Sat.* 1, 2, 108.

8. **urtica**: *nettles*, more often referred to for their medicinal properties; here used only to give a humorous definiteness to the general word *herbis*. — sic: *in the same way*. — **protinus**: of time; 'you

confestim liquidus Fortunae rivus inauret;
10 vel quia naturam mutare pecunia nescit,
vel quia cuncta putas una virtute minora.
Miramur, si Democriti pecus edit agellos
cultaque, dum peregre est animus sine corpore velox,
cum tu inter scabiem tantam et contagia lucri
15 nil parvum sapias et adhuc sublimia cures:
quae mare compescant causae; quid temperet annum;
stellae sponte sua iussaene vagentur et errent;

will go right on living.' — **ut**: concessive; *even though*.

9. The river Pactolus, in which Midas bathed to rid himself of the 'Golden Touch,' had come to be thought of as having the power to gild with its waters, and so is proverbial as a source of wealth. Cf. *Epod.* 15, 20, *tibique Pactolus fluat*.

10. Cf. *Epod.* 4, 6, *fortuna non mutat genus*; in this case, however, the general truth is intended to convey a compliment.

11. This also is complimentary and leads on to the detailed references to the interest of Iccius in philosophical studies.

12-15. 'The stock illustration of the philosopher's absorption in his speculations is feeble compared to your interest.' — **Democriti**: of Abdera, the early teacher of the atomic theory of matter. The story is told in various forms; here the allusion is to his neglect of his farm because he was so intent upon scientific study. — **peregre**: his mind, as it were, separated itself from his body and roamed the universe. — **cum**: adversative. — **scabiem**: the figurative use is rare and is therefore defined by *contagia lucri*; 'contagious itching for pelf' (Wilkins). Iccius, in his work as overseer of Agrippa's estates, was in the closest contact with the money-making instincts. — **nil parvum**: *i.e.*, 'are indifferent to all this,' 'regard all this as petty'; then the thought is repeated in positive form in *sublimia*. — **adhuc**: *still*, 'as you did when I wrote my ode about you.' — **sublimia**: *lofty themes*, both in the general sense and with special reference to astronomical questions.

16. **compescant**: *i.e.*, why the sea, in spite of all the rivers that empty into it, does not rise, but is confined within fixed bounds. Cf. Lucr. 6, 608. — **temperet**: 'divides the year into seasons'; cf. *Carm.* 1, 12, 16.

17. **sponte sua**: the Stoic doctrine was that the planets were self-moved and were therefore

quid premat obscurum lunae, quid proferat orbem;
quid velit et possit rerum concordia discors;
20   Empedocles an Stertinium deliret acumen.
Verum seu piscis seu porrum et caepe trucidas,

themselves divine. The atomic theory brought them under the rule of physical law (*iussae*).

18. obscurum: predicate with *premat*. The question is in regard to the changes of the moon from crescent to full circle (*orbem*).

19. quid velit: in the direct form, *quid vis tibi?* (*Sat.* 1, 2, 69), 'what do you mean?' In the indirect form, *quid . . . ista velit sibi fabula, Sat.* 2, 5, 61. 'What is the meaning and what the powers of . . . ?'— **concordia discors**: cf. *strenua inertia, Epist.* 1, 11, 28. In the atomic theory all motion is the result of two forces, attraction and repulsion, love and hate, which are opposed and yet work out a harmonious result. The expression *concordia discors* is used by many writers.

20. Empedocles: of Agrigentum, a follower of Pythagoras and a physicist; his name is suggested by vs. 19, and he is mentioned as a representative of the school which explained natural phenomena by purely physical causes. — **Stertinium**: a Stoic philosopher, whose supposed discourse on the madness of men forms the main part of *Sat.* 2, 3. He may have been of the Ciceronian period.

He is here used in a humorous spirit as the counterpart to Empedocles, standing for Stoic doctrines. The name is in the adj. form, without change, agreeing with *acumen*. For the epic use of the abstract noun cf. *Sat.* 2, 1, 72, *virtus Scipiadae*. — **deliret**: a Stoic word, used of the madness of *stultitia*, here employed in humorous contrast with *acumen*.

21. 'But whatever may be your mode of living (vss. 5-8) or your philosophical tenets (vss. 16-20), make the acquaintance of Grosphus.'—Many systems of philosophy have run over into dietetic regulations, connected in some cases with the more important doctrines. The Pythagorean doctrine of the transmigration of souls was thus connected with the forbidding of certain articles of food, animal and even vegetable, on the ground that the use of such food involved the taking of life. Many of the allusions are evidently parody, as here *trucidas* is humorous. — **piscis**: standing for good living, vs. 5. — **porrum et caepe**: *leeks and onions*, the *herbis et urtica* of vss. 7-8. The description is in all these cases (5, 7-8, 21) humorously phrased, with no attempt at precision, so that the use of *piscis*

utere Pompeio Grospho et si quid petet ultro
defer: nil Grosphus nisi verum orabit et aequum.
Vilis amicorum est annona, bonis ubi quid dest.
25 Ne tamen ignores, quo sit Romana loco res:
Cantaber Agrippae, Claudi virtute Neronis
Armenius cecidit; ius imperiumque Phraates
Caesaris accepit genibus minor; aurea fruges
Italiae pleno defundit Copia cornu.

for high living is not surprising or doubtful.

22. Pompeio Grospho: *Carm.* 2, 16 is addressed to him, and alludes to his having estates in Sicily. — **ultro**: with *defer*.

24. annona: properly the year's harvest, then the price of grain, which depended on the harvest, and in turn influenced all prices. Here figuratively; 'it costs but little to secure friends, when those who ask the price are good men.' — **dest**: = *deest*. The thought is the same as that in *quid petit*, not that Grosphus would necessarily be asking for help, but that Iccius need not hesitate out of fear that he might make inconvenient demands.

26-29. The news of the day, given in condensed form, with little touches of half-humorous poetic phrasing. — Agrippa, the patron of Iccius, put down an uprising in Spain in the summer of 20 B.C. — The expedition of Tiberius, to which reference is made in many of the Epistles, resulted in the submission of Armenia. — Phraates, king of Parthia, restored to Augustus, through Tiberius, the Roman standards taken long before, when Crassus was defeated. The formalities of the occasion are alluded to in *genibus minor* ('inferior by his kneeling'), and both this event and the conquest of Armenia are commemorated on coins of the period and mentioned by Augustus in the Monumentum Ancyranum. — **defundit**: present tense; the harvest was just coming in. There had been serious trouble from a bad harvest in 22 B.C.

13

The first three books of the Odes were published in the year 23. At that time Augustus was still in Italy, in or near Rome, and Horace sent to him an early copy of the three volumes. The bearer of the gift was Vinnius Asina (or perhaps Asellus), of whom nothing is known except by inference from this letter. The Epistle is supposed to be a hasty note, sent by a messenger to overtake Vinnius before he reached Rome and to remind him again of the author's instructions in regard to the manner in which the gift should be presented to Augustus.

'This is to remind you again, Vinnius, to be careful. Don't make a nuisance of yourself; your name, you see, exposes you to jibes. And do try to be graceful; don't carry my books under your arm like a common bundle. And don't brag about them, either. Remember what I've told you and do be careful.'

This is not an actual letter, sent after Vinnius, but a humorous Epistle handed to him with the books and intended in reality for Augustus. There is not a serious word in it; the elaborate and fussy advice, the permission to throw the book away, the reference to the badness of the road, are all fictitious. Vinnius was not a country clown, but a common friend of Augustus and Horace, who undertook the little commission for the poet, doubtless with pride. Nor was Augustus so remote and great a personage that Horace felt it to be necessary to approach him with elaborate caution. All this belongs to the machinery, as it were, of the little play.

The facts were, in reality, something like this: in sending a copy of his completed lyrics to Augustus, Horace desired to write a note of presentation, like an inscription on a flyleaf. Seeking to avoid the commonplace forms, he hit upon the little fiction of pretending great anxiety about the reception of the gift and of expressing his anxiety in these fussy and exaggerated directions to the bearer. The note was, of course, to be shown to Augustus.

Vt proficiscentem docui te saepe diuque,
Augusto reddes signata volumina, Vinni,
si validus, si laetus erit, si denique poscet;
ne studio nostri pecces, odiumque libellis

1. **proficiscentem**: 'when you were starting,' as if this letter had been sent to overtake him on the journey.

2. **signata**: *i.e.*, 'with the seal unbroken,' in good condition.

3. **si validus**: the conditions are emphatic; 'only in case he is. . . .' Augustus was often ill and under the care of physicians. — **denique**: this changes the condition into a temporal clause; 'and not until he shall ask for it.' — **poscet**: it is implied that Augustus already knew that a copy of the book was to be sent to him.

4-5. The adjuration not to be overzealous is intentionally re-

5   sedulus importes opera vehemente minister.
    Si te forte meae gravis uret sarcina chartae,
    abicito potius quam, quo perferre iuberis,
    clitellas ferus impingas Asinaeque paternum
    cognomen vertas in risum et fabula fias.
10 Viribus uteris per clivos, flumina, lamas;
    victor propositi simul ac perveneris illuc,
    sic positum servabis onus, ne forte sub ala
    fasciculum portes librorum ut rusticus agnum,

peated in various forms in *studio nostri, sedulus minister*, and *opera vehemente*, as if to express the extreme anxiety of the writer.

6–9. The lines are, of course, wholly humorous, to introduce the joke on the cognomen of Vinnius. — **gravis . . . sarcina**: a jest at the books themselves, not unlike the Engl. 'heavy reading.' The three volumes of the Odes would be in fact a very light parcel. — **uret**: *gall*; cf. *Epist.* 1, 10, 43. The word is selected in anticipation of the joke on Asina. — **quo**: supply an antecedent, *ibi*, to go with *impingas*; 'rather than carry it all the way and then dash it down in the very presence of Augustus and his friends.' — **ferus**: 'like an angry mule.' — **Asinae**: both this name and the other form, Asellus, are known to have been in actual use in several families. — **paternum**: *i.e.*, an inherited cognomen and not one given in derision to Vinnius himself. — **fabula**: so *Epod.* 11,

8, *fabula quanta fui*, Juv. 10, 167. *ut . . . declamatio fias*.

10. **viribus uteris**: fut., like *reddes, servabis*; 'use your strength where it is called for, on the road, but when you arrive carry the books gracefully.' — **lamas**: *bogs, mudholes*. The word is found only here in classical Latin and was probably a colloquialism. These references to difficulties on the way are not to be taken literally; they suit the general tone of humorous exaggeration.

11. **victor propositi**: this phrase also is intentionally over-serious, almost epic.

12–13. **sic positum**: 'just as I am arranging it now'; as if Horace were actually showing Vinnius how to hold it and how to carry it properly. — **ne . . . portes**: in form a clause of purpose, but in sense a continuation of the command from *uteris, servabis*. 'don't carry my package under your arm, like a farmer carrying a lamb.'

ut vinosa glomus furtivae Pyrrhia lanae,
15 ut cum pilcolo soleas conviva tribulis.
Ne vulgo narres te sudavisse ferendo
carmina, quae possint oculos auresque morari
Caesaris. Oratus multa prece, nitere porro;
vade, vale; cave ne titubes mandataque frangas.

14. glomus: acc. plur.; the word is a technical term, of wool gathered into a ball for spinning. — **Pyrrhia**: the form of the name is quite uncertain. The Scholiast says that this is an allusion to a scene in a play of Titinius.

15. conviva tribulis: a poorer member of a 'tribe,' invited to dinner for political purposes by a richer fellow-tribesman, would have no slave to carry his cap or to take his sandals when he reclined on the couch. He would therefore carry them under his arm. — The three comparisons are not meant to describe three different ways of carrying things under the arm, but merely to suggest the awkwardness which Vinnius is to avoid.

16-17. 'And don't brag to everybody about your important mission.' The important word in the infin. phrase is not *sudavisse*, but *ferendo*. The exaggeration of *sudavisse* is like that in vss. 4-5, 10, 11.

18. oratus: by Horace, in this letter. — **multa prece**: the whole Epistle is made up of such exhortations and the point is the same as that of *saepe diuque*, vs. 1. 'You have heard all my directions, now go on.'

19. titubes: a very common word in Plautus, in giving directions for the carrying out of a plan; *M.G.* 946, *Pseud.* 764, 939. The literal meaning is here distinctly in mind, with a reference back to vss. 8-9, and is carried on into *frangas*. — **mandata**: not the volumes, but the injunctions, the *multae preces*. The literal and figurative meanings run together; 'don't stumble and break your load,' 'don't make a mistake and forget my directions to you.'

14

The date of this Epistle cannot be determined nor is it of importance for the interpretation. The person to whom it is supposed to be written is the superintendent of Horace's farm.

'Foreman of my nice little farm, we seem to be disagreeing. I am detained here in Rome, longing for the country; you want to be back in Rome. You are inconsistent and I am not, but the real difference is in our tastes. To you my farm seems a desert and a place of hard labor, and you long for pleasures, while I have dropped all that kind of thing and want only peace. Each wants what the other has. But it won't do; the shoemaker will have to stick to his last, according to the old saying.'

This Epistle is in complete contrast to the one which immediately precedes it. It is a little disquisition on the inconsistencies of men, as illustrated by the steward's discontent with the life which he had once greatly desired, and on the attractiveness of the country, which seemed all the stronger to Horace when he happened to be detained in Rome beyond his usual time. These themes Horace had treated before, in *Sat.* 1, 1 and *Sat.* 2, 6, using the satire form. In returning to them at this later time, under the impulse of his longing to escape from the city, he used the epistolary form with which he was then experimenting. The *vilicus* is, of course, a mere figurehead; the letter was not actually sent to him at all; but the advantages of the direct form of address appear in the individual allusions (vss. 2-3, 6-7, 14-15, 19-30), which illustrate the general doctrines that underlie the whole. There is, too, a certain simplicity and directness in the language, though there is, of course, no attempt to come down to the level of the steward's comprehension.

Vilice silvarum et mihi me reddentis agelli,
quem tu fastidis habitatum quinque focis et
quinque bonos solitum Variam dimittere patres,
certemus, spinas animone ego fortius an tu

1. **silvarum**: Horace mentions the woodlands in several allusions to his farm (*Sat.* 2, 6, 3; *Epist.* 1, 16, 9) and evidently regarded them as an important part of the estate. — **mihi me reddentis**: 'that restores me to myself'; cf. *Epist.* 1, 18, 101, *te tibi reddat amicum.*

2-3. **habitatum**: 'though it is large enough to furnish homes to five families'; there is a little half-humorous boasting in the repetition of *quinque.* — **Variam**: now *Vicovaro*, the nearest market town. — **patres**: 'heads of families.' They were *coloni*, who held the lands on lease from Horace and were independent farmers and citizens. On the part of the estate which Horace reserved for himself and of which the *vilicus* had charge, eight slaves (*Sat.* 2, 7, 118) were kept at work.

4-5. **certemus**: *i.e.*, 'I challenge

5   evellas agro, et melior sit Horatius an res.
    Me quamvis Lamiae pietas et cura moratur,
    fratrem maerentis, rapto de fratre dolentis
    insolabiliter, tamen istuc mens animusque
    fert et amat spatiis obstantia rumpere claustra.
10 Rure ego viventem, tu dicis in urbe beatum;
    cui placet alterius, sua nimirum est odio sors.
    Stultus uterque locum immeritum causatur inique;
    in culpa est animus, qui se non effugit unquam.
    Tu mediastinus tacita prece rura petebas,

you to a contest, to see whether . . . .' — **spinas**: for weeds in general; so *filix* (*Sat.* 1, 3, 37) is used both of faults and of weeds. — **res**: *his farm.*

6. **Lamiae**: subjective gen.; 'Lamia's affection and distress,' further explained by the next line. [The single case of an objective gen., *deum pietas*, in a fragment of Naevius, by no means justifies the taking of *Lamiae* as an objective genitive.] — **moratur**: the subjv. is the proper mode with *quamvis*, but the confusion with *quamquam* had already gone so far that Horace uses the indic. more often than the subjunctive. — *Carm.* 1, 26 is addressed to L. Aelius Lamia and he is referred to in *Carm.* 3, 17. He became consul in 3 A.D. Evidently he was one of Horace's most valued friends.

7. The repetition *fratrem . . . fratre* and the assonance of *maerentis, dolentis* give the line a peculiar effect. Cicero (*ad Att.* 12, 28, 2, *maerorem minui, dolorem nec potui*) distinguishes between the two words, but the distinction is here unimportant; *mourning, grieving.*

8. **istuc**: 'to the place where you are,' to the country.

9. **amat**: *longs*; so, with infin., *Carm.* 3, 9, 24. — The figure in the rest of the line is taken from chariot racing; *claustra* are the bars which kept the horses within the *carceres* until the race was started and which may therefore be said *obstare spatiis*, to 'stand in the way of the race course.'

11. **alterius**: sc. *sors*. The thought is that with which *Sat.* 1, 1 opens.

12-13. Cf. *Epist.* 1, 11, esp. vss. 25-27. — **immeritum**: *i.e.*, 'which is not responsible,' as in *Sat.* 2, 3, 7 f. *immeritus . . . paries*. The same thought is expressed also in *inique.*

14. **tu**: this takes up the con-

15   nunc urbem et ludos et balnea vilicus optas;
     me constare mihi scis et discedere tristem,
     quandocumque trahunt invisa negotia Romam.
     Non eadem miramur; eo disconvenit inter
     meque et te. Nam quae deserta et inhospita tesqua
20   credis, amoena vocat mecum qui sentit, et odit
     quae tu pulchra putas. Fornix tibi et uncta popina
     incutiunt urbis desiderium, video, et quod
     angulus iste feret piper et tus ocius uva,
     nec vicina subest vinum praebere taberna
25   quae possit tibi, nec meretrix tibicina, cuius
     ad strepitum salias terrae gravis. Et tamen urgues
     iampridem non tacta ligonibus arva, bovemque
     disiunctum curas et strictis frondibus exples;

trast begun in vs. 6 and expressed in vs. 10. — **mediastinus**: *a common drudge.* — **tacita**: *i.e.*, 'you regarded it as so great a piece of good fortune that you did not dare to ask for it.'

15. **nunc**: 'but now that you have it.' — **vilicus**: a head servant, in contrast to *mediastinus.*

16. **me**: 'but I am consistent in my wishes.'

18. **eo disconvenit**: 'the difference in our tastes explains the fact that you are inconsistent and I am consistent.'

19. **tesqua**: *wilds*; said by the Scholiast to be a Sabine word.

21. **fornix**: *a brothel.* — **uncta**: cf. *immundis popinis, Sat.* 2, 4, 62. The common cook shops would be ill-kept and greasy.

23. **angulus iste**: 'that hole, as you call it.' — **piper et tus**: *i.e.* 'the farm cannot be made to produce good wine (*uva*); you might as well expect to raise tropical plants there.' This and the following lines express the steward's disgust with his occupation and circumstances.

25. **meretrix tibicina**: like the *Copa Syrisca* in Vergil's poem.

26. **tamen**: 'in spite of your having no pleasures, as you say.' — **urgues**: to express the steward's sense of the difficulty of his labors.

27. **non tacta**: and therefore harder to bring under cultivation.

28. **disiunctum**: the oxen are loosed from the plow and their labor is over, but the steward must still take care of them and give them their fodder (*frondibus*).

addit opus pigro rivus, si decidit imber,
30 multa mole docendus aprico parcere prato.
Nunc age, quid. nostrum concentum dividat, audi.
Quem tenues decuere togae nitidique capilli,
quem scis immunem Cinarae placuisse rapaci,
quem bibulum liquidi media de luce Falerni,
35 cena brevis iuvat et prope rivum somnus in herba.
Nec lusisse pudet, sed non incidere ludum.
Non istic obliquo oculo mea commoda quisquam
limat, non odio obscuro morsuque venenat;
rident vicini glebas et saxa moventem.
40 Cum servis urbana diaria rodere mavis,

29. **addit**: and there is even more to do, like directing the flow of the water in a heavy rain. — **pigro**: this is added by Horace.

31. **quid ... dividat**: *i.e.*, 'what makes my view of country life so entirely different from yours.' — **audi**: *let me tell you*, as often; *Sat.* 1, 1, 14.

32. **tenues**: *fine*, 'of fine material'; the opposite was *crassa*, *Sat.* 1, 3, 15.

33. **immunem**: 'though I brought no gift' (Wilkins). — **Cinarae**: cf. *Epist.* 1, 7, 28 and note. The adj. *rapaci* is general, of women of her class, not individual.

34. **media de luce**: to drink before nightfall is often referred to as typical of a rather fast life, *e.g.*, *Sat.* 1, 4, 51 f., or at least a life of pleasure. *Carm.* 2, 7, 6.

36. **nec lusisse pudet**: all this was, by Roman standards, suitable enough for a young man. — **incidere**: *cut short*, 'bring to an end at the proper time.'

37. **istic**: *where you are*, in the country; cf. *istuc*, vs. 8. — **obliquo**: *look askance* with envy.

38. **limat**: literally *files*, *cuts away*, *i.e.*, *lessens*; but the word is more frequently used of polishing and is here chosen for the pun upon *limis oculis*, which is the same as *obliquo oculo*. — **venenat**: envy and hatred are like the bite of a poisonous serpent. Horace frequently alludes to the fact that he was envied and criticized, especially for his friendship with Maecenas.

39. **rident**: 'instead of envying me, my neighbors merely smile in a good-natured way, as they see me trying to work with my own hands about my farm.'

40-44. A summary of the whole; 'every man wants what he has not

horum tu in numerum voto ruis; invidet usum
lignorum et pecoris tibi calo argutus et horti.
Optat ephippia bos, piger optat arare caballus.
Quam scit uterque libens censebo exerceat artem.

— a great mistake, in my opinion.' — **cum servis**: 'like my slaves in the city,' *urbana* going in sense with *servis*. — **diaria**: *rations*, instead of the abundant food of the farm. — **calo**: *my groom*, who had occasionally gone out with his master to the farm; cf. *Sat.* 1, 6, 103. — **argutus**: *i.e.*, 'using all his arguments to persuade me.' — **piger**: the riding-horse thinks that the oxen, moving slowly in plowing, have an easy life. — Vs. 44 is proverbial; Cicero expresses it (*Tusc.* 1, 18, 41) in slightly different form; 'bene enim illo proverbio Graeco praecipitur; quam quisque norit artem, in hac se exerceat.' — **censebo**: inserted in parataxis with *exerceat*. The future does not really belong to *censebo* (for *censeo*), but is taken over from *exerceat*; cf. Plaut. *M.G.* 395, 1209; *Curc.* 493.

15

Of the date of this Epistle it can only be said that it was written after 23, when Antonius Musa introduced the cold-water cure, and perhaps in fulfilment of the intention expressed in *Epist.* 1, 7, 11, to spend a winter on the southern coast. The person addressed is a Numonius Vala, of whom, individually, nothing is known except what is implied in the letter. But there are references in inscriptions and on coins to Numonii, who were of a somewhat distinguished family in Lucania.

'Tell me all about your part of the country, Vala (for my doctor has ordered me to give up Baiae and take to the cold-water business; I don't like it, but I suppose I must do as he says); how about the bread? and the water? (I'll attend to the wine myself.) And what can I get in the way of game and sea food? Oh, yes, I haven't forgotten my own sermons. But you know the story of Maenius, how he used to preach against prodigals, but, when he had a chance, used to return with gusto to his prodigal life again. So I preach simplicity when my bank account is low, but I also know a good dinner when I see it.'

A genuine letter, asking for information and expecting an answer. But the dry questions are interrupted by humorous parentheses which explain the reason for the letter and set forth the cheerful frame of mind of the writer. And the letter is turned into a work of art, worthy of preservation, by the story of Maenius and the humorous application of it to Horace himself.

> Quae sit hiems Veliae, quod caelum, Vala, Salerni,
> quorum hominum regio et qualis via, (nam mihi Baias
> Musa supervacuas Antonius, et tamen illis
> me facit invisum, gelida cum perluor unda
> 5   per medium frigus. Sane murteta relinqui,
> dictaque cessantem nervis elidere morbum

1. quae sit: the letter, down to vs. 25, consists of a series of indirect questions interrupted by two long parentheses (2-13 and 16-21) with vs. 25 as the leading clause. — **hiems**: this has reference to the purpose expressed in *Epist.* 1, 7, 10-11. — **caelum**: *climate;* not really different from *hiems,* which refers to the winter climate. — **Veliae**: a small town on the Lucanian coast, some sixty miles below Naples. — **Salerni**: on the coast of Campania, about fifteen miles from Naples. The family of Vala came from this region.

2. quorum hominum : the two genitives make a kind of compound interrogative adj. corresponding to *qualis;* 'a what-sort-of-people district.' — **qualis** : there was no good Roman road going down to Velia, and off the regular routes the character of the roads was of importance.

3. Musa ... Antonius: *nomen* and *cognomen* are in reversed order, as in *Epist.* 1, 8, 1. This famous physician had recently introduced the cold-water cure, and Horace, either following the fashion or under the orders of the doctor, was giving up his habit of going to Baiae for the warm baths. — **supervacuas**: *superfluous, useless.* — **et tamen**: 'and for that matter,' 'and what is more'; for this sense of *et tamen* cf. Cic. *Cat. Mai.* 6, 16, 'notum enim vobis carmen est; et tamen ipsius Appi exstat oratio'; and at the end of the same section, 'ex quo intellegitur Pyrrhi bello grandem sane fuisse; et tamen sic a patribus accepimus.' [This usage is not infrequent, but is often emended or explained away by all sorts of ellipses. There is a fairly good note on it in Munro's *Lucret.* 5, 1177.]

5. sane: *of course, naturally;* with the whole sentence, but esp. with *vicus gemit.* — **murteta**: these *myrtle groves* on the slope above Baiae are often mentioned.

6. cessantem: *lingering,* therefore chronic. — **nervis**: *muscles,* as always in classical Latin. The

sulfura contemni vicus gemit invidus aegris,
qui caput et stomachum supponere fontibus audent
Clusinis Gabiosque petunt et frigida rura.
10 Mutandus locus est, et deversoria nota
praeteragendus equus. 'Quo tendis? Non mihi Cumas
est iter aut Baias,' laeva stomachosus habena
dicet eques; sed equis frenato est auris in ore);
maior utrum populum frumenti copia pascat,
15 collectosne bibant imbres puteosne perennes

disease was probably rheumatic. — **elidere**: a technical term of medicine; *drive out* would be the modern equivalent.

7. **invidus**: corresponds actively to the passive *invisum*, vs. 4.

8. **supponere**: the treatment was given in part by shower baths. — **audent**: *venture* to take the new-fashioned treatment.

9. **Clusinis**: there is no other mention of baths at Clusium, but in the hill country springs would be found anywhere. The baths of Gabii, near Rome, are mentioned by Juvenal. — **frigida rura**: the country places of Romans were almost all up in the mountains, where the air would be cooler than in the city.

10. **mutandus**: this is the conclusion of the whole matter: 'I've got to take cold baths all winter; I've got to abandon Baiae and duck my head into a cold spring. I don't like it, but it's the doctor's orders.' There is a humorous skepticism in regard to the new cure and a humorous acceptance of the situation in the whole passage, vss. 2–13. — **deversoria nota**: the inns where he had lived before at Cumae and Baiae, known to his horse as well as to himself.

12. **laeva**: the road down to Cumae and the coast towns branched off to the right, and the horse was trying to take this familiar turn. — **habena**: abl. with *stomachosus*; 'expressing his anger by pulling the left-hand rein.'

13. **sed**: *i.e.*, 'but he might as well have spared his words and simply pulled the rein, for a bridled horse hears with his mouth.'

14. The indirect questions go on after the parenthetic explanation of the reason for asking them. — **frumenti copia**: the *supply of grain* stands for all the ordinary kinds of food, perhaps with special reference to the bread (cf. *Sat.* 1, 5, 89–90).

15. **collectos . . . imbres**: in

iugis aquae, (nam vina nihil moror illius orae.
Rure meo possum quidvis perferre patique;
ad mare cum veni, generosum et lene requiro,
quod curas abigat, quod cum spe divite manet
20 in venas animumque meum, quod verba ministret,
quod me Lucanae iuvenem commendet amicae);
tractus uter plures lepores, uter educet apros;
utra magis pisces et echinos aequora celent
pinguis ut inde domum possim Phaeaxque reverti,
25 scribere te nobis, tibi nos adcredere par est.
Maenius, ut rebus maternis atque paternis

some parts of southern Italy the supply of water was scanty (*Sat.* 1, 5, 88, 91, 97) and it was necessary to store rain water in cisterns. — **perennes**: 'good all the year round,' *i. e.*, which do not dry up in summer.

16. iugis: *running*, not from a stagnant pool; cf. *Sat.* 2, 6, 2, *iugis aquae fons.* This is not tautological with *perennis:* 'springs from which there is running water at all seasons.'

16-21. 'About the wine I make no inquiries, for I will bring some with me.' — **nihil moror**: 'I care nothing'; cf. *Sat.* 1, 4, 13. — **rure meo**: in contrast to *ad mare cum veni*; in his own home, contented and satisfied, he does not care what he has to eat or drink. — **perferre patique**: with intentional exaggeration of phrase. — **generosum**: not as 'generous' is used in English, but *of good stock*, *i.e.*, from a good and well-known vineyard. — **lene** · *smooth.* — The following lines are the conventional praises of wine, with slight variations. Compare the corresponding lines in *Epist.* 1, 5, 16-20, with notes there. — **manet**: from *māno*, not from *măneo*.

22. The indirect questions are resumed, becoming now more specific. — **lepores**: *hares* appear in both the gastronomic satires (2, 4, 44; 2, 8, 89). — **apros**: Lucanian boars are often mentioned.

23. echinos: *sea urchins*; they were eaten with very elaborate sauces and were considered a great delicacy (*Sat.* 2, 4, 33).

24. Phaeax: cf. *Epist.* 1, 2, 28 ff. and note.

25. adcredere: because Vala was at home in this region.

26. The story is introduced with an abruptness that is quite in Horace's manner, without any suggestion of the connection with the preceding thought. To a

fortiter absumptis urbanus coepit haberi
scurra, vagus non qui certum praesepe teneret,
impransus non qui civem dignosceret hoste,
30 quaelibet in quemvis opprobria fingere saevus,
pernicies et tempestas barathrumque macelli,
quicquid quaesierat, ventri donabat avaro.
Hic ubi nequitiae fautoribus et timidis nil

Roman reader, however, the name of Maenius, a Lucilian character who had become a type of the reckless and witty spendthrift, would at once suggest the general character of the anecdote and the connection with vs. 24 — 'You smile at my anxiety about my food and my desire to get fat on good living. Yes, I confess it, Maenius is my model, and I'll tell you a story about him.' — **maternis, paternis**: he had gone through two fortunes.

27. **fortiter**: 'like a young man of spirit'; with *absumptis*.

27-28. **urbanus ... scurra**: 'a man about town.' The word *scurra*, which is defined by Plautus (*urbani adsidui cives, quos scurras vocant, Trin.* 202), had always a suggestion of disparagement, but in combination with *urbanus*, which inclines toward a good sense, it is so nearly neutral as to need the definition of the two adjectives and the relative clauses. — **vagus**: not a regular *convictor* at any house, but picking up an invitation where he could. — **praesepe**: *crib, manger*, used humorously. — The order of words must be noticed; 'a roamer, not the kind that has a regular crib.' [The order is too marked in this vs. and in 29 to make it possible to include *vagus* and *impransus* in the relative clauses, as if it had been *qui vagus non ... teneret.*]

29. **civem ... hoste**: *friend from foe*; cf. Plaut. *Trin.* 102, *hostisne an civis comedis parvi pendere.* The older sense (=*peregrinus*) is quite uncalled for here.

30. **opprobria fingere**: this characteristic of the *scurra*, paying for his dinner by insulting witticisms, is well described by Horace, *Sat.* 1, 4, 81-85.

31. A Plautine line; cf. *Capt.* 911, *clades calamitasque intemperies modo in nostram advenit domum*, of a hungry parasite, and *Curc.* 121 b, *age effunde hoc* [*vinum*] *cito in barathrum*. The figure is 'he came upon the market house like ruin, like a hurricane, like an abyss.'

33. **nequitiae**: *worthlessness*, with special reference to a spendthrift's follies: joined with *nugis* and *pravorum amore, Sat.* 2, 3,

aut paullum abstulerat, patinas cenabat omasi
35 vilis et agninae, tribus ursis quod satis esset;
scilicet ut ventres lamna candente nepotum
diceret urendos correctus Bestius. Idem
quidquid erat nactus praedae maioris, ubi omne
verterat in fumum et cinerem, ' Non hercule miror,'
40 aiebat, ' si qui comedunt bona, cum sit obeso
nil melius turdo, nil vulva pulchrius ampla.'

244. — **fautoribus**: *i.e.*, he had for a time found persons to applaud his follies, but they had become afraid (*timidis*) of his savage wit.

34. **abstulerat**: *i.e.*, had reached the point where no one would give him a dinner. — **patinas**: *platters*, he still kept his appetite, though he had to eat coarse food. — **omasi**: *tripe;* spoken of with contempt in *Sat.* 2, 5, 40.

35. **vilis**: with *agninae*. But it is odd to modern taste that lamb should be classed with tripe as coarse and cheap food.

36-37. **scilicet ut**: 'in order, you know, that he might be able to say . . .'; an ironical purpose; cf. *Epist.* 1, 9, 3, and note. — **lamna**: slaves were branded with hot plates (*laminae*) on the member that had been most guilty, as on the hand for stealing. Maenius, being unable to buy dainty and expensive food, filled himself with coarse food and then discoursed with severity on the punishments that ought to be inflicted on people who wasted their money (*nepotum*) on high living. — **cor-**

rectus Bestius: 'like Bestius after his reformation,' or perhaps 'reformed into a regular Bestius.' For *correctus*, cf. *Sat.* 2, 3, 254, *mutatus Polemon*. As Bestius is wholly unknown, it is impossible to understand the allusion precisely; he may have been a reformed prodigal who denounced his former vices, or a type of the severe censor of others' vices.

38. 'And yet this same man, if he had the chance, relapsed into his prodigal ways.' — **praedae maioris**: 'whenever he had made a good haul,' *i.e.*, had succeeded in getting something good out of one of his *fautores*.

39. **fumum et cinerem**: proverbial, esp. of sacking and destroying a captured town. — **hercule**: as an interjection more commonly in the form *hercle*.

40. **comedunt bona**: cf. Catull. 29, 22. *devorare patrimonia;* the literal sense is, of course, also in mind.

41. **vulva**: the matrix of the sow, which was regarded as a delicacy.

Nimirum hic ego sum ; nam tuta et parvula laudo,
cum res deficiunt, satis inter vilia fortis ;
verum ubi quid melius contingit et unctius, idem
45 vos sapere et solos aio bene vivere, quorum
conspicitur nitidis fundata pecunia villis.

42-46. The application of the story to Horace himself is made in phrases which recall the preceding lines without precisely repeating them. *tuta et parvula laudo* = vss. 36, 37; *cum res deficiunt* = vss. 33-34; *ubi quid . . . contingit* = *quidquid erat nactus*, vs. 38; *idem* = *idem*, vs. 37; and the rest is Horace's way of expressing the thought of vss. 39-41. — **vos**: Vala was among the wealthy people of the region. — **conspicitur ... fundata**: to be taken together; 'is plainly seen to be solidly based.'

— **nitidis**: *splendid, gleaming*, like *villa candens, Epod.* 1, 29, with reference to the appearance of the white mass of the house when seen from a distance against the background of trees. — The underlying meaning of vss. 45-46 is, 'then I turn Epicurean, too, and enjoy your fine country houses and your good dinners, just as if I had never preached the Simple Life.' The story thus turns back to its starting-point, the inquiry in vss. 22-23 about game and sea food.

16

The year in which this Epistle was written cannot be determined, and the character of the letter is such that the precise date is not important. It may perhaps be inferred from vs. 16 that it was written in the late summer or the early autumn. The Quinctius to whom the letter is addressed is a man of position in public life (vss. 17-18), of some experience (vs. 25), and perhaps in office at this time (vs. 34). He may be the Quinctius Hirpinus of *Carm.* 2, 11.

'My farm, if you care to know about it, my dear Quinctius, is not so much a source of revenue to me, as a source of pleasure and health. Mountains, woods, streams, and a cool spring make it a perfect retreat from the heats of the city.

'As for you, you are in the midst of the active struggle of life, where reputation seems more important than character. But we must not be misled by popular applause, for it is often insincere and always fickle. Reputation may be taken away; character is our own. But it must be true virtue, not the fear of consequences, that keeps us from doing wrong. We must not be the slaves of our desires, but must stand independent and free from fear. Death itself, the ultimate penalty, comes alike to all.'

This Epistle belongs to the more impersonal class of the letters, like 1, 6 and 1, 10. There is some degree of personality in the first part, vss. 1-16; Horace cannot write impersonally of his Sabine farm. And vss. 17-18 have undoubtedly some special reference to the circumstances of Quinctius. But the latter part of the Epistle is general, a sort of restatement, in Horace's words and manner, of the second Stoic Paradox. This is quoted by Cicero (*Parad.* 2) : ὅτι αὐτάρκης ἡ ἀρετὴ πρὸς εὐδαιμονίαν, *in quo sit virtus, ei nihil deesse ad beate vivendum*, and is discussed and illustrated by him somewhat as it is here treated by Horace, with allusions to popular favor, to the tyranny of the passions, and to death as the *ultima linea*. In the style, also, as well as in the substance, there is an adoption of Stoic teaching by means of short sentences and lively bits of dialogue. No careful reader of the Satires will be surprised to find that Horace, in his later study of philosophy, sometimes accepts the Stoic doctrines ; even in the earlier writings it is possible to see, underneath the flippancy with which he meets the formalism of the Stoics, a considerable measure of sympathy with the essence of their teaching.

Ne perconteris, fundus meus, optime Quincti,
arvo pascat erum an bacis opulentet olivae,
pomisne an pratis an amicta vitibus ulmo ;
scribetur tibi forma loquaciter et situs agri.

1. **ne perconteris**: cf. *Epist.* 1, 1, 13, *ac ne forte roges.* — The questions which Quinctius might have asked relate entirely to the farm as a source of income, while the answering description, vss. 5-16, is concerned only with the estate as a pleasant place to live in during the summer.

2-3. **pascat, opulentet**: *feeds* with grain, *enriches* by the sale of olives and fruit; but the distinction is unimportant and the two verbs are used merely for variety. — The forms of cultivation mentioned were among those generally used in Italy: *arvo*, land plowed for grain; olives and fruit for sale in the city; *pratis*, *meadows* for pasturing cattle; *vitibus*, *vines* trained on elm trees for the making of wine. The four books of Vergil's Georgics deal with grain, vineyards, cattle, and bees.

4. **loquaciter**: *at full length*, with

5   Continui montes, ni dissocientur opaca
    valle, sed ut veniens dextrum latus adspiciat sol,
    laevum discedens curru fugiente vaporet ;
    temperiem laudes. Quid, si rubicunda benigni
    corna vepres et pruna ferant? si quercus et ilex
10 multa fruge pecus, multa dominum iuvet umbra?
    dicas adductum propius frondere Tarentum.
    Fons etiam rivo dare nomen idoneus, ut nec

a jocose admission of his pleasure in talking about his farm.

5. continui montes: sc. *sunt*. — **ni**: introducing an exception; 'mountains in an unbroken stretch, except where they are separated'; 'the continuity would be unbroken, if it were not. . . .'

6–7. sed ut: limiting *opaca*; 'shaded, but lying so that the sun. . . .' — **veniens dextrum**: the valley runs north and south, and in describing the scene Horace thinks of himself as facing the south or southeast. — **vaporet**: *warms*, merely a variation on *adspiciat*. — In connection with this description one should read *Carm.* 1, 17, and the first part of *Sat.* 2, 6, in order to see how deeply Horace loved the scene. The description, however, does not make it possible to determine with certainty the location of the villa.

8–10. temperiem laudes: this is added as a consequence of the mingling of shade and sunlight. — **quid, si**: this form of question is one to which the answer is thought to be obvious. No verb needs to be supplied, but if one were to be added in this case, it would be *dicas*, taken from the answer to the question. — **rubicunda**: he is thinking of the looks of the red berries, rather than of their use for food, while *pruna, wild plums*, are for eating. — **fruge**: *i.e.*, acorns for the swine.

11. Such a line as this can be better paraphrased than translated; 'you would say that Tarentum had been brought hither and that you were looking at its foliage.' The point of the line is in *frondere*; the foliage of green Tarentum was famous.

12. **fons**: it is often taken for granted that this is the *fons Bandusiae* of *Carm.* 3, 13, but in fact the location of that spring is quite unknown. — **rivo**: the Digentia, which flowed down the valley to join the Anio. — **idoneus**: *i.e.*, so large and full that the river might well take its name from the spring which is its source. — **ut**: the clause of result containing the comparative is equivalent to 'so

frigidior Thracam nec purior ambiat Hebrus,
infirmo capiti fluit utilis, utilis alvo.
15 Hae latebrae dulces, etiam, si credis, amoenae,
incolumem tibi me praestant Septembribus horis.
Tu recte vivis, si curas esse quod audis.
Iactamus iam pridem omnis te Roma beatum;
sed vereor, ne cui de te plus quam tibi credas,
20 neve putes alium sapiente bonoque beatum,

cool and clear that even the Hebrus does not surpass it.'

13. **ambiat**: 'winds through Thrace.'

14. **infirmo capiti**: cf. *Epist.* 1, 15. 8 and note. — **alvo**: this may refer to the same treatment or to the excellence of the water for drinking.

15. **latebrae**: so in *Sat.* 2, 6, 16 it is called *arx*, a place of refuge. This is the answer to the questions that might be asked (vss. 2-3) about the productiveness of the farm. — **dulces, amoenae**: the distinctions made in books on synonymy between such adjectives are often forced; each case must be judged singly. Here it is plain that *amoenae* expresses something beyond *dulces*; *dear* (to my feeding) and *delightful* (in itself). — **si credis**: humorously deprecating.

16. **Septembribus**: the worst time of the year in Rome.

17. **tu**: turning from his own affairs to the affairs and situation of Quinctius. — **quod audis**: 'what people call you,' 'what you are said to be.' Cf. *Epist.* 1, 7, 38, *Sat.* 2, 3, 298.

18. **iactamus**: 'we have been declaring,' 'saying openly'; there is no necessary implication of boasting. — **iam pridem**: not, therefore, because of any new honor, but because of Quinctius' high standing. — **omnis ... Roma**: so *dicemus civitas omnis*, *Carm.* 4, 2, 50; *eamus omnis civitas*, *Epod.* 16, 36. — **te ... beatum**: this is *quod audis*.

19. **ne ... credas**: this commonplace of philosophy, which means in essence that one should not be puffed up by popular favor, is first put in general terms and then more specifically explained and illustrated in the next lines. These verses form a transition from the opening of the Epistle to the main thought, that the wise man is one who lives by the precepts of philosophy, and are not to be understood as referring to anything definite in the character or situation of Quinctius. He is merely the man of high position to whom these exhortations may be fittingly addressed.

20. Another form of the Stoic

neu, si te populus sanum recteque valentem
dictitet, occultam febrem sub tempus edendi
dissimules, donec manibus tremor incidat unctis.
Stultorum incurata pudor malus ulcera celat.
25 Si quis bella tibi terra pugnata marique
dicat, et his verbis vacuas permulceat aures:
'Tene magis salvum populus velit an populum tu,
servet in ambiguo, qui consulit et tibi et urbi,
Iuppiter,' Augusti laudes agnoscere possis :
30 cum pateris sapiens emendatusque vocari,

Paradox, to which Horace frequently refers in the Satires.— **alium sapiente**: so *species alias veris*, *Sat.* 2, 3, 208; *alius Lysippo*, *Epist.* 2, 1, 240 and often.

21-23. This is Horace's favorite method of presenting an argument, by means of an implied comparison; 'do not be like a man who....'— **dictitet**: the same in sense as *iactamus*, vs. 18.— **edendi**: *i.e.*, he feels the chill coming on just as he is going to the table, but tries to conceal it from his guests. — **manibus**: where the chill would first betray itself. — **unctis**: the food was taken up with the fingers, and the meaning is, 'after you have begun your dinner,' when it is more inconvenient than it would have been before the dinner began.

24. stultorum: emphatic; 'only fools, not *sapientes*.'— The line is a second argument by comparison; 'do not be like a man who....'

25. tibi: with *pugnata*. This harmonizes with the implication of vs. 18, that Quinctius was a man who had been long active in public life and had taken part in the civil wars.

26. vacuas: 'ready' to listen; cf. *Epist.* 1, 18, 70, *patulae aures*, and, in a slightly different sense, *Epist.* 1, 1, 7, *purgatam aurem*.

27-29. These verses are said by the Scholiast to be taken from a Panegyric of Augustus, by Varius. The quotation of them is therefore a double compliment. — **servet in ambiguo**: *i.e.*, 'I pray that we may never be forced to decide between your safety and the safety of the state.' — **et tibi et urbi**: repeating the contrast of *populus an tu*. — **agnoscere**: both because the verses were so well known and because the praise was suitable only to Augustus.

30. pateris: 'allow yourself to be called,' without protest. For the nomin. after the infin. there are many parallels, *e.g.*, in vs. 32 and

respondesne tuo, dic sodes, nomine? 'Nempe
vir bonus et prudens dici deiector ego ac tu.'
Qui dedit hoc hodie, cras, si volet, auferet, ut, si
detulerit fasces indigno, detrahet idem.
35 ' Pone, meum est,' inquit: pono tristisque recedo.
Idem si clamet furem, neget esse pudicum,
contendat laqueo collum pressisse paternum,

Epist. 1, 5, 15. It is a perfectly natural deviation from the mechanical accus. and not a Grecism. Cf. *Sat.* 1, 1, 19, *licet esse beatis.*

31. **respondesne**: not equal to *nonne respondes,* but with a formal neutrality; 'do you answer or do you not?' — **tuo ... nomine**: *i.e.*, 'for yourself,' by accepting the description as really applicable to you. — **dic sodes**: a formula of appeal, as in *Epist.* 1, 1, 62. *sodes = si audes,* with the earlier meaning of *audeo* (= *avideo, aveo*).

32. **bonus et prudens**: a more modest substitute for *sapiens emendatusque.* — **delector**: intentionally stronger than *pateris.* — **ac tu**: a retort; 'just as you do, in spite of your superior tone.' — The whole line is a restatement of vs. 30, but in terms which satisfy the speaker better than *pateris sapiens emendatusque;* 'of course I like to be called a respectable and sensible man, and so do you.'

33. **qui dedit**: *i.e.*, public opinion. The reply, as so often in Horace, begins without an introductory conjunction, *at* or *sed.* Cf. *Sat.* 1, 1, 36.

34. **fasces**: for any high office.
— **detrahet**: not with reference to any legal impeachment, but merely as a vivid expression for the withdrawal of favor.

35. The figure in this vs. is slightly changed from that of the preceding line; it is the figure of a person taking up an object, any object, and being interrupted by the rightful owner. The subject of *meum est* is not *officium* (from *fasces*) or *nomen,* but is entirely indefinite; 'put that down, it's mine.' The variation of thought in vss. 33, 34, 35, is thoroughly Horatian; 'public opinion may take away reputation, as the voters may take away the office they gave, or as any man may reclaim what is his own.'

36. **idem**: the person who is vaguely thought of as the subject of *inquit,* with a slighter reference back to the subjects of *detrahet* and *auferet.* The force of *idem* is, as often, adversative; 'but when that same man accuses me unjustly, I can regard him with indifference.'

37. **laqueo**: this is a proverbial

mordear opprobriis falsis mutemque colores?
Falsus honor iuvat et mendax infamia terret
40 quem nisi mendosum et medicandum? Vir bonus est
quis?
Qui consulta patrum, qui leges iuraque servat;
quo multae magnaeque secantur iudice lites;
quo res sponsore et quo causae teste tenentur.
Sed videt hunc omnis domus et vicinia tota
45 introrsum turpem, speciosum pelle decora.
'Nec furtum feci nec fugi' si mihi dicat
servus, 'Habes pretium, loris non ureris,' aio.
'Non hominem occidi.' 'Non pasces in cruce corvos.'
'Sum bonus et frugi.' Renuit negitatque Sabellus.
50 Cautus enim metuit foveam lupus accipiterque

form of exaggerated accusation; cf. *Carm.* 2, 13, 5; *Epod.* 3, 1 f.

39. falsus honor: the substance of vss. 25–32. — **mendax infamia**: vss. 36–37.

41–43. This is the answer of the popular judgment to the question of vs. 40, not Horace's own answer, which is given in an indirect way in vss. 73 ff. — **secantur**: *are decided*; cf. *Sat.* 1, 10, 15, *ridiculum . . . magnas plerumque secat res.* — **sponsore**: *i.e.*, as a responsible man in business affairs. — **teste**: his evidence on the witness stand is accepted as decisive. — **tenentur**: used in a general sense with *res* (*are settled*) and in a technical sense, of winning a case at law, with *causae* (*are won*).

45. An allusion to the fable of the Ass in the Lion's Skin, to which Horace alludes also in *Sat.* 1, 6, 22; 2, 1, 64 f., in phrases very similar to those used here.

47. loris: leather thongs for whipping a slave. — **ureris**: so *Sat.* 2, 7, 58, *uri virgis.*

49. The unexpressed thought is 'since I am innocent of these things, I am therefore an upright man.' But this claim the strict judge refuses to admit. The same course of reasoning is followed in *Sat.* 2. 3. 159–162, with the same parody of the Stoic manner. — **Sabellus**: as a type of the strict moralist, who is not satisfied with good conduct unless the motive is also good.

50–51. 'For mere caution in avoiding trouble is shown by birds and animals,' and is therefore not

suspectos laqueos et opertum miluus hamum.
Oderunt peccare boni virtutis amore:
tu nihil admittes in te formidine poenae;
sit spes fallendi, miscebis sacra profanis,
55 nam de mille fabae modiis cum surripis unum,
damnum est, non facinus, mihi pacto lenius isto.
Vir bonus, omne forum quem spectat et omne tribunal,
quandocumque deos vel porco vel bove placat,
'Iane pater,' clare, clare cum dixit 'Apollo';
60 labra movet metuens audiri: 'Pulchra Laverna,
da mihi fallere! Da iusto sanctoque videri!
Noctem peccatis et fraudibus obice nubem!'
Qui melior servo, qui liberior sit avarus,
in triviis fixum cum se demittit ob assem,

a virtuous motive. — **foveam**: *pitfall*. — **miluus**: in three syllables; this variety of fish takes its name from the bird, and the word may be rendered *kite-fish*.

52-53. The ablatives, *amore, formidine*, are the important words.

56. **damnum**: the pecuniary loss, which is trifling. — **facinus**: *the sin*; sc. *tibi lenius*. — **pacto ... isto**: repeating the thought of *cum surripis unum*. *isto* is in the proper second person sense. — The argument is that the sin is not to be measured by the extent of the loss inflicted, but by the motive that prompts it. This is not precisely the Stoic doctrine that all sins are equal and deserve a like penalty.

57. **vir bonus**: still in the ironical sense. as in 41 ff., and therefore defined in the rest of the line,

'the man whom the popular judgment approves.' — **forum**: cf. vs. 41. — **tribunal**: cf. vs. 42.

60. **labra movet**: without uttering any sound; in contrast with *clare, clare*. — **Laverna**: the goddess of theft.

61. **iusto**: cf. *Sat.* 1, 1, 19, *licet esse beatis*, and vs. 30 above, with note.

63. **qui**: *how*, with the indirect question after *non video*. — **servo**: after both *melior* and *liberior*, which are predicates after *sit*.

64. **fixum ... assem**: this is explained by the scholiast on Persius 5. 111; 'quia solent pueri, ut ridendi causam habeant, assem in silice [*the pavement*] plumbatum [*i.e. with melted lead*] figere, ut qui viderint se ad tollendum eum inclinent nec tamen possint evel-

65 non video; nam qui cupiet, metuet quoque; porro
qui metuens vivet, liber mihi non erit unquam.
Perdidit arma, locum virtutis deseruit, qui
semper in augenda festinat et obruitur re.
Vendere cum possis captivum, occidere noli;
70 serviet utiliter: sine pascat durus aretque;
naviget ac mediis hiemet mercator in undis;
annonae prosit, portet frumenta penusque.
Vir bonus et sapiens audebit dicere: 'Pentheu,
rector Thebarum, quid me perferre patique
75 indignum coges?' 'Adimam bona.' 'Nempe pecus, rem,
lectos, argentum: tollas licet!' 'In manicis et
compedibus saevo te sub custode tenebo.'

lere. quo facto pueri etiam acclamare solent.'

65. cupiet, metuet: cf. *Epist.* 1, 6, 12.

67. arma, locum: acts which were proverbially discreditable; but they are really no worse than it is to give up one's life to money making.

69-72. 'Such a man is a mere slave, and should be set to do slave's work.' — **captivum**: this carries on the figure of vs. 67; the coward who has allowed himself to be captured may be made useful as a slave. The verse is a scornful bit of advice, addressed to the conqueror. — **durus**: as a hard-working farm slave. — The *agricola* and the *mercator* (*nauta*) are frequently used as types of men who endure hardship for gain,

e.g., *Sat.* 1, 1, 28 ff. — **annonae**: 'let him help to keep down the cost of living by bringing grain from Egypt.'

73-79. These lines paraphrase a passage of Euripides (*Bacch.* 492-498), as in *Sat.* 2, 3, 262-271, a passage from Terence is transposed into hexameters. The god, Dionysus, in disguise is in the power of Pentheus, king of Thebes. — **bonus et sapiens**: the man who is truly good in heart, and who relies upon his character rather than upon his reputation, or upon the judgment of others. Cf. *Carm.* 3, 3, 1 ff., *iustum et tenacem*. — **perferre patique**: cf. *Epist.* 1, 15, 17. — **lectos**: for all his furniture. — **argentum**: *silver plate*, not money. — **ipse deus . . .**: an exact translation of λύσει μ' ὁ δαίμων

'Ipse deus, simul atque volam, me solvet.' Opinor,
hoc sentit: 'moriar.' Mors ultima linea rerum est.

αὐτὸς ὅταν ἐγὼ θέλω. — moriar: this is, of course, not in the play, but is an interpretation of the scene according to Stoic ideals. To take refuge from the ills of life in self-inflicted death was quite in harmony with Stoic doctrine. Cf. *Carm.* I, 12, 35 f., *Catonis nobile letum.* — ultima linea: the white line which marked the end of the race course.

17

The person to whom this Epistle is addressed is wholly unknown, nor is there anything in the letter to fix the date.

'I know that you need no advice about living with the great, yet perhaps I may be able to say something about it that you will care to hear. If you prefer a retired life, you can find happiness there, but if you seek for something more, you must go where it is to be found. You know the story of Diogenes and Aristippus; the one prided himself upon his rudeness, the other was a man of the world. It was the latter who was truly a philosopher, for if it is a worthy ambition to desire to be distinguished in public life, then it is also a worthy ambition to desire to please the men who are thus distinguished. To refuse to make the attempt is a kind of cowardice; to enter the contest and win a place is honorable.

'But I don't mean that one should be a beggar, always parading his needs and his misfortunes. The Egyptian humbug, pretending to have broken his leg in order to excite pity, fools only the inexperienced.'

There is scarcely anything of the epistolary form or tone in this letter. It is a discourse, partly serious, but largely ironical, on the proper attitude toward men of higher rank. This was a subject which Horace had himself been obliged to consider with serious attention. His relation to Maecenas and Augustus and Agrippa had exposed him to criticism and had been in itself difficult to reconcile with that independence of life and thought which he desired to maintain. It was impossible for him to write on this subject without a consciousness, which reveals itself in several places, of his own personal interest in it. To some extent, therefore, it is seriously meant; the attitude and teaching of Aristippus in regard to social relations command Horace's approval. On the other hand, the relation of the man of humbler rank to the greater men is almost everywhere treated as though the ultimate object of it was profit, not real friendship. This is, of course, ironical, and at the close, from vs. 43 to the end, it becomes pure satire.

It is certainly difficult for the modern reader, accustomed to democratic ideals, to estimate this Epistle quite justly, not taking it too seriously and yet not overlooking the serious meaning. For a full understanding of Horace's attitude on this subject, this Epistle should be compared with the next and both should be read in connection with *Epist.* 1, 7, to Maecenas.

> Quamvis, Scaeva, satis per te tibi consulis, et scis
> quo tandem pacto deceat maioribus uti,
> disce, docendus adhuc quae censet amiculus, ut si
> caecus iter monstrare velit; tamen adspice si quid
> 5 et nos, quod cures proprium fecisse, loquamur.
> Si te grata quies et primam somnus in horam
> delectat, si te pulvis strepitusque rotarum,
> si laedit caupona, Ferentinum ire iubebo.
> Nam neque divitibus contingunt gaudia solis,
> 10 nec vixit male qui natus moriensque fefellit.

1. **quamvis ... per te:** cf. *A.P.* 366 f., *quamvis ... per te sapis;* this is a modest formula to soften the assumption of wisdom that may be involved in proffering advice. *per te,* 'without advice from any one.'

2. **tandem:** frequent in direct questions and then retained in the indirect. — **maioribus:** *the great;* this plain recognition of difference in station is common in all societies where there is an established nobility. — **uti:** *to get along with, to associate with.* There is no suggestion of making use of for one's own advantage.

3. **docendus adhuc:** with *amiculus;* 'a friend who admits that he has himself still much to learn.' This and the diminutive *amiculus,* 'a humble friend,' continue the deprecatory tone of vs. 1.

5. **et nos:** the *amiculus.* — **proprium fecisse:** *to adopt.*

6–10. 'If you choose a retired life, it will bring its own rewards.' — **primam ... in horam:** in contrast to the early rising for the *salutatio;* cf. *Sat.* 1, 1. 10. — **rotarum, caupona:** the discomforts of travel, when the follower was under obligation to attend his patron on a journey, as Horace had attended Maecenas on the journey to Brundisium. — **Ferenti-**

Si prodesse tuis paulloque benignius ipsum
te tractare voles, accedes siccus ad unctum.
'Si pranderet holus patienter, regibus uti
nollet Aristippus.' 'Si sciret regibus uti,
15 fastidiret holus qui me notat.' Vtrius horum
verba probes et facta, doce, vel iunior audi
cur sit Aristippi potior sententia. Namque
mordacem Cynicum sic eludebat, ut aiunt:
'Scurror ego ipse mihi, populo tu; rectius hoc et

num: one of the small mountain towns, selected merely as a type of a retired spot. — natus... fefellit: 'whose birth and death have passed unnoticed.'

11. si: the second and contrasting possibility is introduced, as often, without an adversative particle, the adversative connection being implied in the thought. — prodesse tuis: cf. vs. 46; there is some irony in putting care for one's friends first and *benignius ipsum* second, and in the use of *paullo*.

12. accedes: future almost with impv. force. — siccus: *thirsty*, but implying hunger also; cf. *Sat.* 2, 2, 14, *siccus, inanis.* — unctum: *to a rich table*; cf. *Epist.* 1, 15, 44. The contrast between rich and poor is often expressed, as here, in terms of food and drink; in this case it prepares for the story which follows.

13-15. The dialogue is paraphrased from Diog. Laert. 2, 8, 68. Diogenes the Cynic was washing some vegetables, preparing for his plain meal, when Aristippus happened to pass by. — patienter: *i.e.* 'with the endurance which we Cynics teach and practice.' — regibus: Aristippus lived for a time in the court of Dionysius, the tyrant of Syracuse. — si sciret: *i.e.*, 'if the Cynic knew how to live reasonably with all men, even kings, as my philosophy teaches.' — notat: *censures*; cf. *Sat.* 1, 3, 24, note.

16. verba... et facta: 'their teachings and their lives.'

17. potior: in this particular instance; but all the references to Aristippus (*Sat.* 2, 3, 100; *Epist.* 1, 1, 18) are respectful, and he seems to have stood in Horace's mind as a good type of the mean between Stoicism and Epicureanism.

18. mordacem: this particular adj. is selected because of the derivation of *Cynicus* from κύων, *a dog.* — eludebat: *parried, dodged*; a word used of the movement of a gladiator.

19. scurror: *i.e.*, 'we both play the *scurra*, the parasite and hanger-

20 splendidius multo est. Equus ut me portet, alat rex,
officium facio; tu poscis vilia, verum
dante minor, quamvis fers te nullius egentem.'
Omnis Aristippum decuit color et status et res,
temptantem maiora, fere praesentibus aequum.
25 Contra, quem duplici panno patientia velat,
mirabor vitae via si conversa decebit.
Alter purpureum non exspectabit amictum,
quidlibet indutus celeberrima per loca vadet
personamque feret non inconcinnus utramque;
30 alter Mileti textam cane peius et angui

on, if you choose to put it so, but my way of doing it is the better.' — **mihi, populo**: *i.e.*, 'I do it for my own sake, for my own approval, you for the approval of the crowd.'

20. **equus . . . rex**: a Greek proverb; ἵππος με φέρει, βασιλεύς με τρέφει.

21-22. **officium**: as courtier, but intentionally neutral, so that it might mean 'as *scurra*.' — **poscis**: Diogenes was supported by gifts which he begged from his admirers. — **verum**: 'and yet you are inferior to those who bestow the gifts.' — **fers te**: *boast yourself.* — The point of the retort is that Aristippus gets a real reward, while Diogenes, just as truly a courtier, gets only a petty reward.

23-24. **color**: cf. *Sat.* 2, 1, 60, *vitae color*. — **temptantem maiora**: this line is a free rendering of a doctrine of the school of Aristippus, as vs. 23 is a characterization of him from Greek sources. — **praesentibus**: neut. plur. dat.; 'what he had,' in distinction from *maiora*.

25. **duplici panno**: the διπλοῖς, the cloak of the Cynics, folded over to take the place of both inner and outer garment. It is called *pannus* in contempt, because the philosopher wore old and coarse clothing, to prove his indifference to luxury and his endurance (*patientia*).

26. **vitae via . . . conversa**: *i.e.*, the change from his ostentatious asceticism to ordinary life with other men.

27-28. **non exspectabit**: *i.e.*, he is not dependent upon some particular kind of dress to support his character as a philosopher, but is at ease in any dress (*quidlibet indutus*) and any company. This characteristic of Aristippus was traditional.

29. **utramque**: either the man of the world or the philosopher.

30. **alter**: Diogenes. — **Mileti**:

vitabit chlamydem, morietur frigore, si non
rettuleris pannum; refer, et sine vivat ineptus!
Res gerere et captos ostendere civibus hostis,
attingit solium Iovis et caelestia tentat;
35 principibus placuisse viris non ultima laus est.
Non cuivis homini contingit adire Corinthum.
Sedit qui timuit ne non succederet. Esto;
quid, qui pervenit, fecitne viriliter? Atqui
hic est aut nusquam quod quaerimus. Hic onus horret,
40 ut parvis animis et parvo corpore maius;

the woolen fabrics of Miletus were famous for their fineness. — cane: put in only for the joke on the Cynic; cf. *mordacem*, vs. 18, and note.

32. **rettuleris**: there is a story that Diogenes refused to exchange his coarse cloak for the better garment of Aristippus, preferring to suffer from cold rather than to appear in public in anything but his philosopher's dress.

34. **attingit solium**: cf. the various expressions for this thought in *Carm.* 1, 1, *evehit ad deos, sublimi feriam sidera vertice*, and for *caelestia tentat* cf. *Carm.* 3, 2, 21 f., *virtus, recludens . . . caelum, negata temptat iter via*, all meaning to attain the height of felicity.

35. **principibus placuisse**: *i.e.*, 'to have won the favor of men who have attained to these heights is in itself no small credit.' Though the thought is put in general terms, Horace is also thinking of himself. Cf. *Sat.* 2, 1, 76, *me cum magnis vixisse . . . fatebitur . . . invidia*, and *Epist.* 1, 20, 23.

36. A translation of the Greek saying οὐ παντὸς ἀνδρὸς ἐς Κόρινθον ἔσθ' ὁ πλοῦς, with the general meaning that not every man can succeed in getting the prize, *i.e.*, in winning the favor of men of position.

37. **sedit**: a true perfect, not 'gnomic'; 'the man who was afraid of failure sat still and avoided the contest.' There is a reference, apparently, to the contestants at the games, who are summoned by the herald to enter the race. — **esto**: *very good*; 'suppose he did well to decline the contest, yet we must say that the man who entered and ran to the end was even better.'

38-39. **atqui**: adversative to the interrogative form of *fecitne*; 'but you must not avoid the issue by a question, for this is the very point of the whole discussion.'

39-41. **hic**: a man like Diogenes, one who prefers not to enter the

hic subit et perfert.   Aut virtus nomen inane est,
aut decus et pretium recte petit experiens vir.
Coram rege sua de paupertate tacentes
plus poscente ferent.   Distat, sumasne pudenter,
45   an rapias.   Atqui rerum caput hoc erat, hic fons.
'Indotata mihi soror est, paupercula mater,
et fundus nec vendibilis nec pascere firmus,'
qui dicit, clamat 'victum date'; succinit alter
'et mihi'; dividuo findetur munere quadra.

social contest at all, but to keep wholly out of the activity of life, as in vss. 6–10. — hic subit: a man of the type of Aristippus, one who dares to play his part among men. Cf. vss. 11–12.

41–42. virtus: with a reference back to *viriliter*. — decus: 'the credit of having won favor.' — recte: *justly*. — experiens: *qui omnia experitur*, 'the man who dares make the attempt'; joined by Cicero with *fortis* and *promptus*. — This is a summary of the whole argument from vs. 6. The man who chooses a quiet life, Diogenes in his tattered cloak, the timid man who shuns the contest, represent one side of the argument; the man of some ambition, the philosopher, like Aristippus, who is nevertheless a man of the world, the contestant who risks defeat, these are on the other side, and vs. 42 gives the decision in their favor.

43–61. As many of these satires close with a humorous turn, so the thought of this Epistle turns at this point to a humorous treatment of the theme, which may be compared to the ironical advice of Tiresias to Ulysses in *Sat.* 2, 5, 88–98.

43. rege: the word that a parasite uses of his patron, not as in vss. 13, 14, nor as in *Epist.* 1, 7, 37.

44. distat: *it makes a great difference*.

45. atqui: as in vs. 38; 'and yet this very difference was the point of my argument.' — erat: *i.e.*, all the time, in all the preceding argument.

47. firmus: *suitable*, giving a secure income by pasturing flocks and herds.

48. qui dicit, clamat: *i.e.*, such statements are in effect a beggar's outcry. — alter: *another, a second man*; not *the other*.

49. findetur: 'the result of such shameless begging will be that each man will get half a loaf.' — dividuo: predicate. — quadra: *the loaf, the piece*; there is no sugges-

50　Sed tacitus pasci si posset corvus, haberet
　　plus dapis et rixae multo minus invidiaeque.
　　Brundisium comes aut Surrentum ductus amoenum
　　qui queritur salebras et acerbum frigus et imbres,
　　aut cistam effractam et subducta viatica plorat,
55　nota refert meretricis acumina, saepe catellam,
　　saepe periscelidem raptam sibi flentis, uti mox
　　nulla fides damnis verisque doloribus adsit.
　　Nec semel irrisus triviis attollere curat
　　fracto crure planum, licet illi plurima manet
60　lacrima, per sanctum iuratus dicat Osirim:
　　'Credite, non ludo; crudeles, tollite claudum!'
　　'Quaere peregrinum,' vicinia rauca reclamat.

tion, of course, of dividing into four parts.

50–51. tacitus pasci: the cawing of the crow when it finds something to eat attracts other birds which want a share of the food. There is no allusion to the fable of the Fox and the Crow.

52. Brundisium: cf. *Sat.* I, 5; the naming of this place is one of the many personal touches in this letter which show that Horace was thinking of his own relation to Maecenas and other men of position in public life.

53. salebras: *roughnesses*; only here in Horace.

55. refert: *brings back* to memory. — **acumina**: *tricks*. — **catellam**: diminutive of *catena*.

57. veris: *real*, *i.e.*, different from the trifling matters of vs. 54, which are no more than the ordinary incidents of travel, not worth a moment's notice.

58. triviis: the impostor, pretending to be suffering from an accident, selects a place where many persons would be passing.

59. planum: πλάνος, *an impostor*; not the adj. *plānus*. — **manet**: from *māno*, not from *măneo*.

60. Osirim: the cheat was an Egyptian and swore by his own god. Rome swarmed with foreigners who lived by their wits.

62. peregrinum: *i.e.*, 'try your tricks on some one who doesn't know you.' — **vicinia**: this continues the same thought, that the tricks had been tried too often in that neighborhood.

18

This Epistle was written in the year 20 B.C., as the reference to the recovery of Roman standards from the Parthians (vss. 56 f.) shows, and is addressed to the Lollius to whom *Epist.* 1, 2 was written.

'Lack of independence is a fault to be avoided, my dear Lollius, in your relation to a man of rank, but lack of common sense is worse. The true course lies between. The lack of self-respect makes a man a mere parasite; lack of judgment makes him assert his independence by wrangling about trifles.

'Do not try to rival your patron in extravagance; he will not like you the better for it, and you cannot afford it. The ill-natured witticism of Volumnius, that the best way to ruin a man was to give him a fine coat and let him try to live up to it, has enough of truth in it to serve as a warning. Do not try to learn his secrets and don't betray his confidences. Don't insist on following your own inclinations, even though they may seem to you the better; Amphion, you know, gave up the lyre to please his brother. If your friend likes hunting better than poetry, yield and go with him. It will do you good and you are an athlete; I have seen you on the Campus and I remember that sea fight on your father's estate. Be careful in your speech and in your conduct. Introduce only men that you know well, and if you make a mistake in this, don't refuse to acknowledge it. But stand by your true friends, as you expect them to stand by you. And conform even to your patron's moods; be serious when he is serious, and gay when he is gay, and keep a cheerful countenance at all times.

'But above all fix your mind upon the lessons and ideals of philosophy and learn from them the secret of a peaceful life.

'As for me, I have attained to that peaceful life. I ask of the gods nothing but a continuance of it.'

This Epistle deals, in substance, with a situation like that which is discussed in the Epistle immediately preceding, but with great differences both in form and in tone. The epistolary form is maintained with much skill; there are many personal touches, so that the character and situation of the young Lollius are clearly defined and the unnamed patron is more than a lay figure. And the letter closes with a passage of peculiarly intimate self-disclosure. All this is much superior to the essay form of *Epist.* 1, 17. In the tone, also, there is more of reality. Here, even more distinctly than in the letter to Scaeva, Horace had constantly in mind his own relation to Maecenas and his own efforts to find the middle course between an undue deference and an unwise independence. As he was conscious that he had succeeded in preserving both his friendship and his independence, he can describe his own course, under the guise of advice to a younger friend, with a sense of satisfaction.

> Si bene te novi, metues, liberrime Lolli,
> scurrantis speciem praebere, professus amicum.
> Vt matrona meretrici dispar erit atque
> discolor, infido scurrae distabit amicus.
> 5 Est huic diversum vitio vitium prope maius,
> asperitas agrestis et inconcinna gravisque,
> quae se commendat tonsa cute, dentibus atris,
> dum vult libertas dici mera veraque virtus.
> Virtus est medium vitiorum et utrimque reductum.

1-2. **liberrime**: so *Sat.* 1, 4, 132, *liber amicus, free-speaking, frank.* The word gives the keynote of the Epistle, which is addressed to a man of independent character, of whom it could be said with special force *metues . . . praebere.* — **speciem**: *i.e.*, 'in your great independence you will dislike even the appearance of servility.' — **amicum**: directly after *professus*; the concrete for the abstract; *Carm.* 1, 35, 22, *comitem abnegat.*

3-4. **matrona**: this word has always an especially honorable sense. — **discolor**: a definition of *dispar.* The *meretrix* wore a dark-colored toga, the *matrona* a white *stola.*

5. **est**: the emphatic position gives an adversative effect; 'you need not fear, for an *amicus* is as different from a *scurra* as a *matrona* from a *meretrix.* There is, however, another fault, which your independence may lead you into.' — **huic . . . vitio**: *i.e.*, the fault of servility.

6. **inconcinna**: cf. *Epist.* 1, 17, 29; *disagreeable*, unsuited to pleasant society.

7. **commendat**: the meaning of the verb suggests the ironical turn: cf. *Epist.* 2, 1, 261. — **tonsa cute**: *i.e.*, 'by hair cut close to the scalp,' a fashion affected by the Cynics and by persons who desired to prove themselves superior to the prevailing fashion. — **dentibus atris**: another way of showing independent indifference.

8. **libertas**: with a reference back to *liberrime*, and with the implication that too great freedom of speech is like the *asperitas agrestis.*

9. This vs., taking up at the beginning the word with which

10 Alter in obsequium plus aequo pronus et imi
derisor lecti, sic nutum divitis horret,
sic iterat voces et verba cadentia tollit,
ut puerum saevo credas dictata magistro
reddere vel partes mimum tractare secundas.
15 Alter rixatur de lana saepe caprina,
propugnat nugis armatus. 'Scilicet ut non
sit mihi prima fides et vere quod placet ut non
acriter elatrem? Pretium aetas altera sordet.'

vs. 8 ends, is a well-known definition. Cf. Cic. *de Off.* 1, 25, 89, '... mediocritatem illam, quae est inter nimium et parum, quae placet Peripateticis,' and often in Horace, especially in *Carm.* 2, 10, 5, *aurea mediocritas*.

10–14. **alter**: the *scurra*. — **imi derisor lecti**: so *Sat.* 2, 8, 40 f., *imi convivae lecti*, in the same place in the verse. The parasites were on the *lectus imus* with the host. This whole passage is best illustrated by a reading of *Sat.* 2, 8. — **cadentia**: *i.e.*, remarks which have failed to attract the attention of the guests. — **dictata ... reddere**: cf. *Epist.* 1, 1, 55, *haec recinunt ... dictata.* — **partes ... secundas**: the second actor in the mimes was expected to 'play up to' the leading actor (cf. *Sat.* 1, 9, 46), even repeating his gestures and actions.

15. **de lana ... caprina**: this appears to be a proverbial expression; it is correctly explained by the Scholiast as a trifling question, whether the hair of goats could properly be called wool (*lana*), a mere strife about words.

16. **nugis**: dative after *propugnat.* — **armatus**: absolute; 'with drawn sword,' carrying out the sense of *propugnat*. [*rixatur de lana* and *propugnat nugis* are different expressions for the same thought, as often in Horace, *e.g.*, *dispar atque discolor*, vs. 3 f. The dative after *propugnat* is perfectly normal, though it happens not to occur in classical Latin; the ablative, either with *propugnat* or with *armatus*, gives a wrong sense.] — **scilicet**: cf. *Epist.* 1, 9, 3, note. — **ut non**: a repudiating exclamation, cf. *satin ut* in questions and see Lane, §§ 1568, 1569. With this form of interrogative exclamation *scilicet* is perfectly harmonious, though it is not used in ordinary questions.

17. **prima**: *i.e.*, 'I should be trusted at once,' 'my mere statement should command instant acceptance.'

18. **elatrem**: with a hit at the Cynic philosophy. — **pretium** ...

Ambigitur quid enim? Castor sciat an Docilis plus;
20 Brundisium Minuci melius via ducat an Appi.
Quem damnosa Venus, quem praeceps alea nudat,
gloria quem supra vires et vestit et unguit,
quem tenet argenti sitis importuna famesque,
quem paupertatis pudor et fuga, dives amicus,
25 saepe decem vitiis instructior, odit et horret,

sordet: a condensed expression; 'I should think a second life (the privilege of living two lives) too small a price to pay me for submitting to such treatment.' *pretium* is an appositive to *aetas altera*.

19. **ambigitur**: *i.e.*, 'what is all the row about? Some matter of the most trivial importance.' — **Castor ... an Docilis**: unknown; they were actors or gladiators or other persons then well known, an allusion to whom would be understood by contemporary readers. — Cf., as an example of the same kind of trifling matter, *Sat.* 2, 6, 44, *Thraex est Gallina Syro par?* and 72, *male necne Lepos saltet*. — **sciat**: this would suit either actors or gladiators.

20. The *via Minucia* was perhaps the shorter but rougher road, taken by Maecenas and Horace in *Sat.* 1, 5. The *via Appia*, to Brundisium by way of Tarentum, was longer, but better. — This passage, vss. 15-20, is one of those vivid portraits which Horace often draws; it is the irascible person who is always ready to contend about trifles and whose intolerance of the views of others is so great that any hesitancy in accepting his decisions seems to him like an unbearable insult.

21 ff. The general discussion which started from *liberrime* now passes over into special warnings and injunctions.

21-24. The faults mentioned have in common the characteristic of leading to the desire for money. — **damnosa**: *ruinous*, financially, not morally. — **supra vires**: cf. *Sat.* 2, 3, 179 ff. on the expensiveness of office seeking. — **et vestit et unguit**: *i.e.*, leads into expensive habits. — **argenti sitis**: the love of money for itself produces the same effect as the need of money to pay gambling debts, *i.e.*, it makes a man a less agreeable friend and companion. — **paupertatis ... fuga**: this is, in its results, the same as *avaritia*; cf. *Epist.* 1, 16, 65; 1, 6, 9 and notes.

25. **vitiis instructior**: 'ten times as well provided with faults.' *decem* is a round number. *vitiis*, abl. of degree of difference with the comparative. The whole ex-

aut, si non odit, regit ac, veluti pia mater,
plus quam se sapere et virtutibus esse priorem
vult et ait prope vera: ' Meae, contendere noli,
stultitiam patiuntur opes; tibi parvula res est:
30 arta decet sanum comitem toga ; desine mecum
certare.' Eutrapelus cuicumque nocere volebat
vestimenta dabat pretiosa; beatus enim iam
cum pulchris tunicis sumet nova consilia et spes,
dormiet in lucem, scorto postponet honestum
35 officium, nummos alienos pascet, ad imum

pression is, of course, humorous; the great man, who has had plenty of experience of all sides of life, does not want his friend to bother him with small extravagances, but to be a better man than himself.

26. regit : *advises him.* — mater: parents wish their children to be wiser and better than they have themselves been.

28. prope vera : *i.e.*, not philosophically true, since folly is never good, but true enough in their present application. — contendere noli: parenthetic.

30. arta: the narrow toga is treated as a sign of simplicity, as in *Epod.* 4, 8 the *trium ulnarum toga* is a sign of ostentation.

31-36. Eutrapelus: P. Volumnius, a Roman knight of Cicero's time, a friend of Antony. Two letters (*ad Fam.* 7, 32 and 33) are addressed to him by Cicero, both written in a tone of jesting, and in one he alludes to the εὐτραπελία, from which the name Eutrapelus is derived. The allusion is undoubtedly to some jesting sarcasm of his, to the effect that the best way to ruin an enemy would be to make him a present of some fine clothes; in the attempt to 'live up to' these he would work out his own destruction. But it begins as if it were an anecdote, like that of Philippus in *Epist.* 1, 7, and even as if the joke had been perpetrated frequently (*cuicumque, volebat, dabat*). In sense it is a continuation of vss. 28-31, but it need not be supposed to have been uttered by the *dives amicus*; rather, it is Horace's supplement. — dormiet : *i.e.*, will grow lazy. — honestum officium : general, *his proper duties.* — pascet: *i.e.*, he will increase his debts and thus increase the property of his creditor. — Thraex : a mere gladiator, one of the last refuges of men of fallen fortunes. — Or he will end by hiring himself out to drive the horse of some huckster.

Thraex erit aut holitoris aget mercede caballum.
Arcanum neque tu scrutaberis illius unquam,
commissumque teges et vino tortus et ira.
Nec tua laudabis studia aut aliena reprendes;
40 nec, cum venari volet ille, poemata panges.
Gratia sic fratrum geminorum, Amphionis atque
Zethi, dissiluit donec suspecta severo
conticuit lyra. Fraternis cessisse putatur
moribus Amphion: tu cede potentis amici
45 lenibus imperiis, quotiesque educet in agros

37. **illius**: 'your patron'; the reference goes back over the intervening story to vs. 24 or 28.

38. **commissum teges**: to reveal what had been intrusted to one in confidence is mentioned in *Sat.* 1, 3, 95 (*prodiderit commissa fide*) as a fault to be ranked with theft. — **vino tortus**: cf. *A. P.* 435, *torquere mero, quem perplexisse laborant*. — **ira**: *i.e.*, because he happened for the moment to be angry with his patron.

39–40. **aliena**: in particular the interests of the patron. — **venari, poemata**: these two pursuits may be selected merely for the strong contrast, but they sound like definite allusions to personal interests of an actual patron and of Lollius himself. Hunting was a favorite sport with the Romans and is often alluded to by Horace, and many of his younger friends like Lollius were interested in literature. — **panges**: a rather formal term, such as Lollius might himself use in speaking of his wish to stay at home and devote himself to the high art of poetry.

41–44. The debate between the brothers Zethus and Amphion in regard to the comparative value of music — standing for art in general — and the active life of a herdsman and hunter was in Euripides' *Antiope* and was repeated in the *Antiopa* of Pacuvius. — **dissiluit**: *was broken*. — **severo**: the serious and practical Zethus. — **cessisse**: he is represented in art as in the act of hiding the lyre under his cloak. — **putatur**: *is believed*; *i.e.*, 'if we may accept the story.' In fact, he became in tradition one of the representatives of musical skill, as in *Carm.* 3, 11, 2.

44. **tu**: the chiastic arrangement emphasizes the argument; 'all the more should you yield.'

45. **lenibus**: because they came from an *amicus*; yet they are also

Aetolis onerata plagis iumenta canesque,
surge et inhumanae senium depone Camenae,
cenes ut pariter pulmenta laboribus empta:
Romanis sollemne viris opus, utile famae
50 vitaeque et membris, praesertim cum valeas et
vel cursu superare canem vel viribus aprum
possis. Adde virilia quod speciosius arma
non est qui tractet. Scis quo clamore coronae
proelia sustineas campestria; denique saevam
55 militiam puer et Cantabrica bella tulisti
sub duce, qui templis Parthorum signa refigit

imperiis because the friend is *potens*.

46. Aetolis: the Scholiast understands this to be an allusion to the hunting of the Calydonian boar in Aetolia by Meleager; the story was a familiar one, and perhaps this slight allusion would be sufficiently clear. But it is also quite possible that there is some other meaning in the word. — **iumenta**: cf. the description of such a hunting party in *Epist.* 1, 6, 58 ff.

47. inhumanae: *unfriendly* to all that would interrupt her pursuits; the epithet is used by the poet with a certain humor and with reference to this particular occasion. — **senium**: *moroseness*, also half humorous.

48. pariter: *i.e.*, with your friend. — **pulmenta ... empta**: the thought is expressed more fully in *Sat.* 2, 2, 9-22, and especially in vs. 20, *tu pulmentaria quaere sudando*.

49. sollemne .. opus: in *Sat.* 2 2, 10 f. hunting is called *Romana militia*, in contrast to Greek athletics. — **viris**: with intentional emphasis; 'the manly Roman.'

50-51. The injunctions are at the same time lightened and made more personal by these compliments and by the references to Lollius' early life.

52-54. speciosius: *i.e.*, 'you are especially successful in the sports of the Campus Martius and win the applause of the surrounding spectators (*coronae*)'.

55. militiam, Cantabrica bella: the general term followed by the specific reference. Augustus made campaigns in Spain in 27-25 B.C.; *puer* implies that this was Lollius' first experience as a soldier.

56. Parthorum: with *templis*. There are many allusions to the recovery of the Roman standards taken from Crassus.— **refigit nunc**: this gives the date of the Epistle

nunc et, si quid abest, Italis adiudicat armis.
Ac ne te retrahas et inexcusabilis absis,
quamvis nil extra numerum fecisse modumque
60 curas, interdum nugaris rure paterno.
Partitur lintres exercitus; Actia pugna
te duce per pueros hostili more refertur:
adversarius est frater, lacus Hadria, donec
alterutrum velox victoria fronde coronet.

as 20 B.C. The standards are thought of as having been hung as trophies in the Parthian temples and as being taken down by Augustus from the walls. In fact, they were restored as a result of diplomatic negotiations.

57. **si quid abest**: *i.e.*, 'if anything is still outside the sphere of Roman military power.' — **adiudicat**: as a judge who assigns to the rightful owner that which he has claimed. — **Italis ... armis**: dative; so Cic. *de Off.* 1, 10, 33: *in medio relictum quod erat populo Romano adiudicavit.* — Augustus himself speaks with pride of his extension of Roman influence into the East by diplomacy, and it was the fashion of the time to find in these peaceful successes compensation for the defeat which the Romans had suffered at the hands of the Parthians.

58-60. 'And, to anticipate your saying that a sport like hunting is too trival for one who has been a soldier, let me remind you, though I know that you would do nothing unsuitable, of that sham battle which you and your brother once exhibited in the country at your father's place.' — **ne ... retrahas**: a parenthetic clause of purpose; cf. *ne perconteris, Epist.* 1, 16, 1. — **inexcusabilis**: *without good reason*; cf. *ignobilis = ignotus*. — **extra numerum ... modumque**: *unfitting*, 'unsuitable to your character and position.' The figure is taken from music. The clause is put in to excuse in advance the use of *nugaris*.

61-64. A reminiscence of a mimic naval fight, in which the two brothers had represented a battle like that of Actium, the forces being slaves or boys of the neighborhood and boats being used for galleys. — **partitur**: the game began with a fair division of the skiffs between the two armies. — **hostili more**: *i.e.*, 'as if you had really been enemies.' — **lacus**: a *pond* on the estate. — Such representations of sea fights were often given with much splendor at public shows.

65 Consentire suis studiis qui crediderit te,
    fautor utroque tuum laudabit pollice ludum.
    Protinus ut moneam, si quid monitoris eges tu,
    quid de quoque viro et cui dicas saepe videto.
    Percontatorem fugito; nam garrulus idem est,
70 nec retinent patulae commissa fideliter aures,
    .et semel emissum volat irrevocabile verbum.
    Non ancilla tuum iecur ulceret ulla puerve
    intra marmoreum venerandi limen amici,
    ne dominus pueri pulchri caraeve puellae
75 munere te parvo beet, aut incommodus angat.
    Qualem commendes etiam atque etiam adspice, ne mox

65-66. These vss. resume the main thought, which was interrupted at vs. 49, or at vs. 58, by the complimentary digression on Lollius' skill in games. — **utroque . . . pollice**: a reference, as the words *fautor* and *ludum* show, to the gesture by which approval was expressed in the amphitheater. The gesture had become proverbial (Pliny, *Hist. Nat.* 28, 2, 25, *pollices cum faveamus premere etiam proverbio iubemur*). Both the origin and the precise form of the gesture are in doubt.

68. de quoque viro: = *et de quo viro*, *i.e.*, 'be careful what you say and about whom and to whom.'

70. patulae: the man who is *percontator*, eager to ask questions, will be also eager to hear the answers.

71. A familiar thought, which is found in various forms; cf. *A. P.* 390, *nescit vox missa reverti*.

72-75. non . . . ulceret: an excellent example of *non* with a subjunctive of will, which should not be dodged by twisting the mode into a potential or by connecting *non* with *ulla*. Cf. *Sat.* 2, 5, 91, note. — **pueri, puellae**: with *munere*. — **parvo**: small in comparison to the benefits which might have followed, if the relation with the patron had continued. — **beet**: *i.e.*, the patron would think the gift a full discharge of all obligation or perhaps would be annoyed (*angat*).

76. commendes: *introduce.* — The Romans made frequent use of the privilege of introducing a friend to the attention of men in high position. Cf. especially *Epist.* 1, 9.

incutiant aliena tibi peccata pudorem.
Fallimur et quondam non dignum tradimus; ergo
quem sua culpa premet, deceptus omitte tueri,
80　ut penitus notum, si temptent crimina, serves,
tuterisque tuo fidentem praesidio : qui
dente Theonino cum circumroditur, ecquid
ad te post paullo ventura pericula sentis?
Nam tua res agitur, paries cum proximus ardet,
85　et neglecta solent incendia sumere vires.
Dulcis inexpertis cultura potentis amici;
expertus metuit.　Tu, dum tua navis in alto est,
hoc age, ne mutata retrorsum te ferat aura.
Oderunt hilarem tristes tristemque iocosi,
90　sedatum celeres, agilem navumque remissi;

77. **aliena**: 'of the other person,' the friend thus introduced.

78. **fallimur**: 'it is true that we sometimes make mistakes, in spite of our best care.' — **ergo**: 'since this does happen, be prepared for it.'

79. **deceptus**: with emphasis; 'when it is clear that you have made a mistake.'

80. **penitus notum**: *i.e.*, 'a friend whom you know so well that you cannot possibly be mistaken in him'; the opposite of *non dignum* and *quem . . . premet*. — **crimina**: 'unfounded accusations'; cf. *Sat.* 1, 3, 60 f., *cum genus hoc inter vitae versetur, ubi acris invidia atque vigent ubi crimina*.

81. **fidentem**: the *penitus no-*

tum. — **qui**: connective; 'for when he is attacked, do you not see that you will likewise suffer in the same way?'

82. **dente Theonino**: 'by the tooth of envy.' Cf. *Sat.* 1, 4, 81, *absentem qui rodit*. But the allusion in *Theonino* is obscure; the story told by the Scholiast is quite inapplicable.

86-88. A parenthetic injunction, to enforce what has been said and to introduce the few miscellaneous warnings (89-96) which follow. In these Horace returns to the thought with which he began, the danger of *asperitas agrestis*, to which Lollius was exposed by his independence of temper, and warns him against the error of refusing to conform to the moods of his patron.

[potores bibuli media de nocte Falerni]
oderunt porrecta negantem pocula, quamvis
nocturnos iures te formidare tepores.
Deme supercilio nubem; plerumque modestus
95 occupat obscuri speciem, taciturnus acerbi.
Inter cuncta leges et percontabere doctos,
qua ratione queas traducere leniter aevum;
num te semper inops agitet vexetque cupido,
num pavor et rerum mediocriter utilium spes;
100 virtutem doctrina paret naturane donet;
quid minuat curas, quid te tibi reddat amicum;
quid pure tranquillet, honos, an dulce lucellum,
an secretum iter et fallentis semita vitae.
Me quotiens reficit gelidus Digentia rivus,

91. This verse is not found in good Mss. It was made up out of *Epist.* 1, 14, 34, *quem bibulum liquidi media de luce Falerni*, to supply a subject for *oderunt* in the next line.

92-93. **oderunt**: the subject is implied in *porrecta*. — **quamvis**: *i.e.*, 'however good the excuse you may offer for your refusal.' — **tepores**: the heating effect of wine.

94-95. **nubem**: the figure is still in use, though with reference to the forehead rather than to the eyebrow alone. The thought is more fully explained in the following sentence, to which *deme . . . nubem* is an introduction. — **plerumque**: *often*, not 'generally, usually.' — **occupat**: cf. *Carm.* 4, 9, 46 f., *rectius occupat nomen beati*. — **obscuri**: *secretive*. — **acerbi**: the reserve of a taciturn man may easily be mistaken for disapproval.

96. **inter cuncta**: *i.e.*, 'amid all the chances and changes of life.' — **lĕges**: not *lēges*. — **doctos**: *the wise*, the philosophers.

99. **mediocriter**: with *utilium*.

100. This question was often debated in philosophy.

102. **dulce**: ironical.

103. **fallentis semita vitae**: cf. *Epist.* 1, 17, 10, *qui natus moriensque fefellit:*

104-112. 'For myself, I have known such a life as you are living and have now entered upon the path of a quiet life.' — **Digentia**: the stream which flowed through his valley, *Epist.* 1, 16, 12 — **Mandela**: a village near the farm, the inhabitants of which drew their

105 quem Mandela bibit, rugosus frigore pagus,
   quid sentire putas, quid credis, amice, precari?
   Sit mihi quod nunc est, etiam minus, et mihi vivam
   quod superest aevi, si quid superesse volunt di.
   Sit bona librorum et provisae frugis in annum
110 copia, neu fluitem dubiae spe pendulus horae.
   Sed satis est orare Iovem quae donat et aufert;
   det vitam, det opes, aequum mi animum ipse parabo.

water from the Digentia. — **rugosus**: *i.e.*, in winter. — **sit mihi**: cf. the prayer of *Carm.* I, 31, 17 ff.

'Frui paratis et valido mihi,
  Latoe, dones ac precor integra
  Cum mente, nec turpem senectam
      Degere nec cithara carentem.'

— **mihi vivam**: *i.e.*, 'live my own quiet life.' — **fluitem . . . pendulus**: 'be tossed about like a leaf.' The thought is repeated in *aequum animum*. — **sed satis est**: *i.e.*, 'but I need pray only for those things which I cannot secure myself, for *vitam* (= 107-108) and *opes* (vs. 109); the spirit of the philosopher I will myself provide.'

19

This Epistle was written just before the publication of the collection, in the year 20 B.C. It is fitly addressed, like *Epist.* I, I, to Maecenas, as the most cordial and intimate of the poet's friends and admirers.

'There is an old idea that poets should drink wine. Cratinus held this, and Homer and Ennius, too, and I once laid down the same doctrine. Since then my contemporaries have reeked of wine, as if one could become a Cato by wearing a toga like his. Imitation of eccentricities is not very laudable, nor, in fact, is any kind of imitation. From that fault I have kept myself free. Archilochus was my leader in the Epodes, but I followed him exactly as Alcaeus and Sappho did, learning from him the lyric art, but using it for other purposes than his. So also I followed Alcaeus and Sappho in turn in the Odes, and I claim with pride, as I said at the time when the Odes were published, to have been the first of Romans to carry on the tradition of the lyric poetry of Lesbos.

'If you ask why my poetry has not won greater applause, I can easily answer the question; it is because I have not sought for the favor of critics and cliques. And when I say that I cannot venture to submit my trifles to their learned judgment, they accuse me of laughing at them. The result is that I don't dare to show any contempt at all; I back out of the contest; they might be the death of me, if they knew what I really think of them.'

Under the form of an Epistle to Maecenas Horace is here defending his Odes against the critics, as in his earlier career he had defended himself in *Sat.* 1, 4 and *Sat.* 1, 10 and had made sport of his detractors in *Sat.* 2, 1. Of the occasion for such replies we know little except by inference. Vergil, highly as he was honored during his lifetime, was also severly criticized, so that his friends felt called upon to defend him. That Horace should have been the object of similar attacks, made all the more bitter by his intimacy with Maecenas, is altogether natural. With respect to the Odes, published in 23 B.C., the criticism took the form of a charge of lack of originality. To this Horace replies, first by a kind of definition of servile imitation, and then by a statement of his real relation to the Greek lyric poets. He stood, he says, in precisely the same relation to Alcaeus and Sappho in which they stood to Archilochus; he was an artist of the same school, not an imitator. This is, of course, the true explanation of the relation of any poet or artist to his predecessors; a proper understanding of it would have saved modern critics from repeating the statement that Latin literature is imitative.

> Prisco si credis, Maecenas docte, Cratino,
> nulla placere diu nec vivere carmina possunt
> quae scribuntur aquae potoribus. Vt male sanos

1. **prisco . . . Cratino**: one of the poets of the Old Comedy mentioned in *Sat.* 1, 4, 1. The adj. *priscus* is used because it was the technical rhetorical term for the *prisca comoedia*. Cratinus' fondness for wine was frequently referred to and had become traditional. — **docte**: so of Maecenas, *Carm.* 3, 8, 5, *docte sermones utriusque linguae*; his acquaintance with literature would have made the sayings of Cratinus familiar to him.

2-3. This precise sentiment is not found in any of the fragments of the plays of Cratinus. It is, however, merely a lively expression of the praise of wine which is frequent in all literature; cf. *Carm.* 1, 18, 3, *siccis omnia nam dura deus proposuit.* — **diu**: with *placere*, not with *vivere*, which contains the idea in itself.

3. **ut**: *since.* — **male sanos**: = *insanos, i.e.,* inspired by the Muses. But Horace always uses this adj.

adscripsit Liber Satyris Faunisque poetas,
5 vina fere dulces oluerunt mane Camenae.
Laudibus arguitur vini vinosus Homerus;
Ennius ipse pater nunquam nisi potus ad arma
prosiluit dicenda. 'Forum putealque Libonis
mandabo siccis, adimam cantare severis':
10 hoc simul edixi non cessavere poetae
nocturno certare mero, putere diurno.
Quid si quis vultu torvo ferus et pede nudo

of poets with a humorous or scornful tone; cf. *Sat.* 2, 3, 322; *Sat.* 2, 7, 117, *aut insanit homo aut versus facit.*

4. **adscripsit...Satyris**: 'added them to the list,' 'enrolled them with his satyrs.' This is not a reference to some definite myth, but only a humorous way of saying 'from the beginnings of poetry.'

5. **fere**: *usually.* — **mane**: 'the next morning,' 'the morning after,' from the fumes of the night's drinking.

6. **laudibus**: they are merely the traditional praises, a line here and there. — **vinosus**: predicate; 'is accused of being.'

7. **Ennius**: there was a tradition that he had gout, based perhaps upon a line from one of his *saturae* (*numquam poetor nisi si podager*) the form of which seems to have been in Horace's mind.

8. **prosiluit**: he sprang forward like one of the fighters he described. — **puteal Libonis**: a spot in the Forum which had been struck by lightning and therefore, as sacred, surrounded by a low wall. It is said by the Scholiast to have been the place where the praetor held court. The sense would then be, 'business and public affairs I will leave to water drinkers.'

9. **cantare**: *i.e.*, 'poetry.' — **severis**: the same as *siccis*.

10-11. **edixi**: a formal word used of the edict of the praetor. — **putere**: the expected verb would be *certare*, but *putere* is substituted ironically. — The sentence continues the previous course of thought; 'Cratinus taught that poets should be drinkers; so, it is said, did Homer and Ennius, and when Bacchus enrolled poets among his followers, the very Muses took to hard drinking. Now it is my turn; when I sang the praises of wine, my fellow-poets began to sit up all night over the bottle.'

12-14. 'But bare feet and a scanty toga do not make a Cato.'

exiguaeque togae simulet textore Catonem,
virtutemne repraesentet moresque Catonis?
15 Rupit Iarbitam Timagenis aemula lingua,
dum studet urbanus tenditque disertus haberi.
Decipit exemplar vitiis imitabile: quodsi
pallerem casu, biberent exsangue cuminum.
O imitatores, servum pecus, ut mihi saepe
20 bilem saepe iocum vestri movere tumultus!
Libera per vacuum posui vestigia princeps,

— **pede nudo**: in imitation of the strict fashion of the older time. — **exiguae**: cf. *arta toga, Epist.* 1, 18, 30. — **textore**: abl. of means; 'by the help of a weaver of a scanty toga.' — **repraesentet**: not exactly with the meaning of the corresponding English word, but 'bring before us,' 'show us in his own person.'

15-16. The point of the allusion is that Iarbitas tried to rival Timagenes in rhetorical skill, but succeeded only in imitating his fault of bitterness. This is the same as the point of vss. 12-14, that one cannot acquire the character of Cato by imitating his eccentricities, and the two illustrations are summed up in vs. 17. Timagenes was a Greek rhetorician of considerable ability (*urbanus, disertus*), who fell into disgrace because of the bitterness of his wit. Iarbitas is perhaps the nickname of a certain Cordus, who may be the Codrus referred to by Vergil, *Ecl.* 7, 26, *invidia rumpantur ut ilia Codro*. But the allusion must remain obscure in its details, though the general sense is clear. — **rupit**: a reference to the fable of the Ox and the Frog, to which Horace alludes also in *Sat.* 2, 3, 314 ff. The Scholiast, however, takes it literally. — **Timagenis**: gen. after *aemula*. — **lingua**: i.e., 'the tongue of Iarbitas was his ruin.'

17. **decipit**: the emphatic word: 'we make a mistake when we follow an example by a mere imitation of faults and eccentricities, as when we suppose that we must be hard drinkers in order to be poets.' — **vitiis**: with *imitabile*.

18. **casu**: *by mere chance*; it would have no meaning, any more than Cato's toga had. — **exsangue**: 'to produce paleness.'

19. **imitatores**: primarily the men who imitated Horace himself, but also in a general sense. — **servum**: the adjective.

21. **libera, per vacuum, princeps**: an emphatic assertion of his own freedom from slavish imi-

non aliena meo pressi pede. Qui sibi fidet,
dux reget examen. Parios ego primus iambos
ostendi Latio, numeros animosque secutus
25 Archilochi, non res et agentia verba Lycamben.
Ac ne me foliis ideo brevioribus ornes
quod timui mutare modos et carminis artem,
temperat Archilochi Musam pede mascula Sappho,
temperat Alcaeus, sed rebus et ordine dispar,

tation, which is explained in the following verses, down to 31.

23. **dux reget**: *i.e.*, 'will be the leader of the swarm, like a queen bee.' — **Parios ... iambos**: 'such iambic measures as were used by Archilochus of Paros.' This refers to the Epodes, that is, to couplets of iambic measure used for satirical purposes; both form and spirit (*numeros animosque*) are included in this technical use of the word *iambi*. Iambic senarius is the ordinary verse of Latin comedy and is of course not meant here.

25. **non res**: *i.e.*, 'but the form and spirit were employed upon a wholly different subject-matter.' — **agentia verba Lycamben**: it is the tradition that Lycambes was attacked by Archilochus with so much bitterness that he hanged himself. The phrase must be taken as a whole; Horace means that he did not imitate the savageness of Archilochus' language.

27. **modos et ... artem**: the same as *numeros animosque*, vs. 24.

28. **temperat**: in the rhetorical sense, of regulating and shaping the rhythm of verse or prose. — **Archilochi**: with *pede*; 'by the measures of Archilochus.' — **mascula**: *i.e.*, not a weak woman, but the equal of men in poetry.

29. **Alcaeus**: compare the noble tribute to Alcaeus and Sappho in *Carm.* 2, 13, 24–36. — **ordine**: in the arrangement of different lines to form a strophe, like the Alcaic or Sapphic. In general the thought here repeats the thought of vss. 24–25; *temperat* is the same as *secutus*, *pede* repeats *numeros*, *rebus* corresponds to *res*, and vss. 30–31 expand *agentia verba Lycamben*. This makes complete the parallel between Horace and the two Greek lyric poets; he has done exactly what Alcaeus and Sappho did. To this parallelism he makes a slight exception in *ordine*, because he recognizes fully in the Odes the claim of Alcaeus and Sappho to be considered the originators of the two strophes which bear their names.

30 nec socerum quaerit quem versibus oblinat atris,
nec sponsae laqueum famoso carmine nectit.
Hunc ego non alio dictum prius ore Latinus
vulgavi fidicen; iuvat immemorata ferentem
ingenuis oculisque legi manibusque teneri.
35 Scire velis mea cur ingratus opuscula lector
laudet ametque domi, premat extra limen iniquus?
Non ego ventosae plebis suffragia venor
impensis cenarum et tritae munere vestis;
non ego, nobilium scriptorum auditor et ultor,
40 grammaticas ambire tribus et pulpita dignor.

30. **socerum**: Archilochus had desired to marry the daughter of Lycambes.

31. **sponsae**: used like *socerum*, of the relation which Archilochus desired. The tradition is that she also hanged herself in consequence of the bitterness of the attacks upon her father and herself. — **famoso**: so *famosis versibus*, *Sat.* 2, 1, 68, of the satires of Lucilius.

32. **hunc**: Alcaeus, the last referred to. — **non alio ... ore**: the Alcaic strophe had not been used before in Latin poetry. This repeats the claim made in the epilogue to the Odes, *Carm.* 3, 30, 13 f., *princeps Aeolium carmen ad Italos deduxisse modos.*

33. **iuvat**: i.e., 'I feel pride in what I have done and in the class of readers to whom I appeal.' — **immemorata**: 'things hitherto unuttered'; this is the early sense of *memorare*, 'to tell, to utter.'

34. **ingenuis**: in contrast to *servum pecus*, vs. 19. Horace frequently expresses his pleasure at being recognized by competent judges, e.g., *Sat.* 1, 10, 72 ff.; 2, 1, 74 ff.

35. **opuscula**: this must refer to the Odes.

36. **premat ... iniquus**: to be taken together; 'is unjustly critical.'

37-38. **ventosae**: cf. *Epist.* 1, 8, 12, where Horace uses the word of himself. The belief that democracies were fickle is a very old one and is still held by some persons, in spite of the facts. — **suffragia**: a condensed comparison: 'I am not like an office seeker, who hunts for votes.' The thought is then repeated in plainer words, though still with some figurative expressions, in vss. 39-40. — **impensis ... munere**: ordinary means of indirect bribery.

39-40. 'I do not try to win the favor of other poets by an inter-

Hinc illae lacrimae. 'Spissis indigna theatris
scripta pudet recitare et nugis addere pondus,'
si dixi, ' Rides,' ait, ' et Iovis auribus ista
servas ; fidis enim manare poetica mella
45 te solum, tibi pulcher.' Ad haec ego naribus uti
formido, et luctantis acuto ne secer ungui,
' Displicet iste locus,' clamo, et diludia posco.

change of compliments.' — **nobilium**: ironical, as in *par nobile fratrum*, *Sat.* 2, 3, 243; 'writers who think themselves famous.' — **auditor et ultor**: *i.e.*, 'by listening to their readings from their works and by reading mine to them for their approval.' The best parallel to this is Juv. 1, 1, *semper ego auditor tantum? numquamne reponam . . . ?* The custom of giving readings, which had already become wearisome, tended to form mutual admiration societies, and the attendance at such readings was therefore a kind of bribe to win approval for one's own writings. *Ultor* is intentionally substituted for some word like *recitator*, to make the irony plainer. — **tribus**: this recurs to the figure of 37-38. —**pulpita**: the *platforms* from which the critics lectured.

41. **hinc illae lacrimae**: this phrase was first used in Latin literature by Terence (*Andr.* 125 f.) and had become proverbial, as it has in English, always with an ironical tone. — **spissis . . . theatris**: the halls where public readings were given, which were crowded with poets and literary critics. There is no reference to the performance of plays. — **indigna**: this is said with pretended modesty, like *opuscula*, vs. 35, and *nugis* in the next line.

42. **addere pondus**: *i.e.*, to treat them as if they were weighty utterances.

43. **rides**: *you are ironical*; *i.e.*, 'my critic seems to find my humility merely affected,' as of course it was. From this point to the end the tone is wholly one of scornful and open irony, as in the close of *Sat.* 1, 10. — **Iovis**: Augustus, as the supreme representative of the inner circle of cultivated readers.

44. **fidis**: 'for you feel a conceited confidence in the quality of your poetry.' — **mella**: a cognate accus. after *manare*.

45. **naribus uti**: cf. *naso suspendis adunco*, *Sat.* 1, 6, 5, and note.

46. **formido**: entirely ironical, since he is at this moment expressing his scorn (*naribus uti*) in the very act of pretending to conceal it.

47. **displicet iste locus**: the cry

> Ludus enim genuit trepidum certamen et iram,
> ira truces inimicitias et funebre bellum.

of a contestant, a wrestler or gladiator, who thinks that his opponent has an unfair advantage in position and who therefore demands a pause (*diludia*) to equalize the conditions. The reference to the *pulpita*, 40, and *theatris* is secondary.

48-49. 'For the consequences may be most serious'; still, of course, with irony. Cf. Thackeray, 'The Rose and the Ring,'

'Critics serve us authors thus;
Sport to them is death to us.'

— **ludus**: with reference to *diludia*. — The adjectives are intentionally extravagant, *trepidum*, *truces*, *funebre*, carrying out the irony of *formido*.

20

An Epilogue to the collection of Epistles, written in the year 20, after the other poems were collected for publication.

'You are eager to see the world, my book, like a young slave who seeks to escape from the house of a good master. Go, then, and meet your fate; you will, I think, have some readers, but I do not predict for you an immortality of favor.

'While the favor lasts, tell your readers what I am, a freedman's son who feels himself now coming to middle age.'

This poem is, on the one side, an expression of the writer's hopes and fears, as he sends a new book out into the world. It is done, as one would expect from Horace, without flourish of trumpets; he is quite aware of the fact that the book has merits, but he knows also that it is not the greatest book that was ever written. On this side the poem might be compared with Catullus's address to his new book, with Ovid's *Tristia* 1, 1 and Martial, 1, 3. On the other side, this epistle is like the biographies which were often appended to standard editions, much as the *Vita* by Suetonius is preserved in the Mss. of Horace's complete works. The brief 'Life' of the author gives his birth and origin (20), his rise in life (21-23), his appearance and character (24-25), and his age (26-28), as such things are given in biographies of the standard form. Propertius (1, 22) and Ovid (*Amor.* 3, 15) have followed the same custom.

Vertumnum Ianumque, liber, spectare videris,
scilicet ut prostes Sosiorum pumice mundus.
Odisti clavis et grata sigilla pudico;
paucis ostendi gemis et communia laudas,
5   non ita nutritus. Fuge quo descendere gestis.
Non erit emisso reditus tibi. 'Quid miser egi?
quid volui?' dices, ubi quis te laeserit, et scis
in breve te cogi, cum plenus languet amator.
Quodsi non odio peccantis desipit augur,
10 carus eris Romae donec te deseret aetas;

1. **Vertumnum**: a shrine of this god was in the Vicus Tuscus, a street leading down from the Forum toward the river; there were booksellers' shops along this street. — **Ianum**: this may have been an archway over the Vicus Tuscus or one of the arches in the Forum; cf. *Epist.* 1, 1, 54. The two names together stand for a quarter of the city where books were sold and where also, carrying out the double meaning of the Epistle, there were houses of ill-repute.

2. **scilicet ut**: cf. *Epist.* 1, 9, 3, note. — **prostes**: in a double sense; cf. *prostibulum*, of a harlot. — **Sosii**: a well-known firm of booksellers, mentioned also in *A. P.* 345. — **pumice**: used to smooth the end of the papyrus roll; cf. Catull. 1, 1-2, *... libellum arido ... pumice expolitum.*

4. **gemis**: *i.e.*, 'you are dissatisfied with the admiration of my friends and wish for more admirers.'

5. **fuge**: *i.e.*, 'go quickly then, since you will have your way.' — **descendere**: the regular word for going down from the residence quarters, on the hills, to the Forum, with a secondary reference to the descent in life of the runaway slave.

6. **emisso**: primarily of the slave, but also of the book; cf. *Epist.* 1, 18, 71, *et semel emissum volat irrevocabile verbum.*

7-8. **scis**: = *sentis*; the primary reference is to the book, rolled up (*in breve ... cogi*) and laid aside; with reference to the slave it means 'driven to poverty and hardship.' — **languet amator**: here the slave is chiefly in mind, yet the phrase may be used also of the tired reader.

10. **aetas**: *youth*, the flower of youth; so often of boys and girls. From this point the comparison of the book to the young slave is

contrectatus ubi manibus sordescere vulgi
coeperis, aut tineas pasces taciturnus inertis
aut fugies Vticam aut vinctus mitteris Ilerdam.
Ridebit monitor non exauditus, ut ille,
15   qui male parentem in rupes protrusit asellum
iratus: quis enim invitum servare laboret?
Hoc quoque te manet, ut pueros elementa docentem
occupet extremis in vicis balba senectus.
Cum tibi sol tepidus plures admoverit auris,
20   me libertino natum patre et in tenui re
maiores pennas nido extendisse loqueris,
ut quantum generi demas, virtutibus addas;

less prominent, though occasional words show that the figure is not forgotten.

11. **contrectatus ... manibus**: the buyer could take up the book and look at it as in a modern bookshop; cf. *Sat.* 1, 4, 72, *libellos quis manus insudet volgi*.

12-13. **taciturnus**: this word and *fugies* are selected for their suggestion of the slave, though the rest of the phrase is applicable only to the book. — **Vticam, Ilerdam**: in Africa and in Spain; they are selected as types of provincial towns, where books no longer salable in Rome might find purchasers.

14-16. **monitor**: Horace; cf. *augur*, vs. 9. — **protrusit**: since he could not keep the ass from the cliff, he gave up the effort and pushed him over. — **iratus**: cf. *odio peccantis*, vs. 9.

17. **elementa**: *i.e.*, used as a text-book for children who are learning to read and are too young to be interested in the sense. — **docentem**: sc. *te*.

19. **sol tepidus**: 'the warm sunshine of popular favor'; *i.e.*, 'when you are still fresh enough to have many readers.' [There are many varying explanations of this rather ambiguous phrase, but *tepeo, tepor, tepidus* in Horace always mean warmth in contrast to cold, except in *Sat.* 1, 3, 81, never warmth in contrast to heat. That in connection with *sol* it should mean anything but 'warm' is quite impossible.]

20. **libertino natum patre**: so *libertino patre natum, Sat.* 1, 6, 6; 45: 46, with emphatic repetition. — **in tenui re**: cf. *Sat.* 1, 6, 71, *macro pauper agello*, of his father.

22. **generi**: *birth*. The reason given in this line is one which could not have been expressed in *Sat.* 1, 6, before he felt that his

me primis urbis belli placuisse domique;
corporis exigui, praecanum, solibus aptum,
25 irasci celerem, tamen ut placabilis essem.
Forte meum si quis te percontabitur aevum,
me quater undenos sciat implevisse Decembris,
collegam Lepidum quo duxit Lollius anno.

position was secure, though it was doubtless even then in his mind.

23. belli . . . domique: with *primis*, not with *placuisse*. Cf., in general, *Sat.* 2, 1, 76, *Epist.* 1, 17, 35.

24. corporis exigui: *short of stature*, as is said in the Vita of Suetonius; 'habita corporis fuit brevis atque obesus.' — praecanum: *gray before my time*, as he was only forty-four years old. — solibus aptum: the Romans made less use than we of artificial heating and so arranged their porticoes as to have convenient places sheltered from the wind and open to the winter sun. Many passages show that Horace disliked cold weather.

25. irasci celerem: the *vitium irae* is one to which Horace frequently refers in such a way as to acknowledge his own proneness to it.

27. Decembris: the month in which his birthday came.

28. The year 21 B.C. The peculiar word *duxit* is used because Lollius was at first consul alone and 'brought in' Lepidus as his colleague only after long delay. The birthday named would of course be the last one preceding the time of writing, which was in the summer or autumn of 20 B.C.

LIBER SECVNDVS

I

The date of this Epistle can be determined with a fair degree of precision. It is probable that Horace wrote it, in accordance with the custom which he had followed in publishing other collections of poems, after the other Epistles, 2 and 3 (the *Ars Poetica*), to serve as an introduction and to dedicate the whole collection to the person addressed in this letter. This general probability is supported by a passage in the *Vita* of Suetonius: 'post sermones vero quosdam lectos nullam sui mentionem habitam ita sit questus: "irasci me tibi scito, quod non in plerisque eius modi scriptis mecum potissimum loquaris. An vereris ne apud posteros infame tibi sit, quod videaris familiaris nobis esse?" expresseritque eclogam ad se cuius initium est *cum tot sustineas* . . . .' This story comes immediately after a reference to the Carmen Saeculare and the Fourth Book of the Odes. The *sermones quosdam* and the *eius modi scriptis* cannot have been the Satires, published fifteen years earlier, and can scarcely have been the First Book of the Epistles, which had been before the public for some years. These words must therefore refer to *Epist.* 2, 2 and 3, already known to Augustus before they were formally published. All this falls into proper sequence with the references to the campaigns of 15-14 B.C., referred to in vss. 252-253, and points to 14 or 13 B.C. as the date of composition.

The course of thought is natural and easy, shifting from one aspect of the subject to another without following a formal scheme. Some general divisions will be noticed: vss. 5-92, the overestimate of early writers in comparison with new poetry; 93-117, the historical development which has resulted in the present situation; 118-138, the contributions of the poet to the welfare of society; 139-213, the special disadvantages and defects of dramatic writing; 214-250, the good influence of the patronage of Augustus upon literature; 250-270, Horace's own relation to the patronage of Augustus.

In the Second Book of the Epistles the form of versified letter is somewhat changed. The three Epistles are all long and their very length destroys the illusion of the letter form: they necessarily become essays, addressed, it is true, to an individual, but intended for the public

In this Epistle the personal tone is also subdued by the fact that it was addressed to the Emperor. The opening lines, therefore, though they are concerned entirely with the personal aspect and not at all with the subject of the letter, are distinctly and quite properly formal. The close, from vs. 250 to the end, is also personal, having to do with Horace's own relation to literature and to Augustus, and here there is a lighter tone, especially from vs. 264 to the end. At other points, too, as in 214 ff., there is a certain measure of appeal to Augustus to use his influence for the good of literature. In general, however, Horace has not made any very serious effort to preserve the illusion of a letter.

On the other hand, this is not a formal essay; it is rather the unstudied comment of a veteran man of letters upon the condition and prospects of the literature of his time. The particular subjects selected for comment or criticism are not indeed limited to Horace's own experience, but they are in part suggested by it. The whole of the first third of the Epistle is a protest against the over-valuation of the early Latin poetry and a defense of living writers, including Horace himself, against the disposition to undervalue the present. This is, in some sense, a continuation of the argument of *Sat.* 1, 4; 1, 10; 2, 1, and *Epist.* 1, 19, but it would be pressing it too far to find in it the motive of the whole letter. In other parts, in 118-138, in 139 ff., Horace is writing as a student of literary history, selecting such portions of the rhetorical tradition as suited his purpose and using them to illustrate and define the situation of his time.

This Epistle deserves most careful reading. Much of the subject-matter, it is true, has no immediate relation to modern conditions, though the comments upon the stage are an exception and might have been written for a magazine in this century. The literary history, also, must be taken with much reserve; it is only the current teaching of the scholar and is in many points quite incorrect. But the easy turn of the thought, the mastery of happy expression, the humor and the occasional satire, all show that Horace came toward the close of life with ripening powers — *integra cum mente*, as he had wished.

> Cum tot sustineas et tanta negotia solus,
> res Italas armis tuteris, moribus ornes,

1. **solus**: others (Agrippa, Tiberius) were associated with him, but the real responsibility rested upon Augustus alone.

2. **res Italas**: no more than *rem publicam*, 'the state.' — **moribus**: one of the purposes which Augustus kept most distinctly before

legibus emendes, in publica commoda peccem,
si longo sermone morer tua tempora, Caesar.
5 Romulus et Liber pater et cum Castore Pollux,
post ingentia facta deorum in templa recepti,
dum terras hominumque colunt genus, aspera bella
componunt, agros adsignant, oppida condunt,
ploravere suis non respondere favorem
10 speratum meritis. Diram qui contudit hydram
notaque fatali portenta labore subegit,

him was the need of social reform, which he attempted to bring about by a return to stricter standards. He took great pains to set a good example himself and tried, though with little success, to train his family in the good old ways. — ornes: *provide, furnish*; this is the proper sense of *ornare*.

3. **legibus**: many laws were passed to regulate marriage and divorce, to control bribery, to limit expense, all with very small results.

4. **longo**: this and the other epistles of this book are in fact long, as compared with Horace's other writings. He does not mean, therefore, 'if I should delay you by a long discourse,' but 'if this long epistle should detain you.' The modest suggestion is ' do not allow me to detain you, but put off the reading to a convenient time.'

5-17. 'Other heroes have not been honored till after their death, but we have recognized your worth while you are still with us.'

5. **Liber**: the god Dionysus, as a bringer of civilization, who taught men to cultivate the vine, not Bacchus, as the god of drinking. — The list of beneficent gods and heroes, Romulus, Liber, Castor and Pollux, Hercules, is traditional and occurs with slight variations in many places, *e.g.*, *Carm.* 1, 12, 21-28; 3, 3, 9-16; Cic. *de Nat. Deor.* 2, 24, 62, where Aesculapius is added.

6. **templa**: *i.e.*, into the dwelling places of the gods in heaven; an old sense of *templum*.

7-8. The various steps in advancing civilization. Cf. *Sat.* 1, 3, 99-105.

10. **contudit**: *crushed* with his club.

11. **fatali**: 'decreed by the Fates,' *fated*, not 'fatal.' — **portenta**: he is thinking especially of those labors of Hercules which consisted in the killing of destructive monsters.

comperit invidiam supremo fine domari.
Vrit enim fulgore suo, qui praegravat artes
infra se positas, extinctus amabitur idem.
15 Praesenti tibi maturos largimur honores
iurandasque tuum per numen ponimus aras,
nil oriturum alias, nil ortum tale fatentes.
Sed tuus hic populus sapiens et iustus in uno,
te nostris ducibus, te Graiis anteferendo,
20 cetera nequaquam simili ratione modoque
aestimat, et nisi quae terris semota suisque

12. **invidiam**: this repeats the thought of vs. 9 and leads on to the main theme, the *invidia* which poets encountered. Strictly, the word is not in place in the story of Hercules.—**supremo fine**: *i.e.*, 'only by death,' 'not until after his death.'

13-14. **urit**: transferred from physical pain to the suffering of emotion. Here the physical sense is to *dazzle, blind*, as *fulgore* shows. — **praegravat**: literally, *weighs down*; to be interpreted with *infra se positas*. — **artes**: *powers*, almost the same as *virtutes*. — The whole expression is difficult of analysis, first, because two different figures are used in *urit* and *praegravat*, and, second, because of the mixture of the concrete (*qui, extinctus, amabitur*) and the abstract (*praegravat, artes*). The underlying sense is 'he who is superior to others in his powers and who thus makes others feel their inferiority, excites envy by his greatness.' — **ama-**

bitur: 'but after his death his virtues are recognized,'

15. **praesenti tibi**: 'to you, it is true, recognition has come during your lifetime.' — **maturos**: *i.e.*, 'before it was too late.'

16. **numen**: an unofficial deification of Augustus began early (29 B.C.) in the provinces and was then taken up in some parts of Italy. But the only formal recognition of this in Rome was a cult of the *genius Augusti*, with altars where oaths could be taken. The complete deification was not until after the death of Augustus, who during his lifetime discouraged these extravagances.

18. 'But this recognition of present merit is by no means extended to poets and poetry.'— **tuus**: with reference back to vss. 15-17.

19. **anteferendo**: in apposition with *uno*, anticipating the single exception to *cetera*.

21-22. **terris semota**: 'which

temporibus defuncta videt, fastidit et odit,
sic fautor veterum, ut tabulas peccare vetantes,
quas bis quinque viri sanxerunt, foedera regum
25 vel Gabiis vel cum rigidis aequata Sabinis,
pontificum libros, annosa volumina vatum,
dictitet Albano Musas in monte locutas.

had passed away from the earth.'
— **temporibus defuncta**: 'and had completed the time allotted to them.' The phrases belong strictly to the writers of books, rather than to the writings.

23. **sic fautor**: the verbal force of many nouns was so strongly felt that they may even, in combination with *esse*, take an accusative, or, as here, an adverb. Translate by a verb; 'and so strongly favors ancient writings that. . . .' — **veterum**: neuter, like *cetera*. — **tabulas**: the Twelve Tables.

24. **bis quinque viri**: the Decemvirs.

25. **Gabiis**: governed by the following *cum*. A copy of this treaty, made by Tarquin with Gabii, written in archaic letters on bull's hide, was still in existence in the time of Dionysius of Halicarnassus, in Horace's time. Cf. Livy, 1, 54. Several treaties with the Sabines were preserved. — **aequata**: *ratified*. The implication that they were 'on equal terms' is merely conventional.

26. **pontificum libros**: the records of rituals and of events of religious significance, dating back to the earliest use of writing in Rome. — **volumina**: prophecies and oracles, written in some of the early verse forms like the Saturnian. Livy mentions in 25, 12 certain *carmina* which foretold the battle of Cannae.

27. **dictitet**: the subject is still *populus*. — **Albano . . . in monte**: one of the most sacred spots in early Roman worship; if the Muses transferred their home from Greece to Italy, as such opinions would seem to imply, then the Alban Mount would become their Helicon. — **Musas . . . locutas**: this seems to be a reminiscence of the phrase of Aelius Stilo and Varro, quoted by Quint. 10, 1, 99, 'Musas Plautino sermone locuturas fuisse, si Latine loqui vellent.' — Though these early records are lost, there are fragments enough to show that they were composed in an extremely formal and cramped style, that they were, in fact, not literature at all. Horace is using extreme examples to lay a foundation for his argument against the school of critics who maintained with an excess of zeal

Si, quia Graiorum sunt antiquissima quaeque
scripta vel'optima, Romani pensantur eadem
30 scriptores trutina, non est quod multa loquamur:
nil intra est olea, nil extra est in nuce duri;
venimus ad summum fortunae, pingimus atque
psallimus et luctamur Achivis doctius unctis.
Si meliora dies, ut vina, poemata reddit,
35 scire velim chartis pretium quotus adroget annus.

the value of the early Latin literature.

28-33. 'The fact that the oldest Greek writers are the best does not prove that the same thing is true in Latin literature.'

28. Graiorum: the more poetic word. In the Satires Horace prefers *Graecus*; but the distinction is not sharply made, cf. vs. 90, below.

29. optima: Horace is thinking in a general way of the fact that Greek literature begins with Homer; he is not following out the argument into details, like the comparison of the merits of Archilochus and Alcaeus, and he is not thinking at all of the place of tragedy.

30. trutina: cf. the similar use of this figure in *Sat.* 1, 3, 72, where *ponetur* corresponds to *pensantur*. — **non est quod**: *i.e.*, 'there is no more to be said.' 'it is an end of all rational argument, and we can prove anything.'

31. intra, extra: adverbs. — **olea**: with *in* to be supplied from *in nuce*; cf. *Gabiis*, vs. 25. — **duri**: with *nil*. 'The same kind of argument from analogy would prove that as a nut is hard outside and soft inside, so an olive must be the same.'

32-33. 'By the same reasoning, as we have become masters of the world, we must be masters of the Greeks in all the arts.' This is another illustration, beside that of vs. 31, of the absurdities to which the argument of 28-29 would lead. — **pingimus, psallimus, luctamur**: literature, painting and sculpture, music, and gymnastics are the four liberal arts on which Greek education was based. — **unctis**: with reference only to the last mentioned art, *luctamur*.

34-49. A new argument: 'the measurement of poetry by its antiquity is absurd, because the standard is shifting. How many years are required to make a writer old?'

34. dies: *time*; cf. *Carm.* 3, 6, 45, *quid non imminuit dies?*

35. quotus ... annus: the English idiom requires a plural.

Scriptor abhinc annos centum qui decidit, inter
perfectos veteresque referri debet an inter
viles atque novos? Excludat iurgia finis.
'Est vetus atque probus centum qui perficit annos.'
40 Quid, qui deperiit minor uno mense vel anno,
inter quos referendus erit, veteresne poetas,
an quos et praesens et postera respuat aetas?
'Iste quidem veteres inter ponetur honeste,
qui vel mense brevi vel toto est iunior anno.'
45 Vtor permisso, caudaeque pilos ut equinae
paullatim vello et demo unum, demo etiam unum,
dum cadat elusus ratione ruentis acervi,

36. **decidit**: the figure of the falling leaf.

37. **referri**: *be set down, be counted*.

38. **finis**: a definite line, here a definite figure, like *centum*.

40. The argument is general, as *centum* was of course suggested as a round number; but Horace probably noticed the fact that this limit would exclude from the *veteres atque probi* Lucilius, who was highly praised by the admirers of the early literature. He died in 103 B.C., and would therefore fall short of the time by only a few years.

42. **respuat**: the subjv. means 'should, according to your rule, refuse to accept.'

43-44. 'Such a trifle as a month or even a whole year should not count.' — **iste**: 'the man you mention.' — **honeste**: *with credit, to his honor*.

45-47. The argument called *Sorites*, the argument of the 'falling heap.' Given a sufficient amount of grain to be called a heap (σωρός), will it still be a heap if one grain is taken away? And at what point, if one still continues to take away a grain at a time, will it cease to be a heap? Another form of the argument was to ask how many hairs may be lost before a man can fairly be called bald (φαλακρός). — **permisso**: the concession in vss. 43-44. — **caudae ... equinae**: this is either a confusion of the argument of the φαλακρός with a story about the pulling out of the hairs from a horse's tail one at a time, to show what may be accomplished by patience (Val. Max. 7, 3, 6), or it is some variant of the argument, unknown to us. — **ratione**: *the argument, the reasoning*.

qui redit ad fastos et virtutem aestimat annis
miraturque nihil nisi quod Libitina sacravit.
50 Ennius et sapiens et fortis et alter Homerus,
ut critici dicunt, leviter curare videtur
quo promissa cadant et somnia Pythagorea.
Naevius in manibus non est et mentibus haeret
paene recens? Adeo sanctum est vetus omne poema
55 Ambigitur quoties uter utro sit prior, aufert

48. **redit ad fastos**: 'turns back to the Fasti,' *i.e.*, goes to the record of years and dates for his standard. The general phrase is made more specific in *aestimat* and *miratur*.

49. **Libitina**: the goddess associated with funerals; cf. *Sat.* 2, 6, 19.

50–62. 'But let us look in more detail at the old and greatly admired Roman poets, and at the critical and popular judgments of them.'

50. **sapiens**: a general term of praise used also by Horace of Lucilius (*Sat.* 2, 1, 17). — **fortis**: with reference to his descriptions of wars and heroes. — **alter Homerus**: these words were used of him by Lucilius and expressed with exaggeration the prevalent attitude of critics.

51. **leviter curare**: 'to care but little,' 'to be indifferent.'

52. **quo ... cadant**: 'how they turn out.' — **somnia**: in the beginning of the *Annales* Ennius told how Homer had come to him in a dream and had said that Ennius was a reincarnation of Homer himself, according to the doctrine of the transmigration of souls, taught by Pythagoras. — These lines about Ennius give the critical estimate of students of the early literature like Varro, but with touches of irony, especially in *leviter curare videtur*; 'he is so securely established that he does not need to care — and in fact does not care — whether his performance equals his promise or not.'

53–54. **Naevius**: died in 204; writer of comedies and especially, in this connection, the first of Roman epic poets. His *Bellum Punicum* in Saturnian verse was supplanted by the Annals of Ennius, as that in turn gave way to the Aeneid. — **paene recens**: *i.e.*, 'we read him almost as if his works were still new,' a little hit at the critics, who, in spite of their praise of the old, are as eager as any one to read the last thing that has appeared.

55–56. **uter utro**: such questions were much debated by critics and grammarians; they arranged

Pacuvius docti famam senis, Accius alti,
dicitur Afrani toga convenisse Menandro,
Plautus ad exemplar Siculi properare Epicharmi,
vincere Caecilius gravitate, Terentius arte.
60 Hos ediscit et hos arto stipata theatro
spectat Roma potens; habet hos numeratque poetas
ad nostram tempus Livi scriptoris ab aevo.
Interdum vulgus rectum videt, est ubi peccat.
Si veteres ita miratur laudatque poetas,

writers in lists according to their merits, with some words of comment on each, as here. — **Pacuvius**: died in 132, one of the great tragic writers. — **Accius**: died in 104, also a writer of tragedies. The judgment here expressed was the traditional judgment and is repeated by Quintil. 10, 1, 77.

57–59. Four comic poets, with the conventional estimate of each. Afranius, a contemporary of Accius, wrote comedies on Roman subjects, called by grammarians *fabulae togatae*, but in the manner of the Greek New Comedy. He is said to have used material from Menander, and this is expressed in *toga convenisse*. Plautus (died in 184), the representative of the *fabula palliata*, comedy in which the actors wore the Greek *pallium*. His excellence was held to be in the quick and easy movement (*properare*) of his dialogue, in which he was thought to equal Epicharmus, a Sicilian writer of comedy. The general form of expression pairs Afranius and Plautus off together, though in fact Plautus should be classed with the two following writers. Caecilius (died about 168) was sometimes considered the greatest of the writers of the *fabula palliata*. Terentius (died in 160) was the last of the greater writers in this style. Of all these poets only the works of Plautus (twenty plays) and Terence (six plays) are preserved; the rest are in rather scanty fragments.

60. **arto**: so crowded that it seemed small.

61. **potens**: ironically, like *venimus ad summum fortunae*, vs. 32.

62. **Livi**: Livius Andronicus, the earliest of Latin writers, with whose production of a play, in 240 B.C., Latin literature was thought to have begun.

63. The thought is turning back from the judgment of critics to the popular opinion, connecting thus with vs. 18 ff.

64. **si**: the alternatives are put

65 ut nihil anteferat, nihil illis comparet, errat.
Si quaedam nimis antique, si pleraque dure
dicere credit eos, ignave multa fatetur,
et sapit et mecum facit et Iove iudicat aequo.
Non equidem insector delendaque carmina Livi
70 esse reor, memini quae plagosum mihi parvo
Orbilium dictare, sed emendata videri
pulchraque et exactis minimum distantia miror;
inter quae verbum emicuit si forte decorum et
si versus paullo concinnior unus et alter,
75 iniuste totum ducit venditque poema.

in two conditional clauses, without any indication of the adversative relation; cf. *Epist.* 1, 17, 6, and 11.

66–67. **antique**: in the old and stiff style. — **dure**: with special reference to the versification; cf. *Sat.* 1, 4, 8, *durus componere versus,* of Lucilius. — **ignave**: *flatly,* without making sufficient effort to find attractive and agreeable expression.— **pleraque**: *many things,* not 'most things.'

68. **mecum facit**: *supports my view.*

69. **delenda . . . esse reor**: a periphrasis for another verb like *insector;* 'I am not attacking or desiring-to-destroy . . . .' — **Livi**: selected here partly because he had not been mentioned in the list above, vss. 50–59, partly because his writings illustrate with special clearness the faults of the very early literature.

70–71. **plagosum . . . Orbilium**: the phrase of the pupil has conferred immortality upon the teacher. Suetonius included him in his *de Grammaticis*, with a reference to this passage. This was the school which Horace attended in Rome, *Sat.* 1, 6, 76 ff. — **dictare**: the poetry, probably the Latin translation of the Odyssey, was dictated to the pupils to be written down and learned.

72. **exactis . . . distantia**: *little short of perfect.* — **miror**: in intentional contrast to *insector, delenda . . . reor,* as a very mild expression of judgment.

73–75. **emicuit**: *stands out* above the mass, with *decorum,* as a predicate. — **versus**: Horace frequently refers to the great advance in the art of versification, which is most conspicuous in the hexameter. — **ducit venditque**: to be taken together, 'carries along and sells'; the first verb is, as often, very general and needs the

Indignor quidquam reprehendi, non quia crasse
compositum illepideve putetur, sed quia nuper;
nec veniam antiquis, sed honorem et praemia posci.
Recte necne crocum floresque perambulet Attae
80 fabula si dubitem, clament periisse pudorem
cuncti paene patres, ea cum reprehendere coner,
quae gravis Aesopus, quae doctus Roscius egit;
vel quia nil rectum nisi quod placuit sibi ducunt,
vel quia turpe putant parere minoribus et quae
85 imberbi didicere senes perdenda fateri.
Iam Saliare Numae carmen qui laudat, et illud,

interpretation of the more definite following word.

77. putetur: a verb of thinking is often illogically inserted into a causal clause in which the opinion of some other person than the writer is expressed, in order to emphasize by its meaning as well as by its mode the fact that the writer is not responsible for the opinion.

79. crocum floresque: the stage was sprinkled with saffron, to give a pleasant fragrance, and apparently with flowers, though the custom is not elsewhere alluded to. — **Attae**: T. Quinctius Atta, died in 78 B.C., a writer of comedies, *fabulae togatae*. He is not strictly among the *veteres*, but he illustrates the contrast between the treatment of living writers and of those no longer living.

81. patres: the men of an older generation, who had seen these plays in their youth.

82. Aesopus: a tragic actor of the Ciceronian period, highly esteemed for his acting and his character; hence *gravis*. — **Roscius**: an actor of comedy, also very highly regarded. Cicero's speech *pro Roscio Comoedo* was made in a suit to which he was a party.

83-85. These ordinary weaknesses of age are connected with the general course of thought by the fact that they explain the unreasonable prejudice against the new writers.

86. Saliare . . . carmen: a chant of the guild of the Salii, 'leaping' priests. The fragments are given in Baehrens' Fragmenta, pp. 29 ff. Quintilian (1, 6, 40) says of them *vix sacerdotibus suis satis intellecta*. — **Numae**: this king was traditionally regarded as the founder of many religious ceremonies.

quod mecum ignorat, solus vult scire videri,
ingeniis non ille favet plauditque sepultis,
nostra sed impugnat, nos nostraque lividus odit.
90 Quodsi tam Graecis novitas invisa fuisset
quam nobis, quid nunc esset vetus? Aut quid haberet,
quod legeret tereretque viritim publicus usus?
Vt primum positis nugari Graecia bellis
coepit et in vitium fortuna labier aequa,
95 nunc athletarum studiis nunc arsit equorum,
marmoris aut eboris fabros aut aeris amavit,

88. non favet plauditque: *i.e.*, 'such absurd praise of the past is not what it purports to be; it is in reality nothing but an expression of jealous dislike of the writers of the present.'

92. tereret: frequently used, as in English, of the wearing out of a book by repeated and careful reading. — **viritim ... usus**: a mixture. as in vss. 13-14, of the concrete and the abstract, to express emphatically the universal reading of the Greek writers.

93-117. Contrasts and resemblances in the history of civilization in Greece and in Rome.

93. positis ... bellis: after the great war for existence, the Persian War, was over. — **nugari**: *i.e.*, 'to turn to lighter pursuits.' The word does not necessarily imply censure; it is used by Horace (*Sat.* 1, 9, 2) and by Catullus (1, 4) of their own lyric poetry; yet there is in it and in *vitium* something of the Roman feeling that art is not quite a serious business.

94. labier: = *labi*; Horace uses this old form some half a dozen times. — **aequa**: *favorable*; but the word is selected for the contrast to the figure in *labier*.

95-100. A vivid picture of the lively interest of Greece in all forms of art. The three liberal arts, gymnastics and games (95), sculpture and painting (96-97), and music and dancing (98), are taken up in turn. The verbs, *arsit, amavit, suspendit, est gavisa*, express the intensity of the interest, and the forms of sentence, *nunc ... nunc, aut ... aut*, the sucession of genitives grouped about the noun, express the variety of interest. — **suspendit**: cf. *Epist.* 1, 6, 14, *defixis oculis animoque et corpore torpet*, and *torpes, Sat.* 2, 7, 95, of gazing intently at a picture. — **tragoedis**: the art of acting is connected with dancing and music.

suspendit picta vultum mentemque tabella,
nunc tibicinibus nunc est gavisa tragoedis;
sub nutrice puella velut si luderet infans,
100 quod cupide petiit, mature plena reliquit.
Hoc paces habuere bonae ventique secundi.
Romae dulce diu fuit et sollemne reclusa
mane domo vigilare, clienti promere iura,
105 cautos nominibus rectis expendere nummos,
maiores audire, minori dicere per quae
crescere res posset, minui damnosa libido.
101 Quid placet aut odio est, quod non mutabile credas?

99–100. 'Like a little child, playing at the feet of its nurse, it turned quickly from one plaything to another.' — **sub nutrice**: cf. *Epist.* 1, 16, 77, *sub custode.* — **petiit, reliquit**: the subject is *Graecia*, continued from the preceding sentence; the formal comparison is all contained in vs. 99. — **mature plena**: to be taken together and both with *reliquit*.

102. **hoc ... habuere**: 'such was the result,' going back in thought to vss. 93–94. — **paces**: *times of peace*. [But I do not think that this translation explains the plural. It may be due to *positis bellis*, or, more probably, to *venti secundi*, the plural being regular in this phrase. The single example in Plautus (*Pers.* 753) is inexplicable. See, in general, Langen, Beiträge, pp. 105 ff.] — **venti secundi**: a common figure.

103–110. 'At Rome the history has been a very different one.'

103. **sollemne**: 'the fixed custom.' — **reclusa**: the patron admitted freely all who chose to come to him for help or advice.

105. **cautos**: with *nummos*. — **rectis**: expressing in a different way the same idea as *cautos*.

106. **maiores, minori**: with reference to the strict family discipline and the respect exacted from the young.

107. **damnosa libido**: cf. *damnosa Venus*, *Epist.* 1, 18, 21; the caution is economic, not moral.

The contrast in these verses is double; Greece turned to the arts, and changed quickly from one interest to another, while Rome was severely practical, and for a long time unchanging.

101. 'But there is nothing so fixed that it does not at last change; we have abandoned everything else and plunged into writing.' This line stands in the Mss. after 100, where it breaks the thought, while

Mutavit mentem populus levis et calet uno
scribendi studio; puerique patresque severi
110 fronde comas vincti cenant et carmina dictant.
Ipse ego, qui nullos me adfirmo scribere versus,
invenior Parthis mendacior, et prius orto
sole vigil calamum et chartas et scrinia posco.
Navem agere ignarus navis timet; abrotonum aegro
115 non audet nisi qui didicit dare; quod medicorum est
promittunt medici; tractant fabrilia fabri:
scribimus indocti doctique poemata passim.
Hic error tamen et levis haec insania quantas

at this point it makes a perfect middle step from vss. 103-107 to 108 ff.

108. mutavit: this takes up *mutabile credas*, with emphatic assertion of the reality of it; 'the change has actually occurred.' — **calet**: as *Graecia arsit*, but *uno studio*, not with many.

110. fronde: with the poet's ivy crown, instead of the usual garland of flowers. — **dictant**: they have a slave ready, so that they may dictate their verses even while they are at dinner.

111. ipse ego: 'and I, who am laughing at it, am no better than the rest.' — **adfirmo scribere**: the present tense implies 'in the very act of making the statement I am found to be lying like a Dutchman.'

112. Parthis mendacior: this is merely one of the expressions of national hostility, like *Punica fides* or *perfide Albion*. The Parthians were at this time the traditional enemies of Rome.

113. scrinia: the boxes to put the rolls in when they were finished.

114-116. 'All other trades demand some knowledge and training.'

114. abrotonum: a comparatively harmless household remedy, yet even for giving that some knowledge is considered necessary.

117. scribimus: in the emphatic position; 'but writing may be done by anybody at any time.' — All this is, of course, to be taken humorously. It is the amusement of the trained professional at the zealous eagerness of the amateur.

118 ff. 'Yet this popular craze for poetry has its good side: the poetry may be poor, but it keeps the writer busy with harmless things.'

virtutes habeat, sic collige.   Vatis avarus
120 non temere est animus, versus amat, hoc studet unum;
detrimenta, fugas servorum, incendia ridet;
non fraudem socio puerove incogitat ullam
pupillo; vivit siliquis et pane secundo;
militiae quamquam piger et malus, utilis urbi,
125 si das hoc, parvis quoque rebus magna iuvari.
Os tenerum pueri balbumque poeta figurat,
torquet ab obscenis iam nunc sermonibus aurem;
mox etiam pectus praeceptis format amicis,
asperitatis et invidiae corrector et irae,
130 recte facta refert, orientia tempora notis

119. **sic collige**: so *Sat.* 2, 1, 51, *sic collige mecum.*

120. **non temere**: *not easily,* 'not without strong reason'; so *Sat.* 2, 2, 116; *Sat.* 2, 4, 35; *Epist.* 2, 2, 13.

121. The losses which most people are constantly dreading; cf. *Sat.* 1, 1, 77, *formidare malos fures, incendia, servos, ne te compilent fugientes.*

123. **siliquis**: standing for plain living, as does *pane secundo,* 'bread of an inferior quality of flour.'

124. **militiae**: dative; this is a joking reminiscence of his own brief career as a soldier. — **urbi**: *i.e.,* in peace, as *domi militiae* are used for 'peace and war.'

125. **si das hoc**: *i.e.,* 'unless you deny that so humble a person as a poet can be of use at all to the great Empire.'

From this point, through the enumeration of the poet's services to society, the thought turns to the history of poetry, and especially of the drama.

127. **obscenis**: more general in meaning than the English word; *low, harmful,* in contrast to the lofty thought and expression of poetry. — **iam nunc**: while he is still *puer.*

128. **mox**: at the later stage, when the character (*pectus*) is taking shape. — **amicis**: like a friendly adviser and helper, not with the severity of laws.

129. Faults to which youth is especially prone.

130. **recte . . . refert**: *i.e.,* poetry contains the record of noble action. — **orientia tempora**: *i.e.,* as the young man goes on from one period of life to another, each period in turn rising, as it were, above the horizon of life. Not to

instruit exemplis, inopem solatur et aegrum.
Castis cum pueris ignara puella mariti
discerct unde preces, vatem ni Musa dedisset?
Poscit opem chorus et praesentia numina sentit;
135 caelestis implorat aquas docta prece blandus,
avertit morbos, metuenda pericula pellit;
impetrat et pacem et locupletem frugibus annum.
Carmine di superi placantur, carmine Manes.

be compared with the English 'rising generation.' — notis: the *recte facta*, which, having been made known to us through poetry, become *exempla*.

131. solatur: by raising him above his discouraging circumstances.

132-133. A reference to the *Carmen Saeculare* composed by Horace for the great festival in 17 B.C. It was sung by a chorus of boy's and girls; *C. S.* 6, *virgines lectas puerosque castos*. — disceret: the poet is thought of as himself teaching the song to the chorus. — unde: *a quo*. — vatem: the more formal name for the poet, especially in his religious capacity.

134-137. There were many other occasions when choral songs were used, from early times, in religious ceremonies, *e.g.*, Livy, 27, 37; 31, 12, and they probably formed a part of some of the annually recurring festivals. *Carm.* 1, 21 is such a song to Diana and Apollo, and Catull. 34 to Diana. The function of the chorus is stated in general terms in vs. 134, then more specific instances are given in 135-7, and the whole is summarized in 138. — poscit opem: the general function, as in many places in the *Carm. Saec.* — praesentia . . . sentit: *C. S.* 73 f., *haec Iovem sentire deosque cunctos | spem bonam certamque domum reporto*; the chorus recognizes the presence and favor of the gods to whom it has prayed. — caelestis . . . aquas: prayers for rain were common, and there was a special ceremony, called *aquilicium*, for this purpose. — docta: *i.e.*, the prayer taught in suitable formula by the *vates*. — morbos: the performance of prescribed rites, which often included a choral prayer, was one of the regular methods of averting pestilence. — pericula: dangers to the state, threatened invasion, defeat in battle. — locupletem . . . annum: the *ambarvalia* was a ceremony for this purpose.

138. A summary of the whole, 132-137. — Manes: *i.e., di inferi*.

Agricolae prisci, fortes parvoque beati,
140 condita post frumenta, levantes tempore festo
corpus et ipsum animum spe finis dura ferentem,
cum sociis operum, pueris et coniuge fida,
Tellurem porco, Silvanum lacte piabant,
floribus et vino Genium, memorem brevis aevi.
145 Fescennina per hunc inventa licentia morem

139-155. A history of the rise of poetry in Italy, before the coming in of the Greek influence, leading up to a critical estimate of it. This history is not, however, based upon any knowledge of the development of Italian poetry before Livius Andronicus. That development, whatever it may have been, had passed entirely unrecorded. The account which Horace here gives and the corresponding account in Livy 7, 2 are based upon some Greek rhetorical tradition, adapted to embrace the few facts which were known by inference or tradition, like the *versus Fescennini* (145) and the *lex* of the Twelve Tables (152 f.).

139. fortes parvoque beati: *i.e.*, simple and happy, as in a Golden Age, when song might, as it was thought, originate.

140. condita: the harvest-home festival.

141. ipsum animum: *and even their spirits*. — **ferentem**: *i.e.*, which had borne hardship up to this time.

142. pueris: as Ofellus (*Sat.* 2, 2, 115) labors in the fields with his sons. — **coniuge**: so *Epod.* 2, 39 ff. — These are details of the ideal life of the farmer, cultivating his own fields with the help of his family, not working on the great estate of an absentee landlord.

143. Tellurem: mentioned by Varro (*R. R.* 1, 1, 4) as one of the gods to be worshiped by farmers. — **Silvanum**: called *tutor finium* in *Epod.* 2, 22.

144. Genium: a protecting spirit, born to each human being and accompanying him through life to the end, sharing his pleasures and sorrows. Offerings were made to the Genius, as to a divinity, yet he was mortal and therefore *memorem brevis aevi*, like the man himself.

145. Fescennina . . . licentia: the Fescennine verses survived in historic times in the form of abusive songs sung at weddings and in triumphal processions, apparently to avert the jealousy of the gods, which might be awakened by the felicity of the bridegroom or of the successful general. A modified specimen is given in Catullus, 61, 119 ff. Horace here treats the

versibus alternis opprobria rustica fudit,
libertasque recurrentis accepta per annos
lusit amabiliter, donec iam saevus apertam
in rabiem coepit verti iocus et per honestas
150 ire domos impune minax. Doluere cruento
dente lacessiti: fuit intactis quoque cura
condicione super communi; quin etiam lex
poenaque lata, malo quae nollet carmine quemquam
describi: vertere modum formidine fustis
155 ad bene dicendum delectandumque redacti.
Graecia capta ferum victorem cepit et artes
intulit agresti Latio; sic horridus ille

custom of singing such verses as having been invented for use in rustic festivals (*per hunc morem*), and regards the abusive quality of the songs as the most important element.

146. versibus alternis: Livy, 7, 2, uses almost the same expression: the singers are supposed to have extemporized in turn, somewhat as in the songs in the Eclogues, 3 and 7.

147. libertas: *i.e.*, the *licentia* became customary and so a permitted freedom. — **accepta**: balancing *inventa*. Livy uses this word also.

148. amabiliter: *i.e.*, the *opprobria rustica* were at first merely jocose.

149. honestas: *honorable*, with the Roman feeling of respect for the 'great houses.'

150. impune: with *minax*.

151. dente: the figure of a savage animal is already suggested in *rabiem*. — **intactis**: others beside the *lacessiti*; cf. *Sat.* 2, 1, 23, *timet quamquam est intactus et odit*, of satire.

152-153. lex poenaque lata: Cic. refers to this (*de Rep.* 4, 10, 12), *si quis occentavisset sive carmen condidisset quod infamiam faceret flagitiumve alteri*, but the exact words of the law are not known. — **quae nollet**: *which forbade*.

154. describi: cf. *Sat.* 1, 4, 3, *si quis erat dignus describi.* — **formidine fustis**: the penalty was death by the rods of the lictors.

156. One of Horace's best and most frequently quoted phrases.

157. agresti: referring back to vss. 139 ff. — The whole statement is to be understood in a very general sense. The earliest Greek influences, which came in through Livius Andronicus, Ennius, and their successors in the drama, were

defluxit numerus Saturnius et grave virus
munditiae pepulere, sed in longum tamen aevum
160 manserunt hodieque manent vestigia ruris.
Serus enim Graecis admovit acumina chartis,
et post Punica bella quietus quaerere coepit,
quid Sophocles et Thespis et Aeschylus utile ferrent.
Tentavit quoque rem si digne vertere posset,
165 et placuit sibi natura sublimis et acer ;

at least a century earlier than the conquest of Greece.

158. numerus Saturnius: of this old Italian meter many specimens are extant. It was the national verse until it was displaced by the hexameter. The earliest epic, the *Bellum Punicum* of Naevius, was in Saturnians. Its irregularities justify the adj. *horridus*. — **grave virus**: *i.e.*, the roughness was like an unpleasant liquid, oppressive to the senses.

160. vestigia ruris: ' of the primitive rudeness of rustic Latium.' — This is the point of the argument; ' the early writers, whom critics extol so highly, were in fact only partially affected by Greek influence, while we of the present time have more perfectly learned Greek technique.' It is not to be expected that Horace should share the modern view, which finds so much of interest in the origins and primitive forms of art.

161. serus : this refers backward to *manserunt hodieque manent* and is then made more definite in vs. 162.

162. post Punica bella: these words could not be used with reference to the First Punic War only. We are obliged therefore to suppose that Horace was following an erroneous chronology, of which there are traces in other authors, which made Livius Andronicus a contemporary of Ennius. — The thought here corresponds to vs. 93, *positis . . . . Graecia bellis*; the peace which succeeded a great war gave opportunity for the cultivation of literature.

163. Thespis: traditionally the founder of the tragic drama ; cf. *A. P.* 276. The chronological order is not observed. — **utile**: there is perhaps a touch of the Roman attitude in the use of this word.

164. tentavit rem: *made the attempt*. — **vertere**: used as a technical term of translating or adapting a Greek play.

165-166. placuit sibi: *i.e.*, 'the attempt was successful'; the phrase does not at all imply 'self-satisfaction,' as the context shows. — **natura**: this prepares for the

nam spirat tragicum satis et feliciter audet,
sed turpem putat inscite metuitque lituram.
Creditur, ex medio quia res arcessit, habere
sudoris minimum, sed habet comoedia tanto
170 plus oneris, quanto veniae minus. Adspice Plautus
quo pacto partes tutetur amantis ephebi,

restriction of vs. 167. — **sublimis et acer**: *of lofty spirit*; this is the same as the *acer spiritus ac vis* of *Sat.* 1, 4, 46. — **spirat tragicum**: this figure is especially poetic; it appears in various forms, *spirare bellum, quietem, amores* (*Carm.* 4, 13, 19), *proelia, magnum, maiora*, and has been taken over into English. — **satis**: with *feliciter*. — **feliciter audet**: of the style, as *spirat* is of the spirit. — These opinions in regard to the fitness of Roman character to tragedy are justified by the facts. There was no lack of the lofty and the heroic. But the production of great tragedy requires a very high esthetic and constructive imagination, in which the Romans were lacking.

167. This was a favorite doctrine with Horace (cf. *Sat.* 1, 10, 67-72; *A. P.* 290) and a natural one in the Augustan Age, when the efforts of writers in prose and in verse were directed most earnestly toward perfection of style. Cf., *e.g.*, what is said in the *Vita* of Donatus about Vergil's methods of work.

168. ex medio: *from ordinary* life, in distinction from the mythical and heroic world from which tragedy takes its subjects (*res*).

170. plus oneris: merely another figure for *plus sudoris*; the labor of writing well is like a burden under which the bearer sweats. — **veniae minus**: *i.e.*, it is less easy to win a favorable judgment in comedy than in tragedy, precisely because it deals with ordinary life, so that each hearer can judge for himself of the correctness of the picture. — **Plautus**: the unfavorable judgment here expressed is repeated, from a slightly different point of view, in *A. P.* 270 ff. It is not without justification, but it is one-sided; the merits of Plautus as a writer of comedy were not of a kind to appeal to Horace.

171-172. quo pacto: *i.e.*, 'how poorly.' — **tutetur**: 'plays the part,' transferred from the actor to the writer; the meaning is that the characters are not harmoniously and consistently drawn, as they are in the Greek originals and in Terence. The judgment rests upon too narrow a conception of art in comedy. — **ephebi, patris, lenonis**: standing figures in the

ut patris attenti, lenonis ut insidiosi,
quantus sit Dossennus edacibus in parasitis,
quam non adstricto percurrat pulpita socco.
175 Gestit enim nummum in loculos demittere, post hoc
securus cadat an recto stet fabula talo.
Quem tulit ad scaenam ventoso Gloria curru,
exanimat lentus spectator, sedulus inflat;
sic leve, sic parvum est, animum quod laudis avarum
180 subruit aut reficit! Valeat res ludicra, si me
palma negata macrum, donata reducit opimum.
Saepe etiam audacem fugat hoc terretque poetam,

comedy; the adjectives used with each are also traditional.

173. Dossennus: a character in the *fabula Atellana*, resembling in general the parasite of Plautus. The sense of the line is not quite clear, but appears to be, 'what a Dossennus he is in the part of the hungry parasite.' *i.e.*, 'how much his parasites resemble the Dossennus of popular farces, rather than the more artistic figure of the parasite in the New Comedy.'

174. non adstricto: 'loosely tied,' 'careless.' This is a general expression, summarizing vss. 170–173.

175-176. 'For he was careless and negligent (vs. 167), interested only in the price he got for his play.' — **post hoc**: after he was paid. The leading actor (*dominus gregis*) was the agent of the giver of the games in buying the play from the writer. — **securus**: *careless*. — **stet**: a technical word for holding a place on the stage, but here brought back to its original meaning by *recto talo*, 'stands firm,' 'stands upright.'

177. The thought turns from Plautus to the condition of the stage and dramatic writing. — **Gloria**: cf. *Sat.* 1, 6, 23, *fulgente . . . Gloria curru*. — **ventoso**: as fickle as the wind; cf. *Epist.* 1, 19, 37, *ventosae plebis*.

178-181. The same thought is here expressed three times; first by *exanimat* (takes away his breath) and *inflat* (causes him to take a full breath of self-satisfaction); second, by *subruit* and *reficit* (of pulling down and rebuilding an edifice): and third, in *macrum* and *opimum*. — **lentus**: *unresponsive*, exactly as in *Sat.* 1, 9, 64, *lentissima bracchia*. — **valeat**: *i.e.*, 'I do not care for it.'

182. etiam: with *audacem*; 'even one who might venture to take the risk of failure is daunted by

quod numero plures, virtute et honore minores,
indocti stolidique et depugnare parati,
185 si discordet eques, media inter carmina poscunt
aut ursum aut pugiles; his nam plebecula gaudet.
Verum equitis quoque iam migravit ab aure voluptas
omnis ad incertos oculos et gaudia vana.
Quattuor aut plures aulaea premuntur in horas,
190 dum fugiunt equitum turmae peditumque catervae;
mox trahitur manibus regum fortuna retortis,
esseda festinant, pilenta, petorrita, naves,
captivum portatur ebur, captiva Corinthus.

the poor taste of the audience that is to judge him.'

184. **indocti stolidique**: *i.e.*, 'incapable either by training or by natural sensitiveness of judging correctly.' — **depugnare parati**: not literally, but 'prepared to maintain their position.'

185. **eques**: used also in *Sat.* 1, 10, 76, of the more cultivated part of the audience, with a reference to the law of Otho reserving fourteen rows behind the senators for the *equites*.

186. **aut ursum aut pugiles**: shows suited to their taste. The *Hecyra* of Terence was twice driven from the stage by the superior attraction of boxers and a rope-dancer and a rumored gladiatorial show, and it is to this well-known bit of literary history that Horace is alluding.

187. **equitis quoque**: even the better portion of the audience has been led astray by the spectacular drama.

188. **incertos**: *shifting, changing* from one object to another. — **vana**: the pleasures which come from seeing mere shows are empty, in comparison with the more lasting pleasure of good poetry.

189. **premuntur**: *kept down*; the curtain was lowered, instead of being raised, as in a modern theater.

190. A battle was represented on the stage.

191-193. The triumphal procession after the battle. — **manibus ... retortis**: as captives, with their hands bound behind their backs. — **regum fortuna**: kings, once favorites of fortune, now enslaved; the phrase is epic, like *virtus Scipiadae, Sat.* 2, 1, 72. — The details that follow are merely suggestive of the elaborateness of some triumphal processions. — ' chariots, carriages, wagons, models of ships or

Si foret in terris, rideret Democritus, seu
195 diversum confusa genus panthera camelo,
sive elephas albus vulgi converteret ora;
spectaret populum ludis attentius ipsis
ut sibi praebentem nimio spectacula plura;
scriptores autem narrare putaret asello
200 fabellam surdo. Nam quae pervincere voces
evaluere sonum, referunt quem nostra theatra?
Garganum mugire putes nemus aut mare Tuscum;

figureheads, statues of ivory and Corinthian bronze.'

194. Democritus: by tradition the 'laughing philosopher'; the sense therefore is 'here would indeed be a spectacle for the philosopher who found in the follies of men matter for laughter rather than for reproof.'

195. The giraffe, *camelopardalis*, was supposed to be a cross between a camel and a panther (*pard*), and the confusion of expression here is intended to symbolize the mixture. The expression is, in fact, so confused that it is not clear whether Horace means *diversum genus* to be an accus. with *confusa* (*Sat.* 1, 6, 74, *suspensi loculos*) or an appositive of *panthera*. The first giraffe seen in Rome was brought over for Cæsar's Alexandrian triumph in 46 B.C.

198. nimio . . . plura: *much more*; so, frequently, *plus nimio*, e.g., *Epist.* 1, 10, 30.

199-200. scriptores: of such plays, of plays in which the spectacular element greatly exceeded the poetical. — **asello . . . surdo**: the proverbial expression *surdo fabellam narrare* (Ter. *Heaut.* 222, *nunc surdo narret fabulam*) is strengthened by *asello*, with a reminder of the Greek saying ὄνῳ τις ἔλεγε μῦθον· ὁ δὲ τὰ ὦτα ἐκίνει, 'a man told a story to an ass; the ass only shook his ears.'

201. evaluere: more emphatic than a form of *posse*, and the perfect tense, appealing to the facts of past experience, is more emphatic in a sentence that implies a negative, than the present tense would be; 'no voices have ever had (or now have) power enough to. . . .'

202. Garganum: the same illustration, from the noise of the wind in the oak forests of Garganus (a mountainous promontory on the Adriatic coast not very far from Horace's early home) is used in *Carm.* 2, 9, 7, and references to the storms of the Tuscan sea are frequent.

tanto cum strepitu ludi spectantur et artes
divitiaeque peregrinae! Quibus oblitus actor
205 cum stetit in scaena, concurrit dextera laevae.
' Dicit adhuc aliquid?' 'Nil sane.' 'Quid placet
ergo?'
. ' Lana Tarentino violas imitata veneno.'
Ac ne forte putes me, quae facere ipse recusem,
cum recte tractent alii, laudare maligne,
210 ille per extentum funem mihi posse videtur
ire poeta, meum qui pectus inaniter angit,
irritat, mulcet, falsis terroribus implet,
ut magus et modo me Thebis modo ponit Athenis.
Verum age, et his, qui se lectori credere malunt

203. artes: ironical; *artes* and *divitiae* are together the antecedent of *quibus*, and therefore refer especially to the dress of the actors, not to such things as are mentioned in vs. 193.

204. oblitus: also ironical; lit., 'smeared,' *i.e., loaded down, covered up.*

207. The wool of Tarentum was famous and the dye made from the *murex* of the Gulf of Tarentum was considered second only to the Tyrian. — violas: color comparisons in poetry are to be regarded as mere suggestions. — veneno: this continues the ironical tone.

209. maligne: *grudgingly, ungenerously;* the sense of the English *malignant* is not in the word.

210. per extentum funem: the expression is proverbial. as in English, of an act which requires great skill and involves danger.

211. meum: by putting himself into the position of a spectator and hearer Horace is able to express more easily his admiration for the art of the dramatist and to disclaim all rivalry. — inaniter: *i.e.*, by the stage illusions, which are unreal; to be taken also with *irritat* and *mulcet.*

212. falsis: the same as *inaniter.*

213. ut magus: to be taken with the rest of the vs.; 'and like a magician. . . .' — Thebis, Athenis: the scenes of tragedy, like the Oedipus story, and of the plays of the New Comedy.

214 ff. ' Turn now from the stage and consider the difficulties with which poets labor who write for the reading public.'

214. et his: *these also,* since *age*

215 quam spectatoris fastidia ferre superbi,
curam redde brevem, si munus Apolline dignum
vis complere libris et vatibus addere calcar,
ut studio maiore petant Helicona virentem.
Multa quidem nobis facimus mala saepe poetae,
220 ut vineta egomet caedam mea, cum tibi librum
sollicito damus aut fesso, cum laedimur, unum
si quis amicorum est ausus reprendere versum,
cum loca iam recitata revolvimus irrevocati,

prefixed to another imperative is not usually connected with it by *et*.

216. **curam redde**: a direct address to Augustus as a patron of literature, interested in all forms of poetry and founder of the temple of Apollo, with which the two great libraries, of Greek and of Latin writings, were connected. The words are carefully chosen; *curam*, not merely interest; *redde*, give as something due to them; *brevem*, since Augustus is so much occupied with other cares, vss. 1-4. — **munus**: the library was a gift for public use. The general sense is, 'if you wish to make your gift worthy of the god of poetry by filling it with books that deserve such preservation.' — **addere calcar**: *to set spurs to* without any suggestion of 'adding'; the phrase is common and not different from *admovere calcar, subdere calcar*.

218. **Helicona**: as the home of the Muses. The line is entirely general, merely a supplement to *addere calcar*.

219. **quidem**: with concessive effect; 'it is quite true that we poets are sometimes childish in our expectations.' The completion of the thought begins with *sed tamen*, vs. 229.

220. **ut vineta ... caedam**: the expression is evidently proverbial, of saying or doing something which injures one's own interests. It does not occur elsewhere in this form, but cf. Tibull. 1, 2, 100, *quid messis uris acerba tuis?* and, for the literal meaning, Verg. *Ecl.* 3, 10 f., *cum me arbustum videre Miconis | atque mala vitis incidere falce novellas*.

221. **sollicito ... aut fesso**: cf. the humorously exaggerated carefulness of Horace, when he was sending a copy of the Odes to Augustus, *Epist.* 1, 13. especially vs. 3. *si validus, si laetus erit*.

223. The line refers to the behavior of an author reading his own poetry to an audience; when a passage pleases him, he goes back and reads it over, without

cum lamentamur, non apparere labores
225 nostros et tenui deducta poemata filo,
cum speramus eo rem venturam, ut simul atque
carmina rescieris nos fingere, commodus ultro
arcessas et egere vetes et scribere cogas.
Sed tamen est operae pretium cognoscere, quales
230 aedituos habeat belli spectata domique
virtus indigno non committenda poetae.
Gratus Alexandro regi magno fuit ille
Choerilus, incultis qui versibus et male natis

waiting to be urged. — **revolvimus**: in a literal sense, of the turning back of the scroll. — **irrevocati**: *revocare* is the technical word for recalling an actor or a reciter.

224. non apparere: *i.e.*, 'that the labor we have given to our work is not sufficiently appreciated'; the complaint is intentionally put in a form which reveals its absurdity.

225. tenui deducta ... filo: 'the fineness and subtlety of our work.' The figure is taken from spinning and is often used, *e.g.*, *Sat.* 2, 1, 3 f.

227. commodus: 'you will be so obliging as to ...'— **ultro**: without waiting to be asked.

228. egere vetes: *i.e.*, 'save us from poverty.' The two verbs, *vetes* and *cogas*, carry on the thought of *ultro* and suggest, ironically, the picture of the poet indifferent to poetry and shrinking from writing, but compelled by his patron to accept wealth and assume the task of writing.

229. sed tamen: taking up the thought where it was interrupted by *multa quidem ... facimus*, vs. 219. — **est operae pretium**: 'it is worth your while.' — **cognoscere**: a rather formal word, *to consider carefully*, 'to investigate the question.'

230. aedituos: 'temple attendants,' as if the *virtus Augusti* were a divinity. — **habeat**: more fully expressed this would be *habere oporteat*; the direct question would have been in the subjv., *quales aedituos habeat* (should have) *virtus tua*.

232-234. The story is that Choerilus wrote a poor poem on the exploits of Alexander and was rewarded by him, in spite of the badness of the poetry. These outlines are filled in by the Scholiast with some details which rather detract from the aptness of the illustration. If they are authentic, Horace has intentionally omitted them. A few later allusions (Cur-

rettulit acceptos, regale nomisma, Philippos.
235 Sed veluti tractata notam labemque remittunt
atramenta, fere scriptores carmine foedo
splendida facta linunt. Idem rex ille, poema
qui tam ridiculum tam care prodigus emit,
edicto vetuit ne quis se praeter Apellem
240 pingeret aut alius Lysippo duceret aera
fortis Alexandri vultum simulantia. Quodsi
iudicium subtile videndis artibus illud
ad libros et ad haec Musarum dona vocares,
Boeotum in crasso iurares aere natum.

tius, 8, 5, 8; Auson. *Epist.* 16, 3) show that the story became traditional. — **incultis**: from lack of art. — **male natis**: from lack of natural ability. — **rettulit acceptos**: *i.e.*, 'put them down in his account book on the credit side'; a bookkeeping term used ironically. — **regale nomisma**: because they were called *Philippi*, after the name of the king; cf. the 'Napoleon.' There is perhaps also a suggestion that Alexander 'paid like a prince.' *nomisma* is in apposition to *Philippos*.

235-237. 'But poor poetry really brings discredit upon the hero whose deeds it celebrates.' — **remittunt**: 'give off,' leave upon the hand. — **atramenta**: ink or any black pigment. — **fere**: *often*, not 'generally, usually.' — The comparison ('poor poets stain great deeds, as ink stains the fingers') is good enough in its essential point (*linunt* = *notam labemque remittunt*), but is distinctly lame in the details, which by no means correspond.

237-238. idem: with adversative force, as often. — **tam, tam**: these words take for granted a knowledge of the details of the story, as do *ille* (232), *ille* (237).

239-240. edicto vetuit ne quis: in the legal style; cf. *Sat.* 2, 3, 187. The story was traditional and is alluded to by Cicero (*ad Fam.* 5, 12, 7) and told by Pliny (*H. N.* 7, 37, 125). Apelles and Lysippus were the two most distinguished artists of the period. — **alius Lysippo**: cf. *Epist.* 1, 16, 20; exactly equivalent to *praeter Apellem*. — **duceret**: *cast.* — **aera**: the plur. is significant; *bronzes, i.e.,* bronze figures.

242. videndis artibus: 'arts that appeal to the eye,' painting and sculpture; ablative, Lane, § 2266.

244. Boeotum: gen. plur. with *aere*. — **crasso**: proverbial of the

245 At neque dedecorant tua de se iudicia atque
munera, quae multa dantis cum laude tulerunt,
dilecti tibi Vergilius Variusque poetae:
nec magis expressi vultus per aenea signa
quam per vatis opus mores animique virorum
250 clarorum apparent. Nec sermones ego mallem
repentes per humum, quam res componere gestas,

atmosphere of Boeotia, so that the name of the country had become proverbial for dullness. — The tradition which Horace is here following, that Alexander was a poor judge of poetry, is not in fact consistent with a correct interpretation of the Choerilus story, which, in its full form, is meant to represent him as dealing humorously and good-naturedly with a poem the badness of which he fully understood. A similar tradition, attributing to him ignorance of painting, appears in an anecdote told by Pliny (*H. N.* 35, 10, 85) of his making foolish criticisms in the studio of Apelles. Both traditions probably came from Athenian witticisms, extending the proverbial dullness of Boeotia to the Macedonian conqueror.

245 ff. 'But you do not need this warning, as your patronage of Vergil and Varius shows.'

245. dedecorant ... iudicia: *i.e.*, 'do no discredit to your selection of them.'

246. munera: there is a definite story of the giving of money to Vergil when he read the sixth book of the Aeneid to Augustus, and he left a considerable fortune at his death, which must have come from gifts. Varius also received money from Augustus. — **laude**: *credit, honor*, not 'praise' from the recipients of the gifts.

247. Vergil died in 19 B.C., and Varius was probably not living at this time, though the date of his death is not known.

248. expressi: the figure is taken from the shaping of wax or clay. — **vultus**: 'the expression of the face.'

250 ff. 'I too would join in recording your deeds if only my powers were equal to the task.'

250–251. sermones ... repentes per humum: this often-quoted phrase expresses Horace's habitual attitude toward the Satires and Epistles; they are *Talks*, inspired only by a *Musa pedestris* (*Sat.* 2, 6, 17). It was in the Epodes and the Odes that he felt himself to be a poet. — **res ... gestas**: an historical epic after the manner of Ennius. The title of the work might have been *Res Gestae Augusti*.

terrarumque situs et flumina dicere et arces
montibus impositas et barbara regna, tuisque
auspiciis totum confecta duella per orbem,
255 claustraque custodem pacis cohibentia Ianum,
et formidatam Parthis te principe Romam,
si, quantum cuperem, possem quoque: sed neque parvum
carmen maiestas recipit tua, nec meus audet
rem tentare pudor, quam vires ferre recusent.
260 Sedulitas autem, stulte quem diligit, urget,

252-253. These details evidently refer to campaigns in countries little known to the public and deserving particular description. The phrase *arces montibus impositas* points to the campaigns of Drusus and Tiberius in the valleys of the Alps against the Vindelici, which were carried on in 15-14 B.C., and which Horace had already celebrated in *Carm.* 4, 4 and 14, at the request of Augustus.

254. duella: the epic word. In these lines, as in the similar passage in *Sat.* 2, 1, 12-15, Horace, in the very act of professing his inability to write an epic, indulges in a bit of epic description.

255. claustra: the temple of Janus was closed by Augustus twice before this Epistle was written, in 29 and in 25 B.C., and a third time at some later date. — custodem pacis: the phrase is not quite precise; Janus guards peace within his closed doors.

256. Parthis: cf. *Epist.* 1, 12, 27, note.

257. si . . . possem: the protasis of *mallem*, vs. 250. — quantum cuperem: the thought was traditional in rhetorical criticism. Cf. also *cupidum* in the similar passage, *Sat.* 2, 1, 12.

258. maiestas . . . tua: not, of course, as a title, but with something of formality. — recipit: *admit, permit.*

259. rem tentare: 'to attempt a task,' not quite as in vs. 164. — pudor: the abstract for the concrete, to balance *maiestas.* — The clauses repeat and amplify the thought of *quantum cuperem possem*; 'I do not wish to offer you a poor song, which is all that I am able to do, and I am not able to attempt a great poem, which is what I should wish to give you.'

260. sedulitas: *officiousness*, an ill-regulated desire to please; cf. *sedulus, Epist.* 1, 13, 5. — stulte: with *urget*; 'is foolish in laying a burden upon the very person he desires to please.'

praecipue cum se numeris commendat et arte;
discit enim citius meminitque libentius illud,
quod quis deridet, quam quod probat et veneratur.
Nil moror officium, quod me gravat, ac neque ficto
265   in peius vultu proponi cereus usquam,
nec prave factis decorari versibus opto,
ne rubeam pingui donatus munere et una
cum scriptore meo capsa porrectus operta
deferar in vicum vendentem tus et odores
270   et piper et quidquid chartis amicitur ineptis.

261. praecipue: 'this is especially true of poetry, because poor verses stick in the memory.'

262. discit: the subject is to be supplied from the next clause.

264–265. officium: = *sedulitas*. — **gravat**: = *urget*. — **ficto**: *shaped*. — **in peius**: *i.e.*, 'by a poor artist, who would misrepresent my features, as I, if I tried to write an epic, might misrepresent your deeds.' — **cereus**: wax was used for portrait busts, as for masks (*imagines*) of distinguished ancestors. Cf. *expressi*, vs. 248.

266. decorari: ironical. — There is an implied comparison; 'as I should not be pleased by a poor portrait of myself, so I should not care to be described in bad verses.'

267. pingui: *stupid*, as in *Sat.* 2, 6, 14.

268. scriptore meo: 'the man who wrote about me,' 'my eulogist.' — **capsa porrectus**: like a corpse in a coffin.

269. vicum vendentem tus: the *vicus Tuscus*, with a pun on *tus* — *tuscus*.

2

The subject matter of this Epistle is so general and there are so few allusions to public matters that the date cannot be fixed with certainty. It is clear that so elaborate a renunciation of poetry cannot have been written during the period from 17 B.C. to 13 B.C., when Horace was writing the *Carmen Saeculare* and the Fourth Book of the Odes. There is nothing to show that it might not have been composed after 13 B.C., but the general tone, in which it much resembles *Epist.* 1, 1, and the difficulty of supposing that Horace twice publicly announced his intention of giving up lyrical poetry, makes the earlier date, 20-18 B.C., more probable.

For the young Julius Florus, see Introd. to *Epist.* 1, 3. He was still in the suite of Tiberius and had apparently been long absent from Rome.

'Did you ever buy a slave, my dear Florus, and find yourself prevented from complaining of his faults by the fact that the dealer had expressly mentioned them? Then you must not complain of not hearing from me, for I warned you that I never answer letters. And in spite of this, you call on me for more Odes! Do you remember that story of the soldier of Lucullus? Some thief stole his savings and in a rage he went off and stormed a castle and got honor and more money. But when the general, with most flattering words, invited him to lead another storming party, he declined with thanks and advised the general to get some other man who had just lost his purse. That is just my attitude. I lost my purse at Philippi and, in a rage, I stormed the castle of poetry. But once is enough; I am taking my ease now. There are plenty of reasons for not writing. In the first place, you all ask for different things. And then, how can one write in Rome, where all is confusion? Nor, for another reason, do I like the mutual admiration clubs, which I should have to join. And it is no easy matter, either, to write really good poetry.

'The fact is that I have turned, as I said once before, from lyrics to philosophy, and am trying to learn the secrets of true living. I am considering the nature of possession and how it differs from use and how transient it is, at the best. I am trying to practice the doctrine of the Golden Mean and to become both better and happier, as I grow older.'

In this Epistle, as in *Epist.* 2, 1, the letter form is used at the beginning with considerable skill, and something of the personal tone is maintained for perhaps fifty lines. But from that point the epistle becomes a versified essay, first, on the writing of poetry and, second, on philosophy. The latter part contains nothing that Horace had not said before, though it is here expressed in new forms, but the strictures upon the state of literature in Rome are always interesting. The humorous opening of the Epistle, the bit of autobiography, and the veiled allusion to Propertius are perhaps the best parts of the letter. As a whole it is scarcely equal to the other Epistles of this Book.

Flore, bono claroque fidelis amice Neroni,
si quis forte velit puerum tibi vendere natum
Tibure vel Gabiis et tecum sic agat: 'Hic et
candidus et talos a vertice pulcher ad imos
5 fiet eritque tuus nummorum milibus octo,
verna ministeriis ad nutus aptus eriles,
litterulis Graecis imbutus, idoneus arti
cuilibet; argilla quidvis imitaberis uda;
quin etiam canet indoctum sed dulce bibenti.
10 Multa fidem promissa levant, ubi plenius aequo
laudat venales qui vult extrudere merces.

1. **Flore, Neroni**: cf. *Epist.* 1, 3. 1–2, notes, and *Epist.* 1, 8, 2.

2. **puerum**: *slave*, not 'boy,' though the context shows that he is young.

3. **Tibure vel Gabiis**: any two Italian towns; a slave born in Italy, not a foreign captive. — **agat**: *deal*, i.e., 'present his proposal in these terms.'

4. **candidus**: *fair*, of complexion. — **talos a vertice**: proverbial like the English 'from head to foot.'

5. **fiet eritque**: legal tautology, like 'to have and to hold,' employed here to give an air of definiteness and frankness to the offer. — **milibus octo**: nearly $400, an ordinary price for a fairly good slave. Davus, speaking of himself as a cheap slave, says he was worth $100. The price named is meant to be attractive, but not suspiciously low.

6. **verna**: *a house slave*, not a common field laborer. — **ministeriis**: dative with *aptus*. — **ad nutus**: to be taken closely with *ministeriis aptus*, almost as a modifier; 'quick to perform his duties at a nod.'

7–8. **litterulis ... imbutus**: 'he knows a little Greek'; the depreciatory tone is suggested by the diminutive and expressed in *imbutus*. Cf. Tac. *Dial.* 19, *elementis studiorum etsi non instructus at certe imbutus*. — **arti cuilibet**: there is a description in Ter. *Eun.* 476 ff. of a young slave who knows literature, wrestling, and music. — **argilla ... uda**: the figure of the artist making his clay model is suggested by *arti*.

9. **quin etiam**: i.e., 'in fact he already knows something of one art, singing.' — **indoctum**: this suggests again the frank man who will not praise too highly what he offers for sale.

Res urget me nulla, meo sum pauper in aere.
Nemo hoc mangonum faceret tibi, non temere a me
quivis ferret idem. Semel hic cessavit et, ut fit,
15 in scalis latuit metuens pendentis habenae':
des nummos, excepta nihil te si fuga laedat,
ille ferat pretium poenae securus; opinor
prudens emisti vitiosum; dicta tibi est lex;
insequeris tamen hunc et lite moraris iniqua?

12. res: *pressure, necessity.* — meo ... in aere: in distinction from *aes alienum*; the words explain the first part of the line; 'I'm not rich, but I have no debts.'

13. hoc faceret: 'would make you such an offer as this.' — non temere: 'not without some special reason.'

14-15. This is the point of the whole, dropped in at the end as a matter of no importance, yet distinctly mentioned lest the concealment should invalidate the bargain. — cessavit: cf. *Sat.* 2, 7, 100, *nequam et cessator Davus.* This is the mildest possible way of saying that the young slave shirks his work whenever he can; 'it is a fact that he once lingered about his work and then, fearing a a whipping, hid himself.' So in Plaut. *M. G.* 582 f. the slave says *nam iam aliquo aufugiam et me occultabo aliquot dies, | dum haec consilescunt turbae.* — in scalis: *under the stairs*; he did not really run away. — pendentis: *i.e.*, usually hanging on the wall, ready for use.

16. des: continuing the supposition, without *si*; 'suppose you hand over your money.' — si ... laedat: a secondary condition, with *des*; 'taking it for granted, of course, that you find nothing else objectionable.' — excepta ... fuga: 'the running away having been distinctly mentioned.' *Exipere* is the technical term in law for mentioning a point which is an 'exception' to the general statement; cf. *Sat.* 2, 3, 285, *mentem, nisi litigiosus, exciperet dominus, cum venderet.*

17. poenae securus: *without fear of penalty*, because he had complied with the law in mentioning the slight tendency to 'shirk.'

18. prudens: *deliberately,* 'with your eyes open.' — lex: the statement which the law requires, *semel ... cessavit*, not the written 'law.'

19. insequeris, moraris: 'are you pursuing him, trying to hold him?' The present tense carries the reader over from the story to its application; this is a condensed way of saying 'would you make

20 Dixi me pigrum proficiscenti tibi, dixi
talibus officiis prope mancum, ne mea saevus
iurgares ad te quod epistula nulla rediret.
Quid tum profeci mecum facientia iura
si tamen attentas? Quereris super hoc etiam, quod
25 expectata tibi non mittam carmina mendax.
Luculli miles collecta viatica, multis
aerumnis, lassus dum noctu stertit, ad assem
perdiderat, post hoc vehemens lupus et sibi et hosti
iratus pariter, ieiunis dentibus acer,
30 praesidium regale loco deiecit, ut aiunt,
summe munito et multarum divite rerum.
Clarus ob id factum donis ornatur honestis

a fuss about your bargain and threaten a suit? Yet that is exactly what you are doing to me, though I warned you plainly.'

20. **dixi, dixi**: 'I was just as plain in my warnings as the seller of the slave in my little story.' — **proficiscenti**: on his journey with Tiberius.

It is extremely characteristic of Horace to go through all the details of the story, leaving the application to the end. Compare the detailed description of Tigellius, *Sat.* 1, 3, 2–19, the point of which is not reached till vs. 24.

21. **talibus officiis**: letter writing and other friendly offices; dative with *mancum*, which is a strong word for *haud aptus, inutilis.*

23. **profeci**: *i.e.*, 'what good has my plain warning done?' — **mecum facientia**: cf. *Epist.* 2, 1, 68.

24. **super hoc etiam**: 'in addition to all this,' 'you even go, so far, besides.'

25. **mendax**: 'breaking my promise'; cf. *Epist.* 1, 7, 2.

26. **Luculli**: commander in Cilicia against Mithridates, 74–67 B.C. The story is not told elsewhere. — **viatica**: properly 'traveling money,' then any kind of allowance, from which the soldier had saved what he could.

27. **ad assem**: *i.e.*, all of it, 'to a penny.'

29. **dentibus**: with reference to *lupus.*

30–31. **regale**: *i.e.*, of Mithridates. — **ut aiunt**: with the next line, giving the authority of the story teller for the strong expressions *summe, multarum divite.*

32. **donis ... honestis**: the various insignia, chains, crowns,

accipit et bis dena super sestertia nummum.
Forte sub hoc tempus castellum evertere praetor
35 nescio quod cupiens hortari coepit eundem
verbis, quae timido quoque possent addere mentem:
'I bone quo virtus tua te vocat, i pede fausto,
grandia laturus meritorum praemia. Quid stas?'
Post haec ille catus quantumvis rusticus: 'Ibit,
40 ibit eo, quo vis, qui zonam perdidit,' inquit.
Romae nutriri mihi contigit atque doceri
iratus Grais quantum nocuisset Achilles.
Adiecere bonae paullo plus artis Athenae,
scilicet ut vellem curvo dinoscere rectum,

medals, that were given for conspicuous bravery.

33. **bis dena ... sestertia**: a little less than $1000, a large share of the booty for a common soldier. — **super**: adverb.

34. **forte sub hoc tempus**: a phrase for continuing the narrative, like 'it happened about this time.' — **praetor**: in the old sense, *commander*.

35. **nescio quod**: this also is in the narrative style, passing over unimportant details.

36. **timido quoque**: *even to a coward*. — **mentem**: *spirit, purpose*; this is an unusual sense for *mens*.

37. **pede fausto**: a rather formal phrase, almost in a solemn tone, as if the gods were sure to favor the undertaking.

38. **grandia ... praemia**: so in *Sat.* 2, 1, 11 f., to the lofty motives for writing about Augustus, Trebatius adds, as if by an afterthought, *multa laborum praemia laturus*.

39-40. **catus**: *sharp*; a colloquial, almost vulgar, word to go with *quantumvis rusticus*. — **ibit, ibit**: the shrewd soldier mimics in his reply the lofty tone of the repeated *i, i* of the general's exhortation. — **zonam**: 'money belt,' i.e., 'who has had the same experience that I had,' vs. 27.

41-54. The application of the story.

41. **contigit**: 'it was my good fortune'; this corresponds to the soldier's *collecta viatica*. For the facts compare *Sat.* 1, 6, 76.

42. That is, he learned Greek and read the Iliad.

43-45. 'My good fortune was increased by the opportunity of studying in Athens.'— **bonae**: with *Athenae*. — **artis**: *education*, as in

45 atque inter silvas Academi quaerere verum.
Dura sed emovere loco me tempora grato,
civilisque rudem belli tulit aestus in arma
Caesaris Augusti non responsura lacertis.
Vnde simul primum me dimisere Philippi,
50 decisis humilem pennis inopemque paterni
et laris et fundi paupertas impulit audax,
ut versus facerem. Sed quod non desit habentem

Sat. 1, 6, 77. — **vellem**: *desire, choose.* — **curvo, rectum**: geometrical terms, transferred to ethics, as the use of *dinoscere* shows. — **inter silvas**: the olive trees of the Academy. This spot was outside of the city and one of the most beautiful parks about Athens. — **Academi**: this does not refer to the Academic school, to which Horace shows no inclination, but only to the place, as representative of all philosophy. — **quaerere verum**: this is the more theoretical side of philosophy, including speculations in natural philosophy.

46-48. 'But I lost my chances, as the soldier lost my money.' — **dura . . . tempora**: the period immediately after the death of Julius Caesar in March, 44 B.C. — **civilis**: with *aestus*; cf. *furor civilis*, *Carm.* 4, 15, 18. — **rudem belli**: = *imbellem*; cf. *Epod.* 1, 16. Horace mentions Brutus as his leader only in *Carm.* 2, 7, 2, quite casually, and in *Sat.* 1, 7, which dates from this period of his life.

— **non responsura**: the future expresses the idea of destiny. — **lacertis**: as if in wrestling.

49. Philippi: in 42 B.C. Horace returned at once to Rome, not continuing the contest, as some of his friends did, by joining the army of the younger Pompey.

51. et laris et fundi: with *inopem*. The two words together stand for the estate near Venusia, which was probably confiscated and assigned to some veteran of the army of Augustus. — **audax**: corresponding to vss. 28-29, *vehemens lupus*.

52. ut versus facerem: this corresponds to the soldier's exploit, vss. 30-31. But Horace does not, either here or elsewhere, tell how his writing brought him relief from poverty, except indirectly, through his acquaintance. There is no reason to suppose that an author received a royalty from the sale of his works. — **quod non desit habentem**: this is the modest equivalent of vss. 32-33.

quae poterunt unquam satis expurgare cicutae,
ni melius dormire putem quam scribere versus?
55　Singula de nobis anni praedantur euntes,
eripuere iocos, venerem, convivia, ludum,
tendunt extorquere poemata. Quid faciam vis?
Denique non omnes eadem mirantur amantque.
Carmine tu gaudes, hic delectatur iambis,
60　ille Bioneis sermonibus et sale nigro.
Tres mihi convivae prope dissentire videntur,

53. **poterunt . . . expurgare**: *i.e.*, 'what possible remedy can cure his feverish madness?' — **cicutae**: *hemlock*, which was used not only as a poison, but also in smaller doses as a cure for fever.

54. **dormire**: cf. *Sat.* 2, 1, 7, where the word is used exactly as here.

55. The application of the anecdote of the soldier to Horace's own history and circumstances is carried out into humorous detail and is not to be taken seriously. Cf. the equally exaggerated and humorous explanation of his choice of Satire in *Sat.* 1, 10, 40-47. From this point, however, the reasoning becomes more serious. — **singula**: specified in the next line. This line is an expression of the feeling of the middle-aged man. The thought is repeated in *A. P.* 175-176.

56. Cf. *Epist.* 1, 7, 26-28, where the losses that come with middle age are described somewhat more fully.

57. **tendunt**: the present tense is emphatic; 'they are now going on to take. . . .' — **extorquere**: 'against my will.' — **quid faciam vis?** *i.e.*, 'what can I do but submit?' Greenough well compares *que voulez-vous?*

58. **denique**: introducing a new point, but not the final one; *then, too*. This is a not uncommon use.

59-60. **carmine**: lyric poetry, the Odes. — **iambis**: iambic poems of satirical tone, like many of the Epodes. — **Bioneis**: Bion was a philosopher of the third century, of a biting wit, so that he became a type of the caustic satirist. It is quite unlikely that Horace was influenced by him; at the most it was only in his earliest satires. His name is used here only as a general descriptive term. — **sermonibus**: *satires*. — **sale nigro**: coarse black salt, which would make strong brine. The figure is often used. *e.g.*, *Sat.* 1, 10, 3.

61. **prope**: with the whole sentence or with *videntur*, not with *dissentire*; 'if you have only three

poscentes vario multum diversa palato.
Quid dem? Quid non dem? Renuis tu, quod iubet alter,
quod petis, id sane est invisum acidumque duobus.
65 Praeter cetera, me Romaene poemata censes
scribere posse inter tot curas totque labores?
Hic sponsum vocat, hic auditum scripta, relictis
omnibus officiis, cubat hic in colle Quirini,
hic extremo in Aventino, visendus uterque;
70 intervalla vides humane commoda. Verum
purae sunt plateae, nihil ut meditantibus obstet.
Festinat calidus mulis gerulisque redemptor,
torquet nunc lapidem nunc ingens machina tignum,

guests, it is almost certain that they will differ.'

62. **multum**: with *diversa*.

64. **acidum**: maintaining the figure of guests at the table.

65. **praeter cetera**: still another reason, vss. 65-86, for not complying with the expectation of Florus that he should send him poems. For the general thought, which was habitual with Horace, cf. *Sat.* 2, 6, 23-39.

67. **sponsum**: cf. *Sat.* 2, 6, 23, *Romae sponsorem me rapis.* — **auditum**: *i.e.*, to a recitation, as in *Sat.* 1, 4, 23.

68. **cubat**: *is lying ill*; cf. *Sat.* 1, 9, 18.

70. **intervalla**: the distance would be somewhere between one mile and two, but Horace is not thinking of precise measurements; he names the two hills which were on opposite sides of the city, by way of saying 'clear across the whole town.' — **humane commoda**: so in colloquial Latin, *misere miser, inepte stultus*, and frequently an adjective is strengthened by an adverb of like stem or meaning; instead of either *humana*, 'human, suited to a man,' or *commoda*, 'convenient,' the two are united into the single ironical phrase, 'convenient for a man.'

70-71. 'But perhaps you will say that . . .'; as if put in by some other person, who said 'you can be thinking over a poem (*meditantibus*) as you go.' — **purae**: *empty*, clear of obstacles which would prevent thinking.

72. **festinat**: the answer begins, as often, without an adversative particle, as though a mere statement of facts supplied a sufficient answer. — **calidus**: *hurrying*; this continues the thought of *festinat*, as a predicate.

73. **torquet**: *twists up, winds*

tristia robustis luctantur funera plaustris,
75 hac rabiosa fugit canis, hac lutulenta ruit sus:
i nunc, et versus tecum meditare canoros!
Scriptorum chorus omnis amat nemus et fugit urbes,
rite cliens Bacchi somno gaudentis et umbra,
tu me inter strepitus nocturnos atque diurnos
80 vis canere et contracta sequi vestigia vatum?
Ingenium, sibi quod vacuas desumpsit Athenas
et studiis annos septem dedit insenuitque
libris et curis, statua taciturnius exit

up, the verb being chosen because the lifting of the weight is done by means of wheels and pulleys.

74. Cf. *Sat.* 1, 6, 42 f., where the noise of the Forum is expressed in the same way, by imagining the meeting of funeral processions and heavy wagons.

76. **i nunc**: as in vs. 37. — For this description of the confusion of an ancient city, cf. the similar passage in Juv. 3, 245 ff. Some attempts were made to control the traffic, but they cannot have been very effectual.

77. **scriptorum**: *poets*, as *canoros*, *canere*, and *vatum* show. — **chorus, nemus**: these words suggest the chorus of the Muses in the sacred grove.

78. **rite**: with *cliens*; 'devoted to Bacchus, as is fit.' This is the traditional idea, expressed more fully in *Epist.* 1, 19, 1-11.

80. **contracta**: *i.e.*, 'to follow the steep and narrow path,' the path where only the few have been able to tread. The same thought is in Propert. 4, 1, 14, *non datur ad Musas currere lata via*.

81-86. 'Study and the writing of poetry are incompatible with the excitements and confusions of active life. A man who gives himself up to one unfits himself for the other. The student in the retirement of Athens makes a ridiculous figure in affairs; I, when I am living in the midst of the distractions of Roman life, must not expect to write poetry.'

81. **ingenium**: 'a man of ability.' This is probably not an allusion to some definite person (the presents, *exit*, *quatit*, are general), but, to make it more vivid, an air of definiteness is given to it by *Athenas* (the typical spot for seclusion and study) and by *annos septem* (a long time).

82. **insenuit**: cf. *Epist.* 1, 7, 85, *amore senescit habendi*.

83. **libris et curis**: abl., like *amore* in the passage just quoted.

plerumque et risu populum quatit; hic ego rerum
85 fluctibus in mediis et tempestatibus urbis
verba lyrae motura sonum conectere digner?
Frater erat Romae consulti rhetor, ut alter
alterius sermone meros audiret honores,
Gracchus ut hic illi, foret huic ut Mucius ille.
90 Qui minus argutos vexat furor iste poetas?
Carmina compono, hic elegos. 'Mirabile visu

curae, of studies in philosophy, as in *Carm.* 3, 21, 15, *sapientium curas*. — **statua**: a proverbial comparison, which is used also in English. — **taciturnius**: neut. with *ingenium*. — **exit**: *turns out*, 'comes out at the end'; cf. *A. P.* 22, *currente rota cur urceus exit?*

84-86. **plerumque**: *generally*; this indicates that the whole comparison is in general terms. — **hic**: 'in Rome, not in *vacuae Athenae*.' — **ego**: 'I, not an *ingenium*.' — **motura sonum**: like the English, 'to wake the lyre.' — **digner**: 'consider myself fit,' *i.e.*, 'think it possible that in such a life I should still be capable of writing poetry.'

87-105. This reason for not writing poetry — the fact that one must join the mutual admiration societies in Rome — is introduced abruptly by an allusion, the point of which does not appear till vs. 90, just as this letter begins with a story, vss. 2-19, the point of which is not at first apparent.

87. **consulti**: an office lawyer, a *jurist*. — **rhetor**: a court lawyer, a *pleader*. The two are of the same general profession, but in different branches of it. — The construction of this line and the next is harsh and, indeed, doubtful. As the text stands, it means 'there was an orator in Rome who was the brother of a jurist, a brother so close that each heard from the other nothing but compliments.'

89. **Gracchus**: both the Gracchi were orators, but Gaius, the younger of the two, was especially famous. This compliment was paid of course to the *rhetor*. — **Mucius**: there were three great jurists named Mucius Scaevola.

90. **qui minus**: *i.e.*, 'is there any reason why poets should not show the same fraternal spirit?' — **argutos**: as a standing epithet, *clear-voiced*. — **vexat furor**: these words throw off the ironical tone of the story, vss. 87-89.

91. **carmina**: lyric poetry. — **elegos**: elegy, which was cultivated at this time in Rome with great success, so that it was prob-

caelatumque novem Musis opus!' Adspice primum,
quanto cum fastu, quanto molimine circum-
spectemus vacuam Romanis vatibus aedem,
95   mox etiam, si forte vacas, sequere et procul audi,
quid ferat et quare sibi nectat uterque coronam.
Caedimur et totidem plagis consumimus hostem
lento Samnites ad lumina prima duello.

ably the most admired form of poetry. Horace did not himself attempt it. The allusion here is almost certainly to the elegiac poet Propertius. He was a member of the Maecenas circle, yet he is nowhere mentioned by Horace, who mentions so many literary friends. The suspicion that this silence covers some hostility is strengthened by the great differences in temperament and in literary ideals. Commentators have therefore found veiled allusions to Propertius in various passages (*Sat.* 1, 10, 18, *simius iste*; *Sat.* 1, 9); this is the most distinct and probable.

92. caelatum: the poem is praised in terms which would be used of a highly ornamented work of art. — novem Musis: dat. of agent with *caelatum*; the poem is so perfect that all the Muses must have aided in the writing of it. — adspice: the two poets are pictured standing before the temple of Apollo, exchanging compliments.

93-94. fastu: *pride.* — molimine: a rather rare word, with a suggestion of vastness and effort from its connection with *molior, moles; an air of importance.* — circum-spectemus: a word is run over from one line to the next in a few other places; *Sat.* 1, 2, 62; 2, 3, 117; *A. P.* 424. There may be here an intentional hit at the dignified air of the poets. — vacuam: the temple library was 'open to Roman poets,' as if in expectation of their coming. Cf. *Epist.* 2, 1, 216 f.

95. si . . . vacas: 'if you are quite at leisure,' and have nothing better to do. — sequere: to the hall where the poets are to read their verses to each other. No definite place is thought of; the two poets, having looked proudly at the library where they hope that their poems are to be preserved, pass on to a hall where they hold a *recitatio*.

96. sibi nectat: each is weaving a chaplet for himself by complimenting the other in order to be complimented in turn.

97-98. A condensed comparison; the two poets are like two gladiators and exchange poems as the gladiators exchange blows. —

Discedo Alcaeus puncto illius, ille meo quis?
100　Quis nisi Callimachus? Si plus adposcere visus,
fit Mimnermus, et optivo cognomine crescit.
Multa fero, ut placem genus irritabile vatum,
cum scribo et supplex populi suffragia capto;
idem, finitis studiis et mente recepta,
105　obturem patulas impune legentibus aures.

caedimur: the comparison is introduced without any word of comparison. — **lento, ad lumina prima**: *i.e.*, 'we keep it up all the afternoon, till the first lamps are lit,' till darkness separates the combatants. — **Samnites**: heavily armored gladiators, who would fight long without injury, until both were tired out. — **duello**: here in the original sense, a fight between two persons.

99. **discedo**: *i.e.*, 'when the combat of poems is over, he calls me an Alcaeus.' — **puncto**: the vote was recorded by a mark, *punctum*, on a tablet, which was a kind of tally sheet. — **quis?** Horace's pretended hesitation suggests that he does not know or care what name he shall use, but will call the other poet anything that will please him — say, Callimachus.

100. **Callimachus**: Propertius (5, 1, 64) calls himself the *Romanus Callimachus*. Callimachus was a poet of the Alexandrian school, of the third century B.C. He was regarded as one of the masters of the learned elegy; Catullus translated one of his poems (Catull. 66), the *Coma Berenices*.

101. **Mimnermus**: an earlier (about 600 B.C.) writer of elegiacs, who was considered to be the founder of elegy. — **optivo**: a legal term (= *adoptivo*), expressing with *cognomine* the idea that the name is given as names were given to great generals, *e.g.*, *Scipio Africanus*. Such a *cognomen* increases the poet's sense of importance (*crescit*).

102-105. 'I bear all this kind of thing when I am myself writing, but if I do not write I can escape from it.' This sums up vss. 87-101 and explains how the necessity of paying compliments is an added reason for not writing. — **irritabile**: *i.e.*, sensitive and eager for compliments. — **suffragia capto**: a comparison in brief; 'and seek for hearers as a candidate seeks for votes.' — **mente recepta**: Horace is always half humorous when he refers to the inspiration of poets. — **obturem**: the subj. mode is faintly potential, almost a future. — **patulas**:

Ridentur mala qui componunt carmina, verum
gaudent scribentes et se venerantur, et ultro,
si taceas, laudant quidquid scripsere beati.
At qui legitimum cupiet fecisse poema,
110 cum tabulis animum censoris sumet honesti,
audebit, quaecumque parum splendoris habebunt
et sine pondere erunt et honore indigna ferentur,

i.e., 'which before I had been obliged to keep open.' — **impune**: with *obturem*.

106-128. Besides all the reasons already given for not writing poetry, there is the further reason, the most serious of all, that the work demands the utmost effort and the best powers. 'Some poets, it is true, find pleasure in composing, without regard to the quality of the product, but the poet of high ideals is his own severest critic.'

107. **gaudent scribentes**: 'are full of joy in their writing.' The best parallel to these verses is Catull. 22, on Suffenus; *neque idem umquam | aeque est beatus ac poema cum scribit.* — **ultro**: 'they go on themselves to praise their writings.' — **beati**: with *laudant*.

109. **legitimum**: *i.e.*, 'a poem according to the rules of the art of poetry.'

110. **cum tabulis**: 'when he takes up his tablets to begin writing.' The *tabulae* were used for a first draft, because erasure and change were easy in the waxen surface. The expression partly anticipates the following comparison of the critic to the censor; 'the poet, when he takes up his tablets to write, will feel as the censor does when he takes up the lists.' — **honesti**: defining *censoris* by a predicate addition; 'with all its strictness.' The thought is then further amplified in *audebit*.

The next lines deal almost entirely with that part of the poet's work which has to do with the selection of dignified and expressive words. This was a subject to which Horace had given much thought, and, while he is following the ordinary rhetorical doctrines, he is also illustrating them by expressing his thought with special care.

111. **quaecumque**: sc. *verba*. — **parum splendoris**: = *sordida, humilia;* words that carry with them mean or unpoetic associations.

112. **sine pondere**: = *levia, inania;* words that do not convey much meaning of any kind. — **honore indigna**: this rather general phrase — *unworthy* — is used with special reference to the figure of

verba movere loco, quamvis invita recedant
et versentur adhuc intra penetralia Vestae;
115 obscurata diu populo bonus eruet atque
proferet in lucem speciosa vocabula rerum,
quae priscis memorata Catonibus atque Cethegis
nunc situs informis premit et deserta vetustas;

the censor, who removes from the senatorial list *honore indignos*. — **ferentur**: 'are in circulation,' the words being here in mind, rather than the censor's office.

113. **movere loco**: the technical expression for the censor's act of condemnation is *movere tribu*. — **invita**: properly of those who were removed by the censor: as applied to words rejected by the critical writer it has only a rather vague meaning; 'although such common words recur constantly to the mind and it is hard to avoid their use.'

114. The expression here is selected almost entirely with the thought of the censor's work in mind; 'although they may have been hitherto at home in the most sacred spot in Rome,' 'although they may have had thus far a perfect reputation.' With reference to words it means 'although they have been used in the finest of poetry.' The identification of the object compared with the figure results in some lack of clearness. — **adhuc**: *i.e.*, 'until you bring them under your critical scrutiny.'

115-119. But the office of the critical poet is not merely that of the censor who rejects; he must also enrich the language.

115. **populo**: with *obscurata*, the two together being the opposite of *ferentur, versentur*. — **bonus**: *i.e.*, 'working for good results.'

116. **speciosa**: the opposite of *quaecumque parum splendoris habebunt*, words of vivid meaning and elevated suggestion.

117. **Catonibus, Cethegis**: the plur. means 'men like Cato and Cethegus.' They are again used in *A. P.* 50, 56 as representatives of the early Latin style. Cato was regarded by writers of archaizing tendencies, like Sallust, as a master of vigorous and individual style, and Cethegus (consul 204) is mentioned with praise by Cicero (*Brut.* 15, 57) and was called by Ennius (*Ann.* 306) *Suadae medulla*. It is not necessary, however, to attach to Horace's use of these names any very specific meaning; they are types of the early orator.

118. **situs informis**: as *neglect* results in rust and mold, that disfigures the object, it is itself called *informis*. So *deserta* is

adsciscet nova, quae genitor produxerit usus.
120 Vemens et liquidus puroque simillimus amni
fundet opes Latiumque beabit divite lingua;
luxuriantia compescet, nimis aspera sano
levabit cultu, virtute carentia tollet,
ludentis speciem dabit et torquebitur ut qui

applied to *vetustas*, though it properly describes the result of *vetustas*. — The enrichment of the poetic vocabulary by bringing back into use words which had fallen out was one of Vergil's characteristic merits. Horace, from the nature of his subjects and the character of his lyric poetry, made fewer contributions of this kind.

119. **adsciscet**: primarily a legal word, used of admitting to the enjoyment of legal rights; *enroll*, 'admit to full rights.' — **genitor . . . usus**: the doctrine that usage makes language, brings forward and maintains new words, was fully accepted by Horace and is expressed by him in a classic phrase (*A. P.* 72), *usus, quem penes arbitrium est et ius et norma loquendi.* — This is the second means of enriching the living vocabulary. In the fragmentary condition of Latin literature it is not always possible to tell what writers first adopted a new word into literary style, but Horace certainly made considerable use of this method of giving vividness and novelty to his forms of expression.

120. **vemens, liquidus**: these adjectives, though they go with the subject of *beabit* (*i.e.*, *poeta*), are really a part of the comparison. — **puro . . . amni**: cf. for the opposite, *cum flueret lutulentus*, of Lucilius, in *Sat.* 1, 4, 11. The figure has been often used in English literature, *e.g.*, Tennyson, The Poet's Mind: —

'Clear and bright it should be ever,
Flowing like a crystal river.'

121. **fundet opes**: a rather general phrase, which is immediately explained more precisely in the rest of the line, in which *beabit* and *divite* repeat *opes*.

122-125. These lines go over from the choice of words to the larger aspects of composition, following the order of rhetorical treatises. There is nothing novel in Horace's treatment; what he says can be paralleled by passages from Cicero's rhetorical works and from Quintilian, and the same things are said again, more fully, in the *Ars Poetica*. — **luxuriantia**: the figure of the husbandman, trimming off the foliage of the vine in order to increase its production of

125 nunc Satyrum, nunc agrestem Cyclopa movetur.
Praetulerim scriptor delirus inersque videri,
dum mea delectent mala me vel denique fallant,
quam sapere et ringi. Fuit haud ignobilis Argis,

grapes, is frequently used of the restraint of an exuberant style. — **aspera . . . levabit**: rhetoric paid much attention to the sound of words and phrases, as was natural when prose composition was largely occupied with oratory and when verse was still closely allied to song. *aspera* therefore means primarily 'rough in sound,' but with a secondary reference also to expressions that are too blunt, that do not harmonize sufficiently with the general tone of the writing. — **sano**: since too great polish is itself a fault, the smoothing off of roughnesses must be done with judgment. — **virtute carentia**: this carries on the thought of *sano*; words and phrases which are 'lacking in energy and vigor' must be taken out altogether, and more forcible and expressive words put in their place. For *tollet* in this sense cf. *Sat.* 1, 4, 11, *erat quod tollere velles*, and *Sat.* 1, 10, 51, where *tollenda* and *relinquenda* define each other. — **ludentis**: 'he will look like one who moves with ease and pleasure; his style will seem to involve no effort.' This general expression is elaborated in the figure of the trained dancer; 'he will seem to move with ease, as a dancer turns this way and that and plays now one part, now another.' Cf. *Epist.* 2, 1, 210, where the art of the dramatist is compared to the difficult art of the rope dancer. — **Satyrum, Cyclopa**: this is an allusion to the pantomime of the rivalry of a faun (satyr) and the Cyclops Polyphemus for the love of the nymph Galatea, in which a single actor expressed alternately in his dancing the feeling of the graceful faun and of the clumsy giant. — **movetur**: the passive is equivalent to *saltat* (*Sat.* 1, 5, 63) and retains the cognate accusative.

126–128. 'As I think of all that is necessary to produce good poetry, I could almost wish that I were one of the self-satisfied writers (vss. 106-108) who do not know how badly they write.' — **delirus**: this is one of the synonyms for *insanus* in *Sat.* 2, 3, 107, 293. It is selected rather than *stultus* or *ridiculus*, because the story of 128 ff. is already in Horace's mind. — **iners**: *i.e.*, 'too indolent to meet the requirements of the true poet.' — **ringi**: 'to suffer the discomforts and vexations which necessarily attend upon the effort to be a critical writer (*sapere*).'

128. haud ignobilis: *well known;*

qui se credebat miros audire tragoedos,
130 in vacuo laetus sessor plausorque theatro,
cetera qui vitae servaret munia recto
more, bonus sane vicinus, amabilis hospes,
comis in uxorem, posset qui ignoscere servis
et signo laeso non insanire lagoenae,
135 posset qui rupem et puteum vitare patentem.
Hic ubi cognatorum opibus curisque refectus
expulit elleboro morbum bilemque meraco,
et redit ad sese: ' Pol me occidistis, amici,
non servastis,' ait, 'cui sic extorta voluptas
140 et demptus per vim mentis gratissimus error.'
Nimirum sapere est abiectis utile nugis

but the adjective is meant to characterize the story, which is told by various writers, rather than the person. — **Argis**: the regular Latin form for the dat. and abl. of this word.

129–131. The two *qui* clauses, with *credebat* and *servaret*, illustrate well the effect of the modes in relative clauses.

131. cetera: 'in all other respects' he was perfectly sane.

133. posset . . . ignoscere: a little more general than *ignosceret* would have been: he 'was capable' of acting like a sensible man.

134. signo laeso: *i.e.*, when he found the seal on a bottle of wine broken and therefore knew that some slave had been stealing the wine. Cf. also *Sat.* 1. 3. 80–83.

135. rupem, puteum: this same test of sanity, evidently proverbial, is referred to in *Sat.* 2. 3, 55, *fluvios* being used instead of *puteum*. Cf. 'I can see a church by daylight.'

137. These expressions for madness and for the cure of it by hellebore are used also in *Sat.* 2, 3, 82, 141. — **meraco**: *i.e.*, the strongest kind of a dose was necessary.

138. pol: cf. *Epist.* 1, 7. 92, in a similar ejaculation, expressing the astonishment of the speaker at finding himself where he is.

141. sapere: this resumes the thought of vs. 109 and, more distinctly, the thought and expression of vs. 128, after the digression of the anecdote, and gives it a new turn, toward philosophy. This is the underlying thought of the Epistles, that Horace has given up the writing of poetry and turned to the study of philosophy. —

et tempestivum pueris concedere ludum,
ac non verba sequi fidibus modulanda Latinis,
sed verae numerosque modosque ediscere vitae.
145 Quocirca mecum loquor haec tacitusque recordor:
Si tibi nulla sitim finiret copia lymphae,
narrares medicis: quod quanto plura parasti,
tanto plura cupis, nulline faterier audes?
Si vulnus tibi monstrata radice vel herba
150 non fieret levius, fugeres radice vel herba
proficiente nihil curarier. Audieras, cui

abiectis . . . nugis: *i.e.*, lyrical composition, as in *Sat.* 1, 9, 2, Catull. 1, 4.

142. **pueris**: the word is chosen with reference to *ludum*; cf. *ludicra, Epist.* 1, 1, 10.

143-144. **non verba**: words, in distinction from realities. — **sequi**: as the writing of good poetry requires, vss. 111-119. — **numerosque modosque**: these terms of music and rhythmic art are used to point the contrast; 'I am learning the measures and rhythms of a wise life.'

145. Cf. *Sat.* 1, 4, 133 f., 137 ff., where the same thought is expressed in very similar words. — The rest of the Epistle is an exposition of his philosophy of life, all introduced, as if in direct quotation, by this line. It is occupied chiefly with that false passion which Horace always puts first among the sins of men, the love of money and of many possessions.

146. 'The love of money is like the dropsy, with an unsatisfied thirst for more.' The same figure is used in *Carm.* 2, 2, 13-16.

147-148. 'In the same way, the desire for money increases as it is gratified.' — **nulli faterier**: *i.e.*, 'you should seek the advice of those who can cure your soul,' of the philosophers. — **audes**: *summon courage* to overcome the *pudor malus* (*Epist.* 1, 16, 24) that inclines you to conceal your disease.

149. **monstrata**: *prescribed*. The figure of the physician and his patient is carried on further; 'find the right treatment for your disease.' — **radice**: abl. instrumental, in both lines.

150-151. **fugeres**: governing *curarier*; cf. *fuge quaerere, Carm.* 1, 9, 13, and *mitte sectari, Carm.* 1, 38, 3. — **curarier**: *to be treated*, and of course 'to be cured,' which would be inconsistent with *proficiente nihil*.

151-154. **audieras**: 'you had perhaps been told,' corresponding

rem di donarent, illi decedere pravam
stultitiam, et cum sis nihilo sapientior, ex quo
plenior es, tamen uteris monitoribus isdem?
155 At si divitiae prudentem reddere possent,
si cupidum timidumque minus te, nempe ruberes,
viveret in terris te si quis avarior uno.
Si proprium est, quod quis libra mercatus et aere est,
quaedam, si credis consultis, mancipat usus;
160 qui te pascit ager, tuus est, et vilicus Orbi,
cum segetes occat, tibi mox frumenta daturas,

to *monstrata radice*. The advice would be like that in *Epist.* 1, 1, 65, *rem facias, rem*, or, more precisely, in *Sat.* 2, 3, 95 f., *divina humanaque pulchris divitiis parent.*—nihilo sapientior: like *proficiente nihil*; the treatment produces no effect.

155–157. This thought also is found in *Sat.* 2, 3, 91 ff. Here, however, the desired virtues are more definitely expressed in *prudentem, cupidum timidumque minus*, since the purpose is not caricature, but exhortation. Cf. also *Epist.* 1, 16, 65, *qui cupiet, metuet quoque*; desire and fear are merely the two sides of a single passion.

158 ff. 'Possession consists in use; only the man who uses can be said to possess.'—libra . . . et aere: this was one of the traditional ways of acquiring property by purchase. The scales and piece of brass were preserved as symbols from the early time when brass was money and when it was not coined, but was weighed out for each purchase. This method was called *mancipatio*.

159. 'Yet there is another method, according to the jurists, by which property may be acquired, namely, by *usucapio*, that is, by possession for a certain period.' Horace intentionally uses *mancipat* in this clause, as if to say that *usucapio* was equivalent to *mancipatio*; this is the basis of the argument that follows, in which *usus* is really employed in a double sense, as a legal term and in the more general meaning.

160. qui te pascit: *i.e.*, 'of which you enjoy the profits, the *usus*.'— tuus: = *proprius*, 'your property, because you enjoy it.'—Orbi: unknown. The only point is that he is the 'owner' of the workman, yet the person who profits by the labors of the *vilicus* is the person who finally eats the grain.

161. occat: *harrows*; to stand for all the processes of cultivation.

te dominum sentit; das nummos, accipis uvam,
pullos, ova, cadum temeti: nempe modo isto
paullatim mercaris agrum, fortasse trecentis
165 aut etiam supra nummorum milibus emptum.
Quid refert, vivas numerato nuper an olim?
Emptor Aricini quondam Veientis et arvi
emptum cenat olus, quamvis aliter putat; emptis
sub noctem gelidam lignis calefactat aenum.
170 Sed vocat usque suum, qua populus adsita certis
limitibus vicina refugit iurgia, tamquam

162. **te dominum sentit**: equivalent to *tibi proprium est*, 158. The meaning of *sentit* is not to be pressed; it means only that, in effect, by transferring the products of his toil to you, he acknowledges you, not Orbius, to be his master.

163. **temeti**: this old word is apparently the farmer's term, used here with other words describing farm produce. — **modo isto**: *by so doing*.

165. **emptum**: with emphasis, recurring to the thought of *proprium*; 'and it is then yours.'

166. **numerato**: abl. as if of the noun, but a participle also, having the adverbs *nuper*, *olim*, with it. — **nuper an olim**: the significant words in the sentence; 'whether the money by which you live was paid out recently or some time ago.' If the field had been bought in the beginning, the money would have been paid *olim*; in the daily purchase of supplies the money was, in part, paid *nuper*.

167-169. 'The man who buys the produce, really buys the farm; so, conversely, the man who begins by buying the farm is in reality daily buying his supplies from the farm.' — **emptor**: 'the man who is commonly called the buyer.' — **quondam**: = *olim*, vs. 166; to be taken with the verbal noun *emptor*. — **et**: connecting *Aricini* and *Veientis*. The Latin frequently uses *et* where English usage would have 'or.' These towns, Aricia and Veii, were near Rome and the owner would have the vegetables for his table sent in from his country place. But the vegetables and the firewood would in reality be 'bought,' though he might like to boast that they were not. Cf. *dapes inemptas. Epod.* 2, 48; so 'boughten' things used to be spoken of with apology in New England.

170. **usque ... qua**: 'up to where.' — **pŏpulus**: not *pŏpulus*.

171. **refugit**: the row of pop-

sit proprium quidquam, puncto quod mobilis horae
nunc prece, nunc pretio, nunc vi, nunc morte suprema
permutet dominos et cedat in altera iura.
175 Sic, quia perpetuus nulli datur usus, et heres
heredem alterius velut unda supervenit undam,
quid vici prosunt aut horrea? Quidve Calabris
saltibus adiecti Lucani, si metit Orcus
grandia cum parvis, non exorabilis auro?
180 Gemmas, marmor, ebur, Tyrrhena sigilla, tabellas,
argentum, vestes Gaetulo murice tinctas,

lars 'avoids' disputes. *i.e.*, enables the owner of the land to avoid them.

172. proprium: going back to the beginning of this argument, vs. 158. — **puncto . . . horae**: the phrase is, like all Latin phrases for a brief time, entirely vague, and all attempts to interpret this or *horae momento* (*Sat.* 1, 1, 7 f.) with precision make the mistake of reading into it a modern accuracy.

173. prece, pretio: 'by gift or purchase.' The contrast is natural and the alliterative words are several times used together in this sense. — **morte suprema**: 'death which is the end of all things.'

175. perpetuus . . . usus: 'there is therefore no such thing as the perpetual possession of which lawyers speak.'

176. heredem alterius: *i.e.* 'one heir succeeds an heir of still another heir'; the phrase expresses, perhaps too briefly, the continuity of the succession. Of the four possible changes of ownership (vs. 173) Horace dwells only upon the last.

177. vici: *estates.*

178. Lucani: sc. *prosunt.* This refers to the driving of the herds from the lowlands of Calabria to the mountain pastures of Lucania. — **metit**: a very effective turn from literal to figurative expression. The thought, and, in general, the phrases of this passage find frequent expression in the Odes.

180-182. These possessions of the wealthy stand for wealth itself, as merely a different expression from *vici, horrea, Calabris saltibus,* just as in *Carm.* 1, 31, *armenta, aurum, ebur, rura, aureis, cululis,* are all symbolic of riches. — **sigilla**: small figures, apparently of earthenware, which were found in Etruria and valued for their antiquity. — **argentum**: *silver plate,* not money. — **Gaetulo**: the

sunt qui non habeant, est qui non curat habere.
Cur alter fratrum cessare et ludere et ungi
praeferat Herodis palmetis pinguibus, alter
185 dives et importunus ad umbram lucis ab ortu
silvestrem flammis et ferro mitiget agrum,
scit Genius, natale comes qui temperat astrum,
naturae deus humanae mortalis, in unum

African dye, one of the better kind; cf. *Epist.* 2, 1, 207. — **sunt qui**: the subjunctive after these words is phraseological, not expressive; it came over from negative sentences and sentences with indefinite antecedents, and there is, in most cases, no more essential difference of meaning than there is between *quamvis* with the subjunctive and *quamvis* with the indicative. In this particular instance, however, the difference between the many (*sunt*) and the one (*est*) is strongly marked and is further emphasized by the difference in the mode. — **est qui**: Horace.

183–189. 'Why there should be such differences between men, even between brothers, only the power that made us so can tell.' This passage is parenthetic, yet is not far from the main thought, especially in vss. 185 f.

183. **alter fratrum**: so in the *Adelphoe* of Terence and cf. *Sat.* 2, 1, 26, on the contrast between Castor and Pollux. — **cessare**: absolutely, as in *Epist.* 1, 7, 57, *et properare loco et cessare.*

184. **Herodis palmetis**: Herod the Great, the Herod of the New Testament, who ruled in Judea from 39 to 4 B.C. The palm groves about Jericho were specially famous and were a source of great revenue (*pinguibus*) by the sale of dates.

186. **silvestrem**: *i.e.*, it was wooded land, which was to be cleared and prepared for farming. — **flammis et ferro**: both methods were in use, by burning or by cutting the timber for building material or for firewood. — **mitiget**: the clearing of land is often treated as a sort of conquest or 'breaking in,' like the training of horses. — While the one brother prefers a life of ease to any kind of occupation, however profitable, the other is seeking profit at the cost of any kind of labor.

187–189. **Genius**: cf. *Epist.* 2, 1, 144, and note. The individual and contradictory characteristics of the Genius are dwelt upon as explaining the contradictions in human nature. — **natale ... astrum**: the constellations which by their position at the hour of birth

quodque caput vultu mutabilis, albus et ater.
190 Vtar et ex modico quantum res poscet acervo
tollam, nec metuam quid de me iudicet heres,
quod non plura datis invenerit; et tamen idem
scire volam, quantum simplex hilarisque nepoti
discrepet et quantum discordet parcus avaro.
195 Distat enim, sparsis tua prodigus, an neque sumptum
invitus facias, neque plura parare labores,
ac potius, puer ut festis quinquatribus olim,
exiguo gratoque fruaris tempore raptim.
Pauperies immunda domus procul absit; ego utrum
200 nave ferar magna an parva, ferar unus et idem.
Non agimur tumidis velis Aquilone secundo,

determined character and fate. — **temperat**: the Genius, being divine, could affect the constellations and planets. This passage does not imply a belief in astrology; cf. *Carm.* 1, 11; 2, 17. — **in unum ... mutabilis**: *i.e.*, 'assuming a different form and character for each individual.' This is the important point of the whole description. — **albus et ater**: proverbial; cf. Catull. 93, *nec scire utrum sis albus an ater homo.* The words merely amplify *mutabilis.*

190. **utar**: 'I for my part desire only use, not possession.' This is familiar doctrine, beginning with *Sat.* 1, 1.

191. **heres**: with a general reference only; Horace had no natural heir, but he alludes often to the proverbial feeling between testator and heir.

193. **scire volam**: *i.e.*, 'to be fully aware of the difference' and, it is implied, to act accordingly. — With the following thought, which Horace expresses in many places, cf., *e.g.*, *Sat.* 2, 2, 53 f.

195-198. **neque ... invitus**: to be taken together, as equivalent to *hilaris.* — **Quinquatribus**: the short spring vacation, 'Easter recess,' March 19-23, which, because it is so short, the schoolboy enjoys most eagerly (*raptim*).

199. **domus**: gen. with *pauperies.* — **absit**: the clause with subjv. is a paratactic condition or clause of proviso.

200. The figure is changed somewhat abruptly; literally the thought is, 'if only I am free from sordid poverty, I care not whether I have much or little.'

201-202. The two clauses are in

non tamen adversis aetatem ducimus Austris,
viribus, ingenio, specie, virtute, loco, re
extremi primorum, extremis usque priores.
205 Non es avarus; abi. Quid, cetera iam simul isto
cum vitio fugere? Caret tibi pectus inani
ambitione? Caret mortis formidine et ira?
Somnia, terrores magicos, miracula, sagas,
nocturnos lemures portentaque Thessala rides?
210 Natales grate numeras? Ignoscis amicis?
Lenior et melior fis accedente senecta?
Quid te exempta levat spinis de pluribus una?
Vivere si recte nescis, decede peritis.
Lusisti satis, edisti satis atque bibisti;

paratactic relation; 'I am not borne on by favoring breezes of prosperity, yet I am not struggling with adversity,' for 'though I am not borne on. . . .'

204. The figure again changes to that of the racecourse; cf. *Sat.* 1, 1, 115 f.

205. **non es**: paratactic condition. — **abi**: *good*. This use is colloquial, *e.g.*, Plaut. *Trin.* 830, *abi, laudo*. — For the thought of the line cf. *Sat.* 2, 3, 159 f., *quid, si quis non sit avarus, continuo sanus? Minime.*

208–209. 'All kinds of superstitious fears.' Freedom from these meant much more to the ancients than it can ever mean to modern men. — **sagas**: *fortune tellers*. — **lemures**: 'umbras vagantes hominum ante diem mortuorum et ideo metuendas,' is the comment of the Scholiast. — **Thessala**: this was proverbial, in Greek literature and in Latin.

210. **natales grate**: *i.e.*, 'are you grateful for each added year of life?'

211–212. 'Are you becoming a better man as you grow older? For to get rid of a fault or two is not enough.' The comparison of faults to thorns is used also in *Epist.* 1, 14, 4 f.

213. **recte**: *i.e.*, as a true philosophy teaches. — **decede peritis**: neither this phrase nor *tempus abire* (215) is a suggestion of suicide; the meaning is simply, 'you are through with life, since for you it has no real meaning; leave it to those who truly understand how to live.'

214. The emphasis is not upon the frivolity or self-indulgence of men: this is merely an application of *decede peritis* under the

215 tempus abire tibi est, ne potum largius aequo
rideat et pulset lasciva decentius aetas.

figure of the satisfied guest rising from the table, as in *Sat.* 1, 1, 118 f., *exacto contentus tempore, vita cedat uti conviva satur.*
216. **lasciva decentius**: youth may with more propriety indulge in follies and may laugh at an old man who has not learned to control himself.

3
ARS POETICA

Of all the writings of Horace none has been more carefully studied and more elaborately discussed than this Epistle. Yet it must be said that, in consequence of the insufficiency of *data*, there is still considerable uncertainty in regard to the date, the persons addressed, the occasion and purpose, and even the title.

The internal evidence in regard to the date of composition or publication is both scanty and indefinite. It is to be found in the references to persons, to Vergil and Varius (55), to Cascellius (370), to Tarpa (387), and to Varus (438). But no one of these is precise. The context and the purpose of the allusion is such as to be suitable to a person still living or to one who had passed into literary tradition. There is a like uncertainty in regard to the allusions to public works in vss. 63 ff.; they are too vague to afford material for dating.

The only external evidence of any weight is the statement of Suetonius that Augustus asked for and received *Epist.* 2, 1 *post sermones quosdam lectos* in which he was not mentioned: these *sermones* cannot have been the First Book of the Epistles, where Augustus is frequently referred to; they must have been *Epist.* 2, 2 — the bare mention of Augustus' name in vs. 48 does not stand in the way of this — and this Epistle. The inference from the statement of Suetonius would therefore be that this Epistle was written before *Epist.* 2, 1; that is, in the period between the publication of the First Book and the writing of the *Carmen Saeculare*, between 19 or 20 B.C. and 17 B.C. Fortunately the character of the Epistle is such that a more precise date is not necessary to its interpretation.

The persons to whom the letter is supposed to be sent are a father and two sons, the Pisones. From the merely formal address in vs. 6 and vs. 235 and the words *O Pompilius sanguis* in vss. 291 f. no inference can be drawn as to their identity. In vs. 366 the elder son is specially addressed in terms which imply, though not very clearly, that he was just engaging or might soon engage in poetical composition. These are but scanty indications of identity, and the uncertainty is increased by the frequency of the name Piso; fourteen persons of that name are mentioned in the *Onomast. Cic.*, ten in Tacitus, seven in Suetonius. But there was a Gn. Calpurnius Piso, some years older than Horace, who fought at Philippi and was afterward consul in 23 B.C. His eldest son, consul in 7 B.C., was born about 44 and would have been about twenty-five when this Epistle was written. There was also a younger son. These may be the Pisones addressed, but it is evident that any identification is at best a mere possibility. As nothing definite is known of the literary interests of these persons, the identification, even if it were certain, would contribute little to the interpretation of the Epistle.

The proper title of this poem is also uncertain. It stands in most of the Mss. as a separate composition, just before or just after the *Carmen Saeculare*, as if it had been published by itself; and it certainly was put into circulation, with some degree of publicity, before *Epist.* 2, 1 was written. For such publication its title may have been *Epistula ad Pisones*. But it is referred to by Quintilian, *praef.* 2, in the words . . . *Horati consilio, qui in arte poetica suadet* . . ., and again, 8, 3, 60, *Horatius in prima parte libri de arte poetica fingit*, with a quotation of the first verse. This is the title used by most of the grammarians and by the scholiasts. It is also found in most of the Mss., though it may well have been introduced there from the grammatical tradition. In most printed editions, because of the subject matter and the date, the poem is placed after *Epist.* 2, 2, as the third Epistle of the Second Book, and it is often referred to, for convenience, as *Epist.* 2, 3. If Horace gave it a title, it was probably *Epistula ad Pisones*, perhaps with the addition of *de Arte Poetica* or *Ars Poetica*. Tradition has fixed upon it the name *Ars Poetica*.

The course of thought from sentence to sentence and from one paragraph to another is easily followed, but it resists all attempts to reduce it to a scheme. All that can be said is that the Epistle consists of a series of remarks upon poetry, followed (from vs. 309 to the end) by similar remarks upon the training and ideals of the poet.

The general course of the thought is as follows : —

'A poem, like a painting, must be well composed, not tricked out with inharmonious ornaments; nor should the poet, avoiding one fault, fall into its opposite. Harmony depends in part upon a wise choice of subject, which insures good arrangement. Choice of words also contributes to harmony of effect, for words suffer change, like all human things.

'The meters and style of different kinds of poetry are fixed by tradition, from which it is not easy to break away. Tradition also fixes the outlines of characters, and in all these matters it is best to follow a good model, in order that your characters may speak as befits their nature and their period of life.

'In the drama, too, one should follow the best usage, with five acts and three speakers. As to the chorus, it should take a sympathetic part in the action, and the music and the dress of actors should not be too prominent. The satyric drama presents peculiar difficulties, owing to the mingling of the heroic and the comic.

'In the observance of metrical laws our Roman poets are too careless, a fault for which, as the history of the Greek drama shows, nothing will atone. Inspiration is not a substitute for training; it is a kind of madness and, for myself, I prefer to avoid it and to devote myself to laying down laws for other writers.

'The poet must enrich his mind by reading and observation and train himself to avoid faults. Not that all faults can be avoided; even Homer sometimes nods. Yet, for a poet, mediocrity is failure, and only training can teach us how to escape that. We must listen to the real critics, not to flatterers. Untrained inspiration is mere madness, and I do not want to see you a madman.'

The fact that the course of thought is rambling is the key to an understanding of the Epistle. For this arrangement is not the result of carelessness; Horace followed this unsystematic and yet closely knit succession of topics from deliberate choice. He was not trying to compose a treatise, but to write an *epistula*, a *sermo*. Like any epistle, it is addressed to certain persons, and, like any *sermo*, it follows the line of easy transition by suggestion from one topic to another. This is in itself a form of art, the particular form to which Horace had trained himself, and this Epistle is to be interpreted precisely as *Epist.* 2, 1 and 2, 2 are to be interpreted. That this intentionally unsystematic poem should have been taken for a formal treatise on the art of poetry is indeed surprising; the error was due in part to a too literal understanding of the traditional title, in part to a general tendency among early scholars to overvalue the content of classic literature. It should be valued rather as a beautifully finished *sermo*, to be studied for its skillful turns of thought and expression, its perfect phrasing, its easy and mellow tone.

On the other side, the substance of what is said in the *Ars Poetica* comes from two different sources. Porphyrion says in his brief introduction that Horace has here gathered the teachings of Neoptolemus, a rhetorician of the third century, *non quidem omnia, sed eminentissima*. This may very well be correct; it is at any rate clear that Horace is in part repeating and applying some of the traditional doctrines of rhetoric, in which, as a lifelong student of the art which he practiced, he was certainly interested. To this source is due the large proportion of Greek literary history. Of all this it is fair to say that it is interesting chiefly to students of the history of rhetoric. But Horace does not merely repeat traditional doctrine; he also comments upon it, speaking with the authority of an older poet addressing a younger generation of literary men. Our incomplete knowledge of the tendencies of the period makes it difficult to understand fully the point of some of his warnings, but much of it is of universal application, even to modern conditions. This is the more valuable part of the *Ars Poetica*, centering, as it does, upon the necessity of adequate training for the professional man of letters. It is at the same time a proclamation of Horace's own creed and thus a guide to the interpretation of all his poetry.

> Humano capiti cervicem pictor equinam
> iungere si velit et varias inducere plumas
> undique collatis membris, ut turpiter atrum

1-37. 'Harmony is necessary to a poem, as to a picture.'

1. **Humano**: the general term before the specific, *mulier*, as often. The chiastic order, adj.-noun, noun-adj., is intentional.

2. **velit**: *should choose*, deliberately. — **varias**: *of many colors*, going beyond nature even in this detail. — **inducere**: *lay on*, as if the body were first drawn and then the feathers were spread over it.

3. **undique**: *i.e.*, 'from all kinds of creatures.' — **membris**: dat. after *inducere*. — **ut**: the result of the whole process, especially of *collatis membris*. Strictly taken, this clause should be in the form of another infinitive; but such a use of a clause of result, to express some single characteristic of the whole, is not uncommon. — **turpiter atrum**: to be taken together, to balance *formosa superne*; cf. *turpiter hirtum*, *Epist.* 1, 3, 22. This sense of *turpis*, 'ugly, hideous,' is frequent.

desinat in piscem mulier formosa superne,
5 spectatum admissi risum teneatis, amici?
Credite, Pisones, isti tabulae fore librum
persimilem, cuius velut aegri somnia vanae
fingentur species, ut nec pes nec caput uni
reddatur formae. ' Pictoribus atque poetis
10 quidlibet audendi semper fuit aequa potestas.'
Scimus et hanc veniam petimusque damusque vicissim,
sed non ut placidis coeant immitia, non ut
serpentes avibus geminentur, tigribus agni.

4. **mulier**: he has in mind such a figure as Scylla, in which the hideousness of the whole was increased by the contrast between the beauty of the face and bust and the ugliness of the body.

5. **spectatum admissi**: *i.e.*, admitted to a private view in the painter's studio. — **amici**: general, *my friends*, yet immediately made definite by the address in the next line, as, indeed, the whole point of vss. 1–5 is general, until the application is reached in vs. 6. Cf. the beginning of *Epist.* 2, 2.

7. **vanae**: *unreal*, *i.e.*, fantastic, without any corresponding reality.

8. **species**: *images*, 'conceptions.' — **ut nec pes nec caput**: the expression is not strictly logical; the common phrase *nec pes nec caput* ('neither head nor tail') would properly require something like 'shall be distinguishable' (*adparet*, Plaut. *Asin.* 729) or it should be *ut et pes et caput non*. . . .

9. **reddatur**: *belong to*, 'be suitable to.'

9–10. The objection of an imagined hearer. — **quidlibet audendi**: *i.e.*, 'of using their imagination freely.' — **aequa**: 'a like power,' 'an equal power.' This word merely repeats the implication of *pictoribus atque poetis*, 'poets as well as painters'; the emphasis is upon *semper fuit potestas*.

11. **vicissim**: *i.e.*, 'we poets expect it from painters, and we also grant it to them.'

12–13. **coeant**: in the general sense, *unite*, as in *Epist.* 1, 5, 25 f., *ut coeat par iungaturque pari*; but the general sense is repeated in clearer form in the next verse, where *serpentes* corresponds to *immitia*, *avibus* to *placidis*, and *geminentur*, 'pair,' is a more definite expression for *coeant*. — The pairing of creatures of different species is often used to typify the

Inceptis gravibus plerumque et magna professis
15 purpureus, late qui splendeat, unus et alter
adsuitur pannus, cum lucus et ara Dianae
et properantis aquae per amoenos ambitus agros
aut flumen Rhenum aut pluvius describitur arcus.
Sed nunc non erat his locus. Et fortasse cupressum
20 scis simulare: quid hoc, si fractis enatat exspes
navibus aere dato qui pingitur? Amphora coepit
institui, currente rota cur urceus exit?
Denique sit quod vis, simplex dumtaxat et unum.
Maxima pars vatum, pater et iuvenes patre digni,

unnatural or the impossible, *e.g.*, *Epod.* 16, 30-32.

14. That is, the poem begins as an epic in the grand style, dealing with the heroic.

15-16. purpureus ... pannus: this is one of the phrases that have come over from Horace into modern thought. The allusion is not to the purple stripe on the tunic, which would not suggest incongruity to a Roman, but to a patch of bright color sewed on where it did not belong.

17-18. These examples may very well have been taken from poems then in circulation, so that the allusions would be at once identified; cf. *defingit Rheni luteum caput* (*Sat.* 1, 10, 37) from a poem of Furius Bibaculus.

19. sed: *i.e.*, 'they are all very fine, but. . . .' — **et**: 'and in the same way.'

20. scis: 'the motive which leads to such incongruities is the writer's belief that he has special skill in such descriptions, or, to return to the painter's art, in the painting of certain objects.' — **enatat**: *i.e.*, 'if he is to be represented as swimming ashore.' The reference is to the pictures which were hung in temples to express gratitude for escape from peril, and which represented the scene of escape. Cf. *Carm.* 1, 5, 13 ff., *Sat.* 2, 1, 33 and note.

21-22. aere dato: 'and he has paid good money for it, too.' — **amphora**: the larger vessel corresponds to *magna professis*, vs. 14, and the smaller *urceus*, in a less definite way, to the petty details upon which the poet spends his efforts. This shifts the thought slightly, from the lack of harmony to the lack of consistency and tenacity in the purpose of the writer.

23. A summary of the thought up to this point.

24-30. 'Incongruities are often

25 decipimur specie recti : brevis esse laboro,
obscurus fio; sectantem levia nervi
deficiunt animique; professus grandia turget;
serpit humi tutus nimium timidusque procellae;
qui variare cupit rem prodigialiter unam,
30 delphinum silvis appingit, fluctibus aprum.
In vitium ducit culpae fuga, si caret arte.
Aemilium circa ludum faber imus et ungues
exprimet et molles imitabitur aere capillos,

the result of a desire for variety, as other faults are the result of the desire to attain to some particular virtue of style.'

` 25. **specie recti**: *i.e.*, 'by a perception of some excellence without due regard to the fact that it may lead to a defect.' The characteristics mentioned are all in themselves desirable; the suggestion that they are misleading lies in *decipimur* and, slightly, in *specie*.

26. **levia**: *polish*, as in *nimis aspera sano levabit cultu*, *Epist.* 2, 2, 122 f. — **nervi**: cf. *Sat.* 2, 1, 2, *sine nervis*, of one judgment of the Satires, opposed to *nimis acer*.

27. The danger of falling into bombast in the attempt to write in a lofty style was constantly before the mind of Horace; it is the fault which he most sedulously avoids. — **professus**: not essentially different from *sectantem*.

28. **tutus nimium**: *i.e.*, 'one who is too anxious to be safe.' — **timidus procellae**: = *dum procel-*

las cautus horrescis, *Carm.* 2, 10, 2 f., where also *tutus* is used almost as it is here.

29–30. 'So it is, in seeking variety of ornament, that one falls into the absurdities of which I was speaking above.' — **cupit**: *is anxious*, as the desires are expressed above by strong words, *laboro*, *sectantem*, *professus*. — **prodigialiter**: a rare word, perhaps coined by Horace (cf. *Epist.* 2, 2, 119); to be taken with *variare*; 'to introduce such variety as to be like a miracle,' 'to be wonderfully varied.' — **unam**: with emphasis, at the end of the verse and in contrast to *prodigialiter*. — The instances in vs. 30 are merely vivid expressions of the thought of vss. 16–18 and especially vs. 20 f.

31. A summary, like vs. 23.

32–34. **Aemilium circa ludum**: in the irregularity of an ancient city, where few streets were named and no buildings were numbered, localities could be described only by reference to some known build-

infelix operis summa, quia ponere totum
35 nesciet. Hunc ego me, si quid componere curem,
non magis esse velim, quam pravo vivere naso,
spectandum nigris oculis nigroque capillo.
Sumite materiam vestris, qui scribitis, aequam
viribus, et versate diu, quid ferre recusent,
40 quid valeant umeri: cui lecta potenter erit res,
nec facundia deseret hunc nec lucidus ordo.
Ordinis haec virtus erit et venus, aut ego fallor,
ut iam nunc dicat iam nunc debentia dici,
pleraque differat et praesens in tempus omittat.

ing or statue or arch. The *Aemilius ludus* was a building used for a gladiatorial school, having shops about it opening on the street. In one of these — at the bottom (*imus*), away from the Forum — was a sculptor, whom Horace chooses to designate only by giving the location of his shop. He was successful in details, — even in the difficult matter of representing flowing hair in bronze, — but unsuccessful in the total result of his work. — **ponere totum**: = *componere*, 'to bring the whole into unity.'

37. The beauty of black hair and black eyes appears to be traditional (cf. *Carm.* 1, 32, 11), though they must have been very common among the Romans.

38-45. On the choice and arrangement of material for a poem.

38. **materiam**: literally building material, and this meaning is sufficiently strong in Horace's mind to find half-expression in *umeri*, vs. 40. — **vestris**: any poets, not especially the Pisones. — **aequam**: *suited to.*

40. **potenter**: 'according to his powers,' repeating *quid ferre . . . valeant umeri.*

41. **facundia**: the technical term is *elocutio*; the meaning is given in 46, *in verbis serendis*, in the choice and use of words, *diction.* — **ordo**: this is taken up first, in vss. 42-44, because the treatment of it is to be brief, while much more space, vss. 46-72, is given to *facundia.*

42-44. **venus**: *charm.* — **aut ego fallor**: 'if I am not mistaken.' This conventional phrase is inserted here because the brevity and positiveness of the statement seems to lack modesty. — **differat, omittat**: the expression is doubled for emphasis and to correspond to the emphatic *iam nunc . . . iam nunc.*

46 In verbis etiam tenuis cautusque serendis
45 hoc amet, hoc spernat promissi carminis auctor.
    Dixeris egregie, notum si callida verbum
    reddiderit iunctura novum. Si forte necesse est
    indiciis monstrare recentibus abdita rerum,
50 fingere cinctutis non exaudita Cethegis
    continget, dabiturque licentia sumpta pudenter.
    Et nova fictaque nuper habebunt verba fidem, si
    Graeco fonte cadent, parce detorta : quid autem

46. tenuis: to be taken in sense especially with *amet*, as *cautus* is to be taken with *spernat*; 'he must be critical (fine, subtle) in accepting words, and equally cautious in rejecting.'

45. promissi carminis auctore: *i.e.*, 'in the actual work of composition, when he comes to the carrying out of his intentions.'

47. dixeris egregie; *i.e.*, 'your diction will be particularly happy, successful.' This is only a variation on the form of vs. 42; it might have been *facundiae haec virtus erit*.

47-48. callida . . . iunctura: the skillful putting together of common words, so that the meaning of each is slightly shifted, will often produce all the effect of novelty. Horace was himself particularly successful in this, and many such combinations may be found in the poems, especially in the Odes; perhaps the best known is *splendide mendax*, though the effect is even better seen in less daring combinations.

49. indiciis: *tokens, signs, i.e.,* 'words,' used instead of *verbis* to carry out the figure of *monstrare abdita*. — abdita rerum: a rather frequent form of expression; *Sat.* 2, 2, 25, *vanis rerum*; 2, 8, 83, *fictis rerum*. The meaning is 'to express ideas hitherto unexpressed, by means of words which will necessarily be new.'

50. fingere: the making of new words is most happily illustrated by *cinctutis*, which does not occur before this in the extant literature and was probably coined by Horace. It means 'clad in the *cinctus*,' a kind of loin cloth or kilt which was used before the tunic as an undergarment. — Cethegis: cf. *Epist.* 2, 2, 117 and note.

51. continget: 'you will have occasion to. . . .' — sumpta: a condensed condition.

52. et: *and also*; in addition to the new words like *cinctutis*.

53. Graeco fonte: Horace rarely uses Latinized forms of Greek words and cannot be here recom-

Caecilio Plautoque dabit Romanus, ademptum
55 Vergilio Varioque? Ego cur, acquirere pauca
si possum, invideor, cum lingua Catonis et Enni
sermonem patrium ditaverit et nova rerum
nomina protulerit? Licuit semperque licebit
signatum praesente nota producere nomen.
60 Vt silvae foliis pronos mutantur in annos,
prima cadunt, ita verborum vetus interit aetas,

mending such additions to the Roman vocabulary. He does, however, make large use of words suggested by Greek compounds or derivatives (*centimanus, inaudax*, perhaps *potenter*, vs. 40), in which a new meaning is given to a Latin stem. This slight shift of meaning is expressed in *parce detorta*. The novelty would in such words be essentially the same as that given to Roman words by the *callida iunctura*.

54. dabit, ademptum: the illogical structure (for *datum, adimet*) is intentional and points to some definite criticism; ' he has already refused the right to Vergil. . Is he now proposing to grant it to Plautus?' Both during his lifetime and after his death Vergil was criticized on the ground that his style was not pure Latin, as is evident, for instance, from the parody of *Eclog.* 3, 1, *cuium pecus, anne Latinum?* It is against some critic of this school that this question is directed. — **Romanus**: with emphasis; ' and he a Roman !'

55. pauca: this is the same as *sumpta pudenter*, vs. 51, and the opposite of *ditaverit*.

56. invideor: the usual passive is *invidetur mihi*, preserving in the passive the dative construction of the active voice. This dative, however, is essentially the same thing as an accus., and the use of *invideor* is merely a sporadic instance of the process of adjusting language, by analogy, to prevailing tendencies. It has nothing whatever to do with φθονοῦμαι. — **Catonis et Enni**: cf. *Epist.* 2, 2, 117. Ennius was probably the greatest innovator in the history of Latin literature.

58-59. licuit, licebit: emphatic, with reference to *dabit, ademptum*, 54: ' on the contrary, neither to writers of the past nor to those of the future is this right denied.' — **praesente nota**: = *indiciis recentibus*, vs. 49, with the added suggestion of the figure of coinage, the figure which has become traditional in English.

60-62. ' As in the woods, with the passing years, the leaves change, those of one year falling

et iuvenum ritu florent modo nata vigentque.
Debemur morti nos nostraque, sive receptus
terra Neptunus classes Aquilonibus arcet
65 regis opus, sterilisve diu palus aptaque remis
vicinas urbes alit et grave sentit aratrum ;
seu cursum mutavit iniquum frugibus amnis,

and new ones growing in their place, so words grow old and perish, passing like the generations of men from birth to maturity and then to death.' — **foliis**: abl. with *mutantur*; it does not matter whether it is called an abl. of instrument or of limitation (respect). — **pronos**: the year glides down toward its end; cf. *pronos volvere mensis, Carm.* 4, 6, 39. — **in annos**: 'with each year.' The distributive meaning is common, *e.g.*, *in horas*, vs. 160. — **prima cadunt**: this, in the context, implies the converse, 'and new ones grow,' the two sentences being parenthetical. — **iuvenum ritu**: ' like the generations of men.' Here also a part of the thought — ' and finally perish ' — is left to be supplied from the context.

63-68. 'All things perish, even the greatest works of men.' This general truth is illustrated by allusions to three great pieces of engineering work, planned or undertaken by Julius Caesar or Augustus. The course of thought demands that they should be works which were either carried to completion or at least so far advanced that Horace could think of them as practically completed. The first is either the cutting into the Lucrine Lake to make a harbor (a work of no great magnitude, carried out by Agrippa) or the making of a similar harbor at Ostia (planned by Julius Caesar and perhaps carried on by Augustus). The second was the draining of the Pomptine marshes, also planned by Julius Caesar, but never completed. The third was the straightening of the Tiber to prevent floods and protect the farm lands; this was another large project ascribed to Caesar, and some progress was made upon it under Augustus. So far as we can judge, with our scanty knowledge, Horace is alluding to great works which seemed to be so far advanced that he could regard them as completed. Whether the first was the Lucrine Lake or the port at Ostia does not matter to the sense. — **regis opus**: *a royal work.* — **palūs**: this is a very unusual prosody. — **iniquum frugibus**: this would imply that the work was done on the river either above or below the city.

doctus iter melius: mortalia facta peribunt,
nedum sermonum stet honos et gratia vivax.
70 Multa renascentur, quae iam cecidere, cadentque
quae nunc sunt in honore vocabula, si volet usus,
quem penes arbitrium est et ius et norma loquendi.
Res gestae regumque ducumque et tristia bella
quo scribi possent numero monstravit Homerus.
75 Versibus impariter iunctis querimonia primum,
post etiam inclusa est voti sententia compos.
Quis tamen exiguos elegos emiserit auctor,

68-69. mortalia ... peribunt: repeating *debemur morti nos nostraque*, to summarize the thought and prepare for the application. — sermonum: not exactly *verborum*, but 'habits of speech,' 'ways of speaking.' — vivax: to be taken closely with *stet;* 'maintain their living force.'

70-72. The thought here goes back to the positive statements of vss. 60-62. — usus: *usage*, as in *Epist.* 2, 2, 119, *genitor ... usus*. — arbitrium, ius, norma: *decision, rights, standard*. Horace uses three words to emphasize the thought that the making and unmaking of forms of speech is not, after all, in spite of his injunctions to the poet, determined by any individual, but by general usage. The three nouns merely express a single idea with slightly varying shadings.

73-98. On the forms that are suitable to the different kinds of matter. — This goes back, over the intervening parts, *ordo* and *facundia*, and connects with *sumite materiam*, vs. 38. It is to be remembered that in the forms of poetry, and especially in the meters appropriated to particular subjects, classical literature, both Greek and Latin, was much more strongly traditional than modern literature.

73-74. 'The hexameter is to be used for epic poetry.' — res gestae: *i.e.*, historical events and actions, not mythological or legendary, which belong to tragedy (*regum facta, Sat.* 1, 10, 42 f.). He is thinking of the Roman historical epic, like the Annals of Ennius.

75-78. Elegiac verse, the couplet made up of a hexameter and a pentameter. — querimonia: *laments*, like songs of grief for the dead. — voti sententia compos: *i.e.*, the expression of thanks for the granting of a prayer, which was expressed in the form of a dedicatory epigram. — The rhetoricians (*grammatici*) made it a part of

grammatici certant et adhuc sub iudice lis est.
Archilochum proprio rabies armavit iambo;
80 hunc socci cepere pedem grandesque cothurni,
alternis aptum sermonibus, et populares
vincentem strepitus et natum rebus agendis.
Musa dedit fidibus divos puerosque deorum
et pugilem victorem et equum certamine primum
85 et iuvenum curas et libera vina referre.
Descriptas servare vices operumque colores
cur ego si nequeo ignoroque poeta salutor?
Cur nescire pudens prave quam discere malo?
Versibus exponi tragicis res comica non vult.
90 Indignatur item privatis ac prope socco

their doctrine to determine in the case of each kind of meter who was its 'inventor,' as here Homer is regarded as the inventor of the hexameter, and Archilochus of the lyric iambics. — **exiguos**: in contrast to the hexameter, which was used for large subjects and long poems.

79. **proprio**: *his own* because invented by him. Cf. also *Epist.* 1, 19, 24 f., 30 f.

80. **hunc ... pedem**: the iambus passed over (in the trimeter) to the drama. — **socci, cothurni**: the common designation of comedy and tragedy by the shoes worn by actors in them.

81-82. **alternis ... sermonibus**: dialogue, especially that in which two characters speak alternate lines. — **rebus agendis**: *i.e.*, for accompanying action on the stage.

83-85. **fidibus**: the lyric meters. — The proper subjects are hymns to the gods and heroes, odes commemorating victories in the games, love poems and drinking songs. These are all varieties of lyric poetry recognized in rhetoric.

86-87. **descriptas servare vices**: this connects immediately with the preceding, vss. 73-85; 'these are the accepted canons of poetic form. If through ignorance I fail to observe them, then I am not a poet at all.' — **descriptas**: 'laid down in rhetorical theory and here repeated.'

88. **pudens ... malo**: 'out of false shame.' that *pudor malus* which leads one to conceal his defects instead of seeking a cure for them. Cf. *Epist.* 1, 16, 24.

90-91. **privatis**: with *carminibus*; 'poetry that deals with the affairs of ordinary people,' in dis-

dignis carminibus narrari cena Thyestae.
Singula quaeque locum teneant sortita decentem.
Interdum tamen et vocem comoedia tollit,
iratusque Chremes tumido delitigat ore ;
95 et tragicus plerumque dolet sermone pedestri
Telephus et Peleus, cum pauper et exul uterque
proicit ampullas et sesquipedalia verba,
si curat cor spectantis tetigisse querela.
Non satis est pulchra esse poemata ; dulcia sunto,

tinction from a tragedy involving a king of heroic legend. Atreus gave to Thyestes the flesh of his own children to eat.

92. A summarizing statement at the close of the argument, followed by an acknowledgment that there are exceptional cases. — **singula :** 'each form of poetry,' epic, elegiac, lyric. — **sortita :** the meaning of *sors,* ' lot,' is frequently left out of the verb, which means only 'to obtain, secure, receive.' Here it is 'the place which custom has assigned to them.' — **decentem :** with emphasis; 'and to which good taste confines them.' *locum teneant* of course involves a figure, the literal meaning being, ' let each kind of writing use the meter and style which belongs to it.'

93-94. The kind of scene in comedy where an angry father (*Chremes*) berates his son, which Horace has already used (*Sat.* 1, 4. 48 ff.) in his argument to prove that comedy is not poetry, in the full sense of the word. The example is probably taken from some book on rhetoric.

95-98. 'Tragedy also will occasionally use an ordinary style.' — **tragicus :** with *Telephus et Peleus ;* 'in tragedy,' as in *Sat.* 2, 5, 91. *Davus sis comicus,* 'be like Davus in a comedy.' — **dolet :** *i.e.,* 'expresses his sorrows.' — Telephus and Peleus are illustrations of tragic characters in poverty or exile, in circumstances which reduce them to the level and language of common people. — **ampullas :** *Epist.* 1, 3, 14 and note. — **sesquipedalia :** this word is used literally by various writers; the humorous meaning, when it is applied to words, is strengthened by the length of the word itself and it is only in this use and sense that it has come over into English — perhaps from this passage.

99-111. 'So, in general, the effectiveness of poetry, especially of dramatic poetry, depends upon the use of a fitting style.'

99-100. pulchra, dulcia : 'beau-

100 et, quocumque volent, animum auditoris agunto.
Vt ridentibus arrident, ita flentibus adsunt
humani vultus : si vis me flere, dolendum est
primum ipsi tibi ; tunc tua me infortunia laedent,
Telephe vel Peleu ; male si mandata loqueris,
105 aut dormitabo aut ridebo. Tristia maestum
vultum verba decent, iratum plena minarum,
ludentem lasciva, severum seria dictu.
Format enim natura prius nos intus ad omnem
fortunarum habitum ; iuvat aut impellit ad iram,
110 aut ad humum maerore gravi deducit et angit ;
post effert animi motus interprete lingua.

tiful in themselves, as works of art'; 'charming in their effect.' Catullus, 86, expresses the same difference between two women by *pulchra* and *formosa*. — **sunto et . . . agunto**; paratactic coördination ; 'but if they are delightful, then they will move . . . .'

101-102. 'The emotions felt and expressed by the speaker and actor excite similar emotions in the hearers and spectators.' The thought is not clearly expressed. *humani vultus* means the expression, and therefore the emotions, of the audience, but the word *vultus* is selected really with reference to the mobile face of the actor, to whom *ridentibus* and *flentibus* refer. *Adsunt* is a more general term than *arrident*, used in the second part of the comparison; 'respond to,' 'sympathize with.'

104. The thought goes back for a moment to vs. 96. — **male . . .**

mandata : *i.e.*, 'if the words that the speaker utters sound merely like things he has been told to say (*mandata*), and, still worse, are ill-adapted to his situation (*male mandata*).'

106. **vultum** : as above, both the emotion and the expression of face which accompanies the emotion. In this whole passage Horace is thinking of the effect of a play upon the spectators, and is identifying the expression of the actor with his feeling.

108-111. 'For, by a law of nature, all emotions come from within, and then find expression in words.' This is the reason why the words should correspond to the looks and the emotions. — **format**: this general word is explained by *iuvat, impellit, angit*, expressing the various 'forms' of emotion. — **prius** : 'before we speak'; the sense is completed by *post*, vs.

Si dicentis erunt fortunis absona dicta,
Romani tollent equites peditesque cachinnum.
Intererit multum divusne loquatur an heros,
115 maturusne senex an adhuc florente iuventa
fervidus, an matrona potens, an sedula nutrix,
mercatorne vagus, cultorne virentis agelli,
Colchus an Assyrius, Thebis nutritus an Argis.
Aut famam sequere, aut sibi convenientia finge.

111. — **ad ... habitum**: 'according to the varying circumstances of our lives (*fortunarum*).' — **effert**: the subject is *natura*; 'expresses,' 'brings out from within (*intus*).'

112-113. Line 112 summarizes in negative form the thought which has just been expressed positively, and at the same time introduces a treatment of the same theme from a different point of view. — **absona**: the opposite of vss. 105-107. — **equites peditesque**: Horace frequently uses *eques, equites*, to denote the more cultivated part of the audience or of the reading public. Here, desiring to refer to the whole audience, he uses the customary word, and then humorously adds *pedites*, playing upon the literal meaning of *equites*.

114. **divusne an heros**: *i.e.*, between a god and a man, even a hero such as would appear on the stage with a divinity.

115-118. Classical drama was more limited and conventional in its range of characters than modern fiction, and the persons represented are easily classified, as here. Such lists are given often in rhetorical writings. Horace is merely selecting a few well-known types, in contrasting pairs, the old man and the young man, the mistress of the household and the old nurse, the trader or sailor and the farmer. — In vs. 118 the contrast is carried out rather elaborately; the two barbarians are contrasted with the two Greeks, and then with each other. This corresponds to reality in the contrast of the Colchian (the wilder and more savage type) with the Assyrian (the effeminate Oriental), but there is not, in reality or in tradition, any such distinct contrast between the Theban and the Argive. Horace is probably thinking of the legends which brought the two cities into conflict, like the *Seven against Thebes* of Aeschylus.

119. This line, again, is both summary and transition, carrying the thought on from harmony between the speaker and his words to harmony in the character itself.

120 Scriptor honoratum si forte reponis Achillem,
    impiger, iracundus, inexorabilis, acer
    iura neget sibi nata, nihil non adroget armis.
    Sit Medea ferox invictaque, flebilis Ino,
    perfidus Ixion, Io vaga, tristis Orestes.
125 Si quid inexpertum scaenae committis, et audes
    personam formare novam, servetur ad imum
    qualis ab incepto processerit et sibi constet.
    Difficile est proprie communia dicere, tuque
    rectius Iliacum carmen deducis in actus,
130 quam si proferres ignota indictaque primus.
    Publica materies privati iuris erit, si

120. **scriptor**: closely with *reponis*, which is so general in meaning that it needs a definition. — **honoratum**: *i.e.*, as the great hero of the Iliad, with the characteristics which belong to him in tradition.

122. The two parts of the line say the same thing in two different ways; 'let him refuse to acknowledge laws, but instead appeal always to arms.' The traditional contrast between laws and arms, between peace and war, underlies the form of expression.

123-124. These are typical examples from Greek legends, each character having its descriptive adjective. They illustrate the first part of vs. 119, the following of tradition.

125. **inexpertum**: this takes up the possibility implied in the second half of vs. 119. — **scaenae**: Horace is not here specifically discussing the drama, as a particular poetic form distinct from the epic or the lyric, but, since the delineation of heroic character was to be found chiefly in tragedy, he uses terms of the drama, without, however, intending to exclude epic treatment of the same material.

127. **ab incepto**: logically with *servetur ad imum*. — **processerit**: of coming out upon the stage. — **sibi constet**: this goes back to *sibi convenientia* and closes the brief discussion of that topic.

128-135. **proprie communia**: these somewhat general words express concisely and figuratively what is explained more fully and literally in the rest of the paragraph, by means of which these words must be interpreted. *difficile* is the opposite of *rectius* ('more wisely, more safely'), and *proprie ... dicere* is therefore the opposite of dramatizing a well-known story and identical with

non circa vilem patulumque moraberis orbem,
nec verbum verbo curabis reddere fidus
interpres ; nec desilies imitator in artum,
135 unde pedem proferre pudor vetet aut operis lex,
nec sic incipies, ut scriptor cyclicus olim : .

proferre ignota indictaque. It therefore means 'to write about things which no other writer has handled, things which are not a part of literature, but which belong to common experience, in such a way as to make them your own (*proprie*).' The thought of the whole is, 'it is hard to put the stamp of individuality upon ordinary material, and you will find it easier to dramatize some story from the Trojan cycle than to strike out into unknown fields.' — **tu**: the poet, not one of the Pisones. — **Iliacum carmen**: not necessarily the whole Iliad. — 'Yet a certain measure of originality in the handling of old material may be attained, if you use the right method.' — **publica**: such as the Homeric story. — **privati iuris**: *i.e.*, 'will become your own, will bear your stamp.' This figure, of acquiring private rights in what had been public property, was in Horace's mind from the beginning of the sentence and undoubtedly led to the choice of the rather confusing phrase *proprie communia*. Cf. also *Epist.* 1, 3, 15 ff., where the same figure is used in a different way. — **patulum ... orbem**: primarily of the monotonous path of an animal turning a millstone then of the commonplace path which most writers of little originality follow. — **interpres, imitator**: this appears to have been especially frequent in Roman tragedy, so far as can be judged from the fragments, though even there it is not quite what we understand by a 'word-for-word' translation; Horace is contrasting it with his own freer following of Alcaeus and Sappho. — **desilies in artum**: the phrase seems to be a reminiscence of the fable of the goat that jumped into a well, but the comparison is not to be carried over into the next line. — **pudor**: *i.e.*, an unwillingness to acknowledge your error. — **operis lex**: no more than 'the nature of the work'; a close imitation will bind the writer so closely to the plot of his model that he cannot free himself at all without destroying the unity of the work.

136. The form of sentence, *nec* with the future, goes on, though the subject changes from originality to the treatment of the beginning of a poem. This continuation of grammatical structure is intended to make the transition easy and unperceived, as in all

'Fortunam Priami cantabo et nobile bellum.'
Quid dignum tanto feret hic promissor hiatu?
Parturient montes, nascetur ridiculus mus.
140 Quanto rectius hic, qui nil molitur inepte:
'Dic mihi Musa virum, captae post tempora Troiae
qui mores hominum multorum vidit et urbes.'
Non fumum ex fulgore, sed ex fumo dare lucem
cogitat, ut speciosa dehinc miracula promat,
145 Antiphaten Scyllamque et cum Cyclope Charybdim;
nec reditum Diomedis ab interitu Meleagri,
nec gemino bellum Troianum orditur ab ovo.
Semper ad eventum festinat et in medias res,

his writings Horace avoids formal arrangements of thought. — **cyclicus**: a technical name given by Alexandrine critics to the poets who handled parts of the Trojan story not included in the Iliad or Odyssey; their poems, with the Homeric poems, form a complete circle (*cyclus*).

137-138. The absurdity, as Horace sees it, is in the largeness of the promise, and perhaps in *nobile*. But there is much that is conventional and unreal in this paragraph, vss. 137-142. Cf. the noble opening sentence of Paradise Lost. — **promissor**: apparently coined to ridicule the cyclic poet. — **hiatu**: also a ridiculous suggestion, as if the poet opened his mouth wide to utter such a line.

139. Notice the effect of the monosyllabic close.

141-142. Cf. *Epist.* 1, 2, 19-21, where the first lines of the Odyssey are freely rendered. Horace has simplified Homer by omitting the second line, ἐπεὶ Τροίης ἱερὸν πτολίεθρον ἔπερσε.

143. 'Not like a fire that begins brightly and then dies down into smoke.' *fulgore* and *lucem* are the same.

145. **Antiphaten**: *Od.* 10, 100 ff. — **Scyllam, Charybdim**: *Od.* 12, 87 ff. — **cum Cyclope**: *Od.* 9, 160 ff.; the construction is merely a variation for *et Cyclopem*.

146. Homer does not begin as the writer did who, having for his subject the return of Diomed from Troy, went back by way of introduction and told the other story of the tragic death of his uncle, Meleager.

147. That is, from the birth of Helen.

non secus ac notas, auditorem rapit, et quae
150 desperat tractata nitescere posse, relinquit;
atque ita mentitur, sic veris falsa remiscet,
primo ne medium, medio ne discrepet imum.
Tu, quid ego et populus mecum desideret, audi.
Si plausoris eges aulaea manentis et usque
155 sessuri, donec cantor 'Vos plaudite' dicat,
aetatis cuiusque notandi sunt tibi mores,
mobilibusque decor naturis dandus et annis.

149. notas: *i.e.*, Homer treats his subject-matter as already in part known to his hearers, as in fact it was.

150. tractata: *handled, treated.* The Latin construction here is clumsy and should not be used in translating.

151. mentitur: *i.e., uses fictions.* — veris falsa: this reflects the belief that the Homeric story was in the main historical.

153-177. 'The poet must make his characters consistent and life-like and, in particular, must notice the characteristics of different periods in life.'

153. tu: the poet, as in 128. The abrupt line introduces a new thought, in this case wholly without transition. From this point the drama, which has been frequently alluded to, though not distinctly the subject of discussion, becomes more prominent.

154. plausoris: to be taken closely with *manentis*; 'if you want your audience to stay and to listen with pleasure up to the end.'

155. vos plaudite: the formula with which the plays ended; sometimes *vos valete et plaudite*. It is spoken sometimes by the company (*grex*), sometimes by the last actor, and sometimes (Plaut. *Trin.*, *M.G.*, and all the plays of Terence) there is no indication of the speaker. There is no allusion elsewhere to a *cantor*, nor can anything be inferred from this passage in regard to the usage in the time of Terence.

156. notandi: 'observed with care.'

157. decor: that which is suited (*decens*, vs. 92) to each period, not merely the good qualities; cf. 170 ff.

The description of the different Ages of Man was probably traditional. In Terence there are only two, *adulescens* and *senex*; Aristotle (*Rhet.* 2. 12) has three; Shakspere (*As You Like It*, 2, 7) has seven. Though Horace introduces this as a part of his advice to the dramatist, he does not confine himself strictly to the possi-

Reddere qui voces iam scit puer et pede certo
signat humum, gestit paribus colludere, et iram
160 colligit ac ponit temere et mutatur in horas.
Imberbus iuvenis, tandem custode remoto,
gaudet equis canibusque et aprici gramine campi,
cereus in vitium flecti, monitoribus asper,
utilium tardus provisor, prodigus aeris,
165 sublimis cupidusque et amata relinquere pernix.
Conversis studiis aetas animusque virilis
quaerit opes et amicitias, inservit honori,
commisisse cavet quod mox mutare laboret.
Multa senem circumveniunt incommoda, vel quod

bilities and needs of the drama. The first stage, vss. 158-160, would not be represented in tragedy or comedy, characteristics are mentioned which, though they can be noticed by a writer of novels, could scarcely be indicated within the conventional limits of Greek or Latin drama (164, *tardus provisor*; 165; 167, *amicitias*; 171), and, in general, much stress is laid upon the quickness of change (157; *iam*, 158; 160; 166: 175) from one period to another. Horace has carried his description beyond his first intention.

159-160. signat: *i.e.*, leaves tracks (*signa*) as he walks. — **gestit**: of the child's eagerness for play. — **temere**: *without cause*.

161-165. tandem: *i.e.*, the long-desired time has come and he is his own master. — **custode**: the *paedagogus*, as Horace's father was to him, *Sat.* 1, 6, 81. — **equis canibusque**: this has a Greek sound; cf. Ter. *Andr.* 56 f., *aut equos alere aut canes ad venandum*, of a young man's first interests, when he is out of his father's control. — **cereus**: the figure which this word suggests does not extend to *flecti*; 'impressible as wax and easily turned toward folly.' — **monitoribus asper**: cf. the scene in Plaut. *Bacch.* 109 ff. — **provisor**: 'slow to provide . . .'; the corresponding phrase in Aristotle (*Rhet.* 2, 12) is φιλοχρήματοι ἥκιστα.

166-168. studiis: *his interests*. — **opes**: in the general sense, 'influence and power,' which connects well with *amicitias*, 'alliances' for influence, such as Cicero discusses and condemns; cf. also *Sat.* 2, 6, 75. — **honori**: *office*.

169-174. This picture of old age is found in various places, *e.g.*, in Cic. *de Senect.*, and especially in scenes in Terence. — **vel quod**: not

170 quaerit et inventis miser abstinet ac timet uti,
vel quod res omnes timide gelideque ministrat,
dilator, spe longus, iners, avidusque futuri,
difficilis, querulus, laudator temporis acti
se puero, castigator censorque minorum.
175 Multa ferunt anni venientes commoda secum,
multa recedentes adimunt, ne forte seniles
mandentur iuveni partes pueroque viriles;
semper in adiunctis aevoque morabimur aptis.
Aut agitur res in scaenis, aut acta refertur.

causal, but explicative of *incommoda*. — **quaerit**: absolute. Avarice is traditionally and perhaps actually the vice of old age. — **timet uti**: while youth is *prodigus aeris*; perhaps there is a relation between the two. — **gelide**: a particularly well-chosen word. — **spe longus**: this may be a translation of δύσελπις, the word which Aristotle uses. It would then mean 'slow to entertain hopes.' It is, in fact, not a clear phrase. — **avidus futuri**: *i.e.*, anxious about what of life is left to him. — **minorum**: *of younger men*.

Though much of the substance of this passage (158-174) is traditional, the admirable phrasing, which has made it a classic, is Horace's own.

175-178. Cf. *Epist.* 2, 2, 55. This is, in reality, a comment upon life and its changes and not directly connected with the work of the poet. Horace brings it into connection with his main line of thought by *ne . . . mandentur*, but somewhat awkwardly, since no one would propose to give to a *iuvenis* the words suited to a *senex* or would confuse a *vir* and a *puer* in delineating character. — **ne . . . mandentur**: a parenthetic final clause; 'and so one must not. . . .' — **semper**: with *morabimur*, not with *adiunctis*; the sense is 'character changes, but we poets must always be watchful to note the qualities of each period.' — **adiunctis**: *i.e.*, the qualities that accompany each time of life. — **aevo**: with both *adiunctis* and *aptis*, which are connected by *-que*.

179-188. What scenes should be put upon the stage. — This is one of the traditional subjects of rhetorical discussion.

179. The statement of actual usage precedes the discussion. — **refertur**: 'are described by an actor as having occurred off the stage,' within the palace or elsewhere.

180 Segnius irritant animos demissa per aurem,
quam quae sunt oculis subiecta fidelibus et quae
ipse sibi tradit spectator. Non tamen intus
digna geri promes in scaenam, multaque tolles
ex oculis quae mox narret facundia praesens,
185 ne pueros coram populo Medea trucidet,
aut humana palam coquat exta nefarius Atreus,
aut in avem Procne vertatur, Cadmus in anguem.
Quodcumque ostendis mihi sic, incredulus odi.
Neve minor neu sit quinto productior actu
190 fabula, quae posci vult et spectata reponi.
Nec deus intersit, nisi dignus vindice nodus

180. segnius irritant: 'produce a less vivid impression.' — **demissa per aurem**: *i.e.*, the matters which are merely described.

182. sibi tradit: the spectator has, as it were, seen the action himself and so tells it to himself, instead of having it told to him by the messenger or reporter. — **intus**: in the palace; with *digna geri*.

184. facundia praesens: 'a messenger (speaker) appearing in person.' It is, I think, quite impossible that *praesens* should mean 'who was present when the action occurred.' The point of *praesens* is that it enforces the contrast between that which took place off the stage (*ex oculis*) and that which the spectator is permitted to see, in the person of the actor who comes on to tell the tale.

185. ne: nearly like **ne** of vs. 176. Many *ne*-clauses are like this, indistinguishable in form from pro-

hibitions and not essentially different in sense. — In the Medea of Euripides the children are killed within the palace, but their cries are heard by the audience.

186–187. These myths are not the subject of any Greek plays now extant, but the references are of course to definite plays known to Horace.

188. incredulus odi: expressing in one phrase the two distinct emotions; *incredulus* refers to the impossible metamorphoses of vs. 187, *odi* to the horrible spectacle of vs. 185 or 186.

189. quinto ... actu: this rule Horace got from some grammatical tradition, and it was long current, on his authority, in modern times. It is, however, quite without foundation. The act divisions in Latin comedy are not in the Mss. or in the earliest editions.

191. deus intersit: *i.e.*, natural

inciderit: nec quarta loqui persona laboret.
Actoris partes chorus officiumque virile
defendat, neu quid medios intercinat actus,
195 quod non proposito conducat et haereat apte.
Ille bonis faveatque et consilietur amice,
et regat iratos et amet peccare timentis;
ille dapes laudet mensae brevis, ille salubrem
iustitiam legesque et apertis otia portis;
200 ille tegat commissa, deosque precetur et oret,

means should usually be found for working out the plot. The rule was laid down with reference to plays in which supernatural intervention was unnecessarily employed. — **vindice**: *defender*, one who protects the hero and releases him from the complications of the plot. The phrase *nisi dignus vindice nodus* is classic.

192. **loqui . . . laboret**: the rule was that only three speaking characters should be on the stage at once; a fourth would not easily find a place (*laboret*) in the dialogue. This rule is not without exceptions and in the later comedy was not observed at all.

193. **actoris partes**: *i.e.*, the chorus should be treated as an actor, should have its place in the plot and in the action, and this should be an important part (*officium virile*).

194-195. 'It should not be used merely to sing interludes, odes which do not contribute (*conducat*) to the plot or have any real connection with it.'

196-201. The proper function of the chorus.

196. **bonis faveat**: this is in accordance with the practice of the extant tragedies, that the chorus should support the cause of virtue. — **consilietur**: *advise*. This also is common.

197. **regat**: *i.e.*, 'try to control.' — **peccare timentis**: not the same as *bonis*, but the characters who seem to be shrinking from some wrong act that is presenting itself to them as a possibility. For the expression cf. *Epist*. 1, 16, 52; 2, 1, 23.

198. **mensae brevis**: *i.e.*, 'it should be on the side of simplicity, against luxury.' Cf. *cena brevis*, *Epist*. 1, 14, 35.

200. **tegat commissa**: 'it should play the part of the trustworthy confidant and not betray secrets committed to its keeping.' This situation is not infrequent in Greek tragedy.

ut redeat miseris, abeat fortuna superbis.
Tibia non, ut nunc, orichalco vincta, tubaeque
aemula, sed tenuis simplexque foramine pauco
adspirare et adesse choris erat utilis, atque
205 nondum spissa nimis complere sedilia flatu,
quo sane populus numerabilis, utpote parvus,
et frugi castusque verecundusque, coibat.
Postquam coepit agros extendere victor et urbes
latior amplecti murus vinoque diurno
210 placari Genius festis impune diebus,

201. **redeat, abeat, fortuna,** a partial personification; cf. *Carm.* I, 35, 23 f., *utcumque mutata potentis | veste domos inimica linquis.*
202 ff. The discussion of the function of the chorus suggests easily the music which accompanied the songs.
202. **tibia**: properly a wooden or ivory flute, with few openings, which gave a light and clear sound. When bound with metal — *orichalcum* was an amalgam of copper and other metals — its note was more like that of a brass horn (*tuba*), less clear and simple.
204. **adspirare, adesse**: as an accompaniment to the choral song, without independent force.
205. **nondum**: especially with *erat utilis* to be supplied. — **nimis**: with *spissa*. 'The flute was not yet used, as it is now, to fill with loud blast a crowded theater,' *i.e.*, was not independent of the song.
206. **quo**: the antecedent is *sedilia*, for the whole theater. —
sane: 'of course,' 'you know.' — **utpote parvus**: parenthetic and explanatory of *numerabilis.*
207. The adjectives describe the ideal simplicity and piety of the early time, which Horace here regards as necessary to the purity of art.
208-210. In the preceding discussion of the drama there is nothing to indicate that Horace was thinking exclusively of the Greek tragedy; on the contrary, the advice is of course addressed to writers of Roman tragedy. Yet the tone is almost wholly Greek. As the discussion goes on, however, to the period of luxury, the underlying thought is Roman. This appears in *agros extendere victor*, which is not strictly applicable to Greek history after the Persian Wars, but is accurately descriptive of Roman history after the Punic Wars. The plural *urbes* would suggest Greek cities; *latior murus* is suitable to either; but

accessit numerisque modisque licentia maior.
Indoctus quid enim saperet liberque laborum
rusticus, urbano confusus, turpis honesto?
Sic priscae motumque et luxuriem addidit arti
215 tibicen traxitque vagus per pulpita vestem:
sic etiam fidibus voces crevere severis,
et tulit eloquium insolitum facundia praeceps,
utiliumque sagax rerum et divina futuri

vs. 210 is wholly in Roman terms. — **diurno**: *in the daytime.* — **impune**: *i.e.,* without consideration of the proper restraints.

211. **numerisque modisque**: more complicated music and meters were used. This, according to the traditional doctrine, was regarded as *licentia*, like the increasing license of manners.

212-213. **quid enim saperet**: *i.e.,* 'no standard of taste could be maintained in a population so mixed and so unrestrained.' — **liber laborum**: on festal days labor would be suspended. — **turpis honesto**: where there was no such distinction as that which in Horace's time separated the *equites* — the cultivated part of the audience — from the lower classes.

214-215. **sic**: as a result of this confusion and this increase of luxury. — **motum**: *i.e.,* he moved about the stage (*vagus*), no longer subordinating himself to the chorus. — **luxuriem**: *i.e.,* he trailed his purple robe (*traxit vestem*) about the stage.

216. **voces**: *notes.* The tradition was that the lyre was at first four-stringed, and that the number of strings was gradually increased to eleven.

217. **tulit**: *brought in,* 'brought with it.' — **eloquium**: *style.* — **facundia praeceps**: 'the eager desire to speak, unrestrained (*praeceps*) by considerations of taste.' The same *licentia maior* which had affected music influenced also the style of the choral odes.

218-219. **sagax**: with *sententia*; the thought itself was affected by the same tendencies and came to be full of precepts and sententious maxims of wisdom. — **divina futuri**: the chorus undertook to prophesy, and became as obscure and bombastic as oracles. The precise point of these criticisms is not clear, nor even whether Horace has in mind the later Greek tragedy or the Roman. This whole passage, vss. 202-219, is to be regarded as a bit of the traditional rhetorical doctrine and not as history or direct criticism. The point of view is wholly incorrect.

sortilegis non discrepuit sententia Delphis.
220 Carmine qui tragico vilem certavit ob hircum,
mox etiam agrestis Satyros nudavit, et asper
incolumi gravitate iocum tentavit eo, quod
illecebris erat et grata novitate morandus
spectator, functusque sacris et potus et exlex.
225 Verum ita risores, ita commendare dicaces
conveniet Satyros, ita vertere seria ludo,

220-250. The Satyric drama. This section also is in part traditional, but it is in part a real criticism of forms of drama which were on the stage in Horace's time, like mimes and *fabulae Atellanae*, and which bore enough resemblance to the Satyr plays to justify Horace in treating them all as one kind of drama.

220-221. **certavit**: this is Greek, referring to the dramatic contests at Athens. — **hircum**: the commonly accepted derivation of τραγῳδία was from τράγος, a goat offered as the prize of victory. — **mox**: *i.e.*, the Satyr play is supposed to be derived from tragedy. This is the reverse of the fact; formal tragedy was a development out of the popular Satyr play and the name comes from the use of τράγος of the chorus of the Satyr drama. — **nudavit**: the Satyrs were naked except for a goatskin about the loins. — **asper**: *i.e.*, he was still a tragic poet, with something of the severity of tragedy. The Satyr play, as a fourth play after the dramatic trilogy, was written by the same poet who had written the tragedies.

222. **incolumi gravitate**: 'without loss of dignity' by presenting such plays.

223. **morandus**: *i.e.*, 'it was necessary to provide some amusement and novelty to detain the spectators.'

224. **functus sacris**: 'having already performed the solemn rites of sacrifice, they were released from restraint (*exlex*).'

225. **verum**: 'but, though the spectators were *exlex* and the object of the play was laughter and jesting, there were still restraints imposed upon the characters and the style of the plays.' — **risores**: in effect an adj., *merry*, to balance *dicaces*, *jesting*, **commendare**: *i.e.*, 'present them to the favor of the audience.'

226. **vertere seria ludo**: the Satyr play, coming immediately after the tragedies, changed the spirit from seriousness to lightness. The abl. (*ludo*) is rare with *verto*, but is found occasionally after the analogy of the abl. with *muto*.

ne quicumque deus, quicumque adhibebitur heros,
regali conspectus in auro nuper et ostro,
migret in obscuras humili sermone tabernas,
230 aut, dum vitat humum, nubes et inania captet.
Effutire levis indigna tragoedia versus,
ut festis matrona moveri iussa diebus,
intererit Satyris paullum pudibunda protervis.
Non ego inornata et dominantia nomina solum

228. conspectus ... nuper: the characters of the tragedy, where they had appeared in royal state, might reappear in the Satyr play. In that case the contrast should not be made so startling as to shock the taste or to degrade the heroic tone of tragedy.

229. migret in ... tabernas: the king or hero who has just been seen coming out of his palace must not now be represented as moving to a hovel. The word *tabernas* is chosen with reference to the Roman farces called *fabulae tabernariae*, plays of low life, the scene of which was in some poor place of resort for the common people. — **humili sermone**: this anticipates what is said at greater length in the next lines.

230. nubes et inania: the opposite fault of a tone too lofty for the general spirit of the play.

231. indigna: 'not condescending to ...,' as in *Epist.* 1, 3, 35, *indigni fraternum rumpere foedus*. — **tragoedia**: *i.e.*, the tragic (heroic) character in the Satyr play.

232. moveri iussa: dancing was ordinarily considered quite unsuitable for a woman of dignity, but at some religious festivals the married women took part in the dance as a religious duty (*iussa*). Cf. *Carm.* 2, 12, 17 ff.; 3, 14, 5 f., for references to such dances.

233. intererit ... paullum: 'will have little to do with,' 'will be among them, but will retain the dignity proper to tragedy.' The contrast is emphasized by the juxtaposition of the two adjectives, 'dignified herself, in spite of their frolicsome behavior.'

234. non ... solum: the other half of the thought begins with vs. 240, without a particle (*sed etiam*); 'I should not be satisfied with observing the ordinary laws of colloquial style or even with making some finer distinctions; I should aim at something still higher.' — **inornata**: *plain* words which suggest no figurative meanings. — **dominantia**: a translation of κύρια, *literal*, as *nomina verbaque* is a translation of ὀνόματα

235 verbaque, Pisones, Satyrorum scriptor amabo;
nec sic enitar tragico differre colori,
ut nihil intersit, Davusne loquator et audax
Pythias, emuncto lucrata Simone talentum,
an custos famulusque dei Silenus alumni.
240 Ex noto fictum carmen sequar, ut sibi quivis
speret idem, sudet multum frustraque laboret
ausus idem : tantum series iuncturaque pollet,
tantum de medio sumptis accedit honoris.

καὶ ῥήματα, standing for all language; cf. *Sat.* 1, 3, 103.

235. The address to the Pisones at this point is consistent with the more personal and direct tone of the whole discussion of the Satyr plays, and supports the view that the matter was one of living interest at the time. — **scriptor**: this also maintains the tone of direct interest, but does not, of course, mean that Horace himself intended to write for the stage.

236. nec sic: 'nor should I be satisfied with a mere distinction between the tragic and the comic style, without observing also the finer distinctions between the different characters.'

237-239. Davus: a standing name for a slave in comedy. — **Pythias**: this name for the *arguta meretrix* (*Sat.* 1, 10. 40) happens not to be used in any extant comedy. — **emuncto**: one of the many slang words used in comedy for cheating: perhaps *swiped*. — **Simone**: an old man; Chremes is used as the typical name in the corresponding passage in *Sat.* 1, 10, 40 ff. — The names and the situation all refer to the *comoedia palliata*, like the plays of Terence, the style of which, it is implied, is not to be used in a Satyr play. — **Silenus**: the old guardian and attendant of the youthful Dionysus, fond of wine, but also a kind of philosopher.

240-243. This passage contains a summary of Horace's own ideal in style, of wider application than is given to it here. — **noto fictum**: the same general contrast as that expressed in vs. 151. *sic veris falsa remiscet.* — **speret**: *i.e.*, the style shall seem easy enough to tempt any one to try it. — **idem, idem**: intentionally repeated in the same place in the verse. — **series iuncturaque**: cf. *callida iunctura*, 47 f.; but here the thought is broader, including all the more general characteristics of style, not the meaning of words only. — **de medio sumptis**: ordinary

Silvis deducti caveant, me iudice, Fauni,
245 ne velut innati triviis ac paene forenses
aut nimium teneris iuvenentur versibus unquam,
aut immunda crepent ignominiosaque dicta:
offenduntur enim, quibus est equus et pater et res,
nec si quid fricti ciceris probat et nucis emptor,
250 aequis accipiunt animis donantve corona.
Syllaba longa brevi subiecta vocatur iambus,
pes citus : unde etiam trimetris adcrescere iussit
nomen iambeis cum senos redderet ictus,
primus ad extremum similis sibi : non ita pridem,

words, out of which skillful use can make a style that has distinction.

244. Fauni: the Italian equivalent for the satyrs.

245. innati triviis, forenses: the wild creatures of the woods must not use the language of street boys or even the more cultivated speech of those who attend the law courts.

246. teneris ... versibus: sentimental love songs, expressions alien to the free spirit of the Fauns. — **iuvenentur**: *sport*, play the *iuvenis*; formed like the Greek νεανιεύεσθαι.

247. The Satyr plays were coarse, but they should avoid vicious and indecent expressions.

248–250. equus: with reference to the providing of a horse for the *equites* in the early time, when the word had a military meaning. — **et pater**: the free-born citizens. — **et res**: the persons of property and standing and, presumably, of cultivation. — **fricti**: *parched*; from *frigo*. — **corona**: symbolic, since there were no formal contests at Rome. — It is to be noticed that from vs. 231 the thought is almost wholly Roman.

251–269. On meter and versification.

251. The fact that an iambus consists of a short followed by a long is stated rather formally, in order to make a proper starting point for the discussion of the use of spondees.

252–253. unde: *i.e.*, because it is a 'quick foot.' — The construction is *iambeis nomen trimetris adcrescere iussit*; *iambeis* is dat. after *adcrescere* and *trimetris* is attracted into the same case; 'for which reason it bade the name trimeter attach itself to iambic lines,' although there were six feet and one might expect the name hexameter. Cf. *Sat.* 1, 3, 57. *illi tardo cognomen damus.*

254. similis sibi: all the feet

255 tardior ut paullo graviorque veniret ad aures,
spondeos stabiles in iura paterna recepit
commodus et patiens, non ut de sede secunda
cederet aut quarta socialiter.   Hic et in Acci
nobilibus trimetris apparet rarus, et Enni
260 in scaenam missos magno cum pondere versus
aut operae celeris nimium curaque carentis
aut ignoratae premit artis crimine turpi.
Non quivis videt immodulata poemata iudex,
et data Romanis venia est indigna poetis.
265 Idcircone vager scribamque licenter?   An omnes
visuros peccata putem mea, tutus et intra
spem veniae cautus?   Vitavi denique culpam,

being iambi. — **non ita pridem**: these words are not quite intelligible, since spondees had been used in iambic trimeters from the earliest times. [None of the various explanations is really good. Cic. *Brut.* 10, 41 is not a parallel.]

256. **stabiles**: heavy in comparison with the lightly running iambi. — **in iura paterna**: adopted them legally.

257. **non ut**: 'but not to the extent of admitting them to the second or fourth foot.'

258. **socialiter**: 'like an ally,' like one who made a partnership on absolutely equal terms. The personification of the iambus goes through the whole passage, *iussit, recepit, commodus et patiens, cederet*.

259-262. 'In Roman poets the frequency of spondees makes the verse too heavy.' — **hic**: the iambus. — **nobilibus**: *well-known*, without approval, which would be inconsistent with the context. — **rarus**: this supplies, in thought, the subject of *premit*; 'and the rarity of it in the verses of Ennius.' — **in scaenam missos**: his verses in drama, as distinct from his epic poetry. — **operae**: with *crimine*, as *artis* is, and modified by *nimium celeris* and *carentis*.

263-264. **non quivis**: the meaning of the general phrase appears in *Romanis*. — **indigna**: *undeserved*; strictly, 'pardon that the giver should think it unworthy of himself to bestow.'

265. **idcirco**: *i.e.*, 'because I know that the judge is not strict.'

266-267. **tutus et . . . cautus**: 'or shall I be just careful enough to keep within the law?'

non laudem merui. Vos exemplaria Graeca
nocturna versate manu, versate diurna.
270 At vestri proavi Plautinos et numeros et
laudavere sales, nimium patienter utrumque,
ne dicam stulte, mirati, si modo ego et vos
scimus inurbanum lepido seponere dicto,
legitimumque sonum digitis callemus et aure.
275 Ignotum tragicae genus invenisse Camenae
dicitur et plaustris vexisse poemata Thespis,

268. non . . . merui: 'there is no positive merit in that course.'— vos: emphatic; 'you, who surely desire *laudem merere*.'

270-294. On the need of study and care in the writing of poetry, as shown in the history of the Greek drama.

270. proavi: in a general sense, *maiores*. — Plautinos: for Horace's judgment on Plautus see *Epist.* 2, 1, 170 ff. and note. — numeros: this may be a reference to the verses which were supposed to be Plautus's own epitaph, in which the phrase *numeri innumeri* is used. Plautus was, in fact, an extremely good versifier, but of a sort that Horace did not appreciate.

271-272. patienter: *i.e.*, they should not have endured them, much less admired them.

273. inurbanum lepido: with reference to the *sales*. The word *lepidus*, which Horace uses rarely, is one of the commonest adjectives in Plautus and is chosen here for that reason. The standard of *urbanitas* is better suited to the Augustan age than to the time of the Second Punic War.

274. sonum: the *numeri*. Horace's judgment on this point also, as on the wit of Plautus, is too narrow, like the judgment of a Queen Anne writer on a poet of the Elizabethan period. — digitis: this seems to be traditional; Horace did not count the feet of his Alcaics on his fingers. But it is true that the natural feeling for the free early versification had, in part, died out under the impulse toward finished accuracy.

275. The order of thought here is more important than the grammatical structure; 'tragedy was an unknown kind of poetry before its invention, according to tradition, by Thespis.'

276. plaustris: the source of this curious tradition, which appears only here, is unknown, nor is it possible to discover what error

quae canerent agerentque peruncti faecibus ora.
Post hunc, personae pallaeque repertor honestae,
Aeschylus et modicis instravit pulpita tignis
280 et docuit magnumque loqui nitique cothurno.
Successit vetus his comoedia, non sine multa
laude, sed in vitium libertas excidit et vim
dignam lege regi : lex est accepta chorusque
turpiter obticuit sublato iure nocendi.
285 Nil intentatum nostri liquere poetae;

of interpretation gave rise to it. — **Thespis**: the 'inventor' of tragedy, as Homer was of the epic and Archilochus of iambics. But, properly understood, no form of art was ever invented.

277. canerent, agerent: Horace uses the plural a little carelessly, in speaking of a play in which there was only one actor. — **peruncti faecibus**: this quite uncertain tradition, if it has any foundation in fact, has to do with comedy, not with tragedy.

278-280. The innovations here attributed to Aeschylus are the mask, the special dress, the elevated wooden stage, and the thick-soled tragic boot. There are traces of these traditions in various authors, but the source from which Horace derived them is unknown. — **honestae**: *dignified*; with *pallae* only, not with *personae*. — **modicis**: a qualification of the tradition: the first stage would naturally be thought of as small. — **magnum loqui**: inserted into the account of the stage machinery to go with *niti*.

281. vetus: ἀρχαία; the technical name for the comedy of which Aristophanes is the only extant representative. Cf. *Sat.* 1, 4, 1-2; 1, 10, 16 f.

282-283. libertas: so *Sat.* 1, 4, 5, *multa cum libertate notabant*. 'But this freedom degenerated (*excidit*) into a fault.' — **vim**: the technical word for 'assault,' 'illegal violence.' — **lege**: the accounts are somewhat confused and it is more probable that the law against extreme personalities on the stage had nothing to do with the decline of the chorus.

284. turpiter: with *obticuit*; the silence was discreditable because it was, as Horace understood it, the result of the withdrawal of the right to do harm. — This reference to the loss of the chorus has, in fact, nothing to do with the main thought, and comedy is mentioned only to lead up to the general statement *nil intentatum*.

nec minimum meruere decus vestigia Graeca
ausi deserere et celebrare domestica facta,
vel qui praetextas vel qui docuere togatas.
Nec virtute foret clarisve potentius armis
290 quam lingua Latium si non offenderet unum-
quemque poetarum limae labor et mora. Vos, O
Pompilius sanguis, carmen reprehendite, quod non
multa dies et multa litura coercuit atque
praesectum decies non castigavit ad unguem.
295 Ingenium misera quia fortunatius arte

286. nec minimum: *i.e.*, 'and not the least of their merits is the fact that they have shown independence.'

287. domestica facta: *i.e.*, 'that they have used native material, Roman legends.'

288. praetextas: sc. *fabulas*; tragedies on themes from Roman history, like the *Brutus* of Accius. The name came from the *toga praetexta* worn by the Roman generals and heroes who were represented in the plays. — togatas: comedies in which Roman citizens appeared, wearing the ordinary toga. — docuere: the technical word for the poet's part in preparing the play for presentation by 'teaching' it to the actors.

289-290. virtute . . . armis: a double expression for a single idea. — lingua: for literature in general.

291. This thought is often expressed by Horace; *Sat.* 1. 4. 12 f.; 1, 10, 68-72; *Epist.* 2. 1. 167.

292. Pompilius sanguis: the claim of the Calpurnii (*Pisones*) was that they were descended from Numa Pompilius through a son *Calpus*. This form of address is hardly more than a variation on *Pisones*.

294. praesectum . . . ad unguem: cf. *Sat.* 1, 5, 32, *ad unguem factus homo*; the figure is taken from the testing of the smoothness of a surface by passing the thumb nail over it; the closely cut nail (*praesectum*) would be especially sensitive. — castigavit: general in meaning (*corrected, restrained*), not continuing the figure of pruning, which is faintly suggested by *coercuit*.

295. misera, fortunatius: the words are quoted, as it were, from the poets, who were expressing in vivid language their acceptance of the dictum of Democritus; labor seemed to them wretched and they trusted to their talent for success.

credit et excludit sanos Helicone poetas
Democritus, bona pars non unguis ponere curat,
non barbam; secreta petit loca, balnea vitat.
Nanciscetur enim pretium nomenque poetae,
300 si tribus Anticyris caput insanabile nunquam
tonsori Licino commiserit. O ego laevus,
qui purgor bilem sub verni temporis horam!
Non alius faceret meliora poemata. Verum
nil tanti est: ergo fungar vice cotis, acutum
305 reddere quae ferrum valet, exsors ipsa secandi:
munus et officium nil scribens ipse docebo,
unde parentur opes, quid alat formetque poetam,

297. **Democritus**: Cicero (*de Div.* 1, 37, 80) records it in this form; 'negat sine furore Democritus quemquam poetam magnum esse posse.' — **bona pars**: 'most poets.' — **non ... curat**: 'do not take the trouble.' The neglect of personal appearance seems to them evidence of inspiration. It is most curious that this tradition should still persist among musicians and painters.

299. **nanciscetur**: *i.e.*, 'he believes that he will obtain ...'

300. **tribus Anticyris**: cf. *Sat.* 2, 3, 83, where it is said that all Anticyra must be reserved for the *avari*.

301. **Licino**: there is doubtless some point in the use of a proper name here, but the man is unknown and the point is lost. — **laevus**: 'fool that I am!'

302. **verni**: the time of year when it was held (Celsus, 2, 13) that purgatives should be used.

303. **faceret**: *i.e.*, 'if I were not so foolish as to use purgatives.'

304. **nil tanti est**: 'it isn't worth while,' 'I don't care so much as all that about it'; an expression of indifference; cf. Cic. *Att.* 2, 13, 2; 5, 8, 3. — **cotis**: this is the reply of Isocrates when he was asked why he taught others the art of oratory.

306. This is the literal statement, explaining and applying the anecdote. — **munus et officium**: *function and duty* of the poet; the two words express merely two slightly different sides of one idea. — **nil scribens**: referring to his repeatedly expressed determination to write no more lyric poetry; such a *sermo* as this is not poetry.

307-308. These clauses are not a table of contents of the rest of the Epistle, nor are they a

quid deceat, quid non, quo virtus, quo ferat error.
Scribendi recte sapere est et principium et fons.
310 Rem tibi Socraticae poterunt ostendere chartae,
verbaque provisam rem non invita sequentur.
Qui didicit, patriae quid debeat et quid amicis;
quo sit amore parens, quo frater amandus et hospes;
quod sit conscripti, quod iudicis officium; quae
315 partes in bellum missi ducis: ille profecto
reddere personae scit convenientia cuique.

formal and complete outline of an Art of Poetry. They are merely amplifications of *munus et officium*, specifying certain aspects of poetic art and corresponding only by accident and in the most general way with the discussions that follow. — **opes**: *powers*; *i.e.*, 'what will best furnish him with material and prepare him to write.' — **quid deceat**: 'standards of taste.' — **virtus, error**: in a very general sense, 'the right path and the wrong,' 'a true understanding of poetry and a mistaken judgment about it.'

309. **scribendi recte**: as in *Sat.* 1, 4, 13, with emphasis upon a high standard. — **sapere**: *wisdom*, with secondary reference to philosophy and in contrast to the thought of 295 ff.

310. **rem**: the material, the things to write about; not exactly 'subject-matter,' but the ideas to be expressed. — **Socraticae ... chartae**: these are named for illustration only, not as exclusive sources. The important 'Socratic' writers are Plato and Xenophon. — **poterunt**: 'they will, for example, contain such suggestion as you need.'

311. **rem ... sequentur**: this rule appears in various forms, most concisely in Cato's *rem tene, verba sequentur*, and humorously in the saying of Asinius Pollio, *male hercle eveniat verbis, nisi rem sequantur*.

314. **conscripti**: *councilor*; the word is familiar in the formula *patres conscripti*, but is here used in a more general sense, as in inscriptions (*neve ibi senator neve decurio neve conscriptus esto*, C.I.L., I, 206, 96). This is the only passage except in inscriptions where the word is used alone without *pater*. — **iudicis**: such an official combined some of the functions now divided between the judge and the jury; cf. *Sat.* 1, 4, 23.

316. **personae**: dramatic poetry is here, as in so much of this Epistle, uppermost in Horace's mind. — **convenientia**: *i.e.*, to

Respicere exemplar vitae morumque iubebo
doctum imitatorem et vivas hinc ducere voces.
Interdum speciosa locis morataque recte
320 fabula nullius veneris sine pondere et arte
valdius oblectat populum meliusque moratur,
quam versus inopes rerum nugaeque canorae.
Graiis ingenium, Graiis dedit ore rotundo
Musa loqui, praeter laudem nullius avaris.
325 Romani pueri longis rationibus assem
discunt in partes centum diducere. 'Dicat
filius Albini: Si de quincunce remota est

make the speech of each character suitable to the part he plays in life.

317-318. 'The poet who desires that his work should be a reflection of life (*imitatorem*) and who has learned the principles of life and art from study (*doctum = qui didicit*) will then turn to life itself, to the observation of character (*morum*), and from this, as from a model, will learn to give vividness to the speeches (*vivas voces*) of the persons of his drama.'

319-322. 'For a vivid and lifelike portrayal of character is often more effective than a merely artistic finish.' — **speciosa locis**: *i.e.*, 'which contains vivid and attractive passages (*vivas voces*), speeches that attract the attention of the hearer'; cf. *Epist.* 2. 1, 223. — **morataque recte**: 'in which the speeches conform properly to the characters that utter them,' as is suggested in *exemplar morum*. — **nullius veneris**: 'without the attractiveness of lofty words (*sine pondere*) or artistic polish.' The thought is again expressed by contrast in *inopes rerum nugaeque canorae*.

323-332. 'It is to the Greeks that philosophy and art have given the power to realize these ideals.'

324. avaris: the word is selected in anticipation of the thought that follows; 'for the Greeks are eager only for glory, while we Romans are *avari* in a worse sense.'

325. longis rationibus: 'long calculations' like the 'examples' in arithmetic.

326. centum: the *as* was divided into twelfths, *unciae*, and the Roman reckonings were based in part on a duodecimal system. But they also used a decimal system and *in partes centum diducere* means, in effect, 'to reduce the duodecimal system to decimals.'

327-330. A school recitation in arithmetic; *filius Albini* is the

uncia, quid superat? Poteras dixisse.' 'Triens.' 'Eu!
rem poteris servare tuam! Redit uncia, quid fit?'
330 'Semis.' An, haec animos aerugo et cura peculi
cum semel imbuerit, speramus carmina fingi
posse linenda cedro et levi servanda cupresso?
Aut prodesse volunt, aut delectare poetae,
aut simul et iucunda et idonea dicere vitae.
335 Quicquid praecipies, esto brevis, ut cito dicta
percipiant animi dociles teneantque fideles.
Omne supervacuum pleno de pectore manat.
Ficta voluptatis causa sint proxima veris,
ne, quodcumque volet, poscat sibi fabula credi,
340 neu pransae Lamiae vivum puerum extrahat alvo.
Centuriae seniorum agitant expertia frugis;

pupil who is called upon to recite; the problem is in the addition and subtraction of simple fractions. — quincunce: *quinque unciae*, five-twelfths. — triens: *i.e.*, it is not enough to answer four twelfths; the boy must also be able to reduce the fraction to its lowest terms, one third. — redit: not the putting back of the *uncia* taken away, but a new problem; *is added*.

330. aerugo: *canker, rust*, as consuming the metal; cf. *Sat.* I, 4, 101. — peculi: with *cura* only; the word has here some slighting force, since it is used chiefly of the small property of a child or slave.

332. linenda...: *i.e.*, 'deserving of immortality.' Oil of cedar was used to preserve the papyrus from bookworms. — levi... cupresso: the cypress wood took a high polish, and cases made of it would be especially fine.

334. iucunda, idonea... vitae: these repeat *prodesse* and *delectare* in reversed order.

335. quicquid praecipies: *i.e.*, 'if you choose *prodesse*, *idonea vitae*, to write a didactic poem.' — cito: with *dicta*; = *brevia*.

336. dociles, fideles: predicate.

338. ficta: the other alternatives; 'if you choose *iucunda, delectare,* to write poems to give pleasure only.' — proxima veris: *i.e.*, not at variance with probabilities.

340. Lamiae: a monstrous creature that devoured children alive.

341. centuriae: this word suggests the figure of an election. — seniorum: the citizens above forty-

celsi praetereunt austera poemata Ramnes:
omne tulit punctum qui miscuit utile dulci
lectorem delectando pariterque monendo.
345 Hic meret aera liber Sosiis, hic et mare transit
et longum noto scriptori prorogat aevum.
Sunt delicta tamen, quibus ignovisse velimus:
nam neque chorda sonum reddit, quem vult manus et mens,
poscentique gravem persaepe remittit acutum,
350 nec semper feriet quodcumque minabitur arcus.
Verum ubi plura nitent in carmine, non ego paucis
offendar maculis, quas aut incuria fudit,
aut humana parum cavit natura. Quid ergo est?
Vt scriptor si peccat idem librarius usque,

five. — **expertia frugis**: poems that are not didactic, but *iucunda*.

342. celsi... Ramnes: the knights were the younger citizens, proud of their position and their old name. — **austera**: poems that are merely didactic, not *iucunda*.

343-344. omne... punctum: *i.e.*, both old and young; cf. *Epist.* 2, 2, 99, note. — Vs. 341 corresponds to the first half of vs. 333, vs. 342 to the second half, and vss. 343-344 to vs. 334.

345. Sosiis: the booksellers, already mentioned in *Epist.* 1, 20, 2.

346. This verse returns, as a kind of summary, to the thought of vs. 332.

347. tamen: *i.e.*, 'though I thus hold up the ideal, I recognize the fact that it is difficult of attainment.'

348-350. The comparison, as so often in Horace, is merely implied; 'such failings of a poet are like the mistakes of the musician or the archer.' — **gravem**: *low.* — **persaepe**: there is an apologetic tone in this word; *very often*, so weak is human skill. — **feriet**; the future tense, instead of the present *reddit, remittit*, represents the archer as already excusing his possible miss, before he shoots.

352. offendar maculis: this is the doctrine of *Sat.* 1, 3, 68 ff. and almost the same form of expression as that in *Sat.* 1, 6, 65-67. The use of *maculis* anticipates the comparison of vs. 354. — **fudit**: as if by the spilling of ink.

354. scriptor ... librarius: a slave who copied books, in the Roman way.

355 quamvis est monitus, venia caret, et citharoedus
ridetur, chorda qui semper oberrat eadem:
sic mihi, qui multum cessat, fit Choerilus ille,
quem bis terve bonum cum risu miror; et idem
indignor quandoque bonus dormitat Homerus;
360 verum operi longo fas est obrepere somnum.
Vt pictura, poesis; erit quae, si propius stes,
te capiat magis, et quaedam, si longius abstes;
haec amat obscurum; volet haec sub luce videri,

355. **venia caret**: 'can no longer be pardoned.'

357. **qui multum cessat**: this corresponds to *peccat idem* and *semper oberrat*. — **Choerilus ille**: *Epist.* 2, 1, 233.

358-360. **cum risu miror**: *i.e.*, 'he is generally so poor that, when once or twice he says a good thing, it only makes me laugh and wonder how he came to do it.' — **idem**: with adversative implication, as often; 'and, on the other hand.' — **indignor**: not 'I am angry,' but in its proper sense, 'I count it unworthy of him.' — **quandoque**: = *quandocumque*; the different forms of the indefinite relative were never as clearly differentiated in usage as they are in the grammars. — **bonus**: a standing epithet. — **dormitat**: cf. *dormire*, *Sat.* 2, 1, 7, in a figurative sense not unlike this. — Vs. 360 is a humorous excuse playing upon the literal sense of *dormitat*. — The thought here is only apparently contradictory to vs. 347 and vss. 351 f.; *non ego paucis offendar maculis* means 'I will not condemn a whole poem for a few faults'; *indignor* . . . *Homerus* does not mean 'I am angry with Homer for his few faults,' but rather 'I so admire Homer that, when he makes an occasional slip, my only feeling is that it is unworthy of so great a poet.' The word *indignor* is not the same as *offendar*; it is selected for the contrast with *cum risu miror* and means scarcely more than 'I wonder at it,' 'I am surprised.'

361-365. **ut pictura, poesis**: the comparison is not original; cf. Auct. *ad Herenn.* 4, 28, 39, *poema loquens pictura, pictura tacitum poema debet esse*. It should be noticed that the comparison, which is suggested by the thought of vss. 347-360, concerns only the proper attitude of the critic toward works of art, either pictures or poems, not their essential characteristics. — In carrying a comparison out into details, as is done here, there is

iudicis argutum quae non formidat acumen:
365 haec placuit semel, haec decies repetita placebit.
O maior iuvenum, quamvis et voce paterna
fingeris ad rectum et per te sapis, hoc tibi dictum
tolle memor, certis medium et tolerabile rebus
recte concedi: consultus iuris et actor
370 causarum mediocris abest virtute diserti
Messallae, nec scit quantum Cascellius Aulus,
sed tamen in pretio est; mediocribus esse poetis
non homines, non di, non concessere columnae.

always a tendency to let the mind rest upon one side, sometimes to the exclusion of the other side. The contrast in *propius, longius* is primarily pictorial, not poetic, though it doubtless means, secondarily, to contrast poetry highly finished in details with poetry on a larger scale, like an epic. But *haec amat obscurum*, which is a very just remark about some paintings, is almost meaningless when used of a poem. The last line, vs. 365, is written with poetry primarily in mind (*repetita*), though it applies equally well to a picture.

366. **maior iuvenum**: this is almost the only personal touch in the epistle, and it is not certain that this address to the elder brother means anything more than that he is now old enough to be making his choice of a career.

367. **ad rectum**: in matters of taste; cf. *recte*, vs. 309. — **per te sapis**: a polite phrase to take off the edge of the rather earnest advice, as in the first lines of *Epist.* I, 17, *satis per te tibi consulis*, and *Epist.* I, 18, *si bene te novi*. — **hoc dictum**: in vss. 372 f.

368. **tolle memor**: *i.e.*, 'carry away with you and store in your memory,' as if the epistle were really a *sermo*. — **medium**: not as Horace often uses the word, but 'mediocre,' 'moderately good.'

369. **consultus, actor**: the two branches of the legal profession, the jurist and the pleader.

370. **mediocris**: the emphatic word; 'of only moderate ability.' — **abest**: *i.e.*, 'fails to attain to.'

371. **Messallae**: cf. *Sat.* I, 10, 29, note. He was a man of much distinction in several fields. — **Cascellius**: distinguished in the Ciceronian period as a jurist and an orator. He was probably not living at this time.

372-373. **in pretio**: *of value*; a term of moderate praise. — **mediocribus**: dative in the predicate; cf. *Sat.* I, 1, 19, *licet esse beatis*. —

Vt gratas inter mensas symphonia discors
375 et crassum unguentum et Sardo cum melle papaver
offendunt, poterat duci quia cena sine istis:
sic animis natum inventumque poema iuvandis,
si paullum summo decessit, vergit ad imum.
Ludere qui nescit, campestribus abstinet armis,
380 indoctusque pilae discive trochive quiescit,
ne spissae risum tollant impune coronae;
qui nescit versus, tamen audet fingere. Quidni?
Liber et ingenuus, praesertim census equestrem

This is the *dictum* of vs. 367. — columnae: an intentionally lofty word for the *pilae* (*Sat.* 1, 4, 71), posts in front of the shop where announcements of books or copies of the books themselves were hung to attract buyers. There is also an intentional anticlimax in *homines, di, columnae*.

374-376. 'This is true of any luxury; only the best is really good.' — symphonia discors: to the educated Roman leader, acquainted with Greek, the contradiction in these words would be as obvious as in the phrase *concordia discors*, *Epist.* 1, 12, 19. Music was often played during a dinner. — crassum: *thick, coarse.* — Sardo: of inferior quality. — papaver: the seeds of the white poppy. — duci: *carried on.*

377. natum: so of a wall. *Sat.* 2, 3, 8. — The distinction between the arts which have to do only with pleasure and cultivation and those which serve also a practical end is made by Cicero, in comparing the actor and the orator.

379. ludere: the general sense which this word has when standing alone is immediately made definite by the next words. — campestribus . . . armis: those which are mentioned in the next verse.

380. pilae: *Sat.* 1, 5, 49. — disci: *Sat.* 2, 2, 13, where (in vs. 11) these two forms of Greek athletics are contrasted with hunting and riding.

381. impune: *i.e.*, there would be no ground on which the player who was laughed at could resent the ridicule; *justly, properly.*

382. qui nescit: this is the opinion expressed in *Epist.* 2, 1, 114-117, under a slightly different figure.

382. quidni: *why not, of course?* In this phrase *ni* has no conditional force.

383-384. 'He's a perfectly respectable citizen. Why shouldn't

summam nummorum, vitioque remotus ab omni.
385 Tu nihil invita dices faciesve Minerva;
id tibi iudicium esto, ea mens: si quid tamen olim
scripseris, in Maeci descendat iudicis aures,
et patris et nostras, nonumque prematur in annum,
membranis intus positis.   Delere licebit
390 quod non edideris; nescit vox missa reverti.
Silvestris homines sacer interpresque deorum

he write poetry?'—census: the participle, retaining in the passive the cognate accus. of the active. The construction is rare.—vitio remotus: so *sine crimine* in a similar description, *Epist.* 1, 7, 56.

385. tu: referring back to vs. 366, and returning, after the general remarks of vs. 374 ff., to the personal application.—nihil . . . dices: concessive in force (cf. *tamen*), like *quamvis . . . per te sapis*, vs. 366 f., and with the same courteous intention.—invita . . . Minerva: this phrase was proverbial and is explained by Cicero (*de Off.* 1, 31, 110), *invita Minerva, ut aiunt, id est, adversante et repugnante natura.* Minerva is here the goddess of the intellectual powers.

386. id, ea: *such.* The construction is paratactic for 'such is your judgment that you will say nothing. . . .'

387. Maeci: Sp. Maecius Tarpa, named in *Sat.* 1, 10, 38 as a critic of authority. He is named here merely as a representative of the severe criticism to which the writings of a young man should be submitted.

388. et patris et nostras: as critics also, though perhaps more friendly critics.—nonum . . . in annum: this famous precept is not to be understood literally or definitely. The meaning is that a young writer should hold back his work for mature consideration and revision. The number (*nonum*) was perhaps chosen because the poet Helvius Cinna spent nine years in the writing and correcting of his epic *Smyrna* (Catull. 95, 1-2). But this case was by no means unique; Vergil spent seven years upon the Georgics and left the Aeneid unfinished after ten years of work upon it.

390. vox missa: the expression is figurative; literally, it refers to the spoken word, as in *Epist.* 1, 18, 71, *semel emissum volat irrevocabile verbum.*

391-407. 'But, on the other hand, do not think that poetry is too light an occupation for a serious Roman, for it has contributed

caedibus et victu foedo deterruit Orpheus,
dictus ob hoc lenire tigres rabidosque leones;
dictus et Amphion Thebanae conditor urbis
395 saxa movere sono testudinis et prece blanda
ducere quo vellet. Fuit haec sapientia quondam,
publica privatis secernere, sacra profanis,
concubitu prohibere vago, dare iura maritis,
oppida moliri, leges incidere ligno.
400 Sic honor et nomen divinis vatibus atque

largely to the movement of civilization.' This thought is repeated in substance in *Epist.* 2, 1, 118-138. But the tone there is less historical and more abstract, and there is consequently little repetition of phrases or illustrations.

391. **silvestris**: *i.e.*, men in their primitive state, still living in the woods. — **sacer**: the poet is *vates*, inspired singer, interpreter of the divine will.

392. **victu foedo**: *i.e.*, the acorns and nuts which they lived upon as the animals did. The adj. *foedo* is used in a general way of the kind of life, rather than of anything unpleasant in the food itself.

393. **dictus ob hoc**: 'this is the origin of the legend of his taming tigers.'

394. **dictus**: the repetition of the word at the beginning of the line is meant to suggest that the story of Amphion is also a legend, the real purpose of which is to express in vivid form the power of the singer.

395. **prece**: his song moved rocks as it moved the gods, when it was addressed to them; cf. *Epist.* 2, 1, 135, *docta prece blandus*, of the chorus.

396. **haec**: referring back to the work of Orpheus and Amphion, and then analyzed and explained in the following infinitive phrases.

397-399. Cf. the similar account of the evolution of society in *Sat.* 1, 3, 99-110, where, however, it is used to support the Epicurean doctrine that all moral ideas are derived from *utilitas*. — **concubitu . . . vago**: *venerem incertam rapientis more ferarum*, *Sat.* 1, 3, 109. — **maritis**: 'to husband and wife.' The regulation of marriage was one of the most important matters of Roman law. — **ligno**: perhaps a reference to the tradition that the laws of Solon were made public on wooden tablets. But there is a similar tradition in regard to the Twelve Tables.

400. **sic**: because poets were leaders in all these civilizing movements.

carminibus venit. Post hos insignis Homerus
Tyrtaeusque mares animos in Martia bella
versibus exacuit; dictae per carmina sortes,
et vitae monstrata via est; et gratia regum
405 Pieriis tentata modis, ludusque repertus,
et longorum operum finis: ne forte pudori
sit tibi Musa lyrae sollers et cantor Apollo.
Natura fieret laudabile carmen, an arte,
quaesitum est: ego nec studium sine divite vena,
410 nec rude quid prosit video ingenium; alterius sic
altera poscit opem res et coniurat amice.
Qui studet optatam cursu contingere metam,

401. hos: the *divinis vatibus*, of whom Orpheus and Amphion were the earliest examples.

402. Tyrtaeus: the poet who wrote war songs and marching songs for the Spartans, in the seventh century B.C. — mares: as in *Epist.* 1, 1, 64, *maribus Curiis*.

403. exacuit: the subject is *Homerus*, as well as Tyrtaeus. Horace frequently uses a singular verb with several singular subjects. The thought of the sentence is, 'poets inspired men to deeds of valor,' taking up again the enumeration of the services of poetry to mankind. — sortes: in the more general sense, *oracles*, which were uttered in hexameters.

404. vitae ... via: in didactic poetry, like that of Hesiod. — gratia regum: Pindar, Bacchylides, Simonides were all in some sense court poets.

405-406. ludus ... finis: dramatic poetry. The thought is more fully expressed in *Epist.* 2, 1, 139-142. — ne forte: a 'parenthetic' clause of purpose, summarizing the argument of vss. 391-406.

408-415. 'Both nature and art must contribute to make a good poet — though I know that this is not the accepted doctrine.'

408. natura ... an arte: this was an old question, usually answered as here by saying that both are necessary. Cf., *e.g.*, Cic. *pro Arch.* 7, 15.

409. studium: = *ars*. — vena: of precious metals, as in modern usage.

410. rude ... ingenium: = *natura sine arte*.

411. amice: *i.e.*, 'it is a mistake to oppose nature and skill, as if they were enemies; they are really close friends.'

412-415. The error of attempt-

multa tulit fecitque puer, sudavit et alsit,
abstinuit venere et vino. Qui Pythia cantat
415 tibicen, didicit prius extimuitque magistrum.
Nunc satis est dixisse : ' Ego mira poemata pango ;
occupet extremum scabies ; mihi turpe relinqui est,
et quod non didici sane nescire fateri.'
Vt praeco, ad merces turbam qui cogit emendas,
420 adsentatores iubet ad lucrum ire poeta
dives agris, dives positis in faenore nummis.
Si vero est, unctum qui recte ponere possit,
et spondere levi pro paupere, et eripere artis

ing to write without sufficient training is illustrated in *Epist.* 2, 1, 114 ff. by a comparison with trades and professions, in vss. 379 ff. by a comparison with the players in games of skill, and here by a reference to the practice needed for success in the Pythian games. — cursu : in the foot race, from which so many figures have been drawn. — tulit fecitque : *i.e.,* both passive and active preparation. — puer : ' from boyhood.' — Pythia cantat : cf. *coronari Olympia, Epist.* 1, 1, 50. Musical contests were a regular part of the games. — extimuit : *i.e.*, ' has endured discipline from which, at the time, he shrank.'

416. nunc satis est : ' but nowadays poets are satisfied with their own approval and think courage is the only quality necessary to writing.'

417. occupet ... scabies : ' the devil take the hindmost.' The Scholiast says that this is part of a phrase used by children in a game and gives the whole chant, *habeat scabiem quisquis ad me venerit novissimus* (arranged in metrical order). Cf. *Epist.* 1, 1, 59, note.

418. sane : *at all*, with *nescire.*

420. ad lucrum : ' as the auctioneer summons a crowd who hope to make something by buying cheap, so the rich author invites flattery.'

421. This verse occurs also in *Sat.* 1, 2, 13, where, however, it is not necessary to the sense, as it is here.

422. unctum : *a rich morsel.* — ponere : as a host places a good dinner before his guests.

423. levi : *i.e.*, a poor man who is so lacking in self-respect as to be willing to profit by such help. — The object of *eripere* is to be supplied from *pro paupere.* — artis : ' lawsuits that bind him tight.'

litibus implicitum; mirabor, si sciet inter-
425 noscere mendacem verumque beatus amicum.
Tu seu donaris, seu quid donare voles cui,
nolito ad versus tibi factos ducere plenum
laetitiae; clamabit enim 'pulchre! bene! recte!'
pallescet super his; etiam stillabit amicis
430 ex oculis rorem, saliet, tundet pede terram.
Vt qui conducti plorant in funere, dicunt
et faciunt prope plura dolentibus ex animo, sic
derisor vero plus laudatore movetur.
Reges dicuntur multis urgere cululis

[This is Bentley's conjecture. The reading of the Mss., *atris*, cannot be justified by *atra cura*.]

424. **inter . . . noscere**: cf. *Sat.* 2, 3, 117 f., *unde . . . octoginta*; *Epist.* 2, 2, 93. It is to be remembered that to the Roman feeling the difference between the juxtaposition of two words and their composition into a single word was much less distinct than it is in English. The habit of reading from print prevents us from perceiving actual composition in such a phrase, for example, as *not at all*.

425. **beatus**: 'in his self-satisfaction.'

426. **donaris**: = *donaveris*; 'if you already have some person who is under obligation to you.'

427. **tibi factos**: 'the verses that you, his host and benefactor, have made.'

429. **super his**: 'at this or that passage,' which is intended to excite terror.

430. **saliet**: as an expression of joy, when that is the proper emotion. — **tundet . . . terram**: when he hears of the wickedness of the villain of the drama. — All this is, of course, a humorous exaggeration of natural expressions of emotion.

431. **conducti**: *for hire*. There are various allusions to the custom of hiring women (*praeficae*) to accompany a funeral procession with cries of grief. The masculine is used in order that the phrase may be more directly applicable to the flattering friend.

432. **ex animo**: with *dolentibus*, contrasting with *conducti*.

433. **derisor**: *i.e.*, 'the man who is pretending to admire, but is in his heart laughing at the poet for being so easily fooled.' — **movetur**: 'makes a greater show of emotion,' as already described.

434. **reges**: this is like the allusion in *Sat.* 1, 2, 86, *regibus hic*

435 et torquere mero quem perspexisse laborant,
an sit amicitia dignus: si carmina condes,
nunquam te fallent animi sub vulpe latentes.
Quintilio si quid recitares, 'corrige sodes
hoc,' aiebat, 'et hoc': melius te posse negares
440 bis terque expertum frustra, delere iubebat
et male tornatos incudi reddere versus.
Si defendere delictum quam vertere malles,

mos est, but neither custom is elsewhere mentioned.

435. torquere mero: cf. *Epist.* 1, 18, 38, note. This is the general idea which is expressed in the saying *in vino veritas*. — **laborant**: *are anxious, are striving.*

437. fallent: *i.e.,* 'you need not use such means as these, for your flatterer will reveal himself surely enough.' — **sub vulpe**: the allusion is to the fox who flattered the raven in order to get the bit of cheese (Phaedr. 1, 13), keeping his real purpose (*animi*) out of sight (*latentes*). The phrase *sub vulpe* is therefore a concise expression for 'as the fox hid his purpose in his heart.'

438. Quintilio: the abruptness of the transition gives a strong adversative force; 'Quintilius, on the other hand, will speak his mind plainly.' This is the Quintilius Varus whose death Horace mourned in the noble ode, *Carm.* I, 24, attributing to him *incorrupta Fides nudaque Veritas*. — **recitares**: of the past, as *aiebat*, *iubebat* show, not an ordinary unfulfilled condition.

439. negares: a condition without *si* expressed, but dependent upon *si* of vs. 438, which is again expressed in vs. 442.

441. 'If, on a second or third attempt, the verses prove incapable of improvement, then they must be stricken out and the thought must be expressed in some entirely new form, as a metal worker puts a piece of work that cannot be properly finished back upon the anvil and begins all over again.' The finishing of the metal work was sometimes done on the lathe, and *male tornatos* means 'which come out badly in the finishing process.' Such work would be taken back to the anvil (*incudi*), to be forged over again.

442. vertere: *to change, to amend.* In this general sense *vertere* needs some additional defining phrase, usually *in* with the accus.; here the definition is already given by *defendere delictum*. [It is quite impossible that there should be any connection with

nullum ultra verbum aut operam insumebat inanem,
quin sine rivali teque et tua solus amares.
445 Vir bonus et prudens versus reprehendet inertes,
culpabit duros, incomptis adlinet atrum
transverso calamo signum, ambitiosa recidet
ornamenta, parum claris lucem dare coget,
arguet ambigue dictum, mutanda notabit,
450 fiet Aristarchus, nec dicet, 'cur ego amicum
offendam in nugis?' Hae nugae seria ducent
in mala derisum semel exceptumque sinistre.

vertere stilum, as many good editions say.]

443. **inanem**: predicate; *to no effect*.

444. **sine rivali**: with *solus*; the phrase is used by Cic. (*ad Q. Fr.* 3, 8, 4) as if it were proverbial.

445-449. The attitude of the frank and competent critic, which has been outlined in the reminiscence of Quintilius Varus, is here defined in more general terms, with the *vir bonus et prudens* substituted for Quintilius and with future tenses instead of imperfects. The process of revision is illustrated in details which are undoubtedly drawn from Horace's own experience and practice and which therefore reveal to us something of his method of work. The faults selected for illustration are those which Horace has especially endeavored to avoid; *versus inertes* (flat, lacking in vigor of expression), *duros* (harsh in sound and rhythm), *incomptis* (ill-arranged in order of thought), *ambitiosa* (aiming too directly at effect), *parum claris* (words which do not sufficiently express the thought), *ambigue dictum* (phrases which are capable of more than one interpretation). Some of these have parallels in *Epist.* 2, 2, 122 f. There is a careful variation in the verbs also; *reprehendet, culpabit, arguet* are general, *adlinet atrum signum, recidet, lucem dare coget* are more specific.

450. **Aristarchus**: the famous Homeric critic, who lived in Alexandria in the second century B.C. His name had become typical of the severe critic.

451-452. **hae nugae**: 'these things which you call trifles.' — **derisum semel**: the poet who has once been ridiculed in public for faults which may be in themselves trifling has suffered a loss of reputation from which he can scarcely recover.

Vt mala quem scabies aut morbus regius urget,
aut fanaticus error et iracunda Diana,
455 vesanum titigisse timent fugiuntque poetam
qui sapiunt: agitant pueri incautique sequuntur.
Hic, dum sublimis versus ructatur et errat,
si veluti merulis intentus decidit auceps
in puteum foveamve, licet 'succurrite' longum
460 clamet 'io cives,' non sit qui tollere curet.

453-476. 'Allow me, in conclusion, to hold up to you the picture of the kind of poet you should try not to be — the crazy fool, who thinks himself inspired.'

453. **morbus regius**: this phrase embalms two popular errors, that jaundice was a contagious disease and that it was somehow especially connected with kings or with the rich; to account for the latter various fanciful explanations were given.

454. **fanaticus error**: the frantic dancing of the priests of Bellona (*Sat.* 2, 3, 223, *gaudens cruentis*), who went about the streets cutting themselves in frenzy and begging from the passers-by. The word *fanaticus* (from *fanum*) was used especially of the priests and worship of Bellona and Cybele. — **Diana**: as moon goddess, whose beams were supposed to cause lunacy (*luna*).

455. **vesanum**: = *insanum*.

456. **qui sapiunt**: = *sapientes*; subject of *timent fugiuntque* and contrasted with *incauti*. — **agitant**: at the beginning of the clause with adversative effect. The picture of the poet in the rôle of the madman, tormented by street boys (cf. *Sat.* 1, 3, 133 ff.), while the more reckless of the people follow behind to look on, and the cautious and respectable citizens cross to the other side of the street, is highly effective in its ridicule.

457. **sublimis**: 'with his head in the air.'

458. **merulis intentus**: this reads like an allusion to some well-known story, but no such story has come down to us.

459-460. **longum**: 'so as to be heard afar.' — **non sit**: the grammatical construction is *si ... decidit, licet ... clamet, non sit*; the indicative of the condition would naturally be followed by an indicative *non est* in the conclusion, but the concessive clause *licet ... clamet* comes in and forms a new protasis, under the influence of which the apodosis takes a subjunctive: if 'he falls into a well, even though he should cry out, no one would help him.'

Si curet quis opem ferre et demittere funem,
'qui scis an prudens huc se proiecerit atque
servari nolit?' dicam, Siculique poetae
narrabo interitum. Deus immortalis haberi
465 dum cupit Empedocles, ardentem frigidus Aetnam
insiluit. Sit ius liceatque perire poetis.
Invitum qui servat, idem facit occidenti.
Nec semel hoc fecit, nec, si retractus erit, iam
fiet homo et ponet famosae mortis amorem.
470 Nec satis apparet, cur versus factitet; utrum
minxerit in patrios cineres, an triste bidental

461–463. 'For, as I should point out to any zealous rescuer, most probably he doesn't want to be rescued.' — **dicam**: apodosis to *si quis curet.* — **Siculi poetae**: Empedocles of Agrigentum, philosopher, poet, and statesman of the fifth century B.C. About his life and death various legends grew up, the one of widest currency being this, that he threw himself into the crater of Aetna. The best thing to be said of this story is that it furnished the theme for Matthew Arnold's 'Empedocles on Etna.'

464. **deus immortalis**: this was one of the motives ascribed to him for the deed.

465. **frigidus**: it is possible that this is an allusion to teachings of Empedocles (who was a physicist), in which he identified life with heat. But the allusion would be rather obscure. It is more likely to be 'in cold blood,' for the contrast with *ardentem*.

467. **idem ... occidenti**: 'does the same thing as killing him'; *i.e.*, it is just as bad to prevent him from dying when he wants to die, as to kill him when he wants to live. The construction with the dative is rare, but is found in Lucret.; cf. also the abl. after *alius*. This is the only spondaic hexameter in Horace.

468–469. 'And it will do no good to save him; he has tried it before, and he likes the notoriety.'

470. **nec satis apparet**: *i.e.*, 'we don't know the cause of his poetic madness, but the fact is plain.' — **cur versus factitet**: this is expressed as if it were identical with madness.

471–472. **triste bidental**: a spot struck by lightning, which was therefore considered sacred (*triste*) and was consecrated by a sacrifice of *bidentes* (esp. sheep). It was also surrounded by a wall, and any one who should remove this

moverit incestus : certe furit, ac velut ursus
obiectos caveae valuit si frangere clathros,
indoctum doctumque fugat recitator acerbus ;
475 quem vero arripuit, tenet occiditque legendo,
non missura cutem, nisi plena cruoris, hirudo.

would be unclean (*incestus*). — **certe**: 'at any rate, whatever the cause, he is certainly mad.'

474. indoctum doctumque: a humorous variation on *pueri puellae, et pueros et anus*; the mad poet will make no distinction according to education, if only he can find a hearer. — **fugat**: cf. the story of Ruso, *Sat.* 1, 3, 86 ff.

476. The two objects, that which is compared and that with which it is compared, are, as often, identified in the expression.

To avoid fine, this book should be returned on
or before the date last stamped below

CPSIA information can be obtained
at www.ICGtesting.com
Printed in the USA
LVHW081602211019
634866LV00016B/2162/P